# Majority-Minority Relations 5

## John E. Farley

Southern Illinois University
Edwardsville

PEARSON

Prentice
Hall

Pearson Education, Upper Saddle River, New Jersey 07458

*Library of Congress Cataloging-in-Publication Data*

Farley, John E.
Majority-minority relations / John E. Farley.—5th ed.
    p. cm.
Includes bibliographical references and index.
ISBN 0-13-144412-3 (alk. paper)
1. Ethnology—United States. 2. United States—Race relations. 3. United States—Ethnic relations. I. Title
E184.A1F34 2004
305.8′0973—dc 22

2004040140

*AVP, Publisher:* Nancy Roberts

*Editorial Liaison:* Sharon Chambliss

*VP, Director of Production and Manufacturing:* Barbara Kittle

*Production Editor:* Barbara Reilly

*Copy Editor:* Carol Peschke

*Proofreader:* Alison Lorber

*Editorial Assistant:* Lee Peterson

*Production Assistant:* Kristen Sleys

*Director of Marketing:* Beth Mejia

*Senior Marketing Manager:* Marissa Feliberty

*Marketing Assistant:* Jennifer Lang

*Prepress and Manufacturing Manager:* Nick Sklitsis

*Prepress and Manufacturing Buyer:* Mary Ann Gloriande

*Creative Design Director:* Leslie Osher

*Interior and Cover Designer:* Kathy Mrozek

*Line Art Manager:* Guy Ruggiero

*Line Art Illustrations:* Maria Piper

*Director, Image Resource Center:* Melinda Reo

*Manager, Rights and Permissions:* Zina Arabia

*Manager, Visual Research:* Beth Brenzel

*Manager, Cover Visual Research & Permissions:* Karen Sanatar

*Image Permission Coordinator:* Michelina Viscusi

*Photo Researcher:* Beaura Kathy Ringrose

*Cover Art:* Stock Illustration Source, Inc.

*Media Editor:* Kate Ramunda

This book was set in 10/11 New Baskerville by GGS Book Services, and was printed and bound by Courier Companies, Inc. The cover was printed by Coral Graphics.

For permission to use copyrighted material, grateful acknowledgment is made to the copyright holders listed on page 542, which is considered an extension of this copyright page.

Pearson Education LTD.
Pearson Education Singapore, Pte. Ltd
Pearson Education, Canada, Ltd
Pearson Education—Japan
Pearson Education Australia PTY, Limited

Pearson Education North Asia Ltd
Pearson Educación de Mexico, S.A. de C.V.
Pearson Education Malaysia, Pte. Ltd
Pearson Education, Upper Saddle River, New Jersey

10 9 8 7 6 5 4 3 2 1
ISBN 0-13-144412-3

# BRIEF CONTENTS

# CONTENTS

# PREFACE

## ► ABOUT THE BOOK

This book is designed to enable the reader to understand the principles and processes that shape the patterns of relations among racial, ethnic, and other groups in society. It is not a study of any one racial or ethnic group, although a wide variety of information is provided about a number of groups. Rather, it is intended to enhance the reader's understanding of why such groups interact as they do. The primary emphasis is on the relationships between dominant (majority) and subordinate (minority) racial and ethnic groups in the United States. However, because a thorough understanding of the dynamics of intergroup relations cannot be obtained by looking at only one country, a full chapter is devoted to intergroup relations in other societies. There is also discussion, particularly in Chapter 13, of minority groups other than racial and ethnic ones.

The book is divided into four major parts. In Part I (Chapters 2 and 3) the attitudes and beliefs of the individual concerning intergroup relations are explored through a variety of social-psychological approaches. The concept of prejudice is examined, as well as various theories about its causes, ways in which it may be combated, and the relationship between intergroup attitudes and intergroup behavior. In Part II (Chapters 4 through 8) the emphasis shifts to the larger societal arena. Two major sociological perspectives, order and conflict, are introduced here. These perspectives, and more specific kinds of theories arising from them, are used throughout the book to understand intergroup relations in society. In the balance of Part II, the history of U.S. majority-minority relations is explored and analyzed using the two perspectives, and the theories arising from them are tested and refined. Also introduced here are the concepts of assimilation and pluralism and their roles in the history of American intergroup relations. The theories are further refined through the examination of cross-cultural variations in intergroup relations in the closing chapter of Part II.

The major concern in Part III (Chapters 9 through 12) is present-day intergroup relations in the United States. This part begins with a compilation of data concerning the numbers, characteristics, and social statuses of a wide range of American racial and ethnic groups. The remainder of Part III is an extensive discussion of institutional discrimination, which has become at least as important as individual discrimination in the maintenance of racial and ethnic inequality in America. That fact, however, was not reflected in many of the general works on intergroup relations available when I first wrote this book, and still often receives insufficient attention. This book attempts to remedy that deficiency through extensive discussion of processes that create or maintain such inequality in political, legal, economic, health-care, and educational institutions. All of these areas, as well as housing discrimination and its causes and effects, are analyzed in Chapters 9–12. The purpose of this coverage is not to deny the reality of individual discrimination; in fact the book addresses many ways in which this continues to occur, even today, at the beginning of a new century. Rather, the purpose is to help students understand the reality of institutional forms of discrimination, which are often more subtle and harder to see than individual acts of discrimination.

Part IV explores key issues, trends, and controversies in the present and future of intergroup relations. Chapter 13 addresses majority-minority relations based on gender, sexual orientation, and disability, with special attention to the ways in which racial and gender inequality interact and overlap, thus presenting special concerns and dilemmas for women and men of color. Chapter 14 addresses current trends in majority-minority relations, including diversity and multiculturalism in work and education; the continuing problem of hate group activity and hate crime; debates about how to combat hatred, including issues centering around speech codes and "political correctness"; and the discrimination-testing movement. Chapter 15 explores selected issues in the future of race and ethnic relations in the United States, including the continuing controversy over affirmative action; debates over the desirability of assimilation, pluralism, and separatism; the relative importance of race and class in American society; and the current and future immigration policy of the United States.

To enhance the reader's awareness of essential concepts used throughout the book, important new terms are defined in a glossary at the end of the book. Major ideas throughout the book have been illustrated photographically, and the substantial list of references has been grouped together at the end of this book so any reference can be easily located. For the instructor, a test item file is also available.

## ► CHANGES IN THE FIFTH EDITION

For the most part, the basic approach and organization of this book has been retained through all five editions. Indeed, academic reviewers for this newest edition were unanimous in requesting this.

However, the content has been revised and updated extensively with each edition, with substantial new material added to every chapter for this fifth edition. For the fifth edition, the book has been updated in the following important ways:

1. Data have been updated throughout the book, including extensive incorporation of data from the 2000 census throughout the book.

2. There is extensive updated coverage throughout the book both of current events in majority-minority relations and of new social-scientific research, theory, and writings on majority-minority relations. These updates, as well as those of data noted above, have resulted in the addition of more than 400 new references in the fifth edition, the great majority of them since 2000.

3. The discussion of affirmative action has been rewritten and completely updated to reflect the 2003 Supreme Court decisions on affirmative action arising from the University of Michigan cases (*Grutter v. Bollinger* and *Gratz v. Bollinger*). This discussion appears in Chapter 15, but other parts of the book have also been updated to reflect these cases.

4. There is extensive exploration in several chapters of the impact of the September 11, 2001 terrorist attacks and the societal response to them on intergroup relations, including expanded coverage of issues relating to Arab and Muslim Americans (and the difference between the two).

5. Portions of the education chapter (Chapter 12) have been extensively rewritten to reflect the recent trend toward re-segregation of schools and the reasons for it, the effects of the No Child Left Behind Act, and other important issues.

6. The impacts of welfare reform are discussed extensively, especially in Chapter 11. Also found in Chapter 11 is discussion of evidence of racial discrimination in voting in the 2000 presidential election, and an expanded discussion of the racial consequences (and, likely, motivation) of the "war on drugs."

7. There is expanded coverage in several chapters of recent sociological work on whiteness and the denial of race and racial privilege by whites, as well as discussion of ways in which color-blindness may actually perpetuate racism.

8. Expanded coverage has been added concerning the cumulative costs of racism to minorities over U.S. history, and the related issue of reparations for racism.

## ► ACKNOWLEDGMENTS

An undertaking such as this book would be impossible without the assistance of many people. This assistance goes back to the first edition and has continued with each revision. In the early stages of developing ideas for this book I received encouragement and helpful advice from Hugh Barlow, Joel Charon, and Charles Tilly. Donald Noel, Howard Schuman, Lyle Shannon, Richard Cramer, David Willman, Katherine O'Sullivan See, and Betsey Useem read and commented on part or all of earlier versions of the manuscript. Reviewers for the second edition were Darnell F. Hawkins of the University of Illinois at Chicago and Katherine O'Sullivan See of Michigan State University. Portions of the manuscript for the first edition were typed by Sherrie Williams, Kathy Howlatt, Lynn Krieger, Krista Wright, and Marilyn Morrison. Brenda Eich assisted in the compilation of the reference list. The capable editorial staff at Prentice Hall, including past sociology editors Ed Stanford and Bill Webber, their assistants Irene Fraga and Kathleen Dorman, and past production editors Alison Gnerre and Marianne Peters, have been a pleasure to work with.

In the third edition, acquisitions editors Nancy Roberts and Sharon Chambliss, as well as project manager Virginia Livsey, were most helpful with their continued work and commitment on behalf of this book. Helpful suggestions on portions of the book were received from Thomas D. Hall, DePauw University; David N. Lawyer, Jr., Santa Barbara City College; Pranab Chatterjee, Case Western Reserve University; Alan Siman, San Diego State University; and Vernon McClean, William Paterson College. I am grateful to graduate students Craig Hughey, Cheryl Riggs, and Michelle Ruffner for library assistance during the revision of the third edition, and to Michelle Ruffner and Gina Goodwin for assistance in combining the new references for the third edition with the reference list from the second.

In the fourth and fifth editions, it has been a continuing pleasure to continue to work with Sharon Chambliss. The production editors for the fourth edition, Rob DeGeorge, and for the fifth edition, Barbara Reilly, were very helpful in clearing up the many minor glitches that inevitably occur in an undertaking of this magnitude. Helpful suggestions for the fourth edition were received from Lori A. Brown, Meredith College; and Michael Pearson, University of North Carolina at Charlotte, and for the fifth edition from Mona Scott, Mesa Community College; Lori Brown, Meredith College; and Kwaku Twumasi-Ankrah,

Fayetteville State University. As with earlier editions, comments and suggestions from faculty and students who have used the book were also helpful in the revision. My e-mail address is jfarley@siue.edu, so please keep sending me your comments and suggestions. For the fourth edition, I am also grateful to SIUE graduate student Zhong Lan Yang for assistance in getting the electronic reference file properly styled and formatted. As usual, support and ideas from my colleagues in the Department of Sociology and Criminal Justice Studies at Southern Illinois University at Edwardsville have made an important contribution to the fourth edition. Finally, the most important support of all is the emotional support that I have received from my daughter, Megan, and from my wife, Alice. To them, to everyone else mentioned here, and to anyone I may have forgotten, many thanks.

# ABOUT THE AUTHOR

John E. Farley is Professor and Chair in the Department of Sociology and Criminal Justice Studies at Southern Illinois University Edwardsville, where he has taught a wide range of course, including many years of teaching the race and ethnic relations course. He conducted his undergraduate studies at Michigan State University, where he received a B.A. in political science. He continued his studies at the University of Michigan, where he received an M.A. and a Ph.D. in sociology, as well as the master of urban planning degree. He has taught at Southern Illinois University Edwardsville since 1977.

He is also the author of *Sociology*, Fifth Edition (Prentice Hall, 2003). He is an active researcher in urban sociology and race and ethnic relations, and his articles have appeared in the *American Journal of Sociology*, the *American Journal of Economics and Sociology*, *Urban Affairs Review*, the *Sociological Quarterly*, and a number of other journals. He also regularly presents the results of his research at professional meetings, and has addressed such meetings in Canada and Sweden as well as throughout the United States. He headed a research team studying public response to Iben Browning's prediction of an earthquake in the Midwest in 1990, and was editor of a special issue of the *International Journal of Mass Emergencies and Disasters* on that topic. His book, *Earthquake Fears, Predictions, and Preparations in Mid-America*, which reports the results of the three-year study, was published by Southern Illinois University Press in 1998. Dr. Farley has conducted research on racial housing segregation based on each U.S. census from 1980 through 2000. He has received research grants from the National Science Foundation, the National Institute of Mental Health, and SIUE's Graduate School and Institute for Urban Research.

Professor Farley has received a number of awards for his work, including the SIUE Outstanding Scholar Award for his research on race relations and racial housing segregation, the SIUE Kimmell Community Service Award for his efforts in creating a fair housing organization in the St. Louis metropolitan area, and SIUE's Dr. Martin Luther King, Jr., University Humanitarian Award for his efforts in the community. He has served as president of the SIUE Faculty Senate, the Illinois Sociological Association, the Midwest Sociological Society, and the Metropolitan St. Louis Equal Housing Opportunity Council. Dr. Farley enjoys fishing, snow skiing, travel, and nature and weather photography, especially when sharing these activities with his wife, Alice and his daughter, Megan. In 2004, he became a grandfather, with the birth of his grandson, Justin.

# CHAPTER

# 1

# Orientation: Basic Terms and Concepts

# Overview

## ▶ WHY STUDY RACE AND ETHNIC RELATIONS?

It has now been more than twenty-five years since I began work on the first edition of this book. As the book now enters its fifth edition, conflict, tension, inequality, and misunderstanding between racial and ethnic groups continue in the United States and elsewhere. In early editions, I pointed out that race relations in America are perhaps this nation's most intractable problem, the problem that won't go away. As the book has moved through subsequent editions, we have witnessed a host of events that bear this out. In Los Angeles in 1992, the beating of Rodney King by police led to the deadliest incident of racial violence of the twentieth century. In two 1997 incidents a week apart, racist skinheads killed a West African immigrant and a city police officer in Denver (Boyle, 1997). In 1998, an African American man was dragged to his death behind a pickup truck by whites near Jasper, Texas, a black Marine was permanently paralyzed as a result of a beating by whites near San Diego, California, and a gay student at the University of Wyoming was beaten to death, at least partly because of his sexual orientation.

In addition, the twin specter of domestic and international terrorism has changed everyone's lives in recent years. Though not directly racial or ethnic in nature, both domestic and international terrorism have strong ethnic or racial undercurrents and consequences. The tragedy of September 11, 2001, arose in part from mutual fears and distrusts between the European and Christian parts of the world and the Arab and Muslim parts of the world. Among the many consequences of that event have been increased harassment of Arab and Muslim Americans, severe immigration restrictions applied against immigrants and international students from certain national, ethnic, and religious backgrounds, and support from portions of mainstream America for ethnic profiling of Arab and Muslim Americans, based on a view that anyone who looks Arabic or who adheres to the Muslim faith is a potential security threat. Along with this has come an increase in overt expressions of prejudice, such as the bumper sticker I saw recently that said, "Nuke their ass and take their gas," or another one that showed a man in Arabic dress riding a camel, with a target superimposed.

The current fears and prejudices surrounding international terrorism come on the heels of a surge in the mid-1990s of domestic terrorism by extreme-right antigovernment and militia groups, most tragically evident in the bombing of the Murrah Federal Building in Oklahoma City in 1995, which took 168 lives. Although not all of this terrorism is overtly racist, much of it has racist undertones. Many antigovernment groups are followers of a book titled *The Turner Diaries*, by William Pierce of Virginia, which tells a story of inciting race war through terrorist acts. In addition, many antigovernment groups are linked to white-supremacist groups such as the Aryan Nations. Others advocate the establishment of a white Christian nation in the United States and are suspected of involvement in such incidents as the bombings of a gay bar and abortion clinic in Atlanta and the Atlanta Olympic bombing (Southern Poverty Law Center, 1997).

In the meantime, other incidents have repeatedly reminded us of how racially divided we remain. One of the most dramatic was the differing response of black and white Americans to the trial of O. J. Simpson. Although all were looking at the same evidence, each group saw something different. Most African Americans saw a racist police officer, Mark Fuhrman, who had used a racial slur and had perjured himself when asked about it in court. Because this officer was the source of much of the evidence, they concluded that the case was a racially motivated frameup. On the other hand, most whites saw an African American man (Simpson) who had previously assaulted and threatened his white wife, Nicole Simpson. Conditioned to fear crime by black men, many whites found it easy to believe the charges against Simpson, particularly given his past history of violence against his wife.

As a result, whites and African Americans had very different views of Simpson's guilt or innocence. Even a year after he was found not guilty in the criminal trial, 59 percent of whites thought the verdict was wrong, whereas just 18 percent thought it was right. For African Americans, the result was just the opposite: 58 percent thought the verdict was right; just 16 percent disagreed (*USA Today*, 1997). Thus, although both blacks and whites were looking at the same evidence, what they saw and took note of was heavily influenced by what they had been conditioned to expect, and that conditioning was largely a product of their race.

Two important realities emerge from these observations. First, conflict, discrimination, and inequality between racial and ethnic groups remain deeply entrenched in American society, as they are in many other multiethnic and multiracial societies. In the United States, this remains true despite a decline in open discrimination; despite hundreds of civil rights laws, ordinances, and court decisions at the federal, state, and local levels; and despite the fact that conditions have substantially improved for some minority group members. In spite of all this, the aggregate pattern remains one of racial and ethnic inequality. As will be shown in much detail in this book, this is true whether we talk about income, education, political representation, or any other measure of status in American society. In some regards there has been modest improvement, but in other regards, conditions have actually gotten worse.

Second, intergroup relations in America are becoming increasingly complex, involving more groups and a wider variety of dynamics. When the first edition of this book was written, it was a clear-cut reality that the largest minority group in the United States was African Americans. Hispanic or Latino/a Americans numbered about half the African American population, and aside from a few enclaves such as the Detroit area, most Americans had very limited contact with people of Arab or Islamic backgrounds. Today, the Latino/a population is slightly larger than the African American population, and the Latino/a, Asian American, Native American, Arab American, and Islamic populations in the United States are all growing at rates far greater than those of either whites or African Americans. Therefore, intergroup relations today are more complex than ever before and are marked by tensions that would have seemed quite unfamiliar a quarter century ago.

The continuing reality of racial and ethnic inequality carries serious implications for all Americans. For some minority group members, it means that life is a day-to-day struggle for survival. For all minority group members, it means facing socially imposed disadvantages that they would not face if they were white. For majority group members, it means the continued dilemma of living in a society that preaches equality but in large part fails to practice it. Often, too, it means confronting expressions of anger and frustration from people of color that many white people find difficult to understand. Finally, it means the near certainty of turmoil and social upheaval in the future. As long as the fundamental inequalities that have led to past and present upheavals remain, the potential—indeed, the strong likelihood—of future turmoil remains. All that is needed is the right mix of precipitating social conditions to set off the spark. The conclusion is inescapable: Racial and ethnic relations will affect the life of nearly every American in the coming years.

Another important reality about racial and ethnic relations can be found in the aforementioned changes in the racial and ethnic composition of the United States. Not only is there a greater variety of racial and ethnic groups, but also a growing percentage of the U.S. population will be composed of racial and ethnic minorities in coming years. Today, about 31 percent of the American population is made up of people of color, that is, African Americans, Hispanic or Latino/a Americans, Asian Americans, and Native Americans (U.S. Census Bureau, 2003a). By 2020, this is projected to increase to 39 percent and, by 2050, to 50 percent (U.S. Census Bureau, 2004a, Table 1a). Soon after 2050, people of color will be a majority of the U.S. population (U.S. Census Bureau, 2003a).

As America becomes more diverse—and as it continues to face increased international competition in the world economy—every American has a growing economic stake in reducing racial and ethnic inequality. Today, the talents of millions of Americans are being wasted. Poor education, concentrated poverty, and widespread unemployment in the country's predominantly African American and Hispanic inner cities are making it increasingly difficult for the people who live there to develop the skills needed in today's high-tech economic environment. Conditions on many Indian reservations, as well as for rural African Americans, Hispanics, and poor whites, are as bad or worse. Moreover, the situation of those people of color who live in areas of concentrated poverty has become increasingly bleak since the 1970s (Wilson, 1987, 1991; Massey, 1990).

In addition to the potential for social turmoil that this creates, it has a direct bearing on our present and future productivity. Continued failure to fully utilize the human resources of more than half the population will seriously harm America's productivity precisely when international competition is at an all-time high and continuing to increase. The consequences of such a decline in competitiveness in today's global economy are clear: Fewer people will buy American products, with the result that jobs will be lost and wages will fall. This will affect all Americans, not just people of color. One study estimated the cost of racial discrimination to the U.S. economy (in the form of reduced gross domestic product) in 1991 at $215 billion—nearly ten times what it was in 1967 (Brimmer, 1993). And as the minority share of the population grows and international competition intensifies, this cost can only grow, and it is surely much higher now than a decade ago, when this study was done.

For all of these reasons, there remains a critical need to understand racial and ethnic dynamics in America. The goal of this book is to contribute to such understanding.

The ongoing debate over affirmative action, which reached the U.S. Supreme Court for the second time in 2003, illustrates the continuing importance of race and ethnic relations in the United States.

## ▶ EMPHASIS AND APPROACH OF THIS BOOK

The primary emphasis of this book is on race and ethnic relations in the United States. Nonetheless, this book is not exclusively about American race relations. The fundamental objective is to understand the dynamics of race and ethnic relations, which one could never accomplish by looking at only one society. How ethnic groups interact with one another varies from one society to another according to the social, economic, cultural, and political conditions found in those societies. Racial and ethnic relations—including those in America—can be best understood through a comparison of what has occurred in different times and places. Moreover, patterns and problems similar to some of those in the United States are evident in a number of other industrialized countries with diverse populations. For all these reasons, the emphasis of this book on the American situation includes a comparative analysis of racial and ethnic relations in other societies.

A second major characteristic of this book is that it is concerned with analysis and explanation rather than mere description. In other words, the major concern is understanding *why* race relations work the way they do, not merely describing the pattern of American race relations or presenting a detailed descriptive history of various ethnic groups. (The size of the book would not permit us to do justice to the varied and rich histories of the multiplicity of American ethnic groups, in any case.[1]) If we are to understand and deal with racial and ethnic problems, we must know not only what those problems are but also how they developed and the social forces that cause them to persist. Therefore, we search for principles and regularities in patterns of ethnic relations: For example, what are the social conditions under which segregation develops? What changes are associated with declines in segregation? Only through this approach, which stresses the whys of race relations, can we begin to understand and deal with the problems we face today.

A third important characteristic of this book is that it examines race and ethnic relations on both the individual and societal levels. Some people who study race relations look mainly at the behaviors and prejudices of individuals, asking why a person is prejudiced and what we can do about it. Others look mainly at groups and societies, stressing economic and political systems or such trends as urbanization and industrialization, asking how these large-scale factors influence the interaction of the ethnic groups in a society. This book begins at the individual level, then moves to analysis on a larger scale. We shall examine theory and research about individual thinking and behavior, then theories and research about larger societal factors and their relationship to race and ethnicity. Having laid this groundwork, we will consider the status of various racial and ethnic groups in American society today and the ways in which this status is affected by major social institutions. The book concludes with an examination of contemporary trends in majority-minority relations and issues likely to shape future intergroup relations in the United States.

## ▶ BASIC TERMS AND CONCEPTS

In any field of study, one must understand certain terms and concepts to make sense of the subject. Unfortunately, in the field of racial and ethnic relations, more than most, any particular term may be given a wide variety of meanings by different scholars. Therefore, it is probably impossible to devise definitions on which all would agree. Still, we must know what is meant by the terms we are using. Accordingly, we present the following definitions with these provisions:

- It is unlikely that every social scientist who studies race and ethnic relations would agree on all of these definitions or on any set of definitions.

- The definitions, insofar as possible, reflect current trends in common usage among those who study race and ethnic relations.

- The reasons for using a particular definition will be explained.

- The definitions are stated in such a way that, once they are understood, it should be quite possible for any reader to say who or what fits the definition and who or what does not.

---

[1]For those interested in historical information on a wide variety of racial and ethnic groups in America, an excellent though somewhat dated source is the *Harvard Encyclopedia of American Ethnic Groups* (Thernstrom, Orlov, and Handlin, 1980).

## Race and Ethnicity

The term **race** refers to a socially defined group of people who are generally considered to be physically distinct in some way, such as skin color, hair texture, or facial features, from other groups and are generally considered by themselves or others to be a distinct group. Thus, the concept of race has two components: social and physical. The social component involves group identity: The group must in some way be recognized by its own members or by others as a distinct group or at least as having some characteristics (physical and perhaps other characteristics) in common. Without such social recognition, a group of people will not be identified as a race. The physical component involves the fact that every race is generally regarded as being somehow different in appearance from other races, but it is a social choice to define what physical differences matter.

This definition of race differs from that of many members of the general public (and, at one time, many scientists as well). People often think of race as a matter of physical or biological characteristics, something that is genetically determined. Although it is true that race is *socially* defined on the basis of *physical* characteristics, it is easy to show that it is not fundamentally physical or genetic. One illustration of this is the inability of geneticists, anthropologists, or sociologists to agree on how many races there are in the world's population. The estimates range anywhere from the common notion of three races (black, white, and yellow) to thirty-four races (Dobzhansky, 1962) to more than a hundred. Furthermore, the particular physical characteristics used to define a race are arbitrary and vary from one classification scheme to the next. Racial classifications similarly vary from time to time and from place to place, both in terms of the numbers of groups recognized and in terms of the different ways that people of mixed ancestry are classified. Finally, long-term interbreeding between races has in many cases made the notion of race as a discrete biological category meaningless. As these examples show, physical characteristics

While racial groups are defined on the basis of physical appearance, the process by which any group, such as Chinese Americans, comes to be defined as a racial group is social: Society collectively decides to define a particular group as a race. Absent this, a group will not be considered a race, regardless of physical appearance.

partially define race, *but only in the context of a decision by society to consider those physical characteristics relevant.*

This underlines the fact that race is *socially constructed.* It is based on societal choices about what physical characteristics to pay attention to and about how to classify people on the basis of those characteristics. Such societal choices can and do vary over time and from one society to another.

**Is Race a Meaningful Concept?** For the reasons discussed, increasing numbers of social and natural scientists in recent years have questioned whether the concept of race makes sense at all. In 1994, for example, the American Anthropological Association passed a resolution stating that "differentiating species into biologically-defined 'races' has proven meaningless and unscientific" (Wheeler, 1995). There is no particular gene or precise combination of genes that can be linked to race, and genetic traits, such as antibodies to many diseases, generally do not correspond to racial groupings. Also, genetic variation within one particular racial group (however it may be defined on the basis of appearance) is almost always greater than genetic variation between two different racial groups (Lehrman, 2003). All these reasons together indicate the futility of trying to classify humanity into any set of biologically defined races (Cavalli-Sforza et al., 1994). It is true that some biological characteristics correlate with race. For example, physical characteristics such as skin color and hair texture usually are the products of evolution in response to the climate that groups have experienced over the long term. And it is well known that propensity to certain diseases varies among racial, ethnic, and geographic groupings, in part because when genetic changes that cause disease occur, these changes are reproduced within groups where in-group marriage patterns occur (Duster, 2001). However, these patterns do not fit any particular racial classification system.

One reason that growing numbers of social scientists object to the race concept has to do with the ways in which it has been used: If a scientifically unjustifiable set of racial groupings is treated as if it were real, it can easily be used to make unfounded racial distinctions that support or lead to discrimination (Lieberman and Reynolds, 1991). On the other hand, many social scientists argue that we must continue to pay attention to race because people *do* treat systems of racial classification as if they were real, whether they have a sound biological basis or not. Certainly the fact that race is treated as real has very real social consequences (Duster, 2001), and if we ignore or deny race we risk ignoring or denying the consequences of racism.

Some social scientists distinguish between a race and a **racial group**. This distinction is illustrated by Spencer (1979, p. 274) with the example of an Eskimo girl raised in a white American family in the South, never exposed to Eskimo culture or society. This girl's race might be considered Eskimo (she has physical features and parentage that would define her as Eskimo), but she is not part of Eskimo society or culture, and on first contact with Eskimo society she would not understand it any more than anyone else in the South would. Therefore, she would not be considered a member of the Eskimo racial group. Thus, a racial group can be defined as a group of people of the same race who interact with one another and who develop some common cultural characteristics.

In practice, however, many sociologists question the distinction between a race and a racial group. Pointing out that race is a socially constructed concept, they maintain that races, as well as racial groups, are social groups, not biological ones. Also, others in society may treat the Eskimo girl in Spencer's example as an Eskimo even if she is not familiar with Eskimo culture. Accordingly, *race* and *racial group* will be used interchangeably in this book, although we follow the current tendency in the discipline to use the term *racial group* in preference to *race.* This reflects sociology's recognition that races and racial groups are socially defined and constructed, not defined on the basis of biology. We study race not because the concept of race is biologically sound but rather because people are identified and grouped on the basis of the socially constructed concept of race, and in real life, these groupings make a big difference in people's life experiences (Winant, 1994; R. L. Taylor, 1998; Duster, 2001).

**The Difference Race Makes: Why We Think in Racial Terms.** The difference race makes in people's lives—its social and political consequences—is one of the main reasons why society recognizes race as a key category and why its definition and its social meaning change over time. Omi and Winant (1994) call the process by which society recognizes and defines racial groups *racial formation.* This process defines both who the racial groups in a society are and how the meaning of race is understood. The process of defining and, over time, redefining racial groups is always driven by political interests. For example, as is discussed in greater detail in Chapter 5, the notion of whites as free people and blacks as slaves was *not* there from the beginning of the colonies that later became the United States. At first, most of the colonial population, whether of European or African ancestry, was made up of indentured servants, who served a limited period of servitude and then were set free. Later the plantation owners promoted the idea of permanent slavery *tied to race* to get around the problem of having to periodically free their indentured servants and get new ones.

Furthermore, whites did not initially think of themselves in racial terms; rather, they thought in terms of ethnicity (English, Irish, Scottish) and class (Roediger, 1991). The notion of whites as a distinct racial group is something that developed later. White workers saw it as a way of escaping indentured servitude and of placing themselves above another class, which would be even more disadvantaged (black slaves). Plantation owners, in turn, promoted this notion because they saw it as useful to their own interests once slavery had become tied to being African. Whites became defined as a racial group whose race was associated with power and freedom, and this definition of race became the underpinning of slavery and of an economic system dominated by an elite segment of the white population (Roediger, 1991; Winant, 1997). Europeans in the colonies, including many former indentured servants, began to think of themselves as *whites,* which at least entitled them to some privileges relative to the African American slave population. As a result, however, these poor whites identified with other whites and supported a plantation system that in fact exploited them by denying them landownership and by using them as cheap labor. This was possible because racial thinking led them to align themselves with white plantation owners rather than black slaves (T. W. Allen, 1997). Thus, the definition of whites as a race reflected the power and political interest of precisely the group (plantation owners) that benefited from this definition of race. Thus, the early understanding of race in American society was directly the product of political interests and a political process (Winant, 1997). As we shall see in later chapters, much the same is true of our understanding of race today.

**Ethnic Groups.** A concept closely related to race is that of the ethnic group. An **ethnic group** can be defined as a group of people who are generally recognized by themselves or by others as a distinct group, based entirely on social or cultural characteristics. The most common of these characteristics are nationality, language, and religion. Ethnic groups tend to be, at least to some degree, biologically self-perpetuating. In other words, one's ethnicity is determined largely by the ethnicity (or ethnicities) of one's parents. Thus, ethnicity, like race, is a social characteristic that passes from generation to generation. In the United States, Irish Americans, Jewish Americans, and Italian Americans are examples of ethnic groups. Unlike in races or racial groups, physical traits are not necessarily characteristics of an ethnic group; that is, it is impossible to reliably tell on the basis of appearance alone who belongs and who does not. It is perhaps ironic that Adolf Hitler, who always insisted that Jews are a race, ultimately turned to a classification based on parentage to determine who was Jewish (one was Jewish if one or more of one's grandparents identified with the

## THE CENSUS BUREAU AND RACE

Nothing illustrates the arbitrary nature of racial classification systems more clearly than the changing ways in which the U.S. Census Bureau has classified race in the United States over the years. Look at Table 1.1, which shows how the census handled race (and, more recently, Hispanic origin) for 110 years. Note that the racial categories used were different in every census, although in general they increased in number over time as the U.S. population became more diverse and as more groups have insisted on being recognized and the Bureau has become more sensitive to such demands. Nearly every group has been handled differently over time, and various groups have come and gone as "races."

Mexican Americans are a good illustration of this practice. They were not treated as a separate group early on, but in 1930 "Mexicans" were treated as a race. They disappeared as a classification after that, only to reemerge as an ethnic group under the "Hispanic" classification, which was created in 1970. The Hispanic groups are ethnic groups in that they can be of any race and are expected to separately classify themselves into one of the racial groups. Consistently, about 40 percent have refused to do so, marking the race question "other" and writing in "Hispanic," "Latino," "Mexican," "Puerto Rican," and so on. But the other 60 percent have answered the race question and classified themselves as white, black, or one of the other racial classifica-tions. In hopes of increasing this percentage, the 2000 census asked the race question before the Hispanic origin question because experiments suggested that this way, more Hispanics would classify their race into one of the Bureau's racial categories. However, in the actual census, more than 40 percent again chose the "other" category, although a few of those also chose a second group from the list of racial groups (U.S. Census Bureau, 2001a). This is yet another way in which arbitrary factors enter into racial classifications.

Finally, note the varying ways in which the Census Bureau has handled people of mixed racial background. It used to have a complex set of categories—"mulatto," "quadroon," and "octoroon"—to classify people of mixed white and black ancestry. In deference to the "one drop" rule, by 1920 anyone with black ancestry was classified as "Negro," but this category was subclassified into "black" (supposedly, all-black ancestry) and "mulatto" (mixed ancestry). After 1920 the mixed categories were done away with altogether, more fully formalizing the "one drop" rule. However, pressures from the growing number of Americans with parents of two or more different races led to more changes for the 2000 census (Office of Management and Budget, 1997; see also Wright, 1994). Beginning with that census, Americans could check off more than one race on the race question. About 2.4 percent of the population, nearly 7 million people, did so.

Jewish faith) because it was impossible to tell by appearance. To tell who was Jewish, Hitler required Jews to wear identifying marks such as buttons with the Star of David.

For some, ethnicity is a highly salient feature of life, whereas for others it is not. For example, some Irish Americans view their Irish ancestry as an important part of their identity, whereas others with the same ancestry simply think of themselves as Americans. Thus, psychological identification with a group is an important part of what makes ethnicity real to people. Sometimes, of course, ethnic discrimination by others makes people's ethnicity a salient feature whether they want it to be or not. Hitler's oppression of the Jews is a good example of this, as is the discrimination that many ethnic immigrants encounter when they arrive in a new country in large numbers. In this case, ethnicity becomes salient because others with power have decided to make it so.

Sociologists disagree on whether ethnicity is a broad concept that includes racial groups or whether racial and ethnic groups are two different entities. Some (Gordon 1964; Glazer, 1971) argue that races are a particular type of ethnic group. By this definition, some ethnic groups are not racial groups (for example, Mennonites and Polish Americans), but all races are ethnic groups. Other social scientists make a distinction, arguing that if physical characteristics are involved, the group is a race (blacks or whites), but if the group is based solely on social or cultural characteristics, the group is an ethnic group (French Canadians or German Americans). Examples of this can be seen in the writings of Warner and Srole (1945) and Van den Berghe (1978). In fact, it makes a good deal of difference in terms of intergroup relations whether or not a group is identifiable on the basis of appearance. Accordingly, for purposes of this book, racial groups are defined on

**Table 1.1    Racial and Ethnic Origin Classifications Used by the U.S. Census, 1890–2000**

| One, Chosen by Census Taker | | | | One, Chosen by Respondent | | One or More, Chosen by Respondent |
|---|---|---|---|---|---|---|
| *1890* | *1920* | *1930* | *1950* | *1970* | *1990* | *2000* |
| White | White[3] | White | White | White | White | White |
| Black | Negro | Negro | Negro[4] | Negro/black | Black | Black/African American |
| Mulatto | Black | Mexican | Indian[2] | Japanese | American Indian or Alaska Native | American Indian or Alaska Native |
| Quadroon[1] | Mulatto | Indian[2] | Japanese | Chinese |    American Indian |    American Indian |
| Octoroon[1] | Indian[2] | Chinese | Chinese | Filipino |    Eskimo |    Eskimo |
| Chinese | Chinese | Filipino | Other nonwhite | Hawaiian |    Aleut |    Aleut |
| Japanese | Japanese | Hindu | | Korean | Asian or Pacific Islander | Asian |
| Indian[2] | All other | Korean | | Indian[2] |    Chinese |    Chinese |
| | | Hawaiian | | Other |    Filipino |    Filipino |
| | | Malay | | |    Hawaiian |    Korean |
| | | Siamese | | |    Korean |    Vietnamese |
| | | Samoan | | |    Vietnamese |    Japanese |
| | | | | |    Japanese |    Asian Indian |
| | | | | |    Asian Indian |    Samoan |
| | | | | |    Samoan |    Guamian |
| | | | | |    Guamian |    Cambodian |
| | | | | |    Other A.P.I. |    Malaysian |
| | | | | | Other |    Pakistan¡ |
| | | | | | |    Thai |
| | | | | | |    Other Asian |
| | | | | | | Pacific Islander |
| | | | | | |    Hawaiian |
| | | | | | |    Guamian |
| | | | | | |    Samoan |
| | | | | | |    Other Pacific Islander |
| Hispanic origin (may be of any race; this category not used until 1970; called "Hispanic or Latino" beginning in 2000) | | | | Mexican | Mexican | Mexican |
| | | | | Puerto Rican | Puerto Rican | Puerto Rican |
| | | | | Cuban | Cuban | Cuban |
| | | | | Central/South American | Central or South American | Central or South American |

[1]"Quadroon" and "octoroon" refer to people with varying proportions of white and black ancestry.
[2]Refers to American Indians.
[3]This category was subcategorized into "native-born" and "non–native-born" categories.
[4]Includes people with mixed and black ancestry and people with American Indian and black ancestry unless clearly accepted as Indian.

the basis of both physical and social characteristics, ethnic groups purely on the basis of social or cultural characteristics.

**Measuring Race and Ethnicity.** Because race and ethnicity are socially constructed and change with time, they are difficult to measure. This is illustrated in the box "The Census Bureau and Race," which shows how both definitions of racial groups and the handling of mixed categories have changed over time. Through much of our history, the "one drop" rule has applied to people of mixed black and white ancestry: If there was any black, or "Negro," ancestry, the person was placed in that group (U.S. Bureau of the Census, 1953, p. 35; Wright, 1994). This was done in large part to maintain the system of discrimination and to discourage whites from marrying or having children with African Americans and other minorities. But at one time the census did include categories for people of mixed black and white ancestry, and for the first time, in the 2000 census, people were able to check more than one racial category (2.4 percent did so). This new policy is largely the outgrowth of pressures from people of mixed ancestry, who did not identify with any of the existing census racial categories.

All this has more than academic importance. On one hand, people with multiracial parentage were made to feel like nonpersons by the system used in the past; there was no category that accurately described them. On the other hand, if everyone were classified as multiracial (which in reality a large proportion are, at least to some extent) or if race were dropped from the census as an unscientific concept, there would be serious implications for the enforcement of civil rights laws. Unfortunately, discrimination and segregation are real, even if, in the biological sense, race is not. Census data and other federal data on race permit the measurement of school and housing segregation, racial inequalities in income and employment, and other indicators of discrimination that are all too real. Thus, such data are important tools in the fight against discrimination, despite their many imperfections. For the same reason, some support for omitting the race question on the census has come from groups opposed to affirmative action and other efforts to increase opportunities for people of color (Wright, 1994). Recently, a group opposing affirmative action attempted unsuccesfully to eliminate all collection of race data in the state of California (Glazer, 2002).

## Majority and Minority Groups

Two terms used throughout this book are *majority group* and *minority group*. When sociologists use these terms, they are not speaking in a strictly numerical sense. The sociological meaning of **majority group**, as used in this book, is any group that is dominant in society, that is, any group that enjoys more than a proportionate share of the wealth, power, or social status in that society. Typically, a majority group is in a position to dominate or exercise power over other groups. A **minority group** can be defined as any group that is assigned an inferior status in society, that is, any group that has less than its proportionate share of wealth, power, or social status. Often, minority group members are discriminated against by those in the majority.

A number of important points can be made about these groups. First, majorities and minorities often are determined by race or ethnicity, but they can also be determined by many other relatively permanent factors, such as sex, physical disability, or sexual orientation. Much of what is true about relations between African Americans and whites, for example, is also true about relations between males and females, gays and straights, and people with and without disabilities. I have chosen the title of this book precisely for this reason: The dynamics of relations between majority groups and minority groups are in many ways similar, regardless of how those groups are defined. Thus, although this book is mainly about race and ethnic relations, many of the principles apply to other kinds of majority-minority relations, or intergroup relations, as well.

Second, as noted, the sociological usage of the terms *majority* and *minority* differs from the common numerical usage. It is quite possible for a group to be a numerical majority but still a minority group in the sociological sense. Several familiar examples come to mind. Perhaps the best known is that of blacks in South Africa. Although more than 80 percent of the population is black, until about a decade ago the political system was completely under the control of whites. Racial separation and discrimination were required by law. Since all South Africans were given the right to vote in 1994 and Nelson Mandela was elected as South Africa's

Although women are a slight numerical majority of the U.S. population, they are a minority group in the sociological sense because of disadvantages such as lower pay.

first black president, political control has been in the hands of the black numerical majority. However, even with such free elections, a disproportionate share of the country's wealth has remained in the hands of the white numerical minority, and this probably will likely continue to be the case for many years. Thus, although blacks are an overwhelming majority numerically, until a decade ago they were a minority group in the sociological sense, and in terms of economic position in society, they still are.

Another numerical majority that is a sociological minority group is women in the United States. Women make up slightly more than half of the U.S. population, but relatively few hold offices in the nation's higher political governing bodies (such as the U.S. Congress). They have long been subject to discrimination, and a proposed U.S. constitutional amendment to ban sexual discrimination has still not been enacted. Even today, full-time working women are paid only about 76 percent of the wages of similarly educated working men. Thus, even though they are a numerical majority, women have in many ways been relegated to a subordinate role in American society and can be regarded as a minority group in the sociological sense.

The important point to keep in mind, then, is that it is a group's role and status, not its numbers, that make it a majority or minority group. A helpful way to think of this, suggested by Yetman (1991, p. 11), is to think of *majority* as a synonym for **dominant** and *minority* as a synonym for **subordinate**. Occasionally, a society may have relatively peaceful and egalitarian relations among its racial or ethnic groups, so that no group is dominant or subordinate. However, the more common pattern in diverse societies is for some groups to dominate others; thus, in such societies interracial and interethnic relations usually fall into the larger category of majority-minority relations. Unless we are talking specifically about cases in which the three concepts—race and ethnic relations, majority-minority relations, and intergroup relations—do not overlap, we shall use these terms somewhat interchangeably to avoid repeated use of the same term. This is not meant in any way to negate the important facts that not all race and ethnic relations are marked by domination and subordination and that many intergroup relations besides race and ethnic relations operate according to the majority-minority model.

One final note: In recent years, there has been some criticism of the *majority group* and *minority group* terminology (University of Maryland, 1994; Wilkinson, 2002). A number of objections have been raised, including the following:

- Because such status is not defined on the basis of numbers, *minority* is not a correct term.

- The term *minority* can be a negative label, and defines the groups so labeled from the standpoint of the dominant group.

- Groups with little in common, such as African Americans and white women, are lumped together under one rather meaningless label.

- The criteria used to define minorities are ambiguous and inconsistent.

- The statuses that form the basis of defining minority groups include both true ascribed statuses and statuses that involve an element of choice (e.g., religious belief).

- The term *minority* glosses over the very real impacts of racial, gender, and other forms of discrimination, using an ill-defined term to focus on groups rather than systemic discrimination.

Despite these concerns, the terms continue to be widely used, both in sociology and in popular terminology. In the social sciences, at least, the experiences that lead a group to be considered a minority group are fairly well agreed-upon, including victimization, discrimination, exploitation, and political and economic disadvantage. Although each group considered a minority experiences these processes in a unique way, all such groups experience them to a degree. Moreover, possible alternative terms also pose problems: For example, *subordinate* does not necessarily convey a more positive image than *minority*. But whatever term is used, the purpose of such usage in sociology is not to convey negative connotations but rather to describe a similar and very real situation—minority or subordinate status—that is experienced by a number of different groups. Thus, as used in this book, *majority* and *dominant* are similar in meaning, as are *minority* and *subordinate*.

## Racism

Perhaps no term in recent years has been used in as many different ways as *racism*. Any definition of this term is subject to controversy; for this reason, we have chosen to give this term a very broad definition and then to present further definitions to identify different forms of racism. Accordingly, **racism** can be defined as any attitude, belief, behavior, or institutional arrangement that favors one race or ethnic group (usually a majority group) over another (usually a minority group). By "favoring one group over another" we mean not only intentions but also consequences: If the result of an action or social arrangement is that one race or ethnic group receives a disproportionate share of scarce resources (such as money, education, political power, and social status), it is an example of racism. It is also a case of racism if the consequence of an arrangement is to give one group greater freedom than another. Thus, by this broad definition, something or someone can be racist either on the basis of intentions or on the basis of results. It then follows that sometimes racism (and similar phenomena such as sexism) are conscious and deliberate; at other times they are not. The unfortunate fact is that if one is the victim of racism or sexism, it makes little difference whether the disadvantage was intentionally imposed or not; it is still a disadvantage. (For further discussion of this broad concept of racism, see U.S. Commission on Civil Rights, 1970b; J. M. Jones, 1972; Ridley, 1989; Yetman, 1991, pp. 19–29; Feagin, 2000, pp. 14–27.)

Within this broad definition of racism, we can identify several specific kinds. One is attitudinal and is called racial prejudice. A second, more narrowly defined kind of racism is ideological racism, also called racist ideology. A third type involves individual behavior and is called individual racial discrimination. A fourth type involves institutional or societal patterns; this is called institutional racism or institutional discrimination. Although we present this typology primarily with respect to racism, it is the case that prejudice and discrimination on the basis of other factors—such as sex, sexual orientation, disability status, and in some instances religion—operate similarly and can be similarly categorized.

**Racial Prejudice.** Racial **prejudice**, the attitudinal form of racism, refers to people's thinking—their attitudes and beliefs that tend to favor one group over another or to cause unequal treatment on the basis of race. Prejudice can be direct or overt, such as disliking a group or believing that it is inherently inferior. However, it can also be subtle, such as the belief that a group that has been discriminated against is to blame for its own troubles, the feeling that a group protesting its subordinate status is "causing trouble," and the practice of stereotyping, of assuming that "all of them are alike." Thus, two critical points should be kept in mind about the meaning of *prejudice*. First, the term refers to people's thinking—their attitudes and beliefs—not their behavior. Second, prejudice can be overt and very obvious or it can be subtle and indirect. A more detailed definition of racial prejudice and other forms of prejudice is presented in Chapter 2; the purpose here is to distinguish it from other forms of racism.

**Ideological Racism.** Closely related to the concept of prejudice is the more specific concept of **ideological racism**, or **racist ideology**. These terms refer specifically to the belief that some races are biologically, intellectually, or culturally inferior to others. The term *racism* was originally used to mean this type of ideology, which views various races as superior or inferior to one another, and some social scientists continue to prefer this narrower definition. Racist ideology has been widely advocated and widely believed, particularly in Europe and North America. Such racist ideology often has been elevated to the status of "scientific theory," giving rise to what has been called *scientific racism*. The idea here is that science supposedly proves that some groups are innately superior to others. It is significant that such ideologies always define the race of the "scientist" as superior. An example of this can be seen in social Darwinism, which argues on the basis of "survival of the fittest" that the wealthiest and most powerful groups are biologically the "most fit." This ideology was widely used to justify domination and colonization of the natives of Asia, Africa, the Americas, and Oceania by white Europeans.

In fact, it is an important characteristic of ideological racism that its main function is to justify domination and exploitation of one group by another by showing that group superiority or inferiority is the natural way of things (W. J. Wilson, 1973, pp. 32–35). When it has served dominant-group interests to do so, claims of innate inferiority have been made at various times in the United States against a wide variety of groups, including Irish, Italian, Polish, Portuguese, and Jewish Americans, as well as African Americans, Chicanos, and American Indians. The rise of the anti-immigration and anti-Catholic Know Nothing party around 1850 and the Ku Klux Klan in the early twentieth century marked high points of ideological racism in the United States. Elsewhere, it was at the heart of German Nazism, whose ideology consisted of beliefs that Germans were part of the superior "Aryan" race and that Jews, blacks, and others were innately inferior. Notions of racial superiority were also used by the Japanese to justify expansionism during World War II.

Despite a 30 percent decline in the racial gap in IQ scores in the previous two decades, scientific racism resurfaced in 1994 with the publication of *The Bell Curve*, which sought to revive the belief that race is genetically linked to intelligence.

Despite the advocacy of scientific racism in Europe, America, and elsewhere for more than a hundred years (Gobineau, 1915; Grant, 1916; Stoddard, 1920; Hitler, 1940), careful scientific analysis does not support the notion of innate biological, intellectual, cultural, temperamental, or moral superiority of any racial or ethnic group over another (UNESCO, 1950, 1952; Montagu, 1963, 1964).[2] Recently, scientific racism resurfaced in the form of a book titled *The Bell Curve* (Herrnstein and Murray, 1994), which attempted to revive the argument that race is genetically linked to intelligence. The book received considerable public acclaim but was rejected by most sociologists in the fields of stratification, education, and race and ethnic relations and officially criticized by the American Psychological Association. Although this book is discussed in more detail in Chapter 12, it is important to note here that it made a number of errors that overstated the genetic influence on intelligence (H. F. Taylor, 1995; see also Jencks and Phillips, 1998) and that its argument was undermined by a 30 percent decline in racial differences in intelligence scores in the two decades before it was published—hardly what one would expect if such tests measured innate differences (Hauser, 1995). What is significant, though, is that the attention and public acclaim the book received when first published indicate the continued popularity in some circles of the idea that some groups could be innately superior to others.

In discussions of scientific racism, it is also significant that science has discredited not only the notion of racial superiority but also—as noted earlier—the concept that races can even be defined on a purely biological basis. Therefore, ideological racism is best understood as a means by which members of dominant groups attempt to make acceptable their domination of other groups. Unfortunately, the stamp of science has often been used to legitimize such ideological racism.

---

[2]It is true that average scores on particular tests designed to measure intelligence and achievement vary from group to group. As we shall see in Chapter 12, however, these differences are best explained by the testing process and by cultural variations between groups, rendering any one test useless as a measure for all groups.

Obviously, ideological racism is in many regards similar to some types of racial prejudice. The difference is that ideological racism has become institutionalized (in other words, it has become a widely accepted element of a culture) or it is used to justify behavior whereby one group dominates or exploits another. Prejudice, on the other hand, can exist in the absence of both of these conditions.

**Individual Discrimination.** When we talk about discrimination, we are referring to behavior, not beliefs or attitudes. **Individual racial discrimination** can be defined as any behavior by an individual that leads to unequal treatment because of race or ethnicity. Examples could include a homeowner refusing to sell his or her house to a Jew, a taxi driver refusing to pick up African Americans, or an employer paying lower wages to Chicanos than to Anglos for comparable work. The important distinction here is what people actually do—their behavior—rather than what they think. The two are not always the same. Again, of course, similar types of discrimination occur not only on the basis of race but also on the basis of sex, religion, sexual orientation, disability, and other social characteristics.

**Institutional Discrimination.** Carmichael and Hamilton (1967) pointed out that not all, and perhaps not even most, discrimination is perpetrated by individuals. Our basic **social institutions**—well-established structures such as the family, the state, the educational system, the economic system, and religion, which perform basic functions in our society—play a critical role in the creation and perpetuation of racial inequality. Accordingly, we can define **institutional racism** or **institutional discrimination** as arrangements or practices in social institutions and their related organizations that tend to favor one racial or ethnic group (usually the majority group) over another. Institutional racism sometimes is conscious and deliberate, as in the legally required school segregation that existed in southern states before the Supreme Court ruled it unconstitutional in 1954.

Sometimes, however, institutional racism develops without any conscious racist intent; nonetheless, such practices tend to place or keep minority groups in a subordinate position. An example can be seen in today's high costs of college tuition. The cost of college is one reason that African Americans and Hispanic Americans remain half as likely or less to become college graduates as whites. College tuition is the product of a political decision that students should pay a significant part of the cost of a college education. It has not always been this way: At one time, California's public colleges were tuition-free, and high school—which early in the twentieth century was sufficient for most good jobs—has always been free. But today, students are expected to pay much of the cost of college, and polls show that most Americans approve of this (Selingo, 2003). Although not racial in intent, this practice has more of an impact on African Americans and Hispanics because of their lower average incomes. This may not be the result of any intent to discriminate, and tuition costs keep many whites from attending college as well. However, the results of this policy *are* discriminatory because a higher proportion of African Americans and Hispanics than of Anglos (non-Hispanic whites) are kept out of college by its high cost.

Financial aid only partially offsets this practice. Even among college students from families with incomes below $20,000, 30 percent received no federal aid in the 1999–2000 school year, and the majority got no state or institutional aid (Chronicle of Higher Education, 2003a). For those in the $20,000 to $39,999 category, almost half got no federal aid, and most got no other aid. In addition, even for those who do get aid, in most cases it covers only part of the cost of education, and a growing share has come in the form of loans, which bring long-term indebtedness. Thus, the financial barriers to college attendance are very real, and financial hardship affects a higher proportion of African American, Hispanic, and American Indian students than of white students, although many of the latter are also kept out of college by its high and rising cost.

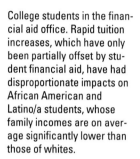

College students in the financial aid office. Rapid tuition increases, which have only been partially offset by student financial aid, have had disproportionate impacts on African American and Latino/a students, whose family incomes are on average significantly lower than those of whites.

Sometimes, such unconscious institutional discrimination operates by perpetuating the effects of past, more deliberate discrimination. Minorities today have low incomes partly because of past discrimination. The cost of college thus often deprives them of education, which in turn deprives them of access to good jobs. Thus, inequality resulting from past discrimination is perpetuated.

Institutional racism, including that which is not necessarily conscious or deliberate, plays a critical role in the continuing pattern of racial and ethnic inequality in the United States. Every available measure shows significant reductions in prejudice in general and in the belief in racist ideologies in particular over the past fifty years in the United States. Deliberate racial discrimination in virtually every form has been illegal for years, although it is clear that it does still occur. Yet, as indicated at the beginning of the chapter and despite laws forbidding deliberate discrimination, racial inequality continues in America today. In fact, for many people of color, the social and economic situation is getting worse. In my judgment, the explanation for this is to be found largely in our social institutions and related organizations. Indeed, there is strong evidence that institutional discrimination continues to be systemic in all of our major social institutions (Feagin, 2000). Thus, our concern in this book cannot focus exclusively on prejudice, racist ideology, or deliberate instances of individual discrimination. We must also examine our political, economic, educational, and other institutions to identify ways in which they unconsciously perpetuate racial inequality. Without such analysis, the problem of racial inequality in America today can be neither understood nor effectively attacked.

## Summary and Conclusion

In this chapter, we have examined some of the reasons for studying race relations in contemporary America and discussed some of the ways this book approaches the study of majority-minority relations. We have also defined some of the basic terms that will be encountered throughout the book. Your understanding of these terms is critical, both because they are used throughout the book and because you must understand their meaning if you are to understand the principles of intergroup relations presented later. As you proceed, you will encounter additional definitions related to each topic. However, the concepts in this chapter are crucial to your understanding of almost all topics in the book. The key terms that appear in boldface in each chapter are defined in the Glossary, which is provided at the end of the book.

In the next two chapters, we are concerned primarily with the first of the four kinds of racism: racial or ethnic prejudice. We shall try to identify what causes prejudice, what can be done about it, and how it is related to the problem of racial and ethnic discrimination.

## *Critical Review Questions*

1. What does it mean to say that race is a socially constructed concept?

2. What is the difference between a race and an ethnic group, and what do the two concepts have in common?

3. Create two lists—one of groups that fit the sociological definition of a *majority group* and one of groups that fit the sociological definition of a *minority group.* Explain briefly why each group belongs on the list where you placed it.

4. What is institutional racism and why is it important?

# Overview

## ► WHAT IS PREJUDICE?

One of the first things most people think of when they think about race and ethnic relations is prejudice. We are all familiar with the concept of prejudice, and we have all seen numerous examples of it, both in people we know and in examples from the popular media. At the most basic level, the term *prejudice* means just what it suggests: attitudes and beliefs involving a tendency to prejudge people, usually negatively and usually on the basis of a single personal characteristic (e.g., race, sex, religion, or hair length), without any objective basis for making such a judgment. This prejudgment takes the form of *overcategorization*: the tendency to think of or react to everyone in some category (say, black, Chinese, female, or gay) in a more or less fixed way, based on the category. Prejudice differs from objective observations about average differences between categories. For example, it would not be prejudice to state that Mexican Americans have a higher rate of unemployment than Anglos. However, it would be prejudice to assume that because a person is Mexican American he or she is unemployed. Such overcategorization can take several forms, and thus there are several types of prejudice, not all of which are found in the same people. The objectives of this chapter are to investigate those different types of prejudice, illustrate some of the ways in which they differ, and try to find at least some tentative answers to the ever-present question, Why are people prejudiced?

## ► FORMS OF PREJUDICE

As described in Chapter 1, prejudice is basically in the mind: The term refers not to behavior but rather to beliefs and attitudes, to what people think. What people think can be divided into at least three dimensions: what they believe is true (*cognitive*), what they like or dislike (*affective*), and how they are inclined to behave (*conative*). This suggests three types of prejudice, each slightly different from the others. Prejudice toward a group may take the form of negative beliefs concerning what is true about a group (cognitive prejudice), dislike of a group (affective prejudice), or the wish to discriminate against or show aggression toward a group (conative prejudice) (B. M. Kramer, 1949; Triandis, 1971). Although the three are related, it is quite possible for a person to be prejudiced in one way without being prejudiced in the others (Stangor, Sullivan, and Ford, 1991; Esses, Haddock, and Zanna, 1992; C. Williams, 1992; Dovidio et al., 1996). For example, a person might believe that most members of a particular race lack intelligence yet feel no dislike toward them and have no desire to discriminate. Or someone might favor discrimination against a particular ethnic group because he or she is in intense competition with some of its members (for scarce jobs, for example) without believing that they are stupid, clannish, greedy, immoral, or anything else bad. The distinction between these types of prejudice can be important because sometimes it is possible to reduce one type without having much effect on another. For example, we might correct a white person's incorrect beliefs about African Americans without reducing his or her dislike for them. Moreover, recent research indicates that such affective prejudices may have stronger effects on people's overall racial attitudes than cognitive prejudices (Stangor, Sullivan, and Ford, 1991). The common factor in each type of prejudice is that the beliefs, attitudes, or tendencies toward discrimination are overcategorized: They are applied to the group as a whole, without recognition of wide variations that exist in individuals in any group (Allport, 1954, Chap. 1).

## ▶ STEREOTYPES

Of special interest to those who study race relations is the form of cognitive prejudice called stereotyping. Various definitions are possible, but Allport's (1954) will do quite well: A **stereotype** is an exaggerated belief associated with a category (a group of people, such as a racial, ethnic, or religious group). This short definition implies several important characteristics. First, it refers to *exaggerated* beliefs. Occasionally, groups are stereotyped in ways that bear absolutely no resemblance to reality. Often, though, there are real cultural differences between racial and ethnic groups, and some stereotypes do contain, as Allport puts it, a "kernel of truth." For example, it is true that African Americans are more likely to support liberal political candidates than are white Americans. However, that does not justify the stereotype that all blacks are liberals; many are not. The difference between a stereotype and a legitimate observation about group differences is that the latter allows for the wide variation in cultural traits that occurs from one individual to another in any group; the former does not.

A second characteristic of a stereotype is that, like other forms of prejudice, it is associated with a *category* of people: blacks, whites, Jews, Americans, Germans, homosexuals, or whatever. The stereotyped thinker tends to categorize people, assuming that they have whatever characteristic he or she associates with the category. For example, if John believes that Jewish people are money-hungry (a common stereotype among people prejudiced against Jews), he will tend, without thinking about it, to assume that any Jewish person he encounters is money-hungry. In other words, he has come to more or less automatically associate the characteristic "money-hungry" with the category "Jew."

Not all stereotypes are negative or derogatory. Often, we form positive or complimentary stereotypes of our own group (what social psychologists call an **in-group**) and negative or derogatory stereotypes of groups of which we are not a member and that are different from our own (**out-groups**). This practice is illustrated by surveys of U.S. college students in the 1930s and 1950s (Katz and Braly, 1933; Gilbert 1951), in which students chose highly positive adjectives to describe "Americans" but much less positive and often negative terms to describe "Chinese," "Jews," "Negroes," and "Turks." (However, more recent studies have shown drastic changes in these stereotyping patterns, which will be discussed in a later chapter.) It is also true that the identical trait may be given positive connotations for an in-group but negative connotations for an out-group. A widely used example suggested by Merton (1949, pp. 426–30) highlights the characteristics admired in Abraham Lincoln: thrift, ambition, and hard work. Stereotyped thinkers often see these same characteristics in Jews, for example, or Asian Americans. However, in these out-groups, the characteristics are seen not as admirable traits but as greed and stinginess, pushiness, and excessive competitiveness. In other words, the same stereotypes that make Abraham Lincoln admirable are labeled to make Jewish or Asian Americans objects of disdain. More recent reseach has confirmed these tendencies. Maass et al. (1989) have shown that people generalize positive traits to in-group members and negative traits to out-group members more quickly than the other way around.

In some cases, stereotypes of minority groups are positive. For example, blacks are often stereotyped by whites as being "musical" or "good dancers." Such stereotypes are mixed blessings at best. First, they rationalize the more common negative stereotypes and make the prejudiced person appear a bit more "reasonable." For example, sports sociologist Harry Edwards (1994) has pointed out that the stereotype that blacks are superior athletes goes hand in hand with the stereotype that they are not as good as other groups in intellectual endeavors. Second, they deny individuals in the group the freedom to be what they are, demanding instead that they live up to the stereotypical expectation. This was graphically illustrated in the television epic *Roots, Part II*, in which a black college president was made to tap dance to please a group of white donors.

Positive stereotypes can also channel minorities away from other areas of activity in which they could excel. For example, the false belief among many young African Americans that sports is the best route to success leads to the pursuit of sports careers that only a tiny percentage will attain while creating a "brain drain" that takes young blacks away from careers in such areas as medicine, law, economics, science, and business (Edwards, 1994). Thus, what many might view as a positive stereotype of African Americans may contribute to economic and professional underdevelopment in the black community.

## ▶ CAUSES OF PREJUDICE

It has been suggested that people form prejudices because they observe characteristics they do not like in members of groups against whom they are prejudiced. If this were true, a researcher who wanted to find out why people are prejudiced against, for example, Turks, might study Turks rather than the people who are prejudiced against them. There are several problems with this line of reasoning. Although it is undoubtedly true that individual encounters shape many people's thinking about out-groups, prejudice involves *unfounded generalizations* about groups and does not allow for individual variations. Many people may have had unpleasant experiences with individual members of out-groups, but only some of those individuals respond with the irrational generalizations that we call prejudice. Moreover, in a fascinating study by Hartley (1946), respondents were asked about their attitudes concerning a variety of ethnic groups, including "Danireans," "Piraneans," and "Wallonians." The study found that people who were antagonistic toward blacks and Jews were also antagonistic toward these other three groups, sometimes even advocating that restrictive measures be taken against them. The catch is that none of the three groups exists! In other words, people who are prejudiced against real groups are also quite capable of being prejudiced against nonexistent groups. This suggests very strongly that the causes of prejudice must be sought in the characteristics and experiences of those who are prejudiced, not in the characteristics of those they are prejudiced against.

In our discussion of causes of prejudice, we shall focus on three general kinds of theories. One views prejudice primarily as a means of meeting the personality needs of individuals with certain kinds of experiences. A second approach views prejudice as an attitude learned from others and that develops largely out of the need to conform to group pressures. A third approach sees the source of prejudice primarily in a person's position in the larger social structure (one's economic position, for example). In the remainder of this chapter, we shall discuss and evaluate each of these approaches.

## ▶ THEORIES ABOUT PERSONALITY AND PREJUDICE

One of the most influential studies ever done on prejudice was published in 1950 in a book by Theodor Adorno and associates titled *The Authoritarian Personality*. This book, which today remains a basic study in the understanding of prejudice, made the fundamental argument that people are prejudiced because their prejudices meet certain personality needs. The questions these researchers sought to answer were, Is a particular personality type associated with prejudice? If so, how is such a personality acquired?

### Is Prejudice Generalized?

Adorno and his associates (1950) began with the assumption that if there is a prejudiced personality type, it ought to be possible to show that a person prejudiced against one out-group is likely to be prejudiced against out-groups in general. In other words, if being prejudiced is a personality characteristic, as the researchers thought, we would expect that a person with this personality characteristic would be prejudiced not just against one particular out-group but against people or groups in general who are culturally or ethnically different. To test this assumption, they developed questionnaires designed to measure two forms of prejudice. One measured **anti-Semitism**, which refers to prejudice against Jews.[1] The other measured a somewhat more complex and generalized form of prejudice called ethnocentrism. **Ethnocentrism** is a tendency to view one's own group as the norm and other groups not only as different but also as strange and, usually, inferior. Thus, one's own ways of doing things are seen as the normal, natural way of doing things, a standard against which the ways of other groups are to be judged. (The concept of ethnocentrism is extremely important in the study of majority-minority relations and is widely used throughout this book.)

Both questionnaires consisted of sets of statements to which respondents could choose one of six responses, ranging from strong agreement to strong disagreement. There was no "neutral" choice. The anti-Semitism (AS) scale included such items as the following:

- "One trouble with Jewish businessmen is that they stick together and connive so that a Gentile doesn't have a fair chance in competition."
- "I can hardly imagine myself marrying a Jew."
- "No matter how Americanized a Jew may seem to be, there is always something different and strange, something basically Jewish underneath."
- "The trouble with letting Jews into a nice neighborhood is that they gradually give it a typical Jewish atmosphere."

The last item suggests the sometimes subtle nature of prejudice. Certainly it does not indicate a fierce hatred of Jewish people or a malicious intent to do harm. Nonetheless, it does reflect some deep-seated prejudices. The phrase *letting into*, for example, suggests that Gentiles are or should be in a position of greater power and also suggests a belief that Jews have a certain "pushiness" or intrusiveness. The term

---

[1]Actually, the term *Semitic* properly refers to a variety of people of eastern Mediterranean stock, including both Jews and Arabs, but in common usage *anti-Semitism* has come to refer to prejudice against Jews.

*nice neighborhood* suggests that the neighborhood might become otherwise if Jewish people move in, and the word *typical* indicates stereotyped thinking.

In the ethnocentrism (E) scale, items are of a similar nature, but they are designed to measure both the in-group's feelings of superiority and its distrust of out-groups, traits that characterize enthocentrism:

- "Negroes have their rights, but it is best to keep them in their own districts and schools and to avoid too much contact with whites."

- "Certain religious sects who refuse to salute the flag should be forced to conform to such a patriotic action or else be abolished."

- "America may not be perfect, but the American Way has brought us about as close as human beings can get to a perfect society."

If prejudice is a generalized attitude, as Adorno believed, then a person prejudiced against Jews would also be prejudiced against African Americans, Mexican Americans, immigrants, and so on. If this were the case, we would expect two things to be true of the AS and E scales. First, the E scale (ethnocentrism) items should be highly correlated with one another; that is, a person agreeing with one of them should tend to agree with most of the rest of them. Second, we would expect that people scoring high on the AS scale would tend to score high on the E scale and that people scoring low on one would tend to score low on the other. It turns out that both of these things were true. In fact, a high correlation (.80) between E scale and AS scale scores was obtained.[2] This finding (along with similar findings) supports the view that prejudice is largely a personal characteristic of the prejudiced person that is directed at a variety of out-groups rather than an attitude resulting from a person's particular experiences with one specific group. If a person is prejudiced against one group, she or he is likely to be prejudiced to some degree against a number of groups. Although Adorno's research was done more than fifty years ago, today's studies continue to show the same pattern. For example, recent studies have shown that prejudices against homosexuals and against people with AIDS are correlated with racial prejudice, anti-Semitism, and sexism (Ficarrotto, 1990; Larsen, Ommundsen, and Elder, 1991; Haslam, Rothschild, and Ernst, 2002; Laythe, Finkel, and Kirkpatrick, 2002). In addition, recent surveys have continued to show a very strong correlation between stereotyping of African Americans and stereotyping of Jews (Sniderman and Piazza, 1993, pp. 51–56).

Adorno and his colleagues (1950) also developed a measure of political and economic conservatism to see whether prejudice might simply be an indication of conservatism. They found that it was not. Conservative people did tend to be somewhat more prejudiced, but it was far from a perfect relationship: Some conservatives were not at all prejudiced, whereas some liberals were quite prejudiced. More recent research findings support the view that conservatism and prejudice are clearly two different things (Sniderman et al., 1991; Sniderman and Piazza, 1993).

## The Authoritarian Personality

At this point, Adorno and his colleagues (1950) were ready to test their theory that prejudice is produced by some particular personality pattern or type. They were able to identify certain themes that appeared with some regularity in the speeches and writings of fascists and anti-Semitic agitators, and they hypothesized that these themes might indicate the characteristics of a prejudiced or authoritarian personality type. A questionnaire similar to the E and AS scales was developed to test for and

---

[2]A correlation, or correlation coefficient, is a statistical measure of the strength and direction of a relationship between any two variables that can be expressed as numbers. It can range from +1.0 (perfect positive relationship) through 0 (no relationship) to −1.0 (perfect negative relationship). Because many studies in the social sciences base their findings on correlations as weak as .20 to .40, a correlation of .80 is considered a very strong positive relationship.

measure this personality type. This questionnaire was called the F scale (for "potential for fascism") but has become commonly known as the authoritarianism scale (R. Brown, 1965). The researchers called this personality type the *authoritarian personality* because they felt that people with it would be likely to support authoritarian political movements espousing prejudice, such as the Nazis in Germany, whom Adorno had fled to the United States to escape. The basic characteristics associated with the authoritarian personality and some of the F scale items used to measure them follow:

1. *Conventionalism:* Rigid adherence to conventional values
   a. "Obedience and respect for authority are the most important virtues children should learn."
   b. "A person who has bad manners, habits, and breeding can hardly expect to get along with decent people."
   c. "The businessman and the manufacturer are much more important to society than the artist and the professor."
2. *Authoritarian submission:* Uncritical acceptance of authority
   a. "Every person should have complete faith in some supernatural power whose decisions he obeys without question."
   b. "Young people sometimes get rebellious ideas, but as they grow up, they ought to get over them and settle down."
3. *Authoritarian aggression:* Aggressiveness toward people who do not conform to authority or conventional norms.
   a. "An insult to our honor should always be punished."
   b. "There is hardly anything lower than a person who does not feel a great love, gratitude, and respect for his parents."
4. *Anti-introspection:* Opposition to the subjective or imaginative; rejection of self-analysis
   a. "When a person has a problem or worry, it is best for him not to think about it but to keep busy with more cheerful things."
   b. "Nowadays more and more people are prying into matters that should remain personal and private."
5. *Superstition and stereotypical thinking*
   a. "Some people are born with an urge to jump from high places."
   b. "Someday it will probably be shown that astrology can explain a lot of things."
6. *Concern with power and toughness*
   a. "An insult to our honor should always be punished."
   b. "People can be divided into two distinct classes: the weak and the strong."
7. *Destructiveness and cynicism*
   a. "Human nature being what it is, there will always be war and conflict."
   b. "Familiarity breeds contempt."
8. "*Projectivity:* Projection outward of unconscious emotions; belief that the world is a wild and dangerous place
   a. "Nowadays when so many different kinds of people move around and mix together so much, a person has to protect himself especially carefully against catching an infection or disease from them."
   b. "Most people don't realize how much our lives are controlled by plots hatched in secret places."
9. *Exaggerated concern with sexual "goings-on"*
   a. "Sex crimes, such as rape and attacks on children, deserve more than imprisonment; such criminals ought to be publicly whipped or worse."

b. "The wild sex life of the old Greeks and Romans was tame compared with some of the goings-on in this country, even in places where people might least expect it."

Unlike the AS scale, which measured attitudes toward Jews, and the E scale, which measured attitudes toward out-groups in general, the F scale does not attempt to measure any one type of attitude. Rather, it measures a set of attitudes and beliefs that do not necessarily follow logically from one another (one does not logically have to be superstitious to be submissive to authority) but nonetheless are believed to occur together in the same people. This is what makes the F scale a *personality* measure, which the others are not: Only the F scale measures a set of logically diverse or unrelated attitudes and beliefs that are nonetheless found together in the same people. Adorno and his colleagues (1950) were able to show that the F scale was indeed a valid measure of personality: The various attitudes and beliefs measured by the scale did tend to occur together as they expected. Specifically, they were able to show that if a person agreed with one of the items, he or she was likely to agree with most of the rest. Furthermore, Adorno found that people who scored high on the F scale were substantially more likely than others to be prejudiced: High F scale scores were strongly associated with high AS scale (anti-Semitism) and E scale (ethnocentrism) scores. Accordingly, Adorno had established significant evidence supporting the following generalizations:

- Prejudice is an attitude or set of attitudes that tends to be generalized to a wide variety of out-groups rather than a specific attitudinal response based on experiences with members of a particular out-group.

- There is a personality type (he called it the authoritarian personality) that tends to be associated with prejudice.

## Explaining Prejudice: Scapegoating and Projection

It should be noted here that Adorno is not without his critics, and some of the major criticisms will be discussed as we look at other theories about the causes of prejudice. Nonetheless, it appears that he was able to mount substantial, if not conclusive, evidence in support of the preceding generalizations. If we were to stop here, however, something would be missing. Although it may be interesting (and perhaps self-satisfying to the unprejudiced person, if such exists) to know that prejudice is associated with a personality type, it leaves unanswered the basic question of how that personality type comes into being. Probably the most useful—and most controversial—part of Adorno's (1950) work addresses this question. His theories illustrate two of the most widely analyzed processes that lead to prejudice: scapegoating, or *displaced aggression*, and *projection*.

**Scapegoating**, or **displaced aggression** (the terms are used almost interchangeably), is a tendency to take out feelings of frustration and aggression on someone other than their true source. Often, this someone is an out-group or a relatively powerless minority group. The process of projection is related but somewhat different. **Projection** is a process in which one minimizes, avoids, or denies undesirable characteristics in oneself by exaggerating those same characteristics in others. Again, these others often are members of cultural or ethnic groups other than one's own.

Adorno was associated with a school of thought called *critical theory*, which applied the theories of Sigmund Freud to issues of societal inequality, such as racism. Like Freud, Adorno felt that adult personalities largely reflect childhood experiences. A major principle of Freudian theory is that people are born with strong innate needs or drives, such as aggressiveness and sexuality. Freud felt that if these drives are too severely repressed in childhood, frustrations result that remain throughout life and are reflected in adult personality problems (see Freud,

[1930] 1962). Adorno (1950) argued that such frustrations produced authoritarian personalities, leading to unusually strong personality needs for scapegoating and projection.

## The Development of Prejudiced Personalities

Using Freud's theory as a starting point, Adorno (1950) explored the childhood experiences and personalities of highly prejudiced and less prejudiced subjects through open-ended questions and projective methods. The latter included the Thematic Apperception Test (TAT), in which subjects were shown pictures and asked to tell stories about them and answered questions such as "We all have times when we feel below par. What moods or feelings are most unpleasant or disturbing to you?" This part of Adorno's study revealed a number of additional findings that are useful in explaining how people may develop a personality type that predisposes them toward prejudice. Among these findings are the following:

- Prejudiced subjects were generally unwilling to acknowledge faults in themselves, whereas unprejudiced subjects tended to be more objective in self-evaluation, seeing both good and bad in themselves.

- Perhaps to an even greater degree, prejudiced subjects tended to idealize their parents, apparently unable to view their parents critically; unprejudiced subjects, in contrast, tended to be able to talk about both desirable and undesirable characteristics in their parents.

- When prejudiced subjects did say something that might appear critical of themselves or their parents, they tended to quickly qualify it or explain it away. In themselves, they tended to view negative qualities as coming from some external force, making statements such as "I let my carnal self get away from me," "It's the Latin in me," or "I got that from the other side of the family." When they criticized their parents, they tended to withdraw or qualify the criticism quickly: "He forced some decisions on me," followed quickly by, "but he allowed me to do as I pleased."

- On the other hand, prejudiced subjects were very likely to find faults in out-groups. Their references, for example, to "oversexed Negroes" and "pushy Jews" showed up in this open-ended part of the research, as well as on the fixed-response questionnaires discussed earlier.

These four findings strongly support the notion that projection is an important process in the thinking of prejudiced people. They downplay faults in themselves and those close to them by exaggerating the same characteristics in others, particularly in others who are culturally, racially, ethnically, or religiously different. Indeed, a wide variety of research (for a thorough review, see Ehrlich, 1973) shows that people who are insecure about their own qualities or are inwardly lacking in self-esteem are the people who are most often prejudiced. It is among such people that the need for projection is likely to be greatest, particularly if they are unable to accept the negative aspects of their personalities. The relationship between feelings of insecurity and prejudice has been documented not only in the United States but in other countries as well (Sharma and Zafar, 1989).

Two other findings from the subjective part of Adorno's (1950) research cast additional light on the dynamics of prejudice. First, the responses to open-ended and projective questions indicate that the prejudiced subjects were highly concerned about status. They had a need to rank people and had learned at an early age to be very concerned about their own status. They often talked about the importance of never doing anything that would reflect negatively on their family. Second, Adorno noticed that nearly all the prejudiced subjects came from very strict homes. As children, they had been severely punished and taught to obey without arguing or asking why.

With these findings, Adorno and his colleagues (1950) felt that they had identified the process by which prejudiced people develop personality needs for projection and scapegoating. The process can be sketched as follows:

1. Very strict child-rearing practices generate feelings of frustration and aggression. This occurs because of the severity of the punishment and the highly restrictive rules characteristic of very strict families.

2. At the same time, children are taught strong norms (rules) about respecting authority. They are also taught to believe in the justness and legitimacy of society's ranking systems. Eventually, they come to internalize (accept in their own minds) these norms and beliefs.

3. These conditions create a situation in which frustration and aggression build up but cannot be released against the authority figures who are the source of the strict rules and severe punishment.

4. As a consequence, a process of displacement, or scapegoating, occurs: The aggression is taken out against those who are low in the person's ranking system (racial, ethnic, or religious minorities or other out-groups).

5. Because of the concern with ranking and the learned need to avoid bringing shame on themselves or their families, people minimize or deny faults in the self by exaggerating those faults in out-groups (the process of projection). This projection is especially noticeable in the areas of sexual behavior and aggression.

## Evaluation of the Personality Theory of Prejudice

Certainly, Adorno's (1950) authoritarian personality study has been subjected to criticism, both of the methods used and the underlying theories on which they are based. For example, the study's methods have been criticized because, on three of the four scales, the prejudiced or authoritarian response was always to agree with the statements presented. Some people, commonly known as "yeasayers," will agree with almost any statement with which they are presented (Cronbach, 1946; Babbie, 2004). Thus, the scales to some degree probably measured yeasaying rather than prejudice or authoritarianism (T. S. Cohn, 1953; but cf. Ray, 1980). A common substantive criticism is that the theory deals only with right-wing or fascist authoritarianism, although it may be true that those on the left—liberals and radicals—can be rigid and authoritarian, too. This has sparked sociological and psychological debate over whether there are authoritarians of the left as well as of the right (for detailed discussions of these and other criticisms, see R. Brown, 1965, pp. 509–44; Kirscht and Dillehay, 1967; Simpson and Yinger, 1985, pp. 78–88).

Despite these criticisms, few social scientists would deny that prejudice meets basic personality needs in some people. It is also widely agreed that displacement, or scapegoating, and projection are important processes that lead to prejudice (see Allport, 1954, Chaps. 21 and 24; Simpson and Yinger, 1985, pp. 73–78). Research has continued to show that authoritarian, restrictive child rearing often causes children to be more prejudiced when they grow up (Hassan, 1987; Hassan and Khalique, 1987). A need to see the world in oversimplified terms has also been clearly linked to prejudice (Hamilton, 1981), as has been a need to deny one's own shortcomings (Fishbein, 1996, pp. 250–51).

Debate continues on the precise means by which people develop authoritarian personality patterns and how such patterns contribute to prejudice. Numerous studies in a wide variety of countries and time periods have linked authoritarianism with prejudice and have shown that this linkage holds for a number of different types of prejudice, including racial prejudice (Morris and Heaven, 1986; Heaven and Furnham, 1987; Ray, 1988; Laythe, Finkel, and Kirkpatrick, 2001), prejudice

Overly strict child rearing may be an important cause of prejudiced personalities because it often leads to a tendency to displace aggression. Minority groups often become scapegoats toward whom such displaced aggression is expressed.

against people with AIDS (Witt, 1989; Cunningham et al., 1991), sexism (Rigby, 1988), opposition to immigrants (Quinton, Cowan, and Watson, 1996), hostility toward people with disabilities (Jabin, 1987), anti-Arab prejudice (S. D. Johnson, 1992), antigay prejudice (Laythe, Finkel, and Kirkpatrick, 2001), and even hostility toward out-groups created briefly in an experiment (Downing and Monaco, 1986). Recent studies have shown strong correlations between authoritarian attitudes and prejudice in South Africa (Duckitt, 1993a, 1994a, 1994b; Schlachter and Duckitt, 2002), Russia (Stephan et al., 1994), the United States (Sniderman and Piazza, 1993; Raden, 1994; Stephan et al., 1994; Quinton, Cowan, and Watson, 1996; Laythe, Finkel, and Kirkpatrick, 2001), Great Britain (Billig and Cramer, 1990), and Canada (Zanna, 1994). Finally, authoritarian attitudes have been linked to both open and subtle prejudice, as well as to racist behavior (Duckitt, 1994a; Raden, 1994) and to stereotyped attitudes toward minorities and toward positions taken on government policies toward minorities (Sniderman and Piazza, 1993, pp. 60–65; Kluegel and Bobo, 1991). Thus, fifty years after the original authoritarian personality studies, evidence of a correlation between authoritarianism and prejudice is stronger than ever.

The major debate today concerns the relative importance of personality needs compared with other causes of prejudice. One example can be found in the observation that people who feel insecure about their status are more likely to be prejudiced. Although this can be readily interpreted as evidence that personality problems lead to prejudice, there are other explanations as well. It could be argued that people who feel insecure about their status often *are* in less secure social and economic positions and that they believe (perhaps with some justification) that any gains by minority groups are likely to come at their expense rather than at the expense of those who are better off. Indeed, people who are in marginal economic positions do tend to be more prejudiced.

It is also hard for personality theory to account for sudden upsurges of prejudice, such as that of anti-Semitism in Germany before and during World War II. Germany had experienced defeat in World War I, followed by economic depression, certainly a situation conducive to frustration, aggression, and even collective scapegoating. In this case, however, the experiences producing these conditions occurred on a societal, not individual scale. It is reasonable, then, to conclude that some of the patterns observed by Adorno et al. (1950) may be the result of the larger social structure rather than entirely the product of individual personalities. We shall turn now to some of the other possible causes of prejudice.

## ▶ SOCIAL LEARNING AND CONFORMITY AS CAUSES OF PREJUDICE

Rather than focus on the personality needs of the individual, social scientists who study *social learning* and *conformity* as causes of prejudice usually look at the social environment. They believe that an environment in which prejudice is the norm tends to produce prejudiced individuals, even if those individuals have no particular personality need to be prejudiced.

One way this occurs is through the childhood socialization process. In a variety of ways, agents of socialization—parents, peers, schools, the media—transmit their values and behavior patterns to the child. One of the most important transmission processes is that of selective exposure and modeling. In this process, children are exposed to certain kinds of values and behaviors but not to others. Sometimes this reflects a deliberate effort on the part of parents, who are seeking to "protect" or shelter their children. However, such exposure often is unintentional, reflecting homogeneity among peer groups, parents, and other agents of socialization. When a child is exposed over a long period of time to one set of values or one way of doing things, he or she is likely to eventually view it as the natural way or the only way. This is particularly true when the models (those from whom the values or behaviors are learned) are people with whom the child feels a close identification, such as parents or close friends (Allport, 1954; Bandura and Walters, 1963). Young children often see their parents—their main source of assistance and support—as all-knowing and all-powerful. Thus, the parents' prejudices are taken as truth by the children, often with very little thought or awareness that they have been taught to be prejudiced (Allport, 1954, Chap. 17; Bergen, 2001). Peers, too, are important. Recent research by Van Ausdale and Feagin (2001) shows that children learn racial prejudices from their peers even at preschool ages. Although such prejudices originate with adults, they are often passed from one child to another through interactions in day care, neighborhood play settings, and school. As they wrote (p. 21), "Most of the young white children in our study are helping to build, or rebuild, a racialized society with their own hands with materials learned from the racial order of the adult world surrounding them."

In addition to these effects of selective exposure and modeling, patterns of reward and punishment also play a role in social learning, including learning of prejudice. All agents of socialization reward behavior and attitudes that conform to their norms, and punish those that do not. As with selective exposure, these patterns of reward and punishment are sometimes very deliberate and planned but at other times very informal and impromptu. Among peer groups, it may be as simple as mild derision, or "kidding," when nonconforming views are expressed. Thus, the message gets across: Conform and you will be rewarded; dissent and you will be punished. Research on the moral and cognitive development of children shows that whereas children may initially conform merely to get rewards or avoid punishment, they will eventually internalize (come to accept as their own) the conforming beliefs, values, and norms about behavior (Piaget, [1932] 1965; Kohlberg, 1969).

Prejudice can be seen as just one of many kinds of beliefs and attitudes that are learned through such socialization processes as selective exposure, modeling, reward and punishment, and internalization. This suggests that one source of prejudice is a prejudiced environment: families, peer groups, schools, and other places where prejudice is the norm. Children growing up in such environments are likely to express prejudice (see Blake and Dennis, 1943; Allport, 1954; Richert, 1974; Mielenz, 1979; Hassan and Khalique, 1987; Garcia-Coll and Vazquez-Garcia, 1995). One recent study suggests that there is a correlation between children's *perceptions* about the beliefs of their parents and peers and their own racial attitudes, even in cases in which the actual correlation is weak (Aboud and Doyle, 1997). Thus, what children perceive to be the attitudes of significant others may be more important than what the actual attitudes are. Finally, growing up in a society marked by sharp racial inequalities in itself produces racial prejudices and discriminatory behaviors in children. In Van Ausdale and Feagin's (2001) study of preschool children, it became evident that the children were largely trying out patterns of racial inequality that they learned from the racial order of the larger society. A key finding of the study was that children learn and act out these racial inequalities at a much younger age than was previously believed.

To the degree that children internalize prejudiced beliefs and attitudes that they learn from their parents and peers, they may retain these biases in their adult lives. Indeed, numerous studies have shown that people's ethnic attitudes, even in adulthood, are substantially influenced by the attitudes of their parents. (For a review of this literature, see Ehrlich, 1973.) Of course, many other factors in adult life will determine the actual level of prejudice, but it does appear that social learning from parents and other agents of childhood socialization lays a groundwork that significantly predisposes people to being more, or less, prejudiced later on.

Not all social learning and pressure for conformity occur in childhood, however. Indeed, social scientists today recognize that socialization is a lifelong process. Moreover, it seems fair to say that the attitudes prevailing in an adult's present social environment can be at least as important as anything learned in childhood. Put simply, most people are concerned about what others think of them and tend to conform to gain or keep the acceptance of others. The strength of this pressure for conformity has been demonstrated in a famous experiment by Asch (1956) showing that people will give a description contrary to what they can plainly see if the pressure for conformity is strong enough. In Asch's experiment, seven confederates

To children growing up around Ku Klux Klan rallies, racial prejudice will seem to be a normal, everyday fact of life. Through the process of selective exposure, it is quite likely that they will grow up to be very prejudiced adults.

(the researcher's accomplices, who posed as subjects) gave an obviously wrong answer about the relative length of lines shown to research subjects. When the real subjects were asked the answer, about a third of them conformed to the unanimous opinion of the others and agreed with the clearly wrong answer. (In a control group in which no confederate gave a wrong answer, fewer than 1 percent of the subjects gave wrong answers.) This tendency toward conformity has been widely confirmed by other research.

The general principle that attitudes tend to conform to those of *reference others* (other people with whom we have contact, who are meaningful to us, and whose judgments are important to us) has been shown to be true for prejudice as well as for other types of attitudes and beliefs. This can be illustrated in several ways. First, it appears that in settings where strong prejudice is the norm, personality factors are less valid predictors of one's level of prejudice. In the southern United States in the 1950s, for example, the pressure to conform was so strong that the overwhelming majority expressed prejudiced views (see Prothro, 1952). In that setting, one did not have to have an authoritarian personality to score high on a scale measuring antiblack or anti-Semitic attitudes and beliefs (Pettigrew, 1971, Chap. 5). Similarly, authoritarian personality theory was not very useful for explaining racial prejudice among whites in South Africa before the country began to move toward majority rule (Louw-Potgieter, 1988), although more recent studies have found more substantial effects (Duckitt, 1994a, 1994b). Even when prejudices are less blatant, society itself can be a powerful teacher of bias. Hence, to some extent in any society, the racial attitudes most people learn are the dominant attitudes of their society, taught not only by parents and peers but also by schools, mass media, and popular entertainment (Ponterotto, Pedersen, and Vontress, 1993, especially chap. 3; Van Ausdale and Feagin, 2001). In this sense, prejudice and discrimination are top-down phenomena that are taught by the society to the individual (Fishbein, 1996).

The tendency to conform on racial and ethnic issues can be seen in a set of studies in which college students were asked to commit themselves to public actions supporting harmonious race relations. Examples included appearing with a person of the opposite race and sex in a newspaper ad supporting tolerance, participating in a civil rights demonstration, and giving a speech on television advocating tolerance. (For examples of this type of research, see DeFleur and Westie, 1958; Fendrich, 1967; Ewens and Ehrlich, 1969.) These studies found that individual attitudes and beliefs could not completely predict willingness to take such actions. The perceived attitudes of reference others—friends, parents, acquaintances—were a significant factor in such willingness. Taken together, the various studies on conformity and prejudice suggest that ethnic attitudes, beliefs, and predisposition to behave are all shaped by the dominant norms of one's reference others. In other words, they are significantly influenced by pressure for conformity.

This suggests two generalizations about prejudice. First, as we have already observed, people who grow up in social settings in which prejudice is the norm tend to be prejudiced both in childhood and in their adult lives. Second, anyone in an environment in which prejudice is the norm experiences pressure to be prejudiced. Thus, they tend to be more prejudiced than people in other settings. Of course, there are rebels: Some people in prejudiced environments are unprejudiced, and some people in tolerant settings are prejudiced. Social learning and conformity clearly do not totally explain human behavior. Nonetheless, in the absence of some social or psychological force to the contrary, people usually tend to conform.

## Personality Theory Versus Social Learning Theory

It is difficult to evaluate the relative importance of personality needs as opposed to social learning and conformity pressure as causes of prejudice. Some have suggested that social learning offers a simpler explanation for some of the relationships observed in the authoritarian personality studies than the rather complex

Freudian theories suggested by Adorno (1950). If authoritarian people are prejudiced, as Adorno found, and prejudiced people tend to have been raised in authoritarian homes, is it not possible that they simply learned prejudice from their parents? This is an appealing suggestion and probably is true in many cases. The problem with it is that some people who grow up in prejudiced homes retain their prejudices throughout life and others do not. One explanation is that people who have a strong personality need to be prejudiced tend to remain prejudiced even when the social environment is not supportive, whereas people who are prejudiced mainly for reasons of conformity tend more often to change as the environment changes. There is good evidence that many people of both types exist (Pettigrew, 1976, pp. 486–89).

Still, in homes where children are strictly raised and severely punished (which leads to personality types that are prone to prejudice), the parents often tend to be more prejudiced (see Allport, 1954, Chap. 18; Hassan and Khalique, 1987). Thus, both personality dynamics and social learning patterns tend to create prejudice in the same people, and it is often difficult to sort out the influences of the two factors. Despite this difficulty, it does seem clear that prejudice that meets some basic personality needs (such as scapegoating and projection) is more difficult to change than prejudice that is mainly the result of social learning and conformity. The latter often can be unlearned in an unprejudiced environment; the former cannot.

Before moving on, we should point to one further pattern that suggests that neither personality theory nor social learning and conformity theory can give us the whole picture of prejudice. This pattern is easy to understand and quite well known: Various social groups differ drastically in their degree of prejudice toward groups and individuals who differ from them. Such group differences cannot be explained on the basis of individual personality differences, and social learning and conformity do not offer a very good explanation either. They can explain why people within a group tend to hold similar attitudes, but they cannot explain how different groups developed different attitudes and beliefs in the first place. In other words, why is it that some social, cultural, and religious groups tend generally to be open and tolerant toward others, whereas other groups tend to be narrow and intolerant? It appears that the answer must be sought in variations in the collective experiences of the groups, that is, in the larger social structure in which the groups exist. This approach is given greater emphasis in later chapters, but we shall explore one aspect of it in the remainder of this chapter.

## ▶ SOCIOECONOMIC STATUS AND PREJUDICE

One of the fundamental criteria by which people in any society tend to group themselves is socioeconomic status (often abbreviated SES). By *socioeconomic status* we mean one's position in society's ranking system as represented by such criteria as income, educational level, and occupation. It has been shown consistently that some forms of prejudice are strongly related to SES. People in lower SES groups tend to report more negative views toward out-groups, to be more ethnocentric, and to express more stereotyped thinking (see R. Brown, 1965, pp. 518–23; Simpson and Yinger, 1985, pp. 66–70). Some critics of this view have suggested that these findings reflect sophistication more than actual prejudice: Middle- and upper-class participants in present-day social research "know better" than to make strongly or clearly prejudiced statements (Brewer and Kramer, 1985, p. 231). For example, it is true that qualitative interviews reveal subtle forms of prejudice that do not show up in responses to survey questions, where better-educated whites often give "politically correct" responses (Feagin, 2000).

However, there are several reasons to believe that the SES-prejudice relationship cannot be entirely dismissed. Many characteristics known to be related to prejudice are also related to social class, such as authoritarianism and its related dimensions, rigidity of thinking and status concern coupled with insecurity (MacKinnon and Centers, 1956; Lipset, 1959). Furthermore, there are two important ways in which socioeconomic status can logically be expected to influence levels of prejudice. The first is through the direct effects of education on prejudice, and the second concerns the nature of one's economic or social position: how secure it is and whether it involves the perception or reality of competition with other groups.

## Effects of Education

Education is widely seen as a way of breaking down stereotyped, oversimplified thinking. It may directly affect how people think about out-groups, but it may also influence prejudice in other ways. As has been noted earlier, by its very nature prejudice involves oversimplification. Prejudiced people react to others on the basis of one characteristic: race, ethnicity, gender, sexual orientation, disability, religion, or whatever. It is certainly true that if we could know everything there is to know about a person from one or more of these characteristics, our world would be tremendously simplified. Of course, reality is much more complex, but for people who cannot tolerate ambiguity or uncertainty, prejudice becomes a way of simplifying reality (Tajfel, 1981, 1969; Billig, 2002). It is no coincidence that prejudice is correlated with a lack of tolerance for ambiguity and uncertainty, which helps to explain why education might reduce prejudice: As we become more educated, we become better able to understand complex ideas and situations, and our tolerance for complexity and ambiguity increases. On this basis alone, we might expect more educated people to be less prejudiced.

Research strongly suggests that this is the case. People with higher levels of education score lower on most measures of prejudice, although the relationship is not always strong (Allport, 1954; Bagley and Verma, 1979). Recent studies show that this relationship holds for a number of different types of prejudice in the United States

As educational levels increase, people tend to be at least somewhat less prejudiced. One reason may be that with greater education, people have less need to oversimplify through mechanisms such as prejudice.

and in a number of other societies (Morris and Heaven, 1986; Case, Greeley, and Fuchs, 1989; Dyer, Vedlitz, and Worchel, 1989; Bolvin, Donkin, and Darling, 1990; D'Alessio and Stolzenberg, 1991; Gibson and Duch, 1992; S. D. Johnson, 1992).

In recent years, the debate over whether the correlation between education and prejudice is real has intensified. It has been more widely suggested that the correlation may appear because people who are more educated know they are not "supposed to" make prejudiced comments and consequently disguise their prejudices. In other words, the more educated person may give the socially or politically "correct" response, whereas the less educated person will more honestly state his or her prejudice. According to this view, education does not really reduce prejudice; it just makes prejudiced people more sophisticated about expressing it. It has even been argued that education may reinforce prejudices by teaching students the ideologies of dominant groups (Jackman and Muha, 1984; Schaefer, 1996).

Recently, some studies have been designed to get around the problem of masked biases, and these studies still suggest some real effect of education. A study by Sniderman and Piazza (1993) used a series of survey-based experiments to examine this question. White Americans of various levels of education, who identified themselves as either conservative or liberal, were asked whether they thought the government should guarantee equal rights for women and for blacks. The test for subtle racism was whether whites displayed a double standard—that is, whether they were more likely to support equal rights for women (who could be of their own race) than to support equal rights for blacks (who, of course, were not). Overall, the answer was "yes": Both liberals and conservatives showed a double standard, being more supportive of equal rights for women than for blacks. In addition, there was a big education effect. Among people with a college degree, there was no double standard: There was just as much support for equal rights for blacks as for women. But at lower levels of education, the double standard became huge: For both liberals and conservatives with a high school education or less, about 60 percent supported equal rights for women, whereas only 20 percent supported equal rights for blacks. In addition, this relationship with education could not be explained away by income. Regardless of income, the more educated people were, the less likely they were to apply a racial double standard.

Sniderman and Piazza (1993) concluded that the reason for this educational effect is that people with higher levels of education are more comfortable with abstract ideas and can better handle "subtlety and complexity of thought and expression" (pp. 84, 87). In other words, they have less need to engage in the kind of oversimplification that prejudice amounts to. Other recent evidence supports this view. A study of college students found that those who came from more educated families made more use of relative thought than absolute categories in their decision making. Not surprisingly, these students had more positive attitudes toward minorities (Glover, 1994). A national study linked both the level of education and the degree of complexity in thought and communication to racial attitudes: Those with higher levels of education and those who were more complex in their thought and communication tended to be less prejudiced (Case, Greeley, and Fuchs, 1989). This research strongly suggests that at least part of the inverse relationship between education and prejudice is real.

Finally, some interesting research findings indirectly support the notion of an inverse relationship between complexity of thinking and prejudice. People are more likely to rely on stereotypes when they are busy, overwhelmed, or even functioning at a nonoptimal time (for instance, early in the morning for night people) (Bodenhausen, 1990; Pratto and Bargh, 1991; Stangor and Duan, 1991; Olson and Zanna, 1993, p. 143). In all of these situations, people's ability to engage in complex thinking or thoughtful reflection is reduced, so they fall back on stereotypes.

Although education does have some real effect of reducing prejudice, that effect is not unlimited, and there is some support for the idea that educated people hide their prejudices. For example, a study of white college students by Bonilla-Silva and Forman (2000) showed that although 80–90 percent of white students expressed acceptance of interracial marriage on a survey question, many raised objections in qualitative interviews on the same subject. Often, white students said they did not object to intermarriage in principle, but if there were children or if people in the area had prejudices, it would be bad because of the likely consequences. The end result, as Bonilla-Silva (2002) points out, is effective opposition to most interracial marriages. Often, these kinds of responses were accompanied by statements such as, "I'm not prejudiced, but . . . ," "I can see both sides of it," or lots of "uh," "um," "well," "you know," and similar indications of hesitancy, caution, and ambivalence. In fact, Bonilla-Silva found that nearly all of the college students he interviewed displayed a noticeable degree of rhetorical incoherence when speaking about race, indicating their nervousness about the subject and desire to say things in a way that would not make them look bad. Bonilla-Silva sees these as arising from efforts to project an image of color-blindness while in fact harboring prowhite or antiblack viewpoints.

## Economic Insecurity and Prejudice

Prejudice can arise from both the perception of and the reality of insecure status. If people who feel insecure about their status are indeed more prejudiced, we could reasonably expect people of lower SES to be more prejudiced: Their position in life is less secure than that of people who are economically better off. As a result, they may attempt to make themselves feel better about their status by invidious comparisons with minority group members: "I may not be much, but at least I'm better than a lousy [fill in the blank]." Still another explanation for the tendency toward an inverse relationship between SES and prejudice is to be found in the structural position of the lower- or working-class person. As this book shows in detail in subsequent chapters, society is organized so that most of the time it is the least advantaged members of the majority group who are forced

Qualitative interviews such as this one often reveal subtler forms of prejudice that are missed by survey research in populations such as white college students.

to compete with minority group members for such resources as jobs, education, and housing. Accordingly, working-class prejudice may arise less from personality or psychological factors than from the fact that working-class whites are structured into competing with minorities in a way that others are not (Ransford, 1972). For this reason, lower-status members of majority groups sometimes see minorities as threats, even enemies, and develop the prejudiced attitudes consistent with that view.

Research findings are inconclusive about the extent to which perceived or real competition contributes to prejudice (Case, Greeley, and Fuchs, 1989; Lynch and Beer, 1990). For example, in some studies, the negative relationship between income and prejudice disappears after education is introduced as a control variable (Case, Greeley, and Fuchs, 1989; see also Oliver and Mendelberg, 2000). This suggests that education, not economic security, is the factor that affects prejudice. However, some studies indicate higher levels of prejudice among lower-income people, a relationship that sometimes persists after controls for education (Dyer, Vedlitz, and Worchel, 1989; Quillian, 1996). A Norwegian study showed that middle-income adolescents were less prejudiced than ones from either elite or (especially) low-income families, with the highest levels of prejudice in low-income teens in areas with large numbers of immigrants (Pederson, 1996). This strongly supports the competition hypothesis. In addition, racist organizations such as the Ku Klux Klan have historically drawn most of their support from working-class and poor whites. Moreover, there is evidence that societies that provide higher levels of social and economic security to their citizens are characterized by lower levels of aggression between groups within their societies (Marmor, 1992).

Social conditions involving a perceived threat have, in fact, been shown to increase authoritarianism and prejudice (Doty, Peterson, and Winter, 1991; Bobo and Hutchings, 1996). Fiske and Ruscher (1992) have shown that out-groups often are assumed to hinder the attainment of goals, and when this happens, prejudice and discrimination often result. Finally, there is a good deal of research suggesting that when the percentage of a minority in an area increases, it is often seen as a threat and is correlated with increases in prejudice (Pederson, 1996; Quillian, 1996). Similarly, violence toward minority groups by members of the dominant group, such as race riots and lynchings, often peaks in times and places where the minority group population is rising most rapidly (Allport, 1954, pp. 59–61). All of these findings suggest that perceived competition and threat can be important causes of prejudice and discrimination.

## Summary and Conclusion

In this chapter we have examined the meaning of prejudice and seen the various forms that prejudice can take. One reason some people are prejudiced is that it meets their personality needs, which have developed as a result of certain kinds of experiences in life. Nonetheless, not all people who are prejudiced have a psychological need for it; some are prejudiced because they learned prejudice from their parents, peers, or other agents of socialization or because they live in a social environment in which prejudice is the norm. Finally, we have introduced the idea—to be explored in greater detail in later chapters—that prejudice can be a result of one's position in the socioeconomic hierarchy. This can occur either because of effects of education, which is believed to make people more open-minded and less likely to oversimplify and overcategorize, or because of structured competition between minority groups and lower-status majority group members. In addition, downgrading of minorities may serve the psychological function of easing dissatisfaction with one's own low status.

This chapter has concerned itself mainly with the nature of prejudice and with its causes; the next chapter turns to two important questions about prejudice that we have not yet discussed: First, how can existing prejudice be reduced? Second, what is the relationship between prejudiced attitudes and discriminatory behavior?

## Critical Review Questions

1. Both social learning theory and personality theory argue that early experiences in life can cause people to be prejudiced. Therefore, what is the difference between these two theories?

2. What is the difference between scapegoating and projection, and how does each explain why some people are prejudiced?

3. A person who is prejudiced against a racial minority group is also more likely than most people to be prejudiced against other racial minority groups and against gay and lesbian people. Why is this the case?

4. It is likely that some of the tendency for more educated people to be less prejudiced is real, and some of it reflects their greater tendency to know and give socially acceptable answers on questionnaires. How might you get a better idea how much is real and how much reflects the latter tendency?

# CHAPTER 3

# Reducing Prejudice: How Achievable? How Important?

# Overview

Having examined some of the causes of prejudice, we shall now examine two other important issues. First, we shall evaluate various approaches to combating or reducing prejudice. Second, we shall look at the relationship between prejudice and behavior and attempt to answer the question, How important is prejudice as a cause of racial and ethnic discrimination and inequality?

## ▶ REDUCING PREJUDICE: SOME PRINCIPLES AND APPROACHES

Two key principles presented in the previous chapter were that (1) there are three different kinds of prejudice—cognitive (involving beliefs), affective (involving dislike), and conative (involving a desire to discriminate)—and (2) that prejudice of any kind has multiple causes, such as personality needs, social learning and conformity, and the nature of a society and its institutions. Taken together, these facts suggest some important principles about combating or reducing prejudice. First, no one approach is *the* solution to the problem of prejudice in society. There are simply too many kinds of prejudice, and too many reasons for it, for any one approach to always work. Thus, such statements as "The answer is education" or "If only people would get to know each other, they'd get along" are oversimplifications. They are true in some situations but clearly not in others.

Second, the approaches that work best vary from individual to individual, depending on the type of prejudice and its main causes in any given case. For example, if some personality need underlies a person's prejudice, neither education nor contact with minorities is likely to reduce it. The most effective approach in such a case may be some type of individual or group therapy to resolve the personality problem that is causing the prejudice. If a person is prejudiced mainly as a result of social learning or pressure for conformity, however, personal therapy aimed at personality change may be ineffective. A better solution in this case could be either an educational effort or an effort to change the environment to make it more supportive of open-mindedness. Another important situation occurs when prejudice serves mainly to justify or support discriminatory behavior. In this case, direct attempts to change the prejudice may not be effective at all. The behavior is the source of the problem, and it is the behavior that must be changed. The important point is that what works to eliminate one type of prejudice may be ineffective against another; therefore, the approach used must always be geared to the particular situation.

**39**

We can identify at least five major approaches that are often suggested as possible ways of reducing racial and ethnic prejudice: persuasive communications, education, intergroup contact, simulation and experiential exercises, and therapy. All share the common assumption that although prejudice may serve some important individual or social functions, it fundamentally involves invalid or irrational thinking and is therefore vulnerable to attack. In addition to the examples shown in Chapter 2 (such as, prejudice against nonexistent groups), it has also been shown that stereotyping is often contradictory. For example, anti-Semitic people view Jews as "pushing in where they don't belong" but also "sticking to themselves and refusing to assimilate" or as being "ruthless capitalists and unfair businessmen" but also "communistic" (Adorno et al., 1950; Allport, 1954). In theory, then, pointing out the fallacies of prejudiced thinking ought to have some potential to reduce the level of prejudice. All five methods seek to do this in some way. Therapy, in addition, may help people try to resolve personality problems that may be causing prejudice. In practice, the effectiveness of each of these techniques varies widely. They can be used well or used poorly, and their effectiveness varies with different types and causes of prejudice. In the following pages, we shall discuss and evaluate each of these five approaches to reducing prejudice.

## Persuasive Communications

**Persuasive communication** can be broadly defined as any communication—written, oral, audiovisual, or whatever—that is specifically intended to influence attitudes, beliefs, or behavior. The key defining characteristic is intent. A speech, movie, or book clearly aimed at reducing prejudice is a persuasive communication; a college course on race relations, designed to impart information, is not, even if it did bring about a change in students' attitudes. (Of course, some courses are designed in part to change people's minds, so in reality, the line between education and persuasion is often fuzzy.) Some social scientists, such as Simpson and Yinger (1985, pp. 387–90) further subdivide persuasive communications into such categories as exhortation (direct pleading, arguing a viewpoint to a person or audience) and propaganda (large-scale and organized efforts, often involving the mass media). Although such a distinction is useful for some purposes, the general principles concerning the effectiveness of the communication are quite similar for either type. Accordingly, in this chapter we treat these two subtypes together under the general heading of persuasive communications.

We begin with some minimum conditions necessary for a persuasive communication to succeed (Flowerman, 1947; Hovland, Janis, and Kelley, 1953; McGuire, 1968). First, it must be heard and paid attention to. This is no small requirement because in a society in which advertising and propaganda are pervasive, most people have learned to avoid or ignore many persuasive communications. Second, the message must be correctly understood. If a pleasant story with the moral that prejudice is bad is understood only as a pleasant story—that is, if the message about prejudice is totally missed—it cannot be effective in changing people's minds. (For research on message reception and persuasion, see Tesser and Shaffer, 1990; Rhodes and Wood, 1992; Eagly and Chaiken, 1993, pp. 505–7). Third, receiving the communication should in some way be a positive experience: The message must be enjoyed or seen as presenting a good idea. Finally, the message must be retained and internalized so that the desired effect lasts. A failure at any one of these points means that the communication will not be successful in changing attitudes or beliefs. The likelihood that these conditions will be met depends on a number of factors, including (1) the source of the communication, (2) the content of the message, (3) the process in which the message is presented, and (4) the characteristics of the audience, that is, the person or people receiving the message (Triandis, 1971).

Having outlined these general principles, we can move to several more specific observations. One is that people tend to expose themselves to messages that are consistent with what they already believe. They also pay better attention to, and retain longer, messages that support their preexisting viewpoints. These tendencies vary according to personality and situation (Triandis, 1971, chap. 6), but overall we see, pay attention to, and remember things that reinforce what we already believe. Thus, those who are most likely to accept an antiprejudice communication tend to be people who are already least prejudiced, and the tendency is for those who are *most* strongly prejudiced to be the least exposed and the most resistant. People usually dislike having their beliefs seriously challenged (so they avoid communications that do so), and they tend to resolve inconsistencies by ignoring or rationalizing away communications that are inconsistent with their attitudes and beliefs rather than by changing their thinking. Moreover, prejudiced people often do not think of themselves as prejudiced and thus see the message as applicable to someone else. As prejudices have become more subtle, such rationalizations probably have become easier (Pettigrew, 1985, p. 338). In short, attitudes tend to be resistant to change, even if they are, *logically* speaking, vulnerable to attack. Thus, the potential of persuasive communication appears to be greatest as a means of reinforcing open-mindedness in relatively unprejudiced people. It can sometimes reduce prejudice in mildly prejudiced people but not usually in ones with strong prejudices (Simpson and Yinger, 1985).

Furthermore, the main sources of information for most people—books, newspapers, television, movies, and the Internet—are generally privately controlled and enjoy constitutional guarantees of freedom of expression. Thus, there is no easy way to force these media to expose people to antiprejudice communications. In fact, the messages people receive tend to reflect the interests and values of those who produce the media and the values already present in the larger culture (because the media producers want to sell their product). Unfortunately, it follows that in times when prejudice is most widespread, the media are least likely to send antiprejudice messages. In recent years, the Internet has broadened the range of messages available to anyone who can access a computer. However, because people who use the Internet mainly seek out views and material they already find appealing, it is doubtful that Internet communications opposing prejudice are going to reach the people most in need of them. On the contrary, the wide range of material on the Internet, including more than 440 Web sites maintained by hate groups as of 2002, often means that any view, no matter how extreme, can be reinforced by material available somewhere on the World Wide Web (Potok, 2003).

The personality characteristics of the person receiving the message also influence the effectiveness of persuasive communications. In general, people who have a strong personality need for prejudice tend to be resistant to persuasion: They are prejudiced mainly because prejudice serves a psychological function for them, not because they are persuaded by the logic of prejudiced arguments. However, there may be some effective ways to use persuasion in such cases. One is to persuade the person to adopt some other viewpoint that meets his or her personality needs more effectively than prejudice, although this can be difficult if the personality need is related to self-image (Triandis, 1971, p. 144), as is often the case. With authoritarian personalities, another approach is to alter the source of the communication. In this case, a message from a respected authority figure might be better received than a message from some other source.

As the last example suggests, the source can be highly important in determining the effectiveness of antiprejudice persuasion. The prestige, credibility, attractiveness, and power of the person or source presenting the message can all influence how the message is received (DeBono and Harnish, 1988; Chebat, Filiatrault, and Perrien, 1990). Of course, the kind of speaker with prestige and power varies with the audience. For conservative whites, the American Legion has high prestige, and its message usually would be more effective for such an audience than an identical one from the National Association for the Advancement of Colored People (NAACP) or the American Civil Liberties Union (ACLU).

The effects of source credibility, attractiveness, and power, as well as those of message content, intensity, and approach, all vary with the personality, attitudes, and experience of the person being persuaded. Among the attributes that influence how people respond to a message or its source are their degree of involvement with the issue (Chebat, Filiatrault, and Perrien, 1990), the extent to which they monitor their own thinking (DeBono and Harnish, 1988), their sense that they can control their situation (Chebat, Filiatrault, and Perrien, 1990), their degree of experience with the issue being addressed (Wu and Shaffer, 1987), the personal relevance of the issue (Petty, Cacioppo, and Goldman, 1981), and their self-esteem (Baumeister and Covington, 1985). A reasonable conclusion from this research is that to maximize persuasion, the source, the approach used, and the content of a persuasive message must all to some extent be tailored to the audience. If the audience is diverse or if the person doing the persuading has limited knowledge of the audience's characteristics, it is almost inevitable that any approach to reducing prejudice through persuasion will work better for some people in the audience than for others.

Research suggests that of the various factors mentioned, the most important one for bringing about long-term attitude change is the credibility of the source (Kelman, 1958). The expertise of the source is especially influential (Cooper and Croyle, 1984, p. 418). Power is less influential because it matters only as long as the source of the message has some control over the audience. In some cases gender may matter; one study showed that attitude change was most likely to occur when both the speaker and those listening were female (Paxton, 2002). Finally, messages are especially effective when their content is unexpected, such as when a well-known segregationist argues in favor of integration (Wood and Eagly, 1981; Maheswaran and Chaiken, 1991).

The ability and motivation of people to process a message are also important. If people are motivated and able to give a message careful attention, its content has greater influence. In this situation, if the content of the argument is strong, attitude change is likely and is often long-lasting. If people are less motivated or distracted, other factors, such as the source and the enjoyability of the message, become more important influences, but attitude change is less likely to last (Eagly and Chaiken, 1993; Petty and Cacioppo, 1986).

A variety of research on persuasive messages shows that receiving the message from multiple sources increases its impact. For example, a study of the impact of HIV-positive speakers on adolescents' attitudes toward people with AIDS found that two different speakers had a bigger and more lasting impact than just one (Paxton, 2002). Getting the same message from several sources is especially effective if the sources are (or at least appear to be) independent of one another (Harkins and Petty, 1987).

Studies have also shown that people can become somewhat less prejudiced as a result of viewing a film with a general theme of tolerance. In one instance, students shown a popular Hollywood movie that took a strong stand against anti-Semitism became somewhat less prejudiced against not only Jews but also blacks, even though antiblack prejudice was not dealt with in the film (Middleton, 1960). As expected, people highly concerned about status—a characteristic associated with authoritarian personalities—were least affected by the film. Although there was no follow-up to see whether the reduction of prejudice remained over an extended time, a similar study (Mittnick and McGinnies, 1958) indicated that if a film was followed by a discussion of prejudice, some of the decrease remained a month later.

A recent review of studies of the effects on schoolchildren of media messages against prejudice is encouraging. Fishbein (1996, pp. 245–46) reviewed several such studies and found that well-designed media messages reduced both racial and ethnic prejudice and prejudice against people with disabilities. Moreover, these effects occurred regardless of the race, age, or gender of the students. In fact, such media messages may be more effective for children than for adults because they can be presented to all children in school, whereas adults who want to do so often can avoid these messages. Still, caution is needed. In many cases, we do not know whether the effect was lasting, and it could be that the children were expressing the attitudes they thought the researchers wanted.

One recent study of racial discussions among children illustrates the possibilities of persuasion in informal discussions, at least for young people. Schoolchildren who had been identified as high and low in prejudice were asked to discuss racial attitudes in pairs, in which one partner was high in prejudice and the other was low. Then their attitudes were measured again after the discussion. The children who had been high in prejudice showed decreases in negative racial evaluations, whereas children who had been low in prejudice showed no increase. This suggests that such discussions may sensitize the more prejudiced children to the negative consequences of prejudice (Aboud and Doyle, 1996).

All in all, we can conclude that under certain circumstances persuasive communications can lead to some reduction in prejudice and can reinforce open-mindedness in those who are already unprejudiced, or at least not extremely prejudiced. However, the effectiveness of this approach seems very limited in the case of highly prejudiced people, especially if the prejudice is meeting some personality need. Such people are least likely to be exposed to the message, and if they are exposed, they are least likely to understand it (Cooper and Jahoda, 1947; Kendall and Wolf, 1949), enjoy it, or be persuaded by it.

## Education

**Intergroup education** is somewhat similar to persuasion in that it imparts information that may help to break down incorrect stereotypes and irrational prejudices. Certainly, it is subject to some of the same limitations as persuasion; for example, it cannot by itself resolve personality needs that cause prejudice. The main definitional difference is that education does not, per se, attempt to change people's attitudes. Its objective is to bring about learning, to impart information. As it is actually practiced, it often does have a latent objective of changing people's minds, although for the purposes of definition, its objective is to teach rather than to persuade. Nevertheless, in real life much of what is called education is in fact a mixture of education and persuasion.

Many of the principles pertaining to persuasion also apply to education, but we can make some generalizations that apply specifically to the latter. Our focus here is mainly on education about intergroup relations; we discuss the effects of overall educational level in Chapters 2 and 12.

Education about intergroup relations is most effective in reducing prejudice when it minimizes the stress associated with admitting previous error. In other words, such education should not make people feel defensive or threaten their egos. The best results are obtained if they feel they are participating in the process of learning new ideas that may be contrary to old ones (Lewin, 1948; Fineberg, 1949). In fact, these principles apply not just to education but also to reducing prejudice through persuasion and through simulation and experiential exercises.

The teachers also make an important difference, both in their own attitudes and in the diversity of the teaching staff. Teachers, like other people, are sometimes prejudiced, a fact that can limit the effect of intergroup relations education (Zeichner, 1995). Also, minority group members are underrepresented at all levels in the teaching profession. In elementary and secondary education, about 7 percent of teachers are African American and about 4 percent are Hispanic, compared with 16 percent and 10 percent of students, respectively (National Center for Education Statistics, 2002a, Chap. 2). At the college level, fewer than 5 percent of all instructors are African American and fewer than 3 percent are Hispanic, compared with 11 percent and 9 percent of students, respectively (Chronicle of Higher Education, 2003c, 2003d).

The evident presence of prejudice or discrimination in the teacher, or a teaching staff that is all or mostly white, can offset any positive effects of the educational program. Thus, it is important that minorities be appropriately represented on intergroup relations teaching staffs and that the teachers in such courses be as free from racial and ethnic prejudices as is humanly possible. School materials also must be free of stereotypical portrayals of minorities and of the equally common pattern of ignoring minorities altogether (see Lessing and Clarke, 1976). These principles apply not only to intergroup relations courses and materials but to the entire curriculum. If the learning that occurs in the race relations course is offset by prejudiced teachers, lack of minority role models, discriminatory practices, and stereotypical books and materials elsewhere in the curriculum, it is unlikely that students will become less prejudiced.

Another problem with the use of education to reduce prejudice—particularly at the college level, where courses often are taken on an elective basis—is the familiar one of self-selection. People who voluntarily take courses in majority-minority relations or related topics tend to be less prejudiced than others to begin with. Thus, as with persuasion, education often does not reach the most prejudiced people. A similar pattern may develop at the elementary and secondary levels, although for different reasons. At those levels, the school districts that do the most to teach intergroup relations tend to be the more liberal or diverse ones, in which prejudice may be somewhat less widespread to begin with. School districts in which prejudice is more widespread (among parents, as well as children) may do less to teach intergroup relations simply because the views of decision makers generally reflect the views of those in the school district. Often, intergroup relations education is seen as an unnecessary distraction from time spent on "reading, writing, and arithmetic" or, worse, as indoctrination aimed at promoting a particular cultural or political viewpoint. For this reason, intergroup relations education often is controversial (Weinstein, 2001), and students are least likely to receive it in districts where the objections to it are strongest.

Nonetheless, increasing numbers of elementary and secondary schools and colleges have been including intergroup or multicultural education as a mandatory part of their curriculum in recent years. At the elementary and secondary school levels, for example, programs such as *A World of Difference* and *Teaching Tolerance* have been used in a growing number of school districts to teach students about cultural differences and to encourage them to value and respect diversity (Golub, 1989).

At the college level, more and more colleges and universities have established requirements that all students take at least one course in intergroup relations or minority group studies. As of 2000, 54 percent of colleges and universities in the United States required one or more courses on diversity, and another 8 percent were developing such requirements (Humphreys, 2000). Often, such courses are designed to show how and why majority and minority groups often have different experiences, perceptions, and beliefs. For example, students of color often experience discrimination and social isolation that white students do not. These differences in experiences lead to very different beliefs about the extent of discrimination in society and the fairness of the social system. By showing how these different experiences lead to different beliefs, such courses are designed to alleviate some of the causes of tension between students of different racial and cultural backgrounds. Although such requirements can be controversial, a 1998 poll showed that about two-thirds of Americans support such a requirement (Humphreys, 2000).

One of the places that has been most successful in reducing intergroup tensions is the U.S. military (Moskos, 1991). Mandatory intergroup education has played a significant role in this success and has been adjusted and made more effective on the basis of social science evaluations of its effectiveness. There appear to be two key reasons for its success. First, it has emphasized role-playing activities aimed at helping whites to see situations from the standpoint of minority group members, and vice versa. Second, the strong emphasis given to it by the military has sent soldiers a message that the military is serious about equal opportunity (Moskos, 1991), so any soldier interested in getting ahead had better take it seriously.

On the whole, research indicates that well-designed educational programs are effective in reducing prejudice. Early studies that showed a reduction in prejudice outnumbered ones that did not by about two to one (Harding et al., 1969; R. D. Ashmore, 1970). More recent studies support this conclusion when such educational programs are comprehensive and designed to address various sources of prejudice, including personality, social structure, culture, and the environment (Lynch, 1987, 1988; Banks, 1995a; 1995c). However, there are methodological problems in some evaluations of the effects of such education, and the evidence that participants in intergroup education *believe* that their attitudes have been changed often is stronger than the evidence of actual change (Kiselica and Maben, 1999; McGauley, Wright, and Harris, 2000).

Some research suggests that prejudice is most easily changed in young children (Rooney-Rebek and Jason, 1986; Banks, 1995b). Common techniques include factual teaching about race and ethnic relations; value-based approaches, including statements that prejudice and discrimination are unacceptable and will not be tolerated; experiential simulations (discussed in greater detail later in this chapter); intergroup contact; and confrontational strategies designed to bring prejudice into the open (Andreoni and Nihas, 1986; see also Beswick, 1990; Banks, 1995b). Care must be taken with the latter strategy; it may be counterproductive, especially if teachers are not adequately prepared to deal with prejudiced statements by students (Fenton and Nancarrow, 1986). In some cases, education programs have also been used to reduce prejudice in teachers and to encourage them to develop multicultural skills and incorporate the experiences of diverse social groups in their classroom teaching (Banks, 1995b). Evaluation studies indicate that such programs have positive effects on teachers' knowledge, attitudes, and behaviors, although the extent of these effects on different teachers varies widely (Bennett, 1989).

As it has become more common for intergroup relations courses to be required at the college level, researchers have begun to evaluate their effects. A study of education students in a required intergroup relations course, showed, for example, that after taking the course, students had become more supportive of policies to increase opportunities for minorities (Davine and Bills, 1992). This effect seems to be greatest when there is one course on diversity that all students are required to take (Fitzgerald and Lauter, 1995), although in many cases it is easier to get faculty and student support for requirements that allow students to choose from a number of such courses. However, choices often include courses without material that seriously analyzes intergroup inequality and its causes (Fitzgerald and Lauter, 1995). The effects of diversity courses on intergroup attitudes appear to be greater for women than for men, and the impact of taking multiple diversity courses is greater than that of just one course (B. Palmer, 2000). Research also suggests that courses that address issues of power and oppression, courses that use discussion-based pedagogy, and courses affiliated with women's studies or ethnic studies programs have greater impacts on attitudes (B. Palmer, 2000). Finally, some research suggests that a service-learning component in courses on diversity may contribute to attitude change (Hanks and Icenogle, 2001).

An advantage of required college courses in intergroup relations is that they avoid the problem of self-selection (discussed earlier). On the other hand, in the short term such required courses may trigger intergroup conflicts by bringing latent racial tensions to the surface. Over the long term, though, it seems better to get the issues on the table and deal with them as fairly and sensitively as possible because it is likely that they will come to the surface in some context anyway, where they will probably be more difficult to address. According to Astin (1993), students who have had courses or workshops on diversity-related material report greater commitment to promoting racial understanding, greater self-reported cultural awareness, and greater satisfaction with the college experience. One model that has been shown to be successful is in-class discussions of diversity issues led by teams of trained minority and majority group student facilitators (Nelson et al., 1994). This model, like many, actually involves a combination of education and intergroup contact, an approach discussed later in greater depth.

One challenge facing intergroup education programs is that often they must address different but related problems at the same time. One problem is that some minority group students have internalized prejudices they have learned from others about their own group (Toomer, 1977; Gonzales and Cauce, 1995). Therefore, intergroup education must try to foster both a more positive self-image and group identity among students of color and more positive relations between these students and white students. A review of studies of this issue by Toomer (1977) shows that the most successful education programs were ones that consciously addressed both of these issues.

Like other methods of reducing prejudice, intergroup education appears to be most effective when prejudices are relatively mild and communities are not highly polarized (Litcher and Johnson, 1969; Lessing and Clarke, 1976). And as suggested earlier, the educational approach appears to be more effective when prejudice does not arise out of personality needs. For example, Dent (1975) found that an education program in intergroup relations was somewhat effective in lowering prejudice in people with relatively low F scale (authoritarianism) scores, but among those with high F scale scores, education made no significant difference. These results suggest that, like persuasion, the educational approach to reducing prejudice can be effective, but only up to a point and only in certain situations. For cases in which prejudice is strongest and most deeply entrenched, the educational approach is least effective.

## Intergroup Contact

One of the most frequently suggested remedies for prejudice is intergroup contact. It is generally believed that intergroup contact, perhaps even more than persuasion and education, can break down people's prejudices by showing them that their stereotypes or fears about out-groups are unfounded. Indeed, some impressive findings from social science lend support to this notion (often called the *contact hypothesis*). Early studies of the contact hypothesis focused on residential settings where people were assigned housing. This provided a close form of contact, but in a situation in which people who were already less prejudiced could not choose integrated settings (thus reversing cause and effect). These studies showed that people assigned to integrated settings in public housing (Deutsch and Collins, 1951; Wilner, Walkley, and Cook, 1955) and to integrated troop units and military barracks (Stouffer et al., 1949; Mandelbaum, 1952) showed reductions in prejudice or became less prejudiced than comparable people in segregated settings.

In studies of areas of life other than housing, the results have been less consistent, but there is evidence of benefits from contact in educational, employment, recreational, and other settings. A national survey showed that school desegregation is associated with greater racial tolerance in both blacks and whites (Scott and McPartland, 1982). A review of a larger number of studies by Fishbein (1996) found mixed results for black children and, in some time frames, for white children as well. For the latter, however, there was a clear improvement in attitudes one to five years after desegregation.

One problem is that increased contact in a particular setting may lead to increased acceptance only in that situation (R. D. Ashmore, 1970; Wilder and Thompson, 1980; Jackman and Crane, 1986; Fishbein, 1996, p. 241). For example,

Intergroup contact often leads to intergroup friendships, as with these children in a Bronx, New York, school. Under the right circumstances, such contact can improve intergroup relations and reduce prejudice.

a white person who works with black people might come to favor integrated work-places but continue to object to integrated neighborhoods. Also, people may define members of other groups that they interact with as "exceptions to the rule," thus rationalizing continued prejudice. However, the more such contacts they have, the more difficult this becomes (Hewstone, Rubin, and Willis, 2002, p. 589). The effects of contact may be greater and longer lasting when it occurs in child-hood. One recent study showed that adults who had experienced extensive inter-racial contact as children were significantly less prejudiced as adults (Wood and Sonleitner, 1996). This suggests that attending integrated schools or growing up in integrated neighborhoods can have long-lasting effects on racial attitudes. Simi-larly, it has been shown that heterosexuals who have had contact with homosexuals are less prejudiced against them than people who have not had contact (Whitely, 1990).

Contact between two racial, ethnic, or social groups does not always lead to reduced prejudice or improved relations. An example can be seen in the intense and sometimes violent conflicts that accompanied school desegregation in the 1970s in Boston; Louisville, Kentucky; Pontiac, Michigan; and elsewhere. Accord-ingly, research exploring the contact hypothesis has sought to identify the condi-tions under which contact is likely to reduce prejudice.

One essential condition is *equal status*. In other words, people from the racial or ethnic groups involved must be similar in status and power and must not be in a position in which one can dominate or exercise authority over the other. People working on the same jobs for the same pay or renting similar apartments in the same building are an example of equal-status contact. A supervisor-employee rela-tionship is a clear case of unequal-status contact. If the people are not of equal sta-tus, contact is likely to foster resentment for those in the subordinate role and to reinforce stereotypes in both majority and minority groups about inequalities between groups. Because in a society marked by racial inequality much intergroup contact is on an unequal basis, often the effectiveness of intergroup contact as a way of reducing prejudice is limited. According to Fishbein (1996, p. 226), this is one reason that school desegregation has in many cases not produced improvements in intergroup attitudes: It has often been marked by unequal contact, such as track-ing, unequal achievement due to unequal opportunity before desegregation, and socioeconomic inequalities. In addition, it is often competitive rather than cooper-ative. Practices such as tracking not only lead to unequal statuses but also often reduce the overall amount of contact that occurs, so that classrooms usually are more segregated than schools (Braddock, Dawkins, and Wilson, 1995).

In some cases, contact designed to create equal status fails to do so because cul-tural or institutionalized status differences are carried into the situation. Thus, groups designed to create equal-status majority-minority contact often end up being dominated by majority group members (E. G. Cohen, 1972, 1982). Accord-ingly, special efforts may be necessary to ensure that truly equal status is created. Research by Cohen, Lockheed, and Lohman (1976) suggests that one way to do this may be to present role models or experiences that contradict the generalized cul-tural pattern, such as having black students act as teachers and white students as learners in training exercises involving unfamiliar tasks or knowledge. If the minor-ity group is perceived as academically disadvantaged, equal-status contact may be possible only if the minority group is highly influential in some other arena, such as the social. Such influence may be enhanced by minority group teachers and admin-istrators and by emphasis in the school on minority group culture (E. G. Cohen, 1984). Also, tasks may be structured to ensure, for example, that women and minorities have the same amount of speaking time as white men. Research on inter-ventions such as these indicates that they generally increase the participation of stu-dents from disadvantaged groups without inhibiting the participation of those from the majority group (F. Cohen, 1993; Cohen and Lotan, 1995). Thus, they are effec-tive in transforming intergroup contact to a more equal-status basis.

Another essential condition is that contact must be *noncompetitive* and *nonthreatening* for both groups involved. Any contact that evokes fear and defensiveness runs the risk of making intergroup relations worse, not better. Racial prejudice sometimes is strong in working-class whites because they fear they will lose their jobs or lose control of their schools or neighborhoods to people of color. Contact that intensifies such fears often makes prejudiced people even more prejudiced. Some conflicts over school desegregation illustrate this point. The city of Boston experienced intense conflict and a number of violent incidents during the implementation of a school desegregation plan in the mid-1970s. Although the plan was city-wide, the violence centered on a very few schools and neighborhoods. The conflict was most intense in the white district of South Boston and in the black neighborhood of Roxbury. These neighborhoods were largely poor neighborhoods, where people had little security or control in their jobs and their economic situations. South Boston was also an ethnic neighborhood (heavily Irish), and ethnicity formed a basis for solidarity. In addition, the neighborhoods were grossly underrepresented in the city's political and educational power structure. However, there was a strong sense of community within the neighborhood, perhaps even a sense of "turf." Indeed, the residents (whites particularly) perceived their immediate neighborhood, symbolized by the neighborhood school, as one of the very few places where they did have control. Finally, there was a widespread belief, among both the poor blacks in Roxbury and the poor whites in South Boston and similar neighborhoods, that they were in intense job competition with the other race. Consequently, each race saw the other as a threat to already limited employment opportunities. And to whites in South Boston, school desegregation took away one of the few remaining areas in which they felt they had control.

The generally insecure position of South Boston whites and their fears and prejudices toward blacks created an explosive mix. Antiblack feelings soared and exploded into violence. African Americans, who felt equally threatened and powerless, responded with violence of their own. The result was several mass attacks on black people in South Boston, followed by attacks on whites in Roxbury. As we shall see when we study the issue of busing in Chapter 12, it is questionable whether much could have been gained by busing children between two of Boston's poorest neighborhoods. Because of the particular characteristics of the neighborhoods, desegregation was viewed as a threat, and intergroup contact led to worse, not better, race relations, at least in the first year or two of the plan. The difference between these neighborhoods and most Boston neighborhoods (where little or no real conflict accompanied desegregation) illustrates well the point that intergroup contact must be noncompetitive and nonthreatening to both groups. If this condition is not met, the contact is unlikely to improve attitudes and can even make them worse.

Even when intergroup contact is highly threatening to both groups, it does not have to remain that way forever. If the initial storm can be weathered, people can sometimes overcome their fears so that they see less threat in a particular kind of contact. An example can be seen in another northern school desegregation case in Pontiac, Michigan. Several years before the Boston controversy, a desegregation plan that, like Boston's, involved busing was implemented in Pontiac under court order. The plan brought intense conflict, climaxed by a bombing of several school buses by Ku Klux Klan members. Within a few years, however, people had adapted to the plan, and many felt that although they would rather have done without it, it did not really pose a great threat to the quality of their lives. Many observers in the community also felt that racial conflict in Pontiac was greatly reduced in the several years after implementation of the desegregation plan.

Another example of delayed positive effects of intergroup contact can be seen in a review of research by Schofield (1995). She found mixed effects in studies of short-term effects of school desegregation on intergroup relations. In some cases intergroup relations improved, in some they got worse, in some they did not change, and in some there were different effects on majority and minority group students. But the more limited literature on longer-term effects is more consistent: Over the long run, school desegregation seems to lead to less segregated housing (Pearce, 1980; Crain, 1981; Pearce, Crain, and Farley, 1984; D. A. Johnson, 1990), a greater likelihood of working in an integrated workplace (Braddock, Crain, and McPartland, 1984; Trent, 1991), and more of a tendency to attend racially integrated colleges (Wells and Crain, 1997). The last study also showed that the majority of white students in a suburban county felt that their education had been enriched by a desegregation plan that brought substantial numbers of African American students to their schools from the central city.

Intergroup contact must also be more than superficial. For example, studies of interracial camping have shown that sharing a room or tent led to a greater reduction in prejudice and stereotyping than merely playing games together. This is probably because people tend to avoid getting to know members of the other race very well if the situation permits such avoidance. This is probably why interracial housing arrangements generally lead to a greater reduction in prejudice than other forms of contact (Harding et al., 1969). It also points to a problem with many prejudice reduction activities: They do not continue long enough to have lasting effects. Close contact over an extended period of time has a greater impact on attitudes than short-term contact in a one-hour or one-day prejudice reduction activity (Pettigrew, 1998, p. 76).

It has become increasingly clear that the most effective contact in reducing prejudice is contact that not only meets all of these conditions but also *creates interdependence* and *necessitates cooperation*. This principle was illustrated in a fascinating study by Sherif et al. (1961), known as the Robbers' Cave experiment. Sherif and his colleagues divided a group of boys attending scout camp into two groups (the Rattlers and the Eagles), then placed the groups in numerous competitive and sometimes frustrating situations. For example, it was arranged that one group would arrive first at a party and thus eat most of the food before the other group arrived. This caused strong group identities to form within each group and considerable hostility to develop between the groups. Eventually, the experimenters ended the competition and brought the groups together in noncompetitive situations. This had no effect. The groups continued to maintain their identities, and members of each remained hostile toward members of the other. It was not until a third stage of the experiment that a significant change occurred. In this stage, the experimenters cleverly created situations in which members of the two groups had to cooperate to achieve some shared goal. For example, on a trip a truck stalled, and members of both groups had to cooperate in pulling it up a hill until it would start. In another instance, the experimenters secretly disrupted the camp's water supply, and members of the two groups had to cooperate in restoring it. After a series of similar incidents, the hostility had almost entirely melted away. No longer were members of the opposite group shunned and ridiculed; instead, friendships developed between members of opposite groups. In this experiment, equal-status contact alone was not sufficient to break down the intense intergroup hostility that had developed. Only when the two groups were interdependent and had to cooperate did the hostilities end.

Although the Sherif et al. (1961) experiment involved groups artificially created by an experimenter rather than real racial and ethnic groups, there is ample evidence that interdependency is important in reducing real-life racial and ethnic prejudices. This is illustrated by the reductions in racial prejudice among black and white soldiers who have depended on one another in combat (Stouffer et al., 1949), perhaps the prototypical case of a situation demanding cooperation for a common goal. Similarly, a series of studies has shown that the use of interracial work groups whose tasks required cooperation led to improved intergroup acceptance (Johnson,

Johnson, and Maruyama, 1984) and that this acceptance extends beyond the immediate work setting. Such cooperative task-oriented groups were found to improve intergroup attitudes concerning gender and religion more readily than groups focusing entirely on intergroup communications (Rich, Kedem, and Shlesinger, 1995). One reason for the effectiveness of such cooperation is that it changes the group orientation of group members. Rather than thinking of themselves as members of two preexisting groups (blacks and whites, males and females, and so on), they think of themselves as members of one group facing a common challenge (Hewstone, Rubin, and Willis, 2002). However, such benefits may occur only if the task is completed successfully (Brewer and Miller, 1984). Additionally, a major difficulty in such interventions is getting the attitude change to carry over outside the group situation, which can be very difficult if the larger society is marked by sharp intergroup inequality or conflict (Connolly, 2000; Hewstone, Rubin, and Willis, 2002, p. 590). This problem may be reduced by making the racial differences visible in the cooperative task-oriented group so members can see that different groups bring different resources to the problem-solving task. However, it is important to design the process in ways that build personal trust among members, or the group may divide on the basis of race and fail to unify in the way intended (Hewstone, Rubin, and Wilis, 2002, p. 591).

A wide variety of research has confirmed that equal-status, cooperative intergroup contact reduces prejudice. This has been shown among young elementary school children (Rooney-Rebek and Jason, 1986), whites who have previously indicated prejudice toward blacks (Cook, 1990), and high school students (McWhirter, Paluch, and Ohm, 1988). It has been shown not only for racial prejudice but also for other prejudices, such as prejudice against people with AIDS or HIV (Paxton, 2002, p. 283). Social psychologists have designed cooperative classroom activities to break down prejudice (Aronson and Patnoe, 1997) and used them successfully with a wide variety of children (Pettigrew, 1998, p. 67). Significantly, though, one study suggests that such techniques may be more effective with younger people, for whom prejudice and competitiveness have had less time to become set and habitual. Rooney-Rebeck and Jason (1986) found that cooperative peer tutoring improved interethnic interaction among first grade children, but by the third grade this was no longer the case. In general, studies have shown that when intergroup contact in schools occurs in a context of cooperative learning (as opposed to the more competitive arrangement typical in many school classrooms), the benefits of contact are more positive and consistent (Banks, 1995c, p. 619; Slavin, 1995a). Similar findings were obtained with college students who interacted with a former mental patient: The biggest attitude changes toward people with a history of mental illness occurred in cooperative learning tasks (Desforges et al., 1991).

To summarize, then, under the right conditions contact can be an important force for reducing prejudice. To be effective, intergroup contact must be on an equal-status basis, it must be more than superficial, and it must be nonthreatening and noncompetitive. It is most effective when the contact is such that members of the groups must cooperate to reach some common goal, and it is important that authorities in the settings where contact occurs support the efforts at better intergroup relations. Research suggests four ways in which such contact breaks down prejudices: learning about the out-group, changing behavior, getting to like people in the out-group, and gaining insights about the in-group through the process (Pettigrew, 1998). Unfortunately, much of the contact between racial and ethnic groups in America today does not meet the conditions noted above, and because of continuing segregation, many whites have very little nonsuperficial contact with minority group members.

Many of the research studies we have discussed focused mainly on the prejudices of majority group members. Indeed, the intergroup attitudes of whites have been studied much more extensively than those of minority groups, partly because the problem of racial discrimination is by its nature mainly a majority group problem. Subordinated minorities simply do not have comparable power to discriminate, even if they are so inclined. Nonetheless, research that has been undertaken in the area of minority group attitudes has yielded some interesting findings. One is that the attitudes of blacks toward whites appear less subject to change by education (Robinson and Preston, 1976) and by intergroup contact (Ford, 1973; Robinson and Preston, 1976) than do the attitudes of whites about blacks. This could be interpreted as meaning that blacks are less flexible in their thinking than whites, but the studies suggest that other explanations are more plausible. These studies show that African Americans were less prejudiced to begin with and so had less room for improvement. It also turns out that what whites see as equal-status contact does not seem equal to blacks, who perceive, often with some basis in fact, subtle acts of condescension or superiority and dominance on the part of whites (see Cohen and Roper, 1972; Riordan and Ruggiero, 1980; E. G. Cohen, 1982). Finally, the "prejudices" among blacks turn out to be mainly the perception that whites will behave in a discriminatory, paternalistic, or egotistical manner toward blacks. Because whites have a disproportionate share of power and because many (though certainly not all) whites do behave in these ways, the negative interracial attitudes of African Americans appear to be largely a cautious approach of withholding trust until they are confident that trust is warranted. These attitudes certainly are qualitatively different from the kinds of prejudice whites often display toward blacks.

## Simulation and Experiential Exercises

Another approach to reducing prejudice that has come into increasing use in recent years involves simulation exercises. These sometimes combine aspects of several other techniques, including education, intergroup contact, and therapy. The exercises set up situations in which people experience discrimination, so they learn about the feelings that result from being discriminated against, and they see in a direct way the irrationality of prejudice and discrimination. Simulation games such as Star Power and Urban Dynamics, in which people are randomly assigned to what turn out to be advantaged and disadvantaged groups, are one example of this approach. Another is the brown eyes–blue eyes exercise, first developed by Jane Elliott, a teacher in a small, rural, all-white town in northern Iowa. In this exercise, participants are assigned to advantaged and disadvantaged groups according to eye color. Hostility and discrimination quickly develop, and people who had been friends in the past become instant enemies. The effects of the hostility created were so profound that there were substantial increases in achievement among the advantaged group of Elliott's students and declines among the disadvantaged group, which were reversed the next day when the groups were switched. First used with elementary school students, this exercise has since been used by a wide variety of groups, ranging from college students to prison guards. A study of the effects of this exercise among teacher education students confirmed that it reduced racial prejudice (Byrnes and Kiger, 1990). Many years after participating in the exercise, Elliott's own students said that it had had lasting effects, making them less prejudiced and more accepting of diversity (Public Broadcasting Service, 1985). A similar exercise in which students were divided into "orange" and "green" groups and subjected to discrimination on alternate days was found to reduce racial prejudice, with reductions still present two weeks after the exercise (Weiner and Wright, 1973).

In another simulation exercise, participants are excluded from group exercises, which simulates the exclusion that occurs with discrimination. Evaluations of this exercise with a group of eight- to ten-year-olds revealed that after being excluded, the children became more sensitive to the feelings of children from other ethnic groups (Ciullo and Troiani, 1988). There are also exercises in which people experience simulations of having disabilities, and these exercises have been shown to improve attitudes toward people who use wheelchairs or are blind (Fishbein, 1996, pp. 247–48).

Other exercises focus on helping majority group members see the discrimination that minority groups experience. One widely used exercise asks people to step forward or back according to various experiences they have had in life that influence their opportunities. This exercise vividly shows how race (and in many cases, gender and class) influence life opportunities; it helps to break down the common but inaccurate perception that everyone has the same opportunity in life, creating empathy for the obstacles faced by groups that experience discrimination. I have participated in a diversity training team that has used this exercise, sometimes in combination with viewing a hidden camera video that catches incidences of racial discrimination. Workshop participants have indicated that these experiences have greatly heightened their awareness of discrimination, although there are no data on the long-term effects of these exercises.

Although much of the research on simulation exercises is encouraging, this approach shares some of the same shortcomings as others we have examined. One is that the most prejudiced people are least likely to be involved, unless the exercises are mandatory, as has been the case in some schools and among some public employees. Additionally, how these exercises are facilitated and debriefed makes a big difference in their effectiveness. Fishbein (1996, p. 248) notes that studies of exercises that included thorough discussion and debriefing indicate significant prejudice reduction, whereas similar simulations without discussion may have little effect. Finally, there is a need for more evaluation of the effectiveness of these techniques. Recent studies of diversity workshops have found that although most who participate report that they found the workshops useful, there is almost no research on whether the workshops had actually changed people's prejudices (Tritelli, 2001; Kiselica and Maben, 1999). A few studies do assess the effects of such exercises on diversity awareness and on awareness among whites of the advantages they receive because of their race, and these studies do find attitude changes in these areas (Kiselica and Maben, 1999). However, it can be difficult to sort out the specific effects of simulation exercises because they are often used in combination with educational activities.

## Therapy

Therapy often is aimed at a different kind of prejudice than are the methods previously discussed. Persuasion, education, and intergroup contact, as we have seen, all appear to be most useful when prejudice arises from causes other than personality needs. When prejudice serves mainly as a way of handling personal feelings of insecurity or low self-esteem, undermining the logic of prejudice is unlikely to have much effect. Instead, some form of individual or group therapy may be the best approach. Such therapy may be aimed at resolving the personality problems that are causing the prejudice or, more conservatively, at convincing the prejudiced person that prejudice is not a rational way of dealing with one's problems and insecurities (a discussion of therapeutic techniques to reduce prejudice may be found in Sandhu and Aspy, 1997).

Although there is evidence that individual therapy can sometimes reduce prejudice (Allport, 1954, Chap. 30), group therapy is most commonly used, partly because people rarely seek individual therapy primarily to change their ethnic attitudes. When individual therapy does deal with ethnic attitudes, it is usually in relation to some other problem that caused the person to seek therapy. Additionally, the intense, one-to-one, and often long-term interaction between patient and therapist necessary in individual therapy simply does not permit the method to reach any sizable proportion of the large number of prejudiced people in the population. Accordingly, group therapy is more widely used to reduce prejudice, and its use for that purpose has been more widely evaluated. There is evidence that both group therapy aimed at personality change (Haimowitz and Haimowitz, 1950; Pearl, 1954; Rubin, 1967) and group therapy that shows that prejudice is a poor way of adjusting by revealing the personality dynamics of prejudice (Katz, Sarnoff, and McClintock, 1956; Stotland, Katz, and Patchen, 1959) can be effective in reducing prejudice.

Research by Grossarth-Maticek, Eysenck, and Vetter (1989) has shown that among people with prejudice-prone personality types, cognitive-behavioral therapy aimed at changing personality patterns can reduce prejudice. Another study evaluated weekly group therapy sessions conducted in a residential setting with nine- to sixteen-year-olds who had a history of maladjustment problems. The therapy, which addressed such topics as racial tolerance, led to declines in prejudice that were sustained three and six months later and at the time the youths left the residential community (Lowenstein, 1985). Another type of therapy is rational-emotive therapy, which uses experimental methods to help people achieve peaceful human relationships and reduce anger and hostility, which are common causes of prejudice (Ellis, 1992). Finally, several studies have shown that individual or group therapy aimed at increasing self-acceptance (in other words, learning to accept rather than deny one's shortcomings) produces both increases in self-acceptance and decreases in prejudice (Fishbein, 1996, pp. 251–52). A more controversial approach is therapy aimed at preventing people from expressing or acting on their prejudices rather than directly attacking the prejudices themselves. The goal of this type of therapy is to help people to control their actions by pursuing a goal of not behaving in a biased manner (Hewstone, Rubin, and Willis, 2002, p. 588). There is some evidence that changing behavior in this way may later lead to reductions in prejudice (Leippe and Eisenstadt, 1994), an idea explored further later in this chapter.

Although group therapy can be effective in reducing prejudice, it can be difficult to distinguish the effects of the therapy itself from the effects of intergroup contact occurring in the therapeutic group. For example, R. D. Ashmore (1970) has pointed out that because the groups in many studies of group therapy are racially diverse, some of the reduction in prejudice probably is a result of the effects of intergroup contact. In some of the studies, the people were relatively well educated and may have been more motivated than the typical person to reduce their prejudices. More typically, highly prejudiced people tend to avoid any kind of therapy because they do not believe they are prejudiced and, as noted in Chapter 2, anti-introspection is a characteristic of authoritarian personalities. Thus, even group therapy probably does not reach many of the people who need it most, and when it does, the reasons for entering therapy may have little to do with prejudice.

Another way that has been suggested to reduce personality-related prejudice is to induce people to change their child-rearing practices. As we saw in Chapter 2, those with prejudiced personalities often grew up in overly strict, authoritarian homes. Unfortunately, however, the parents who are most authoritarian are least likely to be influenced by the child-rearing advice of psychologists and sociologists.

## Overview

We have seen that depending on the situation, the kind of prejudice, the reasons a person is prejudiced, and other factors, persuasion, education, contact, simulation exercises, and therapy can be effective in reducing prejudice. However, none of these approaches offers great promise for reducing the strongest or most deeply entrenched kinds of prejudice. An additional problem is that such interventions often are put in place only after a crisis, such as a racial fight—precisely the most difficult time to change racial attitudes. Fortunately, more businesses and schools today are offering diversity education or training on a routine basis, before trouble begins. But in many instances such interventions occur only after a crisis develops.

Regardless of what method is used to reduce prejudice, research suggests some general guidelines. Hawley et al. (1995) identified the following general principles:

- Strategies should address both individual and institutional sources of prejudice and discrimination.
- Strategies should seek to influence behavior, not just provide information.
- Strategies should address attitudes and behaviors of all racial or ethnic groups involved.
- Strategies should include participants who reflect the diversity of the social context and encourage equal-status, cooperative interaction.
- Strategies should have the support of those with authority and power in the setting.
- Strategies should involve children at an early age and new entrants to the organization at an early stage.
- Strategies should be part of learning activities that are valued and incorporated throughout the organization.
- Strategies should address similarities and differences between and within racial and ethnic groups, including differences related to class, gender, and language.
- Strategies should recognize the value of people with bicultural or multicultural backgrounds and the challenges such people face.
- Strategies should expose the inaccuracies of myths that perpetuate stereotypes.
- Those implementing the strategies should be thoroughly trained and given opportunities to adapt the strategies to their particular setting.
- Strategies should be tailored to the learning needs of participants and evaluated on an ongoing basis.
- It should be recognized that the consequences of prejudice and discrimination for one group may not be the same as for others.

Note that many of these strategies in one way or another address the larger social or organizational environment. Many sociologists believe that the causes of prejudice are to be found mostly in features of the wider society, such as competition between blacks and whites for scarce jobs. Often, too, the unequal division of labor among different groups itself leads to stereotyping. This has been shown to occur even with imaginary groups that were described as having different social roles (Hoffman and Hurst, 1990). Additionally, social roles often carry strong pressures to behave in a discriminatory manner. Consider a department store clerk whose boss believes that Mexican Americans are likely to shoplift. The clerks in the store have been warned that their jobs will be at risk if the rate of theft in the store does not decline, and the boss has made it clear that she thinks Mexican Americans are doing most of the stealing. Consequently, the clerk follows Mexican Americans around to watch for theft. Because he is following Mexican Americans but not Anglos, he is discriminating, especially because in many cases the Mexican Americans have not behaved in any suspicious way. But what is the cause of this behavior? Probably it is not the clerk's own prejudice; rather, it results from his role expectation: "Please the boss." Of course, one could argue that he ought to refuse to do this, even at the risk of getting fired (some of my students have reported quitting jobs over events like these). However, if he needs the job and fears he can't find another one, his own lack of power clearly plays some role.

Therefore, many sociologists believe that the most promising approach to reducing prejudice is to alter the features of society that cause people to be prejudiced or to discriminate. This view is explored extensively in later portions of this book. A closely related view is that prejudiced attitudes are largely produced by discriminatory behavior (Raab and Lipset, 1959). According to this view, prejudiced attitudes develop largely to support or rationalize discriminatory behavior that has become institutionalized in some social settings. This suggests that strategies such as persuasion, therapy, and education are unlikely to succeed unless accompanied by efforts to prevent discriminatory behavior, because it is largely the discrimination that causes the prejudice.

A question that follows is whether prejudice is really an important cause of discriminatory behavior. Although it is popularly believed that attitudes cause behavior, there is some reason to question the extent to which they really do so. In the remainder of the chapter, we shall focus on questions relating to the importance of prejudice as a cause of discrimination and to the reverse possibility, that discrimination may in some cases be a cause of prejudice.

## ► HOW IMPORTANT IS PREJUDICE?

Just how important is prejudice as a cause of discriminatory behavior? A classic study by La Piere (1934) illustrates dramatically that discrimination does not always follow from prejudice. La Piere, a white man, traveled around the United States with a Chinese couple. They visited 66 hotels and motels and 184 restaurants. Of all the establishments, only one refused them service. Six months later, he sent a letter to each establishment, asking whether it would serve Chinese guests. Only about half answered the letter, but of those that did, 92 percent indicated that they would *not* serve Chinese guests. (Obviously, such a response would be illegal today, but at that time it was not.) Kutner, Wilkins, and Yarrow (1952) obtained substantially the same results in visits to restaurants by a group of blacks and whites. It is evident that the operators of the establishments had some racial prejudices and preferred not to serve Chinese Americans or African Americans. When presented with an actual face-to-face encounter, however, they did. Why? There are several possibilities. Perhaps in the actual situation, the proprietors did not have the nerve to say no. Other values—the desire to avoid a scene or to avoid seeming unkind—may have outweighed the prejudice. Perhaps, too, the presence of a white person with the Chinese or black people made a difference. It could be that when the operators of the establishments answered the letters, they did not envision the possibility of a racially mixed group of customers. To a prejudiced white, a Chinese person with a white person may have seemed "safer" to serve (or riskier not to serve) than a Chinese person alone.

Ironically, research has indicated that behavioral intentions such as those measured in these studies may be the kind of attitudes that best predict behavior (Fishbein and Ajzen, 1975; Ajzen and Fishbein, 1980). Studies indicate that stated behavioral intentions explain about half of the variation in actual behavior (Sheppard, Hartwick, and Warshaw, 1988; Tesser and Shaffer, 1990). Still, the specific nature of the situation in which the behavior occurs sometimes has a greater effect on behavior than plans or intentions about how to behave. Group norms influence the behavior and the degree of attitude-behavior consistency, especially if the group is highly important to the individual (Wellen, Hogg, and Terry, 1998). In addition, generalized attitudes, such as prejudice, have been shown to be much weaker predictors of behavior, in part because they do not directly prescribe any given behavior (Eagly, 1992, pp. 695–97). Finally, experiments have shown that even when people are thinking of a particular group, who is called to mind as an example of that group has a big influence on whether they behave consistently with their attitudes (Sia et al., 1997). Thus, it is not surprising that prejudiced attitudes—even ones that directly support discrimination—do not always lead to that behavior.

## Merton's Typology on Prejudice and Discrimination

Robert Merton (1949) developed a useful typology based on the principle that prejudice and discrimination do not always occur together. He developed four classifications concerning prejudice and discrimination (see Figure 3.1). Type 1, the unprejudiced nondiscriminator, or *all-weather liberal*, behaves consistently with his or her beliefs, as does type 4, the prejudiced discriminator or *all-weather bigot*. Many people—perhaps most—do not fit into either of these categories, however. Some (type 2) are *fair-weather liberals*: They are not prejudiced, but they discriminate anyway. Others (type 3) are *timid bigots*: They are prejudiced but do not discriminate. How can the behavior of fair-weather liberals and timid bigots be explained? In both cases, the answer is likely to be found in social pressures that influence people's behavior so that it does not always reflect their beliefs. The fair-weather liberal (unprejudiced discriminator) may discriminate because his or her friends or work associates discriminate and expect others to do so. It is simply easier to discriminate than to risk the ridicule or criticism that could result from doing otherwise. For fair-weather liberals, social policies that create pressure *not* to discriminate or that reduce the pressure to discriminate may be very effective in reducing or eliminating discriminatory behavior. Greater contact with all-weather liberals may also reduce discrimination because such contact would strengthen and reinforce their unprejudiced attitudes and perhaps make them aware of the inconsistency of their behavior. The timid bigots (prejudiced nondiscriminators) are also inconsistent in their behavior. Although they would like to discriminate, they don't because they fear running afoul of civil rights laws or, like La Piere's (1934) subjects, they are simply too uncomfortable to discriminate in the face-to-face situation. If they are businesspeople, they might avoid discrimination for fear of losing minority business. When such people have the opportunity or power to discriminate without suffering any consequences, they usually will, but in the face of consequences, they usually will not. Accordingly, antidiscrimination laws probably are an important way to prevent discrimination by such people, especially if they are well enforced.

Very few people fit unambiguously into any one category all of the time. The lines between categories can be fuzzy, behavior often varies from one incident to the next, and both prejudice and discrimination are partly a matter of degree. Also, prejudice today often is more subtle than in the past and thus harder to detect. Even so, prejudice and discrimination do not always go together. In any particular case, the presence or absence of discrimination is influenced by a number of factors other than prejudice. The pressures of any given situation can affect behavior as much as or more than personal attitudes.

In general, attitude-behavior research supports this interpretation. It suggests that behavior is influenced by attitudes but also by norms—the expectations of oth-

|  | Does Not Discriminate | Discriminates |
|---|---|---|
| *Unprejudiced* | 1. Unprejudiced nondiscriminator (All-Weather Liberal) | 2. Unprejudiced discriminator (Fair-Weather Liberal) |
| *Prejudiced* | 3. Prejudiced nondiscriminator (Timid Bigot) | 4. Prejudiced discriminator (All-Weather Bigot) |

**FIGURE 3.1**    Merton's Typology on Prejudice and Discrimination

*Note:* The shaded boxes represent behavior inconsistent with beliefs.

ers. If attitudes and norms conflict, people may often behave consistently with the norms, not their own attitudes. When norms and attitudes are more similar, people will be more free to behave consistently with their attitudes (Fishbein and Ajzen, 1975; Grube and Morgan, 1990; Olson and Zanna, 1993). In addition, other personal attitudes—for example, the desire to please others—may conflict with one's ethnic attitudes. How one behaves in such situations may be determined largely by which of the conflicting attitudes is stronger or more salient. In some cases, too, the strength of people's own sense of control over their behavior may also be a factor in determining whether they behave in ways consistent with their attitudes or with the norms and expectations of others (Ajzen, 1991).

## Can Behavior Determine Attitudes?

We have established that attitudes do not always determine behavior. We can now go a step further and ask whether behavior can sometimes determine attitudes. A social-psychological theory known as **cognitive dissonance theory** (Festinger, 1957) is relevant to this question. Cognitive dissonance theory says that we want to believe that our behavior is consistent with our attitudes. Accordingly, if—because of social pressure or for some other reason—we repeatedly behave in a manner inconsistent with our attitudes, we tend to unconsciously change our *attitudes* so that the attitudes and behavior are again consistent. For instance, Festinger and Carlsmith (1959) found that laboratory subjects who were asked to do a boring task and did so decided afterward that the task had really been quite interesting, even when given very little reward for doing it. Other subjects, who had been paid more for doing the same task, later said that it had been dull and boring. The difference was that these subjects could say, "It was stupid, but I did it for the money," but the poorly paid subjects could make no such rationalization. They could either say, "I did this dumb task and got almost nothing for doing it" or "That was really fun." Most chose the latter. Since Festinger's original research, a variety of studies have confirmed the principle that behavior influences attitudes. Researchers continue to debate what precise thought processes lead to such attitudinal change, but the general principle that people often change their attitudes in response to how they have already behaved has received strong support from social-psychological research (Eagly, 1992; Eagly and Chaiken, 1993).

The application of these findings to race relations can perhaps be best seen in the American South. The most dramatic declines in prejudice and discrimination in the United States in the decades after World War II occurred in that region. The decline did not occur as a result of voluntary attitude change; rather, the South was forced to change by federal legislation, court orders, and at times intervention of federal marshals and federal troops under the order of the president. *After* overt discrimination had been outlawed and had become less common, attitudes changed to become consistent with behavior. In effect, it was easier to say, "We don't discriminate because we know now that discrimination is wrong" than to say, "We really want to discriminate, but we don't because the Washington bureaucrats told us we can't." The new viewpoint even put southerners in a position to tell whites who protested school desegregation in the 1970s in Boston and Michigan to "practice what you preach; we are." In fact, something much like that occurred, as students from desegregated schools in North Carolina were invited to help students in northern states to adapt to school desegregation. Indeed, the experiences of the South since World War II seriously challenge the old truism that legislation can't change people's minds. Although prejudice has not been eliminated in the South or elsewhere, it has been substantially reduced, and an important cause of this reduction was legislation that forced behavior to change by banning open and deliberate forms of discrimination. In short, a change in behavior led to a change in attitudes (for further discussion of these issues, see Sheatsley, 1966; Bem, 1970, pp. 68–69). This interpretation is supported by findings from social psychology experiments in which nondiscriminatory behavior was elicited in prejudiced subjects, which resulted in a reduction in prejudice (Leippe and Eisenstadt, 1994).

## Prejudice and Discrimination in America Today

Because prejudice is not always accompanied by discrimination and because a reduction in discrimination can cause a reduction in prejudice, many social scientists believe that prejudice is not really an important cause of discrimination. More important, they argue, are characteristics of the larger society, such as the relative power and numbers of different races and ethnic groups and the degree of competition between groups for scarce resources such as jobs and housing. Furthermore, a strong argument can be made that both prejudice and open, deliberate discrimination are much less important today as causes of racial and ethnic inequality than they were in the past.

**Cognitive Prejudice and Stereotyping.** We know that at least the more open forms of prejudice are less prevalent today. Studies of cognitive forms of prejudice show that negative stereotyping of minority groups, once common, declined sharply between about 1930 and 1970. A series of studies of Princeton University students in 1933, 1951, and 1967 illustrates the change. Students were given lists of traits and asked to mark those that were true of each of a variety of ethnic groups. Data from these studies, showing a steady decline in negative stereotyping of blacks, are presented in Table 3.1. The same studies show similar tendencies for stereotypes of Chinese (sharp reductions in "superstitious" and "sly"), Jews (greatly reduced tendency to mark "shrewd" and "mercenary"), and Turks (large reduction in "cruel"). However, there appears to have been an increased tendency to attribute more positive stereotypes to minority groups, such as "musical" for blacks, "ambitious" for Jews, and "loyal to family ties" for Chinese. This suggests that people still think in stereotypes, but they are much less willing today than in the past to stereotype minority groups negatively. The opposite may be true of stereotypes of the majority group. There was a large reduction in marking "industrious" and "intelligent" for "Americans" and an even larger increase in "materialistic." By 1967, this trait was marked more than twice as often as any other. A reduction in cognitive prejudices toward minorities—at least the negative type—can also be seen in the first part of Table 3.2, which shows a huge increase in the percentage of whites who agree that blacks are as intelligent as whites. In 1942, fewer than half of white Americans agreed with such a statement; since the mid-1950s, studies have consistently shown that 70 percent to 80 percent agree with it.

| Table 3.1 | Characteristics Assigned to Blacks by White Princeton University Students | | |
|---|---|---|---|
| | 1933 | 1951 | 1967 |
| Superstitious | 84% | 41% | 13% |
| Lazy | 75 | 31 | 26 |
| Happy-go-lucky | 38 | 17 | 27 |
| Ignorant | 38 | 24 | 11 |
| Musical | 26 | 33 | 47 |

*Source:* Adapted from Marvin Karlins, Thomas Coffman, and Gary Walters, "On the Fading of Social Stereotypes: Studies of Three Generations of College Students," *Journal of Personality and Social Psychology* 13:1–6. Copyright 1969 by the American Psychological Association. Reprinted by permission.

## Table 3.2    Whites' Perceptions of Blacks over Time

| | Year | Percentage of Whites Who Agree with Statement |
|---|---|---|
| "Blacks are as intelligent as whites"[a] | 1942 | 42% |
| | 1956 | 78 |
| | 1976 | 72 |
| | 1978 | 75 |
| "I would not object if a black of the same income and education as mine moved onto my block."[b] | 1942 | 35% |
| | 1956 | 51 |
| | 1968 | 65 |
| | 1972 | 84 |
| | 1986–1987 | 79 |
| | 1997 | 99 |
| "White children and black children should attend the same schools."[c] | 1942 | 30% |
| | 1956 | 48 |
| | 1968 | 60 |
| | 1970 | 73 |
| | 1972 | 84 |
| | 1977 | 85 |
| | 1980 | 87 |
| | 1983 | 89 |
| | 1983–1987 | 91 |

*Sources:* [a]1942–1956: Hyman and Sheatsley (1964); 1976–1978: *Newsweek* (1979).
[b]1942–1968: Skolnick (1969, pp. 179–82); 1972: R. Farley (1977); 1986–1987: Schuman and Bobo (1988); 1997: Gallup Organization (1997). The 1997 figure is based on the percentage (1%) who said they would object if a black family moved next door.
[c]1942–1968: Skolnick (1969); 1970: Greenley and Sheatsley (1971); 1972: R. Farley (1977); 1977–1987: Tuch (1988); National Opinion Research Center (2003).

On the one hand, this change is encouraging because it suggests a real change in attitude: If you express racial stereotypes, you are more likely to anger your friends or colleagues than would have been the case fifty years ago because more people today genuinely disapprove of racial stereotyping. On the other hand, the fact that stereotyping is less socially acceptable today leads some people to mask their stereotyped thinking. This is clear from surveys that ask about racial stereotypes in subtler ways. For example, a national survey on racial attitudes in 1990 showed reductions in prejudice from 1972, but it also revealed that stereotyping may be more widespread than previous surveys suggested (National Opinion Research Center, 1991). Rather than asking people to agree or disagree with a stereotype of a particular group, as earlier surveys had done, this survey asked respondents to rank various groups on a scale of one to seven on how well they fit each of six stereotypes. As Green and Manzi (2002) point out, there may be less pressure to give a "politically correct" answer in a ranking or sorting task than in one in which respondents are asked to label a group negatively. The result: 78 percent in the 1990 survey ranked blacks more likely than whites to prefer welfare over work, and 74 percent ranked Hispanics more likely than whites. In sharp contrast to the findings of surveys that used the old methodology, 55 percent ranked Hispanics as less intelligent than whites, and 53 percent ranked blacks as less intelligent. Blacks and Hispanics were also seen as lazier and less patriotic than whites.

Thus, subtler forms of stereotyping remain much more widespread than some surveys suggest. And other surveys still show considerable evidence of stereotyping. Sniderman and Piazza (1993) found a good deal of negative stereotyping of African Americans by whites. For example, the majority believed that "most" blacks on welfare could get a job if they really tried; nearly half agreed that "if blacks would only try harder, they would be just as well off as whites" and that black neighborhoods are run down because "blacks simply don't take care of their property."

Other studies show that the stereotype of "lazy" African Americans remains widespread among whites and has a strong impact on their political opinions (Gilens, 1995). W. J. Wilson (1996) found a good deal of negative stereotyping of black men by Chicago area employers, which often influenced their hiring decisions. Finally, Kluegel and Bobo (1991) found that white Americans commonly stereotyped not only African Americans but also Hispanic and Asian Americans in several negative ways, including being less hard-working and more prone to violence. Thus, although some types of prejudice have declined, stereotyping remains common, especially beliefs about the degree to which different groups exhibit different cultural traits and especially in surveys that ask about it in subtler ways (Jackman and Senter, 1983; Bobo, 1988).

The latter is evident in another survey on stereotyping. In this study, respondents were asked about stereotypes of "blacks," "Negroes," and "Afro-Americans." Although these terms all apply to the same racial group, people responded to them differently. They were most stereotypical in their responses to "blacks" and least so to "Afro-Americans," with responses to "Negroes" in between (Fairchild, 1985).

**Social Distance.** A trend toward less prejudice does appear evident in measures of *social distance*. Social distance refers to a preference to avoid certain kinds of contact with minority groups. In general, the closer the supposed contact (say, living next door as opposed to shopping in the same store), the greater the tendency to maintain social distance or avoid contact. One commonly used measure of social distance developed by Bogardus (1968) was administered to U.S. college students in 1926, 1946, 1956, 1966, 1977, and 2001. The items on this scale range from "would marry into group" to "would debar from my nation." The results of these studies for selected groups are presented in Table 3.3. The larger the average social distance score shown in the table, the less accepting the students were of a group. These studies show a substantial decline in social distance for minority groups over the seventy-five-year period. An especially sharp decline occurred for blacks between 1966 and 1977, and for all groups between 1977 and 2001. Still, consistent with the stereotyping studies, social distance increased between 1966 and 1977 for the dominant group (white Americans) and also increased slightly for Japanese Americans, but has again fallen since.

**Conative Prejudice and Attitudes Toward Discrimination.** As indicated in Chapter 2, another important form of prejudice is conative, a desire to behave in a discriminatory way toward a group. The findings in Table 3.2 show that there has been a major change here too, at least for some types of conative prejudice. Far fewer whites in recent years than in the early 1940s indicated a desire to discriminate in the areas of schools and housing. However, this trend occurred largely between 1942 and 1972, with somewhat less change thereafter on these two measures. Research by Firebaugh and Davis (1988), the National Opinion Research Center (1991), and the Gallup Organization (1997) indicates that in the overall white population, other measures of conative prejudice against African Americans showed a fairly steady decline from 1972 into the 1990s. For example, the proportion of whites opposing

| Table 3.3 | Bogardus Social Distance Scores for Selected Groups, U.S. National Samples of College Students | | | | | |
|---|---|---|---|---|---|---|
| | 1926 | 1946 | 1956 | 1966 | 1977 | 2001 |
| Americans | 1.10 | 1.04 | 1.08 | 1.07 | 1.25 | 1.07 |
| African Americans[a] | 3.28 | 3.60 | 2.74 | 2.56 | 2.03 | 1.34 |
| Mexican Americans | — | 2.52 | 2.51 | 2.37 | 2.17 | 1.55 |
| American Indians | 2.38 | 2.45 | 2.35 | 2.12 | 1.84 | 1.40 |
| Japanese Americans | — | 2.90 | 2.34 | 2.14 | 2.18 | 1.52 |
| Mean, 30 groups | 2.14[b] | 2.12 | 2.08 | 1.92 | 1.93 | 1.44 |

[a]Referred to as "Negroes" in 1977 and earlier surveys.
[b]Twenty-eight groups in 1926.

*Sources:* Emory Borgardus, "Comparing Racial Distance in Ethiopia, South Africa, and the United States," *Sociology and Social Research* (1968), 52:149–56; Carolyn Owen, Howard C. Eisner, and Thomas R. McFaul, "A Half Century of Social Distance Research: National Replication of the Bogardus Studies, *Sociology and Social Research* (1981), 66:80–98; Vincent N. Parrillo, "Updating the Bogardus Social Distance Study: A New National Survey" (Paper presented at the annual meeting of the American Sociological Association, August 16–19, 2002, Chicago).

laws against racial intermarriage rose from 48 to 76 percent between 1972 and 1990. Also, white support for busing to desegregate schools more than doubled, from 14 percent to 29 percent, although the majority of whites still disapproved of this policy (and this trend may since have reversed as many busing programs have been dismantled since the mid-1990s). For the first time, in 1997, a majority of white Gallup poll respondents indicated a preference for living in a neighborhood "with both black and white familes" rather than "in a neighborhood with white families," although one in four still expressed the latter preference. In a large change from earlier Gallup polls, just two in ten whites said that they would object if blacks "in large numbers" moved to their neighborhood (Gallup Organization, 1997). Also for the first time, the majority of whites said they approved of interracial marriages: This percentage rose from just 4 percent forty years earlier to 61 percent in 1991 (see Figure 3.2). However, about one-fourth of blacks and nearly 40 percent of whites still objected to interracial marriage in 1997.

As noted earlier, survey data must be used with some caution. People often have objections that they do not express in response to quick survey questions, so that the survey data may paint an overly optimistic picture. We know this from qualitative interview studies: People who say in surveys that they do not object to interracial marriage often do express objections to it when asked about it in more in-depth qualitative interviews (Bonilla-Silva and Forman, 2000; Bonilla-Silva, 2002). This may indicate that people are giving survey-takers "politically correct" or socially approved answers, that surveys are simply too "quick and easy" to detect underlying racial attitudes, or both (Feagin, 2000, 2001).

The declines in prejudice that did occur seem to have happened partly because people's attitudes were changing but also partly because less prejudiced younger generations were replacing more prejudiced older ones. However, the generational effect was bigger than the attitude change for several measures of prejudice. Among both blacks and whites, age is a strong predictor of attitudes. The younger the person, the more likely he or she is to approve interracial marriage. Another recent attitude change shown in the Gallup survey is in the willingness of whites to vote for an African American for the U.S. presidency. As recently as the late 1980s, about a quarter of whites said they were unwilling to do this, but by 1997, hardly any

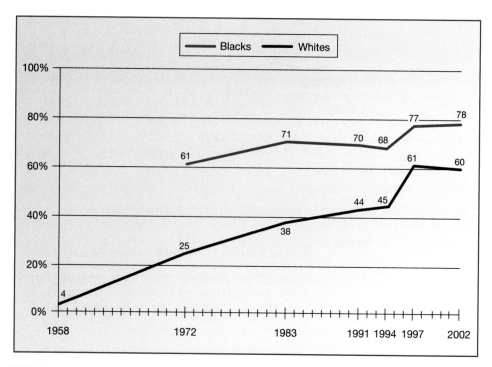

**FIGURE 3.2**    Percentage Who Approve of Marriage Between Blacks and Whites, 1958–2002
*Source:* Gallup Organization, 1997, 2003a.

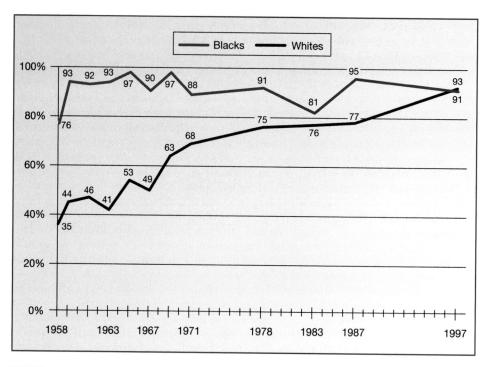

**FIGURE 3.3**    Percentage Who Would Vote for a Black Candidate for President, 1958–1997
*Source:* Gallup Organization, 1997.

said that (see Figure 3.3). Again, though, actual voting patterns often differ from what people say they are willing to do.

**Attitudes Among Minority Groups.**  A related issue that has received growing attention from researchers in recent years is prejudice among minority groups. In some cases, negative stereotypes are so entrenched in society that minorities themselves accept them. Around half of both whites and blacks agreed that blacks are "aggressive," "boastful," and "complaining" (Sniderman and Piazza, 1993, p. 45). Another problem is that minority group members sometimes accept dominant group prejudices toward members of other minority groups, sometimes while accepting more positive stereotypes of the dominant group. For example, one study showed that African Americans and Mexican Americans expressed greater social distance toward each other than either group did toward whites (Dyer, Vedlitz, and Worchel, 1989).

Tensions and prejudices among minority groups, like other kinds of prejudice, often are fed by conflict, competition, and fear. Tensions have risen between black and Hispanic Americans in some areas because each group has perceived the other as taking jobs and economic opportunities, thereby contributing to the continuing poverty of their own group (Fears, 1994). In addition, anger toward Korean shopowners among black and Hispanic customers led to some targeting of Korean businesses during the 1992 Los Angeles riot, and similar resentment toward Koreans who own shops in African American neighborhoods has been noted in New York and other cities. One reason for these tensions is that the minority population in the United States is more diverse today than in the past. In the recent past, the minority population was overwhelmingly African American. Even as recently as 1970, Hispanics and Asians combined amounted to less than 6 percent of the population, whereas 11 percent were black. Today, however, Asian Americans make up about 4 percent of the population and Hispanic Americans nearly 14 percent, whereas African Americans are about 13 percent (U.S. Census Bureau, 2004b). In this situation the perception of competition and threat can lead to intergroup tensions, which in turn can give rise to prejudices. Having said this, it is not clear whether there have been increases in out-group prejudices among different minority groups in the United States because, until recently, very few data on such attitudes were available.

Overall, survey data do not indicate a resurgence of prejudice in the United States since 1980, although it does appear that declines in prejudice have slowed, perhaps in part because the more blatant forms of prejudice have become so rare that there is not much room for further declines. Subtler forms of prejudice are alive and well, however, and surveys do indicate that some forms of prejudice, particularly cultural stereotyping, have remained quite widespread.

## Symbolic Racism

Despite some indications of declining prejudice, a case can be made that more subtle forms of prejudice remain widespread. We have already seen that this is the case for stereotypes. Another example is a type of conative prejudice called *symbolic racism* (Kinder and Sears, 1981) or sometimes *modern racism* (McConahay, Hardee, and Batts, 1981). While rejecting stereotypes and blatant discrimination, this form of racism involves opposition to any social policy that would enable minorities to escape their disadvantaged position in American society (Pettigrew, 1985). In fact, trends in survey responses show very clearly that since around 1950, there has been a widening gap between responses to questions about segregation and integration as a *principle* and questions about social policy. For example, in 1986, 93 percent of whites supported the principle of integrated schooling, but just 27 percent supported government efforts to bring about more integration. Similar gaps exist in the areas of jobs and housing (Bobo, Kluegel, and Smith, 1998).

The more subtle form of prejudice known as symbolic racism appears to be based on a belief, apparently learned in childhood socialization, that blacks are getting unfair advantages that violate basic American norms such as individualism and self-reliance. A key element of this form of prejudice appears to be a denial of the presence of racial inequality in society: Kluegel and Smith (1982, 1986; Kluegel, 1990) showed that the majority of white Americans believe that blacks have equal or greater chances to get ahead in life compared with whites. Recent polls indicate that this perception has persisted into the new century (Helem, 2001; Ludwig, 2003a). A 2001 poll illustrates this persistent pattern: 83 percent of whites believed that blacks have as much access to whites to housing that they can afford, whereas only 48 percent of blacks share this belief (Helem, 2001). Overall, in 2003, 73 percent of whites believed that blacks are treated as well as whites in their communities, compared with just 39 percent of African Americans (Ludwig, 2003). In a society in which nearly one black or Hispanic child out of three lives in poverty and the chance of dying before reaching the age of one is twice as great for a black baby as for a white baby, the belief that whites and blacks (or Hispanics) have the same opportunities in life is preposterous, yet many whites believe it anyway.

Apparently, whites view racism and discrimination differently than do blacks (Blauner, 1989, 1994). Whites tend to see racism and discrimination as individual acts of deliberate discrimination, whereas people of color are much more likely to see racism as an institutionalized system of unequal opportunity (Bonilla-Silva, 2003a, 2003c). In the terminology of this book, whites see racism as individual discrimination, whereas minorities are much more likely to see it as institutional discrimination. Because individual discrimination today has largely gone underground—in other words, people who engage in it generally deny doing so—it is harder to see than in the past, so whites do not readily see it or experience its consequences. Because this is the case and because most whites associate racism and discrimination with such individual behavior, it is easy for them to deny their existence. Yet the experiences of minorities, as well as discrimination-testing studies, show that even individual discrimination remains fairly common. For example, a 2003 Gallup poll showed that, in the past month, about 28 percent of African Americans had experienced unfair treatment because of their race in a store, and more than 20 percent said the same for their workplace, for restaurants, bars, or theaters and for treatment by the police (Ludwig, 2003a).

For whites, believing in the existence of equal opportunity provides a sense of diminished responsibility for racial inequality. Thus, whites can think of themselves as accepting, unprejudiced people without having to acknowledge that they live in and benefit from a society where race makes a huge difference in opportunity. They do this by denying or being unaware of the great inequality in their society (Wellman, 1993; Schutte, 1995), which then they do not have to face. By so doing, they can maintain a myth that society is *color-blind*, and that race not only should not matter but *doesn't* (Bonilla-Silva, 2003c). However, the problem is that ignoring the reality of racial inequality perpetuates that inequality by doing nothing to change it. Bonilla-Silva (2003a, 2003c) has called this phenomenon "color-blind racism."

In this belief system, stereotypes become useful. If whites can believe that blacks, Hispanics, and other people of color are violent or lazy or don't take care of their property, unequal opportunity isn't an issue. Instead, they can blame any disadvantage they see minorities suffer on the minorities themselves (Bobo, Kluegel, and Smith, 1996). Indeed, Kinder and Sanders (1996) have shown that beliefs among whites about the willingness of minorities to exert effort to improve their status have a big influence on white attitudes about policies both directly and indirectly related to race. And as discussed earlier, a variety of studies have shown that stereotyping of African Americans, Latinos, and other people of color remains widespread. Thus, a case can be made that prejudice has changed its form but is still around; it may even be more insidious because it is less obvious. This is further supported by several studies of attitude-behavior consistency showing that, in Merton's terminology, there are more fair-weather liberals than timid bigots. These studies show that although most prejudiced people do discriminate, fewer who score low on traditional prejudice scales behave in a nondiscriminatory manner (Linn, 1965; Fendrich, 1967; Duckitt, 1993b). Additionally, it appears that measures of symbolic racism may be better predictors of whether people discriminate than measures of traditional racism (Duckitt, 1993b).

## Do Attitudes Cause Intergroup Inequality?

Attitude surveys over the past thirty years consistently indicate a reduction in the expression of the more blatant forms of stereotyped thinking and, even more so, in the desire to openly discriminate. Despite this change, racial and ethnic inequalities in America persist. In Chapter 9, we explore in detail the status of a variety of American minority groups. A fair summary of that material is that despite improvement in some areas, very substantial inequalities persist. In some areas there has been no real improvement and, in some cases, inequalities have even worsened. This brings us back to the question raised at the beginning of this chapter: If prejudice has declined but inequality persists, just how important can majority group attitudes be as a cause of racial inequality? Social scientists answer this question in two ways, and there is no unanimous belief about which answer is better.

### The Affirmative Answer: Attitudes Do Cause Inequality.

Several kinds of arguments are made by those believe that white attitudes remain an important cause of minority disadvantage, even today when surveys indicate that a number of prejudices have decreased. First, they point out that the prejudice has by no means been eliminated, despite the changes. The social distance scores for blacks, Chicanos, American Indians, and Asian and Arab Americans remain significantly higher than those for white Americans and for European groups (Kleg and Yamamoto, 1998). And as we have seen, stereotyping about the cultural attributes of racial and ethnic groups remains quite common. In addition, public opinion research shows that racial attitudes do make a difference in what public policies people support. For example, one recent study found that racial attitudes, particularly a tendency to stereotype minorities as lazy, were the best predictor of opposition to welfare among whites (Gilens, 1995). A major reason why many whites oppose efforts to increase opportunities for African Americans is that they do not believe that African Americans are making enough effort to get ahead (Kinder and Sanders, 1996).

Consistent with the notion of symbolic racism, there is indeed a notable unwillingness on the part of most whites to support efforts aimed at undoing the effects of discrimination. For example, just 36 percent of whites in a 2003 Gallup poll said that government should make every effort to help minorities, compared with 67 percent of African Americans. The majority of whites said no special effort was needed (McMurray, 2003). In the two states where referenda to end affirmative action have been put on the ballot (California and Washington), the referenda have passed. Moreover, when whites, who generally deny the existence of black disadvantage, are pressed to account for whatever disadvantage blacks do experience, they often maintain that blacks themselves are mainly responsible, as shown in Table 3.4 (Schuman, 1975; see also Feagin, 1972; Kinder and Sanders, 1996). This goes hand in hand with cultural stereotyping.

The belief that minorities are mainly responsible for their own disadvantages is not grounded in reality. The effects of growing up in poverty are enough to greatly reduce the opportunities one has in life, and African American and Latino children

**Table 3.4    Opinions About Who or What Is Mainly to Blame for Black Disadvantage: Two National Surveys**

| 1974 (white respondents only) | | 1998 (all respondents, multiple responses allowed) | |
| --- | --- | --- | --- |
| Discrimination by whites | 19% | Mainly discrimination | 35% |
| Negroes themselves | 54 | Blacks have less ability to learn | 10 |
| Mixture of both | 19 | Blacks have less chance to get education | 43 |
| Denied disadvantage or refused to answer | 4 | Blacks lack motivation or will power | 42 |
| Don't know | 4 | | |

*Sources:* 1974 data are from Schuman (1975). 1998 data are from National Opinion Research Center (2003).

are more than twice as likely as white children to live below the poverty level. Additionally, African Americans and Latinos continue to experience discrimination, both individual and institutional (Feagin, 2000; Feagin and Sikes, 1994; Ludwig, 2003a). Rather than being based on facts, the belief that blacks and Hispanics are responsible for their own disadvantages appears deeply rooted in an American ideology of individualism, a belief that each individual determines his or her own situation (Sniderman and Hagen, 1985; Kluegel and Smith, 1986). Although it conflicts with reality, this belief appears to be shared even by a large number of blacks (Parent, 1980). It is much more common among whites.

Beliefs such as these have an important effect on people's views about public policy on race relations. Research by Kluegel (1990) shows that when people believe that the system is fair, that is, that African Americans and Latinos have the same opportunity as white Americans, they will usually do two things. First, they will blame minorities themselves for any disadvantages they experience rather than blaming white discrimination or an unfair system (Kinder and Sanders, 1996). Second, and partly as a result, they will oppose policies designed to increase minority opportunities, such as busing for school desegregation, affirmative action in hiring and college admissions, and minority scholarships (Kluegel, 1990; see also Sears et al., 1980; McConahay, 1982; Herring et al., 2000). In one regard, such reasoning seems to make sense: If the system is fair and everyone has equal opportunities, then such programs would amount to an unfair advantage for minority groups. The problem, however, is that the system is *not* fair: Numerous discriminatory processes make it harder for some groups to get ahead in American society. In this context, the widespread myth that society is color-blind leads to the incorrect conclusion that behaving in a color-blind way will promote equal opportunity (Bonilla-Silva, 2003a, 2003b). It does not, because both our social institutions and a significant number of whites in fact operate in ways that are *not* color-blind, reducing opportunities for African Americans, Latinos, and other people of color. If nothing is done to counter or offset this, racial inequality will continue.

Of course, this does suggest a way in which attitudes might be changed so that people would be more supportive of policies to increase opportunities for minority groups: Show them convincing evidence that minorities do not today enjoy equal opportunity. In my own classes and in diversity workshops, I have shown a video of a series of hidden camera tests for discrimination that were conducted in the St. Louis area, not far from our campus, in the early 1990s (ABC News, 1991). A black man and a white man of similar age and education visited a number of businesses and agencies over a period of two weeks. Each day, the camera captured incidents in which the black man experienced discrimination. This occurred in stores, auto dealerships, employment agencies, rental offices, and even on the streets and sidewalks of St. Louis. Before showing the video, I presented to these groups a questionnaire similar to the one used by Kluegel (1990; Kluegel and Smith, 1986) and obtained similar results: Whites typically perceive the American system to be a good deal fairer than blacks do. After viewing the video, however, many of the whites indicated that they would now answer the questionnaire differently, having observed more discrimination than they had expected.

Beliefs that African Americans enjoy greater opportunities than they actually do have also been associated with unwillingness among some whites to vote for black political candidates (Kinder and Sears, 1981; J. E. Farley, 1992a). With a few notable exceptions, such as Carol Moseley Braun's successful 1992 U.S. Senate campaign in Illinois and the election of L. Douglas Wilder as governor of Virginia in 1989, it remains relatively uncommon for African Americans to be elected by predominantly white constituencies. In fact, Moseley Braun is the only African American woman who has ever been elected to the U.S. Senate, and Wilder was the first African American elected governor of any state. Neither remains in office today, as Wilder was precluded by state law from succeeding himself, and Moseley Braun was defeated in her 1998 campaign for reelection. The reluctance of many whites to vote for black candidates largely explains why there are only one-tenth as many elected black officials as would be expected, based on the size of the black population. Thus, a strong case can be made that white attitudes, translated into votes and political pressure, still make a difference by blocking policy changes that could break the cycle of racial inequality and by limiting minority political representation.

All in all, it is clearly an overstatement to say that racial attitudes have no effect on racial inequality: We have seen several areas in which they do have an effect. But open to serious question is how large and how important this effect is. Attitudes should not be ignored as a cause of racial and ethnic inequality, nor should they be overplayed. Other factors may be of equal or greater importance than attitudes, as we shall see in the next section.

Carol Moseley Braun, the first African American woman elected to the U.S. Senate, campaigned unsuccessfully for the Democratic presidential nomination in 2004. It remains unusual for black candidates to win elections in which the large majority of voters are white.

**The Negative Answer: Attitudes Are Not an Important Cause of Inequality.** Some social scientists see larger-scale characteristics of social groups and entire societies as the main cause of inequality, not individual attitudes. This idea is explored in detail in the next few chapters; the main objective here is to outline its reasoning. Basically, two kinds of arguments are made. One argument centers on a fact we examined earlier in the chapter: Attitudes and beliefs often change to conform to behavior (as they have in the South since discrimination was made illegal) rather than the other way around (Leippe and Eisenstadt, 1994). Social scientists who hold this view tend to ask, What came first, the attitude or the behavior? If racist attitudes develop merely to rationalize racist behavior that is already present for other reasons, such as personal gain, the attitudes cannot be the cause of the racist behavior; they are merely a supporting mechanism.

The other argument acknowledges that racist attitudes can sometimes lead to racist behavior but questions where the attitudes came from in the first place. If intergroup competition or social and economic insecurity, for example, is the ultimate cause of people's prejudices, it is not productive to point a finger at prejudice as the cause of racial inequality and conflict; rather, the cause runs deeper. Social scientists who hold this view generally downplay the study of prejudice and in particular do not emphasize personality needs or social learning as its root cause. Instead, they believe that prejudice, discrimination, and intergroup conflict are all caused by larger social forces that can be understood only through awareness of how entire societies operate. Thus, to blame racial inequality entirely on prejudice is, at best, an oversimplification. Whatever importance prejudice may have, we cannot have a full understanding of majority-minority relations without also understanding how the characteristics of whole societies shape the relations between the racial and ethnic groups within them.

Bobo, Kluegel, and Smith (1998) argue that cause and effect run in both directions: In part attitudes about race and ethnicity reflect the larger structural conditions of society, but they also affect race relations. For example, they argue that Jim Crow segregation ended in the South largely because of the decline of the plantation-owning class that was the main beneficiary of it, and consequently popular support for segregation declined as well. But at the same time, the denial by many whites of the reality of unequal opportunity enables that inequality to continue. Hence, the larger structural conditions of racial inequality in society influence attitudes, but attitudes also influence inequality. In part for this reason, even those who favor a largely structural approach to changing racial inequality also recognize the importance of addressing individual attitudes and beliefs (Connolly, 2000; Feagin, 2000, pp. 253–55).

## Summary and Conclusion

We have seen that although there is some correspondence between prejudiced attitudes and discriminatory behavior, it is far from a one-to-one relationship. In any given case, a person's prejudice is only one of several factors that determine whether that person actually discriminates. Moreover, at the larger societal level, there is far from a one-to-one relationship between the degree or prevalence of prejudice and the degree of actual racial inequality. Prejudices, at least of some kinds, have greatly declined in the United States from those of forty years ago, but inequality persists. Thus, factors other than prejudice may account for the persistence, if not for the original development, of racial inequality. Finally, we have seen that attitudes sometimes change to conform to behavior rather than the other way around. For all these reasons, prejudice alone cannot totally explain racial and ethnic inequality and conflict. We must also look at larger societal forces, which we shall do in the next part of the book.

## Critical Review Questions

1. How do the *causes* of prejudice influence the ease or difficulty of changing prejudice?

2. Present a short argument on why people's attitudes are an important cause of discrimination and racial inequality. Then, present a short argument on why people's attitudes *are not* an important cause of discrimination and racial inequality.

3. How can racial discrimination or racial inequality cause people to have racial prejudice?

4. From the standpoint of majority group members *and* from the standpoint of minority group members, why is it important for intergroup contact to be on an equal-status basis in order for it to reduce prejudice?

5. Design an activity to be used at your college that uses interdependency to reduce racial prejudice.

# Sociological Perspectives: The Order and Conflict Models

# Overview_____

## ▶ SOCIOLOGICAL VERSUS SOCIAL-PSYCHOLOGICAL APPROACHES TO MAJORITY-MINORITY RELATIONS

In Chapters 2 and 3, we used a primarily *social-psychological* approach to race and ethnic relations. In other words, our concern was with socially learned attitudes and beliefs in *individuals*. In this chapter, we introduce an alternative approach. This approach is *sociological* because, rather than studying individuals, it focuses on *collectivities* of people: groups and societies. It suggests that the nature of interaction between racial and ethnic groups is determined not by the characteristics of individual members but rather by the nature of the groups themselves and the society in which they are found. Those who study majority-minority relations through a **sociological**, or **social-structural, approach** are concerned with such variables as the social, political, and economic organization of a society; the roles played by various ethnic groups; the social organization within the ethnic groups; and the cultures of both the society as a whole and the various groups that compose it.

The sociological approach assumes that the attitudes of individuals are for the most part shaped by these larger social forces, as are the patterns of ethnic relations. In other words, the general characteristics of a society at a given time, and the position of a social group (for example, Chinese Americans) within that society determine (1) the relationship between Chinese Americans and other groups in society, (2) the pattern of attitudes held by individual Chinese Americans toward other groups, and (3) the attitudes of individuals elsewhere in society toward Chinese Americans. In the sociological view, then, individual attitudes are relatively unimportant in shaping patterns of intergroup relations. Instead, these patterns are caused by the nature of the society as a whole and the nature and social positions of the groups within it. Furthermore, these societal and group characteristics are the major factors in determining individual attitudes. Thus, although attitudes may perpetuate inequalities, the ultimate cause of the attitudes is the structure of society.

Accordingly, those who take this sociological, or social-structural, approach toward studying race relations analyze groups and societies rather than individuals. They seek, first, to describe accurately the pattern of relations between the racial and ethnic groups in a society and, second, to explain the reasons for it. In doing so, they emphasize characteristics of the society and characteristics and positions within society of racial and ethnic groups—not the characteristics of individuals, which are seen mostly as resulting from, not causing, the group- and society-wide patterns (Bonilla-Silva, 1997).

Consider this example. Let us imagine a hypothetical society in which there are two ethnic groups, say, Wallonians and Piraneans. The first task of a social scientist who is studying intergroup relations in this society is to describe the nature of the relationship between the two ethnic groups. Perhaps, for example, the Wallonians generally dominate the Piraneans. Most of the better jobs and positions of authority are held by Wallonians, and Wallonians have higher incomes and better education. Although not all Wallonians are wealthy, nearly all the means of production (such as factories, land, and natural resources) are owned by Wallonians. Furthermore, Wallonians often discriminate against Piraneans, although there is no formal code requiring such discrimination. Sometimes the Piraneans respond with organized protest, but usually they try to adapt and make the best of their situation.

This is an example (abbreviated and simplified) of a description of a relationship between two ethnic groups in a society. Indeed, if one were to substitute *whites* for *Wallonians* and *African Americans* for *Piraneans*, the description would apply fairly well to the present-day United States. As you can see, the emphasis is not on individual behavior but on group characteristics and on interaction between the groups, including their roles and statuses in the larger society. In this example, we might summarize the relationship as subtle but nonetheless real domination of one group by another, with the subordinate group responding to the domination with a mixture of protest and adaptation.

## Factors Shaping Patterns of Majority-Minority Relations: The Sociological View

The next task of the sociologist is to explain the reasons for a particular relationship. These reasons would similarly be sought in the characteristics of the society and of the two ethnic groups. Among the features a sociologist would look for are the following:

- *The basis of economic production.* Is the society an industrial society? An agricultural society? A colony? What is the level of technology and productivity in the society? Is the society complex and specialized or small and simple? Such factors influence the roles that may be played by the social groups within that society and thereby influence how the groups relate to one another.

- *The nature of the political system.* Is it, for example, a democracy, dictatorship, or monarchy? What are the power relationships between groups? What degree of political freedom is permitted?

- *The nature of the economic system.* Is it capitalist, feudal, socialist, or some other system? Of particular importance is the overall distribution of income and wealth, especially ownership of the basic means of production.

- *Characteristics of other basic institutions in society.* These include religion, the family, and education.

- *The predominant culture in the society.* Particularly relevant are the shared beliefs about reality and the value systems in the society.

- *Internal cultural and social characteristics of the various ethnic groups that make up the society.* Examples might be the existence of aggressive or warlike values, a history of doing a certain kind of work, or a shared belief in a particular religion.

- *Historical conditions.* For example, if there are different racial or ethnic groups, did they come into contact with one another as a result of voluntary immigration, or did one group conquer or impose its rule on another?

If we wanted to explain *why* in our imaginary society Wallonians and Piraneans relate to each other as they do, and if our approach was sociological, we would ask questions such as these. All of the questions pertain to characteristics of the society as a whole or of entire groups within that society, not to the characteristics of individual members.

## ▶ PERSPECTIVES IN SOCIOLOGY

Those who study racial and ethnic relations from a social-structural approach may be further divided into at least two differing and often clashing groups, which represent competing *perspectives* within sociology. In this section we shall briefly explain what a perspective is; in the remainder of the chapter we shall describe, illustrate, and compare the two dominant perspectives of the sociological approach.

In the most literal sense, a **perspective** is a way of looking at a question or problem. A "way of looking at a problem" may be divided into at least three parts. The first involves the questions we ask about a problem or issue. (In a sense, the answer we get always depends in part on the question we ask.) The second involves what we believe to be true about the issue. When we put together a complex set of statements that we believe to be true about some topic, we say we have developed a **theory** about that topic. Ideally, a theory is testable: We can gather evidence to evaluate the degree to which it accurately describes reality. The third part implies that we may like or dislike what we see; that is, we may believe that it is "good" or "bad." This opinion is not something that can be proved or disproved; it is a matter of personal preference or ethical viewpoints. When we talk about views that carry notions of good or bad, right or wrong, we are talking about **values**. A perspective, then, usually comprises three elements:

- An approach to a topic that helps to determine the kinds of questions that are asked about the topic
- A theory or set of theories describing what are believed to be the realities of the topic
- Stated or unstated values concerning potentially controversial issues related to the topic

It is sometimes asserted that the social sciences are or should be free of values. In real life, however, this is rarely possible. Even the topic a researcher chooses and the questions he or she asks about it are always determined at least partly by personal values. It will become evident as we examine the major perspectives in sociology and their application to race relations that these perspectives are far from value-free. This does not imply that they are *only* value judgments or "just a matter of opinion"; they do reflect actual theories about the reality of how societies in general, and majority-minority relations in particular, work. However, like most human creations, they also reflect the values of the people who developed them. (For further discussion of the role of values in the sociology of majority-minority relations, see Abalos, 1986, and on theory in sociology generally, see Lord and Sanderson, 1999.)

## ▶ ORDER AND CONFLICT: TWO SOCIOLOGICAL PERSPECTIVES

In macrosociology (the study of large-scale, social-structural issues), two perspectives—order and conflict—have been particularly influential. In the study of racial and ethnic relations, most sociological theorizing has used one perspective or the other or has attempted to synthesize the two. We shall describe in general terms each of the two perspectives, then attempt to show how each has been applied to the study of race and ethnic relations.

## The Order (Functionalist) Perspective

The first perspective we will discuss is known by a variety of names. It has at various times been called the **order perspective**, the **functionalist perspective**, structural-functionalism, consensus theory, equilibrium theory, and system theory. It arises largely from the theories of Emile Durkheim, although it has been further developed and greatly elaborated on by Talcott Parsons and others. It has been widely applied to race and ethnic relations, especially in the United States. This perspective, like others, should not be seen as one clear, unified, all-encompassing theory but rather as a set of related theories (and sometimes value judgments) arising from certain common premises. A central notion underlying this perspective is that society is the way it is not by chance but for very specific reasons. Social arrangements exist because they perform some *function* for society: They meet some need of the society or somehow enable the society to operate more effectively than would otherwise be possible. This perspective involves a number of assumptions related to this basic premise:

1. Society is made up of a number of interdependent parts. The functioning of society depends on the operation and coordination of all these interdependent segments. Because different parts of society depend on one another, a change at one point in society will have an impact elsewhere, especially in large, modern, complex, and specialized societies.

2. Every element of society performs some function for the social system; somehow, it meets a need or helps to make the system work or hold it together. An often unstated but implicit notion is that society usually tends to work for the greatest good of the largest number of its members.

3. Societies tend toward stability and equilibrium because each part is performing a function (making a contribution to society) and is interrelated with other parts. A drastic change anywhere usually would be dysfunctional for the entire system (preventing it from meeting its basic needs).

4. Society tends toward consensus, at least on certain basic values. This consensus is necessary for cooperation, which in turn is necessary because the people and groups in the social system depend on one another to meet their basic needs.

5. Consensus and stability are desirable in society (a value judgment). They facilitate the cooperation necessary to meet individual, group, and system needs.

Largely because of the final assumption, the order, or functionalist, perspective often is associated with political conservatism, or at most with a cautious type of liberalism, advocating minor adjustment but not wholesale change in the social, political, and economic system. Because of its emphasis on stability and its belief that social structure meets basic social needs, the order perspective often values stability over social equality, the attainment of which often involves conflict, change, and struggle. For this reason, critics point out that the perspective reflects values as well as theory (see Horton, 1966), even though some of its proponents claim it is value-free. The functionalist perspective was dominant for a period in American sociology, from around the end of World War II into the early 1960s (Lord and Sanderson, 1999). For a variety of reasons, however, including the fact that order theory did not predict (and had a hard time explaining) the social upheavals of the 1960s and early 1970s, its alternative, the conflict perspective, was "rediscovered" in the 1960s and has taken on greater importance in American sociology since then. It has become particularly influential in the study of race and ethnic relations.

## The Conflict Perspective

The major competing approach to the order perspective is the **conflict perspective**. This approach arises largely, though not entirely, out of the theories of Karl Marx and has been elaborated on by such twentieth-century sociologists as C. Wright Mills, W. E. B. DuBois, and Ralf Dahrendorf. Like the order approach, the conflict perspective is best seen not as one unified, totally coherent theory but as a set of related theories that share certain common premises and assumptions. The basic premise underlying this approach is that society is made up of groups with conflicting self-interests. Often, one such group dominates, and in that case society takes on a form that serves the interests of that dominant group. The conflict perspective involves the following assumptions:

1. Conflict is built into society; that is, societies naturally tend toward conflict because wealth and power are limited or scarce resources and are distributed unequally. Therefore, different social groups have different and conflicting self-interests.

2. Because competing interest groups have unequal power, one group usually becomes dominant. This group uses its power so that most aspects of the social structure operate in a way that serves its interest. As a result, this group (usually a small percentage of the entire population) controls a vastly disproportionate share of such scarce resources as wealth and social status.

3. When consensus does appear in society, it is artificial and unlikely to persist over the long run. The usual causes of apparent consensus are either coercion and repression by the dominant group or an acceptance by disadvantaged groups of ideologies not in their self-interest. The latter occurs because dominant groups exert disproportionate control over information and the media. In either case, the consensus lacks a fundamental stability and is unlikely to persist over the longer run.

4. Conflict in society is desirable (a value judgment) because it makes possible social change, which may lead to a more equitable distribution of wealth and power.

As can be seen from the last assumption, the conflict perspective also makes value judgments. Because social change and equality are valued over stability, the conflict perspective tends toward a radical (or at the very least, strongly reformist) political orientation: It argues that if the social structure promotes the interests of a dominant few at the expense of others, it must be changed, often in very fundamental ways.

One social theorist, Karl Marx, has had an especially strong influence on the conflict perspective. Although not all conflict-oriented theories are based on Marx's thought, his theories are relevant to race and ethnic relations and have influenced many modern conflict theories. A central assumption of Marxist theory is that the distribution of wealth largely determines other aspects of society, such as the political system and the culture, including social norms, values, and beliefs (Marx, [1867–1894] 1964, [1867–1894] 1967, [1859] 1971), which Marx called *ideology*. In particular, he focused on ownership of the *means of production*, by which he meant whatever one had to own or control to produce things of economic value. This varies with technology and the system of production. For example, in an agricultural society, the means of production is mainly land; in an industrial society, it is *capital*: ownership of industries, natural resources, and distribution systems, or the money with which to purchase them. According to Marx, then, the political system, social institutions, and culture all support the economic system. Specifically, they serve the interests of those who control the means of production. In effect, control over the means of production determines the political system, social institutions, and culture. These in turn support and reinforce the economic system and protect the interests of those who control the means of production.

Consider the following example of this principle. In the Middle Ages, there was a common religious belief known as the "divine right" of kings. According to this

Some sociologists would look at this picture and see cooperation, exchange, and interdependency. Others would look at it and see unequal power, possibly even domination. What do you see?

principle, kings were appointed to their royal positions through the will of God. Thus, anyone who challenged the right of a king to rule or objected to the system of royalty and nobility was opposing the will of God. In effect, the royalty and nobility, who amassed wealth by controlling the means of production (land), were able to create an ideology—the divine right of kings—that served their own economic interests. This belief was generally accepted in the societies of the time, even by the peasant class, which provided the labor that enriched the landowners but earned very little reward for its efforts.

According to Marx and his followers, a subordinate group's acceptance of an ideology that goes against its own self-interest is not unusual. It is, in fact, common enough that they have a name for it: **false consciousness**. Its existence among subordinate groups is not limited to societies in the past. In fact, examples can be seen in fairly recent American history. In the 1972 presidential election, the Democratic candidate, Senator George McGovern, proposed a 100 percent tax on all inheritance over $500,000, an amount equivalent in purchasing power to $2.2 million in 2003. The practical effect of the proposal would have been to set a maximum amount that a person could inherit. Although this probably would have benefited the working class through lower taxes or improved services, the strongest opposition to it came not from the elite, which had the most to lose, but from the working class, which stood to gain (Dushkin Publishing Group, 1977). Apparently, blue collar workers wanted to believe that they had the chance of amassing such a fortune and passing it along to their children, even though the real chance of doing so was very small. The consequence is that the attitudes of the masses enabled the very wealthy few to continue to pass their wealth from generation to generation. More recently, a 2002 poll found that 50 percent of all Americans favored President Bush's proposal to completely eliminate the inheritance tax (Gallup Organization, 2003b), even though at the time the tax applied only to inheritances of over $1 million, an amount that very few could realistically expect to inherit. Perhaps all this can be explained by American's unrealistic expectations about their chances of getting rich: A 2003 Gallup poll found that half of all Americans between 18 and 29 expect to sometime get rich, a percentage that steadily falls with experience until age 65, when just 10 percent say they either are rich or expect to become rich (Moore, 2003a).

## A Comparison

In many ways, order and conflict are competing perspectives. The order approach sees society as basically stable and orderly, arranged in ways that meet its basic needs and marked by value consensus. The conflict approach sees society as being arranged in ways that meet the needs of a powerful few, with sharply conflicting values and power conflicts caused by the unequal distribution of resources. Conflict theorists believe that because of these struggles, society tends toward change. Furthermore, the two approaches often involve conflicting values and political orientations. Nonetheless, the fact that the two perspectives often compete and disagree does not necessarily make them completely incompatible (R. Williams, 1977; Schermerhorn, 1978; Deegan, 1991).

This compatibility can be seen in several ways. First, it is possible that any given aspect of social structure or culture may operate as both perspectives say it should. In other words, it may *both* meet some societal need—say, contributing to overall efficiency—*and* tend to keep wealth and power in the hands of a few. The task of sociologists is to determine the extent to which it does each of these things and to identify the processes by which it does so. Second, in any given society there are periods of relative stability and periods marked by conflict and upheaval. Obviously, then, there are both forces for stability and forces for change at work in the same society, albeit in different amounts at different times. The challenge for sociologists is to identify these forces and determine why some predominate at one time and others at another time. Similarly, some societies have relatively equal intergroup relations; others are marked by brutal exploitation and intense conflict. Again, the challenge is to explain why. Throughout much of the rest of this book, we will engage in analyses such as these, using the order and conflict approaches together to identify the basic dynamics of interaction between different racial and ethnic groups in different societies. Because it is anticipated that most readers of this book will be Americans, the greatest emphasis is on intergroup relations in the United States.

## ▶ THE SOCIAL-STRUCTURAL PERSPECTIVES AND SOCIAL PROBLEMS

The sociology of racial and ethnic relations can be seen as one part of a larger area: the study of social problems. We shall begin our study of how the order and conflict perspectives are applied to intergroup relations by determining how they apply more generally to the study of social problems. In the study of social problems, the two perspectives tend strongly toward disagreement in two particular areas. One is in the *definition* of social problems, which is mostly a matter of values; the other is in the *location*, or *cause*, of social problems, which is—or should be—an issue of scientific theory and empirical research.

## The Definition of Social Problems

When we talk about defining social problems, we simply mean asking, What is considered to be a problem? This is primarily a value judgment. Something is a problem if it has (or can be expected to have) some consequence that people don't like or consider undesirable (for elaboration, see J. E. Farley, 1992a, Chap. 1). Thus, it is primarily the human reaction to some fact or event (that is, a substantial number of people do not like its consequences) that makes it a problem. However, this reaction is not the same for everyone. Some people may see a condition as a social problem, whereas others do not. Such disagreement often occurs between sociologists of the order and conflict perspectives. And even when both agree that something *is* a problem, they may not agree on *how serious* that problem is or even *why* it is a problem.

In general, to the order, or functionalist, sociologist, the most serious social problems are those that threaten the smooth or efficient functioning of society or that threaten to cause such drastic social change that a new, less well-adapted form of society may result. For this reason, social protest—especially if it is violent or demands radical change—is seen as potentially a very serious problem. Conflict in society usually is seen as a problem for the same reason (for an example of this viewpoint, see Lipset and Raab's 1973 analysis of social conflicts underlying the Watergate case).

To the conflict sociologist, on the other hand, the most serious social problems involve such concerns as poverty, racism, exploitation, and inequitable distributions of scarce resources. Conflict and social movements generally are not considered social problems, in part because conflict and change are seen as built into society. Conflict theorists view conflict as an ordinary part of society that does not threaten the existence of an otherwise effective society. More fundamentally, however, they believe that *only* conflict and change can bring about a fairer and more equitable distribution of resources. For this reason, then, many conflict theorists view protest and conflict as *desirable*, offering the possibility of reducing social inequality, which the conflict theorist usually sees as the most serious social problem.

## The Location of Social Problems

Whereas the definition of social problems is mainly a matter of values, the *location* of social problems involves a theoretical or empirical question: What is the *cause* of some phenomenon that we have decided is a problem? Because this is a *factual* question, it is—in the ideal sense—a theoretical-empirical question, not a matter of values. However, values still have some influence. First, one can look in different places or ask different questions in seeking the cause of some social problem. An order sociologist and a conflict sociologist probably would begin their analysis of a problem by asking different questions. Second, almost any problem in real life has multiple causes, and functionalists and conflict theorists are apt to emphasize different causes.

On one hand, the order, or functionalist, sociologist often seeks the causes of a social problem mainly in the characteristics of a disadvantaged group. Such a group might be disadvantaged because it collectively lacks the necessary skills to perform a function for which it would be rewarded, or perhaps because its culture is incompatible with the general culture of a society. In each case, the burden of change is placed mainly on the disadvantaged group, not on the dominant group or on the society as a whole. In fact, the functionalist would advise against major changes in the society itself: The society is the way it is because it works well that way (its various elements perform functions necessary to the system as a whole), and if it is substantially changed, this functioning is likely to be disrupted or impaired. Hence, for functionalists, it is important for various groups to "fit in" to society as well as possible.

The conflict theorist, on the other hand, does not seek the source of social problems in the characteristics of disadvantaged groups. These groups are seen as the victims of exploitation by the powerful. Thus, seeking the causes of social problems in these subordinate groups is somewhat akin to blaming the victim for a crime (for a forceful statement of this view, see Ryan, 1971). In the view of the conflict theorist, the source of social problems lies in the exploitative behavior of the dominant or ruling class. It is assumed that if someone is suffering or placed in a disadvantaged position, someone else more powerful probably is benefiting from it (see Gans's 1971 analysis of who benefits from poverty). Furthermore, because conflict theorists often assume that a society's institutions are arranged to serve the needs of the dominant elite, these institutions are seen as an important source of the problem. If such social problems as poverty and racism are to be effectively combated, argue conflict sociologists, the only workable solution is to make fundamental changes in the social, political, and economic institutions.

The positions argued by the order and conflict perspectives are, at least in theory, empirically testable. A supporter of the functionalist view should be able to identify and document the characteristics of a subordinate group that cause it to be disadvantaged and to demonstrate how they place the group at a disadvantage. A conflict theorist should be able to show who is benefiting from the disadvantaged position of a subordinate group and to show how social institutions work both to benefit the dominant group and to hold down the subordinate group. Of course, supporters of each view often try to disprove arguments made in support of the opposing view. Once again, neither perspective is totally right. Social problems may well be caused in part by the behavior of subordinate groups and in part by the behavior of dominant groups and by the structure of society's institutions. The job of the researcher is to answer the question, How much of each, and in what ways? The present state of sociological knowledge leaves room for spirited debate between functionalist and conflict sociologists. In the remainder of this chapter, we shall examine this debate as it applies to race and ethnic relations.

## ▶ THE SOCIAL-STRUCTURAL PERSPECTIVES AND MAJORITY-MINORITY RELATIONS

We can best start a discussion of the order and conflict approaches to majority-minority relations by looking at their definitions of the problem (primarily a matter of values). In other words, in what respect do majority-minority relations constitute a social problem? The different answers given by the order, or functionalist, and conflict perspectives are more a matter of emphasis than of total disagreement. In general, however, functionalist sociologists tend to be most concerned about majority-minority problems because of their potential for serious disruption of society. In other words, it is not rational or functional for society to become severely divided along lines of race, ethnicity, or religion. When such division becomes sufficiently deep, a society can no longer function normally. One might point to Northern Ireland, Lebanon, Bosnia-Herzegovina, the former Soviet Union, Israel and Palestine, Kosovo, or Rwanda in recent years as examples to support this viewpoint.

In contrast, conflict sociologists look at majority-minority relations as a case of domination and exploitation. The problem is that the majority group—or some elite within the majority group—enhances its own position by placing or keeping the minority group in a disadvantaged position. The conflict sociologist is likely to view intergroup relations as a problem because the minority group is treated unfairly or because its members are harmed by the exploitative behavior of the dominant group. From this perspective, racial or ethnic conflict often is seen as desirable because the position of the minority group may be improved.

We turn now to the actual theories about intergroup relations that the two sociological perspectives offer. As in other areas of sociology, the order, or functionalist, approach to race and ethnic relations was much more widely used, especially in American sociology, from the end of World War II until the changes of the 1960s challenged many of its assumptions. This is not to say that the conflict approach had no adherents; some important analyses of intergroup relations in the 1940s and 1950s did use this approach (see Cox, 1948). On the whole, however, it has been much more common since the mid-1960s. Today each approach has its adherents in the sociology of race and ethnic relations, although the conflict approach undoubtedly predominates. There are also number of sociologists attempting to achieve a synthesis of the two approaches.

## Functionalist Theories About Majority-Minority Relations

Such phenomena as racial and ethnic inequality, prejudice, and ethnocentrism can be explained along different lines, depending on one's theoretical perspective. Let us first examine the approach taken by the order, or functionalist, perspective. We shall begin by defining *ethnic stratification*, then explaining, in the view of functionalist theorists, why it occurs. By **ethnic stratification**, or **ethnic inequality**, we mean any system that distributes scarce resources (such as wealth, income, and power) on an unequal basis according to race or ethnicity. *Racial inequality* is a special case of ethnic stratification in which the inequality is based on race. Whereas the conflict theorist tends to see such inequality as mainly a case of domination and exploitation, the functionalist is more likely to suggest that if a society has ethnic inequality, one of two conditions is present. Either the inequality itself is meeting some kind of social need in the society, or, more likely, the inequality is a result of some other social condition that is in some way useful to the society.

We can start by examining social inequality in the general sense (that is, stratification or inequality *not necessarily based on race or ethnicity*). In one of the best-known (and most controversial) sociological articles ever written, Davis and Moore (1945) presented a functionalist theory of stratification (social inequality), arguing that its existence is necessary to create incentives. Some jobs are more critical to the functioning of society and require longer, more difficult periods of training than others. To ensure that these more critical and more demanding jobs are filled by competent people, they must carry greater rewards. Accordingly, socioeconomic inequality is necessary and inevitable in a modern society. Of course, this does *not* explain why stratification should occur on the basis of race or ethnicity (in fact, we will see later that it suggests this should *not* be the case), but it does clearly suggest that any modern society needs and will tend to have socioeconomic inequality.

Taking it as a given (from the functionalist perspective) that a society will have socioeconomic inequality, we still face the question of why that inequality falls along the lines of race. There are several reasons why this may be the case, according to sociologists who identify with the functionalist perspective. One argument suggests that ethnic minorities fill an important need in society by their willingness to work at jobs or wages that are unattractive to others. This may be particularly true of immigrant minorities who view such positions as superior to those available in their place of origin; the same argument is applied to rural migrants to the city. Were it not for such minorities, these necessary but unattractive jobs would not be filled.

An example can be seen in Germany's guest-worker program. Germans, particularly those from what used to be West Germany, have enjoyed a high standard of living and often are unwilling to accept low-wage jobs. To get certain jobs done that native Germans were not willing to do, guest workers from countries such as Turkey were admitted on the condition that they accept these jobs. Many did so because jobs in their home countries paid even less. One result was ethnic inequality: People of Turkish and other non-German ethnic groups had a lower standard of living than ethnic Germans. Later, when the economy worsened and jobs became scarce, the guest-worker arrangement also led to ethnic conflict. As Germany's economy worsened in the early 1990s, many native Germans found it increasingly difficult to find work. They began to perceive Turks and other minorities as taking their job opportunities, even though most Germans were unwilling to work for the wages paid to the guest workers. These resentments contributed to a series of riots and attacks against Turks and other immigrants, guest workers, and other minority groups.

**Ethnocentrism and Ethnic Stratification.**   The guest-worker program in Germany illustrates the argument that ethnic inequality can be directly useful to a society: It may enable the filling of essential jobs. However, the most important explanation of ethnic stratification offered by the functionalist perspective does not focus on this issue. Rather, it sees ethnic stratification as a product of another condition that is useful to society. That condition is *ethnocentrism*, which was introduced in Chapter 2. (It might be helpful to review that section if you are unclear about the meaning of this term.) Although ethnocentrism obviously can be dysfunctional if it causes ethnic conflict that threatens to tear a society apart, a manageable amount often is seen as functional, or useful, for society (Sumner, 1906, p. 13; Catton, 1961; Simpson and Yinger, 1985, Chap. 3). The reason is found in a society's need for consensus and a shared identity, that is, a "we" feeling. Durkheim ([1893] 1964, [1912] 1965) and numerous order theorists since have argued that cooperation within a society is possible only when its members share certain basic values and feel a sense of common or shared identity.

Ethnocentrism can contribute to this sense in several ways. First, it highlights the nature of the common culture and group identity. For example, it helps to illustrate what is "truly American" by illustrating what is "un-American." Furthermore, it can create unity and cooperation within the in-group by defining the out-group as a threat or by promoting hostility toward it. Perhaps the best example is the characterization of "the enemy" in times of war, as is illustrated in the box, "Ethnocentrism and War." For all these reasons there is some tendency for ethnocentrism to

## ETHNOCENTRISM AND WAR

One of the best illustrations of the functions of ethnocentrism can be seen in characterizations of the enemy during periods of war. The image at the left is a U.S. poster aimed at building support for the Allied cause during World War II. Note the menacing appearance of the German soldier and the reflection in his monocle of a person hanging from a gallows. The poster at the right is a German poster intended to demonize Jews and thereby justify the Nazi program of extermination of Jewish citizens. Note the similarities between the two posters. More recently, the connection between ethnocentrism and war can be seen in the words of conservative talk show host Michael Savage, who in the days before the war against Iraq in 2003, stated, "We need racist stereotypes right now of our enemy in order to encourage our warriors to kill the enemy" (*San Francisco Chronicle*, February 6, 2003).

*Left*: Karl Koehler/Victor Ancona, "This is the Enemy," c. 20th Century. National Museum of American Art, Washington, DC/ Art Resource, NY. *Right*: United States Holocaust Memorial Museum.

develop in any society (see R. Williams, 1977, pp. 18–19). But however functional or necessary this may be, it also can create problems. The two most obvious are that it can push a society into conflict with another society when such conflict might not otherwise occur, and—our present concern—it can lead to ethnic stratification (and therefore ethnic conflict) within any society that is racially, ethnically, or culturally diverse. Ethnocentrism in reality is directed not only at other societies that are perceived as enemies but also at minority groups within the society. As a result, the minority groups against whom it is directed are placed in a disadvantaged position. In other words, the result is ethnic stratification.

**Assimilation.**  Most functionalist sociologists agree that ethnic stratification is a problem and that it ought to be minimized. However, many see it as inevitable as long as there is diversity within a society. Because of the need for consensus and group identity, ethnocentrism will always tend to occur, and as long as there are cultural minorities,[1] they will tend to become the objects of enthocentrism. The best ways to minimize this tendency are (1) to reduce the cultural differences between the dominant group and the minorities, (2) to eliminate legal and other barriers set up by the dominant group to exclude the minorities, and (3) to develop in the minority groups any skills they may be lacking to enable them to participate in society. This approach will result in **assimilation**, a process whereby differences between the minority group and the dominant cultural group are reduced, and the minority group gradually becomes integrated into the system. Through this process, the need for drastic changes that threaten the system is avoided. Furthermore, by becoming culturally similar to the majority group, the minority group eliminates itself as a potential target of ethnocentrism. Because functionalists consider both stratification and ethnocentrism to be necessary for society, however, they see some degree of ethnic stratification as unavoidable in any culturally diverse society. The way to minimize it is through assimilation. According to functionalists, assimilation minimizes ethnic stratification because once all groups become culturally similar, their differences are no longer the basis for ethnocentrism and prejudice. When all groups share a common culture, ethnocentrism will no longer divide them; rather, with one common culture, it will unify them.

Because they emphasize the need for assimilation, functionalist theories often have been criticized for placing most of the burden of change on minority groups. If stratification and ethnocentrism are indeed largely unavoidable in any society, it seems to follow that minorities will experience hostility (and probably subordination) as long as they remain different from the majority group. Therefore, it appears to follow from this viewpoint that for equality to occur, minorities must become more similar to the majority. It is not particularly surprising that some people, particularly minority group members, find this view offensive; furthermore, not all sociologists accept it. For an alternative interpretation, we now turn to the conflict perspective.

## Conflict Theories About Majority-Minority Relations

Conflict theorists are much less supportive than order theorists of the idea that ethnic stratification and ethnocentrism are functional and necessary in any society. Ethnic stratification is seen not as an unfortunate byproduct of social diversity but as a pattern that serves the interests of some dominant elite. The basic cause of the problem is to be found in the exploitative behavior of either the majority group as a whole or some very wealthy and powerful (though possibly very small) segment of it. Minority groups are subordinated because doing so provides some benefit to the elite and because the minority lacks either the power or the awareness to prevent such exploitation.

---

[1]Keep in mind that here and throughout the chapter we are using the term *minority* in the sociological sense, as explained in Chapter 1.

Conflict theorists are unconvinced by functionalist arguments about the necessity of economic stratification for a productive, efficient society. Tumin (1953) and others have raised a number of criticisms, arguing that Davis and Moore's (1945) functionalist theory cannot explain the degree of stratification that is found in most societies, particularly the United States, which has greater economic inequality than most other industrialized countries. First, they argue, economic stratification cannot possibly act as an incentive in the way Davis and Moore suggest because much social inequality is inherited rather than earned. For the system to work as the functionalists claim, there would have to be free mobility between generations so that, for example, a well-qualified son or daughter of a sharecropper would have the same chance of becoming a medical doctor as anyone else. In reality, this rarely occurs. In addition, ethnic stratification itself acts as a barrier to the mobility necessary for inequality to work as an incentive in the way that the functionalists argue. If high income is to reward hard work, it must be equally available to anyone who is capable and works hard, regardless of ethnicity.

Tumin (1953) and other critics also argue that there are often shortages of personnel in highly demanding jobs because professional organizations restrict entry into the profession, not because there is a shortage of motivated and capable job seekers. Two other observations can be made. First, some occupations that carry little economic reward in relation to the training required are nonetheless crowded because they are inherently rewarding or because they carry prestige. Social workers and college professors are frequently cited as examples. Second, there is considerable variation in the degree of stratification in societies with similar levels of productivity. Several industrialized countries have lesser extremes of wealth and poverty than the United States yet similar levels of productivity. An analysis by the author of the relationship between social inequality (the ratio of the income of the top 10 percent of the population to that of the bottom 20 percent of the population) and productivity (gross national income per capita) in fourteen major industrial countries showed that, in 2000, inequality explained only 3 percent of the variation in productivity (Farley, 2003a, p. 153). Considering all these arguments, conflict theorists conclude that stratification is much less necessary than the functionalist view suggests and that it exists mainly because it benefits the wealthy and powerful. It is doubtful whether the society as a whole—and particularly those who are in the lower part of the wealth and income distributions, including racial and cultural minorities—really benefits from the degree of social inequality that exists.

According to conflict theorists, then, stratification exists not because it meets the needs of society as a whole but because it serves the interests of some group that is dominant in terms of wealth, income, or power. Similarly, if inequality occurs along the lines of race or ethnicity, it is because such ethnic stratification serves the interests of some advantaged group, usually either the majority group as a whole or some elite among this group. This viewpoint does not see ethnocentrism primarily as a way of promoting social solidarity and thereby contributing to society's ability to function. Rather, it claims that ethnocentrism and other forms of prejudice develop as a way of rationalizing exploitation of minority groups.

In fact, ethnocentrism and prejudice can be seen as just one example of a general principle discussed earlier in this chapter: According to Marx and other conflict theorists, a society's ideology (system of beliefs and values) tends to support its distribution of resources. In general, the elite or advantaged group will promote—consciously or otherwise—the beliefs and values that serve its own self-interests, which usually conflict with those of subordinate groups.

For this reason, among others, many conflict theorists—and many members of minority groups themselves—are skeptical of the argument that racial or ethnic equality can best be brought about by assimilation. If a society's ideology generally supports the interests of the elite over all others, as Marxists argue, it would be foolhardy for any disadvantaged or exploited group to buy into that ideology. Indeed, it would be a classic case of false consciousness: supporting a system of beliefs and values that goes against one's own self-interests. If a social system is built on inequality, domination, and exploitation, the best way for a minority group to achieve equality is not to try to become part of that system, not to adopt the ideologies created by that system, but rather to try to make fundamental changes in the way the system works and in the way resources are distributed. In effect, this means a challenge to the power of the dominant group or elite.

Because the self-interests of subordinate groups (ethnic or otherwise) lie in challenging the power structure, conflict theorists believe that any society with stratification (ethnic or otherwise) will eventually experience social conflict. Thus, if there is racial or ethnic stratification in a society, that society probably will experience conflict along racial or ethnic lines. Conflict theorists do not see anything wrong with this development; indeed, they tend to view it as desirable. The most effective strategy for a minority group, they argue, is to challenge the power structure that keeps the minority group disadvantaged. To accept the ideologies of the dominant society, which may actually be used against the minority group, is not considered a viable strategy; rather, it is counterproductive.

There is another reason why many conflict theorists are skeptical of assimilation: the notion of blaming the victim. If racial inequality results from exploitation of the minority group by the majority group, as those who support the conflict perspective believe, the cause of the inequality is to be found primarily in the behavior of the majority group. However, assimilation typically demands that the minority group make most or all of the changes in behavior; it must change its ways to fit in. Many see this as both illogical and an unfair demand on minority groups, whose subordinate position is, after all, not their fault.

## Varieties of Conflict Theory in Race and Ethnic Relations

In general, conflict theorists agree that (1) there are competing interests in society with unequal power and unequal shares of scarce resources; (2) in diverse societies, power and money are distributed unequally along the lines of social class, race, and ethnicity; and (3) it is not usually in the interests of subordinate groups to adopt the ideology of the dominant group. There are a number of specific points on which conflict theorists disagree among themselves, however, which have resulted in the development of a number of competing conflict theories about race and ethnic relations. One of the areas in which they disagree most intensely is the degree to which social inequality is based on social class (i.e., economics) as opposed to race. This disagreement distinguishes three of the most important types of conflict theory about race: Marxist theory (Cox, 1948), split labor market theory (Bonacich, 1972, 1975, 1976), and a third type consisting of two variants, internal colonialism theory (Blauner, 1972) and critical race theory (Bell, 1992). All are discussed in greater detail in later chapters, along with research that tests hypotheses arising from them. However, we shall briefly introduce them here to illustrate the range of conflict theories about race and ethnic relations. These theories can be arranged in a continuum based on the relative importance they attribute to class and race as causes of inequality.

**Marxist Theory.** At one end is *Marxist theory*, which, as we have seen, maintains that inequality is based mainly on class—specifically, who owns the means of production. Marxist theory considers racism to be a mechanism used by the wealthy to prevent the working class (to Marxists, everyone who works for a wage or salary) from recognizing its own interests. Marxists believe that there are only two true interest groups: those who own the means of production and the rest of society, which works for wages for those who own the means of production. Marxists view racism as a means by which wage earners are manipulated and divided. For example, if white, African American, and Latino workers spend all of their time and energy fighting one another, there is little chance that the working class will unite and demand a bigger share from employers. This keeps wages low and profits high. In fact, wealthy elites often have a vested interest in dividing society along lines such as race, ethnicity, religion, and gender. Such divisions give elements of the working class (majority group, male) a stake in the existing order. They see themselves as better off than their minority counterparts, even though in an economic sense they are exploited by the elite (Tilly, 1998, p. 8). Thus, Marxists believe that the working class would best be served by putting aside racial divisions. Doing so would enable its members to think of themselves as workers first and to act on their common class interests. For this reason, Marxist theorists advocate the development of class consciousness, but they believe that strong racial or ethnic consiousness carries the risk of dividing the working class (Gitlin, 1995).

**Split Labor Market Theory.** In the middle of the continuum is *split labor market theory,* which sees both race and class as the bases of inequality in society. These theorists divide society into three classes, rather than the two envisioned by Marxist theorists: those who own the means of production, higher-paid laborers, and lower-paid laborers. The owners have an interest in getting the best worker for the lowest price, while the higher-paid workers are trying to protect their jobs from competition from lower-paid workers. For this reason, higher-paid workers, who tend to be either from the middle and working classes of the dominant group or from ethnic groups with a "middle" status, feel that they have an interest in protecting their position and often demand discrimination against the minority groups that encompass much of lower-paid labor. Thus, split labor market theory proposes that the working class of the majority group may often demand discrimination to protect its "middle" position, particularly in bad economic times, when that position may be particularly threatened.

**Internal Colonialism Theory and Critical Race Theory.** At the opposite end of the continuum from Marxist theory are *internal colonialism theory* and *critical race theory.* Internal colonialism theory sees societal inequality as being largely racial and ethnic, resulting from a dominant racial group that has established a system of racial inequality for its own benefit. It emphasizes the fact that groups such as African Americans, Mexican Americans, and Native Americans were involuntarily brought under the rule of white Americans of European ancestry and that this was done so that the white population could benefit economically. To establish such a system, whites used force, promoted racist ideologies, attacked the cultures of people of color, and isolated them from mainstream labor markets. These experiences became the basis of the racial inequality that continues today and were rationalized by beliefs about the cultural inferiority of the groups that were exploited. This theory sees race as the primary basis of social inequality and the primary issue dividing such societies as the United States. According to this view, minority groups would be best served by rejecting attacks on their culture, rejecting calls for assimilation, and promoting and maintaining their own set of values supportive of economic development and control of the resources of their own communities.

A newer variant on the same theme is critical race theory. This theoretical movement arose among legal scholars, largely African American and Latino/a, and has gradually spread to other disciplines such as sociology, economics, and women's studies. Like internal colonialism theory, it sees race as the core dimension along which the United States is stratified. It holds that even with today's ideologies of equal opportunity and color-blindness, racism is a normal and everyday, not exceptional or unusual, feature of law and society. In fact, assumptions of white superiority, and mechanisms that perpetuate it, are so ingrained in our laws and our institutions that they are often hard to see and recognize. In part because of the subtlety of these processes, critical

**Table 4.1   Conflict Theories of Race and Ethnic Relations**

| | Marxist Theory | Split Labor Market Theory | Internal Colonialism and Critical Race Theories |
|---|---|---|---|
| Major Interest Groups | 1. Owners of means of production<br>2. Workers | 1. Owners of means of production<br>2. Higher-paid labor (majority group or "middleman" minorities)<br>3. Lower-paid labor (minorities) | 1. Dominant racial group (colonizer)<br>2. Immigrant minorities<br>3. Colonized minorities |
| Key Basis of Inequality in Society | Class | Class and race or ethnicity | Race or ethnicity |
| Functions of Racial and Ethnic Inequality | Divides working class so owners of means of production can control wealth and maintain power | Used by higher-paid labor to protect their "better jobs" from competition by minorities | Means by which dominant racial group maintains wealth, power, and ability to economically exploit colonized minorities |
| Who Gains from Racial Inequality? | Owners of means of production | Higher-paid labor | Dominant racial group |
| Who Loses from Racial Inequality? | Workers in both the majority and the minority groups | Minorities who are kept out of jobs and employers who must pay higher wages to majority group workers | Colonized minority groups |

race theory holds that it is important to examine law and society from the viewpoint of people of color and thus places a strong emphasis on narrative and personal experience. A key point is that the larger society often treats as "objective" what is in fact a majority group viewpoint. Accordingly, important elements of the truth about society can be learned only by understanding how society is experienced by African Americans, Latinos, and other oppressed groups. Finally, because racism is seen as a normal feature of law and society, it tends to be resilient: When progress is made in changing one form of racism, it usually resurfaces in some new way, so that true progress is uncertain and difficult. For more on critical race theory, see E. Taylor (2000), Bell (1992), Delgado and Stefancic (2000), and Valdes, Culp, and Harris (2002).

On the one hand, all of these conflict theories emphasize the ideas that racial and socioeconomic inequalities exist because there are interest groups that benefit from them and that it is often not in the interests of disadvantaged groups to accept the ideology of the dominant group. On the other hand, they disagree on the relative importance of race and class as a cause of inequality in the United States and on whether class consciousness or race consciousness is the best way for subordinate groups to advance their self-interests. The major positions of each of these conflict theories are summarized in Table 4.1, and they will all be discussed in greater detail later in this book.

## Competing Perspectives: Is Synthesis Possible?

To briefly summarize the chapter thus far, we have outlined two competing perspectives in sociology and examined how they apply to majority-minority relations. One, the order, or functionalist, perspective, sees society as basically stable and orderly. Society does tend to have inequality and ethnocentrism, but only because they perform certain functions for society. This often leads to ethnic stratification, which is seen as a social problem for several reasons, most particularly because the resultant conflict can inhibit the effectiveness and productivity of the society and, in severe cases, can even destroy the society. The functionalist perspective considers the best solution to the problem to be a gradual process of assimilation, whereby minorities come to accept and be accepted into the dominant society and culture.

Conflict theory, in contrast, sees society as tending, over the long run, toward instability and change because most societies have marked inequality between those who own and control resources and those who do not. This comes about mainly because such an arrangement favors the interests of the elite, which is powerful enough to hold on to what it has. A society's institutions and culture (ideology) tend to serve the interests of that elite. Accordingly, acceptance of dominant ideologies and institutions is not in the interests of those who lack resources, including racial and ethnic minority groups. Rather, their interests are best served by challenging the power structure and seeking to alter the distribution of resources. Such conflict is both natural and desirable. Rather than viewing it as a threat to society, conflict theorists see it as a way to create a better, more egalitarian society, free of inequality and racism.

Obviously, the two perspectives are fundamentally opposed in many ways. Many strong adherents of each perspective would say that no synthesis is possible between the two: They are stating opposite views, and one is right and the other wrong. Yet, as we have mentioned, many sociologists, including specialists in race and ethnic relations such as R. Williams (1977) and Schermerhorn (1978), have sought such a synthesis. There are probably two ways such common ground might be found. First, it is possible that the two perspectives could, on any given point, each be partially correct. For example, a given institution or ideology might *both* promote the efficiency of the society as a whole (as functionalists argue) and serve the interests of the dominant elite in particular (as conflict theorists argue). The challenge is to identify, as precisely as possible, the ways in which it does each.

The second source of common ground can be found in the fact that under different circumstances, people and societies behave differently. Thus, as Schermerhorn (1978) points out, a society may at one point in its history and under one set of circumstances be stable and orderly, with ethnic minorities seeking—and to some extent gaining—equality through assimilation. At another time, the same society might be marked by disorder and conflict, with minority groups seeking—and again to some extent gaining—equality through conflict and use of power. Here, the key task for sociologists is to identify the circumstances that produce one outcome or the other.

In much of the rest of this book, we will try to answer the following questions:

- In what ways are racial and ethnic relations consistent with the predictions of order theories? Of conflict theories?

- Under what circumstances do racial and ethnic relations tend to follow patterns predicted by order theorists? By conflict theorists?

In the remainder of the chapter, we shall present an example that concretely illustrates the differences and disagreements between the two perspectives and that shows some ways in which sociological research can be used to test competing theories arising from the two perspectives.

## ▶ AN ILLUSTRATION OF THE DEBATE: CULTURE OF POVERTY THEORY AND AFRICAN AMERICAN FAMILIES

A debate that illustrates the arguments of the two sociological perspectives centers around a concept known as the culture of poverty as it relates to African American families. We begin with a general overview of the theory, then proceed to a more specific analysis of the debate over African American family structure.

## Culture of Poverty Theory

The term *culture of poverty* arises from the work of Oscar Lewis (1959, 1965). Lewis and other social researchers have observed certain cultural characteristics among poor people in industrial, capitalist societies. These characteristics have been observed in a number of such societies and across a wide variety of racial and ethnic groups. Furthermore, according to culture of poverty theorists, these cultural characteristics and values are not held by the nonpoor in those same societies. Among these characteristics are

> the absence of childhood as a specially prolonged and protected stage in the life-cycle, early initiation into sex, free unions or consensual marriages, a relatively high incidence of abandonment of wives and children, a trend toward female- or mother-centered families, a strong predisposition toward authoritarianism, lack of privacy, verbal emphasis upon family solidarity which is only rarely achieved because of sibling rivalry, and competition for limited goods and maternal affection. (O. Lewis, 1965, p. xvii)

According to culture of poverty theory, such cultural characteristics are predominant among the poor because they enable poor people to adapt to difficulties arising from poverty. At the same time, however, they make escape from poverty more difficult. Therefore, the net effect of the culture of poverty is to keep poor people poor and to cause poverty to be passed from generation to generation. Many theorists conclude that as long as poor people retain the culture of poverty, they will remain poor. The way to enable poor people to escape poverty, therefore, is to change the culture of poverty.

As you can see, this theory is closely associated with the functionalist perspective. Poor people are kept poor because their culture deviates from the norm; therefore, the solution to the problem of poverty is to change the culture of poor people so that it more closely fits the dominant culture. In other words, poor people need to be assimilated. Not surprisingly, this view has come under both ideological and theoretical attack from social scientists associated with the conflict perspective. They argue that this approach (1) blames the poor for their poverty, when the true cause is to be found in the exploitative behavior of those who benefit from poverty, and (2) suggests an ineffective approach to solving the problems of poverty because accepting an ideology and system that mainly serves the interests of the "haves" cannot possibly serve the interests of the "have-nots." Examples of such criticism can be seen in the writings of Valentine (1968), Ryan (1971), Gans (1973, Chap. 4), and Waquant (2002).

Although such criticisms have resulted in reduced sociological support for culture of poverty theory, elements of its viewpoint can still be seen in recent sociological work. For example, Elijah Anderson (1999) argues that strong pressures from the "street" element of inner-city culture have prevented many young, urban African Americans from behaving in ways that would help them to escape poverty, and William Julius Wilson (1987, 1996) argues that cultural adaptations to joblessness have added to other problems being experienced by minorities in neighborhoods of concentrated poverty. Although both Anderson and Wilson point out that the ultimate causes of inner city poverty are structural, both have nonetheless been criticized for overemphasizing the influence of the cultural factors (Reed, 1996; Waquant, 2002). A more direct recent assertion of culture of poverty theory can be seen in the work of Dinesh D'Souza (1995, 1996), who argues that cultural characteristics are the main cause of black disadvantage in the United States today.

## Family Structure, Poverty, and African American Families

Beginning with a government report written in the mid-1960s, known as the Moynihan Report (U.S. Department of Labor, 1965) and continuing until today in the form of political debates about "family values," both social scientists and the general public have debated the extent to which changing family structure is an important cause of poverty and other social problems in America today. Because African American families have changed the most from the traditional model of the two-parent family, in which the parents raise their children together and stay married until death, much of this debate has focused on the extent to which family structure is a cause of poverty and other problems in the African American community.

The Moynihan Report is named for its author, the late Daniel Patrick Moynihan, a social scientist, advisor to four presidents, and U.S. senator from New York from 1977 until 2001. In the report, Moynihan presented statistics showing above-average rates of divorce, separation, and unwed motherhood in the black community, which together resulted in an above-average proportion of single-parent, female-householder families.

It was not Moynihan's statistics but rather his conclusions that made the report controversial. In effect, he concluded that the structure of the black family was the most important cause of continuing black poverty and that blacks would not be able to escape poverty until their family structure changed. Consider the following quotations from the Moynihan Report:

> At the heart of the deterioration of the fabric of Negro society is the deterioration of the Negro family. . . . It is the fundamental source of the weakness of the Negro community at the present time. (U.S. Department of Labor, 1965, p. 5)
>
> The evidence—not final, but powerfully persuasive—is that the Negro family in urban ghettoes is crumbling. So long as this situation persists, the cycle of poverty and disadvantage will continue to repeat itself. (U.S. Department of Labor, 1965, introduction)

Although the Moynihan Report was written three decades ago and was greeted by a hail of criticism when it appeared, the basic argument it made continues to enjoy the support of a number of sociologists today. Some have even seen it as prophetic because the proportion of single-parent families in the black population is far higher today than it was when Moynihan wrote the report. In 2002, just under half of all black children under eighteen were in single-mother families (U.S. Census Bureau, 2003i). In fact, the percentage of such families has risen among all racial and ethnic groups since the 1960s. However, the rate remains higher among African Americans than among other groups. About one of four Hispanic children and one of six white children lived in a single-mother family in 2002.

A number of sociologists have pointed out that female-householder, single-parent families have a very high poverty rate (Bianchi, 1981; Reimers, 1984; Wilson, 1987; Mare and Winship, 1991). In fact, their poverty rate is more than five times as high as that of married couples, and more than four out of every ten African American families with female householders have incomes below the poverty level (U.S. Census Bureau, 2002f, Table 16a). In addition to Moynihan, other sociologists have recently argued that the growing incidence of divorce and single parenthood is detrimental to children and/or an important cause of poverty (Sampson, 1987; McLanahan, 1988; McLanahan and Bumpass, 1988; Popenoe, 1988, 1996; N. Glenn, 1997a, 1997b; Gottfredson and Hirschi, 1990; for updates of Moynihan's views, see Moynihan, 1986, 1995a, 1995b). These arguments, like Moynihan's original report, have often generated significant sociological controversy, and in the political arena, family structure and family values debates have been very intense, as illustrated by a flap over unwed childbearing by the TV character Murphy Brown, which occurred during the 1992 presidential campaign.

This issue is a good example of a situation in which statistics show the presence of a certain pattern, but the meaning of that pattern is intensely debated. The statistics show racial and ethnic variation in the rates of single parenthood, which are highest among blacks, intermediate among Hispanics, and lowest among non-Hispanic whites. They show a rising incidence of single parenthood among all groups, and they show that the poverty rate of single-parent families is much higher than that of married-couple families among all racial and ethnic groups. But what does this mean? Does it mean that single-parent families are a cause of poverty? Does it mean that the family structure of African Americans is a major reason why their poverty rate is higher than that of whites? In general, functionalists tend to say "yes," and conflict theorists are much more likely to say "no."

Those who see black family structure as a major cause of poverty operate largely from the order perspective and, more specifically, from the culture of poverty theory. They argue that black family structure places African Americans at a disadvantage, partly for the simple reason that it is different from the typical American family structure; that is, it does not "fit in" (U.S. Department of Labor, 1965). Thus, although it may have evolved partly in response to a high rate of poverty (a point culture of poverty theorists generally acknowledge), it now makes it difficult for poor blacks to escape from poverty. In fact, some sociologists have argued that the high rate of female-householder families is the main reason that the poverty rate among African Americans is three times as high as among non-Hispanic whites. The solution, in this view, is to alter black family structure so that it corresponds more closely to the American ideal of the two-parent family. (Of course, this particular argument weakens to the extent that the one-parent family becomes more common among other groups, as it has since the Moynihan Report was written.)

Critics of this view, largely associated with the conflict perspective, argue that it puts the blame for black poverty on African Americans themselves. They argue that identifying the black family as the primary cause of continuing black poverty deflects attention from the real causes of disproportionate black poverty: higher unemployment, lower wages, and poorer educational opportunities. This group of factors, they point out, is associated with processes at work in the larger society—a point that is lost or forgotten when the blame is focused on the black family. It has also been pointed out that the mere fact that female-householder families are *correlated with* poverty does not establish that they *cause* poverty. In fact, the Moynihan Report did not present any actual evidence of a mechanism by which this might occur (although sociologists writing since then have suggested a number of possible mechanisms, many centering around a lesser ability in single-parent families to supervise children and give them needed attention).

Besides their sociological criticisms, conflict theorists and others have also expressed concern about the political effects of emphasizing the black family as a cause of poverty. There is a real risk that whites will conclude, "There is nothing our society can do about the problem of black poverty; it is entirely the product of black family structure, which is up to blacks to take care of." Also, as discussed in the box "The Culture of Poverty Debate and Welfare Policy," it is clear that the culture of poverty theory has had some important effects on legislation pertaining to welfare reform.

Finally, with all the emphasis on single-parent families in the black community, it is easy to forget that married-couple families remain common among African Americans. It is still true today that more black family households are married couples than single-mother families (U.S. Census Bureau, 2002f, Table 16a). It would also be a mistake to associate single parenthood only with African Americans: The percentage of single-parent households among whites today is slightly higher than that observed among blacks when Moynihan first wrote his report. As of 2002, about 20 percent of white children, 30 percent of Hispanic children, and 53 percent of African American children lived in one-parent households, compared with 19 percent of black children in 1960 (U.S. Census Bureau, 2003i). In sheer numbers, there are more single-parent households among white Anglos than among any other group: In 2002, 60 percent of all children in single-parent households were white non-Hispanic (U.S. Census Bureau, 2003i, p. 7).

## Is the Black Family Responsible for Disproportionate Black Poverty?

To evaluate the competing arguments of the order and conflict theories, it is help-ful to consider some statistics. We can get some idea of the importance of family type as an immediate cause of poverty by considering the income data in Table 4.2. As we would expect from the preceding discussion, the table shows that female-householder families have lower incomes than other families, and black and His-

## THE CULTURE OF POVERTY DEBATE AND WELFARE POLICY

The culture of poverty debate is directly relevant to current political disagreements over welfare reform. From the view-point of the functionalist perspective or of culture of poverty theory, two possible arguments can be made on the sub-ject. A liberal variant on this viewpoint can be seen in the views of the late Daniel Patrick Moynihan, discussed in the text. As we have seen, Moynihan argued that high rates of single parenthood are an important cause of poverty. How-ever, he later came to see single parenthood as a pervasive trend in advanced industrial societies, not easily altered by social policy (Moynihan, 1995a). He also argued that the extremely low incomes of poor households in the United States make it necessary to provide extra financial help. Accordingly, just forcing people off welfare will worsen the already severe problem of child poverty. Moynihan sug-gested increasing support for job training and child care for people who leave welfare and requiring welfare recipients to obtain education or job training. In part to shore up the family as much as possible under difficult conditions, he also favored requiring mothers under eighteen who receive welfare to live with their parents (Moynihan, 1995b).

A conservative variant of culture of poverty theory can be seen in the writings of Charles Murray (1984). Murray argued that welfare made it possible for poor people to sur-vive without working and to receive higher benefits by hav-ing babies out of wedlock. Because he saw welfare as rein-forcing a culture of poverty, he argued that it would actually help people get out of poverty and help reduce single par-enthood if welfare were limited, as was done in the 1996 welfare reform legislation. In his view, people had become dependent on welfare in ways that kept them in situations of poverty, unemployment, and single parenthood. If the incentives were different, he argued, more would escape from these situations. There is little doubt that this view-point had a strong influence on the welfare reform legisla-tion that was passed in 1996, which placed national limits on the amount of time people can receive welfare.

Conflict theorists are skeptical of both of these argu-ments. They see the underlying causes of poverty not in the family structure of the poor (although it may add to the poverty) but rather in the higher concentration of poor peo-ple (especially the minority poor) in inner-city neighbor-hoods, where most of the employment opportunities have

disappeared (Kasarda, 1990; Massey and Denton, 1993; W. J. Wilson, 1996). From this viewpoint, the solutions become structural: Create job opportunities in inner cities that have been abandoned by employers or create opportunities for inner-city residents to more easily move to where the jobs are.

Sociological research offers several important insights on this issue. First, certain facts undermine Mur-ray's (1984) argument that welfare contributed to poverty and single parenthood. The level of welfare is not positively correlated to either the poverty rate or the rate of out-of-wedlock births, as was predicted by Murray (W. J. Wilson, 1987, p. 94; Jencks, 1991; Moffit, 1992; Ruggles, 1997a; Lichter, McLaughlin, and Ribar, 1997). Similarly, a study by Rutgers University for the New Jersey government showed that the birthrate was no lower among mothers who were penalized if they had more children while on welfare than among those who were not penalized (M. Kramer, 1995). Second, it is clear that getting people off welfare involves costs, as desirable as it may be. Once single parents go to work, they need day care for their children, job training, and some way to pay for their health care costs, which were previously paid by Medicaid. Research supports this view: Welfare-to-work transitions are most likely to occur when recipients have more education or training and when they get full-time employment, which includes benefits such as health coverage (Harris, 1993). It is true that since the 1996 welfare reform, the welfare rolls have shrunk. The poverty rate fell at first but then rose, both trends probably reflect-ing the ups and downs of the economy more so than the effects of welfare reform.

The real test of welfare reform is beginning to arrive in 2004, as more recipients reach the time limits of their bene-fits and more difficult economic times are making jobs harder to find. (The consequences of welfare reform are explored more fully in Chapter 11.) Rather than welfare, there is evidence that the disappearance of employment opportunities from inner cities is the real cause of poverty there. In a study of a Chicago program in which impover-ished black women were given a chance to move to a sub-urban area, where jobs were more plentiful, the relocation produced significant improvement in employment rates (Rosenbaum and Popkin, 1991).

panic female-householder families have the lowest incomes of all. However, it is clear that the income difference by race persists even among those with the same family type. Note that in every type of family, African Americans and Hispanics have significantly lower incomes than whites. Thus, race clearly is associated with income and poverty above and beyond any effect of family type. However, it is also notable that in some categories, the racial gap is narrowing. In 2001, black married-couple families with both partners in the labor force earned 82 percent of the income of white families in the same category—still a significant gap, but a narrower gap than in some past years and also narrower than for any other family type.

Moreover, it is true that for each racial group, female-householder families have the lowest incomes, suggesting that they may account for part of the racial difference in income because they are more common among African Americans than among whites. Conversely, where the gap is narrowest—married-couple families with both partners working—African American families are underrepresented. Similarly, note that for African Americans and, to a lesser extent, Hispanics, the income gap is wider in the population as a whole than it is within any given family type, although it remains sizable in all family types. Do these facts indeed suggest that the higher rate of single-mother families among African Americans is an important cause of high poverty rates among this racial group? To answer this question, we must address several issues.

**Poverty as a Cause of Single Parenthood.** First, given that there is a correlation between single parenthood and poverty, we must ask about the possible direction of cause and effect. The argument that single parenthood causes poverty assumes that single parenthood is the cause and poverty is the effect. Yet there is a good deal of convincing evidence that poverty causes single parenthood. Poverty both prevents and disrupts marriages. Our society continues to expect men to support their families or at least to be the primary source of support. Yet with the high rates of poverty and joblessness in America's inner cities, this has become difficult for many African American men to do (W. J. Wilson, 1987, 1996; Mare and Winship, 1991; Massey and Denton, 1993). This situation has several consequences. First, it disrupts marriages: Low socioeconomic status is associated with higher divorce rates (Waite and Lillard, 1991; Hoffman and Duncan, 1995) and much higher separation rates than occur among middle- and upper-class families.

Poverty also prevents marriage: Poor women are less likely to marry than otherwise similar nonpoor women (McLaughlin and Lichter, 1997). In part for this reason, poverty is strongly associated with births outside marriage (Jencks, 1991). Poor inner-city women, particularly African Americans, experience a severe shortage of men who would make suitable marriage partners because many are unemployed, imprisoned, or prematurely dead (W. J. Wilson, 1987; Lichter, LeClere, and McLaughlin, 1991). Research suggests that these shortages of partners may explain much of the reason why African American women marry later and less often (Brien, 1997) Yet, like single women of all social classes and ethnic backgrounds today, most of these women are sexually active. This fact, together with the low marriage rates of inner-city women because of a shortage of employed men who could serve as marriage partners, contributes to an elevated rate of childbirth outside marriage (Seeborg and Jaeger, 1993; Stokes and Chevan, 1996). An additional factor is that many of these women have limited knowledge about and access to contraceptives. Like nearly everything else, health care is inadequate in areas of concentrated poverty. As black poverty in particular, but also Hispanic poverty to some extent, has become more geographically concentrated, the problem has become worse. More than in the past, African Americans and Hispanic Americans who live in large cities live in areas where a large proportion of the population is poor (W. J. Wilson, 1987; Massey, 1990; Massey and Denton, 1993). This contributes to the hardships young women experience in their attempt to find employed, nonpoor males who can pro-

### Table 4.2    Median Family Income by Race, Hispanic Origin, and Type of Family, 2001

| | | Married-Couple Families | | | Single-Parent Families | |
|---|---|---|---|---|---|---|
| | All Families | All Married Couple Families | Wife in Paid Labor Force | Wife Not in Paid Labor Force | Male Householder, No Wife | Female Householder, No Husband |
| U.S. Total | $51,407 | $60,335 | $70,834 | $40,782 | $36,590 | $25,745 |
| White Non-Hispanic | $57,328 | $63,862 | $74,071 | $43,423 | $39,979 | $30,062 |
| Black | $33,598 | $51,514 | $60,693 | $29,309 | $31,512 | $20,894 |
| % of White Non-Hispanic | 59% | 81% | 82% | 67% | 79% | 70% |
| Hispanic | $34,490 | $40,614 | $50,437 | $28,682 | $31,635 | $20,547 |
| % of White Non-Hispanic | 60% | 64% | 68% | 66% | 79% | 68% |

*Source:* U.S. Census Bureau, 2002i, Table FINC-01.

vide economic support for a family. Partly because of the resulting decline in marriages, nonmarital births have become more important than divorce as a cause of single parenthood in the African American community. For the reasons discussed, it is clear that poverty does contribute to single parenthood, which accounts for part of the correlation between the two.

**The Wages of Women and Minority Groups.** A second part of the answer can be found by comparing the two kinds of single-parent families shown in Table 4.2. Note that the incomes of the single-parent, male-householder family are consistently higher than those of the female-householder family for all racial groups. In fact, the male version of the single-parent family enjoys very similar incomes to the most traditional American family, a married-couple family in which only the father works outside the home. Why do single-parent, male-householder families do so much better than ones with female householders? Obviously, one reason is that women's wages are far below those of men. Thus, a single-parent, male-householder family has a lower risk of poverty than a single-parent, female-householder family. This suggests strongly that the low wages of women (about three-fourths of those of men, regardless of level of education) may be at least as important a cause of poverty as anything inherent in the family. If sexual (and racial) inequality in wages were eliminated, living in a female-householder family would carry much less risk of poverty. In fact, sociologist Cordella Reimers (1984, p. 901) has pointed out that "the most important single reason for the lower family incomes of Hispanics and blacks than of white non-Hispanics is lower wage rates even after differences in age, education, and regional distribution are controlled." As this suggests, black and Hispanic female-householder families experience a double disadvantage in income: the low wages and high unemployment rates associated with minority group status and the low wages of women. Significantly, neither of these has anything to do with the effects of one-parent, female-headed families per se.

**Two-Worker Families.** One other fact is worthy of note. On the one hand, the double disadvantage of racial and gender inequality, which has nothing to do with family structure, clearly explains much of the economic disadvantage faced by female-householder black families. On the other hand, it is also true that the economic advantage of married-couple families with both partners in the labor force has increased. Regardless of race, married-couple families with both partners in the labor force received about $20,000 to $45,000 a year more than any of the family types with just one adult in the labor force. Thus, if a group is underrepresented in this family type, it will suffer some economic disadvantage simply because the advantage of having two adult workers in the labor force is so great. This is true even though there is also a good deal of racial income inequality that cannot be explained by family type.

**Longer-Term Effects of Single-Parent Families.** Another argument is that the disproportionate number of female-headed families in the black population has longer-term effects—that children who grow up in these families are disadvantaged in ways that put them at a high risk of poverty when they are adults. This was a key point in the Moynihan Report, yet Moynihan presented no direct evidence of any such disadvantage (Gans, 1967; Ryan, 1967). Gans pointed out a number of studies showing that single-parent families are not strongly linked to such problems as poor school performance (mentioned by Moynihan) and mental illness. Research since that time presents a mixed picture: Some studies show effects on child development or long-term outcomes from growing up in one-parent families, whereas other studies do not, at least after control for relevant factors such as the family's income level.

A series of studies of California children whose parents were divorced is fairly representative. Wallerstein and Kelly (1980) found that about one-fourth of these "children of divorce" were very well adjusted, about one-fourth had real problems, and the rest were coping adequately but not totally free from difficulties—a mix probably not much different from the population of children as a whole. In fact, these researchers concluded that a divorced family per se is neither more nor less beneficial for children than an unhappy marriage.

Follow-up research by Wallerstein and Blakeslee (1989) of the children ten years after divorce produced findings similar to those of the initial study. A number of the children did report long-term problems such as low self-esteem, anger, and underachievement. Yet many others developed into well-balanced, competent adolescents or young adults. The authors of the study noted that it was not at all clear that these young people would have been better off if their parents had stayed married; continued exposure to open conflict between parents usually is even worse for children than divorce (Wallerstein and Blakeslee, 1989, p. 305). This conclusion has been supported by several other studies (Peterson and Zill, 1986; Demo and Acock, 1988; Jekielek, 1998).

Lieberson (1980, pp. 183–93) conducted research concerned specifically with the effect of family structure on the educational achievement of black children. He found that very little of the racial gap in school success could be explained by racial differences in family structure. Similar findings were obtained by Patten et al. (1997) with regard to depressive symptoms and by Leve and Fagot (1997) concerning family discipline processes. In fact, if anything, they found such processes to be more positive in single-parent families. Demo and Acock (1996) found only small differences by family type in adolescent well-being. More important was the degree of mother-adolescent disagreement. These studies suggest that families have ways of adapting, and a female-headed family cannot be equated with an unstable family. In particular, the role of the extended family as a source of strength and stability in the black family has been noted by many sociologists, with grandmothers and aunts playing a particularly important role (Frazier, 1966; Gans, 1967; Hill, 1972; Staples, 1973; Hunter et al., 1998). Additionally, recent research shows that even when they do not live with their children, many African American fathers are heavily involved in their children's lives. Even when poverty limits their ability to provide financial support, many African American fathers provide emotional support, assist their children's mothers in providing care, and engage in activities regularly with their children (Hamer, 2001). Even so, poor African American children are somewhat more likely to have little or no contact with their fathers than poor white or Hispanic children (Mincy and Oliver, 2003).

Some research does suggest that single parenthood may have some damaging long-term effects, including a greater risk of early and premarital childbearing, a greater risk of divorce, and lower education and income (McLanahan, 1988; McLanahan and Bumpass, 1988; Upchurch et al., 1999; Ross and Mirowsky, 1999). Growing up in a single-parent home does not increase the risk of having an unhappy marriage, but it does increase the likelihood of maladaptive behaviors and of divorce if the marriage is unhappy (Webster, Orbuch, and House, 1995). Because of its effects on socioeconomic status and divorce, having one's parents divorce during one's childhood indirectly increases the risks of adult depression (Ross and Mirowsky, 1999). However, aside from its effects on socioeconomic status and relationships, experiencing a parental divorce does not have a direct effect on adult depression, nor does it lead to lower levels of social support (Ross and Mirowsky, 1999).

Sampson (1987) found in a study of African American families that family disruption led to increased rates of juvenile crime. Similarly, Paschall, Ennett, and Flewelling (1996) found that for African American boys, living in a single-parent family was a significant risk factor for violent behavior. One reason for this may be that one parent has less time and ability to supervise children than two parents (Stack, 1994). These differences, though real, are in some cases partially offset by other factors, most notably family size. In general, children with more brothers and sisters do more poorly in several regards, perhaps because their parents, like single parents, are busier (Featherman and Hauser, 1978; Jencks, 1991, p. 87). Because one-parent families have fewer children than two-parent families, particularly among the poor, the disadvantages of a one-parent family are in part offset by the advantages of a smaller family (Jencks, 1991; Biblarz and Raffery, 1999). In addition, some of the disadvantages associated with growing up in single-parent families are not so much the result of single parenthood as of low income, suggesting that poverty, more than family type, is the key factor (Aseltine, 1996). One recent study estimates that about half of the disadvantages of children who grow up in single-parent families comes from low income and the rest from the parents' inability to provide adequate parental supervision for the children and their tendency to move frequently (McLanahan, 1994; McLanahan and Sandefur, 1994). Other research suggests that the influence of low income may be more important than that of family type, especially on the socioeconomic status children attain when they grow up (Biblarz and Raferty, 1999).

Some studies suggest that there may be lower school achievement among children raised in single-parent families, particularly if supervision of the children is problematic. For example, Coley and Hoffman (1996) found that lack of supervision and monitoring contributed to low school achievement more in single-parent families than in two-parent families. Some research also suggests that children in single-parent families may be at greater risk for drug use (Suh, Schutz, and Johanson, 1996), but studies that also measured the amount of time spent with the family suggest that family relationships and interactions are more important factors than family type (Adalf and Ivis, 1996).

Finally, there is some evidence that the effects of growing up in single-parent families vary by race. McLanahan (1994) found that the effects of single parenthood were biggest for Hispanics, smaller for whites, and smaller yet for African Americans. For example, family disruption raised the risk of school failure by 24 percentage points for Hispanics, 17 points for whites, and 13 points for blacks. This finding is not consistent with an argument that family background is a major cause of black disadvantage in society.

What does this information, taken as a whole, tell us? First, much of the correlation between single parenthood and poverty occurs because poverty prevents and disrupts marriage. However, single parenthood may contribute to poverty by precluding the possibility of having two parents in the labor force at the same time,

Sociologists have long debated the question of wheter growing up in single-parent families in and of itself creates disadvantages for children. Most studies suggest that other factors are more important.

thereby reducing family income. However, poverty is also clearly an important cause of single parenthood. Second, gender inequality in wages is a major cause of the high poverty rates of single-parent families, and for black and Hispanic single mothers, this is aggravated by racial inequalities. Third, the long-term and developmental effects on children of growing up in single-parent families, though real, are partially offset by the smaller size of these families. In most cases, these effects are relatively small after other contributing factors are controlled for; also, for some kinds of problem behavior, the research presents only a mixed picture of whether there are any effects at all. In the words of McLanahan (1994), if all children lived in two-parent families, problems such as teen parenthood and dropping out of high school "would be less common, but the bulk of these problems would remain." All of this together suggests the following: Whereas the high rate of single-parent families among poor African Americans probably contributes somewhat to the perpetuation of poverty, it is not the main cause. To a large extent, it is a consequence of high poverty rates. Finally, its importance has been overstated in many discussions of minority poverty that have appeared in the media and some that have been written by sociologists. Equally important, high rates of single parenthood among African Americans are not likely to decline much as long as many African Americans live in areas of concentrated poverty and unemployment.

This point is backed by historical analyses. Although female-headed families were somewhat more common among blacks than whites as early as 1900 (Morgan et al., 1993), most of the racial difference in the incidence of single parenthood developed after African Americans began to urbanize on a large scale and consequently encounter the concentrated poverty of inner-city ghettos. Until the mid-twentieth century, the vast majority of black families were two-parent families (Lammermeier, 1973; Furstenburg, Hershberg, and Modell, 1975; Gutman, 1976; W. J. Wilson, 1987). Additionally, recent black migrants from the rural South are *less* likely to have single-parent families than African Americans who have lived longer in big northern cities (Tolnay, 1997). These facts suggest that the one-parent family is not so much a product of African American culture as a product of a particular social and historical experience: living in central city areas with declining job opportunities. Research on Mexican Americans, who also have above-average rates of marital disruption, supports a similar conclusion: Structural opportunities, not group culture, explain divorce and separation among Mexican Americans (Bean, Berg, and Van Hook, 1996).

Considering these findings for African Americans, it is not surprising that a study of single black mothers revealed that their values, aspirations, and concerns are not much different from those of more "mainstream" U.S. families; they just face a much more difficult economic and neighborhood environment (Nandi and Harris, 1997). Overall, research findings do not support the culture of poverty theory's argument that culturally based differences in family structure play a major role in the perpetuation of poverty. Although family differences may play some role, the causes of these differences are more structural than cultural.

## Teenage Pregnancy

In recent years, increased attention has been devoted to another concern: high rates of teenage pregnancy and childbirth. In 2001, the birthrate among unmarried teenagers was 71.4 per thousand among African Americans aged fifteen to nineteen, 71.8 among Hispanics, and 22.9 among non-Hispanic whites (National Center for Health Statistics, 2002a). These rates are down significantly from the mid-1990s, but the higher rates among black and Hispanic teenagers remain a concern because pregnant teenagers and their children are at a very high risk of poverty, even compared with other female-householder families.

Again, however, there is debate over whether a high rate of teenage pregnancy is a cultural characteristic of black, Hispanic, or poor Americans that perpetuates poverty, as has been suggested by culture of poverty theorists. It is true that teenage pregnancy and childbirth are disproportionately common among poor people of all races, and in large part they occur more often among blacks and Hispanics because teenagers in these groups are much more likely to be poor than are white teens. However, is teenage pregnancy a product of the culture of the poor (as culture of poverty theory argues), or is it a response to the situation of poor teenagers (as conflict theory would argue)?

Certain facts about teenage pregnancy are relevant to this question. First, racial and social class differences in the teenage pregnancy rate do not result mainly from differences in sexual activity. Although black teenagers are somewhat more likely than white teenagers to be sexually active, large numbers of U.S. teenagers of all races are sexually active. In 2001, for example, about 43 percent of white high school students, 48 percent of Hispanic students, and 61 percent of black students had had sexual intercourse (Centers for Disease Control, 2003). The group differences in these rates are much smaller than the differences in teenage birth rates.

Thus, racial and class differences in teenage pregnancy and childbearing rates are not primarily the product of differences in the amount of sexual activity. Rather, they are mostly the product of differences in the likelihood that sexual activity will result in a pregnancy. Elijah Anderson (1991) found that in poor neighborhoods, where people have less control over many aspects of their lives, teenagers felt less control over the risk of pregnancy and therefore were less likely to try to prevent it. Also, to some impoverished teenaged girls, having a baby can be a rare source of self-esteem, as well as a sign of adulthood (E. Anderson, 1999, p. 147). Among poor teenage boys, sexual conquest (which is valued to some extent among young males of all social classes) may be one of the few ways they can attain a feeling of accomplishment, given that most opportunities for legitimate achievement are blocked (E. Anderson, 1999, p. 147). Thus, some teenage pregnancies may well result from cultural values that arise as adaptations to poverty. However, it seems unlikely that these values will change for teenagers growing up in neighborhoods where nearly everyone is poor and where unemployment is the norm. Unfortunately, as the black and Hispanic urban poor have become more concentrated in such neighborhoods, the proportion who grow up in these situations has grown (W. J. Wilson, 1987, 1996; Massey and Denton, 1993; E. Anderson, 1999).

Still, the desire to have a child clearly does not account for most teenage pregnancies, even among the urban poor. Research continues to show that most teenage pregnancies are unintentional. In the 1980s, about 80 percent of single black and Hispanic teenagers who became pregnant did not intend to do so (National Research Council, 1987, p. 52), and more recent research suggests little change. In 1995, 78 percent of all teen pregnancies were unintended, and overall black women were much more likely than white women to have unintended pregnancies (Henshaw, 1998). This occurred because they had limited knowledge about or access to contraceptives or did not have a real sense of control over whether they got pregnant.

For those who become pregnant, racial and class differences affect decisions about becoming a single parent. African American teenage girls and poor teenage girls of any race are less likely than their white, nonpoor counterparts to marry the father. We have already seen one reason for this: Given the high unemployment rates of those living in the inner city, the father is unlikely to have a steady job, enabling him to provide financial support. (However, getting married to "legitimize" a baby born out of wedlock is becoming less common among all groups.) At one time, African American teenagers were also less likely than white teenagers to get abortions, but this is no longer true.

The fact that most teenage pregnancies among the minority urban poor are unintentional suggests that greater information and better access to contraceptives might reduce their numbers. In some urban neighborhoods, the severity of this problem has led to the distribution of contraceptives through clinics in high schools and junior high schools. This decision has been controversial because some people, particularly religious traditionalists, have argued that it promotes teenage sexual activity. However, studies of clinics consistently show that sexual activity does not increase (Schorr and Schorr, 1988, p. 53; Kirby, 2001, p. 11), perhaps because these clinics often provide information about human sexuality and advise that teens do not have to be sexually active if they don't want to be (Hayes, 1987a, 1987b). This empowers them to say "no" in situations in which they are pressured to have sex. The degree to which they increase contraception use and prevent pregnancy is less clear, although they probably do to some extent (Kirby, 2001). Although abstinence-only programs have been an increasingly popular alternative to distribution of contraceptives in recent years, there is no evidence that such programs reduce sexual activity or prevent pregnancy, although carefully controlled studies of such programs are few (Kirby, 2001).

Today's teenagers repeatedly receive subtle and not-so-subtle sexual messages from the media and culture, yet frank discussion of sex and contraception is often discouraged. Thus, teenagers become sexually active without being prepared for the consequences. Those with the least education and the least sense of control over their lives—often blacks, Hispanics, and the poor—are the most affected. This is not necessarily the result of their culture, as culture of poverty theory would argue, but because their situation makes them especially vulnerable to society's mixed messages about sex. The effect of these mixed messages can be seen in the fact that teenage pregnancy in the United States is much higher than in other industrialized countries. In fact, even if one considers only the lower teenage pregnancy rate of white U.S. teenagers, it is still higher than the rate in Canada, Great Britain, France, Sweden, and the Netherlands, even though teens here are no more sexually active (Jones et al., 1986). In most of these countries, sex and contraception are discussed more frankly than in the United States, so that teenagers do not get the kind of mixed messages that American teenagers do. Thus, what culture of poverty theorists see as a problem of blacks or the poor turns out to be largely a product of how our society treats sexuality, which has a disproportionate effect on black, Hispanic, and poor U.S. teenagers because of their low educational level and less sense of control over their lives.

## Overview

What, then, do conflict theorists argue is the best approach to race and poverty? Rather than focusing on characteristics of blacks (or of any disadvantaged or exploited group), they emphasize aspects of the social structure that place the group at a disadvantage. Conflict theorists argue that African Americans and other people of color are disproportionately poor because whites (at least some) are benefiting from that fact and have been for years. The differences in family structure that exist between black and white families are largely a product of racial discrimination and the historic exploitation of African Americans. Among these factors are the deliberate disruption of black families under slavery, discrimination and violence against black men (which has weakened their ability to act as leaders of traditional families), and high black unemployment. For all these reasons, it is highly unrealistic to treat the black family as if it were independent of the social forces acting on it.

In the view of the conflict theorist, the solution is to make fundamental changes in the aspects of the economic and political system that place blacks at a disadvantage. This would involve a challenge to the existing power structure. Whatever difficulties this may entail, conflict theorists prefer it urging African Americans or other minorities to conform to the majority group's cultural and institutional patterns. They believe that there is no reason to conclude that such conformity will improve the group's situation or even that there is much chance that such conformity could occur, given the structural conditions that many blacks encounter on a daily basis.

## Summary and Conclusion

We began this chapter by contrasting a sociological approach to majority-minority relations, which stresses social organization, institutions, and culture, with a social-psychological approach, which stresses individual attitudes and beliefs, including racial and ethnic prejudice. We then outlined two major perspectives within the sociological, or social-structural, approach. The order, or functionalist, perspective stresses order, stability, interdependency, and the need for shared values and beliefs in society. The conflict perspective stresses inequality, conflict, and biases that support the dominant group in a society's social structure and culture. We examined how these approaches disagree on definitions and the causes of social problems, first in general, then specifically in the area of race relations. The culture of poverty issue and, specifically, the controversy over the black family illustrates this disagreement. The culture of poverty approach focuses on ways in which minority groups (or the poor in general) do not conform to a society's culture or institutions. This view is closely aligned with the functionalist perspective. The critics of the culture of poverty approach—mostly aligned with the conflict perspective—argue that an emphasis on assimilation, or "fitting in," is misplaced and that minority groups (and disadvantaged groups in general) can improve their position only by challenging the power structure and attempting to change the social institutions or dominant group behavior.

We shall use these two major sociological perspectives (and, where appropriate, the social-psychological approach as well) in following chapters to enhance our understanding of how minorities and majorities relate to one another in a variety of situations.

## Critical Review Questions

1. People often emphasize the attitudes and behaviors of individuals when trying to address social problems such as racial inequality or racial violence. How is a sociological or social-structural approach different from this?

2. Why, from a functionalist standpoint, is ethnocentrism common in most societies? How does ethnocentrism contribute to racial inequality?

3. According to functionalist theory, whose interests are served by social inequality? According to conflict theory, whose interests are served by social inequality? What kinds of research might be useful for resolving this debate?

4. Give three reasons why family structure or family type may be an important cause of high rates of poverty among African Americans or Hispanic Americans Give three reasons why family structure or family type may *not* be an important cause of high rates of poverty among African Americans or Hispanic Americans.

# CHAPTER 5

# Origins and Causes of Ethnic Inequality

# Overview

We all know that in societies with more than one ethnic or racial group, such as the United States, there is often inequality or conflict along the lines of race and ethnicity. We know, too, that the basic patterns of intergroup relations vary over time in any given society and from one society to another. Black-white relations in the United States, for example, are quite different from black-white relations in Brazil. Today's race relations in the United States are also quite different from those before the Civil War, and both today's race relations and antebellum (before the Civil War) race relations differ markedly from those of the period between World War I and World War II.

In the next four chapters, we will examine some of the ways in which race relations differ in various time periods and various societies. We will also explore some of the reasons for these variations. This chapter will introduce some major patterns of race and ethnic relations that have been identified by social scientists and that seem to appear repeatedly in a number of societies. It will also examine the circumstances associated with the development of racial inequality in early American history. Using the theoretical perspectives outlined in previous chapters, we will try to answer the question, How and why did racial and ethnic inequality (also sometimes called *stratification*) first develop in the United States? In Chapters 6 and 7, we will examine how and why race relations have changed in the United States and, in Chapter 8, how and why intergroup relations differ from one country to another in today's world.

## ▶ PATTERNS OF RACE AND ETHNIC RELATIONS

### Caste Versus Class Systems of Stratification

Sociologists who study stratification, or social inequality, often place societies along a continuum or range that runs from *caste systems* at one end to *class systems* at the other. A **caste system** has two or more rigidly defined and unequal groups in which membership is passed from generation to generation. The group into which one is born determines one's status for life. In this type of system, one's legal rights, job, marriage partner, and even where and when one may be present are all determined by caste membership. Caste membership is rigid and cannot be changed at any time throughout life. **Ascribed status**—the group into which one is born—totally determines one's opportunities throughout life. In caste systems, caste membership may be based on religious criteria, as it was in the caste system once legally in effect (and today far from totally eradicated) in India. However, many of the more rigid systems of racial inequality, such as that of South Africa from the late 1940s until the early 1990s, have operated in much the same way as caste systems. In fact, many social scientists consider them to be a slightly different form and call them *racial caste systems.*

At the opposite end of the scale is the **class system**. In a class system, there is also inequality, but—ideally, at least—one's status is not determined by birth; rather, **achieved status** is emphasized. This is the status one gains through one's own actions, not the status one is born into. Theoretically, in class societies people are not born into rigid groups that influence their statuses for life. Rather, everyone has the same chance, depending on what they do.

In reality, however, ascribed status does make a difference, even in class societies. Both the caste system and the class system, in their pure, abstract forms, are ideal types, or hypothetical conceptualizations, that do not exist in a pure form in real life. Most societies lie somewhere between a pure caste system and a pure class system. In all societies that are commonly regarded as class systems, ascribed statuses have important influences on the social and economic positions that people attain in their lives. Even though this is the case, caste and class are still useful concepts in describing real societies.

## Three Common Patterns of Race Relations

Borrowing from the work of sociologists Pierre L. Van den Berghe (1958, 1978) and William J. Wilson (1973, 1978), we can identify three major patterns of race and ethnic relations found in various societies. Initially, Van den Berghe outlined two patterns, which he called paternalistic and competitive systems of race relations. Wilson expanded on the competitive system, dividing it into relatively rigid competitive and fluid competitive systems. We shall discuss in turn each of the three patterns: *paternalistic* race relations, *rigid competitive* race relations, and *fluid competitive* race relations. As with caste and class, keep in mind that these terms represent ideal types and that in real life societies exist along a continuum. Roughly speaking, paternalistic systems are at one end of the continuum, fluid competitive systems are at the other end, and rigid competitive systems are somewhere between.

**Paternalistic Race Relations.**  **Paternalistic race relations** can be seen as a kind of caste system in which one's race pretty well determines one's status for life and that of one's children as well. In a paternalistic system, the roles and statuses that belong to each race or ethnic group are known and understood by all in both the majority group and the minority group. These roles and statuses are supported by a complex system of "racial etiquette," which specifies the manner in which minority group members can speak to and behave toward majority group members. As the terminology suggests, there is a great deal of paternalism toward minority group members. It is often claimed that members of the subordinate group are childlike and helpless, so that dominant group members are doing them a great favor by providing them with shelter and work and teaching them the ways of civilization (Hamilton, 1998, pp. 545–52). The roles of majority and minority groups are structured in such a way that minorities are not permitted to compete with the dominant group for jobs, housing, and so on. In societies of this type, there is usually little or no visible racial conflict or competition, for two reasons. Most important is the fact that the penalty for anyone who steps out of line is severe, often death. Also, the ideology of dominant group superiority, along with the idea that the dominant group is doing the minority group a favor by sheltering and civilizing its members, is sometimes accepted even by some minority group members. In some instances, it is the only mode of thinking to which they have been exposed. Of course, it is often true that minority group members may play along with the system to gain favors or avoid punishment without ever really accepting it.

**Competitive Race Relations.** In competitive systems of race relations, conflict and competition occur between the races in both the rigid and fluid forms. On a number of other criteria, however, these two patterns are quite different.

**Rigid Competitive Race Relations.** **Rigid competitive race relations**, like the paternalistic form, closely resembles a caste system: For the most part, one's social status is determined by one's race. This system differs from the paternalistic system in some very important ways, however. First, majority and minority group members compete in some important areas. For example, they may work at similar jobs in the same factory. Typically, the jobs held by minority group members have different job titles and lower pay than those held by majority group members. There is still at least implicit competition, however, because the two groups are doing much the same kind of work. Thus, there is always the possibility that the factory owner might fire members of the majority group and replace them with lower-paid minority group members. The two groups may also compete for housing if the population of either group (or both) increases rapidly in an area with limited housing. When such competition threatens the dominant group, it often responds by demanding increased discrimination against the subordinate group. In fact, one of the main ways in which this pattern differs from the paternalistic one is that the dominant group usually feels more immediately threatened by minority group competition. Partly for this reason, conflict between majority and minority groups is much more open under this system.

This tendency toward conflict is the second major way in which the rigid competitive system is different from the paternalistic system. In rigid competitive race relations, both groups are aware that despite the discrimination and racial inequality, there is always the possibility of majority-minority competition, which is not the case in the paternalistic system. This makes the dominant group feel more threatened, and it makes the minority group feel more powerful and assertive. Therefore there is more conflict. This conflict carries the possibilities of mass violence between groups and of severe repression of the minority. Perhaps this pattern can be best described as an unstable form of caste system. There is still gross racial inequality and formalized discrimination, but the system is beginning to come under attack by the minority, and the majority knows it. As a result, this pattern, unlike the paternalistic one, is marked by extensive open conflict.

**Fluid Competitive Race Relations.** Considerable conflict and intergroup competition are also found in **fluid competitive race relations**. However, this pattern has more of the elements of a class system, although some castelike qualities remain. The main difference between fluid and rigid competitive race relations is that in the fluid pattern, open and formalized discrimination usually has been outlawed. In theory, members of both groups are free to pursue any endeavor and to be judged on their own merits. In practice, however, minority groups start out with fewer resources because of past discrimination. Furthermore, the majority group usually controls the major social institutions and runs them in ways that serve its own interests first. Finally, for a variety of reasons, some majority group members still discriminate, even though discrimination is not socially approved. People often think and act in terms of their racial identity, so that when jobs, housing, or educational opportunities are in short supply, there is competition between racial groups. Frequently, this leads to racial or ethnic conflict. Another source of conflict is associated with protests by minority group members against their generally disadvantaged position in the system. To summarize, in the fluid competitive system, minorities are much less restricted than in either the paternalistic or rigid competitive systems, but the fluid competitive system is still one of racial inequality. As in the rigid competitive system, there is considerable racial competition and conflict. In fact, the fluid competitive pattern usually has even more competition and conflict because minorities are freer both to compete with the majority and to protest their generally disadvantaged position.

**Some Further Comparisons of Paternalistic, Rigid Competitive, and Fluid Competitive Race Relations.** In the preceding sections we have seen some of the basic elements of each of the three patterns of majority-minority relations. We shall now compare them on the basis of a number of characteristics.

**Economic Systems.** Patterns of majority-minority relations tend to differ according to a society's economic system, or system of production. The paternalistic system is most commonly found in rural, agricultural societies with large-scale landownership. Typically, these are plantation or feudal economies in which much of the population serves as a source of cheap labor for the small elite that owns the land. In a paternalistic system of race relations, minority groups become the source of this cheap labor. The system of slavery in the United States before the Civil War is frequently cited as an example of a paternalistic system of race relations. For reasons we will explore in the next two chapters, a society tends to move to competitive race relations when it urbanizes and industrializes. The rigid competitive pattern is associated with early stages of this process. As society becomes more complex, diverse, and technologically sophisticated, it tends to move toward fluid competitive relations.

**Stratification.** In paternalistic systems, stratification is very much linked to race. There is a large gap between the social and economic status of the majority and minority groups, with very little difference within the minority group, where status is quite uniformly low. In the rigid competitive system, there is also considerable racial stratification. Typically, a few members of the minority group attain relatively high status, but the great majority remain near the bottom of the ladder. In the fluid competitive pattern, there is also racial stratification, but the variation of status within both the majority group and the minority group is wide. A sizable proportion of the subordinate group may attain relatively high status, although the average status remains substantially lower for the subordinate group.

**Relative Size of Majority Group and Minority Group.** Sociohistorical studies have shown that the paternalistic pattern occurs most often when the majority group in the sociological sense (the dominant group) is small in size relative to the subordinate, or minority, group. Often, the dominant group is actually a numerical minority. It is also not unusual for the dominant group to be a numerical minority in rigid competitive systems. In general, when a numerical minority is dominant, race relations tend to be castelike. When a dominant group is outnumbered, it requires more stringent social control to maintain its advantaged position. Any strengthening of the position of the subordinate group could lead to a breakdown of the dominant group's advantaged position. In the fluid competitive pattern of race relations, on the other hand, the dominant group usually is also the numerical majority. Here, superior numbers often are enough to ensure a somewhat advantaged position, even without formal discrimination.

**Division of Labor.** In general, in the paternalistic pattern of majority-minority relations, division of labor is relatively simple because the society is not complex or highly specialized. Furthermore, division of labor is very much along racial lines, so that certain types of work are always or almost always done by members of one group. In rigid competitive race relations, specialization of labor is more complex, and division of labor is less along the lines of race or ethnicity. Although the jobs may carry different titles and pay, members of both groups may do quite similar kinds of work. As a society moves toward the fluid pattern of race relations, division of labor becomes more complex and less tied to race, although even at the fluid competitive end of the continuum, one's race has some influence on the kind of work one does.

**Mobility.**  Both geographic and socioeconomic mobility tend to increase as one moves from paternalistic through rigid competitive toward more fluid race relations. In the paternalistic pattern, the majority group generally determines where members of the minority group will live. It is a rural agricultural society in which there is little residential movement; people know what their social status is from early childhood and pass that same status on to their children. Status tends to be less tied to birth as one moves through the competitive pattern, particularly toward the fluid competitive. Geographic mobility also increases as one moves through rigid competitive relations toward the fluid competitive pattern. However, there can still be considerable restrictions on where minorities can live under the rigid competitive system and, in a less formal way, under the fluid competitive system as well.

**Racial Interaction.**  One of the major differences among the three systems involves how the races interact with one another. In the paternalistic system, a complex racial etiquette specifies exactly how minority group members can speak to and behave toward majority group members. This system also permits majority group members to give orders to minority group members and to extract favors from them, within certain limits. This system can best be described as one in which there is a great deal of contact between the groups, but the contact is always unequal, reminding the minority of its subordinate status. There is relatively little racial separation or segregation other than separate homes. It is so clearly understood that the groups have unequal status that the dominant group feels no need to impose segregation to prove it. Even sexual contact is common, but it reflects both racial and sexual inequality. Minority women must submit to the sexual desires of dominant group men, whereas subordinate group men are strictly forbidden sexual access to majority group females; violation of this rule results in severe punishment.

In the rigid competitive system, the races become much more separated, and jobs and other statuses are not quite as sharply delineated. Consequently, the majority group tries to protect and maintain its favored status by mandating a doctrine of "separate and unequal." It is under a system of rigid competitive race relations that **segregation**—enforced separation of racial groups—becomes most intense as the majority group tries to protect its threatened status. What the majority group has lost in social deference and advantage automatically conferred by race, it tries to make up for by requiring the minority to live in separate (and physically inferior) neighborhoods and to use separate and inferior public facilities.

In the fluid competitive system, strict segregation has broken down under the pressures of a modern, complex, mobile society, and there is more interracial contact than under the rigid competitive pattern. That contact tends much more to be of equal status than in either of the other patterns. Still, to a large degree the groups form separate subsocieties and often live in separate neighborhoods. Thus, close personal contact between racial groups outside of work and business settings is more the exception than the rule.

**Value Consensus Versus Conflict.**  As we have already noted, there is usually little or no open conflict in the paternalistic pattern. It is difficult to tell to what degree this reflects a value consensus or the result of forced conformity. It is probably some of both. In these societies, people usually are exposed to only one way of thinking, so they come to accept it as the natural way. All institutions—scientific, religious, legal, and educational—support the dominant group ideology. Even if people are inclined to disagree with the accepted mode of thought and behavior, the penalties for doing so are severe enough to discourage most people. It is not unusual for minority group members to play along to avoid punishment or to get what favors they can from the dominant group, even when they do not really believe in the dominant ideology. Thus, what appears to be consensus may in fact be conformity for the sake of survival.

In competitive patterns of majority-minority relations, there is usually a good deal of open conflict, and the value systems of majority and minority groups tend to differ on some key points. Although conflict occasionally reaches great intensity in rigid competitive systems, with outbreaks of mass violence between groups, it is probably more widespread and continuous in the fluid competitive pattern. Societies of this type often have *institutionalized mechanisms of conflict resolution,* such as courts, civil rights commissions, and collective bargaining. These mechanisms acknowledge the regularity of conflict and also serve to keep it within acceptable bounds, preventing it from threatening the basic operation of the social system. Nonetheless, conflict sometimes becomes too intense for these mechanisms to handle, and it spills over into collective violence, as happened in many U.S. cities in the middle and late 1960s, in Miami in the 1980s, and in Los Angeles and several other cities in 1992.

These patterns are summarized in Table 5.1 and examples are listed. In the next four chapters, we shall examine American history and compare different countries in today's world to find out why each pattern has appeared in the times, places, and situations that it has.

**Table 5.1    Summary of Characteristics Associated with Three Patterns of Race and Ethnic Relations**

|  | Paternalistic | Rigid Competitive | Fluid Competitive |
|---|---|---|---|
| System of Production | Agricultural, usually plantation or feudal | Early urban industrial | Advanced industrial and corporate |
| Stratification | Caste; group determines status | Unstable caste; group usually determines status with some exceptions | Mixture of caste and class; within-group status variation but still racial stratification |
| Relative Size of Groups | Dominant group usually numerical minority | Variable, but dominant group often numerically small | Dominant group usually numerical majority |
| Division of Labor | By race; simple division of labor | Mostly by race, but some jobs done by both dominant and subordinate groups; more complex division of labor | Complex specialization; race moderately related to type of work; wide variation within all racial groups |
| Mobility | Very low | Low to moderate | Relatively high but not unlimited |
| Racial Interaction | Much interaction, but highly unequal; little separation of races | Little and mostly unequal interaction; almost total separation of races | More interaction than rigid, less than paternalistic; more equal interaction than either of the others |
| Consensus vs. Conflict | Little outward conflict, apparent consensus on most issues | Some racial conflict; occasional violent outbursts | Diverse values; institutionalized conflict in racial and other areas |
| Examples | United States South during slavery; many South American countries during slavery | United States South after slavery; South Africa after World War II | United States today; Great Britain today |

*Source:* Material is drawn primarily from Van den Berghe (1958, 1965) and W. J. Wilson (1973, 1978).

## ▶ THE DEVELOPMENT OF ETHNIC STRATIFICATION

As Table 5.1 indicates, each of the three patterns described has been found in some times and places in American history. In fact, a strong argument can be made that in the history of the United States and some other societies, some very regular sequences of events can be found in which the three patterns appear in fairly regular order. This can be summarized as follows:

1. Diverse racial or ethnic groups come into contact with one another. Usually the initial contact is marked by curiosity and some degree of accommodation. Often, early contact has elements of both conflict and cooperation.

2. Under certain circumstances, one group becomes subordinated. When this occurs, relations between the dominant and subordinate group quickly become castelike, and depending on the social setting, either a paternalistic or rigid competitive system is established.

3. As the society modernizes, urbanizes, and industrializes, race relations become more classlike, with competitive systems replacing paternalistic ones and becoming increasingly fluid. Fewer and fewer formal restrictions are placed on the minority group, and its social movements become larger and stronger.

In the United States, three of the groups that best fit the definition of minority group, or subordinate group, presented in Chapter 1 are African Americans; American Indians, or Native Americans; and Chicanos, or Mexican Americans. We shall examine the history of these groups to see to what degree the general pattern described above fits their particular histories. We shall also try to discover *why* these groups experienced the history of subordination that they did, and we shall use this knowledge to test competing theories about the causes of ethnic stratification.

## Initial Contact Between Racial and Ethnic Groups

Obviously, before any kind of intergroup relations can occur, two or more racial or ethnic groups must come in contact with one another. This can occur in a number of ways, and how it occurs can have a big effect on the subsequent relations between the two groups (Blauner, 1972; Schermerhorn, 1978, Chap. 3; Feagin, 1984, pp. 20–26; Ogbu, 1988a; Zweigenhaft and Domhoff, 1991). Essentially, for any two groups to come into contact, one or both must migrate: Either one group must move into an area where the other group is already present, or both groups must move into the same area. When these migration patterns occur, they can result in several types of contact, which can be classified as colonization, voluntary and involuntary annexation, and voluntary and involuntary immigration. **Colonization** occurs when one group migrates into an area where another group is present and conquers and subordinates that indigenous group. **Annexation** occurs when one group expands its territory to take over control of an area formerly under the control of another group. This can occur through military action (conquest), in which case the outcome may be very similar to colonization, or it can be voluntary, as when residents of an area petition to be annexed. Many cases of annexation, such as land purchases, fall somewhere between fully voluntary and fully involuntary actions. **Immigration** occurs when a group migrates into an area where another group is established and becomes a part of the indigenous group's society. Like annexation, migration may be voluntary, as when people move to a new country in search of better economic opportunity, or involuntary, as when they are imported as slaves. Again, there are intermediate cases, such as contract or indentured labor and political refugees. As we shall see, the degree to which an ethnic group is voluntarily a part of a society has a major influence on that group's status in the society. There is a tendency for greater stratification when contact originally occurred through colonization, involuntary annexation, or involuntary migration. This alone does not always determine the outcome of contact, however, and it is certainly true that contact does not always lead to ethnic stratification.

## Origins of Ethnic Inequality

One way to identify the causes of racial or ethnic inequality (stratification) is to examine how it begins. Recall from previous chapters that different theoretical perspectives offer different explanations of why there is racial inequality. The social-psychological approach stresses individual prejudices and suggests that inequality can occur if a sufficient number of individuals are racially or ethnically prejudiced. The order, or functionalist, approach also stresses attitudes and beliefs but on a larger scale: It suggests that ethnocentrism toward out-groups becomes generalized in a society because it meets the society's needs for cohesiveness and cooperation. This ethnocentrism tends to cause discrimination against those who are racially or culturally different from the majority. Because of this ethnocentrism, stratification occurs along the lines of race or ethnicity in societies that are racially or culturally diverse. The conflict perspective, unlike the other two, does not stress prejudice or ethnocentrism as important causes of ethnic stratification. Rather, it stresses the idea that the dominant group benefits from ethnic stratification and is in a position to impose a subordinate role on the minority group. Thus, majorities subordinate minorities because they can gain from doing so.

Noel (1968) has drawn on both the order and conflict perspectives to develop an important theory of the origins of ethnic stratification. According to Noel, three conditions must be present for intergroup contact to lead to ethnic stratification. First, there must be *ethnocentrism*, as the order perspective suggests, although this alone will not cause ethnic stratification: Noel cites examples of initially ethnocentric groups that have lived side by side in peace over long periods. Second, there must be *competition* or *opportunity for exploitation* between ethnic groups. This occurs whenever two groups both desire the same scarce resource or have mutually exclusive needs or desires, or one group has some resource (such as land or labor) that the other group wants. In short, the situation must be such that one group can benefit by subordinating the other. This is one of the main explanations given by the conflict perspective for social inequality. However, even the presence of ethnocentrism and competition does not guarantee that there will be ethnic stratification. If the groups involved have relatively equal power—if neither can impose its will on the other—ethnic stratification will not occur. Accordingly, the third condition is *unequal power*. One group must be powerful enough to dominate or subordinate the other. To summarize, Noel's theory argues that we cannot explain racial or ethnic inequality on the basis of prejudice or ethnocentrism alone, as the social psychological or functionalist perspectives suggest. There must also be competition or opportunity for exploitation *and* unequal power, as suggested by the conflict perspective. In short, notions arising from both the order and the conflict approaches must be used to understand how racial or ethnic inequality initially develops.

## ▶ ORIGINS OF RACIAL AND ETHNIC INEQUALITY IN THE UNITED STATES

I have argued that initial contact between diverse racial or ethnic groups often does not involve stratification. Ethnic stratification—the dominance of one group by another—occurs only when certain conditions are met, namely, ethnocentrism, competition, and unequal power. When ethnic stratification first occurs, the pattern is frequently castelike: paternalistic or rigid competitive. In the remainder of this chapter, we shall examine the history of interactions between whites and the three minorities mentioned earlier—African Americans, Native Americans, and

Chicanos—to see to what degree the history of each group actually fits the theoretical pattern just outlined.

## African Americans

Historians generally agree that blacks first arrived in what is now the United States in 1619 in the colony of Virginia. Because they were brought here involuntarily, racial inequality existed from the start. However, evidence suggests that the racial inequality in the first few decades was quite mild compared with what developed later. During the first generation or two of black presence in the future United States, many blacks had a status comparable to that of English indentured servants (Franklin and Moss, 2000, p. 65). Although this was certainly involuntary servitude, it was not comparable to the system of chattel slavery that existed later. First, many blacks were servants for a limited period of time, after which they became free and received land of their own (Franklin and Moss, 2000, p. 65). Furthermore, the status of blacks was not very different from that of many whites, who often were under some form of servitude and were sometimes brought involuntarily to the New World. Handlin and Handlin (1950) note, for example, that "nearly everyone" in the Virginia colony in the mid-seventeenth century was under some form of indenture or involuntary servitude (see also Fogleman, 1998). In fact, the status of black and white servants was similar enough that in some instances, mixed groups of the two ran away and worked together to avoid capture (Richard Thomas, 1996, pp. 18–20). Indentured servitude was at times brutal for both whites and blacks, but until the mid-seventeenth century, both were eventually freed (Fredrickson and Knobel, 1980, p. 833). Thus, although blacks were generally not free, their status was also not very different from that of many whites for the first forty or fifty years of colonial settlement. The amount of racial inequality was quite small compared with what came later. (For further discussion of this point see Degler, 1959a, 1959b; Elkins, 1959; Jordan, 1962, 1968.)

Within two or three generations, the situation had changed drastically. By the 1660s, several colonies had passed laws sanctioning the enslavement of blacks, and the principle was rapidly evolving that slaves were property and therefore had few or no legal rights. By this time, slavery had become a status from which one could not escape and which was automatically passed on to one's children.

Why the change? Most sociologists and historians focus on two major factors. First, the plantation system that was evolving in the South could be most profitable only with large amounts of low-cost labor. Second, for various reasons other groups were not as easy to enslave and force to do plantation work as were blacks involuntarily imported from Africa. A third factor was ethnocentrism, although it alone would not have been sufficient to bring about slavery. Let us examine each of these factors in greater detail.

**The Plantation System.** The economic predominance of the plantation system, coupled with the fact that the economic elite that controlled it depended on slavery to amass wealth, is probably the most important reason for the development of chattel slavery in the southern United States. In fact, it is probably safe to say that without the plantation system, slavery in the United States would never have developed as it did. As the plantation system became the dominant mode of economic production in the South, two important changes occurred. First, the plantation-owning class became the dominant economic and political elite. W. J. Wilson (1978, p. 25) notes that "by the end of the eighteenth century, the Southern slaveholders had clearly established themselves as a regional ruling class. The economic system, the political system, and the juridical system were all controlled and shaped by the slaveholding

Although popular illustrations such as this one often portrayed slavery in a somewhat benign manner, the reality was that it was a harsh institution in which slaves were forced to work at hard labor for many hours, and few escaped the whip.

elite." Second, the plantation system required cheap and dependable labor to produce wealth for its owners, which explains why slavery was never institutionalized in the North to the same degree.

In the North, slaves were largely a luxury for a few wealthy individuals; they were not crucial to the power elite for amassing its wealth. Consequently, northern states never passed laws—as the South did—legislating all blacks into slavery. The plantation's need for labor also explains why most southern whites did not own any slaves at all and why most slaves belonged to plantation owners. Only one-fourth of all southern white families owned slaves, and more than half the slaves were owned by planter-class white families that owned more than twenty slaves. Only about 3 percent of the white southern population owned this many slaves, yet this small group, almost totally made up of plantation owners, owned more than half the slaves (Stampp, 1956, pp. 29–31).

It seems clear that the self-interests of a small, wealthy, powerful elite were a critical factor in the creation of black slavery. This can be seen not only in the United States but also throughout the Western hemisphere. Virtually everywhere that a plantation system emerged—the West Indies, Brazil, Venezuela, Mexico—a system of slavery also emerged (Curtin, 1990; J. Thornton, 1992). In fact, just 6 percent of the African slaves brought to the Americas came to the United States or the colonies that preceded it; far more were brought to the Caribbean, Central America, and South America (Curtin, 1990, p. 109). Also, shipment of African slaves to the West Indies—the area most dependent on the plantation economy—had been occurring for more than eighty years before the first slaves arrived in Virginia in 1619 (Curtin, 1990, p. 43). In some areas where it was feasible to do so, Indians were also enslaved for plantation work. In short, in the United States and elsewhere in the Americas slavery was created because an elite could benefit from it. That elite was the plantation-owning class that controlled the U.S. South, as well as much of the Caribbean and Central and South America. Thus one of Noel's (1968) three conditions for the development of ethnic stratification was clearly present: The elite group among the whites could benefit from the subordination and enslavement of blacks in the South.

**Why Blacks?**  But the question remains, Why were black Africans rather than some other groups ultimately enslaved in the United States? One of Noel's (1968) other two conditions, ethnocentrism, suggests part of the answer: The elite needed cheap labor, and blacks became the source because people were prejudiced against them. However, the answer is not that simple. As Noel demonstrates, the prejudice and ethnocentrism among the British colonists were not directed toward blacks a great deal more than toward some other groups, although there were certainly antiblack prejudices (Jordan, 1968, Chap. 1). There was a comparable amount of ethnocentrism toward Indians, and the overriding prejudice of the period was against non-Christian "heathens," be they black, Indian, or otherwise (Boskin, 1965, p. 453; Jordan, 1968, pp. 85–92). Even non-English white Christians such as the Irish were subjected to some, though less, ethnocentrism. In fact, many of the white indentured servants were Scottish, Irish, or Catholic (Fredrickson and Knobel, 1980, p. 841), whereas others were debters or former prisoners, all the objects of prejudice among the dominant colonist population. Additionally, numerous cases can be cited from world history in which slaves were the same ethnicity as their masters— about one out of four slaveholding societies, according to Patterson (1982, p. 179). Thus, there is no automatic connection between race or ethnicity and slavery. For all these reasons, neither ethnocentrism nor racial prejudice alone can account for the enslavement of Africans. Rather, such prejudices contributed to their enslavement *along with* other factors.

Noel's (1968) third factor, unequal power, appears to complete the explanation. Alternative groups that might have been enslaved on the plantations were white indentured servants and American Indians. However, both of these groups were in a better position to resist enslavement than were blacks. If indentured servants were permanently enslaved, there was the very real possibility that the supply of servants would be cut off: English debtors would no longer be willing to come to the colonies to work off their debts. Indeed, the supply of servants was threatened by rumors of harsh treatment and permanent enslavement. Additionally, improved economic conditions and political conditions in England reduced the incentive to come to North America as an indentured servant after about 1650. Moreover, white indentured servants were not racially identifiable if they ran away; black slaves were. Finally, landowners worried about the political effects of having a large number of free but poor and landless former indentured servants, who were showing signs of rebelliousness by the 1670s (Fredrickson and Knobel, 1980). If black slavery was institutionalized, there would be fewer of these, and they could also be convinced to support slavery because it would protect them with direct competition from freed African Americans.

Enslavement of Indians also proved difficult because of the ease with which they could run away and rejoin their tribal groups and the threat that Indians would attack the plantations to free their people. Furthermore, whites in the colonies often depended on Indians for trade. Thus, attempts to enslave the Indians, although they did occur, were rather quickly abandoned in the colonies. However, none of these problems existed with Africans: There was nothing voluntary about their immigration, and once here they were in a strange land with no possibility of running off to rejoin their people. They lacked the group cohesion of the Indian tribes because black family and tribal groupings often were deliberately broken up. In short, the power balance was so heavily weighted against blacks that they were the easiest group to enslave.

Thus, we see that Noel's (1968) third condition, unequal power, was also a crucial factor in the development of black slavery: Both white indentured servants and Indians had certain advantages that made it possible for them to resist slavery in a way that was not possible for black Africans. An additional factor was that Africans knew hot-weather farming techniques unknown to either the Indians or Europeans, which made them even more desirable as a source of plantation labor. Also, they were available in much larger numbers than were Indians, particularly in areas where much of the Indian population was wiped out by exposure to European diseases. And disease may have played a role in another way: Because Africans had better resistance than Europeans to tropical diseases such as malaria and hookworm, they were less likely to become ill in the hot growing seasons in the South (Coelho and McGuire, 1997). For all these reasons, it is clear that economic motives and power considerations—who could be most readily used as a cheap source of labor—explain who was enslaved at least as well as does ethnocentrism. The labor needs of the economic elite and blacks' relative lack of power to avoid enslavement were crucial factors. Thus, neither the order perspective, stressing cultural differences and ethnocentrism, nor the conflict perspective, stressing the dominant group's self-interests and the unequal power between races, is sufficient by itself to understand slavery: Both theories must be used to understand the origins of black-white inequality in the United States.

**Institutionalization of Paternalistic Caste Relations.** Over the two hundred or so years after slavery was legally established in the 1660s, it became increasingly more institutionalized, and the plantation became even more the dominant mode of economic production in the South. For example, the invention of the cotton gin in 1793 altered the economics of southern agriculture further in favor of the large-scale plantation, thereby increasing the demand for black slaves (Franklin and Moss, 2000, pp. 100–101). During the era of slavery, antiblack racism gradually intensified, so that by the mid-nineteenth century a pervasive racist ideology had developed in the South unlike anything that existed when slavery was first established (Jordan, 1968, Chap. 2; W. J. Wilson, 1973, pp. 76–81).

Among the ideologies that became widespread *after* the establishment of slavery were the beliefs that blacks were innately inferior to whites, lacking in intelligence, and incapable of developing a civilized society. As is usually true of racist ideologies, these beliefs arose mainly to justify slavery, which was beginning to come under attack from northern abolitionists. As D. B. Davis (1966) notes, many whites would find unacceptable the enslavement of human beings with the same abilities and human rights as themselves. However, if they could convince themselves that slaves were less than human, heathens and savages incapable of being civilized, they might be able to convince themselves and others that slavery was not so bad. Indeed, they could even claim it was morally good because it taught the slaves as much as they could learn about the ways of "civilized" society. Thus, ideological racism and intense antiblack prejudice were not so much the cause of slavery as the result of it: They developed largely as a way for whites to rationalize or justify to themselves and others slavery's brutal and total subjugation of other human beings. This illustrates again that racial attitudes are as often the result of behavior as the cause and that a common function of racist ideology is to justify racist behavior (see Noel, 1972a).

In contrast to the growing claims that African Americans were biologically inferior to whites during this period, prejudices against other groups were less ethnic and more political or religious. Thus, various white immigrant groups were feared not so much because of their ethnicity as because of fears that they might bring unwanted changes, such as a return of monarchy or, at the opposite end of the scale, radical insurrection. Many also feared that Catholic immigrants wanted to establish a religious state (Fredrickson and Knobel, 1980, p. 841). But beliefs about innate biological inferiority were reserved for blacks, mostly as a way of justifying slavery, because they were far less common before slavery was established. As slavery came under increasing attack, these beliefs were increasingly promoted in order to try to defend it.

In most regards, slavery in the South between the mid-seventeenth and mid-nineteenth centuries closely resembled Van den Berghe's (1958) concept of a paternalistic system of race relations. The status of slaves was determined totally by race, with laws in most southern states aimed at assigning slave status to all blacks. A complex racial etiquette developed, specifying when and how blacks could approach and address whites. In general, there was little outward racial conflict, although serious slave uprisings did occasionally occur. Certainly, the planter class lived in constant fear of such uprisings. Especially during the latter portion of the period of slavery, the fear sometimes approached paranoia. This concern was increased by the realization that in some parts of the South, blacks substantially out-numbered whites, as is often true in the paternalistic pattern of majority-minority relations.

Some historians have made much of the fact that there were relatively fewer slave revolts in the United States than in Latin America. The major reason appears not to be that most blacks accepted their status, although in the controlled setting of the southern plantation, some probably did.[1] Rather, the main reason probably is found in the power situation: There was virtually no opportunity for successful revolt for several reasons. First, blacks in the southern United States were a numer-ical minority overall, even though they outnumbered whites in some smaller areas. Being outnumbered, and with whites controlling the guns, blacks were in a poor position to revolt. In Latin America and the West Indies, however, blacks often were the majority. Second, blacks were highly fragmented and scattered in a white-dominated region. Families and tribal or linguistic groups deliberately were broken up to inhibit the planning of rebellions. Probably for similar reasons, it was against the law in most southern states for anyone to teach a black person to read or to write. Slave codes also forbade slaves to travel except when authorized or accompa-nied by whites, so they lacked the mobility necessary to plan revolts on any regional scale. The lengths to which the slave codes went to control slaves can be seen in the box "The Alabama Slave Code, 1833." As a result of the restrictions mandated by the slave codes, even contact with slaves on a nearby plantation was very difficult.

Third, nearly half the slaves were on small plantations with fewer than twenty slaves, unlike in South America, where the average plantation had about two hun-dred slaves. This further isolated and divided slaves in the United States. Fourth, the agricultural development of the southern United States was such that runaway slaves could never be far from whites who supported slavery (including nonslave-holders). Escaping and plotting a rebellion were very difficult. Again this represents a contrast with some parts of the West Indies and South America, where runaway or rebellious slaves sometimes were able to establish and defend communities in remote areas or in areas where they could form alliances with Native Americans, who were in some cases militarily strong enough to resist Europeans (J. Thornton, 1992, pp. 282–300). The rebellions that did occur in the U.S. South all ultimately ended in failure, and they were often followed by witch-hunts in which any slaves suspected of supporting the uprising were in danger of losing their lives. For these reasons—as is typically the case with paternalistic, castelike race relations—there was little open conflict in the South during the era of slavery. This does not mean that most slaves willingly accepted their status. Subtle resistance in the form of sabotage, playing on white prejudices to avoid work or gain favor, and even self-mutilation that made it impossible to do some kinds of work were not uncommon. In addition, thousands of slaves ran away, despite the severe punishment they faced if caught.

---

[1]A related factor noted by W. J. Wilson (1973) is the relative lack in the United States of newly imported slaves who remembered their freedom, compared with the predominance of such slaves in Latin America.

## THE ALABAMA SLAVE CODE, 1833

Under the slave codes in effect in Alabama in 1833, the following acts were forbidden by law:

Any passage of laws by the general assembly that would emancipate slaves, or prevent people from bringing slaves into the state, so long as they are kept in slavery.

For a slave to testify in any criminal or civil case, except against another slave.

For any slave to go from the tenement of his or her master without a pass; if such slave is found on any plantation, the slave must be returned to his or her master and receive up to thirty-nine lashes.

For any slave to be present on any plantation without permission, unless sent on lawful business.

For any slave to carry any weapon unless ordered to do so by their owner or overseer to take it from one place to another.

For any master, mistress, or overseer to permit any slave not belonging to him or her to remain on their property for more than four hours at a time, or five or more such slaves for any amount of time.

For five or more slaves, with or without passes, to assemble anywhere off the "proper plantation where they belong."

For any "white person, free negro, or mulatto" to be found in company with slaves at any unlawful meeting and for any justice of the peace or sheriff to fail to take action against such a meeting.

For any person to buy, sell, receive from, or give to a slave without the slave owner's permission or for any slave owner to permit a slave to "go at large and trade as a freeman," or to hire him or herself out for work.

For any slave to keep a dog, horse, or mule.

For any free person of color to settle in Alabama after February 1, 1833, with penalties including imprisonment, whipping, and being sold into slavery if such person does not leave the state within specified time frames.

For any person to attempt to teach any free person of color or any slave to spell, read, or write.

For any "free negro or person of color" to associate with slaves without the owner's permission.

For any slave or free person of color to "preach to, exhort, or harangue" any slave or slaves, except "in the presence of five respectable slave-holders."

For less than two-thirds of the jury in any trial of a slave to be composed of slave owners.

*Source:* John G. Aiken, *A Digest of the Laws of Alabama*, 1833 (Montgomery: Alabama Department of Archives and History).

## ▶ LIFE UNDER SLAVERY

To understand majority-minority relations in the United States, one must be aware of the reasons for the emergence of black slavery; however, a sociological analysis cannot describe what slavery was like on a day-to-day basis, nor can it adequately depict what a dehumanizing institution slavery was. Such a description is presented vividly in the box "The Peculiar Institution: Slavery in the Antebellum South."

The box shows that ethnocentrism, competition, and unequal power combined to take blacks from a status not too different from that of white indentured servants to that of being property with no recognized human rights. The value of the labor that was taken from African Americans in this way was enormous. According to Marketti (1990), the value of the labor taken just during the period from 1790 to 1860, in 1987 dollars, was between $0.7 and $40 billion. Adding the interest that would have been paid on a debt of this amount over the years brings the total to somewhere between about two and five trillion dollars—and that does not include the value of labor between 1619 and 1790 or interest between 1987 and today (Feagin, 2000). Using a somewhat different approach based on the relationship of inheritance to wealth, Conley (2002) estimates that about 25 percent of today's large gap in wealth between whites and African Americans can be explained by their relative financial positions at the time slavery was ended.

When it was profitable for the white power elite (remember, most slaves were owned by a tiny percentage of the white population) to do so, and they had the power to do so, blacks were relegated to the status of a minority group in a paternalistic system of race relations. Only after this system of racial inequality and exploitation was established did intense antiblack prejudices become widespread, apparently as a way to justify the exploitation. (For further discussion of the origins

## THE PECULIAR INSTITUTION: SLAVERY IN THE ANTEBELLUM SOUTH

It would not be too much to say that masters usually demanded from their slaves a long day of hard work and managed by some means or others to get it. The evidence does not sustain the belief that free laborers generally worked longer hours and at a brisker pace than the unfree. During the months when crops were being cultivated or harvested the slaves commonly were in the fields fifteen or sixteen hours a day, including time allowed for meals and rest.[1] By antebellum standards this may not have been excessive, but it was not a light work routine by the standards of that or any other day.

In instructions to overseers, planters almost always cautioned against overwork, yet insisted that the hands be made to labor vigorously as many hours as there was daylight. Overseers who could not accomplish this were discharged. An Arkansas master described a work day that was in no sense unusual on the plantations of the Deep South: "We get up before day every morning and eat breakfast before day and have everybody at work before day dawns. I am never caught in bed after day light nor is any body else on the place, and we continue in the cotton fields when we can have fair weather till it is so dark we can't see to work, and this history of one day is the history of every day."[2]

Planters who contributed articles on the management of slaves to southern periodicals took this routine for granted. "It is expected," one of them wrote, "that servants should rise early enough to be at work by the time it is light. . . . While at work, they should be brisk. . . . I have no objection to their whistling or singing some lively tune, but no drawling tunes are allowed in the field, for their motions are almost certain to keep time with the music."[3] These planters had the businessman's interest in maximum production without injury to their capital.

The work schedule was not strikingly different on the plantations of the Upper South. Here too it was a common practice to regulate the hours of labor in accordance with the amount of daylight. A former slave on a Missouri tobacco and hemp plantation recalled that the field-hands began their work at half past four in the morning. Such rules were far more common on Virginia plantations than were the customs of languid patricians. An ex-slave in Hanover County, Virginia, remembered seeing slave women hurrying to their work in the early morning "with their shoes and stockings in their hands, and a petticoat wrapped over their shoulders, to dress in the field the best way they could."[4] The bulk of the Virginia planters were businessmen too.

Planters who were concerned about the physical condition of their slaves permitted them to rest at noon after eating their dinners in the fields. "In the Winter," advised one expert on slave management, "a hand may be pressed all day, but not so in Summer. . . . In May, from one and a half to two hours; in June, two and a half; in July and August, three hours rest [should be given] at noon."[5] Except for certain essential chores, Sunday work was uncommon but not unheard of if the crops required it. On Saturdays slaves were often permitted to quit the fields at noon. They were also given holidays, most commonly at Christmas and after the crops were laid by.

But a holiday was not always a time for rest and relaxation. Many planters encouraged their bondsmen to cultivate small crops during their "leisure" to provide some of their own food. Thus a North Carolina planter instructed his overseer: "As soon as you have laid by the crop give the people 2 days but . . . they must work their own crops." Another planter gave his slaves a "holiday to plant their potatoes," and another "holiday to get in their potatoes." James H. Hammond once wrote in disgust: "Holiday for the negroes who fenced in their gardens. Lazy devils they did nothing after 12 o'clock." In addition, slave women had to devote part of their time when they were not in the fields to washing clothes, cooking, and cleaning their cabins. An Alabama planter wrote: "I always give them half of each Saturday, and often the whole day, at which time . . . the women do their household work; therefore they are never idle."[6]

Planters avoided night work as much as they felt they could, but slaves rarely escaped it entirely. Night work was almost universal on sugar plantations during the grinding season, and on cotton plantations when the crop was being picked, ginned, and packed. A Mississippi planter did not hesitate to keep his hands hauling fodder until ten o'clock at night when the hours of daylight were not sufficient for his work schedule.[7]

Occasionally a planter hired free laborers for such heavy work as ditching in order to protect his slave property. But, contrary to the legend, this was not a common practice. Most planters used their own field-hands for ditching and for clearing new ground. Moreover, they often assigned slave women to this type of labor as well as to plowing. On one plantation Olmsted saw twenty women operating heavy plows with double teams: "They were superintended by a male negro driver, who carried a whip, which he frequently cracked at them, permitting no dawdling or delay at the turning."[8]

Among the smaller planters and slaveholding farmers there was generally no appreciable relaxation of this normal labor routine. Their production records, their diaries and farm journals, and the testimony of their slaves all suggest the same dawn-to-dusk regimen that prevailed on the large plantations.[9] This was also the experience of most slaves engaged in nonagricultural occupations. Everywhere, then, masters normally expected from their slaves, in accordance with the standards of their time, a full stint of labor from "day clean" to "first dark."

Some, however, demanded more than this. Continuously, or at least for long intervals, they drove their slaves at a pace that was bound, sooner, or later, to injure their health. Such hard driving seldom occurred on the smaller plantations and farms or in urban centers; it was decidedly a phenomenon of the large plantations. Though the majority of planters did not sanction it, more of them tolerated excessively heavy labor routines than is generally realized. The records of the plantation regime clearly indicate that slaves were more frequently overworked by calloused tyrants than overindulged by mellowed patriarchs.

That a large number of southern bondsmen were worked severely during the colonial period is beyond dispute. The South Carolina code of 1740 charged that "many owners . . . do confine them so closely to hard labor, that they have not sufficient time for natural rest."[10] In the nineteenth century conditions seemed to have improved, especially in the older regions of the South. Unquestionably the antebellum planter who coveted a high rank in society responded to subtle pressures that others did not feel. The closing of the African slave trade and the steady rise of slave prices were additional restraining influences. "The time has been," wrote a planter in 1849, "that the farmer could kill up and wear out one Negro to buy another; but it is not so now. Negroes are too high in proportion to the price of cotton, and it behooves those who own them to make them last as long as possible."[11]

But neither public opinion nor high prices prevented some of the bondsmen from suffering physical breakdowns and early deaths because of overwork. The abolitionists never proved their claim that many sugar and cotton growers deliberately worked their slaves to death every seven years with the intention of replacing them from profits. Yet some of the great planters came close to accomplishing that result without designing it. In the "race for wealth" in which, according to one Louisiana planter, all were enlisted, few proprietors managed their estates according to the code of the patricians.[12] They were sometimes remarkably shortsighted in the use of their investments.

Irresponsible overseers, who had no permanent interest in slave property, were frequently blamed for the overworking of slaves. Since this was a common complaint, it is important to remember that nearly half of the slaves lived on plantations of the size that ordinarily employed overseers. But planters could not escape responsibility for these conditions simply because their written instructions usually prohibited excessive driving. For they often demanded crop yields that could be achieved by no other method.

Most overseers believed (with good reason) that their success was measured by how much they produced, and that merely having the slave force in good condition at the end of the year would not guarantee re-employment. A Mississippi overseer with sixteen years of experience confirmed this belief in defending his profession: "When I came to Mississippi, I found that the overseer who could have the most cotton bales ready for market by Christmas, was considered best qualified for the business—consequently, every overseer gave his whole attention to cotton bales, to the exclusion of everything else."[13]

More than a few planters agreed that this was true. A committee of an Alabama agricultural society reported: "It is too commonly the case that masters look only to the yearly products of their farms, and praise or condemn their overseers by this standard alone, without ever once troubling themselves to inquire into the manner in which things are managed on their plantations, and whether he may have lost more in the diminished value of his slaves by overwork than he has gained by his large crop." This being the case, it was understandably of no consequence to the overseer that the old hands were "worked down" and the young ones "overstrained," that the "breeding women" miscarried, and that the "sucklers" lost their children. "So that he has the requisite number of cotton bags, all is overlooked; he is re-employed at an advanced salary, and his reputation increased."[14]

*2*

A wise master did not take seriously the belief that Negroes were natural-born slaves. He knew better. He knew that Negroes freshly imported from Africa had to be broken in to bondage; that each succeeding generation had to be carefully trained. This was no easy task, for the bondsman rarely submitted willingly. Moreover, he rarely submitted completely. In most cases there was no end to the need for control—at least not until old age reduced the slave to a condition of helplessness.

Masters revealed the qualities they sought to develop in slaves when they singled out certain ones for special commendation. A small Mississippi planter mourned the death of his "faithful and dearly beloved servant" Jack: "Since I have owned him he has been true to me in all respects. He was an obedient trusty servant. . . . I never knew him to steal nor lie and he ever set a moral and industrious example to those around him. . . . I shall ever cherish his memory." A Louisiana sugar planter lost a "very valuable Boy" through an accident: "His life was a very great one. I have always found him willing and obedient and never knew him to fail to do anything he was put to do."[15] These were "ideal" slaves, the models slaveholders had in mind as they trained and governed their workers.

How might this ideal be approached? The first step, advised those who wrote discourses on the management of slaves, was to establish and maintain strict discipline. An Arkansas master suggested the adoption of the "Army Regulations as to the discipline in Forts." "They must obey at all times, and under all circumstances, cheerfully and with alacrity," affirmed a Virginia slaveholder. "It greatly impairs the happiness of a negro, to be allowed to cultivate an insubordinate temper. Unconditional submission is the only footing upon which slavery should be placed. It is precisely similar to the attitude of a minor to his parent, or a soldier to his general." A South Carolinian limned a perfect relationship between a slave and his master: "that the slave should know that his master is to govern absolutely, and he is to obey implicitly. That he is never for a moment to exercise either his will or judgment in opposition to a positive order."[16]

The second step was to implant in the bondsmen themselves a consciousness of personal inferiority. They had "to know and keep their places," to "feel the difference between master and slave," to understand that bondage was their natural status. They had to feel that African ancestry tainted them, that their color was a badge of degradation. In the country they were to show respect for even their master's nonslaveholding neighbors; in the towns they were to give way on the streets to the most wretched white man. The line between the races must never be crossed, for familiarity caused slaves to forget their lowly station and to become "impudent."[17]

Frederick Douglass explained that a slave might commit the offense of impudence in various ways: "in the tone of an answer; in answering at all; in not answering; in the expression of countenance; in the motion of the head; in the gait, manner and bearing of the slave." Any of these acts, in some subtle way, might indicate the absence of proper subordination. "In a well regulated community," wrote a Texan, "a negro takes off his hat in addressing a white man. . . . Where this is not enforced, we may always look for impudent and rebellious negroes."[18]

The third step in the training of slaves was to awe them with a sense of their master's enormous power. The only principle upon which slavery could be maintained, reported a group of Charlestonians, was the "principle of fear." In his defense of slavery James H. Hammond admitted that this, unfortunately, was true but put the responsibility upon the abolitionists. Antislavery agitation had forced masters to strengthen their authority: "We have to rely more and more on the power of fear. . . . We are determined to continue masters, and to do so we have to draw the rein tighter and tighter day by day to be assured that we hold them in complete check." A North Carolina mistress, after subduing a troublesome domestic, realized that it was essential "to make them stand in fear"![19]

In this the slaveholders had considerable success. Frederick Douglass believed that most slaves stood "in awe" of white men; few could free themselves altogether from the notion that their masters were "invested with a sort of sacredness." Olmsted saw a small white girl stop a slave on the road and boldly order him to return to his plantation. The slave fearfully obeyed her command. A visitor in Mississippi claimed that a master, armed only with a whip or cane, could throw himself among a score of bondsmen

and cause them to "flee with terror." He accomplished this by the "peculiar tone of authority" with which he spoke. "Fear, awe, and obedience . . . are interwoven into the very nature of the slave."[20]

The fourth step was to persuade the bondsmen to take an interest in the master's enterprise and to accept his standards of good conduct. A South Carolina planter explained: "The master should make it his business to show his slaves, that the advancement of his individual interest, is at the same time an advancement of theirs. Once they feel this, it will require but little compulsion to make them act as it becomes them."[21] Although slaveholders induced only a few chattels to respond to this appeal, these few were useful examples for others.

The final step was to impress Negroes with their helplessness, to create in them "a habit of perfect dependence" upon their masters.[22] Many believed it dangerous to train slaves to be skilled artisans in the towns, because they tended to become self-reliant. Some thought it equally dangerous to hire them to factory owners. In the Richmond tobacco factories they were alarmingly independent and "insolent." A Virginian was dismayed to find that his bondsmen, while working at an iron furnace, "got a habit of roaming about and taking care of themselves." Permitting them to hire their own time produced even worse results. "No higher evidence can be furnished of its baneful effects," wrote a Charlestonian, "than the unwillingness it produces in the slave, to return to the regular life and domestic control of the master."[23]

"Chains and irons," James H. Hammond correctly explained, were used chiefly to control and discipline runaways. "You will admit," he argued logically enough, "that if we pretend to own slaves, they must not be permitted to abscond whenever they see fit; and that if nothing else will prevent it these means must be resorted to."[24] Three entries in Hammond's diary, in 1844, indicated that he practiced what he preached. July 17: "Alonzo runaway with his irons on." July 30: "Alonzo came in with his irons off." July 31: "Re-ironed Alonzo."

Hammond was but one of many masters who gave critics of the peculiar institution a poignant symbol—the fettered slave. A Mississippian had his runaway Maria "ironed with a shackle on each leg connected with a chain." When he caught Albert he "had an iron collar put on his neck"; on Woodson, a habitual runaway, he "put the ball and chain." A Kentuckian recalled seeing slaves in his state wearing iron collars, some of them with bells attached. The fetters, however, did not always accomplish their purpose, for numerous advertisements stated that fugitives wore these encumbrances when they escaped. For example, Peter, a Louisiana runaway, "had on each foot when leaving, an iron ring, with a small chain attached to it."[25]

But the whip was the most common instrument of punishment—indeed, it was the emblem of the master's authority. Nearly every slaveholder used it, and few grown slaves escaped it entirely. Defenders of the institution conceded that corporal punishment was essential in certain situations; some were convinced that it was better than any other remedy. If slavery were right, argued an Arkansas planter, means had to be found to keep slaves in subjugation, "and my opinion is, the lash—not used murderously, as would-be philanthropists assert, is the most effectual." A Virginian agreed: "A great deal of whipping is not necessary; some is."[26]

The majority seemed to think that the certainty, and not the severity, of physical "correction" was what made it effective. While no offense could go unpunished, the number of lashes should be in proportion to the nature of the offense and the character of the offender. The master should control his temper. "Never inflict punishment when in a passion," advised a Louisiana slaveholder, "but wait until perfectly cool, and until it can be done rather in sorrow than in anger." Many urged, therefore, that time be permitted to elapse between the misdeed and the flogging. A Georgian required his driver to do the whipping so that his bondsmen would not think that it was "for the pleasure of punishing, rather than for the purpose of enforcing obedience."[27]

Planters who employed overseers often fixed the number of stripes they could inflict for each specific offense, or a maximum number whatever the offense. On Pierce Butler's Georgia plantation each driver could administer twelve lashes, the head driver thirty-six, and the overseer fifty. A South Carolinian instructed his overseer to ask permission before going beyond fifteen. "The highest punishment must not exceed 100 lashes in one day and to that extent only in extreme cases," wrote James H. Hammond. "In general 15 to 20 lashes will be a sufficient flogging."[28]

The significance of these numbers depended in part upon the kind of whip that was used. The "rawhide," or "cowskin," was a savage instrument requiring only a few strokes to provide a chastisement that a slave would not soon forget. A former bondsman remembered that it was made of about three feet of untanned ox hide, an inch thick at the butt end, and tapering to a point which made it "quite elastic and springy."[29]

Many slaveholders would not use the rawhide because it lacerated the skin. One recommended, instead, a leather strap, eighteen inches long and two and a half inches wide, fastened to a wooden handle. In Mississippi, according to a visitor, the whip in general use consisted of a "stout flexible stalk" covered with a tapering leather plait, about three and a half feet in length, which formed the lash. "To the end of the lash is attached a soft, dry, buckskin cracker, about three eighths of an inch wide and ten or twelve inches long, which is the only part allowed to strike, in whipping on the bare skin. . . . When it is used by an experienced hand it makes a very loud report, and stings, or 'burns' the skin smartly, but does not bruise it."[30]

How frequently a master resorted to the whip depended upon his temperament and his methods of management. On some establishments long periods of time elapsed with relatively few whippings—until, as a rice planter explained, it seemed "as if the devil had got into" the hands, and for a time there was "a good deal of it." Or, occasionally, a normally amiable slave got out of hand and had to be flogged. "Had to whip my Man Willis for insolence to the overseer," wrote a Tennesseean. "This I done with much regret as he was never whipped before."[31]

On other establishments the whip was in constant use. The size of the estate may have had some relationship to the amount of whipping, but the disposition of the proprietor was decidedly more crucial. Small farmers, as well as large planters, often relied upon corporal punishment as their chief method of enforcing discipline. Southern women were sometimes equally prone to use the lash upon errant domestics.

Some overseers, upon assuming control, thought it wise to whip every hand on the plantation to let them know who was in command. Some masters used the lash as a form of incentive by flogging the last slave out of his cabin in the morning.[32] Many used it to "break in" a young slave and to "break the spirit" of an insubordinate older one. "If the negro is humble and appears duly sensible of the impropriety of his conduct, a very moderate chastisement will answer better than a severe one," advised a planter. "If, however, he is stubborn . . . a slight punishment will only make bad worse." Slaves had to be flogged, explained an Alabamian, until they manifested "submission and penitence."[33]

In short, the infliction of stripes curbed many a bondsman who could not be influenced by any other technique. Whipping had a dispiriting effect upon most of them. "Had to administer a little rod to Bob this morning," reported a Virginian. "Have seen for more than three months I should have to humble him some, hope it may benefit him."[34]

[1]Gray, *History of Agriculture*, I, pp. 556–57.

[2]Gustavus A. Henry to his wife, November 27, 1860, Henry Papers.

[3]*Southern Cultivator*, VIII (1850), p. 163.

[4]William W. Brown, *Narrative of William W. Brown, a Fugitive Slave* (Boston, 1847), p. 14; Olmsted, *Seaboard*, p. 109; *De Bow's Review*, XIV (1853), pp. 176–78; Benjamin Drew, *The Refugee: or the Narratives of Fugitive Slaves in Canada* (Boston, 1856), p. 162.

[5]*Southern Cultivator*, VIII (1850), p. 163.

[6]Henry K. Burgwyn to Arthur Souter, August 6, 1843, Henry King Burgwyn Papers; John C. Jenkins Diary, entries for November 15, 1845; April 22, 1854; Hammond Diary, entry for May 12, 1832; *De Bow's Review*, XIII (1852), pp. 193–94.

[7]Jenkins Diary, entry for August 7, 1843.

[8]Olmsted, *Back Country*, p. 81; Sydnor, *Slavery in Mississippi*, p. 12.

[9]See, for example, Marston Papers; Torbert Plantation Diary; *De Bow's Review*, XI (1851), pp. 369–72; Drew, *Refugee*; Douglass, *My Bondage*, p. 215; Trexler, *Slavery in Missouri*, pp. 97–98.

[10]Hurd, *Law of Freedom and Bondage*, 1, p. 307; Flanders, *Plantation Slavery in Georgia*, p. 42.

[11]*Southern Cultivator*, VII (1849), p. 69.

[12]Kenneth M. Clark to Lewis Thompson, December 29, 1859, Thompson Papers.

[13]*American Cotton Planter and Soil of the South*, II (1858), pp. 112–13.

[14]*American Farmer*, II (1846), p. 78; *Southern Cultivator*, II (1844), pp. 97, 107.

[15]Baker Diary, entry for July 1, 1854; Alexander Franklin Pugh Ms. Plantation Diary, entry for June 21, 1860.

[16]*Southern Cultivator*, IV (1846), pp. 43–44; XVIII (1860), pp. 304–305; *Farmers' Register*, V (1837), p. 32.

[17]*Southern Planter*, XII (1852), pp. 376–79; *Southern Cultivator*, VIII (1850), p. 163; *Farmers' Register*, I (1834), pp. 564–65.

[18]Douglass, *My Bondage*, p. 92; *Austin Texas State Gazette*, October 10, 1857.

[19]Phillips (ed.), *Plantation and Frontier*, II, pp. 108–11; *De Bow's Review*, VII (1849), p. 498; Mary W. Bryan to Ebenezer Pettigrew, October 20, 1835, Pettigrew Family Papers.

[20]Douglass, *My Bondage*, pp. 250–51; Olmsted, *Back Country*, pp. 444–45; [Ingraham], *South-West*, II, pp. 260–61.

[21]*Farmers' Register*, IV (1837), p. 574.

[22]*Southern Cultivator*, IV (1846), p. 44.

[23]*Southern Planter*, XII (1852), pp. 376–79; Olmsted, *Seaboard*, pp. 58–59; *Charleston Courier*, September 12, 1850.

[24]*De Bow's Review*, VII (1849), p. 500.

[25]Nevitt Plantation Journal, entries for November 9, 1827; March 28, 1831; July 18, 1832; Coleman, *Slavery Times in Kentucky*, pp. 248–49; *New Orleans Picayune*, December 26, 1847.

[26]*Southern Cultivator*, XVIII (1860), pp. 239–40; *Southern Planter*, XII (1852), p. 107.

[27]*De Bow's Review*, XXII (1857), pp. 376–79; *Southern Agriculturist*, IV (1831), p. 350.

[28]Kemble, *Journal*, pp. 42–43; Phillips (ed.), *Plantation and Frontier*, I, pp. 116–22; *Plantation Manual* in Hammond Papers.

[29]Douglass, *My Bondage*, p. 103.

[30]*Southern Cultivator*, VII (1849), p. 135; [Ingraham], *South-West*, II, pp. 287–88.

[31]Olmsted, *Seaboard*, pp. 438–39; Bills Diary, entry for March 30, 1860.

[32]*Southern Cultivator*, II (1844), pp. 169–70; Davis, *Cotton Kingdom in Alabama*, pp. 54–55.

[33]*Southern Cultivator*, VIII (1850), p. 164; William P. Gould Ms. Plantation Rules.

[34]Adams Diary, entry for July 2, 1860.

*Source:* Copyright© 1959 by Kenneth Stampp. Reprinted by permission of Alfred A. Knopf, Inc.

of black-white inequality, including reprints of several articles cited in this section, see Noel, 1972b.)

## Native Americans

**Early Contact.** The history of relations between Native Americans and European whites in North America is incredibly complex, with wide variations in events from one area to another. When the Europeans first arrived in the fifteenth century, North America's native population numbered at least 1 million (J. Collier, 1947, p. 172) and probably several times that (Josephy, 1968, pp. 50–51, 1992; Garbarino, 1976, p. 72; Lord, 1997; R. Thornton, 1997). One of the more widely accepted estimates is that of R. Thornton (1987), who placed the Native American population at around 7 million, which was made up of about 600 independent nations that varied tremendously in culture, social organization, and mode of economic production. Three major national groups of Europeans—Spanish, French, and British—were involved in the conquest and settlement of North America by whites, and here, too, there was great variation within the three groups. Because of this historical complexity, almost any generalization one might make has its exceptions. Nonetheless, certain patterns and regularities in Indian–white relations in North America held more often than not, and these may enable us to understand some of the causes of the oppression and subordination of Indian people in the United States. Of the three major European colonial groups that settled in the United States, the one that had the greatest direct influence on Indian-white relations was the British. The Spanish played an important role in Florida and the Southwest and had an important effect over a wider area because of the spread of horses, first introduced by the Spanish among a variety of Native American groups. The French played an important role for a time in the Northeast. In the United States, however, most white contact with Native Americans involved British colonists or their descendants.

The Spanish, French, and British all had somewhat different objectives in coming to the New World. The Spanish came mainly to seek wealth and secondarily to convert souls to Christianity (Garbarino, 1976). In Latin America, the Spanish also sought to conquer and control land (and the land's population) but basically to extract its wealth rather than to establish a self-supporting system of production (Josephy, 1968, Chap. 25). This led them to immediately conquer whatever populations they encountered in Latin America; plunder the highly developed and often wealthy cities of the Aztecs, Incas, and Mayas; and force the natives into slavery or peonage. This was less common in North America, although it did occur to some extent both in the Southwest and in Florida (T. D. Hall, 1993). More often, Spanish contact with native peoples in North America tended to take one of two forms. When the Spanish periodically sent expeditions through North America seeking wealth, such as those of De Soto and various slave catchers in Florida, Indian people were sometimes brutally attacked, tortured, and killed. (Coronado's famous expedition in the western and plains states was a notable exception to this rule.) The other type of contact was more benevolent and took the form of missionaries who wanted to convert the native peoples to Christianity.

Among both the French and British, trading with the Indians was an important objective. Accordingly, both groups enjoyed relatively harmonious relations with Indian people at first and, in these early years, largely depended on Indian people for their survival. For example, it is unlikely that the Pilgrims at Plymouth could have survived the winter of 1621–1622 without Indian assistance (Josephy, 1968, p. 301). The French depended largely on the fur trade as a source of economic support, and many British settlers also relied on trade with the Indians. Indian people, too, often found the early contact beneficial, particularly the tribes that were hunters and could benefit from the fur trade (Lurie, 1991). This relationship, marked by substantial but not total cooperation, did not last long, however. It soon changed to one of conflict and led to the conquest of the native people by the Europeans, particularly the British. However, the existence of this period of relative cooperation does illustrate one sociological point: Even where there are two greatly different cultural groups and considerable ethnocentrism, ethnic conflict and stratification do not automatically occur. It is clear that the British, especially, took a highly ethnocentric view of Native Americans, sometimes seeing them as ungodly heathens worthy neither of conversion nor of human association. Under the influence of Calvinism, the Protestant British regarded conversion largely as a matter of predestination: Either one was part of God's chosen people or one was not, and attempting to convert those who were not chosen was a waste of time. This generally led to the view that the British were chosen and the Indians were not. Indeed, the same generalized prejudice against non-Christians that shaped British attitudes toward blacks also shaped their attitudes toward Indians.

The Catholic French, on the other hand, were like the Catholic missionaries from Spain: They viewed the Indians as fellow human beings with souls, to whom they felt obligated to bring the message of Christianity. Accordingly, the French had a milder prejudice against the Indians than did the British. Another fact was of even greater importance in shaping the history of European relations with Native Americans. The French were for the most part uninterested in settling land: They were traders, and their livelihood depended on reasonably good relations with the native hunting peoples, who provided their source of wealth. The British, on the other hand, mainly wanted to settle land. They were largely agriculturists, and for British settlers, the opportunity to own land was one of the major attractions of North America (Garbarino, 1976, p. 44). When added to their ethnocentrism, this factor made it inevitable that conflict would eventually break out between the British colonists and Indian people. As more and more British settlers arrived, they forced Indian people off their land (Josephy, 1968, Chap. 26). Because the Europeans controlled the firearms, the balance of power was grossly unequal. The outcome could never have been in serious doubt once the British began to arrive in large numbers. This British power during the colonial era thus sowed the seeds of what would become more than two centuries of conquest and domination of native peoples under the rule of the United States. The basic approaches of making treaties with Indians to gain their land and of establishing Indian reservations were largely established under the British before the Revolutionary War (Garbarino, 1976, p. 440; Lurie, 1991, p. 136).

One disastrous effect of the displacement of Indian people by whites was an increase in rivalries between the various Indian nations (Abler, 1992). At first, conflicts arose over who would control trade with the whites. Later, as Indian people began to be displaced from their homelands, conflicts over land flared between various tribes. A tragic consequence was a tremendous escalation of warfare among the various Native American groups. In the past, conflict had been controlled and somewhat ritualistic; now, struggle was a matter of life and death. Also, this conflict often included the use of firearms obtained from the Europeans (Abler, 1992). In addition to the many deaths, tribal warfare made it nearly impossible for Indian people to mount a unified defense against the incursions of the whites. Largely because of animosities that had built up against Indian allies of the French, the Iroquois nations supported (in fact, if not openly) the British in the French and Indian War (Josephy, 1968, pp. 311–12; Garbarino, 1976, p. 437). This support was critical for the British, and as a result of this war, the French lost control of eastern North America.

In addition to intertribal conflicts, another disastrous result of Indian-white contact was disease. Indian people had no immunity to European diseases. Most historians agree that more Indians died of white people's diseases than were killed in warfare. In some areas, 90 percent of the indigenous population was lost (Garbarino, 1976, p. 438), and in at least one case, an entire tribe was wiped out (Debo, 1970). This was not always accidental: In some cases, Europeans deliberately exposed Indians to disease (Thornton, 1987).

**A Trail of Broken Treaties.** An American Indian protest campaign in the 1970s called itself the Trail of Broken Treaties. This name is a fitting description of Indian-white relations from before the Revolutionary War until the end of the nineteenth century. Again and again, treaties were made with Indian nations, requiring the Indian people to give up their land with only the smallest compensation and move to new land, which was to be theirs forever. Again and again, the demands for land by a swelling white population and by white land speculators led to displacement of the Indian people from the "promised lands." This system of treaties was fundamentally deceptive to Indian people, for two major reasons. First, Indian nations generally had a system of common ownership of land. Often, they believed they were letting whites use commonly owned land, not giving it up. Whites saw the land as strictly theirs and did not even permit Indians to pass through it (Guillemin, 1978, p. 320). Second, Indian people generally signed treaties in good faith, expecting them to be kept. In Indian societies, a person's word was enough. Whites, on the other hand, often saw the treaties as stopgap measures to get the Indians out of the way. Treaties could always be renegotiated later when whites needed more land (Lurie, 1991, p. 139–41). Gradually, as whites increased their population and their desire for land, Indian nations were forced to move farther and farther west, often displacing others in the process. Some were ultimately forced to move as far as from Georgia to Oklahoma. One-fourth of the Cherokees died on one such forced trek (Josephy, 1968, p. 323). Certainly, it is one of history's worst examples of the forced migration of an indigenous population by an invading population.

**Causes of the Subordination of Indian People.** In analyzing the causes of this forced migration and subordination of America's native peoples, the same three factors stand out as in the establishment of slavery. First, there was ethnocentrism, as there usually is when two very different cultures come into contact. This in itself did not lead to widespread subordination of the Native American peoples. Only when population pressures in the land-settling British (and later American) population led to competition with the Indians over land did subordination occur. In other words, whites had something to gain—land—by subordinating the Indians, just as the southern plantation owners had something to gain by enslaving blacks. Firearms gave the whites the power to take land from Indians, and they used it. Thus, the same three factors—ethnocentrism, competition, and unequal power—also explain the displacement and conquest of the Indians. As Lurie (1991, pp. 136–41) points out, this can be illustrated by comparing Indian-white relations in the United States with those in Canada, where white pressure for land was never so great. There, too, Indian people often were deprived of their land, but they were given more desirable land than the American Indian, with reserves "located in the tribes' homelands or nearby ecologically similar areas" (Lurie, 1991, p. 136). Furthermore, once treaties were established, they were generally honored, and Indian people were not forced to move repeatedly from place to place, as they were in the United States. One reason is that there has always been much less pressure for land in Canada, which has both a much smaller population and less reliance on the land-based enterprise of agriculture than does the United States (Guillemin, 1978).

**The Reservation System.** As Native Americans were forced off their land in the United States from the late eighteenth through the nineteenth century, more and more of them had to live on reservations. As the white population increased, the reservations were increasingly relegated to land the whites considered worthless or uninhabitable. The reservations also became more and more prisonlike, with Indian people having fewer and fewer recognized legal rights. In 1871, Congress abolished the practice of making treaties with the Indians. This even further stripped Indians of their rights because whites tended to view the "agreements"

Fort Union on the Missouri. Note the process of white encroachment on Indian land. Gradually, Indians were displaced from most of the desirable locations and forced into small areas on the least desirable land.

made after this exchange as legally and morally even less binding than the earlier treaties (Lurie, 1991). Another development during this period was the government's designation of Indian people as "wards" of the government in 1862. Although paternalism and a general effort to press Indians to surrender their own culture and adopt the white man's ways had always been a key part of European colonial and, later, American policy toward Indian people, they became even more prevalent from the 1860s on. By the late 1800s, most Indians had been forced onto reservations, often after ferocious warfare and great bloodshed on both sides. In California, for example, it is estimated that 70,000 Indians lost their lives in the ten years immediately after the 1849 gold rush, the period of greatest white population expansion (Garbarino, 1976; see also Hurtado, 1988). By the end of this period, most of those who survived had been forced onto reservations.

If it existed today, the Indian reservation of the late nineteenth century probably would be called a concentration camp. The reservations more often than not were heavily guarded by U.S. Army troops, and Indian people could not leave the reservation without a pass. Practice of native religions and other displays of Indian culture were forbidden. The Sun Dance, an annual religious ritual practiced by many plains tribes, was banned (Jorgensen, 1972). The reason given was that the ceremony often involved some elements of self-torture, but the fact remains that it was a freely chosen and crucial aspect of the culture and belief of many tribes and nobody was compelled to participate in the self-torture aspect. Indian children on reservations often were taken from their homes and forced to attend boarding schools run by whites. There they were required to speak only English; if they were caught speaking their native language, they were severely punished. Finally, Indians were denied the right to vote. They could not vote in state and federal elections because they were not regarded as U.S. citizens, and they were allowed no input into the running of reservations, although the reservations were supposedly their land.

Even those who sought to help the Indian people usually ended up exercising social control over them instead. Philanthropists, some policymakers, and missionaries who meant well generally assumed that the best way to improve the conditions of Indian people was to convince them to accept the "civilized" ways of the whites. Beginning in 1887, a policy known as "allotment" was initiated. Its purpose was to set up Indians as individual landowning farmers who would make a living growing and selling agricultural products from their own land. Because it simply attempted to model itself after the social and economic organization of white culture without understanding the situation of the people it was supposed to help, the program was a miserable failure (Garbarino, 1976, p. 442). First, it was applied indiscriminately to all tribes, whether they had any history of agriculture or not. Second, it imposed the white concept of landownership, which was different from the usual Indian concept of commonly owned land. Also, in many Indian cultures, women cultivated while men hunted or were warriors, so European-style farming was contrary to long-held notions about gender roles. Finally, many Indians were encouraged to become indebted to whites, who then took the land for payment (Lurie, 1991, p. 142). All of these factors combined to make this well-intended but highly ethnocentric program a failure. Its main result was to transfer millions of acres of Indian land to whites. Thus, even when intentions were good (and usually they were not), the white people's behavior and policy toward Indian people were so shaped by paternalism and ethnocentrism that they ended up serving white interests rather than those of Native Americans (Guillemin, 1978, pp. 322–23).

## The Indian Reservation and the Slave Plantation: A Comparison

We end our discussion of American Indian history up to 1900 by comparing the Indian reservation of the late nineteenth century with the slave plantation of the early nineteenth century. In some regards, the reservation fits the model of the paternalistic pattern of race relations almost as well as the slave plantation, although it is less often given as an example, and there are some differences. In both systems, status was based totally on racial or ethnic identity. Indians were expected to go to the reservations, just as antebellum southern blacks were automatically slaves. Moreover, neither group could travel freely. In both cases, group culture was severely repressed, and ideologies of paternalism—"we're doing them a favor by civilizing them"—were pervasive. Although such paternalism was typical even among well-intentioned people, it developed first and foremost as a way of justifying the exploitation that was occurring. Thus, the use of paternalism as a justifying ideology was another common element between the slave plantation and the Indian reservation.

Despite these similarities, there was at least one important difference. Blacks were exploited totally for their labor; they had no land in this country that could be taken away. Indian people, on the other hand, were exploited mostly for their land. Although a few were made slaves by British settlers in the Southeast and Spanish settlers in the Southwest (on slavery in the Southwest, see Brooks, 2002), most Indians were not enslaved, for the reasons mentioned earlier. This explains the other major difference between the two systems. Under slavery, there was continuous contact between whites and blacks, who lived in close proximity to each other in a hierarchical system in which everyone was expected to know one's place. This was necessary if whites were to exploit blacks for their labor on the plantation. However, the effort in the case of Native Americans was to separate them from the white population, to force them onto white-controlled reservations. The main objective was to get them out of the way, so whites could safely farm or develop the land that had been taken from them.

Thus, the different economic objectives of the dominant group—land versus labor—led to a difference in the pattern of racial inequality that resulted. The black–white pattern almost totally resembled the paternalistic form; the Indian-white pattern might best be described as basically paternalistic, the one difference being the racial separation that is more characteristic of the rigid competitive model. The important fact remains that when whites were in a position to benefit and when they had the power to do so, they set up rigid systems of inequality, subordinating both black people and Indian people. Despite the many differences in the two histories, the crucial elements of ethnocentrism, competition or potential gain, and unequal power were present in both. In the case of black people, the objective was labor; in the case of Indian people, it was land. In both cases, intense racist ideologies arose as a way of rationalizing or justifying the exploitation. The original ethnocentrism greatly increased after the pattern of exploitation was developed.[2] As G. B. Nash (1970, Chap. 1) points out, the English settlers were aware that they were taking land away from an established people. To justify this, they developed an image of the Native American as a helpless savage who could only benefit from being Christianized, civilized, and brought into a modern agricultural system. As pressures for land increased, so did racist stereotyping, and the image of the Indian as a lawless barbarian replaced the earlier image of the "noble savage."

## Mexican Americans

**Early Contacts.** The first contact between Mexicans and Anglo Americans came about in what is now the southwestern United States. This contact began to occur on a sizable scale in the early 1800s as the Mexican population expanded north and the Anglo American population expanded west. Mexicans were mostly mestizo, a mixture of Spanish and Indian, which by that time made up the overwhelming

---

[2]The different nature of the contact with and exploitation of the two groups resulted in somewhat different racist stereotypes. For further discussion of this point, see G. B. Nash (1970, Chap 1).

majority of the population. There were also some recent white immigrants from Spain, who preferred to think of themselves as Spanish rather than Mexican and were generally so recognized. At that time, the present-day states of Texas, California, New Mexico, Arizona, Nevada, and Utah were all part of Mexico, as were most of Colorado and small parts of three other states. The relationship between white Americans, or Anglos, and Mexicans during this period might best be described as displaying elements of both cooperation and competition but little ethnic stratification. Both groups were landowners, farmers, and ranchers; Mexicans were operating ranches on a large scale in Texas by the late eighteenth century and later in California, especially after Mexico became independent from Spain in 1822 (Meier and Rivera, 1972, Chap. 3). In addition to the general absence of ethnic inequality, the competition was limited and counterbalanced by significant elements of cooperation. One example can be seen in the occasional instances of "filibustering" by some Anglo settlers in Texas. This refers to insurrections aimed at separating from the authority of the Mexican government. When these uprisings occurred, other Anglos generally helped the Mexican authorities put them down. One influential U.S. citizen who received a number of land grants from the Mexican government, Stephen Austin, was instrumental in helping control a revolt of this type in 1826, the Fredonia Revolt, which had the support of a number of recent American immigrants. Austin also ensured that immigrants respected the terms of their land grants and swore an oath of loyalty to Mexico (Meier and Rivera, 1972, p. 58). The relationship was such that one expert in Chicano (Mexican American) history has observed that "the *general* tone of the times was one of intercultural cooperation" (Alvarez, 1973, p. 922). In California in the 1820s and 1830s, there is similar evidence of cooperation. In fact, the Anglo immigrants of this period often were completely assimilated into Mexican life. They often became Mexican citizens, married Mexicans, and received land grants; occasionally they even held public office (Meier and Rivera, 1972, p. 67).

To summarize, Mexican and Anglo residents in the early stages of southwestern settlement lived side by side in similar status, with relatively cooperative relationships. In each of the three major areas (Texas, California, and Nuevo Mexico, which largely comprised present-day Arizona and New Mexico) the lifestyles and modes of production were somewhat different, but in all three the pattern was mostly one of equality and cooperation. Of course, both groups in different ways oppressed the southwestern Indian people, but they treated and regarded each other largely as equals.

## Origins of Ethnic Stratification

**Texas.** In the 1830s, a chain of events began that proved disastrous for Mexicans living in Aztlan, as the region of Mexico that became part of the United States is sometimes called. By the early 1830s, conflict had arisen in Mexico over the role of its national government. Some Mexicans, the centralists, wanted a strong national government that would exercise close administrative control over all of Mexico. Others, the federalists, wanted a looser confederation with greater local autonomy, not unlike the system of the United States (Hamnett, 1996). Most Texans, both Mexican and Anglo, favored the latter approach and sided with the federalists. However, centralists came to control Mexico's national government. This led to conflict with Texas, conflict that was heightened by the Mexican government's 1829 decision to abolish slavery. Many Anglos who immigrated to Texas were southern, slave-owning cotton growers (Estrada, 1985, p. 163; Mirande, 1985, pp. 23–25). The Mexican army came to Texas to control the dissident federalists but in the process spilled so much blood that a revolution was started: For a short time, Texas ended up as an independent nation (Alvarez, 1973). This chain of events upset the balance of power, creating new demands for land by whites in Texas in a way that resulted almost overnight in gross social inequality between Anglos and Mexicans.

Why did this happen? First, Texas's independence from Mexico accelerated the influx of white immigrants, mostly from the South. This influx began in earnest when Mexico opened its northern border to non-Mexicans in 1821 (Nostrand, 1992) and continued after Texas declared independence from Mexico in 1836. The Mexican population of Texas fell to 20 percent in 1830, 10 percent in 1840, and just 6 percent by 1860 (Grebler, Moore, and Guzman, 1970, p. 40; Mirande, 1987, p. 31). The growing numbers of Anglo immigrants brought with them the prejudices of the South and a tremendous demand for land. Outnumbering the Mexicans as they did, they soon appealed for admission to the United States (as a slave state), and in 1845 Texas was annexed. The situation now was totally changed, and the past cooperation of the Mexicans and Anglos was forgotten. Most Mexicans were quickly deprived of their land, either by force or by American law (backed by force), which consistently served Anglo, not Mexican, interests (Mirande, 1987, Chap. 2). By 1900, even the largest and wealthiest Mexican landowners had generally been deprived of their land (Alvarez, 1973).

During this period, there was also a great upsurge in anti-Mexican prejudice, which further contributed to the subordination of the now Mexican American people in Texas. Alvarez (1973) cites three major reasons for this upsurge. First, the warfare with Mexico had led most Anglos to view all Mexicans as former enemies, even though most of them had also opposed Mexico's centralist government and many had fought for Texas's independence from Mexico. Second, as noted, many had learned intense racial prejudice in the South and readily applied notions of racial inferiority to Mexicans. Finally, racist ideology served an economic purpose in supporting and rationalizing the Anglos' actions of taking land from the Mexicans.

**California and Nuevo Mexico.**    Most of the rest of the Southwest—California and Nuevo Mexico—became part of the United States in 1848 as a result of the Treaty of Guadalupe Hidalgo, which ended the Mexican-American War. This war was the result of a number of factors, particularly Mexican objections to the annexation of Texas by the United States, the American desire to expand westward into Nuevo Mexico and California, and border disputes all along the U.S.-Mexican border (Meier and Rivera, 1972, Chap. 4). During this war, Nuevo Mexico surrendered itself to the United States without a fight, in part because of opposition to the centralist government of Mexico. In California, the situation was somewhat different. The cooperation between Anglos and Californios (Mexican settlers in California) in the 1820s and 1830s increasingly turned to conflict in the 1840s as more and more Anglo settlers came to northern California via the Oregon Trail. Here, too, opposition to the centralists among both Anglos and Mexicans was strong enough that California declared its independence from Mexico in 1836. In 1840, however, California returned to Mexican control. But increasingly, the influx of white settlers caused Anglo-Californio conflicts that ended any cooperation between the two, even though both had opposed the centralists in Mexico. In 1846, a new independence movement known as the Bear Flag Revolt arose. This movement came to be controlled mainly by Anglos, who soon antagonized Californios in Los Angeles and nearby areas so strongly that they rebelled against the Anglos, who were openly proclaiming California to be U.S. territory. This led to the only serious fighting of the Mexican-American War that occurred in what is now the United States and by 1847 led to effective American control of California. Meanwhile, the major fighting of the war was occurring in Mexico, which had been invaded by U.S. troops. In 1847, Mexico City was captured, and a year later the Treaty of Guadalupe Hidalgo was signed and ratified. This treaty ceded most of California and Neuvo Mexico to the United States, formally recognized American sovereignty over Texas, and resolved the border disputes along the Texas-Mexico boundary in favor of the United States. In a protocol accompanying the treaty, the United States agreed in writing to recognize the land ownership of Mexicans in the ceded territories. The 80,000 Mexicans living in the ceded territories also were given U.S. citizenship rights, and most became citizens.[3] A few years later, the present U.S.-Mexican border was established when the Gadsden Purchase (1853) ceded the southern parts of present-day Arizona and New Mexico to the United States.

As was the case a few years earlier in Texas, the annexation of Neuvo Mexico and California caused a critical change in the power structure, which eventually proved disastrous for the Mexican people living in these two territories. The familiar pattern was repeated: Once there was a sizable influx of Anglos into an area, the Anglos and Mexican Americans competed over land. The latter were nearly always deprived of their land, despite the international agreement (and numerous verbal promises) that this would not happen. Sometimes the land was simply taken by force; at other times, the legal system accomplished the same result. This was possible because the Mexican and American concepts of landownership were different, as were the methods for legally proving a land claim (Meier and Rivera, 1972). Thus, many Mexicans who could easily have proven their claims in Mexican courts could not do so in American courts. It is also true that judges and magistrates usually were Anglo and protected Anglo interests and that Anglo landowners often were more able to afford good lawyers. Furthermore, even when Mexican Americans did eventually win their claims, they wound up so deeply in debt from the cost of the legal battles—some of which dragged on for as long as seventeen years—that they often lost part or all of their land because of the debt (Meier and Rivera, 1972, p. 80). Put simply, the balance of power was totally on the side of the Anglo Americans (Mirande, 1987).

As stated, competition for land and displacement of Mexican American landowners were closely associated with the influx of Anglos into an area. This first incursion occurred on a large scale in northern California during the Gold Rush, which began in 1849. In southern California, few Anglos were present, so the process occurred more slowly. Californios and new immigrants from Mexico were in the majority until the 1870s, but the building of transcontinental railroads brought more whites to the region; by 1880, three-fourths of the population was Anglo (Meier and Rivera, 1972, Chap. 5). With this influx of whites, Californio wealth, landownership, and cultural influence over the region declined. The process was sped up in the 1860s by floods, droughts, and declining farm prices, which put many Californio landowners in debt (Grebler, Moore, and Guzman, 1970, pp. 49–50). By the 1880s, Anglos were solidly in control of the region. The area slowest to come under Anglo domination was the present-day state of New Mexico, largely because there were fewer whites and a larger Mexican American population there than elsewhere. In 1848, about 60,000 of the 80,000 or so Mexican Americans lived in New Mexico (Moore and Pachon, 1976, pp. 12, 15). Except on the ranchlands of eastern New Mexico near Texas, there was no influx of whites like that seen in Texas and California. A wealthy class of Mexican American urbanites—who usually preferred to think of themselves as Spanish rather than Mexican—was present in New Mexico and highly influential in the region's politics past the turn of the century. Even today, a larger and more powerful Hispanic elite lives there than anywhere else in the country. Even there, however, Anglos eventually came to dominate, although often only after strong resistance by Mexicans (Rosenbaum and Larson, 1987). One example of this domination can be seen in the fact that by 1910, fewer than a third of the parcels of land owned by Mexicans before annexation to the United States remained in the hands of the Mexican owners (N. L. Gonzales, 1967, p. 29). It is easy to see why. Between 1891 and 1904, New Mexico *Hispanos* claimed land grant rights on nearly 35 million acres, but fewer than 2 million acres of these claims were confirmed by the U.S. courts (Nostrand, 1992, p. 124). Nonetheless, more Hispanic landowners in New Mexico were able to keep some of their land than anywhere in the Southwest, largely because Anglos did not outnumber Hispanics until the twentieth century. In New Mexico in 1900, only

---

[3]However, Indians in the ceded territories, who previously had the right of Mexican citizenship, did not receive the right of U.S. citizenship (Meier and Rivera, 1972, p. 70).

about 30 percent of the population was Anglo (Nostrand, 1992). Even in 2000, more than 42 percent of the state's population was Hispanic, and only about 45 percent was non-Hispanic white (U.S. Census Bureau, 2001b).

**Causes of Anglo-Chicano Inequality.** This brief discussion of the early history of Anglo-Chicano relations shows that Noel's (1968) theory about the origins of ethnic stratification can be applied to Mexican Americans as well as to other U.S. minorities.[4] Only in the presence of all three elements cited by Noel—ethnocentrism, competition, and unequal power—did patterns of near total domination of Chicanos by Anglos emerge. Early competition for land and the whites' superior power and numbers brought this about first in Texas. The Treaty of Guadalupe Hidalgo gave political and legal power to whites throughout the Southwest, but this did not immediately cause great ethnic inequality except in northern California, where the Gold Rush began almost immediately after the treaty. In other areas, subordination of the Mexican American population tended to come when there was a sizable influx of whites: the 1870s and 1880s in much of southern California, later in Arizona, and still later in New Mexico. This influx added the element of competition, as whites deprived Mexican Americans of their land claims. It also increased both white ethnocentrism and the inequality of the power balance. As with blacks and Indians, racist stereotypes developed and were used to justify mistreatment of Chicanos. Another form of ethnocentrism was the concept of Manifest Destiny, which was used to justify annexation of Mexican territory and to displace both Mexican Americans and Indians from their lands. This view was that the white man's supernaturally willed destiny was to rule and "civilize" all of North America, from coast to coast. Thus, the conquest of indigenous Indian and Mexican American populations and the taking of their lands could be justified as "God's will." The other factor, unequal power, also increased with a large influx of whites. Whites became a numerical majority, which augmented the legal and political power they already held. For all these reasons, there was a close association between the numerical balance of Anglos and Chicanos and the amount of inequality between the two groups in various times and places throughout the Southwest.

In the words of Mirande (1987, p. 29), "As the Anglo population expanded, so did it gain in political power. Loss of political control by the Californios went hand in hand with economic and occupational displacement." In some regards, the history of Chicanos is very different from that of blacks and Native Americans. Only Chicano history involves the conquest by force of a sovereign, internationally recognized nation-state and the abrogation of rights accorded to its citizens by that nation. Despite this and other differences, however, the origin of Anglo-Chicano inequality seems to involve the same three elements as the other two groups we have examined.

**Exploitation of Chicanos for Labor.** Another way in which Mexican Americans are unique among the three groups discussed is that only they were exploited on a large scale for *both* their land and their labor in this country. Blacks had no land here because they were not indigenous. Indians were never enslaved on a large scale, and their resistance to forced assimilation, as well as their forced isolation on the reservation, generally kept white employers from seeing them as a source of cheap labor. However, Mexican Americans soon were exploited for their labor as well as their land. We have already discussed at length the exploitation of Chicanos for their land and the reasons behind it. In the remainder of this section, we shall examine the ways in which Anglos took advantage of Mexican Americans as a source of cheap labor.

---

[4]For more complete discussions of Chicano history, see the previously cited publications and McWilliams (1949), which is considered by some to be the best general work on Mexican American history in the Southwest.

As Mexican Americans were being displaced from their land by whites between 1850 and 1900, whites in the Southwest were developing an economic system built largely around mining, large-scale agriculture, and railroad transportation. These types of economic activity, especially mining and large-scale agriculture, are highly labor-intensive and are most profitable when there is a large labor supply. The owners of the ranches and mines accordingly sought a supply of laborers willing to do hard, dirty work for low wages (Grebler, Moore, and Guzman, 1970, p. 51). Although bonded laborers from Asia were brought to the West to do some of this work, Mexican Americans became the most important source of such labor. Mexican Americans who were displaced from their land when the United States took over the Southwest were placed in a desperate economic position and became a major source of farm and mine labor in the latter half of the nineteenth century. Later, the Mexican Revolution of 1909–1910 caused widespread displacement and economic distress in Mexico. For political and economic reasons, as well as simply for reasons of personal safety, thousands of Mexicans fled to the United States during and after that upheaval. This massive wave of immigration continued through the 1920s and made even more Mexican Americans available as cheap labor. Furthermore, fears about competition with whites had led to tight restrictions on Asian immigration, so Asians were less available as an alternative source of labor (see Camarillo, 1979).[5]

By the early twentieth century, the Chicano agricultural laborer was in a position only marginally better than that of a slave, in a system that in some ways resembled the paternalistic pattern of race relations. To a large degree, Mexican Americans were restricted to certain low-paying, low-status jobs, so that ethnicity largely determined one's status and economic position. And racial divisions among Mexican Americans, African Americans, and whites were used by plantation owners to keep wages low, as is shown in the box titled "Race and Cheap Labor in Texas Cotton." The total control associated with paternalistic systems often was present for Mexican American farm and mine workers, who were required to buy their goods at inflated prices at the company or ranch store and could be hired only through labor contractors. Frequently, too, the system of labor was more unfree than free because workers often were bound to their employers to work off the debts incurred at these company stores or for housing. And of all workers, only farm workers are not guaranteed the right to unionize under federal law, even today. (A few states, most notably California, do provide such a guarantee, although none did before the 1970s.) Finally, there was the paternalism—the constant assertion by ranch, farm, and mine owners that their Mexican American workers were happy, that the owners had their best interests at heart, and that the workers needed "close supervision" because they were incapable of functioning on their own. And there was the oft-repeated claim that Mexican Americans were incapable of work other than unskilled labor or farm work and that they were especially suited to this type of work. Consider the following quote about Mexican farm workers from a white cotton farmer in the 1930s: "Picking cotton, that's their lot. It don't make any difference whether you pay them 15 or 35 cents an hour. Their women only wear shoes when someone will see them. They buy Buicks and don't know how to spend their money intelligently. They're stupid" (Taylor and Kerr, 1935, quoted in Chacon, 1984, pp. 348–49).

It should be pointed out that in other regards, the pattern did not resemble Van den Berghe's (1958) paternalistic system. For one thing, there was typically a good deal of geographic mobility. Although one's movements might be quite restricted while working at any one ranch, Chicano farm labor in the early twentieth century (and since) was highly migratory, with movement from job to job as different crops needed to be planted or harvested. There was also much movement between the city

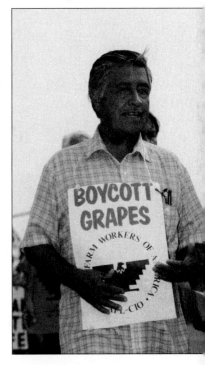

Cesar Chavez, founder and first president of the United Farm Workers (UFW) union, led nationwide boycotts of grapes and lettuce in support of the right of farm workers to unionize—a right still not recognized by federal law.

---

[5]Similar efforts were also directed at Mexicans but had less effect. Immigration across the border was harder to control, and—especially in agriculture—Chicanos largely held jobs whites were unwilling to accept, so whites were less concerned about their competition.

## RACE AND CHEAP LABOR IN TEXAS COTTON

An award-winning book by historian Neil Foley (1997) has recently illustrated how the Texas planter class used race to ensure cheap labor after the Civil War. In an analysis strongly influenced by Marxist theory, Foley shows how race was used to maintain the lower-caste position of Mexican Americans in Texas, as well as to impoverish a segment of the white working class. Foley focuses on cotton, a segment of agriculture that after the Civil War resembled the rigid competitive pattern of race relations more so than did migrant labor. In Texas cotton farming after the Civil War, Mexican Americans, African Americans, and poor whites were all farm laborers. Early after the Civil War, whites were more likely than blacks or Chicanos to be tenants, who had a somewhat better status than sharecroppers, but by 1900 more of them, too, were becoming sharecroppers. As farm laborers (and, after 1900, sharecroppers), these different racial groups shared a common economic interest. But unlike in California, no effective multiracial farm labor movement emerged in Texas in the early twentieth century. In fact, even today,

Texas farm workers are far less unionized than California farm workers because, according to Foley, Texas share-croppers and farm workers were kept divided along the lines of race.

White tenants and sharecroppers thought of themselves as better than black or Mexican farm laborers and therefore avoided labor activism (N. Foley, 1997, pp. 197–200). Mexican Americans, though more supportive of labor organizing, nonetheless thought the way to get ahead was to identify as white; therefore, they supported segregation of blacks even while fighting segregation of Mexicans. Color was also reinforced by the fact that white sharecroppers' wives spent less time in the fields than Mexican women, and the latter spent less time than black women. The consequence of all this color division was that the different groups were unable to unite, so there was no serious challenge to the system of sharecropping and the conditions of extreme poverty it brought to most of the rural African American and Chicano population, and to a significant segment of the white population as well.

and rural areas, with many of the farm workers spending much of the off-season in the city, working at low-skill jobs and living in Mexican American neighborhoods known as *barrios* (Grebler, Moore, and Guzman, 1970). Regardless of just how closely it resembled the paternalistic pattern, it is clear that for Chicano farm workers and many mine and railroad workers, the situation was highly exploitative. Hours were long, pay exceedingly low, food and housing poor, and education virtually nonexistent. Especially in the rural areas, few Chicanos were permitted to rise above this status. The system of stratification thus closely fits the caste model. In the mining and railroad industries and in the city, the pattern was often more like the rigid competitive pattern than the paternalistic, but here, too, Mexican Americans were seen by employers as a source of cheap labor (Camarillo, 1979; Mirande, 1987).[6] In either case, most Mexican Americans in the late nineteenth and early twentieth centuries found themselves in a caste system with little chance of advancement.

### Summary and Conclusion

In this chapter, we have examined different patterns of race relations and the conditions under which these patterns tend to appear. One theory of ethnic stratification argues that three conditions must be present for ethnic stratification or racial inequality to develop: ethnocentrism; competition, or the opportunity for one group to gain at the other's expense; and unequal power. The order perspective stresses ethnocentrism as the major reason for racial inequality when different cultures come into contact. This approach suggests that to reduce racial inequality, assimilation must occur. Minority groups must be absorbed into the system and become culturally similar to the majority (although the majority may also borrow from the minority culture). The conflict perspective argues that racial inequality occurs because one group is in a position to gain by dominating or exploiting

---

[6]The experience of this segment of the Mexican American population is discussed in Chapter 6.

another and because groups are not equal in power. The more powerful group will gain, and the less powerful group will become subordinate. This approach suggests that assimilation cannot solve the problem of racial inequality because cultural differences are not the cause of the problem. Only a change in the balance of power or a redistribution of resources can solve it.

Our examination suggests that each view is partially correct. The histories of the three American groups we have examined vary greatly in many regards, but all support Noel's (1968) thesis that ethnocentrism, competition, and unequal power must all be present before substantial racial or ethnic inequality will appear. Thus, the once-common view that eliminating prejudices and encouraging assimilation can by themselves eliminate racial inequality seems dubious. Prejudices and cultural differences did not *by themselves* cause racial inequality. It is only in the context of competition and unequal power that ethnocentrism seems to result in racial stratification. In other words, racial or ethnic inequality occur only when, in addition to the presence of ethnocentrism, one group can benefit from dominating or oppressing another and is powerful enough to do so. Significantly, research beyond the United States leads us to the same conclusion. In an analysis of persistent intergroup inequality throughout the world, Charles Tilly (1998) concludes that beliefs are less important than social structures and opportunities to gain at another group's expense. This suggests that part of the solution to the problem of racial inequality must be sought in the basic power structure of a society and that changes deeper than simple attitudinal and cultural ones may be necessary.

To illuminate the origins and causes of racial and ethnic inequality in the United States, our discussion focused on three of the minority groups that have encountered the greatest exploitation and discrimination and that continue to occupy a disadvantaged status today. Of course intergroup inequality based on factors other than race or ethnicity (such as gender or sexual orientation) may or may not have causes similar to those of racial and ethnic inequality. It is also true that the causes of racial and ethnic inequality may vary among countries and thus may not be the same elsewhere as in the United States. In later chapters, we shall explore the causes of types of majority-minority inequality other than racial and ethnic inequality, as well as the causes of racial and ethnic inequality in other societies around the world.

In the next chapter, we shall identify some of the factors associated with change in patterns of racial inequality once they have been established. It is clear that majority-minority relations today are different from those fifty or one hundred years ago. In the next chapter, we will find out some of the reasons why.

## Critical Review Questions

1. Explain why there is more racial segregation in a rigid competitive system of race relations than in a paternalistic system of race relations. Also, explain why there typically is more conflict in a rigid competitive system.

2. Explain the following statement: "There is still significant racial inequality in a fluid competitive system of race relations, but it is less visible and works in different ways than in a paternalistic or rigid competitive system."

3. Slavery of African Americans became institutionalized in the U.S. South. Explain why 1) this did not happen in the U.S. North, and 2) why other groups (white indentured servants, American Indians) avoided slavery in the South.

4. Research suggests that ethnocentrism by itself does not necessarily lead to racial inequality, unless there is also scarcity, competition, and unequal power. In what ways does this support explanations of racial inequality offered by the conflict perspective? Also, in what ways does it apply to the early experiences of African Americans, American Indians, and Mexican Americans in the United States?

# Overview

In Chapter 5, we examined the origins of racial and ethnic inequality in the United States. We traced the early development of relations between whites and three minority groups–African Americans, American Indians, and Chicanos—through an era of castelike relationships with gross racial inequality. In this chapter and the next, we shall examine changes over the past 100 years or so, a period in which American race relations have gradually changed to a more fluid, classlike pattern. Though still marked by great inequality, race relations today are in a number of ways fundamentally different from what they were in the late nineteenth century. In these chapters, we shall try to find out how and why we got from where we were then to where we are now.

Where we are now, of course, has been partly determined by our earlier patterns of racial inequality. Accordingly, we shall start this chapter by examining how the origins of ethnic stratification discussed at length in Chapter 5 have influenced majority-minority relations through American history and to the present time. We shall then examine how we got from the castelike patterns discussed in Chapter 5 to the more classlike race relations of today.

## ▶ ORIGINS OF CONTACT AND MODERN-DAY RACE RELATIONS: A THEORY OF INTERNAL COLONIALISM

In Chapter 5, we discussed a number of different ways in which two groups can come into contact, ranging from voluntary to involuntary. Blauner's (1972) theory about the development of American race relations places crucial importance on the nature of this initial contact. This theory of **internal colonialism** distinguishes between conquered peoples who became part of the United States (or any country) involuntarily and those who entered voluntarily. A group that is conquered, or annexed by force, is called a **colonized minority**; one that entered willingly is called an **immigrant minority**. As we have seen, African Americans, Mexican Americans, and Native Americans all fit the category of colonized minorities. The Chicano and Indian people were conquered and forced into subordinate status in much the same way as native peoples in Asia, Africa, Latin America, and Oceania when the Europeans colonized those areas. A major difference is that in the United States, the white Europeans became a majority and declared independence from the mother country more quickly than elsewhere, although they treated the indigenous populations they conquered—Indians and Mexicans—much as colonizers did in other parts of the world.

**133**

Some critics argue that blacks do not fit the model because they were not conquered and enslaved on their own land. Blauner (1972) replies that this does not change the basic fact that they were conquered and forced into a subordinate status in this country. Puerto Ricans (*Boricuas*) also largely fit the model because the United States gained control over Puerto Rico, then a Spanish colony, through warfare. When Puerto Rico and Cuba fought for independence from Spain, the United States eventually joined the conflict in 1898, opposing Spain in what is now known as the Spanish-American War. Once the United States entered the conflict, Spain was quickly defeated. This resulted, eventually, in Cuba becoming independent, but Puerto Rico has remained under American rule as a U.S. territory ever since. For Puerto Rico, the result of this conflict was not its objective of independence but rather a transformation, in effect, from being a Spanish colony to being a U.S. colony. In one sense, however, Puerto Ricans on the U.S. mainland do not fully fit the definition of a colonized minority: Their presence is the result of a decision to immigrate, even though they did not voluntarily come under U.S. rule (Blauner, 1972). Moreover, although Puerto Rico's initial status as a U.S. territory was involuntary, it now has the legal right, if it chooses to do so, to become independent.

Nonetheless, the fact that Puerto Ricans first came under American rule by conquest has been a dominant factor in their subsequent experiences, both in Puerto Rico and on the mainland. The experience of forced entry into American society distinguishes African Americans, Chicanos, Native Americans, and to a large extent Puerto Ricans from all other American ethnic groups. As much discrimination as various immigrant groups may have suffered, their entry was voluntary. They did not take on the status of a conquered people. Blauner argues that this difference between immigrant and colonized minorities created vast differences in their position in American society, some of which persist today. According to Blauner, certain things always occur when ethnic or racial groups are conquered and colonized. First, they are forced to participate in somebody else's society, whether they want to or not. Second, they are subjected to some form of unfree labor, which "greatly restricts the social mobility of the group and its participation in the political arena" (Blauner, 1972, p. 53). Often, the colonized group is isolated in the least advanced sector of the society, away from the areas of growth and opportunity. Finally, the culture and social institutions of the colonized group are subjected to attack by the colonizer. The colonizer's objective is to *force* the group to give up its ways and accept the "superior" ways of the colonizer. As a result, the colonized minority often is subjected to the castelike patterns of intergroup relations discussed in Chapter 5. All of these things happened to blacks, Chicanos, and American Indians. (For further discussion of how this model applies to American Indians, see Snipp, 1986a, 1986b; T. D. Hall, 1989.)

Some have argued (see Murguia, 1975, Chap. 3) that Mexican Americans fall somewhere between the colonial and immigrant classifications, largely because, despite their initial involuntary presence, they have voluntarily been immigrating into the United States ever since the Southwest was annexed. However, the initial mode of contact—which for Chicanos was involuntary—shapes all subsequent contact. Even those who came as immigrants, for example, are influenced by the prejudice and the system of discrimination targeted toward a conquered people. For this reason, including the distinct Chicano history of subordination and subjection to unfree labor, many argue that the internal colonialism model describes very well the Chicano experience (J. W. Moore, 1970; Barrera, 1979; Mirande, 1985, 1987). Thus, despite some debate, Mexican Americans appear to fit the description of a colonized minority more closely than that of an immigrant minority.

The experience of blacks, American Indians, and Chicanos presents a sharp contrast with that of European ethnic immigrants. For whatever reason, these immigrants came voluntarily. In some cases, their culture was closer to America's dominant culture than that of the other groups, but the critical difference is that they *chose* to enter and to learn American culture. As much as they may have been discriminated against, they never experienced the complete social control of the plantation or Indian reservation. They never experienced the unfree labor situation of the slave or the migrant farm worker. Their families and religious institutions were never systematically attacked, as were those of black and Indian people. Finally, they were never restricted to jobs outside the industrial mainstream, as were so many African Americans, Native Americans, and Chicanos.

Additionally, a majority tends to have different and more intense prejudices toward a conquered and subordinated people than it has toward an immigrant people. Blauner's (1972) main point is actually quite simple: These tremendous historical differences place modern-day African Americans, Chicanos, Puerto Ricans, and Native Americans in a very different social position than their counterparts among the European immigrants. They have been subject to a number of socially imposed disadvantages that the immigrant groups have not been, no matter how much they may have been discriminated against. Furthermore, the colonized minorities' relationship to the dominant society always has been fundamentally different, which offers one answer to two oft-repeated questions: (1) Why have blacks, Puerto Ricans, Chicanos, and Native Americans not assimilated to the degree that other groups have? (2) Why do these four groups remain socially and economically disadvantaged when other groups, such as Irish Americans and Italian Americans, have enjoyed rising status? Blauner and others believe that these differences result from the different historical experiences of *immigrant minorities* and *colonized minorities*.

By now, you may be wondering where the various Asian American groups fit in. The answer seems to be somewhere between an immigrant minority and a colonized minority. It is hard to classify their original presence in the United States as either completely voluntary or completely involuntary. The majority of Chinese immigrants during the peak period of migration in the nineteenth century came as indentured laborers or contract laborers. They were bound to creditors in China, to whom they had to pay off debt incurred for travel to the United States. Some of the contract laborers, who were called "coolies," were actually forced into servitude (Barth, 1964, pp. 50–59). The same was true of some, though far fewer, Japanese immigrants, mostly those who came by way of Hawaii (Ichihashi, 1969, Chap. 5). The early immigration of Filipinos, whose homeland was made into a colony of the United States, also was often less than voluntary. More recently, Vietnamese immigrants have arrived as refugees and served as a reminder of a war that many Americans would rather forget.

These groups might be classified as falling somewhere between immigrant and colonized minorities, and their experiences since their arrival in America support that view. Their labor often was unfree, with many tied to a job and employer until their debts, contracts, or indentures were paid off. They were largely isolated in low-paying, labor-intensive sectors of the economy, as were blacks and Chicanos. On the other hand, with one very important exception,[1] they were not forcibly deprived of their land or subjected to the total control of slavery or the Indian reservation, as were the other groups, so they were in a more favorable position to retain their social organization and ways of life. Because many of them did come voluntarily, they were also more inclined to make some voluntary adaptation to American culture and institutions. Moreover, many of the more recent immigrants from Asia have been well-educated professional and managerial workers, who have had little trouble finding an economic niche. In short, both the nature of their arrival and their experiences after arriving in America suggest that the experiences of Asian Americans fall somewhere between the colonialized experience of blacks, Puerto Ricans, Chicanos, and Indians and the immigrant experience of the European ethnic groups.

Regardless of the exact position of any group on this continuum, Blauner's (1972) basic point seems to be correct. The experiences of those who entered

---

[1]This notable exception is the imprisonment of Japanese Americans in concentration camps during World War II, which is discussed later in this chapter.

America involuntarily have been quite different from the experiences of those who entered voluntarily. Not only were they forced into American society against their will in the first place, but colonized minorities have also been subjected to disadvantages, social control, and attacks on their culture that immigrant groups have not (see Lieberson, 1980, on this point with respect to blacks). Even the earliest immigrants from eastern and southern Europe had better social conditions in urban America than did their black counterparts (Lieberson, 1980). These differences have led to less assimilation, greater exploitation, and lower status, even to the present day, among colonized minorities than immigrant minorities. To summarize, the position of any racial or ethnic group in America today cannot be understood without some examination of that group's history, going all the way back to how it first came into contact with American society.

Studies by Ogbu (1988b), Zweigenhaft and Domhoff (1991), and Gibson and Ogbu (1992) show that this is the case not just in the United States but in other countries as well. For example, in Japan, Koreans and the Burakumin—groups colonized and stigmatized in Japan—do poorly in Japanese schools. Yet in the United States, Koreans and descendants of the Burakumin (not recognized as a distinct group here but simply considered Japanese American) do as well as or better than white American children. This suggests very strongly that it is not the characteristics of a group or its traditional culture that determines success but rather how it is treated and viewed in the society in which it lives. Simply put, voluntary or immigrant minorities and involuntary or colonized minorities are treated very differently.

Another reason colonized minorities tend to be less successful than immigrant ones is that the harsh treatment they receive produces in them an *oppositional identity*, including rejection of the dominant group's values and cultural traits, that allows them to maintain a positive self-identity in the face of that treatment and the attacks on their culture. Whites, in turn, use the oppositional identity as a rationalization for rejecting minorities and keeping them in a low status, arguing that "they won't cooperate" or "they can't be trusted" (Fordham and Ogbu, 1986; Matute-Bianchi, 1986; Zweigenhaft and Domhoff, 1991, pp. 148–53). In some cases, an oppositional identity also opposes such things as studying and school achievement because they are seen as giving in to the norms of the dominant group (Zweigenhaft and Domhoff, 2003). Thus, in addition to its other harmful effects, colonization tends to create a vicious cycle of reactions that create other disadvantages that immigrant minorities do not face. As these researchers show, these effects are found not only in the United States but also in a number of other countries, including Japan and Sweden (Zweigenhaft and Domhoff, 1991).

It is important to keep the internal colonialism theory and these studies in mind when considering debates about the status of different groups in the United States today. It is often suggested that cultural differences account for the greater economic success of Asian American and European American immigrants than that of African Americans, Native Americans, Chicanos, and Puerto Ricans. However, cultural differences at best offer only part of the explanation. The experiences of these two sets of groups (immigrant and colonized minorities) in the United States have been fundamentally different, and this difference accounts for much of the difference in socioeconomic status that persists today.

## ▶ EVOLVING PATTERNS OF BLACK-WHITE RACE RELATIONS

### Caste Relations Become Unstable: The Development of Rigid Competitive Race Relations, 1860–1945

As America moved through the latter half of the nineteenth century and into the twentieth, a number of important social changes were taking place. Throughout the Western world, including the United States, urbanization, industrialization, and increasing organizational complexity were occurring. The dominant mode of production was shifting from agriculture, for which ownership of land was crucial, to industry and commerce, for which ownership of capital was crucial. In some ways it was a gradual, evolutionary process. In other ways, there were abrupt, cataclysmic changes. For example, most historians see the Civil War not simply as a struggle to free the slaves but also as a more basic conflict between the rural, agrarian, landowning interests of the South and the rising industrial and commercial interests of the North. The North's victory is sometimes seen as a triumph of capitalism over feudalism, analogous in some ways to the outcome of the French Revolution. Race relations were greatly influenced both by the abrupt changes that came with the Civil War and by the more gradual changes that took place over a longer time. These changes included the transformation of the South from a rural to an urban society and the accompanying transition from a feudal to a capitalist economy. Outside the South, they included a somewhat less dramatic but still substantial rural-to-urban transition and the growth of mass-produced heavy industry. The important changes in majority-minority relations that resulted from these social and economic changes are the main subject of this chapter.

The overall effect was a destabilization of castelike race relations but not—for a very long time—a real move toward their elimination. In the late nineteenth and early twentieth centuries, the dominant pattern of American race relations came to resemble the rigid competitive pattern. This was most clearly true for African Americans, but it was also largely true for Mexican Americans and Asian Americans and partially true for Native Americans and Puerto Ricans. Although the characteristics of rigid competitive patterns of race relations were described in some detail in Chapter 5, they can be briefly listed here:

- Status is determined mostly but not totally by race. Small elites appear among generally disadvantaged minority groups.

- Division of labor is largely but not totally dependent on race. In some situations, both majority and minority group members do the same kind of work, although the latter are nearly always paid less. (This is called a dual-wage market.) Also, the job titles often are different for majority and minority group members even when the work is the same.

- Separation of racial groups, or segregation, is extensive. The majority group imposes this segregation as a way of protecting its status from the upward mobility of the minority group or groups.

- The competition over jobs (because majority and minority group members are sometimes seeking and doing similar work) and other scarce resources carries the potential for severe conflict. Major outbursts of violence—usually attacks by majority group members against minorities—occur periodically.

**The Antebellum North.** The development of this pattern may be most evident in the history of black-white relations in the nineteenth century and the first half of the twentieth. The rigid competitive pattern was already well developed in the North before the Civil War. After slavery was abolished in the North—by 1804 in most of the areas where it had ever existed—blacks and whites, particularly lower-status whites who had recently immigrated from Europe, began to compete for jobs. Numerous discriminatory laws and practices were developed to protect white workers from black competition. In 1862, Irish longshoremen threatened to shut down the port of New York unless all black workers were fired (Bloch, 1969, p. 34). Earlier, laws had been passed in Illinois, Indiana, and Oregon that banned black people from entering those states (W. J. Wilson, 1973, p. 95). By the time of the Civil War, a pattern of race riots was also becoming established in the North. In 1863, the worst riot in American history occurred in New York City as thousands of whites went on a rampage to protest being drafted to fight in the Civil War. It is estimated that up to two thousand people died in the violence (Bahr, Chadwick, and Strauss, 1979). This event, known as the Draft Riot, was depicted in the 2002 film *Gangs of New York*. Although this event was not ostensibly a race riot, it had considerable racial overtones. First, it was largely a protest by whites against what they saw as being forced to fight a war to free black slaves. Second, like later race riots, it involved numerous attacks against blacks. Many blacks were beaten to death, and their homes were destroyed. Clearly, then, racial resentment was a major factor in the violence. (For further discussion of northern race relations before the Civil War, see Litwack, 1961.) Reflecting the increasing competition between immigrants and African Americans, many of the participants in the riot were Irish immigrants, who felt that their insecure economic position would be threatened by any growth in the black population that might result from the abolition of slavery.

**The Postbellum South.** When the Civil War brought an end to slavery in the South, many hoped that it would result in major improvements in race relations in the South. For the brief period known as Reconstruction, there were indications that this was occurring. This period did not last, however, and before long, prejudice and racist ideology in the South intensified, and black-white segregation increased to a level beyond anything that existed under slavery. For several important reasons, the Civil War did not bring an end to pervasive racial inequality in the South.

First, the elite planter class did not disappear at the end of the Civil War, although its power was certainly reduced. It still retained enough influence immediately after the war to pass a series of laws in southern states, sometimes called Black Codes, aimed at keeping the black population in a subordinate status and, more specifically, as a cheap source of labor (Woodward, 1971, pp. 251–52; W. J. Wilson, 1973, p. 99, 1978, pp. 52–53). These laws, passed in 1865–1866, were designed to force all blacks to work whether they wanted to or not; blacks who quit their jobs were subject to arrest and imprisonment, and those who refused to work could be fined or bound out to labor contractors (Franklin and Moss, 2000, pp. 250–51; W. J. Wilson, 1973, p. 99). Laws were also passed that deprived blacks of the right to vote, hold office, serve in the military, sit on a jury, testify against whites in court, and travel freely (Gossett, 1963; Meier and Rudwick, 1970a).

These laws were quickly nullified by federal (that is, northern) intervention, which initiated Reconstruction. Partly for ideological reasons but also in large part for political purposes (to strengthen their position nationally by giving the vote to southern blacks), the Republicans who controlled the U.S. Congress passed a series of laws in 1866 and 1867 that protected the rights of southern blacks. These civil rights laws and Reconstruction bills not only guaranteed protection of the rights of southern blacks and nullified the Black Codes but also established martial law in the South to enforce the federal policy. In addition, the Freedmen's Bureau was established to provide food, education, medical care, transportation, and in some cases land to freed slaves (and to many needy whites as well).

Reconstruction substantially improved the condition of southern blacks, both economically and politically. For example, blacks served in legislatures of southern states, occasionally in large numbers. At various times between 1869 and 1901, two blacks (Hiram R. Revels and Blanche K. Bruce, both from Mississippi) served in the U.S. Senate, and twenty blacks served in the House of Representatives. Despite these improvements, Reconstruction did not last very long and was soon replaced by a new version of the old order of racial inequality.

After about 1875, it became evident that Reconstruction was on its way out. In the North, political changes caused the federal government to lose its will to enforce the policies of Reconstruction. In the South, two important changes occurred. First, old Confederate officials and supporters—many of whom lost the right to vote at the start of Reconstruction—were given back the vote under amnesty or policies of universal male suffrage. This strengthened the political power of antiblack, southern white Democrats. Second, southern whites opposed to Reconstruction took the law into their own hands by forming the Ku Klux Klan and a host of other violent secret societies that kept blacks from voting and exercising other rights. After Rutherford Hayes became president in 1876, federal troops were withdrawn from the South, and the reforms of Reconstruction were gradually undone. In the 1880s, blacks gradually lost the vote; segregation appeared and became widespread in education and public facilities (Franklin and Moss, 2000, pp. 281–91). The Supreme Court began to strike down civil rights legislation that had been passed during Reconstruction and finally gave its full stamp of approval to segregation in *Plessy v. Ferguson* in 1896. In this ruling, the Court established the "separate but equal" doctrine, which upheld segregated facilities as long as those available to each race were equal. As a practical matter, however, very little attention was paid to the "equal" part, and separate and *unequal* facilities became the rule throughout the South. By thirty-five years after the Civil War, a system of segregation existed that was unlike anything that had existed before, even under slavery. Prejudice and ideological racism (the belief that blacks are innately inferior) also rose to levels of intensity beyond even those of the slavery period.

Although historians debate which segment of the white population was responsible for and benefited from the establishment of racial segregation in the South, it is clear that both the upper and lower socioeconomic segments of the white population felt that they were benefiting from the reestablishment of strict racial inequality. There is little doubt that the main strength of the Ku Klux Klan and the greatest demand for segregation laws came from poor and working-class whites in the South. It was these whites who were in direct competition with freed blacks for land, under the sharecropping system, and for jobs. Therefore, they sought to shield themselves from competition through discrimination. The reaction of poorer whites to such competition was even stronger because they had never had to compete directly with blacks in this way before.

At the same time, the ruling class of the South—now comprising both the old planter class and a growing industrial elite—was happy to benefit from racism and at times actively encouraged it. As long as working-class whites and blacks saw each other as the enemy, there was little chance of a united, class-based movement against those who controlled the real wealth of the South. Although the elite occasionally sided with blacks against working-class whites to keep the latter under control, it did nothing to prevent, and sometimes encouraged, the emergence of a system of racial inequality that divided the poor and the working class along racial lines. In Feagin's (2000, p. 30) words, "It was not long . . . before the old elites in the South recovered their positions by aggressively persuading and buying off ordinary white farmers and workers with a renewed racist ideology." Thus, both competition between lower-status whites and freed blacks and the desire of the upper economic class to protect its position by dividing its potential opposition helped to create and maintain the rigid system of segregation. (For further discussion of this period, see Woodward, 1966, 1971; W. J. Wilson, 1978, Chap. 3; Feagin, 2000, pp. 30–31, 82–88.) Divisions and competition between poorer members of the majority and minority groups are critical elements in a rigid competitive system of race relations and are a crucial reason for the emergence of such a system after Reconstruction.

There was also an attempt by whites more generally to maintain a system in which whiteness conferred status—a system of **social distance**. Under slavery, doing so had been easy; everyone knew that whites were masters and blacks were slaves. This in itself created an unequal relationship from which the whites gained psychological and material benefit. If whites were to maintain such a relationship after slavery, however, they would have to find a new way to proclaim and enforce the norm of racial inequality. They did this by establishing segregation—by replacing social distance with physical distance. Now, whites proclaimed their superiority by

Streetcar terminal in Oklahoma City, July 1939. Separate and usually unequal facilities were a predominant characteristic of the period of rigid competitive race relations in the United States.

setting up places and situations where only whites could go and where blacks were defined as unworthy and unacceptable. In effect, society would be remade into a private club that only whites were good enough to enter. Special privilege and physical separation rather than a master-slave relationship were now the indicators of a system of white dominance and white superiority. Along with the policy of segregation came an intensified ideology of racism as whites tried, by promoting notions of biological superiority, to retain the image of dominance and superiority that being slave owners had given them. In short, the intensified racism and the rise of segregation after the Civil War represented an attempt by whites to hang onto the favored social and economic status that was threatened by the end of slavery.

There were some attempts during the post–Civil War period to break through the racial division and unify poor whites and blacks on the basis of class. Probably the most notable of these was the Populist party, which had some degree of success in getting the votes of both blacks and poor whites. The Populist appeal was clearly class-based, arguing that the rural poor of both races should unite to defeat the wealthy elite that ruled them. Consider, for example, the following statement by Populist leader Tom Watson: "You are made to hate each other because upon that hatred is rested the keystone of the arch of financial despotism which enslaves you both. You are deceived and blinded that you may not see how this race antagonism perpetuates a monetary system which beggars you both" (quoted in Woodward, 1966, p. 63). Watson gained substantial black support in Georgia, and a coalition of Populists and the remnants of Reconstruction-era liberal Republican organizations briefly gained control of the North Carolina legislature in 1894, resulting in the appointment of numerous black public officials (Franklin and Moss, 2000, pp. 284–86).

Ultimately, however, the Populists did not succeed. It became clear to them that the wealthy, southern Democratic elite could use laws designed to deny blacks the vote against poor whites, too. The elite's implicit threat to do so if the Populists continued to appeal to the black vote caused the Populists to back off this strategy in most areas. In addition, the Populists in many areas were hurt by the fraudulent use of black votes by conservative Democrats. Thus, the Populists were both weakened and frightened away from the black vote. In short, the strategy of the wealthy white elite to divide and conquer, though briefly challenged, was ultimately successful. As a consequence, black political power was thwarted, and the white working class was kept largely powerless and increasingly resentful of the threat of competition from blacks (for further discussion of the Populists, see Woodward, 1966, pp. 60–65; W. J. Wilson, 1973, pp. 102–3, 1978, pp. 58–59; Franklin and Moss, 2000, pp. 284–86).

Thus, the power of the elite to divide and conquer the poor on the basis of race, combined with the real fear of the black population by working-class and poor whites who were forced into competition with it after the Civil War, led to a pattern of intensified prejudice, racism, and segregation by about thirty years after the Civil War. We can see again that the social-structural factors of unequal power, intergroup competition, and the opportunity for one group to gain by subordinating another played a crucial role in maintaining racial inequality in the South. Because the competition took a new form (the competition between poor whites and blacks for land and jobs) and because of federal intervention, which ended slavery, racial inequality took a new form. The old paternalistic system of slavery was replaced by a rigid competitive system of race relations, marked by strict segregation, heightened prejudice and ideological racism, and more intergroup conflict.

Despite these great setbacks, there were some longer-term effects of Reconstruction. Although they had little impact on the day-to-day life of whites and African Americans in the South between the 1880s and the 1950s, they did lay the legal groundwork for later changes. For example, during Reconstruction, the Thirteenth, Fourteenth, and Fifteenth Amendments to the Constitution were passed. These amendments, respectively, ended slavery, guaranteed due process and equal protection of the law to all citizens, and banned denial of the vote based on race or former servitude. After the end of Reconstruction, the Fourteenth and Fifteenth Amendments were disregarded and mostly unenforced because northern politicians lacked the will to take on nearly unanimous opposition to them among southern whites. However, they did lay the groundwork for later changes. For example, the "but equal" part of the "separate but equal" doctrine was based on the equal protection clause; although it was routinely ignored for many decades, it eventually became the basis of the *Brown* ruling in 1954, which overturned segregation on the grounds that it did not allow equal educational opportunity.

In the 1890s, most southern states went the final step and took measures to deprive blacks of the right to vote. They did this through various techniques, beginning with the "grandfather clause" (a person could vote only if his grandfather could vote, which effectively disfranchised all blacks in the South) and followed by poll taxes, literacy tests, and whites-only primaries. Some of these actions were eventually overturned by the Supreme Court on the basis of the constitutional amendments just discussed. When this happened, however, the states simply moved on to another technique or restriction. Thus, on top of the new system of total segregation and the intensification of prejudice and racial ideologies already mentioned, blacks in the South lost virtually all of their political power. Before long, nearly all of the many blacks who had been elected to public office were gone. The racial caste system of the South was quickly restored in a new form.

Because whites felt threatened by African American competition resulting from the end of slavery and the transition from a plantation economy to capitalism, whites resorted to more violence against blacks than ever before. According to Franklin and Moss (2000, p. 345), there were more than 2,500 lynchings in the last sixteen years of the nineteenth century. Williamson (1984) and Fredrickson (1988) show how these lynchings were related to threat and competition felt by the white population. Before 1889, most lynchings had occurred in the West, and most of the victims were white. As the feudal economy of the cotton plantations declined in the late 1880s and 1890s, whites were displaced economically. They made blacks the scapegoats, and lynchings increased dramatically. By 1890, lynching had become a southern phenomenon, and most of the victims were black. In the 1890s, an average of 138 people a year were lynched in the South, 75 percent of them black. In 1892, there were twice as many lynchings as legal executions in the United States. Between 1900 and 1910, there were fewer lynchings in the South, but 90 percent of the victims were African American (Fredrickson, 1988, p. 176). According to Feagin (2000, p. 147), a total of 6,000 African Americans lost their lives in lynchings between the 1870s and 1960s.

The box titled "The Ethics of Living Jim Crow," drawn from an essay by African American author Richard Wright, provides a graphic description of what black people experienced during the era of Jim Crow segregation, as the strict, legally mandated segregation of blacks and whites came to be known. It also illustrates a number of features we have identified as characteristic of rigid competitive race relations: the white working class's fear of minority competition, the ideology of racial superiority, the segregation of blacks and whites, and the exclusion of blacks from white society.

**The Postbellum North.** In the North, as in the South, the period immediately after the Civil War brought a short-lived relaxation of racial restrictions. The federal government's Reconstruction policies, aimed at transforming the South, had their effects in the North, too. For a time, from about 1870 to 1890, race relations in the North became more fluid, that is, less restrictive. Accounts of racial violence during this period (see Grimshaw, 1959a) focus mainly on the South, and Spear (1971, p. 154) reports that "there was probably more contact between the races [in the North] during this time than at any other time before or since." After 1890, however, northern race relations took an abrupt turn for the worse, with a great upsurge in both prejudice and discrimination. Discriminatory devices of every type were used to keep blacks at a distance from whites and to protect whites from the perceived threat of black competition. It is significant that during this period there were also intensified prejudice and discrimination against other racial and ethnic minorities, notably Chinese Americans, Japanese Americans, and Mexican Americans in the West and Jewish Americans and Catholic Americans in the East. Sentiment against immigration was strong, and ideologies of racial superiority and inferiority were given legitimacy by scientific racists, who argued that science "proved" racial superiority (of their own white race, of course).

There seem to be a number of reasons for this change, and it is striking that most of them in some way arose from the economics of the era, from some form of competition for scarce resources. This was a period of unrestricted capitalism that led to some of the grossest exploitation of labor in American history. Accordingly, deep resentment developed among the working class (which in the North was still overwhelmingly white), and the beginnings of the American labor union movement were under way. At the same time, difficult conditions in the South were causing an increasing number of blacks to migrate to the North. They came to northern cities in sufficient numbers to be seen as a threat by whites but not yet to be a major political force. Also, large numbers of immigrants were arriving or had recently arrived on the East and West coasts. Both migrations were largely consequences of the transition from an agrarian economy to a more urban, industrial, capitalist economy. African Americans and poor whites were being displaced from the South and attracted to the North, while at the same time immigrants were being attracted to the United States in record numbers.

The consequence was intense competition for jobs and housing, especially between white immigrants and blacks. This was made worse by labor and management practices. Most white workers saw blacks as a threat and tried to keep them out of the workplace. As a consequence, most labor unions discriminated against blacks

**THE ETHICS OF LIVING JIM CROW**

There is but one place where a black boy who knows no trade can get a job, and that's where the houses and faces are white, where the trees, lawns, and hedges are green. My first job was with an optical company in Jackson, Mississippi. The morning I applied I stood straight and neat before the boss, answering all his questions with sharp yessirs and nosirs. I was very careful to pronounce my sirs distinctly, in order that he might know that I was polite, that I knew where I was, and that I knew he was a white man. I wanted that job badly.

He looked me over as though he were examining a prize poodle. He questioned me closely about my schooling, being particularly insistent about how much mathematics I had had. He seemed very pleased when I told him I had had two years of algebra.

"Boy, how would you like to try to learn something around here?" he asked me.

"I'd like it fine, sir," I said, happy. I had visions of "working my way up." Even Negroes have those visions.

"All right," he said, "Come on."

I followed him to the small factory.

"Pease," he said to a white man of about thirty-five, "this is Richard. He's going to work for us."

Pease looked at me and nodded.

I was then taken to a white boy of about seventeen.

"Morrie, this is Richard, who's going to work for us."

"Whut yuh sayin' there, boy!" Morrie boomed at me.

"Fine!" I answered.

The boss instructed these two to help me, teach me, give me jobs to do, and let me learn what I could in my spare time.

My wages were five dollars a week.

I worked hard, trying to please. For the first month I got along O.K. Both Pease and Morrie seemed to like me. But one thing was missing. And I kept thinking about it. I was not learning anything and nobody was volunteering to help me. Thinking they had forgotten that I was to learn something about the mechanics of grinding lenses, I asked Morrie one day to tell me about the work. He grew red.

"Whut yuh tryin' t' do, nigger, get smart?" he asked.

"Naw; I ain' tryin' t' git smart," I said.

"Well, don't, if yuh know whut's good for yuh!"

I was puzzled. Maybe he just doesn't want to help me, I thought. I went to Pease.

"Say, are yuh crazy, you black bastard?" Pease asked me, his gray eyes growing hard.

I spoke out, reminding him that the boss had said I was to be given a chance to learn something.

"Nigger, you think you're white, don't you?"

"Naw, sir!"

"Well, you're acting mighty like it!"

"But, Mr. Pease, the boss said . . . "

Pease shook his fist in my face.

"This is a white man's work around here, and you better watch yourself!"

From then on they changed toward me. They said good-morning no more. When I was just a bit slow in performing some duty, I was called a lazy son-of-a-bitch.

Once I thought of reporting all this to the boss. But the mere idea of what would happen to me if Pease and Morrie should learn that I had "snitched" stopped me. And after all the boss was a white man, too. What was the use?

The climax came at noon one summer day. Pease called me to his workbench. To get to him I had to go between two narrow benches and stand with my back against a wall.

"Yes, sir," I said.

"Richard, I want to ask you something." Pease began pleasantly, not looking up from his work.

"Yes, sir," I said again.

Morrie came over, blocking the narrow passage between the benches. He folded his arms, staring at me solemnly.

I looked from one to the other, sensing that something was coming.

"Yes, sir," I said for the third time.

Pease looked up and spoke very slowly.

"Richard, Mr. Morrie here tells me you called me Pease."

I stiffened. A void seemed to open up in me. I knew this was the show-down.

He meant that I had failed to call him Mr. Pease. I looked at Morrie. He was gripping a steel bar in his hands. I opened my mouth to speak, to protest, to assure Pease that I had never called him simply Pease, and that I had never had any intentions of doing so, when Morrie grabbed me by the collar, ramming my head against the wall.

"Now, be careful, nigger!" snarled Morrie, baring his teeth. "I heard yuh call 'im Pease! 'N' if yuh say yuh didn't, yuh're callin' me a lie, see?" He waved the steel bar threateningly.

If I had said: No sir, Mr. Pease, I never called you Pease, I would have been automatically calling Morrie a liar. And if I said: Yes sir, Mr. Pease, I called you Pease, I would have been pleading guilty to having uttered the worst insult that a Negro can utter to a southern white man. I stood hesitating, trying to frame a neutral reply.

"Richard, I asked you a question!" said Pease. Anger was creeping into his voice.

"I don't remember calling you Pease, Mr. Pease," I said cautiously. "And if I did, I sure didn't mean . . . "

"You black son-of-a-bitch! You called me Pease, then!" he spat, slapping me till I bent sideways over a bench. Morrie was on top of me, demanding:

"Didn't yuh call 'im Pease? If yuh say yuh didn't, I'll rip yo' gut string loose with the bar, you black granny dodger! Yuh can't call a white man a lie 'n' git erway with it, you black son-of-a-bitch!"

I wilted. I begged them not to bother me. I knew what they wanted. They wanted me to leave.

"I'll leave," I promised, "I'll leave right now."

They gave me a minute to get out of the factory. I was warned not to show up again, or tell the boss.

I went.

When I told the folks at home what had happened, they called me a fool. They told me that I must never again attempt to exceed my boundaries. When you are working for white folks, they said, you got to "stay in your place" if you want to keep working.

## II

My Jim Crow education continued on my next job, which was portering in a clothing store. One morning, while polishing brass out front, the boss and his twenty-year-old son got out of their car and half dragged and half kicked a Negro woman into the store. A policeman standing at the corner looked on, twirling his night-stick. I watched out of the corner of my eye, never slackening the strokes of my chamois upon the brass. After a few minutes, I heard shrill screams coming from the rear of the store. Later the woman stumbled out, bleeding, crying, and holding her stomach. When she reached the end of the block, the policeman grabbed her and accused her of being drunk. Silently, I watched him throw her into a patrol wagon.

When I went to the rear of the store, the boss and his son were washing their hands at the sink. They were chuckling. The floor was bloody and strewn with wisps of hair and clothing. No doubt I must have appeared pretty shocked, for the boss slapped me reassuringly on the back.

"Boy, that's what we do to niggers when they don't want to pay their bills," he said, laughing.

His son looked at me and grinned.

"Here, hava cigarette," he said.

Not knowing what to do, I took it. He lit his and held the match for me. This was a gesture of kindness, indicating that even if they had beaten the poor old woman, they would not beat me if I knew enough to keep my mouth shut.

"Yes, sir," I said, and asked no questions.

After they had gone, I sat on the edge of the packing box and stared at the bloody floor till the cigarette went out.

That day at noon, while eating in a hamburger joint, I told my fellow Negro porters what had happened. No one seemed surprised. One fellow, after swallowing a huge bite, turned to me and asked:

"Huh! is tha' all they did t' her?"

"Yeah. Wasn't tha' enough?" I asked.

"Shucks! Man, she's a lucky bitch!" he said, burying his lips deep into a juicy hamburger. "Hell, it's a wonder they din't lay her when they got through."

## III

I was learning fast, but not quite fast enough. One day, while I was delivering packages in the suburbs, my bicycle tire was punctured. I walked along the hot, dusty road, sweating and leading my bicycle by the handle-bars.

A car slowed at my side.

"What's the matter, boy?" a white man called.

I told him my bicycle was broken and I was walking back to town.

"That's too bad," he said. "Hop on the running board."

He stopped the car. I clutched hard at my bicycle with one hand and clung to the side of the car with the other.

"All set?"

"Yes sir," I answered. The car started.

It was full of young white men. They were drinking. I watched the flask pass from mouth to mouth.

"Wanna drink, boy?" one asked.

I laughed as the wind whipped my face. Instinctively obeying the freshly planted precepts of my mother, I said:

"Oh, no!"

The words were hardly out of my mouth before I felt something hard and cold smash me between the eyes. It was an empty whisky bottle. I saw stars, and fell backwards from the speeding car into the dust of the road, my feet becoming entangled in the steel spokes of my bicycle. The white men piled out and stood over me.

"Nigger, ain' yuh learned no better sense'n tha' yet?" asked the man who hit me. "Ain' yuh learned t' say sir t' a white man yet?"

Dazed, I pulled to my feet. My elbows and legs were bleeding. Fists doubled, the white man advanced kicking my bicycle out of the way.

"Aw, leave the bastard alone. He's got enough," said one.

They stood looking at me. I rubbed my shins, trying to stop the flow of blood. No doubt they felt a sort of contemptuous pity, for one asked:

"Yuh wanna ride t' town now, nigger? Yuh reckon yuh know enough t' ride now?"

"I wanna walk," I said, simply.

Maybe it sounded funny. They laughed.

"Well, walk, yuh black son-of-a-bitch!"

When they left they comforted me with:

"Nigger, yuh sho better be damn glad it wuz us yuh talked t' tha' way. Yuh're a lucky bastard, 'cause if yuh'd said tha' t' somebody else, yuh might've been a dead nigger now."

### IV

Negroes who have lived South know the dread of being caught alone upon the streets in white neighborhoods after the sun has set. In such a simple situation as this the plight of the Negro in America is graphically symbolized. While white strangers may be in these neighborhoods trying to get home, they can pass unmolested. But the color of a Negro's skin makes him easily recognizable, makes him suspect, converts him into a defenseless target.

Late one Saturday night I made some deliveries in a white neighborhood. I was pedaling my bicycle back to the store as fast as I could, when a police car, swerving toward me, jammed me into the curbing.

"Get down and put up your hands" the policemen ordered.

I did. They climbed out of the car, guns drawn, faces set, and advanced slowly.

"Keep still!" they ordered.

I reached my hands higher. They searched my pockets and packages. They seemed dissatisfied when they could find nothing incriminating. Finally, one of them said:

"Boy, tell your boss not to send you out in white neighborhoods after sundown."

As usual, I said:

"Yes, sir."

### V

My next job was a hall-boy in a hotel. Here my Jim Crow education broadened and deepened. When the bell-boys were busy, I was often called to assist them. As many of the rooms in the hotel were occupied by prostitutes, I was constantly called to carry them liquor and cigarettes. These women were nude most of the time. They did not bother about clothing, even for bell-boys. When you went into their rooms, you were supposed to take their nakedness for granted, as though it startled you no more than a blue vase or a red rug. Your presence awoke in them no sense of shame, for you were not regarded as human. If they were alone, you could steal sidelong glimpses at them. But if they were receiving men, not a flicker of your eyelids could show. I remember one incident vividly. A new woman, a huge, snowy-skinned blonde, took a room on my floor. I was sent to wait upon her. She was in bed with a thickset man; both were nude and uncovered. She said she wanted some liquor and slid out of bed and waddled across the floor to get her money from a dresser drawer. I watched her.

"Nigger, what in hell you looking at?" the white man asked me, raising himself upon his elbows.

"Nothing," I answered, looking miles deep into the blank wall of the room.

"Keep your eyes where they belong, if you want to be healthy!" he said.

"Yes, sir."

### VI

One of the bell-boys I knew in this hotel was keeping steady company with one of the Negro maids. Out of a clear sky the police descended upon his home and arrested him, accusing him of bastardy. The poor boy swore he had had no intimate relations with the girl. Nevertheless, they forced him to marry her. When the child arrived, it was found to be much lighter in complexion than either of the two supposedly legal parents. The white men around the hotel made a great joke of it. They spread the rumor that some white cow must have scared the poor girl while she was carrying the baby. If you were in their presence when this explanation was offered, you were supposed to laugh.

### VII

One of the bell-boys was caught in bed with a white prostitute. He was castrated and run out of town. Immediately after this all the bell-boys and hall-boys were called together and warned. We were given to understand that the boy who had been castrated was a "mighty, mighty lucky bastard." We were impressed with the fact that next time the management of the hotel would not be responsible for the lives of "trouble-makin' niggers." We were silent.

### VIII

One night, just as I was about to go home, I met one of the Negro maids. She lived in my direction, and we fell in to walk part of the way home together. As we passed the white nightwatchman, he slapped the maid on her buttock. I turned around, amazed. The watchman looked at me with a long, hard, fixed-under stare. Suddenly he pulled his gun and asked:

"Nigger, don't yuh like it?"

I hesitated.

"I asked yuh don't yuh like it?" he asked again, stepping forward.

"Yes, sir," I mumbled.

"Talk like it, then!"

"Oh, yes, sir!" I said with as much heartiness as I could muster.

Outside, I walked ahead of the girl, ashamed to face her. She caught up with me and said:

"Don't be a fool! Yuh couldn't help it!"

This watchman boasted of having killed two Negroes in self-defense.

Yet, in spite of all this, the life of the hotel ran with an amazing smoothness. It would have been impossible for a stranger to detect anything. The maids, the hall-boys, and the bell-boys were all smiles. They had to be.

### IX

I had learned my Jim Crow lessons so thoroughly that I kept the hotel job till I left Jackson for Memphis. It so happened that while in Memphis I applied for a job at a branch of the optical company. I was hired. And for some reason, as long as I worked there, they never brought my past against me.

Here Jim Crow education assumed quite a different form. It was no longer brutally cruel, but subtly cruel. Here I learned to lie, to steal, to dissemble. I learned to play that dual role which every Negro must play if he wants to eat and live.

For example, it was almost impossible to get a book to read. It was assumed that after a Negro had imbibed what scanty schooling the state furnished he had no further need for books. I was always borrowing books from men on the job. One day I mustered enough courage to ask one of the men to let me get books from the library in his name. Surprisingly, he consented because he was a Roman Catholic and felt a vague sympathy for Negroes, being himself an object of hatred. Armed with a library card, I obtained books in the following manner: I would write a note to the librarian, saying: "Please let this nigger boy have the following books." I would then sign it with the white man's name.

When I went to the library, I would stand at the desk, hat in hand, looking as unbookish as possible. When I received the books desired I would take them home. If the books listed in the note happened to be out, I would sneak into the lobby and forge a new one. I never took any chances guessing with the white librarian about what the fictitious white man would want to read. No doubt if any of the white patrons had suspected that some of the volumes they enjoyed had been in the home of a Negro, they would not have tolerated it for an instant.

The factory force of the optical company in Memphis was much larger than that in Jackson, and more urbanized. At least they liked to talk, and would engage the Negro help in conversation whenever possible. By this means I found that many subjects were taboo from the white man's point of view. Among the topics they did not like to discuss with Negroes were the following: American white women; the Ku Klux Klan; France, and how Negro soldiers fared while there; French women; Jack Johnson; the entire northern part of the United States; the Civil War; Abraham Lincoln; U. S. Grant; General Sherman; Catholics; the Pope; Jews; the Republican party; slavery; social equality; Communism; Socialism; the 13th and 14th Amendments to the Constitution; or any topic calling for positive knowledge or manly self-assertion on the part of the Negro. The most accepted topics were sex and religion.

There were many times when I had to exercise a great deal of ingenuity to keep out of trouble. It is southern custom that all men must take off their hats when they enter an elevator. And especially did this apply to us blacks with rigid force. One day I stepped into an elevator with my arms full of packages. I was forced to ride with my hat on. Two white men stared at me coldly. Then one of them very kindly lifted my hat and placed it upon my armful of packages. Now the most accepted response for a Negro to make under such circumstances is to look at the white man out of the corner of his eye and grin. To have said: "Thank you!" would have made the white man think that you thought you were receiving from him a personal service. For such an act I have seen Negroes take a blow in the mouth. Finding the first alternative distasteful, and the second dangerous, I hit upon an acceptable course of action which fell safely between these two poles. I immediately—no sooner than my hat was lifted—pretended that my packages were about to spill, and appeared deeply distressed with keeping them in my arms. In this fashion I evaded having to acknowledge his service, and, in spite of adverse circumstances, salvaged a slender shred of personal pride.

How do Negroes feel about the way they have to live? How do they discuss it when alone among themselves? I think this question can be answered in a single sentence. A friend of mine who ran an elevator once told me:

"Lawd, man! Ef it wuzn't fer them polices 'n' them ol' lynch-mobs, there wouldn't be nothin' but uproar down here!"

*Source:* Selected excerpt from "The Ethics of Living Jim Crow" from *Uncle Tom's Children* by Richard Wright. Copyright 1937 by Richard Wright. Copyright renewed 1965 by Ellen Wright. Reprinted by permission of HarperCollins Publishers, Inc.

and would not accept them as members. Blacks arriving from the South, desperately poor, often were willing to work for lower wages than whites. Even white immigrants at this time came from countries where opportunities were greater than those for southern blacks, and in the presence of racial discrimination, they were able to get better-paying jobs (Lieberson, 1980). For these reasons, dual-wage systems developed, in which blacks were paid less than whites for doing the same work. In other cases, blacks were kept out of certain "white jobs," at least until the white workers went on strike. For several reasons, blacks newly arriving in northern cities often ended up working as strikebreakers. First, their poverty often placed them in a position where they had little choice but to take any job that was offered. Second, because most unions excluded blacks, they were distrustful of and unsympathetic toward unions and therefore were sometimes willing to break a strike. Third, being a strikebreaker often was the only way to move into better jobs that were normally reserved for whites. Finally, many employers actively sought out blacks to break their employees' strikes, realizing that their bargaining position would be enhanced if the working classes could be divided along the lines of race. In some cases, blacks in the South were promised jobs if they moved north, without being told that they would be breaking a strike.

The use of blacks as strikebreakers stirred up racial tensions in northern cities large and small in the early twentieth century. In 1910, blacks were brought to Waterloo, Iowa, by the Illinois Central Railroad to break a strike by white workers (Kloss, Roberts, and Dorn, 1976). Railroads repeated that tactic in Chicago in 1916, and in the next ten years blacks were used to break six more strikes in that city (Bonacich, 1976). In East St. Louis, Illinois, the use of blacks as strikebreakers in the meat-packing industry in 1916 and in the aluminum industry in 1917 significantly contributed to that city's bloody race riot of 1917 (Rudwick, 1964; Theising, 2003). The most widespread instance of this practice occurred in 1919, when a nationwide steel strike was broken largely by the importation of an estimated 30,000 to 40,000 blacks into the mills, mostly from the South (Foster, 1920). Of course, not all strikebreakers were blacks, and most black workers were not strikebreakers. Still, their use as strikebreakers was common enough to worsen the already tense relations of the era. The only real winners in these situations were the owners of the plants, mills, railroads, and so on. Because of their mutual fear and mistrust of one another—and their inherently weak bargaining position in an era of low wages and surplus labor—black and white workers were easily played off against each other.

These conflicts and similar ones over housing and other resources led whites—especially working-class and immigrant whites—to take drastic measures to protect their status from the real or perceived threats that blacks represented. Blacks were forced out of white neighborhoods by every means, from boycotts to bombs. Juries and public officials stopped enforcing civil rights laws (W. J. Wilson, 1973, p. 104), and most public and private facilities became segregated. Even churches pushed out their black members. In short, there was a shift in the North after 1890 toward the segregation characteristic of rigid competitive systems of race relations.

In a variety of ways, the federal government became an active participant in the policies of segregation. Formalized segregation in the U.S. government began largely with the Woodrow Wilson administration in 1912 and 1913 and in many ways continued past the end of World War II. Often, policies of segregation were established in response to pressures from whites, who objected to working with or being supervised by African Americans, and from southerners who favored segregation. These policies came to include segregation of workers in government offices and the disproportionate placement of blacks in custodial, menial, and junior clerical positions (D. King, 1995). Federal prisons and armed services were also segregated, and by the 1940s the federal government was actively supporting racial segregation and discrimination in housing.

Another unfortunate characteristic of this pattern was periodic, severe outbursts of violence. Lynchings increased in the North, and the period from 1917 to 1919 included some of the bloodiest race riots in American history. Unlike the riots of the 1960s and 1970s, these involved mass fighting between blacks and whites, and the targets of the mobs were people, not property. Usually the riots broke out in cities where the black population was increasing and blacks and whites were competing for jobs. Fears of a sexual nature were also significant: Some of the riots started after rumors of attacks by blacks on white women were circulated in the white community. Nearly always the riots began with white mobs attacking blacks, and most of the victims were black. The two worst were in the Illinois cities of East St. Louis in 1917 and Chicago in 1919. The death toll of the East St. Louis riot (forty-eight, of whom thirty-nine were black, according to official statistics) was exceeded among U.S. riots only by that of the New York City Draft Riot in 1863 and the Los Angeles riot in 1992. However, the true death toll from the East St. Louis riot may have been much higher than the official toll (Theising, 2003) and may have exceeded that of the Los Angeles riot. The chilling accounts of the East St. Louis riot described the actions of whites as having a visible coolness and premeditation: "This was not the hectic and raving demonstration of men suddenly gone mad" (Rudwick, 1964, p. 46, quoting reporters describing the violence).

Two years later, in Chicago, the violence was repeated. This riot was touched off when a group of black children swam into a white area on a Lake Michigan beach and were attacked by a white mob. Three days of violence ensued, with white mobs attacking blacks and black mobs striking back at whites. In this mayhem, thirty-eight people were killed: fifteen whites and twenty-three blacks. In both riots—and in most of the other two dozen or so riots that occurred during this era—the police did little or nothing to stop the white mobs from attacking blacks; they moved in only when the blacks began to strike back.

Although the tensions eased somewhat after the early 1920s, the general pattern of discrimination, segregation, and periodic violent outbursts associated with the rigid competitive pattern of race relations continued until World War II. In 1943, in a situation of racial competition similar to the earlier one in East St. Louis and Chicago, a bloody race riot erupted in Detroit. In this violence, twenty-five blacks and nine whites were killed.

It is notable that racial violence in the United States has closely corresponded with periods of war (Grimshaw, 1959b, 1969; Rudwick, 1964; Farley, 1994b). In fact, one study showed that of 210 major outbreaks of racial violence in the United States in the twentieth century, 202 occurred in just nine years during and immediately after World War I, World War II, and the Vietnam War (Schaich, 1975). Whereas the specific causes of racial violence have varied in different periods, there do appear to be some ways in which war precipitates it (Farley, 1994b). During World War I and World War II, for example, the growth of wartime industries led to large-scale migrations of African Americans to several American cities, which in turn led whites in those cities to feel threatened. This was probably a factor in the East St. Louis, Chicago, and Detroit riots.

Wars may also lead to heightened minority group assertiveness—with minorities feeling that if they fight and risk their lives for their countries, they should receive some measure of equal opportunity in return—which makes them seem more threatening to the dominant group. Sometimes, the dominant group responds to this perceived threat with violence and repression. Finally, war may heighten aggression and foster a vicarious desire to participate. Domestic minority groups may be substituted for "the enemy" and attacked, a behavior pattern Mazón (1984) called "symbolic annihilation." It is important to stress that war does not by itself cause racial violence, but it may make it more likely when conditions are otherwise favorable, as was the case during the era of rigid competitive race relations that prevailed in the North during the first half of the twentieth century.

## ▶ RIGID COMPETITIVE RACE RELATIONS AND OTHER RACIAL AND ETHNIC GROUPS

We have discussed the pattern of rigid competitive race relations mainly in terms of black-white relations, but from about 1880 to 1945 the pattern applied to a number of other minorities as well. In both the East and the West, immigration was seen as a threat to the status of white workers and was widely opposed. Eastern Europeans and—largely by association—Catholics and Jews were the target in the East and Midwest, Asian Americans and Mexican Americans in the West. For example, less two weeks after the East St. Louis riot, Hungarian mine workers were the target of rioting in nearby St. Francois County, Missouri (Theising, 2003, p. 151). In the East, strong opposition to immigration and accompanying surges of anti-Catholicism and anti-Semitism arose during periods of economic instability or downturn: in the 1830s and the 1850s, from 1880 to 1900, and in the 1920s and 1930s (Simpson and Yinger, 1985).

## Asian Americans

It was in the West that anti-immigrant sentiments were the strongest, probably because that was the region in which the largest number of Asian immigrants arrived. The opposition became so strong that the U.S. Congress eventually passed laws forbidding Asians to immigrate to the United States. The first such law, passed in 1882, banned Chinese immigration. It was to last ten years but was repeatedly renewed until 1904, when it was made permanent. Immigration by Japanese was also gradually restricted after 1900 until it was ended entirely in 1924 by a quota system that banned all Asians from migrating to the United States.

Although ethnic prejudices played an important role in the development of exclusionist sentiment, economic competition between whites and Asian Americans probably was the biggest cause. Of course, this competition was also a major cause of the prejudice. There was intense competition for jobs between whites and Asian Americans from the 1870s on. Asians, often in debt for passage to the United States, often were willing to work for lower wages than whites. This greatly aggravated the tensions between the two groups, and among most whites highly negative stereotypes ("deceitful," "opium smugglers," and "clannish") replaced the earlier, more positive ones. As had happened to blacks, violence and mob action were directed against Asian Americans. Anti-Chinese riots broke out in San Francisco, Los Angeles, and a number of other areas. In San Francisco, white laborers rioted against the presence of Chinese workers in certain industries (Barth, 1964, p. 143). The Los Angeles riot of 1871 resulted in the death of twenty Chinese Americans (Kitano, 1985, p. 220). In the mid-1880s, mobs attacked and killed Chinese Americans in Seattle and in Rock Springs, Wyoming. The Japanese were also sometimes the victims of violence: In 1890, fifteen Japanese cobblers were violently attacked by members of the shoemaker's union (Ichihashi, 1969). Boycotts of Japanese restaurants and other businesses were common in the early 1900s; in one case, the boycotters handed out matchboxes bearing the slogan "White men and women, patronize your own race" (Ichihashi, 1969, p. 235).

In 1906, the city of San Francisco banned all Japanese, Chinese, and Korean children from attending school with white students. Asian American students were required to attend a separate "Oriental school." In general, not only in education but also in a number of other areas, whites enforced a system that segregated Asian Americans much as blacks had been. These developments set the stage for one of the most disgraceful events in American history. During World War II, all people of Japanese ancestry (defined as one-eighth or more Japanese) in the western United States were required by presidential order to be relocated to prison camps. By November 1942, nine months after the order, some 110,000 West Coast Japanese, most of them American citizens, were in the camps. They remained there for more than two years. Many lost their incomes and possessions during the ordeal. One did not have to show any evidence of questionable loyalty to be put in the camps; one only had to be Japanese. It is also significant that no such imprisonment was used against German Americans, even though the country was also at war with Germany. Racism appears to have been the crucial factor in the imprisonment of Japanese Americans (Grodzins, 1949; Hane, 1990).

With the one very serious exception of the internment of Japanese Americans, it is important to note that the severity of discrimination against Asians living in the United States gradually subsided after Asian immigration was banned. The apparent reason for this is that as the banning of Asian immigration brought an end to rapid growth in the Asian population, the tendency of whites to see Asians as a serious economic threat subsided (Lieberson, 1980).

## Mexican Americans

The patterns of competition, segregation, and occasional violent attacks that marked Asian-white relations were also evident in Anglo-Chicano relations. As with other groups, competition for jobs was an important cause of friction. Because many employers used a dual-wage system, paying Mexican Americans less than Anglos, many whites believed that Mexicans were responsible for low wages. Anglo labor unions also opposed Mexican immigration on the grounds that it created a labor surplus that held down wages and raised unemployment. In some cases, Chicanos, like African Americans, were recruited to break strikes by Anglo labor unions, although in other cases they were very involved in the labor movement themselves (Cortes, 1980, p. 710). As with blacks and Asian Americans, segregation in housing, schools, and public accommodations was imposed on Chicanos. In California, a "foreign miners' tax" was applied not only to aliens but also to conquered Mexicans who had been born in California. Several discriminatory policies were pursued by the federal government, including the *bracero* guest-worker program of 1942–1947 and 1951–1964. Under this program, hundreds of thousands of Mexican workers were allowed to temporarily enter the United States to provide low-cost labor in the agriculture and transportation industries but were forbidden to permanently relocate to the United States. During much the same period, the federal "Operation Wetback" rounded up 3.8 million Mexicans for expulsion in raids at their workplaces, in restaurants and bars, and even on the streets and highways and in their homes. Technically, the raids were directed at illegal immigrants, but in some cases the people expelled were elderly Mexican Americans who had lived in the United States for many years, having entered when border crossing policies were far more informal than they had become by the 1940s (Cortes, 1980).

Chicanos sometimes were the victims of mass violence, as other minorities had been. The worst was a week-long series of disturbances in Los Angeles in 1943, which have come to be called the "zoot suit riots." The trouble began when gangs of white servicemen attacked Chicano youths who were wearing zoot suits, a flashy form of dress especially popular among young Mexican Americans. To many whites, zoot suits were a symbol of disrespect and lawlessness at a time when, because of World War II, national unity and sacrifice seemed especially important (Mazón, 1984). As the riots worsened, civilian whites joined the servicemen, and Mexican Americans were indiscriminately set on and beaten, whether or not they were wearing the zoot suits that supposedly were the target of the rioters. Chicanos—and some blacks and Filipinos as well—were dragged from streetcars and theaters and beaten. The police generally did not interfere with the rioters, but they did arrest a number of injured Mexican Americans after they had been beaten.

The press played a major role in inciting the race riot; for more than a year it had been headlining crime by Mexican youths and appealing to white fears. During the riots, the servicemen were presented in the papers as heroes, giving the "lawless youth gangs" a well-deserved lesson. The press also announced that Mexican "gangs" were planning a counterattack and even published the times and places. These places then became the assembling points for mobs of whites, who rampaged through the downtown area and Chicano neighborhoods, beating and stripping the people. The newspapers did not present the events as a race riot but rather as an attempt by servicemen to restore law and order. The true character of these events—a race riot initiated and sustained by whites, in which only about half the Chicano victims were even wearing zoot suits—came out later. A committee appointed by the governor of California to investigate concluded that it was a race riot, that Anglos were the main aggressors, and that the newspapers were largely to blame for the whole thing. This riot triggered a number of similar disturbances in other western and midwestern cities and is seen by some as a contributing factor in Detroit's bloody race riot in 1943. (For a full account and analysis of the zoot suit riots, see McWilliams, 1949, Chaps. 12 and 13; the psychological factors contributing to this riot, including those related to World War II, are explored by Mazón, 1984.)

## Overview

To summarize briefly, we can say that the general period from the end of the Civil War to World War II is a classic case of rigid competitive race relations. Urban populations of African Americans, Asian Americans, and Chicanos increased rapidly at various places and times during this period, but their numbers were not yet great enough to give them much political power. All these groups were seen by whites as competitors for jobs, housing, education, and public facilities. They were limited to restricted, low-wage job markets as whites attempted to maintain the advantages they received in a racial caste system. However, the caste system was threatened by the increasing industrialization of this period. Employers saw the advantage in playing off white and minority workers against each other. Dual-wage systems were set up in which minorities were paid less for the same work than whites. In addition to blatantly exploiting minority workers, this pattern also angered whites, who saw their wages and jobs threatened. They tried to protect their status by segregating and excluding minorities; African Americans, Asian Americans, and Mexican Americans all experienced segregation during at least part of this period.

White ethnocentrism, combined with fears of minority competition, and white economic and political power produced not only segregation but also violent outbursts against minorities, with the minorities receiving little or no protection or support from the law or the news media (for a summary, see Table 6.1). Thus, all the minorities became the targets of race riots, suffered most of the casualties, and often were blamed for the riots, which in fact were initiated by whites. These riots

**Table 6.1    Major Riots in Which Whites Attacked Minority Group Members, 1860–1945**

| Date | Place | Notes |
|------|-------|-------|
| 1863 | New York | Draft riot: mass attacks by whites on blacks; total death toll 1,000 to 2,000 (see text). |
| 1871 | Los Angeles | Attacks by white mobs on Chinese Americans; 20 Chinese Americans killed (see text). |
| 1898 | Wilmington, N.C. | White attacks on blacks. |
| 1906 | Springfield, Ohio, and Atlanta, Ga. | Attacks by white mobs on blacks (Boskin, 1969). |
| 1908 | Springfield, Ill. | Mass attacks by whites on blacks: black neighborhood burned; 2 blacks lynched, 4 whites killed by stray bullets (Crouthamel, 1969). |
| 1917 | East St. Louis, Ill., and other cities | White attacks on blacks; 48 deaths (see text); disturbances also occurred in Philadelphia and Chester, Penn. |
| 1919 | Chicago; Washington, D.C.; and other cities | White attacks on blacks and interracial fighting; 39 deaths in Chicago (see text); 2 whites and 2 blacks killed in Washington. Other riots in Omaha; Knoxville; Charleston; Elaine, Arkansas; and Longview, Texas (Franklin, 1969; U.S. National Advisory Commission on Civil Disorders, 1968). |
| 1921 | Tulsa, Okla. | Mob attacks on blacks by whites, including, by some accounts, bombing from airplanes; 21 blacks, 9 whites killed (Franklin, 1969). |
| 1943 | Los Angeles, Detroit, and other cities | Zoot suit riots; interracial fighting; 25 blacks and 9 whites killed in Detroit (see text; Franklin, 1969). |

tended to occur when a city's minority population was growing rapidly and when white and minority workers were competing for jobs (Allport, 1954, pp. 59–61). They were also particularly common around World Wars I and II, when ethnocentrism reached a fever pitch. Although more peaceful at other times, race relations were still unequal and mostly segregated. Despite periods of relative fluidity and rigidity, the overall pattern changed little until after World War II: Segregation was still the rule. However, it has changed significantly since that time, a change that will be explored in the following sections.

## ▶ A SHIFT TO FLUID COMPETITIVE RACE RELATIONS: AMERICA SINCE WORLD WAR II

Since World War II, dramatic changes have taken place in American race and ethnic relations. Debate continues over whether and to what degree race relations today are *better* than in the past, but there can be no question that race relations are substantially *different*. Today's majority-minority relations in the United States are an example of what W. J. Wilson (1973, 1978) calls fluid competitive race relations. Briefly, this can be classified as a system that is a mixture of caste and class, with more open and less restricted intergroup competition and decreasing amounts of open discrimination. In fact, open discrimination may even be illegal in such a system, as it is in the United States. Unfortunately, although discrimination is illegal and open discrimination is less common, "discrimination with a smile" remains common: Minority group members are politely told there is no job or no vacancy, whereas whites are told the job or apartment is still available and are encouraged to apply. In the next few pages, I outline some of the major characteristics of present-day American intergroup relations and describe how they represent a change from the past.

### Changes in the Law: The Banning of Discrimination

Racial segregation and discrimination were the rule in most of the United States until World War II. In some areas, they resulted from formal or informal practices in the private sector, such as the unwillingness of many employers to hire blacks and other minority group members (or hiring them only for certain jobs), refusals of homeowners or realtors to sell to blacks, and segregated businesses such as lunch counters. In other instances, discrimination was written into law. The laws of many southern states *required* discrimination in public facilities and education, and numerous state universities refused to accept blacks. These conditions remained largely in effect until the late 1940s to mid-1950s and, in some cases, well beyond. In addition to this legally required discrimination, a great deal of private sector discrimination operated with the support of the legal system. An example was the restrictive housing covenant. When a person purchased a house, she or he was often required, as a condition of purchase, to agree to a legally binding commitment not to sell the house to blacks, Jews, or other minority group members. This agreement had the backing of the law, so that it was actually illegal and punishable for the homeowner to sell to a minority group member. Without the backing of the law, the agreement would have been meaningless; thus, this private sector discrimination was made possible by the action of the public sector.

Beginning in the late 1930s, the law that at worst required and at best tolerated racial discrimination began to change. Although they did not challenge segregation, court rulings in 1936 and 1938 put some teeth in the "but equal" part of the old "separate but equal" doctrine. In 1936, the appellate court required the University of Maryland Law School to admit a black applicant because there was no comparable state-supported facility for blacks. In 1938, the Supreme Court ruled the same way in a case involving the University of Missouri Law School (C. S. Johnson, 1943). In 1946, federal courts ruled that segregation on interstate travel regulated by the federal government was illegal (Simpson and Yinger, 1985). In 1948, the Court ruled that states could no longer enforce restrictive housing covenants, although the writing of such agreements was not banned.

The most crucial ruling came in 1954, in *Brown v. Board of Education* of Topeka, which abolished the concept of "separate but equal." The Court ruled unanimously that separate schools could not be equal because segregating children on the basis of race "generates a feeling of inferiority as to their status in the community that may affect their hearts and minds in a way unlikely ever to be undone." In this and a related case, the Court ruled that the equal protection clause of the Fourteenth Amendment and the due process clause of the Fifth Amendment forbade school segregation. Various legal rulings in the remainder of the 1950s and into the 1960s extended the *Brown* principle to all publicly operated programs and facilities, although some cities and states in the South defied these rulings well into the 1960s. In many cases, direct protest was a significant factor in getting local and state governments in the South to comply with the federal law. In general, the action of the courts was a critical factor eliminating segregation and overt discrimination by state, federal, and local bodies of government.

The banning of overt discrimination and segregation in privately owned businesses came later, and legislation and direct protest were both important factors in bringing about this change. After the 1954 *Brown* decision, important civil rights laws were passed by Congress in 1957, 1960, 1964, 1965, and 1968. These laws protected the voting rights of blacks and other minorities, which in some parts of the country had been almost totally blocked by various tactics such as poll taxes and literacy tests. (As noted earlier, such tactics as grandfather clauses—one could vote only if his or her grandfather had been a voter—and the white primary had been also used to restrict black voting, but these had been ended by previous court decisions.) These laws also extended the protection against discrimination beyond the public sector to the private sector: Employers were not to discriminate in hiring, businesses were not to discriminate in the sales of goods or services, and real-estate owners and brokers were not to discriminate in the sale or rental of housing. These laws generally forbade discrimination on the basis of race, religion, color, or national origin. In general, they did not deal with discrimination on the basis of other characteristics, such as sex, age, disability, or sexual orientation, with the important exception that the 1964 law banned sex discrimination in employment. (More recent federal legislation has banned many types of discrimination based on age and disability.)

At the local level, numerous ordinances and laws were also passed against discrimination on the basis of race and ethnicity and, in some cases, other characteristics as well. Although these laws have not always been effective, it is indeed significant that by 1968 the clear position of American law was against racial and ethnic discrimination. This represents a near total reversal of the situation twenty-five to thirty years earlier, when the position of American law was somewhere between tolerating and requiring such discrimination. The change came about first through the action of the courts and later through legislation by elected lawmaking bodies, with the help of court rulings that legitimized and enforced the legislation. It is important to stress that the court rulings and especially the legislation came largely in response to a powerful, articulate, and well-timed protest movement by American minorities—a development that will be discussed at greater length in Chapter 7. (The stance of American government and law toward minorities past and present is discussed in Chapter 11.)

## Changes in Economics: The Development of Substantial Middle Classes Among Minority Groups

One of the major changes in minority group status since World War II is the presence of a sizable and growing middle class. There have always been some members of each American minority group who have attained middle-class or elite status. Until around World War II, however, pervasive racial discrimination kept that proportion very small. After World War II, this began to change. The educational gap between Chicanos and whites closed between 1950 and 1970, and the proportion of Chicanos in white-collar (professional, managerial, clerical, and sales) jobs increased, although improvement here was less extensive than in the educational area (Moore and Pachon, 1976, pp. 64–67). Somewhat greater improvements were noted in the black population, especially in the job structure. Among black men, the percentage in white-collar jobs more than doubled, from 8.6 percent in 1950 to 20.2 percent in 1970 (W. J. Wilson, 1978, p. 128). The comparable figure for Chicano men in the Southwest in 1970 was 21.6 percent (Moore and Pachon, 1976, p. 64), a rise from around 16 percent in 1950.

It should be pointed out that despite the development of a substantial middle class among African Americans and Latinos, the comparable figures for white Anglos are much higher, even today. More than half of white men hold middle-class, white-collar jobs. In 2002, for example, about 35 percent of non-Hispanic whites held managerial or professional jobs, the best, highest-paying work. However, this was the case for only about 23 percent of African Americans and 14 percent of Hispanics (U.S. Census Bureau, 2003h, 2003k). Among Chinese Americans and Japanese Americans, who were also victims of segregation and discrimination—which dissipated earlier and more completely—the change has been such that by most criteria, both groups would be considered predominantly middle class today.

With the growth in the middle class has come some increase in social mobility among minorities. No longer are certain jobs reserved for whites, as they often were before World War II. In theory, there is free competition for jobs, unrestricted by rules of discrimination, although in reality much informal discrimination persists. This continued pattern of informal discrimination has been demonstrated both by surveys of employers and housing providers (Kirschenman and Neckerman, 1991; Lake, 1981) and by testing studies in which socially similar whites and blacks apply for jobs or housing or attempt to make purchases (H. Cross, 1990; ABC News, 1991; U.S. Department of Housing and Urban Development, 1991; Ahmad, 1993; Yinger, 1995; Bendick, 1996; Bertrund and Mullainathan, 2002; Turner et al., 2002; Turner and Ross, 2003; Pager, 2003a, 2003b, 2002). These studies show that blacks and whites often are treated differently when they shop, apply for jobs, or attempt to rent or buy housing, even though it is rare for people to openly say that they will not rent or sell to blacks (Feagin and Sikes, 1994).

W. J. Wilson (1978) summarized changes in the class structure of the black population by noting that today there is more class stratification *within* the black population than ever before. In other words, we have to some degree shifted—as is ordinarily true when competitive race relations become more fluid—from a *racial caste system* toward a *class system*. That is not to say that we have moved all the way. Although Wilson sees race itself as declining in economic significance, he points out that there remains in the black population a large group, sometimes called the *underclass*, that is not enjoying the benefits of this fluidity of race relations. Much the same is true of Chicanos and Puerto Ricans, despite their growing middle classes, and the underclass is even larger in the American Indian population. This impoverished underclass is trapped in poverty, apparently unable to move up. (We shall examine the reasons for this in later chapters.) Still, class stratification has increased within minority populations, and a portion of the black and Hispanic populations has experienced increased social mobility. (The debate over the relative importance of race and class as causes of minority group disadvantage are explored in greater detail in Chapter 15.)

### Changes in Attitudes: Changes in the Kind and Degree of Prejudice Among Whites

Another clear trend in the past forty to fifty years has been an apparent change in the kind and degree of racial and ethnic prejudice. These changes were discussed in greater detail in Chapter 3, but the major points can be restated here. First, overt racial prejudice of all three types has declined: Cognitive prejudice (stereotypical or racist beliefs about minorities) has decreased somewhat. Americans today show less tendency to agree with stereotypical statements about racial and ethnic groups, although more subtly worded questions and qualitative techniques still show a fair amount of stereotyping. Affective prejudice (dislike of minorities) has also declined as people report more willingness to associate with minorities on a friendly basis. Finally, conative prejudice (desire to act in a discriminatory way) has declined as fewer and fewer whites express support for segregation and discrimination. This does not mean that prejudice has been eliminated, and part of the change might be a result of greater "sophistication" or unwillingness to openly express prejudice. Still, the change in what people say, at least, has been quite dramatic. The second change is in the kind of prejudice or, more precisely, the kinds of racist ideologies or beliefs that are accepted. Fifty years ago, it was widely believed among whites that blacks and other minorities were biologically or genetically inferior. Today, these beliefs have greatly declined, despite the arguments in support of genetic racial intelligence differences by a few advocates such as Jensen (1969, 1973), Herrnstein and Murray (1994), and Shockley (1971a, 1971b).

However, another form of racism, which W. J. Wilson (1978) calls *cultural racism*, has come to predominate. This view argues that minorities have developed cultural characteristics that in some way place them at a disadvantage. In more extreme forms, this view holds that groups are culturally inferior; in milder forms, minorities are believed to be at a disadvantage because of some of their cultural characteristics. In other words, if people are poor (or a minority group is disproportionately poor), it is their own fault. Feagin (1972), Schuman (1975), Bonilla-Silva (2003a, 2003c), and Kluegel (1990; see also Kluegel and Smith, 1986) have demonstrated that this view is very widespread among whites—even those who consider themselves unprejudiced—and that it is specifically used by many whites to explain black poverty. This allows whites to escape the responsibility for causing minority poverty through discrimination and exploitation by placing the blame for that poverty on minorities. This leads readily to the *symbolic racism* discussed in Chapter 3, which is marked by unwillingness to make the changes that would be needed to eliminate the disadvantages that blacks and other minorities in our society experience (Pettigrew, 1985; Kluegel, 1990).

## ► FACTORS CAUSING THE CHANGES: THE EFFECTS OF URBANIZATION AND INDUSTRIALIZATION

The twentieth century was a period of dramatic urbanization and industrialization in the United States. This process was already under way by 1900, but at that time the United States was still a predominantly rural society. Today, it is overwhelmingly urban. Industry and technology expanded tremendously in the twentieth century, and increasingly the productive capacity of the country came to be owned by massive corporations. For minority groups, the transformation was even more rapid. Early in the century, blacks and Mexican Americans were more rural than the white population; today, they are more urban. Much of the urbanization of these groups occurred between World War II and about 1970, although the process had begun earlier. Only American Indians are less urban than the white population.

Urbanization, modernization, and industrialization have influenced majority-minority relations in numerous ways and can directly or indirectly explain much of the change. We have already noted that as urbanization proceeds, societies often move from castelike toward increasingly classlike race relations, and we have seen that this type of change has corresponded to urbanization and industrialization in the United States—which, of course, does not prove that they caused the change. Nonetheless, a number of consequences of urbanization and industrialization do seem to push in the direction of more fluid race relations.

## Need for Greater Mobility and the Economic Irrationality of Discrimination

To operate effectively, industrial societies require greater mobility than do agricultural societies. Especially in the modern era of giant corporations and complex technology, employees often are recruited on a nationwide basis. Geographic and social mobility is required to achieve the best match of person and job, and such considerations as race, religion, and parentage—ascribed statuses—should not influence the hiring decision. Only job qualifications should matter because considering ascribed statuses can only interfere with the best match. The same can be said of other kinds of activities and transactions. It does not make sense for a seller of goods or services to cut off potential buyers because of race, religion, or some other irrelevant factor. In short, a complex, modern society is most efficient when all irrelevant factors such as race are disregarded. This was recognized by the classic sociological theorist Max Weber ([1922] 1968), who argued in the early twentieth century that this *rationalization* is the critical element in the emergence of industrial society. Many theorists of race and ethnic relations see it as a key force, leading to the breakdown of discrimination as societies modernize.

If rationalization had been the only social force at work, however, it might not have been sufficient to cause the changes that have taken place. Social psychologist Herbert Blumer (1965), in a widely cited article titled "Industrialization and Race Relations," argues that the forces of modernization and rationalization do not always lead to more fluid race relations. Even with industrialization (and sometimes because of it), some elements within society perceive that they are gaining from the subordination of minorities, and these elements press for continued discrimination (as when white workers tried to shield themselves from black, Chicano, or Chinese competition). Thus, were it not for other changes, which reduced majority demands for discrimination and created a situation conducive to the development of strong and effective minority group movements, the changes in majority-minority relations might never have occurred, even with industrialization. Moreover, had rationalization been the only factor at work, the influence of race might have declined much more than it has, as many sociologists of an earlier era incorrectly predicted that it would (McKee, 1993).

## Generally Rising Educational Levels

Another trend that has occurred throughout the twentieth century and became especially pronounced after World War II is a rising educational level. Among minority group members, this has tended to promote greater assertiveness, as we shall see in Chapter 7. Among whites it has undoubtedly led to some increase in tolerance as the irrationality of prejudice is revealed. We have already seen that there is some tendency for prejudice to decrease at higher levels of education. Thus, the increasing educational level of the population probably has played some role in the reduction of prejudice and overt discrimination.

## Postwar Economic Growth and Relaxation of Intergroup Competition

We have already seen that intergroup competition is an extremely important cause of intergroup prejudice, discrimination, and conflict. It therefore follows that when intergroup competition is reduced, intergroup relations should improve. W. J. Wilson (1978) makes a strong case that this is what occurred in the 1950s and 1960s. In general, this was a prosperous time. The economy was growing rapidly, for the most part unemployment was fairly low, and the number of jobs was increasing, especially in the white-collar sector. This resulted in a number of changes, all of which tended to bring about more fluid race relations. First, new opportunities were opened to blacks and other minorities in the expanding economy. Second, the position of minority group members was more secure, so it was safer for them to make demands for more equality. Third, whites—especially the middle class—were less threatened by minority gains than in the past, which meant they could be less prejudiced, more receptive to the demands made by minorities, and more accepting of court rulings against discrimination and segregation. In short, the expanding economy and reduced intergroup competition of the postwar period made the climate favorable for easing the strict racial barriers of the prewar period.

## Increased Assertiveness by Minorities

Much less change in race relations would have come about were it not for what is probably the most important factor of all: the increased assertiveness of minorities, most notably the African American civil rights movement of the 1950s and 1960s and the legal efforts of the National Association for the Advancement of Colored People (NAACP). These changes, too, arose in large part from postwar urbanization, industrialization, and economic growth. Both in itself and as a means of understanding the changing pattern of race relations after World War II, the rise of minority group social movements is of special importance, and this is a major focus of Chapter 7.

### Summary and Conclusion

In this chapter, we have seen that urbanization, industrialization, and the Civil War brought important changes in U.S. race relations. Although slavery ended, racial inequality did not, and segregation became more widespread than ever, remaining so for well over half a century. White Americans clashed with African Americans, Asian Americans, and Mexican Americans in some of the worst domestic violence in U.S. history. As in earlier periods, economic factors continued to have an important effect on intergroup relations, as various groups of whites used segregation, minority group strikebreaking, lynchings, and race riots to try to hold on to their economic advantage. Thus, competition and unequal power continued to be important forces in intergroup relations.

After World War II, however, formal policies of segregation began to be abolished, for a number of reasons. Among the most important were expansion of the economy and an upsurge in minority group social movements, which have continued to be a major force in American life ever since.

As we end this chapter, it is important to emphasize that racial discrimination and inequality have not disappeared from society, but their forms have changed. In fact, the persistence of racial inequality and race consciousness among both majorities and minorities has defied the predictions of many Weberian sociologists, who predicted that race and ethnicity would become insignificant as society modernized and rationalized (McKee, 1993). This has not happened, although patterns of race relations have changed. Color lines in society today are less clear-cut than in the past, the mechanisms of racial discrimination are more subtle, and patterns of racial inequality are less rigid and more fluid.

### Critical Review Questions

1. Why did the U.S. South become more racially segregated after slavery was abolished?

2. How does the concept of rigid competitive race relations apply to the history of Latino/a and Asian ethnic groups in the United States?

3. Present arguments for and against the idea that urbanization and industrialization lead to a decline in racial prejudice and discrimination.

4. What is meant by *cultural racism*? According to some sociologists, this form of racism has become more common in recent decades. What might be some of the causes for an increase in this type of racism?

# Overview

In the first part of this chapter, we shall see why the black civil rights movement and other minority group movements became so influential in the 1950s and 1960s. Later, we shall consider the ways in which minority group movements have changed since then and how the attitudes and beliefs of minority group members in America have changed along with them.

For any social movement, such as the civil rights movement, to emerge, people must decide that they want to make some change in society. Such a decision is only one of two major ways people can respond when they find themselves in a situation that they do not like: to *adapt* to the situation—to attempt to get along as best they can in a bad situation—or to try to *change* the situation. The responses of minority group members to the undesirable situation of being subordinated fit into one of these two approaches. Either they are *adaptive* strategies, which try to make the situation as tolerable as possible, or they are *change-oriented* strategies, which seek to change the situation for the better. In different historical periods with different social conditions, the mix of responses has varied widely. In the following section, we shall discuss some responses that fit into each category.

## ▶ ADAPTIVE RESPONSES

Four common ways of responding to subordinate or minority status are mainly adaptive: feigned or real *acceptance* of the status, *displaced aggression*, *avoidance* of the status, and *assimilation* into the majority group. Each of these responses takes the system of unequal status as a given and attempts to adapt to or live with that system. Let us discuss each in more detail.

### Acceptance

The response involving the greatest degree of resignation to a socially imposed position of disadvantage is to just accept it. When minorities choose simply to accept their lower status, several things may be happening. One possibility is that they really have become convinced of the ideology of dominant-group superiority and that minorities deserve an inferior role. This response is certainly not unheard of among relatively powerless people. Clark and Clark's (1958) doll studies (discussed in detail in Chapter 12) suggest that racism did result in a lower self-image among some black children in the 1950s. Also, the fact that some women opposed the passage of an Equal Rights Amendment to the Constitution often is seen as an example of internal acceptance of a subordinate role.

More commonly, however, people do not agree that they should have a lower status or that they are inferior, yet they believe that they can do little to change their situation. In this case, the usual response is to put up with the situation and try to make the best of it.

A third response of this type is to *pretend* to accept the status and play on majority group prejudices. In effect, it says, "If they think we're all stupid, then we'll pretend to be stupid, fool them, and use it to our advantage." It calls to mind the story (of unknown truth) about a white southern sheriff who stopped a black man for running a red light. The man responded, "But sir, I didn't want to go on the white folks' light [green]. I thought us black folks was supposed to wait for the other one." The sheriff, completely fooled, responded, "Well, OK, I guess you meant well. But from now on, I'm going to let you go on the white folks' light," and he got into his car and drove off.

## Displaced Aggression

You will recall from Chapter 2 that when people feel frustrated, and consequently aggressive, but cannot take it out against the person or thing causing the frustration, they will take it out against some easier or more available target. This is called *displaced aggression*, or *scapegoating*, and as we have seen, it is a common cause of prejudice among majority group members. Such displacement of aggression also frequently occurs among minority group members. If they are oppressed by members of the dominant group and the power structure does not permit them to strike back, they may well displace the aggression. This helps to explain the tragic fact that minority group members frequently commit violence against one another and, more generally, the fact that their crime rates often are high. Most crimes are committed against others of the same racial group; in the 1980s and early 1990s, as the plight of the urban underclass worsened, rates of black-on-black and Latino-on-Latino crimes rose in America's inner cities, particularly certain types of street crimes, such as assaults and robberies. Much of this crime appears to represent displaced aggression, as hopelessness and frustration worsened in areas of chronic, concentrated poverty (E. Anderson, 1990; W. J. Wilson, 1996). Fortunately, as the economy improved in the 1990s, these crime rates fell, but black-on-black and Latino-on-Latino crime remains a serious problem. Displacement of aggression may also explain high suicide rates among some ethnic minority groups, as frustration and aggression may even be turned inward.

## Avoidance

Another way of dealing with a bad situation is to try to avoid reminders of it or to try to escape reality entirely. Minority group members may avoid contacts with the majority group, which may remind them of their subordinate status. Others may turn to a more generalized kind of avoidance, using alcohol or drugs, for example. Alcoholism and drug abuse rates often are high among subordinate ethnic groups; apparently, substance abuse offers the hope of escape from an unhappy situation not of one's own making. In recent years in the United States, the percentage of minorities who are using illegal drugs has in fact been *lower*, not higher, than the percentage of whites using illegal drugs. However, the kinds of drugs that are more often used by urban, low-income African Americans and Latinos are sometimes stronger and more addictive and therefore may result in serious problems of drug dependency. Whereas young, middle-class whites most often use marijuana, minority youths more commonly use stronger drugs such as heroin and crack cocaine, particularly in areas of concentrated poverty. Among rural, poor, and working-class whites, methamphetamine use has become a serious problem in recent years. In addition, alcoholism has always been a problem among the poor of all races.

## Seeking Assimilation

This response might best be seen as accepting the system but attempting to deny one's role within it. In effect, the minority group member seeks either to become a member of the majority group or to become accepted in its culture or social institutions. In this case, no real attempt is made to change the system of majority-minority relations. Rather, the minority group individual attempts to change his or her individual position or role.

The most extreme form of this response is the practice of "passing." Sometimes minority group members who are close in appearance to whites have presented themselves to the world as white, or passed as white. This has enabled them to enjoy the advantaged status that is reserved for members of the majority group. It is not known how many people do this, but it does happen at least occasionally. (For discussions of the extent of the practice among American blacks, see Stuckert, 1958; Simpson and Yinger, 1985, pp. 139–140, 507.)

Other, nonracial minority groups often engage in similar practices, and it can be easier for them to do so. For example, some homosexuals choose to remain "in the closet"—in other words, to deny to the outside world that they are gay. In some societies, persecuted religious minorities have practiced their religions in secret to avoid discrimination. All of these closely related strategies have a disadvantage: They tend to produce great psychological stress because they force people to deny who they are. This constant denial of one's identity is both stressful and degrading, but some people feel that it is necessary when they are faced with intense discrimination. Even today, there are situations in which members of some nonracial minorities are virtually forced into such behaviors. The 1993 compromise policy on gays in the military, dubbed "don't ask, don't tell," forbids gays in the military to publicly acknowledge their sexual orientation: Those who do so are supposed to be discharged immediately.

More common than these practices, however, is that of seeking cultural assimilation with the majority: adopting the lifestyles, fashions, and values of the majority group. Often, this is aimed at gaining acceptance by the majority group. This practice has been more common among the minority group middle classes than among the poor or working classes. In fact, minority middle-class people may attempt to put distance between themselves and poor people of the same group. For example, some black middle-class neighborhoods have resisted the introduction of low-cost, subsidized housing as strongly as have white middle-class neighborhoods. Historically, Booker T. Washington's accommodationist policies in the late nineteenth and early twentieth centuries are an excellent example of the assimilationist response. Washington believed that by becoming better educated and proving their abilities through hard work, African Americans could show whites that they could make a valuable contribution to society (Washington, 1900). He thought that this would lead whites to value African Americans to a greater degree and that such an approach was more effective than challenging the system. Toward this end, he generally avoided protest movements, but he founded Tuskegee Institute, an African-American college, and did what he could to encourage African Americans to become better educated.

Other, more recent evidence of assimilationist tendencies may be seen in the popularity of straightened hair ("process" haircuts) among many blacks in the 1950s and early 1960s and the practice in that era and earlier among a number of groups of "Americanizing" ethnic names. Although some people in minority groups still seek assimilation into the majority, there has been some movement away from this pattern since the mid-1960s. Trying to "look white" has been intensely criticized in the African American community in more recent times, and some children of immigrants have gone back to their original ethnic names. We shall examine the reasons for changes such as these later in this chapter.

## ▶ CHANGE-ORIENTED RESPONSES

The alternative to trying to live with an unpleasant position is trying to change it. Change-oriented responses attempt to change the nature of majority-minority relations in a society or to change the role or position of the minority group in that system. These efforts vary in both their goals and strategies. The *goal* of such a movement may be to bring about a systemwide assimilation—to create a society and culture that are common, shared, and equal among the former dominant and subordinate groups. This results in a cultural and social coming together of the two groups, although in practice the new culture and society usually resemble that of the old majority group more than that of the old minority group. Other change-oriented responses seek a different outcome: to build alternative, minority-controlled institutions. This approach aims to preserve and strengthen minority group culture and to build an independent power base that ultimately will make the minority politically, socially, and economically stronger. To some degree, this encourages movement toward separate or distinct social structures rather than the single shared structure sought by assimilation. Of course, these goals are ideal types; real-life social movements usually fall somewhere in between, with some elements of each approach.

The *strategies* of movements seeking change also vary. They may be legal and within the system or illegal and outside it. Examples of the former include legal campaigns such as lawsuits and judicial appeals, legislative campaigns (attempting to pass favorable legislation), voter registration and election efforts, legal strikes and boycotts, and peaceful legal protests that appeal but do not disrupt. Outside-the-system strategies include peaceful but illegal protests aimed at disruption (non-violent sit-ins are a good example) and violent forms of protest such as riots and bombings.

## ▶ A SHIFT TOWARD CHANGE-ORIENTED RESPONSES

Minorities have always responded to subordinate status with both adaptive and change-oriented responses, and they continue to do so today. In the early twentieth century, for example, there were intense debates among African Americans over this issue as they faced the strict segregation and discrimination of the rigid competitive era. On one hand, Booker T. Washington advocated an accommodationist approach, as previously noted. On the other hand, W. E. B. DuBois, a cofounder of the NAACP, supported a political action approach aimed at creating social movements to press for equal opportunity (DuBois, 1903). Yet another approach could be seen in Marcus Garvey's Back to Africa movement, which essentially took the position that African Americans would be best served by withdrawing from a white-controlled society and creating their own. Each of these positions represented a different choice in dealing with socially imposed disadvantages, and there was a good deal of debate about their relative merits.

Although these debates have been going on for more than a century, there was a definite shift over the course of the twentieth century. Particularly after World War II, opinions shifted away from adaptation and toward efforts to bring about change. Largely because the power structure made it difficult or impossible to do otherwise, the earlier responses by minorities fell more often in the adaptive category than in the change-oriented one. This is not to say that most minorities were satisfied with their roles; they were not. Furthermore, important efforts to change the system had been made by all minorities. We have already discussed slave rebellions before the Civil War; here we shall briefly note some of the protest movements of the period between the Civil War and World War II. In the late 1860s and again from 1900 to 1906, boycotts and protests were carried on against segregated streetcars in southern and border cities (Meier and Rudwick, 1969; W. J. Wilson, 1973). The first wave of protest ended such segregation in New Orleans, Louisville, Charleston, Richmond, and Savannah. The later campaign, though less successful, involved twenty-six cities. In the 1870s, the Negro Convention movement became an important political force that protested violence against blacks and sought civil rights enforcement of the Fifteenth Amendment, which forbade racial discrimination in voting. In the early twentieth century, the social movements led by Marcus Garvey and W. E. B. DuBois were important and influential. Garvey's separatist Back to Africa movement enjoyed widespread support among low-income blacks, and DuBois's militant movement for racial integration and equality helped lead to the founding of the NAACP.

The amount of pre–World War II protest activity by Mexican Americans was less than that of blacks (Simpson and Yinger, 1985, pp. 427–29) but still significant, especially in the labor movement. In the 1880s, the Caballeros de Labor sought to unionize Chicano workers and protest the taking of Chicano land by Anglos. In the 1910s, 1920s, and particularly the 1930s, Chicano farm workers struck in California; the movement to unionize farm workers, then as now, was largely led and coordinated by Mexican Americans. In 1929, a number of organizations combined to form the League of United Latin American Citizens (LULAC). This organization combated segregated schools, exclusion of Mexican Americans from jury duty, and exploitation of farm labor (Meier and Rivera, 1972, pp. 241–43).

However, movements since World War II have been considerably more significant. Those by African Americans, Latinos, Native Americans, and a number of other ethnic groups have been larger, more powerful, more widely supported, and more successful than ever before. Furthermore, more people of color have rejected various ways of adapting to subordinate status. To them, adaptation is unacceptable because subordinate status is unacceptable. Since World War II, they have demanded change to an unprecedented extent.

## ▶ THE RISING TIDE OF PROTEST

It is impossible here to provide a detailed history of the protest movements of minority groups during the postwar era; to do so would fill volumes. However, I will attempt to present a brief overview of some of the major events since World War II.

African American activity during and after the war focused largely on the courts. The NAACP began to pursue legal efforts against discrimination more vigorously and more effectively in the 1940s and 1950s, and this effort led to most of the important court rulings discussed in Chapter 6, including the 1954 *Brown* decision. There were other efforts, too, most notably A. Philip Randolph's threat to organize a massive march on Washington if President Roosevelt did not ban job discrimination in military supply industries during World War II. (Under the threat of such an internationally embarrassing demonstration, Roosevelt did issue this order.)

Gradually, as the 1950s gave way to the 1960s, such actions became more widespread. Court rulings were important, but their effectiveness was limited for two reasons. First, local governments—especially in the South—seldom complied promptly with the court orders. Typically, they stalled and looked for loopholes; sometimes they even defied the orders more or less openly as in the Little Rock, Arkansas, school desegregation case. Governor Orval Faubus defied a federal court order in 1957 to desegregate a high school in that city; President Eisenhower had to send federal troops to carry out the order. A second limitation of the courts was that their orders—before the civil rights laws of the 1960s—generally applied only to public sector discrimination, not discrimination perpetrated by private businesses or organizations. For these reasons, the civil rights movement had to change its tactics to include direct action.

A crucial event took place in 1955 that precipitated a move toward direct-action protest movements. A black woman named Rosa Parks refused to give up her seat on a bus in Montgomery, Alabama, to a white man. This led to a campaign to desegregate the city's bus system. The campaign was joined by a young minister named Dr. Martin Luther King, Jr. Months later, and bolstered by a federal court order, the battle was won. This victory led to similar campaigns around the country and helped catapult Dr. King into a position of national leadership. Applying the principles and philosophy of nonviolent resistance developed in India by Mahatma Gandhi, King led similar campaigns around the country. Notable was the 1963 struggle in Birmingham, Alabama, in which hundreds of peaceful protesters were jailed, beaten, and fire-hosed by police and in which the motel where Dr. King was staying was bombed, as was his brother's house. These protests and others, along with a demonstration by about 250,000 blacks and whites in Washington later that year, helped bring about the Civil Rights Act of 1964. It was at this demonstration that Dr. King gave his famous "I Have a Dream" speech. Other major events in the civil rights movement included the student sit-ins at lunch counters and various public facilities in the early 1960s and the freedom rides to protest segregated transportation facilities. In 1965, Dr. King's famous march from Selma to Montgomery, Alabama, helped to pass the 1965 Voting Rights Act.

Not all the action was in the South. Campaigns against discrimination were also carried on in a number of northern cities. A 1966 protest march against housing segregation led by Dr. King on Chicago's southwest side was attacked by a mob of angry whites, leading him to say he had never seen such racial hatred anywhere in the

Dr. King delivers his famous "I Have a Dream" speech to a crowd of 250,000 in Washington, D.C., in 1963.

South. By the mid-1960s, white resistance to civil rights had grown so strong that many blacks felt new tactics were needed; furthermore, a repeated pattern of violent attacks against peaceful protesters was raising tensions to a critical point. The objectives of the protesters began to change, and "black power" replaced desegregation as a goal. During this period, leaders with a new, more militant message began to emerge. Malcolm X and Stokely Carmichael, for example, began to stress survival, economic equality, and political power as the immediate goals of the black movement. These goals required changes far more drastic than civil rights laws, but they spoke directly to the immediate concerns of impoverished blacks in big-city ghettos.

At the same time, many blacks were beginning to question the value of nonviolence in light of the strong and often violent resistance to change by whites. The failure of civil rights laws to change the day-to-day lives of poverty-stricken urban blacks also led to heightened frustration. Given the increasing anger and frustration of African Americans, it is not surprising that a wave of violent rebellions spread across the country from 1964 to 1968. Violence broke out in hundreds of cities, and the rebellions resulted in scores of deaths (mostly blacks killed by law-enforcement officials) and millions of dollars in property damage. The worst of these outbreaks were in the Watts district of Los Angeles in 1965 (thirty-four deaths) and in Newark (twenty-five deaths) and Detroit (forty-three deaths) in 1967 (U.S. National Advisory Commission on Civil Disorders, 1968). In 1968, Dr. King was shot to death on the balcony of a motel in Memphis, Tennessee, where he was supporting a garbage collectors' strike. To many, this violent attack on a man who had won the Nobel Prize for his advocacy of peaceful protest was the last straw. Violent outbursts occurred in numerous cities, with especially severe ones in Washington and Chicago. More than ever, the effectiveness of peaceful protest was called into question. (For further discussions of the black civil rights and Black Power movements of the 1950s, 1960s, and early 1970s, see Killian, 1968, 1975; Meier and Rudwick, 1970b; Pinkney, 1975; Morris, 1984.)

African Americans were not the only ones turning to change-oriented movements during this era. After World War II, Mexican American veterans, returning home to find discrimination, formed the G.I. Forum, which became one of the most influential Chicano organizations of the 1950s and 1960s (Meier and Rivera, 1972, pp. 245–47). This organization fought discrimination at the local level and conducted voter registration drives and lobbying efforts throughout the Southwest. In the 1960s, Chicanos increasingly turned to direct-action protest. Student walkouts and protests over discrimination, biased materials, and prejudiced teachers occurred in a number of areas. In California, a campaign begun by Cesar Chavez to unionize agricultural laborers led to massive strikes in 1965 and subsequent years and to nationwide boycotts of grapes, lettuce, and certain wines. Like King, Chavez practiced Gandhian nonviolence and even went on an extended fast (with some damage to his health) to protest violence in his movement. Like King's, Chavez's efforts were met with considerable violence by Anglos. However, his efforts were also successful as never before in unionizing a large segment of farm labor.

Chicanos were also carrying on other, more militant action. In New Mexico a movement seeking restoration of land to Mexican Americans claimed 20,000 members in the mid-1960s. Its leader, Reies Lopez Tijerina, led an occupation of Forest Service land in which several Forest Service rangers were taken captive. Tijerina and several others were arrested, but on June 5, 1967, they were freed in an armed raid on a New Mexico courthouse by a group of their followers. A force of 600 state troopers and National Guardsmen eventually captured them (Meier and Rivera, 1972; see also Knowlton, 1985). Tijerina represented himself in court and was acquitted by an Albuquerque jury of charges in the courthouse takeover; however he later served several years in prison on a federal conviction for the Forest Service incident. As with blacks, continuous resistance by Anglos was causing frustration and stimulating a move toward violence. The most serious outburst occurred in Los Angeles in 1970. A large demonstration called the Chicano Moratorium was held to protest the Vietnam War and its effects on Chicanos. Violence broke out between protesters and police, spread across the barrio, and continued for hours. At least one person, a Chicano journalist, was killed by police fire, and property damage was heavy.

Among Indian people, too, social action and protest increased. The incidence of such protest gradually rose during the 1960s, often focusing on treaty rights to unrestricted fishing. This issue has led to conflicts in Michigan, Minnesota, and the Pacific Northwest. In 1968, the American Indian Movement (AIM) was founded in Minneapolis. It started out as a local organization but soon became national in scope and played a role in several major protests, most notably the 1973 occupation at Wounded Knee, South Dakota, which led to violent confrontations with federal authorities and to two deaths. Other major protests by Native Americans included a takeover of Alcatraz Island, a former federal prison on San Francisco Bay, under an 1868 treaty providing that surplus federal property could be claimed by the Sioux. This takeover lasted nearly two years. Indian protesters also occupied Fort Lawton, a military base in Washington State, after it was declared surplus in 1970, and they eventually were granted part of that property (Bahr, Chadwick, and Strauss, 1979). One of the most widely publicized protests, called the Trail of Broken Treaties, took place in 1972 in Washington and led to a takeover of the Bureau of Indian Affairs building.

Some of these Native American demonstrations were harshly repressed, particularly during the Nixon administration and on South Dakota's Pine Ridge Lakota (Sioux) Reservation. Later investigations revealed concerted efforts to discredit Indian protest leaders, false charges of violence against AIM members, and cover-ups of violence by AIM opponents and government agents (Matthiessen, 1983; Churchill, 1994, especially pp. 173–206). For example, Churchill (pp. 180–81) notes incidents in which Federal Bureau of Investigation (FBI) officials made allegations about AIM activists that were widely reported in the press, then later admitted, sometimes in sworn testimony, that the statements were not true. From 1973 through 1976, there were dozens of unsolved murders—possibly as many as seventy—of AIM supporters on the Pine Ridge Reservation (Churchill, 1994). Most of these murders were never investigated (Matthiessen, 1983; Churchill, 1994). At least sixty have been documented by name and date of death (Johansen and Maestas, 1979; Churchill, 1994, pp. 197–205). If we count only the murders of AIM supporters, the homicide rate on the Pine Ridge Reservation was eight times that of Detroit, the city with the highest homicide rate at the time.

Clearly, then, these three minority groups and others gradually changed their response to subordinate status from trying to adapt to it toward trying, with increasing insistence, to change it. Let us now examine some of the reasons why.

## ▶ NECESSARY CONDITIONS FOR SOCIAL MOVEMENTS

An important sociological question concerns why this large-scale change from adaptive to change-seeking responses occurred when it did. Although there has always been debate over how to respond to discrimination, change-oriented responses have been much more common since around the late 1950s or early 1960s. To explain why, a logical starting point is to ask, What are the conditions under which social movements get started? Social scientists have identified five major conditions that must be present for social movements to develop.

### Collective Dissatisfaction (Relative Deprivation)

The first condition is dissatisfaction. People must feel that they are being taken advantage of in some way or that their situation is unsatisfactory. Such feelings are not always present where people *are* the worst off in absolute terms. Rather, they are found when people *feel* worse off than others or feel deprived of what they should have. This condition is called **relative deprivation**, and helps to explain why social movements develop most readily when poverty is found in the midst of wealth or when conditions begin to improve (for further discussion of the notion of relative deprivation, see Geschwender, 1964). Importantly, this sense of deprivation must be *collective*, that is, it must be tied to an identity shared by a sizable number of people, such as a racial minority that has been singled out for discrimination (Polletta and Jasper, 2001).

## Communication Network

The second condition needed for a social movement to develop is a network of communication within the dissatisfied group. It does not matter how dissatisfied people are if they cannot communicate with one another. Without communication, they cannot act collectively. To form a movement, dissatisfied people must be able to share their dissatisfaction, develop a group consciousness, and decide what they are going to do to change the source of their dissatisfaction (see Morris, 1984, especially pp. 275–86). Communication also helps in the formation of a collective identity that supports movement participation (Tindall, 2002).

## Resources

A communication network is one example of a resource that can be used to organize social movements. A recent approach to the study of social movements is known as *resource mobilization theory* (McCarthy and Zald, 1973, 1977). According to this theory, movements develop and spread when people who are dissatisfied have resources they can use to build a social movement and, equally important, are aware that they have the resources and can use them in this way. Resources include money, influence, and personal communication networks, as well as modern mass media, which can be used both to facilitate communication among potential movement participants and to generate bad publicity about the groups or institutions that the movement opposes (J. Freeman, 1973, 1979; Lofland, 1985; Snow et al., 1986; McAdam, McCarthy, and Zald, 1988, pp. 722–23).

## Sense of Efficacy

Assuming that a group is dissatisfied and has adequate means of internal communication, it must still have what social scientists call a *sense of efficacy*. Put simply, this means that people must feel that they have something to gain by protest and that the potential gains outweigh any possible negative effects. No matter how dissatisfied people are, they are unlikely to become involved in a movement if they think doing so will make them even worse off than they already are. At the same time, once they do become involved, research has shown that participation in social movement can heighten people's efficacy (Hasso, 2001). Thus, a sense of efficacy and participation in social movements can be mutually reinforcing.

One factor in a sense of efficacy is the extent to which a social or political system is, in fact, vulnerable to protest. This is one of the main points of another fairly recent approach to the study of social movements: *political process theory*. When people realize that the system is vulnerable to change through protest, they are much more likely to become involved in social movements (Jenkins and Perrow, 1977). For example, the antinuclear power movement grew and prospered in Germany, whereas it atrophied in France, even though it started similarly in both countries. This happened because German government review procedures provided opportunities for intervention by those opposed to nuclear power plants; French procedures did not (Nelkin and Pollak, 1981).

## Leadership

The final condition that must be present for social movements to develop is leadership. Somebody has to plan strategies, inspire the rank-and-file participants, and do the day-to-day work. There is some question of whether this factor is as critical as the other four—some say that under those conditions effective leadership will emerge—but it is clear that leadership is important both in getting a movement started and in making it effective once it is under way.

## ▶ DEVELOPMENT OF THESE CONDITIONS AND THE FORMATION OF MINORITY SOCIAL MOVEMENTS IN THE UNITED STATES AFTER WORLD WAR II

In the twentieth century, and particularly after World War II, a number of changes occurred that helped bring about these movement-facilitating conditions of collective dissatisfaction, communication, movement-related resources, sense of efficacy, and effective leadership. The most important were the trend toward urbanization and industrialization, economic expansion, mass communications, rising education levels, and international changes. Each helped in important ways to bring into being conditions favorable to the development of social movements among oppressed minorities.

### Urbanization and Industrialization

We have already discussed the general trend of urbanization in the United States and the fact that most minority groups have undergone an even greater and more rapid transition from rural to urban than the white Anglo population (see Table 7.1). The pattern of rapid urbanization is particularly notable for blacks and Mexican Americans, who as recently as 1930 were more rural than the overall population but today are more urban. Rapid urbanization is also notable among Japanese Americans and, since 1950, among Native Americans.

One of the effects of urbanization was to increase feelings of relative deprivation or dissatisfaction. Minority group members arriving in large cities were exposed to affluence and lifestyles many had not seen before, an experience that undoubtedly made them more conscious of what they could have and, consequently, less satisfied with their share. The mobility that goes with urbanization and industrialization also helps to raise expectations (R. Williams, 1977, p. 28). If peo-

| Table 7.1 | Percentage of Urban Residents in Various American Ethnic Groups | | | | | |
|---|---|---|---|---|---|---|
| Year | Total Population | Blacks | Chicanos | American Indians | Chinese Americans | Japanese Americans |
| 1910 | 46% | 27% | 32% | 4% | 76% | 49% |
| 1930 | 56 | 44 | 51 | 10 | 88 | 54 |
| 1950 | 64 | 62 | 66 | 16 | 93 | 71 |
| 1970 | 74 | 81 | 85 | 45 | 96 | 89 |
| 1990 | 75 | 87 | 89 | 56 | 96 | 94 |
| 2000 | 79 | 90 | 92 | 58 | 98 | 95 |

*Source:* U.S. Bureau of the Census, population figures for the years 1910, 1930, 1950, 1970, 1990, and 2000.

ple enjoy greater freedom and have higher expectations but find that they must still accept a subordinate status, the potential for dissatisfaction becomes very great. In a society with racial inequality, urbanization has exactly this effect. Urbanization in the United States also increased competition between whites and minorities for the same jobs. Often whites were hired ahead of others or received higher pay for the same work, adding to dissatisfaction among minority groups.

Urbanization also made it easier for minority group members to communicate their dissatisfaction to one another and to discuss what could be done. In the urban ghettos and barrios, masses of people with similar ethnic backgrounds were brought together with many others who had the same sense of dissatisfaction. The urban ghettos established a base for black churches and colleges, which became key forces in organizing the civil rights movement (Morris, 1984, pp. 4–12). In addition, the greater freedom and independence of the urban setting made it safer to promote antiestablishment ideas. This presents a sharp contrast to the rural setting (especially on large-scale plantations and fruit and vegetable farming operations), where close social control made even talking about protest risky. Thus, both the concentration of minority group members and the greater freedom of the city made it easier for people to communicate with one another about their dissatisfactions and what they could do to remedy them (Morris, 1984, pp. 3–4).

It is also probably true that a social movement has, all else being equal, a greater chance of success in an urban setting than in a rural one, partly because of the weaker social control in large cities. There are simply too many people for any authority to be aware of what everyone is doing. The large numbers of people mean that, almost by definition, there must be more variety of opinions and lifestyles. Thus, a social movement in an urban area is less likely to be repressed by authorities than a similar movement in a rural area. Furthermore, it is possible to mobilize large numbers of people in the city. People can vote, they can boycott businesses, they can pack public meetings, and they can tie up city traffic. These actions are a source of power for a social movement, and all are more effective when masses of people are involved. Thus, not only is a movement easier to organize in the city, but it is also more likely to have some positive results. Undoubtedly, these factors go a long way toward explaining why social movements and protests are nearly always disproportionately urban events (Tilly, 1974).

All of these considerations point to the same conclusion: A society that attempts to maintain a pattern of racial inequality when it is urbanizing is likely to experience considerable minority group protest. Urbanization helps to create most of the conditions necessary for social movements: feelings of dissatisfaction, ability to communicate among the dissatisfied, and a reasonable chance of success. It probably also helps to develop leadership; even movements in rural areas, such as the United Farm Workers and the Wounded Knee protest, have had leaders with a largely urban background. Another look at Table 7.1 will show not only that minorities became much more urbanized in the twentieth century but also that the period 1950–1970 was a time of particularly rapid urbanization among the black, Chicano, and American Indian populations. It is hardly surprising that this period was an era of social movements among groups seeking change in their subordinate status.

## Economic Expansion

Although the trend toward urbanization and industrialization played an important role in facilitating ethnic protest movements, it has not been the only factor. Another reason can be found in the economic expansion of the postwar period. W. J. Wilson (1973, 1978) has shown that both the extent and militancy of racial protest and its degree of success tend to be greater in times of economic expansion. In times of economic decline, minorities have tended to protest less and often have difficulty protecting their status against attacks by members of the majority group.

The 1950s and early 1960s were generally a time of economic expansion in the United States. Given W. J. Wilson's historical observations, it is hardly surprising that this was a period of rising ethnic protest. First, such expansion tends to raise expectations by opening up new positions to minority group members. At the same time, it makes the minority groups less of a threat to the majority, so that the latter are more inclined to respond favorably to minority protest, increasing its chance of success. Thus, one of the important conditions necessary for social movements to develop is brought about: a belief that the movement can succeed. Wilson argues that one reason for both the size and effectiveness of the civil rights movement of the 1950s and 1960s is the fact that African American leaders correctly perceived that the social and economic climate was favorable for a successful movement. Of course, once one campaign has been successful, others often follow.

In addition to these factors, good economic times also tend to increase the resources that social movements can bring to bear. In the growing economy of the 1950s and 1960s, the civil rights movement was able to develop substantial resources such as money and legal assistance, receiving support from both the small but growing black middle class of that era and a sizable number of sympathetic whites (Zald and McCarthy, 1975; McAdam, 1982; Morris, 1984; Jenkins and Eckert, 1986).

## Mass Communications

P. J. Williams (1977) and others have commented on the importance of mass communications in stimulating social protest. The media can easily raise dissatisfaction by making people more aware of the contrasts between the haves and the have-nots. This can facilitate the exchange of ideas among the dissatisfied, if only by exposing more people to the ideas of protest leaders. Finally, it can stimulate protest by making people aware of movements elsewhere. In effect, it helps people to realize that "we could do that, too." Through the spread of radio and television (and, more recently, the Internet) and the nearly universal availability of telephones, mass communications since World War II have created a revolution in how people receive and exchange information. This change has been an important stimulus for racial and other kinds of protest since World War II.

## Rising Educational Levels

We have already discussed ways in which rising educational levels of all groups in the United States have contributed to the increasing fluidity of race relations in the twentieth century. More specifically, they have also contributed directly to the rising incidence of protest demanding social equality. As in most movements, the leaders of the civil rights and other social movements have tended to be people of above-average education. More education also has tended to increase feelings of relative deprivation as people became more aware of inequalities and unfair treatment.

Increasing levels of education in the population have also influenced the thinking of the white population. As we have seen, education tends to lower the level of prejudice. It also may make whites more aware of unjust treatment of minorities, undoubtedly making whites more responsive to minority demands (see Hall, Rodeghier, and Useem, 1986). Furthermore, it helps to explain the involvement by whites in protest movements on behalf of minorities. Thousands of whites were involved in the civil rights movement, in protests to increase numbers of minority students in universities in the 1960s, in the United Farm Workers' boycotts of grapes and lettuce in the 1960s and 1970s, and in other efforts. In the 1980s and early 1990s, many white Americans were involved in the campaign against South African apartheid. In recent years, growing numbers of whites have been involved in efforts to promote diversity at work and school and in various efforts opposing hate groups. In general, white college students and more highly educated whites have been most involved in these efforts.

## International Changes

A final factor can be found in certain international changes. Most important is the emergence of independent nations in former colonies in Africa and other Third World areas. This trend has had two important effects. First, it has presented minority Americans with important examples, or role models, of the successful exercise of power and self-governance by people of color. For example, the emergence of self-determination for black Africans has strengthened the hopes of African Americans for greater self-determination. Second, it has forced the American government to be more supportive of the demands for equality by its own people of color. The United States is competing with other countries for friendship and economic relations with Third World nations. If it loses such friendship and economic ties, its position in the world may be seriously weakened. One important facet of such relationships is how people of color are treated in America. If the United States discriminates against blacks, it can hardly expect to maintain good relations with African nations. If it mistreats Chicanos, it can hardly expect cooperation from Mexico. Thus, the position of people of color in the United States has been helped by these concerns, particularly from the 1950s to the 1980s, when the United States was in constant competition with the Soviet Union for influence in the world.

To summarize, a number of changes helped bring about the conditions necessary for the development of minority group social movements. Particularly notable since World War II are urbanization and industrialization, economic expansion, the spread of mass communications, rising educational levels, and international changes. Together, these changes heightened feelings of relative deprivation among minority groups, enabled communication and planning, improved the hopes of success, increased the resources of such movements, and facilitated the development of effective minority leadership. The result was a turn toward change-oriented social movements by African Americans, Mexican Americans, American Indians, and other groups after World War II.

## ▶ CHANGING VALUES AND GOALS: RACIAL AND ETHNIC GROUP MOVEMENTS AND ATTITUDES FROM THE 1960S TO THE NEW CENTURY

In the early stages of minority group movements, the goals were, for the most part, to eliminate the policies of open and deliberate discrimination that were widespread in the 1950s and earlier and to eliminate barriers that kept minority group members from participating fully in American society. These movements were fairly successful in attaining the first goal, but the second proved much more elusive. Even with open discrimination on the wane, blacks, Hispanics, and Native Americans did not come close to full participation in American society. As we shall see in greater detail in Chapter 9, all of these groups remain distinctly disadvantaged in income, health, employment, education, political representation, housing, and a host of other indicators of the quality of life. In short, the mechanisms of inequality today are more subtle than in the past, and there has been a clear decrease in some types of inequality, but a good deal of racial and ethnic inequality nonetheless remains.

As the mechanisms of intergroup inequality in American society have changed, both the tactics and goals of minority group members have also changed. Indeed, the diversity of minority viewpoints—which has always been present—has increased tremendously since the late 1960s. One example can be seen in the issue of school desegregation. In the era of *de jure* segregation in the 1950s, virtually all blacks in the United States favored integrated schools. Today, however, a significant number of blacks are skeptical about the benefits of integrating schools, and many more object to the methods proposed to bring it about. Partly for this reason, the number of districts using busing to desegregate schools has decreased.

This change in attitude is just one of many examples. At least in part, it reflects a change in what some blacks consider to be an ideal or model pattern of race relations. It could also be seen as a change in what is considered to be an appropriate goal for social movements. On one hand, there has been debate about the appropriateness of these goals through much of U.S. history. For example, although W. E. B. Du Bois and Marcus Garvey rejected accommodationist strategies, they disagreed on whether African Americans should press their demands for full inclusion in American society (Du Bois's position) or strive to set up their own separate society (Garvey's position). On the other hand, debates of this type have been more pronounced since the late 1960s, when it became evident that passing civil rights laws and breaking down legal patterns of segregation did not always reduce racial inequality. In the remainder of this chapter, we shall turn our attention to these changes in additudes. We shall examine changes, and increasing diversity, in the goals and values of minority (and majority) group members concerning what constitutes a desirable pattern of intergroup relations. Specifically, we shall explore changing attitudes toward three models: assimilation, pluralism, and separatism.

## ▶ THREE IDEAL MODELS OF INTERGROUP RELATIONS

### Model 1: Assimilation

The general concept of assimilation was first introduced in Chapter 4 and has been referred to a number of times since. In this section, we discuss the concept in greater detail and delineate several distinct types. By way of review, assimilation occurs when (1) the dominant group accepts the minority group or groups (at least in some aspects of social life), and (2) the majority and minority groups become integrated into a common culture and social structure. In many cases, the common culture and social structure are for the most part those of the dominant or majority group, although they may incorporate some features of the minority group as well. In other cases, however, the minority group influence is quite substantial. Accordingly, the balance of dominant and minority group cultural influences varies considerably from society to society.

Sociologists distinguish between two major kinds of assimilation: cultural and structural (Gordon, 1964, pp. 70–71). As the name suggests, **cultural assimilation** occurs when two or more groups come to share a common culture; that is, they develop common attitudes, values, and lifestyles. Often, they also increasingly think of themselves as one common group. When cultural assimilation occurs, the resultant common culture often is mainly that of the dominant group, although, as noted, certain aspects of minority group culture usually are also adopted.

**Structural assimilation** occurs when two or more social groups come to share one common social structure; that is, they share common social institutions, organizations, and friendship networks. When structural assimilation is complete, the groups hold roughly equal positions in these social structures. Partly for this reason, structural assimilation tends to be more difficult to achieve than cultural assimilation (Gordon, 1964, p. 77). A minority group may change its culture (attitudes, beliefs, and lifestyles) to conform to the dominant society, but such conformity does not guarantee that the group will be accepted into equal-status roles in the society, which remains in the control of the dominant group. Also, both majority and minority group members may prefer to develop friendships within their own group, even when cultural differences are not great. For these reasons, structural assimilation tends to occur to a significantly lesser degree than cultural assimilation.

Perhaps the most difficult type of structural assimilation is what Gordon (1964, p. 71) calls *marital assimilation*, which occurs only when there is widespread intermarriage between two racial or ethnic groups. If marital assimilation occurs and persists for an extended period of time, the assimilation of the groups becomes complete, and they gradually lose any identity as separate groups, an outcome known as **amalgamation**.

Although there has been much resistance in the United States to true structural assimilation, American ideology has always strongly supported the idea of cultural assimilation. Great emphasis has been placed on the idea of America as a "melting pot" in which citizens cease to think of themselves as German, Irish, Polish, Italian, African, or Mexican and regard themselves instead as American. Assimilation is also highly valued by the functionalist perspective in sociology because it helps to bring about the common values and shared identity that functionalists believe are necessary in any society.

Assimilation can indeed lead to a system of racial and ethnic equality. For this to occur, however, there must be *structural* assimilation as well as the often more superficial cultural type. In addition, assimilation is more likely to lead to intergroup equality if it involves a true blend of the cultures and institutions of both groups. Unfortunately, because assimilation often means that the minority group largely adopts the culture and social structure of the dominant group, the process is unbalanced from the start. As we shall see in more detail later in the chapter, this has been largely true of assimilation in the United States, although in some other societies, such as Mexico (see Chapter 8), the assimilation process has been much more balanced. For these reasons, the existence of cultural assimilation in a society does not guarantee that the society will have intergroup equality.

## Model 2: Pluralism

A second model of intergroup relations is *pluralism* (Higham, 1974). In pluralism, some aspects of culture and social structure are shared in common throughout society; other aspects remain distinct in each racial or ethnic group. There is a common culture and set of institutions throughout society, but only up to a point. To a large degree, each ethnic group maintains a distinct subculture; a distinct set of social institutions such as churches, clubs, businesses, and media; and a distinct set of *primary group* relations such as friendship networks and families. Thus, under pluralism there exists one society made up of a number of distinct parts. In contrast to the melting pot, the pluralist model often is compared to a mosaic, in that it is one unit made up of many distinct parts.

As was the case with assimilation, we can subdivide the concept of pluralism into cultural pluralism and structural pluralism. **Cultural pluralism** occurs when each group in society retains certain sets of attitudes, beliefs, and lifestyles while sharing others. Similarly, **structural pluralism** exists when groups retain some social structures and institutions of their own but share others. An example can be seen when several groups all willingly give allegiance to one government, speak the same language, and share the same monetary system but at the same time go to their own churches, have different patterns of occupations, and marry within their own groups.

In recent years, *multiculturalism* has been widely advocated as a model for intergroup relations in the United States, Canada, and other countries. Because it emphasizes the preservation of the distinct cultural characteristics of different racial, ethnic, and religious groups, multiculturalism is similar in meaning to cultural pluralism.

In the sense that it involves sharing some common cultural and social structural features throughout a society, the pluralist model is in part consistent with the functionalist perspective in sociology. In other respects, however, the pluralist model is more closely aligned with the conflict perspective. Specifically, it denies the need for complete consensus, suggesting instead that society can benefit from diversity and the opportunity for change that diversity can offer. The distinct cultures and distinct sets of institutions found in a pluralist society offer a power base for the various racial and ethnic groups. In the view of conflict theorists, social groups in any society do not all share the same self-interests. By retaining its own culture and set of social institutions, each group potentially has a power base to protect its legitimate interests.

As with assimilation, a pluralist society can be a society of racial equality. This tends to occur if the power position of the various groups is fairly similar and if the institutions they control have fairly similar resources. If these conditions are not present, equality will not exist either, although conflict theorists might argue that having distinct groups with distinct cultures and social institutions provides a power base, which makes social change more possible than when assimilation is complete.

## Model 3: Separatism

A third model of intergroup relations, at the opposite end of the scale from assimilation, is racial or ethnic separatism. Under **separatism**, two or more racial or ethnic groups occupying an area have their own cultures and their own separate sets of social institutions and primary group relationships. Little or nothing is held in common by the groups. If there is contact between them, it is the type of contact that occurs between two distinct societies or independent nations.

In many instances, separatism could occur only with *population transfer* because separatism is impossible unless each group has a distinct geographic base—a territory of its own. Therefore, unless the population distribution in a society is such that each group lives in a distinct area, it is necessary for many members of one or both groups to move to bring about separatism. Because people often are unwilling to do this, separatism can be very difficult to implement.

Like assimilation and pluralism, separatism may or may not be a means of bringing about intergroup equality. If separatism is voluntary on the part of the minority group, as in secession (in which the minority group withdraws from the dominant group's society), if the two groups are able to gain similar levels of power, and if the geographic areas to which the groups move have similar resources, separatism can offer an opportunity for intergroup equality. However, if these conditions are not present, separatism not only may fail to bring equality but also may lead to even more inequality, particularly when it is imposed on the minority group against its will. An example is South Africa's policy in the 1970s of resettling the black population in *bantustans*, or "independent" black states. This policy delayed any real movement toward black-white equality because (1) it was imposed on the black population by the dominant whites, (2) the areas assigned to the black population were small and limited in resources, and (3) the bantustans were not allowed the power associated with true independence. When majority rule was established in 1994, they were eliminated.

More broadly, the difficulties of separatism are illustrated by the division of the former Yugoslavia into separate territories for Yugoslavia's major ethnic groups: Croatians, Serbs, Bosnians, Albanians, and Macedonians. No matter how the country was divided, some ethnic groups faced the choice of moving, living under the rule of another ethnic group, or fighting. Consequently, it was impossible to draw any set of boundaries on which everyone agreed. A number of groups, but particularly Serbs, engaged in a practice known as "ethnic cleansing," an attempt to force other groups out of a territory so that the group that makes up the numerical majority (or that is most powerful) could control the territory. Murder, rape, destruction of cities and towns, and imprisonment in concentration camps were among the tactics used to force out unwanted groups. Although virtually all ethnic groups engaged in these tactics to some extent, Serbs used them on the largest scale by far. Thousands of people died in the early and mid-1990s as a result of these actions, large portions of Sarajevo and other cities were destroyed, and international intervention was needed in Bosnia and Kosovo.

In general, sociologists of the functionalist viewpoint tend to frown on separatism because of the divisions within society that separatist movements create. Some conflict theorists, however, see merit in some forms of separatism, taking the view that if it is voluntary on the part of the minority group, separatism can free the subordinate group from the control of the dominant group and give it the independent power base it needs.

Each of these three models—assimilation, pluralism, and separatism—has had varying levels of support in the United States. In the following section, we shall explore changing attitudes toward the three models among the American population and, in particular, how the goals of minority groups and their social movements have changed.

## ▶ ASSIMILATION, PLURALISM, AND SEPARATISM IN AMERICAN SOCIETY

### Assimilation and Anglo Conformity

In any discussion of alternative models for race and ethnic relations, it must be noted that the dominant norm in the United States through nearly all of its history has been cultural assimilation. The dominant cultural group in the United States has been the so-called WASPs: white Anglo-Saxon Protestants. Such has been the influence of this group on American culture that many social scientists describe the cultural pattern of the United States as *Anglo conformity*: All other groups in America have been expected to adopt the language, culture, and social structure of the white, northern Europeans (Gordon, 1964, p. 85). As Feagin and Feagin (2003, Chap. 3) illustrate in a thorough chapter on English Americans and the Anglo-Saxon core culture, the most influential group has been British Protestants. A somewhat altered British Protestant culture came to be accepted as the dominant American culture, and all ethnic groups in America have been expected to conform to this culture and its attendant institutions. Thus, although the United States is a nation of immigrants, English remains the language that everyone has always been expected to learn and speak, regardless of one's native language. In fact, about half the states and a number of localities have passed legislation designating English as the only official language; California did so by public referendum in 1986. (As Latino political power has increased, however, some areas, such as Dade County, Florida, have repealed this legislation.) Bilingual education, an innovation of the 1960s originally aimed at improving the schooling of Hispanics and immigrants, has become highly controversial because many people feel it gives educational sanction to languages other than English. In 1998, such sentiments led California voters to pass another referendum, banning bilingual education even as a way of teaching English.

Indeed, education has played a central role in the assimilation of a variety of immigrant groups into the so-called WASP culture. Not only was American education based largely on a British model and heavily under the control of elite English Americans during its formative years, it also placed intense pressure on children to conform to the dominant Anglo culture. In Feagin and Feagin's (2003, p. 69) words, "Whether the children were Irish, Jewish, or Italian, Anglicization of the children was designed to ferret out non–Anglo-Protestant ways and assimilate the children to Anglo-Protestant manners, work habits, and values."

Although we have seen that schools and other agents of socialization have placed a great deal of pressure on immigrant groups to culturally assimilate, in many cases not all that much pressure has been needed: Many immigrants have very much wanted to give up their old ways and assimilate into the dominant Anglo-American culture. This tends to be especially true of the children of immigrants, who generally have oriented themselves much more closely to the American ways of their peers and the school system than to the Old World culture of their parents (see Gordon, 1964, pp. 107–8). Still, these tendencies have largely resulted from the strong pressure to assimilate in American society (Gordon, 1978, Chap. 7). In general, the view that cultural assimilation is expected of American immigrants has rarely been challenged, and the overwhelming majority have assimilated to a substantial degree.

Although cultural assimilationist tendencies have always been strongest among immigrant minorities, they have also existed among colonized minorities. Such a theme can be seen in the Negro self-help movement of Booker T. Washington around 1900. Washington, one of the very few blacks to gain widespread credibility among whites during that era, argued that rather than challenging white society, blacks should demonstrate their value to American society through improved education, hard work, and demonstrations of loyalty (Hawkins, 1962; Washington, 1900). Washington hoped that by emulating the values and work habits of middle-class white society, blacks could eventually gain a greater degree of acceptance. Of course, part of the reason for such an emphasis on assimilation and accommodation was Washington's belief that a more direct challenge to the white power structure would not have been tolerated.

Even in the 1950s and early 1960s, when the civil rights movement blossomed, assimilationist tendencies remained evident. True, the movement did seek to persuade, pressure, or force whites to accept social change, and it challenged the power structure through civil disobedience and direct action. Nonetheless, it is clear that the goals and objectives of the early civil rights movement were in many ways assimilationist. The major issues of this era centered largely around desegregation: the elimination of "whites only" schools, lunch counters, buses, railroad stations, and so on. In effect, the demand was for full participation by black Americans in all aspects of the white-controlled society. During this period, the goal was not to build new or radically different social institutions; rather, it was for blacks to be able to participate in American social institutions on the same basis as whites.

There have been debates about appropriate goals among African Americans throughout U.S. history. We have already mentioned the differing positions that Booker T. Wasington, W.E.B. Du Bois, and Marcus Garvey advocated 80 to 100 years ago. And throughout the assimilationist period of the civil rights movement, the Nation of Islam offered an alternative, separatist view. Nonetheless, its influence was far more limited then than it is today, reflecting much more widespread assimilationist beliefs among African Americans at that time.

Although their continuing loyalty to the Spanish language reflects a significant tendency toward cultural pluralism, Mexican Americans have in many ways sought assimilation into American society as well. For example, Alvarez (1973) notes strong assimilationist tendencies in what he calls the "Mexican American generation." These children of migrants from Mexico, born in the United States and coming of age in the 1950s and 1960s, generally lived an urban life somewhat better than that of their parents. Consequently, most of them began to think of themselves as more American than Mexican and as moving toward full participation in American life. Unfortunately, the acceptance by Anglos that would have been necessary for full Chicano participation was still missing.

Probably the one major racial or ethnic group that presents a clear exception through most of its history to the pattern of seeking assimilation is Native Americans. Over the years the U.S. government has used about every technique imaginable to get Indian people to give up their ways and to seek assimilation into white culture and society. Among these have been attempts to set up Indian people as small farmers, to isolate their children from native culture in white-controlled boarding schools, and to get them to leave the reservation to take industrial jobs in urban areas. Native rituals and languages have been banned in some cases (for further discussion of U.S. policy toward Indian people, see Chapters 5 and 6).

All of these efforts have been notably unsuccessful, in part because American Indians have, until very recently, lived in predominantly rural and predominantly Indian social settings. Thus, they have been able to maintain much of their culture, even in the face of sometimes powerful attacks. More recently, even despite rapid urbanization of the Native American population, Indian people have continued to resist pressures for assimilation. C. H. Steele (1972, 1985) has demonstrated the strong resistance by many urban Indians to white social and cultural influences, apparently because of their close contact with nearby Indian reservations. Thus, Native Americans probably are the one major exception to the general pattern whereby nearly all racial and ethnic groups in America have sought assimilation into the dominant culture and society during at least a significant portion of their history in the United States.

In one sense, even Native Americans have undergone considerable assimilation. A substantial number through the years have married whites, and to a large extent, people of mixed European and Native American ancestry have culturally blended into the white population. In part because they are a smaller percentage of the population than other groups, American Indians are more likely than most other racial groups to marry outside their group. This is especially true in areas with small Indian populations (J. Nagel, 1995).

The result has been a large and growing population of American Indian ancestry mixed with other groups. The number of Americans reporting some Indian ancestry grew from about 6.7 million in 1980 to 8.7 million in 1990 (R. Farley, 1991; U.S. Bureau of the Census, 1993c, p. 51), or about 3 percent of the population. In 1990, the number of Americans who reported some American Indian ancestry was nearly five times as great as the number who indicated that their race was American Indian or Native American. Most of these people of mixed ancestry live in urban areas and have little or no knowledge of Native American culture or connection to the reservation. Until recently, most thought of themselves as white, although increasing numbers today are identifying with their Native American ancestry. Among relatively assimilated people of mixed ancestry, most have substantially more white than Native American ancestry. Still, the number of them reporting their race as American Indian or Native American has been growing (J. Nagel, 1995). When the 2000 census for the first time allowed people to report more than one race, more than 4 million people (1.5 percent of the population) reported their race as American Indian, either alone (2.5 million) or in combination with another race (1.6 million) (U.S. Census Bureau, 2002e).

## Critique: Have Social Scientists Exaggerated the Degree of Assimilation in American Society?

Americans from a wide variety of racial and ethnic groups have shown signs of turning away from assimilation since the mid-1960s. Furthermore, some social scientists have questioned whether there was ever as much assimilation in America as was widely believed. For example, Glazer and Moynihan (1970, p. xxxiii) found in their study of the six major ethnic groups in New York City (blacks, Puerto Ricans, Jews, Italians, Irish, and WASPs) that ethnic groups remained important throughout the twentieth century, developing and retaining "distinctive economic, political, and cultural patterns." These patterns may not have been particularly similar to the culture of the "old country," but they were distinct in American society.

To this we must add Gordon's (1964, 1978) reminder that *structural assimilation* occurs much less easily than cultural assimilation. Thus, family and other primary group relations continue to be influenced to a substantial degree by race and ethnicity. Interracial marriage remains quite rare, although it has increased in recent years. The issues of interracial marriage and dating are explored further in the box titled "Interracial Relationships in the New Century." Despite these recent changes, it remains true that majority group members associate, form friendships, and marry

### INTERRACIAL RELATIONSHIPS IN THE NEW CENTURY

Although interracial marriages and relationships remain the exception today, their number has increased sharply since the 1960s. In 1960, there were just 157,000 interracial couples in the United States; by 2000 there were 1.34 million, more than eight times as many (U.S. Census Bureau, 2001c, Table FG4; *St. Louis Post-Dispatch*, 1998a). This represented 2.4 percent of all married couples in 2000, up from 0.4 percent in 1960. In other words, about more than one of every forty married couples is interracial—still a small minority but far more than in the past—although most of them are not black-white couples. In 2000, there were 307,000 black-white couples, less than one of four interracial couples. Still, about 7 percent of couples with one African American partner are black-white couples. The majority of interracial couples are white and either Asian American or Native American. As of the 1990 census, there were 334,000 couples in which one partner was Native American and the other white, although this may be overstated because many of these people may already be of mixed white and Native American ancestry. The largest number of interracial marriages involve Asian Americans and whites: 465,000 in the 1990 census. Clearly, with the growing number of interracial marriages, the proportion of the population with mixed racial ancestry is bound to grow, which is one reason that beginning in 2000, the Census Bureau permits people to report more than one racial background.

Additionally, a large and growing number of marriages are between Hispanics and non-Hispanics. In 2000, 1.71 million couples, or 3.1 percent of all married couples, were composed of a Hispanic person married to a non-Hispanic person (U.S. Census Bureau, 2001c, Table FG4). Thus, 5.5 percent of all marriages in 2000 were either interracial or were composed of Hispanic and non-Hispanic partners.

The growth in interracial marriages is almost sure to continue. A 1997 poll showed that 57 percent of teenagers in a national sample who go on dates had done so with a person of a different race. (Unlike the Census Bureau, this survey treated Hispanics as a racial group.) This figure represented an increase from 17 percent in 1980, although the 1980 poll did not include Hispanics (K. Peterson, 1997). If Hispanics are excluded from the 1997 poll, the figure is still 31 percent, well above the 1980 rate. As with marriages, the poll indicates that interracial dating between blacks and whites is less common than other combinations. However, acceptance of interracial dating had become pervasive among U.S. teens by 1997: 66 percent of African Americans, 74 percent of Latinos, and 75 percent of whites said that interracial dating was "no big deal" at their schools. Thus, although interracial marriage remains very much the exception today, it could become much less so in the future. The percentage of teens who said that they had no objections to interracial marriage was actually higher than the percentage saying that interracial dating was "no big deal": 91 percent approved marriage between blacks and whites, 93 percent between Asians and non-Asians, and 94 percent between Hispanics and non-Hispanics (Lyons, 2002). However, these percentages may be overstated: One study found that many college students who gave such responses to survey questions expressed reservations about interracial marriage in subsequent qualitative interviews (Bonilla-Silva and Forman, 2000; Bonilla-Silva, 2003a).

In the past, people who entered interracial relationships sometimes were motivated partly by factors associated with racial inequality. For example, some theorists have suggested that whites tend to marry minorities of higher socioeconomic status or physical attractiveness than their own because these traits "offset" their minority status. Similarly, minorities who marry whites will marry "down" in status or attractiveness because they consider the person's majority group status more important. Kalmijn (1998) found that highly educated African Americans are more likely to marry whites, whereas less-educated whites are more likely to marry African Americans. However, other recent studies suggest that such patterns may not occur in dating. Yancey and Yancey (1998) studied the racial preferences indicated in personal ads. The theory would predict that whites seeking or open to interracial partners would emphasize financial status more than would minorities, but they did not. It would also predict that whites seeking interracial partners would value attractiveness more than would either minorities or whites seeking

By 2000 there were 1.34 million interracial couples—eight times as many as there were in 1960. About one in four interracial couples in 2000 were composed of an African American and a white person.

whites. However, none of these relationships were found. This suggests that people dating today may be less swayed by concerns about racial inequality. What Yancey and Yancey did find was that people who date interracially are more concerned about attractiveness and less so about financial security, regardless of race. These findings may reflect differences in conventionality between those who date within and outside their own group. More conventional, conservative people worry more about financial security and are also less willing to date outside their group. Less conventional people worry less about financial security, are more concerned about their partner's looks, and are more willing to date outside their own group. However, some caution should be used in generalizing from these findings because not all who date use the personal ads. Moreover, the limited number of studies of interracial dating and marriage remind us how limited our knowledge of these phenomena is—a limitation that may increase in importance as interracial dating and marriage continue to become more common.

mainly within their group. For example, when whites were asked in a recent survey to name their good friends and afterward were asked the race of the people they had named, it turned out that only 6 percent had named an African American (T. Smith, 1999). Similarly, though to a slightly lesser extent, minority group members associate mainly with other members of their group. Although interethnic marriage is not uncommon, the image of one great melting pot does not fit very well here, either. A study of eighty years of marriage data in New Haven, Connecticut, by R. J. R. Kennedy (1944, 1952) revealed that patterns of interethnic marriage were far from random. In fact, there seemed to be three distinct marriage pools: a Protestant one among British, Germans, and Scandinavians; a Catholic one among Irish, Italians, and Poles; and a Jewish one (see also Greeley, 1970). Although this tendency has decreased over time (Alba, 1981; Yetman, 1985, pp. 233–34), it has not disappeared.

Major occupational distinctions also exist, as can be seen in the well-known specialization of many Irish Americans in police work, manufacturing, and politics; of Greek Americans in fishing and the restaurant business; of Jewish Americans and Arab Americans in small business; and of Chinese Americans in services, restaurants, and specialty shops. Research by Greeley (1974, pp. 51–55, 1977) and Cummings (1980) confirms that different ethnic groups have different occupational structures, although Neidert and Farley (1985) have shown that these differences decrease as time passes after immigration. Overall, indicators of structural assimilation such as occupation, marriage and friendship patterns, and religious affiliation do reveal a lower level of assimilation than we would expect if we considered only cultural assimilation. Thus, assimilation, although considerable, has definitely had its limits, especially structural assimilation. Structural assimilation has occurred to a significant extent among "old" immigrant groups (British, Scots, Germans, Scandinavians, and Irish), less so among "new" immigrant groups (eastern and southern Europeans, Asian Americans, and Arab Americans), and only to a very limited extent among minority groups (African Americans, Hispanics, and Native Americans), who, as we have seen, remain largely outside the institutional power structure of America.

## ▶ CHANGING ATTITUDES TOWARD ASSIMILATION AND PLURALISM

As we have seen, most racial and ethnic groups have sought cultural assimilation throughout most of American history. Even minority group social movements were substantially assimilationist in their goals until around the mid-1960s, although, as always, there were debates and some important exceptions to the rule. Since that time, however, important changes have taken place, which we shall examine in the remainder of this chapter.

## African Americans

**The Years 1965 to 1975: The Black Power Movement and a Shift Toward Pluralism.**
Probably the earliest and most important indicator of a shift away from seeking assimilation was the Black Power movement, which began in the 1960s. Although it was never a cohesive, single, centrally organized movement with a totally agreed-on set of goals, certain viewpoints and objectives were fairly well agreed on by the various groups and individuals who identified with the general concept of Black Power. On the whole, the goal of black-white integration was deemphasized. Rather than integration, the major goals of the Black Power movement were (1) self-determination, whereby blacks would have full control of their own lives instead of having their roles and statuses defined by whites, and (2) full social and economic equality. There was increasing skepticism among African Americans that the goals of self-determination and equality could be achieved through assimilation. More and more blacks began to believe that as long as society's institutions remained under the control of whites, black people could not realistically expect to gain equality through integration into those white-controlled institutions.

As a result of these changing perceptions, Black Power proponents developed objectives and priorities quite different from those of the earlier civil rights movement. A central objective was that blacks should have much greater (in some cases, total) control over institutions that affected black people. Examples of this were the community control movement in education and, in higher education, the widespread demand for black studies and black culture programs *under the control of blacks*. The Black Power movement also placed great emphasis on pride in the accomplishments and culture of African Americans. More and more African Americans began to say, "We will determine our own reality and our own concept of ourselves as a people rather than having it defined for us by white people."

All this added up to a distinctly more pluralistic and less assimilationist set of goals than had existed in the past. There was a good deal of serious discussion about African Americans building their own institutions and organizations to serve their own interests. At the same time, the distinct features of black culture and an African heritage attracted considerable interest. A growing number of black people came to believe that by promoting assimilation, many white people were seeking to impose white culture on African Americans as a precondition for social equality. Not surprisingly, this perception aroused considerable opposition to assimilation.

Thus, not only pluralist but also separatist goals enjoyed a surge of support. Although they were not supported by the majority of black people, separatist movements such as Elijah Muhammad's Nation of Islam (commonly known as the Black Muslims) enjoyed greatly increased support from the mid-1960s into the 1970s. Of course, separatism was not a new idea in 1960: Marcus Garvey's Back to Africa movement had gained support in the 1920s, and the Nation of Islam, under Elijah Muhammad's leadership, existed as early as the 1930s (Pinkney, 1976, p. 156). By the 1960s, however, it began to enjoy more widespread support among African Americans than earlier separatist movements. By the 1970s, membership had reached somewhere between 100,000 and 250,000 (membership statistics were not released), but its influence was broader. By the mid-1970s, its weekly newspaper, *Muhammad Speaks*, had a circulation of 600,000, the largest of any black-owned newspaper in the United States (Pinkney, 1976, pp. 159–60).

Throughout most of its history, the Nation of Islam has been distinctly separatist in its goals and practices. Until a brief period beginning in the late 1970s, membership was limited to blacks, and Elijah Muhammad argued that whites were an evil and inferior race. The emphasis of the organization was always on building separate, membership-controlled institutions rather than relying on those of the dominant society. It operated its own school system and financed its operations through ownership of numerous business enterprises, including supermarkets, restaurants, a publishing house, and thousands of acres of farmland in several states (Pinkney, 1976, p. 162). In the 1960s and early 1970s, a major objective of the organization was to establish a separate, African American–controlled region in the United States. Although the Nation of Islam never came close to attaining this goal, it did succeed in amassing a good deal of wealth and property, the benefits of which were shared among the membership. One estimate by the *New York Times* (1973) placed the value of the organization's holdings in 1973 at $70 million. (More recent directions of the Nation of Islam are discussed in a later section on contemporary trends in African American thought and social action.)

The Black Muslim movement gave rise to one of the most influential spokespersons for a new, more militant view that rejected assimilation as the route to success for African Americans: Malcolm X. Although Malcolm X eventually broke with the Nation of Islam over its separatist tendencies, he constantly spoke of the need for African Americans to develop their own institutions and their own power base. He argued persuasively that nobody else would do that for African Americans, and he was greatly admired for his willingness to stand up to threats from the police, the FBI, and his political opponents. In his autobiography, he pointed out that from the standpoints of economics, quality of life, and political power, the civil rights movement had done little or nothing for impoverished, inner-city blacks (Haley, 1964). To make a difference in these areas, he argued, African Americans would have to build their own social institutions and their own power base. Malcolm X was assassinated while speaking at a rally in New York City in 1965.

Along with a shift away from assimilation, important changes in the tactics used by the black movement were occurring. Although the civil rights movement of the 1950s and early 1960s often used civil disobedience as a tactic, in nearly all cases it was nonviolent. Dr. Martin Luther King, Jr. carefully studied the philosophy and tactics of the great nonviolent leader of India's struggle for independence, Mahatma Gandhi. With the coming of the Black Power movement in the mid-1960s, however, there were some important changes in tactics. Younger black activists were particularly dissatisfied with the "turn-the-other-cheek" philosophy. The Black Muslims, the Black Panthers, and many leaders in the movement began to argue that when whites use violence against blacks, black people should fight back. For example,

The failure of the civil rights movement to bring increased economic opportunity to inner-city blacks contributed to the growing influence in the 1960s of leaders such as Malcolm X, who offered a more militant message than earlier civil rights leaders.

Malcolm X said, "We should be peaceful, law-abiding, but the time has come to fight back in self-defense whenever and wherever the black man is being unjustly and unlawfully attacked." This statement was frequently quoted by Black Panther leaders Huey Newton and Bobby Seale, who explained that the black panther, chosen as the symbol of their movement, symbolized an animal that will not attack but will tenaciously defend itself (R. L. Hall, 1978, pp. 123, 124).

Despite this philosophy, the white media often exaggerated the violent tendencies of the Panthers, Muslims, and other groups associated with the Black Power movement. The number of violent incidents involving either the Muslims or the Panthers was in fact relatively small, nearly always involving shootouts or other confrontations between group members and police, with some doubt about who initiated the violence. In some cases, there is good reason to believe that the police were the instigators, such as the incident in 1969 in which fifteen armed law officers raided the Black Panther office in Chicago, resulting in the deaths of party leaders Fred Hampton and Mark Clark and the wounding of four others. Subsequent investigations of the incident indicate that contrary to police reports of a shootout, it is likely that the Panthers were attacked while sleeping. Ultimately, a lawsuit led to the payment of nearly $2 million in damages to the survivors of the raid and to relatives of Hampton and Clark (Simpson and Yinger, 1985, p. 424). Both the American Civil Liberties Union and a staff report of the National Commission on the Causes and Prevention of Violence concluded that police action against the Panthers was widespread, was excessive, and often violated the group's rights (Pinkney, 1976, pp. 109–10).

**Urban Racial Violence.** Most of the violence committed by blacks in the 1960s was not initiated by any organized group such as the Muslims or Panthers but rather took the form of spontaneous ghetto uprisings with little organization or planning. That these uprisings were as widespread as they were between 1964 and 1968 indicates a major change in black attitudes toward violence. Indeed, nearly every city with a sizable black population (except some in the South) experienced at least one disorder during this period, and many had several. The worst outbreaks were in Los Angeles in 1965 and Newark and Detroit in 1967. According to the U.S. National Advisory Commission on Civil Disorders (1968), however, in 1967 alone, 164 disorders took place in all parts of the country. The following year also brought widespread violence. About 125 cities experienced disorders after the assassination of Martin Luther King, Jr., in April 1968, and outbreaks of violence continued intermittently throughout the summer and early fall of that year. After 1968, the level of violence subsided, and the 1970s were quieter, with the exception of widespread outbreaks of looting and arson in New York City's minority neighborhoods during a citywide power blackout in 1977.

The riots of the 1960s were different from earlier riots in the United States in several important ways. Most previous riots involved mass fighting between whites and blacks or other minorities, nearly always starting when white mobs attacked minority group members. The main targets of the rioters were people, not property, as the mobs sought to beat and in some cases kill members of the other racial group. In the riots of the 1960s, however, the target of the rioters was mainly property, not people. The violence primarily took the form of window breaking, looting, and arson. Few whites were involved, as either victims or participants. The instances of personal violence that did occur between blacks and whites took place mainly between white police and black rioters. Resentment of the police by ghetto residents was a significant factor in the rioting of the 1960s, and many of the outbreaks began with incidents between police officers and black citizens (U.S. National Advisory Commission on Civil Disorders, 1968, Chap. 11). Most of the deaths and injuries in the disturbances resulted from police action against citizens in the riot areas. Other than the confrontations with the police, personal violence between black and white citizens was rare during the urban violence of the 1960s (see Feagin and Hahn, 1973).

Contrary to beliefs among whites at the time, there was no evidence of any national organization or conspiracy behind the riots, and most of those arrested were long-time residents of the cities where they lived (Campbell and Schuman, 1968; U.S. National Advisory Commission on Civil Disorders, 1968; Fogelson, 1971; Williams, 1975). Rioters were no more likely than similarly aged blacks to have a previous arrest record, and rather than being concentrated among the poorest blacks, participation in the disturbances occurred across the full range of income and occupational levels (Geschwender and Singer, 1968; Fogelson, 1971). Studies of a dozen of the cities with the most serious violence suggest that, on average, about ten percent of black residents participated in some active way (Fogelson, 1971; see also Fogelson and Hill, 1968).

Attitude surveys of urban black Americans indicate that the rioting had the support of far more than a tiny "riffraff" element. Research by Campbell and Schuman (1968) revealed that about a third of blacks believed that the riots helped the cause of black rights, whereas only a quarter felt that they hurt. Most of the rest either thought they both helped and hurt or thought they made no difference. The majority of ghetto residents felt that the riots had a purpose (Feagin and Hahn, 1973, p. 271). Thus, the position of the black majority appears ambivalent: The majority did not "favor" riots but did see them as resulting mainly from discrimination and unemployment (Campbell and Schuman, 1968), as having a definite purpose, and as being of at least some potential benefit. All this suggests that rioting was not created by a criminal riffraff and was not caused by militant activists. Rather, it was an outburst of protest against what was, to a great many blacks, an intolerable situation that had not been much changed by earlier, more moderate forms of protest.

It is now clear that there were some fairly major changes in the thinking of African Americans during the 1960s. Many blacks, both those who were actively involved in protest and those who were not, turned away from assimilation as a goal and toward a more pluralist model. For some, the turn was more radical; as we have seen, support for separatism increased substantially. The turn away from universal acceptance of nonviolence indicates a similar change in attitudes and behavior, although the violence committed by blacks in the 1960s and since pales in comparison to the violence directed toward blacks by whites in earlier years.

**The Reasons Behind the Changing Goals and Values of Black Americans.** There were a number of reasons for the shift away from assimilation and other changes in the 1960s. Among those most commonly mentioned are the inconsistent behavior of even progressive whites, who did not always live up to what they preached; the violent response by the white power structure to civil rights protest in the South; a growing realization that civil rights laws were not bringing real racial equality; a rejection of the culture of poverty and cultural deprivation models that had become popular among white social scientists; and the continuing influence of black nationalism in Africa. Let us examine each of these factors in greater depth.

To blacks, the behavior of whites by the 1960s did not seem to reveal a serious or consistent commitment to the kind of open opportunity that true integration of black people in American society would have required. While white supporters of civil rights were urging other white people to open up their schools and businesses to blacks and telling black people that assimilation was the answer, other whites were doing everything possible to prevent meaningful participation by black people in American society. By the mid-1960s, even the moderate policies of the federal government in support of civil rights (regarded as totally inadequate by most blacks) were under heavy attack from whites (Skolnick, 1969, p. 134). Furthermore, even whites who professed support for equal rights often did not live up to those ideals in their own behavior. A prominent example of this was the failure of the Democratic National Convention in 1964 to seat the delegation of the Mississippi Freedom Democratic party (Carmichael and Hamilton, 1967; Skolnick, 1969), an integrated delegation formed to challenge the all-white delegation of the regular party in Mississippi. Despite the self-proclaimed position of the national Democratic party against racial discrimination, it seated the all-white delegation. The only so-called compromise was an offer—viewed by most blacks as an insult—to seat two members of the challenge delegation along with the segregated regular delegation. To many black people, actions spoke louder than words, and this was a clear message that even liberal whites could not be trusted to practice what they preached.

Closely related was the widespread violence by whites against civil rights workers in the South and the inability or unwillingness of the federal government to do anything about it. As Skolnick (1969, p. 132) writes, "Freedom Riders were beaten by mobs in Montgomery; demonstrators were hosed, clubbed, and cattle-prodded in Birmingham and Selma. Throughout the South, civil rights workers, black and white, were victimized by local officials as well as by nightriders and angry crowds." In most cases, the federal government—notably the Justice Department, whose duty it is to enforce federal law—did little. Eventually, African Americans in the South and elsewhere got tired of turning the other cheek or relying on the protection of a government that was not willing to protect them.

By the mid-1960s, it was also becoming clear to many African Americans that the passage of civil rights laws was not bringing about racial equality. Black unemployment continued to run twice as high as white unemployment, and black family income remained far below that of whites. In the North especially, schools and neighborhoods remained as segregated as ever. To the poor or unemployed northern urban black, the civil rights movement of the 1950s and early 1960s had made almost no difference. Although this group had never been as involved in that movement as the black middle class and sympathetic whites, they had had their hopes raised by the promises to end discrimination and poverty that came with the civil rights movement and the Johnson administration's War on Poverty. When these hopes proved to be false, this group was deeply disillusioned. It is accordingly not surprising that militant separatist organizations such as the Muslims gained most of their support from this segment of the African American population. To the poor urban black, it did little good to integrate a lunch counter if you were unemployed and couldn't afford to buy a lunch. Leaders such as Malcolm X and groups such as the Muslims and the Black Panther Party weren't talking about integrated lunch counters; they were talking about economic survival and self-defense, and these themes had great appeal to the urban black, trapped at the bottom.

Among African American intellectuals, important changes in thinking were also taking place. It was during the early and mid-1960s that culture of poverty and cultural deprivation theories were gaining great popularity among white social scientists and intellectuals. What we have called the functionalist, or order, perspective was dominant in American social science at that time, and it seemed to offer a logical explanation of black disadvantages to the white social scientists of the era: Because of past discrimination, black Americans had never had the opportunity to develop the values, habits, and skills necessary to get ahead in American society. This seemed reasonable and not at all racist to most white social scientists, but black social scientists and intellectuals heard a different message. To them, this amounted to saying that because of their culture and attitudes, African Americans were at fault for their own disadvantages. (As we have seen, many avowedly racist whites used these theories to make exactly that argument.) Furthermore, this explanation placed the burden for change on African Americans: They had to change their ways before they could hope to enjoy the benefits of American society, even though the cause of their disadvantages, as admitted by white social scientists, was past discrimination by whites. This hardly seemed fair. Finally, all this seemed like a putdown of black culture precisely when blacks were proving their capabilities through the civil rights movement. Many African Americans felt a great need for pride in their race, and black accomplishments were becoming more visible than ever. (They had always been there but had been kept largely hidden by white society.) Nothing that seemed like an attack on the culture and accomplishments of African Americans was going to be tolerated. By the mid-1960s, assimilation to many educated blacks seemed to be a message from whites that said, "Do it our way or don't do it." This was no longer acceptable.

A final factor that led to increased emphasis on black self-help and Black Power was the continuing development of independent black nations in Africa (Skolnick, 1969, pp. 137–39). This development served as a model to blacks in the United States. Through their own efforts, African Americans could throw off the domination and influence of whites, run their own affairs, and build their own power base.

**Recent Trends in Black Attitudes and Actions: 1975 to the Present.** After the mid-1970s, the level of protest abated somewhat, but there was again a resurgence of political action by African Americans in the late 1980s and early 1990s that in large part has continued into the new century. This resurgence was also marked by a renewed shift in black opinion away from assimilationist viewpoints. In 1987, there was a major civil rights march in Forsythe County, Georgia. Just one week after a small group of marchers commemorating Dr. King's birthday was attacked by Ku Klux Klan members, more than 20,000 people from all over the United States marched peacefully through the all-white county. Around this time, a student movement to get colleges and universities to disinvest in South African spread throughout the country, and major black student protests (which received some support from white students) occurred at the University of Michigan in 1987, the University of North Carolina in 1992, and Penn State in 2001. And in 2003, students intervened in the University of Michigan affirmative action cases (discussed in Chapter 15) to insist that part of the legal argument be based on the presence of discrimination against blacks and other minorities. They organized a march on the Supreme Court that drew 50,000 participants.

The largest marches of all, however, occurred in the 1990s: the Million Man March in 1995, which drew an estimated 840,000 participants (and possibly as many as 1 million), and the Million Woman March in 1997, for which crowd estimates ranged from 300,000 to 1 million (Lorant, 1995; Camia, 1997). These marches, held in Washington and Philadelphia, respectively, were among the largest ever in the United States; indeed, the Million Man March was probably the largest gathering ever of the many that have occurred in the nation's capital. These marches were distinctly pluralist or even separatist in their orientation, with only African American men encouraged to participate in one and only African American women in the other. The organization of the Million Man March was led by Minister Louis Farrakhan of the Nation of Islam. Much of the appeal of both events was their emphasis on black pride and self-help. These events placed somewhat less emphasis on political demands than most other marches organized by African Americans and somewhat greater emphasis on self-help and self-improvement. Clearly, the participation of such large numbers of African Americans showed the broad appeal of the themes of black pride, Afrocentrism, and self-improvement.

Whereas these events were entirely peaceful, there have been intermittent violent outbreaks over the past three decades. Serious racial violence occurred in Miami in 1980 and 1989, in New York's Crown Heights neighborhood in 1991, in Cincinnati in 2001, and in Benton Harbor, Michigan, in 2003. Racial polarization also was cited as a factor in annual outbreaks of arson in Detroit around Halloween in the mid-1980s and a Mardi Gras riot in Seattle in 2001. However, the most serious violence occurred in 1992, when the acquittal of four police officers in the videotaped beating of Rodney King led to the deadliest violence of the twentieth century. More than fifty people died in Los Angeles, and serious violence spread to several other cities as well, including Atlanta, Las Vegas, San Francisco, and Seattle. These outbreaks were similar to the ghetto rebellions of the 1960s in that they involved widespread looting, vandalism, firebombing, and fighting between crowds of civilians and police. However, they differed in two important ways: First, the participants in the Los Angeles, San Francisco, and Seattle riots came from a variety of racial and ethnic backgrounds. Although the violence started in black neighborhoods, large numbers of Hispanics, substantial numbers of whites, and some Asian Americans also participated. This led one Los Angeles sociologist to comment, "This was not a race riot. It was a class riot" (Joel Kotkin, quoted in T. Mathews, 1992).

The second difference suggests that in some ways, the Los Angeles riot was a race riot. In the rebellions of the 1960s, most of the violence was directed against property and the police; few civilians were attacked. This presents a sharp contrast with the race riots earlier in the twentieth century, which involved mass attacks by whites against blacks and other minorities and sometimes retaliatory attacks by the minority groups. Research by McPhail (1994) indicates that in the Miami riot of 1980 and the Los Angeles riot of 1992, something of a move back toward the earlier pattern took place, although this time most of the crowd violence was committed by minority group members. In Miami and Los Angeles, the percentage of deaths caused by crowd attacks against civilians was much higher than in the 1960s, although not as high as in the earlier race riots. This suggests that the violence of the 1980s and 1990s was targeted against civilians to a greater extent than in the riots of the 1960s, and much of this violence appears to have been racially motivated. An example is the videotaped beating of a white truck driver, Reginald Denny. However, it is important to point out that although he was severely beaten by African Americans, he was also rescued by other African Americans, who intervened to stop the violence.

Although both violent and nonviolent protest increased again in the 1990s, the most important political trend among African Americans in the past three decades appears to be increased political action through the ballot box. By 1986, four of the country's largest cities had black mayors, and by 1993, nearly all of the country's largest cities had at some time elected a black mayor. The 1980s and 1990s brought the election of the first African American governor in any state (Douglas Wilder in Virginia) and the first African American female U.S. senator (Carol Moseley Braun of Illinois). Jesse Jackson ran for the Democratic nomination for the presidency in 1984 and again in 1988, receiving as much as 95 percent of the black vote in some areas (Walton, 1985, p. 107). In 1988, he outlasted all but one of his white opponents, finished second in the delegate count, and won in a number of states through a combination of overwhelming black support and, in some states, a substantial part of the white vote (Farley, 1990). Both the Jackson campaign and some of the local campaigns brought blacks to the ballot box as never before. The black turnout in the 1984 primaries was a record, and in some mayoral elections involving black candidates in the last decade, black voter turnout has exceeded white turnout, reversing the historical pattern. The continued interest in black candidates among black voters can be seen in early polls for the 2004 presidential election, when 38 percent of the black Democrats (compared with just 4 percent of white Democrats) supported one of the two black candidates, Al Sharpton or Carol Moseley Braun, in a June 2003 Gallup poll (Gallup Organization, 2003c).

The increased tendency of black voters to support black candidates and to vote in greater numbers when there is a black candidate are only two indications that the attitudes of African Americans today in recent years have remained less assimilationist than in the past. The massive turnouts for the Million Man March and the Million Woman March suggest the same thing. This view is confirmed by studies of black public opinion. Surveys of black intellectuals showed that by the 1980s, they were deemphasizing such issues as school desegregation and placing greater emphasis on what could be called Black Power, even though they did not use that specific term. Concerns included more black elected officials, more black-owned businesses, greater black political control, and greater support for predominantly black schools (Conyers, 1986). A series of surveys in the mid- and late 1980s of African American students in black American studies courses at Southern Illinois University at Carbondale revealed similar trends (Tripp, 1992). For example, the surveys showed increased support for a black political party and for the idea of working to build "a separate black nation." The survey also showed that between 1984 and 1989 there was a shift away from the view that through reform, American society could accommodate the demands of black people for racial justice and equality. Instead, the view that the only real alternative for blacks is radical change became more common. The percentage favoring the reform option fell from 64 percent to 38 percent, and the percentage favoring a concerted effort for radical change rose from 36 percent to 62 percent.

The trend in the attitudes of black college students apparently mirrors that of the larger society. The 1993–1994 Black Politics Study, conducted by University of Chicago researchers, showed a sharp increase in support of black nationalism between 1988 and 1994. By 1994, about half the black population supported an independent black political party, which was the highest level ever observed in surveys (Michael Dawson, quoted in Strong, 1994). Why? Many blacks perceived that the mood and temper of the country were such that efforts at integration could not bring about true acceptance or social equality. Thus, growing numbers of blacks turned to black nationalist ideologies and separatist ideas in the early 1990s.

More recent evidence suggests this trend may have peaked in the early 1990s, following the Rodney King case in Los Angeles. A series of Gallup surveys (Gallup Organization, 2003a) found trends of falling optimism about race relations among blacks between 1980 and 1992, followed by increased optimism again between 1992 and 2003. The percentage that felt that the quality of life for blacks had gotten better in the last ten years fell from 54 percent in 1980 to just 15 percent in 1992, after the trial for the police beating of Rodney King. It rose again to 33 percent in 1997 and 49 percent in 2003—still lower than in 1980. Even so, in 2003 African Americans remained just half as likely as whites to say that that civil rights for blacks had "greatly improved" in their lifetimes. And in some areas, blacks remain distinctly pessimistic, with the percentage saying that black children have the same chance for a good education as white children reaching a forty-year low in 2003 (H. Mason, 2003). Also feeding pessimism was a widespread perception among African Americans that the result of the 2000 presidential election was unfair and that (as was in fact the case) black voters were less likely to have their votes counted in the disputed Florida results than white voters (Simmons, 2000).

An important contemporary movement that reflects a more nationalist viewpoint is **Afrocentrism**, an effort by African Americans to emphasize African history, philosophy, and culture, particularly but not only in education. Afrocentrism received strong backing from a number of leading black intellectuals in the early 1990s and has become a model for curricula in predominantly black schools in many parts of the country. It represents a rebellion against the Eurocentric aspects of much of American culture and education, with its emphasis primarily on the culture, philosophy, and history of Europeans and people of European ancestry. Those who favor Afrocentrism see Eurocentrism as both destructive to the collective self-image of African Americans (by sending a message that only that which is European is worthy of serious study) and irrelevant to peoples of African ancestry. (Afrocentrism as an educational movement is explored further in Chapter 12.) The emergence of Afrocentrism in the 1990s is one more indication that pluralist and separatist strains of thinking are once again gaining influence among African Americans.

In reviewing trends such as these, it is important not to get the impression that assimilationist or integrationist viewpoints hold no sway among African Americans today. In fact, public opinion polls show clearly that most blacks recognize the need to get along with and interact with whites and want to do so (Kilson and Cottingham, 1991). Moreover, most African Americans continue to favor neighborhood

One area in which the trend toward cultural pluralism since the 1960s is evident is in dress and hairstyles. Observe the African influence on the dress of this African American family celebrating Kwanzaa.

integration, oppose the idea that blacks should always vote for black candidates, and do not object to interracial dating (Kilson and Cottingham, 1991; Gallup Organization, 1997). Thus, in many ways blacks continue to support integration to a greater extent than whites. Nonetheless, a substantial proportion of blacks oppose these positions and instead support such ideas as learning an African language and patronizing black-owned businesses whenever possible. Thus, African American attitudes today, as in the past, reflect a mix of integrationist, pluralist, and separatist ideas.

The resurgence of nationalist thinking in the early 1990s led to an increased following for black leaders who express militant or separatist themes, such as the Reverend Al Sharpton of New York City and Nation of Islam minister Louis Farrakhan. In the mid-1980s, there was a split in the Black Muslim movement between Farrakhan's Nation of Islam and another segment of the movement led by Elijah Muhammad's son Warif, who adopted the beliefs of orthodox Islam and opened his group's membership to people of all races. Under Farrakhan's leadership, the Nation of Islam enjoyed a resurgence in the late 1980s and 1990s. Although Farrakhan was at times criticized for being antiwhite and anti-Semitic, he also gained recognition as the most outspoken advocate of black pride, black power, and black self-help in the 1980s (*New York Times*, 1985). For this reason, his movement gained a large following in big-city ghettos around the country, and his appearances reliably packed large arenas in major cities with sizable African American populations.

Farrakhan's influence reached an even higher level with his successful organization of the Million Man March in 1995. As noted, this was the largest public gathering ever to occur in the nation's capital. It expressed a distinctly separatist theme in that only African American men were encouraged to participate. It also highlighted another ongoing discussion in the African American community: To what extent should African Americans strive for changes in public policy rather than self-improvement? Although Farrakhan was and is intensely critical of U.S. public policy and social institutions, self-help is also a major theme in his speeches and was a major focus of the Million Man March. Significantly, in the Gallup survey of African Americans in 1997, 54 percent said that blacks should focus more on improving themselves, and 31 percent said they should focus more on changing the system.

This is a continuation of a discussion that dates back to debates between W. E. B. DuBois and Booker T. Washington early in the twentieth century. Although he remained an influential figure, Farrakhan made fewer public appearances after about 2000 because of medical problems.

Another leader expressing a separatist theme is Marcus Garvey, Jr., who spoke on numerous college campuses in the 1990s, repeating his father's emphasis on the African roots and heritage of black Americans, whom he calls Africans in the United States. The increased use of the term *African American* as an alternative to *black* in recent years reflects similar thinking. In a 2003 Gallup poll, most blacks did not indicate a strong preference for either *black* or *African American*, although more preferred *African American*, and these two terms were heavily preferred over any other (Gallup Organization, 2004).

Farrakhan, Garvey, and others have placed considerable emphasis in recent years on the themes of Malcolm X in the 1960s: African Americans cannot and should not count on whites or anyone else to take steps that will lead to the betterment of the black community. This can be accomplished only by blacks, taking control of their own destiny by building their own institutions and power structure. For example, Farrakhan and the Nation of Islam argue that only by creating their own separate state can African Americans grow and prosper to the fullest extent (Nation of Islam, 1998). Although leaders with this particular viewpoint clearly do not have the unqualified support of the black community, it is clear that this general viewpoint has substantial support, even among the majority of African Americans who do not entirely reject the concept of integration and who favor trying to get along with whites whenever possible. In summary, it is fair to say that assimilationist, pluralist, and separatist tendencies are all present to some extent in current African American thought, as has been the case for the past century, although the emphasis has shifted back and forth over time. It also seems accurate to say that today the need for an independent black political and economic base is being emphasized by a significant number of African Americans.

## Pluralism and Militancy Among Chicanos, Latinos, and American Indians

In the 1960s, Mexican Americans also turned away from assimilation as a goal and began to emphasize such concepts as self-defense and building an independent power base. *Chicanismo*—pride in Chicano culture and heritage and a struggle to combat forced assimilation—became a widespread ideology, particularly among younger Mexican Americans. There was growing emphasis during this period on preserving the Spanish language and unique Chicano dialects that mixed Spanish and English. One manifestation of this trend was the demand for bilingual education, not only as a way of helping Chicano children to speak English but also as a way to ensure the preservation of the Spanish language among young Mexican Americans.

Important changes also occurred in the 1960s in the tactics used by the Chicano movement. In the early 1960s, Chicano political involvement was marked by the Viva Kennedy movement, which was basically an effort to get Chicanos involved in the traditional American political process, which they have always shunned to some degree. This effort often is credited with carrying the crucial state of Texas for the Kennedy-Johnson ticket in 1960 (Acuña, 1972, p. 223). In the mid-1960s, Cesar Chavez's use of Gandhian nonviolence to unionize Mexican American and Filipino farm workers was probably the most widely known effort of the Chicano movement. Though a more direct challenge to the system than the earlier voter registration efforts, Chavez's movement retained a belief that Chicanos could be integrated into basic American institutions, in this case the labor movement. Today, voter registration and voter turnout efforts and the United Farm Workers (UFW) remain important parts of Mexican American political involvement. For example, the UFW succeeded in unionizing a sizable portion of California's agricultural labor force and led to significant improvements in wages and working conditions for Chicano farm workers. It has continued to win new labor contracts for farm workers, and in 2002, succeeded in passing legislation strengthening California's Agriculture Labor Relations Act by requiring growers to bargain in good faith or face binding arbitration.

Nonetheless, by the late 1960s, many Chicanos were starting to turn away from traditional electoral participation and Gandhian nonviolence. The year 1967 saw the formation of the Brown Berets, a group stressing militant self-defense tactics similar to those of the Black Panthers. A number of militant Chicano student groups were also formed in that and subsequent years (Moore and Pachon, 1976, p. 151). The imagination of younger Chicanos was captured by the militant actions of Reies Tijerina in New Mexico (see Chapter 6). By the late 1960s, younger Chicanos in particular had given up on integration and sought to build an independent Chicano power base. At least some felt that violence or the threat of violence was the only way to get the Anglo power structure to take the demands of Chicanos seriously. The turn away from assimilationist tendencies could also be seen in the formation of a Chicano political party, La Raza Unida. This party won control of the school board and city council in Crystal City, Texas, and other nearby communities in 1970 and captured about 6 percent of the vote for governor in Texas in 1972 (Acuña, 1972, p. 236; Moore and Pachon, 1976, p. 153). The party was also on the ballot in Colorado in 1970.

Several factors contributed to these changes in attitudes. A very important one was the development of the Black Power movement during this period. It provided a role model, illustrated that legal equality did not guarantee social equality, and "legitimized an ideology that rejected assimilation and fixed the blame on the larger society" for racial inequality (Moore and Pachon, 1976, p. 49). In addition, it demonstrated that blacks could at least get attention and promises by rioting, which at the time was more than Chicanos were getting. In addition to the Black Power movement, the antiwar movement and the general atmosphere of protest and rebellion helped to produce a situation conducive to a militant Chicano protest movement. The Chicano movement represented a response to the failure of assimilation, as did the Black Power movement. However, the frustrations of Chicanos may have even been greater than those of blacks. The promises of the Kennedy and Johnson administrations and the War on Poverty had led to raised expectations, but Chicanos soon learned that the government bureaucrats for the most part thought of poverty and intergroup relations in terms of blacks and whites. Chicanos were almost entirely forgotten in the early stages of the War on Poverty, and this proved an important stimulus for the militant Chicano movement (Acuña, 1972, pp. 226–27).

Today, the ideology of Chicanismo continues to influence Mexican Americans, as seen in the continuing use of the Spanish language in the home by many Chicanos (Pachon and Moore, 1981) and widespread support for bilingual education, partly as a means of teaching English to non–English speakers but also partly to preserve Hispanic culture. For example, Latino advocacy groups such as the National Council of La Raza and the Puerto Rican organization Aspira have continued into the 1990s to support bilingual education on the grounds that they enhance Latino culture, bolster self-esteem among Latino students, and offset the Eurocentric focus of many schools (R. P. Porter, 1991).

Bilingual education spread rapidly in the 1970s, and despite some efforts by the Reagan administration to curtail it in the 1980s, it remained quite widespread through the mid-1990s. However, it came under unprecedented attack in 1998 with the passage, by a margin of 61 to 39 percent, of Proposition 227 in California. This ballot proposition abolished bilingual education in favor of an English immersion approach, providing a year of intensive instruction in English and then a transition into regular classrooms. National survey data in 1998 showed that public opinion on the issue mirrored the California vote (F. Newport, 1998), but by 2003, national public opinion supported bilingual education by a margin of 58 to 40 percent (Gallup Organization, 2003a). In California, there was also strong opposition among Chicano voters to eliminating bilingual education. Both Mexican Americans and college students (of a variety of ethnic backgrounds) were very active in the opposition to Proposition 227. (The issue of bilingual education is discussed further in Chapter 12.)

According to Pachon and Moore (1981), three factors tend to promote cultural pluralism among Hispanic Americans: proximity to the homeland (Mexico or Puerto Rico, for most), the recent general emphasis among American racial and ethnic groups on cultural identity, and bilingual education. (As noted, however, bilingual education came under increasing attack in the 1990s and was eliminated in some areas.) Two other factors might be added. First, Hispanic Americans are very geographically concentrated: Most live in just five states. Second, the proportion of Spanish-speaking people among current immigrants is larger than the proportion of immigrants speaking any one language at any time in our history (Domestic Policy Association, 1986). Both of these facts make it easier for Hispanics than for past immigrants to maintain their culture.

Although Hispanics continue to maintain their culture, recent surveys suggest that they are fairly optimistic about their opportunities in the United States. For example, in a 2003 Gallup poll, 70 percent of Hispanics believed that the quality of life for Hispanics has improved over the past 10 years (Gallup Organization, 2003a). In fact, more Hispanics believed this than either whites or blacks. Nearly 85 percent of Hispanics described relations between whites and Hispanics as somewhat or very good. (About 80 percent of both blacks and Hispanics said the same about relations between blacks and Hispanics.) Support for integration and good relationships with other groups are also strong among Latinos. One example can be seen in a recent survey on teenage interracial dating: Hispanic teens were more likely than whites, blacks, or Asians to date people outside their own ethnic group, even as interracial and interethnic dating became more common among all groups (K. Peterson, 1997). Despite these generally positive responses, the 2003 Gallup poll showed that Hispanics were about evenly split on whether they were satisfied or dissatisfied with treatment of Hispanics in the United States.

An important new development in recent decades is the emergence of what Padilla (1985) has called *Latino ethnic consciousness*. This trend represents a move toward common identification among different Latino or Hispanic groups, particularly Mexican Americans and Puerto Ricans. Padilla sees this trend as partly the result of political necessity. Even combined, the various Hispanic or Latino groups make up only about 14 percent of the population, even though their numbers are growing and they are now the nation's largest minority group. Still, they are a numerical minority, even in places such as Chicago, where there are large populations of both Chicanos and Puerto Ricans. For a group (or set of groups) this size, Padilla argues, unity is essential, and he presents strong evidence that there was an increasing common identity among various Latino groups in the 1970s, at least in Chicago, where he conducted his study.

As has been the case with African Americans, activism among Chicanos appears to have increased in the 1990s. In 1993, a series of protests, including an extended hunger fast by a number of students and faculty, as well as rallies and sit-ins, sought the establishment of a department of Chicano studies at the University of California at Los Angeles. Hunger fasts by Chicano students spread to a number of other college campuses during the 1993–1994 school year. The UFW undertook a number of new campaigns in the 1990s and 2000s, resulting in the new contracts and legislation mentioned earlier. Cesar Chavez died in 1993 and was succeeded as president of the UFW by Arturo Rodriguez. He used techniques of nonviolent protest similar to those of Chavez to gain passage of the 2002 legislation, including marches on the state capital in Sacramento.

Other data support the impression of increased activism in the 1990s. For example, voter turnout increased sharply. The proportion of actual voters who were

United Farm Workers president Arturo Rodriguez leads a march to Sacramento in 2002 in support of legislation requiring employers of farm workers to bargain in good faith or face binding arbitration.

Hispanic rose from 2 percent in 1992 to 5 percent in 1996 and 1998 (Powell, 1998; Powell and Helm, 1998). Hispanic votes, which a 1998 poll showed to be shifting toward the Democrats, were a major reason that President Clinton, in 1996, became the first Democratic presidential candidate to carry Arizona since 1948 and the first to win Florida since 1976. The 1998 poll of Hispanics, commissioned by the Hispanic TV broadcaster Univision, also showed strong support among Latinos for affirmative action in employment and higher education and for bilingual education. However, more recent polls suggest some shift toward the Republican party, and in 2003, President Bush enjoyed levels of support among the Hispanic population that were about three-fourths of those among the white population.

As is the case with the African American community, a wide range of opinions exists among Hispanic Americans, all the more so because of the ethnic diversity within the broad Hispanic category. On economic issues and international policy, for example, Cuban Americans have tended to be much more conservative and thus more likely to support Republicans than other Latinos. They were probably crucial in the 2000 election; without them, Florida probably would have been clearly in the Gore column. A survey showed that Latinos in Texas (who are mostly Mexican Americans) were more likely to perceive that they had equal job opportunities than Latinos in other states (Tomas Rivera Center, 1998). This may be one reason why a large minority of Texas Chicano voters supported Republican George W. Bush for election as governor in 1998 and for president in 2000, despite the overall tendency of Hispanics to support Democrats (Powell, 1998).

Finally, to a greater extent than other groups, Hispanics seem to accept some negative stereotypes of their own group and engage in some self-blame. For example, a poll showed that Latinos were more likely than Anglos to attribute their problems to "lack of motivation and an unwillingness to work hard" and to the breakup of the Hispanic family. This is true even though actual statistics show that Hispanics have an above-average level of participation in the work force (Constable, 1995).

Among Native Americans, the picture is somewhat different. Indian people never sought assimilation to the degree that blacks or Mexican Americans did, so a turn away from assimilation was not possible. However, important changes did occur in the 1960s and early 1970s. The most important was the upsurge in protest, which had been rare among Native Americans until the late 1960s. By 1970, Indian people had become much more involved in protest, and much of it took on a very militant tone. From the beginning, the protest was largely separatist in nature, as Indian people reasserted land claims and their historic status as independent nations. Thus, the thrust of Indian protest since the 1960s has been mainly the return of Indian land and the reassertion of treaty and fishing rights, not the elimination of barriers to participation in American society. As with the other groups, militant protest has had the greatest appeal among younger Indians. Also as with other groups, urbanization (even though it was less extensive for Native Americans than for other groups) appears to have contributed to the protest, in part by allowing Indians from different tribal backgrounds to come together and form a common American Indian consciousness (J. Nagel, 1995).

Throughout much of the 1970s, both legal means, such as lawsuits demanding the enforcement of old treaties, and illegal means, such as occupations of land and buildings (discussed previously), were used. Although these actions did not result in the return of large land areas, Indians had some important successes. For example, there have been some large cash settlements in lieu of land claims, and historic Indian fishing rights have been reestablished in a number of states, despite strong opposition from sport fishers and state fish and game departments. Among the broader Indian population, a reemphasis of traditional culture emerged in the 1970s. By the early 1980s, nearly every tribe was making strong efforts to teach its younger generation its language, crafts, skills, and tribal history. This cultural revival included urban Indians, too: By the early 1980s, nearly every city with a sizable Native American population had an Indian center offering cultural and recreational activities (Deloria, 1981). These efforts have continued to the present. And AIM membership continued to grow, to the point that by the early 1990s AIM existed in some form in almost every native community in North America (Churchill, 1994, p. 99).

An issue receiving new emphasis by all minority groups today, but particularly by Native Americans, is **environmental racism**. This term, coined in 1983 by Benjamin Chavis, president of the NAACP in the early 1990s, refers to the tendency for people of color to be placed at particular risk of suffering the harmful effects of environmental contaminants. We have already seen an example of this in the high incidence of cancer among Chicano farm workers and their families, which apparently results from exposure to dangerous pesticides. For Native Americans, a major issue has been the disposal of radioactive and other hazardous wastes on Indian reservations. In many cases, government agencies and waste disposal companies that have encountered opposition elsewhere have sought to take advantage of the poverty of the reservations by offering tribal councils large sums of money in exchange for disposal of this waste on reservations. Another issue related to environmental racism has centered around the actions of mining and oil corporations on Indian reservations, which often threaten the environment and destroy the traditional economic base of Indian tribes, such as the wild rice harvest, spearfishing, and agriculture.

These issues have generated considerable controversy and a strong movement against environmental racism on a number of reservations. In many cases, tribal councils have rejected monetary offers from waste disposal, mining, or oil companies; in other cases, their acceptance has led to deep divisions. And in still other cases, strong movements involving coalitions of Native Americans and environmentalists have prevented the establishment of mining or oil operations (Gedicks, 1993, 2001).

Other issues in recent years include the use of Indians as team mascots, the abuse of Indian burial grounds and remains, and the often careless imitation of Native American religious rituals by non-Indians. Most Native Americans regard

A key issue among Native American activists in recent years has been the disturbance of burial grounds for construction or research.

Indian-like team mascots as highly degrading, along with such behaviors as the "tomahawk chop," which Indian people see as mocking their culture and traditions. Ward Churchill (1994) shows striking similarities between the appearance of the Cleveland Indians mascot and caricatures used in Germany in the 1930s to degrade Jews. He points out how silly it would sound to call a team the Blacks, Whites, Jews, or Hispanics, yet many teams are called the Indians, Redskins, or Braves. In response to these concerns, more than 170 schools, colleges, and universities have eliminated Indian symbols, nicknames, or mascots (American Indian Sports Team Mascots, 2003). Among the colleges and universities that have eliminated such symbols are Dartmouth, Marquette, Stanford, Syracuse, Eastern Michigan, and Eastern Washington Universities, and Miami University of Ohio. Others, however, such as the Universities of North Dakota and Illinois and Florida State University, have resisted strong pressures for change.

With respect to burial grounds, Native American activists ask non-Indians how they would feel if their great-grandparents' bones were dug up and put in a display case for people to look at. Protests in recent years have largely curtailed this practice, although as recently as June 1994, ground containing Indian bones was dug up and used as fill for construction of a freeway in Illinois after state archeologists said the bones were "of no archeological significance."

Although the civil rights and Black Power movements played an important role in stimulating protest among American Indians (see Day, 1972), the distinctive history of the Indian people also made a difference. The resistance among Indians to forced assimilation probably helps to explain why, although protest was slower to come to Indians than to some other groups, it was more militant and separatist from the start.

## Discrimination and Rising Group Consciousness: Arab Americans

A group that has received increased attention, and undoubtedly grown in collective consciousness, in recent decades is Arab Americans. Like Hispanics and American Indians, Arab Americans are not one group but many: They come from many different countries, including Lebanon, Syria, Egypt, the Palestinian territories, Jordan, and some parts of the Persian Gulf region. However, like Hispanics and American Indians, Arab Americans have been largely treated by the rest of American society as one group, and they have encountered growing amounts of discrimination and hate crime. Although Arab Americans have long been stereotyped negatively (Shaheen, 1984, 2001), discrimination, stereotyping, and hate crimes against Arab Americans have increased as a result of conflicts in the Middle East and the September 11, 2001, terrorist attacks.

In the year after the September 11, 2001, terrorist attacks, there was a 1,600 percent increase in hate crimes against Arab Americans according to the Federal Bureau of Investigation (2002). In addition, there were numerous reports of racial profiling by airlines aimed against Arabs and Arab Americans, based on a stereotype that if a person is Arab, he or she must be dangerous. Although racial profiling is discussed in greater detail in later chapters, the core issue is the same for Arab Americans as it is for black or Hispanic Americans: It is discrimination to assume that someone is going to commit a crime based on their race or ethnicity.

In the case of Arab Americans, we can add two points. First, although the September 11 terrorists were Islamic extremists, such a viewpoint cannot be generalized to all Muslims, most of whom are peace-loving and law-abiding. To do so would be the same as to assume that all Christians are like Eric Rudolph, the Christian fundamentalist extremist who has been charged with bombing the Atlanta Olympics, a gay bar, and two health care clinics where abortions are performed. Second, the majority of Arab Americans are not Muslim. Rather, the majority are Christian (*Detroit Free Press*, 2001). The double fallacy of equating all Muslims with terrorists and viewing all Arabs as Muslims comes down to one word: *discrimination*.

The American-Arab Anti-Discrimination Committee notes an irony: In an age when discrimination against most groups seems to be decreasing, it is increasing against Arab Americans.

This discrimination has created heightened collective consciousness among Arab Americans, as evidenced by the growth of organizations such as the American-Arab Anti-Discrimination Committee. It has also led Americans of various Arab national ancestries, such as Lebanese, Egyptian, Syrian, and Palestinian, to give greater emphasis to their common Arab ethnicity. For example, they have increasingly adopted cultural symbols such as clothing. The veil worn by some women is not an Arab symbol but an Islamic one, and not all Muslim women wear it. But for those who do, many see it as a symbol of religious veneration, whereas others see it as promoting modesty or as a feminist symbol that rejects the objectification of women (Nichols, 2001; Walker, 2001). Although its origins are religious, it has also come to have a more secular meaning in recent years, representing to some who wear it a symbol of independence and nationalism and rejection of colonialism. Among men, the checkered garment sometimes worn on the head, called a *kafiyyeh*, is worn as a cultural symbol, not a religious one. It is worn as a symbol of ethnic pride, much like the African dress that has become popular among some African Americans. While it is true that the need to unify in the face of discrimination has brought greater cultural awareness to Arab and Muslim Amercans in recent years, it is also true that discrimination has made their lives more difficult.

## The "Ethnic Revival" Among White Americans

White ethnic groups also placed renewed emphasis on ethnicity beginning around the late 1960s. Much has been written about the "ethnic revival" among various white ethnic groups. There is much debate over its nature and extent, but it seems clear that outwardly, at least, Americans from a wide variety of groups have emphasized ethnicity and ethnic culture to a greater extent in recent decades. This can be seen in the proliferation of ethnic festivals, the celebration of ethnic holidays, and so on. Much debate also centers on whether the change is superficial; relatively few participants (but some, nonetheless) have learned the language of their ethnic place of origin, for example. There is also debate over whether the changes were really based on ethnicity or whether they mainly reflected social class (Gans, 1974, pp. xi, xii). The ethnic revival in the 1960s and 1970s was most notable among Catholic, Jewish, eastern European, and predominantly working-class groups, and it often took on political overtones.

In two ways, these changes seem to have grown out of the Black Power movement. First, this movement served as a role model. It showed all other groups that racial or ethnic group consciousness is a way of getting the political system to listen to their collective concerns. Second, many white ethnic groups, especially in the working class and lower middle class, perceived blacks' gains as a threat: They believed that any gains made by blacks would come at their expense, not at the expense of those with higher socioeconomic status (Goering, 1971; Novak, 1971; Rieder, 1985). There was some basis in reality for this perception. Rarely were middle-class, suburban white children bused, and rarely were middle-class neighborhoods blockbusted. Unfortunately, the anger of working-class white ethnics was sometimes turned against blacks and the gains they made rather than against the larger power structure (see Ransford, 1972).

Thus, it is ironic that a trend that is in part a product of the Black Power movement became a threat to the position of blacks. Indeed, this group has vigorously opposed such programs as affirmative action and bilingual education (Kluegel and Smith, 1986; Lipset, 1992), significantly backing efforts by the Reagan and both Bush administrations to reverse these policies and supporting California referenda in the 1990s opposing affirmative action, bilingual education, and welfare benefits for children of illegal immigrants. Nonetheless, some observers such as Novak

(1971) argue that the dominant thrust of the white ethnic movement was against a power structure that had ignored the concerns of working-class white ethnics. Perceptions that the power structure pays more attention to "minority" issues than to concerns of the white working class were and are a major source of resentment among white ethnics. Issues such as these suggest that the "ethnic revival" was partly a social class phenomenon and partly a matter of ethnic solidarity.

Another school of thought suggests that the ethnic revival of the 1970s is not entirely an outgrowth of the Black Power movement but rather partly a result of the length of time that some ethnic groups have been in the United States. Marcus L. Hansen (1952, 1966) developed a theory that an ethnic revival typically occurs in the third generation. The second generation tries to get rid of all trappings of the ethnic background of its parents and to become fully assimilated. The third generation, generally more socially and economically secure, wants to rediscover its ethnic culture and heritage. Hansen based his theory partly on his observations of Swedish Americans. Studies of other groups (see Sandberg, 1974; Abramson, 1975) call into question the universality of a third-generation ethnic revival, although Greeley (1971) sees the ethnic revival of the 1970s as largely an affirmation of Hansen's third-generation hypothesis. According to Greeley, the fact that many white ethnic groups had become more secure and affluent than they were in earlier years enabled them to assert their ethnicity and investigate their origins. (Concerning the increased affluence of white ethnic groups, see also Greeley, 1974.)

Although there is debate about its degree (see Gans, 1974, 1979), there is little doubt that there was a revived interest in ethnicity and group culture in the late 1960s and the 1970s. This was true for virtually every racial, ethnic, and cultural group in America, and it has had lasting cultural effects. The blank in the statement, "I'm _____ and proud" could be filled in with *black, Chicano, Indian, Polish, German, Italian, Greek, Arab, Muslim, Irish, Jewish,* or numerous other labels. It could even go beyond ethnic groups and read *female, gay,* or perhaps *physically challenged.* The extent and meaning of the change may be debatable, but there can be little doubt that cultural pluralism became very fashionable in the United States in the late 1960s and early 1970s and, to a large extent, has remained so since.

## *Summary and Conclusion*

In this chapter, we have seen that cultural assimilation has been the dominant mode of adaptation for racial and ethnic minority groups in American society. The dominant group has always demanded it, and for the most part minorities have gone along with it, although there have been notable cases of resistance. In the early stages of the black civil rights movement—which brought political action by blacks on an unprecedented scale in the 1950s and 1960s—the movement's goals were largely assimilationist. As some of those goals proved elusive, a shift toward more pluralist thinking emerged. Moreover, assimilation in American society has never been complete, particularly at the structural, as opposed to the cultural, level. Indeed, substantial structural pluralism has been maintained even when cultural assimilation has been quite general. Thus, the ideology of Anglo conformity probably has led many to believe that America has been more of a melting pot than in fact it ever was. A noticeable shift away from cultural assimilation toward cultural pluralism has taken place since the 1960s. An important stimulus for this shift was the Black Power movement, which was at least partly the result of the failure of the assimilationist efforts of the civil rights movement to bring equality for black Americans. In the 1980s and 1990s, diversity of attitudes among people of color became more evident, in part because they had become more numerous, more educated, and more diverse in social class.

We have also seen that assimilation occurs less readily for exploited minorities of the colonized type (Blauner, 1972) than for immigrant minorities. In the United

States, this has meant that African Americans, Hispanic Americans, and Native Americans have experienced less cultural and structural assimilation than have immigrant groups from Europe such as Irish Americans, German Americans, and Polish Americans. As a general rule, racial minorities are also assimilated less easily than ethnic ones because their distinct appearance makes discrimination easier. Both these factors suggest that a big reason blacks, Hispanics, and Indians have never been fully integrated into American society is that many whites have not wanted or permitted them to participate as equals. Another reason for a lack of assimilation is that colonized groups are likely to perceive the dominant group as an oppressor and for that reason to resist its culture. Colonized groups have also seen that group consciousness can build an important base for political power.

Other factors not mentioned in this chapter (but discussed elsewhere; see Chapter 8) affect the likelihood of assimilation or pluralism. For example, cultural and structural assimilation are less likely when a minority group is relatively large than when it is very small. A large group is both more likely to be perceived as a threat (and thereby resisted by the dominant group) and more capable of reinforcing and preserving its own culture. In the long run, however, this factor is probably less important than others: Irish Americans and German Americans are both more numerous and more assimilated than the typical ethnic group in America. A final factor is proximity to one's homeland. Groups that live near or on their homeland are generally more able to maintain their group culture than groups who are very distant. In the United States, the two minorities living on or near their homeland are American Indians and Chicanos. It is striking that these are probably the two groups that have preserved their group cultures and institutions to the greatest degree in the United States.

America has been marked by substantial elements of both assimilation and pluralism. Separatist movements have occurred and exist today, but separation in the strict sense of choosing to live in separate territories has never enjoyed the support of the majority of blacks or other people of color. Whereas cultural assimilation mixed with structural pluralism has been the norm, there have been important variations both from time to time and from group to group. The consequences of these shifts continue to be debated. Functionalist theorists see a serious threat to national unity in pluralism and therefore urge assimilation and consensus (see Thernstrom, 1980). Conflict theorists, on the other hand, see potential for a fairer power balance if pluralism can enhance the power base of such minorities as blacks, Chicanos, and Indians. They worry, however, that racial divisions could play the white and minority working classes against one another, thus enhancing the power of the elite. (For further discussion of assimilation and pluralism in the United States, see Abramson, 1980.)

## *Critical Review Questions*

1. Choose one or more of the following, and explain how it contributed to social movements against racial or ethnic inequality during the period from around 1955 to 1970: urbanization, economic expansion, mass communications, rising educational levels.

2. Why, after about 1965, did social movements among African Americans shift away from an emphasis on integration and assimilation toward an emphasis on pluralism, power, and in some cases, separatism?

3. What is *environmental racism*? How does this concept apply to the experiences of Native Americans? To the experiences of African Americans?

4. What trends have occurred recently in the attitudes of minority group members regarding assimilation, pluralism, and separatism? What might account for these trends?

# Overview

In the previous three chapters, we have examined the changing patterns of majority-minority relations over the history of the United States and the earlier British colonies, and we have identified a number of basic principles. By studying different periods of American history, we have seen some of the conditions that have led to racial or ethnic inequality, and we have seen that the form of inequality varies with the social and economic conditions at the time. However, there is a limit to how much we can learn by looking only at American history. American society and, consequently, American race relations have been very different at different times, but we are still talking about one society. In a world with thousands of different societies, large and small, there are all kinds of social conditions that have never been seen in the United States. To fully understand the dynamics of race and ethnic relations, we must see them in a wide range of social and cultural settings. In this chapter, we plan to (1) use international evidence to further test and refine major principles already identified in earlier chapters and (2) use cross-cultural comparisons to identify additional principles about the dynamics of majority-minority relations.

## ▶ CROSS-CULTURAL EVIDENCE ON THE EFFECTS OF COLONIZATION

One principle we have identified in American race relations is that the racial or ethnic groups that have experienced the greatest disadvantages and that have had the greatest conflict with the majority are those whose initial entry into American society was through conquest or colonization. This would seem to suggest that one very important cause of both racial and ethnic stratification and conflict is the conquest or colonization of one group by another. At least, that is what U.S. history suggests. But is it true throughout the world?

Consider for a moment the racial or ethnic conflicts you have read or heard about. Among the best known are those between blacks and whites in South Africa; between Catholics and Protestants in Northern Ireland; between English speakers and French speakers in Quebec, Canada; among various groups in the former Soviet Union; among Serbs, Croats, Albanians, and Bosnians in the former Yugoslavia; between Arabs (particularly Palestinian Arabs) and Jews in the Middle East; and between Hindus and Muslims in India and Pakistan. These groups and societies vary tremendously, but if we examine the situation closely, we find one common denominator: In each place, the intergroup conflict can be traced back to the colonization or conquest of one racial or ethnic group by another.

## South Africa

No other nation in recent world history has been known for a system of racial inequality as rigid as that which existed in South Africa until the early 1990s. By law, South Africans were classified as black, white, Asian, or colored (that is, a mixture of black and white). Until the early 1990s, South African law attached to these racial categories specified rights and restrictions affecting all aspects of life. In the 1980s and early 1990s, most restrictions were gradually repealed, but until 1994 the right to vote and hold office were denied to blacks, who constitute more than two-thirds of South Africa's population. An agreement was reached in mid-1993 to extend these rights to blacks, and the country's first nonracial elections were held on April 27, 1994. Nelson Mandela was elected South Africa's first black president, under the banner of the African National Congress (ANC) party. The election of a black president and a black majority parliament in a free election in which all could vote represented a dramatic turnaround for a country in which the right to vote had been systematically denied to the black majority throughout its history. However, the challenging task of undoing decades of institutionalized racial inequality remained: Nearly all wealth in South Africa was in the hands of the white minority, and the average income of blacks was a tiny fraction of that of whites.

Beginning in 1949 and continuing through forty years of South Africa's history, *apartheid,* a legally mandated system of racial classification, segregation, and discrimination, restricted far more than the right to vote. It defined who could live where, who could work at what job, and even who could be present in a given area at a particular time of day. For a long time, only the poorest jobs were open to blacks, although the need for labor changed that restriction somewhat as time passed. Although constituting more than two-thirds of South Africa's population, blacks were limited to ownership of only 13 percent of the land—and the worst land at that. At one time, it was illegal to even conspire to have sex with someone of a different race, much less to actually do so. Whites, who number less than 20 percent of the population, used their total control of the political system to ensure that they would continue to own virtually all the wealth while the overwhelming majority of blacks remained segregated and trapped in poverty.

This severe racial inequality led to violent uprisings, particularly in the 1960s and thereafter, as well as an increase in underground acts such as sabotage. The roots of this inequality and conflict began with the conquest of the indigenous black African population by white Europeans. Although apartheid was the law only since 1949, racial inequality had been deeply institutionalized since the Dutch began to colonize the area in the mid-1600s. The first Dutch settlers were interested mainly in supplying their ships in the area, but agricultural settlers later began moving inland, or "trekking." This brought conflict with the natives and ultimately their conquest. It also brought genocide to the native population. Close to the coast, a paternalistic system of slavery was developed, although the slaves usually were imported from other parts of Africa.

Gradually and after a series of conflicts, the British gained control of the area from the Dutch and attempted to treat the native population more liberally. This was not the actual result, however, for several reasons. First, the Dutch were pushed inland in further "treks" to avoid the British, conquering and subordinating still more of the native population. Included in this group was the large and well-organized Bantu nation, which fought fiercely and effectively for many years before its final conquest. Second, the British ultimately became as dependent as the Dutch on white supremacy, and their attempts at liberalization always stopped well short of a point that could have threatened the white power structure. In addition, the descendants of the Dutch settlers, known as Afrikaners, viewed the British as outsiders who threatened their way of life with their attempts at racial liberalism, and the Afrikaners responded by becoming even more repressive of the native population. Thus, the establishment of apartheid in 1949, when the Afrikaners regained full control, was by and large a codification of what had already developed: a strict caste system of racial inequality that had changed mainly from paternalism to segregation (the rigid competitive pattern) as the society changed from agricultural to urban. The caste system actually became more rigid as the society urbanized because whites came to see the black majority as an ever greater threat to their supremacy as a result of economic competition and the increased threat of rebellion. (For further discussion of South Africa, see Van den Berghe, 1965, 1978, Chap. 5; Hunt and Walker, 1974, Chap. 6; Thompson and Thompson, 2001) Although the pattern of conflict and inequality changed over time and in many ways became worse, its roots can be traced directly to the country's colonial origins.

## Northern Ireland

Not all instances of severe intergroup conflict or stratification involve different races. In Northern Ireland, a violent intergroup conflict between Catholic and Protestant whites flared in the late 1960s and continued through most of the 1990s until a peace agreement was approved in 1998. Since then, there has been much less bloodshed, but the underlying conflict remains unresolved, and occasional bombings and other violent incidents continue. Between 1968 and 1992, approximately 3,000 lives were lost in that conflict (Dyer, 1992). By the mid-1980s, a wall had been built to separate the Catholic and Protestant sectors in Belfast. All participants in this conflict have been white and European. By outward appearances, it is a religious conflict between Catholics and Protestants. However, a closer analysis shows that there is much more to it than that. Indeed, the roots of the conflict go back to the sixteenth century, when Britain gradually asserted control over Ireland. Initially, an English colony was established in Ireland mainly for military and political reasons because control of Ireland was advantageous in military conflicts with mainland European countries. Later, economic motivations also became important, as the English colonists established themselves as feudal landlords over the Irish population.

The English colonists were Protestant (Anglican), and the Irish whom they conquered were Catholic. Later, the English settlers were joined by Scottish ones, who were also Protestant but Presbyterian. Accordingly, an ethnic conflict took on religious overtones. Many of the Scots settled in the six northern counties, which are today Northern Ireland. The Irish people never accepted domination by the British, and revolts and upheavals occurred intermittently. The Scottish Presbyterians, who occupied an intermediate position between the Anglicans from England and the Irish Catholics, also rebelled against the English periodically, but by the late eighteenth century the two Protestant groups were drawn together by the threat of increased Irish Catholic political power (R. Moore, 1972). In addition, the British government played on the prejudice of the Presbyterians to ensure that they would never form a coalition with Irish Catholics against the British crown (See, 1986, pp. 45–46). Eventually, polarization between English and Scottish Protestants on one side and native Irish Catholics on the other led to violent and bloody conflict, which resulted in the division of Ireland. The six northern counties, known as Ulster or Northern Ireland, remained under partial British control and Protestant domination. The remainder of the country, heavily Catholic, became the Republic of Ireland.

Since that time, the arena of conflict has been in the north. There the Protestant majority retained general, though at times indirect (through the British government), political control and have kept social and economic advantages. Not all Protestants are wealthy or even middle class, but most of the wealth is in Protestant hands. The Catholics demand equality, but lacking effective political power until recently, they have been kept in a subordinate status. However, their numbers—never less than one-third of the population and projected to be a majority by 2020—facilitate collective action. The result was a violence-ridden stalemate for many years.

By the 1990s everyone was wearying of the violence, which had lasted more than a quarter of a century. With the encouragement of a more supportive British government, serious peace talks began in the mid-1990s. The result was a historic agreement, approved by 71 percent of Northern Ireland's voters (and by more than 90 percent in the Republic of Ireland, where approval was also required) in 1998. The agreement provided for a Northern Ireland Assembly including both Catholic (nationalist) and Protestant (unionist) proportional representation, along with guarantees for minority rights. This was implemented in 1999, but this "devolved government" was suspended four times due to crises in the peace process between 2000 and 2002, when direct rule by Great Britain was reimposed.

Significantly, when the first parliament was elected in June 1998, the majority of both Catholics and Protestants voted for moderates who supported the peace agreement. Overall, 75 percent of the deputies in the newly elected parliament came from parties that supported the peace agreement (de Breadun, 1998). These voting results suggest that the agreement has the potential, though not the certainty, of finally bringing about peace between the two major ethnic groups in Northern Ireland (Sinnott, 1998). However, the subsequent conflicts and the reimposition of British direct rule indicate that true peace will not be easy. The country remains highly segregated and highly divided: A 2001 survey in Belfast showed that segregation was as great as or greater than ever, and two-thirds of young people between eighteen and twenty-five said that they had never had a meaningful conversation with a person on the other side of the "troubles" (Shirlow, 2002). As of July 2003, the assembly remained suspended, British direct rule continued, and elections that had been scheduled for May 2003 had been postponed. Still, the level of violence remained less than in the past, and leaders on both sides continued to express hope of a permanent agreement.

Segregation remains as great as ever in Northern Ireland. These wall paintings in Protestant *(left)* and Catholic *(right)* neighborhoods illustrate the opposing stances: support of Protestants for continuing union with Britain; support of Catholics for the Irish Republican Army (IRA).

This necessarily brief and somewhat superficial discussion[1] is sufficient to illustrate one very important point: The roots of the conflict are to be found in colonialism. Today's Irish Catholics (North and South) are descendants of the native Irish who were conquered and colonized by British (Scottish and English) Protestants. Today's Irish Protestants are the descendants of the British colonizers and view the Irish Catholics as an inferior but dangerous and treacherous people. The history of conquest, rebellion, and conflict has remained central to both groups in Northern Ireland throughout its history, and the two groups largely retain the statuses associated with colonizers and colonized minorities. As a result, majority-minority relations in Northern Ireland, even though between two white, European, and Christian ethnic groups, have in many ways closely resembled race relations between blacks and whites in such countries as South Africa and the United States (R. Moore, 1972).

## Quebec, Canada

Quebec Province in Canada is unique among the areas we have discussed; not only is the conflict between two white, European, and Christian groups (English- and French-speaking Canadians), but also it is between two groups whose original presence in Canada was that of colonizer rather than indigenous population. Neither the British nor the French were native to Canada, and both (in somewhat different ways) colonized the native Indian population. The dominance of the English-speaking population (a 20 percent minority in Quebec) over the much larger French-speaking population originated with the conquest of the French colonists by the British in 1759. Since that time, English-speaking Canadians have had a dominant social, economic, and (until fairly recently) political position. Although the English-French conflict has been muted by class divisions that exist within the French population (Ossenberg, 1975), it did increase in the 1960s and 1970s and has been evident to varying degrees since then. There was violence by militant Quebec separatists in 1970, and later in the 1970s the Parti Québécois, which advocated separation of Quebec from the Canadian confederation, was voted into power. In 1980, a referendum on separation failed, and the position of the Parti Québécois weakened somewhat. In the 1970s and 1980s, however, increasingly strict laws mandated that French was to be the province's only official language, despite Canada's national policy of bilingualism (English and French). Quebec's language laws require that signs posted outside businesses be in French.

The question of separation again came to the fore in the late 1980s and early 1990s as efforts were made to amend Canada's constitution in ways that would recognize Quebec as "a distinct society" within the Canadian confederation. In 1992, agreement was reached on such a constitution (which also provided for autonomy for Canada's native Indian population). However, the agreement failed because it was not ratified by the required number of provinces: Quebec rejected it because it did not go far enough in guaranteeing Quebec's autonomy, and a number of other provinces rejected it because in their view it went too far and gave Quebec (or the native population) special privileges that other provinces did not enjoy.

The failure of this agreement raises some questions about Canada's long-term ability to function as a unified nation. In 1994, the Parti Québécois returned to power, and it remained in power until 2003. The failure of the autonomy agreement led to a second referendum on separation in 1995, and this time it came very close to passing. It did gain majority support (60 percent) from voters of French ancestry, but strong opposition from English-speaking voters led to a narrow defeat: The "no" majority vote was just 50.6 percent in this second referendum on Quebec independence. After this narrow defeat, the Parti Québécois pursued policies of

---

[1]For more extensive discussions, see Barritt and Carter (1962), Rose (1971), R. Moore (1972), See (1986), and Doherty and Poole (1997).

greater autonomy for Quebec but did not propose another referendum. Because the Parti Québécois was voted out in 2003 (in an election in which issues such as health care, education, taxes, and urban mergers dominated the debate), there is no immediate likelihood of Quebec separating from Canada. However, its long-term role in Canada remains uncertain. For example, even at the time of the Parti Québécois defeat in 2003, polls still showed that about 40 percent of Quebec's residents favored Quebec sovereignty (Pratte, 2003).

Once again, the example of Quebec shows that considerable ethnic stratification and conflict can result from conquest and colonization, even when one colonizing group conquers another colonizing group and they are of the same race and only moderately different in cultural values. As we shall see later, language differences such as those in Quebec can greatly aggravate ethnic conflicts but, in the absence of colonization or conquest, often do not do so. The inequality and conflict in Quebec arise largely out of a situation in which one group conquered and colonized another more than 200 years ago.

## The Former Soviet Union

In 1991, the Soviet Union was abolished after the failure of a coup attempt against the government of President Mikhail Gorbachev, who had dramatically altered Soviet politics through the introduction of freedom of expression, a free press, and, to a limited extent, free elections. When the plotters of the coup attempt failed in their efforts to reestablish an authoritarian communist government, the end of the old Soviet Union came quickly, with all fifteen of its republics establishing themselves as independent countries. Eleven of them chose to remain very loosely connected as the Commonwealth of Independent States.

Given the freedom to pursue old ethnic rivalries, and separated into fifteen countries based largely on ethnic groupings, the former Soviet Union plunged into a bewildering variety of ethnic conflicts, some of which became very violent. Two of the former republics, Armenia and Azerbaijan, immediately plunged into a war that to a large extent had already been under way before the breakup of the Soviet Union and continued into 1993 with heavy casualties. In other parts of the former Soviet Union, disputes arose among former republics over control of nuclear weapons and of installations such as naval bases. In a number of former republics, ethnic minorities rebelled against the government, seeking to establish their own independent, ethnically based nations much as the former republics had done. The most serious and ongoing of these rebellions has been in Chechnya, a region of the Russian Republic, the largest of the countries formed when the Soviet Union split up. As is discussed in greater detail later on, warfare between Chechen rebels and the Russian army has dragged on for years, and Chechen rebels have been responsible for a series of terrorist attacks in Moscow, the Russian capital.

As recently as the late 1980s, the Soviet Union was one of the two strongest military powers in the world. Its population was the third largest of any country, and its military and political influence extended to all parts of the world. For more than seventy years, the Soviet Union had ruled a vast, ethnically diverse territory, extending from eastern Europe across northern Asia all the way to the Pacific Ocean—a bigger territory than any other country in history. How could it be that in just a few years, such a superpower could break up into fifteen countries, many of which were in conflict with one another or deeply divided within, each of which was ruled by a different ethnic group, and most of which were of relatively minor military or economic significance in the modern world?

As in other ethnic conflicts around the world, the answer lies to a large extent in a history of conquest and colonialism. When the Soviet Union was created in 1917, its territory coincided largely with that of the old Russian empire, which was created through a series of annexations and conquests beginning in the sixteenth century and continuing into the late nineteenth (Nahaylo and Swoboda, 1989). Among the conquered or annexed groups were Lithuanians, Latvians, Estonians, Byelorussians, Ukrainians, Moldavians, Georgians, Armenians, Azerbaijanis, Tatars, Kazakhs, Kirghizes, Uzbeks, Chechens, and Tadzhiks.

In 1917, the czar (the monarch of the Russian empire) was overthrown in the Bolshevik revolution, led by Vladimir Lenin. A few months before the revolution, Lenin had reiterated his support of a nation's right to secede from the empire through a process of referendum (Nahaylo and Swoboda, 1989, p. 15). However, Lenin also believed that most regions could be induced to voluntarily remain in the new nation created by the revolution, the Soviet Union. He believed that this could be accomplished in part by allowing each ethnic region to retain its own language and culture: "We want free unification; this is why we must recognize the right to secede (without freedom to secede, unification cannot be free)" (Lenin, 1960–1970). At the same time, he believed that the advantages of having one national language would eventually lead most regions to voluntarily choose to speak Russian if it was not imposed on them against their will.

In reality, however, the right to secede was not respected by the Soviet Union. The test came less than a month after the Bolshevik revolution, when the Ukraine announced that it did not recognize Soviet rule and proclaimed independence. Although Lenin at first recognized its right to secede, the Soviet Union soon invaded the Ukraine after it refused to allow Russian Red Guards free passage through it. Russian troops, with the support of ethnic Russians in the Ukraine, occupied almost all of the Ukraine and established Soviet rule within about three months. Soviet control was similarly established over almost all former Russian territory in Europe. In the next few years, control was similarly established over Islamic regions of the former Russian empire. In effect, Soviet policy proclaimed the legitimacy of the various ethnic states in former Russian territory, whereas in reality it created a centralized, unitary state that denied any opportunity for real independence (Rakowska-Harmstone, 1992).

The only real exceptions to this pattern were the three Baltic States: Latvia, Estonia, and Lithuania. In part because they were or had been occupied by the Germans or Poles, these countries were able to become independent and remain so for about twenty years after the creation of the Soviet Union. Georgia also briefly gained independence but lost it ten months later when the Soviet army invaded. At the end of World War II, the Baltic states were brought back under Soviet rule. The Soviets also gained effective control of Poland and several other eastern European nations that remained nominally independent.

In compelling more than 100 ethnic groups—many of them living in clearly distinct territories—to live under a common state, the Soviet Union to a large extent sowed the seeds of its ultimate destruction and of the ethnic turmoil that erupted into violence in the 1990s (Rakowska-Harmstone, 1992, p. 523). The Russians were clearly in charge in the Soviet Union, even though a large minority (about 50 percent by 1990) of its population was non-Russian. Moreover, for the most part non-Russian minorities occupied a clearly subordinate economic position (Huttenbach, 1990). Thus, non-Russian ethnic groups were, in effect, forced into a subordinate status under Russian rule, under both the old Russian empire and the more recent Soviet Union.

This pattern only intensified when Joseph Stalin gained control of the Soviet Union after Lenin's death. Stalin imposed a harshly dictatorial state that suppressed all signs of independent thought, including expressions of ethnic consciousness and the practice of traditional religions. Although himself Georgian, Stalin pursued a policy of Russian hegemony because he had seen how regional independence movements could threaten the power of the centralized government. This led to repeated purges of non-Russian, ethnic-oriented elements in the Communist party and government.

The consequences of all this were (1) to make expressions of ethnic solidarity or independence as impossible as they had been under czarist Russia and (2) to build tremendous resentment of conquest and outside rule that simmered for years, then came to the surface once freedom of expression was finally allowed in the 1980s. As the country modernized, higher educational levels gave rise to better-educated elites among the various ethnic groups, who became leaders in the struggle for ethnic autonomy. After Stalin's death, the Soviet government tried to accommodate the desire for ethnic autonomy by tolerating some increases in regional autonomy. Loyalty to the national government was still demanded, however, and any secessionist moves were harshly suppressed. Thus, true autonomy was impossible, and as soon as conditions allowed, the republics and ethnic groups rebelled against central rule. Once the Soviet Union was abolished, they also rebelled in any situation in which one ethnic group lived in an area ruled or dominated by another. For example, Armenians in the Nagorno-Karabakh region of Azerbaijan did not want to become free of Russian rule only to fall under Azerbaijani rule. This led to the war between Armenia and Azerbaijan. With no powerful, authoritarian Soviet government to repress them, ethnic groups were free to use whatever means they could to advance their causes, and in most cases they did.

In addition to the war between the former republics of Armenia and Azerbaijan, conflicts have flared in other ethnically mixed republics. In Russia, the largest of the former republics, this has been particularly intense as Tatars, Bashkirs, Yakuts, Buryats, Ossetians, and others have all rebelled against Russian rule, many declaring independence (Rakowska-Harmstone, 1992). An example of the complexity of ethnic tensions in Russia can be seen in the Chechen-Ingushetia region of southern Russia, which declared independence in 1991. Subsequently, Ingushetia broke away from Chechen and fought over territory with neighboring North Ossetia (Elliott et al., 1993). The rebellion in the Chechen region led to a bloody civil war in Russia in the mid-1990s. In the former Russian republic, the potential for tension is especially great because the group that continues to rule the minority groups there, the Russians, is the one that conquered them in the first place.

Thus, in the former Soviet Union as elsewhere, the roots of today's ethnic violence and conflict lie in the past conquest and colonization of a host of ethnic groups. In this case, colonization by the Russian empire came first, but it was followed by the continued imposition of a basically colonial model of Russian domination under the Soviet Union for seven decades (Huttenbach, 1990). The effect of these historical influences can be seen in a statement made at a rally of Tatars who were seeking independence from Russia in March 1993: "Russia occupied us in 1552 and must beg forgiveness. Now Russia is falling apart, and we must hurry to make them recognize our independence" (Marat Mulyakov, quoted in Elliott et al., 1993).

The explosive long-term consequences of colonization became most evident in the Chechen region of Russia. Chechnya, a predominantly Muslim region conquered long ago by the Russians, declared independence from Russia after the breakup of the old Soviet Union. Russian President Boris Yeltsin responded in 1994 by sending the army to retake the Chechen capital of Grozny, which it did after a bloody two-month campaign. But the Chechen rebels simply moved to the country and staged a guerrilla war against the Russian troops, occasionally attacking inside Russia as well. By late 1996, the rebels had filtered back into the city and largely pinned down the larger but demoralized Russian forces. By the time Russia backed down, withdrew its army, and allowed the Chechens to hold elections in 1997, more than 30,000 people had been killed. In the elections, all thirteen presidential candidates favored Chechen independence (Womack, 1997). Russia did not agree to full independence, however, and Chechen rebels undertook a campaign of terrorism, including multiple bombings of apartment buildings in Moscow. In addition, Chechen rebels also entered the neighboring Russian area of Dagestan to support

A victim is carried from the Moscow theater taken over by Chechen rebels in 2002. More than 100 Russian civilians were killed.

fellow Islamic rebels there. After these events, Russian troops returned to Chechnya in 1999, and a good deal of blood was spilled on both sides.

In 2002, war-weary Chechens voted for a constitution that provided for autonomy but kept Chechnya in the Russian Republic and provided for elections, but on no set timetable. The violence continued, in both Chechnya and Russia proper. Later in 2002, a theater takeover in Moscow by Chechen rebels ultimately took 128 civilian lives (mostly when the Russian military and police used gas to regain control, inadvertently killing many of the 700 theatergoers being held hostage). In 2003, a suicide bombing by two Chechen women at a Moscow rock concert killed fifteen people. Throughout 2002 and 2003, many more died in Chechnya as guerilla warfare continued between Chechen rebels and Russian troops.

## The Former Yugoslavia

As in the old Soviet Union, a variety of new ethnic nations were created when the old country of Yugoslavia began to dissolve in 1991. Here, too, ethnic conflict flared when the unifying force of the central Yugoslav government was eliminated. One by one, Slovenia, Croatia, Bosnia-Herzegovina, Macedonia, Montenegro, and Kosovo declared independence or voted to secede from Yugoslavia. The Serbian-dominated Yugoslav government at first intervened militarily to prevent Slovenia and Croatia from seceding, although both eventually did secede. (However, Serbs regained control of a substantial part of Croatian territory.) The most serious violence occurred in Bosnia-Herzegovina and Kosovo. In Bosnia, the effort to establish an independent Bosnian state met resistance not only from Serbia (as eastern Yugoslavia again became known after the breakup) but also from ethnic Serbs and Croats within Bosnian territory. Bosnia is much more ethnically diverse than Yugoslavia's other former republics. While a narrow majority of its population is Bosnian and Muslim, sizable portions are composed of Serbs and Croats, both of whom are predominantly Christian, though of different denominations. As a result, Bosnia's move toward independence was opposed not only by the Serbian government but also by ethnic Serbs and Croats in Bosnian territory who did not want to live under Bosnian rule. The result was civil war and the worst case of ethnic genocide in Europe since World War II.

In Bosnia, where 30 percent of the population is ethnically Serbian, the Serbian army and militias made up of ethnic Serbs living in Bosnia began a campaign in early 1992 that they called *ethnic cleansing*. This meant eliminating the Bosnian Muslim population from areas of Bosnia that had Serbian majorities and establishing Serbian control. This was accomplished through a variety of brutal techniques, including concentration camps, where Bosnians were tortured and sometimes killed and Bosnian women systematically raped; forced relocations of Bosnians, sometimes accomplished by burning their homes; and a series of sieges in which Bosnian cities and neighborhoods were blockaded, rocketed, and shelled. The violence was finally brought under control by a peace agreement in November 1995, but only after as many as 250,000 people were killed and up to 2 million displaced (Benkoil, 1997). A major reason the peace agreement held was the presence of 30,000 North Atlantic Treaty Organization (NATO) troops, including up to 8,000 Americans.

In 1998 and 1999, trouble flared again in former Yugoslavia, this time in Kosovo, a province of Serbia. Ninety percent of the population of Kosovo is ethnic Albanian, and like other ethnic groups who have lived under Serbian rule, ethnic Albanians want independence for Kosovo. Serbia opposed such independence and asserted tighter control over Kosovo than was the case under the old Yugoslavian government. Fighting began in early 1998 when Serbian President Slobodan Milosevic sent forces to put down the movement for independence. By early 1999, more than 2,000 had been killed, and NATO began a bombing campaign to try to stop Milosevic. By May, 840,000 refugees had been displaced from Kosovo, but under the pressure of NATO's air strikes, Milosevic agreed to withdraw Serbian troops from Kosovo. A NATO peacekeeping force, including up to 7,000 Americans, was sent in to protect Kosovo's autonomy. In 2001, Milosevic was arrested and taken to The Hague, Netherlands, where he was placed on trial under the auspices of the United Nations for war crimes in Kosovo, Bosnia, and Croatia. The trial continued in 2004.

The roots of the ethnic conflict in the former Yugoslavia, as elsewhere, are imbedded in histories of domination and colonialism. For hundreds of years, the Croats were ruled by Hungary, and all of Yugoslavia's other ethnic groups were ruled by the Turks. In 1878, Montenegro and Serbia managed to gain their independence, but all of the other regions remained under foreign rule until Yugoslavia was formed in 1918 (McFarlane, 1988, pp. 3–4). From then until 1939, Yugoslavia was dominated politically by the Serbs and economically by foreign (French, British, and German) capital investment (McFarlane, 1988). In 1939, a Serb-Croat coalition took charge of the country until 1941, when disorder resulted from both a Nazi invasion and civil war. In 1943, under the leadership of Josip Broz Tito and with the backing of the Soviet Union, Yugoslavia was reconstituted as a socialist republic. Tito's army was the only one of the various factions in Yugoslavia during World War II that fought on the basis of equality for all of Yugoslavia's component ethnic groups.

During and just before World War II, ethnic massacres were committed by virtually all of Yugoslavia's ethnic groups against one another. In 1941, Croats, cooperating with the Nazis and angry over decades of rule by Serbs, undertook a campaign of extermination, with one of their military commanders proclaiming, "I have given orders for the total extinction of Serbs [on Croatian territory]. Annihilate them wherever you can find them" (Joffe, 1992). Another group, known as the Chetniks, an alliance of Serbs and Montenegrins, similarly engaged in systematic extermination of both Croats and Bosnians. Tito's partisans did not have clean hands, either.

After World War II, they engaged in mass executions, and in at least two cities they massacred thousands of people. Although these actions were motivated more by politics than by ethnicity, they added to the resentment and the feelings, which persisted into the 1990s, that every group in Yugoslavia had scores to settle (Joffe, 1992).

Strains between Croatian nationalism and Serbian attempts at central rule occurred throughout the history of Yugoslav communism (McFarlane, 1988). Whereas Tito himself was of Slovenian and Croatian ancestry, Serbs dominated the military, the government bureaucracy, and the secret police (Joffe, 1992). This domination was resented by Croats, Slovenians, Albanian Kosovars, and Bosnians, but given the power of Tito's government and his willingness to use the secret police to stifle dissent, this resentment was kept in check. An additional factor helped to hold Yugoslavia together throughout Tito's life and beyond: fear of its bigger and more powerful communist neighbor, the Soviet Union. Yugoslavia was the only communist country in eastern Europe that was able to remain free of Soviet domination. It did so through a combination of enough strength to put up a fight if it were militarily invaded and Tito's skills in leading a movement of "non-aligned" nations that played off the Soviet Union and United States against each other in a contest for influence. Because nobody in Yugoslavia wanted to be ruled by the Soviets, the fear of being conquered by them to a large extent kept internal tensions among Yugoslavia's ethnic groups in check. Tito died in 1980, however, and a decade later the Soviet Union was on the road to collapse and was clearly no longer a threat to Yugoslavia's independence. With neither Tito's central power nor the fear of the Soviet Union to hold it together, Yugoslavia was torn apart in the early 1990s by its long-standing ethnic conflicts.

Several historical factors are important in understanding the recent ethnic warfare in the former Yugoslavia. First, through much of its history *every* ethnic group had been conquered by other groups and denied any rights of autonomy or statehood. Second, during the twentieth century, Serbians, by force, dominated every other group in Yugoslavia—even as they themselves had been similarly dominated in the past—and they saw power and dominance as ways of preventing their own loss of independence. Third, all of these conflicts and resentments were worsened by a twentieth-century history in which nearly all ethnic groups in Yugoslavia were both perpetrators and victims of massacres and extermination campaigns. Finally, ethnic groups are so scattered and mixed in some parts of former Yugoslavia that it is virtually impossible to create ethnic nations in which some group does not end up being involuntarily ruled by another. For example, the 30 percent of Bosnia's people who are Serbs and the 17 percent who are Croats do not like living under Bosnian rule. Thus, they sought to force out Bosnians and link themselves to Serbia or Croatia. But to Bosnians, the consequence of that would be to place large parts of Bosnia under Serbian or Croatian rule, an option that is equally unacceptable to them. Without a history of conquest, colonialism, and massacre, these ethnic distinctions might not matter so much, but with such a history, each group sees them as matters of national and ethnic survival.

## The Middle East

Another potentially explosive area of intergroup relations in the modern world has been the Middle East. Conflict here is not entirely an issue of ethnic or racial relations, or even of majority-minority relations, because the conflict is in large part an international issue between Israel and several of its Arab neighbors. However, it is worth considering in a book on majority-minority relations for several reasons. First, the conflict is both internal and international: One fundamental question is the status of Palestinian Arabs within the boundary of Israel, some of whom are even Israeli citizens. Second, the conflict is partly ethnic, in the sense that being

Jewish or Arab will almost certainly determine where one stands. Third, even the international aspect of the conflict centers around jurisdiction over land areas to which both Jews and Palestinian Arabs feel they have a historical and legitimate claim and which each group regards fervently as its true homeland.

The origins of this conflict are more complex than some of the others we have examined. First, both the dominant group (Jews) and the subordinate group (Arabs) in today's Israel had some historical claim to the land prior to the establishment of the Israeli state in 1948. Israel, or Palestine, was the historic home of the Jewish people and has been the focal point of their religion throughout history. Nonetheless, until modern times no significant Jewish presence was there after the conquest of Jerusalem in A.D. 70 (Douglas-Home, 1968, p. 14). During this long period, the only Jewish population was a handful of students and scholars of the Holy Writings (Dodd and Sales, 1970).

The Arab dominance can be traced at least to the establishment of the Turkish and Islamic Ottoman Empire's rule in the sixteenth century, although some trace it to the spread of Islamic and Arabic culture to the region in the seventh and eighth centuries (Epp, 1970). In any case, the area had unquestionably been predominantly Arab for hundreds of years before the Zionist movement of the twentieth century, even though it was often governed from outside and did not exist as a distinct Arab or Palestinian state. It should also be noted that the area has major religious significance for both Christians and Muslims as well as for Jews. It is certainly fair to say that at the time Israeli control was established, both the Jewish and Arab populations viewed the area as their homeland and felt they had a legitimate claim to it. The same cannot be said for majority and minority groups in America or in the African colonies.

The Israeli situation also differs from the others in that the group that established dominance—the Jews—was in large part a displaced population that had experienced centuries of worldwide persecution. It had just suffered perhaps the worst incident of genocide in the history of the world: the murder of 6 million Jews in the Holocaust. Thus, the impetus for the Jewish settlement came not from the expansionist desires of a colonial power but in large part from the desire of a persecuted people for a safe homeland.

In these regards, then, the origin of the Israeli state and the present-day Arab-Jewish conflict differ from the patterns of colonialism and conquest we have seen in other societies. But there are also important similarities. When Zionism first became a serious movement in the late nineteenth century, the population of what is now Israel was overwhelmingly Arab and had been so for hundreds of years. Furthermore, the establishment of the Jewish state of Israel was imposed against the will of the indigenous Arab population. It was accomplished through the actions of the United Nations, European powers (notably Britain and France), and ultimately the armed struggle of the Jewish immigrants against the indigenous Arab population. In the end, much of that population fled, and those who stayed behind have occupied a subordinate role in Israeli society (though not to nearly the extent that blacks did in South Africa, for example). Thus, the problem did arise as a result of an indigenous population coming under the domination of a new population through the use of force.

In 1993, an important step toward resolution of the bitter dispute in the Middle East was reached when, for the first time, Israel and the Palestine Liberation Organization (PLO) recognized each other diplomatically and in effect accepted that each had some historic claim to land in the Middle East. Although the 1993 agreement was promptly rejected by the more extreme elements on both sides, it was historic in that it was the first time that Palestinians and Jews mutually acknowledged and accepted, however grudgingly, each other's aspirations for a homeland. For this reason, it laid a groundwork that could become the basis for a more extensive agreement and a more lasting peace. Since 1993, progress on further agreements has

A repeated cycle of violence has frustrated efforts to achieve a peace agreement between Israel and the Palestinians. *Left:* Palestinian victims of an Israeli Air Force bombing; *right:* Israeli victims of a Palestinian suicide bomber.

been irregular. In 1998, a new agreement, the Wye River Memorandum, was reached between Israeli Prime Minister Benjamin Netanyahu and Palestinian President Yasir Arafat, with help from President Clinton and Jordan's late King Hussein, who served as mediators. The agreement specified that Israel would return additional land to Palestinian control and free additional Palestinian prisoners, in return for heightened security guarantees from the Palestinians. However, disagreements arose quickly over implementation of the accord, the agreement was suspended in late 1998, and tensions were heightened by the continued establishment of Israeli settlements in Palestinian territory beyond the borders of Israel and by periodic attacks on Israeli civilians by Palestinian guerrillas opposed to the agreement. Opposition to the agreement within Israel was tragically demonstrated in 1995 when a Jewish fundamentalist assassinated Prime Minister Yitzhak Rabin, a leading architect of the 1993 peace agreement. In 2000, a peace agreement, largely brokered by Clinton, was nearly reached between the leaders of Israel and the Palestinians at that time, Ehud Barak and Yasser Arafat. But talks broke down after Arafat rejected parts of the proposed agreement, Barak was replaced by Ariel Sharon, and Clinton was replaced by George W. Bush. For more than two years, violence flared again on both sides, leading to about 1,900 Palestinian fatalities and 700 Israeli fatalities. In 2003 the two sides agreed to cease-fires and pullbacks as part of a "road map" to peace proposed by President Bush. This occurred after Arafat shifted to a mainly ceremonial role, ceding power to Mahmoud Abbas, who was appointed to the new Palestinian position of Prime Minister. However, by mid-2004 this peace process had become stalled, as both sides again resorted to violence. Abbas resigned in September 2003, and attacks and counterattacks led to a steadily rising death toll on both sides.

## Some Comparisons and Contrasts

Sociologist Stanley Lieberson (1961) has examined majority-minority relations both historically within certain societies and comparatively among a number of them. Lieberson concluded that when an *indigenous group*—one that is established in or native to an area—is subordinated to another group entering from the outside, the result usually is conflict and ethnic inequality. Assimilation and intergroup cooperation are very difficult in this situation, which usually originates with the conquest or colonization of the indigenous population. In the reverse situation, in which the indigenous group is dominant over the immigrant group, conditions usually are different. Unless the immigrant group was forced to immigrate, as in the case of slaves, a trend toward assimilation usually emerges, with only mild and occasional ethnic conflict.

The societies we have examined in this section all fit Lieberson's (1961) first type, in which the indigenous group was made subordinate to an immigrant or outside group. With the possible exception of Israel, they all have a history of colonialism. And they have all been among the world's most volatile areas of intergroup conflict. A history of colonialism, conquest, or domination of an indigenous population by an immigrant population appears to be one of the factors most closely associated with ethnic conflict and inequality in today's world.

Not every country with such a history has a serious majority-minority problem, and not every country with such a problem has that type of history. Despite their history of colonialism, Mexico and Brazil often are cited as cases of better than average intergroup relations. On the other hand, Hitler's genocidal campaign against Jews occurred in a situation with no colonial history. This reminds us that no one factor taken alone can explain the pattern of intergroup relations in any society. Nonetheless, if we examine the broad range of societies in the world, it does seem clear that *all else being equal,* the presence of a colonial history is associated with greater than average amounts of intergroup inequality and conflict. (For further discussion of this issue, see Mason, 1971, pp. 81–86; Kinloch, 1974, 1979, pp. 175–88.)

In some cases, as in the former Soviet Union and Yugoslavia, these conflicts related to past conquest and colonization have come to the surface when the strong central states that once held them in check collapsed. More broadly, Crawford (1998a) argues that the current trend of economic globalization, which generally lessens the influence of governments as worldwide economic and political forces come to predominate, may be weakening social controls that have kept ethnic conflict in check in many places. Thus, although the former Soviet Union and Yugoslavia are extreme cases, they may to some degree represent a worldwide trend, especially in countries with a history of colonialism or conquest. Still, it is important to remember that the weakening of governments by globalization and other forces does not *cause* racial and ethnic conflict. Rather, it creates a situation in which it can come to the surface as underlying conditions associated with a history of colonialism, conflict, and domination cause social divisions to occur along ethnic or racial lines (Crawford, 1998a, pp. 5, 18–20).

## Great Britain: Another Effect of Colonialism

Great Britain illustrates another way in which colonialism can lead to intergroup conflict and inequality. About 4 percent of Britain's population is made up of immigrants (or their children) from former British colonies, mainly in Asia, Africa, and the Caribbean (Richmond, 1986). These immigrants, nearly all people of color, have experienced discrimination and social inequality. In such key areas as housing, education, and employment, they have disadvantages much like those of blacks and Hispanics in the United States. As in the United States, this racial inequality has at times resulted in violence. During the 1980s, a series of violent uprisings spread through major British cities, including Liverpool, Birmingham, Bristol, and London. Although the violence in the 1980s was unprecedented in extent, violent racial or ethnic conflict in Britain can be traced at least to the turn of the century. And serious incidents have continued to occur since the 1980s: the murder of a black teenager by a gang of white youths in 1993, bombings by a neo-Nazi group in multiracial and Asian neighborhoods in 1999, and serious rioting between white and Asian youths in several northern England cities in 2001.

Britain's immigrant groups, then, have not yet experienced the assimilation and rising status that are typical of immigrant groups in many places. Like Puerto Ricans in the United States, they do not fit the usual historical experience of immigrant groups. Rather, they were originally colonized elsewhere and eventually took advantage of their status as commonwealth citizens to migrate to Great Britain. Once there, however, they were treated by many British as colonized peoples, and they found escape from the disadvantages associated with that status difficult. In this way, too, their experience is much like that of Puerto Ricans in the United States. (For a general discussion and review of several major works about intergroup relations in Great Britain, see Richmond, 1986; for more information on immigration and racial violence in Great Britain, see Panayi, 1996, 1999).

## ► SOCIETIES WITH PEACEFUL INTERGROUP RELATIONS

The importance of history to contemporary intergroup relations can also be illustrated by looking at the opposite end of the scale. One example, cited by Hunt and Walker (1974, pp. 41–45), is Switzerland, which has a number of different nationalities and religions, and many of these groups do not even speak the same language. Despite this diversity, relations among groups are for the most part harmonious, mostly because each of the various and ethnically diverse parts of the country came into the confederation voluntarily, largely to seek protection. One rare exception is the Jura region, which is the one part of Switzerland where intergroup relations are not harmonious. This area was taken from France and made a part of Switzerland in 1815, against the will of its residents. As recently as the 1960s and 1970s, a social movement to separate the area from Swiss rule sparked violence.

Another relevant example is Hawaii. Although Hawaii did experience external colonization, it was quite different from that of South Africa, Ireland, or the mainland United States. Berry and Tischler (1978, pp. 158–63) discuss Hawaii as an example of a society with relatively harmonious intergroup relations. It has greater ethnic diversity than any other state, yet it sets an admirable example of racial and ethnic harmony for the rest of the country. In the 1940s, for example, while race continued to divide segments of the labor movement on the mainland, Hawaii's workers organized into one large, unified union with a consciously interracial identity (Jung, 1999). This is not to say that there is no racial problem: Native Hawaiians do occupy a position subordinate to that of several newcomer groups, with rates of poverty, mortality, and imprisonment that exceed those of other groups in Hawaii. In addition, there is a history of inequalities among Asian and European groups in Hawaii, including Portuguese, Japanese, and Filipinos (Jung, 1999, 2002). Nonetheless, racial harmony and tolerance seem more the rule than in the rest of the United States. Certainly, norms against prejudice and discrimination have been stronger and existed earlier than on the mainland, and contact among various racial groups is more common and more harmonious.

According to Berry and Tischler (1978), much of the reason for this can be found in the islands' history. Although subject to colonial influences, the local population was never conquered and subordinated in a manner similar to, for example, the native populations of the mainland United States or South Africa. Although there was considerable outside interest in Hawaii from 1778 on, the native population was well organized and had effective leaders who represented their interests well to outsiders. The whites who came to Hawaii, in turn, respected and cooperated with the leaders. Indeed, friendship and marriage between the two groups were common and socially supported, in part because the early contact was with whites interested in trade rather than conquest. A variety of groups, such as Chinese, Japanese, and Filipinos, arrived later to meet the islands' labor needs, but no outside group ever took control and dominated the indigenous population. Consistent with Lieberson's (1961) theory, Berry and Tischler argue that this history is an important factor in Hawaii's relatively harmonious racial and ethnic relations.

Thus, the first general pattern that we see from examination of intergroup relations elsewhere is that colonization or conquest of an indigenous population tends to leave a legacy of majority-minority inequality and conflict that can persist for years, even centuries. In countries where groups have come together peaceably, intergroup relations tend to be more harmonious. Of course, this is not the only factor in intergroup relations, and other factors can and often do create exceptions. Still, the general rule holds more often than not.

## ▶ CROSS-CULTURAL EVIDENCE ON THE EFFECTS OF URBANIZATION AND MODERNIZATION

In American history, urbanization, industrialization, and modernization have been associated with a decrease in rigidity in race relations, especially since World War II, although the shift from an agricultural society to an industrial one began to have important effects much earlier. In this section, we explore the degree to which parallel changes have been taking place throughout the world. Of course, we cannot explore the history of every country in even the limited detail we have given to the United States. Nonetheless, some important worldwide trends seem to be related to one another, and they may provide some answers to the question of whether and how modernization and urbanization affect intergroup relations.

### Industrialized Countries

In countries of the world that have subordinate ethnic or racial minorities, two changes have tended to occur. First, the minority groups have increasingly turned to protest and to social and political action to improve their position. We have already discussed this trend in some detail for the United States, and it is equally evident in a number of other developed countries. In Canada, the French-speaking minority, about 30 percent of the population, became highly vocal in the 1960s and 1970s. Among the results were legislation making French the only official language in Quebec Province, where most of the French-speaking population lives, and the 1976 election victory of the Quebec separatist Parti Québécois. Although Quebec voters have since voted against separation from the Canadian confederation and the Parti Québécois has been in and out of power, its victories in 1976 and 1994, the passage of the language legislation, and continued pressure by Quebec for recognition in Canada's constitution as a "distinct society" all clearly indicate heightened assertiveness by Canada's French-speaking minority. The causes underlying this political change have long existed, but the protest has surfaced only in the last forty years.

Although Northern Ireland has a long history of conflict, its conflict began to escalate substantially around 1968. Other examples of minority groups that have become increasingly vocal in recent decades include blacks and Asians in Great Britain; the Flemish in Belgium (who have become a numerical majority but have historically been a subordinate group); the South Moluccans, who turned to terrorism in Holland; and the Jurans in Switzerland. In Great Britain, minority group dissatisfaction was an important factor in widespread urban violence for several years in the 1980s.

Second, there has been a reduction in overt discrimination and prejudice and a move toward legal protection of the rights of minorities. The United States, Great

Britain, Canada, and other Western countries have passed legislation banning racial and ethnic discrimination. The open expression of racial prejudice is generally frowned on, although most of these countries continue to have significant racial and ethnic inequality.

An exception to this general pattern in both Europe and North America has been greater opposition to immigration in recent years, as the number of immigrants identifiable by skin color has grown. In some countries, this opposition has become quite violent, and in many a resurgence in hate group activity has taken place. The worst violence has been in Germany, where right-wing, neo-Nazi mobs in 1992 and 1993 attacked Turks and other immigrants and refugees, resulting in a number of deaths, many injuries, and considerable homelessness as a result of arson.

In a number of other countries, including the United States, Canada, and Great Britain, opposition to immigration has grown, although the type and level of violence found in Germany have not developed. Nonetheless, the intensity of opposition to immigration can be seen in proposals made in 1993 by then-governor Pete Wilson of California, who argued for harsh crackdowns on illegal immigration, including changes in the law to revoke automatic citizenship for children born in the United States if their parents were present illegally and to deny such children the educational and nutritional benefits they were entitled to. The latter move was approved by California voters in 1994 as Proposition 187, but it was overturned by a federal court because immigration policy is the responsibility of the federal government, not the states. Similar sentiments were evident in 1998 when California voters approved another referendum to end bilingual education. In addition, hate group activity increased in the early and mid-1990s not only in Germany but also, to a lesser extent, in France, Great Britain, the United States, and elsewhere.

The severity of these problems is greater in Germany than elsewhere, reflecting a combination of circumstances. First, Germany has admitted more immigrants than most Western countries, a number that was greatly increased by floods of refugees from Romania, former Yugoslavia, and elsewhere in the early 1990s. (Until 1993, Germany was extremely open in granting asylum to refugees, a policy designed to repay Germany's debt to other countries that accepted refugees from Germany during the Nazi era. However, opposition to immigration in recent years has led to some tightening of this policy.) Second, and at the same time, Germany experienced serious economic difficulties arising from attempts to absorb the unproductive East German economy and to some extent from worldwide recession in the early 1990s. Consequently, hopes on the part of East Germans that union with the West would bring rapid economic improvement were unfulfilled, and many began to look for scapegoats. Third, unlike other Western countries such as France, Canada, Great Britain, and the United States, Germany has never accepted or acknowledged the concept of a multicultural society. In the words of German sociologist Erwin Scheuch (quoted in Nagorski, 1993, p. 39), "Britain and France are former empires, but Germans are entirely European. Anything outside of Europe for them is close to Mars." In such demographic, economic, and cultural circumstances, it was easy to view immigrants as a threat and to make them into scapegoats. (In a later part of this chapter, we shall examine how changes in the amount of immigration in a country may affect its intergroup relations.) Finally, the process of unification disrupted the political system in what had been East and West Germany, but especially in the East, where the old social controls of communism were eliminated. This breakdown of social control eliminated constraints that normally kept such ethnic conflict in check, and widespread violence against immigrants broke out in the East and then spread throughout Germany (Leslie, 1998).

Despite conflicts over immigration, discrimination today is illegal in most Western nations, and open discrimination and prejudice are less common than in the past. It is sometimes argued that discrimination is economically irrational in such societies because it interferes with hiring the most productive workers. Furthermore, as Kinloch (1979) points out, social differentiation in the more developed nations has become more complex and is based on a wide range of factors, with some decline in the importance of race and ethnicity, although both remain linked to opportunity and social status in subtler ways than in the past.

## Increasing Fluidity? Or Rigidity with Conflict?

Despite these general patterns, it would be an overstatement to say that modernization always leads to increasingly fluid intergroup relations. South Africa and Northern Ireland, and to some extent Germany, show that rigid intergroup inequality and intergroup conflict can continue and even worsen in societies that have experienced considerable modernization and urbanization. A widely cited essay by Blumer (1965) argues that industrialization is no guarantee of improved race relations because certain social forces tend to maintain inequality, even if discrimination is economically irrational in a modernizing society. Important elements of the traditional structure remain, including a desire for discrimination on the part of many majority group members, some of whom benefit directly from discrimination. An example of this would be the white industrial laborers in the early twentieth century in the United States, who saw discrimination as a way of protecting themselves from competition from minority workers (for further discussion, see Chapter 6). Thus, in societies with a history of rigid discrimination, Blumer argues that dominant group members exert strong pressure for discrimination as a way of shielding themselves from potential competition. As a result, it is often more economically rational for industrialists to continue discriminating than to put up with the conflict and protest they would get from elements of the majority group if they stopped. And in some cases, they know that they can use race or ethnicity to divide their workers and keep them from forming strong unions or otherwise making demands on them.

This suggests that there are two directions a country's intergroup relations can take as it modernizes. One is that they may become increasingly fluid, though sometimes after a period of rigid competitive relations, as in the United States. The following conditions make such a pattern more likely:

- Minority groups are in a position to generate effective protest. Among other factors, such protest is more likely to be a result of urbanization in countries allowing greater freedom of expression.

- There is external pressure for more equal race relations. Blumer (1965) cites the pressures of northern liberals and the federal government on the South as examples. The desire of the United States, Britain, and other Western countries for good relations with African countries is another example because it exerted pressure on them to improve race relations at home.

- The economy or social system is such that gains by minority group members are not viewed as a threat by the majority. W. J. Wilson (1978) argues that this was the case in the United States in the late 1950s and much of the 1960s because it was a period of economic growth with room for everyone to benefit. Thus, it was largely during this period that the United States moved from rigid to fluid competitive race relations. Bastide (1965, pp. 14–18) argues that one reason for Brazil's relatively harmonious intergroup relations is that until very recently, blacks were not seen as competitors by most whites. They largely did different kinds of work. For example, whites had little desire to work in crafts or manual labor, so there was little objection to the movement of blacks into these jobs (Mason, 1971, p. 314). Even when blacks did compete with whites, they were not seen as a real threat because whites could shield themselves from blacks in their family settings, even if not in their work settings, and the family, not the economy, has historically been the central institution in Brazil's social system. Recently, as blacks and whites have begun to compete more in the work setting and as the family has declined somewhat in importance, there has been more noticeable racial conflict.

• The country does not have a history of highly rigid racial inequality. Blumer (1965, p. 23) suggests that ethnic distinctions in the United States have blurred more than racial ones in part because they did not have the same degree of rigidity to begin with. He cites the mingling of racial groups in southeast Asia as another example. Crawford (1998b) similarly argues that where social institutions provide benefits based on cultural group membership (as with race in the United States), group identities sharpen and conflict results. Where institutions deemphasize group membership and do not give rewards on that basis, intergroup conflict is less likely and intergroup relations will be more fluid as long as those institutions remain effective.

The other possibility that can result from modernization, urbanization, and industrialization is continued rigid intergroup inequality but with rising levels of conflict, protest, and often violence. South Africa until very recently is probably the best example, although Northern Ireland (also until recently) is another, and for a time this was the pattern in the southern United States. Recently, elements of this pattern have developed in Germany also. The following conditions make this pattern most likely:

• The dominant group has great power relative to the subordinate group.

• The dominant group sees the subordinate group as a strong threat.

• There is no effective source of external pressure for more fluid intergroup relations.

• The country has a history of very rigid racial distinctions.

• The dominant group is smaller in number than the subordinate group.

Not surprisingly, all these conditions were very clearly present in South Africa until recently. Historically, the power was always on the side of whites, first through the possession of firearms and later through control of the government and the military. Blacks in South Africa had essentially no civil or political rights until the early 1990s. They did not enjoy freedom of assembly, free speech, and free press, and until the elections in 1994, they were never allowed to vote. Until 1984, when they were granted separate parliaments, coloreds and Asians also had no political rights. In fact, nobody of any race enjoyed truly free speech until around 1990. During much of the 1980s, government sanctions often were applied even to whites who opposed apartheid. It was only after the release of political prisoners, including ANC leader Nelson Mandela in 1990, that South Africa began to move toward allowing free expression and negotiating to bring about majority rule.

Despite the harsh repression of dissent in South Africa in the apartheid era, violent outbursts of protest occurred regularly from the 1960s on. Outnumbered four to one, whites came to see these protests as a very serious threat to their monopoly on power, and they repressed them severely for many years. Dominant whites in fact felt threatened for a long time in South Africa. For many years, whites tenaciously fought to protect apartheid because they saw its exclusion of blacks from the political process as the only way they could maintain power and status in a society in which they were outnumbered by such a great margin. As the forces of urbanization and modernization fed growing protests by black South Africans and as whites struggled to repress these protests and hang on to their advantaged status, the level of violence escalated. Even in 1993 and early 1994, as the government of President Frederick Willem de Klerk negotiated to bring about majority rule, a great many South African whites intensely opposed this move. In 1993, a group of armed whites opposed to the negotiations broke into buildings and, for a time, held government officials hostage.

A final factor in this example is the absence, until the mid-1980s, of any effective outside pressure on South Africa to change. In the southern United States, pressure from the North was an important cause of liberalization during the 1960s. In what was then known as Rhodesia (now Zimbabwe), pressure from Britain and the United States (along with an escalating civil war on the home front) helped to force the white, minority government there to give up power in 1978. Until the mid-1980s, however, no comparable pressure was placed on South Africa. Although opposed to its minority rule, its African neighbors were not militarily strong enough to interfere, although some supported the idea of economic sanctions by Western nations (see Mason, 1971, pp. 218–19; Legum, 1975, pp. 103–4).

The first real pressure came in the form of economic sanctions in the 1980s. After many Third World countries and several Scandinavian countries imposed economic sanctions, the U.S. Congress adopted strong sanctions during the 1980s, overriding the veto of President Ronald Reagan. Eventually—and despite some smuggling and breaking of the sanctions—most of the world joined the sanctions, creating significant economic pressure on South Africa. With the combination of rising internal violence and worsening economic difficulties because of the sanctions, South Africa's white, minority government began to feel increasing pressure for change. When President de Klerk took office in 1989, he began to dismantle apartheid and to support negotiations for majority rule. Following a series of steps in this direction, the negotiations were successful and the elections were held, resulting in the election of President Nelson Mandela.

To summarize, change in South Africa came about when the combination of internal violence and external economic pressure became too strong for the white government to withstand. But until that occurred, apartheid was able to survive for more than forty years, despite modernization. The result was a rising tide of violence and internal conflict, as is usual when societies try to maintain rigid systems of discrimination in the face of modernization. Ultimately, apartheid was abolished, but South Africa will continue to feel its effects, particularly in the form of economic inequality, well into the future.

## Developing Countries: Two Major Trends

In developing countries, the change has been more dramatic than in the West, although its direction has been perhaps less uniform. Here, two major trends can be observed. First, there has been a great movement away from colonialism toward national independence. The great colonial empires of the British, French, Portuguese, and Dutch have disappeared. In some cases, the colonies were relinquished voluntarily, but in others independence came about only after long periods of warfare.

Once direct colonial rule had largely disappeared, two alternative forms often replaced it for a time. Sometimes a small minority of people ethnically associated with the colonial power dominated an indigenous majority population. The ethnically British whites who dominated Zimbabwe until the late 1970s and the descendants of Dutch and British colonialists in South Africa until the 1990s are two examples. In other countries, a government was established and heavily influenced by a colonial power, even though the country involved may never have been a colony of that power. Examples in fairly recent history include the Thieu government in Vietnam and the monarchy of Shah Mohammad Reza Pahlavi in Iran, both of which were established by actions of the Central Intelligence Agency (CIA) and heavily supported and influenced by the U.S. government. In both of these types of "pseudocolonial" situations, there was a marked increase in indigenous opposition after World War II, making this type of situation temporary in most places where it appeared. In all of the examples just mentioned, colonial governments or ones supported by European powers collapsed in the face of indigenous opposition.

Since the collapse of white rule in South Africa, almost all governments throughout Asia and Africa have been under the political control of indigenous populations, not colonizing powers. And when western powers do attempt to assert control, as in the U.S.-led invasion of Iraq in 2003, the action is highly controversial. Throughout the Middle East and Africa, as well as most of Europe, polls showed overwhelming public opposition to the U.S. action, and the United States was unable to gain majority support for military action against Iraq even in the Western-dominated UN Security Council. (The opposition would have been even more overwhelming had the United States sought a vote in the General Assembly, where every country has one vote.)

Despite this changed *political* climate, however, Europe and North America exert considerable *economic* power throughout the world. Multinational corporations based in the United States and Europe extract natural resources and use inexpensive labor throughout much of Asia, Africa, and Latin America. This tendency is sometimes called *globalization* or the *global economy*, and it has been heavily dominated by multinational corporations based in North America and Europe. As this has occurred, indigenous people have often been heavily exploited, but it occurs through economic processes rather than through overt processes of racial or ethnic discrimination or direct outside political control. Thus, in South Africa and elsewhere throughout Africa, Asia, and Latin America, indigenous populations remain disproportionately poor and European populations disproportionately wealthy, even in the absence of formal discrimination. And in many cases, indigenous populations have lost land, suffered economic exploitation, or been deprived of their traditional ways of making a living through environmental damage caused by the actions of multinational corporations (Bornschier and Chase-Dunn, 1985; Nolan, 1987; Wimberly, 1990; Gedicks, 2001).

These changes came about during a period of rapid urbanization and modernization. Certainly, many parts of the world remain rural and traditional, but even they are undergoing rapid change. By 2002, the world's population was 47 percent urban, and even the two most rural continents, Africa and Asia, were 33 perent and 38 percent urban, respectively (Population Reference Bureau, 2002). Even predominantly rural countries today often have large cities. For example, Bangladesh is only 23 percent urban, yet it has a city, Dhaka, with a population of 8 million. China, India, Pakistan, Indonesia, Myanmar (Burma), and Vietnam all have cities among the world's fifty largest; all of these countries are less than 40 percent urban, and none but Indonesia is more than one-third urban (United Nations Population Division, 1995; Population Reference Bureau, 2002). Between 1950 and 1975, the proportion of the world's population living in places with a population of 20,000 or more increased by nearly 50 percent. In the less developed parts of the world, the increase was greater (Frisbie, 1977), and it has continued since then. Also notable has been social and technological modernization. The complexity of social organization increased throughout the world; mass communications such as radio, television, and the Internet spread to even some of the least developed parts of the world; and modern economic systems such as capitalism continued to spread, supplanting agrarian feudal systems. In most parts of the world, there has been more and more influence from outside the local area, both national and international (Schermerhorn, 1978, p. 165).

Of course, the fact that the changes in majority-minority relations around the world have been occurring at the same time as the urbanization and modernization does not prove that the changes were *caused* by those trends. Nonetheless, a thoughtful analysis of the issue does suggest some reasons they probably were, at least in part. One of the most important changes has been the move toward more minority assertiveness in developed countries and toward nationalism and anticolonialism in developing countries. We can identify a number of ways in which urbanization and modernization have brought these changes. Urbanization has brought people together in the cities, where they can share ideas and organize protest. Mass communications have helped make people aware of inequalities and have contributed to rising expectations by showing subordinate peoples what life could be like. They have provided role models by showing protests and revolutions over similar issues in other places. Finally, mass communications have facilitated communication and the use of propaganda by protest movements.

Industrialization and technological modernization have had more general effects. They have created demands for labor, thus opening new opportunities to members of the native or colonized population, even when the colonial leadership would rather not create such opportunities. For example, the white leaders in South Africa had to face the question of whether to leave jobs unfilled and suffer lowered productivity or train and hire blacks for what were formerly "white jobs" (Hunt and Walker, 1974, pp. 187–91). Modernization and industrialization also created a need for higher educational levels, which has had a number of important effects both on minorities in developed countries and on indigenous populations in less developed, colonial societies. One general effect has been to raise expectations by heightening awareness of inequalities. Another, particularly in the developing countries, has been to provide leadership for protest movements. It is not unusual for leaders in revolutionary Third World movements to have been educated in developed Western nations. Another important trend associated with modernization has been greater contact among the nations of the world, tending to expose people to a wider range of social, religious, and political ideologies than ever before. This alone is likely to have had some unsettling effects.

Finally, in this era of international contact and mass communications, the spread of minority and anticolonial protest since World War II has developed a momentum largely of its own. This is not unlike the "contagion effect" on domestic protest in the United States, discussed in Chapter 7. A successful protest or revolution in one place raises hopes for a similar action in another place where similar conditions exist. Thus, the rise of protest against one colonial or racist regime, particularly if successful, can lead to similar protest against others, given the amount of international contact and the extent of mass communications in today's world. This does not mean that protests are always successful, and globalization and the rise of multinational corporations have in many cases muted the effects of eliminating colonial governments. Nonetheless, the dynamics of intergroup relations have changed considerably since the days of colonial governments, sometimes in ways that have improved the lives of indigenous populations and sometimes in ways that have not.

## ▶ COMBINED EFFECTS OF COLONIALISM AND DEGREE OF MODERNIZATION

Kinloch (1979, Chap. 12) developed a useful model that combines the effects of a nation's colonial history or lack of one and its degree of development or modernization. Kinloch, along with most sociologists of race relations, argues that societies with a history of colonialism or conquest have more majority-minority inequality and more conflict than do countries without such a history. Within this group of societies, race and ethnicity are more important in the less developed, less modernized countries. As such countries modernize, they tend to become differentiated less on the basis of race and ethnicity and more on the basis of a wide range of factors, including economics, behavior, sex, and age. Among countries without a colonial history—for example, Switzerland—there tends to be less division, and race and ethnicity are less important. Again, the degree of inequality and the lines along which society is divided vary with the degree of development. Among less developed societies with no history of colonialization, there may be very little stratification. There is barely enough to go around, and everyone shares fairly equally. As Kinloch notes, such societies are an extreme rarity in today's world: Only some scattered tribal groups really fit this pattern. More common is the noncolonial developed society, which has less racial or ethnic inequality than in the past but does tend to have inequalities based on class, behavior, sex, age, and so on.

## ► NUMBER OF RACIAL AND ETHNIC GROUPS

Although many social scientists feel that the two most important factors in comparative studies of majority-minority relations are the nature of the original contact—whether or not it involved colonialism or conquest—and the degree of modernization and development of a society, other factors also seem to make important differences. One that many experts have emphasized is the number of racial or ethnic groups. In general, when a society has many groups that are generally recognized as distinct, it tends to have less racial and ethnic conflict and less inequality than when it has only two groups (Hunt and Walker, 1974, p. 235). When there are several groups, there is often no one group large or powerful enough to dominate the others. Furthermore, any group that discriminates against or shows hostility toward out-groups runs the risk of being treated the same way itself. When there are only two groups, it is much easier for one to discriminate against the other. It is also common for each group to see the other as the enemy and the cause of its troubles in the us-versus-them mentality that can easily develop in the two-group situation.

According to W. C. Smith (1942), one reason for Hawaii's harmonious race relations is that it has a large number of racial and ethnic groups rather than just two. As of the 1990 census, no racial group accounted for more than about a third of the population, and the population included large numbers of whites, Japanese Americans, native Hawaiians, Filipino Americans, and Chinese Americans (U.S. Bureau of the Census, 1998b). Also present, in relatively small numbers, were African Americans, Korean Americans, Vietnamese Americans, and American Indians. The fact that no group is a majority makes the situation in Hawaii particularly conducive to harmonious racial and ethnic relations. To a lesser degree, the presence of multiple ethnic and linguistic groups in Switzerland probably helps to explain that country's relative racial harmony.

This principle may also apply to other parts of the western region of the United States, though to a lesser extent than in Hawaii. For example, in California, the 2000 census showed that no longer is any racial or ethnic group a numerical majority. At 47 percent of the population, non-Hispanic whites were the largest, with 32 percent of the state's population being Hispanic. There are also sizable numbers of Asian Americans (11 percent) and African Americans (7 percent) (U.S. Census Bureau, 2001b). Relative to whites, African Americans in California fare slightly better in terms of income than in the United States as a whole, and there is less racial segregation in the West than in other regions. On the other hand, the larger Hispanic population there actually fares worse than Hispanics in some other parts of the country, which may reflect either a larger number of recent immigrants or discrimination based on fear of competition.

In other examples, complex racial classification systems, recognizing a number of distinct classifications, have been suggested as causes of racial and ethnic harmony in Mexico and in the French Antilles (Hunt and Walker, 1974, pp. 155–56, 235). In Mexico, a multiple-classification system that contained from ten to forty-six categories (Roncal, 1944, p. 533; Hunt and Walker, 1974, p. 139) became so confusing that it was generally disregarded, and the bulk of the population came to be regarded as *mestizo* (mixed Indian and white), or simply "Mexican." Ultimately, the result was considerable *amalgamation*: biological mixing that eliminated distinct racial categories. In the French Antilles (Guadalupe and Martinique), racial animosities were reduced as a result of a multiple-classification system that treated people of mixed black and white ancestry as a separate group. This practice, which is also common in Latin America, helps "to blur racial distinctions rather than to sharpen them" (Hunt and Walker, 1974, p. 214). In general, if a society has multiple racial and ethnic groups or multiple racial and ethnic classifications, it will—all else being equal—tend to have more harmonious intergroup relations. As the Hispanic and Asian American populations have grown, and as intermarriage has increased, some sociologists have suggested that race relations in the United States may be shifting toward a pattern more like that of Latin America (Bonilla-Silva, 2003a). This does not mean that racial inequality will disappear, but it may continue to become more subtle, taking the form of a gradual hierarchy of average group socioeconomic positions as opposed to sharply delineated statuses for different racial groups.

Often, it is not so much the number of groups present as it is the number of classifications that is important. In the United States, people of European, African, and North American ancestry have historically been classified in three major groupings: whites, blacks, and American Indians. In Mexico, however, the same population would be divided into at least six groups: whites (*Hispanos*), blacks (*Negros*), Indians (*Indios*), *mestizos* (Indian and white), *lobos* (Indian and black), and *mulattos* (white and black). In fact, the Mexican classification system has tended to be more complex than that, with mixtures such as Indian-mulatto recognized as separate groups and with region and birthplace also related to classification. Historically, in the United States mixed groups have not been recognized, and the "one drop" rule has applied: If you had any minority group ancestry, you were regarded as a member of that minority group. This was especially true for African Americans. Today, however, interracial marriage is becoming more common, and more people are identifying themselves as "biracial" or "multiracial." Partly in response to pressures from people who indentify themselves in this manner, the U.S. Census in 2000 for the first time allowed people to classify themselves as belonging to more than one race (Perlmann and Waters, 2002). Nearly 7 million people, 2.4 percent of the population, did so (U.S. Census Bureau, 2001f). Thus, the number of racial categories being formally recognized in the United States (63 in the 2000 census, including combinations) is increasing, and some think this could have effects similar to what has occurred in Mexico and other Latin American countries (Bonilla-Silva, 2003a).

The propensity for conflict may be especially great where the majority of the population falls into one of two classifications. Although both South Africa and the United States have multiple classifications, historically the great majority have been either black or white in both countries. In the United States, this is now changing, but a population that was mostly either white or black until recently may help to explain the sharp racial inequality throughout U.S. history. In fact, one way that this racial inequality was maintained was through efforts by European immigrant groups to be regarded as white (not as "Irish," "Italian," or "Polish"), and the success of these efforts sharpened black-white inequality in the United States (Ignatiev, 1995). The effect of two main classifications can be seen in other countries, too. Canada has many racial and ethnic groups, but in Quebec Province, the great majority is either English or French. Finally, in Northern Ireland, nearly everyone self-identifies as either Catholic or Protestant. Overall, the division of most of a population into two major groups appears to heighten the potential for polarization, whereas a multitude of classifications—with no one or two groups forming a large majority—often seems to blur and soften intergroup divisions.

## ►CULTURAL AND DEMOGRAPHIC CHARACTERISTICS OF MAJORITY AND MINORITY GROUPS: BRAZIL AND MEXICO

The cultural and demographic characteristics of the groups involved also help to determine the kinds of relations that develop. We shall illustrate this general principle with two examples from Latin America: Brazil and Mexico.

Brazil has sometimes been cited as an example of successful assimilation between diverse groups. Extensive assimilation, including widespread intermarriage, took place between the white population and the native Indian population and between blacks and whites, even though blacks were originally brought to Brazil as slaves. Forty percent of Brazil's population is of mixed (mostly African and European) ancestry (sometimes called *pardo*). This does not mean that there is an absence of racial stratification in Brazil: In general, darker skin color is associated with lower status, and blacks and *pardos* have lower incomes than those with exclusively European ancestry. Brazil did have a long period of slavery, and both blacks and Indians were forced to live under a paternalistic system of race relations (Van den Berghe, 1978, pp. 63–65). The blacks were slaves on the *fazendas*, or feudal plantations, as were some Indians. However, most of the Indians experienced paternalism in the *aldeas*, or Jesuit mission villages. Although these had more benevolent objectives than the slave plantations, they too were a despotic system that forcibly took children from their parents and resocialized Indians to the Jesuits' view of the ideal culture. Nonetheless, there was no U.S.-style segregation and little overt discrimination. Indeed, to Brazilians the major "problem" in intergroup relations historically was concern about groups that were unwilling to assimilate (Berry and Tischler, 1978, pp. 156–58).

Recently, though, there has been increased awareness of the economic disadvantages of those with darker skins and more African ancestry, and programs of affirmative action, including in some cases minority quotas, have been implemented in education and employment to reduce color inequality (*Economist*, 2003). Similarly, the persistence of the color hierarchy in Brazil has recently led to stronger social movements emphasizing black identity, affirmative action, and community-based schools. As this *Movimento Negro* (black movement) has flourished in Brazil, and as open racial discrimination has been replaced by subtler forms of racial inequality in the United States, the two countries have become more similar than in the past (Jones de Almeida, 2003).

Several characteristics of the ethnic groups involved (the majority group in particular) help to account for Brazil's pattern of greater assimilation than in the United States, despite its color hierarchy. One is the very uneven sex ratio among the Portuguese who settled in Brazil: They were overwhelmingly male, which encouraged intermarriage with Indian women. Later, when more women arrived, the pattern of intermarriage had become well established. This mixing of groups led to a considerable blurring of racial distinctions. In contrast to the Brazilian pattern is that of the United States, in which English settlers much more often came over as families. As a result, intermarriage has been much less common.

Another factor that supports a tendency toward assimilation in Brazil is the history of Moorish influence in Portugal (Pierson, 1942). According to Pierson, this led to a tolerance of darker-skinned people, perhaps even a tendency to view dark skin as a source of prestige. In Brazil, for example, brown skin and straight hair are standards of beauty, again reflecting the mixed composition of the population. To the degree that this was true, it certainly would have led the Portuguese colonists in Brazil to be more supportive of intermarriage and assimilation. Intermixing was also supported by the common Portuguese custom of concubinage, which often brought regular and somewhat institutionalized relationships between white men and racially mixed women.

A final factor, noted by Kinloch (1974), was the Catholic religion of the Portuguese colonists, which caused them to seek the assimilation of the Indians and black slaves rather than to isolate and subordinate them. The Catholic religion emphasized human equality and conversion. Consequently, some effort was made to integrate the Indians and blacks into Portuguese society. In contrast, some Protestant religions view people as being either saved or not saved and encourage members to avoid the latter. This has often been suggested as a reason for the lack of acceptance of racial minorities and the much greater segregation in the majority-Protestant United States than in countries like Brazil.

These cultural characteristics have helped lead to subtler and possibly milder forms of intergroup inequality, and more harmonious intergroup relations, in Brazil than are found in many other countries with a history of colonialism. As suggested, they made possible a greater degree of cultural assimilation and more amalgamation than is typically found elsewhere. Such cultural assimilation and interbreeding with whites (called *blanchiment*, meaning "bleaching" or "whitening") became a potential route of upward mobility for blacks and mulattos (Bastide, 1965, pp. 15–17).

Even so, assimilation has been a limited source of mobility, and one that entails a loss of one's racial identity. Nonetheless, it was sufficient, for quite some time, to prevent widespread protest by blacks and to preserve the widespread image of Brazil as a racial paradise. In reality, it is not a racial paradise. There is racial inequality, albeit in subtler forms than elsewhere, and the old view that class, not race, explained social inequality in Brazil has fallen out of favor with social scientists. Recently, both social scientists and Brazil's black and mixed populations have placed greater emphasis on this reality (Reichmann, 1999; Baranov, 2000; Jones de Almeida, 2003). The result, as noted earlier, has been an increase in race consciousness and protest by the black and mixed population. Undoubtedly, the movement of the country toward a competitive, industrial system has also contributed to this trend.

Another country often cited for successful assimilation is Mexico. There, the assimilation and intermarriage were largely between American Indians (*Indios*) and the Spanish. Some of the reasons are the same as in Brazil: The colonizers (Spanish) were mostly Catholic, so they believed that Indians had souls and that, accordingly, there was an obligation to convert them. They were also mostly male, which encouraged racial mixing. Important characteristics of the indigenous or subordinate group also contributed to the pattern of assimilation. In Mexico, the Aztec Indians had a highly developed and in many ways modern culture before the Spanish *conquistadores* arrived. Their chief city, Tenochtitlán (now Mexico City), had a population of more than 300,000 and was one of the great cities of the world at that time. Although the Indian society was quickly crushed by Spanish military forces, the influence of its highly developed culture lived on. Mexico's unique mixture of Spanish and Indian culture became a national symbol, the more so as intermixing continued over time. The evolution of a Mexican, or mestizo, culture that was neither Spanish nor Indian but a mixture of both became a symbol of national unity and helped to contribute further to the disappearance of distinct racial categories. Thus, we see from this example that cultural- and social-organizational characteristics of both the majority group and the minority group had important effects on their relationship. In this case, it led to an amalgamation of the two groups into one new group, which became a symbol of national unity.

It became the rule in Mexico that one's group identity was determined by one's social roles and cultural attributes rather than one's genetic composition or physical appearance. A mestizo who married into a prominent Spanish family could be seen as a Spaniard. An Indian who moved to the city and adopted the Spanish language, style of dress, and customs would be regarded as a mestizo, or Mexican, whereas one who remained in the rural village and kept the Indian culture would be regarded as a member of the *Indio* group. Today, most of the Mexican population identifies with the mestizo, or simply Mexican, group, and it is this group that is regarded as representative of the Mexican culture. Nonetheless, despite a view that in Mexican history the Spanish are seen largely as villains and the Indians as heroes, higher status attaches to Spanish appearance and culture than to Indian (Mason, 1971, p. 249). The 15 percent or so of Mexico's population that retains the *Indio* identity is the least well off and is somewhat looked down on by the rest of the population. Thus, in Mexico, as in Brazil, movement toward the European group's culture is an important requisite for upward mobility. On the other hand, the group boundaries in both countries have been greatly blurred, and Mexico is one of the closest approximations of the amalgamation model (loss of group distinctions through interbreeding) in the world.

## ▶ OVERLAPPING VERSUS CROSSCUTTING CLEAVAGES

Divisions, or cleavages, in society are sometimes described as either overlapping or crosscutting. *Overlapping cleavages* occur when, for example, racial, religious, class, and language divisions all cut the same way. Imagine a fictitious society made up of blacks and whites. Assume that all the blacks are wealthy, Muslim, and speak Swahili and that all the whites are poor, Protestant, and speak German. In a society like this, the potential for conflict would be very high: Whether it occurred over race, religion, language, or economics, the division would always be the same. Nobody would have mixed loyalties, and such a society would quickly divide into two mutually hostile and distrustful groups. The opposite kind of society is said to have *crosscutting cleavages*: There is little or no relationship among race, income, religion, language, and so on. In a society like this, knowing that a person was black would tell us nothing about his or her income, language, or religion. Divisions along the lines of religion would be different from those along the lines of income, and both would be unrelated to racial divisions. In this kind of society, there would be little conflict because everyone would have mixed loyalties.

Although few societies are as closely delineated as these, real-life societies do differ in the degree to which they have overlapping or crosscutting cleavages, and there is evidence that the latter do reduce intergroup conflict. This can be illustrated by two examples. We have already discussed the general pattern of ethnic harmony in Switzerland, which has two religious groups, three nationalities, and four language groups. However, two of the three nationality groups, Germans and French, are religiously divided. Hunt and Walker (1974, p. 42) believe that these crosscutting cleavages are an important reason for Switzerland's relatively harmonious ethnic relations because those united by religion often are divided by language.

Another society in which crosscutting cleavages have muted ethnic conflict is Canada. The conflict between English- and French-speaking Canadians heated up in the 1960s and 1970s, but before that time it was very difficult for French-speaking Canadians to develop a unified movement because of the existence of class divisions within that population (Ossenberg, 1975). Although the French-speaking population as a whole was of lower socioeconomic status than the English-speaking population, and the latter controlled the wealth, there was also a fairly wide range of status within the French-speaking population. This tended to prevent a unified French position against the dominant English-speaking group and thereby reduced the amount of English-French conflict. Moreover, after the English gained control of Quebec, they exploited these class divisions by protecting the French-Canadian upper class, in what amounted to a tacit deal designed to avoid upper-class support of Quebecois nationalism. For the most part, this worked for a full century, until the worldwide social upheavals of the 1960s helped to create a social climate conducive to the growth of Quebec separatism. Significantly, when the English-French conflict temporarily subsided in the mid-1980s, economic issues were again predominant in Quebec politics (Martin, 1985).

The contrasting case, overlapping cleavages, can be seen in the bloody conflicts in Northern Ireland and Bosnia-Herzegovina. In both of these countries, ethnic background, religion, and to some extent social class overlap in ways that have worked to heighten conflict. In Northern Ireland, nearly all Protestants are of British (that is, either English or Scottish) ancestry, and nearly all Catholics are of Irish ancestry. Furthermore, among the Protestants, those of English ancestry are mainly Anglican, and those of Scottish ancestry, Presbyterian. Finally, social class also overlaps with ethnicity to a large extent: The wealthy are mainly English and Anglican, and nearly all of the Irish-ancestry Catholics are working class or poor. The Scottish-ancestry Presbyterians fall somewhere in the middle. Thus, whether the battle lines are drawn on the basis of ethnicity or religion, they are largely the same, and class in many regards also divides the population similarly.

In Bosnia, ethnicity overlaps strongly with religion: Croats and Slovenes are mainly Catholic, Bosnians are Muslims (in fact, they are often referred to as "Muslims" rather than "Bosnians"), and Serbs are Orthodox Christians. As a practical matter, ethnic and religious identity in Bosnia are virtually indistinguishable. Whether people think in terms of religion or ethnicity, the divisions are identical. Thus, for these two variables, divisions clearly overlap. Social class is not as strongly linked to ethnicity and religion as in Northern Ireland, but given Bosnia's history not only of conquest but also of brutal ethnic massacres as recently as World War II, the overlapping cleavages based on nationality and religion have proved sufficient to cause one of the worst outbreaks of intergroup conflict in recent world history.

Because of overlapping cleavages, the conflicts in Bosnia and Northern Ireland have been particularly difficult to resolve. In Northern Ireland, as noted, an agreement was reached and seemed to have the clear support of the majority on both sides. But it had opponents on both the Irish Catholic nationalist side and the British Protestant unionist side, and issues as seemingly simple as where marches could be routed were cited in 1998 as possible threats to the agreement (*St. Louis Post-Dispatch*, 1998b). Indeed, in 2004 some elements of the agreement remain unimplemented or suspended, as discussed earlier. In Bosnia, nearly everyone agreed that the presence of NATO troops was a major reason the peace agreement held and that the mere removal of the troops could lead to a rekindling of the ethnic civil war at almost any time, at least for the first several years after the agreement was reached. About 12,000 NATO troops remained in Bosnia at the beginning of 2003.

### ▶ TERRITORIAL ETHNIC BASE

Another factor that can influence the intensity of racial or ethnic conflict is whether ethnic minority groups are territorially based. When a subordinate group is concentrated in one part of a country and is a numerical majority there, its ability to mount an effective social movement often is strengthened, even though it is subordinate in the nation as a whole. Accordingly, if ethnic conflicts exist, they may become more intense when the subordinate group is territorially based. Once English-French conflict in Canada came out into the open, the strength of the French-speaking group was increased by its concentration in Quebec Province. This enabled the French speakers to elect leaders supportive of their cause and to change the province's language laws. As often happens when minorities are territorially based, a secessionist or separatist movement developed. As discussed earlier in this chapter, the Quebec secessionist movement has surged and faded at various times since it emerged strongly in the 1960s. But despite such fluctuations, conflict between English- and French-speaking Canadians is likely to continue in the future because migration patterns within Canada are increasing the geographic separation of the two groups (Kaplan, 1994).

Other minorities that have used a territorial base to develop powerful social movements include the Basques in northern Spain, the Flemish and Walloons in Belgium, and the Kurdish population in northwestern Iran and northern Iraq. Territorial ethnic bases obviously have also played an important role in the conflict in the former Yugoslavia. Each former republic of Yugoslavia—Croatia, Slovenia, Serbia, Bosnia-Herzegovina, Montenegro, and Macedonia—represents a territory historically occupied by a particular ethnic group. Undoubtedly, the fact that Yugoslavia's ethnic groups were so territorially distinct is why its ethnic conflicts were able to persist through many decades of centralized Yugoslavian rule and resurface so intensely as soon as the Yugoslav national government lost its power. If ethnic groups are sufficiently geographically concentrated, severe conflict can occur even when there are many different ethnic groups, a condition that usually mutes intergroup conflict.

One of the very few former Yugoslav republics that is not overwhelmingly made up of a particular ethnic group is Bosnia. Even today, the Bosnians, or Muslims, who live there are only a bare majority of Bosnia-Herzegovina's population, and in the past, Croats and Serbs together outnumbered them (Banac, 1984; Joffe, 1992). Within Bosnia-Herzegovina, however, there have always been different areas of Serbian, Croatian, and Bosnian settlement. Even though some areas such as the capital city of Sarajevo have been multicultural, each group has had its territorial base. This fueled the conflict because (1) each group has had a base from which it can organize and operate, and (2) those who live in the Serbian and Croatian ethnic territories do not want to live under Bosnian rule.

## ▶ LANGUAGE

When two ethnic groups speak different languages, the potential for conflict between them increases. Language has been the major bone of contention between French- and English-speaking Canadians; it has also been a major source of conflict between the Flemish and Walloons in Belgium. In the United States, a growing Hispanic population has increasingly demanded bilingual education; has often continued to use Spanish, especially at home and among friends; and has demanded ballots, social service materials, public documents, and product labels in Spanish. The intensity of debate on this topic in my own race relations classes suggests that, as the Hispanic population has become America's largest minority group, the potential for language-based conflict in the United States may further increase. Indeed, there are already signs that this is happening, as seen by the recent passage of a California ballot proposal to end bilingual education.

Further evidence can be seen in the passage in recent decades of official language legislation in several places in the United States. In 1980, Dade County, Florida, voters reacted to the growing Latino influence by voting to make English the county's only official language. Their objective was to end the county's practice of doing business on a bilingual basis. This legislation remained in effect for more than a decade, until it was repealed when Latinos gained a majority on the county's legislative board. Since 1980, however, similar laws have been established in several states, including California, where in 1986 voters overwhelmingly passed a law to make English the state's only official language.

## ▶ INTERNATIONAL RELATIONSHIPS

Within any country, race and ethnic relations can be greatly affected by international relations. In a nation that is in conflict with the country associated with one of its minority groups, members of that group often are in an unenviable position. One of the clearest examples is the mass internment of Japanese Americans—many of whom were U.S. citizens—in detention camps in the United States during World War II. In addition to being imprisoned for up to two years without a trial or hearing, many American citizens of Japanese descent lost most of their possessions. Other groups placed at a disadvantage because of international conflicts include Chinese in Vietnam, Arabs in Israel, and Jews in Arab countries. In 1979, a number of Iranians (as well as some Latin Americans mistaken for Iranians) in the United States suffered physical attacks or destruction of their property to avenge the American hostages in Iran, even though some of the Iranians attacked did not even support the Iranian government.

Similar events occurred during the 1991 Persian Gulf war. Nationally, hate crimes against Arab Americans, as recorded by the American-Arab Anti-Discrimination Committee, tripled in 1991 from 1990 (*Belleville News-Democrat*, 1992). Incidents of harassment, death threats, and violence against Arab Americans took place in late 1990 (after Iraq's invasion of Kuwait) and in 1991 in Boston, Detroit, San Francisco, Washington, Toledo, the Los Angeles area, and elsewhere (Butterfield, 1990; Shaheen, 1990; D. Arnold, 1991; Stertz and Miller, 1991). In the Los Angeles area, an increase in attacks on Arab Americans after the 1990 invasion of Kuwait pushed hate crimes to a record level (Katz, 1991). These incidents occurred despite the fact that nearly every Arab country besides Iraq sided with the United States in the Gulf war.

The most serious cases of such incidents in recent memory occurred after the September 11, 2001, terrorist attacks. For example, there were sixteen times as many anti-Islamic hate crime incidents in 2001 as there had been the year before (Federal Bureau of Investigation, 2002b, p. 1). There were more than 700 violent incidents against Arab Americans, Muslims, or people believed to belong to one of these groups in the first nine weeks after September 11 and a total of almost 900 violent incidents in the year after September 11. In addition, there were eighty cases in which Arabs or Arab Americans were illegally put off airplanes before departure, based on their ethnicity rather than their behavior. Reports of job discrimination against Arab Americans increased fourfold during the year after September 11, and discrimination in housing and public services also increased (Ibish and Stewart, 2003). Official harassment increased also. The USA PATRIOT Act allowed indefinite detention of foreign nationals without due process, and thousands of young Arab men were called in for "voluntary questioning." Some were detained secretly for extended periods of time.

Such incidents of violence and discrimination against, and sometimes official harassment of, groups associated with "the enemy" are more likely when the targeted group is one against which there is already significant racial or ethnic prejudice (J. E. Farley, 1994b). Examples of such groups include Japanese Americans during World War II and Arab Americans during the two wars against Iraq and after the September 11 terrorism. In contrast, there was no imprisonment of German Americans during World War II, even though the United States was also at war with Germany. It is important to stress that there is a difference between racial or ethnic profiling and acting against those who have behaved in some way that arouses suspicion. The problem with racial and ethnic profiling is that it automatically casts suspicion on a person because of his or her race or ethnicity and results in action being taken against that person for no other reason. Most Arab Americans are not even Muslims, and the overwhelming majority of Muslims in the United States were just as appalled by the September 11 attacks as everyone else. Yet with racial profiling, "Arab" or "Muslim" is equated with "terrorist," and Americans who happen to be Arab or Muslim are deprived of their rights for no reason other than their ethnicity or religion. It is not coincidental that, like the Japanese Americans who were imprisoned because of their race during World War II, Arabs and Arab Americans have been the object of prejudice and discrimination in the United States for more than a century (Shaheen, 2001).

## Surges of Immigration

Ethnic prejudice and violence against minorities can also be triggered by surges in immigration. In the United States, two major surges occurred in the twentieth century: one in the first two decades of the century, from around 1900 to about 1920, and another beginning around the mid-1970s and continuing to the present time. Both were accompanied by substantial opposition to immigration, particularly that of non-Europeans. Concern on the West Coast about growing numbers of Chinese and Japanese immigrants in the early twentieth century led to legislation that completely banned immigration of Asians. By 1921, the Ku Klux Klan had nearly 100,000 members and had made opposition to immigration a central element of its program. In 1925, 40,000 Klan members marched through Washington, D.C. (Southern Poverty Law Center, 1988). Also around this time, President Herbert Hoover wrote a letter to an Italian-American congressman (Fiorello La Guardia) stating that Italians are "predominantly our murderers and bootleggers . . . foreign spawn [who] do not appreciate this country" (Morganthau, 1993). By the mid-1920s, such views had shaped U.S. immigration policy to the point that immigration was almost entirely cut off.

Immigration began to increase again in the 1960s after the law was liberalized and rose sharply in the 1970s, partly because of surges of refugees from Vietnam, Cuba, Cambodia, and Haiti and partly because of the burgeoning population in economically impoverished countries in Latin America, Asia, and the Caribbean. From 1971 to 1990, 10.5 million people—an average of about half a million a year—immigrated to the United States legally. If a conservative estimate of 3 million illegal immigrants is added to the total, the annual number of migrants during this period was about the same as in 1900–1920 (Morganthau, 1993). The annual total continued to climb, to more than 800,000 legal immigrants annually by the early 1990s. In 1996, it reached 915,000 (U.S. Immigration and Naturalization Service, 1998), and from 2000 through 2002, net immigration reached 3.28 million, or an average of more than a million per year (U.S. Census Bureau, 2002c).

Again, the growth in immigration since the 1970s has been accompanied by a growth in opposition to it. In the 1970s, robed Ku Klux Klansmen harassed Vietnamese fishers in Texas, and the growth of the Latino/a population in Florida and California sparked the passage of the official language legislation discussed earlier. It is also in Florida and California, which together receive nearly half of all immigrants to the United States, where opposition to immigration has become the hottest political issue. In 1993, public opinion polls clearly indicated rising opposition to immigration not only there but throughout the United States, much of it because most of today's immigrants come not from Europe but from Asia, Latin America, or the Caribbean. For example, a 1993 *Newsweek* poll showed that whereas 59 percent of Americans agreed that immigration had been a good thing in the past, 60 percent also agreed that immigration is a bad thing today (Morganthau, 1993). The poll showed much more opposition to immigration from Haiti, Asia, Africa, and Latin America than from eastern Europe. The strongest opposition of all was to immigration from the Middle East. Undoubtedly, this political climate helps to explain actions of voters in the 1990s in California, where the largest number of Mexican American and Asian immigrants have arrived. California voters approved measures in the 1990s to eliminate government programs for children of illegal immigrants, to end affirmative action, and to end bilingual education. These public opinion data are also helpful in understanding many of the harsh immigration actions taken after September 11, 2001: Well before the terrorism occurred, there was already strong opposition to immigration from the Middle East. Among the actions taken have been rounding up and detaining at least 1,200 Arab immigrants for technical visa violations (of a type routinely overlooked in the case of non-Arab immigrants) and requirements that anyone from five Islamic countries register, give fingerprints, and apprise the government of their movements (Ibish and Stewart, 2003, pp. 31–32). Of those detained, about half were held without charges for more than forty-eight hours, and some were held without charges for more than a month (Ibish and Stewart, 2003, p. 32).

Although growing immigration in the United States has led to growing opposition to immigration—particularly that of non-European people of color—the harshest response in recent years occurred in Germany in the early and mid-1990s. Earlier in this chapter, I discussed the rise of neo-Nazism in Germany and the violent attacks against minorities and immigrants. An important factor in these attacks was the growing opposition to immigration, which, relative to the country's population, was at an all-time high in the early 1990s and on that basis exceeded immigration in virtually all other industrialized countries, including the United States. Germany also has admitted a large number of guest workers, many from Turkey, who generally work at jobs most Germans do not want. All told, about 8 percent of Germany's population is legally classified as foreign, reflecting both a high rate of immigration and Germany's unwillingness to admit people of non-German ancestry to citizenship: Neither refugees nor guest workers, nor even their children born in Germany, are admitted to German citizenship.

Germany's "foreign" population was largely blamed for the economic hardship that resulted from absorbing the troubled economy of the former East Germany, together with the effects, in the early 1990s, of a worldwide recession. Turks, Gypsies, and other minority groups became targets of violence. Opposition to immigration became the primary organizing issue of Germany's neo-Nazi groups. Although most Germans continued to reject Nazism, opposition to immigration became widespread. In fact, it had become so strong by 1993 that the German parliament moved to repeal Germany's liberal asylum provisions (Nagorski, 1993). Thus, both the German and American experiences suggest that large surges of immigrants breed both opposition to immigration and heightened hate group activity and ethnic prejudice.

## ▶ RACIAL VERSUS ETHNIC DIVISIONS

All else being equal, racial divisions tend to be more intense than ethnic divisions, if for no other reason than that race makes discrimination easier. It is possible to distinguish a racial group by appearance, something that is not possible with ethnic groups. Thus, most of the long, seemingly intractable intergroup conflicts in the world involve racial rather than ethnic divisions. Of course, this does not mean that ethnic conflicts can never become intense; Northern Ireland and Quebec prove otherwise. The point is that race, because of its visibility, can become a basis of discrimination and conflict more easily than ethnicity.

## ▶ INTERNATIONAL PRESSURE

It is important to note another effect of international relations on majority-minority relations. In a highly complex world, where no nation can afford to be isolated, international pressure can have important effects on race and ethnic relations within a country. Although just how effective such pressure can be is debatable, its importance cannot be totally discounted, as two cases in Africa show. One case is Zimbabwe (formerly Rhodesia), whose white minority government was replaced with a system of majority rule in the mid-1970s. The United States, England, and even to some extent South Africa applied strong pressures on the white minority government to negotiate a settlement because they feared a bloody civil war that might well have resulted in a pro-Soviet government hostile to Western interests. These pressures were an important source of change, although the direct threat of internal revolt probably was an even greater factor. In the second case, South Africa, international sanctions played a key role in bringing about the settlement that brought majority rule in 1994. However, the unwillingness or inability of international powers to apply effective pressure on South Africa until well into the 1980s is one reason that country's white minority government lasted as long as it did.

### Summary and Conclusion

In this chapter, we have examined intergroup relations in a wide range of societies throughout the world. This examination has given rise to a number of generalizations. The most important is that no one factor can explain the pattern of intergroup relations in any society: The factors involved in shaping a society's intergroup relations are always multiple and complex. Therefore, none of the generalizations we have made will hold for all societies. In any society, there are counterforces that modify the influence of any factor. Thus, whereas intense racial conflicts (that is, conflicts between groups different in appearance) develop more easily than intense ethnic conflicts, the particular history and social conditions in Quebec and Northern Ireland have given rise to severe intergroup conflicts, even though both groups in both societies are white. With this caveat, we can summarize the generalizations as follows:

1. Societies in which the dominant group gained power through conquest or colonialism tend to have more racial or ethnic stratification and more intergroup conflict than societies without such a history. This may be especially true if the subordinate group is indigenous to the area.
2. Modernization, urbanization, and development tend to facilitate the development of minority or indigenous group movements. Depending on a number of factors, this may lead either to increased fluidity of intergroup relations or to continued rigidity, with rising levels of conflict. Typically, greater fluidity leads to social differentiation on the basis of a wider range of characteristics.
3. Societies with a large number of racial and ethnic classifications tend to have more harmonious intergroup relations than those in which the bulk of the population is classified into two major groups, especially when no group is a numerical majority.
4. The cultural and demographic characteristics of the two or more groups have important effects on the pattern of relations between them.
5. Societies with crosscutting cleavages have less intergroup conflict than those with overlapping cleavages.
6. Ethnic groups with a territorial base tend to be in a stronger power position and resort more readily to conflict than do groups without a territorial base.

7. Ethnic conflicts tend to be more intense when the groups involved speak different languages.

8. International conflicts with a nation associated with a minority group tend to result in hostility toward and subordination of that minority group.

9. Surges of immigration often lead to increased ethnic prejudice and conflict and to heightened opposition to immigration.

10. Racial divisions tend to be more intense than ethnic divisions.

11. International pressure can cause dominant groups to change their treatment of subordinate groups, although the degree to which this is true is uncertain.

12. Long-standing ethnic conflicts that have been dormant may surface and lead to intense conflict when institutions such as government change or weaken.

These generalizations help us to further evaluate the social-psychological, functionalist, and conflict perspectives. Item 4 and, to a lesser extent, items 7, 8, and 10 suggest that the attitudes in a society are important, as the social-psychological perspective suggests. However, attitudes relevant to these generalizations are determined to a considerable degree by large-scale characteristics of the society. Clearly, much that is attitudinal is a product of society; only through an understanding of culture and social structure can the pattern of intergroup relations in any society be understood. Within the broad area of social-structural effects, some support is found for both the functionalist and conflict perspectives. In support of the functionalist view, item 2 recognizes that patterns of intergroup relations that may be functional in modern societies differ from those that are functional in traditional societies. Items 4, 7, 8, and 10 implicitly recognize the importance of ethnocentrism, which is stressed by the functionalist perspective as a cause of ethnic inequality and conflict. On the other hand, there is also considerable support for the importance of competition and conflict in majority-minority relations, as stressed by the conflict theory. Item 1, which is crucial, recognizes the importance of one group's (the colonizer) opportunity to benefit at the expense of another (the indigenous group) in a context of unequal power. Items 2, 3, 6, and 11 all stress the importance of power, as, less directly, does item 12.

Thus, three general conclusions regarding the major perspectives seem warranted. First, variations in large-scale social structure and culture seem to be the most important factors in determining what kind of intergroup relations a society will have. Second, both the order (functionalist) and conflict perspectives make important contributions to the understanding of intergroup relations in a worldwide context. Third, the power relationship between two groups and whether or not one has ever been in a position to gain at the expense of the other probably are the most important factors in determining the kind of relations any two groups will have.

### Critical Review Questions

1. How do comparisons of race and ethnic relations among different countries around the world support the view that colonization is a major cause of inequality and conflict along the lines of race or ethnicity? Give examples of countries to support your argument.

2. What accounts for the long history of violence between Protestants and Catholics in Northern Ireland, whereas Protestants and Catholics have no such problems in the United States and a number of other countries today?

3. Describe two different kinds of changes in intergroup relations that may result from urbanization and modernization. What are some factors that influence which of these two different possible outcomes occurs in any given country?

4. How and why may the number of racial and ethnic groups in a country influence the degree to which intergroup relations in that country are marked by inequality and conflict?

5. Why has assimilation among racial groups occurred to a greater extent in Mexico and Brazil than in the United States?

6. Why is there a tendency for opposition to immigration to increase during periods of increased immigration? To what extent are public perceptions of the effects of immigration accurate?

# Overview

## ► MAJOR RACIAL AND ETHNIC GROUPS: OVERVIEW AND GENERAL STATISTICS

In this chapter we shall examine the major racial and ethnic groups in American society today: who they are, their numbers and geographic distribution, and their social status. We shall also explore the current debate over whether the status of minority groups in American society is improving and, if so, by how much and in what areas.

### Minority Groups: African Americans, Latinos/as, and Native Americans

As indicated in Chapter 1, the three groups that most closely fit the definition of *minority group* are blacks, or African Americans; Latinos/as, or Hispanic Americans (actually made up of several distinct subgroups); and Indians, or Native Americans (again, a larger grouping comprising many distinct subgroups).

**African Americans.** Through most of U.S. history, African Americans were the largest minority group in the United States. Today, their numbers, though at a record high, have been slightly eclipsed by the number of Hispanic Americans. Nonetheless, the African American population continues to grow faster than the overall U.S. population. In mid-2003, there were approximately 37.1 million people whose race was only African American, or 12.8 percent of the population, according to Census Bureau estimates (U.S. Census Bureau, 2004b). Additionally, another 1.6 million were black in combination with some other race, yielding a total of 13.3 percent of the population that was black alone or in combination with another race. This statistic reflects a new procedure, begun with the 2000 census but continued in subsequent estimates and surveys, of allowing people to identify themselves as belonging to more than one race. The African American population grew by a little over 1 million between the 2000 census and mid-2002. In the past, the census has missed a considerable number of African Americans, but this has improved with recent censuses. It is estimated that the 1960 census missed 8 or 9 percent of the African American population, and as recently as 1990, around 4.4 percent was missed, compared with about 1.6 percent of the total population (O'Hare, 1992, p. 10; U.S. Bureau of the Census, 1979b, p. 10). In the 2000 census, it is estimated that only about 1.8 percent of the African American population was missed. By contrast, there was an estimated *overcount* of about 1.1 percent of the non-Hispanic white population and 0.5 percent of the total

**235**

population (U.S. Census Bureau, 2003r). Although there remains a slight under-count of the black population, the 2000 figures for African Americans (and for most other groups) are more accurate than in any previous census.

Today as in the past, the majority of African Americans live in the South. The percentage living there fell throughout much of the twentieth century until the early 1970s, reflecting the migration of blacks into other parts of the country. How-ever, this percentage never fell below half of the black population. Since the early 1970s, at least as many blacks have moved into the South as have moved out, as many who had moved to other parts of the country have returned to the South. Thus, the percentage of blacks living in the South has remained steady or risen slightly since the early 1970s. This return movement in recent decades reflects sev-eral factors. First, many blacks came to realize that the North was not the racial par-adise some of them had believed. Second, many found it sensible to return to the South, where their families resided and where the mores, lifestyles, and undoubt-edly the climate were more familiar to them. Third, the general nationwide pattern of jobs and population was moving to the Sunbelt. In recent decades, economic growth has been greater in the South than in the North, and blacks, as well as oth-ers, have moved south to take advantage of the newly created opportunities.

In 2000, 54.8 percent of all African Americans lived in the South. The remain-der were fairly evenly divided between the Northeast (17.6 percent) and the Mid-west (18.8 percent); a smaller number (8.9 percent) lived in the West (U.S. Census Bureau, 2003h). These percentages refer to people who gave their race as African American only; if people who are African American combined with other races are included, the percentages are a little larger in the Northeast and West and a little smaller in the South.

The black population is now highly urbanized, even though it was more rural than the population as a whole during the early twentieth century. As of 2000, 89.7 percent of blacks lived in urban areas, compared with 74 percent of non-Hispanic whites and 79 percent of the overall population (U.S. Census Bureau, 2003f). The African American population is particularly concentrated in the large industrial cities of the Great Lakes and Northeast regions, as well as in the cities of the South (although there are more rural blacks in the South than anywhere else). The black population is more highly concentrated in large central cities and less suburban-ized than the population as a whole. More than half (53 percent) of all blacks live in central cities, compared with only 30 percent of the overall population. In contrast, just one-third of African Americans live in the suburbs, compared with half of the total population. Reflecting the highly urban character of the black population, fewer than 14 percent live in nonmetropolitan areas (U.S. Census Bureau, 2000f). Although African Americans are less likely than other groups to live in the suburbs, the percentage that does live there is rising. Among blacks who live in metropolitan areas, the proportion who live in suburbs rose from 27 percent in 1980 to 32 per-cent in 1990 and more than 38 percent in 2000 (O'Hare, 1992; U.S. Census Bureau, 2003f).

Finally, the black population of the United States is younger than the popula-tion as a whole. In 2000, 31.4 percent of all African Americans were under age eigh-teen, compared with 22.6 percent of non-Hispanic whites and 25.7 percent of the total population. The median age in 2000 was 30.2 for blacks, 38.6 for non-Hispanic whites, and 35.3 for the total population (U.S. Census Bureau, 2000b).

**Hispanic Americans.** The largest minority group in the United States is now His-panic Americans, also known as Latinos and Latinas. This umbrella label covers at least four distinct groups: Mexican Americans, or Chicanos; Puerto Ricans, or Boricuas; Cuban Americans; and Central and South Americans. There are also a number of Hispanic Americans who do not fit neatly into any of these categories. In mid-2003, there were 39.9 million Americans of Spanish origin, or 13.7 percent of the U.S. population (U.S. Census Bureau, 2004b). This represents a dramatic increase from 14.6 million, or 6.4 percent of the population, in 1980. Thus, by 2003, there were almost three times as many Hispanic Americans as there were just a little more than two decades earlier. As shown in Table 9.1, which is based on census data from 1980 through 2000, the majority of Hispanic Americans are Chicanos, with Puerto Ricans the next largest group. As with African Americans, the census in the past undercounted Hispanic Americans. However, by 2000 the undercount of Hispanics was less than 1 percent, and given the degree of statistical accuracy possible in making such estimates, there may have been no undercount at all (U.S. Census Bureau, 2003r).

The Hispanic population is one of the fastest-growing population groups in the United States, partly because Latinos have a relatively high birthrate and partly because their immigration rate has been among the highest of any group in recent years. The population of Latinos more than doubled between 1980 and 2000, reaching roughly the same size as the black population by the 2000 census. (Whether it was larger or smaller depended on whether or not people who indicated a combination of black and another race were included in the total black population.) However, by 2002 more people identified as Hispanic than even the number of people who reported their race as either black alone or black in combination with other races.

We must remember that census procedures affect these numbers. Just as procedures for counting African Americans and other races have changed, so have procedures for counting Hispanics. At one time, for example, Mexicans were considered to be a race, and at other times, the census collected little or no data on Hispanics. However, in recent censuses the Census Bureau has treated Hispanics as an ethnic group (or more accurately, a set of ethnic groups) who may be of any race. Thus, race and Hispanic origin are considered to be two distinct concepts. Accordingly, the census asks separately, "What is your race?" and "Are you Spanish, Hispanic or Latino?" (a yes-no question). Because public opinion, including among Latinos, is unclear on whether Latinos/as should be thought of as a race or an ethnic group, people answer these questions in a variety of ways. For example, 42 percent of the Hispanic population opted out of the race question by rejecting all of the categories provided by the census, marking "other" on the race question and writing in "Hispanic," "Latino," "Mexican American," "Chicano," "Puerto Rican," "Cuban," or something similar. The other 58 percent, though, did place themselves in one or more of the Census Bureau's racial categories. About 48 percent identified their

**Table 9.1    Hispanic or Latino/a Americans, 1980–2000**

| Group | Number (in millions) | | | Percentage of Hispanic Population | | |
|---|---|---|---|---|---|---|
| | *1980* | *1990* | *2000* | *1980* | *1990* | *2000* |
| Chicanos (Mexican Americans) | 8.74 | 13.50 | 20.64 | 59.8% | 60.4% | 58.5% |
| Puerto Ricans | 2.01 | 2.73 | 3.41 | 13.8 | 12.3 | 9.6 |
| Cuban Americans | .80 | 1.04 | 1.24 | 5.5 | 4.7 | 3.5 |
| Other Hispanic or Latino/a | 3.05 | 5.09 | 10.02 | 20.9 | 22.4 | 28.4 |
| Total | 14.61 | 22.35 | 35.31 | | | |

*Sources:* U.S. Bureau of the Census (1983, pp. 20–21, 1992c, U.S. Census Bureau 2001e).

race as white, 2 percent as black, and just over 1 percent as Native American. Another 6 percent chose more than one race, often combining one of the "other" categories with white, black, or Native American.

The Hispanic population is even more urban than the black population. In 2000, fully 93 percent of the Spanish-origin population lived in metropolitan areas (U.S. Census Bureau, 2003f). Although there is some variation among the groups, all Hispanic groups are more than 85 percent urban. Many people associate them with agricultural labor, but 89 percent of all Mexican Americans live in metropolitan areas. This percentage is higher than that of either the white or black population. Like African Americans, Latinos are heavily concentrated in central cities; 47 percent lived in central cities in 2000, a figure that is almost as high as that for blacks and well above the figure for non-Hispanic whites. Hispanic Americans are more suburbanized than blacks but less suburbanized than non-Hispanic whites; 44 percent of the Hispanic population lived in suburbs in 1990 (U.S. Census Bureau, 2003f). Just 9 percent of Hispanic Americans lived outside metropolitan areas in 2000.

The Chicano population is heavily concentrated in a limited number of states. The seven states with the largest Hispanic populations are California, Texas, New York, Florida, Illinois, Arizona, and New Jersey. Each of these states has at least 1 million Hispanic residents, and together these states account for more than three-fourths of the Hispanic population of the United States (U.S. Census Bureau, 2001f). Two of these states, California and Texas, account for half the nation's Hispanic population. The state with the largest percentage of Hispanics in its population is New Mexico, where more than 42 percent of the population is Hispanic. In all of the aforementioned states except New Jersey, New York, and Florida, the largest Hispanic group is Mexican Americans.

The Puerto Rican population is heavily concentrated in the urban Northeast, particularly the New York City area, including nearby New Jersey. As a result, about

Cinco de Mayo Festival at the Civic Center Plaza in Los Angeles. Although Chicanos often are associated in the public mind with farm labor (and many farm workers are Chicanos), most Chicanos, like all other Hispanic Americans, are more urbanized than the U.S. population as a whole.

10 percent of the total Latino/a population lives in New York State, which has the third largest Latino/a population of any state, behind only California and Texas (U.S. Census Bureau, 2001f). There are also large Puerto Rican populations in several other northeastern cities, such as Boston.

The Cuban American population, largely refugees from the Castro government and their descendants, is heavily concentrated in Florida, particularly the Miami area. According to the 2000 census, more than 2.6 million Hispanic people lived in Florida, the fourth-largest total of any state. About 846,000 of these were Cuban American. There are also large numbers of Cuban Americans in some parts of the Northeast.

As a whole, Latinos/as are one of the youngest ethnic groups in the United States. As of 2000, 35 percent were less than eighteen years old, which is a higher proportion than for blacks and almost one and a half times as high as for whites. The median age of Hispanic Americans in 1998 was 25.8, about nine and a half years younger than that of the American population as a whole (U.S. Census Bureau, 2003b).

**Native Americans.** In the 2000 census, 2.66 million Americans identified their race as American Indian or Alaska Native alone (U.S. Census Bureau 2003b). This is up from Native American populations of 1.96 million in 1990, about 1.5 million in 1980, and 800,000 in 1970 (O'Hare, 1992; U.S. Bureau of the Census, 1972). About an additional 1.6 million Americans reported their race as Native American in combination with another race. This gives a total in 2000 of 4.26 million Americans—1.5 percent of the population—who reported their race as American Indian or Alaska Native alone or in combination with another race. The Census Bureau estimates that by 2003, this number had risen to 4.37 million, still about 1.5 percent of the population (U.S. Census Bureau, 2004b). In part these figures represent real growth, but much of the increase probably is the result of people of mixed parentage classifying themselves as Indian rather than white (the census determines race on the basis of self-reports) or, once the census permitted it, reporting their race as both Indian and white (see Nagel, 1995). In recent years, people of mixed parentage have increasingly come to think of themselves as Indian. The total today nonetheless reflects substantial and real growth in the Indian population from a low point of around 250,000 just before the turn of the century (Driver, 1969). However, it is still probably substantially less than the Native American population before their decimation by warfare and, especially, European diseases that followed the arrival of whites to the continent (Kroeber, 1939; Dobyns, 1966; Driver, 1969).

In 2000, 48 percent of the American Indian population[1] lived in the West, 29 percent in the South, 16 percent in the Midwest, and 7 percent in the Northeast. However, just three states, Oklahoma, California, and Arizona, account for nearly one-third of the Indian population (U.S. Census Bureau, 2002a). (The regional distribution of various racial and ethnic groups is illustrated in Figure 9.1.)

American Indians are the only minority group that is less urbanized than the population as a whole. As recently as 1970, fewer than half, 45 percent, lived in urban areas; 55 percent lived in rural areas. By 2000, a 60 percent majority of Indian people lived in urban areas—still a lower percentage than that of any other racial group. The 2000 census found a little over a half million Native Americans living on reservations (U.S. Census Bureau, 2003f). The largest of these is the Navajo Reservation and Trust Lands in Arizona, New Mexico, and Utah, with a Native American population of about 173,000.

---

[1]These figures refer to people whose race is American Indian or Alaska Native alone or in combination with another race. Among those whose race is American Indian alone, somewhat more (48%) live in the West, and somewhat fewer (6.6%) live in the Northeast.

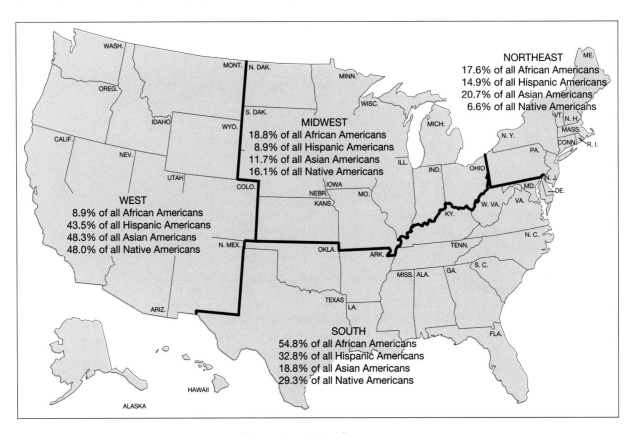

**FIGURE 9.1** Geographic Distribution of Minority Groups in the United States, 2000

For all groups except Native Americans, these figures are for people who reported this race only. Because more people reported Native American in combination with other races, the figures for Native Americans are for people who reported that race alone or in combination with others.

*Source:* U.S. Census Bureau (2001e, 2002a, 2002b, 2003h).

Not only are Indian people more rural than any other group, they also tend to become less permanently linked to the city even when they do move there. Urban Indians often live in cities near the reservation where they grew up. They tend to maintain close ties with the reservation, often remaining active in its cultural, social, and religious affairs. They also return to the reservation frequently for weekend visits and are visited by friends who still live there (C. H. Steele, 1972, 1985). Urban Indians often view their residence in the city as a temporary sojourn, after which they return to the reservation.

The Indian population is among the youngest of any major American racial or ethnic group. As of the 2000 census, about 40 percent of all Indian people were under eighteen. The median age of Native Americans was twenty-eight in 2000, more than seven years younger than the overall population (U.S. Census Bureau, 2003b).

**African Americans, Latinos, and Indian People as Minority Groups.** The three major groups we have been discussing best fit the definition of *minority group.* It is important to note that these groups, more than any others, have less than their proportionate share of virtually all resources in American society today. They have less wealth and lower incomes, less education, and less political power. They are accorded lower social status and live shorter lives than any other groups. Although some other groups suffer low status in some of these areas, these are the only groups that on the whole (there are many individuals who are exceptions to the general pattern) suffer low status across the board.

## Groups with Intermediate Status: Asian, Jewish, and White Ethnic Americans

A number of racial and ethnic groups in the United States hold a status that is in some ways like that of a minority group but in other ways is not. These groups are near, or even in some cases above, the overall societal norm in some areas, such as income or education. However, each has in the past been or is now subject to widespread discrimination. Furthermore, to a large degree each has been excluded from the upper echelons of American corporate power structure, or what Mills (1956) called the power elite. Among these groups are various Asian Americans, Jewish Americans, and a variety of white ethnics of eastern and southern European origin.

**Asian Americans.** The six largest Asian American groups in the United States, as of the 2000 census, are Chinese, Filipinos, Asian Indians, Vietnamese, Koreans, and Japanese. As shown in Table 9.2, each of these groups exceeded a million people in 2000 (at least in combination with other groups), and all are growing rapidly. Together, 10.6 million people identified their race as Asian in the 2000 census, and 12 million indicated Asian in combination with some other race. This represents a sharp increase from the 7.3 million in 1990, which in turn was twice the 1980 Asian population. As of mid-2003, it was estimated that 11.9 million Americans were Asian alone (4.1 percent of the U.S. population), and 13.5 million (4.6 percent) were Asian alone or in combination with another race (U.S. Census Bureau, 2004a).

Asian populations are heavily concentrated in the West, particularly in California and Hawaii. There is also a large concentration of Chinese Americans, more than 280,000, in New York State. Lesser but substantial numbers of the other groups are also found in New York State, Illinois, and Texas. Overall, in 2000, 48.3 percent of Asian Americans lived in the West, 20.7 percent in the Northeast, 18.8 percent in the South, and 11.7 percent in the Midwest (U.S. Census Bureau, 2002f).

### Table 9.2    Asian American Groups, 2000

| Group | Number in This Group Alone* | Number in This Group Alone or in Combination with Other Groups or Races |
|---|---|---|
| Chinese Americans | 2,314,537 | 2,734,841 |
| Filipino Americans | 1,850,314 | 2,364,815 |
| Asian Indians | 1,678,765 | 1,899,599 |
| Vietnamese Americans | 1,122,528 | 1,223,736 |
| Korean Americans | 1,076,872 | 1,228,427 |
| Japanese Americans | 796,700 | 1,148,932 |

*All census racial classification is by self-identification. Beginning in 2000, respondents had the option of identifying themselves as belonging to one race or more than one race.

*Source:* U.S. Census Bureau (2002b).

All Asian American groups are highly urban. In 2000, more than 97 percent of all Asian Americans lived in urban areas. The least urban of the Asian groups are Japanese Americans, and the most urban are Chinese Americans, with the other four groups falling in between. However, the differences are small: More than 94 percent of each group is urban. Chinese Americans live predominantly in central cities, and four urban areas account for the majority of the Chinese American population: San Francisco–Oakland, New York City, Honolulu, and Los Angeles–Long Beach. Many of these urban Chinese Americans live in the central-city neighborhoods known as Chinatowns, although the Chinese population has suburbanized in recent decades. Chicago and Boston also have sizable Chinatowns.

Other Asian Americans are more suburbanized than the Chinese, but many of them live in central cities as well. Overall, 45 percent of Asian Americans lived in central cities in 2000, and 51 percent lived in suburbs. Only 4 percent lived outside metropolitan areas (U.S. Census Bureau, 2003f).

On average, Japanese Americans are older than the population as a whole, whereas Chinese Americans and Filipino Americans are somewhat younger than the population as a whole (U.S. Bureau of the Census, 1992a). In 2000, 24 percent of Asian Americans were under the age of eighteen, compared with just under 26 percent of the overall population. The median age of Asian Americans was 32.7, a little younger than the overall population median of 35.3.

**Jewish Americans.** Accurate data on Jewish Americans and other white ethnic groups are more difficult to obtain and less reliable than data on the other groups we have been discussing. The census does not ask people their religion, and only incomplete data (first- and second-generation immigrants) were obtained on nationality before the 1980 census.

Depending in part on whether one counts only actively religious Jews or all people of Jewish ancestry, the Jewish population of the United States has been estimated anywhere from 3.1 to 6.2 million (Bedell, 1997; World Jewish Congress, 1998; Singer, 2002; see also Goren, 1980, p. 571). The higher figure may be more accurate because some people who are not religious nonetheless identify themselves as Jews. Based on this figure of about 6 million, slightly more than 2 percent of the U.S. population is Jewish. This is about 45 percent the world's Jewish population. The U.S. Jewish population is growing less rapidly than the population as a whole, if indeed it is growing at all. Its limited growth results from its relatively low birthrate, and also many people have lost their Jewish identity over time because of an intermarriage rate estimated at more than 50 percent in recent decades.

The Jewish population is highly urbanized. About nineteen out of every twenty Jewish Americans live in urban areas. In particular, a sizable proportion lives in the New York City metropolitan area. This is reflected in the regional distribution of Jewish Americans: About 64 percent live in the Northeast; the remainder are somewhat evenly distributed throughout the Midwest, South, and West. However, recent data show that, like the rest of the population, Jews have been moving out of the Northeast and Midwest and into the South and West, although the majority still live in the Northeast.

**Eastern and Southern European White Ethnics.** The term *white ethnics* is applied to a wide variety of groups from eastern and southern Europe. As a general rule, these groups have immigrated to the United States somewhat more recently than the groups from northern and western Europe. The bulk of eastern and southern European migration took place after 1900, in the early twentieth century. For example, much of the Italian population came in one decade, 1901–1910. In contrast, immigration from Ireland peaked in the 1850s, and immigration from Germany peaked in the 1880s (Thomlinson, 1976).

The eastern and southern European white ethnics include, among others, Italian, Polish, Greek, Russian, Hungarian, Czechoslovakian, and Ukrainian Americans. The 1980 census—the first recent census to ask everyone a question about ancestry—indicated that the largest of these groups was Italian Americans. Next came Polish Americans and Russian Americans. Those remained the three largest groups in 1990 and 2000 (see Table 9.3).

The majority of these ethnic groups are concentrated in the Northeast and in the Great Lakes states: Massachusetts, New York, Rhode Island, Connecticut, and New Jersey are all among the states in which the percentage of the population that is foreign-born exceeds 10 percent (U.S. Census Bureau, 2003c). Although some of this population is made up of recent, non-European immigrants, a sizable part of it is also made up of older immigrants from eastern Europe who arrived in the early twentieth century.

Eastern and southern Europeans also make up a substantial portion of the population of Illinois, Michigan, Wisconsin, and the northern parts of Ohio and Indiana. For the most part, these ethnic groups are highly urban and are heavily concentrated in the large industrial cities of these regions.

Members of these groups generally belong to religions outside the Protestant majority in the United States. The majority of eastern and southern Europeans are Catholic, particularly Italians and Poles, although a sizable portion of the latter are Jewish. A large part of the Russian American population is also Jewish; much of the remainder is Russian Orthodox. The various Slavic groups tend to belong to one of the Eastern Orthodox churches, as do Greek Americans, who typically belong to the Greek Orthodox church.

**Table 9.3    Americans of Eastern and Southern European Ancestry, 1980, 1990, and 2000**

| Ancestry[a] | Number | | | Percent | | |
|---|---|---|---|---|---|---|
| | *1980* | *1990* | *2000* | *1980* | *1990* | *2000* |
| Italian | 12,184,000 | 14,715,000 | 15,723,555 | 6.5%[b] | 5.9% | 6.9% |
| Polish | 8,238,000 | 9,266,000 | 8,977,444 | 4.4 | 3.8 | 4.0 |
| Russian | 2,781,000 | 2,953,000 | 2,652,214 | 1.5 | 1.2 | 1.2 |
| Czech | 1,892,000 | 1,615,000 | 1,262,527 | 1.0 | 0.6 | 0.6 |
| Hungarian | 1,777,000 | 1,582,000 | 1,398,724 | 0.9 | 0.6 | 0.6 |
| Portuguese | 1,024,000 | 1,153,000 | 1,177,112 | 0.5 | 0.5 | 0.5 |
| Greek | 960,000 | 1,110,000 | 1,153,307 | 0.5 | 0.4 | 0.5 |
| Ukrainian | 730,000 | 741,000 | 892,922 | 0.4 | 0.3 | 0.4 |
| Slovak | 777,000 | 1,883,000 | 797,764 | 0.4 | 0.8 | 0.4 |
| Lithuanian | 743,000 | 812,000 | 659,992 | 0.4 | 0.3 | 0.3 |

[a]Includes both single and multiple ancestry. People who reported more than one ancestry group may be counted in more than one category.
[b]In 1980 and 2000, the percentage of those who reported ancestry in that census; in 1990, the percentage of the total population.

*Sources:* 1980: U.S. Bureau of the Census (1983, pp. 12–14); 1990: U.S. Bureau of the Census, *1990 Census of Population, Social and Economic Characteristics, United States*, p. 12; 2000: U.S. Census Bureau (2003c).

**Arab Americans.** In the 2000 census, about 1.2 million Americans—0.5 percent of the population—reported an Arab ancestry, including Lebanese, Syrian, Egyptian, Palestinian, Jordanian, Morrocan, Iraqi, or other Arab (U.S. Census Bureau, 2003c). However, in light of the high levels of discrimination Arab Americans have experienced in recent years and the tendency of the government to view them as potential terrorists, it is widely suspected that these numbers reflect significant underreporting of Arab ancestry. Some estimates place the Arab American population as high as 3 million (*Detroit Free Press*, 2001). The diversity of Arab Americans lies not only in their national origins but also in their religion. The majority of Arab Americans are Christian, contrary to common associations of Arabs with Islam (*Detroit Free Press*, 2001). Among Christian Arab Americans, most are Catholic or Orthodox. A large and probably growing minority of Arab Americans are Muslim. Arab Americans immigrated to the United States during two main time periods: between 1875 and 1920 (when immigration was severely curtailed), and since World War II. Most of those who came in the first wave of immigration were Christian; more recent immigrants have included more Muslims. The latter have encountered discrimination because of both their nationality and their religion, but it is important to recognize that *Arab* and *Muslim* are two different categories: The majority of Arab Americans are not Muslims, and many Muslim Americans are not Arabs (rather, they are Persian [Iranian], Turkish, African American, or, in growing numbers, European in ancestry).

As a whole Arab Americans are well educated and are represented disproportionately in management, the professions, and small businesses. This has helped them to organize against the growing discrimination and hate crime they have experienced in recent years and to respond to it with an increasing common consciousness, despite their ethnic and religious diversity. Arab Americans can be seen as occupying a middle status: They enjoy above-average education and, in large part, good jobs. On the other hand, they probably experience more open discrimination today than any other ethnic group, and as discussed in Chapters 7 and 8, have faced growing levels of hate crime in recent years. This reality makes their social position as an intermediate-status group somewhat uncertain (Bonilla-Silva, 2003a).

## Whites from Western and Northern Europe: A Dominant Group Within a Dominant Group

In contemporary America, the groups that most clearly fit the definition of *majority* or *dominant group* are whites from western and northern Europe. Certainly, whites as a whole are in a dominant position relative to African Americans, Chicanos, American Indians, and to a lesser degree Asian Americans. Within that white population, however, the most advantaged groups are those from western and northern Europe. Table 9.4 shows the population from 1980 through 2000 of various western and northern European ancestries in the United States. By far, the three largest are the Germans, Irish, and English. In 2000, 43 million Americans, or 19 percent of the population, reported some German ancestry; nearly 31 million, almost 14 percent of the population, reported some Irish ancestry; and nearly 25 million, or 11 percent of the population, reported some English ancestry. At least one-third of the U.S. population can trace part or all of its ancestry to one or more of these three groups. Still, in 2003, fewer Americans, in both numbers and percentage of population, reported these ancestries than in either 1980 or 1990.

Despite the large numbers of these three groups, there are many other groups of western or northern European ancestry. The largest are the French,

**Table 9.4   Americans of Western and Northern European Ancestry, 1980, 1990, and 2000**

| Ancestry[a] | Number | | | Percent | | |
|---|---|---|---|---|---|---|
| | 1980 | 1990 | 2000 | 1980 | 1990 | 2000 |
| English | 49,598,000 | 32,556,000 | 24,515,138 | 26.3%[b] | 13.1% | 10.9% |
| German | 49,224,000 | 57,986,000 | 42,885,162 | 26.1 | 23.3 | 19.0 |
| Irish | 40,166,000 | 38,740,000 | 30,528,492 | 21.3 | 15.6 | 13.6 |
| French | 12,892,000 | 10,321,000 | 8,309,908 | 6.8 | 4.1 | 3.7 |
| Scottish | 10,049,000 | 5,394,000 | 4,890,581 | 5.3 | 2.2 | 2.2 |
| Dutch | 6,304,000 | 6,227,000 | 4,542,494 | 3.4 | 2.5 | 2.0 |
| Swedish | 4,345,000 | 4,681,000 | 3,998,310 | 2.3 | 1.9 | 1.8 |
| Norwegian | 3,454,000 | 3,869,000 | 4,477,725 | 1.8 | 1.6 | 2.0 |
| Welsh | 1,665,000 | 2,034,000 | 1,753,794 | 0.9 | 0.8 | 0.8 |
| Danish | 1,518,000 | 1,635,000 | 1,430,897 | 0.8 | 0.7 | 0.6 |
| Swiss | 982,000 | 1,045,000 | 911,502 | 0.5 | 0.4 | 0.4 |
| Austrian | 948,000 | 871,000 | 735,128 | 0.5 | 0.4 | 0.3 |
| Finnish | 616,000 | 659,000 | 623,573 | 0.3 | 0.3 | 0.3 |
| French Canadian[c] | 780,000 | 2,167,000 | 2,349,684 | 0.4 | 0.9 | 1.0 |
| Canadian[c] | 456,000 | 561,000 | 647,376 | 0.2 | 0.2 | 0.3 |

[a]Includes both single and multiple ancestry. People who reported more than one ancestry group may be counted in more than one category.
[b]In 1980 and 2000, percentage of those who reported ancestry in that census; in 1990, percentage of total population.
[c]Included because most Canadians and French Canadians are of western or northern European ancestry.

*Sources:* 1980: U.S. Census Bureau (1983c, pp. 12–14); 1990: U.S. Census Bureau, *1990 Census of Population, Social and Economic Characteristics, United States*, p. 12; 2000: U.S. Census Bureau (2003c).

Scots, and Dutch, along with the Scandinavians (Swedish, Norwegian, and Danish). Together, Americans of western and northern European ancestry account for perhaps half of the U.S. population. Since about two-thirds of the U.S. population is made up of non-Hispanic whites, as of mid-2002, it still remains true that the majority of white Americans have ancestry from western or northern Europe.

As a general rule, these groups immigrated earlier than most of the eastern and southern Europeans, although Scandinavians are something of an exception. Therefore, these groups tend to be more assimilated into American society and less conscious of ethnicity than other groups we have discussed, although some ethnic awareness persists in all American ethnic groups and may be on the rise in many.

The British groups (English, Scots, and Welsh), a sizable proportion of the Germans, and the Scandinavians and Dutch are predominantly Protestant. These are the groups that form the core of the so-called WASP (white Anglo-Saxon Protestant) population. Most of the rest of the Germans and the majority of the Irish are Catholic, although many Irish, particularly in the South, belong to fundamentalist Protestant churches.

For the most part, these groups are widely distributed geographically. The most notable exceptions are the Scandinavians, who are concentrated largely in the upper Midwest and parts of the Pacific Northwest.

These groups are generally in a dominant socioeconomic position. They tend to have relatively high economic, educational, and occupational levels and low rates of poverty, although there is some variation by both nationality and religion. Data from large-scale surveys by the National Opinion Research Center indicate that among eleven white Catholic and Protestant ethnic groups, the four highest prestige ratings for occupations were held by British Protestants, Irish Catholics, German Catholics, and German Protestants, in that order (Greeley, 1977, p. 60). In urban areas outside the South, Scandinavian Protestants also ranked close to these four groups (Greeley, 1977, p. 61; see also Greeley, 1974).

## Whiteness as a Racial Identity

Although whites from western and northern Europe represent an elite within the dominant majority group in the United States, it is important to recognize that whiteness is an important part of the identity of people in all subgroups within the white population. Whiteness has always been a key racial identity in the U.S. South, but there is reason to believe that this has become more true in other parts of the country today. One reason may lie in the movement of African Americans out of the South in the first half of the twentieth century; this meant increased economic competition from growing numbers of blacks in the Northeast and Midwest, who were also increasingly demanding better treatment. Developing a common white identity was one way to resist the competition and demands arising from this growing black population (Guterl, 2001). Consciously or, more often, unconsciously, many white Americans today identify with other whites regardless of ethnicity, so that when it comes to thinking about racial issues, it may make less difference whether they are of eastern or western European ancestry; whether they are Catholic, Protestant, Jewish, or nonreligious; or whether they are male or female (Frankenberg, 1993; Ignatiev, 1995; Winant, 1997). Regardless of these differences, they may share a common perspective and identity, particularly with respect to racial issues such as affirmative action, busing, minority scholarships, or interpretations of race-related events in the news such as the O. J. Simpson trials. Several studies suggest that an important part of this process is so-called race blindness, in which the denial of racial differences is used to deny the reality of racial inequality (Frankenberg, 1993; Ignatiev, 1995; Bonilla-Silva, 2003a, 2003c). Through such denial, whites are able to create a rationalization that the system is fair and that reform is not needed. Many whites believe this rationalization because they do not personally have the experience of being excluded and discriminated against, so they assume that the experiences of blacks, Latinos, and others are the same as their own (J. Farley, 2000). However, by affirming the fairness of the system and thus denying a need for reform, whites continue to receive the racial privileges that result from systemic racial inequality (Feagin, 2000, pp. 123–129; Bonilla-Silva, 2003b)

To some extent, this white social and political identity has been the outgrowth of efforts by politicians to manipulate racial fears and divisions in order to gain votes. For example, former California governor Pete Wilson sought to gain support and divide his opposition through vigorous and outspoken opposition to illegal immigration and affirmative action, knowing that these were emotional issues with the potential to evoke racial resentment among whites. In 2003, the George W. Bush administration intervened on the side of two white plaintiffs who sued the University of Michigan to overturn its affirmative action admission policies after they were denied admission. In the 1980s and 1990s, a series of Missouri attorneys general, both Democrat and Republican, built careers by opposing "unfair desegregation payments," meaning busing. Among them were John Ashcroft, now U.S. attorney general, and the current Missouri attorney general, Jay Nixon. Whereas politicians today generally avoid overt racial attacks, use of code words such as "illegal immigration," "reverse discrimination," and "unfair desegregation payments" amounts to a thinly veiled appeal to the racial fears of whites and thereby contributes to the formation of a white racial identity and viewpoint centered around issues related to race (Omi and Winant, 1994; Winant, 1997).

## ▶ STATUS OF MINORITY GROUPS IN AMERICA TODAY

In the following sections, we shall focus in greater detail on the racial and ethnic groups in American society that we have identified as minority groups. We shall examine in detail their social and economic status, especially whether it has significantly improved.

### Evidence of Improvement in Minority Status

Some social indicators suggest substantial improvement in the status of minorities between about 1940 and today. Some of the trends are fairly recent; others have been under way since around World War II.

One indication of improved status can be seen in occupational structure, that is, the proportion of group members who hold professional or managerial positions. In 1980, blacks held twice as large a share of the professional and managerial jobs as they did in 1960 (R. Farley, 1984, p. 194), and that share increased by another 50 percent between 1983 and 2001 (U.S. Census Bureau, 2003q, p. 381). In other words, the number of blacks in high-status jobs grew at a faster rate than did the number of whites in such jobs. Latinos/as, too, experienced a more rapid growth in high-status jobs than did whites both between 1960 and 1980 (Moore and Pachon, 1976, p. 64; U.S. Bureau of the Census, 1979a, p. 26) and since. Between 1983 and 2001, the share of professional and managerial jobs being held by Hispanics doubled (U.S. Census Bureau, 2003q, p. 381). Thus, a substantially higher proportion of the black and Latino/a populations held high-status occupations in the United States today than ever before.

Despite this trend, the percentage of African Americans and Latinos/as in higher-status occupations still lags behind the percentage for whites. By 2001, about 23 percent of employed African Americans and a little under 15 percent of employed Hispanic Americans were in professional or managerial occupations (computed from U.S. Census Bureau, 2003q). This represents significant improvement over the past, especially for African Americans. However, it is still well below the 31 percent of all employed workers in the United States who were in such occupations in 2001 (U.S. Census Bureau, 2003q, p. 381).

The gap in individual incomes between employed African Americans and whites has decreased substantially since about 1950. As shown in Figure 9.2, the racial gap in annual incomes has closed over time, though to different degrees and at different times for men and women. The median income of African American men employed year-round full-time rose rather steadily from 63 percent of that of comparable white men in 1961 to about 78 percent in 2001. Among women, the racial gap narrowed sharply during the 1960s. In 1961, the median income of year-round full-time black female workers was just 66 percent of that of comparable white females; by 1971 it was 88 percent. However, since then it hasn't changed much, standing at 88 percent of that of full-time white female workers in 2001. Relative to the incomes of white male workers, the income gap for black female

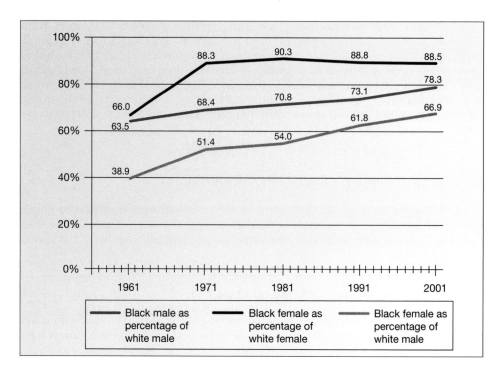

**FIGURE 9.2**    Median Income of Black Full-Time Workers as Percentage of That of White Full-Time
Workers, 1961–2001
*Source:* U.S. Census Bureau (2002g).

workers is wider, but it has narrowed more steadily, from just 39 percent in 1961 to
67 percent in 2001 (U.S. Census Bureau, 2002h). For African Americans (but not
for Latinos/as, as we shall soon see), these figures represent significant improvement over the past, but the racial gap remains quite large.

Part of the remaining racial gap in income is a product of educational differences. If we examine only full-time workers with comparable educational levels, the
gap in income is even smaller than it is in the overall population. Among recent college graduates with year-round, full-time jobs, for example, the median income of
black men is 87 percent that of white men, and the median income of Latino men
is 81 percent that of white men. Among women who have recently graduated from
college, the income of black year-round, full-time workers is 94 percent of that of
comparable white women, and that of Latinas is 93 percent. However, black, white,
and Hispanic women all continue to receive only around three-fourths as much
income as white men even among recent college graduates with full-time jobs (computed from U.S. Census Bureau, 2002d, Table PINC-03). However, it is important to
remember that both African Americans and Latinos/as are less likely to be college
graduates and more likely to be unemployed. Thus, they remain underrepresented
relative to non-Hispanic whites among college-educated, year-round, full-time
workers.

There is also substantial evidence of minority gains in political representa-
tion. Between 1970 and 2000, the number of black elected officials in the United
States rose from fewer than 1,500 to more than 9,000 (Bositis, 1998, 2002; Joint
Center for Political Studies, 1977, 1985, 2000). Between 1984 and 1994 the num-
ber of Latino/a elected officials rose from fewer than 3,100 to more than 5,400
(U.S. Bureau of the Census, 1997b), but it fell to 5,200 in 2001, mostly due to

fewer city and county officials and judges (U.S. Census Bureau, 2003q, p. 252). There are more than 450 black mayors and 585 black state legislators. Nearly every major city in the United States has elected a black mayor at some time in the past two or three decades, including New York, Chicago, Los Angeles, Detroit, Philadelphia, Atlanta, Washington, D.C., New Orleans, St. Louis, and Birmingham, Alabama, a city that was a symbol of resistance to black rights in the early 1960s. Another such city, Selma, Alabama, elected a black majority to its city council in 1993. In 1981, San Antonio became the first major city to elect a Latino mayor, Henry Cisneros (who later became secretary of Housing and Urban Development in the Clinton administration). Two Hispanic governors were elected in the 1970s (in Arizona and New Mexico); the first African American governor (L. Douglas Wilder of Virginia) was elected in the 1980s, and the 1990s brought the election of the first black woman (Carol Moseley Braun of Illinois) and the first Native American (Ben Nighthorse Campbell of Colorado) to the U.S. Senate.

In 1998, Illinois Senator Carol Moseley Braun was narrowly defeated in her bid for reelection to a second term. Additionally, Governor Wilder was prevented by Virginia's term limits law from running for reelection. Because no other African Americans have been elected as governors or U.S. senators since then, there are today no black governors and no African Americans in the U.S. Senate. As of this writing, however, an African American man, Barack Obama, was running for the U.S. Senate in Illinois as the Democratic nominee for the November 2004 election. After the 2002 elections, there were 37 African Americans in the U.S. House of Representatives, down from the peak number of 39 after the 1992 elections but still higher than in most of the 1970s and 1980s. The number of Hispanics in the U.S. House reached a record high of 23 after the 2002 elections, and the first Latino governor in two decades, Bill Richardson in New Mexico, was elected. Hence, it is clear that minorities have made considerable gains in political representation over the past three decades. However, it is also important to note that the percentage of elected officials from minority groups is much lower than the percentage of minorities among the general population. If African Americans and Latinos/as were represented in proportion to their population, there would be more than 55 members of each of these groups in the U.S. House and about 13 members of each group in the U.S. Senate, where neither group is currently represented.

Finally, it is important to reiterate that deliberate racial discrimination is illegal today, and although it still occurs, it is less common and certainly less open than in the past. This in itself is a dramatic change, considering that as recently as fifty years ago, such discrimination was not only legal and widespread but also, in some parts of the country, required by law. When discrimination does occur, it is usually not open and acknowledged—expressed as "We have no space" as opposed to "You can't rent here because of your race." This makes it more difficult to detect, but it also reflects the reality that discrimination today is both illegal and much less socially acceptable than in the past.

It seems clear from these data, then, that in at least some areas there has been substantial improvement in the status of minority group members in America. An important factor in this improvement has been the rise of minority group social movements, discussed at length in Chapter 7.

Despite these apparent gains, some hard questions must still be asked. First, despite whatever progress has occurred, how much inequality and racism still persist? More specifically, what is the standing of minorities relative to that of whites in America today? The fact that minorities have gained in certain areas does not necessarily mean that they have caught up or that all minority group members have gained at all. Finally, we must ask, what is the absolute level of living of minorities today?

## Evidence of Continuing Inequality

**Economics.** Despite the progress we have seen among some segments of the minority population, the overall picture today continues to be one of serious majority-minority inequality in the economic arena. One important indicator of economic well-being is median family income. The median family income for all white, black, and Hispanic families in 2001 is shown in the left column of Table 9.5. These data clearly indicate that whatever gains have been made, the family income of Latinos/as and blacks remains substantially below that of whites. Indeed, the figure for blacks represents only a small gain over the past forty years: In the 1940s, median family income for blacks was about 50 percent of what it was for whites. Today, it is less than 59 percent.

It has been commonly argued that the recent increase in female-householder families with no husband present is a major reason for the lack of improvement in median black family income since these families have low incomes among all races (Bianchi, 1981; R. Farley, 1984, pp. 199–200). This is correct, but it is only one part of the answer. As Table 9.5 shows, substantial racial differences in income exist for each type of family, although the gap is the smallest among married-couple families in which both the husband and wife are employed. For these families, the median income of black families is about 82 percent of that of white families; this compares with about 72 percent in 1967, indicating that for this type of family, the income gap has narrowed over the past four decades, although it has actually again widened slightly since the late 1990s (U.S. Bureau of the Census, 1992b, 1997b; U.S. Census Bureau, 2002i, Table 4).

For all other types of families, including married-couple families in which only the husband is employed, the black-white gap in income is wider. For families where only the husband works, the median black family income is just two-thirds that of similar white families, and in male-headed single-parent families, the median black family income is about 79 percent of the median white family income as of 2001. Black female-householder families receive a little under 70 percent of the income of white female-householder families. Some of these figures represent modest improvement since around 1990, but all indicate a large racial gap; in all cases, even two-worker married couples, the racial gap in family income is wider than the gap in income for comparably educated year-round full-time workers. This reflects the lesser access of African Americans to both a quality education and to full-time employment.

### Table 9.5    Median Family Income by Race, Hispanic Origin, and Type of Family, 2001

|  | All Families | Married-Couple Families | | Male Householder, No Wife | Female Householder, No Husband |
|---|---|---|---|---|---|
|  |  | Wife in Paid Labor Force | Wife Not in Paid Labor Force |  |  |
| White, Non-Hispanic | $57,328 | $74,071 | $43,423 | $39,979 | $30,062 |
| Black | $33,598 | $60,693 | $29,309 | $31,512 | $20,894 |
| % of White Non-Hispanic | 58.6% | 81.9% | 67.5% | 78.8% | 69.5% |
| Hispanic | $34,490 | $50,437 | $28,682 | $31,635 | $20,547 |
| % of White Non-Hispanic | 60.2% | 68.1% | 66.1% | 79.1% | 68.3% |
| Total Population | $51,407 | $70,834 | $40,782 | $36,590 | $25,745 |

*Source:* U.S. Census Bureau (2002i, Table 4).

Although there is a substantial black-white income gap for every type of family, female-householder families are at a particular disadvantage. This family type has the lowest income for every racial group, and black overrepresentation in this group has continued through the 1990s and into the new century. In 2001, about 43 percent of black families were female-householder families, compared with 23 percent for Latino/a families and 13 percent for non-Hispanic white families (U.S. Census Bureau, 2002i). So, in addition to the across-the-board income inequality faced by black families, the economic situation of black families is further worsened by their overrepresentation in the low-income female-householder category. This also helps to explain why the overall racial income gap is wider than the gap within any given family type.

Hispanic families also have lower incomes than Anglos in all types of families. Unlike blacks, however, Latino families have clearly lost ground over the past two decades: In 1978, the median Hispanic family income was 68 percent of the white median; today it is about 60 percent. As with African Americans, part of the reason for the large income gap can be found in family type, as Hispanics are overrepresented among female-householder families. About 23 percent of Hispanic families, and only 13 percent of Anglo families, are female-householder families. However, unlike blacks, Hispanics make no gain relative to the income of comparable white families when they are in married couple families with two full-time workers. The income of this type of Hispanic family is only about two-thirds that of comparable Anglo families, whereas black families of this type receive about four-fifths the income of comparable white Anglo families. Among all family types combined, the median Latino/a family income is just 60.2 percent that of whites and is only slightly higher than the median income of African American families (U.S. Census Bureau, 2002i). As with blacks, the overall income gap is wider than the gap within any family type, reflecting the overrepresentation of Latinos/as in family types with lower incomes. But as with blacks, Hispanic families are also at a consistent income disadvantage regardless of family type.

Another indicator of the economic position of a group is the proportion of its members who are below the federally defined poverty level (in 2002, approximately $18,300 for a family of four and $9,300 for a single individual), which is adjusted annually for inflation. As shown in Table 9.6, African Americans, Latinos, and

| Table 9.6 | Percentage of Population Below Poverty Level by Race and Hispanic Origin, 2001 | | |
|---|---|---|---|
| | All Ages | Children Under 18 | People in Female-Householder Families |
| White | 9.9% | 13.4% | 24.3% |
| Non-Hispanic White | 7.8 | 9.5 | 19.9 |
| Black | 22.7 | 30.2 | 37.4 |
| Hispanic | 21.4 | 28.0 | 37.8 |
| Asian[a] | 12.6 | 14.3 | — |
| Native American[a] | 25.7 | 31.6 | — |
| Total Population | 11.7 | 16.3 | 28.6 |

[a]Data are for 1999, taken from the 2000 census.

*Sources:* U.S. Census Bureau (2002f, Table 1; 2003c, Tables P159c and P159d).

Native Americans all have far greater percentages of their populations living below the poverty level than do white Americans. In fact, the poverty rates of all three groups are around three times as high as that of non-Hispanic whites. Poverty rates of all groups tend to rise during recessions and fall during better economic times. However, the poverty rates of African Americans and Native Americans have quite consistently been around three times the white rate over the past decade or two, and the Latino/a rate has actually risen somewhat relative to the rate of non-Hispanic whites, from about twice the rate of non-Hispanic whites in the 1970s to around three times that rate today. And note that the poverty rate for Native Americans, according to the 2000 census, was even higher than that of African Americans or Latinos/as.

A final indicator of economic status is the unemployment rate. Here, too, substantial intergroup inequalities are evident. In mid-2003, the unemployment rate of whites stood at 5.6 percent. For African Americans, it was 12 percent, and for Latinos/as it was 8.2 percent (U.S. Bureau of Labor Statistics, 2003). Thus, the unemployment rate of African Americans is about twice that of whites, and that of Hispanic Americans is about one and a half times the white rate. Among Hispanics, unemployment rates are highest for Puerto Ricans, whose rate in 1996 was about one percentage point above the overall Latino rate (U.S. Bureau of the Census, 1998c). According to the 2000 census, the unemployment rate of American Indians and Alaska Natives was about 2.85 times as high as that of non-Hispanic whites (U.S. Census Bureau, 2003c, Tables P150c and P150i).

Research by Snipp (1988) has shown that even when valuable resources are developed on Indian reservations, Native American unemployment remains high. Even following the energy crisis of the 1970s, the unemployment rate on reservations with energy resources was about the same as that on reservations without energy. One reason for this is that, to date, mainly non-Indians have benefitted from the development of resources on reservations. Coal is a good example: Between 1978 and 1979, the value of coal produced on reservations nearly doubled, but the amount of royalties paid to Native Americans actually fell, from 6.6 percent in 1972 to just 4.0 percent in 1979 (Snipp, 1988, pp. 14–16). And on some reservations, such as that of the Navajo in Arizona, coal mining has resulted in the displacement of many Indians who had been engaging in agriculture.

Black unemployment generally has been at least twice as high as white unemployment since the end of World War II. Earlier, in the 1920s and 1930s, blacks and whites had very similar unemployment rates (W. J. Wilson, 1978). Since the war, however, there has been a drastic reduction in the number of low-skill, low-paying jobs that many blacks had occupied. A sizable segment of the black population has continued to be excluded from the opportunity to learn skills necessary for better jobs, and the disappearance of unskilled jobs has left many of these people unemployed (W. J. Wilson, 1978, 1987).

The problem of minority unemployment becomes even clearer if we focus on particular segments of the minority population. Among black, urban teenage boys, for example, the unemployment rate is believed to be between 40 and 50 percent. Overall, for African Americans in the labor force who were sixteen to nineteen years old, the unemployment rate was more than 43 percent in mid-2003, and even seasonally adjusted to consider the effects of school being out, it would still have been 39 percent (U.S. Bureau of Labor Statistics, 2003).

Taken as a whole, these economic data indicate that substantial inequalities between whites and minorities persist. Although a segment of the black and Hispanic population today enjoys relatively high incomes and good jobs, a large segment is trapped at the bottom of the socioeconomic structure. For this group, things are not getting better; indeed, relative to everyone else, their situation probably got worse throughout the 1980s and early 1990s, improved only slightly during the boom economy of the mid-1990s, and is worsening again now. If we examine

In the United States today, there is a large and growing minority middle class. At the same time, however, other minority group members remain poor, and the proportion of minorities in the impoverished underclass is far greater than the proportion of whites in the underclass.

the minority population as a whole, two conclusions are evident. First, among the black and Hispanic populations, there is increasing stratification and a growing gap between a segment that is relatively well off and another that is impoverished and struggling for survival. Second, the average economic positions of blacks, Latinos/as, and American Indians have improved only marginally and remain substantially lower than the average position of whites.

**Political Representation.**  As we have seen, the political representation of black and Hispanic Americans has risen dramatically over the past few decades. Nonetheless, it remains well below their share of the population. Even with the larger numbers of minorities in the House of Representatives, it is less than 9 percent black and only about 5 percent Hispanic, even though each of these groups is over 13 percent of the population. When Carol Moseley Braun was elected to the Senate in 1992, she became the only African American in that body and the first since 1978, and she was defeated for reelection in 1998. Only one black person has ever been elected governor of a state, and with the exception of one white woman, Geraldine Ferraro, who was nominated for vice president by the Democrats in 1984 (her ticket lost), only white men have ever been nominated for president or vice president, much less elected. The closest any person of color has come to the presidency was when the Reverend Jesse Jackson finished second to Michael Dukakis in the 1988 race for the Democratic nomination. After an earlier run in 1984, he improved this showing substantially in 1988, carrying about half a dozen states and the District of Columbia and outlasting all candidates except the eventual nominee, Michael Dukakis. In early 2004, two black candidates, the Reverend Al Sharpton and former Senator Carol Moseley Braun, were running for president in the 2004 Democratic primaries and caucuses. Overall, however, only about 1.8 percent of all elected U.S. officials are African Americans and only about 1 percent are Latinos/as—even though, together, these groups make up more than 25 percent of the population. Thus, even though the number has grown, people of color remain very underrepresented among U.S. elected officials.

**Education.** Data on educational attainment in 2002 for whites, African Americans, Latinos/as, and Asian Americans are presented in Table 9.7. This table shows the proportion of high school and college graduates among young adults aged twenty-five to twenty-nine and for the entire population over the age of twenty-five. The gap in high school graduation rates between blacks and whites is narrower than in the past: There is a difference of about five percentage points between young, non-Hispanic blacks and whites and just under a ten-point gap in the population over twenty-five. However, African Americans are somewhat more likely to obtain their diplomas through general equivalency diploma (GED) programs than are whites. About seven out of eight African Americans in their early twenties are high school graduates, a substantially greater percentage than in the overall adult black population. On the other hand, young Hispanics are making no such gains: Their high school graduation rate is more than thirty percentage points lower than that of the young white Anglo population, only a little higher than in the Hispanic population over twenty-five. Even among the young, only 62 percent of Latinos are high school graduates.

**Table 9.7   High School and College Graduation Rates by Race and Hispanic Origin, 2002**

| | Percentage Who Are High School Graduates | |
| --- | --- | --- |
| | 25–29 Years Old | 25 and Over |
| White | 85.9% | 84.8% |
| Non-Hispanic White | 93.0 | 88.7 |
| Black | 86.6 | 78.7 |
| Non-Hispanic Black | 87.6 | 79.2 |
| Hispanic | 62.4 | 57.0 |
| Asian and Pacific Islander | 95.1 | 87.4 |
| Native American[a] | | 70.9 |
| Total Population | 84.7 | 84.1 |

| | Percentage with Bachelor's Degree | |
| --- | --- | --- |
| | 25–29 Years Old | 25 and Over |
| White | 29.7% | 27.2% |
| Non-Hispanic White | 35.9 | 29.4 |
| Black | 17.5 | 17.0 |
| Non-Hispanic Black | 18.0 | 17.2 |
| Hispanic | 8.9 | 11.1 |
| Asian and Pacific Islander | 54.8 | 47.2 |
| Native American[a] | | 11.5 |
| Total Population | 26.9 | 26.7 |

[a]Data for Native Americans are for 2000.

*Sources:* For all groups except Native Americans, U.S. Census Bureau (2003j, Table 1a). For Native Americans, U.S. Census Bureau (2003c, Table P148c).

The data on college graduation in Table 9.7 indicate little gain by either African Americans or Latinos/as relative to whites. Although blacks ages twenty-five to twenty-nine are now almost as likely as non-Hispanic whites to have completed four years of high school, they are less than half as likely to be college graduates. More than one of three non-Hispanic whites, but only a little over one in six blacks, are college graduates by the time they are twenty-five to twenty-nine years old. Even fewer Hispanics, about one in eleven, are college graduates by this age. Moreover, the likelihood of African Americans earning college degrees, relative to whites, has not increased much in recent years, and Hispanics have actually lost ground. Shockingly, Hispanics have only one-fourth the chance that non-Hispanic whites do of becoming college graduates by their early twenties. The black-white gap has persisted for two decades, although it is somewhat narrower than in earlier decades. The Hispanic-Anglo gap is actually widening. Asian Americans present a stark contrast to all other groups; more than half of Asian Americans are college graduates by the time they reach the twenty-five to twenty-nine age group.

Although fewer data are available for Native Americans, 2000 census data, also shown in Table 9.7, present a fairly current picture. These data show that Native Americans, like Hispanic Americans, experience a large educational disadvantage relative to the white population and lag behind the African American population as well. About 71 percent of Native Americans over age 25 are high school graduates, a higher percentage than among Hispanics but lower than among any other group. And like Hispanics, only about one in nine Native Americans over 25 is a college graduate.

Data on current college enrollment are also instructive. In fall 2000, 13.7 percent of college students were black, based on survey data for 2000 (U.S. Census Bureau, 2001g, Table 1). This figure continues to indicate a slight underrepresentation because 14.3 percent of the college-aged population is black (U.S. Census Bureau, 2003b). Also in 2000, just 9.0 percent of college students were Hispanic, whereas Hispanics made up 16.8 percent of the college-aged population (U.S. Census Bureau, 2001g, Table 1; 2003b). This figure of about 9 percent represents an all-time high, but it reflects growth of the Hispanic population more so than increased access to college. This can be seen in the large gap between the percentage of college students and of the college-age population who are Hispanic.

In 2000, 39 percent of black high school graduates between the ages of eighteen and twenty-four were enrolled in college. The corresponding figure for Hispanics was 36 percent (National Center for Education Statistics, 2001). Both of these figures are substantially lower than the 44 percent of non-Hispanic white high school graduates the same age who were in college; recall that Hispanics are less likely to graduate from high school as well. Thus, the overall percentage of college-aged blacks and Hispanics who are in college (around 31 percent for blacks and 22 percent for Hispanics) is considerably less than that of white Anglos (about 39 percent). In general, the African American percentage among college students increased sharply in the early 1970s, peaked in the mid-1970s, fell until the mid-1980s, and began to rise again after about 1988, but with only modest increases since 1997 (National Center for Education Statistics, 1992a, 1992b, 2001). The percentage of Hispanic high school graduates enrolled in college also dipped between the mid-1970s and mid-1980s and rose again until reaching a peak in 1997. It then dipped and rose again, reaching about the same level in 2000 as in 1997. The percentage of undergraduate students who are black or Hispanic at the beginning of the new century appears to be at an all-time high, but for reasons discussed below, the future trend remains uncertain.

It is also noteworthy that minority students are disproportionately likely to enroll in two-year colleges rather than four-year colleges. In 1999, for example, 12.3 percent of students in two-year schools were black and 13.3 percent were Latino/a, compared with just 11.0 percent and 6.6 percent, respectively, in four-year schools (National Center for Education Statistics, 2002a, Table 189). The concentration of African Americans and especially Hispanics in two-year schools is one reason why their college graduation rates are lower than those of whites.

Even fewer African Americans and Hispanics are among graduate and professional (such as medical, law, and dental) students. Among graduate students, just 9.3 percent were black and 5.7 percent were Latino/a in 1999 (National Center for Education Statistics, 2002a, Table 208). As in undergraduate schools, black enrollment in graduate school fell in the late 1970s and early 1980s but has been on the rise again in recent years. Still, the proportion of both blacks and Hispanics in graduate school is well below their percentage in the young adult population as a whole. The picture is not very different in professional schools, where 7.6 percent of the students in 1999 were black and 5.0 percent Hispanic (National Center for Education Statistics, 2002, Table 208). And as low as these percentages are, both of them are record highs.

Taken together, these statistics indicate clearly that African Americans, Latinos/as, and Native Americans remain well behind whites and Asian Americans in educational attainment. Of particular significance are the much smaller proportions of college graduates among minority groups, even among young adults. This indicates that in an era when college graduation is increasingly a prerequisite for good jobs, blacks, Hispanics, and American Indians all continue to have a much smaller chance of obtaining that important credential. Equally important, the data in Table 9.7 suggest that they are not even catching up: The gap is similar among young adults to that among adults of all ages.

This reality is particularly disturbing in light of certain political developments that have reduced the number of African American and Latino/a college students in some states, including the two most populous states, California and Texas. In several states, including Texas, the *Hopwood* ruling by a federal district court in 1996 interrupted affirmative action for minority students in college admissions. This ruling, which was effectively reversed by the U.S. Supreme Court in a later case in 2003, stated that the 1978 *Bakke* ruling by the Supreme Court, which had allowed consideration of race along with other factors in admissions in order to have a diverse student body, was no longer valid. Although it applied only in that court's district and is no longer a valid or enforceable ruling, it did eliminate affirmative action in public college admissions in Texas, the nation's second most populous state, for the period between 1996 and 2003. Also of concern are referenda and legislative developments in some states. In California, a ruling by the University of California Board of Regents and a subsequent 1996 referendum (Proposition 209) put an end to minority preferences in college admissions there, and a similar referendum was passed in Washington state in 1998. Affirmative action opponents began a similar effort in Michigan in 2003, after the Supreme Court upheld its legality in cases involving the University of Michigan. However, that effort faltered after a lawsuit by affirmative action supporters led to a state court ruling that the petition was illegally worded.

In Texas and California, once colleges had lost their ability to compensate in the admissions process for unequal opportunities in elementary and secondary education, the percentage of minority students fell. Three of the five campuses of the University of California experienced sharp drops in minority enrollment in the fall of 1997, when the new rules took effect. At the University of California at Berkeley, the number of black and Hispanic first-year students fell by 52 percent, and the number of Native Americans also fell. Professional schools also had large declines in minority enrollment; the fall 1997 entering class at Berkeley's law school had only one African American student, and the entering class at the University of Texas law school had none (Chronicle of Higher Education, 1997c; Haworth, 1998; Healy, 1998a, 1998b). In Texas, however, the legislature partially compensated for the effects of the ruling on undergraduates by passing a law guaranteeing admission to the University of Texas to anyone in the top 10 percent of one's high school class, which included many students in largely black and Hispanic schools who might not otherwise have been admitted. A more restrictive version of this legislation later also passed in California, but it applied to only the top 4 percent of the state's high school graduates. These laws resulted in a partial recovery of minority enrollments, but at the most selective institutions, they remained below their levels in the past under affirmative action. (Affirmative action issue and the debates surrounding it are addressed more fully in Chapter 15.)

Of course, statistics about educational attainment cannot begin to tell the whole story of how well any group is being served by the educational system. Quality of education is as important as quantity, and statistics about educational levels say nothing about educational quality. For example, we know that black students are underrepresented in prestigious private colleges and major state universities and overrepresented in community colleges and smaller regional or commuter state colleges and universities. (In Chapter 12, we shall explore the entire issue of how the operation of our educational system and the roles of minorities within it shape the status of minority groups in America today.)

**Health and Mortality.** So far, we have seen evidence of continuing serious racial and ethnic inequality in economics, political representation, and education. However, one area, probably more than any other, shows the human dimension—and indeed the human tragedy—of racial and ethnic inequality. In the United States today, the racial or ethnic group to which one belongs partially determines how long one will live. It also affects the amount of time that a person can expect to be ill in his or her lifetime and the likelihood that one or more of his or her children will die in infancy. As we shall see in more detail in Chapter 10, these differences exist not because of biology but rather because of social inequalities associated with race or ethnicity. We turn now to the grim statistics.

On average, African Americans live about five and a half years less than whites. In 2000, the life expectancy for African Americans was 71.7, compared with 77.4 for whites. For black women it was 74.9, compared with 80 for white women, a difference of about five years. Among men, the racial gap in life expectancy is wider. In 2000, life expectancy for white men was 74.8 and just 68.2 for black men, a difference of more than six and a half years (National Center for Health Statistics, 2002b, p. 33). The continuing gap between white and black life expectancies reflects overall age-adjusted mortality rates that are 33 percent higher among African Americans than among white Americans (National Center for Health Statistics, 2002b, p. 18). Between 1996 and 1998, life expectancy for American Indians was 70.6, slightly less than for African Americans at that time and six years less than for whites (Indian Health Service, 2002). Unfortunately, life expectancy data are not published for Hispanics, but in recent years, death rate statistics have been (National Center for Health Statistics, 1997a, 1997b, 2002b). These statistics indicate that among Hispanics in 2000, mortality rates were about 20 percent higher than for non-Hispanic whites below the age of thirty-five. Among older Hispanics, reported rates are lower than for other groups, but this may reflect underreporting. In both 1995 and 1996, mortality rates among American Indians under the age of fifty-five were about 40 percent higher than for whites. Indian children aged one to four are more than twice as likely to die as white children in this age range.

Infant mortality is also higher among minority groups than it is among whites. The infant mortality rate (number of deaths per year of infants under one year old per thousand live births) was 5.7 for whites in 2000 but 14.1—almost two and a half times as high—for blacks (National Center for Health Statistics, 2002b, p. 100).

Consistently for a number of years, black babies have been at least twice as likely to die in the first year of life as white babies. The rate for Native Americans, 8.3 per thousand, is lower than for African Americans but nearly 50 percent higher than that of whites (National Center for Health Statistics, 2003, Table 46). Among Hispanics, on the other hand, the infant mortality rate was about the same in 2000 as it was for the white population as a whole (National Center for Health Statistics, 2003, Table 598).

In addition to living shorter lives and having a greater risk of infant death, African Americans have more illness on average than whites. In 1996, African Americans experienced an average of 16.4 days a year of restricted activity because of illnesses, whites 14.3 days. This racial difference increases with age and is most notable above the age of forty-five. For example, African Americans aged forty-five to sixty-four experience an average 25 days of restricted activity, whites less than 18. Also, black adults overall are bedridden 10.9 days, whites just 6.3 days (Adams, Hendershot, and Marano, 1999, p. 109). In addition, almost 15 percent of African Americans, 13 percent of Latinos/as, and about 17 percent of Native Americans in 2001 described their health as "fair" or "poor," compared with fewer than 8 percent of non-Hispanic whites (National Center for Health Statistics, 2002c, p. 192).

## Summary and Conclusion

In this chapter we have seen that very serious racial and ethnic inequalities remain in the United States. It is true that prejudice and discrimination have decreased significantly in the last four decades, although they certainly have not disappeared. It is also true that more African Americans and Latinos/as today have attained middle-class status, and some are wealthy or highly educated. However, large segments of the black, Hispanic, and American Indian populations still have not shared in that progress and are trapped at the bottom of the socioeconomic ladder. For them, things are not getting better; indeed, in many regards, conditions worsened sharply in the 1980s and early 1990s (Massey and Denton, 1993; W. J. Wilson, 1996) and at best have modestly improved since. Consequently, the overall position of the minority population remains one of substantial disadvantages. In some aspects of the quality of life, the gap between the minority populations as a whole and the white population has narrowed only slightly, if at all. In a few areas, such as life expectancy, the gap has actually widened in the last few years.

The facts in this chapter carry some important implications about the social forces that affect majority-minority relations in America today. Considering that deliberate discrimination has decreased, although not disappeared, it would appear that *open and easily visible* acts of discrimination are not as important as they once were. Deliberate discrimination does still occur, but it is rarely acknowledged and often denied. In addition, much of today's continuing intergroup inequality is the result of two other factors. The first is the continuing effects of past discrimination. This has left a large portion of the minority population—particularly those near or below the poverty level—without the resources necessary to enjoy a reasonable standard of living or to offer their children much chance for upward mobility. The second factor involves a host of institutional, social, and economic processes that have the effect (though often not the intention) of maintaining and sometimes worsening the racial and ethnic inequalities in our society. These processes, which are the legacy of past discrimination and exploitation, affect the underclass particularly heavily. Because they are so institutionalized and because some advantaged segments of the population benefit from them, there is often fierce resistance to any attempts to alter them in a way that would bring about greater equality. These institutional, social, and economic processes are a major concern of the remainder of this book.

## Critical Review Questions

1. In what regard may it be an overgeneralization to speak about the situation of "Latinos/as" or of "Asian Americans" in the United States?

2. Why is there some confusion or disagreement among Latino/a groups about how to respond to the race question on the census?

3. What is meant by an identity of whiteness, and how may this concept have increased relevance for understanding race relations in the United States today?

4. In what ways has the status of African Americans, Latinos/as, and American Indians improved in recent years? In what ways has it not improved? Are there ways in which the situation has worsened for some members of these groups?

5. In what regards might it specifically be argued that the racial gap in the opportunity to obtain a college education is *not* closing?

# CHAPTER 10

## The American Economic System and the Status of Minority Groups Today

# Overview

We shall continue with the theme of institutional discrimination introduced in Chapter 1 and revisited at the end of Chapter 9. In this chapter, the first of three on major American institutions and majority-minority relations, we shall examine further the economic status of people of color, with special attention to how the economic system affects their status and opportunities. More broadly, we shall look at theories and evidence about how the economic system influences majority-minority relations in the United States.

As we have seen, a large gap remains between the average economic position of white people in America today and that of minority groups, most notably African Americans, American Indians, and Hispanic Americans. For some—particularly the younger, college-educated segments of the minority population—the racial disparity has decreased. Nonetheless, if we look at minority populations as a whole, the economic disparity is evident and not even greatly reduced from the past. A major factor in this disparity, as noted in the previous chapter, is the existence within the minority population of a large, impoverished, and underemployed or unemployed underclass. Between 20 and 25 percent of the Latino/a population, the African American population, and the Native American population have incomes below the federal poverty level. A smaller but sizable portion of each of these groups experiences persistent poverty and unemployment. In addition, minorities in the United States face yet one more difficult economic reality: Minority groups have been largely excluded from ownership or control of the major means of production in today's complex corporate economy.

## ▶ ASSET OWNERSHIP IN AMERICA TODAY

America's productive capacity today is overwhelmingly in the hands of a relatively small number of very large national or multinational corporations, exemplified by those in the *Fortune 500*. Both the ownership and control of these organizations are in the hands of a relatively small elite from which minority group members have been almost totally excluded. This is part of a larger pattern whereby *wealth*—the total value of what people own—is distributed much more unequally than income.

For example, if we examine ownership of the corporations, we may think at first that it is fairly dispersed among the population. A great many Americans own corporate stock, including thousands of blacks and Hispanics. However, African Americans and Latinos/as are only a third as likely as non-Hispanic whites to own stocks or mutual funds, and most of those who do own only a small amount. In 2000, for example, about 32 percent of non-Hispanic whites owned stock or mutual funds, compared with about 10 percent of blacks and 9 percent of Hispanics (U.S. Census Bureau, 2003g, Table 2). Among those who did own such assets, the average amount owned was twice as great for non-Hispanic whites ($110,973) as for Hispanics ($52,125) and nearly three times as great as for blacks ($38,680). Half of the blacks who owned stock owned less than $8,000, and half of the Hispanics owned less than $10,000 (U.S. Census Bureau, 2003g, Table 1). A major reason that African Americans and Latinos/as are less likely to own stocks or mutual funds is that they have less discretionary income for such investments. However, the consequence is that it is harder for blacks and Hispanics than it is for whites to generate additional wealth through investment (Oliver and Shapiro, 1995, p. 105). The great bulk of stock is owned by a small number of stockholders, and they are both very wealthy and overwhelmingly white. The majority of all wealth other than cars and houses is owned by just 5 percent of the U.S. population (Oliver and Shapiro, 1990). Very few blacks, Latinos/as, or American Indians fall in the very high income levels in which most of the corporate stock is owned. Thus, it appears safe to conclude that only a tiny proportion of America's total corporate wealth is in the hands of minority group members.

With corporate ownership overwhelmingly white, minorities in the United States have found it difficult to attain ownership of even more common forms of wealth such as houses. As shown in Figure 10.1, the median non-Hispanic white household in the United States is about ten times as wealthy as the median black or Hispanic household. A major reason is that whites are far more likely to own their homes than are African Americans or Latinos/as. In 2000, for example, 73 percent of non-Hispanic white Americans owned their homes, but only 47 percent of African Americans and 48 percent of Hispanics did so (U.S. Census Bureau, 2000l,

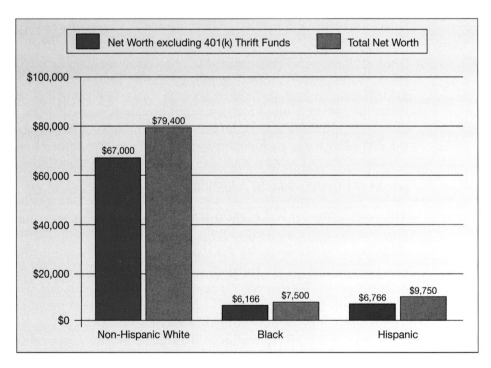

**FIGURE 10.1**   Median Net Worth by Race and Hispanic Origin, 2000

*Source:* U.S. Census Bureau (2003g, Table 1).

Table 2). Because owning a home is the major source of wealth for most households, these differences add up to a huge gap in wealth. In fact, 29 percent of African American households and 28 percent of Hispanic households in 2000 had zero or negative net worth; the figure for non-Hispanic white households is just 11 percent (U.S. Census Bureau, 2003g, Table 4).

Increasingly, research is showing just how harmful the consequences of these racial inequalities in wealth are. Conley (1999) has shown that wealth is even more crucial than income in explaining African American disadvantage in several different areas of life. For example, black high school graduates are less likely than white high school graduates to complete college, even when their families' incomes are similar. But it turns out that wealth, more than income, is what determines who can afford to live in areas with the best schools and enter and remain in college. Among white and black families with similar levels of wealth, young people who graduate from high school are equally likely to complete college (Conley, 1999). But the problem is that most black families have much less wealth than most white families, even at the same level of income. Conley found similar effects of wealth on racial gaps in other indicators of how well-off people are, including employment, illegitimacy rates, and rates of welfare dependency.

Reasons for the lack of wealth among African Americans and Latinos/as, even with higher incomes, include the fact that members of these groups often are relative newcomers to the middle and upper classes. Thus, unlike white Anglos, they have not had generations to accumulate and pass down wealth. For this reason, wealth is a better indicator than current income of the long-term economic impacts of discrimination (Conley, 2002; Feagin, 2000, pp. 186–88). Additionally, housing discrimination has largely excluded African Americans from the neighborhoods in which housing values have grown the fastest, and lending discrimination makes it harder for African Americans and Hispanics to buy homes and businesses. Consequently, the racial gap in wealth is much wider than the racial gap in income, with devastating results for many African Americans and Latino/a Americans.

Similarly, very few minority group members are in positions of true power in the major corporations. As recently as 1970, there were no black senior executives or members of boards of directors among the nation's largest industrial, retailing, and transportation companies and utilities and just a handful among the largest banks and insurance companies (Egerton, 1970). A study of 5,000 positions on boards of directors and other positions of authority in 1976 found just 15 blacks (Dye, 1979). Since then, the number of blacks in such positions has grown somewhat. By 1996, 3 percent of all corporate directors were black. About 37 percent of all major companies had at least one African American on their board of directors (Caudron, 1998a, 1998b). In 2001, 93 out of nearly 5,000 directors of Fortune 500 companies were African American women, and women of color held 2.6 percent of the board seats (Catalyst, 2002; Norment, 2002). The small number of African American directors is particularly striking considering that a few prominent blacks serve on several different corporate boards. For example, Dr. Shirley Jackson, president of Rensselaer Polytechnic Institute, sits on the boards of six different Fortune 500 corporations (Norment, 2002). For top managers, the picture is much the same. Although the number of women and minorities in management has grown, the representation of these groups in top management remains minuscule. In 1995, for example, the Federal Glass Ceiling Commission reported that among the 1,000 largest U.S. companies, at least 95 percent of senior managers were male and 97 percent were white (Caudron and Hayes, 1997). On the whole, it is not an overstatement to say that minority group members remain severely underrepresented on the boards of directors and in the senior executive positions that form the center of power in the corporate structure.

## ▶ THE ECONOMICS OF DISCRIMINATION: THREE THEORIES

Because major racial inequalities persist in the area of economics, it is important to ask, What causes economic inequality or discrimination? In this section, we shall discuss and evaluate three major theories about the economics of discrimination.

### Gary Becker's Theory

The first major effort to construct an economic theory of discrimination was made by Gary Becker (1957), who drew on some important insights from both the social-psychological and functionalist perspectives. His starting point is that some people have a "taste for discrimination"—what we have called conative prejudice—and if this attitude is held by employers, employees, or potential customers, it results in minority group members not being hired or not being hired for certain (usually better) jobs. In effect, the employer chooses to discriminate either as a result of his or her own prejudice or because of his or her concerns about the reactions of white employees or customers.

Such discrimination in hiring, however, is *dysfunctional* for both the employer and the society as a whole because it stands in the way of getting the best-qualified employee. This harms the productivity or efficiency of both the employer's enterprise and the society at large, and it wastes valuable human resources. Of course, it also directly harms minority workers, who end up underemployed, underpaid, or unemployed. The only potential beneficiaries are the white workers who get better jobs and more pay than they would in a rational, nondiscriminatory hiring system. However, even they are negatively affected by the lower overall productivity of the system.

Becker's (1957) theory implies that over the long run, discrimination in a complex industrial society should gradually disappear because it is dysfunctional both for the employer and for the overall society. Accordingly, firms that do not discriminate should gain a competitive advantage over those that do (Welch, 1967; Arrow, 1972; Masters, 1975). We would therefore expect the discriminatory firms either to stop discriminating or to go out of business, with the overall result being a gradual reduction in the amount of discrimination. This is consistent with the broader view of the functionalist perspective that the economic system operates according to principles of the market that reward efficiency and rationality and penalize irrational behaviors such as discrimination. Hence, functionalists generally believe that if left alone, the economic system will tend to work in ways that are productive and that will benefit the largest number of people.

In actual fact, the predicted reduction in discrimination has occurred, but only to a limited degree. Open, deliberate policies and acts of discrimination have become illegal over the past forty years and have become less common. However, less visible forms of discrimination, both intentional and unintentional, continue to occur. Kirschenman and Neckerman (1991) found substantial evidence of discrimination against blacks, particularly black men, in their study of Chicago-area employers. Much of this discrimination was based on stereotypes about black workers. Similarly, studies in which black and white testers, comparable in all regards except race, seek employment have found discrimination against blacks by employers and employment agencies (ABC News, 1991; Bendick, 1996; Bendick, Egan, and Lofhjelm, 1998; Feagin, 2000, pp. 160–62). White job seekers are told that jobs are available, whereas black job seekers are told that there are no openings. In addition, employers and employment agencies often interact differently with black and white applicants, lecturing the former but not the latter about laziness, drug use, and so forth. Testing studies have also shown discrimination against Latino job applicants (Cross, 1990; Bendick, Jackson, and Reinoso, 1994). In part because of discrimination such as this, the overall amount of economic racial inequality remains substantial.

In a critical evaluation of Becker's (1957) theory, we must also question the central role he attributes to *attitudes*. Whereas studies such as Kirschenman and Neckerman's (1991) show that attitudes do frequently underlie discrimination, many other things can result in discriminatory practices and arrangements. We saw in earlier chapters that attitudes often are only weakly linked to discrimination. Economic motivations and pressures from workers and customers may be at least as important as a "taste for discrimination" in causing discrimination. We now turn our attention to two conflict theories that stress just that point: Perceived economic gain can motivate people to discriminate, whether they are prejudiced or not.

## Split Labor Market Theory

One answer to the latter criticism of Becker's (1957) theory may be found in another theory of the economics of discrimination known as **split labor market theory** (Bonacich, 1972, 1975, 1976; W. J. Wilson, 1978; see also Blumer, 1965; Brown and Boswell, 1995). This theory notes some of the same patterns as Becker's theory but attributes them to social structure rather than to individual preferences. It is a form of conflict theory in that it sees discrimination as a result of the clash of competing interest groups. In general, conflict theories argue that the structure of the economy is determined by different groups with competing interests and by their relative power.

This model, unlike Becker's (1957), argues that the business owner or capitalist recognizes that racial discrimination is dysfunctional for the business enterprise and therefore often prefers not to discriminate. The objective of the capitalist is to get the best worker for the lowest wage, and it is therefore in the capitalist's interest not to discriminate because discrimination limits the pool of workers available for the position. Accordingly, those doing the hiring discriminate not because they have a taste for discrimination but rather because they are forced or pressured to do so by another interest group that does benefit from discrimination. This interest group is white laborers. In the view of this theory, discrimination is in the interest of white laborers because it insulates them from potential competition from minority group workers. Accordingly, if they are powerful enough to do so, white workers demand the exclusion of minority group workers from certain more desirable jobs (or from industrial jobs altogether), in effect creating a system of "white jobs" with high pay and "black jobs" or "brown jobs" with low pay.

In such a split labor market, the cost of white labor is higher than the cost of minority labor, still another reason why nondiscrimination would be in the interest of the employer or capitalist. But this is also largely why higher-paid white labor demands discrimination: Discrimination keeps white workers' wages high by protecting them from the competition of lower-paid minority labor. Higher-paid white labor may be able to impose a system of discrimination in a number of ways. It might prevent minority group labor from obtaining skills by demanding educational discrimination. It might seek to exclude minority group members from a territory entirely: If they cannot move into an area, they cannot compete (W. J. Wilson, 1978, p. 7). It may also attempt to keep minority laborers out of its segment of the labor market by keeping them out of labor unions. Exclusion of blacks from labor unions was common in the United States before World War II (Wesley, 1927, pp. 254–81; Bonacich, 1975, p. 38). Brody (1960, p. 186) has also documented that in 1917 several steel firms refused to hire blacks because they were afraid of the reaction of white workers. In another part of the world, the system of apartheid in South Africa had its roots partially in the demands of white labor unions for the exclusion of black workers during the 1920s (Van der Horst, 1967, pp. 117–18; W. J. Wilson, 1973, p. 168).

Apparently, such strategies were effective for white laborers, at least in the short run (Marshall, 1965, pp. 22–23). Over the long run, however, one must question their effectiveness: A common consequence of such discrimination was to so antagonize black laborers that they acted as strikebreakers, greatly weakening the position of the white workers' labor unions. This was especially common in the 1920s (Bonacich, 1976, p. 40; W. J. Wilson, 1978, p. 74), and it contributed significantly to the weakening of labor unions during that period (W. J. Wilson, 1978, p. 76; C. Brown, 2000). Thus, split labor market theory, too, appears to have some limitations or, at the very least, to describe some periods of history better than others.

## Marxist Theory

A third theory, arising from a general Marxist perspective, differs from both theories we have examined thus far. It has one element in common with split labor market theory: It is a conflict theory arguing that racial discrimination in employment is the result of the clash of competing interest groups. However, it disagrees with both of the other theories on who gains and who loses as a result of discrimination. Recall that both Becker's (1957) theory and the split labor market theory argue that white laborers gain and employers or capitalists lose as a result of discrimination. The **Marxist theory of discrimination** argues precisely the opposite: Employers or capitalists gain and white workers lose as a result of discrimination (Baran and Sweezy, 1966; Reich, 1986), mainly because racial antagonisms divide workers and thereby weaken their power relative to that of employers. Hence, from the perspective of Marxist theory, racism is seen as one of the many tools that owners of wealth use to keep the work force divided and weak. A prime example can be seen in the strikebreaking of the early twentieth century. White unions excluded blacks, and blacks responded by acting as strikebreakers when the whites went on strike.[1] The consequence was the weakening of unions and lower wages for both blacks and whites. Eventually, many unions realized this, particularly the industrial unions of the Congress of Industrial Organizations (CIO), and with some encouragement from the Roosevelt administration they changed their policies to oppose discrimination. The result was a stronger union movement: Once workers were able to stay unified and overcome the "divide and conquer" efforts of employers, they were in a stronger position.

Reich (1986) argues that the theory continues to be relevant in more recent periods, as conflicts over school busing and neighborhood racial change involve mainly working-class blacks and whites (see also Rieder, 1985; E. Anderson, 1990). According to Reich, the consequence is that working-class whites and blacks often see each other as the enemy. Consequently, they fail to recognize their common interests and are unable to cooperate with each other to influence the political system or to protect their common interests against the opposing interests of their employers or, more generally, the wealthy elite. In fact, this type of thinking has been used quite consciously by some conservative political strategists, who have referred to issues such as affirmative action as "wedge issues" designed to divide the working class and liberal base of the Democratic party (Germond and Witcover, 1996).

A key assumption underlying Marxist theory is that class divisions have more to do with how well people live than do divisions between racial and ethnic groups. Thus, argue Marxists, the working class and the poor are disadvantaged regardless of their race. Race becomes significant in that it is used by the wealthy and powerful to divide the working class and the poor. Thus, if lower-income blacks and whites,

---

[1]It is important to note that this was not the only reason for black strikebreaking. Many did so out of desperation, and some took jobs in distant areas without being told that they were breaking a strike until they arrived at the job site. Of course, many whites were also strikebreakers, and most blacks never worked as strikebreakers.

for example, blame one another for their troubles, neither will challenge the wealth of the upper classes, and both will remain poor. Hence, race becomes a means by which class inequality is perpetuated, allowing the wealthy to maintain their disproportionate wealth and income.

**A Note on Internal Colonialism Theory.** Another conflict theory, which challenges the Marxist theory's emphasis on the primacy of class divisions, is internal colonialism theory, discussed in Chapter 6. This theory views racial divisions—particularly those between the dominant group and colonized minorities—as more important than class divisions, arguing that everyone in a colonized minority is at a potential disadvantage because, regardless of class, they are subject to discrimination and exploitation (Mirande, 1987). Moreover, entire groups, such as Native Americans and African Americans, have been made to suffer as a result of economic exploitation by the dominant group. Like Marxists and split labor market theorists, internal colonialism theorists believe that discrimination exists because someone benefits from it, specifically people in the dominant group. However, they do not directly address the question of who within the dominant group benefits. Thus, internal colonialism theory is not directly relevant to the debate between Marxist and split labor market theories over this issue. For this reason among others, the main discussion of internal colonialism theory is in in Chapter 6 rather than here.

## Evaluating Theories About the Economics of Discrimination

Gary Becker's (1957) theory, split labor market theory, and Marxist theory each offer a different reason for the existence of economic racial and ethnic discrimination. According to Becker, discrimination occurs because some people have a taste

These girls are being screened for health problems caused by exposure to lead-based paint. Lead poisoning is a common problem among children of impoverished families in urban areas. Sociologists of the conflict perspective believe that such poverty and suffering exist because, somewhere in the social system, some more advantaged group of people benefits from it.

for discrimination; in other words, the cause lies in people's attitudes. According to split labor market theory, discrimination occurs because white workers benefit from it by eliminating minority competition. According to Marxist theory, discrimination occurs because capitalists benefit from the divisions it creates in the working class, which weaken the bargaining position of workers and lead black and white workers to blame each other rather than the capitalist class for their difficulties. With three such different explanations, who is right?

Under different social conditions, each of the three theories can be correct. Discrimination can result from prejudiced attitudes, particularly when the culture is supportive. Certainly a culture that favored prejudice and discrimination led some employers to discriminate, regardless of the economic consequences, in the "Old South." Another example can be found in my personal experience while conducting interviews for a survey of employers in the Detroit area in 1972. One plant owner claimed that if the government told him he had to hire a certain number of blacks (at the time, he had no black employees), he would simply close the plant and go out of business. It is hard to conclude that this employer was acting mainly on calculations of his possible gains; he simply had a very strong opinion that made him willing (or so he said) to go out of business rather than change.

In other cases, however, individual attitudes probably are not the major cause of discriminatory behavior. We have noted cases in which pressures from white labor caused employers to discriminate, and when white labor was able to effectively control the hiring process, the strategy appears to have worked. Marshall (1965, pp. 22–23) notes that certain strong craft unions were able to keep blacks out and thus to maintain high wages and high membership during a period in the 1920s when most unions were losing ground. However, most unions do not have enough control over hiring to make such a strategy work. Both Reich (1986) and W. J. Wilson (1978, p. 78) have noted that the one main element of white labor that has been able to use discrimination to its advantage is the craft unions, such as the building trades, which control hiring through the union hiring hall. A study by Mladenka (1991) has shown a second situation in which this can occur: In some cities, municipal labor unions have largely kept blacks out of city employment. But his study also showed that this occurred only in unreformed city governments, those in which the unions were powerful enough to influence who was hired.

The majority of workers, however, do not have such control over hiring, and in these cases Marxist theory may offer the best explanation for the causes and consequences of race discrimination. Racial divisions were disastrous for many unions in the 1910s and 1920s, and since that time most unions (particularly industry-wide unions such as the United Auto Workers) have taken an official stance against racial prejudice and discrimination (C. Brown, 2000). (Of course, white members do not always go along with the official position.)

There is also evidence that racial divisions continue to harm the economic position of the working and lower classes today. As we have seen, prejudice is strongest among these groups, at least by the usual measures of attitudes about intergroup relations. Moreover, social organizers often lament the degree to which racial divisions keep poor blacks, whites, Latinos/as, and others from recognizing a common interest. A study by Reich (1981, 1986) sheds some empirical light on the issue. Reich examined 1960 and 1970 census data on the forty-eight largest metropolitan areas in the United States. For each area, he determined the ratio of median black family income to median white family income as a measure of economic racial inequality or discrimination. He also obtained two measures of income inequality within the white population. He found that where black-white inequality or discrimination was great, income within the white population was more concentrated: The wealthier segment had higher income and the poorer segment lower income than in areas with less racial inequality. In Reich's judgment, this finding supports the theory that wealthy whites and employers benefit from racism and the less wealthy and working-class whites are hurt by it. However, there are other possible interpretations of Reich's findings. All his variables could be measuring the same thing: the overall amount of inequality in an area, an inequality that falls along both class and racial lines.

Studies by Norval Glenn (1963, 1966), George Dowdall (1974), and J. E. Farley (1987b) seem to support the view that both the Marxist and split labor market interpretations may be correct, depending on the situation. These studies showed that, given the level of discrimination in American society, whites in areas with more blacks enjoyed higher occupational status, income, or employment rates. To the degree that this was true because blacks took the burden of unemployment and underpaid work, leaving the better jobs available for whites, the results appear to support the split labor market theory. On the other hand, Dowdall (1974, p. 182) argues that the findings support Marxist theory in that it seems to be those at the top who benefit most from discrimination.

A more direct test of the effects of discrimination on the overall white population is provided by Szymanski (1976). He showed that in states with relatively high racial inequality in income, whites had lower average incomes and had a more unequal income distribution, especially in states with larger-than-average minority populations. This relationship was explained only partially by region; Szymanski's data indicated that the main reason for the pattern was that unions were weaker in states with great racial inequality. Similarly, Reich (1981, 1986) found that as income inequality between blacks and whites increased, white workers' wages decreased and employers' profits increased. Like Szymanski, Reich found unions to be weaker in areas with greater racial inequality. These findings provide significant support for the Marxist theory of the economics of discrimination.

Even so, there is still room for debate. For example, a study by Beck (1980) found that comparisons made over time rather than across places suggest that to some degree the economy operates according to the split labor market model. Beck's study showed that at different times, from 1947 to 1974, periods of relatively high unionization were accompanied by high black-white inequality and vice versa. However, part of Beck's findings may result from the fact that changes in the job structure toward white-collar jobs have both reduced unionization and, as W. J. Wilson (1978) argues, opened new opportunities for the expansion of a black middle class.

Finally, some sociologists and economists believe that a portion of the minority population is now so far out of the economic mainstream that it is almost irrelevant to the economic welfare of whites. In this view, the poorest segment of the black and Hispanic population is so chronically unemployed and so completely excluded from opportunities to learn job skills that it can neither threaten the jobs of employed whites nor be used by employers to divide the white working class (Willhelm, 1980; see also W. J. Wilson, 1978, especially pp. 151–53, 1987). This observation is probably true for the poorest of the poor, but several related points must be made. First, only a small minority of the black population or the Hispanic population can be considered part of this so-called "underclass," so most of these populations are anything but irrelevant economically. Second, if white workers *perceive* minorities to be a threat, they may demand discrimination, even though discrimination may in reality raise corporate profits at the expense of white workers' wages. It is the perception, not the reality, that determines how people behave. At the least, it is very clear that many white male workers have opposed initiatives to increase the proportion of minority and female workers, fearing that their own jobs or economic security could be jeopardized. For example, white men voted heavily in favor of California's Proposition 209, which ended affirmative action in state hiring and college admissions, whereas Latinos/as, African Americans, and to a lesser extent white women opposed it (Germond and Witcover, 1996).

## Discrimination and Economic Productivity

We conclude our discussion of theories about the economics of discrimination by returning to one idea raised in Becker's (1957) theory: Discrimination hurts the overall productivity of society. Whereas we have thus far emphasized debates about what interest groups get a bigger or smaller share of the pie as a result of discrimination, it is important to note that discrimination does reduce the size of the pie. This economic impact arises in part from employment discrimination, which directly keeps minority group members from contributing to the productivity of the economy. However, it also arises indirectly from racial inequality in education, which can keep minority group members from developing the skills they need to contribute to that productivity. By 2000, 39 percent of children and 31 percent of the working-age U.S. population were people of color: African Americans, Latinos/as, Asian Americans, or Native Americans (computed from U.S. Census Bureau, 2003b). By about 2040 it is projected that 53 percent of children and 44 percent of working-aged adults will be people of color. How well we educate this emerging majority and how well its members are given the opportunity to use their skills in the workplace will have a huge effect on the productivity of the U.S. economy in the next half century.

In today's global economy, the United States faces greater international economic competition than ever before. If the United States continues to relegate a large part of its black and Hispanic population to unemployment or underemployment and does not do a better job of developing high-tech skills in its minority population, the consequences could be serious for the entire U.S. economy. A number of studies and reports have warned about this risk, ranging from the Workforce 2000 report (U.S. Department of Labor, 1987) to academic studies, such as Schwartz and Disch's (1975) *White Racism: Its History, Pathology, and Practice.* The latter uses the example of Latinos/as to point out that if people are not allowed to develop and use their skills, productivity is hurt and, in addition, costs are imposed on society in the form of poverty and the social problems it brings. Similar points were also made in a brief submitted by twenty large corporations in support of the University of Michigan's defense in the Supreme Court of its affirmative action admissions policies (Hurd, 2000). The Court largely endorsed this reasoning in its *Grutter* ruling upholding affirmative action, stating:

> These benefits are not theoretical but real, as major American businesses have made clear that the skills needed in today's increasingly global marketplace can only be developed through exposure to widely diverse people, cultures, ideas, and viewpoints. What is more, high-ranking retired officers and civilian leaders of the United States military assert that, "based on [their] decades of experience," a "highly qualified, racially diverse officer corps . . . is essential to the military's ability to fulfill its principal mission to provide national security."

Thus, quite independent of whether or not some interest groups gain from discrimination, there is strong evidence that the society as a whole loses from discrimination and benefits from full participation by all groups.

## ▶ RECENT TRENDS AND THEIR EFFECTS ON ECONOMIC INEQUALITY

Whatever the underlying causes of racial economic discrimination may be, there are some things we know about the mechanisms that maintain racial economic inequality today and the effects of recent social trends on patterns of economic inequality and discrimination along the lines of race. In the remainder of this chapter, these two closely related issues will be the focus of our discussion.

## Rising Educational Demands and the Employment of Minorities

As we have seen, the expansion of white-collar jobs has created the opportunity for a sizable minority middle class to develop. However, because of the increase in educational requirements for employment that have accompanied it, this expansion has also created problems for a large segment of the minority population. These problems have been aggravated by the tendency of employers to demand higher levels of education for jobs, whether or not the education is actually needed for the job. The tendency of employers to make such demands increases as the average educational level of the population increases, as it has over the past few decades. It also increases during periods of high unemployment, and unemployment was relatively high from the late 1960s to the early 1990s. For a variety of reasons, an employer may want to hire a person with more education than is necessary to do the work. One very important factor—which will be discussed at greater length in Chapter 12—is that employers often try to hire workers with cultural values and work habits similar to their own. Thus, they prefer more educated employees not because these employees know more about the job but because they will "fit in" better.

Although usually not deliberately racist, this practice does end up being racist in its consequences. As we have seen, average educational levels among blacks, Latinos/as, and American Indians are well below that of whites. When more education is demanded than the job requires, many people capable of doing the work are excluded (Berg, 1971), and a disproportionate number of them are members of minority groups. Thus, inflated educational requirements can be identified as one cause of the high levels of unemployment and poverty among the black, Hispanic, and American Indian populations. In addition to the practice of inflating educational requirements, there has been an increase in jobs that do actually require higher educational levels, and automation has reduced the number of unskilled jobs. As a result, the proportion of jobs available to people with limited skills and education has become extremely small in many of the large metropolitan areas where many people of color live (Moss and Tilly, 2001b, pp. 459–463). The result of this, combined with educational racial inequality, is that minorities—particularly minority men—have less chance of getting hired (Moss and Tilly, 2001a, 2001b). Thus, increased educational job requirements clearly help to explain why the black unemployment rate rose to twice as high as the white unemployment rate after World War II and has been at least that high ever since.

In principle, practices that have the effect of discrimination, such as unnecessary educational requirements, were banned by the 1991 Civil Rights Act. This law, which was passed in large part to reverse several Supreme Court decisions in the 1980s that made it harder for minorities to sue for job discrimination, also expanded the rights of minorities, women, and the disabled to take legal action against discriminatory policies and actions in the workplace. Specifically, it guarantees the right to take legal action against requirements, such as educational requirements and strength requirements, that have the effect of discriminating, unless employers can show that the requirements are "job-related for the position in question and consistent with business necessity." The extent to which this legislation will actually prevent employers from engaging in practices that are discriminatory in effect but not intent remains to be seen and probably will depend on how many discrimination cases are brought under the law and how the courts interpret it. Obviously, the degree to which a requirement is relevant to a job involves some subjective judgment. As of mid-2004, there had been no major, ground-breaking court decisions resulting from this law, although the number of employment discrimination complaints filed in U.S. courts did increase sharply after its passage (Litras,

2000, 2002). However, one recent study found that the law had little impact on diversifying industries where minority groups were underrepresented (Oyer and Schaefer, 2002).

## Job Decentralization and Housing Segregation

As we have seen, the majority of black Americans and nearly half of Hispanic Americans, but fewer than a quarter of the non-Hispanic white population, live in the central cities. The black and Latino/a populations became increasingly concentrated in the central cities between World War II and the 1970s.

During the same period and continuing ever since, however, employment opportunities have been moving out of those central cities. This is true for business and retail sales jobs, as well as for the industrial jobs that in the past were especially important as a source of relatively high-paying work for black and Latino/a workers. In addition to the shifts in the locations of jobs, there has been a major decline in the overall number of such manufacturing jobs as a result of automation and globalization, a trend often called *deindustrialization*. Because most of these disappearing jobs were located in central cities, the impacts of deindustrialization have been especially severe there and thus for the disproportionately African American and Latino/a populations that live there. These trends have been especially notable in the larger metropolitan areas, which are also the home of a disproportionate share of African Americans and Latinos/as (Sternleib and Hughes, 1976, p. 30). Whereas the number of jobs simply stopped growing in some of the smaller cities, it actually fell in many of the larger cities and in some smaller ones with large minority populations, especially in the 1970s and in some cases earlier. For example, New York City lost 600,000 jobs between 1970 and 1980, and Chicago lost 200,000 (W. J. Wilson, 1981). East St. Louis, Illinois, a small industrial city that is overwhelmingly black, lost more than half of its manufacturing jobs between 1950 and 1970 (Illinois Capital Development Board, 1977). Nationally, between 1947 and 1967, manufacturing employment in central cities declined by 4 percent; it rose by 94 percent in the suburbs during the same period. A similar movement to the suburbs can be seen in wholesale and retail trade (Barabba, 1976, p. 56).

The rate of overall job loss declined in some central cities in the 1980s and 1990s, but in most cities there has continued to be a major shift away from the higher-paying industrial jobs that had been an economic mainstay for many blacks and Hispanics (particularly men) and toward much lower-paying service jobs. For example, Chicago lost about 50,000 jobs between the 1977 and 1987 economic censuses—still a large number but a considerably slower rate of loss than in the 1970s. However, there was a dramatic shift in the kinds of jobs available, with about 90,000 fewer manufacturing jobs and about 80,000 more service jobs. Service jobs pay only a small fraction of the pay of manufacturing jobs, so the shift from manufacturing to service employment in the city contributed to the further impoverishment of Chicago's African American and Latino/a populations (W. J. Wilson, 1987, 1996). Chicago is typical in that only service jobs grew in the city. This trend continued between 1992 and 1997, with economic censuses indicating that overall employment changed little, but service jobs grew while manufacturing, wholesale trade, and retail trade jobs declined in the city (Oregon State University Libraries, 2002; U.S. Census Bureau, 2003e).

While jobs continued to disappear in the city of Chicago, they continued to grow in the suburbs and fringe areas, which are overwhelmingly white. In the portion of the Chicago consolidated metropolitan statistical area outside the city, the number of jobs grew by about 150,000 between 1977 and 1987, even as it fell by about 50,000 in the city. Job growth in this area continued through the 1990s, while the number of jobs in the city remained flat. This shift to the suburbs harms minority group members because, just as they are overrepresented in the central cities, they are underrepresented in the suburbs. Thus, jobs leave areas where blacks and Latinos/as live and to move into areas where white Anglos live. Because a sizable segment of the urban minority population cannot afford to own an automobile and many cities lack adequate mass transportation, many minority workers cannot get employment unless they can move to the areas where jobs are growing. Housing segregation often makes this difficult, restricting minorities to areas with increasingly fewer jobs. Studies of St. Louis, Chicago, Cleveland, and Detroit indicate that housing segregation has kept the numbers of blacks in the suburbs far below what would be expected on the basis of the black and white income distributions.[2] Exclusionary zoning practices make it even more difficult for lower-income minority people—the ones most in need of decent employment—to move to where the jobs are.

Numerous studies suggest that these factors are an important cause of high black unemployment (Kain, 1968; Mooney, 1969; Hutchinson, 1974; Shanahan, 1976; S. Raphael, 1998; for extensive reviews of this literature see Kain, 1992; Ihlanfeldt and Sjoquist, 1998). My studies (J. E. Farley, 1981, 1987b), using data from all U.S. metropolitan areas, show that black and Hispanic unemployment in 1970 and 1980 was higher relative to white unemployment in areas where black and Hispanic populations were more concentrated in the central city and where jobs were more suburbanized. In 1980, this remained true even after adjustment for racial differences in education. Moreover, research by Kasarda (1989a, 1989b, 1990) indicates that minority group members living in the central cities have higher unemployment rates than minorities in the suburbs, and as increasing numbers of jobs have left the city, this gap has widened. This tendency has been aggravated by urban sprawl, which has increased the distance many people must travel from home to work (Brookings Institution, 2000). Research by Holzer and Ihlanfeldt (1996) has shown that firms closer to black residences and to public transportation are more likely to have black employees, again emphasizing the importance of the relative location of employers and the minority population.

These studies and others (such as Lichter, 1988) indicate that today's high unemployment rates among blacks and Hispanics are in part the result of a growing *geographic mismatch* between job opportunities and the residence locations of many African Americans and Latinos/as. The effects are particularly great for black and Hispanic men, many of whom once relied on manufacturing jobs for good-paying, stable employment. Today, many or most of those jobs have been eliminated or relocated out of the central city. According to Marcuse (1997), this process has reached the point where many central city minority neighborhoods have been effectively "excluded from the economic life of the surrounding community" (p. 314). Marcuse calls these neighborhoods as "excluded ghettoes." The effects of geographic mismatch are also large for minority youths. In the sixteen to nineteen and twenty to twenty-four age groups, between 15 and 35 percent of the unemployment gaps between blacks and Latinos and whites can be explained by differences in access to job locations (Ihlanfeldt and Sjoquist, 1990, 1991; Ihlanfeldt, 1992, 1993). A more recent study by Steven Raphael (1998), emphasizing access to locations where jobs are growing, found even bigger effects, with access accounting for up to 50 percent of the racial gap in youth unemployment.

Clearly, the movement of jobs from minority neighborhoods and the inability of these workers either to commute to distant jobs or to live near them is one more major handicap imposed on many urban blacks and Latinos/as. Even if

---

[2]These studies are discussed in detail later in this chapter.

there were little or no deliberate racial discrimination by employers, the result of the increasing separation of minority neighborhoods and job openings is still fewer opportunities for blacks and Latinos to obtain meaningful employment. Moreover, research now indicates that a similar pattern may be developing in suburbia: As black neighborhoods have developed and grown in suburban areas, job growth has tended to be greater in predominantly white suburbs than in those with sizable black populations (Schneider and Phelan, 1990). If this pattern continues, it may eventually place many suburban minority populations in a situation similar to that of their counterparts in the central cities: They may face rising unemployment because of separation from the areas that have the most job openings.

There is little doubt that job shifts in recent decades have reduced opportunities for minority group members. This pattern raises two important questions: Why have these detrimental changes occurred? What, if anything, can minority group members do to minimize the effects of these job shifts?

**Reasons for Job Shifts.** There are numerous reasons why employment opportunities have moved out of central cities. Some have nothing to do with race or ethnicity, but others suggest at least some race consciousness on the part of corporate decision makers.

One reason is that modern manufacturing is more efficient in sprawling, one-level factory complexes than in the once typical multistory factory. The one-story complexes occupy much more land than the old factories, and this land is available and affordable only in urban fringe areas and rural areas. Nonetheless, the shift to such areas probably would never have happened without the development of truck transportation and the interstate highway system. Because transportation is crucial to manufacturing, it was at one time necessary for industry to locate on a major waterway or near a rail junction. Generally, this meant locating in a major city. Today, however, most industries can locate wherever there is an interstate highway because much more shipping is done by truck. It is significant that the greatest growth in manufacturing activity and in population in rural areas has been in counties with an interstate highway.

Also, the loss of manufacturing jobs in the central cities reflects a decline in the importance of manufacturing in the U.S. economy generally, a trend often called *deindustrialization*. This trend has occurred for a number of reasons, including (1) continued automation of manufacturing processes; (2) relocation of manufacturing jobs to other parts of the world, part of a general trend of *globalization*; and (3) a decline in the importance of manufacturing relative to other kinds of economic activity, most notably services. All of these trends have had a disproportionate effect on inner cities because there the manufacturing plants are the oldest and most economically vulnerable. Consequently, deindustrialization has had disproportionate effects on African American and Latino/a workers, although many whites have also been affected (W. J. Wilson, 1987, 1996).

Other factors in the loss of industrial jobs may be more directly linked to race and ethnicity. Some movement of jobs out of central cities probably is the result of prejudices and fears on the part of whites that make them reluctant to keep their businesses in predominantly black or Hispanic areas (Kirschenman, 1989, 1990; Kirschenman and Neckerman, 1991; Tilly et al., 2001). Some employers have also complained about the work habits and lifestyles of inner-city employees, which may be significantly different from their own (Holzer, 1996; Tilly et al., 2001; Moss and Tilly, 2001a, 2001b). Finally, some of the movement seems aimed at avoiding unionization, and in some cases, this probably means deliberately avoiding black areas. In the South, particularly, white workers are less prounion than black workers, which may be one reason that companies largely move to white areas (W. Thompson, 1976, p. 190).

Moreover, much of the movement of jobs out of the United States is really an effort to cut costs by using cheaper labor. About half a million jobs were shifted between 1994 and 1998 to just south of the Mexican border, for example (Gruben, 1998), as American companies relocated plants to take advantage of low wages and weak labor and environmental protection laws. A job that might pay twelve dollars per hour in an industrial city in the Great Lakes region will pay just one to two dollars an hour in Mexico; consequently, 3,900 *maquiladora* manufacturing plants are now operating near the Mexican border (Quinones, 1998). Similar or greater labor cost savings can be attained by shifting jobs to China or any number of other countries, which have also received large numbers of jobs shifted from the United States and other industrialized countries. These jobs shifts have been facilitated by free trade agreements such as the North American Free Trade Agreement (NAFTA) and the Global Agreement on Trade and Tarrifs (GATT); the Bureau of Labor Statistics estimates that in the textile and apparel industries alone, 650,000 U.S. jobs were lost by 2003 through free trade agreements (Neff, Wagner, and Rives, 2003). Many of these jobs were held by African Americans and Hispanic Americans. Although it is true that free trade has also created jobs by enhancing international markets for U.S. products, most job growth has occurred outside the areas where most minority group members live, as discussed earlier.

Not only manufacturing jobs are leaving U.S. central cities. The movement of retail and wholesale trade to the suburbs appears largely to be the result of the movement of population—especially wealthier (and mostly white) people with money to spend—to the suburbs. Fear of crime and the reluctance of white consumers to shop in minority neighborhoods may also be a factor in the decentralization of these businesses.

Whatever the intent of those who decide to relocate business and industry, the result clearly contributes to racial inequality by taking jobs out of the areas where minorities live and (when jobs are relocated to suburban and rural areas) putting them into the areas where whites live. In the following section, we shall examine the alternatives available to minorities to adjust to this changing distribution of job opportunities.

**Adjustment to Job Shifts.** Two responses to job shifts are possible. One is increased commuting from city to suburb. Undoubtedly, some minority workers have responded in this way, but many others cannot. Only a few American cities have rapid transit systems, and for many minority group members, private transportation is simply not an alternative. A surprising number cannot afford to own an automobile. In 2000, about one out of four African American households and more than one out of six Latino/a households had no motor vehicle (U.S. Census Bureau, 2003c, Tables HCT33a–g), and among those who live in central cities, the numbers are higher. Among those who do have cars, the cost of gasoline sometimes limits the feasibility of long-distance commuting.

The other alternative is to move to the areas where the jobs are located. In fact, a Chicago study in which impoverished black women were given an opportunity to relocate from the central city to subsidized housing in the suburbs showed that relocation produced significant increases in employment rates (Rosenbaum and Popkin, 1991). A second study in Cincinnati obtained similar findings (Fischer, 1995). The cost of moving to the suburbs is often prohibitive, however, and in many cases African Americans and Latinos are steered away from predominantly white areas, as is explained in greater detail later in this chapter. Furthermore, restrictive zoning and public opposition to low-income housing have largely kept the minority poor out of the suburbs. In fact, the relocation opportunities given to African Americans in the studies just mentioned resulted from settlements of lawsuits against the concentration of low-income housing in inner-city areas (Yinger, 1995, pp. 152–53). There has been an increase in migration of blacks to the suburbs in recent years, but much of it has been into "suburban ghettos," large concentrations of black population, mostly in the older parts of the suburbs, which are also losing employment opportunities. Also, much of it has involved blacks who have already attained middle-class status and are least in need of employment opportunities. Probably the most important factor is the pervasive pattern of discrimination and segregation in housing. This issue is of such importance, both in itself and as a factor in reducing employment opportunities, that we shall discuss it separately in the next section.

## ▶ HOUSING DISCRIMINATION AND SEGREGATION

When sociologists talk about housing segregation, they are referring to the tendency for people in any two groups or races to live in separate areas. For example, when all the blacks in a city live in one neighborhood or set of neighborhoods and all the whites live in other neighborhoods, the city is highly segregated. Sociologists have a number of measures of residential segregation, but probably the most widely used is the **index of dissimilarity**, sometimes called the *segregation index*. This index can range from 0 to 100, with 0 being no segregation and 100 being total segregation. As we use it here, this measure is based on urban neighborhood areas called *census tracts*. For any two groups, such as blacks and whites, the segregation index tells us what percentage of a city's black or white population would have to move to another census tract to have no segregation at all.

### Housing Segregation Between Blacks and Whites

This measure has been computed for every U.S. metropolitan area, using census data, from 1950 through 2000. In 2000, the average black-white segregation index for all 331 metropolitan areas in the United States was about 50, down from about 54 in 1990 and the low 60s in 1980 (U.S. Census Bureau, 2003m, Table C1; *USA Today*, 1991). For metropolitan areas with a black population of at least 3 percent or 20,000—the cities for which the index is most meaningful— the average segregation index was 55 in 2000, a reduction of about 4 points since 1990 (U.S. Census Bureau, 2003m, Table C1). Segregation levels are higher in cities where most blacks live, however. When the averages are weighted for race, a more segregated picture emerges. With such weighting, the average rises to about 64 in 2000, meaning that the average African American living in a metropolitan area lives in an area with a segregation index of 64. In other words, the average African American lives in an area that is nearly two-thirds of the way toward the segregated end of the scale. This is down from about 68 in 1990 and 73 in 1980. Segregation has been declining since about 1970, but there was a bigger decline in the 1970s than in either decade since (Glaeser and Vigdor, 2001, Figure 1; see also Logan, 2001).

Housing segregation largely arose in the twentieth century. The foundations of segregation were laid in the 1920s and 1930s, when many urban areas began to experience large increases in their African American populations. As is discussed elsewhere in this book, the African American population was predominantly southern and rural at the start of the twentieth century, but after that time it began to move northward and from the rural South to cities. As a result, the racial composition of large metropolitan areas began to change. In Chapter 6, we examined ways in which the rigid competitive system of race relations, involving extensive segregation, was institutionalized in the late nineteenth and early twentieth centuries. The establishment of racial segregation in housing was part of this pattern, and it can clearly be traced to the time in the early twentieth century when the African American population of large urban areas was growing most rapidly. Massey and Denton (1993, p. 21) have shown that nearly every large city had a dramatic increase in racial segregation between 1910 and 1940. In the North, the average index of dissimilarity rose from 59 to 89 during this time period; in the South it rose from 38 to 81. According to Massey and Denton, these increases reflect the reactions of whites to a growing black population in the cities, especially in a period of industrialization and competition for jobs. White workers saw the African Americans as an economic threat, and whites of all classes were prejudiced against them. These reactions were often heightened by employers who played off black and white workers against one another. When the black population rose, the fears and prejudices of whites became more salient, and they tried to control blacks and isolate themselves from them by instituting a system of segregation. Consequently, black-white housing segregation increased sharply between 1910 and 1940, and despite some declines in recent decades, the average African American today lives in a much more segregated area than a century ago. Compared with today's average of 64, the average African American living in a metropolitan area a century ago lived in an area with an index of about 50, or 14 points less segregated than today.

In general, levels of black-white segregation are higher in the Midwest and Northeast and in larger, older cities with larger black populations (Jakubs, 1986; Massey and Denton, 1987, 1988, 1989; *USA Today*, 1991; Farley and Frey, 1992, 1994; O'Hare, 1992; Glaeser and Vigdor, 2001; Logan, 2001; U.S. Census Bureau, 2003m). Regionally, the lowest levels of segregation are found in the West (O'Hare and Usdansky, 1992; Farley and Frey, 1994; Glaeser and Vigdor, 2001), reflecting large declines in many western metropolitan areas in the 1970s. Data for selected metropolitan areas, from 1960 through 2000, are shown in Table 10.1. As can be seen in this table, a number of U.S. cities, including some of the largest, such as New York, Chicago, and Detroit, still have extremely high black-white segregation indices above 80, and numerous large cities have indices above 70.

As noted earlier, one result of housing segregation has been to largely exclude African Americans from the suburbs. The percentage of African Americans living in the suburbs has risen in recent decades, reaching 33 percent of the black population by 2000 (U.S. Census Bureau, 2003c). However, blacks are still very underrepresented there relative to whites, more than half of whom live in the suburbs. Increased black suburbanization has brought a little more interracial contact because blacks and whites are somewhat less segregated in the suburbs than in the central cities (Hwang and Murdock, 1983; Logan and Schneider, 1984; J. E. Farley, 1987c, 2002b; Massey and Denton, 1988, 1993). Also, research based on the 1990 census indicates that in highly segregated metropolitan areas such as St. Louis, many neighborhoods that had been all white became at least minimally integrated (J. E. Farley, 1993). Nonetheless, many blacks in suburban areas still live in areas that are extensions of black neighborhoods in the central city (J. E. Farley, 1983, 2002b; see also Winsberg, 1983).

It is obvious from these data that the level of housing segregation of blacks and whites in most American cities is quite high and that in many cities there has been little reduction over the past decade or two. How can this persistence be explained? A number of possible explanations have been offered, and the topic has been researched widely enough to suggest some fairly clear answers.

## Economic Explanations of Housing Segregation

One explanation frequently offered for housing segregation is economic. As we have seen, the black population has a significantly lower average income than the white population. Accordingly, some people have argued that a major reason for

### Table 10.1   Segregation Indexes for Selected Metropolitan Areas, 1960–2000

| Metropolitan Area | 2000 | 1990 | 1980 | 1970 | 1960 |
|---|---|---|---|---|---|
| Atlanta | 65.6 | 67.7 | 81.7 | 77.1 | |
| Birmingham | 72.9 | 71.7 | 64.1 | | |
| Boston | 65.7 | 69.4 | 79.3 | 80.8 | |
| Buffalo | 76.7 | 81.7 | 80.0 | 85.7 | 86.8 |
| Chicago | 80.8 | 85.5 | 87.2 | 91.2 | 91.2 |
| Cincinnati | 74.8 | 75.7 | 78.1 | 81.8 | 83.2 |
| Cleveland | 77.3 | 85.0 | 87.7 | 90.2 | 89.6 |
| Dallas | 59.4 | 63.1 | 77.5 | 86.9 | 81.2 |
| Denver | 61.8 | 64.0 | 68.5 | 84.7 | 84.6 |
| Detroit | 84.7 | 87.6 | 87.5 | 88.9 | 87.1 |
| Indianapolis | 70.7 | 74.2 | 78.8 | 83.8 | 78.7 |
| Little Rock | 61.3 | 60.5 | 64.2 | 70.8 | 65.0 |
| Los Angeles | 67.5 | 72.8 | 79.1 | 88.5 | 89.2 |
| Louisville | 64.5 | 69.4 | 73.6 | 82.8 | 80.4 |
| Milwaukee | 82.2 | 82.6 | 83.8 | 89.5 | 90.4 |
| Newark | 80.4 | 82.2 | 80.4 | 78.8 | 72.8 |
| New Haven | 69.0 | 70.2 | 69.6 | 67.0 | 65.4 |
| New Orleans | 69.3 | 68.7 | 71.0 | 74.2 | 65.0 |
| New York | 81.8 | 81.5 | 77.5 | 73.8 | 74.4 |
| Philadelphia | 72.3 | 77.1 | 78.3 | 78.0 | 77.1 |
| Phoenix | 43.7 | 50.2 | 59.6 | 75.4 | 81.1 |
| Pittsburgh | 67.3 | 71.0 | 72.9 | 74.5 | 74.4 |
| Portland, Oregon | 48.1 | 66.3 | 68.4 | 80.2 | 81.3 |
| Richmond | 57.0 | 59.0 | 76.6 | 74.9 | |
| Sacramento | 56.0 | 55.6 | 66.1 | 72.1 | |
| St. Louis | 74.3 | 76.9 | 81.9 | 86.5 | 85.9 |
| San Diego | 54.1 | 57.9 | 61.9 | 76.2 | 79.5 |
| San Francisco | 60.9 | 63.8 | 71.1 | 77.3 | 79.4 |
| Seattle | 49.6 | 56.1 | 67.4 | 78.1 | 83.3 |
| Tucson | 38.8 | 42.0 | 46.6 | 63.6 | 73.0 |

*Sources:* Indexes for 1960 and 1970 reprinted from Thomas L. Van Valey, Wade Clark Roof, and Jerome E. Wilcox, "Trends in Residential Segregation: 1960–1970," *American Journal of Sociology* 82:830–35, by permission of The University of Chicago Press. Copyright 1977 by the University of Chicago. Indexes for 1980 prepared by John F. Jakubs and printed by permission. Indexes for 1990 are from U.S. Bureau of the Census, Residential Segregation Summary Tables, World Wide Web, http://www.census.gov/hhes/www/housing/resseg/sumtabs.html. Indexes for 2000 are from Lewis Mumford Center (2002).

housing segregation is that most blacks cannot afford to live in many of the neighborhoods where whites live. It turns out that it is possible to measure the extent to which this is the case. Through use of a measure called *indirect standardization*, sociologists can estimate quite precisely the number of blacks and whites that one would expect to live in each neighborhood of a city based on the neighborhood's income distribution. From these estimates, it is possible to compute what the segregation index for the city would be if income differences between blacks and whites were the only reason for housing segregation. A different way of answering the same question is to compute segregation between whites and blacks of the same income or who live in similar-priced housing. If affordability were the main cause of segregation, we would expect these segregation indices to be much lower than overall areawide segregation indices.

Studies using both of these methods have been very consistent in showing that very little racial housing segregation can be explained by socioeconomic differences between blacks and whites. Consistently, segregation indices expected on the basis of income or housing cost are much lower than actual segregation indices. Also consistently, segregation indices among whites and blacks of similar income or in similarly priced housing are very close to overall areawide segregation indices. Studies using one or both of these techniques have been performed on data for various cities and metropolitan areas from the 1940, 1950, and 1960 censuses (Taeuber and Taeuber, 1965), the 1970 census (Hermalin and Farley, 1973; Schnare, 1977; Logan and Stearns, 1981; J. E. Farley, 1982); the 1980 census (J. E. Farley, 1986; Darden, 1987; Kain, 1987), the 1990 census (J. E. Farley, 1995; Clark and Ware, 1997; Darden and Kamel, 2000), and the 2000 census (J. E. Farley, 2003a). Although there are minor variations in the findings depending on which methods are used and which geographic areas are studied, all except one of these studies found that only a small proportion of housing segregation between whites and African Americans could be explained by either income or housing cost differences between whites and African Americans. The only study reflecting an exception to this pattern is Clark and Ware's (1997) study of the Los Angeles region, and it is only a partial exception. This study found lower levels of segregation within income categories in the suburbs, but in the city it found high segregation levels within income categories, just as most other studies have. It must be remembered that Los Angeles is unusual in that its suburban areas are less segregated than in most large metropolitan areas, and it is in the least segregated part of the country, the West. Overall, then, these many studies give strong support to the conclusion that racial housing segregation is tied to race and cannot be explained by income differences between African Americans and whites. For example, my data for the St. Louis area in 2000 indicate that if income differences were the only reason for housing segregation, the segregation index between white and black households would have been 10.8. In fact, it was 73.0 (J. E. Farley, 2003a, Table 2).

## Black Preferences

Another explanation offered for housing segregation is that black people prefer to live in all-black neighborhoods. Undoubtedly many do, but research suggests that this factor, too, probably cannot account for anywhere near the level of segregation that really exists. Teams of researchers headed by Reynolds Farley (Farley et al., 1978, 1993, 1994; Farley, Bianchi, and Colasanto, 1979) conducted large-scale surveys of the housing and neighborhood preferences of blacks and whites in the Detroit metropolitan area in 1976 and again in 1992. These surveys were replicated in Boston, Atlanta, and Los Angeles between 1992 and 1994 as part of the Multi-City Study of Urban Inequality (Zubrinsky Charles, 2001; Ihlanfeldt and Scafidi, 2002, 2004). Those responding to the surveys were shown cards depicting various combinations of blacks and whites in hypothetical neighborhoods (see Figure 10.2). They were then asked about their willingness to live in the neighborhoods and their neighborhood preferences. In all the surveys, blacks expressed a clear preference for integrated neighborhoods: Most picked neighborhoods that were either 50 percent black or two-thirds black as their first choice, and only small minorities chose either an all-black neighborhood or an all-white neighborhood. The most common reason given for preferring integrated neighborhoods was the need to get along with whites. A similar study done in New Jersey suburbs by Lake (1981, p. 132) also

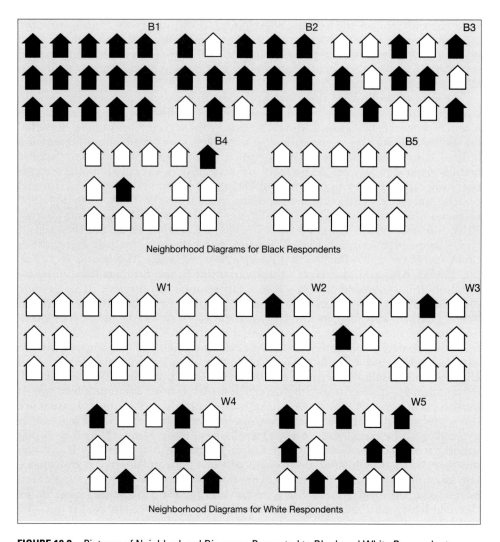

**FIGURE 10.2**    Pictures of Neighborhood Diagrams Presented to Black and White Respondents.

*Source:* Reprinted from "Barriers to the Racial Integration of Neighborhoods: The Detroit Case," by Reynolds Farley, Suzanne Bianchi, and Diane Colasanto in volume 441 of *The Annals of the American Academy of Political and Social Science.* Copyright © 1979 by the American Academy of Political and Social Science.

found that blacks overwhelmingly preferred integrated neighborhoods over mainly black neighborhoods.

This 1992 Detroit survey showed a slight shift toward a preference for neighborhoods with more African Americans compared with the 1976 survey, but the dominant preference was still clearly for integrated neighborhoods. Almost all blacks in all four cities indicated a willingness to move into neighborhoods anywhere from one-fifth black to three-quarters black, and only 20 percent indicated a preference for an all-black neighborhood—more than in 1976, but still a small minority. However, there was some increase in resistance to being the first African American in an all-white neighborhood: 38 percent in Detroit were willing to do this in 1976, but only 31 percent were in 1992 (Farley et al., 1993, 1994), although the percentage was a little higher in the other three areas. Research by Clark (1991) also found that blacks in several cities preferred neighborhoods with roughly equal numbers of blacks and whites.

Clearly, then, housing segregation cannot be explained primarily by black preferences, and the studies' findings are quite consistent with those of a number of previous studies (for a review, see Pettigrew, 1973, pp. 43–58). Whereas blacks in recent years probably have been a little less enthusiastic than in the past about residential integration, that is still clearly their dominant preference.

## White Preferences

Another commonly suggested explanation for housing segregation is that white residents prefer all-white neighborhoods and behave in such a manner as to exclude blacks from their neighborhoods. The Detroit studies by Farley and his associates (1978, 1979, 1993, 1994) and the studies in the 1990s in Los Angeles, Boston, and Atlanta reported by Zubrinsky Charles (2001) and by Ihlanfeldt and Scafidi (2004) provide significant evidence for this explanation. When whites who answered the surveys were shown cards depicting various neighborhood racial mixes, they expressed preferences very different from those of blacks. Sizable minorities of the white respondents would not be willing to move into a neighborhood that was 20 percent black, and some were unwilling to move to a neighborhood with even one black household. The majority of the whites across the four cities in the 1990s indicated that they would not be willing to move to a neighborhood that was one-third black, and many said they would try to move out of such a neighborhood if they already lived there.

Although the 1992 Detroit survey showed some change, there was still significant resistance to integration, there and in the other three cities studied in the 1990s. The percentage of Detroit whites willing to move into a neighborhood that is 20 percent African American rose from 50 percent in 1976 to 69 percent in 1992. This level was similar to that found by Zubrinsky Charles (2001) in the other three cities between 1992 and 1994. However, in Detroit, for example, this still means that 31 percent of whites were unwilling to move into a neighborhood that reflects the overall racial composition of the Detroit area. In addition, the majority of whites across the four cities were still unwilling to move into a neighborhood that was one-third black in the 1990s, although it was a smaller majority then in Detroit and elsewhere than it was in 1976 in Detroit. In 1992, three out of ten Detroit whites said they would try to move out of their neighborhood if it reached a racial composition of three blacks out of ten residents, and the majority said they would try of move out of a neighborhood that was 50 percent black and 50 percent white (Farley et al., 1994). Similar findings about white attitudes were obtained in suburban New Jersey by Lake (1981), although Lake's study found whites' expectations about the future racial mix of the neighborhood to be more important than its current mix. And research on the actual behavior of whites shows that they often move out once substantial numbers of African Americans begin to move in (Cummings, 1998).

These findings are instructive in several respects. Although they do show that some whites—and more today than in the past—are willing to live in minimally integrated neighborhoods, they also show that there are definite limits to the degree of integration that most whites will accept. In addition, many whites prefer exactly the kind of neighborhood that most whites now live in: all white or nearly all white. Ihlanfeldt and Scafidi (2004) show that such preferences do influence the racial composition of the neighborhoods in which whites choose to live. Furthermore, the studies show that the integrated neighborhoods that most blacks prefer to move into—around 50 percent black—are exactly the kind of neighborhoods that most whites want to move out of and, even more so, refuse to move into. This can be illustrated by findings from Clark's (1991) study. As noted, he found that most blacks prefer neighborhoods with roughly equal numbers of whites and blacks. He also found that a large number of whites are willing to live in integrated neighborhoods, but *integration* means something different to whites than to blacks. Most whites who indicated a preference for integrated neighborhoods wanted to live in an area about 20 percent black. Thus, neighborhoods with 30 or 40 percent black populations are highly attractive to blacks but not to whites, even whites who want to live in integrated neighborhoods. In part because a large proportion of whites oppose even this much integration, the actual neighborhood percentage of blacks that whites will accept usually is well under 20 percent. Based on actual patterns of residency, Massey and Gross (1991) argue that because of white resistance to living in mixed areas, the average white person will live in a neighborhood that is not more than 5 percent black in most metropolitan areas. They demonstrate from census data that segregation in most cases does not fall below the level needed to limit the percentage of blacks in the average white person's neighborhood to about 5 percent or less. Research from the 2000 census shows that this remains true in most large metropolitan areas, although there are some, mostly in the South, where the majority of whites live in areas with larger percentages of African Americans (J. E. Farley, 2003b).

It appears that once a neighborhood becomes integrated, the following sequence of events often occurs: (1) The neighborhood becomes more attractive to blacks, so blacks move in at an accelerated rate. (2) Whites stop moving into the neighborhood. (3) In some neighborhoods, whites may move out at a faster than normal rate. Taken together, these processes tend to turn the neighborhood rather quickly from all white to all black or nearly all black. Because so many whites are unwilling to move into integrated neighborhoods, it becomes difficult for neighborhoods to remain integrated once they have become integrated. For the neighborhood to stay integrated, both blacks and whites must continue moving in. The data show that most blacks will continue moving into an integrated neighborhood; most whites will not. Even in the absence of white flight, the failure of whites to move into the neighborhood guarantees that it will become predominantly black (see Molotch, 1972; Cummings, 1998). There is evidence that this kind of racial turnover is not as rapid, abrupt, or universal today as it was in the past, but it still commonly occurs.

Similarly, it appears that whites have become somewhat less resistant to neighborhood integration in recent years. This is suggested by the attitudes expressed in the studies in the four cities discussed earlier: More whites than in the past were willing to live in neighborhoods that are 20 to 33 percent black, with the majority indicating that they would be willing to live in a neighborhood that is 20 percent black. Studies of racial change in neighborhoods suggest the same thing. A study of St. Louis, one of the most segregated metropolitan areas in the country, found that between 1980 and 1990, much less change took place in the racial composition of mixed areas than had occurred in the preceding decade. In the 1970s, some municipalities in the St. Louis areas had increases in their black population of 30, 40, or even 50 percentage points. In the 1980s, changes were much smaller: almost always less than 20 percentage points, and usually a good deal less (J. E. Farley, 1993). Similar results were also obtained in a study of five cities by Wood and Lee (1991): After 1970, racial turnover decreased and the stability of racially mixed neighborhoods increased. The St. Louis study also showed a dramatic decline in the proportion of whites living in areas that were less than 1 percent black, suggesting a real decrease in the number of all-white neighborhoods. Despite these changes, however, the overall pattern in St. Louis and in most other large, industrial cities in the Midwest and Northeast remains one of racial segregation. Moreover, in St. Louis, the pace of change in the 1990s was slower than in the 1980s (J. E. Farley, 2002b).

Another factor that undoubtedly preserves the pattern of housing segregation is harassment by whites of blacks who move into all-white neighborhoods. Incidents of this nature have been reported in most large metropolitan areas in the past and continued to occur in various areas through the 1990s. Many such incidents are violent, with vandalism to homes, automobiles, and other property; in some cases, shots have been fired through windows and houses burned down. In the spring of 1993, for example, blacks living in or moving into predominantly white areas encountered vandalism, harassment, or cross burnings in nine cities in Ohio, California, Oregon, Alabama, Kentucky, and North Carolina (Southern Poverty Law Center, 1993a). Such incidents undoubtedly have blocked the integration of some all-white neighborhoods. The 1976 Detroit study (Farley, Bianchi, and Colasanto, 1979) found that 90 percent of the blacks who were reluctant to move to all-white areas expressed the view that whites would not welcome them, and one-sixth expressed fears of serious violence against themselves or their house. And in the 1990s, the growing minority of blacks who preferred all-black neighborhoods usually explained their preference by saying such things as "because white people are prejudiced against us." Similarly, many black respondents, when asked to explain why housing segregation exists, gave such answers as "whites don't want to live around us" (Farley et al., 1994, p. 767).

## Practices in the Real-Estate Business

Not all racial segregation can be explained by the behaviors and preferences of white residents, however. Although many whites do not want to live in integrated neighborhoods, a significant and apparently growing minority clearly is willing and in some cases even desires to live in racially integrated neighborhoods (Farley, Bianchi, and Colasanto, 1979; D. G. Taylor, 1979; Lake, 1981; Farley et al., 1994). In fact, when whites in the four cities studied in the 1990s were asked to describe the ideal mix of white, black, Latino/a, and Asian residents in a neighborhood, the average composition picked was around 52 percent white and around 14 to 15 percent each black, Latino/a, and Asian (Zubrinsky Charles, 2001, p. 259). Furthermore, a significant portion of the white objection to living in integrated neighborhoods arises from fears that the neighborhood will "tip" and become all black (D. G. Taylor, 1979; Lake, 1981).

This suggests that there may be other important reasons for the pattern of housing segregation, and one that has been most often suggested is the behavior of some real-estate agents and speculators. Discrimination in the sale and rental of housing has been illegal in the United States since 1968, but there is ample evidence that this discrimination continues. One common practice is the selective showing of houses to blacks and whites, commonly called **racial steering**.

One of the first studies of this practice, conducted by Diana Pearce (1976), showed that this practice was widespread in the Detroit area. Couples with similar social characteristics except race approached a number of real-estate agents. Each real-estate agent was approached a few weeks apart by a black couple and a white couple. The results were striking: The white couples were shown more houses, on the average, and blacks and whites were shown houses in different areas. The whites were shown houses in white neighborhoods, usually in the same community as the real-estate agent's office. The black couples were shown houses in either racially mixed or all-black neighborhoods, usually outside the community where the real-estate agent's office was located. A CBS news team, conducting an investigation for the program *60 Minutes*, found essentially the same pattern in the Chicago area, also by sending black and white couples to real-estate agents.

More recently, widespread discrimination and racial steering were found in both sales and rental housing in government-sponsored studies in the 1970s and again in 1989 and 2000 (U.S. Department of Housing and Urban Development, 1979, 1991; Turner et al., 2002). The 1989 and 2000 studies were specifically designed to detect racial steering, and showed that steering continues to be common. These studies found that black home seekers were directed toward neighborhoods with higher percentages of blacks than were white home seekers.

African Americans also encountered other forms of discrimination, such as being kept waiting longer and being told about fewer houses available for sale (Yinger, 1995; Turner et al., 2002). According to Yinger, these findings are consistent with the findings of about thirty-five studies of steering conducted in the 1970s and 1980s. Many found that houses shown to African Americans were in neighborhoods with higher percentages of blacks than houses shown to whites. The studies also found that real-estate agents made comments to whites that discouraged them from living in integrated areas in a number of cities, including Chicago, Grand Rapids, Cincinnati, and Boston (Yinger, 1995, p.56; Turner et al., 2002).

Lake's (1981) survey of both homebuyers and real-estate agents uncovered considerable evidence of racial steering in New Jersey suburbs. The responses of the agents were especially enlightening. Most indicated that they would warn blacks about the prejudice they would encounter if they bought in white neighborhoods—clearly something that discourages blacks from buying in such areas. They also indicated that they often provided more advice and assistance to whites than to blacks. Such patterns of behavior are illegal, and to its credit, the National Association of Realtors, which once opposed fair-housing laws, has in many areas undertaken training programs in recent years to instruct agents about their obligations under the law. However, many real-estate offices are not affiliated with the association, and even among those who are, many offices and individual agents continue to disregard the law. Indeed, it is often difficult for whites willing to buy in integrated or mostly black neighborhoods or for blacks willing to buy in all-white neighborhoods to do so: Many real-estate agents still actively discourage such home buying.

Although illegal, racial steering is difficult to prove to a court or civil rights commission: To do so would require a careful and time-consuming study, such as those discussed earlier, and of course, most potential complainants do not have the resources to do such a study. As an alternative, some communities (mostly in racially changing areas) have proposed affirmative marketing ordinances to require people of all races to be made aware of available houses in areas with the full range of racial composition. These efforts have led to charges of reverse steering or discrimination by some whites and blacks, particularly those who are associated with the real-estate industry. However, unless effective measures are taken to curb the practice of racial steering, substantial reduction in the amount of housing segregation is unlikely.

Because of the difficulty of enforcing the 1968 Fair Housing Act, efforts began in 1979 to strengthen its enforcement mechanisms. After several unsuccessful attempts, these efforts came to fruition in the passage of the 1988 Fair Housing Act Amendments. The new law makes suing for housing discrimination easier and increases the damages that can be collected. It also gives the Department of Housing and Urban Development greater authority to enforce the law by establishing a system of administrative law judges to review discrimination complaints, which can be brought either by the department or by an individual. If discrimination is found, the administrative law judge can issue injunctions, order payment of damages, and impose civil fines of $10,000 to $50,000. Either party can appeal a decision to the federal courts. Finally, the 1988 amendments contain new provisions that protect the rights of people with disabilities to accessible housing and forbid discrimination on the basis of familial status. The latter means that it is now illegal to discriminate against families or individuals with children in the sale or rental of housing, except in the case of housing complexes developed specifically for senior citizens.

After the results of the U.S. Department of Housing and Urban Development's (1991) study of steering were released, the Department of Justice announced that it would undertake a new program to investigate violations of the fair-housing law and to enforce the law. In 1993 and 1994, investigations con-

Although the National Association of Realtors today offers fair housing training for real-estate agents, studies have continued to show that some agents steer African Americans toward neighborhoods with larger minority populations, keep them waiting longer, and show them fewer houses.

ducted under this program resulted in fines and settlements totaling more than $1 million for several Detroit-area apartment complexes that were caught in acts of illegal discrimination. The program also resulted in discrimination lawsuits by the department in St. Louis; Los Angeles; Sioux Falls, South Dakota; and other cities. Several apartment complexes in these and other cities have paid substantial fines or settlements. More actions have been taken against racial steering in recent years, often by nonprofit fair-housing organizations. For example, in St. Louis, a fair-housing organization with which I work closely, funded largely by the Department of Housing and Urban Development, recently took legal action together with a local municipality against two real-estate offices (Equal Housing Opportunity Council, 1998). Both offices, and others in the municipality, had been warned previously after discrimination testing showed that white and black home seekers were being directed to different parts of the municipality. Further testing showed that even after the warning, agents in the two offices continued to steer blacks to one side of a major thoroughfare in the community, whereas whites were shown housing on the other side. Ultimately, a substantial settlement was paid (Parish, 2001), and the real estate offices agreed to obtain fair-housing training for their staff.

Although enforcement of fair-housing law has improved somewhat, most acts of discrimination still go undetected. An inherent problem is that home seekers know only what they are told about, not what they are not told about or whether someone of a different race is treated differently. For example, an African American who is seeking an apartment may be told that there are no vacancies. He or she has no way of knowing whether a white visiting the same rental office would be told the same thing. Similarly, black and white home seekers who are steered have no way to know that people of a different race are being directed toward different housing. The only way to detect this is through testing studies such as those of Pearce (1976), the CBS news team, and the U.S. Department of Housing and Urban Development (1991). More studies of this type, tied to enforcement actions against those caught discriminating, are clearly needed if fair-housing law is to be effectively enforced. There were modest increases in federal funding for such efforts in the 1990s; as a result, fair-housing organizations were able to do more testing for discrimination. Still, the resources of these organizations remain too limited for such efforts to occur on a scale sufficiently widespread to greatly reduce the amount of discrimination. The discrimination-testing movement is discussed in greater detail in Chapter 14.

At one time, it was common for real-estate agents to openly profit from discrimination through a practice known as **blockbusting**, which played on the fears of whites and the housing predicament of blacks to make a fast buck by encouraging rapid racial turnover. It occurred in all-white neighborhoods near black neighborhoods or in areas undergoing racial change. Agents would approach people living in the neighborhood and tell them that blacks were about to move in and that property values would go down. They pressed whites to sell quickly, while they could still get their money, intending to panic whites into selling their houses at a low price. Commissions were collected, and the house could often be sold to a black family at an inflated price because of the limited market of housing available to blacks. Of course, such practices are illegal under the 1968 and 1988 laws against housing discrimination. It is illegal for the real-estate agent to even volunteer information about the racial composition of the neighborhood because that can be a form of racial steering. As a result, the incidence of open blockbusting has been reduced since 1968. There are ways of getting around the law, however. In some cities, anonymous letters have been distributed in the middle of the night; anonymous phone calls, saying "sell now," are not unheard of. In addition, both blockbusting and racial steering can be accomplished through subtler comments such as "You'll get better appreciation on the value of your house if you buy elsewhere than you will if you stay here" or "You really wouldn't be interested in looking south of the freeway."

The Marxist theory of the economics of discrimination (Reich, 1986) appears to apply to blockbusting. Both black and white homeowners are harmed by the practice: Whites sell their houses for less than they are worth, and blacks pay an inflated price. Furthermore, the practice would not work were it not for the fears and prejudices of the white population. If whites did not believe that blacks in the neighborhood lead to lower property values, they could not be frightened into the panic selling that creates falling property values. In short, racial prejudice appears to serve the interests of the real-estate speculators and unscrupulous agents at the expense of both black and white homeowners. Although blockbusting is less common today than in the past, its effects linger in the form of segregated neighborhoods and white fears about the consequences of racial change.

To summarize briefly, we have seen that income differences between blacks and whites and the preferences of blacks are relatively unimportant as causes of housing segregation. The main causes appear to be the preference of most whites not to live in substantially integrated neighborhoods and real-estate practices such as racial steering and blockbusting, which preserve the pattern of racial housing segregation.

## Housing Segregation Among Latinos/as, Asian Americans, and Native Americans

Thus far, we have addressed only black-white housing segregation because it is the most severe and persistent form of racial housing segregation. Historically, though, Latinos/as and Asian Americans have also encountered considerable housing discrimination and segregation, although not usually on the scale encountered by African Americans. In 2000, the average segregation index between Hispanics and non-Hispanic whites for all 333 metropolitan areas was 37.3. Among metropolitan areas at least 3 percent Hispanic or with at least 20,000 Hispanics, the average index was 43.2. Again, however, segregation tends to be higher where there is a larger minority population, so that the average Hispanic individual in 2000 lived in a metropolitan area with a Hispanic-Anglo segregation index of about 51, about 13 points lower than the comparable average for African Americans (U.S. Census Bureau, 2003m, Table C-1). On the other hand, whereas the African American index has been declining, the index for Hispanics has changed very little over the last three censuses. (However, it did fall prior to 1970 and before notable declines in black-white segregation occurred.) In general, Puerto Ricans—who are more likely than other Hispanic groups to also be black—experience higher levels of segregation than other Latino/a groups such as Mexican Americans (Guest and Weed, 1976; Hershberg et al., 1978; Kantrowitz, 1979; M. M. Lopez, 1981; Hwang and Murdock, 1982; O'Hare, 1992, p. 27). In most large cities with sizable Latino/a populations, the segregation index for Latinos/as and Anglos is between about 45 and 65 (U.S. Census Bureau, 2003m, Table 6-4). However, in no case is the index for a large city in the 70s or 80s, as is commonly the case for African Americans.

Although they are significantly less segregated than African Americans, Latinos/as remain somewhat more segregated than Asian Americans (*USA Today*, 1991; Farley and Frey, 1992; Harrison and Weinberg, 1992a, 1992b; Alba and Logan, 1993). Although like Hispanics, Asian Americans were the targets of open housing discrimination in the past, today they are the least segregated group among people of color in the United States. In 2000, for example, the average Asian American lived in a metropolitan area with a segregation index between Asian Americans and non-Hispanic whites of about 41, a level about 10 points lower than that experienced by the average Latino/a and 23 points lower than that experienced by the average African American (U.S. Census Bureau, 2003m, Table C-1). As with Hispanics, this level of segregation has changed little over the past three censuses.

In metropolitan areas with large Asian populations, such as Los Angeles, New York, and Chicago, Asian Americans are less segregated than Hispanics; in all three of these cities, the Asian segregation index was at least 15 points below the Hispanic index in 2000. In San Francisco, the Asian index was about 5 points lower than that for Hispanics. In each of these cities, African Americans experienced the highest level of segregation from non-Hispanic whites, followed by Hispanics, with Asians the least segregated (U.S. Census Bureau, 2003m, Tables 4-4, 5-4, and 6-4). One study of Asian Americans in the suburbs of New York City found that for practical purposes, they were fully integrated in suburban neighborhoods. In contrast, Hispanics were only somewhat integrated, and blacks remained largely segregated (Alba and Logan, 1993). In light of these findings, it is significant that recent research on attitudes regarding housing shows that, among all groups, whites are always seen as the most desirable out-group neighbors, then Asians, then Hispanics, with African Americans least preferred. The fact that the attitudes match the degree to which Asians, Hispanics, and African Americans are segregated suggests strongly that racial attitudes play a significant role in perpetuating segregation (Zubrinsky Charles, 2001, p. 260).

Because the Native American population is a small percentage of the U.S. population and less urban than other groups, there has been little research on the residential segregation of Native Americans. However, the Census Bureau has recently computed segregation indices for the Native American population, with detailed analyses for the thirteen metropolitan areas that are at least 3 percent Native American or that have at least 20,000 Native Americans. These indices, computed for the last three censuses, show that Native Americans are becoming less segregated in most areas. Although their segregation indices are quite variable, ranging from around 61 in Yakima, Washington, to just 21 in Oklahoma City, the average levels of segregation experienced by Native Americans are similar to those of Asian Americans. In the thirteen metropolitan areas with sizable Native American populations, the average Native American lived in an area with a segregation index of 39. Among all Native Americans living in metropolitan areas, the average was about 33 (U.S. Census Bureau, 2003m, Tables 3-1, 3-4)

In summary, Hispanic Americans and, even more so, Native Americans and Asian Americans today are much less segregated than African Americans. Nonetheless, in some areas, recent studies or investigations have found evidence of discrimination and steering targeted against Latinos/as, Asians, and Native Americans. However, this discrimination is not as pervasive as that encountered by African Americans. In fact, both Asian Americans and Hispanic Americans are more segregated from blacks than they are from whites, again illustrating that housing segregation has increasingly become a pattern that applies distinctively to African Americans. This is consistent with survey data showing that blacks are less preferred as neighbors by whites, Asians, and Latinos than other groups (Schuman and Bobo, 1988; Feagin, 2000, p. 156; Zubrinsky Charles, 2001), although many indicate no preference. Taken together, data on segregation, discrimination, and attitudes indicate that there is greater white resistance to black-white neighborhood integration than to integration with Hispanics, Asians, or Native Americans.

## Impacts of Segregation

Obviously, housing segregation is in certain ways harmful in itself: It deprives people—especially black people—of their free choice of places to live and restricts the housing available to blacks and other minorities. But housing segregation can also have an impact in two other important ways. First, it can lead to segregated schools. Second, as we have already seen, it can aggravate the minority unemployment problem by restricting minorities to exactly the areas where employment opportunities are disappearing (Kasarda 1989a, 1989b, 1990; Ihlanfeldt and Sjoquist, 1998). Both blacks and Hispanics have higher unemployment rates than whites when they are more concentrated in the central city (J. E. Farley, 1987b).

In addition to whatever harmful effects housing segregation has on minority employment opportunities, it has probably affected the racial attitudes of both whites and minorities. It greatly restricts the amount of day-to-day neighborly contact between the races, and contact can be an important source of improved race relations. In its absence, prejudices and stereotypes often go unchallenged. Furthermore, when housing is segregated, the racial contacts that do occur can be of a highly destructive type. Sometimes, the racial composition of a neighborhood changes rapidly, as with blockbusting, creating a situation that is highly threatening to both blacks and whites and probably ends up making intergroup relations worse. Finally, controversies over school desegregation and busing are largely rooted in the pervasive pattern of housing segregation in American cities.

Research by Massey and his colleagues has identified two additional impacts of housing segregation. First, based on a study of Philadelphia in 1980, they conclude that segregation reduces the quality of life of the black middle class. Because of segregation, middle-class blacks must live in neighborhoods with fewer resources and amenities, poorer schools, and higher rates of poverty, crime, and mortality than do whites of comparable background (Massey, Condran, and Denton, 1987).

Second, a strong case can be made that residential segregation is a major reason poor blacks are so much more likely than poor whites to live in neighborhoods where many or most of their neighbors are poor. As is noted elsewhere in this book, black poverty is much more concentrated than poverty among other groups, especially whites, and Massey argues that housing segregation is a major reason. A residential location pattern that segregates any group with a high rate of poverty, such as African Americans, tends to produce concentrated poverty. Computer models suggest that black poverty is more concentrated than it would be were it not for housing segregation (Massey, 1990; Massey and Eggers, 1990; Massey and Denton, 1993). The fact that black poverty is concentrated produces additional problems: It deprives young, poor blacks of role models of economic achievement and subjects blacks to increased risks of problems associated with poverty, such as crime and drug abuse (W. J. Wilson, 1987, 1996). Many social scientists have argued that if poverty among African Americans were less geographically concentrated, it would be easier to escape. Concentrated poverty also results in fewer services, such as stores and hospitals, because people who are poor can purchase fewer goods and services. Lack of medical facilities in areas of concentrated poverty is discussed elsewhere in this chapter, but it is important to note here that there is a connection with segregation. To the extent that segregation concentrates poverty, it also reduces the availability of health care in the neighborhoods affected. Research has shown that mortality rates of African Americans are higher when they live in segregated areas (Guest, Almgren, and Hussey, 1998).

Some social scientists have argued, contrary to Massey's analysis, that integration has led to this increased concentration of poverty, as middle-class African Americans have moved out of inner-city neighborhoods. On one hand, it is certainly true that middle-class blacks have left inner-city neighborhoods and that this has increased the concentration of poverty there (W. J. Wilson, 1987). However, there are several flaws with attributing this to integration. Most important is that middle-class blacks are only modestly more likely to live in intergrated neighborhoods than poorer blacks. For example, the segregation index for high-income blacks and whites in most areas is only slightly lower than it is for blacks and whites as a whole, and in some places it is even higher (see J. E. Farley, 1995; 2003a). Thus, although they are moving out of inner-city areas into more affluent neighborhoods, middle-class blacks are not necessarily moving to white neighborhoods. Also, the most important cause of increasing concentration of poverty among inner-city African Americans is that jobs have left their neighborhoods. As this has occurred, wages have fallen, unemployment has risen, and the percentage of poor has increased (W. J. Wilson, 1996). Finally, it is true, as Massey has argued, that if a population has an above-average poverty rate, concentration of that population in one area will produce a neighborhood with an above-average poverty rate. The effects of concentrated poverty and the relative importance of class and race in producing it are discussed further in Chapter 15.

Finally, segregation may reduce job opportunities for African Americans in other ways. For example, it may be that in predominantly white areas, employers are more likely to discriminate against African American or Latino/a job applicants because they fear antagonizing white workers or neighbors (Yinger, 1995, p. 151). It is true that suburban employers hire fewer blacks, relative to the number who apply, than central-city employers (Moss and Tilly, 2001a, pp. 144–46). Even when jobs are close enough to black residents to get to, blacks are less likely to be employed when an employer is located in an all-white area (anonymous, 1997). This finding is also consistent with the idea that blacks may avoid employers in white areas for fear of discrimination or that prejudiced employers may seek out areas that are all white. Presumably, all of these processes would be less likely if there were not the kind of housing segregation that results in all-white neighborhoods within racially mixed metropolitan areas.

For all these reasons, housing segregation is widely viewed as a problem that worsens race relations and adds to the difficulties faced by the black community. Not everyone agrees, however. Some point out that it enhances black political power by making possible cities and suburbs where blacks are in the majority and can elect their own political leaders. Also, some blacks clearly prefer to live in all-black or nearly all-black neighborhoods, although surveys show that most favor mixed neighborhoods. On the other hand, it is also true that because of the concentration of poverty, mostly black cities often lack the tax base to effectively address their problems. Cities such as Detroit; Gary, Indiana; and Newark have faced difficult economic situations, requiring them to cut city services and lay off city workers because of a poor tax base, a condition that obviously limits the ability of black elected officials to improve the quality of life of their constituencies.

Ultimately, the key issue may turn out to be one of encouraging choice, making it possible for people to move to and live in a neighborhood with whatever racial composition they prefer, uninhibited by racial steering, sales and rental discrimination, and resistance from white neighbors. Judging from public opinion polls, segregation would decline at least somewhat if people were free to move where they wish, uninhibited by such practices. Expanded efforts to enforce fair-housing laws would be an important step toward such free choice. For a different approach to encouraging neighborhood integration, see the box, "Supporting Integrative Moves: One State's Initiative."

Finally, it should be noted that not all the housing difficulties that minority group members face are the result of discrimination and segregation, as important as these factors are. Another crucial housing issue is the lack of affordable, high-quality housing, which has a disproportionate effect on African Americans, Latinos/as, and Native Americans because of their lower average incomes and higher poverty rates. The dream of a decent home for every American, articulated when the Department of Housing and Urban Development was created in the 1960s, has never been realized and is especially elusive for people of color. Because the issue of housing affordability is so closely tied to government policy and housing programs, this issue will be discussed in detail in Chapter 11.

## SUPPORTING INTEGRATIVE MOVES: ONE STATE'S INITIATIVE

In response to the high interest rates of the early 1980s, the state of Ohio established a mortgage revenue bond program to offer low-interest home loans to first-time buyers. In 1983 and 1984, about $750 million of mortgage revenue bonds were issued and used to finance such low-interest loans. By making loans available at rates of less than 10 percent (compared with rates of 15 percent and higher that were typical at that time), the program enabled people to buy homes who otherwise could not afford to. In the 1980s, many states established programs similar to the one in Ohio, but Ohio's program had one important difference: In response to pressures from the fair-housing groups that were and are very active in Ohio, along with support from the governor, the program included a component designed to encourage housing integration. In 1985 and again from 1988 to 1991, a portion of the money allocated for the program was set aside for "integrative moves." Integrative moves are moves that increase the diversity of a neighborhood, for example, when a black family moves into a predominantly white area or vice versa. Because there were far more applicants than the number of loans that could be subsidized under the state program, a strong incentive for people to make integrative moves was created: A portion of the scarce mortgage-subsidy money could be obtained only by people willing to make such moves.

Evaluations of the program showed that it accomplished several things: It increased the proportion of black families participating in the mortgage-subsidy program, led black families to extend their housing search beyond traditionally black neighborhoods, and led white families to make moves that reinforced racial integration in areas where it existed (Bromley, 1992). Significantly, however, the program aroused the opposition of both white and black real estate agents, who saw it as social engineering that infringed on their rights to do business as they saw fit. It was this opposition that led to the temporary elimination of the program in 1986 and 1987. In fact, were it not for the support of the governor and his staff and the ability of program supporters to generate data showing that the program worked, it probably never have would been reinstated (Bromley, 1992). Nonetheless, the Ohio program offers an interesting model for other states in that it supports the reduction of housing segregation by creating incentives for people to take voluntary actions that promote integration rather than relying exclusively on enforcement of laws against discrimination. Moreover, evaluations of the program indicate that its incentives were successful in encouraging integrative moves and reduced the previous underrepresentation of blacks among those receiving state-financed mortgage subsidies.

## ► THE FISCAL TROUBLES OF CITIES AND THEIR IMPACT ON MINORITIES

Thus far we have seen how a number of trends, practices, and patterns in contemporary society have contributed to the maintenance of economic inequality: rising educational demands, loss of jobs from central cities, and widespread housing segregation in major metropolitan areas. We shall next examine another significant economic pattern with especially dire implications for American minority groups: the fiscal difficulties of American cities. The reasons for such difficulties are complex, but to a large degree they arise from a tax system that requires local financing of city services and from two trends: the loss of industry and middle-class population and the increasing concentration of lower-income population.

Cities receive significant state and federal financial aid, but because of changing politics, federal aid shrank in the 1980s and 1990s, and state aid is severely threatened now by state fiscal difficulties. In state after state in 2003, cities cut services and laid off employees, such as police officers, as states cut aid to cities to try to balance their own budgets, which were out of balance by 10 percent or more in nearly half the states. According to W. J. Wilson (1996), federal funding fell from 18 percent of city budgets in 1980 to just 6.4 percent in 1990. These trends have forced cities to raise most of their revenues locally. As Table 10.2 shows, municipalities raise almost two-thirds of their revenue locally, mainly through taxes, but also through such utilities as water, sewer, and sometimes electric power. Note that the overall proportion of the budgets covered by federal aid is about one-third as much today as it was in 1983. This has been partially offset by state aid, but the fiscal crises of the states in 2003 brought an abrupt end to state aid in

**Table 10.2   Sources of Municipal Revenue, United States, 1970–1999**

| Source | Percentage of Total Municipal Revenue | | | | |
|---|---|---|---|---|---|
| | *1970* | *1983* | *1990* | *1995* | *1999* |
| General revenue | 81.4% | 77.8% | 78% | 89.3% | 88.1% |
| Intergovernment | 24.2 | 25.8 | 22 | 34.2 | 34.4 |
| State | 18.9 | 15.0 | 17 | 30.7 | 31.1 |
| Federal and other | 5.3 | 10.0 | 5 | 3.5 | 3.3 |
| Local government revenue | 57.2 | 52.0 | 56 | 55.1 | 53.7 |
| Taxes | 41.7 | 32.0 | 34 | 34.5 | 33.2 |
| Property | 27.9 | 16.7 | 17 | 25.6 | 24.0 |
| Sales | 7.4 | 9.0 | 10 | 5.3 | 5.4 |
| Income and other | 6.4 | 6.4 | 7 | 3.6 | 2.2 |
| Miscellaneous charges | 15.5 | 20.0 | 22 | 20.6 | 20.5 |
| Utilities | 15.8 | 18.0 | 16 | 8.6 | 8.1 |

*Sources:* U.S. Bureau of the Census (1986, p. 288; 1992b, p. 298; 1998e); U.S. Census Bureau (2003q, p. 286).

many areas. School districts raise about half of their revenues locally. For both school districts and municipalities, the property tax is the most important source of local general revenue. In addition, both state and federal governments cut back on key assistance programs in the 1980s as they struggled to balance their own budgets.

Because cities must raise most of their revenue locally, the areas with the greatest need for services (and often the largest minority populations) are the least able to raise the revenue to pay for them. For example, the ability of the property tax to raise revenue depends directly on the value of the property in the city. As we have seen, business, industry, and the middle-class population have all left central cities (especially in the Midwest and Northeast) in large numbers since World War II. Their departure has left less high-value property to tax in the city relative to the rate of growth in the cost of urban government. Consequently, many central cities have had to raise their tax rates per dollar of assessed valuation substantially but are still less able to raise revenue than the wealthier suburbs, which have much more property to tax. One example is East St. Louis, Illinois, a city whose population is 98 percent black and in large part poor. The city's tax effort (that is, the tax rate per total per capita assessed valuation) was found by a state study to be six and a half times as great as the average for the county in which it is located (Illinois Capital Development Board, 1977, p. 56). Nevertheless, the city's revenues fell well below those of neighboring communities, and for many years it has been chronically unable to raise enough revenue to meet its expenses, leading to the crisis in which it nearly lost ownership of City Hall. Recently, East St. Louis's economic situation has been improved by the presence of a riverboat casino, but this has produced the undesirable situation of being highly dependent on one revenue source. By 1998, the city was getting half its municipal income from taxes on the casino; were the gambling industry (or for that matter, the particular casino located in East St. Louis) to experience hard times, the city would again be in serious financial trouble. Its revenues did in fact decline after 2000 as its casino faced growing competition from new casinos in nearby Missouri.

Many of the difficulties associated with the property tax also pertain to other local taxes, such as the local sales tax and local income tax. If retail business moves out of the city, there is less sales tax revenue. If the wealthier population moves out, there is less income tax revenue. Thus, the need to raise revenue locally has become a crucial fiscal handicap to large cities with large minority populations, particularly in the Midwest and Northeast.

As local sources of revenue, along with state and federal aid, have been shrinking in large cities, their expenses have been rising, in large part because cities have increasingly become the home of the poor. This in turn has created a rising demand for welfare and for various programs and services aimed at reducing the harmful effects of poverty. In large part, too, this demand has increased because functions that once were performed by someone else have been left to the local government in recent decades. As Piven (1977, p. 134) notes, "In the era of the big city machine, municipal authorities managed to maintain a degree of consensus and allegiance among diverse groups by distributing public goods in the form of private favors. Today public goods are distributed through the service bureaucracies." In other words, they are distributed at the expense of local governments rather than at private expense, as they once were.

As a result of all this, it costs big-city governments more today than ever before to provide even a low level of services to the needy. At the same time, the sources of revenue have been drained to a greater degree than ever before in many cities. The consequence has been sizable cuts in services in the cities where much of the black and Latino/a population of the United States lives. Police and fire protection have been reduced, education has been cut back, library hours have been reduced, and day-care centers and public hospitals have been closed. Black and Latino/a Americans have been disproportionately harmed for a number of reasons. Most obviously, a disproportionate number of them live in the cities where the cutbacks have taken place. Beyond this, however, because they are disproportionately poor, they tend to be more reliant on public services than are others who can buy services such as health care and education in the private sector. The recent tax-cutting mood of the American public has made the problem even worse because the most fiscally fragile communities are most harmed by the revenue losses resulting from tax-slashing efforts such as California's Proposition 13 and similar measures in other states and from attempts to balance the federal budget after repeated federal tax cuts that disproportionately benefitted the wealthy.

Again, all this may well have occurred with no conscious and deliberate intent to discriminate. Nonetheless, it appears certain that as long as the current trend in the distribution of population, industry, and business continues, the present system of taxation will work against the interests of black and Hispanic Americans, who are concentrated in America's central cities. They will continue to pay higher tax rates and receive lower levels of service. It appears that only some major change in the system of raising local revenues could meaningfully alter this pattern.

## ▶ HEALTH CARE AND MINORITIES

As we saw in Chapter 9, minority group members suffer more significant disadvantages than whites in health status. They live shorter lives, are more likely to die in infancy, and suffer more frequent and more serious illnesses. A brief review of the figures from that chapter will remind us that on the average, African Americans live about five and a half years less than whites, as did Native Americans the last time statistics were available on their life expectancies. A black baby is two and a half times as likely as a white baby to die in the first year of life, and the situation is almost as bad for American Indian babies, who are about one and a half times as likely to die in the first year of life as white babies. African Americans are also more likely to be disabled than whites and more often have illnesses that limit their normal daily activities.

Of course, there are many possible causes of health and mortality differences between majority and minority groups, and some have nothing to do with the health care system. For example, some jobs are more dangerous than others, and minority group members are overrepresented among many of the manual occupations that carry a danger of injury or exposure to toxic substances. The latter is an example of **environmental racism**, a pattern whereby minorities are disproportionately exposed to hazardous substances both at work and at home. Examples of environmental racism abound. In California, farm workers (most of whom are Chicanos) are routinely exposed to a variety of pesticides that are widely believed to cause cancer and the safety of which has never been established. Among farm workers in recent years, there have been a large number of *cancer clusters,* unusual numbers of cases that are occurring in small localities. A disproportionate number of America's black communities are located adjacent to industrial facilities that release dangerous pollutants into the air and water. In urban America, both blacks and Hispanics are more likely than other groups to live in older housing, with its heightened risk of illness from lead-based paint. On America's Indian reservations, pressures have been strong in recent years for tribal councils to accept much-needed cash from major waste disposal and energy companies in exchange for allowing the reservations to become dumping grounds for nuclear waste and other hazardous substances.

Other factors are the poor nutrition and inadequate shelter that are frequently associated with poverty. (As we have seen, blacks, Latinos/as, and Indians are much more likely than whites to be poor.) Life is often stressful for minority group members, and they frequently suffer from stress-related diseases such as

One reason for higher mortality among minority groups is that their disproportionate poverty rates often expose them to unsanitary conditions and environmental contaminants.

ulcers and hypertension (high blood pressure). Among the black population, the problem of hypertension is especially widespread. Between the ages of twenty-five and forty-four, blacks are fifteen to seventeen times as likely as whites to die of hypertension (Cockerham, 1978, p. 34). Recent research suggests that anger over racism may be one cause of the high rate of hypertension. For example, a study of black college students found that their blood pressure rose three times as much when they watched racist scenes as when they watched other anger-provoking scenes. And doctors have reported that black patients with no history of hypertension experience increases in their blood pressure after encountering situations in which they experienced racism, such as being assigned a racist supervisor (Goleman, 1990; Leary, 1991). In addition, research reported in 1996 shows that African American professionals had lower blood pressure if they either encountered relatively little discrimination or encountered discrimination but fought back against it, but they had higher blood pressure if they encountered discrimination but did not fight back. Working-class blacks who did not challenge racism had higher blood pressure regardless of the amount of discrimination they encountered. Other studies found that racist comments could trigger increases in blood pressure among African Americans and that minorities who encountered more acts of discrimination showed more medically verified health problems (Elias, 1996, 1997).

Behavioral factors may also play a role in racial differences in health and life expectancy. Among males, blacks are somewhat more likely than whites to smoke, behavior that may be a response to stress and that is known to be harmful to health. Finally, we have seen that minority group members are more likely than whites to be the victims of violent crimes. Between 1960 and 1988, for example, homicide was by far the largest cause of death among black males between the ages of fifteen and twenty-four. At these ages, black males were six to seven times more likely to die as a result of homicide than white males (Snyder, 1991).

Despite these factors, there is reason to believe that a good deal of the differences in health and mortality between minorities and whites do result from the ways in which these groups are treated by the health care system. In the following sections, we shall examine how the health care system treats majority and minority groups unequally.

## Cost of Health Care and Health Insurance Coverage

In the United States, health care is expensive and is in large part based on ability to pay. It is provided by the public sector only for the elderly through Medicare and for some of the poor (about 11 percent of the population) through Medicaid. For most of the population, including millions with low and moderate incomes, getting health care is a matter of buying or arranging for private sector insurance, paying out of one's pocket, or, most likely, some combination of the two. In this respect, the U.S. health care system is virtually unique: Among the major industrialized nations of the world, only the United States and South Africa retain systems of health care based on ability to pay, and South Africa has made attempts since majority rule was established to shift toward a more public system. The remainder of the industrial countries have either a system of socialized medicine, as does Great Britain, or of national health insurance, as does Canada. Under socialized medicine, doctors are essentially salaried employees who are paid out of tax revenues. This system is similar to a large-scale health maintenance organization (HMO), in which a group of people join together to pay the salaries of medical personnel who provide them with health care services. The national health insurance system retains the fee for service (that is, so much paid for each service, such as an office visit, lab test, or operation), but the fee is paid by a government insurance agency. Generally, the entire population is required to participate in this public insurance program.

Today, the United States spends more money per capita on health care than any other country in the world, even though as of 2001, more than 41 million Americans—14.6 percent of the population—lacked health insurance at any time during the year (U.S. Census Bureau, 2002g, Table HI01). Statistics show that measures such as life expectancy and infant mortality in the United States are significantly worse than those of many other industrialized countries, all of which spend less on health care. In 1999, the United States spent 13.1 percent of its gross domestic product on health care, compared with about 10 percent or less in all other industrialized countries (National Center for Health Statistics, 2002c, p. 287). On a per-person basis, the United States spends over 50 percent more than any other country.

This kind of system can be expensive for everyone; for example, medical expenses are the top cause of personal bankruptcies (Blumenthal and Fallows, 1974), accounting for more than 40 percent of such bankruptcies in 1999 (Warren, Sullivan, and Jacoby, 2000). Furthermore, health care is rapidly becoming even more expensive: The rate of inflation in health care costs has outstripped the overall rate of inflation in most years since the 1970s. The burden is especially heavy for groups with low incomes. In 2001, more than 30 percent of the poor had no insurance of any kind, twice the rate for the overall population (U.S. Census Bureau, 2002g, Table HI03). Fewer than half of all poor people were covered by Medicaid at any time during in 2001, and only half received coverage from *any* government plan.

Disproportionate rates of poverty, part-time employment, and unemployment among minorities are reflected in statistics on health insurance among minority groups. In 2001, 33.2 percent of Hispanic Americans and 19.0 percent of African Americans had no health insurance at all, compared with 10.0 percent of the non-Hispanic white population (U.S. Census Bureau, 2002g, Table HI01). Asian Americans were also more likely than the white population to lack health insurance: 18.2 percent of Asian Americans lacked insurance in 2001. Among those in minority groups who do have insurance, many encounter out-of-pocket expenses not covered by insurance (nationally, about 30 percent of health care expenses are paid out of pocket), and many more rely on Medicaid. In 2001, 22.2 percent of the black population and 18.9 percent of the Hispanic population were covered by Medicaid, compared with just 7.7 percent of the non-Hispanic white population. In contrast, 78.4 percent of non-Hispanic whites have private health insurance, compared with just 56.5 percent of blacks and 46.3 percent of Latinos (U.S. Census Bureau, 2002g, Table HI01). In part because of recent legislation, children are somewhat less likely than adults to totally lack insurance and more likely to be covered by Medicaid, and they are less likely to be uninsured than was the case in the mid-1990s. Still, black, Hispanic, and Asian American children are more likely than white children both to lack insurance and to be covered by Medicaid if they do have insurance, as is shown in Figure 10.3.

To summarize the evidence presented here, it is clear that minorities are less likely to be covered by medical insurance and less able to afford to pay for health care out of pocket but more likely to have to do exactly that. This represents a serious barrier to the ability of minority Americans, and poor Americans in general, to obtain needed health care services.

## Frequency of Seeking Medical Care

An obvious factor in people's health is the frequency with which they seek medical care, including preventive care, which can keep them from getting sick when they otherwise might. Because of their poverty, minority group members on the average receive medical care, and particularly preventive care, less often than whites. In 2000, blacks, Hispanics, Native Americans, and Asian Americans were all more likely than whites to go through the entire year without seeing a doctor, and whites

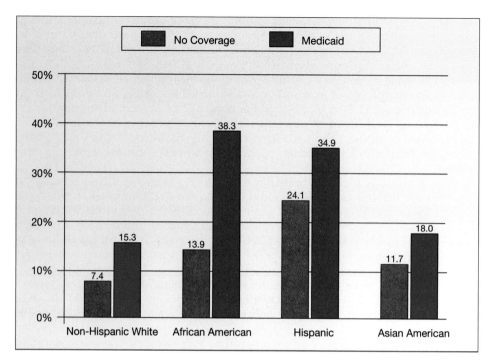

**FIGURE 10.3**    Children's Health Coverage, 2001
*Source:* U.S. Census Bureau (2002g, Table HI01).

were more likely than all of these groups except Native Americans to see a doctor four or more times (National Center for Health Statistics, 2002c, p. 217). Strikingly, most of the racial difference in doctor visits is among children: About 20 percent of Latino/a and American Indian children and about 15 percent of African American and Asian American children did not see a doctor all year, compared with only about 12 percent of white children. This gap widened between the 1997–1998 period and the 1999–2000 period (National Center for Health Statistics, 2002c, p. 224). For the poor person, it often comes down to a choice of what will be the greater burden: being sick or paying money that one cannot afford in order to see the doctor. This is especially true if the patient suspects that the doctor will merely tell him or her to "wait and see what happens" (Blumenthal and Fallows, 1974).

The extent to which medical costs prevent people from seeking care is well illustrated by an experiment in Saskatchewan Province, Canada. As a way of deterring unnecessary visits to the doctor, the province instituted a $1.50 fee per visit (it had been free). Much to their surprise, provincial officials found that it did not reduce visits to the doctor; it merely changed the characteristics of those who came. Poorer patients, especially with large families, in large part stopped coming to the doctor. Wealthier patients took up the slack and came more often, figuring that they would not have to wait as long. In short, all the fee did was keep poor people away. The fee was subsequently abolished (Blumenthal and Fallows, 1974). A similar experiment in California under Medicaid also showed that very small charges to the poor can have major effects on use of health care (Helms, Newhouse, and Phelps, 1978).

Insurance plays a big role in how often people see the doctor: Among people with no insurance, 36.6 percent did not see a doctor all year in 2000, compared with just 14.1 percent of those with insurance (National Center for Health Statistics, 2002c, p. 218). Often, these are people whose incomes are just high enough that they cannot qualify for Medicaid, and their jobs do not provide insurance plans. Although welfare reform legislation in the 1990s did include provisions to keep children covered when their mothers left welfare and went to work, coverage for adults is spottier. As is the case with the lowest income categories, African Americans and Latinos/as are overrepresented in this "working-class" income range.

Other factors may also keep minority Americans from seeing doctors. Both blacks (Hines, 1972) and Mexican Americans (Moustafa and Weiss, 1968; Madsen, 1973) have tended to avoid contact with professional medicine to some degree. Some view this as cultural, reflecting use of folk medicine or the advice of friends and relatives. Some African Americans use healers (sometimes also known as root workers, readers, or advisors), who do not make distinctions between religion and science in the treatment of illness (Snow, 1978). These healers view symptoms as relatively unimportant, emphasizing instead causes that are seen as either natural (consequences of abusing the body or the natural environment) or unnatural (often meaning the product of sorcery, evil influences, or curses). Some black folk religion is influenced by Caribbean approaches, involving rituals, charms, herbs, and prayer aimed at healing the soul or spirit as well as the body. These forms of folk religion are more directly connected to native African beliefs and arrived in the United States by way of the Caribbean's past slave culture (Cockerham, 1992).

Similar beliefs and practices exist among Mexican Americans in the form of *curanderismo*, which centers around folk healers known as *curanderos*. Like black healers, *curanderos* address causes of disorders, not symptoms. Compared with black folk medicine, *curanderismo* uses religion to a greater extent. Suffering is seen as a worthwhile experience offered by God as a way of learning. Illnesses can also be seen as imbalances in the body, such as between "hot" and "cold" influences or as the product of witchcraft. Herbs are prescribed for the former; the "good" power of the *curandero* is used to offset the latter (Kiev, 1968). Native Americans also often attribute illness to such conditions as loss of the soul, evil spirits, or improper behavior. A study of Navajo medicine by Levy (1983) showed that it, too, classified diseases on the basis of such causes rather than symptoms. However, Native Americans also use medicines that have been shown by subsequent medical research to have demonstrable medical benefits.

The extent to which use of such traditional medicine keeps African Americans, Mexican Americans, and Native Americans away from doctors probably has been overstated. A study of small-town blacks in Mississippi by Roebuck and Quan (1976) and a study of Navajo Indians by Levy (1983) produced strikingly similar results: About half used only regular medical doctors, about 40 percent used a combination of traditional healers and physicians, and 10 percent or fewer used only traditional or folk medicine. Also, some research suggests that African Americans use unconventional medicine no more, and possibly less, than whites (Eisenberg et al., 1993). A study by Higginbotham, Trevino, and Ray (1990) found that over a twelve-month period, fewer than one in twenty Mexican Americans in the U.S. Southwest had visited a *curandero* or other folk healer, and those who did were no less likely than others to have seen a regular physician. For those who use traditional or folk medicine along with scientific medicine, as most do, there can be benefits because of traditional medicine's positive effects on mental outlook. On the whole, folk medicine probably is not an important reason why minorities are less likely to see doctors. More important are lack of insurance and additional issues discussed in the sections that follow.

## Availability of Health Care Personnel

Once minority group members decide to seek medical assistance, they sometimes find that medical services are not readily available. Inner-city neighborhoods with large minority populations usually have relatively few practicing physicians.

Nationally, metropolitan areas have about 1 doctor per 500 people. In the inner-city ghettos, however, the picture is quite different. Although the country as a whole has a surplus of physicians, severe physician shortages continue in poor urban neighborhoods and some rural areas (Brink, 1998). In the central district of Baltimore, there is only one doctor per 3,000 people, and in one neighborhood with about 100,000 residents the figure is one per 6,600 residents. In the South Bronx, New York City, one of the nation's poorest areas, in 1968 there was only one doctor per 10,000 residents. Studies of Chicago and Los Angeles showed similar patterns of doctor shortages in low-income minority neighborhoods (Haynes and Garvey, 1969). A study of St. Louis in the early 1980s focused on primary care physicians, the doctors people see first when they have health problems. In one poor neighborhood, it found only one such doctor per 34,000 residents, compared with the national average of one per 3,000. Several other poor neighborhoods had fewer than one per 10,000 (Confluence St. Louis, 1985). Nationally, 46 million people lived in areas designated by the U.S. Department of Health and Human Services as health professional shortage areas in 1998 (Brink, 1998). More than half of these 46 million people lived in inner cities, where the population is disproportionately black or Hispanic. According to the Department of Health and Human Services, these areas need a minimum of 5,300 more doctors than they have, and ideally they should have 12,000 more to fully meet community medical needs (Brink, 1998).

There are a number of reasons for this shortage. In a system in which health care is based on ability to pay, a low-income ghetto is not an attractive place for doctors to locate; they can earn more money in middle- or upper-class (and often predominantly white) neighborhoods. In addition, health care personnel in large part locate according to the availability of health care facilities. The best-equipped hospitals tend to attract the most doctors and the best doctors, who prefer to locate where they can take advantage of the most up-to-date and elaborate technological innovations. Such well-equipped hospitals are rarely found in the ghetto or barrio. In fact, the hospital facilities available to the minority poor have recently decreased in many cities. In New York City, Philadelphia, St. Louis, and other cities, public hospitals serving minority populations were closed during the 1970s and 1980s as a result of the cities' fiscal problems. And in the 1990s, a number of urban, university-affiliated hospitals were sold to for-profit hospital companies. Because university hospitals provide a disproportionate amount of subsidized care for the poor, health care advocates expressed concern that these sales to for-profit companies would threaten this subsidized care because of the drain it can create on profitability. Finally, some studies suggest that racial factors may play a direct role in doctor shortages in minority neighborhoods. For example, Komaromy et al. (1996) found that communities with large African American or Latino/a populations tend to have physician shortages regardless of average income.

Once established, the pattern of doctor shortages in minority neighborhoods tends to perpetuate itself. Physicians often want to locate their practices in proximity to other physicians, partly because of the convenience of referrals but also because physicians, like other professionals, enjoy interaction with professional colleagues and want to avoid situations that deprive them of that opportunity.

## Lack of Minority Physicians

There is another important reason for the lack of doctors in urban minority neighborhoods: There are simply very few minority doctors. This is important because research has shown that minority doctors are more likely to locate in minority neighborhoods and medically underserved areas than are white doctors. For example, research by Komaromy et al. (1996) showed that African American and

Latino/a doctors practiced in areas with fewer doctors per capita than did non-Hispanic white doctors. African American doctors served far more Medicaid patients than did white doctors, and Latino/a doctors cared for more uninsured patients than did doctors of other ethnic groups. Similarly, a national survey showed that nearly 40 percent of black, Chicano, Puerto Rican, and Native American medical graduates planned to practice in underserved areas, compared with fewer than 9 percent of white graduates (Association of American Medical Colleges, 1994). Minority physicians are also more likely to enter primary care specialties, to serve uninsured and medically indigent patients, and to serve minority patients (Moy and Bartman, 1995; Cantor et al., 1996; Saha et al., 1999; Association of American Medical Colleges, 2002).

The shortage of minority doctors is evident in statistics on the ethnic composition of the medical profession. In 2001, 5.6 percent of doctors in the United States were African American, compared with nearly 13 percent of the population. Hispanics represent 4.6 percent of doctors, also compared with about 13 percent of the population (U.S. Census Bureau, 2003g, p. 381). Mexican Americans and Puerto Ricans are even more underrepresented in the medical profession than these figures suggest because some Hispanic doctors are recent immigrants from a variety of countries, not Mexican Americans and Puerto Ricans, who are the most medically underserved portions of the Latino/a population. Data on medical school enrollment confirm the underrepresentation of these groups: Whereas 6.5 percent of medical students in the 1999–2000 school year were Hispanic, only 2.6 percent were Mexican American and only 0.7 percent were Puerto Rican (National Center for Health Statistics, 2002c, p. 276). These percentages are well below those of Mexican Americans and Puerto Ricans in the overall population.

In the 1999–2000 school year, 7.6 percent of students in medical school were black, the same as five years earlier, in the 1994–1995 school year. This is more than the 5.6 percent of doctors who are black, but it is far below the percentage of people in their twenties (the usual age of medical enrollment) who are black. In 1994, 8.9 percent of graduates from medical school were from underrepresented minorities (Steinbrook, 1996), but this remains small compared with more than 25 percent of the population that comprises these groups. These statistics are significant because they show that despite efforts over the past two decades by a number of medical schools to recruit and admit more minority students, they continue to be seriously underrepresented. In addition, such efforts were stalled in 1996 by votes and rulings on affirmative action in Texas and California, the nation's two most populous states. This may explain why the percentage of minority medical students stopped growing after about 1995, although the ruling that affected Texas was effectively reversed by the U.S. Supreme Court in 2003. Statistically, white men and Asian Americans remain far more likely than other groups to attend medical school.

Native Americans also remain seriously underrepresented in the medical profession. The American Medical Association (2003) estimates that less than one tenth of one percent of physicians are American Indian, but this is a rough estimate because their statistics do not include all physicians. Better data are available on the number of Indian people enrolled in medical school, and they show underrepresentation similar to that of other minorities. In 1999–2000, just 0.6 percent of medical students were American Indians (National Center for Health Statistics, 2002c, p. 276), compared with around 1 percent of the population in their twenties.

These figures indicate a serious need to increase the number of minority doctors. Such action probably would improve access to health care among blacks, Hispanics, and Native Americans because, as noted, minority physicians are more likely than others to locate in minority areas (although they, too, are subject to some of the economic and professional pressures that tend to keep physicians away). Obviously, the participation of minority students in medical education today is a crucial determinant of the number of minority doctors in the future. This, in turn, has at least some bearing on access to health care among minority group members generally. Thus, legal decisions such as the *Bakke* and *Grutter* rulings, which upheld the use of affirmative action, with certain limitations, to increase minority admissions to professional schools, probably will have important effects on the future health of minority Americans. The crucial issue of who is admitted to medical schools, as well as the legal and social implications of these cases and California's abolition of affirmative action, will be discussed in Chapter 15.

Thus far, we have explored a number of factors related to the ability of black, Hispanic, and Indian people in the United States to get needed health care. The cost of care, the availability of health care facilities and personnel in minority areas, the cultural incompatibility between middle-class medicine and some minorities, and the lack of minority physicians have all combined to create a situation in which minority group members do not, on average, get health care to the extent that members of the dominant white group do. However, even when they do get health care, it is sometimes quite different from that which the white middle class is accustomed to. We shall explore these differences next.

## Places and Types of Care: Race and Class Differences

Not everyone goes to the same kinds of facilities to get medical care, nor does everyone get care of comparable quality. Indeed, there are very important differences along the lines of social class and race both in where people go for care and in the kind of care that they get. Because minority Americans are so overrepresented among the lower-income groups, even class-based differences also tend to occur largely along the lines of race and ethnicity.

Middle-class people are likely to have a private personal or family physician who is their regular source of medical assistance. This carries a number of advantages. First, the doctor's office maintains records with a detailed medical history of the patients. This is helpful in diagnosis because a new symptom may be related to a past problem and thus explained more readily than it would be if a medical history were not available. It is also helpful in treatment because treatment for one condition can sometimes adversely affect another. The physician who has available a complete and detailed medical history is more likely to be aware of existing conditions that may be worsened by treatment for some new condition. Finally, the regular personal or family physician is more likely to get to know the patient as a person. Because we are becoming increasingly aware of the social, psychological, and emotional aspects of illness, we know that such personal knowledge and concern can be of great importance in the treatment of illness.

The poor, however, receive their treatment not from private physicians but from other types of facilities: emergency rooms, hospital clinics, public hospitals, and sometimes so-called Medicaid mills. We shall explore the treatment of the poor under the Medicaid program in a following section; our focus here is on the various hospital facilities in which the poor often receive treatment.

In 1996, 18.6 percent of physician contacts with African Americans occurred in hospital emergency rooms or outpatient clinics, compared with just 11.1 percent among whites. Low income and lack of insurance are a major reason for this difference. Among families with incomes below $20,000, 14 to 15 percent of doctor contacts occurred in emergency rooms or outpatient clinics, compared with just 10 percent among families with incomes of $35,000 or more (computed from Adams, Hendershot, and Marano, 1999, pp. 113–14).

One problem common to emergency rooms and hospital clinics is that the patient tends not to see the same doctor on a regular basis and thus loses all the advantages of having a regular doctor. Emergency rooms present particular problems. Because they are readily available, to some degree even without insurance, and one does not have to "know" a doctor to go there, they are becoming important sources of primary care, particularly among the poor (Gibson, Bugbee, and Anderson, 1970; Satin and Duhl, 1972; Satin, 1973; Cockerham, 1992). (Primary care is health care that is sought out by the patient, as opposed to care that results from referral by a physician.) All in all, however, emergency rooms are far from ideal as a source of primary care. They tend to be concerned with the relief of immediate symptoms and any seriously threatening conditions rather than the exploration of underlying causes. Detailed medical histories are not taken, and the use of lab tests in diagnosis usually is minimal. In addition, emergency room physicians (often rotating interns or residents) usually have no medical history of the patient. Thus, emergency room care often is fragmented and commonly fails to get to the root of the problem. Partly because of the kind of care they get—fragmented, with little or no explanation of what is being done, long waits, and little or no preventive care— poor people are less likely than others to seek treatment when they get sick. Thus, they are hurt both because of the quality of care they get and because their experiences discourage them from seeking care, even when they need it (Rundall and Wheeler, 1979; Dutton, 1986; Cockerham, 1992).

When their condition requires hospitalization, low-income patients often find themselves in public hospitals or Veterans' Administration hospitals; middle-class patients usually are hospitalized in private hospitals. As a general rule, private hospitals are better staffed and better equipped than public hospitals, which must operate on very limited funds. Understaffing is a common problem in public hospitals, and the limited money available for salaries may keep the best-qualified medical personnel away. In addition, public hospitals often lack the sophisticated, up-to-date diagnostic and treatment equipment found in many private hospitals. In recent years, many public hospitals have closed, partly because of budget crises in the government units that support them and partly because Medicaid patients, who might have gone to public hospitals before Medicaid, now go elsewhere. When public hospitals close, another source of care for the poor who do not have Medicaid is eliminated. St. Louis provides a good illustration. Three large public hospitals there closed during the 1980s, two in the city and one in suburban St. Louis County. Those three were replaced with one publicly funded (but privately operated) regional hospital for the medically indigent, which had fewer beds than any one of the three hospitals it replaced. A few years later, it closed, too.

Sometimes, when they are sick enough, low-income people are able to get admitted to university hospitals as ward patients. When this happens, they receive the most technically advanced treatment available. Even here, however, important differences exist between the way poor and nonpoor patients are treated. Nonpoor patients typically have a private or semiprivate room, and one physician is responsible for overseeing their care. Poor patients, on the other hand, are likely to be placed on a large ward shared with a number of other patients, and they are generally treated by interns and residents, sometimes on a rotating basis, rather than by a regular private physician. These practices led to a suit against one large midwestern university hospital for racial discrimination. The hospital put poor patients admitted through its clinic on certain floors and patients admitted by private physicians on others. The former were so predominantly black and the latter so predominantly white that a pattern of de facto floor-by-floor segregation of patients developed.

Attitudes of medical personnel toward low-income patients also are less than ideal. Indeed, in the hierarchy of roles within the hospital, the role of patient generally is at the bottom of the ladder, regardless of class (Reynolds and Rice, 1971; Coe, 1978). The position of the lower-status patient is even worse: Because of cultural differences between patient and practitioner and because practitioners at the bottom of the hierarchy among physicians (interns and residents) are responsible for their treatment, low-income patients often are viewed as burdens and tend to remind interns and residents of their own low status within the hierarchy.

To summarize, the poor patient (and because of poverty, very often the black, Latino/a, or Indian patient) is generally hospitalized in a different kind of hospital and, within the hospital, in a different kind of setting. These differences often mean that the minority group patient receives lower-quality care, more fragmented care, or in some cases both. Of course, this occurs once the patient has reached the stage of hospitalization. However, the lower-income patient often goes longer before reaching the hospital, which sometimes makes the treatment of conditions more difficult because they become more advanced.

Finally, a number of studies suggest that there are racial biases in the health care system above and beyond the socioeconomic biases that have such disproportionate effects on minorities (Geiger, 1996). A study of the treatment of patients, all of whom were enrolled in the Veterans' Administration medical system, showed sharp racial disparities. For example, blacks were 33 percent less likely to get heart catheterizations, 44 percent less likely to undergo angioplasty, and 54 percent less likely to get coronary artery bypass grafting (Peterson et al., 1994). Whites covered by Medicare were also three times as likely to get the latter medical treatment as blacks covered by Medicare (Goldberg et al., 1992). Recent research also shows that the racial composition of hospitals' patients influences the care provided at the hospital. The higher the proportion of patients who are black, the less intensive the procedures that are provided and the higher the mortality rate. These relationships hold true even for white patients (Nichols, 2003).

A fascinating experiment designed by Dr. Kevin Schulman of the Georgetown University Medical School shows how often doctors treat patients of different races differently. He made videotapes of similarly dressed actors reporting identical symptoms. The actors also reported having the same occupations and incomes. The only difference was that one of the actors was white and one was black. The symptoms reported by the actors involved chest pain of a type that

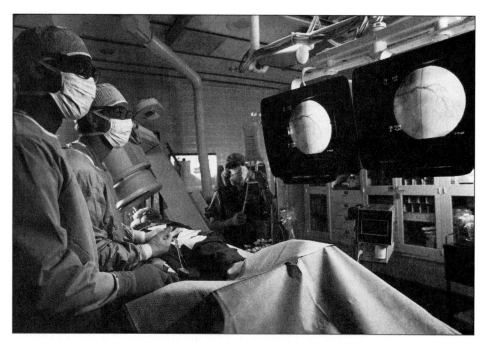

A patient receives a cardiac catheterization. Multiple studies have shown that, even among patients with the same symptoms, African Americans are less likely to receive cardiac catheterizations than whites.

might indicate a serious heart problem. Dr. Schulman then showed the video-tapes to 700 doctors in what was described to them as a government study on clinical decision making. At the end of the showing of the tape, the doctors were asked whether the patients needed further advanced medical treatment. The black actors were 40 percent less likely to be referred for cardiac catheterization—the main diagnostic test for heart disease—than were the white actors (ABC News, 1999; Schulman et al., 1999).

Perhaps because of such differences, one recent study found that race had even bigger effects than class on mortality among Medicare patients in 1993 (Gornick et al., 1996). Again, African Americans were found less likely to get angioplasty and bypass graft surgery. The reasons for these differences are not clear but seem to involve some perhaps subtle but certainly real cultural and racial biases. As Escarce et al. (1993) put it, "Race . . . may influence physicians' clinical decisions in ways that physicians do not even recognize, but that are not justified by medical need."

## The Medicaid Program

In recent decades, an important source of health care for lower-income Americans has been the **Medicaid program**. This program, established by the federal government in 1965, along with the **Medicare program** for the elderly, provides federal funding (with required state matching funds) for medical treatment of the poor. At a minimum, the program must cover people receiving welfare; under welfare reform, it has also been extended to some of the working poor, including those who have recently undergone the transition from welfare to work. In some states, it is limited to those whom the federal law requires to be covered, but others may be included at the discretion of the states, subject to various limitations. The program is administered by the states, which of course means that there is wide variation from state to state. Originally, Medicaid was targeted at a small and very poor segment of the population, but with welfare reform its coverage has been expanded to a somewhat broader population. Also, growing numbers of people have lost coverage under private insurance plans because of increases in part-time and temporary work.

The percentage of the population covered by Medicaid rose from 8.4 percent in 1987 to 12.1 percent in 1995 before falling to 11.8 percent in 1996 and 11.1 in 2001 (U.S. Bureau of the Census, 1997a, 1997b; U.S. Census Bureau, 2002g, Table HI01). Despite some increase in coverage, only a minority of the population below the poverty level is covered by Medicaid: 40.5 percent in 2001 (U.S. Census Bureau, 2002g, Table HI03). Inclusion of those covered by Medicare, the government program for the elderly, brings to about 51 percent the proportion covered by some government program. Thus, Medicaid fails to cover millions of needy Americans, leaving more than 41 million people uninsured in 2001. More than 10 million poor people, or more than 30 percent of all poor people, had no health insurance at all in 2001 (U.S. Census Bureau, 2002g, Table HI03). Many with incomes just above the poverty level also fell through the cracks; nearly one person out of four in households with incomes below $25,000 had no medical insurance at any time in 2001—not even Medicaid.

As in other areas we have examined, because of their disproportionate poverty, minority Americans are more reliant on Medicaid than are white Americans. In 2001, 22.2 percent of black Americans and 18.9 percent of Hispanic Americans were covered by Medicaid, compared with only 7.7 percent of non-Hispanic whites, who are much more likely than minorities to be covered by private insurance (U.S. Census Bureau, 2002g, Table HI01). Even among the minority poor, many (26 percent of poor blacks and 44 percent of poor Hispanics) are not covered by Medicaid or any other kind of insurance. Even so, the Medicaid program is the main source of payment for health care for a large number of minority Americans.

Medicaid has clearly improved access to health care. People with incomes below the poverty level today see doctors more often than before Medicaid was established. In addition, indicators sensitive to the effects of health care access, such as the infant mortality rate, showed dramatic improvements after Medicaid was established. In 1960, five years before Medicaid was established, the infant mortality rate in the United States was 26.0. By 1980, fifteen years after the program began, it had fallen to 12.6. In absolute terms, it fell by more than thirteen points; in relative terms, it fell by more than 50 percent (National Center for Health Statistics, 1992, p. 141). Since 1980, however, gains have been more modest, particularly among minorities. The black infant mortality rate has consistently been more than twice the white rate for many years, and between 1988 and 1989 it actually rose slightly before resuming its long-term decline. The black infant mortality rate per thousand fell from more than 44 in 1960 to about 21 in 1980, but it remained near 18 in 1989 before falling again to 14.1 by 2000 (National Center for Health Statistics, 1992, p. 141; 1997b; 2002b, p. 100).

There is no question that public health improvements result from a variety of factors, of which the Medicaid program is only one. Furthermore, it is equally clear that major inequalities remain, as we have seen. However, there is little doubt that the Medicaid program has resulted in some improvement in access to health care for poor and minority Americans, and it has probably led to some improvement in their health status. Having said this, it must also be said that the program is far from perfect and that the care provided to the Medicaid patient is in many cases not as good as that provided to the middle-class patient. Let us examine some of the reasons for this difference.

First, the Medicaid recipient must find a doctor willing to treat Medicaid patients. This is not always easy. Although the majority of the nation's physicians have at least one Medicaid patient, up to 80 percent of specialists in some areas are not accepting new Medicaid patients (L. Taylor, 2003). Nationally, half of all doctors turned away at least some new Medicaid patients in 2001, and 20 percent turned away all new Medicaid patients (Cunningham, 2002). A major reason is financial: Medicaid pays at lower rates than private insurance and does not allow doctors to bill their patients for the difference (because most cannot afford to pay). Additionally, the introduction of managed care into Medicaid plans in most states has further reduced payments to doctors. Thus, Medicaid patients are less profitable than other patients.

Second, some physicians operate "Medicaid mills," practices specializing in Medicaid patients. These practices attempt to offset Medicaid's lower rates of reimbursement by treating (and sometimes mistreating) large numbers of patients in an assembly-line fashion. These practices sometimes try to give as many treatments as possible (sometimes, whether needed or not) to as many patients as possible in the shortest time possible. This can result in quick, superficial examinations and missed problems. Some doctors specializing in Medicaid have engaged in outright fraud, such as charging for more expensive procedures than the ones actually performed, double-billing for the same service, "ping-ponging" patients back and forth between different doctors for unnecessary visits, and ordering unnecessary visits and procedures (Jesilow, Geis, and Pontell, 1991). Such unnecessary procedures are bad for people's health and in some cases downright dangerous, and because of their disproportionate poverty, minorities often are the victims. For example, one California ophthalmologist received $1 million for Medicaid recipients, many of whom were told that their cataracts, real or imagined, were contagious (cataracts are not contagious). After the doctor was imprisoned for the blinding of one of his patients in an unnecessary operation, the judge had this to say about the doctor and his attorney: "They seem to think the whole trial is a contrivance by the attorney general's office. In not one of the letters has there been one word of sympathy for the true victims in this case, the uneducated, Spanish-speaking people, some of whom will never see a sunrise or sunset again" (Jesilow, Geis, and Pontell, 1991).

All this is profitable for doctors, who are paid once for each service they perform, but it is at best dehumanizing for the patient and at worst downright bad for the patient's health. Unnecessary operations and medical procedures apparently are fairly common in American medicine generally (Cockerham, 1978, pp. 140–41), but the problem is especially widespread among Medicaid patients. Not only does this waste public money; it also threatens the lives and health of the patients because almost no medical procedure is entirely without risk. On the other hand, real problems may be missed because some Medicaid mills tend to run through as many patients as possible in a day. Thus, some Medicaid patients receive unneeded, costly, and potentially dangerous medical treatment; others do not get treatment they really need. In fact, one physician reports that when she opened a clinic in Chicago's inner city, many patients were so conditioned to "Medicaid mill" doctors who wrote prescriptions without examinations or follow-up that they were startled by such basics as doctors taking medical histories and performing medical examinations (Dr. Susan Erlenborn, quoted in Brink, 1998). The government attempted for a time to limit this by restricting managed-care plans to 25 percent Medicaid patients, but this federal rule was lifted in 1997 (Ellerman, 1998), and between then and 2001 the proportion of high-volume Medicaid providers increased, creating a greater concentration of Medicaid patients in fewer providers (Cunningham, 2002).

In summary, we can say that the Medicaid program has made medical care available to millions of poor, largely minority Americans to whom it was not available in the past. However, the quality of that care often does not reach the quality of care enjoyed by middle-class Americans, and doctors can be hard to find for new Medicaid patients. Moreover, many still fall through the cracks, even with Medicaid.

## The American Health Care Institution: A Conclusion

As we have seen, health care in America is economically and racially stratified for two main reasons. First, poor people generally, and in particular a disproportionate number of blacks, Hispanic, and Native Americans, have limited access to medical care: They do not seek or cannot get care as readily as their white, middle-class counterparts. Second, when they do get care, it is often more fragmented, more rushed, less thorough, and less holistic than the care received by the white middle class. Thus, the American health-care institution must be held at least partly responsible for the excessive health difficulties of black, Latino/a, and Indian people in the United States.

It has been said that the American health care system (or nonsystem, as some call it) has been designed to fit the needs of the physician more than those of the patient or the general public (Stevens, 1971). This observation is strikingly similar to the more general position held by the conflict perspective: Social institutions tend to serve the interests of the dominant and powerful elite that controls them. In the United States, at least until recently, physicians have wielded great political power through their national organization, the American Medical Association (AMA). This organization has vigorously resisted any government effort to regulate or control the fees that doctors charge for their services. In the 1980s, soaring medical costs led business and government (which pay many medical expenses through employee insurance, Medicare, and Medicaid) to assert greater control over American medicine. They did so mainly by limiting the kind and amount of care they pay for. The trend toward managed care, mentioned earlier, is one outcome of these cost control efforts. Although this has reduced the power of doctors somewhat, it has done more to help employers and insurance companies—also powerful interests—than to help patients, particularly poor ones. Instead, it has made it harder for poor patients without insurance to get care because cost control measures have reduced the money that hospitals have to cover charity care. As a result, the plight of poor people without medical insurance became significantly worse during the 1980s and 1990s, and a large share of these medically indigent people are black, Hispanic, or American Indian.

The limited reforms of Medicaid and Medicare, though helpful, have not been able to change these basic truths. It appears that to obtain racial and economic equality in health care, the minimum necessary step would be to establish some form of national health insurance, as Canada and so many other countries have done. (Indeed, the United States is virtually the only industrialized country that has not.) The health finance reform plan proposed by President Clinton in the 1990s but rejected by Congress, along with some others proposed at the time, would have guaranteed health insurance coverage to every American, regardless of income, employment status, or health history. A plan of this type would help a wide variety of Americans with their health costs because so many have no coverage or very limited coverage. African Americans, Latinos/as, and American Indians are very overrepresented among this group and therefore would be particularly helped by such a plan. However, it seems clear that even a plan that provides universal insurance coverage would not address all the causes of racial inequality in health care. As noted, a number of studies show that even among people of similar incomes with similar insurance coverage, whites and minorities often receive different treatment. Thus, in addition to reform in health care financing, a plan is needed to identify and correct the processes that produce direct racial inequality in the treatments received (Escarce et al., 1993; Geiger, 1996). Because the causes of racial inequality in health care are both economic and racial, any effort to correct these inequalities must be both economic and racial. But given the failure of even the limited Clinton reform proposals (which did not challenge the notion of medicine as a private sector, largely fee-for-service activity), there is little reason to believe that such an effort is likely to occur on a large scale soon. Also of concern are continuing attacks on affirmative action, which has clearly increased the number of minority doctors. Although the Supreme Court again upheld its legality in 2003, affirmative action remains under attack in the political arena. As long as this remains true, and as long as no plan of national health insurance is enacted, racial inequality in health care is almost certain to continue.

## Summary and Conclusion

We began this chapter by examining competing theories on the causes of economic racial discrimination and on who benefits from it. The causes are complex, and the relative importance of various factors has changed with time. Although deliberate discrimination has decreased since the end of World War II, economic inequality has persisted. Clearly, minorities are harmed by such inequality, and a plausible argument can be made, based on studies such as those of Reich and Szymanski, that many whites are also harmed by it.

Recognizing that the causes of inequality have changed, we then examined practices and patterns that have become institutionalized in modern society and that harm the economic positions of minority group members: the use of inflated educational requirements in hiring, the movement of employment opportunities out of minority areas, and the pervasive pattern of discrimination in housing. The latter two, along with the system of raising revenue through local taxes, have helped to create fiscal problems in America's great cities, which have also been disproportionately harmful to the minority populations that are heavily concentrated in those cities. All of these processes have tended to preserve racial inequalities resulting from past discrimination. In the case of the inner-city poor segment of the minority population, these processes probably have made matters worse. Finally, the problem of racial economic inequality is unlikely to be resolved until these institutionalized practices and patterns are altered. Eliminating deliberate discrimination, although necessary, does not appear to be enough. Further improvement in the status of minorities (and any real improvement in the status of the inner-city poor) will require more fundamental types of change.

Much the same is true of the health status of minority group members. Certainly not all of their health disadvantages can be attributed to the health care system. Nonetheless, it is clear that a health care system based heavily on the ability to pay cannot serve the disproportionately low-income minority population as well as it serves the higher-income white population. Thus, it appears that to eliminate racial and ethnic inequalities in access to quality health care, it will be necessary to make fundamental changes in the system of health care financing or, more basically, to eliminate substantial racial inequalities in income and wealth. Thus, both the problem of economic racial inequality and the more immediate (but largely economic) problems of poorer health and higher mortality among the minority population appear to necessitate basic and far-reaching changes in our social institutions.

## *Critical Review Questions*

1. Split labor market theory and Marxist theory are both associated with the conflict perspective. What is it about these theories that ties them to the conflict perspective? Given this common link, how are these theories different from one another?

2. How do urban sprawl, the decentralization of jobs, and housing segregation elevate the unemployment rate of African Americans relative to that of whites? What can be done about this problem?

3. African Americans experience more housing segregation than any other racial or ethnic group. Why?

4. Examine the roles of social class inequality and racial discrimination in producing racial and ethnic differences in life expectancy and infant mortality.

# The American Political and Legal System and Majority-Minority Relations

# Overview

In this chapter, we turn our attention to the American political and legal systems and examine their impact on majority-minority group relations in the United States. Although the chapter focuses on political and legal processes, it is important to recognize that they are closely intertwined with the economic processes described in Chapter 10.

There is clearly some link between economic wealth and political power. Although the strength of this relationship is debatable (see Riesman, 1961; Mills, 1956; Domhoff, 1967, 1983), clearly, those who are wealthy exercise considerably more power, both directly and indirectly, than those who are poor, and political power can enable a group to protect or advance its economic position. Thus, we see something of a vicious circle: If a group is generally poor, it will tend to have less than its share of political power, which will tend to further weaken its economic position, and so on.

Political processes are also linked to the economic process through the unintended economic effects of decisions made in the political arena. Such effects may work either to the advantage or disadvantage of minority groups. This can be illustrated by two examples from twentieth-century American history. Under the Roosevelt administration, various laws were passed to protect the rights of workers to organize into labor unions and to prohibit employers from engaging in unfair labor practices. According to W. J. Wilson (1978), these laws tended to reduce job discrimination against blacks and other minorities, even though this was not their main purpose. It happened because strikebreaking was made more difficult (and subsequently occurred less often), so that discrimination associated with the use of minority group members as strikebreakers decreased. In heavy industry particularly, a new environment developed in which white and minority workers cooperated in labor unions rather than struggled to undercut each other's position.

Government actions can also have a negative impact on economically disadvantaged minority groups. In Chapter 10, we discussed the impact of current urban fiscal difficulties, which are in part a product of federal government policies that sometimes had unforeseen consequences. Tax deductions, loan guarantees, and subsidies provided housing assistance to millions of middle-class (and mostly white) Americans after World War II and in large part made possible the flight of the middle class to the suburbs, which depleted central cities of their tax base. The construction of urban expressways, financed mainly by the federal government under the interstate highway program, had similar effects, contributing to suburbanization

An urban freeway. More often than not, it is poor people and minorities who are displaced by the construction of such freeways, and they are rarely if ever paid the full cost of their forced move. Furthermore, such freeways have enabled the middle-class populations to flee to the suburbs, leaving the central cities too poor to meet the needs of their growing low-income and minority populations.

of both residences and jobs (Kasarda, 1976, p. 119; Long and Glick, 1976, p. 40). Furthermore, the costs of the freeway system were disproportionately borne by blacks and other minorities, whose central-city neighborhoods often were bulldozed for freeway construction (Downs, 1970). Thus, the economic welfare of minorities was affected both directly and indirectly by government housing, taxation, and highway construction policies that outwardly had nothing to do with race relations.

It is clear, then, that decisions made in the political system can influence the position of racial and ethnic minorities in a wide range of areas and can do so for better and for worse. In the following section, we shall examine ways in which political decisions and the American political system itself have affected the well-being of American minority groups.

### ▶ GOVERNMENT IN AMERICA: AGENT OF THE WHITE OPPRESSOR OR PROTECTOR OF MINORITY RIGHTS?

As is the case with other institutions, the functionalist and conflict perspectives offer very different views about the role and functions of government and the political system. From a functionalist viewpoint, government is the means by which various political interests are represented and given a way to protect their interests. From this point of view, no one group can dominate the system, and many different groups can exercise *veto power,* that is, they can stop proposed government actions that might threaten their interests. In this way, each group has a stake in the system, and each group is ensured some influence and some ability to challenge actions that would seriously threaten it. This viewpoint is evident in the writings of David Riesman (1961) and much of the work of Robert Dahl (1961, 1981, 1982). An alternative viewpoint, associated with the conflict perspective, is that there is a *power elite* of wealthy Americans who, often working behind the scenes, exercise the real decision-making power. This view emphasizes that much of the real decision making is done not by elected bodies but rather behind the scenes by professional bureaucrats in the executive branch of government and the military and through lobbying and influence peddling with both the legislative and executive branches of the government. This viewpoint is associated with the work of C. Wright Mills (1956) and G. William Domhoff (1967, 1978, 1983, 2001). This debate has important implications about how the government and political system influence race and ethnic relations in the United States. The functionalist view suggests that minorities can exercise real political power, whereas the conflict view suggests that this is unlikely to occur because they are largely absent from the wealthy elite that holds the real power.

## Historical Patterns: Government Policies of Discrimination

Throughout American history, there is no doubt that African Americans, Chicanos, and Native Americans have been directly affected by policies and actions of federal, state, and local governments. As was described in some detail in Chapter 5, the U.S. Army, acting on the orders of the federal government, played a critical and central role in the conquest and subordination of both the Indian people and the Mexican citizens who lived in what is now the southwestern United States. Similarly, until the Civil War, the federal government recognized the legality of black slavery in the southern states, and a number of U.S. presidents themselves owned slaves. For the purpose of apportionment of Congress, the U.S. Constitution regarded each black slave as three-fifths of a person, one of many federal "compromise" decisions that recognized the legality and legitimacy of slavery in the southern states (Franklin and Moss, 2000, p. 94). Other such "compromises" provided for the return of runaway slaves to their owners, even when the former had established residence in states where slavery was illegal. Thus, it is no exaggeration to say that from the very beginning, the federal government played a central role in creating and maintaining racial and ethnic inequality in the United States, particularly for the three colonized groups (see Chapter 6): blacks, Chicanos, and American Indians. In various ways the U.S. government has also clearly maintained formal policies of discrimination against people of Asian ancestry. Two of the most blatant examples are the ban on immigration from Asian countries, in effect in the early twentieth century, and the imprisonment of Japanese Americans during World War II.

In addition to the position of the federal government, state governments during the early history of the United States also took strong antiminority positions. In the South, all states had laws protecting slavery. Furthermore, some had slave codes requiring freed slaves to leave the state and forbidding slaves to be taught to read or write or to conduct any business with whites.

Lest there be any confusion, however, we should recognize that openly racist state and local legislation was not limited to the South or to the pre–Civil War era. For example, Pennsylvania denied the vote to blacks in 1838; Indiana did the same in 1851. In "liberal" New York, blacks were subjected to property ownership and length-of-residence voting requirements not applied to whites (Franklin and Moss, 2000, p. 171). Indeed, the predominant stance of state and local legislation concerning race and ethnic relations was supportive of discrimination until around World War II, and in some areas it remained that way for a long while after.

As noted in Chapter 6, the brief period immediately after the Civil War, known as Reconstruction, was something of an exception. During this short period, laws pertaining to race relations were liberalized in both the North and the South, although liberalization in the latter came mainly from federal intervention. During this period, the Fourteenth Amendment (equal protection) and Fifteenth Amendment (no denial of vote because of race) to the U.S. Constitution and federal civil rights laws were passed. Numerous blacks were elected to southern state legislatures, and between 1870 and 1901, twenty blacks were elected to the U.S. House of Representatives and two to the U.S. Senate (C. S. Johnson, 1943; Franklin and Moss, 2000, pp. 264–71). However, this period did not last long. Beginning with a political deal struck between Democrats and Republicans in 1876 (McWilliams, 1951, p. 265; Simpson and Yinger, 1985, p. 230), the control of the South was returned to white supremacists. A very important step in this process was the *Plessy v. Ferguson* ruling of the Supreme Court in 1896, which upheld the doctrine of "separate but equal" facilities. As a result, in many parts of the country, public facilities quickly became separate but rarely, if ever, equal. In addition, the federal Civil Rights Act of 1875, one of the civil rights laws passed during Reconstruction, had been declared unconstitutional, so that before the turn of the century government had returned largely to the position of sometimes tolerating and sometimes requiring discrimination. Government-supported discrimination was most important in the first half of the twentieth century in the areas of voting rights, education, segregation of public facilities, housing, and immigration.

**Voting Rights.** Although the Fifteenth Amendment to the U.S. Constitution, enacted in 1870, prohibited denial of the right to vote on account of race, many of the states, particularly in the South, developed ingenious ways of getting around the amendment. Probably the earliest was the "grandfather clause," which provided that people could vote only if they, their father, or their grandfather had been entitled to vote at some date prior to emancipation (Simpson and Yinger, 1985, p. 230). These laws, passed by several southern states in the late 1890s, kept blacks from voting because they or their fathers or grandfathers had been slaves—and therefore ineligible to vote—on the date specified. These clauses had the effect of making previous condition of servitude (slavery) a condition of voting, which was forbidden by the Fifteenth Amendment, and in 1915 the Supreme Court declared them unconstitutional. In the meantime, however, they were used to eliminate black voting rights in a number of states for nearly twenty years.

Two other practices that were, for a time at least, accepted as constitutional were the poll tax and the "white primary." Both practices became widespread in the South. In many southern states, the only real election in the first half of the twentieth century was the Democratic primary. These states were so heavily Democratic that whoever won the primary always won the general election. In Texas and several other states, voting in the Democratic primary was, with legislative permission, restricted to whites. This practice was based on a 1921 Supreme Court decision that primaries were not elections but rather party matters; after two initial Texas laws were struck down, the Court approved in 1935 a decision by the Texas Democratic party convention to restrict the primary to whites as long as the party, not the state, paid for it. In 1944, the Court reversed itself again and struck down all forms of the white primary, but by then the practice had been in effect in one or more southern states since 1923—a period of more than twenty years.

Around the turn of the century, ten southern states instituted poll taxes, designed to keep blacks, who were disproportionately poor, from voting by attaching an unaffordable cost to voting (Simpson and Yinger, 1985, p. 230). In Texas the poll tax, in effect for about sixty years, also prevented Mexican Americans from voting (Moore and Pachon, 1976, p. 142), as well as numerous poor whites. This discriminatory practice remained in effect in five states until 1964, when it was finally outlawed by the Twenty-Fourth Amendment to the U.S. Constitution.

Another way of limiting minority voting in southern states has been to give voting registrars discretion in deciding whom to accept and whom not to accept. Scruggs (1971, p. 85) argues that this was one of the most important ways in which blacks were kept from voting.

Probably the most widespread requirement used to limit minority voting has been the literacy test, which has existed in various forms in numerous states in the South, West, and Northeast, such as New York, California, and Massachusetts. Literacy tests have tended to reduce voting opportunities for blacks, Hispanics, and Native Americans, all of whom have suffered extensive educational discrimination. Because they were exclusively in English, the literacy tests in New York and in several southwestern states had especially strong effects on Puerto Ricans and Chicanos, respectively, although the New York test was revised to recognize Spanish in 1965. In many instances, literacy tests were applied unequally, with more stringent demands being made of minorities than of whites (see Chief Justice Warren's opinion in *South Carolina v. Katzenbach*, 383 U.S. 301, 1966, quoted in Dorsen, 1969).

These practices were largely ended by the Voting Rights Act of 1965. In 1975, this law was revised to require bilingual ballots in specified areas with large numbers of non–English speakers. Nonetheless, even in the late 1960s and 1970s, some states engaged in practices that reduced minority voter participation. Reports by the U.S. Commission on Civil Rights (1968, 1975) indicate that in some southern states, blacks were kept from registering by limited hours for registration, harassment by registrars, and more stringent identification requirements than were set for whites. Another common practice is the periodic purging of voters who do not vote. In Arizona, for example, this is done every two years (that is, for every state and federal election), and it has had very disproportionate effects on Indian and Chicano voters (U.S. Commission on Civil Rights, 1975, pp. 85–86).

Over the past forty years, court rulings, the Twenty-Fourth Amendment, and the 1965 Voting Rights Act have made discrimination in access to the ballot box considerably more difficult. Nonetheless, even in years since these rulings and laws went into effect the problem has not entirely disappeared, as the 1975 Civil Rights Commission report demonstrates. As a result, when the Voting Rights Act came up for renewal in 1982, Congress added new provisions, prohibiting states from changing voting procedures in such a way that the *effect* would be to discriminate against minorities. In areas with a history of discrimination, such changes must be preapproved by the Justice Department or by a federal court. This is significant because discriminatory effect is much easier to demonstrate than discriminatory intent.

Nonetheless, major problems arose in Florida and other states during the 2000 elections, and it is likely that violations of the Voting Rights Act occurred. As a result of an overzealous and inept effort to purge felons from the voting lists, many Florida blacks with no criminal records were told they could not vote because they were felons. Voters in predominantly black precincts were also turned away on the grounds that they had voted by absentee ballot when they had not. Overall in Miami-Dade County, the state's largest, two-thirds of the people on the purge lists were black, even though African Americans are only 20 percent of the county's population. Also, blacks were sometimes required to present multiple forms of identification, whereas whites were not asked for ID. And when they were allowed to vote, black voters were much more likely to have their ballots rejected. Statewide, blacks were almost ten times as likely as nonblack voters to have their ballots rejected: This happened to 14.4 percent of black voters, compared with 1.6 percent of other voters (U.S. Commission on Civil Rights, 2001).

**Public Facilities.** Throughout the South and in some border states, such public facilities as libraries, museums, parks, swimming pools, golf courses, and public transportation were strictly segregated through most of the first half of the twentieth century. Such segregation was required by both state law and local ordinances

(Myrdal, 1944, Chap. 29). The length to which such rules of segregation sometimes went can be seen in examples presented by Woodward (1966, pp. 117–18). In 1932, Atlanta passed an ordinance forbidding amateur baseball clubs of different races to play within two blocks of one another. In the 1930s, Texas passed a law prohibiting "Caucasians" and "Africans" from boxing or wrestling together, and federal law was used to hinder the circulation of films showing interracial boxing. In Oklahoma, state law even required segregated fishing and boating. In general, segregation of public facilities was the law in the South and in some border areas until the 1950s.

State and local governments in the South were not always content with requiring segregation in publicly owned facilities. In many instances, legislation also required the operators of privately owned facilities and services open to the public to discriminate. For example, the laws of Florida, Tennessee, and a number of other states required segregation of passenger trains (Scruggs, 1971, p. 84).

As a general rule, government-mandated segregation of public facilities was much more widespread in the South and border states than it was in the North (Myrdal, 1944, Chap. 29). Nonetheless, the North was also highly segregated, and the segregation often existed with subtler forms of support and encouragement from state or local government. Although some northern states had civil rights laws before the 1950s, others did not, and even where there were such laws, enforcement often was weak or nonexistent. Often public facilities were de facto segregated by being placed in all-white or all-black areas rather than in borderline or racially mixed areas. In Chicago, police enforced segregation of city beaches even though there was no law or ordinance requiring such segregation (Drake and Cayton, 1945, p. 105). The absence of civil rights laws in some states made it perfectly legal for businesses to post signs such as "whites only," and many did (Myrdal, 1944, Chap. 29). Such practices sometimes occurred without interference even in states that had civil rights laws. Especially in smaller northern cities, rigid patterns of discrimination often existed without government interference. Lynd and Lynd (1929) noted a pervasive pattern of racial segregation in Muncie, Indiana, for example, at the local YMCA. In his biography, Malcolm X reports telling Michigan State University students about his experiences while growing up in East Lansing, the town where that university is located. "In those days," he told the students, "Negroes weren't allowed after dark in East Lansing proper" (Haley, 1964, p. 3).

The best overall description of the stance of state and local governments toward discrimination in public facilities in the first half of the twentieth century would be something like the following: In the South, public facility segregation was generally required by law. In the border states, such discrimination typically was encouraged and often required. In the remainder of the country, the position of state and local governments varied. In some states, there was a formal prohibition of at least some types of discrimination, although enforcement was often weak. In many nonsouthern states, however, there was no law against discrimination in the private sector, and subtler forms of public sector discrimination and segregation were common, particularly at the local level and in smaller communities. With the exception of an occasional Supreme Court ruling, the federal government did little or nothing to stop discrimination before World War II and in some ways encouraged it.

**Housing.** In numerous ways, the actions of federal, state, and local government promoted discrimination in housing. Past actions of government are an important cause of the pervasive pattern of housing segregation that is found in the United States today. One of the most important such actions was to enforce restrictive housing covenants. A restrictive covenant is a provision attached to a deed or sales contract in which the buyer must agree not to sell or rent to a member of a specified group, such as blacks, Chicanos, or Jews. To be enforceable, these restrictive covenants needed the backing of law. Until 1948 they got it: State courts, North and South, enforced these agreements by ordering a buyer of the "wrong" race or creed to give up the property. Thus, state enforcement was the crucial link that made the restrictive covenant an effective force in maintaining discrimination. At one time, this practice was so widespread that it has been estimated that up to 80 percent of all vacant land in Chicago and Los Angeles was closed to blacks (Abrams, 1971, p. 218). In 1944, 11 square miles of Chicago and 5.5 square miles of St. Louis were covered by restrictive covenants against blacks (Vose, 1959). In 1948, the Supreme Court ruled in the *Shelly v. Kramer* case that state courts could not enforce these covenants, but the covenants themselves did not entirely disappear. Rather, they continued to appear on many deeds to older housing, as was vividly illustrated in 1986 when Senate hearings revealed that the chief justice designate of the U.S. Supreme Court and several U.S. senators unknowingly owned houses that still bore restrictive covenants (unenforceable, of course).

Federal actions also contributed to housing segregation. The present-day pattern of predominantly minority cities and white suburbs is a legacy of the tax subsidies and the Federal Housing Administration (FHA) and Veterans' Administration (VA) programs that made suburban housing available to the middle-class masses after World War II. Most of the benefits of these subsidy programs went to whites; comparable levels of aid were not available to lower-income residents, who were more likely to be minorities. Thus, a situation was created that enabled whites to buy new housing in the suburbs and restricted minorities for the most part to poorer-quality housing in the central cities. There is evidence that this did not all occur by chance. The official manuals governing FHA policy from 1935 to 1950 contained warnings against "the infiltration of inharmonious racial and national groups," "a lower class of inhabitants," "the presence of incompatible racial elements," and "a lower level of society" (Larson and Nikkel, 1979, p. 235). In fact, FHA materials even included a model restrictive covenant, with the name of the unwanted group left blank, to be filled in later (Larson and Nikkel, 1979, p. 235). Thus, federal housing policy emerges as a major culprit in the problem of housing discrimination and segregation.

Local governments also promoted housing discrimination. Louisville, Richmond, Baltimore, and Atlanta all had local ordinances in the early twentieth century that required housing segregation, with blocks designated as black or white (Franklin and Moss, 2000, p. 343). Later, many local housing authorities used federal dollars to run segregated public housing developments. According to Franklin (1969, pp. 537, 610), this practice was widespread until around World War II. It was the rule in all southern cities that had public housing, and in some northern and border cities as well. As late as the 1950s, formally segregated public housing developments remained in some parts of the country.

Another approach widely used against minorities at the local level is zoning, used primarily in two ways. One is the use of rezoning to block proposed housing developments that would house minority group members, attempt to create an interracial environment, or be built for low-income populations. The other way is through what is known as "snob zoning," which uses such devices as minimum lot sizes and prohibition of certain types of housing to keep out "undesirables." Both practices have been widespread in American local communities, and both remain a problem today. For example, research shows that the larger the percentage of blacks is in nearby communities, the more likely a suburban community is to use zoning to restrict multifamily housing development (Burnell and Burnell, 1989). Moreover, such practices are legal, even in all-white communities, unless it can be proved than their purpose is to exclude minorities or that they are being applied differently to people of different racial groups.

Clearly, then, despite fair-housing legislation in the 1960s and since, federal, state, and local governments have been actively involved in housing discrimination over the years. Although many of the discriminatory practices have been curtailed, some, such as snob zoning, continue to play a significant role in housing segregation today. Thus, governments at all levels bear a significant responsibility for the pervasive pattern of segregation and inequality in housing in American urban areas today.

**Education.** Although education is discussed in detail in a later chapter, we shall briefly show that government policies—particularly state and local—generally ranged from accepting discrimination to requiring it up to the time of the 1954 Supreme Court ruling against segregated schools. In the South and border states, no fewer than seventeen states and the District of Columbia at one time had laws requiring school segregation (Myrdal, 1944, p. 632). In addition, many local school boards implemented a policy of segregation even where it was not required by state law. State-mandated educational discrimination has been used not only against blacks but against other minorities as well. For example, an 1860 California law excluded Chinese and Indians, as well as blacks, from that state's public schools. In 1906, the city of San Francisco took action to segregate the Chinese and Japanese in its school system (Bahr, Chadwick, and Strauss, 1979, pp. 81, 85). In much of the Southwest, Chicanos were also segregated from Anglos (Moore and Pachon, 1976, p. 81). In at least some instances, school boards in Texas responded to court orders to desegregate schools by mixing black and Chicano students, leaving white Anglo students in all-Anglo schools (Moore and Pachon, 1976, p. 81).

Another area of discrimination has been the refusal in some cases to provide bilingual teachers who could communicate with Spanish-speaking students. At one time, for example, it was against the law in California for teachers to use Spanish in the state's public schools. The state has moved in this direction again recently as the result of passage by initiative and referendum in 1986 of a new law specifying English as California's only official language and a 1998 initiative ending bilingual education.

As we have seen in this chapter, there has been a widespread pattern of discrimination through much of American history, involving in various ways the local, state, and federal levels of government. Although we have emphasized voting, use of public facilities, housing, and education, publicly supported or required discrimination has not been limited to these areas. In earlier chapters, we discussed legal restrictions on the freedom of travel of reservation Indians, laws forbidding Chinese and Japanese to enter the United States at times when other immigrants were accepted, the use of American law to deprive Mexican Americans of their land in the Southwest, and the blanket imprisonment of Japanese Americans during World War II. A careful examination of American history can yield only one answer: Government at all levels in the United States has engaged in discrimination in thousands of ways and must bear a substantial part of the responsibility for racial and ethnic inequality in America today.

## Contemporary Patterns: Government and Majority-Minority Relations Today

As was described in Chapter 6, the position of governments in the United States shifted gradually to an antidiscrimination stance, beginning around the time of World War II. The major legislation, presidential decisions, and court rulings against racial and ethnic discrimination are summarized in Table 11.1.

It is clear that the formal position of the federal government today, as well as that of state and local governments, is, on the whole, opposed to racial and ethnic discrimination. Nonetheless, a strong case can be made that in subtler ways, government continues to operate against the interests of minority group members. As we have seen, government has played a major role in creating and maintaining racial and ethnic inequality and today is doing very little to undo the effects of this discrimination.

## Table 11.1  Major Federal Actions Against Discrimination Since 1935

| Year | Action |
|------|--------|
| 1938 | *Missouri ex. rel. Gaines v. Canada*, 305 U.S. 337. Supreme Court rules that University of Missouri must admit a black applicant to law school because the state provided no comparable law school open to blacks. |
| 1941 | President Roosevelt issues presidential order against discrimination in defense plants and government agencies. |
| 1946 | Two federal courts rule that segregation in interstate travel is illegal. |
| 1948 | President Truman issues a presidential order to integrate the U.S. armed forces. |
| 1948 | *Shelley v. Kraemer*, 334 U.S. 1. Supreme Court rules that racially restrictive covenants in housing are not legally enforceable. |
| 1954 | *Brown v. Board of Education*, 347 U.S. 483. Supreme Court ends "separate but equal" doctrine and rules that school segregation is illegal. |
| 1957 | President Eisenhower orders federal troops into Arkansas to enforce a court order to desegregate Little Rock schools. |
| 1957 | Civil rights Act of 1957 gives certain enforcement powers to a Civil Rights Division in the U.S. Department of Justice and provides penalties for failure to obey court orders in voting rights cases. |
| 1960 | Civil Rights Act of 1960 strengthens voting rights enforcement provisions of 1957 Civil Rights Act. |
| 1964 | Civil Rights Act of 1964 bans racial, ethnic, and sex discrimination in employment and union membership. It prohibits discrimination by privately owned businesses providing public accommodations, such as hotels, restaurants, and theaters. It strengthens enforcement provisions against discrimination in education. |
| 1965 | Voting Rights Act of 1965 suspends use of literacy tests and permits federal review of requirements attached to voting or registration. It authorizes federal registration of voters where states are discriminated. |
| 1968 | Civil Rights Act of 1968 bans discrimination in the sale and rental of housing. |
| 1975 | Voting Rights Act expands to protect linguistic minorities. |
| 1982 | Ten-year extension and strengthening of Voting Rights Act of 1965 takes place. |
| 1988 | Fair Housing Act Amendments of 1988 strengthen fair-housing enforcement mechanisms of 1968 Civil Rights Act, ban discrimination based on familial status, and require new housing to be accessible to disabled. |
| 1991 | Civil Rights Act of 1991 reverses several Supreme Court rulings in 1989 that made it more difficult for minorities to sue for discrimination. It bans job tests and practices that have the effect of excluding minorities or women unless these requirements are demonstrably related to job performance and consistent with business necessity. |
| 1993 | President Clinton eases military ban on homosexuals by no longer allowing recruits to be asked about their sexual orientation. However, a more restrictive policy than Clinton's original proposal is approved by Congress. |

**Government Spending.**  One way to assess the priorities of any government is to see where it spends its money. Examination of government expenditures in recent years clearly shows that contrary to popular opinion, programs to improve the status of minority Americans have not been given high priority. A series of recessions from the 1970s into the new century have reconfirmed the old adage that minority group members are the "last hired, first fired." Throughout this period, the proportion of blacks unemployed has been two to two and a half times as high as for whites, with black unemployment sometimes reaching 20 percent during the worst recessions. Nevertheless, programs to provide jobs and assist the poor have remained a low priority for federal spending. In fiscal year 2000, for example, all programs providing cash and noncash benefits to low-income people amounted to only about 17 percent of the federal budget, about the same as a decade earlier (computed from U.S. Census Bureau, 2003q). Over the years, there have been both gains and losses. On the one hand, welfare reform legislation in the 1990s eliminated many programs targeted to assist the poor. The purpose was to encourage people to be more self-reliant, but as is discussed in greater detail later, the consequences have been more complicated than that.

On the other hand, some changes have also strengthened the safety net designed to protect people from the effects of poverty (Primus and Porter, 1998). For example, more low-income children with disabilities became eligible for Supplemental Security Income (SSI) in the early 1990s. More important, the Earned Income Tax Credit (EITC) program was expanded in 1986, 1990, and 1993, under three different administrations: Reagan, Bush, and Clinton. This program reduces the taxes of working poor families with children and, if their income is sufficiently low, results in a check from the Internal Revenue Service (IRS) to the family rather the other way around. There is little doubt that the EITC is one of the most efficient programs there is for reducing poverty among working families (Bluestone and Ghilarducci, 1996). As a result of these changes, the percentage of families who would otherwise have been poor but were not because of government help rose from 38.8 percent in 1987 to 46.6 percent in 1996. Although the 1996 figure is still not as high as that for 1979, before cuts that were made in the early 1980s, it is a notable improvement over 1987. Research also shows that the EITC significantly increased employment among single mothers and reduced their reliance on welfare (Elwood, 2000; Meyer and Rosenbaum, 2001; Grogger, 2002).

The EITC has been especially effective in reducing poverty among African Americans and Hispanics because poor people in these groups are more likely to fall into the category of nonelderly, working poor families. In 1996, for example, more than 40 percent of poor whites were elderly, and just 19 percent were children. But among blacks and Hispanics, fewer than 13 percent were elderly, and more than 41 percent were children. Unfortunately for minorities, other government programs work in opposite ways, so that the overall racial effect of government antipoverty programs is just the opposite of the EITC. Overall, government programs in 1996 lifted 56 percent of whites who would otherwise have been poor out of poverty, but just 36 percent of blacks and fewer than 34 percent of Hispanics (Primus and Porter, 1998). This is true despite the fact that African Americans and Latinos/as are about three times as likely as whites to be poor. The reason is again age: Overall, the government programs with the biggest impact on poverty are targeted to the elderly, and poor blacks and Hispanics are much less likely than poor whites to be elderly. Consequently, the overall effect of government programs benefits poor whites much more than poor African Americans or Latinos/as, even though the latter groups are much more likely to be poor. One final note of caution: Although the success of government programs in reducing poverty did increase overall between 1987 and 1996, these changes occurred before the welfare reform legislation of 1996 could have any effect. As is discussed later, this legislation has reversed certain aspects of the trend of 1987–1996. For example, food stamps have become less available to the poorest of the poor.

The news on job-creation programs is even less encouraging. In response to the difficult economic conditions of the early 1990s and to the severe inner-city conditions that gave rise to the 1992 Los Angeles riot, the Clinton administration proposed a jobs and economic stimulus package of more than $16 billion in early 1993. However, Congress cut this proposed package to less than $2 billion. One part of the package that was cut was a summer job program for inner-city teenagers; a sample of forty major cities revealed that more than twice as many eligible inner-city youths were registered for jobs as the number of jobs the reduced program was able to provide (Claiborne, 1993; Krauss, 1993). Because the years after 1992 did not bring repeats of the urban violence of 1992, job stimulus programs for urban youth quickly became a forgotten issue. By mid-2003, the unemployment rate for African American youth was again hovering around 40 percent (U.S. Bureau of Labor Statistics, 2003).

Government cutbacks in spending for low-income housing have also had disproportionate impacts on African Americans and Latinos/as, especially when combined with the effects of increasing inequality in incomes. The shortage of affordable housing has increased sharply over the last three decades. In 1970, there were actually 300,000 more low-rent housing units available than the number of low income renters (Daskal, 1998). However, by 1995 there were more than 4.4 million fewer low-cost housing units than the number of low-income households. This occurred mainly because incomes became more unequal, resulting in more poor households, and also because in much of the country, inflation in housing costs outstripped the overall rate of inflation. For a while, expansion of federal housing assistance kept the housing gap from growing even wider. However, this trend was reversed in the 1980s, so that by 1997 the number of new housing subsidies funded by the government was just one-seventh of the amount funded in 1977 (Daskal, 1998). Welfare reform legislation has aggravated this decline because most jobs obtained by those leaving welfare do not provide enough income to pay for decent housing, yet few receive housing subsidies. Even so, appropriation bills for fiscal 2004 contained additional cuts that would result in thousands more low-income families losing their housing subsidies (Sard and Fisher, 2003) as Congress struggled to deal with record deficits caused by the costs of the war in Iraq and efforts to combat terrorism, poor economic times, and massive tax cuts that went disproportionately to the wealthy.

**Welfare Reform.** For many years, the welfare system of the United States was criticized for keeping poor people dependent and unable to become self-supporting. It did this by failing to provide incentives to work: Recipients lost their welfare if they worked, along with their Medicaid coverage, and were faced with the added expense of child care. Consequently, by working, they were little better off and sometimes worse off. It was also widely accepted that the welfare system tended to break up families by taking needed aid away from women because of the presence of a man in the household. Because of these concerns, and especially because of a public perception (incorrect in the case of most welfare recipients) that people were choosing to stay on welfare for years, Congress passed and President Clinton signed comprehensive welfare reform legislation in 1996.

Despite the legislation's laudable goal of encouraging people to become self-supporting rather than dependent on welfare, there are aspects that raise serious questions and concerns. The worst fears have not been realized to date, but the reform per se has not made much difference in the incomes of those affected by it, despite reductions in welfare rolls that have resulted. The major features of the legislation are as follows:

- A strengthening of the national child support enforcement system.

- Increased federal funding for child care, to make it easier for women leaving welfare to have their children cared for while they work. Medicaid coverage was also expanded so that coverage was no longer automatically lost if a mother went off welfare.

- Stricter qualification requirements for benefits for children with disabilities under Supplemental Security Income (SSI), including a requirement for medical examinations, not just functional assessments.

- A lifetime limit of five years for the total amount of time a person can receive welfare. (Up to 20 percent of recipients can be waived by the states from this limit, based on inability to work.) States may impose shorter, but not longer, time limits if they want. In fact, some states established shorter time limits, sometimes as short as two years, but most set the limit at five years (Jencks, 1997; Bernstein and Greenberg, 2001).

- A requirement that people receiving welfare must accept employment.

- A reduction to one year in the amount of time that education may be substituted for employment and exclusion of all types of education (including college attendance) other than vocational education. (Legislation to relax this restriction was passed by the Senate in 1998 but failed in the House of Representatives.)

- The replacement of a federal welfare program, guaranteeing a right to receive welfare to all who meet federally specified qualifications, with block grants to the states. There is no longer any requirement that people who meet any set of criteria qualify for welfare; the only rule is that states must have objective and equitable criteria for deciding and an appeal process. But it is explicitly stated that nobody has any entitlement to benefits.

- Exclusion of legal immigrants from most benefit programs. (This provision was partially rescinded by subsequent legislation.)

- Reduction of food stamp benefits and limitation of unemployed adults without disabilities or dependents to three months of food stamps in any thirty-six–month period.

- Instead of matching federal funds, as was required, states are now required only to maintain state funding of welfare at 80 percent of its 1994 level, without subsequent adjustment for inflation. The federal block grant is also essentially fixed, so that if a state wants to spend more than in the past because of inflation or increased numbers of poor, it must pay all the additional cost itself. On the other hand, if welfare rolls shrink, the block grant does not.

Some features of the legislation, such as the increased support for child care, have made it easier for some people to become self-supporting. However, there are also aspects of the legislation that create challenges for poor families and children. First, it is dubious, based on past experience, whether all but the 20 percent of welfare recipients who can be waived from the time limit are really capable of working. For example, when welfare reform was passed half of welfare recipients were high school dropouts. For this group, employment possibilities are very limited (Moss and Tilly, 2001b). The majority of welfare recipients at the time reform was passed reported a history of abuse, more than 20 percent had been raped or beaten within the past year, and more than a quarter said they were depressed (Allard et al., 1996; Christensen, 1997; Grunwald, 1997). In fact, studies show that those who have been "sanctioned" under welfare reform (cut off welfare for failing to meet requirements such as work or attendance at job training) are more likely to be victims of domestic violence, more likely to be mentally ill, and have less education and work history than other welfare recipients. Among this group, a study in three cities found an 89 percent poverty rate (Bernstein and Greenberg, 2001).

Research on the overall effects of welfare reform show that it has been effective in moving sizable numbers of poor people from welfare to work, but it is dubious whether they are economically better off as a result of welfare reform. Under welfare reform, the proportion of single mothers receiving welfare has been about cut in half, from more than 30 percent in the early 1990s to about 15 percent in 1999. Overall, welfare rolls fell by about 59 percent between 1993 and 2000 (Grogger, 2002, p. 6). Obviously, much of this reduction has been the result of welfare reform, but some was also the result of the booming economy of the 1990s, and some also was the result of the expansion of the EITC, which created incentives to work because it applies only to earned income.

Although some welfare reforms, such as enhanced support for child care and enhanced Medicaid coverage, seem to have increased income, the welfare time limits themselves did not lead to either increased earnings or increased income (Grogger, 2002, pp. 22–23). This is because the time limits may have pressed people to accept less desirable and lower-paying jobs. In fact, they may even have depressed wages by increasing the supply of low-skill labor, at least in some areas. One study of welfare reform found that getting a job, but not entering or leaving welfare, led to increases in family income (Chase-Lansdale et al., 2003). In general, studies of the overall effects of welfare reform on family income have given mixed results, with some studies showing modest gains (Bloom et al., 2000), others showing income declines as families leave welfare for low-paying jobs (Brauner and Loprest, 1999; National Research Council, 1999), and yet others showing little difference (Holcomb et al., 1998). One explanation for some of these contradictory findings lies in different methods of the studies used, but another may be that the effects varied over time. Studies of the incomes of poor families overall show increases between 1993 and 1995 but declines in 1996 and 1997 (Primus et al., 1999).

Although income measures present conflicting results but suggest little overall effect of welfare reform one way or the other, there is evidence from purchasing patterns that the purchasing power of the poor may have increased somewhat during the 1990s as a result of welfare reform (Meyer and Sullivan, 2001). Still, it must be kept in mind that the incomes of most who made welfare-to-work transitions are low. Typically, hourly wages run between $6 and $8 per hour, and a number of studies of annual incomes of former welfare recipients showed average incomes only around $10,000 to $11,000 per year, well below the poverty level (Bernstein and Greenberg, 2001). The EITC has raised family incomes of the working poor, and it closes some but not all of this gap, since the poverty level for a family of four in 2002 was about $18,300. Most who leave welfare (about 70 percent) do find jobs, but only about 40 percent remain on those jobs throughout the year (Bernstein and Greenberg, 2001). In addition, the condition of some families has been worsened by the reduced availability of food stamps. It must also be remembered that there are costs that households incur when they shift from welfare to work. Mothers leaving welfare often have to pay for transportation to work and for their children to day care, even if the day care itself is subsidized.

Studies of welfare reform have also examined outcomes among children. In three cities between 1999 and 2001, an extensive survey was conducted of mostly black or Hispanic families who were affected by welfare reform. It found that for preschool children, employment and welfare transitions resulting from welfare reform made no difference one way or the other for cognitive achievement or behavior problems among the children. Such transitions didn't make much difference for adolescents in the families either, except that stress and anxiety declined modestly when their mothers got jobs (Chase-Lansdale et al., 2003). However, other studies have found higher rates of school problems among teenagers whose mothers made welfare-to-work transitions under welfare reform; specifically, they are more likely to be held back in a grade at school. Possible reasons include less supervision and greater responsibilities for taking care of younger siblings (Gennetian et al., 2000). Other studies suggest that the effects of welfare reform on children depend on the levels of support given to mothers who leave welfare and return to work (Morris, Duncan, and Chase-Lansdale, 2001). Where income from jobs is supplemented with some form of assistance, so that the family increases its income upon returning to work, positive effects on children's achievement occurred. Where the mother was required to take a job with no support, no improvements occurred.

It is important to keep in mind that these studies were done mainly in the 1990s, when the economy was growing to the greatest extent it had in 30 years. In that context, most former welfare recipients were able to find jobs, and their incomes, if not improved, for the most part did not fall greatly, either. However, the effects of welfare reforms in today's more troubled economy could be less positive. Unfortunately, the downturn of the economy after the 2001 terrorist attacks and the fall in the stock market came just about the time that many recipients were beginning to reach the six-year time limit on welfare. Although unemployment levels as of mid-2004 had not reached levels as high as in many previous recessions, jobs have become notably scarcer than in the 1990s, so that the effects of welfare reform in the new decade may be more negative. Additionally, by 2003 welfare rolls were increasing in many states for the first time since welfare reform went into effect, although nationally there was a slight decline in welfare rolls between 2001 and 2004. In the same period, though, there was a 35 percent increase in the number of people receiving food stamps (Pear, 2004).

To a large extent, the success of the reform depends on high-quality job-training programs to prepare people for employment. And this doesn't mean just job skills; it also means basic habits such as punctuality, reliability, and speech. There are successful job-training programs (usually somewhat selective) that do teach such skills and have placed former welfare recipients in the work force; two examples are One with One in Boston and a statewide welfare reform program in Vermont that was started before the federal reforms. But these programs are expensive and contrary to the trend of reducing welfare expenses that has taken hold in some states (Zengerle, 1997).

Overall, although welfare reform has succeeded in freeing many people from welfare dependency, it has, in and of itself, led to little or no improvement in the overall economic condition of the poor, especially net of the economic boom of the 1990s. When welfare reform effects are combined with those of the EITC, however, many poor families have experienced gains (Jencks, 2002). In harder times and over the longer run, the full consequences of welfare reform remain uncertain. In addition to the greater difficulty of finding jobs, poor families may face reduced subsidies for child care and health care as states struggle to balance their budgets (Jencks, 2002). As noted earlier, about half the states in 2003 were experiencing severe budget crunches, and most of the rest were under some fiscal pressure. Because single-parent poor families with children—the main group affected by the legislation—are disproportionately composed of African Americans and Latinos/as, the effects of welfare reform, good and bad, will have a disproportionate impact on these groups. And the effects are not always the same for all groups: For example, studies show that blacks leaving welfare report receiving less government support than whites leaving welfare, and a few studies have found disturbing evidence of unequal treatment of blacks and whites (Weil, 2002).

Whatever its advantages and disadvantages, the welfare reform law is unlikely to be repealed. Given this reality, Jencks (1997) has suggested several steps to lessen its harmful effects and increase its benefits. Among them are raising the minimum wage back to 50 percent of the average wage for blue-collar manufacturing workers, its level through the 1950s and 1960s. He also suggests increasing child care subsidies beyond the levels in the welfare reform bill, because for most mothers these do not cover the additional costs associated with leaving welfare and going to work, and increasing housing subsidies to close the gap between income and expenses, especially in high-cost areas such as New York and California. Especially during recessions, he suggests the government becoming an employer of last resort, and he also points out that a national health care plan, such as that proposed by President Clinton but rejected by Congress, would be helpful because most low-wage jobs do not include health care benefits. For example, only about one-third of the jobs held by former welfare recipients include health insurance (Weil, 2002). Finally, better information would be helpful in some cases. It has been found that many who are eligible for food stamps or Medicaid do not receive benefits because once they no longer are receiving welfare, they are less likely to be given information about such programs (Weil, 2002).

**Wage and Labor Law, Minorities, and the Growing Income Gap.**  Despite the intense debate over welfare reform, more poor people are working than are on welfare. This was already true before passage of welfare reform and is even more true now. Importantly, the lot of the working poor grew worse between 1973 and 1993, during which time the average income of the lowest 20 percent of households fell almost 23 percent (Bluestone and Ghilarducci, 1996). Most of this decline occurred because the wages of lower-paid workers did not keep up with inflation and because more households in the 1990s than in the 1970s were headed by a single mother, and women still receive lower wages at any given level of education than do men. In the boom economy of the 1990s, this trend was partially reversed, but the situation of the working poor remains grim. As more women enter the low-wage labor pool because of welfare reform, the glut of workers in this labor pool will increase, and even more of them will be women. And again, a disproportionate number of African Americans and Latinos/as will be affected because these groups are over-represented among the working poor and among those who are making transitions from welfare to work.

One reason for the falling real wages of lower-income households is that minimum wage law has not been adjusted to keep up with inflation, as it was from 1950 to the 1970s. In 1968, when it was at its peak in real (inflation-adjusted) dollars, it provided 118 percent of the poverty level for a family of three. In other words, if a wage earner worked year-round, the family would have had an income 18 percent above the poverty level. But by 1995, the minimum wage had fallen so far behind inflation that this same family would have had an income 28 percent *below* the poverty level (Bluestone and Ghilarducci, 1996). Although the minimum wage was raised to $5.15 in 1996, it was still not adequate to get a family of three supported by one wage earner up to the poverty level; to do so would have required a minimum wage of $6.06 per hour. As of May 2004, the minimum wage remained at $5.15. After adjustment for inflation, this amounts to almost a 25 percent decline in the minimum wage over the past twenty years.

Although some argue that raising the minimum wage will lead to more unemployment, actual studies suggest that it has little or no effect. Studies from the 1970s and 1980s indicate that raising the minimum wage 10 percent can lead to an increase of 1 to 3 percent in youth unemployment but just 0.3 to 0.7 percent in adult unemployment (Bluestone and Ghilarducci, 1996). However, studies of the actual behavior of fast-food restaurants and other low-wage employers indicate that there is no effect at all on employment when the minimum wage is raised (Card and Krueger, 1995).

Allowing the minimum wage to fall behind inflation since the early 1970s is just one of a number of areas in which the federal government has weakened labor protection and unions, contributing to the fall in wages for lower-paid workers. Labor unions were seriously weakened when President Reagan fired air traffic controllers because this sent a signal to other employers that they could fire striking workers and replace them. This behavior became much more common in the 1980s. Consequently, workers became reluctant to strike for fear of losing their jobs, and by 1996 the number of strikes was at a record low (LeDuc, 1996). In the 1980s, the National Labor Relations Board (NLRB) also reversed a number of earlier decisions that had been favorable to workers, creating a more difficult situation for unions. A later chair of the NLRB described that period: "There was a systematic plan to reverse labor-law precedent . . . [and] there was also inattention given to the expeditious processing of cases" (William Gould, quoted in LeDuc, 1996). Finally, the passage of the North American Free Trade Agreement (NAFTA) without any assurance that Mexico's inadequate labor laws would be strengthened created an incentive to move thousands of jobs south of the border at much lower wages. Because of their historic concentration in manufacturing industries, African Americans and Hispanics were particularly affected by these job shifts, as discussed in Chapter 10. Other jobs have been created by NAFTA, but this does not necessarily help manufacturing workers whose plants have been moved to Mexico.

The collective result of the slowdown of wage growth has been a shift in wealth from workers to the wealthy. The share of corporate income going to profits and to executive salaries rose significantly in the 1980s and 1990s, whereas the share going to wages fell. If profit rates in the 1980s and 1990s had simply remained the same as in earlier decades, workers' hourly wages would have been 3.6 percent higher in 1996 than they were (Mishel, 1997). This may not sound like much until you realize that the entire growth in hourly pay, after adjustment for inflation, was just 2.8 percent between 1989 and 1996. In other words, if the share of income going to wages and profits had stayed the same as in the past, the average hourly worker would have gotten twice the increase.

What does this have to do with race relations? It affects workers of all colors and ethnic backgrounds, but not equally. Minority groups—African Americans, Latinos/as, and American Indians—are overrepresented among hourly workers and underrepresented among stockholders and corporate executives. And they are most overrepresented among the lowest-paid workers, who, as we have seen, have fared the worst. They are also overrepresented both among those who will be affected most by welfare reform and among the lower-paid workers, whose wages probably will be lowered further by a surplus of workers because of the move from welfare. Thus, whereas policies such as minimum wage law, labor law, NAFTA, and welfare reform have no *direct* relationship to race and ethnicity, their effects on the average minority group member are very different from those on the average white person.

**Public Transportation and Health Care.** Two other areas that the U.S. government has neglected are public transportation and health care. Among the industrialized nations of the world, the United States ranks near the bottom in these areas. The efficient subway systems of London, Paris, Stockholm, and Moscow present a striking contrast to the crowded freeways and the limited and financially insecure bus systems in many U.S. cities. Over the past decade or so, several major cities such as Pittsburgh, St. Louis, and Los Angeles have, with federal aid, built new mass-transit rail systems, and these have significantly improved access to employment for minority group members—many of whom lack cars—who are lucky enough to live near the transit lines. However, in some cases those who do not live near the transit lines have been hurt as bus lines have been eliminated, in part to pay the expenses of the rail transit systems (Ahmad, 2001). Mass-transit systems in all but a handful of major cities such as New York, Boston, and Chicago are very small compared with those found in most other industrialized countries. In addition, reductions in federal subsidies for operation of these systems once they are constructed has forced fare increases and, in some areas, service cutbacks and employee layoffs in recent years.

One of the major supporters of national health insurance in the United States, Senator Edward Kennedy, is fond of pointing out that aside from South Africa, the United States is the only industrialized nation in the world without some kind of national health care coverage. This is changing, however, as a result of the shift to majority rule in South Africa, which has led to efforts to bring national health insurance to that country. In fact, one of the first actions of the new government there was to extend universal public health care to children under six years of age and to pregnant mothers (Haffejee, 1995). Given the failure of the Clinton administration's proposal for national health insurance in the United States during his first term, any change will be slower to come in the United States. The issue of health care and how it is linked to race and ethnic relations is discussed in Chapter 10.

Government failure to provide public transportation and health care protection once again affects minority group members more than other Americans because their disproportionate poverty leaves them less able to afford private transportation or private health care. Statistics on auto ownership show that minority group members are less likely than whites to own automobiles (U.S. Census Bureau, 2003c, Tables HCT33a–g), and health coverage statistics show that they are also less likely to have health insurance (U.S. Census Bureau, 2002g, Table HI01).

## Barriers to Greater Minority Political Power

Obviously, a group's interests may be ignored by government if the group has insufficient power to force the government to pay attention to it. Minority groups have greater political power today than in the past, but clearly their power is still quite limited.

One way to get power is through *influence*: gaining favor and popular support among groups other than one's own. When the issue was clear—that is, when the problem was defined as deliberate discrimination, such as segregated lunch counters—minority group members had significant influence among the white population. Thus, in the 1950s and 1960s, when discrimination was open and blatant, it was possible to mobilize large numbers of whites against what they saw as an obviously unfair system. (For greater detail, review Chapters 3 and 6.) However, as the issues became less clear-cut and many whites began to believe that the problem had been solved (or at least the white part of the problem had been solved) by the civil rights laws of the 1960s, minority influence began to wane. Since the late 1960s, various opinion polls have shown that whites no longer blame themselves or our social institutions for racial problems, and whites for the most part do not favor any further major actions to solve such problems. This pattern of public opinion among whites, discussed in detail in Chapter 3, has been very persistent from the 1970s into the new century. Most whites from the 1970s on have felt little or no personal need to try to solve racial problems, and there has been limited support among whites for new government initiatives in that area. As was noted in Chapter 3, the unwillingness of most whites to support public policies aimed at eliminating the disadvantages of minority groups—or even to acknowledge that such disadvantages exist—has been referred to by social scientists as "symbolic racism" or "modern racism" (Kinder and Sears, 1981; McConahay, Hardee, and Bates, 1981; Kluegel and Smith, 1982, 1986). More recently, some social scientists have also called it "color-blind racism" because many whites conflate the idea that society should be color-blind with the myth that it actually is (Bonilla-Silva, 2003a, 2003c).

A major cause of attitudes such as these is a perception among the white population that the American system, for the most part, offers equal opportunities to people of all races. National surveys and qualitative interview studies show that it is widely believed by white Americans that minorities have much the same opportunity as whites (Kluegel and Smith, 1982, 1986; Kluegel, 1990; Blauner, 1989, 1994; Bonilla-Silva, 2003c). Apparently, these beliefs are based largely on the fact that laws against deliberate racial discrimination have been passed. However, the reality (as is detailed in Chapters 10 and 12) is that subtle and sometimes unintentional, but nonetheless real, forms of institutional discrimination persist in most major American social institutions. Moreover, discrimination testing studies have also shown a good deal of intentional individual discrimination, although few people openly proclaim that they discriminate on the basis of race. However, these forms of discrimination are not experienced by most whites, nor are they easily visible. Thus, many white Americans are unaware of them, and it is relatively easy to deny that they exist. The significance of these beliefs is this: When whites incorrectly believe that minorities have the same opportunities in life that they do, they oppose policies designed to increase opportunities for minorities (Kluegel, 1990; Herring et al., 2000). Thus, the political constituency to support such programs is limited outside minority communities.

## Voting and Political Participation

Another source of power is obtained through voting strength, particularly if a group votes as a bloc, as minority group members sometimes do. This can be seen in several presidential elections. In 1964, 97 percent of the black vote went to the Democratic candidate, Lyndon Johnson. In 1972, 87 percent went to Democrat George McGovern, even though he lost badly in the total vote. In 1976, 82 percent of blacks voted for Democrat Jimmy Carter. In 1992, the African American and Latino/a votes went heavily for Bill Clinton (80 percent and 62 percent, respectively), and as in close elections in earlier years, they are a major reason that the Democratic ticket won. For example, John F. Kennedy in 1960 and Jimmy Carter in 1976 would have lost had it not been for the black vote, which provided more than the margin of victory in a number of big states. In 1992, the race between Bill Clinton and George Bush would have been a dead heat among white voters; in contrast, black and Hispanic voters voted heavily for Clinton. In 1986, the black vote was the determining factor in a number of close U.S. Senate contests and was a major reason that the Democrats regained control of the Senate that year.

The disputed presidential election in 2000 presents particular problems, because serious questions arose about the validity of the vote count in Florida and about violations of the Voting Rights Act in Florida and other states. It is quite possible that those violations tipped the election result, because if black voters had not been turned away or had their votes disqualified at rates far above those of white voters, it is likely that Al Gore would have had a clear-cut win in Florida. More than 90,000 ballots cast by black voters were rejected, and around 90 percent or more of the black vote went for Gore, both in Florida and nationwide. This means that, had black voters been allowed to vote and had their votes counted at the same rate as whites, Gore would have had about an 80,000 vote margin in Florida, and there would have been no uncertainty about who carried the Florida vote. Nationally, Gore got about half a million more votes than Bush, but he lost the deciding Electoral College vote when the Supreme Court ended recounts after Bush had been declared the winner by state officials in Florida. Clearly, it was the votes of minorities that made this a close election rather than a Bush landslide. Although Gore got 48.7 percent of the vote and Bush 48.6 percent nationally, there were sharp racial differences in the vote. A postelection Gallup poll found that Bush carried 55 percent of the white vote, compared with 43 percent for Gore and 3 percent for Nader. However, Gore got an overwhelming 96 percent of the black vote, compared with 3 percent for Bush and 2 percent for Nader (Gallup Organization, 2001). CNN estimated a slightly lower margin but still showed 90 percent of the African American vote going to Gore. There was also a gender gap among whites; among white women, the vote was close, but among white men, Bush had a lead of 20 points or more. The Hispanic vote nationally also went heavily for Gore, with CNN (2000) estimating that the 62 percent of Hispanics voted for Gore, 35 percent for Bush, and 2 percent for Nader. Gore also carried the Asian American vote, 55 percent to 41 percent for Bush and 3 percent for Nader (CNN, 2000). Thus, it is clear that it was the heavy vote for Gore among people of color that made this election a cliffhanger.

However, it is important not to overestimate the voting power of minorities. The combined racial and ethnic minority population in the United States is under 35 percent of the total, less among the voting-aged population, and still less among those registered to vote. Thus, minorities have enough votes to make a real differ-ence only when the election is relatively close, as was the case in 1960, 1976, 1992, and 2000. In landslide elections of 1964, 1972, 1984, 1988, and 1996, however, the minority vote made no difference. The black vote was not enough to save George McGovern in 1972 or Walter Mondale in 1984 from two of the worst defeats ever. Despite getting a large majority of the black vote, Michael Dukakis lost badly to George Bush in 1988. In 1964, Lyndon Johnson's win was so overwhelming that he would have won easily without any minority votes. Much the same is true of Bill Clinton in 1996, although his margin of victory in the white vote was much nar-rower than his overall margin. Even in the relatively close election of 1968, an over-whelming black vote for Democrat Hubert Humphrey did not save him from a loss to Richard Nixon. It is clear that any time the electorate divides racially (as it did to an unusual degree in 1972, 1984, and 1988), minorities will come out on the losing side.

One factor that does help strengthen the voting power of minorities is that even though they are a relatively small percentage of the total population, they are con-centrated in certain geographic areas; in these areas, they may be a majority or near majority of the population. In cities such as Washington, Atlanta, Detroit, Newark, New Orleans, and a number of others, the black electorate has become large enough to control or heavily influence the local political apparatus. These cities and many others like them have elected black mayors over the past two or three decades, and black majorities have begun to appear on such elected bodies as city councils and school boards. Similarly, Chicanos have been able to gain control of the politi-cal apparatus in some towns and counties in south Texas, where they are the major-ity of the electorate (Moore and Pachon, 1976, pp. 153–54). In New Mexico, where Chicanos are not only numerous but also have long been politically involved, many Hispanic officials have been elected over the years, even to such high offices as gov-ernor and U.S. senator.

But even where they are in the majority and have elected members of their group to public offices, the power of minority group members is limited. One of the most important limitations is that areas of minority concentration often are low-income areas, which places severe restrictions on their tax bases. Consequently, they are often unable to provide needed services without outside help, and such help, if it is available at all, frequently comes with strings. Thus, minorities are in solid polit-ical control, but the cities they govern often are in a constant position of fiscal inad-equacy. In such situations, a black mayor is confronted with the same choices as a white mayor in the same situation: Cut jobs and services to make the budget bal-ance, accept outside aid with undesirable conditions attached to it, or both. This reality often places a serious limit on the extent of black or Chicano political power, even when blacks or Chicanos are in the majority and have elected members of their own group to public office.

All of these factors combine to create a situation that leaves minorities seriously underrepresented in the political system, despite some improvement in recent years. The unwillingness of whites to further support major action to improve the position of minorities means that current officials have little or no incentive to pursue such pol-icy. It also makes it very difficult for outspoken minority group members to be elected in mostly white areas, although black mayors have been elected in predominantly white cities such as Los Angeles; Spokane, Washington; Minneapolis; Battle Creek, Michigan, and Clinton, Iowa. A small number of minority group members have been elected to statewide offices, which involve mostly white constituencies. Edward Brooke, an African American, represented Massachusetts in the U.S. Senate during the 1970s, and in 1992, Carol Moseley Braun of Illinois became the first African Amer-ican woman elected to the U.S. Senate. However, her 1998 reelection campaign was unsuccessful. Also in 1992, the state of Colorado elected the first Native American U.S. senator, Ben Nighthorse Campbell. In 1989, L. Douglas Wilder of Virginia became the first African American elected governor of any state. Campbell remains in office; Wilder was prevented by term limit rules from running for reelection.

However, most of these officials have held quite moderate views on intergroup relations. More outspoken officials, such as former mayor Richard Hatcher of Gary, Indiana, or Coleman Young, who served for many years as mayor of Detroit, would have a difficult time getting elected without the large black electorates that exist in their cities. For example, in 1984 and 1988 polls showed that the majority of white Democrats were unwilling to vote for the Reverend Jesse Jackson had he received the party's nomination for the presidency. Similarly, polls in 2003 showed the Reverend Al Sharpton and former U.S. senator Carol Moseley Braun near the bottom among whites in the race for the 2004 Democratic presidential nomination, although both enjoyed greater support among African Americans. Among black Democrats, Sharpton was the leading candidate in June 2003 at 24 percent, with Moseley Braun third at 12 percent. In contrast, just 4 percent of white Democrats supported Moseley Braun, and just 1 percent supported Sharpton (Gallup Organization, 2003d). Ultimately, neither Sharpton nor Moseley Braun won any primaries. In addition, when local politics become racially polarized, black elected officials with majority white constituencies are sometimes voted out. In New York City in 1993, after angry confrontations between Hasidic Jews and African Americans, the city's first African American mayor, David Dinkins, was voted out and replaced by a conservative white candidate, Rudolph Giuliani, whom he had defeated in the previous election.

In any case, an examination of the districts from which black officials have been elected reveals that many have predominantly black constituencies. In 2000, for example, about 40 percent of black big-city mayors and 70 percent of black congressional representatives were elected by mostly black constituencies, although the number coming from areas without black majorities grew modestly in the 1990s

Clinton, Iowa, mayor LaMetta Wynn enjoys a meeting with citizens. Although less so than in the past, Mayor Wynn remains something of an exception to the rule: Majority-white constituencies such as Clinton usually do not elect African Americans to positions of top leadership.

(Bositis, 2002). It is largely for this reason that (as noted in Chapter 9) less than 2 percent of all elected officials are black, even though almost 13 percent of the U.S. population is black. The underrepresentation is especially severe at the state and federal levels, at which most of the important and far-reaching decisions are made. Given current voting and belief patterns, it is unlikely that the U.S. political system can soon produce any major change: Nearly all statewide offices and all but a handful of congressional districts have electorates in which the majority of voters (usually a large majority) are white. In most cases, these voters simply will not elect a minority group member who speaks out in favor of major policy changes to improve the status of minorities.

Thus, with the exception of a handful of big-city mayors and congressional representatives from districts with large minority populations, such input is severely underrepresented in the political system. Recent polls suggest that whites are becoming less reluctant than in the past to vote for African Americans and other minorities, and the number elected from majority-white districts has increased somewhat, as noted. However, it remains rare for African Americans to be elected to top offices from predominantly white constituencies. In all U.S. history, there has been only one African American governor: former Virginia governor Douglas Wilder. And today, there is no African American in the U.S. Senate; Carol Moseley Braun of Illinois was defeated in the 1998 election. However, at the time of this writing, an African American man, Barack Obama, was the Democratic nominee for U.S. senator in Illinois in the 2004 election.

In the search for alternatives to this lack of minority representation, one can be seen in the internal policies of the Democratic political party since 1972. To ensure representation of women and minorities, the party established guidelines concerning the percentage of convention delegates that should be female and that should be minority. This led to a substantial increase in female and minority representation in the party's presidential nominating conventions. By the 1984 convention, 18 percent of the delegates were black and half were women, compared with just 5 percent black and 16 percent women in 1968, before the reforms. The pattern of diversity continued in 2000, when half the delegates were women, 20 percent were African American, 10 percent were Latino/a, 3 percent were Asian American, and 1 percent were Native American. Such an approach or something similar might be possible in the larger political system as well (e.g., by requiring parties to use such percentage guidelines in their nominations of candidates for public office). In fact, this is already done with respect to gender in Norway, where party rules specify that between 40 percent and 60 percent of people nominated to run for public office must be women (W. E. Schmidt, 1991). However, based on white reactions to such proposals as busing and affirmative action in hiring for minorities, there would undoubtedly be intense opposition to such a proposal. In fact, when the Voting Rights Act was renewed, it specifically stated that such proportional representation was not required.

A few states have passed laws mandating diversity in appointments to state boards and commissions, but these have focused on gender, not race or ethnicity. For example, Iowa requires equal numbers of men and women on state boards and commissions, and North Dakota requires equal representation "to the extent possible" (Gross, 1990). This legislation is effective in increasing diversity among public officials: The percentage of women in state appointive jobs rose from 30 percent to 49 percent after the Iowa law was passed. However, it is significant that laws requiring proportional representation of women have passed only in states with small minority populations, such as Iowa and North Dakota. In more diverse states, such as California and Pennsylvania, they have bogged down amid debates over "quotas," and a campaign promise to support such a law contributed to Diane Feinstein's defeat when she ran for governor of California in 1990 (although she was later elected to the U.S. Senate). Experience with these laws reveals a problem, however:

Although they do succeed in making public officials more diverse, they generate strong opposition in areas that are racially diverse, especially if racial representation becomes an issue, as it did in California.

Another approach that was attempted for a while was to try to draw election districts in a way that would increase the chance of underrepresented minorities being elected. This was done by a number of states, with the encouragement of the federal government, as a way of complying with the 1965 Voting Rights Act. This law requires corrective measures to be taken where minorities had been systematically denied their full voting rights. However, a series of decisions by the Supreme Court in the 1990s struck down the use of race as a criterion for drawing congressional districts, especially if the result was odd-shaped districts or **gerrymandering**. Consequently, a number of African American congressional representatives who had been elected by majority-black districts faced majority-white districts in 1996. As it turns out, all of these representatives were reelected. Some have taken this as a sign that white resistance to voting for black candidates is decreasing, and it may well be. On the other hand, there are advantages in incumbency, and although these African American representatives were reelected, it may still be more difficult for nonincumbent African Americans to be elected in the new majority-white districts. This interpretation is supported by the fact that the number of blacks in Congress has remained flat around forty or so the last few elections.

To summarize briefly, it is clear that the American political system still leaves much to be desired in its treatment of racial and ethnic minorities. Although deliberate discrimination is for the most part illegal today, the government is doing little to undo the effects of past discrimination, much of which was required or encouraged by laws and policies established by governments at various levels.

Undoubtedly, part of the reason for the lack of effort to undo the effects of discrimination is that despite considerable improvement, minorities are still seriously underrepresented among elected officials. Furthermore, there appears to be a definite limit to how much more this underrepresentation can improve in the context of present white attitudes, the distribution of voting power, recent legal rulings, and the system by which we elect representatives. Thus, we must conclude that a sizable degree of institutional discrimination (though probably mostly of the nonconscious type) remains in the U.S. political system. Despite the ban against open and deliberate discrimination, the system continues to operate in a way that permits, and in some ways encourages, the continuation of the racial and ethnic inequalities it played a central role in creating.

## ▶ THE AMERICAN LEGAL SYSTEM AND MAJORITY-MINORITY RELATIONS

Closely related to and substantially influenced by the American system of government is the nation's legal system. In the remainder of this chapter, we shall examine the present-day treatment of minority group members by the American legal system. We shall attempt to determine the degree to which the legal system protects the rights of minority group members and also the degree to which it keeps them in a disadvantaged position.

As we have already seen, a number of important decisions by the federal courts in recent decades have declared deliberate discrimination illegal and have thereby worked to protect the rights of minority group members. Of course, it is important to point out that in the past, many decisions of the courts went the other way. Our concern in the remainder of this chapter, though, is different: Here we shall examine the day-to-day operations of our criminal justice and judicial systems to see how they influence the well-being of black, Hispanic, and Indian people on a day-to-day basis. We shall emphasize two areas: first, the criminal justice system and the process by which it accuses, assesses guilt, and assigns punishment, and second, the effectiveness of the police and courts in protecting minority group citizens from crime and illegal exploitation.

## The Criminal Justice System and the Minority Accused

Serious questions have been raised about the U.S. criminal justice system and its treatment of minorities. African Americans are about seven times as likely as whites to be incarcerated, and about one of every four African American men in their twenties is under criminal justice control (Tonry, 1995, p. 4): in prison, in jail, on probation or parole, or awaiting trial. In some large cities, a majority of all black men between eighteen and thirty-five are under criminal justice system control (Tonry, 1995, p. 4). As shown in Figure 11.1, imprisonment is an area where racial inequality has gotten *worse* since the 1980s. By the 1990s, an African American man in his twenties was more likely to be in jail or prison than in college. Because of the widening racial gap in imprisonment and because the proportion of blacks in prison is rising while the proportion of blacks among those arrested is not, there is strong evidence that the criminal justice system has become more biased against blacks. Disproportionate numbers of Hispanics are also imprisoned, and these percentages are rising, too. In part, these patterns represent different types of crimes committed by whites and minorities. Because different types of crime are treated differently by the criminal justice system, outcomes are different for whites and minorities. But these outcomes also represent inequalities that come into play even when the crimes are comparable, for reasons that will be explained in the remainder of this chapter.

There are numerous steps in the criminal justice process. At each of these steps, decisions must be made, and at each step there is the potential for either fair and equal

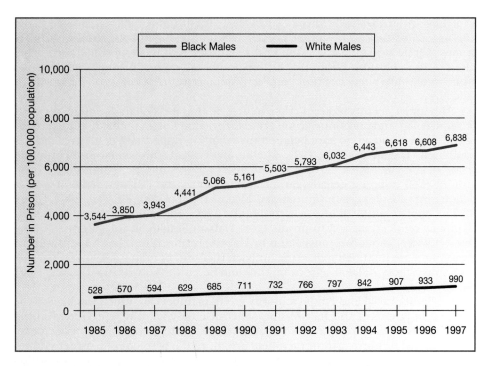

**FIGURE 11.1**    Male Imprisonment Rates (per 100,000 adult population), 1985–1997
*Source:* Bureau of Justice Statistics, (2001b).

treatment under the law or for unfair and discriminatory treatment, whether intentional or not. Among the major steps in the criminal justice process are the following:

1. Detection of a crime
2. Decisions by police to arrest a suspect
3. Setting and administration of bail for the accused person
4. Decision by the police or prosecutor about whether to press charges in court and, if so, in what type of court
5. Decision of the judge, judicial panel, or jury about whether the accused is guilty or innocent
6. Sentencing, that is, a decision about the nature and severity of penalty

**Detection, Public Fear, and Police Priorities.** One cause of unequal justice is that the criminal justice system detects the crimes committed by some kinds of people but fails to detect the crimes committed by others. A look at conventional sources of data on crime, such as the FBI's *Uniform Crime Reports*, quickly confirms that the arrest and conviction rates of minority group members are far above those of whites. Other sources of data, such as criminal victimization surveys and self-report studies, agree that minority group members commit more crime than do whites, although the proportion of minority offenders reported in victimization surveys (around 25 percent black and 9 percent other minority races) is significantly lower than the proportion arrested (almost 38 percent black, for example) (Bureau of Justice Statistics, 2002a, Table 40; Federal Bureau of Investigation, 2002a, Table 43). However, all of these conventional sources of data share one crucial limitation: They focus only on certain kinds of crime. The major crimes in the FBI Crime Index (often called index crimes) include homicide, rape, robbery, assault, larceny, burglary, and auto theft. All are in the so-called "street crime" category. They are disproportionately committed by people of relatively low socioeconomic status, and they are crimes with known and clearly identifiable victims. However, the importance of these and similar crimes may be overstated compared with other crimes that do not appear as often in the statistics, that is, white-collar and corporate crime, including tax fraud, bribery, embezzlement, insider stock trading, antitrust and job safety law violations, and selling products known to be unsafe or defective.

Although the costs of street crime in lives, injury, and dollars are huge, the costs of white-collar and corporate crime are even greater. For example, the dollar costs of consumer fraud alone have been estimated at five times those of all street crimes combined (Hagan, 1985, p. 103). The annual cost of white-collar and corporate crime in the late 1990s has been estimated at more than $339 billion, up from around $200 billion a decade earlier and far above the FBI's estimate of a $3.8-billion cost of street crime (Simon and Eitzen, 1993, p. 290; Reiman, 2004, Chap. 3). The human costs can be great, too. In the 1970s, for example, the A. H. Robins Company reduced its cost to produce the Dalkon Shield, an intrauterine contraceptive device, about five cents a unit by knowingly substituting less expensive, bacteria-conducive multifilament string for bacteria-resistant monofilament string. The result was almost 200,000 serious injuries and at least twenty deaths (Eagan, 1988, pp. 23–30).

Obviously, racial and ethnic minority group members are much less likely to be involved in crimes of this nature simply because they are not represented in the boardrooms where these crimes occur. Because of their relatively low socioeconomic status, minority group members are more likely to commit street crimes; whites, with their higher socioeconomic status, are more likely to commit white-collar and corporate crimes. Because conventional measures of crime focus on street crimes rather than white-collar crimes, they emphasize crimes more likely to be committed by minority group members rather than ones more likely to be committed by whites.

There are a number of reasons for this emphasis. Certainly, the cause lies largely in the economic and political institutions in our society and their supporting ideology. As the dominant economic institution, the corporation exercises tremendous political power (Domhoff, 1967), which gives it substantial influence over the criminal justice system, including the reporting of crime. Societal values and beliefs are strongly influenced by the dominant groups and institutions, and this tends to direct the public's attention toward crimes committed by those from subordinate groups and away from crime in the dominant elements of society (see Quinney, 1979, pp. 41–52; Barlow, 1993, pp. 256–62). Occasionally this changes because of highly publicized corporate crimes such as those that occurred at Enron, Worldcom, and Tyco, but usually the daily reporting in the media of murders, robberies, and carjackings—by far the most frequently covered type of story on local television news (Center for Media and Public Affairs, 1998)—shifts concerns back to street crime and away from corporate crime rather quickly.

Beyond these considerations, the ease of detection plays an important role. When there is a murder, rape, robbery, burglary, or assault, there is usually little or no doubt that a crime has taken place and little or no question of who has been the victim. This is usually not true of white-collar or corporate crime. Although we are all aware that we are continuously paying the cost of these crimes, we usually do not know when and where we have been victimized. For example, if the price of a product is inflated because of price-fixing conspiracies in violation of the antitrust laws, we are usually unaware of it. Illnesses arising from exposure to pollutants encountered in the workplace or the release of dangerous substances into the environment may not be identified as such. Even when employers are the victims of white-collar crime, it often goes undetected. A good example is theft by computer, an increasingly common crime that is very difficult to detect.

Perhaps because of this greater awareness of street crimes, people are generally more afraid of street crimes than they are of white-collar and corporate crimes. They worry more about the possibility of being robbed, shot, or raped than about the possibility of losing money due to insider stock trading, being killed in an automobile that was known to be unsafe, or getting cheated by antitrust law violations. Also street crimes tend to be more sensational. This greater public fear of street crimes puts law-enforcement agencies under more pressure to control them, although this may be changing to some degree. Incidents such as the Love Canal and Times Beach toxic waste disasters and the sale of autos with exploding gasoline tanks may have made the public more aware of the dangers from corporate crime, and corporate scandals such as that at Enron have made people more aware of the economic costs.

Difficulty of detection, combined with political, attitudinal, and ideological influences, has created a situation with important racial and ethnic implications. First, there is a greater public awareness of types of crimes committed disproportionately by minority group members than of crimes committed disproportionately by whites. Because the crimes that people are most afraid of are the ones most likely to be committed by minority group members, a racial dimension is added to the process. The perception that crime is perpetrated by blacks and Hispanics reinforces fears that arise from racial prejudice and lack of experience with members of other racial groups. In the public mind, violent crime often is particularly associated with black men, an image that is reinforced by the sensationalistic manner in which the media often report it. Thus, fears about violent crime have become highly focused on black men, as illustrated by several well-publicized events.

In the 1988 presidential campaign, a man named Willie Horton became the focus of a debate about crime between the major party candidates. Horton was a convict in Massachusetts who had been released from prison under a furlough system much like that of other states. While he was out on furlough, he committed a murder. The Republican candidate, George Bush, attacked the Democratic candidate, Massachusetts governor Michael Dukakis, for being soft on crime and argued that his furlough program proved it. Bush's supporters repeatedly aired an ad showing photos of Horton, a black man. Although this ad was widely criticized for playing on white fears about black crime and for reinforcing stereotypes about black men, these fears and stereotypes were all too real for many whites, and the ad was effective.

The extent of these fears and stereotypes can be seen in another incident in Massachusetts, in 1989, in which a young, white businessman, Chuck Stewart, called police on his car phone and reported that he and his pregnant wife had been shot by a black man in a jogging suit who invaded their car on a Boston street. She died, and he was admitted to the hospital with a gunshot wound. The press widely reported the case as another incident of out-of-control urban crime, and nobody in the media doubted the young white man's story. However, it later came to light that he had murdered his own wife, shot himself to look like an innocent victim, and made up the story about being attacked by a black man because he thought people would find that story believable (Martz, Starr, and Barrett, 1990). He was right.

In 1992 and 1993, two events occurred that dramatically illustrated white fears about black crime. One was the 1992 acquittal of police officers videotaped in the Rodney King beating in Los Angeles. Because of publicity, the trial had been moved to Simi Valley, an overwhelmingly white suburb northwest of Los Angeles. There, a jury with no black members found the police not guilty of beating King. Although a racially mixed jury in Los Angeles later found some of the police officers guilty of federal civil rights violations, the actions of the white jury were widely seen as reflecting the fears of white suburbanites about black and Hispanic crime. To many whites in Simi Valley, the police represented the "thin blue line," protecting them from the crime of the inner city, and their tendency was to give the police every benefit of the doubt.

The same dynamic was at work in Belleville, Illinois, a mostly white St. Louis suburb just east of the nearly all-black city of East St. Louis. Investigations by the local newspaper and by the CBS News program *60 Minutes* in the early 1990s revealed that Belleville's all-white police force, on the orders of its chief, was systematically and selectively stopping cars driven by blacks in the west end of Belleville, the part of the city closest to East St. Louis. Rather than being outraged at the police for engaging in racial discrimination, most Belleville residents turned their anger on the media for exposing the police actions. Hundreds of people canceled their subscriptions to the newspaper and criticized the *60 Minutes* program as unfair, even though the police chief had admitted on the air to a policy of racial profiling. Again, the police were viewed by white suburbanites as the line protecting them from inner-city crime, which they automatically associated with African Americans.

Finally, in 1995, the O. J. Simpson trial focused the nation on racial issues in both crime and criminal justice. It involved an alleged killing of a white woman by a black man, historically the type of crime most feared and most harshly punished by whites. It reinforced the same image of black men that had been driven home by the Willie Horton ads and, in most areas, by repeated sensationalized reports on local TV news of violent acts by African American men. It also involved a white police officer, Mark Fuhrman, who was discovered to have used a racial slur and then lied about it. To African Americans, this brought to mind the much feared and resented image of racist and dishonest police. In this context, it is not surprising that this case was viewed in diametrically opposite ways by white and black Americans and that it brought to light deep racial tensions that had long been simmering just below the surface.

Incidents such as these illustrate the extent to which public fear and concern about crime focus on street crime and, in particular, on street crime committed by blacks and, in some parts of the country, Hispanics. This image of crime has become so strong that several observers argue that the crime issue has become racialized and politicized (Monteiro, 1994). In this view, the racialization of the crime issue has defined blacks in the (white) public mind in a way that undermines support for equal opportunity. Rather than seeing African Americans or Hispanics as groups that have been mistreated, the white public has been taught to view them as a threat. Consequently, federal legislation gradually shifted from civil rights laws in the 1960s to "get tough on crime" laws in the 1980s and 1990s: minimum sentences, increased use of the death penalty, the "war on drugs," and "three-strikes" legislation. Tonry (1995) argues that the war on drugs is a perfect example: Although surveys show that whites are more likely than blacks to have used every illegal drug except heroin, blacks are arrested and imprisoned for drugs at rates many times their share of the population. Much of this is a recent phenomenon; as the war on drugs began during the 1980s (a time when drug use was already falling), the rate of drug arrests among whites remained flat, whereas for blacks it more than doubled. Thus, the war on drugs was really a war on blacks who used or sold drugs; whites who did the same thing were pretty much left alone. Among youths, white drug arrest rates actually declined, whereas black drug arrest rates again more than doubled. These trends probably are the main reason why the proportion of blacks in prison has risen relative to that of whites.

Street crime, including drug-induced crime, committed by blacks and Hispanics is nonetheless a serious problem, and it has undoubtedly been worsened by the concentration of black and Hispanic poverty (W. J. Wilson, 1987, 1996). In fact, this concentration of poverty undoubtedly explains much of the reason why minority rates of street crime are so high: The concentration of poverty increases its effects, including exposure to crime. Consider these statistics: Among people who were young adults in the 1990s, *half* of all African Americans had experienced at least four years of poverty during childhood; only one white in twelve had experienced this much poverty. And when whites and blacks are poor, there is an important difference in the experience: Black and Hispanic poor people are a good deal more likely to live in neighborhoods where many of their neighbors are poor than are white poor people. Although the trend of increasing concentration of poverty in the 1970s and 1980s appears to have reversed in the 1990s, racial differences in the likelihood of a poor person living in a neighborhood with a high poverty rate have persisted (Kingsley and Pettit, 2003, Table 3). Given these differences, who do you think will be more likely to live in situations with pressures and opportunities to commit street crimes?

Still, street crime is just one part of the overall crime problem, and the statistics on white-collar and corporate crime show that it is not even the biggest part. It is important to emphasize that non-Hispanic whites are not the usual targets of crimes committed by blacks or Hispanics; in most crimes, the victim is of the same race as the offender. However, white fears about crime are heavily focused on street crime committed by minorities, and these fears have a strong influence on what is expected and demanded of the police. Moreover, it is easier to detect and solve the street crimes that are disproportionately committed by minorities than the white-collar and corporate crimes that are disproportionately committed by whites. Police are rewarded for solved crimes, whereas there is no reward and possible criticism and rebuke for unsolved crimes. As a result, more police effort is devoted to street crimes.

Class differences also influence the likelihood that crime will be detected. Such activities as drug violations and drunkenness are more likely to come to the attention of police when committed by the poor because they are more likely to occur in public settings. Surveys show that overall, whites are more likely to use illegal drugs than blacks or Hispanics (Office of Applied Studies, 2001, Table 1.26b; National Institute on Drug Abuse, 1989, 2003), but a disproportionate number of people arrested for drug violations are black and Hispanic, and as noted, this disproportionality increased when the drug war began in the 1980s.

One reason for this overrepresentation may be that blacks are more likely to use riskier drugs such as heroin and crack cocaine, which attract greater police attention. Another reason, however, is that because of their higher poverty rate, they are more likely to lack the access to private space that protects drug use by the middle and upper classes from easy detection. For example, Tonry (1995) points out that in the highest-poverty (and most disproportionately minority) neighborhoods, drug selling is likely to occur on the street, whereas everywhere else it is more likely to occur behind closed doors. Also, drug deals involving strangers are more likely to occur in such neighborhoods, whereas in working-class and middle-class neighborhoods, drug deals are more likely to occur between people who already know each other. Thus it is much easier for undercover agents to catch people in the high-poverty, minority neighborhoods, and they tend to concentrate their efforts where it is easiest to make an arrest. For example, studies of marijuana arrests in the Chicago area have shown that blacks are two to four times as likely to be arrested for marijuana violations as whites (National Commission on Marihuana and Drug Abuse, 1972; Johnson, Peterson, and Wells, 1977). Nationally in 1995, blacks were more than 2.5 times as likely as whites to be arrested for marijuana possession (Gettman, 2000). Another example can be seen in arrests for drunkenness, a condition that by itself usually gets one in legal trouble only if it occurs in public. A study by J. Q. Wilson (1978) found that blacks were two to three times as likely as whites to be arrested for drunkenness. Again, racial differences in alcohol abuse rates are not large, but because of higher poverty rates, blacks are more likely to be drunk in public, which explains their higher arrest rates. Another reason appears to be a tendency in many cities for police to view black drunks, but not white drunks, as homeless or derelict (J. Q. Wilson, 1978, p. 160).

**Racial Profiling, Decision to Arrest, and Police-Minority Relations.** One of the most critical stages of the criminal justice process is the police officer's decision about whether to make an arrest when an illegal act is suspected. Unfortunately, this is also one of the most poorly understood stages of the process because it is one of the most difficult to study. Clearly, the police can and do exercise considerable discretion in making these decisions (Mann, 1993). They cannot and do not arrest every person they suspect of committing an illegal act (Goldstein, 1960; La Fave, 1965; Kadish and Kadish, 1973).

Apparently, *police expectations* concerning the behavior and motivations of suspects heavily influence their decision on whether or not to make an arrest. Such expectations are shaped by two major factors: First, there are beliefs about the kinds of people who may commit crimes and about how citizens should behave toward the police. Social class, race and ethnicity, age, dress, and appearance influence these judgments. Police officers will "find" and "solve" more crime among groups they are suspicious of, for example, at least partly because they investigate more closely the activities of people in these groups. Thus, if the police are generally suspicious of a particular racial or ethnic group, they will be more likely to investigate, stop, or arrest its members. And research shows that, even as students in the police academy, police believe that African Americans are more likely than other groups to commit crimes (McMorris, 2002).

It is quite clear that police officers stop and investigate people of color on the streets more than they stop whites (Moss, 1990; Barlow, 1993, pp. 358–61). This is evident from personal interviews (Roddy, 1990; Feagin, 1991; Feagin and Sikes, 1994, pp. 64–71), from surveys (Bureau of Justice Statistics, 2001a), and from testing studies in which black and white testers have received different treatment from the police on public streets and highways (ABC News, 1991). Compilations of data on stops by state police also strongly suggest that officers are selectively stopping minority group members. For example, in a stretch of I-95 in Maryland where 17 percent of the drivers are black, 70 percent of those stopped by the state police from 1995–1997 were black (Barovick, 1998). (Supposedly this stretch of highway was an area of concentrated drug enforcement, but the percentage of motorists actually caught with drugs was about the same for blacks and whites.) The practice of **racial profiling**, or stopping and questioning people on the basis of their race, has led critics to accuse police of stopping people for "driving while black." It appears that Latinos/as may also encounter similar practices. In Illinois, a study by the American Civil Liberties Union found that on highways in southwest Illinois, more than 14 percent of the drivers stopped by the state police between the mid-1980s and mid-1990s had Hispanic names, even though only 2 percent of the drivers in that area were Hispanic (McDermott, 1999). As mentioned, one police chief admitted on national television that he had instructed his officers to stop all cars with two or more African Americans in them in certain parts of town. Significantly, this chief was in Belleville, Illinois, a majority-white community adjacent to the mostly black community of East St. Louis. According to Mann (1993, p. 144), police officers are most likely to stop and question minorities, even if they do not do anything suspicious, where police perceive them to be "off their turf."

In fact, it appears that "by the time they are in their twenties, most black males, regardless of socioeconomic status, have been stopped by the police because 'blackness' is considered a sign of possible criminality by police officers" (Feagin, 1991, p. 113). In one recent survey, 40 percent of black adults and more than 70 percent of black men between 18 and 34 replied "yes" to a question about whether they had ever been stopped by police "just because of your race" (Weitzer and Tuch, 2002). This is quite different from the experiences of whites because police officers view blacks and other minorities as potential criminals, stop them more, and investigate them more. As a result of this greater attention, police often manage to find some violation that becomes the basis for an arrest. This is partly because, even in areas where police do not *stop* minorities disproportionately, they may *search* them disproportionately (Petrocelli, Piquero, and Smith, 2003). In response to criticisms of racial profiling, more states and localities are now requiring police to record the race of everyone they stop. It is too early to tell what the impact of this will be on the amount of racial profiling.

Police expectations about citizens are also influenced by the demeanor and behavior of the citizens themselves toward the police. In one study (Piliavin and Briar, 1964), police officers reported that in juvenile cases, the demeanor of the suspect was the main factor in determining how they handled the situation in 50 to 60 percent of their cases. This is consistent with recent research findings by Lundman (1996), who reports that demeanor is indeed a factor in whether or not police officers make arrests, although there are also effects of race above and beyond differences in demeanor. Of course, citizens' demeanor toward the police is shaped by their perceptions of the police: Citizens who do not trust the police are more likely to behave in a negative manner toward them.

Unfortunately, racial, ethnic, and class factors can affect the ways in which both police and citizens perceive one another. Police officers do often have prejudiced or stereotypical attitudes and beliefs about minority group members (Black and Reiss, 1967, pp. 132–39). However, one should not be too quick to place all the blame on the individual police officers. The structure of the situation in which they must operate probably tends to make them prejudiced: The crimes they can most readily detect and are expected to detect are mainly street crimes, which are disproportionately committed by the poor and by members of racial and ethnic minority groups. This leads to a situation in which a "criminal stereotype" of certain class and ethnic groups easily develops.

Despite some recent improvement, minority groups remain underrepresented on police forces. As suggested by this photo, greater diversity on police forces might improve perceptions of the police in African American and Latino/a communities.

The situation is worsened by the fact that minority groups are substantially underrepresented on many police forces in the United States, although in recent years court orders and increased minority voting power have begun to change that. Black and Hispanic representation on police forces has increased significantly in many cities. Among all cities with populations of 250,000 or more, police forces in 2000 were 20.1 percent African American and 14.1 percent Latino/a (Bureau of Justice Statistics, 2002b, Table 3). However, these numbers in nearly all cases are well below the minority percentage of the city's population because as the minority proportion on police forces has risen, the minority percentage of the city's population also has risen. Although police forces became slightly more representative of the populations of cities they patrol between 1990 and 2000, significant gaps remain. Overall, big-city police forces had 63 percent of the number of minorities that would have been expected based on their populations. African Americans fared a little better, with about three-fourths the number of black police officers that would be expected based on the city's African American population. On the other hand, Hispanics were barely more than half the expected number of officers, and Asian Americans and American Indians were even scarcer (Bureau of Justice Statistics, 2002b).

Race and ethnicity also influence the ways in which citizens view the police. National surveys from the 1970s through 1990s show that minorities have a much less positive perception of the police than whites (Ackerman et al., 2001; see also Parisi et al., 1979). These data are presented in Table 11.2. Blacks are substantially more likely than whites to express dissatisfaction about inadequate patrol of or investigations in their neighborhoods, a lack of promptness, courtesy, and concern, and discrimination. After a series of qualitative interviews with African Americans, sociologist Joe Feagin (1991, p. 113) concluded, "It seems likely that most black men—including middle-class black men—see white police officers as a major source of danger and death." Notably, this was written *before* the Rodney King beating and before a 1992 incident in which a black man was beaten to death by white police officers in Detroit.

### Table 11.2  Opinions of Police Honesty and Ethics, 1977, 1985, and 1995

| Year | | Very High or High | Low or Average | Very Low | No Opinion |
|------|--|-------------------|----------------|----------|------------|
| 1977 | Whites | 38% | 50% | 11% | 1% |
|      | Minorities | 34 | 44 | 21 | 1 |
| 1985 | Whites | 48 | 41 | 9 | 2 |
|      | Minorities | 35 | 42 | 22 | 1 |
| 1995 | Whites | 44 | 44 | 11 | 1 |
|      | Minorities | 25 | 41 | 32 | 2 |

*Source:* Ackerman et al. (2001, p. 51).

There are a number of reasons for these dissatisfactions. Minority group members are well aware of the stereotyping and prejudice among the police, and many have apparently experienced discourtesy or excessive use of force. Accordingly, some minority group members tend to counterstereotype the police. This may lead to a mutual **self-fulfilling prophecy**: The white police officer and the black or Hispanic citizen, each expecting the worst of the other, speak or behave in some negative way toward each other. This "confirms" the other's beliefs, "proving" the correctness of the stereotype (Kuykendall, 1970). Given this mutual distrust, it is easy to see how encounters between white police and minority citizens can escalate into confrontations that lead to arrest (for further discussion, see Bayley and Mendelsohn, 1968, pp. 162–66; Black, 1970). Mann (1993, p. 144) put it this way:

> By the 1960s and 1970s, black hostility and lack of cooperation had become so great that it influenced the decisions of narcotics police with regard to . . . where they would work and whom they would arrest. In other words, demeanor that resulted from violation of arrestees' rights and admitted police brutality had become an influential factor in law enforcement.

Another factor that creates hostility is the role of police as agents of control during minority protests. Regardless of the target of the protest, it is the police who must control it, and this frequently places them in an adversarial position to groups that are seeking change through protest. Because of this role, the police have become protectors of the status quo (Quinney, 1979, pp. 265–69), as indeed has the entire criminal justice system (Balbus, 1973). In addition, police officers often overreact or treat people of different groups differently in situations of social unrest. We have already mentioned the tendency of police to arrest minorities but leave whites alone in the racial clashes of the 1910s and 1940s. In the riots of the 1960s, most of those killed died as a result of police action, often including indiscriminate firing into buildings. For example, Conot's (1967) study of the 1964 Los Angeles riots showed that most of the people killed were black, were killed by police, and were unarmed. Such situations surely create considerable hostility. Research on riots in Miami in the 1980s and in Los Angeles in 1992 shows that fewer of the deaths in these riots were caused by police actions, indicating that the police may have learned some lessons from the riots of the 1960s (McPhail, 1994). However, it is also notable that the Miami and Los Angeles riots, like many of the riots of the 1960s, were precipitated by incidents between the police and citizens: specifically, the acquittal of police officers who had been involved in violence against black citizens. It is significant that hostility toward the police has been observed not only among minorities but among other groups seeking social change, including labor unionists in the 1930s and student and antiwar protesters in the 1960s.

Experiences that people and their friends and family have had with police officers are the best predictor of minority attitudes toward them (Scaglion and Condon, 1980). In this study, minority group members were asked to describe their actual personal experiences in encounters with the police. When they reported positive experiences, they had positive attitudes; when their experiences had been bad, their attitudes were more negative. Both this study and others (such as Browning et al., 1994) have found that minorities report high rates of bad personal experiences with the police. Weitzer and Tuch (2002) found that experience with racial profiling was one of the strongest predictors of attitudes toward the police, as well as of beliefs about the amount of racial profiling that occurs.

The processes just described apparently do lead to disproportionate arrest rates for minorities. An observational study of twenty-four police departments in three metropolitan areas by Smith and Visher (1981) found that routine encounters between police officers and citizens led to arrests of minority group members more often than of whites, even adjusting for the seriousness of the crime and the presence or absence of hostile behavior toward the police. In crimes with victims or complainants, the race of the complainant also made a difference: When the complainant was white, an arrest was more likely (Smith, Visher, and Davidson, 1984). Similar evidence comes from research by Bachman (1996), who found that in robberies and assaults of strangers in which the victim was white and the alleged assailant black, police exerted more effort at the scene than in cases of other racial combinations of victim and assailant. There is some evidence that class plays a role in the arrest process, too, and this has some racial effect. Research by Sherman (1980) and Hollinger (1984) found that people of lower socioeconomic status were more likely to be arrested in similar situations, regardless of race. However, because the average socioeconomic status of minority groups is lower, these findings mean that they are more likely to be arrested (Mann, 1993, p. 147).

Surveys comparing self-reported juvenile delinquency with police arrest rates also indicate disproportionate arrests of blacks and Hispanics, although if the data are controlled for the frequency and severity of crime, the difference decreases (Elliott and Ageton, 1980). As noted earlier, the percentage of African Americans among people arrested for violent crimes is significantly higher than the percentage of offenders who are reported in victimization surveys to have been black (Bureau of Justice Statistics, 2002a, Table 40; Federal Bureau of Investigation, 2002a, Table 43). This strongly suggests that blacks are arrested in numbers out of proportion to the number of crimes they commit. Also remember that whereas blacks and Hispanics are disproportionately likely to commit these street crimes, whites, because of their middle-class status, are more likely to commit white-collar crimes, which lead to arrest less often. In general, minorities are more likely to be arrested in part because they are more likely to commit street crimes, in part because they are arrested out of proportion to the amount of such crime they commit, and in part because their crimes are less likely to be the corporate and white-collar crimes that rarely lead to arrests.

**Bail.** Potential for unequal treatment also exists in the setting and administration of bail. The purpose of bail is to guarantee that an accused person who has been released from jail will show up for his or her trial. It is a sum of money held by the court to ensure appearance for trial. Once the defendant appears, the money is returned; if he or she does not appear, the court keeps the bail. In some states, the law permits private bail bonders to collect fees of 10 to 20 percent of the bail amount. In others, the defendant may be permitted to put up 10 percent of the bail amount. Either way, many see bail as a form of economic discrimination: The wealthier the accused person is, the more likely he or she is to be able to afford the bail. Studies have shown that depending on the crime, the locality, and the amount of bail, the proportion of people unable to afford bail can range from 25 to 90 percent of the suspects (Foote, 1958; Silverstein, 1966; Bureau of Justice Statistics, 1991). Because black, Hispanic, and Indian people have lower incomes than whites, these groups probably are overrepresented among those who cannot make bail. This becomes more significant when one considers research showing that when defendants were given supervised pretrial release without bail, the overwhelming majority did not flee and were not rearrested. Three-quarters of the defendants in this study were minorities (Austin, Krisberg, and Litsky, 1985).

As Barlow (1993, pp. 399–400) notes, numerous factors besides the likelihood that a defendant will fail to appear (the basic legal consideration) influence the setting of bail. At one time, deliberate abuse of bail to control and oppress minorities was common in some parts of the country. A study by the U.S. Commission on Civil Rights (1970a, pp. 48–52) illustrates this. Bail was sometimes used to harass Mexican Americans by keeping them in jail over the weekend. In one case, a group of Chicano students and a teacher were arrested on a Friday night, with bail set at $1,200 each. On Monday, the bail was lowered to $500 and eventually changed again to permit release on personal recognizance (no bail required). Similar tactics were used in Texas against United Farm Workers union organizers. In many cases, the bail set was much greater than the maximum fine for the violations the organizers were accused of. The following passage from the Civil Rights Commission report indicates that the violations sometimes went far beyond mere harassment:

> Mr. Trujillo [an investigator for the Alamosa, County, Colorado District Attorney's Office] disclosed another and more serious problem resembling involuntary servitude or peonage [both of which are forbidden by federal law under a penalty of fine up to $5,000, up to five years' imprisonment, or both]. He stated that during the harvest season local farmers would go to the jails in the towns of Center and Monte Vista, Colorado, on Monday mornings and inquire about the number of Mexican American laborers arrested over the weekend. The farmers would select the best workers and pay their fines for them. Upon their release, the men would have to repay the farmer by working for him. According to Trujillo, in Monte Vista the men were told by the police magistrate that if they did not remain on the farm and work off the amount owed to the farmer, they would be returned to jail. In addition, he said, the police magistrate would sometimes give the farmer a "discount." If the fine was set at $40, he would only require the farmer to pay $25. The magistrate, however, would tell the worker that the fine paid by the farmer was $40 and that he owed the farmer $40 worth of work. According to Mr. Trujillo, once the worker was released from jail, he usually was at the mercy of the farmer and often was ill-treated while on the farm. The chief of police and a patrolman in Center, and the police magistrate in Monte Vista confirmed the fact that workers are bailed out of jail or have their fines paid by local farmers and are obligated to work off the ensuing debt.

Another study (U.S. Commission on Civil Rights, 1965) showed that bail was also used to harass black civil rights workers in the South during the 1960s. Discrimination in bail is not always so blatant, however. Often, such factors as property ownership, employment, and middle-class status come into play. Korfhage (1972) found that in Seattle whites were more likely than either blacks or Indians to be released on personal recognizance when charged with misdemeanors. In another study of a large western city, Bynum (1982) found the same. More recent data demonstrate that such inequalities continue to occur. A national study of more than 5,600 male felony defendants by Albonetti et al. (1989) showed that even after control for legally relevant factors, white defendants fared better in bail decisions than black defendants. Gottfredson and Jarjoura (1996) found evidence of racial bias in bail decisions in Marion County, Indiana. In part, racial differences in bail did reflect differences in risk, but in part they also reflected bias. Finally, a recent national study showed that Hispanics were less likely than either whites or blacks to be released before trial, even after controls for relevant legal factors (Demuth, 2001).

Both because it inherently discriminates on the basis of income and has at times been used in a discriminatory way, it seems fair to conclude that the bail system has generally served the interests of the white accused better than it has served the interests of black, Chicano, and Indian people accused of illegal behavior.

**Prosecution and Conviction.** Another step that has great potential for discrimination is the decision of whether or not to prosecute or refer a case to the court system. These decisions are influenced by the police, by district attorneys or prosecutors, and, when applicable, by juvenile delinquency officials and probation officers. At this stage in the process, there seems to be significant discrimination in some places but little or none in others. Moore and Roesti (1980) found no effect of race on the frequency with which juvenile offenders in Peoria, Illinois, were referred to the court system, and Terry (1967) obtained similar findings with data from Racine, Wisconsin. Similar findings were also obtained in a study by Fagan, Forst, and Vivona (1987) of decisions to prosecute juveniles as adults. On the other hand, evidence that blacks accused of crimes are referred to the courts more often than whites has been found in a medium-sized southern city (W. R. Arnold, 1971), in Philadelphia (Thornberry, 1974), in New Jersey (Dannefer and Schutt, 1982), and in a medium-sized northern city (Ferdinand and Luchterhand, 1970). A review of seventeen studies by Liska and Tansig (1979) reveals that a number, though not all, found evidence of racial bias in the decision to prosecute. Recent passage of "habitual offender" legislation may have aggravated racial inequalities in prosecution; a study in Florida found that when offenders were eligible for such treatment, blacks were more likely than whites to be prosecuted and convicted as habitual offenders (which leads to a much harsher sentence). This was especially true for drug violations and for property crimes with high victimization rates for whites (Crawford, Chiricos, and Kleck, 1998). Although racial inequality in prosecution is not a problem in every part of the country, it does exist in many areas, North and South, and therefore must be seen as a fairly widespread problem.

Interestingly, one study in California (Petersilia, 1983) found the opposite result: Blacks and Hispanics were less likely than whites to be forwarded to the courts by the prosecutor. The apparent reason is that prosecutors have a harder time building a case against minority arrestees than white arrestees. Similarly, Holmes, Daudistel, and Farrell (1987) found that in two counties in Arizona and Pennsylvania, minorities were less likely to be convicted and more likely to have their charges reduced. As in the California study, the apparent reason was initial overcharging of minority as compared with white arrestees. Demuth (2001) obtained similar findings for African Americans in a recent national study.

Racial inequality also sometimes occurs in judgments of guilt or innocence, although it may be less common than bias in the decision to prosecute (Dannefer and Schutt, 1982). Bias in conviction decisions may be especially likely when they are made by juries rather than by judges (Bahr, Chadwick, and Strauss, 1979, pp. 393–94; see also Holmes and Daudistel, 1984). Underrepresentation of minorities on juries is a major cause of the problem and a major complaint of minority group members about the criminal justice system. All-white juries, the conviction of a prominent black educator, and the acquittal or nonfiling of charges in several cases of police violence against blacks were precipitating issues in the 1980 Miami riots that took fifteen lives. Similarly, the acquittal of police officers in the Rodney King beating case by a jury with no black members was the precipitating factor in the worst riot of the twentieth century. The Los Angeles riot that followed the acquittal in May 1992 took more than fifty lives.

Studies of jury composition show that minority group members are underrepresented in juries throughout the United States (Overby, 1972, pp. 268–70; Fukurai, Butler, and Krooth, 1991a). In Seattle, for example, juries are 89 percent white, compared with 75 percent of the population; in Montgomery, Alabama, they are 78 percent white, compared with 59 percent of the population; and in Dallas, they are 77 percent white, compared with 55 percent of the population (Monagle, 1992). One reason for the exclusion of minorities is that they often encounter socioeconomic barriers to jury participation because on the average their incomes are lower and their jobs are less flexible. Other reasons include jury selection criteria that exclude minorities and the combined effects of housing segregation and the ways in which boundaries of court districts are drawn (Fukurai, Butler, and Krooth, 1991a, 1991b). At one time, it was common for lawyers to use peremptory challenges to exclude people from juries on the basis of their race, but this practice was struck down by a series of Supreme Court rulings beginning in 1986. Nonetheless, it can be hard to prove a racial motivation in a lawyer's challenge to a potential juror, even if such a motivation is there.

**Sentencing.** Probably the most widely studied aspect of the criminal justice process, as far as majority-minority inequality is concerned, is sentencing. Do black, Hispanic, and Native Americans receive longer or more severe sentences than whites in comparable circumstances? In many areas, they do. A recent study of sentencing in the Chicago, Kansas City, and Miami areas found that both blacks and Hispanics were more likely to get prison sentences than comparable whites in Chicago, and the same was true for Hispanics but not blacks in Miami, but there was no difference in Kansas City (Spohn and DeLone, 2000). The studies by W. R. Arnold (1971) and Thornberry (1974) discussed in the previous section also show black-white inequality in the sentencing of juvenile offenders. Black-white sentencing inequality was found by Thomson and Zingraff (1978, 1981) in Florida in 1977 and in North Carolina for assault and armed robbery in 1969 and 1977. Petersilla (1983) found that blacks and Hispanics received more severe sentences than whites in California, Texas, and Michigan. Hall and Simkus (1975) found more severe sentencing of American Indians than of whites in a western state. All of these studies show that the sentencing of minorities was still disproportionately severe after controls for such factors as the seriousness of the crime and past criminal record.

In some areas, though, there is little evidence of discrimination (Welch, Gruhl, and Spohn, 1984). Hindelang's (1969) literature review and research by Humphrey and Fogarty (1987) suggest that the problem is more widespread in the South than in the North. Hagan (1974) reviewed seventeen studies published before 1974 (including some cited earlier) and found that although some showed racial effects on sentencing after control for other relevant factors, the effect in most cases was quite small. A recent study of juvenile decisions in Atlanta obtained similar findings (Ruback and Vardaman, 1997).

Other studies, including some in northern cities, have revealed larger effects. A study by Grams and Rohde (1976) in Minneapolis is especially striking. This study found that among 3,390 convicted felons between 1973 and 1975, blacks and American Indians were twice as likely as whites to receive straight jail sentences as opposed to some form of reduced sentence, even after control for type of crime, criminal record, education, and occupation. One reason is that minorities lacked the money for private attorneys, relying instead on court-appointed public defenders (see also S. Nagel, 1969). Grams and Rohde found that Minneapolis blacks and Indians were three times as likely to get jail sentences when they were represented by public defenders rather than private attorneys. Similarly, in Detroit, the Saul R. Leven Memorial Foundation (1959) found that defendants with court-appointed attorneys were twice as likely as others to get prison sentences. However, the Minneapolis study produced an even more disturbing finding: *Blacks and American Indians represented by public defenders were four times as likely to get straight jail sentences as whites represented by public defenders.* Thus, minorities with public defenders apparently received less effective representation than did whites.

The likelihood of racial inequities in sentencing depends in part on whether the evidence and circumstances in the case are clear-cut or ambiguous, as illustrated by a study of convicted drug offenders in Miami by Unnever and Hembroff (1988). When legally relevant or case-related attributes all point to probation or they all point to imprisonment, similar decisions are made for whites and minorities. However, when the case-related attributes are inconsistent, racial or ethnic inequities are likely to occur.

Although many studies indicate racial discrimination in sentencing, some find no discrimination after controls for legally relevant factors such as past records (Kleck, 1985). There is variation from place to place and from time to time in the extent of discrimination. As we have already seen, some studies suggest greater racial inequity in sentencing decisions in the South than elsewhere (Chiricos and Crawford, 1995). Some studies also find harsher sentencing of minorities where they are a larger part of the population (Chiricos and Crawford, 1995). Also, it appears that the trend toward determinate sentencing—that is, fixed rules about the penalties that reduce the discretion of judges to decide how severely a convicted defendant should be sentenced—may have initially reduced racial disparities in sentencing, but with today's emphasis on toughness and mandatory minimum sentencing, disparities are increasing. When Petersilla (1983) studied sentencing disparities before California adopted determinate sentencing, she found evidence of racial inequities. However, when Klein, Petersilla, and Turner (1990) studied sentencing after implementation of the California Determinate Sentencing Act, they found that sentencing decisions were racially equitable after controlling for relevant legal factors such as past criminal records. More recent studies suggest that the recent emphasis on toughness may have changed this, however.

### Minimum Sentencing and the "War on Drugs": A War on Minorities?

A comprehensive study of sentencing in Pennsylvania by Ulmer and Kramer (1996) found that race did have a significant effect on whether or not convicted criminals were sentenced to jail or prison instead of probation and on whether they were sentenced to prison (a much harsher result in Pennsylvania than a jail sentence). This remained true even after controlling for a wide variety of factors that could have been legally relevant, including a detailed prior record scale and detailed data on severity, type, and number of charges involved in the offense. Although it is true that Pennsylvania's determinate sentencing law allows more discretion than those of other states, it does show that attempting to "rationalize" the criminal justice process does not eliminate unfairness. And when it is combined with efforts to "get tough," it may have the opposite effect.

Free (1997) points out that the imposition of mandatory minimum sentences under federal law has widened the racial gap in sentencing. Blacks are more likely than whites to be convicted under these minimum provisions and more likely to be sentenced at or above such minimums. In part, this is because the penalty for crack cocaine (more often used by blacks) is more severe than the penalty for powder cocaine (more often used by whites). Similarly, Schiraldi (1995) found that under California's "three strikes" legislation, which mandates a twenty-five–year sentence for a third felony offense, blacks were accused of a third strike at a rate seventeen times as high as whites in the Los Angeles area.

Also relevant are studies showing that the passage of more punitive minimum sentencing laws has been correlated to states' minority populations (McGarrell, 1993). Specifically, the larger a state's African American population, the harsher the law and the larger the percentage of the population that is imprisoned. This remains true even after controlling for the crime rate and for whether or not the state is located in the South (McGarrell, 1993). These findings are consistent with the ideas that crime has been made into a racial issue and that the war on drugs was largely racial in its motivation and especially in its consequences. The extent to which this is true can be seen in a recent study showing that blacks are incarcerated for drug violations at a rate *seventeen times that of non-Hispanic whites,* and Hispanics at a rate *eight times that of non-Hispanic whites* (Brownsberger, 2000). This is despite the fact that, as noted earlier, national data show whites are more likely to use illegal drugs than either blacks or Hispanics. The result is that whereas about 70 percent of drug *users* are non-Hispanic whites, 78 percent of the people *imprisoned* for drug use are African American or Hispanic (Office of Applied Studies, 2001, Table 1.26b; Brownsberger, 2000).

**Victim's Race and Sentencing.** The race of the victim, as well as that of the offender, often influences severity of sentence. One would hope that things have changed since the early 1960s, when a southern police officer told a writer, "In this town there are three classes of homicide. If a nigger kills a white man, that's murder. If a white man kills a nigger, that's justifiable homicide. If a nigger kills a nigger, that's one less nigger" (Banton, 1964, p. 173). Studies in Virginia and North Carolina (G. B. Johnson, 1941; Garfinkel, 1949) seem to confirm that many criminal justice officials took this view, and blacks accused of killing whites got the death sentence or life imprisonment about half the time, whereas whites accused of killing blacks never did.

The problem is not entirely one of the past, however. A study of sentencing in Philadelphia by Zimring, Eigen, and O'Malley (1976) found that blacks who killed whites were twice as likely to receive life imprisonment or death sentences as were blacks who killed other blacks. A study of homicide cases in Florida from 1973 to 1977 found the most severe treatment of cases occurred when blacks killed whites, and the least severe treatment occurred when blacks killed other blacks (Radelet and Pierce, 1985). Research by Paternoster (1983) in South Carolina produced similar results, indicating that (1) interracial murders were more likely to be treated as capital murders (eligible for death penalty) and to lead to death sentences than same-race murders, and (2) both whites and blacks were more likely to be charged with capital murder and to be given the death sentence when they killed whites than when they killed blacks. Capital murder charges and the imposition of the death penalty were most likely when a black killed a white, next most likely when a white killed a black, somewhat less likely when a white killed a white, and least likely when a black killed a black. Subsequent studies have obtained similar findings in Arizona (Thomson, 1997), Kentucky (Keil and Vito, 1995), Louisiana (M. D. Smith, 1987), New Jersey (Bienen, 1987), and a group of eight states in the Midwest and South (Gross and Mauro, 1989). The Arizona study found a similar pattern for whites and Hispanics (Thomson, 1997).

In fact, the evidence that the race of the victim makes a difference in homicide sentencing is so strong that the U.S. Supreme Court in 1986 agreed to hear a case arguing against the death penalty on the grounds that it is applied more often to people who kill whites than to people who kill blacks. By a five-to-four vote, however, the Court ruled in 1987 that overall patterns of bias in the application of the death sentence were not sufficient cause to overturn a death sentence in any given case. Nonetheless, in 2002, when he commuted all death sentences in the state of Illinois, Governor George Ryan stated,

> "In fact the most glaring weakness is that no matter how efficient and fair the death penalty may seem in theory, in actual practice it is primarily inflicted upon the weak, the poor, the ignorant and against racial

minorities." That was a quote from former California Governor Pat Brown. He wrote that in his book—"Public Justice, Private Mercy." He wrote that nearly 50 years ago—nothing has changed in nearly 50 years. . . . Of the more than 160 death row inmates, 35 were African American defendants who had been convicted or condemned to die by all-white juries. More than two-thirds of the inmates on death row were African American. (SFGate.com, 2004)

Studies also indicate that for types of crime that are often interracial, such as larceny and armed robbery, there is greater racial inequality in sentencing than for typically same-race crimes such as assault (Nagel, 1969; Thomson and Zingraff, 1978; Crawford, Ciricos, and Kleck, 1998).

A final source of inequality in sentencing is related to the different types of offenses committed by majority and minority group members. White-collar offenses, committed by the predominantly white middle and upper classes, are almost always prosecuted in *civil* court. Street crime usually is prosecuted in *criminal* court. This is a very important difference because only criminal court can put a person in prison, and only criminal court can give a person a record that labels him or her for life. The fact that white-collar and corporate offenders usually are white, whereas street offenders are more often black, Hispanic, or American Indian, is another source of racial inequality in the definition and punishment of crime.

## Conclusion

At each step of the criminal justice process, biases against blacks, Hispanics, and American Indians appear to occur in some situations but not others. The type of crime, whether the accused is an adult or juvenile, locality, and the particulars of judicial procedure in a given case all appear to make a difference. Despite this variation, there is enough bias in enough places at each step of the process that even though the effect at any step may be small or none, the cumulative effect over the entire course of the criminal justice process can be substantial (Thomson and Zingraff, 1981). Research by Blumstein (1982, 1993) compared the proportion of blacks in prison to the proportion arrested. If arrests were equally valid and if the criminal justice system were unbiased after arrest, one would expect that the percentage of blacks in prison would mirror the percentage arrested. It did not; rather, it was 20 percent to 25 percent higher, and this was *before* the "war on drugs" and fixed sentencing made racial inequalities even greater.

One could argue that this reflects a tendency of blacks to commit more serious crime, but this is easily tested by comparing the rates for particular crimes. When this is done, the proportion of blacks among arrestees and prisoners is similar for the most serious crimes: homicide, aggravated assault, and, to a lesser extent, robbery. But for all other crimes (which account for the majority of prisoners), blacks are a *much* higher percentage of prisoners than they are of arrestees. This suggests a sizable cumulative effect of biases after arrest, even though the bias may be neither large nor pervasive at any given point in the process. In fact, some studies have found that the population of accused is quite racially mixed at the point of arrest but that the proportion of minority group members rises substantially as one moves through the criminal justice process to the imprisoned population (Liska and Tansig, 1979). As we have seen, for some kinds of offenses, such as illegal drug use, the racial mix of the prison population is not even close to that of offenders.

The effects of this bias can go far beyond the criminal justice system itself because of the labeling process associated with a criminal record. The person with a criminal record frequently experiences rejection in the areas of employment, credit, and social opportunity; this, in turn, can lead the person back to crime, and soon he or she is caught in a vicious circle. For the most serious street crimes such as murder and aggravated assault, disproportionate minority imprisonment probably represents disproportionate involvement in these crimes. But these are relatively infrequent crimes. More people are imprisoned for other, less serious crimes, where racial and ethnic biases in criminal justice are stronger. This has been especially true in recent years for drug crimes, where racial biases are the strongest and imprisonment rates grew the fastest in the 1980s and 1990s (Tonry, 1995). Thus, given the lasting effects of these inequalities, it is no exaggeration to say that inequality in the criminal justice system is a significant force in keeping minority groups in an inferior social and economic position.

## Protecting Minority Rights

In the previous section, we explored the treatment of majority and minority offenders (and accused offenders) in the criminal justice system. But what of the "average citizen," not accused of any crime but with certain fundamental rights as an American citizen, which he or she relies on the police and legal system to protect? It is this concern to which we turn in the remainder of this chapter. Our emphasis is on three areas: police protection, courteous and legal treatment of citizens by the police, and protection of citizens' rights by the civil courts.

**Police Protection.** As we have seen, two of the most common complaints by Americans of color are that the police fail to adequately patrol minority neighborhoods and they do not respond adequately to calls for assistance. J. Q. Wilson's (1978, pp. 158–66) study of police behavior indicates that this is indeed a problem in at least some cities. In Newburgh, New York, interviews with both black citizens and white police officers confirmed that officers often were slow or reluctant to intervene in response to complaints from the black community. This occurred partly because of police fears about intervening and partly because the police believed that blacks preferred to solve their problems themselves (a perception that interviews with black citizens suggest is often incorrect). A study in Denver by Bayley and Mendelsohn (1968) showed that black and Chicano citizens were less likely than whites to be satisfied with the police's actions when called for help. Specifically, 47 percent of whites, 34 percent of blacks, and 31 percent of Chicanos were satisfied (Bayley and Mendelsohn, 1968, p. 177). A national telephone survey showed that blacks were less satisfied than whites with police contacts, less likely to view police as fair and friendly, and more likely to see police brutality as a serious problem (Laville-Wilson and Sheppard, 2001).

Without being an "insider" to observe how officers respond to requests for assistance, it is hard to know exactly how much these perceptions reflect reality. However, studies such as J. Q. Wilson's (1978) described earlier show that there is some basis for such perceptions. Grossman (1974) reports a case in which a police dispatcher decided not to send a car in response to a call for assistance partly because the caller's voice sounded Indian, and that group was known for its disproportionate use of police resources. Subsequently, an assault took place that might well have been prevented had police been sent. Although it is difficult to tell how widespread such incidents are, there is reason to believe that such inequalities may be fairly common. Several studies show that the police are more likely to investigate or make an arrest when the person making a complaint is white rather than a member of a minority group (Bynum, Cordner, and Greene, 1982; Smith, Visher, and Davidson, 1984; Bachman, 1996). We also know that the styles of policing vary among different types of neighborhoods and communities. In minority communities, police tend to adopt either a legalistic style or a "watchman" style that combines toughness on serious crime with avoidance of lesser matters, sometimes accompanied by corruption. These styles contrast with a service style often found in white, affluent, or suburban communities, where responding to calls for assistance is a top priority (Barlow, 2000, p. 220–21).

An event illustrating these differences occurred when Milwaukee police officers missed a chance to arrest mass murderer Jeffrey Dahmer. One of Dahmer's victims (most of whom were young African American or Asian American males) was a four-teen-year-old Laotian boy who managed to escape, with Dahmer in hot pursuit. A black woman reported to police that a man was attacking a teenaged boy. When the police arrived at the scene in Dahmer's predominantly black neighborhood, Dah-mer (a white man) told them that he and the "young man" had been having a homosexual lovers' quarrel. He also said that the boy, who was wobbly from injuries he had already suffered at Dahmer's hand, was drunk. The police released Dahmer and allowed him to take the boy back to his apartment. Dahmer killed the boy that night and murdered several other people before he was eventually caught. The fail-ure of the police to take seriously complaints from black women (others had also complained about Dahmer) and from the Laotian boy allowed Dahmer to continue to murder.

In part because of inadequate police protection and in part because of the link between poverty and street crime, minority Americans are significantly more likely than whites to be the victims of crime. In 2001, 47 percent of murder victims were black, compared with just 13 percent of the population (Federal Bureau of Investi-gation, 2002a). African Americans were also more likely than whites to be victims of robbery and aggravated assault. Overall, one in thirty-one blacks, compared with one in forty whites, were victims of violent crime in 2001 (Bureau of Justice Statis-tics, 2002a, Table 6). Minorities, people living in cities, and people who rent rather than own their homes also experience above-average property crime victimization.

**Police Brutality.** It is difficult to define exactly what is and what is not police brutal-ity. Perhaps the most common definition is the use of force beyond what is neces-sary to make an arrest, subdue a violent suspect, or protect the police officer from injury. However, even this definition is imprecise because in many instances there is a wide range of disagreement on how much force is necessary. Moreover, many argue that brutality is not always physical. Verbal abuse, racial epithets, and listen-ing to only one side of the story are regarded by many people as a form of brutality (Bayley and Mendelsohn, 1968, pp. 122–25; Barlow, 1993, pp. 384–87) and, at the very least, as improper harassment of citizens.

However defined, police brutality is a major issue among people of color throughout the United States (Jeffries, 2002). Indeed, incidents between citizens and police officers have been the trigger for many, if not most, outbreaks of racial violence from the 1960s through the 1990s (see U.S. National Advisory Commis-sion on Civil Disorders, 1968). Complaints about police brutality are much more widespread among black, Hispanic, and Indian Americans than among white Americans (Bayley and Mendelsohn, 1968, pp. 122–29; Parisi et al., 1979, p. 301; Laville-Wilson and Sheppard, 2001). As with arrest decisions, the circumstances sur-rounding minority-police encounters often contribute to the likelihood of violent police behavior. This behavior is especially likely when citizens challenge police authority or when the police hold citizens in low regard (Lundman, 1980, pp. 160–65).

In addition, there is a tendency for more incidents of police brutality during periods of social unrest and political protest (Quinney, 1979, pp. 288–89). Because such protest has often involved minority group members, they have experienced more than their share of such police violence. In fact, a large proportion of the injuries and deaths during these disturbances is the result of police action, and this action often is far beyond that required by the situation.

Examination of the circumstances surrounding the deaths and injuries in two Los Angeles riots (Watts in 1964 and the Chicano Moratorium in 1970) confirms that police action was the main cause of death and injury and that many of those killed or injured were unarmed. In the Watts riot, indiscriminate firing by police officers into buildings, at vehicles, and into crowded areas caused a large proportion of the thirty-four deaths (Conot, 1967, pp. 245–375). In the 1970 Chicano Moratorium, a massive protest by Chicanos against the Vietnam War, there is also evidence of excessive use of force by the police. The event had been mostly peaceful until the police swept the park where the demonstration was being held after minor incidents around the fringes of the crowd. Most people in the crowd were not even aware of any trouble until the police moved in. The three deaths that occurred in the subsequent riot all resulted from the actions of the police. One of those killed was a TV reporter who had been critical of police action in previous incidents; he died when his head was pierced by a 10-inch tear gas projectile fired into the bar where he was sitting, even though there had been no disturbance in the bar (Acuña, 1972, pp. 258–63).

Still, civil disturbances are the exception rather than the rule, and brutality toward minority citizens is fairly widespread at other times as well. In a participant observation of police behavior in Chicago, Washington, D.C., and Boston, Reiss (1968) found that about 3 percent of alleged offenders suffered unnecessary violence. For a city of 500,000, this rate would mean 2,000 to 4,000 incidents of police brutality per year. Both black and white suspects were victimized—indeed, white suspects at a somewhat higher rate than black suspects. But because, as we have seen, the black citizen is more likely to become a suspect than the white citizen, blacks are more likely to suffer police brutality than whites. Interview studies of police themselves are informative: Weisburd et al. (2000) found that 25 percent of the officers they interviewed in Illinois and 15 percent in Ohio had seen an officer harassing a citizen "most likely" because of his or her race. This problem affects other minorities as well and occurs in both cities and rural areas. A 2000 Amnesty International report stated,

> Human rights groups have documented long-standing brutality by law enforcement agents towards people of Latin American origin along the US-Mexican border and in states with large immigrant populations such as California and Texas. There have been complaints of brutality and discriminatory treatment of Native Americans both in urban areas and on reservations. Complaints include indiscriminate brutal treatment of native people, including elders and children, during mass police sweeps of tribal areas.

Minorities are more often the victims of deadly force by police than are whites (Takagi, 1979). Of the more than 4,700 people killed by the police from 1952 to 1969, 49 percent were nonwhite (Kobler, 1975). If the threat of death or severe injury to a police officer or to a third party is regarded as the criterion of justifiability, it appears that about 40 percent of killings by police are unjustified, and another 20 percent are questionable. Moreover, it appears that blacks are more likely to be shot in situations in which it is not obvious that there is such a threat to life (Fyfe, 1982). Awareness of these patterns may be making some difference, however, as police use of deadly force against minorities has decreased (Mann, 1993, pp. 154–55). During the period from 1978 to 1998, the percentage of people killed by the police who were black declined from 49 percent to 35 percent (Brown and Langan, 2001).

Even so, the findings reviewed in this section suggest very strongly that minority group members experience more unnecessary violence by police than do whites. Again, individual police officers do not bear all the responsibility. The structure of the situations in which they come in contact with minority group members virtually ensures that people of color will experience disproportionate police violence, just as it ensures that they will be arrested more frequently than whites. Until there is a fundamental change in the ways wealth, income, and power are distributed between majority and minority groups, this situation is likely to continue.

**Protection of Legal Rights in the Court System.**  Ultimately, it is the judicial system that protects the rights of citizens in a democracy. If a citizen feels that his or her rights have been violated by another citizen or by an agent of the state, the court system that is called on to protect that citizen's rights. As we have seen, the laws of the

United States today provide for equal rights regardless of race, creed, color, sex, or disability. As a practical matter, however, there is serious reason to question whether the judicial system actually operates in that way on a regular, day-to-day basis.

An investigation of the civil court system by a man who was himself a U.S. Court of Appeals justice raised serious questions (Wright, 1969). Ordinarily, a citizen turns to the civil court system when there is a reason to believe that her or his rights have been violated by another citizen or by the government. These courts have the power to award payments for damages and to issue injunctions against actions that illegally deprive citizens of their rights.

Wright's investigation found several ways in which the courts have failed to protect the rights of poor Americans. One widespread problem is the failure of the courts to protect the minority poor from abuses by ghetto merchants. He cites one example in which a court allowed a creditor to repossess property worth six times the cost of the item a customer had failed to pay for, even though the other items repossessed had been paid for. This action was based on a line of fine print on the sales contract that any unpaid balance on any item purchased from the store would be distributed among all items previously purchased. Several lower courts upheld the contract and ordered the woman to return all the items. Only when the case reached the U.S. Court of Appeals did the court reverse and rule that only the original item could be repossessed.

As disturbing as this case is, the woman was fortunate in certain regards. Many poor people lack both the awareness of how the legal system operates and the money to hire a lawyer. To have legal representation, they must find a legal aid lawyer who is willing and able to represent them. Unlike the criminal courts, civil courts in most cases make no presumption of the right to a lawyer, so indigent plaintiffs often are unrepresented. Appeals through several levels of the court system are costly and time consuming, so very few poor people can go as far as this woman was able to.

Additionally, had the contract been sold to a finance company, the woman might have had an even more difficult time in the courts. Under the doctrine of "holder in due course," in most jurisdictions a finance company can purchase installment payments free of any responsibility for fraudulent practices by the dealers (a standard clause in the fine print of sales contracts). Thus, the interests of the finance company are protected but those of the buyer are not, unless the buyer can prove that the finance company knew the dealer was fraudulent (which is almost impossible in most cases).

Another widespread practice criticized by Wright (1969) and others is wage garnishment. It is possible under certain conditions in many states for a creditor to collect on past-due amounts by obtaining a court order to take part of the person's wages. If multiple garnishment orders are issued, the debtor often loses his or her job. The employer may be embarrassed by the garnishment orders or may simply consider the required procedures too much of a bother. Thus, a poor person who fails to make payment on property may lose his or her job, a condition that beyond doubt perpetuates poverty. Federal law prohibits firing an employee if wage garnishment is for only one debt, but if there are garnishment orders for two or more debts, an employee can still be fired (U.S. Department of Labor, 2003).

In some ways, the biases of the civil courts against the poor may have worsened since Wright's (1969) study. A more recent study found that poor people were even less likely than in the past to be represented by lawyers when involved in civil legal disputes. In 1996, there were 2 million more poor people in California than in 1980, but there were 130 fewer legal aid attorneys available to serve them. This resulted in a "legal services crisis which has deprived three out of four poor Californians of representation by an attorney when facing such problems as an eviction, a child custody dispute or a life-threatening domestic violence situation" (California Bar Association, 1996). The reasons for this are cutbacks in federal funding of legal aid for the poor and, in many states, state cutbacks as well. In California, for example, support received from the federal government for legal aid was cut by 40 percent in 1996 alone, and limits were also imposed on the types of cases that legal aid attorneys could take. Nationally, 300 legal aid offices closed as a result of the 1996 budget cuts, and in 2002 federal funding remained about $70 million below the 1995 level (National Legal Aid and Defender Association, 2002). The California Bar Association (1996) noted that among industrialized countries, "the majority—England, France, Germany, the Netherlands, the Scandinavian countries and Canadian provinces—fund civil legal services for the poor by providing lawyers at state expense." Thus, as in other areas such as health insurance, the United States stands virtually alone in its failure to provide guarantees of legal aid for those who cannot afford it.

One innovation established in many areas as a way of better protecting the legal rights of the poor is the small claims court system. In these courts, a citizen can sue for amounts up to a few hundred dollars without legal counsel. The idea is to enable those too poor to hire lawyers to receive legal protection when the amounts involved are not excessive. In practice, however, most of those suing in small claims courts have been landlords and businesses. Often those sued have been poor. Thus, the system has had the opposite effect from that intended: It has largely helped wealthier interests extract debts from the poor, without helping to protect the poor from abuses by landlords and businesses, as had been intended. The apparent reason for this is that the wealthy are more aware of and used to operating in the system. Some landlords and, in states where they are allowed to, collection agencies use it on a routine basis. Some states have acted to prevent this practice by limiting the number of times per year that a person can sue in small claims court. In contrast to landlords and businesses, the poor are largely unaware of their rights and do not know how to sue in small claims court.

Our discussion of the court system has focused mainly on economic rather than racial factors. However, because black, Hispanic, and Indian people are so much more likely than white people to fall into the lower-income brackets, all of these class-related inequalities create de facto racial and ethnic inequalities as well.

A final area in which the courts have in significant ways failed minorities in America is in protecting them from abuses by the state. Of particular salience here is the issue of police abuse of minority citizens. The failure of the judicial system to punish acts of violence by police against citizens has been a major source of tension from the 1970s through the 1990s in Houston, Philadelphia, Los Angeles, and other cities. As we have already noted, it was a major precipitating factor in the 1980 Miami riot and the 1992 Los Angeles riot. In Philadelphia, federal action against police violence failed in the courts in 1980. In a highly publicized case in Houston, a Chicano man, Joe Campos Torres, was taken to a vacant area by police, beaten, and thrown or forced to jump into a swift-flowing stream, where he drowned. The verdict in the case was misdemeanor negligent homicide, and the sentence was one year in prison. The police involved were also convicted of felony violations of federal civil rights laws, but the federal conviction added only one day to their sentence even though the law provided for a penalty of up to life imprisonment (*New York Times*, 1980).

Although only a few cases such as the Houston case and the Rodney King case in Los Angeles have been highly publicized, they represent a much more widespread pattern. Kobler's (1975) study of 1,500 homicides by police officers found only three cases in which any criminal punishment resulted, despite the fact that about 40 percent of the killings appeared to be unnecessary. Because about half those killed were nonwhite, this must be regarded as a failure of the courts to protect the rights of minorities. Conot's (1967, pp. 396–409) examination of the inquests into deaths during the 1964 Watts riot also found that homicides by police officers were rarely questioned. Virtually all cases involving killings of citizens by police or national guardsmen were adjudicated justifiable, although many almost certainly were not. Much the same can be said of lesser offenses by police officers against citizens: They are rarely tried, and convictions are even rarer.

## Summary and Conclusion

We have seen that a good deal of institutionalized racial inequality persists in the political and legal systems. Open and deliberate discrimination in these institutions has been greatly reduced, if not totally eliminated. However, subtler and often unintentional forms of inequality remain, limiting opportunities for African Americans, Hispanic Americans, and Indian people to improve their standing in the political and legal systems. Thus, minorities remain underrepresented on juries and among political officeholders, the legal profession, and police officers. They are overrepresented among those arrested, convicted, and imprisoned. Often, institutionalized policies and practices, though not openly discriminatory, nonetheless have the effect of helping whites or holding down minorities.

Some, though not all, of these inequalities arise from economic inequalities among racial and ethnic groups. Nonetheless, the economically disadvantaged position of minorities is in large part the result of past discriminatory actions by government, as detailed earlier in this chapter. Although the more blatant forms of discrimination have been outlawed, their effect lingers. As an illustration, imagine the government as the organizer of a 20-mile foot race. The race is started with one of the runners required to wear a 10-pound weight on each foot. Halfway through the race, the organizer decides that this is not fair and decides to remove the weights. By now, however, the runner with the weights is exhausted and far behind, but the organizer says that she must nonetheless continue the race from her present position. Because the weights are gone, says the organizer, there is no more discrimination. In your judgment, has the organizer run a fair race? Does government inaction today, in the context of a history of nearly 200 years of government discrimination against African Americans, Native Americans, and Hispanic Americans, make for a fair race in society?

Additionally, when access to government services is unequal, whether for reasons of class or race, there are implications for racial inequality. If public universities are more available to white students than to black, Latino/a, or American Indian students—even if this is not the result of intentional racial discrimination—is racial equality served? If a political decision is made to have a health care system based on ability to pay, and African Americans and Hispanics are far more likely to lack insurance in such a system, has government had no impact on racial inequality? If budget cuts eliminate bus routes that are used mainly by people of color, is government being race-blind?

This chapter's analysis leads to some suggestions on how to, and how not to, try to solve the problem of political, legal, and judicial inequality between the races. On one hand, the more overt forms of prejudice and open acts of discrimination seem less important today. On the other hand, certain individual beliefs and actions remain important. For example, many whites continue to be reluctant to vote for African Americans and other minority candidates for public office. This tendency has decreased in recent years, but it has not entirely disappeared, particularly when those candidates are outspoken in their advocacy of minority group interests. Similarly, a self-fulfilling prophecy continues to occur in which police officers and minority civilians expect the worst of one another and behave accordingly. In these regards, attitude change could clearly make a difference.

However, much of the intergroup inequality in the political and legal systems is a product of institutional or systemic processes, not individual attitudes and beliefs. How political boundaries such as those of congressional districts and city wards are drawn makes a big difference in how well represented minorities are, for example. As a result of the 1982 extension of the Voting Rights Act, congressional boundaries drawn after the 1990 census were designed in a way that gave minorities a better chance to be elected to Congress, and the number of people of color elected to Congress in 1992 rose significantly as a result. But the Supreme Court subsequently ruled against such efforts, and since then minority congressional representation has remained flat. Thus the Court probably has ensured the continuing underrepresentation of African Americans and other minorities.

Another example can be seen in the criminal justice system. No one stage can be identified as the main cause of racial inequality in the treatment of accused criminals. Rather, it is a number of sometimes small inequalities scattered throughout the process, combined with differences in treatment of the types of crimes committed by majority and minority group members, that add up to substantial racial differences in the punishment of crime. Thus, to eliminate the racial inequality, the entire process must undergo significant change, which may threaten dominant elements of the majority group. One example would be to give the same emphasis to white-collar crime that is now given to street crime and drug violations. Although street crime is a serious problem, the costs of white-collar crime are even greater, yet it is not penalized in the same ways. Similarly, the war on drugs has worsened racial inequality. Although drug use is widespread among all racial and socioeconomic groups—and is more widespread among whites than among African Americans—the drug war has been carried out in ways that have led to imprisonment mainly of the minority poor. To target white-collar crime to an extent proportionate to its cost, or to fight the drug war in a racially equitable way, would eliminate significant sources of inequality in the criminal justice system. However, such changes would also threaten much more wealthy and powerful groups of criminals than the ones targeted by present practices.

According to Feagin and Feagin (1978), it is because of just such threats to the advantaged that there has not been a concerted attack on the problem of institutionalized racism. Privileged whites, and the owners of wealth in particular, do not want to think of themselves as racists, hence the reduction in openly expressed prejudice and open discrimination. Yet, Feagin and Feagin argue (1978, p. 178), these dominant elements are unwilling to give up the advantages they enjoy as a result of systemic racial inequality and often fail to acknowledge or even be aware that their advantages result from systemic racial inequality. This is in large part why institutionalized racism, even though it is often unconscious and unintentional, persists.

## Critical Review Questions

1. What methods have been used in the past to keep minority group members from voting in the United States? To what extent are minority group members still denied equal access to voting today?

2. How did government action contribute to the creation of segregated housing in the United States?

3. In what ways was the welfare reform legislation that was passed in 1996 successful? In what ways was it unsuccessful?

4. Describe some ways in which the criminal justice system works that have the effect of discriminating on the basis of race and class. What would it take to create a criminal justice system that does not discriminate?

# Education and American Minority Groups

# Overview

As was discussed in Chapters 6 and 11, a series of court cases and federal actions, highlighted by *Brown v. Board of Education* in 1954, placed the legal position of the government clearly against segregated education. For a variety of reasons, however, these actions did not put an end to institutional discrimination in the educational system. First, there was strong resistance to school desegregation in parts of the South, and actual change was slow to come in many areas. Second, the legal rulings applied only to open and deliberate policies of school segregation. In both the North and South, residential segregation and subtler forms of discrimination in the drawing of school district boundaries have resulted in de facto segregation, that is, segregation in fact if not by law. Third and most important, there are a number of ways in which schools can discriminate without being segregated. The debate over segregation, though important, has often turned public attention away from the numerous practices institutionalized in the educational system that may—often unintentionally—place minority students at a disadvantage. Also often ignored but possibly very important is the role of education in the larger social and economic structure in which it exists. In this chapter, we shall seek to understand these relatively subtle and complex issues in the education of minority groups in America, as well as the more widely debated issue of school segregation.

## ▶ A BRIEF HISTORY OF SCHOOL SEGREGATION SINCE 1954

The Supreme Court's 1954 ruling requiring desegregation of public schools met widespread resistance in the South. Probably the most dramatic was in 1957, when Governor Orval Faubus tried to use the Arkansas National Guard to block court-ordered school desegregation in Little Rock. To enforce the law, President Eisenhower had to order U.S. Army paratroopers into the city and federalize the state's National Guard. In many other parts of the South, resistance took subtler forms. Legislation was passed in an attempt to avoid the jurisdiction of courts ordering desegregation; efforts were made to block the NAACP's desegregation drives (six states passed laws prohibiting the NAACP from providing legal aid); students were given "tuition grants" to attend segregated private schools; pupil assignment laws were written that provided access to desegregated schools only on request for reassignment; and compulsory attendance laws were repealed (Simpson and Yinger, 1985). Some districts went so far as to close their public schools entirely. Such resistance continued for years after the 1954 *Brown* decision.

It was in 1963 that Alabama governor George Wallace (later a presidential candidate) declared, "I say segregation now, segregation tomorrow, and segregation forever!" in his inaugural address.

Despite such resistance, legally segregated education did gradually disappear in the border states in the late 1950s and early 1960s, and in the deep South later. By the mid-1970s about two-thirds of the nation's school districts had taken some action to desegregate their schools (U.S. Commission on Civil Rights, 1976). These efforts led to some decline in school segregation, which continued at a slower pace through the 1980s, until segregation began to rise again after 1988. The percentage of black students in schools with more than 90 percent minority enrollment fell from 65 percent in 1965 to about 40 percent by 1974 and 32 percent by 1988 (Armor, 1992). In 1988, about one of three black students attended schools that could be classified as racially segregated, and nearly two of three attended schools with student bodies that were more than half minority (Armor, 1992).

Since around 1988, school segregation has been increasing again, and the percentage of black students in schools with more than 90 percent minority students rose from a low of 32 percent in 1988 to 37.4 percent in 2000 (Frankenberg, Lee, and Orfield, 2003, p. 31). In contrast to black students, who experienced some decline in segregation in the late 1960s and early 1970s, Latino/a students became steadily more segregated as their proportion of the population grew. Between 1968 and 2000, the percentage of Latino/a students in over-half-minority schools rose from 54 percent in 1968 to 76 percent in 2000—even higher than the percentage of blacks in such schools (Frankenberg, Lee, and Orfield, 2003, p. 33). About 37 percent of Latino/a students—the same as for black students—attend schools that are more than 90 percent minority. In these 90-percent-minority schools, the poverty rate is also very high. In fact, about 45 percent of the students in schools attended by the average black or Hispanic student are poor, compared with about 19 percent for the average white student (Frankenberg, Lee, and Orfield, 2003, p. 35). On

Federal troops escort African American students into Little Rock Central High School in 1957.

average, white, black, and Latino/a children all attend schools where their own race is in the majority. The average white student in 2000 attended a school that was about 80 percent white; on average both black and Latino/a students attended schools where about 54 percent of the students were of their own group. About the only trend that showed a move toward greater integration was the percentage of children attending schools where at least three different racial groups represented 10 percent or more of the student body. For all racial groups the percentage attending such schools increased in the 1990s. Only about 14 percent of whites attended such multiracial schools in 2000, but 29 percent of African American students, 39 percent of Latino/a students, and 75 percent of Asian American students attended such multiracial schools (Frankenberg, Lee, and Orfield, 2003, p. 29).

As we saw in Chapter 3, most Americans agree that children of different racial groups should attend the same schools. And time-series data show that the percentage who think that more should be done to integrate schools rose from 37 percent in 1988 to 59 percent in 1999 (Frankenberg, Lee, and Orfield, 2003, p. 15). We are thus faced with a perplexing question: If Americans overwhelmingly favor the principle of integrated education, why did one-third of the nation's black students still attend segregated schools in 1988, and why did most indicators of school segregation increase between 1988 and 2000?

The problem is largely what is commonly called de facto segregation, combined with a reduced commitment since the mid-1980s to desegregating the nation's schools. Unlike de jure segregation, which involves an official policy of segregated schools, de facto segregation results from subtler processes, the most important of which is housing segregation. Where housing is highly segregated, the system of neighborhood schools often amounts to a system of segregated schools (Wilson and Taeuber, 1978; J. E. Farley, 1984). School segregation may also contribute to housing segregation: Some whites select all-white neighborhoods or suburbs to avoid schools with large numbers of blacks (Levin et al., 1976; Taeuber, 1979; D. G. Taylor, 1981). Among reasons cited by Frankenberg, Lee, and Orfield (2003, p. 16) for the increases in segregation in recent years is changing demographics. As the black and Hispanic populations grow, the proportion of students in these groups who attend schools where most students are black or Hispanic also tends to grow. This has been particularly important in the increase of Hispanic segregation, as the Hispanic population has grown rapidly throughout the past two decades.

More important, the courts in recent years have turned away from orders mandating desegregation (Orfield and Eaton, 1996; Frankenberg, Lee, and Orfield, 2003). In 1991, the Supreme Court changed its definition of what school districts had to do to resolve past policies of discrimination and segregation. It ruled that it was not the result that mattered so much as whether the school district had been consistent in obeying court orders and had done what was feasible to reduce segregation (Frankenberg, Lee, and Orfield, 2003, p. 18). Court-ordered desegregation plans in place since the 1970s or 1980s have been ended in numerous areas, including Kansas City; Oklahoma City; Denver; Norfolk, Virginia; Cleveland; Minneapolis; Miami; Fort Worth; Buffalo; Louisville; and Houston. Others, including those in St. Louis, Indianapolis, and Prince Georges County, Maryland, were significantly scaled back or under gradual phase-out plans (Kunen, 1996; Hansen, 1998). It is striking that although demographic trends (increasing minority population and slowly declining housing segregation) have been steady since around 1970, school segregation fell until around 1988, then has risen since—from around the time the courts began rescinding school desegregation orders.

In general, regional differences in segregation have decreased in recent years, but for black-white segregation, the Northeast is by most measures the most segregated region and the South the least segregated. By some measures, the Midwest is also relatively segregated, and the border states generally less so. In all regions, however, schools have become more segregated since 1988. For segregation between

Anglos and Hispanics, the Midwest and border states are less segregated than other regions, but again, all regions are becoming more segregated (Frankenberg, Lee, and Orfield, 2003, pp. 38–46).

Segregation also appears to be greatest in cities, particularly large cities. In 14 of the 26 largest cities in 2000, the average black student attended a school with 10 percent or fewer non-Hispanic whites. In Detroit, Chicago, New Orleans, and Washington, the figure was 3 percent or less. In six of these cities, the average Latino/a student also attended schools with 10 percent or fewer non-Hispanic whites. (Frankenberg, Lee, and Orfield, 2003, p. 54). For both blacks and Hispanics, segregation levels are much higher in cities than in either suburban or rural school districts, although the latter districts have fewer minority students. Keep in mind that all these statistics refer to segregation *within* school districts. Much of the segregation that exists today is *between* districts, as when a city whose school population is 75 percent minority borders on a suburban district that is 95 percent white.

Table 12.1 summarizes the trend over time in school segregation, showing how black-white segregation fell in the 1970s, then rose again after 1988, while segregation of Hispanic students increased more steadily. Thus, the mere fact that deliberate segregation is illegal does little to eliminate the kind of segregation that remains today. Only more drastic remedies, such as busing, redrawing school districts to combine cities and suburbs, or really doing something about housing segregation hold any real hope of further reducing segregation in U.S. schools.

The reality is that popular concern about school segregation as a social problem has faded in recent years. The courts have ruled in a number of recent cases that school districts have done all that they could reasonably do to reduce discrimination, so they can be released from court-ordered busing (Coughlin, 1991; Armor, 1992; Seligman, 1992; Frankenberg, Lee, and Orfield, 2003). The Supreme Court supported this interpretation in *Board of Education of Oklahoma v. Dowell* in 1991, and in 1992 it ruled in *Freeman v. Pitts* that districts could be partially released from desegregation requirements even if their desegregation plans had been only partially fulfilled. It ruled in *Missouri v. Jenkins* in 1995 that restoration of local control should be the goal in any court-ordered desegregation plan (Hansen, 1998).

Public opinion runs largely against busing, among both blacks and whites, and controversy about it has arisen even within the NAACP, which was once its staunchest supporter (Kim, 1997). However, research shows that such desegregation plans can significantly increase the opportunities of minority students and that abandoning them could have serious educational consequences. We shall return to this issue later in the chapter, exploring in some detail the degree to which desegregation, through busing or otherwise, may offer improved educational opportunities to minority students. In the meantime, we shall explore other aspects of the

### Table 12.1  Percentage of Black and Hispanic Students in Predominantly Minority Schools, 1968–2000

| School Minority | Black Students | | | | | | Hispanic Students | | | |
|---|---|---|---|---|---|---|---|---|---|---|
| | *1968* | *1972* | *1980* | *1988* | *1992* | *2000* | *1960* | *1980* | *1992* | *2000* |
| 50%+ Minority | 76.6% | 63.6% | 62.9% | 63% | 67% | 71.6% | 54.8% | 68.1% | 73% | 76.3% |
| 90%+ Minority | 64.3 | 38.7 | 33.2 | 32 | | 37.4 | 23.1 | 28.8 | | 37.4 |

*Sources:* 1968–1980 statistics: Orfield (1983, pp. 4, 10); 1988 statistics are from Orfield and Monfort (1992); 1992 statistics: Gary Orfield, quoted in *St. Louis Post-Dispatch*, (1993d, p. 3a). 2002 statistics: Frankenberg, Lee, and Orfield (2003).

educational system that influence the educational opportunities of racial and ethnic minority groups in the United States.

## ▶ THE ROLE OF EDUCATION: TWO VIEWS

Sociology offers two contrasting viewpoints concerning the role of the educational system in American society. The traditional view, linked closely to the order, or functionalist, perspective in sociology, is that education provides a source of social mobility in society. In other words, it offers to everyone the opportunity to move up in society, and how far one moves depends on his or her ability and motivation. The educational system also serves as an efficient way of allocating people to professions by giving them the training they need. Thus, education provides employers with qualified workers, and it offers individuals the opportunity for mobility by rewarding them on the basis of what they know and what they can do (achieved characteristics) rather than on the basis of who they are or what their background is (ascribed characteristics). (For further discussion, see Davis and Moore, 1945; Parsons, 1959.)

A contrasting view that has gained increasing support among sociologists of education is that education does not operate in a way that offers much opportunity for upward mobility to the poor. Rather, education reflects and reinforces the social inequality in society. This viewpoint, more consistent with the ideas of the conflict perspective, challenges the popular idea that "education is the answer." Rather, education cannot be expected to bring about equality when the larger social and economic system is based on inequality. One strong proponent of this viewpoint is Christopher Jencks (Jencks et al., 1972), who has argued that if society wants to move in the direction of social equality, the way to do it is not to "educate" everyone but rather to pursue changes in the economic system that would bring about equalization of income. Jencks should not be misunderstood as opposing high-quality education for all; he does not. Rather, he argues that economic advantage is more important than mere access to education, and making everyone a high school or college graduate would not necessarily alter the basic forces that result in economic inequality in the United States.

Conflict theorists argue that education may not provide much opportunity for mobility because the true function of the educational system is to reinforce and preserve the inequalities that exist in society. According to this view, education, as Marxist theory says is true of all institutions, exists to serve the interests of the dominant or advantaged elite that reaps most of society's benefits. The true purpose of education, then, is not to provide social mobility but rather to *channel* students into roles and statuses relatively similar to those of their parents. Thus, the children of the affluent receive more and better education, and the children of the poor get less and worse education. This serves two functions for the dominant group. First, it ensures that they can pass along their advantages to their children. Second, it provides employers with "appropriately" socialized middle-class workers who will fit into their work organizations, work with a minimum of supervision, and not cause trouble.

There is some merit in this view. First, many studies show that predominantly middle-class and predominantly working-class or poor schools tend to stress different kinds of values. Schools with students predominantly from the lower classes stress mainly conformity and obedience; middle-class schools also stress control over one's situation and the ability to work independently, although within a context of hierarchical supervision (Friedenberg, 1965; Bowles, Gintis, and Meyer, 1999; Cohen and Lazerson, unpublished). These value differences between the social classes are already present to some extent when children enter school. They reflect the different experiences in life and work of middle-class and working-class or poor parents and the effect of these experiences on how parents raise their children (Miller, Kohn, and Schooler, 1986). However, the schools reinforce and enlarge these differences in ways that channel middle- and upper-class children toward more education and professional and managerial employment and channel working-class and poor children toward less education and manual, clerical, or blue-collar employment (Bowles and Gintis, 1976, 1999; Bowles, Gintis, and Meyer, 1999). Furthermore, the higher one goes in the educational system (from grade school to high school to college to graduate school), the higher the average family income of the students and the closer the educational approach approximates the middle-class model (Binstock, 1970; Bowles, Gintis, and Meyer, 1999). Thus, the educational system nurtures and reinforces the "appropriate" values of the middle class and "cools out" the aspirations of working-class students and prepares them for lower-paying, manual jobs (Lauter and Howe, 1970).

This function of education can also be illustrated by the behavior and preferences of those who do the hiring for the better jobs. Studies suggest that the *affective* characteristics gained in school (values and habits) are more linked to income and occupational status than is *cognitive* learning (the learning of skills and content). A review by Gintis (1971) of a number of studies shows that whereas years of school were strongly related to a person's job status and income, measures of what the person actually knew added very little to the explanation of job status or income (see also Bishop, 1987; Rosenbaum and Kariya, 1991). Similarly, several studies show that employers do not view school grades, transcripts, or other indicators of academic achievement as a good indication of who will make a good employee (Bills, 1992; Granovetter, 1995; Miller and Rosenbaum, 1997; Sommerfeld, 1995). Clearly, employers prefer educated workers for high-status jobs for reasons other than cognitive knowledge, although for some jobs there are minimum levels of cognitive knowledge that they require, such as basic mathematic and English skills (Rosenbaum and Binder, 1997; Moss and Tilly, 2001a). Gintis argues strongly that what employers are really looking for is middle-class values and work habits—exactly the kinds of things that the school system teaches. Also consistent with this observation is the fact that education pays off better for the white middle class than for minorities and the poor, and better for academic training (mostly middle class) than for vocational training (mostly working class) (Super and Crites, 1962; Weiss, 1968; Harrison, 1972; Boyd, 1995; Friedman and Krackhardt, 1997). Apparently, it is what is learned in the so-called *hidden curriculum* that employers are looking for in applicants for higher-status jobs: values and work habits that will "fit in" rather than any concrete factual knowledge.

Surveys of employers confirm that this is the case. Beyond the need for basic skills, their preference for more educated applicants for higher-status jobs is in many cases not related to what such applicants know in areas related to the job. Usually, this is taught on the job. Rather, more educated employees are preferred because of their values, beliefs, and work habits (Hamilton and Roesner, 1972). As Ivar Berg (1975, p. 308) puts it, employers believe that with increased education, "the worker's attitude is better, his trainability is greater, his capacity for adaptation is more developed." It does not really matter that such employees are not necessarily more productive (I. Berg, 1971, 1975); it is the belief of employers that "desirable" values and work habits are found among more educated employees that counts (Bowles and Gintis, 1976).

All this raises serious questions about the role of the educational system as a source of mobility in American society. Undoubtedly, it does operate that way for some individuals, but these studies suggest there is strong reason to believe that the overall effect of the American educational system is to preserve inequality rather than to reduce or eliminate it. Since economic inequality in the United States falls largely along racial and ethnic lines, education may well be acting in ways that preserve racial and ethnic inequality as well.

Data on the correlation between race and students' achievement also support this interpretation. As recently as 2002, data continue to show black, Hispanic, and American Indian students trailing behind white students on average scores on the National Assessment of Educational Progress. Among eighth-graders in 2002, for example, black students on average scored twenty-six points lower than non-

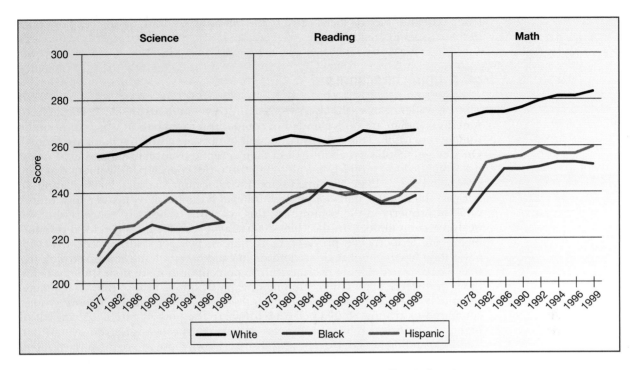

**FIGURE 12.1**    National Assessment of Educational Progress (NAEP) Test Score Trends, Age 13
*Source:* National Center for Education Statistics (2002b).

Hispanic white students in reading, and Hispanic students scored twenty-four points lower (National Center for Education Statistics, 2003a).

The time trend data in Figure 12.1 shows that gaps in achievement between whites and both blacks and Hispanics decreased from the 1970s until the mid- to late 1980s, but after that progress stalled and the gaps widened again in the early to mid-1990s. For reading, the gap narrowed somewhat again in the late 1990s, although it remained wider in 1999 than in the mid-1980s. For math, the gap narrowed slightly in the late 1990s for Hispanic students but continued to widen for black students. For science, the gap narrowed slightly for Hispanic students in the late 1990s but widened further for black students. Inequalities in education, which fall along lines of both race/ethnicity and income, are a major cause of these ongoing racial and ethnic differences in achievement. Also, as we have seen earlier, poor blacks and poor Hispanics are also more likely than whites to go to schools where many other children are poor. Consequently, low-income minorities, to a greater extent than poor whites, typically experience the disadvantages associated with schools where most of the students are poor.

If it is true that educational institutions reinforce patterns of social class inequality—and by so doing also reinforce racial inequality—we face the question of what specific means are used. Two major possibilities have been suggested by educational sociologists: First, more money is spent, and thus the quality of education is presumably greater, in areas where the students are white and middle class than in areas where they are black, Hispanic, American Indian, or poor. Second, there are important cultural and behavioral differences between many minority students and the people who teach them and prepare their educational materials, and minority students are held back because of these cultural differences, which may be based on either race or social class. In the following sections, we shall explore both of these issues in greater detail.

## ▶ FUNDING OF SCHOOLS

There is evidence that schools in which many of the students are black, Hispanic, or American Indian are underfunded in comparison to schools in which most of the students are white. This is partly a function of the way in which schools are funded. On average, schools get about half of their revenue from state aid and most of the rest from the local property tax, although this varies considerably from state to state (Pisko and Stern, 1985; National Center for Education Statistics, 2003b, Graph 4). Because the amount that can be raised through the property tax depends on the value of property in the community, this tax tends to bring in more revenue in wealthier communities. In the 1999–2000 school year, for example, local revenue, mainly the property tax, provided more than $5,900 per student in districts with fewer than 5 percent of their students below the poverty level, compared with less than $2,100 per student in districts with 35 percent or more of their students below the poverty level. State school funding only partly offsets this, so that total general revenue is around $8,000 per student in the districts with the lowest poverty rates compared to around $6,000 per student where the poverty rate is 15 percent or higher. Categorical funds—grants for specific purposes—raise the overall per-student spending level of high-poverty districts above those where the poverty rate is between 15 and 25 percent, but the highest total expenditures per student, even after the categorical funds are added in, are found in the districts with the lowest poverty levels. Where 5 percent or fewer of the students are poor, the average total spending per pupil in 1999–2000 was about $9,000 per year, higher than in all categories of districts with higher poverty rates (National Center for Education Statistics, 2003b, Indicator 21).

Because minorities have lower incomes on the average than whites, we would expect that less money is spent per student on the education of minorities than on the education of whites. But the actual picture is more complex. The lowest levels of spending are in districts with 20 to 49 percent minority school-age children. This is consistent with the expectation that districts with above-average minority enrollment spend less. However, the highest levels of spending are in districts with 50 percent or more minority children. Districts with less than 20 percent minority enrollment fall in the middle ranges between these extremes (National Center for Education Statistics, 1998). However, figures for districts with more than 50 percent minority children are misleading for two reasons. First, these are mainly in the largest cities, and costs tend to be higher in such areas. Therefore, the greater expenditure does not necessarily mean better education because a given level of spending buys less. For this reason, a recent study found that states with large minority populations often rated low on adequacy of financial support for education once these costs are taken into account. Among states where the minority student population was around 50 percent or more, five out of seven states, including the two states with the numerically largest minority populations, California and Texas, were in the bottom 15 of all the states in adequacy of educational funding (Rubenstein, 2003). There was less evidence of within-state inequities, but in some states, including California, Pennsylvania, Nebraska, and Illinois, the percentage of minorities in districts with inadequate spending is much higher than where spending is adequate (Rubenstein, 2003). Overall spending statistics are misleading for a second reason: Relative to the value of their property, central-city residents must pay significantly higher tax rates because there is so little value to tax. For example, the highest property tax rates in poverty-stricken East St. Louis, Illinois, are the highest in the Illinois part of the St. Louis area.

Jonathon Kozol (1991) examined levels of school funding and the quality of school facilities in districts with large minority populations such as Detroit; East St. Louis; and Camden, New Jersey. He found dramatic funding inequalities and woefully inadequate facilities. In Detroit, for example, in 1988 per pupil school spending was $3,600 per year. In several affluent nearby suburbs, per pupil funding ranged from $5,700 to $6,400. In several inner-city districts, students went weeks or months into the school year without receiving textbooks. A 1994 report by the *St. Louis Post-Dispatch* found much the same situation in the St. Louis area, where per pupil spending ranged from around $3,100 in the poorest districts to more than $8,700 in the wealthiest. And in East St. Louis, one physics lab teacher commented, "It would be great if we had water" (Kozol, 1991).

In some states, efforts have been made, often in response to lawsuits, to eliminate some of the inequities arising from property taxation and state matching formulas. Collectively, though, the lawsuits, settlements, and attempts at reform haven't made a great deal of difference in the funding formulas of most states. More than 80 percent of the states have been sued over this issue over the past thirty years, but the resulting reforms have been limited. The gap between the poorest and wealthiest districts still varies widely among the states, depending in part on how much effort they have made to equalize funding. In West Virginia, where extensive equalization efforts had been undertaken, wealthy districts on the average spent just 4 percent more per student than poor ones in the early 1990s. In Illinois, where reform had not yet occurred, wealthy districts spent 67 percent more per student than poor ones (General Accounting Office, 1998). In some cases, however, efforts at equalization failed because when the state acted to equalize funding, poor districts reduced their excessive tax burdens or wealthy districts raised taxes to make up the difference (General Accounting Office, 1998).

An exception is Michigan, where the state legislature voted in 1992 to eliminate the local property tax as the primary source of funding for schools. After a long political battle, it was decided by referendum in 1994 to replace the property tax with a 50 percent increase in the state sales tax and a tripling of the cigarette tax. At the same time, the minimum required per pupil spending was increased from $3,277 to $4,200. Wealthy districts were allowed to continue to fund their schools at a higher level, although upper limits were imposed. The guaranteed level of state funding gradually rose to $6,700 by 2003 (A. Lockwood, 2002). This brought the state share of total school spending to nearly 80 percent, among the highest of all the states. Before the reform, the ten highest-spending districts spent nearly three times as much per student as the ten lowest-spending districts; by 2002 they spent less than twice as much (A. Lockwood, 2002). Still, inequities have not been totally eliminated. Detroit, where the student body is 90 percent African American, did not gain as much as some other districts because its funding was above the minimum level when the change was made. Its funding grew by about 31 percent between 1994 and 2003; some others grew by more than 100 percent (A. Lockwood, 2002). Yet Detroit's spending levels represent the high costs of a large city and do not buy as much as similar levels of expenditure in smaller districts. A particular problem is the many aging schools in Detroit and other large cities, and one thing that the Michigan school reforms did not provide for was state aid to replace aging buildings (Johnston, 1998a).

In addition to inequities *between* school districts, there are also inequities *within* school districts (Rothstein, 2000). Put simply, school boards allocate more money for some schools than they do for others. For example, one study in Detroit compared spending for teachers' pay in schools that were 90 percent or more black with those that were 10 percent or less black in 1970. The finding: Schools that were mostly white spent about 14 percent more per pupil than schools that were mostly black (Michelson, 1972).

As serious as funding deficiencies are, it will take more than money to bring about truly equal educational opportunity. Although many districts with large

African American, Latino/a, or Native American enrollments are underfunded to the point that they lack necessities, there are also problems in education that cannot be addressed by money alone. An important source of evidence is a massive survey of 570,000 students and 10,000 teachers and principals in more than 4,000 schools in the United States. This study, which came to be known as the Coleman Report (Coleman et al., 1966), was mandated by the 1964 Civil Rights Act to explore the quality of education received by minority students, and it revealed a number of startling findings. Among the most important was that traditional measures of educational quality—class size, educational level of teachers, facilities and programs available in the schools, and so on—explained relatively little of the variation in what students actually knew, as measured by tests of ability and achievement. Overall, these factors appear to explain about 5 percent of the variance. There was some racial difference, however: These factors explained about 10 to 15 percent of the variance in achievement and ability for black students but only about 2 to 6 percent of the variance for white students (Coleman et al., 1966, p. 294). In short, although school quality did make more of a difference in learning for blacks (and probably for other minorities as well) than for whites, it did not make a great deal of difference for anyone.

What *did* explain how much students learned? Coleman was able to identify two main factors. The first was a set of background factors, including urban or rural background, parents' education, family size and composition, facilities and educational resources in the home, and parents' interests and desires concerning the child's education. These factors explained 15 to 25 percent of the variance in student learning—more for whites than for blacks (Coleman et al., 1966, p. 300). The other important source of variation was the attitudes of the students themselves. Coleman measured three kinds of attitudes: interest in learning, self-concept, and belief that the individual can control his or her environment. Again, he found a significant relationship: These individual attitudes explained 15 to 20 percent of the variation in learning for blacks and 25 to 30 percent for whites. In the overall sample, these individual attitudes correlated more closely to student achievement scores than anything else measured (Coleman, 1966, pp. 319, 321). Coleman's overall finding was quite clear: The background and attitudes of students were more strongly correlated to what they learned in school than was anything about the school that was measurable or that varied substantially from school to school.

These figures contain some overlap; that is, school characteristics, background factors, and student attitudes all tend to be associated with one another. Thus, it can be difficult to estimate just how much of the effect on student learning is a result of each variable. However, through a method known as stepwise regression, it is possible to add one variable at a time to the analysis and thus measure the additional effect of that factor after all others are taken into consideration. Using such methods Coleman was able to identify the effects of various factors on twelfth-grade verbal achievement, as shown in Table 12.2.

These data reveal that all variations between schools that were not related to the background of their students accounted for only 2 percent of the variation in achievement for Asian students, 7 percent for white students, and 15 percent for black students. Variation linked to backgrounds and attitudes was much more important for Asians and whites, and somewhat more important for blacks. Attitude and background together accounted for 33 percent of the variation in achievement for whites, 30 percent for Asians, and 23 percent for blacks. Thus, the importance of schools seems to be less than many believed, although it is undoubtedly greater for blacks than for whites. The other groups are a bit different. For Chicanos and American Indians, variations between schools seem about as important as differences in attitude and background in explaining students' learning. Only for Puerto Ricans did differences in schools seem more important than individual differences. Even when school differences were important, however, differences in the attrib-

## Table 12.2  Racial and Ethnic Variation in Achievement

| Group | School-to-School Variation | | Individual Variation | | |
|-------|---------------------------|---|---------------------|---|---|
| | Not Linked to Students' Backgrounds | Linked to Students' Backgrounds | Linked to Students' Backgrounds | Linked to Students' Attitudes | Variation Explained by All Factors Combined |
| White | 7.41% | 2.08% | 16.94% | 13.38% | 40.09% |
| Black | 14.83 | 6.07 | 6.41 | 10.87 | 38.18 |
| Puerto Rican | 22.69 | 0.71 | 3.35 | 4.79 | 31.54 |
| American Indian | 23.42 | 0.71 | 10.68 | 8.80 | 43.61 |
| Chicano | 17.75 | 2.32 | 6.02 | 8.24 | 34.33 |
| Asian | 2.20 | 0.13 | 19.66 | 10.05 | 32.04 |

*Source:* Coleman et al. (1966, p. 229, Tables 3.221.1 and 3.221.2).

utes of their student bodies seemed to make more difference than did either teacher quality or school facilities (Coleman et al., 1966, p. 302).

These results should not be taken to mean that school funding and quality of facilities and teachers are unimportant. The Coleman Report clearly showed that these factors make more difference for minority students than for white students. This finding was confirmed a decade later in research by Summers and Wolfe (1977). Undoubtedly, one reason for this is that minority students are more likely to encounter serious inadequacies that could be addressed by better funding. Moreover, the Coleman Report did find one school resource that made a sizable difference, although it was not given great emphasis in the report: When teachers scored higher on a vocabulary test, their students did better (Thernstrom, 1991). The main message to be derived from the Coleman Report (and similar studies since, such as Jencks et al., 1972, and Bowles and Gintis, 1976; for a recent extensive discussion, see Hanushek, 1998) is that more money and better facilities will not *by themselves* solve all of the problems faced by American students, particularly students of color.

## ▶ CULTURAL AND BEHAVIORAL FACTORS IN THE EDUCATION OF MINORITIES

The Coleman Report shocked the American educational establishment because it seemed to suggest that schools do not make as much difference in how much students learn as had been previously believed. Regardless of the apparent quality of schools, it seemed that students with certain kinds of attitudes and backgrounds were learning and those with other kinds of attitudes and backgrounds were falling behind. However, subsequent research has shown that schools can make more difference than one might be led to believe by the Coleman Report. What makes more difference than money alone (although money can be important when schools lack necessities, as many in minority areas do) is the interaction between teachers and students. When teachers interact with students in certain ways, those students tend to learn, and when they interact with students in other ways, the students fall behind. For example, comparisons of impoverished inner-city students in the classes of good and bad teachers in Gary, Indiana, showed that teachers in a given school year consistently made a difference of a full grade year in how far students advanced (Hanushek, 1992). In other words, students with a good teacher might advance by 1.5 grade years in a school year, whereas students with a bad teacher might advance only 0.5 years. Thus, even though more money and better facilities are needed by some schools, they will not by themselves solve the problems. What is also needed is greater attention to cultural, attitudinal, and interactional factors and the role they play in the learning process.

The finding that cultural and background factors are closely associated with learning in American schools can be interpreted in two quite different ways. One interpretation, aligned with the functionalist perspective, identifies the source of the problem in "dysfunctional" attitudes and beliefs among poor people and among racial and ethnic minorities. The other view, aligned with the conflict perspective, sees the source of the problem in the educational institution. According to this view, the educational system demands conformity to an arbitrary norm and punishes those who do not or cannot conform, or it expects poor performance from low-income and minority students and then treats them in ways that ensure that this expectation comes true. In the following sections, we shall explore the evidence concerning the functionalist view that the problem is one of *cultural deprivation* and the conflict theory view that the problem is *cultural bias*.

## Cultural Deprivation?

Recall Coleman's finding that absence of facilities and educational materials in the home was associated with poorer performance in school. Specifically, Coleman found lower levels of achievement among children from homes that lacked a television, telephone, record player, automobile, vacuum cleaner, and so on. He also found that the lack of reading materials—books, magazines, daily newspapers, encyclopedias, and dictionaries—was correlated with lower levels of learning. This (along with other data on family structure and parental interest and encouragement of children's education) suggested to Coleman that children from certain kinds of homes entered school at a disadvantage. That is, they were deprived of many of the learning opportunities that other children enjoyed and thus could not compete on an equal footing. This disadvantage was in many cases worsened by the lack of parental encouragement of education and finally by the attitudes of the children themselves. Underachieving children, Coleman found, tended to (1) have a poor self-image, (2) be relatively uninterested in school, and (3) believe that they could not control their environment, that is, that success was a result of "good luck," not "hard work." Of these three, self-image and belief in control of one's environment had much stronger effects than interest in school, especially among black students; and for students from minority groups (and probably poor whites), the most important factor was belief in control over one's environment (Coleman et al., 1966, pp. 319–24).

To Coleman, this strongly suggested that the lack of facilities and encouragement in the home, *combined with* the attitudes that minority students brought to school, placed those students at a very substantial disadvantage to whites. The solution: Change the attitudes of disadvantaged students so that they could develop a positive self-image and believe that they can control their environment. Coleman was able to present one additional piece of evidence that lent further support to his argument: He found that "as the educational aspirations and backgrounds of *fellow students* increase, the achievement of minority group children increases" (Coleman et al., 1966, p. 302). In short, he found that all else being equal, a minority student who was attending school with students from advantaged backgrounds who had positive attitudes did better than a comparable minority student who was attending school with students from disadvantaged backgrounds who had negative attitudes. The apparent reason: The students conformed to the attitudes and beliefs of their peers, so minority students attending schools where students had more positive attitudes and study habits developed similar attitudes and habits themselves. Of equal significance, the evidence did not show any harmful effect on the more advantaged students of attending school with students of less positive attitude and background. A finding that was to have great political importance in later years, and that follows quite logically, is that racially and socioeconomically integrated schools were associated with higher achievement among minority group children. The suggestion was clear: Desegregation of schools might lead to improved learning among minority students as they took on the attitudes and study habits of their more advantaged white, middle-class peers. As we shall soon see, the findings of the Coleman Report became an important part of the battle over school busing for racial integration that began in the late 1960s and has continued for much of the time since then.

Essentially, Coleman's interpretation of his findings was consistent with the functionalist perspective. He focused on the idea that minority students (and lower-income students in general) come to school with attitudes and backgrounds that do not "fit in" with the school system's expectations. Studies that show a strong link between background and school achievement have led to an emphasis on helping minority students to fit in and develop the attitudes they need to get ahead in the school system. Examples of such efforts include Head Start and school busing for racial integration. The degree to which busing has been successful in improving the achievement of minority students will be explored in the final section of this chapter, which focuses on educational social policy. In the meantime, we shall turn to another interpretation of Coleman's findings that clashes with the functionalist viewpoint.

## Cultural Bias?

Conflict theorists, including a number of minority group spokespersons, argue that the cultural deprivation viewpoint reflects the biases of the white middle class, the group to which most social scientists belong. According to conflict theorists, the problem is to be found not in the characteristics of the minority groups but rather in the schools. According to this view, the reason for low achievement among those with certain attitudes and backgrounds is that the schools demand certain values, attitudes, and habits and, in effect, punish those who do not conform. Conflict theorists believe that schools operate in this way for two reasons: First, it allows the dominant elements in society to pass their advantage along to their children. Second, it provides employers with a well-socialized work force that will "fit in" and not cause trouble (Bowles and Gintis, 1976). Thus, the schools serve the interests of the advantaged, despite the widespread ideology that they serve everyone's interest. Social scientists who hold this viewpoint say that it is not surprising that the Coleman Report and other studies found that more of the same kind of education does not do much for minority students' achievement. The problem is not the amount or quality (as traditionally measured) of education; rather, it is the *kind* of educational system we have and the role it plays in the larger society.

If there is merit in this viewpoint, it should be possible to identify some specific ways in which the educational system penalizes minority students. In the following section, we shall examine the educational institution to see whether we can identify practices or structures that do in fact hold down minority students.

## Biased or Limited Coverage of Minority Groups in School Materials

Both white and minority schoolchildren form important impressions about their own racial group and others based on what they are exposed to in schools. Until very recently, what they have been exposed to has been quite stereotypical and biased. Two distinct tendencies can be noted: The first is simply to exclude minorities from materials discussing U.S. history or from general educational materials, such as "Dick and Jane" grade school readers. This pattern was commonplace until recently and has not yet been completely eradicated. One study done in the 1960s found that of forty-five social science textbooks, only eight even mentioned Spanish-speaking Americans. The largest Hispanic group, Chicanos, was mentioned in only two of the books (M. B. Kane, 1970). Research by Bowker (1972) indicates that Indian people were similarly neglected in history books and that the problem actually got worse between 1960 and 1972. One study of forty-nine major school textbook series from 1958 to 1976 showed that there was only a small increase in the number of minority characters (Britton and Lumpkin, 1977). Another study found African Americans underrepresented even in college psychology of women texts, a type of book one would expect to be sensitive to minority concerns (Brown et al., 1985). Furthermore, the Britton and Lumpkin study showed that minority characters were depicted in a much more limited range of occupational roles than were white characters. A study of science books showed that although minorities were generally well represented in the books, they were underrepresented in the pictures of adults in scientific occupations, thus missing the opportunity to present a positive minority role model (Powell and Garcia, 1985). McCutcheon, Kyle, and Skovira (1979) identified another problem: a tendency to portray everyone, including minority characters, according to a white, middle-class role model. Thus, skin color or names may be changed, but no real effort is made to display the great cultural diversity of the U.S. population.

The second major problem—which many view as more persistent—is distorted or stereotypical presentations of Americans of color. At one time, for example, American Indians were referred to in many school textbooks by derogatory adjectives, including "filthy," "murderers," "lecherous," "dumb," "stupid," and "barely human" (Bahr, Chadwick, and Strauss, 1979, pp. 237–38). Chicanos were similarly stereotyped. For example, M. B. Kane's (1970) study showed that they were often portrayed as "wetbacks," crossing the border illegally, or as lawbreakers and bandits who are not wanted in this country.

Gradually over the past few decades, awareness of these problems has increased, and minority group members have begun to appear in school materials in greater numbers and in less stereotyped roles than in the past (J. Garcia, 1993). Most major textbook publishers have added recommendations to their authors' guides concerning inclusion of minorities and women (Britton and Lumpkin, 1977). Over the past two decades, a number of textbooks and other school learning materials have been specifically designed to be *multicultural*, that is, to represent the full diversity of groups, cultures, and traditions that make up the American population. This type of effort can be seen in California's mandate that the social studies curriculum make a number of changes designed to (1) increase emphasis on history and geography, (2) use a narrative approach to bring history to life and explain why things happened (rather than the memorization of names and dates), and (3) bring problematic issues such as race and religion to the forefront, with material on minority cultures woven into the mainstream narrative of history rather than being presented as peripheral to the main events (Kirp, 1991). For example, world history should pay more attention to non-European regions; discussions of the United States should deemphasize the "melting pot" idea in favor of the image of a "mosaic" of distinct cultural traditions that continue to thrive; and American history should emphasize the long-standing tension between the principle of equality and the reality of the oppression of minorities. Textbooks developed for the California curriculum have been adopted not only in California but also in Arkansas, Virginia, and other states (Kirp, 1991).

Despite the increased emphasis on cultural diversity in today's school materials, however, many critics argue that they are still *Eurocentric*; that is, they give undue emphasis to European historical and cultural influences or describe other groups from the standpoint of the European experience (Ratteray, 1988; Honeman, 1990). For example, Banks (1992) points out that African, Asian, and American histories often are studied under the topic "The Age of Discovery," meaning when Europeans first arrived in these continents. Similarly, debates among scholars about the extent to which African or Afro-Asian societies may have influenced the development of Western civilization often are kept out of the classroom, whereas Banks (1992) argues that in a truly multicultural educational system, such debates would be introduced and discussed. In addition, even recent studies show that minorities are still sometimes absent or stereotypically portrayed in schoolbooks and materials. This is particularly the case for Native Americans and Hispanic Americans (Charles, 1989; Michigan State Board of Education, 1989; Romero and Zancanella, 1990; Ashley and Jarratt-Ziemski, 1999). In teaching about American Indians, for example, it is common for them to be presented as if they existed in the past but not the present, and exotic stereotypes such as that of the "noble savage" also remain common (Almeida, 1996). African Americans sometimes are underrepresented or stereotyped, and curricular bias occurs at the college level as well as K–12. For example, a recent study of fundamental nursing textbooks found racial stereotyping and few portrayals of African American leaders (Byrne, 2001).

The absence or distortion of minority groups in educational materials (coupled with similar omissions and distortions in the media) can have serious effects on all children. Among the majority, prejudices and stereotypes about members of other groups can be created or reinforced. Among minority group children, the result can be serious damage to their self-image or to their beliefs about the racial or ethnic group to which they belong. The symbolic-interactionist school of social psychology has shown that reality is socially constructed. In other words, we acquire our knowledge, beliefs, and self-images through what we are told by others (Cooley, [1909] 1964; Mead, [1934] 1967). For majority group children, this means that their beliefs about minority groups are formed by what they hear and read at home, at school, and in the media—especially when, as very often happens, the children grow up in segregated neighborhoods and attend segregated schools. (For further discussion of the role of social learning in the perpetuation of prejudice, see Chapter 2.)

The relative absence or distorted presentation of minorities in school materials can also seriously harm the self-image of minority group children. Cooley's ([1909] 1964) concept of the *looking-glass self* is highly relevant here. According to this concept, our beliefs about ourselves are based on the messages we get from others. If these messages are negative, the self-concept will tend to be negative. It is not surprising, then, that a large body of evidence shows that black children have in the past developed serious problems in the area of self-image. Among the most widely cited studies are the doll studies by Clark and Clark (1958) and by Radke and Trager (1950). When given a choice of otherwise identical black and white dolls, black schoolchildren (as well as white children) showed consistent preferences for the white doll. In the Clarks' study, for example, two-thirds of the black children chose the white doll as the one they wanted to play with. On the other hand, when asked which doll "looks bad," 59 percent of the black children chose the black doll. The study also showed that the children were aware of racial differences: More than 90 percent made the correct choice when asked which doll "looks white" and which doll "looks colored." Significantly, however, fully one-third of these same black children picked the white doll when asked which doll "looks like you"—an apparent denial of their own racial identity. Doll studies with Chicano children also found a fairly widespread preference for white dolls (Werner and Evans, 1968).

Studies asking children to draw pictures of themselves or tell stories about themselves produced similar findings (Porter, 1971). Black children and, often, poor white children expressed less positive themes and more often drew small pictures or pictures with missing limbs or features. Using pictures of white and American Indian children, B. G. Rosenthal (1974), found that the preference for white children was even stronger among Indians than it was among other groups, such as blacks and Asians, and that unlike some other groups, the pattern did not decrease with age. (However, Rosenthal's data apply only to Chippewa Indians and may not be true for other groups.)

More recent studies suggest that these patterns have changed since around 1970. A later doll study (Katz and Zalk, 1974) found that the preference among black children for the white doll no longer existed. In addition, when Rosenberg and Simmons (1971) administered paper-and-pencil self-esteem scales to both black and white schoolchildren, they found that the black children had self-images at least as positive as those of the white students. Other studies by Baughman (1971), Zirkel

(1971), Zirkel and Moses (1971), Bachman and O'Malley (1984), Richman, Clark, and Brown (1985), and Solorzano (1991) suggest the same thing. The evidence is much more fuzzy and limited on Chicano and Indian children, in part because studies with different methods have produced different findings. Still, some studies show very little difference in self-esteem between them and white children (T. P. Carter, 1968; Fuchs and Havighurst, 1972). There is little doubt that at least for black children, self-esteem since the 1970s has been significantly higher than in the past.

This has important implications because self-esteem tied to race seems to influence achievement. A recent study of black middle school students found lower achievement among two groups: those who identified excessively with whites and avoided their African American identity, and those who identified with African American culture in a surface way as a reaction to white stereotyping and systemic discrimination. An example of the latter would be students who wore Malcolm X caps or Martin Luther King T-shirts but knew little about the contribution of either to black history. On the other hand, youths who identified with African American culture in a way that truly valued that identity (For example, knowing the contributions of Malcolm X or Dr. King) had modestly higher achievement (Spencer et al., 2001). Also, as is discussed in greater detail later in this chapter, when racial stereotypes specifically regard achievement, their impact can be quite harmful to achievement.

Undoubtedly, one factor in the improved self-image of minority students has been the more balanced presentation of minorities in educational materials, even though there remains much room for improvement. Perhaps even more important is the emphasis on black pride and self-identity that came with the Black Power movement in the 1960s and 1970s and again with the Afrocentrism movement of the 1990s, which emphasizes learning about and taking pride in one's African cultural heritage. Both these movements emphasized a rejection of the negative black image presented by whites and a corresponding emphasis on the notion that black people can and should define their own identities. These movements appear to have succeeded in bringing about a distinctly more positive self-identity, and when this leads to more than a surface identity with the history and culture of one's group, student achievement appears to grow. It seems likely that a similar process has taken place among Hispanic Americans, Native Americans, and Asian Americans. Of course, these positive developments cannot undo the harm that was done to minority children in the past, but they do represent positive changes.

## Teachers' Expectations and Tracking

**Teacher Expectations.** Teacher expectations about their students have important effects on student performance, often acting as a **self-fulfilling prophecy** in the classroom. In this process, teachers expect more of some students and less of others, their expectations affect how they interact with the students, and as a result the expectations come true. Rosenthal and Jacobson (1968) studied this process in a book titled *Pygmalion in the Classroom*. In this famous experiment, the researchers began by giving a test to children in a California elementary school. The teachers were told that the test was a new instrument designed to identify "academic spurters": children who would greatly improve their performance in the coming academic year. Actually, the test was an ordinary IQ test, and the 20 percent of the children who were identified as academic spurters, supposedly on the basis of the test, were in fact randomly selected. Of course, the teachers did not know this.

At the end of the year, the children were given another IQ test. The results in the first and second grades were striking: The children who teachers thought were "spurters" showed improvements in IQ of 10 to 15 points more than the other children. Recall that these children were in fact no different from the other children; they had been randomly selected. The only difference was that their teachers thought they were going to do better. The effects of teacher expectations appeared to occur mainly in the first and second grades. Older children seemed less susceptible, maybe because they were more intellectually developed and therefore less subject to such influences or because they had by then established reputations with the teachers that affected expectations more than did the supposed test results.

Apparently it is the content, not the amount, of teacher-student interaction that causes the expectancy effect. Teachers did not spend more time with the children identified as spurters, but apparently they gave them more positive messages. Another study by Brophy and Good (1970) also found that teachers were more critical of those they believed to be poorer students and more praising and encouraging toward those they believed to be better students. These messages affect the students' self-images, which in turn influence their achievement (Brophy, 1983).

Research also shows that when teachers believe their students to be disadvantaged or less capable, they teach in fundamentally different ways. They are more directive, are more likely to walk students through tasks step by step, and give the student less opportunity to engage in higher-order thinking and problem solving (Means and Knapp, 1991). Although this may help students learn basic skills, it deprives them of opportunities to develop the skills of comprehension, problem solving, and reasoning. Growing evidence shows that most students labeled as disadvantaged are capable of these skills but are deprived of the opportunity to develop them because teachers don't think they can and as a result don't try to teach them (Knapp and Shields, 1990). Several experiments have shown that when teachers make efforts to teach higher-order problem-solving skills and believe their students can learn the skills, dramatic improvements in the students' achievement occur. These experiments have produced learning of problem-solving skills by minority and low-income students at grade levels from kindergarten to college, sometimes to the point that students in such programs surpass the average achievement of white, middle-class, suburban students (Selvin, 1992; see also U.S. Department of Education, 1987).

Despite methodological criticisms of the Rosenthal and Jacobson study (Thorndike, 1969) and some inconsistency in the findings of similar studies (Boocock, 1978), an impressive array of studies suggests that teachers' expectations influence students' performance (see Beez, 1968; Brophy and Good, 1974; R. Nash, 1976, especially Chap. 3; Smith, 1984; Brophy, 1983; Nolen and Haladyna, 1990). Effects of labeling are especially large in early education. In a school observed by Rist (1970), students were assigned during the first eight days of kindergarten to three tables according to their teacher's beliefs about their ability. For many children, the assignments were inconsistent with reading readiness scores. By second grade, not one of the children who remained in the class had moved to a higher group, and those in the low group had fallen far behind in reading and had become socially labeled as "the clowns." Thus, the assignment of children to groups, with little regard to available ability measures, had a long-standing effect on their performance. Such effects of teacher expectations may be larger for minority group students than for others. A study by Jussim, Eccles, and Madon (1996) found that effects of teacher expectations on later test performance were nearly three times as great for black students as for white students and also larger for girls and for students from low-income families. And the effects were cumulative: Teacher expectancy effects were especially large for low-income African Americans.

In addition to teacher expectations having bigger effects on minority students' achievement, a large and growing body of evidence shows that teachers often form expectations of students at least partially on the basis of race and class (Ferguson, 1998). In a study by Harvey and Slatin (1975), for example, teachers were given photographs of children and asked to evaluate their chances of success. The result: Teachers had substantially higher expectations of white children and of children whom they perceived to be from the middle or upper classes. In fact, a review of sixteen studies similar to this found that nine showed that teachers had higher expectations of whites, and just one found the reverse; in about a third of the studies the difference was statistically significant, and in these studies, whites were always favored (Baron, Tom, and Cooper, 1985). Research by Leacock (1969) found racial and class effects on teachers' expectations, so much so that expectations of black students were actually *negatively* related to their IQ. And both experiments and classroom observations have shown differences in teacher treatment of students that favor whites, such as more coaching and positive responses to correct responses, perhaps because of race-linked perceptions student ability or effort (Ferguson, 1998, pp. 294–297). Rist's (1970) study also found that the students were placed at the "low" or "high" tables in kindergarten largely on the basis of social class, even though both the students and the teacher in this study were black.

To summarize, research clearly supports two conclusions. First, what teachers expect of students influences how much those students learn and their progress in the school system. One literature review (Brophy, 1983) estimated the average effect on achievement at 5 to 10 percent, but depending on the teacher and student in any given interaction, it is occasionally much larger. Second, teachers' expectations are formed at least partly on the basis of race and class, although the extent to which this is true varies greatly from classroom to classroom (Brophy and Good, 1974; Hurn, 1978; Brophy, 1983; Alexander, Entwisle, and Thompson, 1987; Didham, 1990; Gaines and Davis, 1990). Thus, it does seem clear that teacher expectations perpetuate racial and ethnic inequality in the American educational system.

Teacher expectancy effects can also occur on a schoolwide level. Often, teachers form generalized expectations about the learning potential of their entire class, and these affect students' achievement. A national study known as *High School and Beyond* illustrates this fact dramatically (Coleman, Hoffer, and Kilgore, 1982; Greeley, 1982; Hoffer, Greeley, and Coleman, 1987). This study included public, Catholic, and nonreligious private schools. It found that in both types of private schools, overall achievement exceeded that of public schools. In the Catholic schools, black, Hispanic, and low-income students did better relative to middle-class whites than they did in the public schools. This difference increased as students moved from the tenth to the twelfth grade (Hoffer, Greeley, and Coleman, 1985; Haertel, 1987), although there is some debate about the size of the difference (Jencks, 1985; Alexander and Pallas, 1987; Willms, 1987). Similar successes were also found in a small group of public schools. A key reason for the success of these schools is that they expected and demanded more of their students, and did so *regardless of race or social class* (Hoffer, Greeley, and Coleman, 1987). In short, low-income and minority students are doing very well in some schools, and the ones they do well in are the ones that expect them to do well. As a teacher told Fuerst (1981, p. 90) in his study of successful all-black schools in Chicago, "The belief that children can succeed is more than half the battle."

Unfortunately, the opposite belief, that "students like these can't be expected to learn much," often develops among teachers in predominantly black, Hispanic, or low-income, central-city schools. For example, Kozol (1991) quotes a Chicago teacher as saying, "It makes no difference. Kids like these aren't going anywhere." And when Kozol asked an East St. Louis teacher whether her class was preparation for employment, the teacher replied "Not this class." When teachers expect and demand less from students, they usually get less, and ultimately the learning of minority students is seriously impaired (Moore and Pachon, 1985). In a review of the literature on teacher expectancy effects, Brophy (1983) concluded that they are maximized in racially or socioeconomically homogeneous schools, where low expectations often become generalized. When a school district can break from this usual pattern and form generalized high expectations of their students, however, results can be dramatic. Examples can be found in Jacksonville, Brooklyn, and a group of schools in Atlanta, where student achievement went from far below grade norms to levels at or above the norms as a result of district initiatives to raise expectations and teachers' beliefs about what their students could achieve (U.S. Department of Education, 1987; Howard, 1995).

An encouraging recent trend has been the growing use of programs designed to encourage teachers to develop high expectations of all their students. One such organization is the Efficacy Institute, based on the notion of, in the words of its founder, "an approach to education built on confidence—the belief that normal American children, in all their diversity, have the innate ability to learn at very high levels" (Howard, 1995). Training Tacoma teachers in the Efficacy model, along with other reforms, led to large increases in students' achievement (Finn, 1996). Similar programs include the Gender/Ethnic Expectations and Student Achievement (GESA) program, operated by the Midwest Desegregation Assistance Center at Kansas State University, and the Great Expectations initiative in Oklahoma. Teachers in the latter program report substantial improvements in their students' achievement and standardized test scores, along with increased satisfaction with their own teaching jobs (Ferguson, 1998, pp. 303–11).

**Tracking and Ability Grouping.** A closely related issue is that of tracking and ability grouping. These are common educational practices whereby students believed to be similar in ability are grouped together either in separate classes with different curricula (tracking) or in different classes with the same curricula or different groups within a class (ability grouping). A survey of middle school principals in the early 1990s revealed that 82 percent of the schools were using some form of tracking (Jet, 1993a). The idea is to enable students to proceed at a pace consistent with their abilities, preventing the better students from becoming bored and the poorer ones from being left behind. However, critics have claimed that this practice holds down the educational attainment of minority, poor, and working-class students by acting as a self-fulfilling prophecy, much like teacher expectations (Howard, 1995). Minority and lower-status students are placed into less advanced tracks, on the basis of race or class, and this inhibits their later learning and academic advancement.

Although, again, it is not clear just how strong the effects are, there appears to be fairly wide agreement in the literature that placement in tracks is influenced by race, Hispanic origin, and especially class (Schafer, Olexa, and Polk, 1972; Brischetto and Arciniega, 1973; U.S. Commission on Civil Rights, 1974; Alexander and Eckland, 1975; Alexander and McDill, 1976; Alexander, Cook, and McDill, 1978; Boocock, 1978; England, Meier, and Fraga, 1988; Useem, 1991; Gamoran, 1992a; Oakes, Gamoran, and Page, 1992; Lucas, 1999). Some of the reasons for the overrepresentation of minority and low-income students in lower tracks is that the tests used for placement produce scores that are correlated with race and class (Haller, 1985; Baker, 2001), but some studies show that even when the test scores are the same, lower–socioeconomic status students are placed in lower tracks (Hallinan, 1992). One reason for this may be that college-educated parents are more likely to intervene to get their children into a higher track (Useem, 1992). Similarly, research has shown the wider the variety of socioeconomic statuses in a school, the more rigid the tracking (Lucas, 1999). A recent government report concluded that in about 10 percent of public middle schools, ability grouping verged on outright racial discrimination (Armstrong, 1991).

Once students have been placed in a low track, their future educational experience is largely determined: They stay in the same track and have less opportunity to enter higher education, regardless of their initial ability (McGinley and McGinley, 1970; Schafer, Olexa, and Polk, 1972; Esposito, 1973; Rosenbaum, 1976; Bredekamp and Shepard, 1989; Gamoran, 1992a, 1992b). They are often deprived of opportunities to take the courses they need to enter and succeed in college. Adelman (1999) found that one of the best predictors of graduating from college was whether students had two years of algebra, and low-income students who take algebra and geometry are three times as likely to attend college as those who don't

(Office of Postsecondary Education, 1998). However, in schools with large numbers of students of color or low-income students, most are often tracked away from the courses leading to these levels of math education. In Illinois, for example, barely more than half of high school students take the core courses required for college (Illinois Board of Higher Education, 2001), and urban minority students and rural students are especially likely *not* to get these courses. Urban minority students often are tracked away from college prep courses, and rural students often attend small schools with limited offerings. Significantly, Adelman (1999) also found that the effects of high school curriculum on college graduation were greater for black and Latino/a students than for white students. So those who are hurt the most by not getting core courses are precisely the students least likely to get them.

The tendency for students to remain in the track in which they are originally placed is particularly destructive (Brophy, 1983; Gamoran, 1992b; Hallinan, 1992). In the rare cases in which students move regularly from track to track, tracking may have positive effects. For example, Fuerst (1981) found that in all-black schools that used tracking and changed the track assignments yearly, students' achievement was high. Usually, though, low track placement becomes a social label that stays with a student throughout his or her educational career. Coleman, Hoffer, and Kilgore (1982) concluded that a major reason for the greater success of black, Hispanic, and low-income students in the Catholic schools is that these schools often lack the vocational tracks into which such students are frequently placed in the public schools. When these schools do have tracking, they usually use it in a more flexible manner. Both public and Catholic schools with more mobility and flexibility in their tracking systems produce higher overall achievement and less inequality in achievement (Gamoran, 1992b).

The effects of track placement on children's performance and educational plans have also been noted. Effects on actual learning probably are greatest in the lower grades, where teacher expectations exert their greatest influence. In high school, on the other hand, tracking seems mainly to affect the plans of students: Those placed in lower tracks generally lower their expectations and do not plan on (and therefore do not attend) college. Track placement, then, has effects on future educational attainment even when we compare students who are in different tracks but have similar abilities and achievement levels (Hauser, Sewell, and Alwin, 1976). Alexander, Cook, and McDill (1978, p. 60) found that "enrollment in a college preparatory track increases by about 30 percent the probability that students will plan in their senior year to continue their education in comparison to equally able, motivated, and encouraged youth in nonacademic programs."

Taken as a whole, the literature raises serious questions about the usefulness of tracking unless the placements are carefully reevaluated and changed on a regular basis. It must be stressed that the decision to place students in tracks is haphazard at best. Two studies of high school track placement found that ability, achievement, and background variables combined explained only 30 to 40 percent of the variation in track placement, leaving 60 to 70 percent unexplained (Hauser, Sewell, and Alwin, 1976, p. 318; Alexander, Cook, and McDill, 1978, p. 55). For a process that is supposed to be a rational decision based on students' aptitude and performance, these figures are not impressive. Moreover, we are talking about a process that contains racial and class biases and that arbitrarily influences the future educational attainments of students. Viewed from this perspective, the practice appears highly questionable.

**The Detracking Movement.** In response to extensive research showing the problems associated with tracking, some schools have moved to eliminate it in recent years. This movement, known as *detracking*, is showing some positive results, although it also faces some challenges. Most research on detracking shows that it raises the achievement of students formerly in lower tracks. For example, a New York study showed that when low tracks were eliminated and the students were placed in classes that took challenging regents' exams, most of them were able to pass, and some earned above-average grades in their new, more challenging courses (F. Cohen, 1993, 1995). One reason may be that more disruption occurs in low-track classrooms than in detracked classrooms (Mekosh-Rosenbaum, Spade, and White, 1996). Overall achievement in detracked schools is at least as high as in tracked schools (McDermott et al., 1995; Slavin, 1995b), and a San Diego study found that 50 percent of students in a detracked high school went on to college, compared with citywide and national averages of 38 and 39 percent, respectively (Mehan et al., 1992). In one eastern detracked high school where more than 80 percent of the students are African American or Latino/a, more than 90 percent of the graduates go to college (Gamoran and Weinstein, 1998). One reason is that in detracked schools, more students are enrolled in a curriculum that prepares them for college (Alford, 1997). The most successful detracked schools combine high demands with support for students who need help in meeting these demands (Gamoran and Weinstein, 1998). Students generally appear to like detracking, appreciating the greater diversity in the classroom (Cooper, 1997). The beneficial effects of detracked schools appear to be greatest when cooperative learning and active learning techniques are used, and their use appears to be more common in such schools (Ovando and Alford, 1997; Rothenberg et al., 1997).

Still, detracking is not a cure-all. The interactions that occur between teachers and students probably are more important than whether or not tracking is used (Gamoran and Weinstein, 1998; Jaeger and Hattie, 1995; Lockwood, 1996), and how detracking is implemented makes a big difference in its likelihood of success (Ovando and Alford, 1997; Rothenberg et al., 1997; Gamoran and Weinstein, 1998). In some cases, ability grouping has continued in schools that are supposedly detracked, and in others, generalized low expectations have persisted (Gamoran and Weinstein, 1998). In some cases, though, detracked schools have presented a rigorous and demanding curriculum to students from a variety of backgrounds, and these schools have been most successful (Gamoran and Weinstein, 1998). In some detracked schools, overall achievement remains the same or improves, but the achievement of the top students may be less (Argys et al., 1996; Brewer et al., 1996). There is debate about the reasons for this, and whether or not they have to do with the actual mix of students in the class (Ascher, 1992). But this concern has led to a good deal of opposition to detracking among white, middle-class parents, and this opposition has slowed its implementation in some areas (Wells and Serna, 1996). Some districts have responded to this criticism by eliminating low-track classes and merging the students into more challenging, college preparatory classes but keeping the highest-track classes such as honors classes (F. Cohen, 1993, 1995; Gamoran and Weinstein, 1998). Others have kept tracks but allowed more student choice and different placements in different subjects, an arrangement that seems to offer more opportunity than use of similar tracks across all subjects (Lucas, 1999).

Wells and Serna (1996) found that some opposition to detracking was racially motivated: Affluent white parents supported policies that kept their children from being in class with substantial numbers of African Americans or Latinos/as. For example, one mother who chose a district with an "advanced program" said she would not have moved there had her children not been accepted into the program. Instead, she said, she would have moved into a nearby area with a larger percentage of whites. Significantly, she did not know whether that district had an advanced program (Wells and Serna, 1996).

## Linguistic Differences

Another area of difficulty arises from linguistic differences between minority students and their teachers. This has in various ways been a problem for black students, who often speak varieties of the form of English commonly called "Black English" or "Ebonics"; for Spanish-speaking students; for Asian American students (especially immigrants); and for American Indian students, who may be penalized for speaking their native languages. Contrary to some media depictions, the key issue is not whether students should be able to speak standard English. Virtually all educators, white and minority, agree that not being able to speak standard English is a serious disadvantage and that students should learn how to speak standard English if they do not know how. Rather, the issues concern negative and incorrect labels attached to minority children because they do not enter the school speaking standard English and the failure of the school system in many cases to teach minority group children standard English (Smitherman, 1997).

**Black English and the "Ebonics" Debate.** We shall begin our examination of this issue with an exploration of Black English. Traditionally, Black English was regarded by many educators as an inadequate or poorly developed version of English, linguistically inferior to standard English (Deutsch, 1963). This occurred largely because the educators' cultural and linguistic backgrounds did not give them the knowledge necessary to understand Black English. More recently, however, sociolinguistic research has discredited the idea that Black English is inferior. In fact, Black English has standard rules (although there is some regional variation) concerning tenses, subjects and verbs, and so on, a fact that has been recognized by the Linguistic Society of America (Heller, 1998). Put simply, Black English is different from standard English but equally regular in its rules (Baratz and Baratz, 1970). One difference is in the use of tenses: Black English has a wider variety of tenses than does standard English (Dillard, 1972, pp. 39–72; Seymour, 1972; Fickett, 1975, pp. 67–75). One example is the "habitual" tense, a pattern that exists in Black English but not in standard English. Apparently, this tense, like a number of other features, such as substituting other sounds for the "th" sound, has its roots in West African languages (Smitherman, 1997; see also Turner, 1949). Silverstein and Krate (1975, pp. 146, 166) present two examples of the habitual tense. In Black English, there is an important difference in meaning between "he workin" and "he be working." "He workin" (the present tense) means that he is working right now, whereas "he be working" (the habitual tense) means that he works regularly or habitually. Similarly, "she sick" means she is sick today but will probably be over it soon, whereas "she be sick" means that she is seriously or chronically ill; the illness is likely to be of long duration.

Fickett (1975, p. 77) presents a similar example from research in a Buffalo high school. She found that nearly all the black students knew that "I been seen him" was longest ago, "I done seen him" more recent, and "I did see him" most recent. White students, however, either could not answer the question or guessed wrong. Interestingly, the black students were surprised that white students did not know the difference; some commented, "Those kids gotta be dumb." The findings of these and other studies, then, refute the traditional view that Black English is less developed or less capable of expressing concepts and ideas. The problem is that white educators did not understand Black English. (Some might say that these educators were "culturally deprived.")

Because of these misconceptions on the part of educators, including even some middle-class black ones (Gouldner and Strong, 1978), black children have frequently been, and sometimes still are, incorrectly labeled as "slow" or "illiterate"—with all the consequences these labels carry—because of their use of Black English (P. J. Williams, 1997). For example, Cecil (1988) found that teachers expected lower achievement, intelligence, and reading success from students who used Black English. This misper-

White teachers often incorrectly label black students as withdrawn, noncommunicative, or unable to verbalize, based on their behavior in the white-dominated classroom. If such teachers could communicate with their students in a more comfortable, less threatening setting, they would see a very different pattern.

ception often is compounded in white or middle-class environments where the norm is standard English because black children feel inhibited and become withdrawn, answering questions from the teacher slowly and as briefly as possible. On the other hand, when given a less formal environment, a speaker who communicates with them in their own language, and topics they find more familiar and interesting, the same students become highly verbal and compete with one another for a chance to talk (Labov, 1972, pp. 60–62). Recently, methodologies have been developed that are effective in distinguishing students who speak Black English from students with real linguistic deficiencies (Washington and Craig, 1992; Craig and Washington, 2000). Although research with larger samples is needed to develop norms for these new measures, they offer strong promise for developing more culturally neutral ways of assessing the language needs of children (Craig and Washington, 2000).

In addition to the labeling problem, many teachers apparently are not successfully teaching some of their black students standard English. This problem apparently is most serious for black students of lower socioeconomic status. Middle-class black students often become adept at using both Black English ("everyday talk") and standard English ("school talk") (Wood and Curry, 1969). Although some middle-class blacks have little familiarity with Black English, many others use Black English among their friends and family but standard English in formal or work situations and in other white-dominated settings. Wood and Curry's study indicated that middle-class, black high school students in Chicago were quite adept at this type of "code switching." Apparently, for many blacks who know standard English but prefer to speak Black English, the use of the latter reflects an affirmation of black culture and a rejection of white cultural dominance (K. J. Taylor, 1978).

For black students from poor families, however, the picture is apparently different: Many of these students do have trouble learning standard English. Wood and Curry (1969) found that black students from poor families in the high school they studied were not adept at code switching: Even when they were asked to speak in "school talk," their responses more closely resembled Black English than standard English. One difference may be that the middle-class child's parents speak both Black English and standard English, whereas the poor child's parents speak only Black English (Labov and Cohen, 1967). In any case, it appears that the schools are not too successful at teaching standard English to those black students who are not familiar with it. One problem is that many of the teachers do not know how to speak Black English (Baratz and Baratz, 1970; Fickett, 1975, p. 94). If a teacher cannot communicate with a pupil in language that the pupil understands, it is difficult for that teacher to explain to the student a new form of language. The situation is somewhat analogous to that of a person who knows absolutely no English attempting to teach an English-speaking person to speak Spanish. Although the linguistic differences between standard and Black English are less extensive, the difficulties involved are much the same.

Thus, both inappropriate labeling of some black students and failure of the schools to teach some black students standard English have become barriers to the education of black students. In 1979, the implications for equal educational opportunity became a legal issue when a court ruling required the Ann Arbor, Michigan, school system to take steps to meet the educational needs of students who speak Black English. The court concluded that the previous failure of the school system to deal with this issue threatened the educational opportunities of the city's black students.

Similar concerns led the Oakland, California, School Board in 1997 to pass a resolution mandating the use of Ebonics (another term for Black English) to teach standard English to children in the school system. The term *Ebonics*, coined at a St. Louis conference on black studies in 1973, combines the words *ebony* (black) and *phonics*. In part because it mistakenly attributed the use of Black English to genetic factors, the Oakland resolution prompted a furor of criticism and ridicule. Yet much of its basis has been shown to be sound by academic literature. First, there is no doubt that Black English has constant rules and structures and that it is just as capable of expressing ideas as any other language structure. Second, it is equally clear that many poor, inner-city African American children are able to communicate in Black English but have serious deficiencies in standard English, which is necessary to get ahead in the educational and professional worlds (Smitherman, 1997). Third, research shows that the use of Black English to teach standard English can be a highly effective technique. In a research project called Bridge, students were started with readers using Black English and transferred to readers using standard English. These students were compared with a control group using traditional methods based only on standard English. Five hundred forty students in five school districts in Chicago, Phoenix, Washington, Memphis, and Macon, Alabama, participated in the experiment. According to the Iowa Test of Basic Skills, the Bridge students made an average gain in reading scores of 6.2 months over the four-month experiment, whereas the control group taught only in standard English improved by only 1.6 months (Simpkins and Simpkins, 1981). Results such as these tell us that the furor over the Oakland proposal was based on politics, not sound academic research. The attacks on the Oakland Ebonics proposal are best understood in terms of the political atmosphere at the time, which in the following year led to a vote to abolish all bilingual education in the entire state of California. This vote is discussed further in the coming pages.

**Hispanic and Asian American Students and Bilingual Education.** Much of what has been said about the difficulties imposed by the educational system also holds true (in some cases, even more so) for Hispanic students and for some Asian American students. With the rapidly growing Latino/a and Asian American populations, more and more students are being affected by these issues. McLaughlin and McLeod (1996) put it this way:

> If students were distributed evenly across the nation's classrooms, every class of 30 students would include about 10 students from ethnic or racial minority groups. Of these 10, about 6 would be from language minority families (homes in which languages other than English are spoken); 2–4 of these students would have limited English proficiency (LEP), of whom 2 would be from immigrant families.

The majority of Hispanic Americans speak at least some Spanish in their homes, although most also know English (Moore and Pachon, 1985, pp. 52, 119). However, some have limited English proficiency (LEP). Some 3.2 million U.S. students have been identified as having LEP, and 73 percent are Hispanic (M. H. Lopez, 1998). About one in six students from homes where English is not spoken are Asian American (McLaughlin and McLeod, 1996). Some schools, however, continue to strongly discourage any speaking of Spanish or other non-English languages in school, and opposition to bilingualism in the schools has been growing. It was a big factor in the passage of a 1986 referendum making English California's official language, and in 1998 California voters voted, in Proposition 227, to eliminate bilingual education in the state's schools. Since then voters have approved similar proposals in Arizona and Massachusetts but rejected one in Colorado. In all three states that have voted to eliminate bilingual education, there are provisions for exceptions, and limited pockets of bilingual education continue.

In some cases, teachers look down on students who speak Spanish, which leads to negative labeling of Latino students (Moore and Pachon, 1985, pp. 148–49). This negative attitude in part reflects the development of dialogues that are neither distinctly English nor Spanish. Switching and mixing the two languages is common among Hispanic Americans, as is the use of Spanish forms of English words (*pochismos*) such as *el troque* (the truck) or *huáchale* (watch it!) (Moore and Pachon, 1985, p. 121). This has led to negative labeling by English-speaking teachers and sometimes also by educated Mexican Americans concerned with preserving standard Spanish. Nonetheless, this *caló* (mixed language) has come to be recognized by many in the Chicano movement as a symbol of a distinct Chicano culture that is neither totally Mexican nor totally American. Still, many Hispanic students have been held back by an educational system that labels them negatively because they speak Spanish or mixed Spanish-English dialects yet often fails to teach them standard English. As with black students, it appears that the nonlearning of standard English is most common among the least affluent.

Part of the problem is that some teachers are not able to communicate with the children in Spanish. From the late 1960s to the mid-1990s, this problem was increasingly addressed through bilingual education programs, which teach children in both English and Spanish; of course, teachers must be proficient in both languages. However, these programs have become increasingly controversial since the mid-1990s. Part of the growing debate represents a clash of values. People who favor cultural assimilation oppose it on grounds that it promotes divisions within society. This factor clearly was a major issue in the passage of the referenda. On the other hand, those who favor cultural pluralism argue that bilingual education contributes to a positive self-image among Hispanics and other linguistic minorities and to increased appreciation of U.S. society's diverse heritage (Moore and Pachon, 1985, pp. 122, 153–55). Thus, where one stands on the social uses of bilingual education depends in part on one's values concerning assimilation and pluralism, an issue that will be explored further in Chapter 15.

In contrast, the effectiveness of bilingual education in achieving its *educational* purposes is a matter that can be tested scientifically. Nonetheless, the value clash around bilingual education has influenced the scientific debate about its effectiveness. To some extent, researchers and their sponsors have set out to prove either that bilingual education or its opposite—English immersion, in which LEP students are taught only or almost entirely in English—is more effective (Schnaiberg, 1997; Seder, 1998). For this reason, but also for others, the research findings are somewhat conflicting (Krashen, 1991; Schnaiberg, 1997). Another reason is that the methodology of the studies varies, as does the type of approach used in both bilingual education and English immersion. The conflicting results can be seen in one review of the research that found eight studies showing bilingual educaton to be more effective than English immersion, six studies showing English immersion to be better, and fourteen studies showing no difference (Krashen, 1991). However, the more carefully designed studies that more closely approximate true experiments do tend to show some positive effects on learning from the bilingual approach (Gonzalez and Maez, 1995; Kenji Hukata, quoted in Schnaiberg, 1997).

Longitudinal research on the effects of bilingual education was conducted between 1983 and 1988 for the federal government by a California research firm. The study, which included about 4,000 students, mainly Spanish-speaking, showed that strong bilingual education programs were preferable to either partial bilingual education or English immersion programs. Students in the strong bilingual programs tend to become more proficient in English and receive stronger parental support (Ramirez, 1991; see also A. C. Lewis, 1991). Notably, however, LEP students in all three kinds of programs fared better than with no intervention (Cummins and Genzuk, 1991; Seder, 1998). The findings of this study are consistent with earlier research results reported by Flores (1978). A study even larger than the California study included more than 700,000 student records between 1982 and 1996, examining some records at one time and others over an extended period (V. P. Collier, 1992; Thomas and Collier, 1997; see also Seder, 1998). This study found substantial long-term effects of some types of bilingual education, to the point that within four to seven years students had achieved parity with native English speakers.

Particularly effective are two-way bilingual programs, which equally emphasize the importance of English and the LEP student's native language; often they also teach native English-speaking students the other language. As of mid-1996, 169 schools in eighteen states had two-way bilingual programs (McLaughlin and McLeod, 1996). Significantly, the Massachusetts referendum banning bilingual education exempted this type of program.

Some studies seem to suggest that bilingual education is neither better nor worse than instruction in English (such as Medina, Saldate, and Mishra, 1985; see also Baker and de Kanter, 1981), whereas other research finds it superior in one or more regards (such as Valenzuela de la Garza and Medina, 1985). One study that analyzed twenty-three earlier studies, making adjustments for various statistical inadequacies, found modest positive effects on learning when students were tested in either English or their native language (Willig, 1985). There are some studies that suggest negative effects. For example, a recent study by M. H. Lopez (1996, 1998; Lopez and Mora, 1998) suggests that years after participating in bilingual education programs, the students may attain lesser educational levels or incomes than those who participated in immersion programs. However, this study, like some others addressing this issue, may suffer from methodological problems such as noncomparability of students in the two groups (Seder, 1998). A widely cited series of literature reviews by Rossell (1991; Rossell and Ross, 1986) found that the majority of studies showed either no effect of bilingual education or negative effects compared with immersion. However, questions have been raised about whether some of the programs labeled immersion actually used some of the techniques of bilingual education (Krashen, 1991; see also Seder, 1998). The most thorough and definitive studies probably are the two large-scale studies by Ramirez (1991) and Thomas and Collier (1997), which each involved thousands of students. They both found at least modest beneficial effects of bilingual education. More recently, studies have examined what happened when bilingual education was eliminated in California. In general, scores of both LEP students and native-English speakers have improved, perhaps due to smaller class sizes resulting from other educational initiatives. However, contrary to the predictions of English immersion advocates, the gap has not narrowed between LEP students and native English speakers (Thompson et al., 2002). There is also some evidence suggesting that students in schools that used waivers to keep bilingual education experienced gains similar to those of students in schools that eliminated it (Butler et al., 2000).

However, it is clear that how any approach is implemented makes a big difference. There are good and bad bilingual education programs, and there are good and bad immersion programs (Seder, 1998). And as in other areas of education, the effectiveness of the teacher is crucial (Schnaiberg, 1997; Seder, 1998; E. E. Garcia, 1991). Also essential are teacher fluency in both languages, keeping students in the program for a sufficient length of time, and careful selection of students to participate. Unfortunately, each of these conditions is sometimes missing (see P. Schmidt, 1992). And as with desegregation programs, bilingual programs seem to work best when they involve cooperative and participatory education (McLaughlin and McLeod, 1996). These studies show that bilingual education, properly done, can be educationally beneficial to children who speak Spanish and other languages. However, as illustrated by the referenda eliminating it in three states, its future remains uncertain. One factor that may influence its future is the changing composition of the U.S. population, as the Latino/a and Asian American populations continue to grow. Research has shown that where these two groups are a larger share of the population, adoption of bilingual education programs is more likely (Leal and Hess, 2000). This appears to reflect the wishes of Asian and Latino/a parents (Shin, 2000).

Most of what has been said about language differences and the education of Hispanic Americans is also largely true of the education of American Indians. Through much of our history, Indian education has emphasized the assimilation of Indians into the dominant white culture. In practice, this long meant placing Indian students in boarding schools, separating them from contact with their tribal culture, and allowing them exposure only to English in the schools. Such practices were common as recently as the 1940s and 1950s (Ogbu, 1978, p. 230).

Today, more than three-fourths of Native American students are in public schools; most of the rest are in either Bureau of Indian Affairs (BIA) Indian Schools or tribal schools (Pavel, 1999; Gehrke, 2001). In response to repeated failure of assimilationist educational programs in the past and to increasing demands of Indian people for self-determination, Indian education has begun to change, and many schools attended by Indian students now have bilingual education programs. Nonetheless, there is a long way to go, and Indian students in many white-dominated schools continue to be labeled slow learners simply because of linguistic differences, just as are many black and Latino/a students.

## Test Bias

One of the most controversial issues in the social sciences in recent years concerns differences in ability and achievement test scores between whites and various minority groups in the United States. There is no question that on average, blacks, Hispanics, and American Indians score lower than whites on standardized tests, although, of course, some individual members of all minority groups score far above the white average. Why are the average scores lower?

Some, most notably Arthur Jensen (1969, 1973), argue that the cause is genetic; those who hold this viewpoint have not been able to demonstrate any genetic factor associated with a racial difference in intelligence (Ogbu, 1978, p. 60). Another attempt to show that the racial gap in test scores is genetic was made by Herrnstein and Murray (1994) in a book titled *The Bell Curve*, and this effort gained widespread media attention. However, like other studies purporting to show such an explanation, this one had serious flaws, as can be seen in the box, "*The Bell Curve*: A Debate on Education, Intelligence, Genetics, and Achievement." The large volume of research the topic of race and IQ test scores indicates rather clearly that a more

## THE BELL CURVE: A DEBATE ON EDUCATION, INTELLIGENCE, GENETICS, AND ACHIEVEMENT

In 1994, Richard Herrnstein, a psychologist long known for his beliefs that race is genetically linked to intelligence, and Charles Murray, a political scientist, published *The Bell Curve*. In this book, the authors argued that intelligence is determined mostly by genes, that success in our society is largely and increasingly a product of intelligence, and that racial and economic inequality are largely the result of racial and class differences in intelligence. Therefore, they argued, efforts to bring about greater equality of opportunity, such as Head Start and similar compensatory education programs, as well as affirmative action, are doomed to fail.

In the conservative political atmosphere of 1994—when Newt Gingrich and the Republicans swept the elections to control Congress for the first time in decades—*The Bell Curve* was met with an unprecedented media hoopla. It was discussed on *Nightline* and in the *New York Times, Forbes, Newsweek*, and the *Wall Street Journal*. It received attention from the media and the public that went far beyond anything that usually occurs for an academic book. However, from those knowledgeable about its subject matter, it received a far more critical response. Sociologists in the fields of stratification, education, and intergroup relations have rejected it overwhelmingly (for examples, see Duster, 1995; Hauser, 1995; Massey, 1995; H. F. Taylor, 1995; Nisbett, 1998). In October 1994, the Science Directorate of the American Psychological Association issued a "media advisory" to the effect that the book had misstated research evidence about the effects of early childhood education programs such as Head Start.

What, precisely, did the experts find wrong with the book? Quite a number of things, it turns out. Sociologists and psychologists who have criticized the book have pointed out the following shortcomings, errors, and distortions:

- The book claims that IQ tests predict success in many areas of life, but the authors show only that they are correlated. Specifically, they almost never present numbers showing how much of the variation in school grades and other indicators can be explained by IQ. (None of my graduate students would get away with this!) In fact, IQ almost always explains less than 20 percent of the variation in such measures, and usually less than 10 percent (Duster, 1995; H. F. Taylor, 1995). Moreover, the authors present no data on the intelligence of people who hold positions in the occupational elite, and other studies show that intergenerational correlations of occupational success are declining—just the opposite of what Herrnstein and Murray's argument predicts (Hauser, 1995).
- The authors claim that IQ is genetically determined and that racial differences in IQ are mostly the result of

genes. But other data show that the black-white difference in average IQ test scores narrowed by about 30 percent in just twenty years between about 1970 and 1990. A genetically determined difference would be unlikely to change that much in such a short time (Hauser, 1995; Nisbett, 1995). Finally, the limited amount of research directly addressing the issue of genetic factors in the racial IQ difference is quite consistent in finding no effect that can be attributed to inherent or genetic racial differences (Nisbett, 1995). For example, the amount of white ancestry that African Americans have does not correlate significantly to their IQ scores, as would be the case if the difference were genetic (Nisbett, 1998, pp. 89–93). Also, black and white children raised in the same enriched institutional setting have similar IQs, while black children raised in different settings have different IQs correlated to the different settings (Nisbett, 1998, pp. 93–94).

- According to *The Bell Curve*, measured IQ is not much changed by education or by socioeconomic influences, but in the data used for the study, IQ was measured among people old enough (fourteen to twenty-three) that whatever effects these factors might have had would have already have taken place (Massey, 1995). By the age of fourteen, a person's IQ might be rather unchangeable not because of genetics but because it reflects fourteen years of social, economic, and educational influences. In general, educational research shows that achievement is much more subject to influence in early grades than in later grades.
- The authors claim that 60 percent to 70 percent of intelligence is genetically determined. But other research, based on identical twins (who share the same genetic background) placed in different social environments, suggests that 25 percent to 45 percent is a more reasonable range (H. F. Taylor, 1995). Recent research suggests it is even lower among poor and minority children (Turkheimer, 2003). In addition, even genetic conditions like Huntington's disease and sickle-cell anemia vary widely in their actual development, according to environmental conditions (Duster, 1995). Even a single neuron can respond in a variety of ways as its environment changes (Harris-Warrick and Marder, 1991). Similarly, a dietary supplement can lead to substantial improvements in mental development (Wahlsten, 1995).
- Although it is well known that the level of education has stronger effects than IQ on occupational success (Bowles and Gintis, 1976; Wolfe, 1995), the authors do not report the direct effects of education on occupa-

tional outcomes, nor do they control for the level of education when they report correlations between IQ and occupational outcomes (Gartrell and Marquez, 1995; Hauser, 1995).

- Finally, it is claimed that early childhood education does not change IQ. That may be largely true, but it does not negate the findings of many studies that early childhood education does have long-term effects on achievement (Duster, 1995). In fact, the reality that early childhood education does improve achievement without IQ changes undermines Murray and Herrnstein's argument that achievement is mostly a matter of IQ.

*The Bell Curve* may tell us more about our culture and attitudes than it does about intelligence and achievement. Despite its many flaws, the book clearly struck a chord. In part, this reflects a clever marketing strategy, in which advance copies were made available to expected supporters (including prominent media figures) but not to expected critics (Clawson, 1995). But it also reflects something more basic: a continuing belief that people pretty much get what they deserve and a backlash against programs intended to increase opportunities for minorities and the poor. In Massey's (1995) words, "Strong views about race, intelligence, and culture were widely held by the general public and politicians and formed the basis for much social policy, especially after 1980." In the context of such views, the book's success, despite its many flaws, is not surprising.

*Source:* The majority of this material is reprinted by permission from John E. Farley, *Sociology*, 5th ed. Upper Saddle River, NJ: Prentice Hall, 2003

fruitful place to look for an explanation is in the tests themselves, the testing situation, and the wider environment. Among the important factors that are known to influence IQ test scores are the following:

- Culture-specific content in the tests.
- The test situation
- Teachers' expectations
- Health and nutritional factors
- Perceived usefulness of doing well on the test

The differences that can be created by these factors appear to be more than enough to explain the differences in the average IQ score, about ten to fifteen points, that have been noted between whites and various minority group members. Indeed, even identical twins (twins with the same genetic makeup) raised apart sometimes display IQ differences of this order. Let us explore the various factors that affect IQ test scores.

**Culture-Specific Content.** Although IQ tests are designed to assess ability (what one is capable of learning, not what one already knows), ability cannot in fact be directly measured (Vernon, 1969). All that any test can measure directly is knowledge or task performance: what the person knows or does. It is hoped that the knowledge measured by IQ tests is associated with innate ability, but this assumption has come increasingly under question. What IQ tests in fact seem to measure is the knowledge, habits, skills, and modes of thinking (all *learned* characteristics) that are valued by the dominant cultural group in any society (Berger, 1978; Ogbu, 1978, pp. 30–37). In other words, IQ tests are designed to predict school achievement, and they do correlate modestly with that attribute. The reason is that they largely measure the attributes and skills needed to get ahead in the school system. Jencks (1998, pp. 60–64) calls this *developed capacity*, reflecting things one has actually learned, not just what one *can* learn. This can be illustrated in several ways. Today, most Americans would not take seriously the notion that people of Italian, Russian, or Polish heritage are inherently less intelligent than those of British or German heritage, nor do test scores today suggest this. However, in the early twentieth century, when these immigrant groups were new arrivals unfamiliar with American culture, they *did* score lower on the tests. Furthermore, much of the intellectual community of the time incorrectly believed that these groups were genetically inferior. For example, one author argued that 83 percent of Jewish and 79 percent of Italian immigrants were "feeble-minded" (Henry Goddard, cited in Kamin, 1974). Obviously, the reason for their low scores was cultural, not genetic.

Another example can be seen in the Goodenough Draw-a-Man IQ test. Although the test was designed to be culture-free, it has not turned out that way. In general, groups whose cultures stress art do well on this test. Southwestern Indians—who have highly developed arts—are generally shown by this test to be more "intelligent" than whites. However, the same Indians tend to score lower than whites on verbal IQ tests, which are geared to the white culture. Thus, the differences in "intelligence" between whites and Indians as measured by these tests are cultural, not genetic (Ogbu, 1978, p. 218). It is a matter of what abilities are *developed*.

The cultural biases in intelligence tests and their effects on blacks and other minority groups are well illustrated by an example given by black psychiatrist Alvin Poussaint (1977; see also Kagan, 1971, pp. 92–93). On one IQ test, there was this question: "Your mother sends you to the store to get a loaf of bread. The store is closed. What should you do?" The "correct" answer: Go to the next-closest store and get it there. There were important group differences in response to this question. Rural children got it "wrong" because the next-closest store might be 10 miles away. Inner-city black children also got the question "wrong" because they answered that they would go back home and ask what to do. Poussaint argues that for these children, this was the right answer. Interviews with the children indicated that some felt that going to another store might be unsafe because of dangers associated with gangs who controlled that "turf." Thus, these children were penalized even though they gave what *for them* was the most intelligent answer. Pouissant, Kagan, and others argue that questions followed by interviews with students about their answers would give a more reliable measure of IQ than straight test items. Many in the field of intelligence testing agree, and some of the better tests follow this model. However, time and expense limitations do not always permit such a careful approach.

This item was eventually removed from the test, and many of the more obviously discriminatory items are now gone from IQ tests. Supporters of the tests back this claim by showing that minorities and low-income children no longer do particularly poorly on any given items relative to their overall test scores (Sandoval, 1979; Sattler, 1982, pp. 357–58; Jencks, 1998). Supporters also argue that the tests are not biased because they do not underpredict minority achievement. In other words, a black with an IQ test score of 100 will do no better in school than a white with a score of 100, and if the tests were really unfair, he or she would do better.

Critics of the tests reply that this does not prove that the tests are unbiased—only that, to the extent that they predict school success, the tests may be measuring the same knowledge, beliefs, and habits that the school system rewards. If this is true, the tests could have some success in predicting school success but would still be far from unbiased indicators of innate ability. In fact, even Sattler (1982), who generally supports the use of intelligence testing, acknowledges that tests do not measure innate intelligence but rather an interaction of intelligence and environmental effects (p. 54) and that a number of factors associated with socioeconomic status and race, but unrelated to ability, do affect test scores (pp. 52–56). A survey of testing psychologists showed that nearly all agreed with this view (Snyderman and Rothman, 1987). Among the relevant factors are language models in the home, strictness of upbringing, and family emphasis on achievement and independent thinking, all of which have been shown to vary by social class. This interpretation is very consistent with Jencks's (1998) concept of tests as measures of developed capacity.

A related problem is that even the best tests are limited in their ability to predict later success. Partly for this reason, racial differences in the tests are almost always larger than racial differences in the performance they are trying to predict. For example, high school grades predict college grades better than ACT or SAT scores, and college grades do not vary by race to the same extent that test scores do (Jencks, 1998). This problem is even worse for employment tests: Racial differences in measures of on-the-job performance are far smaller than racial differences in scores on tests used in hiring. In both cases, the results are that many qualified people of color are excluded (Jencks, 1998).

Similar criticisms have been made of the standardized "readiness tests" that are sometimes used to determine whether young children should enter kindergarten, be delayed a year, or be assigned to a two-year developmental kindergarten program. To a large extent, these tests measure skills and knowledge that reflect past opportunities to learn, not inherent ability (Medina and Neill, 1988; Bredekamp and Shepard, 1989). As with IQ and job tests, early childhood developmental tests contain considerable error as predictors of later performance. For example, one widely used kindergarten readiness test misidentified between one-third and one-half of the children said to be unready (Bredekamp and Shepard, 1989).

*Within* any group, inherent differences undoubtedly do account for part (not all) of the variation between individuals in IQ test scores. This does not follow when we are looking at differences in average IQ test scores *between* groups, however. Rather, group differences in familiarity with the culture-specific knowledge and modes of thinking measured by the test probably offer much of the explanation of such group differences in scores.

**Test Situation.** In addition to the content of the test itself, certain aspects of the test situation have also been shown significant. Some studies have shown that the typical formality of the test situation tends to lower the scores of poor and minority group children. When the test is given in an informal, supportive setting or in the context of play, the IQ scores of such children rise significantly (Haggard, 1954; Golden and Birns, 1968; Palmer, 1970; Zigler, Abelson, and Seitz, 1973) and racial and social class differences are reduced or eliminated. Even Jensen (1980) noted increases of eight to ten points in the IQ scores of low-income children as the result of play therapy.

One reason for this is that a formal testing situation may call to mind stereotypes and labels and lead to a self-fulfilling expectation of poor performance (Steele and Aronson, 1998). Steele and Aronson (1995) found that when a standardized test on math was described as a test of intellectual ability, black college students did less well on the test than similarly qualified white students. But when the same test was described as a "problem-solving task," the black students did as well on average as the whites. The reason: A "test of intellectual ability" called to mind negative societal stereotypes about blacks, leading to a condition Steele calls "stereotype threat" in which being reminded of a negative label hurt the performance of the black students. In fact, Steele and Aronson found through a word association task that blacks thought about race and expressed anxiety and self-doubt more with the "intellectual test" description than with the "problem-solving task" description (Steele and Aronson, 1998). When the test was described in a way that did not call stereotypes to mind, their performance was much better. Of course, the term "test" is much more widely used than "problem-solving task," so such stereotype threat effects may be quite common. Interestingly, Steele (1999) and Aronson et al. (1999) found that under some conditions, stereotype threat can also lower the scores of white males, who are generally regarded as "good" at math. They found that if the math test was described as one on which Asian American students do well (a commonly believed stereotype of Asian Americans), the white males felt threatened by the stereotype that Asian Americans were better at math, and their scores went down.

Another problem is linguistic differences, which can lead to testing bias, as well as to the types of general classroom bias we have already examined. For example, some Hispanic children have been labeled as having low intelligence because they were given intelligence tests in English rather than Spanish. Such imputation of low intelligence on the basis of linguistic differences is both inaccurate and harmful to the child.

**Teacher Expectations.** We have already discussed this topic at some length, but it is important to remind ourselves that Rosenthal and Jacobson's (1968) classic study used IQ test scores as the dependent variable and found ten- to fifteen-point IQ differences in the first and second grades as a result of differences in teacher expectations. Although the particular test used by Rosenthal and Jacobson is especially sensitive to social influences, it seems reasonable to expect that when IQ tests or other kinds of standardized tests are given to students who have been in school a year or two (so that teachers have had some time to form and act on expectations), the results may to some degree be influenced by teacher expectations—which, as we have seen, are in turn related to the race and social class of the child.

**Health and Nutritional Factors.** Even primarily hereditary physical characteristics such as height are significantly affected by nutrition and other factors related to physical health. Thus, it hardly comes as a surprise that these factors can also influence IQ scores. Because minority groups are greatly overrepresented in the nation's impoverished population, they are more likely than others to suffer prenatal and childhood deficiencies in nutrition that can later inhibit their ability to do well on tests.

**Perceived Usefulness of High Test Performance.** Ogbu (1978) has raised another interesting factor that may help to explain low scores by minorities on standardized achievement tests. His theory focuses on the fact that there is less payoff for education for minorities than for whites. Put simply, educational success provides a greater return in the form of high-paying jobs for whites than it does for minorities. R. Farley's (1984, pp. 84–88) analysis of 1980 census data on income showed this, and data as recent as 2001 show it is still true, despite gains from affirmative action. In 2001, white full-time workers with bachelor's degrees earned about $18,800 more than white workers with a high school diploma. For African Americans and Hispanics, respectively, the corresponding income gain was only about $14,900 and $14,650 (computed from U.S. Census Bureau, 2003n, Tables 8, 9, 10). Whites also gained slightly more on a percentage basis by getting a college degree. Research by Tienda, Donato, and Cordero-Guzman (1992) has documented that in terms of employment, women of color receive fewer returns for education than white women, a gap that widened between 1960 and 1987. Ogbu (1978, p. 37) argues that this affects the scores of minority students on all types of educational tests and tasks: "Doing well on these tests, like doing well on academic tasks generally, is not as rewarding for caste minorities as it is for the dominant group. Thus, caste minority children often do not take such tests seriously enough to try for the best scores they can get."

According to Ogbu (1978, pp. 235–36), white Anglo parents teach their children to "persevere in school regardless of the boredom and unpleasantness involved *because they will be rewarded in the future with desirable social positions and jobs.*" Minority children may not be so encouraged by their parents because the experiences of minority group parents "are different: education has not usually brought the same desirable social and occupational rewards." Ogbu (1978, p. 37) notes that there is real evidence of such underachievement on tests. Observations by psychologists generally indicate that minority children communicate with their peers, solve problems, and use concepts in ways typical of children who have Binet-type IQs ten to fifteen points higher than theirs.

A related problem, suggested by Ogbu and others, may lie in a common reaction to discrimination and oppression by members of groups we have called *colonized minorities* (Fordham and Ogbu, 1986; Zweigenhaft and Domhoff, 1991; Gibson and Ogbu, 1992). Because they were originally forced into American society involuntarily, then subjected to exploitation and discrimination through the generations, these groups may have developed an *oppositional* culture or identity that views the dominant culture and institutions with distrust and sometimes outright resistance. Ogbu argues that in some circumstances, this leads black and other minority students to view working hard in school as "acting white," so that peer pressures may oppose efforts by minority students to do well in school. However, this argument probably is more debatable than the idea that minority students make less effort on tests because they do not see the payoff. Studies of broader attitudes toward school generally show that these attitudes do not vary much by race among adolescents (Ainsworth-Darnell and Downey, 1998; Cook and Ludwig, 1998; Carter, cited in Tyson, 2002), although it is not uncommon for students of any race to disparage academic achievement (Steinberg, 1996). Among younger students, attitudes toward achievement may be more positive, and the limited research available does not suggest peer pressure opposing school achievement among black children (Towson, 2002).

## Testing Bias: Summary

To summarize briefly, we have seen that numerous factors unrelated to ability tend to cause minority children to receive lower than average scores on intelligence tests and other kinds of standardized tests. If the tests are given to entire classes and used to compare children, or if they are the major criterion for decisions about higher education admissions or employment, serious harm is likely for two reasons. First, it leads to incorrect labeling of minority children as "slow learners," which hurts their ability to learn, their self-image, and their relationships with their peers. Second, it leads to their placement in "slow" tracks or ability groups or to denial of admission to students who could succeed, with harmful consequences for their future opportunities. Thus, if tests are used, they should be used as a way of learning about and helping individual students who are already having problems, *not* as a way of screening, classifying, or comparing children (Sattler, 1982, p. 384).

However, test bias has more general harmful implications for minority groups. First, it has tended to reinforce racist thinking about the intelligence of minority groups by creating the belief that it can be "scientifically proven" that some groups are genetically inferior to others, even though there is in fact no genetic basis for the different scores (Nisbett, 1995, 1998). Moreover, test score differences can be well explained by the biases and situational factors we have discussed.[1] Unfortunately, the public is often not exposed to the scientific critiques of work such as Jensen (1969) or Herrnstein and Murray (1994). Thus, claims based on tests purported to measure intelligence often are taken at face value by the public, even though they have recieved widespread scientific criticism.

Another problem follows directly from such works. Jensen (1969), Herrnstein and Murray (1994), and others have argued that the supposed hereditary aspects of the racial IQ score difference make any effort at compensatory education largely hopeless. Although they are correct in pointing out that many compensatory education programs have not been successful, it is quite another thing to argue that no program to improve the educational opportunities of minorities *can* be successful. An example of how the public can react to such arguments occurred just five days after Jensen's article was widely publicized. In Virginia, it was used in a federal court case by opponents of school desegregation to "prove" that black students could not

---

[1]In addition, critics of the hereditary explanation note that neither blacks nor whites in America are genetically "pure," because there has been extensive racial interbreeding, and that the IQ scores of blacks and other minorities vary across the same range as those of whites.

be helped by integration (Brazziel, 1969). Thus, a real danger in the use of biased tests is that they will reinforce public beliefs that some races are superior to others and that efforts to improve minority education are doomed to failure.

Nonetheless, standardized testing has become more widely used than in the past. In particular, there has been a dramatic increase in standardized testing of younger children, from kindergarten entry through second grade, since the 1970s (Perrone, 1991). This growth in testing is a product of efforts such as the 2002 No Child Left Behind Act to make schools more accountable for what children learn, but it creates problems for reasons outlined earlier. Standardized testing is particularly problematic when children are labeled at such early ages because group placements and decisions to retain children based on these tests have effects that can linger throughout a child's educational career. These effects occur because the tests misclassify many children and contain cultural biases, because tracking and grouping based on such tests often are inflexible, and because the effects of delayed entry into kindergarten or the increasingly common practice of flunking kindergarten are long-standing (Bredekamp and Shepard, 1989; Perrone, 1991). The result is that children who are negatively labeled by the tests are held back for reasons that often have little or nothing to do with their true abilities. And, of course, it is low-income children and children of color who are most likely to be held back in this manner.

Additionally, the punitive aspects of the No Child Left Behind Act may lead to new forms of discrimination. As part of its accountability provisions, the law allows children in districts where average test scores are low to transfer to nearby districts. School funding follows them, which could mean the districts that need the most help actually lose funding. However, there are also unintended incentives that may deny opportunities to poor and minority children. In 2003, for example, the majority-white Belleville, Illinois, district refused to take transfers from the nearby predominantly African American East St. Louis district because of fears that doing so would get Belleville added to the list of deficient districts. The superintendent argued, "It would be virtually impossible to get them to perform adequately on the tests in just one year," and if they didn't, the district would be penalized in the same ways that East St. Louis is now. He also noted that it is a national problem, a view echoed by the president of the American Association of School Administrators, John Lawrence, who expressed fears that the federal law may lead to the unintended perception that some students are hurting entire

Teacher-student interactions have important effects on student learning. One example of this is the self-fulfilling prophecy: When teachers expect students to do well, they tend to actually do better. When teacher expectations are lower, student performance is not as good.

**Table 12.3  Representation of Blacks and Hispanics in the Teaching Profession, 1983, 1991, 1994, and 2000**

| Population | Percentage Black | | | | Percentage Hispanic | | | |
|---|---|---|---|---|---|---|---|---|
| | *1983* | *1991* | *1993–1994* | *1999–2000* | *1983* | *1991* | *1993–1994* | *1999–2000* |
| All employed people | 9.3% | 10.1% | 10.8% | 10.0% | 5.3% | 7.5% | 8.5% | 10.3% |
| College teachers | 4.4 | 4.8 | 4.7 | 5.1 | 1.8 | 2.9 | 2.2 | 3.3 |
| High school teachers | 7.2 | 7.3 | 6.0 | 6.5 | 2.3 | 3.4 | 3.4 | 5.1 |
| Elementary school teachers | 11.1 | 8.9 | 8.6 | 9.7 | 3.1 | 3.3 | 5.0 | 7.7 |

*Source:* U.S. Bureau of Labor Statistics (1984); U.S. Bureau of the Census (1992b, 1999); National Center for Education Statistics (1997; 2003b, Tables 68, 72, 231); U.S. Census Bureau (2003c, Tables P43, P150b, h, i).

schools or districts (Aguilar, 2003). Thus, although the intent of the law is good, its overreliance on testing may end up worsening the very problems it was intended to solve. It is perhaps time for a more objective appraisal by educators and policymakers of the true costs and benefits of standardized testing, despite its great popularity.

## Lack of Minority Role Models

A final factor in the education of minorities is the lack of role models. As shown in Table 12.3, blacks and Hispanics at all levels of education are underrepresented in the teaching profession. Only in the case of black elementary teachers does the minority proportion among teachers come close to that among all workers. At the elementary and secondary levels, there are relatively fewer African American teachers than there were twenty years ago. Compared with other professions, teaching has historically been relatively open to minorities and women. But more recently, as opportunities have opened in other fields paying higher salaries, such as accounting and management, growing numbers of minorities and women have turned away from teaching toward these higher-paying fields (Shenker, 1992).

It is also true that the higher the position in the educational system, the fewer the minority members there are. Thus, there are proportionately fewer minority principals and superintendents than minority teachers. Similarly, the percentage of minority teachers declines from elementary school to high school to college. Surely this gives an important message to all students about the roles to which they might aspire.

## ► RACIAL BIAS IN THE EDUCATIONAL SYSTEM: AN EVALUATION

All of the evidence we have reviewed, taken as a whole, strongly suggests that the present educational system operates in certain ways that prevent minority students from achieving their full potential. This impression is supported by findings that the minority-white gap in learning increases over the course of the educational process (Phillips, Crouse, and Ralph, 1998). As we have seen, a big piece of the problem is related to the fact that those who control our educational institutions and a great many minority students are, quite simply, culturally different from one another. To some degree, the problems of bias in educational materials, linguistic differences, teacher expectations, tracking, and testing all arise from these cultural differences. Given this reality, it is not surprising that research shows that merely spending more money, or increasing the "quality" of minority education, will not do much good. The problem, at least in part, is that schools demand and reward certain values, beliefs, and habits and that they (often unconsciously and unintentionally) hold back students who do not have these values.

How can we resolve the problem of incompatibility between the attitudes and habits demanded by the schools and the diverse cultures of American ethnic and socioeconomic groups? Several answers are possible, some associated with the functionalist perspective, some with the conflict perspective, and some falling somewhere in between. One answer, of course, is that we cannot resolve the problem of incompatibility—and, curiously, this answer has been offered for different reasons by social scientists who identify with both the functionalist and conflict perspectives.

Another answer—an *assimilationist* answer offered by some of those associated with the functionalist perspective—is that the schools must find ways to teach middle-class values and beliefs and must oppose symbols of difference such as distinct languages and dialects. This view counsels against any drastic changes in the educational system itself but suggests that the system do what it can to help minority and poor children learn the skills, attitudes, and habits they need to succeed.

Yet another answer, which stands in opposition to the assimilationist view, is held by a variety of experts, including some conflict theorists. This *multiculturalist* view holds that American society is made up of a variety of distinct cultures and group experiences and that students should not have to conform to that of the dominant group, Anglo-Europeans. Thus, the distinct cultures and experiences of children from different groups must be recognized and valued by the schools. If this is done, achievement can be encouraged through role modeling and the enhancement of self-esteem.

Finally another view draws on insights from both the functionalist and conflict theories but is best classified as *interactionist* because it sees the source of the problem in interpersonal processes between teachers and minority and poor students. This view agrees with the conflict perspective insofar as it believes that part of the problem arises from the unfounded negative judgments about minority and poor students, based on their culture, that are made by teachers and other school personnel. However, it agrees with the functionalist perspective in seeing certain middle-class values, such as achievement motivation and independent thinking, as socially useful, although it does not necessarily favor assimilation in other areas. What is different about this view is that it sees the *process* of education as the critical factor. In other words, what really matters is how teachers think and behave toward their students (which is shaped by the students' cultures and how school personnel react to them) and how students respond to that behavior by their teachers. In the remainder of this chapter, we shall explore the varying approaches to minority group education as suggested by each of these four general viewpoints.

## ▶ RESOLVING PROBLEMS OF MAJORITY-MINORITY INEQUALITY IN EDUCATION: FOUR APPROACHES

### Approach 1: The Problem Does Not Lie in the Educational System

**Conservatism: "Blaming the Victim."** As we have seen, unequal test scores and the failure of some programs to improve minority education have led some people to conclude that it is hopeless to try to improve the educational opportunities of minority students by reforming the educational system. There is both a conservative and a radical version of this viewpoint. The conservative variant often makes the mistake of assuming that the tests are true indicators of ability—an assumption that, as we have seen, is largely incorrect because of various forms of bias in the process and content of "ability" testing. A slightly different version of this view holds that the culture of blacks and other minorities is the cause of the problem. They adopt the culture of poverty or cultural deficit model, arguing—as do a wide range of functionalist theorists—that the values, beliefs, family structure, and so on of minority group members make it impossible for them to advance educationally and that there is little that can or should be done to change this situation (see Banfield, 1968, 1974). This view is clearly racist in the sense that it blames minorities for their disadvantages, when the true source of that disadvantage is a long and continuing history of discrimination, and because it regards as completely acceptable—perhaps even desirable—a continuing pattern of racial inequality in education and most other areas. Nonetheless, it would be a mistake to underestimate the popularity of this view: As we have seen before (see Feagin, 1972; Schuman, 1975), a great many Americans do believe that minorities are to blame for their own disadvantages.

**Economics Versus Education.** The radical version of the view that education can't make much difference holds that the attitudes and values of the minority underclass are a product of its situation, and because of the incompatibility between these attitudes and those of the school personnel, change through the educational system is unlikely. In essence, the roots of educational inequality lie in an economic system that produces great inequality. These scholars, including Jencks et al. (1972), Bowles and Gintis (1976), and Ogbu (1978), argue that the only way to bring meaningful change is to change the economic system, not education. As we shall see shortly, however, other researchers, including conflict theorists, have shown that the educational system can make a difference.

## Approach 2: Assimilation—Compensatory Education and Desegregation Through Busing

**Compensatory Education.** Whereas a great many social scientists do hold views consistent with the culture of poverty or cultural-deficit theories, many of them are not in favor of neglecting the problem of racial inequality. Instead, they favor programs to bring about *cultural assimilation*: to teach to minority students the values and habits they need to get ahead in school and in life. This viewpoint is clearly aligned with the order perspective in that it does not question the need to maintain consensus on dominant (middle-class) values and beliefs. However, it is more liberal than the "blaming the victim" viewpoint because it seeks to bring about more equal educational outcomes rather than accepting racial and class inequality as a given. One approach arising from this liberal version of the order perspective is *compensatory education*: preschool programs for low-income and minority children and, in some cases, supplementary programs within the regular classroom. The idea is to expose disadvantaged children to educational materials and to teach them skills, habits, and values related to education, compensating for what is believed to be missing in the home. The largest and best-known example is the Head Start preschool program.

Early research appeared to show that Head Start and similar compensatory education programs were ineffective in bringing about improved learning (Cicirelli, Evans, and Schiller, 1969; White, 1970; Little and Smith, 1971; Stanley, 1973; for a review see Ogbu, 1978). This led some conflict theorists to argue that such programs are ineffective because they do not change the basic operation of the educational system but simply offer "more of the same" (Baratz and Baratz, 1970; Bowles and Gintis, 1976; Ogbu, 1978). In other words, conflict theorists believed that the programs were attempts to "teach" minority or poor people cultural characteristics that were contrary to their experiences and that they were failing for that reason.

However, more recent research has found that the proclamations of failure in the 1970s were premature. Because one problem with early research was small samples, several researchers in early childhood education decided in 1975 to pool their data to generate a much larger sample. At the same time, early studies were being reanalyzed with more sophisticated methodology, and many new data were being collected. By the late 1970s, these more comprehensive research efforts were generating different and more scientifically sound findings (B. Brown, 1985). By 1978, a review of ninety-six valid studies revealed clear gains among students in early childhood compensatory education programs compared with other students (Brown et al., 1978). Later research (Lazar et al., 1982, 1997; Consortium for Longitudinal Studies, 1979, 1983) showed that early education programs

- Reduce the number of children who need to be placed in special education, even among children of similar background and initial ability
- Reduce the number of children who have to repeat a grade
- Raise IQ and achievement, at least through the early years of elementary school
- Produce a higher achievement self-image and higher parental aspirations

Studies of one program found such effects to be quite long term, extending into adolescence and early adulthood in the form of reduced delinquency, unemployment, and teenage pregnancy (Berrueta-Clement et al., 1984; see also Weber, Foster, and Weikart, 1978; Lazar, 1981).

Nonetheless, there continues to be debate about the long-term effects of Head Start and similar programs as they are usually implemented (Zigler and Muenchow, 1992). Some studies have focused on the best-designed programs, which do appear to have such benefits (M. Kramer, 1993). Long-term studies of more representative samples of Head Start programs generally show little if any effect on achievement test scores after about two years, but they also show that students with Head Start experience are more likely to be in the proper grade (as opposed to being held back) and less likely to be placed in special education classes (McKey et al., 1985; Zigler and Muenchow, 1992). When they reach high school age and beyond, they are less likely to become involved in delinquency, more likely to graduate from high school, and more likely to be employed a year after high school graduation (Helmich, 1985). Thus, Head Start and similar programs may not increase test scores, but they do appear to increase the amount of education that their participants ultimately get and to have other benefits in employment and delinquency.

As a result of Head Start's success, it has been steadily expanded in recent years, serving 450,000 children in 1985 and around 700,000 in 1993. As noted, some of these children are better served than others. Among the suggestions to improve Head Start are to increase accountability, so that all programs function more like the best ones; to address attendance problems; to lengthen the average Head Start day from four hours to a full day to facilitate mothers' employment; and to increase the program from one year (as it is for many children) to two because research shows that two-year programs produce more long-term benefits (A. C. Lewis, 1992; Zigler and Muenchow, 1992; Besharov, 1993; M. Kramer, 1993). It is important to keep in mind that, despite its benefits, compensatory education alone has not fully ended educational inequality along the lines of race and class, nor is there evidence that by itself it could reasonably be expected to do so (Zigler and Muenchow, 1992).

**Desegregation Through Busing.** Another, quite different approach to minority education is the effort to combat urban de facto school segregation through busing. Although some see busing as a radical proposal, it basically arises from the functionalist perspective's ideas on cultural deprivation and the need for assimilation. Much of the theoretical argument behind busing can be traced to the Coleman Report (Coleman et al., 1966). Recall that the study found that the background characteristics of *fellow students* were an important factor in the learning of minority and low-income students. Specifically, the more "advantaged" their fellow students, the better the minority students did. When their fellow students were more exposed at home to books, newspapers, and television, and their fellow students had attitudes and beliefs associated with educational success, minority and low-income students also did better (Coleman et al., 1966, pp. 302–5). Minority students also generally learned more in racially and economically integrated schools than in segregated schools (pp. 307–12, 330–31). In integrated schools, the learning of white students was as good as in segregated schools, and the white students generally appreciated the intergroup contact. Coleman suggests that minority students do better in integrated schools because they adopt the attitudes, beliefs, and study habits of their fellow students and consequently do better. In short, assimilation of minorities occurs. Thus, Coleman's suggestion fits well within the functionalist perspective and its emphasis on cultural assimilation.

The finding that minority students do better in integrated schools—coupled with a theory that explains why—was seen by many as convincing proof that equal educational opportunity could occur only through the creation of an integrated school system. But because schools have neighborhood attendance districts, and neighborhoods are segregated, the only way to bring about school desegregation in many urban areas was to bus minority children to schools in white neighborhoods or vice versa.

The Coleman Report was frequently cited in court cases over school desegregation as "proof" that equal educational opportunity for minorities required that schools be integrated, by means of busing if necessary. During the two decades after the Coleman Report was published in 1966, busing for school desegregation was initiated, on varying scales, in many cities. This often occurred as a result of lawsuits. However, as noted earlier, many court-ordered busing plans were ended by the courts in the 1990s, and others are now under legal challenge.

While the legal and political debates continue, sufficient research has been done on school busing to draw some conclusions about whether desegregation has benefitted minorities in the ways the Coleman Report suggested it might. The answer appears to be that it does have such benefits, but not to an unlimited degree and only under certain circumstances. Some of the many studies have shown that desegregation has beneficial effects on the achievement and education of minority students, and some have not. Among the areas in which a number of studies show improvement are the academic achievement (and in some cases, also IQ scores) of minority students (Pettigrew et al., 1973; St. John, 1975; Crain and Mahard, 1982; Wortman and Bryant, 1985; Rossell and Glenn, 1988; Orfield et al., 1991) and the probability that minority students will go on to attend college or get better jobs (Armor, 1972; Braddock, 1985; Janyes and Williams, 1989). Not all studies show improvement in these areas, but few if any show minority students in desegregated schools to be less well off. Some studies show very substantial results.

Wells and Crain (1997) studied the city-suburb voluntary transfer program in St. Louis, which has provided opportunities for about 14,000 African American students to attend integrated schools in the St. Louis suburbs. The study found that these students have had dramatically better chances of graduating and going to college. Black students transferring to the suburbs were twice as likely to graduate as those who stayed in city schools, and the differences in going to college were even bigger. Of 100 African Americans entering St. Louis public high schools as freshmen, just 13 graduated and went to college. But of 100 African Americans who transferred to the suburbs as freshmen, 40 percent graduated and went to college—three times as many as in the city (Wells and Crain, 1997, p. 198). This difference can be seen in Figure 12.2. According to Orfield (1997; Orfield and Eaton, 1996), peer expectations and pressure are a big reason for this improvement. When a student attends a school where 75 percent of his or her classmates are going to college, this student is much more likely to stay in school and plan on college than would be the case if he or she stayed in a school where more than 70 percent of the students

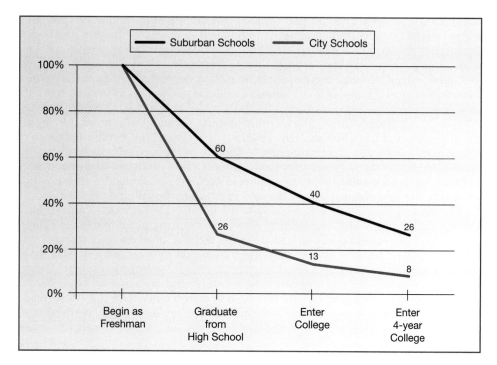

**FIGURE 12.2**    Experiences of 100 African American Freshmen from St. Louis City in City and Suburban Schools

*Source:* Wells and Crain, (1997).

will not even graduate from high school, as is in the case in the city of St. Louis. The high percentage who do not graduate in St. Louis city reflects the concentrated poverty in many inner-city neighborhoods; in St. Louis and other large cities, attending schools where many other students come from poor families is a major cause of the academic difficulties of African American students (Trent, 1997).

When an expert panel convened by the National Institute on Education analyzed a number of studies on effects of school desegregation, it concluded that the best-designed studies showed an average two-month educational gain by black students when they went from segregated to desegregated schools (Wortman and Bryant, 1985). Moreover, the research is quite consistent in showing that the achievement of white middle-class students does not decline when they attend desegregated schools (Orfield et al., 1991). Another benefit of desegregation is that it often triggers beneficial reforms in curriculum and teaching methods (Beady and Slavin, 1980; Center for Education and Human Development Policy, 1981; D. M. Foley, 1993).

As noted, studies find widely varying effects. Some show large effects of desegregation, some small effects and some no effects. One reason for this is that the effects of desegregation vary under different conditions. It appears that improving the achievement of minority students depends on how the desegregation is carried out, the racial and political climate in which it occurs, and social and demographic characteristics of the urban area in which it occurs.

**Effects of How Desegregation is Carried Out.**    In terms of how desegregation is carried out, some of the key issues are the age of the children in the desegregated schools, the geographic scope of the area in the desegregation plan (particularly whether it includes both city and suburban schools or just city schools), and whether there is mandatory busing or parental choice. Other key issues are the preparation of the school staff for desegregation and the degree of integration or segregation *within* schools whose student bodies have been desegregated. In general, desegregation appears to have the largest benefits for student achievement when it occurs in the early grades. For example, one review of the literature showed that every study of desegregated kindergarteners indicated achievement gains (Crain and Mahard, 1982). Overall, it appears that the more grades that are covered, the better desegregation plans work (Orfield et al., 1991).

In general, metropolitan-wide desegregation plans are more effective than plans that involve only central-city children. Metropolitan-wide plans eliminate the opportunity for whites to flee to all-white suburban schools, and they also produce greater gains in achievement and IQ (Crain and Mahard, 1982). Based on findings such as these, a group of fifty-eight desegregation experts recommended to the Supreme Court in 1991 that desegregation plans should encompass as large a geographic area as possible (Orfield et al., 1991).

The degree of segregation *within* schools that have been desegregated also has significant effects on minority student achievement. For example, if a formerly all-white school becomes racially mixed but such practices as inflexible tracking put black and white students into different classes, the benefits of desegregation may be lost. In desegregated schools with no tracking or with flexible tracking, mixed learning groups, and group rewards for learning, minority achievement is enhanced (Epstein, 1985; Slavin, 1985). Pettigrew (1969a, 1969b) draws a distinction between mere desegregation—simply altering the proportion of white and black students attending the schools—and true integration, where real efforts are made to bring about closer and more friendly relations between the races. In some cases, the use of materials that teachers did not realize were degrading to minority groups has caused problems in newly desegregated classrooms, so sensitivity to this issue is needed. It is also important that teaching staffs, as well as students, be integrated, so that there are minority teachers and principals. In short, true integration requires extensive planning, preparation, effort, and in many cases changes in established practices.

To improve the educational performance of minority students, *socioeconomic* desegregation, as well as racial desegregation, is desirable. The original findings of the Coleman Report strongly support this view: The habits and beliefs that relate to academic achievement were associated with social class, just as they were with race and ethnicity. Subsequent experience has supported this view, as the case of South Boston (see Chapter 3) illustrates: Transferring poor black and poor white students between two schools that have always been characterized by low levels of learning can be expected to do little or nothing to help the learning of either black or white students. Sociologist Gary Orfield (quoted in Kunen, 1996, p. 18), put it this way: "The whole discussion of desegregation is corrupted by the fact that we mix up race and class. You don't gain anything from sitting next to somebody with a different skin color. But you gain a lot from moving from an isolated poverty setting into a middle-class setting." In the 1992–1993 school year, the nearly all-white LaCrosse, Wisconsin, school district became the first in the nation to implement a program designed to reduce socioeconomic segregation in its schools.

A major purpose of school desegregation, besides bringing about more equal educational opportunity, has been to improve intergroup relations. The evidence on the effectiveness of school desegregation in improving intergroup relations seems mixed (Fishbein, 1996, pp. 218–26), but predominantly positive over the longer run. In some cases, the short-term effects have been quite bad, but long-term positive effects are common. Desegregation's success or failure in improving intergroup relations, particularly in the short term, depends largely on conditions discussed in Chapter 3 regarding effects of intergroup contact: equal status, interdependency, and the absence of threat and excessive competition. Interdependency may be particularly important: A review of thirteen studies of cooperative interaction in the classroom showed that it nearly always reduced discrimination in the school, and these reductions were lasting (Fishbein, 1996, pp. 234–41). There was less impact on attitudes, but the consistency with which cooperative interaction led to less discrimination is striking.

**Racial and Political Climate of the Community: The Role of Leadership.** In communities where busing led to serious violence—such as Boston; Louisville, Kentucky; and, several years earlier, Pontiac, Michigan—the actions of community leadership apparently played an important role in creating the trouble. A national survey of 532 school districts (U.S. Commission on Civil Rights, 1976, p. 175) shows that in the 411 districts that had no serious disruptions, 65 percent had business leaders who were generally supportive of or neutral toward desegregation, and 67 percent had political leaders who were supportive or neutral. On the other hand, among the 95 districts that did have serious disruptions, only 27 percent had generally supportive or neutral business leaders, and only 30 percent had supportive or neutral political leaders. Boston, Louisville, and Pontiac were all to some degree marked by local leadership that emphasized its adamant opposition to busing rather than the need to cooperate with the program (U.S. Commission on Civil Rights, 1976, pp. 179–83). In cities where the local leaders took the view that regardless of its popularity, busing was inevitable and that violent opposition would harm the schoolchildren and worsen the situation, even large-scale desegregation programs were implemented without serious disruption; Detroit and Columbus, Ohio, are two examples. Communities where the political, business, labor, and religious leaders make a vigorous effort to prepare the community for desegregation are less likely to have problems.

**Social and Demographic Characteristics of the Community.** In general, the literature on school desegregation suggests that its benefits can be expected to be the greatest when the minority population is somewhere in the general range of 20 to 55 percent—enough to go beyond mere tokenism (Rist, 1978) but not so great as to represent a lack of true desegregation. In many large cities, however, the public school enrollment is too overwhelmingly minority to meaningfully integrate a large proportion of the city's schools unless schools from nearby suburban districts are also included in the desegregation plan. Minority enrollments have long exceeded 80 percent in Chicago, Washington, and Baltimore and 70 percent in San Antonio; Newark, New Jersey; Phoenix; Birmingham, Alabama; New York City; Detroit; Philadelphia; and St. Louis. One approach tried in some places is busing between predominantly black central cities and nearby white suburbs, but in 1974 the Supreme Court ruled in the *Milliken v. Bradley* case that cross-district busing was not required by law unless deliberate government action had been taken to create city-suburb segregation. There are a few areas, such as Louisville and St. Louis, where a history of such action led, at least for a time, to metropolitan-wide desegregation plans, but more often only the central city is included.

In several cities, including St. Louis and Hartford, Connecticut, metropolitan-wide desegregation plans have involved parental choice. Black parents in the central city have the option to have their children bused to the suburbs, and white parents in the suburbs may choose to have their children bused to magnet schools in the central city. This approach has generally aroused less opposition than mandatory city-suburb busing programs, but it also leaves many schools segregated, particularly when the minority percentage in the inner city is very high. However, there is some evidence that parental choice programs bring greater integration than city-only busing programs. One study, in Cambridge, Massachusetts, even found that a parental choice busing program led to greater integration than earlier mandatory busing within Cambridge only (Rossell and Glenn, 1988; Rossell, 1990). Ironically, even as school choice has become popular around the country, the plan in St. Louis has come under attack in part because it was labeled a "desegregation plan" (Wells and Crain, 1997, p. 74). There and elsewhere, many desegregation plans have been scaled back since the mid-1990s, as noted earlier in this chapter. One result has been increasing levels of segregation in public schools.

In smaller cities without large minority populations, desegregation often occurred more smoothly than in larger ones. Studies by the U.S. Commission on

It is important that teaching staffs, as well as students, be integrated when schools are desegregated. A diverse staff serves as a model of diversity for all students, provides personal role models for minority students, and helps to break down stereotypes among majority group students.

Civil Rights (1976) indicate that cities such as Berkeley, California; Colorado Springs, Colorado; Kalamazoo, Michigan; Newport News, Virginia; and Waterloo, Iowa, were able to desegregate their schools the most quickly and effectively. Despite their diversity in some regards, all these cities have relatively small populations (75,000 to 175,000) and small to moderate minority school enrollments (16 to 37 percent). Even large cities with relatively small minority enrollments can have very successful desegregation: Minneapolis (population 424,000, minority enrollment 21 percent) has been cited as a city in which desegregation has been very successful (U.S. Commission on Civil Rights, 1976). However, even in some of these cities where desegregation has been successful, including Minneapolis, it came under attack in the 1990s and has in some cases either ended or been scaled back.

The problem of white flight—both that induced by desegregation and that which would have happened anyway—made the desegregation of predominantly minority school systems in large suburbanized cities more difficult than in smaller cities or ones with smaller minority populations. One possible solution is cross-district desegregation between city and suburbs. It is for this reason that voluntary city-suburb and parental choice plans have been used in St. Louis; Hartford, Connecticut; and elsewhere. These plans have been effective in integrating suburban schools, but they leave many central-city schools segregated because relatively few whites from the suburbs volunteer to be bused to the city, even when magnet schools are offered. In St. Louis, for example, fourteen times as many blacks have chosen to be bused from the city to the suburbs as the number of whites who have chosen to be bused from the suburbs to magnet schools in the city. Some critics of busing have pointed out that this is fairly typical of most desegregation programs in another regard: Most of those who end up riding the bus to schools outside their own neighborhood are black. This has led to some black, as well as white, support for ending desegregation plans in recent years.

City-suburb busing for desegregation is unlikely to be implemented in many places besides the few metropolitan areas where it already exists, and it has been abolished in increasing numbers of places. Despite its effectiveness in many regards, busing for desegregation is not popular: 65 to 85 percent of the white population and half or more of the black population oppose it. Ironically, those most directly affected by desegregation often become its strongest supporters (Wells and Crain, 1997), but this support has not generally spread to the larger population.

Some of the opposition relates to two additional concerns have been raised about busing by a number of educators and social scientists. First, when large numbers of black students are bused out of their neighborhoods, neighborhood stability is reduced and neighborhood institutions are weakened. For example, Dempsey and Noblit (1993) describe how one African American neighborhood in Milwaukee was disrupted by the closure of its neighborhood school as part of the effort to desegregate Milwaukee schools. Second, black students are sometimes isolated and rejected by their peers when they are bused to mostly white schools (R. L. Miller, 1989, 1990). This is what Pettigrew (1969a, 1969b) meant by an absence of true integration. A related problem is that the curriculum in such schools emphasizes and reflects the culture, values, and history of the white students and teachers, who are in the majority, leading to self-doubt and identity problems among black students (Gerard, 1988).

Because of these concerns, because of the difficulty of desegregating schools in large metropolitan areas with large minority populations, and because of continuing public opposition to busing, some educators are asking whether other alternatives are available for improving the education of minority schoolchildren. There is also some evidence of a decline in support for busing among African Americans, who have expressed growing concerns about its impact on the African American neighborhoods that the children leave behind. Even the NAACP, once the staunchest supporter of busing, has become divided on the issue. Today, some educators and some members of minority group communities hold that different

Middle school students board a bus as they participate in the St. Louis voluntary city–county transfer program. Although the St. Louis plan is a school choice plan and has received strong support from both black and white parents, it is being scaled back to settle a suit brought by the state of Missouri. The state opposed having to pay for the plan and objected to what several Missouri politicians called "unfair desegregation payments."

institutional attitudes and teaching practices in all-black or all-Latino/a schools will benefit students of color more than desegregation. We turn now to some educational approaches based on that premise.

## Approach 3: Multiculturalism and Cultural Immersion

Some social scientists and educators criticize both compensatory education and busing for desegregation because they are based, in part, on a cultural deficiency model. In effect, they are based on a "transmission-of-values" theory, holding that if blacks and other minorities are placed in a predominantly white, middle-class setting, they will absorb its academically oriented values (Hacker, 1992, p. 165). Such an approach clearly falls within a functionalist or assimilationist model, as opposed to a pluralist or separatist one. A problem is that at least under some circumstances this can lead to isolation, rejection, self-doubt, and identity problems among students of color. Moreover, compensatory education and desegregation do nothing, in themselves, to alter the Eurocentric approach to education that is present in many schools. Such an approach disregards the contribution of minorities, fails to discuss the uglier side of American history such as genocide against Indian people, or examines intergroup issues and history primarily from the perspective of people of European ancestry (Hilliard, 1988). The related but different approaches of *multiculturalism* and *cultural immersion* are efforts to correct this problem. Multiculturalism may be practiced in schools or preschool programs of any racial or ethnic composition; cultural immersion is practical only in schools in which most or all of the students come from a common racial, ethnic, or cultural background. For these reasons, multiculturalism is sometimes seen as placing greater emphasis on cultural pluralism, whereas cultural immersion is sometimes seen as placing greater emphasis on separatism.

**Multiculturalism.** **Multiculturalism** can be defined as an approach that recognizes and values cultural differences and attempts to include all racial, ethnic, and cultural groups in the content and examples used in the classroom and to teach history, literature, and other subjects from the perspectives of multiple groups rather than just the dominant group (Banks, 1992). Multiculturalism is different from traditional education in that it seeks cultural pluralism rather than cultural assimilation. The extent to which this should be done is a key source of debate among educators, however. There is an ongoing debate about how much stress should be placed on the experiences and traits that different groups have in common relative to those that are distinct to each group. And to some extent, this debate reflects an underlying disagreement about the extent to which different groups have similar experiences and traits. Some critics argue that multiculturalism goes too far when it questions the idea that the United States is "one nation, many peoples" or suggests that there is more than one history to be told (Kirp, 1991). These critics, influenced to varying degrees by a functionalist or assimilationist viewpoint, hold that when it questions a common national history, multiculturalism threatens to divide society on the basis of race, ethnicity, and culture and to inhibit cooperation by encouraging each cultural group to place its own concerns above the common interest.

Those who support the pluralist approach underlying multicultural education reply that colonized minorities—those who entered American society involuntarily, including African Americans, Native Americans, Mexican Americans, and Puerto Ricans—never have sought to assimilate to the extent that the larger society expected them to. Nor, for that matter, have they ever sought to assimilate to the extent sought by immigrant minorities who came to the United States voluntarily (Lieberson, 1980; Gibson and Ogbu, 1992). In this view, multicultural education is seen as a much-needed legitimization of the values and experiences of groups that have been historically devalued and abused in American society. Moreover, it is not seen as divisive because racial and ethnic divisions are already present in society as a result of past oppressive actions by the dominant group.

Such an approach has three potential benefits. First, it is believed that this more positive approach to the cultures and experiences of people of color in the United States will lead to better self-images, stronger identities, and greater self-confidence among students of color. Second, it is intended to broaden the knowledge of all Americans about groups other than their own and to help students to understand how the different experiences of other groups have led to the development of different viewpoints. In this way, students will be better prepared for living in a society that is in fact multicultural, even if multiculturalism was not the approach favored by society in the past. Third, it will correct a distorted presentation of American history and culture that has been present in the schools for too long. Rather than presenting these issues from the viewpoint of only European Americans, it will also present them from the sometimes very different views and experiences of non-European groups such as Native Americans and African Americans.

**Cultural Immersion.** Some argue that particularly in areas of concentrated minority poverty, such as inner-city ghettos and Indian reservations, multiculturalism is not enough (see Leonard Jeffries, quoted in A. Sullivan, 1990). In such areas, poverty has become more concentrated and jobs harder to find. And as traditional sources of institutional support have been eliminated through a variety of economic processes and cultural assaults, positive role models have become harder and harder to find. As was described in earlier chapters, Native American culture was systematically attacked by such means as taking children from their parents and placing them in boarding schools. In inner-city black neighborhoods, the combined forces of the massive job exodus and the departure of the middle class (in many cases, both black and white) have undermined institutions and deprived many adults of the opportunity to serve as positive role models for their own and other neighborhood children through regular employment, organizational and religious participation in the neighborhood, and so forth (W. J. Wilson, 1987).

Some hold that job loss and unemployment, along with stereotypical images in the media and elsewhere, have subjected black males in particular to cultural attack and deprived young black males of positive role models (American Council on Education, 1988). Often, the harsh reality in the inner city is that it is easier in the short term to make money by engaging in an illegal activity than a legal one. Yet the long-term consequences of such actions are devastating, and they further undermine the economic stability of the black community by directing young black males away from professional or managerial employment and often toward an ultimate outcome of imprisonment or even early death. By the early 1990s, more African American men were in jail or prison than were attending colleges and universities (Hacker, 1992, p. 177).

What is needed under such conditions as these, some claim, is **cultural immersion**, an educational approach that directly promotes positive role models of the students' own racial or ethnic background and that promotes collective self-worth by teaching students to value their cultural heritage, which has been subjected to attack by the larger society. By establishing such role models and promoting collective self-worth, they argue, this approach can enhance the achievement of students of color (Bell, 1988).

In Milwaukee, Detroit, New York, Baltimore, and other cities, schools based on the cultural-immersion model have been developed and targeted toward black male students. One example is the Matthew A. Henson School in Baltimore, named for the African American man who served as Admiral Peary's navigator to the North Pole. In this school, black male teachers serve as role models for their students, teaching a variety of matters including self-defense, self-control, and personal appearance; using games as a way of learning in the classroom; and taking their students on Saturday outings to museums and libraries (Farley, 1994a, p. 389). This and similar schools also emphasize achievements by African Americans (hence the school's name), and some of them use an Afrocentric curriculum—one centered around African history, culture, art, and literature. At Aisha Schule in Detroit, a private school using an Afrocentric curriculum, students learn about African American poets, greet one another in Swahili, and recite African folktales. At the same time, they also complete standard coursework in such subjects as geometry. By the early 1990s, about 200 such private schools around the country were targeted toward African American children (DePalma, 1990), and their approaches have been emulated in some public school systems with large numbers of black students as well.

Some people have criticized these schools for fostering racial and sexual segregation. In Detroit, plans for such schools in the public school system were altered (but not eliminated) after the American Civil Liberties Union (ACLU) successfully sued the district for proposing a school that would admit only male students. However, the law does not prohibit schools with curricula targeted toward or designed to enhance the achievement of black males, as long as admissions are not restricted on the basis of sex or race. And Hacker (1992, p. 174) points out two key differences between today's cultural-immersion schools and the segregated schools of the past: Those proposing today's schools seek voluntary enrollment, and these schools are under black control.

Does this approach work? Early signs are that it can indeed be effective. At the Matthew A. Henson School, for example, attendance of black male students improved measurably. Graduates of Aisha Schule in Detroit include engineers and medical students. One of the longest-standing experiences with the cultural-immersion approach to education comes from Hawaii, where the Kamahamena Early Education program was established in 1972 to deal with below-average performance of Native Hawaiian children on standardized tests. Students were allowed to speak spontaneously rather than raising their hands, in keeping with their more expressive culture. (This innovation has also been used in a number of immersion schools targeted to African Americans, for similar reasons.) They were also encouraged to assist one another in the tradition of the Hawaiian-Polynesian style of conversation and were allowed to answer questions in their native language, even though the questions were asked in English. Scores on achievement tests rose sharply (DePalma, 1990).

One factor that may contribute to the success of such schools is that the teachers and administrators have faith in the abilities of their students and expect and demand high levels of achievement—elements in the fourth approach discussed in the next section. We can loosely characterize this approach as interactionist because it focuses on student-teacher interactions and because it is based largely on the idea, arising from symbolic-interactionist theory, that the messages we get from others about our abilities and personalities have major effects on how we in fact behave and achieve.

## Approach 4: The Interactionist Approach

This approach has gained momentum as a result of research published in the late 1970s and 1980s. As we have seen, the approach is not clearly associated with either the functionalist or the conflict approach. Like the conflict approach, it rests on the assumption that schools have failed minority students, but like the functionalist approach, it does not *necessarily* demand a substantial change in the organization or power structure of education. However, it does require significant changes in the behavior of teachers and, ultimately, of minority students as well. This interactionist approach is based largely on the fact that low expectations by teachers lead to low student achievement. When teachers have low expectations of students, they demand only a low quality of work. Thus, the solution is to convince teachers that low-income and minority students can learn as well as anyone else and to get those teachers to demand such learning from their students. It is striking that essays advocating this approach have appeared in both the conflict theory–oriented periodical

*Social Policy* (Edmonds, 1979) and in the functionalist *Public Interest* (Coleman, 1981; Fuerst, 1981). These studies, along with other studies and experiences based on efforts at innovative education (G. Weber, 1971; Brookover and Lezotte, 1979; Means and Knapp, 1991; Selvin, 1992), strongly suggest that minority students do better under these conditions:

- Teachers believe that the students are capable of success and believe that their efforts can make a difference in what the students learn.

- The class is a pleasant place, relatively quiet and orderly. The most effective teachers are those who can maintain reasonable order without spending a great deal of time and effort on keeping order.

- There is emphasis on the learning of basic reading and math skills, both in how teachers spend their time and the level of performance that they require of their students.

- There is also emphasis on the learning of higher-order skills, such as comprehension, composition, and mathematical reasoning.

A study by Fuerst (1981) of all-black schools in Chicago showed that the schools where black students excelled (in some of these schools, average reading scores substantially exceeded the norms in white suburban schools) displayed the patterns just described. Although different schools used various innovations, all demanded high-quality performance—students could not be promoted without it—and all had teachers who believed that black students could learn as well as anyone else, a pattern that as we have seen is not typical of most urban schools. Unfortunately, about five out of every six black students in Chicago at that time were in less advantageous settings, benefitting neither from these educational reforms nor from integration (Fuerst, 1981, p. 91).

Similar findings can be seen in the experiences of the Algebra Project, a program designed under a MacArthur Prize "genius grant" to Bob Moses, a civil rights activist who had become concerned because his daughter and other black children were not being taught algebra as early in their schooling as white children typically are. Now implemented in more than 100 schools in thirteen states, this program, focusing primarily on grades six through eight, has demonstrated that supposedly disadvantaged children can be just as successful as others in early algebra education. The program is based on the concepts that its students can learn algebra as well as anyone else if given the opportunity to do so and that algebra is best taught in a step-by-step manner that builds on the students' real-life experiences (Moses and Cobb, 2001). In a Kentucky school with 90 percent of its students below the poverty level, the percentage scoring above the national average on standardized math tests rose to 39 percent. In Cambridge, Massachusetts, where the program began, eighteen eighth-graders in a predominantly black school took a test to get credit for high school algebra after participating in the program. Fifteen of them passed; no student from that school had ever passed the test before (Selvin, 1992). In Jackson, Mississippi, average math test scores rose in 80 percent of the schools that implemented the program, and a sharp decrease in discipline problems also occurred (*NEA Today*, 1996). The beneficial effects in Mississippi were confirmed by the National Science Foundation (Watson, 1996), and the project was so successful that Cambridge mandated that pre-algebra be taught city-wide to all sixth and seventh graders and algebra to all eighth graders. At nearly all-black Lanier High School in Jackson, Mississippi, the percentage of ninth graders taking algebra rose from 12 to 67 percent. The percentage taking algebra, geometry, and advanced math was above the city-wide average, and student test scores were similar to those at nearby, more affluent high schools. And in San Francisco, graduates of the Algebra Project in a school so poverty-stricken that 70 percent of students qualified for free lunches enrolled in post-algebra high school courses at twice the city-wide rate

(Davis and West, 2003). In Mississippi, many graduates of the program return as young adults to assist its efforts to teach math to the next generation (Moses and Cobb, 2001).

A 1987 U.S. Department of Education report titled *Schools That Work: Educating Disadvantaged Children* documents numerous cases of schools where high and uniform expectations, along with a belief that poverty need not be a barrier to achievement, have led to high levels of achievement. Examples include a Dayton, Ohio, elementary school where a principal's insistence that all students can achieve led to rapid increases in the percentages of students performing at grade level; a public high school in the inner city of Los Angeles whose graduates are more likely to go to college than the national average; and an all-black Catholic high school in Chicago where nine of ten graduates go to college. Such success can occur not just in one school but also throughout a school system. In Jacksonville, Florida, a program called Blacks for Success in Education, which emphasizes critical-thinking skills, was begun after it was discovered that three-fourths of the nation's students were scoring above the average Jacksonville black student on the Stanford Achievement Test. By 1985, the typical Jacksonville black student got a score close to the national average. And in Brooklyn, community superintendent J. Jerome Harris insisted on higher expectations and promoted the notion that students in the district, despite their poverty, could succeed. During his tenure between 1973 and 1986, the proportion of students in the district reading at or above grade level rose from 21 percent to more than 65 percent. Subsequently, he obtained similar results in some of Atlanta's poorest schools (Howard, 1995).

Recall also the High School and Beyond study (Coleman, Hoffer, and Kilgore, 1982; Hoffer, Greeley, and Coleman, 1985, 1987; Haertel, 1987), which found that minority students of comparable socioeconomic status do better in private schools than in public schools and that in Catholic schools, particularly, there is much less inequality in achievement along the lines of race and social class than in public schools. The reasons, according to Coleman, Hoffer, and Kilgore (1982), are that these schools expect and demand higher levels of achievement and that they maintain better order. Furthermore, public schools that have these characteristics are also marked by better student achievement. What all this suggests is that minority students can do as well as anyone in school and that when teachers *expect* and *demand* it, the students will. According to Edmonds (1979), there are a variety of ways in which such a situation can occur. It may be the result of an informed and dedicated teaching staff or of a demanding principal. It may also be a result of parental pressure, so that it could be an outcome of an effective community control program.

To summarize, the approach of increased rigor in minority education, like immersion, compensatory education, and desegregation through busing, shows promise where it has been implemented. On the other hand, it is also true that just as very few schools are truly integrated, as Fuerst's (1981) Chicago study shows, few schools really expect and demand high performance from minority students. Thus, despite this promising new development, most of our schools are continuing to fail in their quest to eliminate racial inequality in education.

## Summary and Conclusion

In this chapter, we have seen that educational inequality has persisted despite the elimination of formal discrimination. We have also explored functionalist (cultural deprivation) and conflict (cultural bias) theories about the causes of educational inequality. We have seen a number of mechanisms by which schools subtly (and often unintentionally) discriminate against minority children, including culturally biased educational materials and tests, teacher expectation effects, and tracking. Despite the very different theories and philosophies on which they are based, several approaches to improving the education of minority children have been shown to be effective if properly implemented. These include compensatory education, desegregation, multicultural education, cultural immersion, and higher demands on and expectations of minority students. We know today that schools do make a difference, and we know a number of good ways to make them work better for minority students. Unfortunately, none of these approaches has been implemented on a scale sufficient to greatly reduce racial, class, and ethnic inequality in education, particularly in the biggest cities, where most blacks and Hispanics live. The failure to institute large-scale reforms in education, along with the similar failure to reform the economic system (see Chapter 10), means continuing educational inequality for black, Hispanic, and Native American children, despite the elimination of formal discrimination and official de jure segregation.

## *Critical Review Questions*

1. Why have U.S. schools become more segregated over the past two decades or so? What consequences may this have?

2. How and why do teachers expectations influence student achievement? What groups of students are most likely to be harmed by low teacher expectations?

3. What would be some ways to change education so that students are not harmed by the effects of teacher expectations and tracking? What groups might support or oppose the changes you propose, and why?

4. Discuss the advantages and disadvantages of bilingual education.

5. How do social factors influence test scores in ways that make the tests inaccurate predictors of what the students taking them can accomplish? How do these procedures work against African American, Latino/a, and American Indian students?

6. What accounts for the widespread political popularity of testing, despite the limitations discussed in the question above?

7. Of the four broad approaches to resolving problems of majority-minority inequality in education that are discussed in this chapter, which do you see as most promising and why?

# Majority-Minority Relations Based on Gender, Sexual Orientation, and Disability

Early in this book, we noted that the principles of majority-minority relations can be applied to social groups other than racial and ethnic ones. Women, people with disabilities, and gay men and lesbians have been compared, in terms of their roles in society, with racial groups such as African Americans. All of them have been the targets of discrimination in such areas as employment and housing. On the other hand, there are differences in the nature and type of discrimination these groups encounter, as well as differences between their roles in society and those of racial minorities. In this chapter, we shall examine the nature of discrimination against women, people with disabilities, and gay men, lesbians, and bisexuals, as well as the roles of each of these groups in society. We shall also examine legislation and court rulings concerning such discrimination. In addition, we shall look at the ways in which various minority roles intersect and interact, particularly race and gender. For example, we shall see that the nature of racial discrimination varies by gender, and the nature of gender discrimination similarly varies by race.

### ▶ THE NATURE OF GENDER INEQUALITY

From a sociological standpoint, women quite clearly fit the definition of a minority group. This is the case because the United States and many other societies are characterized by **gender inequality**; that is, different and unequal roles in society are defined on the basis of whether one is a man or a woman, with the result that men enjoy greater power, status, and economic security than women do. The different and unequal roles of men and women are called **gender roles**. Gender inequality is evident in a number of ways. On average, women are paid less for the work they do (even compared with men with the same level of education), and they have less autonomy on the job, less leisure time at home, and less political representation than men. So entrenched is the notion of male power in Western society that until recently, marriage rituals typically included a promise by the bride to "love, honor, and *obey*" her husband. Even today, with deliberate sex discrimination forbidden by law, evidence of gender inequality in the United States abounds. In 2001, the average female, year-round, full-time worker received only about 76 percent of the income of her male counterpart. This did not vary much by education: At all levels of education between some high school and a masters degree, as well as a doctorate degree, women were paid between 71 and 75 percent of the pay of men.

Women with professional degrees fare worse, receiving only about 62 percent of the income of men with professional degrees. At the very lowest (eighth grade or less) educational levels, women are paid about 78 percent of what men earn (U.S. Census Bureau, 2002h, Table PINC 01). Partly because of the low pay of women, people in female-householder families had a poverty rate in 2001 of more than 26 percent, about two and a quarter times the overall poverty rate of 11.7 percent (U.S. Census Bureau, 2002f, Tables 1 and 9).

The power structure of the United States also remains heavily male-dominated. In both the public and private sectors, nearly all of the positions at the top, such as corporate officers, members of boards of directors, and high elected officials, are held by men. Even though the number of women in the U.S. Senate and House grew quite rapidly at times from the mid-1980s into the new century, both remain overwhelmingly male. In 2003, only 14 of 100 senators and only 59 of 435 representatives were women (Center for the American Woman and Politics, 2003).

Some critics of feminism—an ideology and movement supporting equal rights for women—have argued that the situation of women is not comparable to that of racial minorities in two senses. First, they have not been segregated in the same way, and second, their social class composition is not as different from the overall population as is the case for racial and ethnic minority groups. This viewpoint often sees a need to protect women from dangerous and "dirty" occupations, heavy physical labor, and military combat duty. People who feel this way often see the changing roles of women today as a threat to family life, noting that mothers have less time to spend with their children and citing today's higher rates of divorce and nonmarital childbearing.

Feminists counter these arguments in a variety of ways. They point out that even when men and women share the same family income, many women are dependent on their husbands' income. When they get divorced, their economic standard of living quickly falls, whereas that of newly divorced men changes less and by some measures actually rises (Weitzman, 1985; R. Peterson, 1996; Smock, Manning, and Gupta, 1999; McManus and Deprete, 2001). Although the decline for divorcing women is less today than a decade or two ago, it remains substantial (McKeever and Wolfinger, 2001). Also, women who must support a family on their income alone have a far higher poverty rate than other families, including those in which there is only one earner but that earner is male.

Feminists also note that women have paid a high price in the form of low income and lack of power for whatever workplace protection is associated with traditional gender roles. They argue that women should be able to choose dangerous or physically demanding work if they want, the same as anyone else. Finally, they point out that although employed women have a higher divorce rate than stay-at-home wives (Waite, 1981; Ruggles, 1997b), research also shows that families with the wife in the labor force are just as happy as those in which she is not (Thornton and Freedman, 1984) and that when both partners are happy, there is no correlation between the wife's employment and marital disruption (Schoen et al., 2002). Instead, research confirms that the main reason for higher divorce rates among employed women is that they are more financially able to leave bad marriages (Schoen et al., 2002).

In fact, a good deal of research shows that unequal power between men and women remains a fact not only in the larger society but in the home as well. For example, families are far more likely to relocate for a job opportunity for the husband than for the wife; even women with good jobs often must put their husbands' jobs first when questions of relocation arise (Bielby and Bielby, 1992). Research has also shown consistently that women spend many more hours a week on household work than their husbands, even when both the husband and the wife work full-time (Peskin, 1982; Hochschild, 1989; Stockard and Johnson, 1992; South and Spitze, 1994; Zhang and Farley, 1995; Kamo and Cohen, 1998; Dalmia, 2002). This unequal division of household labor has become a source of conflict between husbands and wives in some households (Townsend and Walker, 1990) and may be a factor in today's high divorce rates.

Research has shown consistently that married women spend many more hours a week on household work than their husbands, even when both the husband and wife are employed full-time.

## ▶ CAUSES OF GENDER INEQUALITY

A basic question that sociologists ask is, Why is there gender inequality? Why do men and women have different and unequal roles in society? As in other areas of sociology, the functionalist and conflict perspectives offer different answers.

## Functionalist Explanations of Gender Inequality

Functionalists argue that having men and women play different roles in society may be useful to society in some ways, and it certainly was in the past. Until about a century ago, most women spent much of their young adult lives either pregnant or taking care of young children. Infant and child mortality was high, so to have two or three children survive to adulthood, it was often necessary to give birth to five or six. Because there was no baby formula, all of these children had to be breast-fed. Thus, women had to stay near their children, which usually meant staying at home and avoiding activities such as hunting or any work that involved travel. Also, men are on average larger and physically stronger than women. Much work at that time required physical strength, making men, on average, more able to do it. For these reasons, a gender division of labor made a certain amount of sense.

One view among sociologists is that gender roles survive today because of *cultural lag*. The arrangement once was useful and became engrained in the culture, so it persists even though its original purpose no longer exists. (Today, women have fewer children; overpopulation is a greater risk than underpopulation; alternatives to breast-feeding exist; and most jobs do not require great physical strength.) Some functionalists also believe that in some ways, gender roles may still be useful today. Parsons and Bales (1955) argued that families benefit from the presence of both *instrumental leadership*, which focuses on getting things done, and *expressive leadership*, which addresses people's feelings and relationships. They argue that in general the husband and father fills the need for instrumental leadership, while the wife and mother fills the need for expressive leadership. Other sociologists have been critical of this formulation, however, pointing out that even if families do need both kinds of leadership, there is no clear reason why one type has to come from the husband and the other from the wife.

Some functionalists also hold that families are more stable when there are clear gender roles. These sociologists point out that rates of divorce and nonmarital childbearing have risen as increasing numbers of women have entered the work force. In turn, they argue, children have suffered because they have received less adult attention, have encountered an increased risk of parental divorce, and are more likely to be born to a young single mother without the economic or personal resources to give them a good home environment (Moynihan, 1986; Popenoe, 1988; Glenn, 1997a, 1997b). From this viewpoint, then, gender roles are useful to the family, and recent moves toward eliminating distinct gender roles have undermined its stability.

In response, other sociologists point out that many of the trends that seem to threaten the family have little to do with feminism or changing attitudes about the roles of women. The entry of women into the work force, for example, is tied at least as much to economic need as to feminism; the entry of women into the labor force is the only thing that kept most families from suffering a serious reduction in their standard of living during the 1970s and 1980s (Olsen, 1990). In the early 1990s, many families saw their incomes fall even as wives worked more hours to offset the falling wages of their husbands (Economic Policy Institute, 1996). In addition, the notion that work keeps mothers from having close contact with their children is not well supported by research. A variety of studies show that full-time working mothers interact with their children about as much as full-time homemakers do (J. E. Farley, 1977, pp. 197–202; Robinson, 1977; Goldberg, cited in Hodgson, 1979; Nock and Kingston, 1988; Benokraitis, 1993, pp. 318–19). Recent research also indicates that children in both one- and two-parent homes where the mother works do at least as well on a variety of measures of school success and well-being as children whose mothers do not work and better on some (Hoffman and Youngblad, 1999; see also Jackson, 2003). Overall, children in organized day care appear to develop about as well as children raised at home by their mothers (Hayes and Kamerman, 1983; B. J. Berg, 1986; Hoffmann, 1989; Viadero, 1997). Children with less adequate day-care arrangements do less well, but this is more attributable to the unavailability of good day care than to changes in the role of women per se. (Unlike the United States, most industrialized countries provide subsidized day care, available to any working parent who needs it.)

It is true that day care and home care present different benefits and challenges for young children (Clarke-Stewart, Gruber, and Fitzgerald, 1994) and that children do better when the quality of their day care is better (Burchinal et al., 1996; Broberg et al., 1997; Viadero, 1997). Among the characteristics of good day care are a stimulating environment, adults reading to children, affection, and moderate use of discipline. Of course, these are also the characteristics of good home care (Clarke-Stewart, Gruber, and Fitzgerald, 1994). Good day care is also characterized by the recognition that different children have different needs, interests, and learning styles; by supportive relationships between day-care staff and children's family members; and by ongoing training programs for staff (Dodge, 1995). Research also shows that if a mother responds sensitively to a child's wants and needs when the mother and child are together, the child will develop a normal attachment with her whether or not the child is in day care (Rosen, 1996).

Finally, as we saw in an earlier chapter, staying in a bad marriage is not necessarily any better for the children than getting a divorce. And in response to Popenoe's (1988) argument that adults often put their own priorities and concerns ahead of those of their children, it can be noted that this tendency exists among both men and women and cannot simply be tied to changing gender roles.

## Conflict Theory Explanations of Gender Inequality

From the standpoint of conflict theory, gender inequality, like other forms of inequality, exists because an interest group benefits from it, and because that interest group has the power to shape society in ways that suit its self-interests. The group that has benefitted materially from the subordinate status of women is men (R. Collins, 1971; Reskin, 1988). Because of gender inequality, men have greater incomes, more political power, and more spare time than women. They also, on average, enjoy greater status, autonomy, and authority on the job and generally greater mobility and choice over how to spend their time. Thus, in all these ways, men benefit in a material sense from gender inequality. It is true that there are also costs, mainly in socioemotional areas: Men experience greater pressure to be "in control" and not to show emotion, greater difficulty sharing and expressing feelings, and lack of time to interact with their families and children. These, in turn, have costs in health, as men are more subject to such diseases as high blood pressure, ulcers, and heart conditions, and partly for this reason, they live shorter lives. Nonetheless, the overall material benefits of sexism to men are quite clear in terms of time, money, power, and autonomy. Consequently, it is not surprising that through much of human history in many societies, men have used their power to maintain these benefits. Conflict theory, then, holds that gender inequality exists mainly because it materially benefits men and because men have the power to establish and maintain this system of inequality.

What are the sources of male power? Conflict theorists point to several. One explanation, which draws on both the functionalist and conflict perspectives, is based on the fact that gender role specialization, as we saw earlier, was once useful to society. It may have originally developed for that reason, but conflict theorists point out that once it did, it gave men certain kinds of power that women did not have, such as greater freedom of movement and greater contact with the outside world. It also made women dependent on them for food because men did the hunting in most hunting-and-gathering societies. Once men had gained power through their mobility and outside contacts and women's dependency on them for food, they began to use that power to their own advantage. The result was that society became increasingly male-dominated. Eventually, the societal need for this gender role specialization largely disappeared, for reasons discussed earlier. But because men benefitted from these arrangements and because the arrangements gave men power they could use to their advantage, men acted to maintain the system even after it had outlived its usefulness to society as a whole.

Conflict theorists also point to another source of male power: their greater average size and physical strength. The fact that men can use force against women has been and continues to be a means by which men exercise power over women. At one time in the United States, China, and a number of other societies, women were seen largely as property of their husbands. Thus, rapes, assaults, and even in some cases murders by husbands went unpunished and sometimes were not even recognized as crimes.

This has changed in the legal sense, but as a practical matter change has been slower. The police and courts take domestic violence more seriously today than in the past, but they are still sometimes reluctant to become involved when violence occurs within the family. This reluctance can be seen in the highly publicized O.J. Simpson case in 1994, in which police had been called to the Simpson home at least nine times before the murders of Nicole Simpson and her friend Ronald Goldman in June 1994, but only one of these calls resulted in an arrest. Although Simpson was then convicted of assault, his sentence consisted only of an unenforced public service requirement and a requirement that he see a counselor of his own choice. Similar reluctance can be seen in the ruling in 1995 by the Fourth Circuit Court of Appeals against the Violence Against Women Act. The Court stated, "The legislation could involve the federal courts in a whole host of domestic relations disputes" (National Legal Research Group, 1999). Indeed, in 2000, the Supreme Court struck down key provisions of the Act.

It remains true today that when a woman is assaulted or murdered, the most likely assailant is her husband or boyfriend. In 1998, 33 percent of women who were murdered were killed by their husbands or boyfriends or by ex-husbands, whereas just 4 percent of men who were murdered were killed by their wives, girlfriends, or ex-wives (Rennisan and Welchans, 2000). In general, attacks on wives or girlfriends by husbands or boyfriends are far more common than the reverse (Straus, 1980; Makepeace, 1981; Rennisan and Welchans, 2000). Thus, the use or threat of violence has historically been an important source of men's power over women, and this continues to be the case today.

Finally, the disproportionate economic and political power of men has a self-sustaining effect: Men use this power to ensure continued advantage. As we have seen, Congress, the executive branches of state and federal governments, and corporate boardrooms and executive suites remain overwhelmingly male. It may be unreasonable to expect that public and private policies and arrangements that favor men over women, such as the system of unequal wages between predominantly male and female occupations, will change much as long as the key seats of power are so male-dominated. However, there are a few signs that male domination of positions of power may be starting to change. The Clinton administration appointed a record number of women to the executive branch of the federal government, including such important positions as Attorney General and Secretary of State. Fewer women were appointed by George W. Bush, but women were appointed for the first time to several key posts including National Security Advisor. A handful of states (such as Iowa and North Dakota) have passed laws encouraging or requiring that about half of appointed state officials be female (Gross, 1990). Nonetheless, positions of power in both the public and private sector remain overwhelming occupied by men, and as long as this is the case, conflict theorists argue, it will be easy for men to maintain social policies and institutional arrangements that maintain the advantages they enjoy.

## ▶ THE INTERSECTION OF RACE, GENDER, AND CLASS INEQUALITY

### The Meaning of Gender for Women of Color

Although gender inequality exists in the United States between men and women in virtually all social classes and all racial and ethnic groups, the form and meaning of this inequality vary among different groups and classes. The challenges and problems faced by working-class women, for example, are different from those faced by middle-class women. And African American and Latina women are confronted by different issues and different forms of gender inequality from those faced by most white, non-Hispanic women.

**Gender, Race, and Labor Force Participation.** One way in which these experiences have been different is the extent to which the role of women has been linked to the home as opposed to work outside the home. Among middle-class women, the industrial era brought about a *housewife role*. The expectation was that the husband would be the breadwinner, and the wife would remain at home, raising the children and taking care of the house. From the emergence of the industrial era until about three decades ago, this was the experience of most women in middle- and upper-income families (Degler, 1980). The justification was that this role protected women from the dangers and the often strenuous labor of the workplace. With the emergence of the modern feminist movement in the 1960s and early 1970s, women rebelled against this role and entered the labor force in record numbers. (Remember, though, that economic necessity played at least as big a role in the entry of women into the labor force as did feminism.) Even more fundamentally, women began to seek professional careers that had been male-dominated, attending law school and other forms of professional education in record numbers and dramatically changing the gender composition of some professions.

For low-income women and for many women of color, however, the housewife role never really became the norm (Seifer, 1973; E. M. Glenn, 1980; J. Jones, 1985). These women never had the option of leaving the paid labor force to become housewives because economic necessity demanded that they work for pay even at a time when most women did not. When most white, middle-class women were housewives, for example, most African American women were working for pay, often in household service jobs and other service occupations or in low-paying industrial jobs in such places as textile mills. Thus, the rebellion against the confinement of the housewife role that characterized much of white middle-class feminism in the 1960s and early 1970s was not an issue for poor women and women of color. Rather, their concerns focused on such areas as sexual harassment and abuse, racial and gender discrimination in hiring and pay, and the general low pay and powerlessness of women in service jobs and other working-class occupations (Cotera, 1980; hooks, 1981). Many of these women have juggled multiple low-paying jobs to support their families, often with long commute times because they must rely on public transportation, while at the same time struggling to ensure that their children receive adequate care (A. Jones, 2002). In many cases, African American and Latina feminists have criticized white middle-class feminists, who formed the core of the contemporary feminist movement during its early years, for not paying sufficient attention to these issues (Cotera, 1980; Zinn et al., 1986; A. Y. Davis, 1989; P. H. Collins, 1991).

Differences in labor force participation by gender, race, and ethnicity have decreased somewhat, but they can still be seen in today's statistics. As shown in Table 13.1, African American women remain more likely than either white, non-Hispanic women or Latina women to be employed full-time the year-round. In part this reflects a long-standing pattern for African American women, but it also reflects the more recent pattern whereby a high proportion are single mothers who are the main source of support for their families. In contrast, a somewhat larger proportion of white women work part-time rather than full-time, and a significant minority of Latina women do not work outside the home at all. In contrasting these patterns with the labor force statistics for men, it can be seen that African American men are the least likely of all groups to work full-time the year-round. This is largely because many black men are employed in industries and occupations where employment is decreasing and jobs often are unstable.

These labor force patterns mean, among other things, that gender roles relating to employment vary in different ways in different groups. For white and Hispanic Americans, men remain significantly more likely than women to work full-time the year-round, although more and more women have entered the labor force

## Table 13.1  Income and Year-Round Work, by Race, Sex, and Hispanic Origin, 2001

|  | Non-Hispanic White Male | Black Male | Hispanic Male | Non-Hispanic White Female | Black Female | Hispanic Female |
|---|---|---|---|---|---|---|
| People with income | 95% | 85% | 87% | 92% | 86% | 75% |
| Have income, but not year-round full-time worker | 39 | 38 | 31 | 56 | 45 | 41 |
| Year-round full-time worker | 56 | 47 | 57 | 36 | 41 | 34 |

*Source:* U.S. Census Bureau (2002d, Table PINC-01).

Many black and Latina women are employed in service industries such as fast food. Although this service employment has lowered their unemployment rate relative to black and Latino men, it has also trapped many women of color in low-wage employment.

in all groups. But for African Americans the difference between men and women in labor force status is much smaller. This is because among men of all races, black men are the least likely to work full-time year-round, whereas among women of all races, black women are the most likely to do so.

**Gender, Race, and Occupation.** In recent years, black and Hispanic women have increasingly been working in non-household service occupations, such as fast-food workers and hotel housekeeping. These jobs have proliferated as the economy has shifted away from heavy industry and toward a service economy. As black and Hispanic men have been displaced from the better-paying industrial jobs, black and Hispanic women often have been able to find jobs in these service industries. Thus, in recent years there has been somewhat less unemployment among women of color than among men of color in large urban areas. In fact, there is some evidence that women are preferred in some of these occupations because they are perceived as being less threatening, better able to relate to others, and, in some cases, more skilled than men (Kirschenman and Neckerman, 1991; W. J. Wilson, 1996; Moss and Tilly, 2001a). Women may also be preferred because on average they are paid less than men, making them an attractive source of cheap labor for jobs of this type.

The occupational distribution of white, black, and Hispanic men and women is shown in Table 13.2. Note that compared with whites, African Americans and Hispanics, both men and women, are underrepresented in the most desirable jobs: the managerial and professional occupations. In contrast, African Americans and Hispanics are overrepresented in service, production, and transportation occupations, mostly lower-paid manual occupations. Service occupations are the most common occupations for black men and the second most common for Hispanic men. Hispanic men are well represented in construction, but black men are seriously underrepresented in this relatively well-paying occupation. Women of all races often are employed in the office and administrative support category, which includes clerical

**Table 13.2  Occupation by Race and Hispanic Origin, 2000**

|  | Non-Hispanic White Male | Black Male | Hispanic Male | Non-Hispanic White Female | Black Female | Hispanic Female |
|---|---|---|---|---|---|---|
| Management, business, and financial operations | 16.7% | 8.2% | 6.8% | 12.9% | 9.7% | 8.0% |
| Professional | 18.0 | 11.8 | 7.8 | 25.8 | 20.0 | 14.9 |
| Service | 10.1 | 19.4 | 19.0 | 16.1 | 24.2 | 25.6 |
| Sales | 11.6 | 7.2 | 7.4 | 12.2 | 10.2 | 12.1 |
| Office and administrative support | 6.7 | 11.0 | 7.4 | 25.5 | 24.6 | 22.8 |
| Farming, fishing, and forestry | 0.8 | 0.6 | 3.6 | 0.2 | 0.1 | 1.4 |
| Construction, extraction, and maintenance | 17.3 | 13.3 | 21.9 | 0.7 | 0.8 | 0.9 |
| Production | 10.1 | 12.5 | 14.3 | 4.8 | 7.5 | 11.0 |
| Transportation and material moving | 8.9 | 15.9 | 11.8 | 1.8 | 2.8 | 3.3 |

*Source:* U.S. Census Bureau (2003d, Table PCT86).

work. But for black and Hispanic women, service work is just as common or even more so, and these women are even more likely to work in such jobs than black and Hispanic men. Many of these jobs are in the hotel, restaurant, and health care industries.

Whereas service work has reduced the unemployment rate of women of color, it has also largely trapped them in low-wage employment (P. H. Collins, 1991, Chap. 3) because most hotel and restaurant service jobs pay at or near the minimum wage. This has a particular impact on women of color because the proportion of women who are single parents—and therefore the only source of income for their families—is higher among the Latina population than among the non-Hispanic white population and is even higher among the African American population. When a white, non-Hispanic woman works at a low-wage job, it is more likely that she is either supporting only herself or is combining her income with her husband's (typically larger) income to support a family. Black and Latina women, on the other hand, are both more likely to work in low-wage service occupations and more likely to be the sole source of support for a family.

**Special Concerns of Women of Color.** Sexual harassment and violence against women have been matters of particular concern for African American women. Historically, black women often were expected to submit sexually to white men. Thus, they were sexual victims of both gender inequality and racial inequality (hooks, 1981). For example, slave women were required to submit to the sexual desires of white plantation owners. (This presented a sharp contrast to the inviolable taboo against sex between male slaves and white women; if this occurred, both partners were punished severely.) According to P. H. Collins (1991, p. 54), the sexual victimization of black women by white men "contributed to images of black women as fair game for all men." Sexual violence against African American women has in some cases been exacerbated by the anger and frustration of black men, many of whom have been largely deprived of opportunities to successfully play the traditional male role of economic provider and protector of their families. Culturally, this violence against women is both reflected and reinforced through the language of youth gangs, whose members often call women "bitches" or "hoes," and by media images in popular films about inner-city life and some forms of musical expression such as gangsta rap. For all these reasons, sexual violence has been a focus of major attention among African American feminists (hooks, 1981; P. H. Collins, 1991).

One special problem for black and Latina feminists is the question of how to advance the interests of women without threatening the position of black and Latino men, who are also highly disadvantaged in American society. When men of any race abuse, mistreat, or exploit women, it is always a problem from a feminist standpoint. Yet black and Latina feminists face important debates about the extent to which the subordinate role of women of color results from actions of men of color as opposed to actions of the majority group and institutional arrangements in the larger society. They must also face the reality that even when black or Latino men behave in unacceptable ways toward women, which must be confronted and addressed by feminists, the men, too, are victims of societal discrimination. This complicates the issue, adding a dimension not experienced by white feminists. For all these reasons, African American and Latina feminists, to a greater extent than most white feminists, have emphasized racial and class inequality, as well as gender inequality, as problems to be addressed by feminism (A. Y. Davis, 1981, 1989; hooks, 1981, 1991; P. H. Collins, 1991; Higgenbotham, 1992; Lorde, 1992). Some call themselves *womanists* or, among black women, *Africana Womanists*, distinguishing their viewpoint from feminism (A. Walker, 1983; Ntiri, 2001; Hudson-Weems, 1993, 2001). The difference is that whereas feminism primarily emphasizes gender inequality, womanism emphasizes racial and class inequality as much or more so. Often, black and Latina feminists or womanists argue that race, class, and gender oppression—although they work in different ways and affect various groups of people in different ways—are part of an interlocking social relationship of domination, which oppresses various groups while giving unfair advantage to an elite that is made up of white, upper-class, heterosexual men (hooks, 1989, p. 175; P. H. Collins, 1991, p. 226).

## Black Men in American Society

Whereas women of color face problems arising from both racism and sexism, there are also problems of particular concern to men of color, especially black men, whose situation has been the focus of growing concern in recent years. As noted earlier, one problem they face is that because of racism, they have often been denied the opportunity to fulfill the male role in the ways expected in American society. A long history of slavery, job discrimination, low wages, and high unemployment rates has made it difficult or impossible for many black men to provide for their families, as has been expected of men in American society. For some African American men who have been fortunate enough to be part of the growing black middle class, economic hardship has eased in recent decades. At the same time, however, it has worsened for many other black men, particularly those who reside in central cities, where massive numbers of industrial jobs have been eliminated. As recently as 1974, nearly half of all young, employed black men worked at relatively well-paying jobs in manufacturing. By 1984, however, only about a quarter of employed black men were working in such jobs and, by 2000, just one out of eight (U.S. Census Bureau, 2003d, Table PCT86). Between 1973 and 1984, the average earnings of black men under age thirty with four years of high school fell by more than 50 percent, largely due to loss of manufacturing employment (Gordon Berlin and Andrew Sum, cited in Newport, 1992). As manufacturing jobs disappeared, black male unemployment rates soared, and many black men gave up looking for work and dropped out of the labor force (W. J. Wilson, 1987, 1996). As of the 2000 census, more than 30 percent of black men in their twenties were out of the labor force entirely, more than twice as many as among white men the same age (calculated from U.S. Census Bureau, 2003d, Table PCT86).

Some young black men have responded to the loss of job opportunities by turning to crime or drugs. In many instances, young, inner-city black males can make more money in an illegal activity than in any legal one. As anthropologist Phillippe

Bourgeois (quoted in J. P. Newport, 1992) put it, "Crack has created a new Horatio Alger myth for inner-city kids searching for meaning and upward mobility. It's really their American dream. . . . Compared to earning chump change working for the white man at McDonald's, the drug trade can seem more realistic and even noble." In short, the immediate economic incentives are to engage in illegal activity rather than legal. However, as we shall see, the long-term consequences have been devastating for inner-city African American males, especially given the racial inequalities in enforcement of drug laws, discussed in Chapter 11.

According to West (1993), a number of young black men are turning to crime for another reason: The loss of job opportunities in the inner city, along with other recent changes, has exacerbated a long-standing problem in the black community that West calls "nihilism." He defines *nihilism* as a "sense of psychological depression, personal worthlessness, and social despair that is so widespread in black America" (p. 13). The consequences of nihilism include detachment from others, a self-destructive disposition, and a mean-spirited outlook that "destroys both the individual and others" (p. 15). West blames unrestrained capitalism and corporate market institutions for this problem. On the one hand, he argues, American capitalism has marketed the pursuit of pleasure in a variety of ways, constantly promoting products on the basis of comfort, fun, convenience, and sexual stimulation. Like all Americans, blacks have been heavily influenced by this promotion. At the same time, these same market forces have reduced job opportunities and elevated unemployment, worsening the social conditions of blacks in the inner city. Thus, blacks are subject to the hedonistic, pleasure-seeking tendencies of modern America but lack legitimate means to pursue them. And for inner-city blacks, objective conditions have worsened, leading to greater anger, more pressure in the direction of nihilism, and fewer means to legitimately pursue the pleasures that advertising constantly encourages.

According to West (1993), the destructive consequences of nihilism in the black community were once held in check by strong black institutions and by fear of reprisals from whites. Today, however, many of those black institutions have been undermined by the loss of jobs in the black community and by the departure of the black middle class to the suburbs (on these points, see also W. J. Wilson, 1987). Also, some middle-class blacks have pursued the individualistic goals of making more money and have focused less on service to the black community. (Nonetheless, college-educated African Americans generally devote greater effort to community service activities than comparably educated whites [Bowen and Bok, 1998, pp. 257–58; see also Zweigenhaft and Domhoff, 2003, pp. 162–63].)

In addition, black anger, the expression of which was once held in check by fear of white reprisals, can be more freely expressed today. A result, according to West, has been that many young blacks, particularly males, have become more violent and more hedonistic. One of the few ways a young black man with little hope of employment can gain any feeling of power is by provoking fear in others. In West's (1993, p. 89) words, "to be 'bad' is good . . . because it imposes a unique kind of order for young black men on their own distinctive chaos and solicits an attention that makes others pull back with some trepidation." For the most part, violence by young black men has been directed toward other blacks because they are the easiest targets. Black women have been particularly victimized (West, 1993, p. 18), often by beatings and sexual assaults. On the other hand, fights and shootings among black men have become common in poor, inner-city neighborhoods. According to sociologist Elijah Anderson (1999), a consequence of this is that for reasons of safety and self-respect, even law-abiding African American males must show a "tough" front on the streets, and young males can easily "be sucked up by the streets" (Anderson, 1999, p. 98). To gain respect, a "decent" kid may fight or "roll on" others. In so doing, he does gain respect on the street, but he also changes as a person, becoming a part of the "street" culture he was originally defending himself against (Anderson, 1999, pp. 100–106).

Another consequence, of course, is that blacks are more likely to be victims of street crime. About half of the people murdered in the United States are black (compared with 13 percent of the population that is black). Violent crime increased sharply between the early 1980s and mid-1990s, but since then it has fallen significantly. However, it is still true that African Americans are much more likely to be murdered than whites and that homicide is the most common cause of death for young black males (R. Anderson, 2002). Another consequence of this violence, as well as of drug dealing and racial inequality in the enforcement of drug laws, is that large numbers of black men are imprisoned. It should be again emphasized, as is discussed in greater detail in Chapter 11, that African Americans who use illegal drugs are far more likely to be imprisoned than whites who do so. As a result of all these factors, a commonly cited statistic in recent years has been that more young black men are in prison than are in college.

The last statistic points to another problem: limited educational attainment among many black men. Black men are less likely to attend college today than they were twenty-five or thirty years ago. The proportion of black college students who are male fell from 50 percent in the 1960s to just 39 percent in 1990 (Sudarkasa, 1991). By 2000, it was below 37 percent, whereas men make up about 44 percent of all college students (Chronicle of Higher Education, 2003c). The percentage of all college students who are black males fell from 4.3 percent in 1976 to just 3.5 percent in 1990, then partially recovered to 3.8 percent in 2000 (Chronicle of Higher Education, 1997b; 2003d). This figure, 3.8 percent, is far below the roughly 6.5 percent of the college-age population that is black male (U.S. Bureau of the Census, 1998d). There are several reasons for this. As employment opportunities have worsened in the inner cities, growing numbers of black men entered the military or enrolled in private trade schools that promised (but rarely delivered) quick placement into attractive jobs (Sudarkasa, 1991). Some have been attracted by the temptation of easy money from selling drugs and have ended up in jail. Finally, because of the lack of black male role models and because of a variety of other problems, the proportion of black men with the academic qualifications to get into a four-year college is smaller than that of black women (Sudarkasa, 1991).

Several African American social scientists, including West (1993) and W. J. Wilson (1996), have been critical of both liberals and conservatives for the ways in which they have addressed (or avoided) behavioral problems of black males. Liberals (including many sociological conflict theorists) have said little about crime and drug abuse among blacks for fear of contributing to stereotypes. These stereotypes are a real problem: Despite the high crime rates, most black men are law-abiding citizens, yet they are often harassed by the police, tailed by store employees, and denied jobs (E. Anderson, 1990; Kirschenman and Neckerman, 1991; Feagin and Sikes, 1994). Nonetheless, West, W. J. Wilson, and others argue that we cannot address a problem if we do not discuss it, and they argue that liberals should acknowledge that conditions such as crime, substance abuse, and family disruption are genuine problems in the black community and are increasingly inhibiting its development.

At the same time, West, Wilson, and others are even more critical of conservatives (again, including some sociological functionalists) for their tendency to speak simplistically about these conditions as if they are the only or ultimate cause of African American problems. Both Wilson and West point out that whereas problems such as crime, drug abuse, and family disruption are very real, they can be understood and addressed only as responses to the social conditions in which a large part of the African American community lives. As we have seen, job loss, lack of opportunity through legitimate channels, pressures for consumption and hedonism in the larger society, and role expectations that cannot be fulfilled have all created conditions that foster anger, crime, and substance abuse among inner-city black males. For example, if crime pays more than any available job in the short run or if no job is available at all, it is not surprising that some people turn to crime. Although it is necessary to directly address these problems, West and Wilson argue that this by itself is not enough. Society must also find ways to address the larger social conditions that have contributed to the growth and development of these problems. These include joblessness, low wages, unrestrained market forces, poor education, and the various forms of institutional discrimination that have been addressed in earlier chapters of this book.

Wilson, West, and others have argued for a two-pronged approach. One part would try to address the behavioral problems of black males and to motivate them to pursue education and seek legitimate employment. School programs targeting black males, such as the immersion schools discussed in Chapter 12 and mentoring programs, are examples (Whitaker, 1991; Majors and Billson, 1992). Organizations such as Concerned Black Men, based in Washington, are being established to provide young, fatherless black boys with monitoring and mentoring from black men who act as surrogate fathers (H. Dyer, 1992). Similarly, promoting more responsible behavior on the part of African American men was a major objective of the Million Man March in 1995. At the same time, part of the approach must also be targeted to changing the social structure and institutions in ways that provide greater opportunities for employment and education and that meet basic needs, such as health care, that have not been met in the black community. It is likely that such a two-pronged approach offers the best hope for addressing the plight of inner-city African American males. There have been modest signs of improvement since the early 1990s, as the strong economy of that decade and efforts such as those just described have had some impact. Crime rates have fallen, and the proportion of black men in college has risen slightly. Nonetheless, black men remain more likely to be imprisoned and less likely to attend college than almost all other demographic groups.

We conclude this discussion with a cautionary note. Although it is true that disproportionate numbers of black males face serious difficulties, it is important not to stereotype. Dunier (1992) argues that in attempting to bring problems of racism and poverty to the attention of the public, many sociologists and journalists have inadvertently contributed to stereotypes of black males. Like all groups, black males vary widely in their attitudes, behaviors, and characteristics. In *Slim's Table*, Dunier studies a group of black men who meet regularly for lunch at a Chicago cafeteria. The men Dunier studied were not unemployed, not homeless, and not in trouble with the law. Dunier reminds us powerfully that although many black males do face real difficulties, most are law-abiding and employed and do not face poverty. This is important to keep in mind because stereotyping appears to be a significant reason for discrimination against black males (W. J. Wilson, 1996). If discussion of the real problems of some black males turns into stereotyping that affects how people think about all black males, things could be made worse, not better.

## ▶ PREJUDICE, INEQUALITY, AND DISCRIMINATION BASED ON SEXUAL ORIENTATION

Besides race and gender, prejudice, inequality, and discrimination are based on a number of other social characteristics. Two of the most important, addressed in the remainder of this chapter, are sexual orientation and disability.

### The Applicability of the Majority-Minority Model to Sexual Orientation

There is no question that prejudice and discrimination against homosexual men and women are widespread. So strong are the prejudices that laws protecting homosexuals from discrimination have been repealed by popular referendum in Miami, Colorado, Maine, and several Oregon counties, although many of these referenda have later been overturned by court rulings or legislation, and not all such proposals have been approved by voters. Name calling and physical attacks against gay men and lesbians have long been commonplace, and the latter increased, at least for a time, in the early 1990s (Southern Poverty Law Center, 1993b). Sometimes the results have been deadly, as in the cases of Matthew Shepard, a University of Wyoming student who was kidnapped and beaten to death in 1998 because he was gay, and of Gary Matson and Winfield Mowder, a California gay couple who were murdered in 1999 by two brothers who also set three Jewish synagogues on fire. For many years, a number of states had laws banning sexual relations between people of the same sex or forms of sex other than vaginal intercourse, often referred to in legal terms as sodomy. Although many states eventually repealed these laws, they remained on the books in others, until they were overturned in 2003 by the U.S. Supreme Court in the *Lawrence v. Texas* case. In this case, the Court found that laws restricting the private sexual behavior of consenting adults were an unconstitutional violation of the right to privacy.

Federal law today still discriminates against gay men and lesbians, most notably by banning them from service in the military. (This ban has not always existed; it was instituted in 1943.) An attempt by President Clinton in 1993 to end this discriminatory policy was met with a firestorm of opposition in Congress and among some segments of the general population. In the end, the discriminatory law was retained, supposedly softened by a "don't ask, don't tell" compromise that Congress weakened even beyond the initial compromise proposed by Clinton. Although military recruits no longer have to state their sexual orientation, current policy still provides for discharge of military personnel who are found to be homosexual. In fact, more people have been discharged from the military since this policy was put in place than were under the old, supposedly harsher rules. In fiscal year 1996, 850 people were discharged, more than had been discharged for homosexuality in any of the five years before "don't ask, don't tell" became policy (Servicemembers' Legal Defense Network, 1997).

Historically, one of the ugliest and deadliest cases of discrimination occurred during the Holocaust, when tens of thousands of homosexuals or suspected homosexuals were killed in Hitler's death camps (Humm, 1980; Plant, 1986; K. Muller, 1993). Although this deadly campaign against homosexuals is acknowledged more widely today than in the past, accounts of the Holocaust still often omit any reference to it. Yet the fact is that homosexuals were systematically targeted for imprisonment and brutalization and, aside from Jews, probably suffered the highest death rate of any group systematically imprisoned by the Nazis (Plant, 1986).

Efforts to combat discrimination on the basis of sexual orientation have been widespread since the gay and lesbian rights movement emerged in the 1960s. A galvanizing event was a raid by New York City police in 1969 on the Stonewall Inn, a gay bar in Greenwich Village. This event resulted in a spontaneous protest by homosexuals, who felt that they were being singled out for police attention simply because of their sexual orientation. Since then, gay men, lesbians, and bisexuals have organized to oppose discrimination and prejudice, and public support has grown for laws that protect homosexuals from discrimination. By 2003, fourteen states (California, Connecticut, Hawaii, Maryland, Massachusetts, Minnesota, Nevada, New Hampshire, New Jersey, New Mexico, New York, Rhode Island, Vermont, and Wisconsin) and the District of Columbia had passed laws banning discrimination on the basis of sexual orientation in employment, education, public accommodations, or housing, and in one additional state, Oregon, state courts had ruled employment discrimination illegal (Gay Rights Info Homepage, 2003). More than fifty counties and two hundred cities, including Washington, Baltimore, New York, Albany, Boston, Philadelphia, Pittsburgh, Chicago, Minneapolis, St. Paul, Detroit, Cleveland, Des Moines, St. Louis, Kansas City, Atlanta, Louisville, New Orleans, Orlando, Tampa, Dallas, Fort Worth, San Francisco, Los Angeles, Tucson, and Seattle, and, in Canada, Toronto, have passed local ordinances forbidding at least some forms of discrimination on the basis of sexual orientation. Many, if not most, public colleges and universities have such policies.

By the end of the 1980s, after a brief period of backlash attributable to AIDS, polls showed that most Americans opposed discrimination against homosexuals, and the percentage has grown since. For example, by a margin of 71 percent to 18 percent in a 1989 Gallup poll, Americans agreed that homosexuals should have equal job opportunities, and by May 2003, the margin had widened to 88 percent in favor of equal job opportunities to just 10 percent opposed (Gallup, 1990, pp. 215–18; Gallup Organization, 2003e). In fact, time series Gallup polls show that more than half the change in opinions toward equal employment opportunities over the past twenty-five years occurred after 1989, since the AIDS backlash (Gallup Organization, 2003e). As recently as 1989, the majority opposed hiring gay individuals for some kinds of jobs, such as elementary and high school teachers and members of the clergy. However, by May 2003, substantial majorities in Gallup polls supported the hiring of homosexuals for all of these jobs (Gallup Organization, 2003e).

At the same time, there are some areas in which the public remains cool to homosexuals. For example, just over half of those surveyed in a 1992 *Newsweek* poll rejected the idea that homosexuality is an acceptable lifestyle (Turque, 1992). By a margin of 49 to 46 percent, respondents in a 2003 Gallup poll took the same position, although some Gallup polls between 1999 and 2002 did show a majority viewing it as an acceptable lifestyle (Gallup Organization, 2003e). Additionally, a 1996 "feeling thermometer" survey, in which people were asked to rate their feelings toward homosexuals, produced a mean rating of only 40 (Yang, 1998), and 50 percent in the 2003 Gallup poll indicated support for a constitutional amendment defining marriage as being between a man and a woman. By a margin of 55 to 39 percent, these respondents opposed legal recognition of marriages between homosexuals. Even so, about two-thirds of the population in the 1990s expressed no objection to private, consensual sex between adults of the same sex (Yang, 1998). However, this percentage shrank at least temporarily in mid-2003, falling to just under 50 percent in an apparent backlash against the Supreme Court's *Lawrence* ruling (Gallup Organization, 2003e).

It is clear that many Americans still do not agree that homosexuals are a minority group that should be protected from discrimination by law. This is evident in a 1992 referendum passed in Colorado and a 1998 Maine referendum. The Colorado referendum sought to overturn laws that several Colorado cities had passed forbidding discrimination on the basis of sexual orientation. Although the referendum

Bishop Gene Robinson at his consecration ceremony. Bishop Robinson, of New Hampshire, became the Episcopal Church's first openly gay bishop in 2003. Some Episcopalians objected so strongly to his appointment that they threatened to leave the Church.

was later declared unconstitutional, the fact that it passed shows that the majority did not view homosexuals as a minority that deserved legal protection. Moreover, Maine voters used a referendum in 1998 to repeal an antidiscrimination law that the state's legislature had passed before it even went into effect. One argument commonly made by opponents of such legal protection is that unlike racial or ethnic minorities, women, or the disabled, homosexuals are defined as a group on the basis of behavior, that is, sexual interest in and contact with people of the same sex. Therefore, they argue, homosexuality is a choice freely made (again, unlike race, sex, or disability), and if people don't want to face disapproval, they should avoid this behavior.

However, there is one very fundamental flaw with this argument: Research does not back up the idea that homosexuality is a choice. Whereas homosexual *behavior*, that is, sexual relations with a person of the same sex, is a choice in the sense that any sexual behavior is a choice, homosexuality or a homosexual *orientation*, that is, sexual attraction to people of the same sex, is not a choice. Rather, it is an attribute that people gradually discover that they have, as demonstrated by much research. For example, there has been no increase in the extent of homosexual behavior as homosexuality has become more accepted in American society (Karlen, 1971; Levin, 1975; McCary, 1978; Bell, Weinberg, and Hammersmith, 1981). In fact, some recent surveys have reported lower levels of homosexual behavior in recent years than were observed in the Kinsey studies in the 1940s, when social taboos against it were much stronger than they are today (Barringer, 1993; Schmalz, 1993). The most statistically reliable surveys on homosexuality have been conducted since the late 1980s, a time when social acceptance of homosexuality has increased, yet there is no evidence of significant change in the extent of homosexual behavior (T. Smith, 1998). Similarly, younger men are no more likely than older men to be gay, although there may be a small difference among women. If homosexuality were truly a freely chosen behavior, its frequency probably would increase as social support for it increased, as is the case with most forms of behavior. And as we have seen, this has not happened to any significant degree with homosexual behavior. Even when young people know that a teacher or parent is gay, their own likelihood of becoming homosexual does not increase (McCary, 1978).

Recent medical and biological research has discovered increasing evidence that sexual orientation is, at least to a large extent, biologically determined. These studies have found differences in the brains of homosexuals and heterosexuals (Levay, 1993) and evidence of genetic differences between them for both men and women (Suplee, 1991; Bower, 1992; Wheeler, 1991, 1992, 1993; Hamer et al., 1993; Pool, 1993; Pillard and Bailey, 1998). Rather than choosing to be homosexual, it appears that gay and lesbian people gradually discover that they are homosexual. Based on this discovery, along with interaction with other people, both gay and straight, they gradually come to think of themselves as gay or lesbian (Cass, 1979, 1983–1984, 1984; Newman and Muzzonigro, 1993).

Although homosexual orientation is not chosen, people who are not primarily homosexual do at times engage in sexual relationships with people of the same sex. Some people are *bisexuals*; that is, they are attracted to or engage in sex with people of both sexes. Although a homosexual orientation—that is, being primarily or exclusively attracted to people of the same sex—is largely a product of biological and genetic factors, it is also true that how one *behaves* with respect to sexual preference is influenced by both sociocultural and biological and genetic factors. Nonetheless, it is becoming increasingly clear that at least for many homosexuals, biological or genetic factors are important influences, which further negates the idea that a homosexual orientation is a matter of choice.

It can be argued that even if homosexuality were a freely chosen behavioral pattern, which it is not, it would be inappropriate to pass laws against homosexual behavior as long as it occurs between consenting adults. Thus, just as feminists argue that nobody has the right to tell women what role they must fill in society, advocates of gay and lesbian rights argue that nobody has the right to tell others what their sexual preference should be. And because—as we shall see later in more detail—norms against homosexuality in the United States have their roots largely in religious doctrine, antigay discrimination and rules can be seen as violations of the separation of church and state. In other words, such laws can be viewed as attempts by the state to impose a particular religious viewpoint or set of beliefs on its citizenry. The dangers of this were evident in the religiously repressive eighteenth-century English society that many colonial Americans wanted to escape by coming to North America, and they can also be seen in the excesses of a handful of the most fundamentalist Islamic societies more recently, such as the regimes of Ayatollah Khomeini in Iran and of the Taliban in Afghanistan, both of which brutally enforced religious doctrines and rules with harsh treatment of those who spoke or behaved in ways that were not religiously "correct."

Because growing evidence refutes the notion that homosexuality is voluntary, it must be viewed as an ascribed status much like race, ethnicity, sex, or disability—and equally irrelevant to a person's ability to be an effective worker or soldier. Despite the ban on homosexuals in the U.S. military, for example, there is no evidence that gay, lesbian, or bisexual people are less effective soldiers than anyone else. On the contrary, homosexuals who have kept their sexual orientation secret have been serving effectively in the U.S. military for years (Shilts, 1993a, 1993b). Other countries that do not ban homosexuals from military service have not experienced difficulties (Kier, 1998; Blacker and Korb, 2000), and some of history's most influential and effective military leaders, including the Roman emperor Hadrian, King Richard the Lion-Hearted, King Edward II, and the British soldier and author T. E. Lawrence, have been gay (Wallechinsky and Wallace, 1975, p. 1006; Boswell, 1980, p. 25). In the United States, an early military leader who was gay was General William Frederich Wilhelm von Steuben, the army's first inspector general, one of the two most influential generals of the Revolutionary War and the person who first conceptualized the idea of the West Point Military Academy (Shilts, 1993a). A major argument that doomed President Clinton's proposal to end the ban on homosexuals in the military was the claim that doing so would hurt military performance by weakening "unit cohesion," that is, the sense of oneness and cooperation among military units. However, actual social research has repeatedly shown that the correlation between cohesion and military performance is weak, and that, in any case, the inclusion of gay and lesbian personnel has no impact on unit cohesion (Kier, 1998).

On the contrary, the ban on gay and lesbian people in the military may itself represent a threat to national security by preventing people with much-needed abilities to serve. For example, during the year after the September 11, 2001, terrorist attacks, nine linguists, six of whom specialized in Arabic, were dismissed from the U.S. military because they were gay. This occurred at a time when the U.S. military had a shortage of linguists, needed for critical intelligence work after September 11 and in the run-up to the 2003 war in Iraq (M. Mason, 2002). At the time, Donald Hamilton, author of a National Commission on Terrorism report to Congress on the need for linguists, stated, "We face a drastic shortage of linguists, and the direct impact of Arabic speakers is a particular problem" (Mason, 2002).

Given that homosexuality is not a freely chosen status and is not linked to ability to do a job, the majority-minority model can be very appropriately applied to gay men and lesbians. Like minorities defined on the basis of race, ethnicity, and gender, they are the objects of prejudice and discrimination on the basis of a status they did not choose. Given these realities, to fail to legally protect them in the same ways that other groups are protected seems patently unfair and, in fact, discriminatory. Sociologically, of course, we are faced with the question of why homosexuals are the objects of prejudice and discrimination, an issue to which we now turn.

## Causes of Discrimination Against Gay Men and Lesbians

Prejudice against homosexuals today (sometimes called **homophobia** or, in its institutional form, **heterosexism**) is expressed more openly than most other kinds of prejudice. It is probably one of the few kinds of prejudice that remains socially acceptable to express in many circles, even though it is clearly less acceptable today than in the past. In this sense, prejudice against homosexuals is engrained in culture in the same way that prejudice against other minorities once was but no longer is to the same extent. One reason for the persistence of prejudice against homosexuals is linked to people's religious beliefs. Most Christian religions condemn homosexual behavior, although some have changed in this regard in recent years. Almost all of the more fundamentalist religions continue to condemn sexual contact between people of the same sex. Because the United States is more religious than most other Western countries, religion has played a stronger role in shaping norms about sex in the United States than, for example, in most of Europe (Jones et al., 1986). U.S. norms about homosexuality reflect this: Whereas most U.S. states had laws against homosexual behavior until fairly recently, this is not the case in much of Europe. For example, Holland has had no such law for more than 190 years (Weinberg and Williams, 1974, Chaps. 5–7). In some societies, it has even been valued, at least for parts of the population. For example, the ancient Greeks—who are today regarded as an especially civilized society—valued homosexuality in their leaders and in some ways institutionalized it (Licht, 1932).

The Christian ban on homosexual behavior, like other aspects of traditional American attitudes and rules about sex, can be traced to three historical periods: the biblical era, early Christianity, and the Victorian era, which influenced British and American thought in the nineteenth century (F. Cohn, 1974; McCary, 1978). In each of these periods, but particularly the earlier two, a ban on forms of sex that did not result in pregnancy was functional: In many societies, only about half of all babies born could be expected to live to adulthood. Therefore, a high birthrate was necessary for societies to replace themselves and survive. In this context, forms of sex that could not lead to reproduction, including homosexual sex (also masturbation and heterosexual oral and anal sex), were dysfunctional. This was the source of the biblical concern about "wasting seed," and it explains why religions that developed in this time developed strong norms against homosexuality and other forms of sexuality that could not lead to conception.

Because prejudice and discrimination against homosexuals are so strongly rooted in religious beliefs, they have been quite resistant to change, particularly in a highly religious country such as the United States. Nonetheless, there has been increased recognition that even if such discrimination may once have been functional, it no longer is today. The threat faced by today's world is not loss of population but overpopulation. Thus, in the modern world, it can no longer be argued that homosexuality and other forms of sex that cannot lead to reproduction are dysfunctional. On the contrary, it could in fact be argued that they are functional because they may help to reduce the birthrate in a world that is already overpopulated (Vidal, 1992). But because these norms and prejudices are so deeply rooted in religion, and because a number of religions maintain rules against homosexual behavior, the open expression of homophobic attitudes remains somewhat common today even as open expression of other kinds of prejudice has become less common.

It has also been argued that prejudice and discrimination against homosexuals are closely linked to gender inequality. For gay men, homosexuality involves rejection of a key element of the male role as it has traditionally been defined in our society: sexual relationships with women, often including elements of domination and sexual conquest. For men to reject this role involves an implicit threat to the dominant role in society that men enjoy, and those who reject it by being homosexual are seen by other men as traitors who have broken rank (Pharr, 1992). Thus, males historically have exerted strong peer pressure on any males who appear to reject a traditionally masculine role involving, among other things, the sexual conquest of women. This process starts at a young age: Peer condemnation is stronger for boys who are labeled "sissies" than for girls who prefer a "tomboy" role (Hartley, 1974; see also Avicolli, 1992). Perhaps a major reason for the ban on gays in the military is to preserve "its image as the upholder of traditional notions of masculinity" (Shilts, 1993a).

Lesbianism, too, has been rejected by society for reasons linked to male dominance, and this factor may have become more significant as lesbians have become more outspoken about their sexuality in recent years. By asserting a sexual orientation that does not include the need for a male partner, lesbians are viewed as sending a message that men are unnecessary to their sexual fulfillment or economic support (Pharr, 1992). This threatens the traditional male role as the initiator and controller of sexual encounters and relationships, as well as the economic provider on whom women historically have had to depend. Thus, like male homosexuality, lesbianism may be socially disapproved largely because of the threat it poses to the traditional dominant-male role (Griscom, 1992; Pharr, 1992).

For a time, fear of AIDS played a major role in homophobia in the United States, and when the AIDS epidemic first broke out, some public opinion polls indicated that attitudes toward homosexuals became more negative. However, more recent polls suggest that this trend has reversed and that more people than in the past oppose discrimination on the basis of sexual orientation (Gallup, 1990; Yang, 1998). It appears that a growing proportion of the population has become aware that (1) AIDS cannot be transmitted through casual contact such as at school or work; (2) the disproportionate number of gay men among people with AIDS is specific to the United States but is not the case in some other societies; and (3) AIDS can be transmitted through either homosexual or heterosexual sexual contact, as well as through contact with blood, as when drug addicts share needles. However, fears about AIDS undoubtedly still contribute to homophobia for some people.

## ▶ PEOPLE WITH DISABILITIES AS A MINORITY GROUP

Another group increasingly viewed according to a minority group model is people with disabilities. Estimates of the number of people with disabilities vary. At the high end, about one out of three adults report some type of chronic activity limitation (National Center for Health Statistics, 2002d), not all of which would be regarded by most as constituting a disability. According to the 2000 census, 19.3 percent of all Americans and 18.6 percent of nonelderly adults had disabilities of some type, with just under 12 percent having employment disabilities (meaning any disability that made employment difficult, according to the person answering the census). The majority of adults with disabilities, about 18.5 million people, were employed at the time of the 2000 census (U.S. Census Bureau, 2003c, Table P42).

People with disabilities have come to believe that it is not mainly their physical disabilities that place them at a disadvantage but society's *reaction* to their disabilities. For example, employers are sometimes reluctant to hire people with disabilities, even when their disabilities in no way keep them from doing the job. People with physical disabilities must also frequently deal with nondisabled people who expect them to have mental disabilities, as well as physical ones, and therefore talk down to them, talk about them in their presence, or assume that they are incapable. The nondisabled often view people with disabilities in a unidimensional manner—as *disabled* people rather than as whole people—so that the single characteristic of disability becomes foremost in their minds. This is typical of all forms of prejudice: The characteristic about which a person is prejudiced becomes the foremost characteristic in that person's mind, and other characteristics are ignored. People with such prejudices often stare, maintain an uncomfortable silence, or ask endless questions about the disability. Such behaviors continuously remind people with disabilities that they are "different" (Schuchardt, 1980). These reactions occur not only to adults with disabilities but also to children with disabilities (Fleitas, 2000). In effect, the stigma the rest of society places on people with disabilities, sometimes from the youngest ages on, often can become a greater handicap than the disability itself. This stigma occurs in part because nondisabled people make a number of incorrect assumptions about people with disabilities (Link and Phelan, 2001). According to Fine and Asch (1988), common incorrect assumptions are that biological problems are the only source of difficulty for people with disabilities, that they are victims and "need help," and that their disability is the most important thing in their lives. Even the physical disability is often more of a handicap than it need be because of actions of the larger society. For example, it is not particularly difficult to design sidewalks and buildings so that most people with disabilities can use them. Until recently, however, this was rarely done. Today it is required in new construction by the Americans with Disabilities Act.

Because of various prejudices and socially imposed handicaps such as hiring discrimination, many people with disabilities have come to view themselves as a minority group and to behave accordingly. People with disabilities have held demonstrations and engaged in political lobbying similar to that done by racial and ethnic minorities and women. For example, the threat of a lawsuit led to the captioning of part of the TV broadcast of the 1980 Democratic National Convention for hearing-impaired viewers. Since then, closed-captioning systems have been developed and expanded to include a large proportion of TV programming. Increasingly, legislation and labor contracts have forbidden discrimination on the basis of disabilities not related to job performance. Such discrimination was forbidden in 1973, for example, in federal employment and among private employers under contract with the federal government (Bruck, 1978). Since 1990, this protection has been extended to most private employment. People with disabilities have also come to be regarded as a protected group under affirmative action programs, and many employers have made special efforts to hire and promote them. There is little doubt that these changes have allowed greater opportunities: Today, people with disabilities are obtaining greater levels of education, more challenging employment, and greater independence. In part, this comes as a result of equal opportunity legislation and of increased societal emphasis on what people with disabilities *can* do rather than on what they *cannot* do.

Nonetheless, such changes have not yet entirely eliminated prejudices and fears toward people with disabilities. Much of the disadvantage that people with disabilities still encounter arises from one-to-one interactions with people who have prejudices, fears, and misunderstandings like those just described. Greater awareness of the perspectives of people with disabilities is needed. Even good intentions are not enough; well-meaning expressions of concern often seem patronizing and make the disabled person feel powerless or unaccepted (Gliedman, 1979). For example, it is much better to ask people with disabilities whether they need help, as with getting a door open, than to assume that they either do or do not.

For people with disabilities, as with other minorities, the black civil rights movement served as an important role model and provided some worthwhile lessons both about how society responds to groups who are "different" and about how to deal with that response. (For further discussion of this subject, see S. Cohen, 1977; Stubbins, 1977; Bruck, 1978; Shaw, 1994; Linton, 1998.) An excellent discussion of how the roles of people with disabilities have changed as a result of the disability rights movement can be found in Treanor (1993).

## Access and the Americans with Disabilities Act

As more overt forms of prejudice and discrimination against people with disabilities have diminished somewhat and as legal protection against discrimination has been extended to people with disabilities, their efforts have increasingly shifted to issues of access. Many public buildings, educational institutions, and retail stores are not designed to be easily usable (or in some cases, usable at all) by people who are visually impaired, whose activities are limited by chronic conditions such as arthritis or heart trouble, or who use wheelchairs. Curbs without curb cuts, signs that are printed but not in Braille, and lack of nearby parking places are common design problems that limit access. Thus, it has been difficult in many cases for people with disabilities to gain access to education, work, shopping, and entertainment, even when their disabilities do not impair their actual ability to study, work, shop, or enjoy entertainment facilities. Rather, they are thwarted by design characteristics that make it hard or impossible for them to get in or move around once they do.

In 1992, a major piece of legislation, the Americans with Disabilities Act (ADA), was passed to deal with this and other problems. The law broadens protection of people with disabilities against discrimination, requires that employers accommodate them, and requires public facilities to be accessible. Among the specific provisions is a ban on discrimination against people with physical and mental disabilities in hiring and promotion. This ban applies to all employers with more than fifteen employees. It also outlaws tests that have the effect of screening out job applicants with disabilities unless it can be shown that the tests relate to a worker's ability to perform the job (Traver, 1990). Before the passage of ADA, people with disabilities were protected from discrimination by the Rehabilitation Act of 1973, but unlike ADA, it applied only to organizations that receive federal funds (Jaschik, 1993). Also, ADA allows people to directly sue the organizations that discriminate. Under the old law, all they could do was file complaints to federal agencies, who then decided whether to take action and what action to take (Jaschik, 1993).

In addition to strengthening the ban on discrimination, ADA requires that workplaces and public accommodations be made accessible to people with disabilities. This includes physical accessibility, such as doors wide enough for wheelchairs and ramps or lifts for wheelchairs (Traver, 1990). Restaurants, colleges and universities, transportation systems, theaters, retail stores, and government offices are among the kinds of public facilities that must now be accessible. In addition to accessibility, employers are also required to make "reasonable accommodations" for employees with disabilities, such as providing readers for blind workers and signers or caption systems for the hearing-impaired and arranging modified work schedules. Of course, the word *reasonable* is subject to various interpretations, and it will probably take some time and a number of court rulings to discover exactly what it means in a practical sense (Jaschik, 1993). Many people with disabilities have interpreted this and other provisions to mean that they are to be *integrated*: For example, in colleges, this would mean no separate classes, dorm rooms, or buses for students with disabilities. In some areas, the new law is quite explicit: For example, it specifies that in public transportation systems, *all* new buses must be accessible to people with disabilities; it is no longer enough to merely operate a special "handi-van" service, although such services may be provided in addition (Traver, 1990).

It is too early to tell what all the effects of the ADA will be. Debates continue on how much of the costs employers and organizations providing public accommodations should incur to accommodate the disabled. Questions have also arisen about how far the right to sue under ADA and similar laws goes when it is a state that is being sued, as in the case of accessibility or workplace discrimination in a public university. In the 2001 case *University of Alabama v. Garrett*, the Supreme Court found that states' rights protect states from having to pay damages in lawsuits for violations of ADA. Notably, though, the Court did not rule that states did not have to obey ADA, only that they could not be compelled to pay monetary damages for violations. Presumably, they could still be ordered by the courts to cease any discrimination that was found to occur (N.A.M.I., 2001).

According to national polls of people with disabilities, most say that their living conditions improved after the passage of ADA (U.S. Commission on Civil Rights, 2000). The greatest improvements were reported in access to buildings and to

The Americans with Disabilities Act (ADA) mandates that classrooms and workplaces be accessible. Many have interpreted this to mean that people with disabilities are to be integrated into regular work and school settings.

transportation and fuller inclusion in the community, with up to 80 percent of the poll respondents reporting improved access to businesses and public facilities (United Cerebral Palsy Associations, 1996). Less improvement was noted in employment, and a 1998 and 2000 Harris polls continued to show greater satisfaction with life among people without disabilities than those with disabilities (National Organization on Disability, 2001).

We also know that ADA has uncovered a substantial number of violations and resulted in significant benefits to those whose rights have been violated. From the time the law went into effect in 1992 through 1998, more than 91,000 formal complaints of violations were received by the Equal Employment Opportunity Commission. About 11,000 of these were resolved, resulting in more than $225 million in payments to people whose rights had been violated (U.S. Commission on Civil Rights, 2000). The most common causes of complaints were discharges of employees (54 percent), failure to make reasonable accommodation (32 percent), and harassment (14 percent). Claims of discrimination against people with back ailments, emotional or psychiatric impairments, neurological impairments, or hand or foot disabilities each accounted for more than 10 percent of all complaints. Other disabilities that were often associated with alleged discrimination were heart impairments, diabetes, hearing impairments, vision impairments, and substance abuse (Equal Employment Opportunity Commission, 1998). Although the costs can be high when the law is violated, the actual costs of compliance were found to be relatively low. For example a study of Sears showed that three-fourths of accommodations made for people with disabilities cost nothing, and the overall cost averaged only $30 per accommodation (U.S. Commission on Civil Rights, 2000).

The passage of the ADA indicates one thing quite clearly: More than ever before, Americans recognize that people with disabilities can do many of the same things, and should have the same rights, as people without disabilities. Thus, they increasingly reject discrimination, and this position has been written into law. As with other groups, however, it remains to be seen to what extent such legislation is successful in bringing about truly equal opportunity for people with disabilities.

## Summary and Conclusion

In this chapter, we have seen that the concepts of majority and minority groups can be applied to a wide variety of groups besides those characterized by race and ethnicity: groups based on gender, sexual orientation, and disability, for example. It is clear that women, gay men and lesbians, and people with disabilities have been widely discriminated against in American society, and all of them continue today to be placed in a subordinate position with respect to wealth, income, status, or power, although the forms of discrimination vary among groups. We have also seen that there is a complex interaction among race, class, and gender inequality, so that whereas women of all races and social classes occupy a subordinate role in American society, its nature varies according to race and class. Similarly, racial inequality has imposed unique difficulties on black men in the United States, who experience racial inequality in different ways than do black women. A particular problem has been increasingly difficult access to employment, which has made it impossible for many black men to play the male role as our society expects. The consequence has often been self-destructive violence, arising from frustration and lack of opportunity.

In recent years, Americans have been increasingly cognizant of these forms of intergroup inequality, although all of them persist today. Federal legislation has banned discrimination against women and against people with disabilities in employment and public accommodations, and several states and many cities have also extended such legal protection to gay men and lesbians. However, there has been significant resistance, especially concerning sexual orientation. Much of this opposition is based on religious beliefs, which are a stronger influence in the United States than in other industrialized countries. In recent years, however, some religious denominations in the United States have reevaluated and altered their traditional position that homosexuality is sinful, and some have supported antidiscrimination legislation.

## Critical Review Questions

1. Describe wage and salary inequalities between men and women. What would it take to eliminate gender inequality in wages and salaries?

2. How does gender inequality occur in the home? What would it take to change it?

3. How are discrimination and inequality based on gender, sexual orientation, and disability similar to and different from discrimination and inequality based on race?

4. Does your city or state have a law forbidding discrimination on the basis of sexual orientation? Does your college or university provide benefits to same-sex partners of faculty and staff? What groups support such laws and policies and what groups oppose them? Why?

5. How accessible is your campus to people with disabilities? How might you go about investigating this question?

# Current Trends in Majority-Minority Relations

# Overview

In this chapter, we shall examine several current issues and trends in intergroup relations. These include the diversity and multiculturalism movements in the workplace and in education, the resurgent problem of hate group activity, and the continuing debate over how to respond to it, which has centered on hate crime legislation, speech codes, and so-called "political correctness." In this chapter, we shall also address the growing movement to combat discrimination by testing for discrimination in housing, lending, retail sales, and other business activities.

## ▶ DIVERSITY AND MULTICULTURALISM IN WORK AND EDUCATION

As noted in earlier chapters, the population of the United States is becoming more diverse. Projections indicate that people of color will make up nearly half of the U.S. population by the year 2050 and a majority by 2060. For example, official projections are that non-Hispanic whites will be less than 53 percent of the population by 2050 and less than 50 percent by 2060 (U.S. Census Bureau, 2002j). By the end of this century, it is projected that only about 40 percent of the U.S. population will be composed of non-Hispanic whites. One out of three Americans are projected to be Latino/a by then, and about 13 percent each will be African American and Asian American (U.S. Census Bureau, 2002j). As the population is becoming more diverse, so are American workplaces and educational institutions. White males born in the United States, once a sizable majority of the labor force, were already a numerical minority by 1990, and their proportion of the work force will continue to decline throughout the twenty-first century.

The younger segment of the population is even more diverse than the overall population, in part because birthrates among people of color in the United States are somewhat higher than among whites. Already today, 37 percent of students at all levels, kindergarten through college and graduate or professional school, are people of color (U.S. Census Bureau, 2003p). As in the workplace, the composition of student bodies at all levels will continue to become more diverse in coming years. The educational needs of these increasingly diverse student bodies, along with the need to address the cultural conflicts and social tensions that sometimes accompany diversity, have led to a growing movement for multiculturalism in American education. This movement is discussed in the context of education in Chapter 12, and for that reason, the main emphasis in this chapter's discussion of the diversity movement is on the workplace. Later in this chapter, in the context

429

of debates on "political correctness," some attention is also given to diversity programs in higher education, because in many cases they seem to be a more effective approach than efforts to regulate insensitive or hateful speech.

As the work force continues to become more diverse, all Americans have a growing stake in equal opportunity and harmonious intergroup relations. If racism, sexism, and other forms of discrimination prevent people of color, women, people with disabilities, and gay, lesbian, and bisexual people from becoming fully productive workers, the entire economy will suffer. Moreover, this will occur in a global economy in which international competition demands efficiency and productivity. If the United States does not fully utilize all its talents its productivity will suffer, as will any company that does not fully utilize the human resources of all its diverse employees.

For these reasons, increasing numbers of companies today see diversity as an issue they must address not merely out of principle but also because the productivity and success of the company depend on it (Galagan, 1993). They also realize the need to address racial and cultural tensions and conflicts among their workers. These conflicts can disrupt the work process and cause minority group workers to feel isolated and unwanted, resulting in unnecessary attrition. For example, attrition rates of women and people of color were two to four times that of white men at Monsanto before the company initiated its diversity management program. A survey revealed that the main reasons for this attrition included poor relations with supervisors and a perception among women and people of color that they were being given work that would not lead anywhere (Galagan, 1993).

Attrition among minority and female workers also occurs when they encounter **glass ceilings**: limited upward mobility that keeps them from moving into top executive and managerial positions. Such glass ceilings not only limit opportunities for minority and female employees but also deprive the company of the talents of people with the ability and experience to be good managers (R. R. Thomas, 1990). For example, among female professionals and managers who leave their jobs, 73 percent do so because they see limited opportunities for women in their companies

As illustrated by this meeting of corporate executives, America's work force is becoming more diverse. The most effective work organizations will be ones that create an environment in which diverse people work cooperatively and all feel that they are making a valued contribution.

(Morrison, 1993). This perception appears to reflect reality: The higher the rank in an organization, the greater the disparities in promotions along the lines of race, ethnicity, and gender. Dovidio (1993) has shown this to be true for the U.S. armed forces, the federal government, and the 1,000 largest corporations. For example, African Americans make up 13 percent of the U.S. Navy but only 5 percent of the officers and 1.5 percent of the admirals. These differences cannot be explained by differences in the backgrounds of blacks and whites in the Navy. However, a survey conducted by Dovidio may offer the answer. When applicants have weak credentials, whites rank black and white applicants similarly: Both are ranked low. However, when black and white applicants present similar strong credentials, whites still tend to rank both applicants positively, but they rank the white applicant higher than the black applicant (Dovidio, 1993, p. 56). This is consistent with a subtle form of modern racism in which whites do not assign negative characteristics to minority groups more than they do to whites, but they do assign to whites more positive characteristics than they assign to minorities.

This behavior may occur because managers have a greater comfort level dealing with people who are similar to themselves. Morrison (1993) lists such prejudices and "comfort-level" concerns as being among the greatest barriers to the advancement of women and people of color in the workplace. One recent study suggests that the glass ceiling problem is especially salient for women, with the largest effects for African American women, whereas African American men experience discrimination at all levels and not disproportionately in promotion to the best positions (Cotter et al., 2001). However, the results are much the same. For example, statistics on General Motors closely correspond to those for the Navy: 14 percent of GM's workforce is African American, but only 3.8 percent of its corporate officers are African American (Bodipo-Memba and Butters, 2002).

## Diversity Management in the Workplace

Because of these concerns, a growing number of employers have initiated **diversity management** programs, whose objectives are to empower all employees, particularly women and people of color, to work, produce, and advance in the organization to their full potential. They also aim to address intergroup tensions and conflicts in the workplace that interfere with productivity. By 1996, three out of four of the 500 largest companies in the United States had some kind of diversity program in place, and more than half had staff members dedicated to such programs (Caudron, 1998a, 1998b). Significantly, more than 60 percent of these programs had been started since 1991. Similar programs have been established in many government, nonprofit, and educational organizations, as well as the U.S. military. Among employers recognized for having particularly strong and effective diversity management programs are Monsanto, Corning, American Express, Xerox, DuPont, Allstate Insurance, the Fairfax County (Virginia) public schools, the Palo Alto (California) police department, Procter and Gamble, Avon, Digital, Hewlett-Packard, and U.S. West (R. R. Thomas, 1990; Laporte, 1991; Morrison, 1993; Caudron, 1998b; Hildebrand, 1998; EthnicMajority, 2003).

Diversity management programs are designed in a variety of ways, reflecting different ideas about what works best. For example, there are debates about the extent to which programs should focus on attitudes as opposed to behavior. Some experts argue that much of the problem lies in prejudices and that to be effective, programs must address them. Howard Ehrlich, director of the National Institute Against Prejudice and Violence (quoted in Solomon, 1992), points out that bad economic conditions often give rise to economic fears among many workers, who then focus their fears on competition from other racial, ethnic, or cultural groups. Such fears led to a sharp increase in hate crimes and hate group activities during the recession of the early 1990s. They also can trigger prejudice and discrimination in the workplace, often by white male workers who fear loss of their jobs and who feel threatened by improvements in the status of women, African Americans, Latinos/as, and others. Ehrlich argues that such feelings and prejudices must be dealt with directly and that if employers do not do so they will probably be expressed in the form of hate acts and disruptive and potentially violent incidents in the workplace.

The workplace is also affected by the different experiences and views of whites and of people of color concerning opportunity in American society. Whites often do not recognize that, because of their race, they have enjoyed advantages that make their daily life and work life easier than that of minorities. This lack of recognition of racial inequality affects their reactions to minorities in the workplace. For example, whites often see minorities as demanding workplace privileges based on their race, whereas minority workers view the same demands merely as efforts to offset their unequal opportunities. Thus, some experts on diversity training believe that efforts to address these different experiences and perceptions, including encouraging whites to recognize the advantages and privileges they often enjoy because of their race, must be part of any diversity-training program (Ashmore, 1998).

Others argue that the main focus of diversity management should be on behavior, not attitudes (Janet Himler, quoted in Solomon, 1992; Elsie Y. Cross, interviewed by Cutler, 1993; Hemphill and Haines, 1997; Caudron and Hayes, 1997), because it is behavior that directly affects the opportunities of minority employees and creates incidents and conflicts in the workplace. An employer can say, "Think whatever you want, but intolerant behavior will not be permitted here." For example, at Ethcon, a company that developed a diversity management program in the late 1980s, an outside consultant at a sales meeting made fun of the company's diversity guidelines and told an off-color joke during his presentation. The consultant was dismissed on the spot, sending a powerful message that behaviors unsupportive of diversity would not be tolerated in the company (Ehrlich, 1990). Of course, the most effective approach may be to address both discriminatory behaviors and the feelings, beliefs, and prejudices that give rise to such behaviors. In fact, that is what most diversity management programs do. Also, as was discussed in Chapter 3, changing behavior can often lead to changing attitudes. If people work cooperatively with others of a different race, gender, ethnicity, disability status, or sexual orientation, their attitudes often will change to match their behavior.

An example of addressing both behaviors and attitudes can be seen in a Monsanto program (Laabs, 1993). Employees volunteer and are trained to serve as members of "consulting pairs," which have two main functions. One is to facilitate "join-up" meetings between supervisors and employees who are newly assigned to one another. The gender and ethnic composition of the consulting pair is matched to that of the employee and supervisor. In the join-up meeting, the consulting pair helps the employee and supervisor address mutual expectations and mutual understanding of developmental needs. The meeting helps the supervisor to see what skills the employee would like to develop and where the employee would like to go in the company, and it also helps the supervisor to identify interests and skills in the employee that can be utilized to the company's advantage. The join-up meeting also addresses organizational norms and personal "hot-button" issues of the supervisor and employee (such as annoyance when people show up late for meetings), so that inadvertent conflicts and misunderstandings can be avoided. This is important because in a culturally diverse environment and in a polarized society, conflicts that may initially have nothing to do with race, gender, or culture quickly become defined in those terms.

This reality is demonstrated in a case involving the other use of the consulting pairs: mediation and resolution of disputes in which diversity issues may play some role (Laabs, 1993). In this example, a dispute arose between a white male senior manager and a black male manager under his supervision. The white senior manager saw the black manager as unresponsive to his requests and consequently felt that the manager was not learning his job as he should be. The manager felt that his boss was watching him too closely and hovering over him in a way that would not be done with white managers. He saw this as interfering with his ability to work and take initiative, which he highly valued. When the consulting pair met with the two, it came to light that the white senior manager loved to teach and to get his hands on the work of middle-management employees under his supervision. It also came out that the black middle manager wanted to work independently and perceived the senior manager as interfering and mistrustful of him. It became clear that the issue did not have a racial basis at the start but simply reflected the different and somewhat conflicting work styles of the two managers. In a racially divided society, however, the conflict was quickly perceived in racial terms. Once the two managers understood that the basis of their conflict was a difference in their work styles, they were able to work out their differences, and from that point on, they worked well together without further conflict. Cummins points out that in the absence of the consulting pair, the conflict would have festered. The results could have been increased racial conflict and tension, a bad working relationship between the two managers, and possibly the loss of the black manager. With the consulting pair, none of this happened.

Another company that has had a successful diversity management program is Allstate Insurance. And as shown in the box "Allstate Insurance, Diversity, and Business Success," Allstate, along with other companies, has shown how an effective diversity effort is good for the bottom line.

## ALLSTATE INSURANCE, DIVERSITY, AND BUSINESS SUCCESS

When the publication *Black Enterprise* asked for companies willing to have it assess their diversity management programs, Allstate Insurance stepped forward. When the assessment was completed, it got high marks, and the magazine publicized those high marks. In addition, Allstate also received an award from Denver's Latin American Research and Service Agency for support of community activities and for offering employment opportunities in Denver's Latino/a community and a 1997 Catalyst Award, given to companies that contribute to the advancement of women. As much as Allstate valued this recognition, however, its biggest motivation for its diversity program was the bottom line: Awareness of diversity was profitable for the company.

Allstate launched its diversity program in 1993, with goals of expanding career opportunities for minorities and women and of fostering greater customer growth, retention, and satisfaction. Every employee in the company received diversity training, with feedback sessions six months later to see whether the training was being put into practice. When positions opened in the company, managers were required to present a diverse list of candidates for each important position. Progress toward diversity goals was measured twice a year, and an online feedback system measured employee satisfaction. A percentage of each manager's performance bonus was based on progress toward diversity goals. By 1998, 21 percent of its executives and managers were minorities, including 14 percent who were African American.

The company found that employees who went through the diversity training program reported higher levels of overall job satisfaction. And Allstate's employees took action to change organizational structure, language, and programs to meet the various needs of diverse customers. That is where the bottom line came in. A prime example can be seen in Denver, where Gilbert Villarreal applied to the company because he saw its commitment to diversity and later became Colorado's first Hispanic sales manager. Later, when he returned to operating his own agency, he relocated the agency into a Latino/a neighborhood where Allstate previously had not sold many policies.

He made this move after analyzing data showing that predominantly Latino/a census tracts in Denver had few agencies of large insurance companies such as Allstate. In doing this, he found a large untapped market. There were many people in the neighborhood who, although good insurance risks, were buying high-priced policies from companies specializing in high-risk insurance. This was because those companies had offices in the neighborhood; big companies such as Allstate did not. Now, Allstate is developing a plan to move policyholders from high-risk companies to Allstate, and reaping a profit in the process: It is attracting low-risk policyholders it had ignored in the past. Consequently, the Denver office outperformed the national rate for attracting new customers.

Because they have led to changes like this, Allstate's diversity efforts are not only promoting greater opportunities for minorities but are also increasing the profitability of the company. As Allstate vice president Ron Rex put it, "The people who come to us as customers flourish, and we do, too. People that come to us as employees flourish, and we do, too. . . . We're very excited about this. It's about business success, and it's the right thing to do."

*Sources:* Hildebrand (1998), Caudron (1998a).

## Characteristics of Effective Diversity Management Programs

**Diversity Among the Diversity Program Staff.** The Monsanto example points out some important principles for any diversity management program. One is that those involved must themselves be diverse. One ingredient of the success of the consulting-pairs program at Monsanto is that the pairs are set up to match the characteristics of the people they assist. Thus, each party is assured of having someone with similar characteristics on the consulting pair. Also, the diversity training staff must be diverse, because people will sometimes accept a message from a member of their own group that they would not accept from a member of another group. Thus, diversity-training or management programs work best when those carrying out the program have the same mix of characteristics as the people in the organization.

**Beginning with an Assessment.** There is no one-size-fits-all diversity program. Every organization is different, even though the underlying problems often are similar. Therefore, any program to some extent must be tailored to the needs and situation of the particular place in which it is implemented. For this reason, most diversity-programming experts believe that the first step is to assess the organization—its strengths, problems, and needs and its atmosphere with respect to diversity issues (American Society for Training and Development, 2001). This usually involves collecting data on how employees of different social groups perceive their opportunities. It also may involve identifying and addressing obstacles that a diversity program may encounter in a particular organization (Owens, 1997; American Management Association, 1998).

**Dealing with Issues Promptly.** Another key principle, also illustrated by the Monsanto example, is the importance of dealing with issues promptly rather than letting them fester. In fact, the opportunity to do so is a major advantage of having a diversity management program. Diversity consultant Bob Abrams (quoted in Solomon, 1992) illustrates this by describing a racial incident between a radio dispatcher and a truck driver who could not see each other. Observing that the loading dock was empty, the driver informed the dispatcher that materials he was supposed to pick up were not ready. The dispatcher, who did not know the driver, replied, "Even a one-eyed nigger can see that. They certainly don't have the material ready to go." Nobody reported the incident, and it festered for more than four years until a diversity-training workshop, in which the truck driver, an African American, reported it and described the pain of living with such an ethnic slur, even though the dispatcher had not aimed it at him personally. According to Abrams, a good diversity management program would have given the driver an opportunity to report the incident and express his hurt and would have provided a way to address the issue promptly. According to Abrams, "You can't let this stuff slide, because it impairs team ability to function. If you don't have a willingness to address these problems, you'll have serious problems in a team, working together." According to Solomon, such problems, if left unaddressed, often fester until they are expressed in diversity workshops, discrimination complaints, lawsuits, or exit interviews.

**Use of Case Studies in Training Programs.** Effective diversity-training programs ususally include case studies related to the organization's situation and encourage employees to discuss effective ways of handling difficult situations. For example, a medical center used a case study in which workers discussed what to do if a white patient objected to being treated by an African American medical worker. A university had workers discuss a case in which an Asian American student insisted on being seen by an Asian American counselor who was in the middle of a session with another student at the time. At a school, teachers and other employees were asked what they might do if they saw an overweight child, an Asian child, and a child with a speech impediment sitting by themselves day after day in the cafeteria. In all of these cases, employees discussed the issues involved and came up with creative methods that could be applied to similar situations encountered in the workplace (Labich, 1996; Rodriquez, 1998).

**Goals and Objectives, with Top-Level Support.** Another vital concept is setting specific, clear, and quantitative goals, articulated and actively supported by top management. There must be a way of determining whether or not the program achieved what it was supposed to, and there must be a message that it is important to top management that these goals are attained. Morrison says, "I believe that diversity efforts that don't have statistical goals are doomed. The reluctance of managers to hold themselves and others to some numbers has probably done more damage to diversity efforts than anything else" (Morrison, 1993, p. 43).

Closely related to this, top management must show a strong commitment to diversity. It must articulate diversity as a key organizational goal and involve itself in the diversity program, for example, by being the first to participate in any diversity-training program, by insisting that diversity goals are met, by issuing periodic bulletins on the progress of the diversity program, and by making diversity part of the reward structure. If these things are done by top management, a diversity program has a strong chance of success; if they are not done, it is unlikely to succeed (Owens, 1997; American Management Association, 1998). A study by the American Management Association has shown that diversity training, taken alone, has little impact. But when it is combined with an organization-wide program backed by management, its impact is much greater (Caudron and Hayes, 1997). Accordingly, the American Society for Training and Development (2001) identifies top-level support as a feature critical for the success of diversity initiatives.

**Accountability.** Holding managers accountable for the success of diversity efforts has received growing emphasis in both business and education. In business, most of the companies with effective diversity management programs have included diversity issues in annual employee evaluations. In some cases, a fraction of the annual performance bonus for managers is based entirely on diversity criteria. In higher education, diversity criteria have begun to be included in recent years in evaluations of schools for accreditation. In 1994, for example, the Western Association of Schools and Colleges approved the inclusion of diversity guidelines in its review procedure for accreditation of colleges and universities (Leatherman, 1994a). The guidelines were designed to assist the association in evaluating the extent to which schools were complying with a 1988 standard requiring colleges to foster ethnic diversity on their campuses. Although fourteen member colleges protested the guidelines—sometimes quite loudly—as intrusions on their autonomy, 83 percent of the member colleges supported them.

Along with accountability—and as a means of ensuring it—there must be ongoing efforts to assess and evaluate the effectiveness of the diversity program. Is it accomplishing what it was designed to do at all levels of the organization? This includes but is not limited to such things as keeping track of the diversity of the work force at all levels, assessing the organizational atmosphere and employees' perceptions about whether the workplace is open and supportive, and assessing the effects of the diversity program on the organization's overall effectiveness. For example, has the program led to new markets or new clients in areas with populations that the organization had previously not reached?

**Research and Use What Works.** The American Society for Training and Development (2001) emphasizes that organizations can learn from one another and from social science. It urges employers to *research best practices*, that is, to learn about what has worked for other employers and to use these techniques rather than trying to reinvent the wheel. It also urges employers to use various kinds of methods and media: role plays, storytelling, videos, simulations, small group discussions, and

Web-based materials, for example. This recommendation is consistent with a wide variety of social science research showing consistently that people are most likely to respond to messages that they receive in multiple forms from multiple sources (Mileti and Fitzpatrick, 1993; Mileti et al., 1993).

**Addressing the Concerns of White Men.** Finally, successful diversity management programs must both address the concerns of and raise the awareness of white men, who often feel threatened or attacked and often do not understand why such programs are needed. White men do not experience discrimination as other groups in society do, and consequently they often do not understand the realities of discrimination and inequality that people of color and women regularly encounter (see Kluegel, 1990). Thus, effective diversity management programs, such as that at Monsanto, place substantial emphasis on using examples to help white men become more aware of the realities experienced by other groups (Galagan, 1993, p. 49). As long as they are not aware of these realities, there is a good chance that white men will behave in ways that counteract diversity efforts and will oppose or feel threatened by such efforts. Thus, effective diversity management programs (1) develop minority employees by ensuring that they get the support, encouragement, and opportunity that they are often denied in predominantly white male organizations and (2) prepare the white male employees to accept and work effectively with minority and female employees (Galagan, 1993).

In this context, it should also be noted that highly confrontational diversity training programs, which were fairly common at one time, have been almost universally found to be unsuccessful (Cannedy, 1998). Programs that seek to induce personal guilt or use accusation tend to produce backlash. It is one thing to show employees ways in which whites benefit from unequal opportunity structures in society, which can be a useful technique. It is quite another thing to pointedly accuse whites of personal responsibility for these social conditions. This kind of personal accusation only blocks communication, and there is even evidence that some efforts to induce guilt among whites have further insulted people of color. For example, one Chicago company tried to induce white guilt by having employees repeatedly sit through a film of lynchings of blacks by whites, and it tried to assess racial attitudes by asking whether employees agreed with various insulting statements about African Americans and Puerto Ricans. The result was that a black worker sued the company for discrimination, alleging that it created a hostile workplace by subjecting minority employees to such material (Lubove, 1997). One problem with diversity training is that there is no certification process for trainers. Because some have used counterproductive techniques, other trainers are being hired to undo the harm done by earlier well-intentioned but misguided efforts.

## Diversity Management and Multiculturalism

Workplace diversity programs reflect a recognition that U.S. society is becoming more multicultural or pluralist and less assimilationist. In other words, racial, ethnic, and cultural groups today are placing a stronger emphasis on affirming and retaining their own distinctive cultures. This is reflected in the comment of one leading diversity manager that "as people begin to celebrate being different, they're no longer willing to get into that melting pot" (Roosevelt Thomas, quoted in Nicklin, 1992). Some people have criticized the tendency toward multiculturalism and pluralism on the ground that it creates divisions that inhibit cooperation in society. As we saw in earlier chapters, however, such pluralism probably is inevitable in a society such as the United States, where much of the population consists of groups whose initial entry into American society was involuntary.

A related but more fundamental criticism of the diversity management and training movement has been raised in a recent book by Lasch-Quinn (2001). She argues that by framing the problem as the attitudes and behaviors of individuals rather than societal inequality, diversity training and management programs miss the true causes of the problem. Thus, the problem is not so much that *individual employees* have prejudices as it is that the *social system* works in ways that create and maintain inequality. In her view, the current approach to diversity occurred when the civil rights and minority empowerment movements that arose in the 1960s combined influences with the therapeutic and encounter group movements of the same era. This enabled a substantial industry of race experts to develop who designed diversity-training programs, sometimes based on ineffective and individually targeted guilt-inducing approaches like those described earlier. In her words, "It was no longer about making everybody equal on the basis of true egalitarianism and a universal outlook, but became about saying 'I'm different, you're different, so let's just manage those differences and we'll be happy.'" In part, Lasch-Quinn's argument is similar to other critiques of multiculturalism in that she thinks too much attention is paid to cultural differences. But a more fundamental argument she makes is that the problem lies not with individuals but rather with societal arrangements, and unless those are made more equal, racial divisions will persist.

For this reason, the part of the diversity management movement that emphasizes greater opportunities for people of diverse backgrounds within work organizations may be the most important part. Clearly such efforts, if successful, move society toward equality of opportunity in ways that efforts to change individual attitudes may not. In addition, more equal opportunity can also lead to more effective work organizations. Over the long run, a more diverse work group often is more effective because it can offer a wider variety of ideas and ways of dealing with issues and problems and because it can better address the needs of an equally diverse base of potential customers and clients. A study comparing homogenous and diverse work groups found that although the diverse groups did have more difficulty working together at first, they were more productive over the long term (Watson, Kumar, and Michealsen, 1993). The main reason was that diverse groups did a better job of examining different viewpoints and devising possible responses.

Matching the diversity of the work force to that of customers can also be important. Livingston (1991) cites Nadia Ali, southwest regional manager for the gift store chain Things Remembered. Ali discovered that although nearly half the customers in her region were Spanish speaking, nearly all the retail staff spoke only English. She addressed this by making the ability to speak Spanish a hiring criterion for new recruits and offering free Spanish lessons to present employees. The results increased both the diversity of the work force and the effectiveness of the business. Sales rose by 13 percent, and employee turnover fell to less than one-fourth the companywide rate. Thus, as these examples show, diversity and multiculturalism in the workplace not only are inevitable realities but also can help a company become more adaptable and more in tune with its customers or clients.

## ▶ HATE GROUP ACTIVITY AND HATE CRIME

Hate crime remains a serious problem in the United States. Surges in hate crime and hate group activity occurred in the early 1990s and again just after the start of the new century. In 1992, the number of hate crimes in the United States was the highest since systematic records were first kept in 1979 (Southern Poverty Law Center, 1993b). Since then, hate crime appears to have leveled off for a time, followed by another increase through the second half of the 1990s, with an apparent peak in hate crime in 2001 and in hate group activity in early 2002. In 2002, for example, the nation's largest neo-Nazi group was drawing nearly a million dollars a year and had a staff of seventeen, and Nazi, racist skinhead, and Ku Klux Klan groups were having the largest rallies in years (Potok, 2003). Of particular concern was the

Aryan Nations Internet site. In recent years, the Internet has become an important means by which hate groups reach wider audiences with messages of prejudice and racial division. By 1998, more than 160 Web sites were operated by hate groups.

takeover of Confederate history groups by racist extremists; in one group, the Sons of Confederate Veterans, about 350 members who opposed racism were forced out (Potok, 2003). However, increased attention to hate group activity by law enforcement began to pay off in 2002 and 2003, when arrests not only disrupted a number of hate groups but also led to serious internal conflict in many of the groups. Several notorious hate groups, including the Aryan Nations and the World Church of the Creator (COTC), suffered splits that further weakened the hate movement. Still, the overall number of hate groups and hate-oriented Web sites remained about the same in 2003 as in recent years (Potok, 2003). Another change is that, since the terrorism of September 11, 2001, Arab, Middle Eastern, and Muslim Americans have more often been the target of hate crimes. Also of concern is academic racism: groups making claims that science supports ideas of racial superiority. As discussed earlier in the book, recent scientific discoveries have increasingly invalidated the notion of race as a genetic concept. But even so, groups trying to use science to support racism have thrived in recent years, enjoying increased funding and wider circulation of their publications (Potok, 2003).

In 2002, the FBI reported just under 7,500 hate crimes, down from a peak of more than 9,700 in 2001 (Federal Bureau of Investigation, 2003a, 2003b). The 2002 figure was also below the roughly 8,000 hate crimes in 2000 and 9,000 in 1996 but higher than the numbers reported in the some earlier years (Reno, 1997, 1998; CNN, 2003). About half of all hate crimes in 2001 were racially motivated, about one in five were based on religion, and about one in six on sexual orientation. About 15 percent were based on ethnicity, and 7 percent on disability (Federal Bureau of Investigation, 2003a, 2003b). Although only 10 to 15 percent of hate crimes can be directly linked to organized hate groups, it is clear that many people are encouraged to commit hate crimes as a result of the activities and propaganda of these groups. A disturbing trend is that the proportion of bias crime perpetrators who are teenagers has risen sharply in recent years (Southern Poverty Law Center, 1998a).

Hate crimes are aimed at a very wide variety of groups, but those most commonly targeted are African Americans, Jews, and homosexuals. In 2002, more than 3,000 hate crimes were targeted against African Americans, about 1,400 against gay, lesbian, bisexual, or transgendered people, and about 1,000 against Jews. There were also about 875 hate crimes against whites, about 600 against Latinos/as, about 260 against Asians or Asian Americans, and about 170 against Muslims (Federal Bureau of Investigation, 2003a, 2003b). The latter figure, like the overall hate crime rate, is down significantly from 2001, when a surge of violence was targeted against Arab, Middle Eastern, and Muslim Americans after the September 11 terrorist attacks. As was noted in Chapter 7, the number of hate crimes against Arab Americans increased by a factor of sixteen following September 11, 2001, but the number of attacks on Arabs and Muslims seems to have decreased in 2002. However, it may have increased again in 2003 during the war against Iraq.

Some examples will show the types of hate crimes that occur and the connection of organized hate groups to this violence. In Portland, Oregon, in 1988, a group of skinheads beat an Ethiopian college student to death. The courts later found that Tom Metzger, leader of the White Aryan Resistance (WAR), had played a key role in inciting this crime. Relatives of the man who was murdered were awarded $12.5 million in damages, to be paid by Metzger and WAR. A similar legal action led to the disbanding of a Klan faction known as the Invisible Empire after its members severely beat a group of civil rights marchers celebrating Martin Luther King's birthday in Forsythe County, Georgia, in 1987. In Japan, an enlistee in the U.S. Navy was beaten to death in 1992 by fellow sailors because he was gay. In separate but similar incidents in St. Louis, Missouri, and West Palm Beach, Florida, in 1993, white drivers chased, ran over, and killed black men. Also in 1993, gay men were killed in New Orleans; Everett, Washington; and Azusa, California. In 1992, a homeless black man was stabbed to death when a group of skinheads with connections to several hate groups, including a Klan faction and a renegade chapter of WAR, went out to "bash" minorities, homosexuals, and Jews after a drunken celebration of Adolf Hitler's birthday (Southern Poverty Law Center, 1993b). Two of the most notorious hate crimes happened in 1998. In Jasper, Texas, three white men dragged an African American man, James Byrd, Jr., to his death behind a pickup truck. Two of them had previously had involvement with racist prison gangs, and two of them became the first whites in more than 150 years to be sentenced to death in Texas for killing an African American (King, 2002). Also that year, two men beat to death a gay Wyoming college student, Matthew Shepard. The killers acknowledged that they chose him to beat and rob because he was gay. The killers were sentenced to life in prison; in one case, this sentence was given instead of the death penalty at the request of Shepard's mother, Judy Shepard.

Groups such as the Klan (which is actually composed of about twenty factions that often compete with one another for membership and publicity), WAR, COTC, and others have sought to increase their visibility in recent years by setting up Web sites and through the sales of racist music, art, and literature. About 500 World Wide Web sites were operated by hate groups as of early 2004 (Southern Poverty Law Center, 2004). And a major source of income for the National Alliance, one of the largest white supremacist groups, is its music and merchandise label, Resistance Records, which the group claims brings in a million dollars a year (Moser, 2003). One consequence of these uses of marketing and technology is that messages of hate and bigotry are being seen by more people today than a decade or two ago. As Joe Roy of the Southern Poverty Law Center's Intelligence Project (which tracks hate group activity) put it, "The tentacles of the hate movement are reaching places where they've never been before. Mainstream America is being targeted in a way that this country hasn't seen in decades." A former racist skinhead who now works for an antiprejudice organization said the following:

> If I filled a room with 1,000 neo-Nazi Skinheads and asked them, "What's the single most important thing that influenced you to join the neo-Nazi Skinhead movement?" probably 900 of them would say the music. The Internet is also extremely important. Before, the kid you were going to get, eight out of 10 times, was going to be a street soldier, a kid ditching school, basically a thug. But now with the Net, you're getting the bright kid, the 11- or 12-year-old who knows how to surf [on the World Wide Web]. I'd say there are probably as many racist recruiters on the Net as there are on the street now. (T. J. Layden, quoted in Southern Poverty Law Center, 1998b).

Nearly all white supremacist organizations use newsletters or Web sites to communicate with their members and to recruit new members. Typically, they portray whites as an oppressed group in society, the victims of a conspiracy that is said to involve Jews, blacks, communists, homosexuals, and others. Often they use the language of religion to support their message. The Knights of the Ku Klux Klan (one of many Klan organizations that is currently active), for example, refers to itself as a "white Christian organization" and argues that the United States was founded as a "white Christian society." This is said to justify the segregation of blacks, Jews, Latinos, homosexuals, Arabs, Asians, and anyone else who does not fall within the Klan's definition of "white Christians." Some of these organizations have become media savvy, denying that they are hate organizations while giving whites the message that their troubles in life are attributable to minorities. Their newsletters and Web sites often reflect this viewpoint, and they actively seek interviews with the mainstream media to deny that they are hate organizations while spreading the message that working-class whites suffer because of gains by minority groups. Others advocate violence and hatred much more openly. For example, an anti-Semitic diatribe in a December 1993 WAR newsletter called for guerrilla warfare:

> First, we have men willing to wage this war, though in a disassociated state. Second, we have free access to small arms and ammunition, again in a disassociated state. . . . In any case, where a Jew or an ally of the Jews is found, and they can be easily recognized by their class-distinctive possessions, he will be dispatched. . . . The last phase of the operation will be the use of heavy weapons against the enemy's citadels and residences. We will be in no hurry to negotiate with him in light of his treacherous nature.

## Causes of Hate Group Activity

Although there is no evidence that prejudice has increased over recent decades, it does seem that at various times since around the mid-1980s, hate groups have been both more visible and more active than they were in the 1970s and early 1980s. In some cases, these groups, particularly when they are media-savvy, have also been successful in drawing the support of a sizable segment of the white population. In 1991, for example, David Duke, a former leader of the Knights of the Ku Klux Klan, won the Republican primary election for governor of Louisiana and received the majority of the white vote in the general election. Only overwhelming opposition from black voters kept him from being elected. And the year before, Duke got about 40 percent of the vote as a candidate for the U.S. Senate. Why have these changes occurred?

There are a variety of reasons, including periods of bad economic conditions, increasing socioeconomic inequality in the United States, effects of more general societal violence, and irresponsible statements and actions by many political leaders.

**Bad Economic Conditions.** In the 1980s and early 1990s and again in the year 2000 and the next few years, the economic situation of many Americans—particularly those in the middle, working, and lower classes—worsened. For example, in 1988—about when the increase in hate crimes began to be evident—real (that is, inflation-adjusted) hourly and weekly wages in the United States were lower than at any point since before 1970 (U.S. Bureau of the Census, 1990, p. 407). In part, people compensated by working longer hours, and in many families, wives entered the labor force for the first time (Olsen, 1990). Because of this increase in work, real household incomes have risen even as hourly and weekly wages have fallen, but during recessions, even real household income has fallen. This was the case between 1989 and 1993 and again between 1999 and 2002 (U.S. Census Bureau 2003n, p. 8). With the more recent downturn, as with the one a decade ago, hate group activity surged. This often occurs because when people's economic situation worsens, they feel more threatened.

**Growing Economic Inequality.** For many workers in the lower and middle ranges of income, wages have fallen in recent decades after adjustment for inflation because increasing economic inequality has shifted income away from those in the middle- and lower-income ranges toward those at the top. For example, the share of total income received by the top 5 percent of U.S. households rose from about 16 percent in 1975 to about 19 percent in 1989 and more than 22 percent in 2001. During the same time, the share received by the bottom 20 percent of families—four times as many families— fell from 4.4 percent in 1975 to 3.8 percent in 1989 and 3.4 percent in 2002 (U.S. Census Bureau, 2003l, Table IE3; 2003n, p. 15). In other words, the lower 20 percent lost nearly a quarter of their share of income, while the share going to those at the top increased by more than one-third. In plain terms, the rich got richer and the poor got poorer (Bartlett and Steele, 1992). In a practical sense, this redistribution of income from the poor to the rich worsened the effect of stagnant economic growth on those in the lower ranges of income. At the same time as the overall size of the economic pie was getting smaller, so was the share of the pie going to those on the bottom. In addition, many Americans, particularly in the middle and working classes, found it increasingly difficult to afford sending their children to college, which has become increasingly necessary for the better jobs. This is the case because tuition has risen faster than the cost of living, and financial aid has not kept pace.

In effect, what all this meant was more competition and greater scarcity, especially for those not fortunate enough to be in the top income brackets. Many Americans could no longer be sure that they would be able to hang on to the standard of living that they had enjoyed in the past or to help their children to enjoy a good standard of living when they grow up. This has had several effects. It has led people to perceive groups different from themselves as potential competitors, to be feared and looked at as a threat. It has also led people to feel less secure and to look for scapegoats to blame for their declining fortunes. It is no coincidence that competition and perceived threat, feelings of personal insecurity, and a need to scapegoat have all been identified as factors that contribute to prejudice (see Chapter 2). Perhaps for these reasons, the highest levels of prejudice generally have been found in people who are experiencing downward economic mobility, that is, people whose economic situations are getting worse (Wilensky and Edwards, 1959). Thus, support for hate groups such as the Ku Klux Klan often is strongest when economic conditions worsen.

It is not surprising, then, that as the conditions of much of the U.S. population worsened in the early 1990s and again in 2000 and the years just after, hate group activity and hate violence rose. Many viewed minorities as the source of their economic difficulties and believed that if only there were no civil rights laws and affirmative action, their economic lot would be better. In particular, many white males began to believe that they are a persecuted group, being made to pay for past injustices to women and minorities.

In fact, there is no evidence that gains by minorities had anything to do with the economic difficulties of the white working and middle classes. Statistics such as median family income reveal quickly that minorities have not, overall, gained economic ground relative to non-Hispanic whites. The ratio of the black median household income to that of whites has not changed much in recent decades. For example, in 1972, the median black household income was about 58 percent that of non-Hispanic white households; in 2002 it was about 62 percent—not much change over a period of thirty years. Similarly, the income of Latino/a households has remained around 68 to 70 percent of that of non-Hispanic white households (computed from U.S. Census Bureau, 2003n, pp. 18-20). Thus, the reality is that there has *not* been a substantial redistribution of income from whites to minorities. Rather, it has been from lower-income people of all races to upper-income people, most of whom are white. Similarly, it is also true that whites remain more likely to be employed and more likely to attend and graduate from college than either African Americans or Latinos/as.

Finally, there is no objective basis for the view that white men are being singled out and made to pay for "sins of the past." In fact, white males continue to enjoy higher incomes than any other group, even when comparisons are made between people with identical levels of education. They also remain greatly overrepresented in the political and corporate power structures. White men may not enjoy the same degree of advantages over other groups that they once did, but in terms of economics and political power they remain more advantaged than any other group. Reality does not matter as much as perception, however, and the *perception* of many whites (particularly white men) is that they are losing jobs, income, and opportunities for education, all of which are being gained by minorities.

**Statements and Actions of Political Leaders.** One reason for such perceptions lies in irresponsible statements and actions by political leaders, who have often used the economic fears of whites as a way of getting votes. This can be illustrated by several of the statements and actions of the elder George Bush, who campaigned for the presidency in 1988 and served from 1989 through 1992. In his 1988 campaign, Bush supporters bought TV ads showing Willie Horton, a black man who had committed a crime after being furloughed from the Massachusetts prison system. The photos, designed to make Horton look as threatening as possible, were used to tell voters that if Bush's Democratic opponent, the governor of Massachusetts, were elected, people like Horton could be running loose and committing crimes everywhere. The Bush ads did not mention that nearly every state, including Bush's home state of Texas, which at the time had a Republican governor, had a similar program. They also did not mention that at least half of the people furloughed under such programs were white. Rather, they played on the criminal stereotype of blacks that had been reinforced by the media for so long that much of the public believed it. The strategy worked and helped Bush win the election.

Bush and other politicians used similar tactics in the following years. From 1989 until 1991, Bush referred to what eventually became the 1991 Civil Rights Act as a "quota bill." In fact, this law, discussed earlier in this book, at first said nothing at all about quotas. It was instead designed to reverse several Supreme Court decisions, including one that stated that job qualification requirements with the effect of discriminating against minorities were entirely legal unless their intent was to discriminate. What the civil rights law actually said was that such discriminatory requirements would be made illegal unless it could be shown that they relate in some way to the employee's ability to do the job. Even after the bill was amended to state that quotas were not to be used in hiring, Bush and a number of other politicians continued to call it a quota bill.

This pattern continued through the 1990s and in some cases beyond as politicians intensified their campaigns against affirmative action. Although this issue had always been controversial, there was a marked increase in organized efforts to oppose it in the 1990s, often led by politicians who tried to use the issue to enhance their careers. For example, California Governor Pete Wilson vigorously supported a ballot initiative to eliminate affirmative action in state programs. Similar ballot initiatives were also voted on in other states, and lawsuits and proposed legislation targeted affirmative action in several states. One such lawsuit led to a temporary lower-court reversal in Texas of the Supreme Court's 1979 *Bakke* ruling, which permitted the consideration of race as a factor in college admissions for the purpose of diversity in higher education. The Texas ruling was reversed by the Supreme Court's 2003 *Grutter* ruling, which upheld consideration of race for purposes of diversity in admissions in a case arising from the University of Michigan (discussed in detail in Chapter 15). However, despite its stated intent to downplay racially divisive issues, the administration of President George W. Bush intervened in the case to oppose the university's affirmative action admission policy.

For the reasons just noted, the image of the "angry white male" has been per-vasive since the 1990s, and many politicians—both mainstream and on the racist fringe—have been happy to stir up such resentments for political purposes. For example, the statements of many public figures made it easy for whites to believe that their economic hardships were caused by policies that were helping minorities. Although this had no basis in reality, hearing politicians constantly talking about "quota bills" and "reverse discrimination" made it easy for many whites to believe that minorities were the cause of their troubles. Moreover, this viewpoint was con-stantly repeated by hate groups and their leaders. When David Duke, the former Klan leader, ran for the U.S. Senate and for governor of Louisiana, for example, he made this a central part of his campaign.

A related practice is the use by many political candidates of racial "code words." These are words that indirectly refer to race and call on racial prejudice. This is done indirectly because open racism is no longer socially acceptable and generates contro-versy. Less direct appeals to racial fears and prejudices, are less likely to generate con-troversy and may get votes. For example, in the 1992 campaigns for governor of Mis-souri candidates in both parties used such tactics. The Republican nominee for governor, along with another candidate running for attorney general, used the phrase "unfair desegregation payments" repeatedly in almost every campaign com-mercial. They did not directly say that schools should be segregated, but by repeating the phrase the candidates were able to appeal indirectly to people who felt that way. In fact, every attorney general in Missouri since the mid-1980s, Democrat or Republi-can, has sought rural white votes by loudly opposing school desegregation plans in St. Louis and Kansas City, despite evidence that these plans had enhanced educational opportunities for minorities and had gained the support even of many white subur-ban parents who saw the benefits of a diverse education for their children (for survey data, see Wells and Crain, 1997). These campaigns have been largely successful, with the Kansas City plan ended in 2003 and the St. Louis plan substantially scaled back.

Racial code words are used the other way around, too. In the 1992 Missouri Democratic primary, a white candidate tried to patch up past bad relations with the black community by using a reverse form of racial code. When campaigning in a black neighborhood in St. Louis, he referred to his opponent as the "redneck from Rolla," thus implying that the opponent's rural background meant that he would be prejudiced against blacks. When political leaders are willing to exploit racial fears and divisions in such ways to get votes, the fears, divisions, and tensions are often height-ened. Given the common use of racial code words and similar uses of race by politi-cians, it is not surprising that racial tensions are sometimes heightened to the point that they boil over in the form of hate crimes and increased hate group activity.

**Reaction to Change?** It may also be that in some ways, the current surge in hate crime represents something of a reaction to progressive changes that are occurring in our society. This has happened in the past. For example, the Ku Klux Klan enjoyed a surge in membership during the 1960s as whites reacted to the passage of civil rights legislation. Something of the same thing may now be occurring in response to renewed efforts in the 1990s and since to increase diversity in the work-place and in colleges and universities, as well as to the changing racial and ethnic composition of the population. For example, some workplaces and colleges that were once all white have become more racially diverse in recent years (in part because of diversity efforts and in part because society has become more diverse). In a related vein, there has also been a reaction to increased public support for the rights of homosexuals and the increased tendency for cities, states, and private employers to institute antidiscrimination policies. People who do not want such changes sometimes resist. Moreover, when people who have lived all their lives in segregated environments encounter diversity for the first time, some will respond with fear, and incidents may begin simply because people do not understand what behavior may or may not be acceptable to people of different backgrounds. Often, such incidents escalate as mutual misunderstanding mounts.

Additionally, efforts to promote greater sensitivity to diversity have sometimes been derided as "political correctness" in recent years, and this reaction may be fueling a backlash. Both students and colleagues have suggested to me that one reason that some people engage in hate speech is because it has become socially taboo in some circles; therefore, it becomes a form of rebellion. At the same time, however, there are many other forms of rebellion in today's society that do not involve hatred, and it appears likely that those who engage in hate speech have significant attitude differences from those who rebel in other ways. For some people rebellion may combine with fears and prejudices to produce hate speech, hate group activity, and, in extreme cases, hate crimes. For others, without such fears and prejudices, rebellion is more likely to take other forms.

**Societal Violence.**   Finally, it must be noted that violence of all types increased in the United States in the late 1980s and early 1990s. The total rate of violent crime had reached an all-time high by 1989 (Federal Bureau of Investigation, 1990), and many cities experienced record homicide rates in the early 1990s. It appears that as society became more violent, so did the expression of racial and cultural prejudices and tensions (Southern Poverty Law Center, 1993b). Significantly, when crime rates peaked and then began to decline by the mid-1990s, so did hate crime and hate group activity—although only temporarily.

## ▶ COMBATING HATRED ON CAMPUS: CURRENT DEBATES AND ISSUES

As hate group activity increased in the late 1980s and early 1990s, debates arose about what is the best way to respond. A good deal of hate group activity occurred on college campuses, leading to ugly and sometimes violent incidents. Consequently, since then, much of the debate over how to respond has focused on colleges and universities. In many cases, this has occurred because students, faculty, and administrators, outraged by acts of hatred, have insisted that something be done about the problem. One of the first such incidents occurred in 1987 at the University of Michigan, when a racist joke was told on the campus radio station, followed quickly by other incidents in which racist flyers were passed under the doors of black students' rooms in a dormitory. Outraged by these events, African American students and some white supporters staged a series of demonstrations that lasted nearly two months, leading to a renewal of an unfulfilled 1970 commitment by the university to raise black enrollment to the black percentage of the state's population. However, the incidents continued to spread to other campuses, and some of them have been violent. At the University of Massachusetts, a white mob beat several black students after they expressed support for the Boston Red Sox's opponent in the World Series, the New York Mets. Three Jewish students were attacked at Brooklyn College, and homosexual students were attacked on several campuses, including a fatal attack near the University of Wyoming in 1998.

Other incidents did not involve violence but did involve threats, name calling, and other forms of ethnic harassment. At Dartmouth University, many people on campus were outraged when a conservative campus newspaper, the *Dartmouth Review*, wrote a derogatory article about an African American professor, among other things calling him a "Brillo pad." The paper also printed a sarcastic column in "Black English" and an anti-Semitic quote from Hitler's *Mein Kampf*. An African American homecoming queen was booed at the University of Alabama, thirteen Asian American faculty members received anonymous hate letters at the University of Minnesota, and at the University of Florida, a white student union was formed and quickly established contact with a former Ku Klux Klan official. Such white student groups usually seek to maintain the advantages whites enjoy in society and are often fronts for hate groups. At Penn State in 2001, an African American student reporter and the president of the University's Black Caucus received hate letters, one of which contained death threats. Other black students also received hate letters and threats. In 2003, graffiti on walls at Northwestern University portrayed lynchings and swastikas, along with racial and anti-Semitic slurs. At both Penn State and Northwestern, the incidents led to large-scale student protests.

Incidents such as these have occurred on campuses throughout the United States and have targeted African Americans, Latinos/as, Asians, Jews, women, and homosexuals. They have also occurred on a continuous basis since the late 1980s. In some cases, the offensive statements and actions have come not from students but from professors and administrators. At the University of Washington, the president of the university, while presenting an award for academic achievement to a Latino engineering student, commented that the student may have acquired his interest in the highway system "while driving down the highway at 70 miles per hour in the middle of the night to keep ahead of immigration officials." Later, a faculty member at the same university wrote a journal article alleging that the president had been unfairly criticized for this remark (Alexander, 1990). And at Harvard in 2002, a law professor told his class that "feminists, Marxists, and the blacks" had contributed nothing to tort law theory. When role models such as university presidents and faculty members engage in behavior that says stereotyping is acceptable or even true, it may not be surprising when students express their own prejudices.

Such incidents clearly make college and university campuses unwelcoming and unsupportive places for the groups that are targeted. In fact, they often are one more factor in an atmosphere that minority college students find unwelcoming and unsupportive and in which they feel just plain outnumbered. Studies of African American students on predominanlty white campuses show that many do not feel welcomed or fully accepted. One such recent study reported the following:

> Black students on the campus were routinely confronted in their daily lives with racial discrimination, racial exclusion, and racial segregation. Furthermore, many told stories about pervasive, negative attitudes toward Blacks by professors: "You have this feeling that if I were White, I would get more opportunities. Even Asian and Indian professors don't think you will do as well." Another student reported that a professor told his friend, "If you are not doing well, just drop the class. I can't help you." The ultimate effect was to create a climate in which "race has been on people's minds a lot." A climate existed where a Black student "always senses subtle racism . . . and sometimes experiences overt racism." (Allen, Hunt, and Gilbert, 1997)

Because harassment and unconscious insensitivity have contributed to this problem, many faculty members, administrators, and students have undertaken efforts to prevent such incidents. The most controversial efforts involve *hate speech codes*, which have sought to prevent people from using racial, ethnic, or cultural slurs, insults, and name calling. After more than 150 incidents, the University of Wisconsin decided to ban racist comments, pledging to provide students with an environment free of hostility and intimidation. Other campuses followed suit, and a number of local and state governments also passed laws against ethnic intimidation. These actions have been controversial for two main reasons. First, many people believe that they improperly restrict free speech, setting a precedent that could be used against anyone who says something that someone else deems offensive. A related charge is that they involve an effort to enforce what many people have called "political correctness," a term that is notoriously ill defined but often refers to efforts to ban anything that liberals, diversity advocates, minority groups, or feminists find offensive. (As we shall see shortly, conservatives, religious fundamentalists, and opponents of minority rights are at least as guilty of imposing their viewpoints on others, but to a large extent they have successfully placed the "political correctness" tag on their opponents.) Second, speech codes are controversial because it is very doubtful whether they work.

As a result of the free speech concerns, the American Civil Liberties Union filed suit against the University of Wisconsin, and the code was overturned in court. From a legal standpoint, speech that clearly constitutes threat or intimidation (e.g., "If I see you here again, I'm going to shoot you") can be regulated, but the mere expression of prejudice cannot. At other campuses, political pressures have led to changes in speech codes. At the University of Pennsylvania, a white student was suspended after calling a group of black women "water buffalo." Supporters of the student argued that his free speech rights were violated and that the university was merely trying to enforce an arbitrary standard of political correctness. Eventually, the speech code was modified.

The outcry by conservatives that such speech codes restrict free speech and attempt to enforce arbitrary standards may well be valid, but it is worthwhile to ask why the "PC" ("political correctness") label has been applied only in instances aimed at preventing insensitivity to minority groups. After all, there are numerous other incidents in which groups of all political viewpoints have attempted to impose their views on others and restrict views opposed to their own. In early 1994, for example, the Belleville, Illinois, school board banned a sex education book, which had been used in the Belleville schools for a number of years, when church groups objected that the book did not say that premarital sex and homosexual behavior were morally wrong. The book did not express what the church groups viewed as the politically correct viewpoint, but nobody referred to its banning as a case of PC. Other examples may be seen in efforts to prevent the National Institute for the Humanities from funding gay-oriented art and in efforts to ban popular music with lyrics some find offensive. A flagrant incident of "politically correct" behavior by conservatives occurred in 2003, when they pressured CBS to drop a program on Ronald and Nancy Reagan that conservatives regarded as too critical. Incidents such as these suggest that opponents of diversity may object less to the idea of enforcing "political correctness" than to efforts to promote sensitivity to diversity itself.

Having said this, there are valid questions both about the constitutionality of hate speech codes and about whether they work. Some opponents of speech codes have argued that they make martyrs of those who are charged with violations. For example, the student who made the "water buffalo" remark at the University of Pennsylvania gained considerable media attention and was often portrayed as a victim. To the extent that people who express prejudices come to be seen as victims of the system, speech codes may have the opposite effect from what is intended. For these reasons, as well as the constitutional challenges such as at the University of Wisconsin, most of the speech codes that have been implemented have later been modified or relaxed.

An alternative approach is to establish a requirement that to graduate all students must have some course dealing with diversity, minority groups, multiculturalism, or intergroup relations. As of 2000, 54 percent of U.S. colleges and universities had some requirement of this nature, and another 8 percent were in the process of developing such a requirement (Humphreys, 2000). About two-thirds allowed students to choose one course from a list of diversity courses; the next most common arrangement was one diversity course for all students with a common syllabus. The idea of requiring courses on diversity or intergroup relations is based on research (discussed in Chapter 3) showing that education about diversity and intergroup relations often is an effective way of reducing prejudice. A common and long-recognized problem is that people most in need of such education often avoid it (Allport, 1954), which is why such courses have been made mandatory on so many campuses. A requirement is seen as the only way to get the people into such courses who need them the most.

On some campuses that have established or considered establishing such requirements, the "political correctness" argument has come up. It has been argued

College students at a class on diversity. Coursework in diversity, multiculturalism, or intergroup relations is required for graduation at the majority of colleges and universities in the United States.

that rather than containing sound academic content, these sources aim mainly at getting students to think in a certain way about diversity issues or represent capitulation to politically motivated demands by activist students and faculty (Leatherman, 1994b, 1994c). Such arguments have not prevailed at most campuses, however, in part because intergroup relations has long been recognized as an area of specialization within several traditional academic disciplines, including sociology, psychology, anthropology, and speech communication. If they are based on the substantial body of research on issues related to race, ethnicity, gender, and sexual orientation that has been developed in these disciplines, these courses are as academically valid as courses in any other area. Additionally, as American society has become increasingly diverse and is expected to continue to do so, knowledge about intergroup relations and about the experiences of social groups other than one's own becomes increasingly essential, both in the workplace and in the larger society.

Research has shown that such requirements are effective and that they enjoy substantial and growing public support, despite the "political correctness" argument that some have raised. Studies have shown that courses on diversity increase openness to racial understanding and lead to greater overall satisfaction with college, to increased cognitive development, to increased support for equal educational opportunity, and to greater appreciation of works of culture in different societies (Institute for the Study of Social Change, 1991; Astin, 1993; G. E. Lopez, 1993; Adams and Zhou-McGovern, 1994; Villalpando, 1994; Tanaka, 1996; Smith et al., 1997; Gurin, 1999; Hurtado, 2001). Taking diversity courses also leads to increased positive interaction with social groups different from one's own and to increased commitment to social action (Laird, Engberg, and Hurtado, 2002), as well as to improvements in critical thinking (Gurin, 1999). And contrary to the image of a revolt against "political correctness," a 1998 nationally representative survey by the Daniel Yankelovich polling firm found majority support for such requirements. For example, 55 percent of respondents in the survey agreed that "every college student should have to study different cultures in order to graduate." Similarly, a full 80 percent agreed that "the changing characteristics of America's population make diversity education necessary." And when confronted with a statement that "college courses like women's studies, African American, or Chicano studies take valuable resources away from the education and training that young people need to make it in today's economy," 58 percent *disagreed* (DYG, Inc., 1998).

In addition to courses, many colleges and universities have developed conflict resolution teams, involving students in a manner somewhat similar to that of the consulting pairs at Monsanto. In some racial and ethnic incidents, both parties may feel that their ethnic group has been insulted or that they have been ridiculed or humiliated because of their ethnicity. Such perceptions were evident in an incident at the State University of New York at Stony Brook. A Jewish student wrote an editorial in a student paper describing anti-Semitic name-calling by black students, adding that he was "at times, downright revolted by African Americans." The student who wrote the editorial felt that he had been insulted because he was Jewish; African American students felt that they had been insulted because they were black. Conflict resolution teams generally acknowledge the validity of such feelings while helping the people involved to communicate in ways that meet one another's needs and do not lead others to feel that their ethnicity is being ridiculed.

Finally, many colleges and universities have undertaken diversity-training programs or workshops similar to those of many companies and workplaces. As of 2001, about 70 percent of colleges and universities were offering some form of diversity workshops; nearly all of these schools offered them to their students, but only about half for their faculty and staff (Tritelli, 2001). In general, the issues, concerns, and results of these programs have been similar to those found in the private sector. One challenge, as in business, is that the people who need them the most are often the most reluctant to participate. There have been arguments for and against compelling all employees to attend in both college and business settings. The argument for requiring attendance is that it ensures that those who need the training most will experience it. The counterargument is that compelling attendance can cause resentments that may offset the benefits of the program. In addition, it can be very difficult to compel college faculty to attend such a program, especially if they have tenure. In part for this reason, many colleges have not made diversity training compulsory, even when these programs have been made available to faculty and staff. Furthermore, there is less evidence on the effectiveness of these workshops and training programs than of diversity courses for students; there has been very little effort to evaluate diversity workshops for college faculty and staff (Tritelli, 2001).

Although both intergroup education and conflict resolution efforts can be effective, neither these strategies nor hate speech codes are likely to entirely prevent incidents of harassment and hate group activity on college campuses. To a large extent, the campus, like any other organization or institution, reflects the larger society in which it exists. If there are racial, ethnic, and cultural tensions in the larger society, they probably will surface on college campuses as well. Hate speech codes appear to have been a well-intentioned effort to deal with these tensions, but legal and practical problems have led to their repeal or scaleback on many of the campuses that once had them. Mandatory courses on diversity or intergroup relations and conflict resolution programs offer somewhat more hope and have been somewhat less controversial.

## ▶ THE DISCRIMINATION-TESTING MOVEMENT

Another important trend in majority-minority relations in recent years is the emergence of the *discrimination-testing* movement. Testing for discrimination is a technique for determining whether discrimination on the basis of race, ethnicity, gender, or other characteristics is occurring in some situation. This technique can be used either for research purposes, to see whether, where, and to what extent discrimination is occurring, or for purposes of law enforcement, to detect and punish illegal discrimination. Although the technique has existed for a long time (see Pearce, 1976), it has come into increasing use in recent years because it is the most effective tool for discovering hidden discrimination. Today, civil rights laws have driven discrimination underground; few will openly admit to discrimination because most forms of it are illegal. However, testing studies show that a good deal of it still occurs.

In a discrimination-testing study, two people are sent to whatever business or organization is being tested, perhaps a store, real-estate office, lending institution, auto dealership, or apartment rental office. The two people are chosen to be as similar as possible except for the characteristic on which discrimination might be based. They are instructed to behave similarly and to carefully record what happens as soon as the test is completed. They might shop, try to rent or buy housing, or ask about a car for sale, depending on the type of business. In some cases, testers have been wired with hidden microphones or surreptitiously videotaped so that there is direct audiovisual evidence of any discrimination.

The process can be illustrated by describing a fair-housing test for racial discrimination in rental housing. A black tester and a white tester of the same gender and similar age might visit an apartment rental office about an hour apart. Both would request similar types of apartments, and both would report similar family characteristics (for example, divorced; one child, of whom they have custody) and similar incomes. They would carefully observe what information they were given, whether they were shown apartments and if so how many and what kinds, what they were told about the availability of apartments, what rent and deposit rates they were quoted, and whether any information was volunteered about the neighborhood. After the test, a test supervisor or study director would review the information to see whether they were treated similarly or differently. Because virtually everything about the two testers was the same except their race, discrimination on the basis of race would be suspected if the two were treated differently in any important way. Suppose, for example, that both testers were told that the kind of apartment they wanted was available, but the white tester was told that she could move in with a $200 damage deposit and the African American tester was told that she would have to deposit two months' rent, which would come to $700. This would be very strong evidence of racial discrimination.

The discrimination-testing movement began mostly with fair-housing tests and has since spread to a variety of other areas. Testing can be used either to determine the extent of discrimination or to enforce antidiscrimination laws. Testing studies to determine the extent of discrimination have been undertaken by sociologists (Pearce, 1976), economists (Bertrand and Mullainathan, 2002), the mass media (ABC News, 1991), and by governments and government-sponsored organizations (U.S. Department of Housing and Urban Development, 1979, 1991; Turner et al., 2002; Turner and Ross, 2003).

All of these studies have detected racial discrimination, although in some areas antidiscrimination efforts are showing signs of payoff. One common practice in the real-estate industry is *racial steering*: Whites are more likely to be directed toward all or mostly white areas, and blacks are more likely to be directed toward racially mixed or predominantly black neighborhoods, even when both approach the same real-estate office on the same day and have similar income and family characteristics (Pearce, 1976; Department of Housing and Urban Development, 1991). As recently as 1989, a black homebuyer visiting four real-estate agents had about a 58 percent chance of encountering discrimination, and a Hispanic homebuyer had a 51 percent chance. In rental housing, a black renter had a 65 percent chance of encountering discrimination, a Hispanic renter a 34 percent chance (Yinger, 1995, p. 42).

Today, the probabilities are less but still substantial, according to a national study conducted in 2000 (Turner et al., 2002). This is partly because today, discrimination occurs both ways, for and against minorities. To see the full picture, it is important to look at two measures: *net discrimination* and *consistent adverse treatment* (Turner et al.,

A woman applies to rent an apartment. In a fair-housing test, two individuals or couples of different races who are similar in other regards (age, gender, income) visit a rental office to see whether they are treated similarly or differently.

2002). Net discrimination is the percentage of situations in which the minority tester is discriminated against, minus the number in which the white tester is discriminated against. This offers a lower-bound estimate of the amount of discrimination minorities encounter relative to whites. Consistent adverse treatment is the percentage of situations in which the minority tester is discriminated against in more than one way while not being favored in any way. Instances where this occurs are clear-cut cases of discrimination against minorities. The trend between 1989 and 2000 in the consistent adverse treatment measure is shown in Figure 14.1. The figure shows that there was significantly less housing discrimination against African Americans and Hispanics (except for Hispanic renters) in 2000 than there was in 1989, but discrimination still occurs on 15 to 25 percent of visits to a rental office or real-estate agent. Figure 14.1 also shows the net discrimination measure, the most conservative estimate of discrimination. Even by this lower-bound measure, the net chance of a black or Hispanic person encountering discrimination on any given visit ranges from about one in twenty to more than one in seven. Obviously, in a typical housing search involving multiple visits to several rental or real-estate offices, the chances of discrimination are considerably greater than on one visit, though not as high as they were in 1989, except for Hispanic renters, who experience even more discrimination today than in 1989. Discrimination does not end with rental of an apartment or purchase of a home. Often, it also occurs when homebuyers seek loans or insurance. For example, a recent study in suburban Philadelphia found that 60 percent of the tests revealed unequal treatment on the basis of the race of the tester or the predominant race of the neighborhood (Fair Housing Council of Suburban Philadelphia, 2001).

Two media-sponsored studies—a *60 Minutes* study in Chicago in the late 1970s and a *Prime Time Live* study in St. Louis in 1990—found widespread evidence of discrimination. In the latter study (ABC News, 1991), a black man and a white man, both young college graduates, conducted tests for two weeks in a variety of different businesses around the St. Louis area over a period of two weeks. The black man

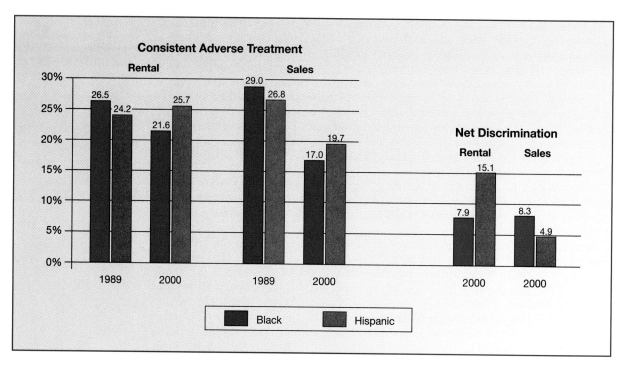

**FIGURE 14.1** Housing Discrimination Against Blacks and Hispanics, 1989 and 2000
*Source:* Turner et al. (2002, p. iii, 8-2).

encountered clear-cut discrimination every day of the two-week period. In Washington, D.C., in 1988, the Lawyer's Committee for Civil Rights had testers hail Washington taxicabs and found that blacks were nine times as likely as whites to be passed by (J. Mathews, 1992). In the same city, tests by the Fair Employment Council of Greater Washington, D.C., found that Hispanic job applicants encountered discrimination 22.4 percent of the time (J. Mathews, 1992). In a creative study of employment discrimination by Bertrand and Mullainathan (2002), employers were sent résumés that were similar except that in some the applicant had a white-sounding name (such as Emily Walsh or Brandon Baker) and in others, a black-sounding name (such as Lakisha Washington or Brandon Jones). The white names resulted in about 50 percent more callbacks for interviews than the black names. Also, whites with better qualifications got more callbacks than less-qualified whites, but this was not true for African Americans. Additional dramatic findings were obtained in an employment-testing study in Milwaukee by Pager (2003). In this study, similar white and black applicants applied for jobs. Additionally, half of the time each tester reported having a criminal record, and half of the time the tester indicated no criminal record. The study found strong effects of both race and criminal record on whether or not the applicant was called back by the employer. However, the race effect was particularly strong—so strong that a white with a prison record was more likely to be called back than an African American without a record. A problem, though, is that other than in housing, most testing research has been conducted in a handful of areas. For example, half of all testing for employment discrimination up to 1998 was done in one metropolitan area, Washington, D.C. (Fix and Turner, 1998a). For this reason, researchers have called for a national report card on discrimination, based on nationwide testing for discrimination in housing, employment, and public accommodations (Fix and Turner, 1998b).

In recent years, testing has increasingly been used both by the government and by private civil rights and fair-housing organizations for purposes of civil rights law enforcement. In 1991, the Fair Employment Council of Greater Washington, D.C., sent male and female testers to an employment agency that had been accused of sexual harassment. The female tester was offered a job if she would let the director of the agency be her "sugar daddy," whereas a male tester encountered no harassment (J. Mathews, 1992). Tests of employment agencies in the San Francisco Bay area in the late 1990s showed that about half of the agencies studied favored white job applicants the majority of the time, with whites about three times as likely to be favored as similarly qualified African Americans (Nunes and Seligman, 1999).

In the early 1990s, the U.S. Department of Justice undertook a series of fair-housing rental tests in several cities, leading to housing discrimination lawsuits in Michigan, South Dakota, Missouri, Illinois, and California. In Detroit, two apartment complexes that had been caught discriminating against black testers were ordered to pay a total of $350,000 in damages (Ahmad, 1993). Increasingly, testing has also been used to investigate discrimination in the availability and pricing of home insurance. In 1998, testing by a Virginia fair-housing organization revealed racial discrimination by the Nationwide Mutual Insurance Company, and a Richmond jury awarded damages of more than $100 million. Although there had been settlements in cases of alleged insurance discrimination, this case was the first to have a jury award damages (*Washington Post*, 1998a).

Testing has also been used in recent years to enforce settlements in cases in which restaurants, hotels, and other public accommodations had been found guilty of discriminating against minority customers. Additionally, some lending institutions such as savings and loans, employers, and apartment rental companies are employing testers to ensure that their own employees are complying with the law.

Sometimes testing is a way of validating complaints about discrimination and is undertaken specifically in response to a complaint about a particular business. Private fair-housing organizations, sometimes working cooperatively with the Department of Housing and Urban Development, have done this type of testing for years.

Increasingly, however, testing is being done on a random basis, and this is important especially if the testing is being done for research purposes to determine the amount of discrimination occurring. The rationale for testing is that discrimination today usually is done surreptitiously. In the ABC *Prime Time Live* program, for example, a rental agent and an auto dealer who have just been caught discriminating on videotape can be seen vigorously protesting that "we don't discriminate." When discrimination occurs in this manner, the victim often does not know that he or she has been discriminated against. Most businesses that discriminate know better than to say they won't do business with a person on the basis of race or gender or that they charge higher rates for blacks, Latinos/as, or women than for white men. Yet they often do: Research by the American Bar Foundation found that blacks and women are charged hundreds of dollars more for cars than are white men buying comparable cars (Ayres, 1990). The only way to know whether discrimination has occurred is through a test in which otherwise similar people either are or are not found to have been treated differently on the basis of their race or gender.

U.S. Justice Department official James Turner (quoted in Ahmad, 1993) uses the Detroit fair housing case to illustrate this principle. Before the Justice Department began random testing in Detroit and found widespread evidence of discrimination, only seven housing discrimination cases had been filed there in the first twenty years of the Fair Housing Act, despite the fact that Detroit has consistently ranked as one of the most segregated metropolitan areas in the United States. The Justice Department tests confirmed that discrimination was widespread, supporting the suspicion that such discrimination is an important reason why Detroit is so segregated. Yet until the department began its random testing there, almost none of that illegal discrimination was being detected and punished.

Some critics of the testing movement, particularly as it relates to enforcement of civil rights laws, have argued that testing constitutes entrapment because the testers do not really intend to rent an apartment, accept a job, or buy a car (M. A. Kennedy, 1992; Mathews, 1992). Supporters reply that this technique is no different from undercover techniques that have long been used to enforce a variety of other laws, and they question why civil rights laws should be treated any differently. They also point out that the legal definition of entrapment is to actively induce someone to break the law, then arrest him or her for the violation—for example, to say, "Come on, smoke a joint with me!" and then charge that person with marijuana use if he or she did so. This type of inducement is not used in a well-designed testing study. Testers do not try to get businesses to discriminate; they only apply for a job or housing or try to buy something and then note how they were treated. An example of entrapment would be for a white tester to say, "Rent to me; I'm white and won't cause you trouble like some of those other folks would." No properly trained tester would do this, and if one did, the test probably would be thrown out in court.

From a legal standpoint, then, the entrapment argument carries no weight in well-designed testing programs. The use of testers has been approved by the courts, including the U.S. Supreme Court (in *Havens Realty Corp. v. Coleman* in 1982), in housing cases. In employment cases, the issue appears to be somewhat in dispute—not so much over entrapment but whether or not testers have standing to sue because they do not really want to work at the places they are testing. Several court rulings, as far back as 1971 and as recent as 2000, have backed the legal standing of testers in employment cases, but there has never been a Supreme Court ruling on the issue. Still, the EEOC formally set forth a position in 1996 that testers and organizations that send testers may file charges of employment discrimination and litigate their claims (Equal Employment Opportunity Commission, 1996). This reiteration of an earlier 1990 ruling was based on court rulings that testers or organizations that send testers do have standing to sue in employment cases, as well as on the increased use of testers to uncover all types of discrimination. In 1997, the EEOC followed up by commissioning nonprofit organizations to conduct testing for employment discrimination.

Because of the difficulty of detecting subtle discrimination, both private civil rights organizations and the federal government are using testing today to a greater extent than in the past. For example, the Department of Housing and Urban Development has placed increased emphasis on testing for mortgage lending discrimination since the mid-1990s. The Office of Federal Compliance Programs also announced in the mid-1990s that it would begin a job discrimination testing program. And in 1998, as noted, a large award was granted by the courts in an insurance discrimination case based on testing. Given the difficulty of detecting discrimination by any means other than testing and given the continuing reality of widespread subtle or surreptitious discrimination, the likelihood is that the discrimination testing movement will continue to grow in the new century.

## Summary and Conclusion

In this chapter, we have examined current trends that include both the continuing reality of prejudice and discrimination and new ways to deal with it. Subtle and institutional discrimination continues to limit the opportunities of minorities in the workplace and to hurt productivity. But a growing number of employers with an enlightened sense of self-interest are dealing with these realities through diversity management programs.

Hate group activity and hate crime have fluctuated in recent years, for a number of reasons including the condition of the economy, the actions of political leaders, and incidents precipitated by terrorism and international conflicts. Yet as hate activity has surged and faded at various times, people and organizations have struggled to come up with new ways of dealing with the problem. Some, such as speech codes, have been highly controversial and of dubious effectiveness. Other techniques, such as the growing tendencies of colleges to require courses on diversity and to encourage the development of conflict resolution techniques, show promise. Nonetheless, colleges, companies, and local communities are likely to continue to experience some tension and divisiveness as long as intergroup inequality and racial segregation remain widespread in the larger society. Although hate group activity remains a problem, most organizations and businesses today do not practice open discrimination. The discrimination that persists has been largely driven underground by civil rights and fair-housing laws. For this reason, the testing movement has developed as an important tool for detecting, and sometimes punishing, more subtle forms of discrimination. Diversity management, hate activity and how to respond to it, and discrimination testing have emerged as major trends and issues in intergroup relations in the past decade and may well remain so in the foreseeable future.

## Critical Review Questions

1. How can accountability be built into diversity plans at colleges and universities? To what extent is accountability a factor in your college's diversity efforts?

2. How is a hate crime different from any other kind of crime? What is the most effective strategy for preventing hate crimes?

3. Find an organization in your area that does testing for racial discrimination. Interview someone there or see if it would be possible to have someone speak to your class. Find out what the organization has discovered about racial discrimination in your area.

4. How do the findings of testing studies differ from the belief among many whites that civil rights laws have put an end to discrimination? Why are popular beliefs often inconsistent with what the studies show the reality to be?

# Affirmative Action and Other Issues for the Future of Majority-Minority Relations in the United States

# Overview

In this chapter, we turn to the future, focusing on issues that are not only current, like the ones discussed in Chapter 14, but also likely to remain at the forefront in U.S. intergroup relations well into the new century. We shall focus on four such issues: the desirability of different models for intergroup relations (assimilation, pluralism, and separatism), the controversy over affirmative action, the immigration policy of the United States, and the relative importance of race and class in American society. As the issue of affirmative action has heated up, extensive material has been added on that topic, which now constitutes about half of the material in this chapter. We turn first to the debate over assimilation, pluralism, and separatism, which carries implications for most of the other issues discussed here.

## ▶ ALTERNATIVE MODELS FOR INTERGROUP RELATIONS

As we have seen in several previous chapters, one major debate in majority-minority relations concerns this question: What is the ideal model or pattern of intergroup relations? In other words, what is the ultimate goal we seek when we try to bring about "better" race and ethnic relations? And is it possible or desirable for different racial groups with different and sometimes competing interests to agree on what constitutes an ideal model? As we saw in Chapter 7, three major models have been proposed: assimilation, pluralism, and separatism. If you do not recall these clearly, you may wish to review the material on pp. 172–75. Today, there remains much debate over which of these three models we ought to be striving toward. In this section, we shall briefly explore the arguments for and against each one.

### Assimilation

**The Case for Assimilation.** The idea that cultural assimilation is desirable arises largely from the view that a society needs to share common values and beliefs: a common culture. This facilitates solidarity, unity, and cooperation, which are needed for society to grow and prosper. This idea, as you probably recognize, is closely aligned with the functionalist, or order, perspective. The underlying premise is that a society with severe internal divisions along the lines of race, ethnicity, or religion cannot work well as a society. Too much energy goes into infighting, people place their own group ahead of the good of the larger society, and cooperation becomes impossible. Functionalists believe the way to avoid this is for all people to identify with the

455

society as a whole and move toward a common culture. The increased support for pluralism in recent decades has been a matter of great concern to many functionalists, who perceive that more and more Americans in recent years have put their own group needs ahead of the needs of the larger society. These sociologists believe that America is becoming a nation of special interest groups, with nobody much concerned about the larger good. (For examples of this viewpoint, see Thernstrom, 1980; J. J. Miller, 1998; a somewhat different take on why common values are necessary can be found in Gitlin, 1995, and W. J. Wilson, 2001.)

Some also believe that assimilation is the only realistic way to obtain racial and ethnic equality (see Patterson, 1977). This viewpoint holds that people's tendency toward ethnocentrism is so strong that wherever racial and cultural differences exist, prejudice and discrimination will occur. This is especially true when there has been a long history of discrimination. This view argues that these evils can be eradicated only by eliminating the cultural differences that are the basis for prejudice and discrimination. In its most extreme form, it holds that *amalgamation*—the elimination through repeated intermarriage and interbreeding of distinct racial groups—is the most effective long-term solution. The advocates of this viewpoint sometimes point to certain Latin American countries where long-term mixing of the white, black, and Indian populations has reduced racial distinctions and prejudices (although cultural differences not totally linked to race remain significant). Others argue, in a more moderate vein, that the widespread acceptance of racial intermarriage would be a crucial step toward the solution of racial problems in this country. Indeed, interracial marriage is becoming more common in the United States, but it remains relatively uncommon.

**The Case Against Assimilation.** A common argument against assimilation is that it amounts to forced conformity. Some advocates of assimilation view it, ideally, as a process of culture sharing, with the majority group adopting some aspects of minority group culture and vice versa. Thus, a new culture and social structure emerges that is neither that of the majority group nor that of the minority group. Critics argue that, in reality, the process is seldom that balanced. As we saw in Chapter 7, the norm throughout most of U.S. history has been Anglo conformity: a demand that all immigrant and minority groups conform to the expectations of the dominant, white Anglo-Saxon Protestant group. Other groups have certainly had some influence, but that of the dominant group has been disproportionate.

Other critics of assimilation see danger in promoting cultural homogeneity rather than heterogeneity. First, a move toward homogeneity would bring a loss in freedom of choice. In a plural, or heterogeneous, society, a person has a wide range of values and lifestyles to choose from. To the degree that this heterogeneity is lost, freedom of choice is lost: There is no choice but to conform to the dominant values and lifestyle. The critics also argue that heterogeneity is an important source of adaptation and innovation in society. If we all become the same, the diversity that produces new ideas may be lost and society may stagnate. For example, the research noted in Chapter 14 shows that diverse groups, over the long run, are more productive than homogeneous ones.

## Pluralism

**The Case for Pluralism.** Many of those who see in assimilation the dangers just discussed support cultural pluralism as the ideal model of intergroup relations. First, they see a need in society for diversity or cultural heterogeneity, and pluralism facilitates it. In other words, a certain amount of diversity—as long as it does not create deep divisions—is good for society because it provides a basis for innovation and for adaptation to new situations. On the other hand, some critics such as Patterson

(1977) have argued that group diversity can lead to individual conformity because of pressures to conform to group norms.

Second, some conflict theorists see a different advantage in pluralism: Racial or ethnic group awareness can form a power base through which a group can act on behalf of its self-interest. Thus, if members of a racial or ethnic group develop a shared identity, it can become a source of social and political power. This can occur through the ballot box (observe how candidates must court the votes of various racial and ethnic groups) or through collective protest. Either way, an ethnic or racial group can potentially gain power if it can develop a common identity and take political action. For groups not well represented in the traditional political process, this kind of group consciousness may be the only real chance to gain political influence. Thus, by providing such a potential power base, cultural pluralism gives minority groups a way to act on behalf of their self-interests. Furthermore, when a group has been subjected to widespread attacks on its culture, as have several minority groups in the United States, group identity can be an important source of self-esteem.

Third, advocates of pluralism point out that preserving the distinct cultures of various racial, ethnic, religious, and social groups is desirable in itself. Such diversity provides a richness in society that would be absent if everyone were culturally the same. Furthermore, this view holds that it is nobody's business to tell a group that it must change its ways to conform to some dominant norm.

In recent years, support for pluralism has increased, as is evident in the growing multicultural movement. This has occurred for the reasons just discussed, as well as for one additional reason: It is increasingly evident that it is unrealistic to expect complete assimilation. As was noted in Chapter 7, conquered or colonized minorities are particularly unlikely to assimilate (Blauner, 1972; Ogbu, 1978; Lieberson, 1980; Zweigenhaft and Domhoff, 1991). Immigrant minorities often do seek assimilation, at least up to a point, largely because they have chosen to enter the society where they now live. Because they want to be there, they probably will have some motivation to learn and fit into the new culture and society. However, colonized minorities involuntarily entered the society—were brought into it to be exploited—and therefore have no automatic reason to want to fit in. Therefore, groups such as African Americans, Chicanos, and Native Americans have been more resistant to assimilation, and all of these groups are growing at a faster rate than the white Anglo population. Examples of support for pluralism can be seen in the growth of Afrocentric education and declining African American support for school desegregation, both discussed in Chapter 12, as well as the growing interest of urban Native Americans in traditional rituals, pow wows, and other cultural expressions. Finally, support for assimilation has always had its limits even among immigrant groups, who have in fact sought to preserve some aspects of their culture. Thus, there is a growing belief among experts on intergroup relations that some degree of pluralism in a society as diverse as the United States is inevitable.

**The Case Against Pluralism.**  The most common argument against pluralism is that it creates divisions in society, which can be harmful in several ways. To the functionalist, any significant division is potentially harmful because it threatens societal consensus and solidarity and thereby inhibits cooperation. Furthermore, given the usual social tendency toward ethnocentrism, the existence of cultural differences makes prejudice and discrimination likely. Although pluralism may sound like a good idea in the abstract, say the critics, it will not work in real life. As an example they point out that the emphasis in America in recent years on black culture, Italian culture, Jewish culture, and so on is dangerous because it emphasizes what is different about us (and therefore a potential basis for conflict and discrimination) rather than what is the same.

An example can be seen in some objections to multicultural education (discussed in Chapter 12). Critics have objected to forms of multicultural education that question the idea of a common national history shared by all ethnic and cultural groups. Such education holds that the experiences of different groups in American society (such as English Americans and African Americans) are quite different. Thus, each group has a distinct national history that is not the same as that of other groups, which helps to explain the role, status, and values of each group today. Writers such as Kirp (1991) have criticized this view on the grounds that it tends to divide society on the basis of race, culture, and nationality. They argue, along the lines of the functionalist perspective, that such divisions inhibit societal cooperation by leading each group to place its own concerns above the common interest.

Some conflict theorists also see dangers in pluralism. For one thing, different racial and cultural groups rarely have equal power. Thus, if people organize and mobilize on the basis of race or ethnicity, the groups with greater political and economic resources are favored. Along this line, Patterson (1977) argues that the Black Power movement, by making ethnic political movements acceptable again, made it easier for the Irish of South Boston to organize an ethnically based movement to keep them in control of their community, which translates to keeping blacks out of the neighborhood.

A related argument can be seen in Marxist theory, which argues that growing awareness of racial and ethnic differences makes people ignore the divisions in society that are really important. A working class in which people think of themselves above all as black or white, Anglo or Chicano, or perhaps (as in Northern Ireland) Catholic or Protestant cannot act together on behalf of its interests as a class. Thus, the masses of blacks and whites (and so on) are hurt by ethnic awareness because it divides them and prevents them from acting on behalf of their larger common interests. Todd Gitlin (1995) and William Julius Wilson (2001) argue that this is largely what has occurred in recent decades. As different ethnic, racial, and cultural groups have battled over cultural issues such as Afrocentrism, bilingualism, gay rights, and affirmative action, socioeconomic inequality in the United States has increased sharply over the past thirty years. In virtually all racial groups, the rich have gotten richer and the poor have gotten poorer. This, of course, has disproportionately affected minority groups because they are overrepresented among the poor. The result has been no coherent or organized voice on the part of working class and poor people, and all of them have suffered as a result.

To remedy this problem, Gitlin (1995) and Wilson (2001) call for a broad-based effort involving people from all races to address growing economic inequality in the United States and for a deemphasis of issues that divide along the lines of race, ethnicity, and other group characteristics. These ideas build on Wilson's (1996, Chap. 7) earlier argument that, of various public policies that would improve the situation of minorities in the United States, the ones most likely to gain popular support are ones that would also benefit a broad (and largely working-class) segment of the white population, in contrast to those that are specifically race-targeted:

> Programs created in response to these concerns—programs that increase employment opportunities and job skills training, improve public education, promote better child and health care, and reduce neighborhood crime and drug abuse—would, despite being race-neutral, disproportionately benefit the most disadvantaged segments of the population, especially poor minorities. (p. 205)

## Racial and Ethnic Separatism

**The Case for Separatism.** Obviously, separation of the races is one mechanism by which a dominant group can maintain its advantages over a subordinate group, as the experience in the U.S. South during the Jim Crow era so clearly illustrates. For this reason, racial separation often has been advocated by racists as a way of maintaining dominant group advantage. In the modern era, examples include the position of the Ku Klux Klan in the United States and, until fairly recently, the systems of apartheid in South Africa and Jim Crow segregation in much of the United States.

However, other arguments for separatism do not arise from the desire of one group to dominate another. Historically, separatist movements have arisen among minority groups (especially those with a geographic base within the larger society) as a way of trying to escape the inequality they have experienced. (Black separatist movements in the United States were discussed in Chapter 7, and French separatism in Canada was discussed in Chapter 8.) In these cases, the main argument for separatism is that it allows each group to control its own social institutions and to make its own political decisions rather than having them controlled by outsiders.

Support for this viewpoint can be seen in the results of a survey conducted as part of the 1993–1994 Black Politics Study at the University of Chicago. In a news interview before its release, its coauthor, Michael Dawson, said, "We were stunned by the magnitude of change in support of black nationalism since 1988. Right now, half the black community supports the idea of an independent black political party. It has never been that high" (quoted in Strong, 1994, p. 7a). Similarly, there is little doubt that one reason for the massive turnouts for the Million Man March in 1995 and the Million Woman March in 1997 is that they were of, for, and by African Americans. This can be seen in the following comments by participants in the Million Man March (Redmond, Fowler, and Atkins, 1998, pp. 103, 107, 124):

> "I've never seen so many Black people together in unity. It really did my heart good."
> "One big difference was that the crowd was all Black men, too, right?"
> "Absolutely."
> "So it makes an even bigger statement."
> "I'm very proud of our Black men coming together for once, because I'm tired of seeing us pull each other down. It is so nice to see us all stand up with so much love, and I think people should recognize what's going on and what could happen."

These trends and statements suggest that in today's society, where many people of color believe that progress in race relations has stalled, there is considerable appeal in ideas of community control and of building institutions and a power base within the group. This does not necessarily reflect a full-blown separatist movement, but it does indicate a widespread priority on community building as opposed to repeated and often unsuccessful efforts for integration into the institutions of the dominant group. The argument is summed up in this statement from the Nation of Islam's Minister Louis Farrakhan (1998): "My future does not depend on a benevolent white person in the White House or in the mayor's mansion or in the governor's mansion. We must get past looking to a benevolent Caucasian to save us. They have not saved us and they will not save us because they can not save themselves."

Some people also support separatism because they see it as the only way to create consensus from a deeply divided society—to create two separate societies, each with its own set of values and its own way of doing things. Thus, consensus and cooperation would be possible within each separate society, whereas they would not have been possible in the previous, larger society. The division of the Indian subcontinent into the separate religiously and ethnically distinct countries of India, Pakistan, and Bangladesh is sometimes cited as an example. This thinking is also reflected in the Quebec separatist movement in Canada, which resulted in the near passage in 1995 of a referendum proposing separation from Canada. The "yes" vote in the referendum was above 49 percent, and the majority of French-speaking Québécois supported it.

**The Case Against Separatism.** Those opposed to separatism counter that in theory the concept may work, but in practice it usually does not. They cite the violent history of Ireland, which was partitioned, in effect, into a Catholic section and a Protestant section, or the volatile situation in the Middle East, which arose out of an attempt to create separate Jewish and Palestinian states after World War II. Additionally, India and Pakistan, both nuclear powers, have gone to the brink of war at times in recent years. Where conflict is deep, there is a genuine risk that the two sides may become warring countries after the separation occurs. If the separation is not complete (as in the continued presence of many Catholics in the "Protestant" section of Ireland, or of Serbs and Croats in Bosnia), internal conflict and violence are also likely. Separatism is nearly impossible to achieve when the groups do not have distinct and nearly exclusive geographic bases. Canada approximates this model to some extent (Quebec is 80 percent French speaking, and the rest of the country is almost totally English speaking), and it has moved somewhat in the direction of separatism in recent years. Even there, however, strong opposition from English-speaking and immigrant populations has been a factor in its defeats at the polls. In contrast to Quebec, the United States does not even come close to having such a geographic distribution.

Quebec illustrates another difficulty: Even those who want separatism for themselves often are unwilling to allow other groups over whom they have power to separate, and separatist movements make such demands more rather than less likely. In Canada, Canadian Indians in northern Quebec have said, in effect, "What about us?" They have argued that just as French-speaking Quebec demands the right to separate from English-speaking Canada, the native peoples of Quebec should have the same right to separate from the Europeans, who took their land. In this regard their history is similar to that of the French Québecois, who came under English and later Canadian rule as a result of their defeat by British military forces in the eighteenth century. Yet the French-speaking Quebec separatists have adamantly opposed the right of the Indians to create their own independent territorial government. Of course, some oppose the entire concept of separatism on the grounds that it gives rise to exactly this kind of fragmentation. Yet it is ironic that sometimes those who seek to separate reject the same demand when others make it of them.

If separatism presents difficulties in Canada, where the English, French, and Native populations do to a large extent live separately from one another, imagine the challenge in the United States, where populations in every part of the country are becoming more diverse. Creating a racial or ethnic territory anywhere would force people of other groups to move. Thus, despite growing advocacy of separatism among some African and Native Americans, full geographic separation would be virtually impossible to implement in the United States. What may happen is a move toward separate political organizations and perhaps economic institutions, as illustrated by the business network and farmland owned by the Nation of Islam and the expansion in recent years of Native American casinos.

Given the practical difficulties of obtaining either complete assimilation or complete separatism, it is likely that the true decisions faced by American society will center around the degree and type of pluralism. Whether there should be a pluralism in which much is shared and only a little is distinct or one in which relatively little is shared and different groups become more distinct and independent probably will be a matter of debate long into the future. Where people stand on this question will be influenced by their values, by their beliefs about how society operates, and undoubtedly by their group identities.

For example, people of different races often have had opposing views about these issues and continue to do so today. In the past, whites fiercely opposed integration, in effect making true assimilation impossible even as they often insisted that minorities accept their values, beliefs, and ways of doing things. Today, it appears that many whites are much more in favor of integration, at least in principle. Public opinion polls suggest this, and so do the comments of white students in my race and ethnic relations classes. However, this integration often takes the form of advocating a "race-blind" approach that, although well intended, does not match up with the reality of unequal opportunities (Bonilla-Silva, 2003c). In contrast, African Americans and other people of color vigorously advocated integration and for the most part supported assimilation in the past but in recent years have moved away from it. This has created a somewhat new situation in which it is sometimes (though by no means always) the whites who seek integration and the people of color who object. For example, the liveliest discussion in my race relations class one recent semester ensued after one African American student expressed an objection to whites who try to "act blacker than the blacks" or to "become something they are not." A white student responded by asking, "What's wrong if we adopt some of the good things we learn from blacks?" This led to a thoughtful but lively discussion of a variety of issues related to integration, group boundaries, and culture. The discussion made it clear that many of the African American students had a strong need to maintain group boundaries and to emphasize certain social and cultural features as being distinctly their own. It was equally evident that some white students saw this as an affront to their efforts to reach out and break down barriers of racial separation.

The debate about assimilation, pluralism, and separatism matters a great deal for a variety of issues in American life. It will influence public thought on bilingual and multicultural education, school desegregation, workplace diversity, political organization, and immigration policy (discussed later in this chapter).

## ▶ AFFIRMATIVE ACTION

Another controversy in intergroup relations is more political, more concrete, and, especially in recent years, seen much more frequently in the headlines. This debate concerns **affirmative action**. The concept dates back to 1967, when the term was first used in an executive order by President Johnson concerning enforcement of antidiscrimination requirements for agencies and businesses under contract with the federal government (Seabury, 1977, p. 99). The order said, "The contractor will not discriminate against any employee or applicant because of race, color, religion, sex or national origin. The contractor will take affirmative action to ensure that employees are treated during employment, without regard to their race, color, religion, sex or national origin." This meant, in effect, that contractors were supposed to make special efforts to ensure that they were not discriminating. In subsequent orders, the emphasis of affirmative action shifted toward the *result* of hiring practices and decisions. Specifically, a requirement was added for "goals and timetables to which the contractor's good faith efforts must be directed to correct the deficiencies and thus, to increase materially the utilization of minorities and women, at all levels and in all segments of his work force where deficiencies exist." Thus, the requirement was added that contractors not only avoid discrimination but also make an active effort to increase the number of female or minority employees where they are underrepresented and develop a specific set of goals and timetables that would serve as targets and as a measure of a contractor's success in hiring more minorities and women.

Organizations doing business with the federal government (including most colleges and universities) undertook various forms of affirmative action in the late 1960s and 1970s to comply with these requirements, and since then many businesses, unions, and nonprofit organizations have taken similar measures voluntarily. Affirmative action programs exist in some colleges and universities in student admissions. They are most common in professional schools, such as law and medical schools, but exist in other areas as well, including undergraduate admissions at a number of colleges and universities. The objective of these affirmative action admissions programs is to increase the number of students from underrepresented groups such as African Americans, Chicanos, American Indians, and women. However, the means used have varied widely.

In the 1990s, affirmative action programs came under unprecedented attack. They have always been controversial, but they became progressively more so during the 1980s and 1990s. The attacks began to take form during the Reagan and first Bush administrations. After a long internal debate, during its second term, the Reagan administration dropped the requirement for goals and timetables. In the later years of the Reagan administration and throughout the administration of the elder President Bush, U.S. Justice Department representatives were ordered to argue against affirmative action preferences in several Supreme Court cases. These positions represented a reversal of positions that had been taken by every presidential administration, Democratic or Republican, from Lyndon Johnson through Jimmy Carter. In another reversal, the first Bush administration also announced its opposition to minority scholarships for college students, no matter how underrepresented the targeted minority group might be in the college's student population. Increasingly, too, the Reagan and Bush administrations sought to portray affirmative action as nothing but "quotas," a position that undoubtedly led to increased public opposition to affirmative action. In 1991, former Ku Klux Klan leader David Duke received the Republican nomination for governor of Louisiana, in part by campaigning strongly against affirmative action. In the general election, Duke received the majority of the white vote, but he lost because an overwhelming majority of the state's sizable African American population voted against him.

Recently, the position of the federal government on affirmative action seems to change with each administration. The Clinton administration returned to the pro–affirmative action position of earlier administrations and also dropped all objections to minority scholarships. George W. Bush said he was for "affirmative opportunity" but opposed affirmative action when the issue went to the Supreme Court in 2003. As is discussed in the next section, affirmative action has been challenged in recent years both in the courts and through the initiative and referendum process, with mixed results.

In the next few pages, we shall explore arguments on both sides of this issue, which has been debated nearly everywhere in America over the past two decades: in classrooms, newspapers, workplaces, union halls, and the U.S. Supreme Court. Later, we shall examine the legal and political status of affirmative action after the various referenda and court rulings of the past decade or so.

## Undoing Discrimination?

The fundamental argument for making special efforts to hire more minority workers or to admit more minority students—even to the point of a preference for the minority applicant—is that this practice is the only way to undo the harmful effects of past and present discrimination. According to this view, past discrimination has left minorities in a disadvantaged position, so that race-blind admission or hiring is not really fair: After generations of discrimination, minority applicants simply do not have all the advantages that white, male applicants have. Recall the analogy in Chapter 11 about the two runners, one of whom had to start with weights tied to her feet. Removing the weights halfway through did not make a fair race: The runner was by then far behind. Removing the weight of discrimination today but doing nothing else to make the competition fair will not, in the eyes of affirmative action supporters, eliminate the disadvantages suffered by minority group members. This analogy was used by President Lyndon Johnson to explain the need for affirmative action when Johnson first proposed the idea, and it remains relevant today.

The effects of past discrimination are not the only reason the supporters of affirmative action give for having such a program. In Chapters 10, 11, and 12, we explored a number of ways in which modern American social institutions discriminate, often without even being aware of it. Until such subtle mechanisms of discrimination are eliminated, race-blind (as well as sex-blind) competition cannot really be fair. Minorities and women are held back by institutional discrimination in ways that whites and men are not. According to this view, the only way to get some semblance of racial or sexual equality today is to have some kind of racial or sexual preference in hiring or admissions. To fail to do so is to keep minorities and women in a position where, through no fault of their own, they have less than their proportionate share of jobs, education, political representation, and so on.

In effect, the supporters of affirmative action argue that the only way to break through the continuous cycle of discrimination is to pay attention to the result. This was done in the South after the *Brown v. Board of Education* case: Schools were given guidelines about what percentage of black and white students constituted an integrated school. In general, supporters of affirmative action see it as a temporary tactic for offsetting the effects of past and institutional discrimination. They argue that once the cycle of inequality has been broken and minorities and women enjoy the same educational and occupational advantages that white men do, the need for special consideration on the basis of race and sex will disappear. Unfortunately, however, that point has not yet been reached.

## Reverse Discrimination?

However, many people see any preference for minority or female applicants as discrimination in reverse, just as unfair as is discrimination against blacks, Chicanos, or women (see Glazer, 1976; S. Steele, 1990). People with this viewpoint argue that preferential treatment of minorities is especially unfair when there is no evidence that the firm or school to which they are applying has deliberately discriminated in the past. They feel this practice forces many whites (or men) who are not guilty of discrimination to unfairly pay the price for past discrimination, which they had nothing to do with. In short, it is seen as unfair to such people to be passed over, through no fault of their own, in favor of women and minorities who are less qualified than they are, at least by traditional measures of qualifications.

The question of qualifications has become a central issue in the debate. Those against affirmative action, in addition to the aforementioned arguments, say that it undermines the quality of work forces and student bodies by giving positions to people other than the most qualified applicants. If one accepts the traditional measures of qualifications as valid indicators, one could claim that this sometimes occurs. In many law schools and medical schools, for example, minority applicants have been accepted with test scores or undergraduate grade point averages (GPAs) significantly lower than those generally required of whites (see Sindler, 1978; D'Souza, 1991; *National Review*, 1994; Thomas, 2003, pp. 22–23).

Another barrage of criticism has been directed at affirmative action on the grounds that it amounts to an unfair quota system. This view holds that the goals and timetables end up as quotas that must be filled regardless of the qualifications of the candidates. Thus, if a firm has a goal of hiring a 10 percent black work force in three years, it will end up having to hire some minimum number of blacks regardless of their qualifications. Negative perceptions have been increased by incidents in which employers have told white male applicants that they have been passed over in favor of less qualified women or minorities to meet affirmative action goals (Nisbet, 1977). The use of quotas is of special concern to some ethnic groups: For example, Jewish Americans remember that many Jews were kept out of American colleges and professional schools by quotas that specified a maximum percentage of Jewish students. In part for this reason, many Jews and others see a dangerous precedent in what they view as a reintroduction of quotas (Raab, 1978).

Finally, there are those who argue that affirmative action is nothing more than discrimination in reverse. They believe that the way to eliminate the effects of discrimination is not to practice what they view as another form of it. They have in some cases adopted the language of the civil rights movement, arguing, for example, that people should be evaluated not on "the color of their skin but rather on the content of their character" (S. Steele, 1990).

## An Alternative View on Quotas

Supporters of affirmative action generally do not agree that a preference for women or minority applicants amounts to reverse discrimination or that affirmative action programs have brought about the widespread use of quotas. On the issue of quotas, they argue that goals and timetables have never been intended as rigid quotas but rather as a target and a standard against which the performance of government contractors can be measured. It is acknowledged that there are sometimes good reasons for an unmet goal. The key criterion is good-faith effort and some indication of progress (Pottinger, 1972). It is also argued that unlike the quotas that limited the numbers of Jews in American universities in the 1950s and earlier, the purpose of affirmative action (whether it involves quotas or not) is to get people *into* employment or school, not to keep them out.

## Considering the Net Outcome

To summarize, then, traditional admission criteria for minority applicants are considered unfair and inappropriate by supporters of affirmative action because they do not compensate for the effects of discrimination (unintentional as well as intentional) that the applicants have previously experienced. People who support affirmative action believe that the net effect of failing to consider race in admissions and hiring decisions is to discriminate against minorities. Nothing is done to compensate for the effects of past discrimination and the subtle processes of institutional discrimination that place the minority applicant at an unfair disadvantage. Hence, affirmative action is not reverse discrimination but rather a way of reversing the effects of institutional discrimination that minority applicants have already experienced. Under affirmative action, the white male applicant may suffer some disadvantage at the point of decision, but this is offset by disadvantages suffered by the minority applicant at earlier stages, such as primary and secondary education (see Chapter 12). Thus, according to this view, the only way to avoid net discrimination is through affirmative action.

## How Accurately Do We Measure Qualifications?

The second reason that traditional measures of qualifications may not accurately measure the potential of minority applicants has to do with the measures themselves. The tests and criteria may contain cultural biases that favor white, middle-class, male applicants and work to the disadvantage of others. (The issue of test bias is discussed in detail in Chapter 12.) Women and minorities may score lower on such criteria, but this does not indicate that they have lower potential. For example, the minority applicant may score lower on these criteria because of disadvantages arising from past and institutional discrimination, not because of lesser ability (Fish, 1993). In addition, most of the tests in popular use are poor predictors of success. In other words, most of the variation in such measures as college grades or work success is left unexplained by the standardized tests.

For this reason, supporters of affirmative action deny that it leads to the hiring or admission of less qualified applicants. Society imposes handicaps on minorities that are not imposed on white men; thus, the criteria measure the effects of this discrimination better than they measure the applicant's true potential. Discriminatory processes in education in particular make it more difficult for minorities to become "qualified" according to the traditional measures. These discriminatory processes include unequal funding of schools, unequal expectations of student achievement, biased or Eurocentric content in educational materials, and tracking and ability grouping influenced by race, ethnicity, and socioeconomic status. All of these processes reinforce and perpetuate racial inequalities already present in society and make it more difficult for minority students to do well on tests used for college admissions and for screening of applicants for employment. It is also important to note that these disadvantages did not just occur in the past; they continue today.

In addition, Jencks (1998, pp. 77–84) points out that *selection bias* occurs any time that there is a greater average racial difference on a measure, such as an SAT or ACT score, than there is on the thing it is being used to predict, such as college GPA or graduation rates. For example, of 1982 high school graduates, about 11 percent overall got a GPA of 3.5 or higher in college. Thus, a college seeking to pick the top 11 percent of students might pick the top 11 percent of SAT scores. If it did this, though, only 2 percent of black applicants would be admitted. This would have excluded the majority of black students who actually got college GPAs above 3.5! This because the racial gap on the test scores is more than the racial gap in college GPAs and because the SAT is in fact a weak predictor of college GPA.

Thus, the inflexible use of traditional qualifications may exclude many minority applicants who in fact have the ability to succeed in school or on the job. Indeed, with the best criteria available, it is possible to make only rough estimates of how good a student or employee an applicant will turn out to be. For example, law school admission criteria typically explain only about 25 percent of the variation in first-year academic performance of law students (Sindler, 1978, pp. 115–16). And college entrance tests such as the SAT are weaker predictors of academic performance in college than high school grades or class rank, yet they exclude a larger proportion of minority applicants (FairTest, 1998). Even by the SAT's own report of validation studies, the SAT score alone explains only 27 percent of the variation in college GPA, whereas high school grades alone explain about 29 percent (College Board, 1999). Even high school grades and SAT scores *together* leave two-thirds of the variation in college GPA unexplained. Jencks (1998, p. 82) argues that because there are no really good predictors of college grades, and because measures such as the SAT contain racial gaps greater than racial gaps in actual college grades, the only way to offset selection bias is to consider race as a factor in admissions.

Some critics of affirmative action have argued that the lower graduation rates of minority students than those of white students show that affirmative action in college admissions has resulted in the admission of students who are not as capable and hence have less chance of success. But a number of facts undermine this argument. First, the racial gap in graduation rates is smallest at the schools that make the *most* use of affirmative action: the elite schools that are hard to get into. A recent study by Cross (1998) shows that at sixteen of the most exclusive schools—including Harvard, Wake Forest, Princeton, Yale, Brown, and Georgetown—the average graduation rate for black students was between 85 and 90 percent, within five points of the rate for white students. It is precisely in these highly selective schools that affirmative action preferences are most widely used, yet the black students there were just about as likely to graduate as the white students (on this point, see also Bowen and Bok, 1998).

In contrast, it was at state colleges and universities that admitted most applicants regardless of race, *without* using affirmative action, where the black-white graduation gap was widest. At a sample of these schools, where around 90 percent of all applicants are admitted, the gap in graduation rates was much wider, typically 20 percentage points or more. During the 1990–1996 period, probably the period in which affirmative action has been most widely used in U.S. colleges and universities, there was a substantial increase in the graduation rate of black students, even as the percentage of new black students who were admitted increased (Cross, 1998). This is totally inconsistent with an argument that affirmative action results in the admission of students who do not have the ability to succeed. Rather than ability, Cross argues that the key factors in the lower graduation rates of black students in many colleges are the social isolation that many minority students experience in predominantly white colleges, and, especially, financial problems. The families of black students have far less wealth than those of white students, and contrary to popular belief, scholarships do not compensate for this lack: Only 4 percent of all scholarships in the United States as of the early 1990s were set aside for minority students (General Accounting Office, 1994). Consequently, black students were much more likely than white students in a national survey to report dropping out of college because of high debts (Cross, 1998, p. 98). Strikingly, the black-white gap in college graduation rates disappears when one compares students from families with similar levels of wealth, that is, the total assets that families own (Conley, 1999). And with regard to Cross's other point, social isolation, numerous studies have shown that African American students experience social isolation and discrimination on college campuses (Feagin, Hernan, and Imani, 1996; W. Allen, 2001; for a review and discussion of actions to address the problem, see J. Farley, 2002a). In testimony for the University of Michigan affirmative action case, which led to Supreme Court rulings in 2003, sociologist Walter Allen (2001, p. 86) stated the following:

> Further research has in many of its aspects demonstrated that African-American students on historically white campuses, predominantly white

At predominantly white colleges and universities such as the University of Michigan, students of color often experience discrimination and social isolation. This creates challenges and impediments to success that white students do not have to deal with.

campuses, report experiences of those campuses as being racially hostile, as being environments that communicated to them that they were interlopers, or aliens or not welcomed on the campuses.

As Allen and many other sociologists have pointed out, these experiences have significant effects on both the graduation rates of black students and other measures of their success, such as grade point averages.

## Does Affirmative Action Stigmatize Minority Group Members?

Affirmative action has come under attack from some African American conservatives in recent years, as in the writings of S. Steele (1990) and Sowell (1977, 1990) and in the legal opinions of Supreme Court Justice Clarence Thomas. Their main objection is that it devalues minority or female employees and students. For example, black professionals and college students commonly encounter the view from some whites that "you're only here to fill a quota; you're not really qualified." Thus, the credentials of even the best-qualified minority employees or students are questioned. Steele and others (such as S. L. Carter, 1992) argue that affirmative action has the unintended effect of reinforcing negative stereotypes about minorities among the dominant group and creating self-doubt among minority group members, who constantly find their abilities and talents questioned. Steele also argues that the perception among whites that affirmative action amounts to reverse discrimination creates resentment, which will be damaging to African Americans and other minorities in the long run.

Supporters of affirmative action offer several responses to these arguments. Some whites do view minorities as unqualified no matter how well they do, and affirmative action undoubtedly contributes to this. However, a good many of today's minority professionals and managers point out that they would not have received the opportunity to prove themselves had it not been for doors opened by affirmative action. They acknowledge the problem that some whites refuse to recognize their abilities and accomplishments, but they also point out that the alternative would be worse: no opportunity to prove themselves at all. In other words, because of past and institutional discrimination, they would not have been given the opportunity to get the managerial or professional job and to show that they could succeed (Olojede, 1991). Bryan Fair (1997), an African American law professor and author, makes a similar argument about affirmative action in higher education:

> Some critics of affirmative action point to decisions by schools like Duke [Fair's alma mater] to admit people like me with test scores substantially below the school's standards. They allege such a mismatch is harmful to people like me, presumably meaning that my test scores preclude my competing with other students at Duke and that when students like me fail, we lose the little confidence and self-esteem with which we began.
>
> I disagree. First, Duke gave me a great opportunity, one that did not hurt me in any way. . . . I learned that its high standards were not beyond my capacity but, rather, only beyond my training. . . . I would never pull up the ladder that helped me climb out of racial poverty.

Thus, many minority group members who have achieved professional status argue that the answer is not to eliminate affirmative action, because that has opened doors for them that would otherwise have been closed. Rather, the challenge is to make sure that the genuine accomplishments of minority students and employees are recognized and known so that doors opened by affirmative action will not be closed. In fact, survey data suggest that minorities and women do not generally feel stigmatized by affirmative action. A survey by M. C. Taylor (1995) found that African American men and women and white women who worked at firms that practiced affirmative action were just as happy with their job situation as their counterparts who worked at firms without affirmative action. In addition, a 1995 Gallup poll found that just 8 percent of white women, 19 percent of African American women, and 29 percent of African American men had ever felt that their colleagues at either work or school had questioned their abilities because of affirmative action (Crosby and Herzberger, 1996).

## Affirmative Action and Majority Group Resentment

Just as it is important to make known the achievements of minority group students and employees, a similar argument can be made about addressing the problem of white (and especially white male) resentment toward affirmative action. It was noted in earlier chapters that white opposition to affirmative action and other policies to increase opportunities for minorities is strongly linked to a belief that the system is fair. In other words, whites who believe that blacks and whites have essentially the same opportunities in American society (a clear majority of all white Americans) generally oppose affirmative action and similar measures (Kluegel and Smith, 1986; Kluegel, 1990; Herring et al., 2000).

The opposition of most whites to affirmative action has been borne out both by surveys and in elections, although the response varies widely by question wording. Surveys have consistently shown that the majority of whites oppose affirmative action if it involves any consideration of race as a factor in hiring or admissions. And many whites view it as unfair, reverse discrimination. For example, one 1994 survey showed that about three-fourths of whites believe that affirmative action sometimes results in discrimination against whites (Steeh and Krysan, 1996), and nearly half in a 1997 survey said that whites losing out to minorities because of affirmative action was a bigger problem than minorities losing out because of discrimination (Verhovek, 1997). However, with other question wording, results can be quite different. For example, when asked, "Do you generally favor or oppose affirmative action programs for racial minorities?" 44 percent of whites in a June 2003 Gallup poll said "yes," and 49 percent said "no" (Gallup Organization, 2003a). (Among African Americans, 70 percent said "yes," and among Latinos, 63 percent.) However, the same poll asked respondents which came closer to their view: "Applicants should be admitted solely on the basis of merit, even if that results in few minority students being admitted" or "An applicant's racial and ethnic background should be considered to help promote diversity on college campuses, even if that means admitting some minority students who otherwise would not be admitted." By a margin of 75 to 22 percent, whites said "solely merit." (African Americans favored considering race by 49 to 44 percent, and Hispanics preferred "solely merit" by 59 to 36 percent.) This suggests that at least a large minority of whites (and most African Americans and Latinos) do recognize the need to do something to increase minority opportunities in work and education but that, at the same time, most whites and even many people of color are uncomfortable with the idea of considering race as a factor in hiring or admissions.

Winant (1997) argues that such opinions show both the success and the limitations of the civil rights movement of the 1960s. Since then, most whites have genuinely rejected racial discrimination and notions of innate racial superiority. However, as discussed in much of this book, institutional discrimination and subtler forms of deliberate individual discrimination have persisted. But because these forms of discrimination are harder to see and because whites are not the ones who experience them, most whites believe that opportunities have become relatively equal. On one hand, the victory of the civil rights movement is that most whites now oppose racial discrimination. On the other hand, its limitations can be seen in the persistence of the subtler forms of discrimination and the failure of whites to recognize these forms of discrimination. Consequently, the ideology that decisions should be race-blind has become an underpinning of opposition to affirmative action because most whites deny or do not recognize that the system does not work in a race-blind way (Bonilla-Silva, 2003c). Therefore, a large majority of whites oppose affirmative action as inappropriate discrimination if it involves any consideration of race. And the race-blind ideology seems to have influenced even the opinions of some minority group members, given that many Hispanics and some, but not most, African Americans indicate opposition in surveys to consideration of race, even to increase opportunity (Gallup Organization, 2003a).

Referenda to end affirmative action in state government (including higher education) were approved by California voters in 1996 and by voters in Washington State in 1998. Specifically, the referenda banned any consideration of race in hiring or public college admissions in those states, even when it was used as a way to diversify the campus or work force or to offset societal discrimination. Exit polls reveal that opposition to affirmative action was a good deal stronger among white men than among white women. In the 1998 Washington referendum, for example, white women were about evenly split, whereas white men supported the abolition of affirmative action by a two-to-one margin (CNN, 1998). Not suprisingly, support for ending affirmative action was also stronger among people whose financial situation had recently gotten worse and among people with lower educational levels.

Some of this opposition is based on fears that any gains by minorities will be at the expense of whites, and some may even reflect more direct racial prejudice. In a fascinating experiment, the Gallup poll alternated the order of questions about affirmative action based on sex and race, using the "Do you favor or oppose affirmative action?" wording described earlier (Moore, 2003b). When asked first about sex and then about race, Americans favored affirmative action for women by 62 to 30 percent and for minorities by 56 to 39 percent. But when asked first about race, they opposed affirmative action for minorities by 48 to 45 percent while favoring it for women by only 53 to 38 percent. This tells us that although people try to give consistent answers, they object much more to affirmative action for minorities than for women. And how much support they state for either kind of affirmative action also depends on whether the first question calls to mind affirmative action for racial minorities or for women.

Even so, research by Kluegel and Smith (1986; Kluegel, 1990) and by Herring et al. (2000) shows clearly that some whites do recognize the reality that blacks and other minorities have less opportunity and that these whites are much less likely to oppose policies such as affirmative action. There is also evidence that when people study and learn about the nature of racial inequality in the United States, they become more supportive of such policies (Davine and Bills, 1992). Thus, supporters of affirmative action acknowlege that some whites resent it, but they argue that the answer is not to eliminate it but to make people more informed about intergroup relations in the United States so that they better understand the reasons for maintaining it. In fact, the Advisory Board to the President's Initiative on Race (1998, p. 46) made this a major recommendation when it issued its report to President Clinton in September 1998:

> To understand fully the legacy of race and color with which we are grappling, we as a Nation need to understand that whites tend to benefit, either unknowingly or consciously, from this country's history of white privilege. Examples include being able to purchase an automobile at a price lower than that available to a comparable minority or person of color, not being followed through department stores by clerks or detectives . . . being offered prompt service while minorities and people of color are often made to wait. . . . One of the lessons of our experience is the significant degree of unawareness by whites today of the extent of stereotypes, discrimination,

and privilege. One of our conclusions is the importance of educating all people of the continuing existence of prejudice and privilege.

Before leaving this topic, it is important to note that whereas many whites do oppose affirmative action, especially if it involves consideration of race in hiring or admissions, those with the greatest experience with affirmative action are the most supportive of it. For example, M. C. Taylor (1995) found that whites whose employers used affirmative action were more supportive of it than were whites whose employers did not use affirmative action. Similarly, a study of elite colleges and universities—the colleges that make the greatest use of affirmative action—found that their alumni were overwhelmingly in support of affirmative action (Bowen and Bok, 1998). Both black and white students in these institutions agree that colleges and universities should devote even more attention to having a racially and ethnically diverse student body than they do. Research clearly shows that among whites, support for affirmative action is greatest among those who have the most education, those who are most knowledgeable about the realities of race and opportunity in the United States, and those who have had personal experience with affirmative action programs at work or at school.

## Affirmative Action and Minority Professionals

A final and related issue raised by the supporters of affirmative action is the need for minority professionals. As we saw in Chapters 10 and 11, a serious shortage of minority doctors and lawyers is one important reason why minority Americans have less access to medical care and legal representation. Without affirmative action in law and medical school admissions programs, this condition would be even worse. In 1992, the dean of the University of Texas Law School estimated that without affirmative action, there would have been only 20 to 30 minority students in the entering class of 500, instead of the 100 there actually were (Mark G. Yudof, quoted in Jaschik, 1992). This estimate was put to the test when a court ruling temporarily ended affirmative action at that university in 1996. As the dean had predicted, the next fall, the number of new black law students fell from 31 to 4, and the number of new Latino/a students fell from 48 to 26. At the university's four medical schools, minority enrollment fell by 25 percent after the ruling (Lederman, Crissy, and Mealer, 1997). Remember that before any of these enrollment decreases occurred, minorities were already underrepresented in law school and medical school, even with affirmative action.

The pipeline of minority students coming out of top undergraduate schools into professional schools is affected, too. When a public referendum and action by the Board of Regents ended any consideration of race in the University of California, the number of African American, Latino/a, and American Indian students admitted to Berkeley fell from 1,676 (19.1 percent of the freshman class) in the previous year to 744 (9.0 percent). More than 750 minority students with GPAs of 4.0 or higher were turned away. By 2002, the minority percentage at Berkeley was still below what it had been in 1997, before affirmative action was eliminated (Laird, 2002). Statewide in California, the number of underrepresented minority students in medical schools fell by 32 percent between the mid-1990s and 1998 (Mangan, 1999). Numbers like these show that without affirmative action, the supply of minority attorneys, doctors, and other professionals decreases sharply. Moreover, the notion that affirmative action leads to the admission of unqualified law school or medical school applicants is simply not supported by the data. For example, more than 90 percent of all minority medical students graduate (Petersdorf et al., 1990; Lee, 1992).

As stated earlier, underrepresentation of minorities in law and medicine is an important reason why minorities lack access to medical care and legal representation. Minority physicians are more likely to have a high proportion of minority patients in their practices, are much more likely to locate in areas of low socioeco-

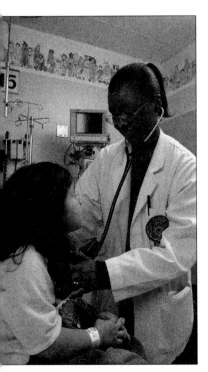

In law schools and medical schools that have dropped affirmative action, the enrollment of minority students has fallen. By reducing the number of minority doctors and lawyers, this has a broader impact, because minority professionals are more likely than others to locate in underserved minority communities.

nomic status, and are somewhat more likely to specialize in primary care (Nickens, 1992; Komaromy et al., 1996; Steinbrook, 1996). They are often more culturally sensitive to minority populations and more likely to schedule evening office hours so that low-income patients don't have to miss work to see the doctor (Nickens, 1992).

## Practical Consequences of Affirmative Action: Empirical Evidence

Examining data on the employment and income of recent minority and white college graduates is helpful in assessing the actual effects of affirmative action hiring programs. These data suggest that among recent college graduates (and people who have recently finished postgraduate work), African Americans and Latinos/as are earning incomes close to but still below those of whites. Thus, the notion that affirmative action has given minorities a net advantage over whites is a myth. In 2001, college-educated black male year-round full-time workers were receiving 87 percent of the annual earnings of comparable white workers, and Hispanic workers were receiving about 81 percent (computed from U.S. Census Bureau, 2002d, Table PINC-03). In 2001, college-educated African American and Latina women who worked full-time each received about 93 to 94 percent of the annual earnings of their white female counterparts. Moreover, women of all racial and ethnic groups have continued to lag well behind white men in income, even among college graduates. Thus, although affirmative action has moved things in the direction of equality among recent college graduates who are working full-time, white men continue to enjoy higher incomes than anyone else, even among this group. And it is this group, recent college graduates, in which minorities have benefitted the most from affirmative action.

Research also does not bear out the view that affirmative action leads to admission of students who are not qualified. This finding is illustrated by research by two former Ivy League university presidents, William Bowen and Derek Bok (1998). Like other researchers, they found that minority students admitted to top colleges and universities under affirmative action graduated the great majority of the time. In fact, for African American students with any given SAT score, they found that the higher the average SAT score of other students in the university, the better the chance of graduation. This was true even for black students whose SAT scores were lower than those of most of the students at their school (Bowen and Bok, 1998, p. 259). Studying a wider sample of colleges, T. J. Kane (1998) found that among black students with any given SAT score, graduation rates were *higher* in the more selective schools and were actually lower in the less selective schools. Findings like these destroy the argument that affirmative action has led to the admission of unqualified minority students to selective schools; the data show decisively that this has not occurred.

In addition, by tracking graduates after college, Bowen and Bok (1998) found that African American graduates of selective colleges became the core of a growing middle class, succeeding in their professions, in many cases earning advanced graduate or professional degrees, and making significant civic contributions. For example, black and white graduates of top colleges were equally likely (56 percent of graduates in each racial group) to obtain graduate or professional degrees. African American graduates of these top colleges, like their white counterparts, are more likely to get law, medical, advanced business, or doctoral degrees than either black or white students from less selective schools. This fact shows that affirmative action in undergraduate admissions to the selective schools, over the longer run, had a big effect on the supply of minority professionals, as suggested earlier. And African American students who had been admitted under affirmative action were just as successful in getting these graduate and professional degrees as their white counterparts, again showing the fallacy of the argument that affirmative action leads to the admission of unqualified minority students.

The two black families in these photos depict the widening gap between affluence and poverty within the African American population. Affirmative action has opened opportunities for minorities with sufficient education to take advantage of the opportunities but has done little for poverty-level minority group members.

Clearly, the ability of affirmative action programs to help more people of color enter and graduate from college has contributed to the growth of the African American and Latino middle classes. Overall, then, the research shows that affirmative action has contributed to the growth of the minority middle class and has narrowed income gaps along the lines of race, ethnicity, and gender among recent college graduates. However, none of the data support the claim that it has given minorities or women an advantage over white men. Even among college graduates, white men still get higher incomes than anyone else. White graduates of the elite colleges studied by Bowen and Bok (1998, p. 124) still had higher earnings than black graduates, although both had incomes well above the national average.

For less educated minorities, the benefits of affirmative action have been fewer, although certain groups have nonetheless benefitted. Minority workers with less education have made some gains as a result of affirmative action in a variety of public employment positions, such as police officers and firefighters. Building trade contractors who are involved in government contracting have hired more minorities, in part because of set-aside programs designed to ensure that some work is done by minority-owned construction firms. In fact, between 1982 and 1991, the overall number of federal contracts going to minority-owned businesses rose by 125 percent, while the overall number of contracts grew by only 24 percent (Holzer and Neumark, 2000, p. 43). Similar patterns can be seen in local government contracts in some areas. Gains have also occurred in some blue-collar manufacturing firms that have labor contracts calling for affirmative action; however, overall employment has declined sharply in these firms because of automation, relocation overseas, and international competition. Consequently, many minority workers who once had good jobs in manufacturing have lost them despite affirmative action and antidiscrimination efforts. Nonetheless, the net overall effect on minority and female employment has been positive: Based on reviews of many studies of affirmative action, Holzer and Neumark (2000, p. 37) estimate that firms that adopt affirmative action increase their employment of minorities and women by a few percentage points, although the increase for women probably is larger.

On the other hand, affirmative action has had almost no effect on low-income, poorly educated, chronically unemployed minorities (W. J. Wilson, 1978, pp. 99–121; 1987). Despite the benefits of affirmative action for more advantaged minorities and some in the working class, minority groups taken as a whole remain substantially disadvantaged in income, employment, and education compared with whites as a whole, even with affirmative action. Even minorities who have benefitted from affirmative action may be less economically secure than whites (S. M. Collins, 1993). For example, middle-class blacks are more likely than comparable whites to be employed in government or in government-supported programs. Thus, they are more vulnerable to government cutbacks.

Research by S. M. Collins (1993) has revealed another reason for the vulnerable position of minority group members with good jobs. Studying black executives in major, white-owned corporations, she found that they are often employed in positions in human relations, affirmative action, urban affairs, or diversity management. To some extent, the amount of resources that corporations devote to activities of this type depends on the amount of social and political pressure they receive to address problems of race relations and minority underrepresentation. As long as companies feel pressure to address these issues, they undoubtedly will do so. But when these pressures ease, as they did for a time in the 1980s, corporations may devote fewer resources to them, making such jobs vulnerable to cutbacks. In fact, many companies did make such cutbacks during the 1980s. To the extent that this occurs, black executives are more vulnerable than white executives because of their area of specialization.

Recent studies have also examined the effects of affirmative action on the institutions where it has been used, particularly the workplace and higher education. Reskin (1998) studied affirmative action in employment and found clear evidence that it has increased workplace diversity. Workplaces that practice affirmative action are more diverse than ones that do not, and workplaces that have instituted affirmative action plans have become more diverse. Overall, the occupational distributions of men and women and of whites and blacks became less segregated between 1970 and 1990, meaning that there is now a reduced tendency for women and African Americans to be channeled into different jobs than men and whites (Reskin, 1998, p. 53).

Research does not support the claim that affirmative action hurts productivity by resulting in the hiring of people who are not qualified. A study of about 3,200 new workers at firms in Boston, Atlanta, Los Angeles, and Detroit showed that there was no difference in the performance evaluations of female and minority workers hired under affirmative action programs from those of either white male workers or minority or female workers hired without affirmative action programs (Holzer and Neumark, 1999). The companies that had affirmative action plans hired female and minority workers with slightly lower educational levels, but the workers performed equally well. It was noted that this is not surprising because educational level is just one of many factors that affect how productive a worker will actually be, and it appears that the employers using affirmative action looked more carefully at some of the other factors and consequently were able to hire more diverse employees who were just as effective. Similarly, Reskin (1998, pp. 76–77) reviewed a number of studies assessing the productivity of workplaces with varying proportions of female or minority employees. All of the studies found that productivity was equal or greater in the workplaces that had more diverse work forces, including a number of employers who had achieved diversity at least in part through affirmative action.

Finally, Holzer and Newmark (2000) reviewed a number of studies of affirmative action and found that minority workers hired under programs of affirmative action generally were evaluated as performing about the same as white workers. Thus, research clearly negates the argument that affirmative action reduces the quality of the work force.

## Legal Aspects of the Affirmative Action Controversy

Not surprisingly, an issue as controversial as affirmative action has been widely debated in the courts. Those who are against it have argued that it violates the Civil Rights Act of 1964 and the equal protection clause of the Constitution by discriminating against whites or men. Those who support it argue that affirmative action is not discrimination against anyone but rather an effort to *include* underrepresented groups, and therefore it is not illegal. In general, because of the equal protection clause and the civil rights laws, the courts view race as a "suspect category." In effect, this means that anyone who in any way uses race as a basis of consideration must demonstrate that some compelling interest is served by doing so and that the purpose is not to discriminate against or exclude anybody on the basis of race. Because most affirmative action programs do in some way involve a consideration of race, an early court test of their legality was inevitable, and since 1971 a series of rulings have resulted in a constantly changing picture, made somewhat clearer, but not entirely so, by the Supreme Court's *Grutter* ruling in 2003.

The first case in which the Supreme Court ruled on the legality and constitutionality of affirmative action was the *Bakke* case in 1978. Rather than settling the affirmative action issue, *Bakke* proved to be the first of a number of Supreme Court cases on affirmative action. What emerged from these rulings is that it makes a difference if the case involves student admissions, hiring, contracting, or layoff decisions and that the legal standing of affirmative action is clearer in some of these situations than in others. In addition, initiative and referendum votes have also changed the picture in at two states, California and Washington, and there is talk of similar attempts elsewhere.

In part, the legal status of affirmative action has shifted over time as the compositions of the Supreme Court and of federal appeals courts have changed because of retirement and new appointments. In the 1980s, appointments by Reagan and Bush led to a Supreme Court less sympathetic to affirmative action. In 1989, several Court rulings were made that limited, but did not reverse, earlier Court support for affirmative action. However, some of these rulings were reversed by the 1991 Civil Rights Act. In a 1995 ruling, the Supreme Court seemed to say that it would require more justification than in the past for any use of race as a factor in decisions made by governments. But in the *Grutter* case in 2003, it found sufficient justification for using race as one factor in public university admissions decisions for purposes of ensuring a diverse student body, just as it had done twenty-five years earlier in the *Bakke* case.

Today, exactly what is permitted in the way of affirmative action varies among hiring, promotion, and student admissions, between the public and private sectors, and among different parts of the country. It also depends in some cases on the degree and type of discrimination that has occurred in the past. Let us now briefly examine the various situations and what the current position of the law appears to be. (Major Supreme Court rulings on affirmative action are outlined in Table 15.1.)

**Higher Education Admissions.** The first Supreme Court ruling on higher education admissions is *Bakke*, decided in 1978. The validity of this case was temporarily in question as a result of the 1996 *Hopwood* ruling by the Fifth U.S. Circuit Court of Appeals. This decision, which directly affected Texas, Louisiana, and Mississippi, was reversed in 2003 in the *Grutter* case, so that the basic principles of the *Bakke*

### Table 15.1    Summary of Major Supreme Court Decisions Concerning Affirmative Action

| Year | Case and Decision |
|---|---|
| 1978 | *Allan Bakke v. Regents of the University of California.* Racial preferences ruled legal in higher education admissions for educational purpose of having a diverse student body. Racial quotas forbidden by Constitution. |
| 1979 | *Weber v. Kaiser Aluminum and Chemical Corporation.* Racial preferences, including the use of quotas, are legal in private employment hiring decisions as a means of compensating for societal discrimination. |
| 1984 | *Memphis Firefighters v. Stotts.* (Not discussed in text because this case was clarified by later *Wygant* decision.) Seniority system for layoffs could not be abrogated to help individuals who were not proven victims of discrimination. |
| 1986 | *Wygant v. Jackson Board of Education.* Struck down minority preference in public school teachers' layoffs for purposes of diverse role models for students. Ruled that stronger case was needed to justify layoff preferences than hiring preferences, but proof of individual discrimination against beneficiaries of preferences was not required. |
| 1986 | *International Association of Firefighters v. City of Cleveland.* Upheld racial preferences in public employment as a remedy for discrimination and ruled that court-approved settlement of discrimination lawsuits could include racial preferences. |
| 1986 | *Sheet Metal Workers v. Equal Employment Opportunity Commission.* Courts can order racial preferences, including goals and timetables for minority employment, if it is found that private employers have engaged in "egregious discrimination." |
| 1987 | *United States v. Paradise.* Use of minority quotas in hiring and promotion by public employers can be ordered by courts when employer has engaged in severe discrimination. |
| 1987 | *Johnson v. Transportation Agency.* Women or minorities can be hired or promoted by public employers ahead of slightly more qualified men or whites for the purpose of making the work force more representative of the area's population. (This ruling was based on the 1964 Civil Rights Act.) |
| 1989 | *Croson v. City of Richmond.* Ruled that government programs that set aside a certain proportion of contracts for minority-owned contractors must be based on documented patterns of past discrimination. |
| 1989 | *Wards Cove v. Antonio.* For an employer to be found guilty of discrimination, it must be proved that there is no business reason for imposing a job requirement that has the effect of excluding minorities or women. Makes it harder for women and minorities to win discrimination cases based on statistics showing employment disparities. This decision was later reversed by the 1991 Civil Rights Act, which states that employers must prove there is a business reason for requirements that have discriminatory effects. |
| 1989 | *Martin v. Wilks.* Even when they have been previously approved by the courts, affirmative action settlements can be reopened by white men who claim reverse discrimination. |
| 1989 | *Patterson v. McLean Credit Union.* Court ruled that whereas the 1966 Civil Rights Act forbids racial discrimination in making contracts, it does not apply to racial harassment on the job or other forms of discrimination after a person has been hired. This part of the ruling was reversed by the 1991 Civil Rights Act. |
| 1995 | *Adarand Constructors Inc. v. Pena.* In another case arising from minority set-asides (similar to the *Croson* case), the Court ruled that use of racial preferences in federal programs must be subjected to "strict scrutiny," meaning that they must serve a "compelling need" and must be "narrowly tailored." |
| 2003 | *Grutter v. Bollinger et al.* The Court reaffirmed *Bakke* principle that race may be considered along with other factors in public higher education admissions for the educational purpose of having a diverse student body. |
| 2003 | *Gratz v. Bollinger et al.* The Court ruled that in public higher education admissions, it is not acceptable to award a fixed number of points toward admission for applicants belonging to underrepresented minority groups. Together with *Grutter*, this case established that consideration of race may occur only in a flexible manner, along with other factors. |

remain the law of the land (except as altered by referenda in California and Washington). In the *Bakke* case, a white medical school applicant, Allan Bakke, challenged an affirmative action plan at the University of California's Davis Medical School. The plan set aside 16 of the school's 100 admissions slots for "economically and/or educationally disadvantaged persons." Although whites were eligible for the special admissions program, only minorities had actually been admitted under it. Bakke contended that the program amounted to illegal discrimination against whites; the university argued it did not because its purpose was to promote the inclusion of groups that were underrepresented in the student body. The Court struck a middle ground in this, its first affirmative action ruling, which had drawn tremendous attention from the media and from advocacy groups on both sides. In a five-to-four vote, it ruled that the Constitution, which governed the actions of a public university, forbade quotas and that the university was operating under a quota system. Thus, it ordered Bakke's admission. However, it also ruled by a different five-to-four vote that public universities could, for the valid educational purpose of having a diverse student body, use racial preferences as long as race was considered along with other factors. Thus, racial preferences were legal; quotas were not.

In the 1996 *Hopwood* case, however, the Fifth U.S. Circuit Court of Appeals ruled, in a case filed by four rejected white applicants to the University of Texas Law School, that the *Bakke* ruling was no longer valid. The circuit court argued that recent Supreme Court rulings showed that the Court had changed its thinking and that the Court had been wrong to rule, as it had, that a diverse student body fostered exposure to diversity of opinion in the classroom. Although the Supreme Court did not accept an appeal of this case, it did subsequently hear two cases, *Grutter v. Bollinger et al.* and *Gratz v. Bollinger et al.*, which involved challenges by rejected white applicants to affirmative action admission policies at the University of Michigan. The *Grutter* case challenged the University of Michigan Law School's admissions policy, which, following the *Bakke* precedent, considered race as one of many factors in order to ensure a diverse student body. The *Gratz* case challenged the university's undergraduate admissions policy, which used a numerical formula that added a fixed number of points for students who were members of underrepresented minorities. (There were a number of other criteria not related to grades or test scores that also added fixed numbers of points, such as being an athlete, from an underrepresented part of the state, or of low socioeconomic status.) The Supreme Court heard these two cases together, and in 2003 it reaffirmed the *Bakke* principle that race could be considered along with other factors in order to ensure diversity in the student body. Thus, it upheld the law school's admissions policy and found that a diverse student body was a sufficiently compelling interest to justify the consideration of race, as long as it was done in a flexible way along with other factors considered in admissions. However, it ruled against the affirmative action plan used in undergraduate admissions. It found that awarding a fixed number of points for being a minority was unacceptable, so that in the *Gratz* case it ruled that the university was using race in an unconstitutional way and ordered the development of a new undergraduate admissions policy. Hence, race can be considered in a flexible way along with other factors, but it cannot be simply awarded a fixed number of points in a formula.

The Supreme Court's *Grutter* ruling permits but does not require affirmative action in public higher education admissions. In California in 1996 and in Washington State in 1998, however, such affirmative action was explicitly banned by referenda. (In California, the referendum passed after the University of California Board of Regents had already voted to end minority preferences in admissions in the University of California system.) Thus, at the end of 2003, consideration of race in higher education admissions for purposes of having a diverse student body is legal in forty-eight states but illegal in California and Washington because of the referenda passed there. However, this could be changed by referenda or legislation in other states; a few such efforts were under consideration in late 2003.

**Private Employment: Hiring Decisions.** A year after its *Bakke* ruling, in 1979 the Court made another major affirmative action decision in *Weber*. In this case, the suit was brought by a white employee against Kaiser Aluminum because of an affirmative action plan that Kaiser and its union, the United Steelworkers, had agreed to. This agreement provided that when minorities were underrepresented in skilled labor positions relative to the local population, one-half of the people trained for placement in these positions would be minorities until the racial mix of the skilled labor force approximated that of the local population (Dreyfuss and Lawrence, 1979). The white employee, Brian Weber, claimed that this amounted to illegal discrimination against whites, but the Court ruled (by a five-to-two majority, with two justices not voting) that it did not. It ruled that if past societal discrimination has caused the underrepresentation of minorities in a work force, racial preferences, including even a quota such as Kaiser's 50 percent provision, is legally permissible. It ruled differently in this case than in *Bakke* because private employers are covered not by the Constitution (which regulates *government* bodies) but by the 1964 Civil Rights Act. Because the purpose of that law was to improve opportunities for minorities, actions consistent with that purpose were found permissible (*New York Times*, 1979a). In general, the principle that past societal discrimination can justify affirmative action has not been accepted as a valid justification for affirmative action by governments, however; in that situation some other justification is required.

In a 1986 ruling, *Sheet Metal Workers*, the Court held that there are even circumstances in which courts may *order* racial preferences in private employment decisions. In this case, hiring occurred through a union hiring hall, and the union involved had been found guilty of racial discrimination. The union had been ordered by a lower court to establish a hiring goal of 29 percent minorities by 1987 to remedy a pattern of discrimination. The Supreme Court upheld that order, ruling six-to-three that where there had been a pattern of "egregious discrimination" the courts could order hiring preferences for minorities as a remedy. It also ruled five-to-four that such court-ordered preferences could include goals and timetables. Thus, not only are minority preferences, goals, and timetables in private employment legal under certain circumstances, but if there is sufficiently strong evidence of discrimination, the courts can even order them.

An important ruling in 1989 was *Ward's Cove v. Antonio*. Although this case did not bear directly on affirmative action, it did have effects that many saw as antithetical to its goals. In part, affirmative action is designed to offset or eliminate subtle practices and employment requirements that have the effect of discrimination. But in *Ward's Cove*, the Court ruled that job requirements that have the effect of excluding minority or female applicants are illegal only if it can be proved that their intent is discriminatory. That is, this ruling said that such requirements are legal unless the person claiming discrimination can prove that there is no valid business reason for the requirements (Dwyer, 1989). However, this ruling was reversed by the 1991 Civil Rights Act (Saltzman and Gest, 1991). This legislation states specifically that job requirements that have the effect of excluding minorities or women are legal only when it can be shown that they have a valid business purpose. The burden of proof falls on any employer who has a job requirement that has such exclusionary effects. For example, if a college degree were required of someone being hired to wash dishes, this requirement might be called into question because it would have the effect of excluding minorities, who are underrepresented among college graduates. Unless it could be shown that having a college degree makes a person a better dishwasher, which is highly dubious, the requirement would be illegal. The 1991 Civil Rights Act also explicitly bans racial and sexual harassment on the job.

### Public Employment Hiring Decisions.

In public employment, race and gender may be considered in hiring if the purpose is to address past discrimination *by the employer.* In the absence of such discrimination, however, consideration of race or gender may be hard to justify. The Supreme Court made its first ruling on public employment hiring decisions in *Firefighters v. Cleveland* in 1986. In this case, the city of Cleveland and a group of minority employees suing it for discrimination had agreed to give black and Hispanic firefighters preferences over whites, even if the whites had more seniority or higher test scores. The firefighters' union sued against the settlement, but the Court ruled that it was a valid way to settle the discrimination suit as long as the two original parties agreed to it. However, the Court indicated that stronger evidence of discrimination would be required for courts to *order* racial preferences than was needed to make such a settlement legal. In 1987, the Court ruled in *United States v. Paradise* that use of quotas in hiring and promotions by public employers is legal and can even be required if the employer (in this case, the Alabama State Police) had a past history of severe discrimination. A month later, in *Johnson v. Transportation Agency,* the Court ruled that either women or minorities could be promoted ahead of slightly more qualified white men to make the work force more representative of the area's population. (This was the first ruling on affirmative action for women.) However, in light of subsequent rulings, it is doubtful whether such a plan would be upheld today unless there was evidence that the employer had engaged in discrimination.

What appears to be a somewhat different viewpoint was outlined in the *Adarand Constructors Inc. v. Pena* case in 1995. Although this case concerned minority set-asides (discussed later), it also addressed federal programs more broadly and clarified and reaffirmed an earlier ruling limiting consideration of race in state and local government programs. In a five-to-four ruling, the Court held that federal affirmative action programs using racial preferences are lawful only if they can withstand the "strict scrutiny" legal test, which means that the reason for using a racial preference must be "compelling" and that the way in which it is used must be "narrowly tailored." Historically, these standards have been difficult, though not always impossible, to meet. These standards were applied in the University of Michigan cases, and the "narrowly tailored" standard was found to have been met in the law school's consideration of race but not in the number formula used in undergraduate admissions. In the case of public employment, these standards mean that consideration of race could be difficult to justify unless the employer itself has discriminated. Finally, it should be noted that state laws are beginning to have some effect. Two states, California and Washington, passed referenda in the 1990s that forbade the use of any racial preference in public hiring. On the other hand, a similar public referendum failed in the city of Houston in 1997. Similar efforts have been started unsuccessfully in other states, suggesting that additional efforts may occur.

### Public Employment: Layoff Decisions.

Also in 1986, about two months before the *Sheet Metal Workers* and *Firefighters* cases, the Court ruled on racial preferences in layoffs. In *Wygand,* a group of white teachers sued over an agreement between the Jackson, Michigan, school board and its teachers' union. The agreement specified that minorities would receive special protection against layoffs. The reasoning was that most of the minority teachers had been recently hired, and if the district was to keep the teaching staff ethnically diverse in the face of layoffs, there would have to be some special protection for minorities, or students would be deprived of diverse teachers. The Court found that this was not a sufficiently strong justification for racial preferences in layoffs, whose effect on innocent whites is more severe than that of hiring preferences. Thus, the Court established that stronger justification is needed in layoff cases than in hiring cases.

**Minority Set-Aside Programs.** Another method of affirmative action that came into common usage in the 1970s and 1980s was the *minority set-aside program.* Under programs of this type, state and local governments set aside a certain portion of their business for companies that are owned by minorities or women. For example, a city that is constructing a new municipal stadium might require that at least 10 percent of the expenditures on the project go to minority-owned companies and at least 10 percent to female-owned companies. These programs are designed to encourage the development of businesses owned by minorities and women, who historically have been largely excluded from business ownership. By 1989, when the Supreme Court first ruled on the legality of this practice, 36 states and 190 cities had some form of set-aside program.

In that ruling, *Croson v. City of Richmond,* the Supreme Court struck down the set-aside program of Richmond, Virginia, on the grounds that the city had not presented sufficient documentation of the need for the program. To justify such programs, the Court ruled, it is necessary to document that there has been past discrimination that limited the opportunities of minorities for business ownership or for minority-owned businesses to effectively compete for government business. This position was reaffirmed by the Court in 1995 in the *Adarand* case, when once again the Court ruled against the use of set-asides unless clear proof of discrimination could be demonstrated. The Court remanded the case back to the lower courts to determine whether the "strict scrutiny" standard had been met. The lower courts found that such strong proof as the Supreme Court ruling required had not been established. Although it is still uncertain just how much proof it takes to justify a set-aside program, it does seem that this form of affirmative action may be difficult to justify because in many cases it will run afoul of the requirement that any government use of racial preferences must be narrowly tailored.

**Minority Scholarships.** Perhaps the least clear area of the law involves minority scholarships. In the *Banneker* case, the Fourth U.S. Circuit Court of Appeals ruled that a scholarship program at the University of Maryland that was limited to African Americans was illegal unless the university could specifically prove that the effects of past discrimination still existed at that specific university (*Journal of Blacks in Higher Education,* 1996/97). In 1995, the Supreme Court refused to hear an appeal of the case but did not rule on its merits. At least in the Fourth U.S. Circuit Court states (Maryland, North Carolina, South Carolina, Virginia, and West Virginia), this ruling may limit the use of minority scholarships. However, its real impact is unclear, for two reasons. First, the case was eventually settled. Second, the student who filed the lawsuit was Hispanic. One could reasonably argue that the program was unfair because it singled out African American students when Hispanic students were also disadvantaged because of societal patterns of discrimination. The end result is that the legal standing of minority scholarships is questionable, especially in the Fourth Circuit states. However, for the various reasons mentioned, no definitive legal standard was set against scholarships for students from underrepresented racial groups. Therefore, they can continue to be used, especially outside the fourth circuit, but could at some time in the future be subject to legal challenge. However, their use has been reduced somewhat in recent years in response to threats of lawsuits by groups opposed to affirmative action, some of which have written to universities and threatened to sue unless the scholarship criteria were changed.

**Overview and Impact of Recent Changes.** As of mid-2004, no Supreme Court ruling has involved a blanket rejection of affirmative action. In its most recent rulings, *Grutter* and *Gratz,* the Court upheld the need for a diverse student body as a compelling interest and clarified what is and is not a narrowly tailored (and therefore legal) consideration of race in affirmative action plans. Still, the Court does seem to be requiring stronger justification for affirmative action and requiring more narrowly tailored plans than in the past. In effect, the rulings since the late 1980s place limits on affirmative action that had not been in effect before. Precisely what all of those limits are may await future court cases and possibly legislation.

We do know, though, that how far affirmative action preferences can go depends on a variety of factors: whether hiring, student admissions, or government contracting is involved and also the specific circumstances of any particular case. Many of the Court decisions on affirmative action have been divided. Often, as was the case in *Grutter*, they have been based on five-to-four votes, and in some cases the justices have written as many as six different legal opinions. Accordingly, what happens in future rulings may depend in part on who is appointed to the Court when future vacancies occur. And, as noted earlier, the standing of affirmative action can also be changed by state referenda and legislation.

We already know that there have been significant impacts on opportunities for minorities in states where affirmative action was at least temporarily curtailed by court rulings or referenda. Overall, in the four states in which affirmative action preferences in public university admissions were banned in 1996, minority applications to medical school fell 17 percent from the previous year (Campbell, 1997). As described earlier, there were sharp declines in the number of minority students entering the University of Texas Law School. Overall, the enrollment of underrepresented minority students at Texas's four state medical schools fell by 25 percent. Nationally, the number of minority students admitted to all medical schools fell from 2,000 in 1994 to 1,770 in 1997 (Chenoweth, 1998). This led a congressional advisory committee to declare in 1998 that members of minority groups had become "critically underrepresented" in medical schools (Mangan, 1998). Since the *Grutter* ruling, the University of Texas has indicated that it plans to resume affirmative action, beginning in fall 2005. However, Texas A&M has indicated that it will not.

After California's ban on affirmative action went into effect in 1997 (after a legal battle over the referendum that banned affirmative action), sharp drops in minority undergraduate enrollment were noted on five University of California campuses. At San Diego, Berkeley, and Los Angeles, the number of African Americans admitted dropped by nearly half (Haworth, 1998; Healy, 1998b). At Berkeley, the number of Hispanic freshmen also dropped by nearly half, and the law school freshman class in 1997 had just one African American (*Chronicle of Higher Education*, 1997c). Statewide, the enrollment of African American freshmen in U.C. law schools fell by 63 percent, and the number of Latino freshmen fell by 36 percent (Basinger, 1998). Some of these declines have since been reversed, but on the flagship campuses, African American and Latino/a enrollment remains significantly reduced. In the U.C. medical schools, on the other hand, there was little change in the number of African American and Latino/a first-year students. California's medical schools have not relied heavily on test scores and grades in making offers of admission, looking instead at a wider range of factors. Therefore, they were less affected by the abolition of affirmative action preferences (Basinger, 1998).

## Alternatives to Affirmative Action: Are There Other Routes to Equal Opportunity?

As discussed earlier, the consideration of race to bring about greater diversity in hiring and college admissions has been abolished by law in California and Washington. Such affirmative action in higher education admissions was temporarily interrupted by court rulings, now overturned, in several other states. Largely for these reasons, there has been considerable interest in other ways to increase opportunities for underrepresented groups and to make work forces and student bodies more diverse. Two possibilities have generated increasing discussion in recent years. One applies to higher education admissions; the other could be used in any type of decision in which preferences for underrepresented racial groups may have been used in the past.

The approach focusing specifically on higher education admissions involves changing admissions criteria to those that do not produce the same disadvantage for minority groups as some of the criteria currently in use. For example, high school grades or class rank are as good as or better than standardized test scores at predicting college grades, but their use will not exclude minorities to the same extent that standardized tests do. In Texas, after the *Hopwood* decision, the legislature passed a law that any student in the top 10 percent of his or her high school class would be eligible for admission to the University of Texas and Texas A&M University regardless of SAT score. (Now that *Hopwood* has been reversed, however, this law may be changed. The University of Texas, but not Texas A&M, is planning to resume affirmative action.)

In the state's many schools that are overwhelmingly black or Hispanic, the number of students eligible for admission to the University of Texas was increased by the 10 percent law. It was also increased in working-class and rural schools with predominantly white populations. Even so, the percentage of black and Hispanic students admitted to both Texas and Texas A&M under this law in 1998 was lower than it had been in 1996, when affirmative action was used. However, it was higher than in 1997, the year it was eliminated (Creech, 1998). Thus, the top 10 percent policy did raise minority enrollment from its level under traditional admissions criteria, but it did not increase it to the level that had been attained under affirmative action. One reason may be that some predominantly African American and Latino high schools are also predominantly poor, and in many cases students, even if admitted, can afford to attend only if they are also given financial aid (Healy, 1998a). Also, this approach does not help good minority students in integrated schools with high average achievement levels, and like affirmative action, it has been criticized as unfair to white students with high test scores. Finally, Bowen and Bok (1998, p. 273) point out that over the longer run it could create an incentive for students to take easier courses or to attend less competitive high schools, which could actually reduce students' preparation for college. However, screening tests showed that very few of the minority students admitted under this policy needed any remedial education (Guinier, 1998). Another problem is that it has eliminated virtually all flexibility in admissions decisions: By 2003, about 70 percent of University of Texas freshmen were automatic admits under the 10 percent law.

Because it may increase opportunities for minorities without considering race, this approach has been considered in other areas where minority preferences are no longer legal. For example, the University of California decided in 1999 to admit all students in the top 4 percent of their high school classes. However, because the California policy, unlike the one in Texas, applied only to getting into some school in the system, not any specific school, it had little impact on admissions to top campuses such as Berkeley and UCLA, where minority enrollment continued to lag behind levels before affirmative action was eliminated. Similar limitations hampered a new admissions system in Florida, whose current governor opposes affirmative action. Like California's, the Florida policy does not guarantee admission to any particular institution. And at the top two campuses, the Univeristy of Florida and Florida State, black enrollment remained lower in 2003 than it had been in 2000, before the new policy replaced affirmative action (*Journal of Blacks in Higher Education*, 2003, p. 48).

Another widely proposed alternative is to base affirmative action preferences on social class (socioeconomic status) rather than race or ethnicity (Schrag, 1995;

Kahlenberg, 1996). Some argue that this is more fair because it gives no preference to a minority student from a wealthy, highly educated background while offering some help to working-class white students who also face significant barriers to their education. In addition, it is more likely to survive a legal challenge because the courts have not historically viewed socioeconomic status as a "suspect category" like race because it is not addressed by civil rights laws or by the Constitution. However, critics of this approach have pointed out that it does nothing to address discrimination that has specifically occurred on the basis of race, ethnicity, or gender and that need-based scholarships have been less successful in attracting minority students than minority-targeted scholarships (National Women's Law Center, 1998). Critics also note that a preference for people of low socioeconomic status or high economic need would in practice be difficult to accomplish, as is indicated by the complex formulas being used for student aid. To incorporate such formulas into admissions decisions would make the process even more complex and difficult than it already is.

Some programs have also targeted underrepresented areas, without regard to race. At UCLA, a scholarship program was targeted toward top students in Los Angeles County high schools that historically had sent few students to UCLA. This program was credited with recruiting a significant number of excellent minority students (AAD Project, 1998). Nonetheless, the number of African American and Hispanic students admitted to UCLA was still lower than it was when the university was able to include a preference for underrepresented minority groups in its admission process. Thus, whereas such geographically targeted programs appear to offer some possibilities of increasing the number of minorities admitted, they do not seem to be as effective as affirmative action.

## ▶ IMMIGRATION POLICY

Immigration policy has long been controversial in the United States and has at times been used in openly racist ways. For about the first half of the twentieth century, Oriental Exclusion Acts kept people from China, Japan, and other parts of Asia from migrating to the United States. Quota systems, dating back to 1921, were also used until the 1960s to limit the number of southern and eastern Europeans. About 84 percent of the national quotas went to northern and western Europe (Great Britain and Germany alone accounted for about 60 percent), 14 percent to southern and eastern Europe, and 2 percent to the rest of the world (Thomlinson, 1976, p. 301).

In part, opposition to immigration is based on the belief that immigrants contribute to the unemployment problem and—because they will sometimes work for relatively low wages—put Americans out of work and hold down their wages. However, because of the money they spend, immigrants in fact usually create more jobs than they take (McCarthy and Valdez, 1985; Muller, 1985). With the possible exception of education, they also generally pay more in taxes than they take back in the form of government services (McCarthy and Valdez, 1985). Exceptions to these patterns do occur, though, when very large surges of poorly educated immigrants come into localized areas, as happened in California in the late 1980s and early 1990s (McCarthy and Valdez, 1997).

However, much of the opposition to immigration arises from plain and simple ethnocentrism. Some Americans simply do not want to admit people who are "different from us," even though they or their ancestors were once immigrants, too. Thus, it is hardly surprising that anti-immigration groups such as the Know Nothing party and the Ku Klux Klan have been not only anti-immigration but also anti-Jewish, anti-Catholic, and antiblack. It also explains why immigration quotas in the past heavily favored western Europe.

Immigrants arriving in an Atlantic liner. Many Americans who favor a restrictive policy in immigration seem to forget that they too are the children of immigrants.   Courtesy Library of Congress

In 1965 new legislation phased out the quota system over a three-year period. The annual limits on immigration were changed to 120,000 from the Western Hemisphere and 170,000 from the Eastern Hemisphere, with a maximum of 20,000 from any one country in the latter. This policy has obviously made immigration much more open to people from outside northern and western Europe than was previously the case. In 1978 the hemisphere distinction was dropped, and immigration was simply limited to 290,000 per year, with not more than 20,000 from any one country. In 1990 the annual limit was temporarily raised to 700,000, then set at 675,000 for 1994 and years thereafter. The actual number of legal immigrants per year has been larger, however, because some immigrants are exempted from these limits. The parents, spouses, and unmarried children of U.S. citizens could enter the United States without numerical restrictions until 1996, when family was added as a category of admission under the larger annual quotas. Exceptions to the limits are still made for political refugees. Thus, legal immigration averaged around 450,000 per year in the 1970s, around 740,000 per year in the 1980s, around 900,000 in the 1990s, and nearly a million a year in the first few years of the twenty-first century (U.S. Citizenship and Immigration Service, 2003c, Table 1). These figures include about a million of the immigrants who were admitted under an amnesty in the late 1980s and early 1990s.

Today's immigrants are far more likely than in the past to come from non-European countries. In 2002, for example, about 32 percent of all immigrants came from Asia. Nearly 21 percent came from Mexico, 13.5 percent from elsewhere in Central or South America, and 9 percent from the Caribbean. The top five countries from which immigrants arrived were Mexico, India, China, the Philippines, and Vietnam (U.S. Citizenship and Immigration Service, 2003b, Table 1). Although immigration from Europe is less common than in the past, refugees from the turmoil in eastern Europe have raised the percentage arriving from Europe to around 17 percent in the mid-1990s, and this percentage remained above 16 percent in

2002. Because most immigrants today are from Asia, Latin America, or the Caribbean, they are more racially diverse than ever before, and immigration is one of the most important reasons for America's increasing diversity.

## Illegal Immigration and the 1986, 1990, and 1996 Immigration Reform Laws

We know that actual immigration into the United States is well above the legal limits, although we do not know by how much. For example, some estimates are based on the numbers caught trying to enter illegally, but there are two common problems with such estimates. First, they are often too high because some of the same people are caught two or more times. Second, most who enter illegally across the Mexican border return to Mexico on their own rather than remaining permanently in the United States. The best estimates are that in 2000, there were around 7 to 8 million undocumented aliens in the United States, with the U.S. Citizenship and Immigration Service (2003a) favoring the lower end of this range and the U.S. Census Bureau (2001d, p. A6) favoring the higher end. (The actual census estimate was about 10 million, but that includes 2 million whose status the Citizenship and Immigration Service does not regard as illegal.) These estimates suggest net illegal immigration of around 350,000 per year in the late 1990s (U.S. Citizenship and Immigration Service, 2003a).

Illegal immigrants enter the United States in two main ways. One is the Mexican border, which at one time was not particularly well patrolled but has become more so in recent years. The other, which may be of equal importance, is that people enter legally and then overstay their visas or, less often, present forged documents at ports of entry. Vining (1979) found that in the 1970s, about 500,000 to 700,000 more people were arriving by air in the United States than were departing each year. If every legal immigrant arrived by air (which is not the case), these figures would still suggest more than 100,000 illegal arrivals by air each year, and they do not take into account people who arrive by land or sea and overstay their visas. As noted earlier, the best estimates are that in the late 1990s a net total of about 350,000 people per year were entering the United States illegally—a large number but well below estimates often reported by the popular press.

Because of the continuing problem of illegal immigration, adjustments were made in immigration laws in 1986 and again in 1990 and 1996. The 1986 Immigration Reform and Control Act (IRCA) attempted to resolve the problem of illegal immigration in two ways: to legalize through an amnesty program those who were already here and to eliminate the main incentive for illegal immigration by preventing employers from hiring illegal aliens. About 2.5 million people were admitted under the amnesty provision between 1989 and 1991 (U.S. Bureau of the Census, 1993a, p. 10). For the first time, IRCA established penalties for employers who knowingly hire illegal aliens, putting the burden on employers to ascertain that their employees are legally present in the United States. A key part of the 1996 legislation was to strengthen requirements for employers to verify the legality of people they hire. The idea behind these rules is that the main reason people enter the United States illegally is economic and that if illegal immigrants cannot get jobs, they will have no reason to immigrate.

Although the theory behind this provision is appealing, its effectiveness has been limited and its side effects substantial. A joint study by the Rand Corporation and Urban Institute (1990) shows that illegal immigration fell by about 15 percent the first year IRCA was in effect, but after that there was little decline (see also Stevenson, 1990). On the other hand, it appears that the law did lead to an increase in hiring discrimination. When the law was being debated, concern was expressed that it might lead to an increase in ethnic discrimination against people who looked or sounded "foreign." For this reason, Congress mandated a study, which found that during the first year IRCA was in effect, about one in ten employers in the United States discriminated on the basis of foreign appearance or accent. In cities such as New York, Los Angeles, and Chicago, which have large Asian and Latino/a populations, 18 to 29 percent of all employers discriminated (General Accounting Office, 1990; Pear, 1990). Another study found that actual discrimination may not have increased, but the real wages and benefits of Mexican American workers declined after IRCA went into effect, apparently because fear of discrimination kept workers from looking for higher-paying jobs (Davila, Pagan, and Grau, 1998). Thus, the discouraging evidence is that IRCA's ban on hiring illegal immigrants had only a small effect on illegal immigration but did lead to increased job and wage disadvantages for Mexican Americans and possibly to more discrimination against Latino/a and Asian workers in some parts of the country.

Why didn't the law work? There appear to be three reasons. First, there are too many different forms of identification that job applicants can use to demonstrate legality, some of which are easily forged. A national identification card has been suggested as a remedy, but this has been criticized on the basis of civil liberties because such a card could be used to keep track of political dissenters. Second, there is a more fundamental reason for IRCA's ineffectiveness. Given the great disparities in income and wealth between the United States and its neighbors to the south, there are very strong incentives for people to look for a better economic future in the United States. This is exacerbated by the rapid population growth of Mexico and other Latin American countries. Over the next forty-five years, for example, Mexico's population is expected to soar from its present level of 105 million—to more than 150 million—an increase of more than 40 percent (Population Reference Bureau, 2003). As this population pressure increases, so will pressure for immigration to the United States. If the North American Free Trade Agreement (NAFTA), approved in 1993, had succeeded in its goal of encouraging economic development in Mexico, some of this pressure could have been offset. However, economic difficulties in Mexico and elsewhere in Central America have prevented this from happening. Even at the time that IRCA was passed in 1986, however, many of its critics argued that the immigration limits then in effect were too low and should have been raised. They were not raised because of popular opposition to immigration in much of the United States.

Third and finally, the incentive for illegal immigration remains because employers, including U.S. corporations, want the cheap labor that illegal immigrants provide. Often, big companies try to avoid direct responsibility by contracting work out to subcontractors who use illegal immigrants. Thus, in 2003, when Wal-Mart was caught using cleaning subcontractors who employed 250 illegal immigrants at sixty of its stores in twenty-one states (CNN, 2003), the corporation could claim that it was the contractors, not Wal-Mart, who were at fault. Nonetheless, the use of such labor by contractors is widely known to occur in janitorial services, agricultural labor, clothing production, and other business activities dependent on cheap labor.

By 1990, it was evident that IRCA had done little to reduce illegal immigration and that it was continuing to rise. Consequently, in 1990 Congress passed amendments to the act to raise the immigration limits, in an attempt to set a realistic limit for immigration of all types. The new overall number to be accepted each year was set at 700,000, which is higher than the numbers admitted annually throughout the 1980s. Some spaces were reserved for immigrants with occupational skills that are scarce in the United States or who are in a financial position to hire employees once they arrive here. Visas were also set aside for immigrants from thirty-five countries—who had been largely shut out because priority had been given to people with families already in the United States—with a special provision for people from Ireland, many of whom had arrived illegally in the 1980s. The limit of 700,000 immigrants per year ran through 1994, with the limit "permanently" set at 675,000 per year beginning in 1995 (Weeks, 1992). Exemptions for family members to enter above the limits were eliminated and were replaced by a provision making family an admission category in the larger annual limit. Exceptions for refugees remained, however. Additional legislation passed in 1996 focused on better enforcement of immigration laws. This legislation strengthened requirements that employers verify the legality of people they hire and doubled the number of border patrol agents. It also sought to curb the use of fraudulent documents and gave some financial assistance to states and public hospitals for costs associated with illegal immigrants.

## Immigration Realities and Immigration Policy

Not only the United States but all affluent countries are experiencing increased immigration pressure. As long as a majority of the world's population lives in countries with high poverty rates and low standards of living, people will try to immigrate to countries such as the United States, Canada, and those in western Europe. Many will try to enter illegally; with borders as extensive as those of the United States, it will be impossible to stop anywhere near all of them. Also, until fairly recently the limits on immigration in the United States were more restrictive than those in some other industrialized countries. As recently as the 1980s, several countries, including Canada, the Netherlands, Sweden, and Norway, admitted immigrants at a higher rate (computed from Europa Publications, 1989). Because of upheaval in eastern Europe, Germany admitted refugees in 1992 at a very high rate, in addition to ordinary immigrants and guest workers. Since then, however, immigration has increased in the United States and decreased or been restricted in many European countries. Between 1995 and 2000, the net rate of immigration (in-migrants minus out-migrants) per 1,000 was 5.1 in Canada, 4.5 in the United States, between 2 and 2.6 in Germany, the Netherlands, Italy, Great Britain, and Norway, and lower in Sweden, France, and Japan (United Nations Population Division, 2003). Because economic pressures for immigration remain strong, undocumented immigration has continued, even though the U.S. has both increased its legal immigration limits and increased enforcement of immigration laws.

Should the legal level of immigration be raised further in the United States, to make it more consistent with the actual pressure for immigration? Some answer yes, based on both the difficulty of enforcing present laws and on the fact that immigration brings important benefits to society. Immigrants fill jobs for which trained workers are in short supply in the United States, and new jobs are created by their buying power. Even some studies of illegal immigrants have shown that they have no downward effect on wages (Massey, cited in Bean and Tienda, 1987). In general, the wages of native-born workers, whether male or female, minority or nonminority, and skilled or unskilled, are only weakly correlated to the amounts of immigration in different areas of the country (Smith and Edmonston, 1997).

There has been much research on the fiscal effects of immigration, with mixed findings. For example, Simon (1990) found that the average immigrant family receives $1,404 per year in all forms of publicly funded assistance during the first five years and $1,941 thereafter. In contrast, the average nonimmigrant family receives more, $2,279. However, more recent data including only need-based assistance show that immigrants do receive more need-based assistance (Food Stamps, Medicaid, Temporary Assistance to Needy Families [TANF]) than nonimmigrants: about $1,980 per immigrant household and $1,325 per nonimmigrant household in 2001 (Camarota, 2003). The overall percentage of immigrants receiving some form of public assistance, around 23 percent, is higher than for the nonimmigrant population, about 15 percent. The main reason is that immigrants often have low-paying jobs that include no health insurance, so they are more likely to receive Medicaid. However, they are not much more likely to receive either food stamps or TANF, and 79 percent of immigrants who receive public support work, compared with 67 percent among nonimmigrants (Camarota, 2003). Immigrants' education levels often are low, which relegates them to low-paying jobs with few if any benefits.

Still, the long-run national fiscal impact of immigration is usually positive. Over their lifetimes, the typical immigrant and his or her children pay about $80,000 more in taxes than they receive in benefits at the federal, state, and local levels combined (Simon, 1990). It is true that without federal assistance, some states such as California, which receive large numbers of immigrants, may incur net fiscal burdens, especially in the short run (Smith and Edmonston, 1997). However, studies underestimate the true effects of immigration on tax collection because they do not count taxes paid by businesses formed by immigrants. When these taxes are added to the total, the net fiscal benefits of immigration become even larger (S. Moore, 1998). Studies also indicate that economic growth is correlated with population growth, and immigration is one way to maintain population growth in the face of the low U.S. birthrate. Finally, many believe that the cultural diversity brought by immigrants is an important source of adaptability and innovation in society.

Nonetheless, a great many Americans would like to see immigration reduced. Indeed, this tendency is seen in nearly every country in the world that admits substantial numbers of immigrants—which, if nothing else, certainly illustrates the near universality of ethnocentrism. Assimilationists are concerned about both the overall number of immigrants and the fact that a few countries account for an especially large share. Large numbers from one country may make it easier for immigrants to retain their own culture rather than blend in.

Unfortunately, some opposition to immigration is, and always has been, motivated by a desire to keep out racial groups different from the majority. This is why, for most of the first half of the twentieth century, immigration was closed to Asians and to nearly everyone else who was not from western or northern Europe. This opposition also played a role in an initiative and referendum, Proposition 187, passed in California in 1994. This law prohibited giving state-financed services, including health services and public education, to illegal immigrants and their children. However, the law was never allowed to take effect because the federal courts declared it unconstitutional as an attempt by a state to regulate immigration, which is the exclusive right of the federal government. A 1982 Supreme Court ruling, *Plyler v. Doe*, had found it unconstitutional to deny public education to children because their parents were illegal immigrants. Although the official arguments made by organizations supporting Proposition 187 focused on enforcing the law and on supposed economic effects of immigration, comments made by its supporters showed that some of the opposition was racially motivated. The founder of Stop Immigration Now, for example, said, "I have no intention of being the object of conquest, peaceful or otherwise, by Latinos, Asians, Blacks, or Arabs." Another supporter said, "Ninety percent of the crimes around here seem to be by Hispanics. Last year I went back to Michigan and I did not hear a thing in Spanish, and it felt good" (Hasian and Delgado, 1998). The ruling that Proposition 187 was unconstitutional was appealed for a time, but the appeal was dropped after the California governorship changed hands in 1998.

In this context, it is important to recognize, as these statements show, that some opposition to immigration is motivated by racial and ethnic prejudice. It is also important to keep in mind that the United States is a nation made up almost entirely of immigrants and that—aside from sudden floods of immigrants that overwhelm an area's ability to absorb them—those who are already here gain from immigration a number of benefits, which is sometimes forgotten amid the worry about increased competition for jobs and the fears about cultures different from our own. Thus, it may well be that the benefits of immigration outweigh the costs. Finally, many argue that it is hardly fair for a nation with the great wealth of the United States, and a nation that consumes such a large share of the world's wealth, to post a "Keep Out" sign at its boundaries, particularly when that nation itself is populated by immigrants and the sons and daughters of immigrants.

## ▶ THE RELATIVE IMPORTANCE OF RACE AND CLASS IN AMERICAN SOCIETY

The final issue, to which we now turn, is an intellectual debate more than a policy debate, but it carries important implications for public policy as well: the relative importance of *racial discrimination* versus *social class* as causes of inequality in American society today.

The controversy began with the publication of William J. Wilson's (1978) *Declining Significance of Race*, discussed in various parts of this book. The controversial part of Wilson's book was his conclusion, suggested by the title, that disadvantages linked to social class (income, education, and occupation) have become much more important than racial discrimination as a cause of black social disadvantages today. He based this conclusion on the following major observations. First, there has been a significant decline in open employment discrimination in the United States since World War II. In other words, it has become much less common (as well as illegal) for employers to openly refuse to hire someone because he or she is black or to have a policy of paying blacks less for the same work. (This change is discussed at greater length in Chapters 6 through 9.) However, it should be noted that the extent of true change is debatable; there is still considerable racial discrimination today, but it is more subtle and more underground (Feagin and Sikes, 1994; Feagin, 2000). This is one of the points that has made Wilson's argument controversial.

As we saw in Chapter 9 and again in our discussion of affirmative action in this chapter, recent black college graduates have become the base of a growing black middle class, largely because previously closed opportunities have been opened by affirmative action. Thus, Wilson concludes that the younger members of this class in particular are doing quite well economically. However, Wilson acknowledges that they still experience considerable discrimination in the residential, social, and educational arenas.

Totally apart from this growing middle class is a large and perhaps growing segment of the black population that Wilson called an *underclass*. This group, mostly falling below the poverty level and living in the inner cities, is beset with problems of unemployment and underemployment and has probably become worse off, not better off, since the 1970s. However, Wilson argues that it is not racial discrimination but poverty itself that is this group's main problem. Thus, although blacks are overrepresented in this group because of past discrimination, it is not present-day discrimination that is *keeping* them in their unfortunate position, according to Wilson. Rather, changes in the economy make this group in large part unemployable. (For a different analysis that reaches a somewhat similar conclusion, see Wilhelm, 1980, especially pp. 108–109.) As manufacturing employment has declined, the availability of low-skill jobs has also decreased (Holzer, 1996; Moss and Tilly, 2001a). Because of past discrimination, however, lower-class, inner-city blacks lack the skills needed for jobs that are growing, and there are fewer and fewer low-skill jobs for which they can compete. Thus, they experience high unemployment, often have to move from one short-term, dead-end job to another, and have little chance to escape from this unfortunate situation. According to Wilson, the problem is not the refusal of employers to hire them because they are black but rather their lack, because of past discrimination, of any marketable skills. Therefore, class, not race, is the primary cause of black disadvantage today, according to Wilson.

Wilson has elaborated on this argument in *The Truly Disadvantaged* (1987) and in *When Work Disappears* (1996). In these books, he argues that continuing losses of manufacturing employment, because of economic shifts, have had both direct and indirect effects on inner-city blacks and to a sizable but lesser extent on Latinos/as. There have also been several important indirect effects. One is the disruption of social institutions in the inner city. As jobs have left and conditions have worsened in the inner city, the economic conditions of those living there have also worsened, and the middle class—of all races—has fled. One effect has been to disrupt and undermine neighborhood institutions such as churches and businesses. For the same reasons, poverty and unemployment among African Americans and Latinos/as, who live disproportionately in the inner-city areas that are losing jobs, have become concentrated. In other words, if you are black or Hispanic and poor, it is far more likely that many or most of your neighbors will be poor than if you are white and poor, and it is far more likely that many of the people in your neighborhood will be out of work (W. J. Wilson, 1987). According to Wilson, this concentrates the problems associated with poverty and, for young people, reduces the number of role models they see working in stable jobs. Concentrated poverty heightens the problems of the neighborhood and makes it harder for people to escape poverty. Finally, according to Wilson, it leads to other conditions, such as family disruption and nonmarital childbearing, which, although not the cause of inner-city poverty, may well make it worse.

*The Declining Significance of Race* (W. J. Wilson, 1978) was a controversial book. One reason was because it was easily misinterpreted to suggest that America's racial problem had been solved (Pettigrew, 1980). As the critics emphatically point out, there is nothing approaching economic equality between the races in America (on this point, see Chapter 9). However, a careful reading of Wilson will clearly show that he certainly never intended to claim there is racial equality, although his title does encourage misinterpretation (Payne, 1979, p. 138; Pettigrew, 1980). As Willie (1979, p. 16) points out, such broad generalizations as "economic class is now a more important factor than race in determining job placement for blacks" (W. J. Wilson, 1978, p. 120) also encourage the interpretation (which many whites would like to make) that America's racial problem is largely solved. In my judgment, a careful reading of Wilson's entire book would not support such an interpretation, although the title and some overly broad generalizations probably do.

The more empirical criticisms of Wilson's work focus on somewhat different issues. Wilson does not disagree with his critics that blacks on the whole have lower incomes than whites[1] or that serious and rapid action is needed on the problem of black poverty (see Wilson, 1979, p. 175). The real argument, as has already been suggested, is over the *reasons* for black poverty and over the degree to which middle-class blacks have really gained a socioeconomic status comparable to that of middle-class whites. On the latter point, it is quite clear that although the income gap has narrowed for younger, highly educated blacks and whites, it has not disappeared. Recent data from a national study of black graduates of elite colleges and universities show that even when they graduate from such top schools, blacks *still* receive lower incomes than white graduates (Bowen and Bok, 1998). Another analysis by R. Farley (1984), shows that even if they had the typical social characteristics of white men and worked the same number of hours, black men would still have received only 88 percent of the white male income. The incomes of women of both races were substantially lower. More recent data show little change. For example, among young adult college graduates working full-time in 2001, black men earned only about 87 percent of what white men earned, and black women earned about 94 percent of what white women earned and 73 percent of what white men earned (calculated from U.S. Census Bureau, 2002i). The figures for Hispanics are similar to those for African Americans, showing that even at the same level of education and working year-round, black and Hispanic workers are paid less than non-Hispanic whites.

All of this research suggests significant racial inequality *independent* of class inequality (as Wilson's critics claim). Furthermore, both R. Farley (1984) and Bowen and Bok (1998) found that the black-white gap persisted after controls for

---

[1]Although he does argue that treating blacks "as a whole" masks important socioeconomic differences within the black population.

A white male manager interviews an African American male applicant. Recent studies using discrimination testing, interviews with middle-class black men, and interviews with employers have shown that black men still experience considerable discrimination in the workplace.

other factors even in the most highly educated group, although, again, the gap did narrow. Thus, evidence has been found for a declining *but continuing* "significance of race." The reason may be that although it is more subtle and more underground than in the past, racial discrimination continues to occur. This has been clearly documented by discrimination-testing studies, like those described in Chapter 14, and by interview studies of African American managers and professionals, almost all of whom report personal experiences of discrimination (Feagin and Sikes, 1994). Even W. J. Wilson (1996) has ackowledged that members of his own research team found considerable evidence of discrimination against black male job seekers by Chicago employers that they surveyed (Kirschenman and Neckerman, 1991). And Massey and Denton (1993) have presented strong evidence that one reason for the concentration of African Americans in neighborhoods with high poverty rates is racial discrimination in the sale and rental of housing (see also Yinger, 1995; Turner et al., 2002).

Part of the racial difference in unemployment appears to be linked to race, not class. Educational differences alone cannot account for the disproportionate unemployment of either blacks or Hispanics. Part of it appears to be a product of the segregation that restricts minority groups to areas with limited job opportunities (J. E. Farley, 1987b; Kasarda, 1989a, 1989b, 1990; Holzer and Ihlanfeldt, 1996) and the potential gains to some whites from keeping African Americans unemployed (J. E. Farley, 1987b).

Edwards (1979), S. M. Collins (1993, 1997), and Marrett (1980) have pointed to another potential problem in W. J. Wilson's (1978) argument: Even though the black middle class has grown and has narrowed the gap with the white middle class, the position of blacks and other minorities in the middle class is much less secure than that of the white middle class. Historically—as Wilson himself stresses—blacks and other minorities have tended to gain in good economic times and to lose in bad. And through the economic ups and down of the 1990s and the first years of the twenty-first century, attacks on affirmative action and other policies aimed at helping minorities have continued. Affirmative action considering race among other factors to promote diversity in higher education was upheld by the Supreme Court in 2003 by the thinnest possible margin, five to four, and even then was subject to a number of restrictions. Given these facts, there is certainly a risk of minority losses. Any additional retreat on affirmative action would further limit black entry into the middle class, and even with affirmative action, the principle of last hired, first fired still holds true. In Detroit, for example, when layoffs became necessary in the city's police force, seniority rules required that most of them would be black because they were the ones most recently hired (under the city's affirmative action program). Despite affirmative action, African Americans and, even more so, Hispanics remain less likely than non-Hispanic whites to attend and graduate from college. Rapid cost increases in higher education caused by state funding cutbacks in the early 2000s are likely to have disproportionate impacts on black and Hispanic students. Thus, it seems a fair criticism of Wilson's work to warn that however much race may have declined in importance relative to class, there is a very real danger that it could increase in importance again, especially given the intermittent economic difficulty the country has experienced in recent years.

Another point on which Wilson has received criticism concerns the reasons for the disproportionate number of blacks in the impoverished underclass and the reasons that the people in this underclass cannot escape from it. It is Wilson's claim that blacks are overrepresented in the underclass because of past discrimination and that it is very hard to escape from the underclass because of the lack of low-skill jobs in today's economy. Accordingly, Wilson argues that present-day racial discrimination is *not* very important as a cause of disadvantage among the black underclass. On this point, Wilson is vulnerable to criticism. Past racial discrimination and present-day class discrimination (including the institutionalized variety) are, as Wilson says, important reasons for continuing black (and other minority) overrepresentation in the impoverished underclass. However, Wilson is widely and correctly criticized for failing to note the importance of present-day institutionalized racial discrimination as a cause of the problem (Payne, 1979, pp. 134–37; Feagin, 2000, pp. 20–21). Consider our own exploration of institutional discrimination in Chapters 10 to 12 of this book. There is no question that much of the discrimination discussed there occurs on the basis of social class, affecting minorities disproportionately because they are overrepresented among the poor. However, there is also a good deal of institutional discrimination, specifically along the lines of race. In education, we have seen de facto school segregation, linguistic biases against minority students, low teacher expectations of minority students, distorted presentations of minorities in texts and materials, and racial inequities in tracking. Although there certainly are strong class biases in the educational system (Bowles and Gintis, 1976), all of the inequities mentioned here are specifically racial.

Because Wilson notes that the lack of good education plays a central role in perpetuating the minority underclass, it seems clear that institutionalized racial inequalities in education contribute to the problem. The same is true in other areas. To cite one example, we can point to housing discrimination. W. J. Wilson (1980, p. 23) himself states that "the lack of opportunity for underclass blacks forces them to remain in economically depressed ghettoes," which, along with poor ghetto education, "reinforce(s) their low labor market positions." Wilson is right about the effects of ghettoization on black employment when jobs have largely left the ghetto (see, for example, J. E. Farley, 1987b; Kasarda, 1990; Holzer and Ihlanfeldt, 1996). However, he is incorrect in ignoring the crucial role of racial discrimination as a cause of ghettoization (Massey and Denton, 1993; Yinger, 1995; Turner et al., 2002). As we saw in Chapter 11, economic differences between blacks and whites are less important than race as a cause of black-white housing segregation. Because such housing segregation restricts black opportunities in both employment and education, it is, as Wilson notes, an important cause of the problems of the minority underclass. However, Wilson fails to recognize the degree to which racial, as opposed to economic, factors produce that segregation. Thus, we see here, too, an example of the continuing significance of race.

These and other processes of institutional racial discrimination do help to explain why African Americans and other minorities are so overrepresented in the impoverished underclass and why they have so much trouble escaping from it. Further evidence of racial discrimination can be seen in the fact that the minority underclass is worse off than the white underclass. At the lowest levels of occupation and education, blacks and other minorities have substantially lower incomes than whites (Willie, 1979, pp. 62–63). In addition, both African Americans and Hispanic Americans are about three times as likely as non-Hispanic whites to fall below the poverty level, and this pattern has not changed significantly in recent years (U.S. Census Bureau, 2003l, Table 2).

Wilson's critics also point out that deliberate employment discrimination, both individual and institutional, remains more common than appearances might suggest. As described in Chapter 14, discrimination-testing studies have found racial discrimination to be quite common in employment and in other areas of life. Even members of Wilson's own research team have found considerable evidence of employment discrimination in surveys of major Chicago-area employers. Much of this discrimination was based on racial stereotypes, particularly about black men (Kirschenman, 1989, 1990; Kirschenman and Neckerman, 1991; see also Moss and Tilly, 2001a, Chap. 4). W. J. Wilson (1996) has argued that these stereotypes are based partly on reactions by employers to the angry response of black men to the joblessness they have encountered because of deindustrialization in the inner city. Thus, he argues that to some extent, the social and economic forces that have taken jobs from the inner city play an indirect role in discrimination by employers. However, by anyone's definition, including Wilson's, these employers are engaging in racial discrimination.

Perhaps Payne (1979, p. 136) has hit on the best description of the reasons for racial inequality in recent decades: "It is entirely possible that the processes sustaining differentials in racial privilege have become a good deal more fragmented than they once were." In other words, there is now a wider variety of factors causing racial inequality. Today's inequality is a product of a combination of acts of discrimination, the effects of past discrimination, economic disadvantages, and institutional discrimination. Wilson is right about the changes in the economy and their impact on minorities, about increasing class differentiation in the African American and Latino populations, and about the decline in open racial discrimination. However, he understates the effects of institutional discrimination and of subtler forms of individual discrimination, and he does not recognize the relative insecurity of much of the minority middle classes. Thus, it is fair to conclude that both race and class remain economically significant, contributing to a situation in which the *average* economic condition of black and Hispanic Americans is little improved over the past, and the plight of the minority underclass has worsened.

## Summary and Conclusion

In this chapter, we have explored some of the issues in intergroup relations in the United States today: affirmative action, assimilation versus pluralism, immigration policy, and the relative importance of racial discrimination and social class. These and a host of other issues relating to intergroup relations remain unresolved. The outbreaks of racial violence in Los Angeles and other cities in 1992 and in Cincinnati in 2001; the continuing pattern of disproportionate poverty and homelessness among African Americans and Hispanics; the ongoing problem of hate crimes and racial incidents around the country; and continuing political attacks on affirmative action, bilingual education, and immigration all remind us that problems of intergroup relations remain deeply rooted in American society. An intelligent and effective response to these problems will require both compassion and informed knowledge on the part of the American public. Neither by itself is sufficient. It is hoped that this book will help in some way to make people more informed about intergroup relations. Americans must be aware of the historical patterns and the present-day institutional processes and discriminatory behaviors that keep minority groups in a disadvantaged position in present-day society. Furthermore, Americans, particularly those in the majority group, who are least often compelled to do so, must be able to look at the problem from a perspective other than that of their own group. If this book has helped to accomplish these things, its author will regard it as a worthwhile endeavor. Although knowledge and understanding are necessary, however, they alone are not enough. Americans of all racial and ethnic groups must be *motivated* to solve problems of intergroup relations; they must *care* about what happens to people in groups besides their own, including those less fortunate than themselves. No book can make that happen. Only the American public, including you, the reader, can do that.

## Critical Review Questions

1. You are on a committee forming an admissions policy for your college. Design a policy that will ensure that your college has a diverse student body, while at the same time remaining in compliance with the *Grutter* and *Gratz* rulings of the Supreme Court.

2. Would it be better to have affirmative action based on social class instead of or in addition to affirmative action based on race? Why or why not?

3. What have been the actual effects of affirmative action on opportunities for African Americans and other underrepresented minorities? For women? For white men?

4. Discuss some ways in which question wording influences the opinions people express about affirmative action? What does that tell you about these opinions?

5. Discuss the impacts of immigration on American society in recent years. Consider ways in which immigration may either be beneficial or present challenges. Should U.S. immigration policy be changed in any major way?

6. On a scale of 1 to 10, how important is race inequality relative to class inequality as a factor determining the quality of life for African Americans? Why? How about Latino/a Americans? Native Americans?

# GLOSSARY

**achieved status** A position of status attained by something a person does or accomplishes rather than by birth. In class systems, social standing is determined largely by achieved statuses, although *ascribed statuses* also have a sizable influence.

**affirmative action** Any deliberate effort to increase minority representation, such as in a work force or student body. Affirmative action may be limited to more vigorous efforts to recruit minorities or may be extended to preferences in hiring or student admissions. This sometimes includes the use of specific goals and timetables for minority representation.

**Afrocentrism** An effort by African Americans to emphasize and value African history, philosophy, and culture, particularly (but not only) in education. In education, it often involves developing a curriculum centered around African experience and culture.

**amalgamation** The combination of two racial or ethnic groups into one through marriage or other sexual contact. Gradually, the distinction between the two groups becomes blurred, and they come to be regarded as a single group.

**annexation** An expansion of territory by one group to take control over territory formerly under control of another group. This may occur through military conquest, in which the outcome is much the same as in *colonization.* It may also be voluntary, as when residents of an area ask to be annexed. Some cases, such as purchases, fall somewhere between.

**anti-Semitism** *Prejudice* and discrimination against Jewish people.

**ascribed status** Any characteristic or status determined by birth, such as race, sex, or who one's parents are. In *caste systems,* one's social standing is determined by ascribed statuses.

**assimilation** A process whereby a *minority group* and the *dominant group* gradually become integrated into a common culture and social system. Although the dominant group may adapt itself to the minority or absorb certain of its cultural characteristics, more often the minority group must adapt to fit into the culture and social system of the majority. See also *cultural assimilation* and *structural assimilation.*

**attitudinal racism** Racial or ethnic prejudice. See *prejudice.*

**blockbusting** A practice by real-estate agents or speculators that attempts to scare whites into selling their houses at low prices because blacks are supposedly moving into the neighborhood. The speculator purchases the house and then sells it to a black family, often at an inflated price. This practice exploits both black and white homeowners and encourages racial segregation and rapid racial turnover in urban neighborhoods.

**caste system** A system of social inequality with two or more rigidly defined and unequal groups, membership in which is determined by birth and passed from generation to generation. There is ordinarily no opportunity for a person in one group to move into another group of higher status.

**class system** A system of loosely defined, unequal groups in which there is significant but not unlimited opportunity to move into a higher or lower status.

**cognitive dissonance theory** A theory that says we strive to make our attitudes consistent with our behavior, often by developing attitudes to support or justify preexisting behavior. This theory suggests that nondiscriminatory behavior (perhaps to comply with the law) may lead to unprejudiced attitudes. Similarly, racist behavior (say, for personal gain) may lead to racist attitudes as a justifying mechanism.

**colonization** A form of intergroup contact that occurs when one group migrates into an area occupied by another group and subordinates that indigenous group.

**colonized minority** A *minority group* that initially became a part of the society it lives in through conquest or annexation. Colonized minorities usually are subjected to some form of unfree labor and to attacks on their culture and social institutions.

**conflict perspective** A sociological perspective that sees society as dominated by a powerful elite, which controls most of the wealth and power, to the disadvantage of other, less powerful members of the society. Because of this inequality, society tends toward conflict and change, although the power or prestige of the dominant group may for a time lead to a consensus or to the appearance thereof. However, this consensus is temporary: The long-term tendency is toward conflict and change.

**cross-cutting cleavages** The situation in which societal divisions such as race, language, religion, and class all cut along different lines; for example, there are religious divisions within racial groups. Cross-cutting cleavages tend to hold down the amount of intergroup conflict because people have divided loyalties.

**cultural assimilation** A type of *assimilation* in which two or more groups gradually come to share a common culture, that is, similar attitudes, values, language, beliefs, lifestyles, and rules about behavior. Often, the shared culture is much more similar to that of the *majority group* than of the *minority group*, although this is not always the case.

**cultural immersion**  An educational approach whereby children in a *minority group* are systematically exposed to positive role models of the student's own racial or ethnic background and that promotes collective self-worth by teaching students to value their cultural heritage. Schools based on the cultural immersion model have most commonly been developed for black males because of the especially severe risk they face, particularly in impoverished inner-city neighborhoods.

**cultural pluralism**  A pattern in which different racial, ethnic, or other groups retain cultural features that are specific to each group but hold some others that are common to all groups in society.

**de facto segregation**  School *segregation* that is the result not of an official policy of separate schools for different racial groups but of other processes. The main cause is housing segregation, which leads to neighborhood school attendance districts that are, for example, all white or all black.

**de jure segregation**  School segregation that is the result of an official or deliberate policy of having separate schools for different racial groups.

**displacement**, or **displaced aggression**  Similar in meaning to *scapegoating*.

**diversity management programs**  Workplace programs designed to empower all employees to work, produce, and advance in the organization to their full potential by addressing intergroup tensions and conflicts that inhibit productivity and often limit opportunities on the basis of *race*, ethnicity, gender, disability status, or sexual orientation.

**dominant group**  Similar in meaning to *majority group*.

**environmental racism**  A tendency for *minority groups* to be placed at disproportionate risk of exposure to hazardous substances and environmental contaminants. Occurs because relatively powerless minority communities often become locations of hazardous waste disposal sites and sources of labor for work involving exposure to dangerous substances.

**ethnic group**  A group of people who are generally regarded by themselves or others as a distinct group, with such recognition based on social or cultural characteristics such as nationality, language, and religion. Ethnicity, like *race*, tends to be passed from generation to generation and is ordinarily not an affiliation that one can freely drop.

**ethnic stratification**, or **ethnic inequality**  A pattern under which social inequality falls along the lines of *race* or ethnicity. In other words, one or more racial or ethnic groups enjoy an advantage over another group or groups with respect to income, wealth, power, prestige, and so on.

**ethnocentrism**  A tendency to view one's own group as the norm or standard and to view out-groups as not just different but also strange and usually inferior. The ways of the in-group are seen as the natural or the only way of doing things and become a standard against which out-groups are judged.

**false consciousness**  The acceptance—usually by a *subordinate group*—of values, beliefs, or ideologies that do not serve the self-interest of that group. In Marxist analysis, false consciousness often occurs when subordinate groups accept ideologies promoted by the wealthy elite to serve the interests of the elite at the expense of the subordinate groups.

**fee-for-service system**  A system of health care payment in which a fee is collected by a physician for each service performed, such as an office visit, operation, or reading of an x-ray. The doctor is paid for each service in this manner regardless of whether the payment is made by the person receiving the treatment, a private insurance company, or a government program. This system can be contrasted with those in which physicians receive fixed salaries, such as health maintenance organizations (HMOs) or systems of socialized medicine.

**fluid competitive race relations**  A pattern of race relations best described as a *class system* with racial inequalities remaining from a past racial *caste system*. There is little official segregation but often much *de facto segregation*. Minority groups have middle classes but are disproportionately poor. Racial conflict is present but usually kept to a controlled level.

**functionalist perspective**  A sociological perspective stressing the notions that society is made up of interrelated parts that contribute to the effectiveness of the society and that society tends toward consensus, order, and stability. These tendencies are seen as necessary if society is to be effective and efficient. According to this perspective, the absence of these conditions can pose a serious threat to the quality of life in the society and even to the society's ability to continue to function.

**gender inequality**  Inequality between men and women in society, which results in men having greater power, status, and economic security than women.

**gender roles**  Different and unequal roles of men and women. In other words, men and women are expected to behave differently and to carry on different kinds of activities, and men typically are accorded higher status and given greater economic rewards.

**gerrymandering**  The practice of drawing odd-shaped school attendance districts as a way of promoting racial or ethnic *segregation* in the schools. The term has also sometimes been applied to the drawing of odd-shaped election districts to influence the outcome of the election.

**glass ceiling** An informal upper limit that keeps women and minorities from being promoted to the positions of greatest responsibility in work organizations. Glass ceilings may exist without any formal or deliberate attempt to discriminate and for a variety of reasons, including *stereotypes*, cultural conflicts, and favoritism.

**heterosexism** *Institutional discrimination* against homosexuals, male and female, and bisexuals.

**homophobia** *Prejudice* and discrimination against homosexuals, male and female, usually also including prejudice and discrimination against bisexuals.

**ideological racism**, or **racist ideology** The belief that one *race* is superior to another biologically, intellectually, culturally, temperamentally, or morally. Such ideologies usually exist to rationalize or justify domination of one race or *ethnic group* by another and tend to become institutionalized or widely accepted within a culture.

**immigrant minority** A *minority group* that voluntarily migrated into the country or society in which it lives. Ordinarily, these minorities are more readily assimilated than are colonized minorities.

**immigration** Migration of one group into an area controlled by another group. The entering group becomes a part of the *indigenous group's* society. Immigration may be either voluntary or, as in the case of slave importation, involuntary. Bonded or indentured laborers and political refugees fall somewhere between.

**index of dissimilarity** A measure of the amount of housing *segregation* between any two groups, such as blacks and whites. It indicates the percentage of either group that would have to move to attain complete integration (the same mix of the two groups in every block or neighborhood). It can range from zero (fully integrated) to 100 (totally segregated). It is also sometimes called the segregation index.

**indigenous group** A *racial* or *ethnic group* that is well established in an area before the arrival of some new group. An indigenous group may be, but does not have to be, native to the area in which it is established.

**individual racial discrimination**, or **individual behavioral racism** Any behavior by individuals that leads to unequal treatment on the basis of *race* or ethnicity, such as a restaurant owner's refusal to serve Chinese Americans.

**in-group** A group of which a person is a member or with which he or she identifies.

**institutional racism, institutional discrimination** Any arrangement or practice within a social institution or its related organizations that tends to favor one *racial* or *ethnic group* (usually the majority group) over another. It may be conscious and deliberate, as in discriminatory voting laws, or subtle and perhaps unintended, as in industrial location decisions that favor suburban whites over inner-city blacks.

**intergroup education** Any effort, by whatever means, to bring about factual learning about intergroup relations. Education is not intended primarily to change attitudes or opinions, although this may be a common result and is sometimes a latent objective.

**internal colonialism** A theory that argues that *colonized minorities* experience discrimination different in kind or degree from that experienced by *immigrant minorities* and as a result have less upward mobility and less assimilation. Also, a process whereby such minorities are exploited for the economic benefit of the majority group or some segment of it.

**majority group** Any social group that is dominant in a society; that is, it enjoys more than a proportionate share of the wealth, power, or social status in that society. Although majority groups in this sense often are a numerical majority, this is not always the case.

**Marxist theory of discrimination** A theory based on the ideas of Karl Marx. It claims that discrimination hurts working-class whites, as well as *minority group* members, by creating racial divisions within the working class.

**Medicaid program** A federally funded program administered by the states that provides medical care to the poor. The program is limited mostly to the poorest of the poor, excluding many households with incomes below the official poverty level.

**Medicare program** A social insurance program, funded under the Social Security system, that provides medical insurance for the elderly.

**minority group** Any group that is assigned to a subordinate role in society; that is, it has less than its proportionate share of wealth, power, or social status. Minority groups are often but not necessarily a numerical minority in society. Blacks in South Africa were, until recent changes, an example of a minority group that is a numerical majority.

**multiculturalism** An approach, often in education, that explicitly recognizes and values cultural differences and attempts to be inclusive of all racial, ethnic, and cultural groups. In education, this inclusiveness applies to course content and classroom examples and also includes the idea that history, literature, and other subjects can and should be taught from the perspective of a variety of different groups rather than only that of the *dominant group*.

**order perspective** See *functionalist perspective*.

**out-group** A group to which one does not belong and with which one does not identify. Often, this group is culturally or racially different from or in competition with the *in-group*.

**overlapping cleavages**   The situation in which societal divisions such as race, religion, class, and language all cut along the same lines. There tends to be a great deal of conflict because no matter what the issue, people are always on the same side.

**paternalistic race relations**   A pattern of intergroup relations usually found in agricultural, preindustrial societies. It is a form of *caste system* characterized by clearly defined and well-understood racial roles, little outward conflict, much contact between races but also much ritual or etiquette that denotes inequality, and considerable paternalism.

**perspective**   A general approach to or way of looking at an issue; a set of questions to be asked about a topic, a *theory* or set of theories about realities concerning that topic, and a set of *values* concerning potentially controversial issues related to the topic.

**persuasive communication**   Any communication—written, oral, audiovisual, or otherwise—that is specifically intended to influence attitudes, beliefs, or behavior.

**prejudice**   A tendency to overgeneralize in some way, usually negative, toward an entire group. Prejudice can be cognitive (beliefs about a group), affective (dislike of a group), or conative (the desire to behave negatively toward a group).

**projection**   A process whereby people minimize or deny characteristics they see as undesirable in themselves by exaggerating these same characteristics in others. Because such characteristics often are projected onto members of *out-groups*, projection appears to be a significant factor in the dynamics of prejudice.

**race**   A group of people generally considered to be physically distinct in some way from others and regarded by themselves or others as a distinct group.

**racial group**   A group of people who develop a group identity or common culture based on race. The main difference between a racial group and a race is that one need not have a strong group identity or be part of a cultural group to be a member of a race.

**racial profiling**   The practice by law enforcement personnel of stopping and/or searching people on the basis of their race or ethnicity.

**racial steering**   A practice whereby real-estate agents show white customers houses in all-white areas and show black customers houses in all-black or racially mixed areas.

**racism**   Any attitude, belief, behavior, or institutional arrangement that tends to favor one *racial* or *ethnic group* (usually a *majority group*) over another (usually a *minority group*). See also the four types of racism: *prejudice, ideological racism, individual racial discrimination,* and *institutional racism.*

**relative deprivation**   The experience of having less of scarce resources than other individuals or groups, or less than what is believed to be a fair share. It is relative deprivation, not the absolute state of poverty, that often contributes to the development of social movements.

**rigid competitive race relations**   A pattern of race relations resembling an unstable *caste system. Race* largely but not totally defines roles and statuses; division of labor is more complex than in the *paternalistic* pattern, with majority and minority workers sometimes competing because they do similar work, although usually at different wages. Strict *segregation* usually accompanies this pattern as a way the *majority group* protects its threatened social status. The potential for major conflict is nearly always present. This pattern usually is found in newly industrializing societies.

**scapegoating**   A tendency to take out one's feelings of frustration and aggression against someone or something other than the true source of the feelings. Often, racial, ethnic, or religious minority groups become the target of this displaced aggression.

**segregation**   The segregation of two groups into separate neighborhoods, schools, workplaces, and so on. This may be the result of open and deliberate policies calling for segregation, as in *de jure segregation,* or of subtler processes, as in *de facto segregation.*

**self-fulfilling prophecy**   Any situation in which the expectation of some event or outcome contributes to its occurrence. In education, for example, teachers often expect a lower quality of work from minority students than from white students. As a consequence, they treat minority students in ways that tend to produce the expected outcome.

**separatism**   The establishment of, or attempt to establish, entirely separate societies made up of distinct racial, ethnic, or other groups that formerly existed within one society. Examples include efforts by some French Canadians to divide Canada into two independent countries, one English and one French, and efforts by some African Americans to establish separate black states in what is now the U.S. South.

**social distance**   This term has two common uses or meanings. One refers to a preference among members of one group to avoid contact with members of another group. Social distance is said to be relatively small if only very intimate contact is resisted but greater when more superficial types of contact are also resisted. The other meaning denotes a pattern whereby the unequal status of two groups is clearly established and understood by both, no matter how closely they may interact, as in a master-slave relationship. Typically, rules governing interaction between two groups remind both groups that one is *dominant* and the other is *subordinate.*

**social institution**   A well-established structure, form, or organization, with supporting norms and values, that performs a central function in society, such as religion, the family, and the economic, political, legal, educational, and health care systems.

**sociological**, or **social-structural, approach**   An approach to the study of majority-minority relations that emphasizes the characteristics of collectivities of people (such as groups or societies) rather than the characteristics of individuals. Issues of interest concern how a group or society is organized, its base of economic productivity, its power structure, its social institutions, and its culture.

**split labor market theory**   A situation in which laborers are divided into two groups, one higher paid (often a *majority* or *dominant group*) and one lower paid (often composed of *minority group* members). The higher-paid group attempts to maintain an advantaged status by excluding the lower-paid group from certain kinds of employment.

**stereotype**   An exaggerated belief associated with a category such as a group of people. It is a tendency to believe that anyone or almost anyone who belongs to a particular group will have a certain characteristic, for example, that Jews are money hungry.

**structural assimilation**   A type of *assimilation* in which two or more groups gradually come to share a common social structure; that is, they share common institutions, organizations, and friendship networks and have roughly equal positions within these structures. If structural assimilation is complete, widespread intermarriage (marital assimilation) will also occur.

**structural pluralism**   A situation in which two or more groups operate within a common social structure up to a point (e.g., a common government and economic system), but some institutions, organizations, and patterns of interpersonal contact are distinct and separate for each group.

**subordinate group**   Similar in meaning to *minority group.*

**theory**   A set of interrelated propositions about some topic or issue that is believed to be true. Ideally, a theory should be testable, that is, possible to evaluate in terms of its accuracy in describing reality.

**value**   A personal preference or an opinion or moral belief concerning goodness or badness, right or wrong, and so on. A value, being a matter of personal preference, cannot be tested, proved, or disproved.

# REFERENCES

AAD PROJECT. 1998. "New Admissions Data Show UCLA to Enroll Largest UC Freshman Class for Fall, 1998." World Wide Web, http://humanitas.ucsb.edu/projects/aa/docs

ABALOS, DAVID T. 1986. *Latinos in the United States: The Sacred and the Political.* Notre Dame, IN: University of Notre Dame Press.

ABC NEWS. 1999. "Health Care and Race," *Nightline.* February 24. Transcript available on World Wide Web, http://abcnews.go.cam/onair/nightline/transcripts.n1990224_trans.html

———. 1991. "True Colors," *Prime Time Live.*

ABLER, THOMAS S. 1992. "Beavers and Muskets: Iroquois Military Fortunes in the Face of European Colonization." Pp. 151–74 in R. Brian Ferguson and Neil L. Whitehead (eds.), *War in the Tribal Zone.* Santa Fe, NM: School of American Research Press.

ABOUD, FRANCES E., and ANNA BETH DOYLE. 1997. "Parental and Peer Influences on Children's Racial Attitudes." *International Journal of Intercultural Relations* 20: 371–83.

———. 1996. "Does Talk of Race Foster Prejudice or Tolerance in Children?" *Canadian Journal of Behavioural Science/Revue Canadienne des Sciences du Comportement* 28: 161–70.

ABRAMS, CHARLES. 1971. *Forbidden Neighbors.* Port Washington, NY: Kennikat Press.

ABRAMSON, HAROLD J. 1980. "Assimilation and Pluralism." Pp. 150–60 in Stephan Thernstrom, Ann Orlov, and Oscar Handlin (eds.), *The Harvard Encyclopedia of American Ethnic Groups.* Cambridge, MA: Harvard University Press.

———. 1975. "The Religio-Ethnic Factor and the American Experience: Another Look at the Three-Generation Hypothesis." *Ethnicity* 2: 163–77.

ACKERMAN, GEORGIA, BOBBIE ANDERSON, SCOTT JENSEN, RANDY LUDWIG, DARREL MONTERO, NICOLE PLANTE, and VINCE YANEZ. 2001. "Crime Rates and Confidence in the Police: America's Changing Attitudes toward Crime and Police, 1972–1999." *Journal of Sociology and Social Welfare* 28: 43–54.

ACUÑA, RODOLFO. 1972. *Occupied America: The Chicano's Struggle Toward Liberation.* San Francisco: Canfield Press.

ADALF, EDWARD M., and FRANK IVIS. 1996. "Structure and Relations: The Influence of Familial Factors on Adolescent Substance Use and Delinquency." *Journal of Child and Adolescent Substance Abuse* 5, 3: 1–19.

ADAMS, M., and Y. ZHOU-MCGOVERN. 1994. "The Sociomoral Development of Undergraduates in a 'Social Diversity' Course: Developmental Theory, Research, and Instructional Applications." Paper presented at Annual Meeting of the American Educational Research Association, New Orleans, April.

ADAMS, PATRICIA F., GERRY E. HENDERSHOT, and MARIE A. MARANO. 1999. "Current Estimates from the National Health Interview Survey, 1996." *Vital and Health Statistics* 10, 200. Hyattsville, MD: National Center for Health Statistics. Also available online at http://www.cdc.gov/nchs/data/series/sr_10/10_200_1.pdf (downloaded July 25, 2003).

ADELMAN, CLIFFORD. 1999. *Answers in the Toolbox: Academic Intensity, Attendance Patterns, and Bachelor's Degree Attainment.* Washington, DC: U.S. Department of Education.

ADORNO, THEODOR W., ELSE FRENKEL-BRUNSWICK, D. J. LEVINSON, and R. N. SANFORD. 1950. *The Authoritarian Personality.* New York: Harper & Row.

ADVISORY BOARD TO THE PRESIDENT'S INITIATIVE ON RACE. 1998. *One America in the 21st Century: Forging a New Future. The Advisory Board's Report to the President.* Washington, DC: U.S. Government Printing Office.

AGUILAR, ALEXA. 2003. "Local Fallout from Federal School Reform: Schools Struggle for Answers." *St. Louis Post-Dispatch* (September 3): A1, A9.

AHMAD, ISHMAEL LATEEF. 2001. "Metrobus or Metrobust?" *St. Louis American* (August 9). Available online at http://www.acorn.org/acorn10/otheracornwork/OtherACORNWorkpressclips/metrobus.htm (downloaded July 30, 2003).

———. 1993. "Redliners Better Beware: Discrimination in Housing Hits Pocketbooks." *St. Louis American* (July 1–7): 1A, 7A.

AINSWORTH-DARNELL, JAMES W, and DOUGLAS B. DOWNEY. 1998. "Assessing the Oppositional Culture Explanation for Racial/Ethnic Differences in School Performance." *American Sociological Review* 63: 536–53.

AJZEN, I. 1991. "The Theory of Planned Behavior." *Organizational Behavior and Human Decision Processes* 50: 1–33.

AJZEN, I., and M. FISHBEIN. 1980. *Understanding Attitudes and Predicting Social Behavior.* Englewood Cliffs, NJ: Prentice Hall.

ALBA, RICHARD. 1981. "The Twilight of Ethnicity Among American Catholics of European Ancestry." *Annals of the American Academy of Political and Social Science* 454: 86–97.

ALBA, RICHARD, and JOHN LOGAN. 1993. "Minority Proximity to Whites in the Suburbs: An Individual-Level Analysis of Segregation" *American Journal of Sociology* 98: 1388–1427.

ALBONETTI, CELESTA A., ROBERT M. HAUSER, JOHN HAGAN, and ILENE H. NAGEL. 1989. "Criminal Justice Decisionmaking as a Stratification Process: The Role of Race and Stratification Resources in Pretrial Release." *Journal of Quantitative Criminology* 5: 57–82.

ALEXANDER, EDWARD. 1990. "Race Fever." *Commentary* 90, 5: 45–48.

ALEXANDER, KARL L., MARTHA COOK, and EDWARD L. MCDILL. 1978. "Curriculum Tracking and Educational Stratification: Some Further Evidence." *American Sociological Review* 43: 47–66.

ALEXANDER, KARL, and BRUCE K. ECKLAND. 1975. "School Experience and Status Attainment." Pp. 171–210 in S. D. Dragastin and G. H. Elder (eds.), *Adolescence and the Life Cycle: Psychological Change and Social Context.* Washington, DC: Hemisphere.

ALEXANDER, KARL L., DORIS R. ENTWISLE, and MAXINE S. THOMPSON. 1987. "School Performance, Status Relations, and the Structure of Sentiment: Bringing the Teachers Back In." *American Sociological Review* 52: 665–82.

ALEXANDER, KARL L., and EDWARD L. MCDILL. 1976. "Selection and Allocation Within Schools: Some Causes and Consequences of Curriculum Placement." *American Sociological Review* 41: 963–80.

ALEXANDER, KARL L., and AARON M. PALLAS. 1987. "School Sector and Cognitive Performance: When Is a Little a Little?" Pp. 89–112 in Edward H. Haertel, Thomas James, and Henry M. Levin (eds.), *Comparing Public and Private Schools. Vol. 2: School Achievement.* New York: Falmer.

ALFORD, BETTY. 1997. "Leadership for Increasing the Participation and Success of Students in High School Advanced Courses: Implications for Rural Educational Settings." In *The Many Faces of Rural Education: Proceedings of the Annual NREA Convention* (Tucson, Arizona, September 24–27). Fort Collins, CO: National Rural Education Association.

ALLARD, MARY ANN, RANDY ALBELDA, MARY ELLEN COLTEN, and CAROL COSTENZA. 1996. *In Harm's Way? Domestic Violence, AFDC Receipt, and Welfare Reform in Massachusetts.* Boston: University of Massachusetts at Boston, with the McCormack Institute and the Center for Survey Research.

ALLEN, THEODORE W. 1997. *Origins of Racial Oppression in Anglo-America.* London: Verso Books.

ALLEN, WALTER. 2001. Expert Testimony in U.S. Federal District Court, February 7 and 8, 2001, in *Grutter v. Bollinger,* Bench Trial Transcript Vol. 9, pp. 82–110, 134–160, 174–181. Available online at http://www.umich.edu/~urel/admissions/legal/grutter/gru.trans/gru2.07.01a.html, http://www.umich.edu/~urel/admissions/legal/grutter/gru.trans/gru2.07.01b.html, and http://www.umich.edu/~urel/admissions/legal/grutter/gru.trans/gru2.08.01a.html (downloaded November 26, 2003).

———. 1985. "College in Black and White: Black Student Experiences on Black and White Campuses." Summary of report prepared for the Southern Educational Foundation Monograph Series. Ann Arbor: Center for Afroamerican and African Studies, University of Michigan.

ALLEN, WALTER, DARNELL M. HUNT, and DERRICK I. M. GILBERT. 1997. "Race-Conscious Academic Policy in Higher Education: The University of MD Banneker Scholars Program." *Educational Policy* 11, 4 (December): 443–78.

ALLPORT, GORDON W. 1954. *The Nature of Prejudice*. New York: Addison-Wesley.

ALMEIDA, DEIRDRE. 1996. "Countering Prejudice Against American Indians and Alaska Natives Through Antibias Curriculum and Instruction." *ERIC Digest*, Accession Number ED400146.

ALVAREZ, RODOLFO. 1973. "The Psycho-Historical and Socioeconomic Development of the Chicano Community in the United States." *Social Science Quarterly* 53: 920–42.

AMERICAN COUNCIL ON EDUCATION. 1988. *Minorities in Higher Education, Seventh Annual Status Report*. Washington, DC: American Council on Education.

AMERICAN INDIAN SPORTS TEAM MASCOTS. 2003. "Trailblazers." World Wide Web, http://aistm.org/fr.trailblazers.htm (downloaded July 3, 2003).

AMERICAN MANAGEMENT ASSOCIATION. 1998. "Seven Strategic Steps." *HR Focus* 75, 7 (July): S3.

AMERICAN MEDICAL ASSOCIATION. 2003. "Total Physicians by Race/Ethnicity: 2001." World Wide Web, http://www.ama-assn.org/ama/pub/article/168-187.html (downloaded July 25, 2003).

AMERICAN SOCIETY FOR TRAINING AND DEVELOPMENT. 2001. "How to Create Effective Diversity Training." *T+D* 55, 12: 27.

AMNESTY INTERNATIONAL. 2000. "Rights for All, United States Report." Chapter 3, "Police Brutality." World Wide Web, http://www.rightsforall-usa.org/info/report/r03.htm (downloaded August 6, 2003).

ANDERSON, ELIJAH. 1999. *Code of the Street: Decency, Violence, and the Moral Life of the Inner City*. New York: W. W. Norton.

———. 1991. "Neighborhood Effects on Teenage Pregnancy." Pp. 375–98 in Christopher Jencks and Paul E. Peterson (eds.), *The Urban Underclass*. Washington, DC: The Brookings Institution.

———. 1990. *Streetwise: Race, Class, and Change in an Urban Community*. Chicago: University of Chicago Press.

ANDERSON, ROBERT. 2002. "Deaths: Leading Causes for 2000." *National Vital Statistics Report* 50, 16. Hyattsville, MD: National Center for Health Statistics.

ANDREONI, HELEN, and VASILIKI NIHAS. 1986. "A Rationale for Intercultural Education." NACCME-Commissioned Research Paper No. 4. Woden, Australia: National Advisory and Coordinating Committee on Multicultural Education.

ANONYMOUS. 1997. "Why Blacks Don't Get Suburban Jobs They Can Reach: The Relationship Between Racial Patterns of Residence and Employment in Chicago and Buffalo, 1980." Unpublished paper anonymously reviewed by author for possible publication.

ARGYS, LAURA, et al. 1996. "Detracking America's Schools: Equity at Zero Cost?" *Journal of Policy Analysis and Management* 15: 23–45.

ARMOR, DAVID J. 1992. "Why Is Black Educational Achievement Rising?" *Public Interest* 108: 65–80.

———. 1972. "The Evidence on Busing." *Public Interest* 28: 90–126.

ARMOR, DAVID J., and DONNA SCHWARTZBACH. 1978. "White Flight, Demographic Transition, and the Future of School Desegregation." Rand Paper Series P-5931. Paper Presented to Annual Meeting of the American Sociological Association, San Francisco, California.

ARMSTRONG, LIZ SCHEVTCHUK. 1991. "Report Attacks Enforcement of Ability Grouping Practices." *Education Week* (May 1): 20.

ARNOLD, DAVID. 1991. "Increase in Bias Reported." *Boston Globe*, January 31, p. 17.

ARNOLD, WILLIAM R. 1971. "Race and Ethnicity Relative to Other Factors in Juvenile Court Dispositions." *American Journal of Sociology* 77: 211–27.

ARONSON, ELLIOTT, and S. PATNOE. 1997. *The Jigsaw Classroom*, 2d ed. New York: Longman.

ARONSON, JOSHUA, MICHAEL J. LUSTINA, CATHERINE GOOD, KELLI KEOUGH, CLAUDE M. STEELE, and JOSEPH BROWN. 1999. "When White Men Can't Do Math: Necessary and Sufficient Factors in Stereotype Threat." *Journal of Experimental Social Psychology* 35: 29–46.

ARROW, KENNETH J. 1972. "Models of Job Discrimination." In Anthony H. Paschal (ed.), *Economic Life*. Lexington, MA: Heath.

ASCH, SOLOMON E. 1956. "Studies of Independence and Conformity: A Minority of One Against a Unanimous Majority." *Psychological Monographs* 70, 9 (whole no. 416).

ASCHER, CAROL. 1992. "Successful Detracking in Middle and Senior High Schools." *ERIC/CUE Digest* 82. New York: ERIC Clearinghouse on Urban Education.

ASELTINE, ROBERT H., JR. 1996. "Pathways Linking Parental Divorce with Adolescent Depression." *Journal of Health and Social Behavior* 37: 133–48.

ASHLEY, JEFFREY S., and KAREN JARRATT-ZIEMSKI. 1999. "Superficiality and Bias: The (Mis)Treatment of Native Americans in U.S. Government Textbooks." *American Indian Quarterly* 23, 3/4: 49–62.

ASHMORE, KAREN. 1998. "Is Your World Too White? A Primer for Whites Trying to Deal with a Racist Society." *Career Magazine* Forum on Diversity, World Wide Web, http://www.careermag.com/diversity/divart.html

ASHMORE, RICHARD D. 1970. "Prejudice: Causes and Cures." Pp. 244–339 in Barry E. Collins (ed.), *Social Psychology*. Reading, MA: Addison-Wesley.

ASSOCIATION OF AMERICAN MEDICAL COLLEGES. 2002. Brief as *Amica Curae* in Support of the Respondents, *Grutter v. Bollinger* case, United States Supreme Court. Available online at http://www.aamc.org/diversity/amicusbrief.pdf (downloaded July 24, 2003).

ASSOCIATION OF AMERICAN MEDICAL COLLEGES. 1994. *Minority Students in Medical Education: Facts and Figures, VIII*. Washington, DC: Association of American Medical Colleges.

ASTIN, ALEXANDER W. 1993. *What Matters in College? Four Critical Years Revisited*. San Francisco: Jossey-Bass.

AUSTIN, JAMES, BARRY KRISBERG, and PAUL LITSKY. 1985. *Evaluation of the Field Test of Supervised Pretrial Release: Final Report*. Washington, DC: U.S. Government Printing Office.

AVICOLLI, TOMMI. 1992. "He Defies You Still: The Memoirs of a Sissy." Pp. 201–7 in Paula S. Rothenberg (ed.), *Race, Class, and Gender in the United States: An Integrated Study*. New York: St. Martin's Press.

AYRES, IAN. 1990. "Fair Driving: Tests of Race and Gender Discrimination in Retail Car Negotiations." American Bar Foundation Working Paper 8903. Chicago: American Bar Foundation.

BABBIE, EARL. 2004. *The Practice of Social Research*, 10th ed. Belmont, CA: Wadsworth.

———. 1992. *The Practice of Social Research*, 6th ed. Belmont, CA: Wadsworth.

BACHMAN, GERALD G., and PATRICK M. O'MALLEY. 1984. "Black-White Differences in Self-Esteem: Are They Affected by Response Styles?" *American Journal of Sociology* 90: 624–39.

BACHMAN, RONET. 1996. "Victim's Perceptions of Initial Police Responses to Robbery and Aggravated Assault: Does Race Matter?" *Journal of Quantitative Criminology* 12: 363–90.

BAGLEY, CHRISTOPHER, and GAJENDRA K. VERMA. 1979. *Racial Prejudice, the Individual, and Society*. Westmead, England: Saxon Books. (Distributed in the United States by Lexington Books.)

BAHR, HOWARD M., BRUCE A. CHADWICK, and JOSEPH H. STRAUSS. 1979. *American Ethnicity.* Lexington, MA: Heath.

BAKER, KEITH, and ADRIANA DE KANTER. 1981. *Effectiveness of Bilingual Education: A Review of the Literature. Final Draft Report.* Washington, DC: U.S. Department of Education, Office of Planning, Budget, and Evaluation.

BAKER, R. SCOTT. 2001. "The Paradoxes of Desegregation: Race, Class, and Education, 1935–1975." *American Journal of Education* 109, 3: 320–43.

BALBUS, ISAAC D. 1973. *The Dialectics of Legal Repression: Black Rebels Before the American Criminal Courts.* New York: Russell Sage Foundation.

BALDRIDGE, J. VICTOR. 1976. *Sociology: A Critical Approach to Power, Conflict, and Change.* New York: Wiley.

BANAC, IVO. 1984. *The National Question in Yugoslavia: Origins, History, Politics.* Ithaca, NY: Cornell University Press.

BANDURA, ALBERT, and RICHARD H. WALTERS. 1963. *Social Learning and Personality Development.* New York: Holt, Rinehart & Winston.

BANFIELD, EDWARD C. 1974. *The Unheavenly City Revisited.* Boston: Little, Brown.

———. 1968. *The Unheavenly City.* Boston: Little, Brown.

BANKS, JAMES A. 1995a. "Multicultural Education: Historical Development, Dimensions, and Practice." Pp. 3–24 in James A. Banks and Cherry A. McGee Banks (eds.), *Handbook of Research on Multicultural Education.* New York: Macmillan.

———. 1995b. "Multicultural Education: Its Effects on Students' Racial and Gender Role Attitudes." Pp. 617–27 in James A. Banks and Cherry A. McGee Banks (eds.), *Handbook of Research on Multicultural Education.* New York: Macmillan.

———. 1995c. "Multicultural Education and Modification of Students' Racial Attitudes." Pp. 315–39 in Willis D. Hawlen and Anthony W. Jackson (eds.), *Toward a Common Destiny: Improving Race and Ethnic Relations in America.* San Francisco: Jossey-Bass.

———. 1992. "Multicultural Education: For Freedom's Sake." *Educational Leadership* 49, 4 (December 1991–January 1992): 32–36.

BANTON, MICHAEL. 1964. *The Policeman in the Community.* London: Tavistock.

BARABBA, VINCENT P. 1976. "The National Setting: Regional Shifts, Metropolitan Decline, and Urban Decay." Pp. 39–76 in George Sternlieb and James W. Hughes (eds.), *Post-Industrial America: Metropolitan Decline and Interregional Job Shifts.* New Brunswick, NJ: Rutgers University Center for Urban Policy Research.

BARAN, PAUL A., and PAUL M. SWEEZY. 1966. *Monopoly Capital.* New York: Monthly Review Press.

BARANOV, DAVID. 2000. *The Abolition of Slavery in Brazil: The "Liberation" of Africans Through the Emancipation of Capital.* Westport, CT: Greenwood Press.

BARATZ, STEVEN S., and JOAN C. BARATZ. 1970. "Early Childhood Intervention: The Social Science Base of Institutional Racism." *Harvard Educational Review* 40: 29–50.

BARLOW, HUGH D. 2000. *Criminal Justice in America.* Upper Saddle River, NJ: Prentice Hall.

———. 1993. *Introduction to Criminology,* 6th ed. New York: HarperCollins.

BARON, REUBEN, DAVID Y. H. TOM, and HARRIS M. COOPER. 1985. "Social Class, Race, and Teacher Expectations." In Jerome B. Dusek (ed.), *Teacher Expectations.* Hillsdale, NJ: Erlbaum.

BAROVICK, HARRIET. 1998. "DWB: Driving While Black: Incidents in New Jersey and MD Heat Up the Issue of Racial Profiling by State Highway Patrols." *Time* 151: 23 (June 15). Also available on World Wide Web, http://cgi.pathfinder.com/time/magazine/1998/dom/980615/nation_driving_while.html

BARRERA, MARIO. 1979. *Race and Class in the Southwest: A Theory of Racial Inequality.* Notre Dame, IN: University of Notre Dame Press.

BARRINGER, FELICITY. 1993. "Sex Survey of American Men Finds 1% Are Gay." *New York Times,* April 15, sec. A.

BARRITT, DENIS F., and CHARLES F. CARTER. 1962. *The Northern Ireland Problem.* London: Oxford University Press.

BARTH, GUNTHER. 1964. *Bitter Strength: A History of the Chinese in the United States, 1850–1870.* Cambridge, MA: Harvard University Press.

BARTLETT, DONALD L., and JAMES B. STEELE. 1992. *America: What Went Wrong?* Kansas City, MO: Andrews and McMeel.

BASINGER, JULIANNE. 1998. "Most Minority Enrollments Fall This Year at U. of California Professional Schools." *Chronicle of Higher Education* (January 12).

BASTIDE, ROGER. 1965. "The Development of Race Relations in Brazil." Pp. 9–29 in Guy Hunter (ed.), *Industrialisation and Race Relations.* London: Oxford University Press.

BAUGHMAN, E. E. 1971. *Black Americans: A Psychological Analysis.* New York: Academic Press.

BAUMEISTER, ROY F., and MARTIN V. COVINGTON. 1985. "Self-Esteem, Persuasion, and Retrospective Distortion of Initial Attitudes." *Electronic Social Psychology* 1: Article 8501014.

BAYLEY, DAVID H., and HAROLD MENDELSOHN. 1968. *Minorities and the Police: Confrontation in America.* New York: Free Press.

BEADY, CHARLES, and ROBERT SLAVIN. 1980. "Making Success Available to All Students in Desegregated Schools." *Integrateducation* 18, 5–6: 107–8.

BEAN, FRANK D., RUTH R. BERG, and JENNIFER V. W. VAN HOOK. 1996. "Socioeconomic and Cultural Incorporation and Marital Disruption Among Mexican Americans." *Social Forces* 75: 593–617.

BEAN, FRANK D., and MARTA TIENDA. 1987. *The Hispanic Population of the United States.* New York: Russell Sage Foundation.

BECK, E. M. 1980. "Labor Unionism and Racial Income Inequality: A Time-Series Analysis of the Post–World War II Period." *American Journal of Sociology* 85: 791–814.

BECKER, GARY S. 1957. *The Economics of Discrimination.* Chicago: University of Chicago Press (rev. ed. 1971).

BEDELL, KENNETH. 1997. "1997 Yearbook of American & Canadian Churches: U.S. Religious Bodies with More Than 60,000 Members." World Wide Web, http://www.dnaco.net/~kbedell/ybstats2.htm

BEEZ, W. V. 1968. "Influence of Biased Psychological Reports on Teacher Behavior and Pupil Performance." *Proceedings of the 76th Annual Convention of the American Psychological Association* 3: 605–6.

BELL, ALAN P., MARTIN S. WEINBERG, and SUE KIEFER HAMMERSMITH. 1981. *Sexual Preference: Its Development in Men and Women.* Bloomington: Indiana University Press.

BELL, DERRICK. 1992. *Faces at the Bottom of the Well: The Permanence of Racism.* New York: Basic Books.

———. 1988. "The Case for a Separate Black School System." *Urban League Review* 11, 1–2: 136–45.

*BELLEVILLE NEWS-DEMOCRAT.* 1992. "Crimes Rise Against Arab Americans in 1991." February 21, p. 5a.

BEM, DARYL J. 1970. *Beliefs, Attitudes, and Human Affairs.* Belmont, CA: Brooks-Cole.

BENDICK, MARC, JR. 1996. *Discrimination Against Racial and Ethnic Minorities in the United States: Empirical Findings from Situation Testing.* Geneva, Switzerland: International Labour Office.

BENDICK, MARC, JR., MARY LOU EGAN, and SUZANNE LOFHJELM. 1998. *The Documentation and Evaluation of Anti-Discrimination Training in the United States.* Geneva, Switzerland: International Labour Office.

BENDICK, MARC, JR., CHARLES W. JACKSON, and VICTOR A. REINOSO. 1994. "Measuring Employment Discrimination Through Controlled Experiments." *Review of Black Political Economy* 23, 1: 25–48.

BENKOIL, DORIAN. 1997. "Fighting Could Easily Break Out Again if They Leave: U.S. Troops Bring Peace." ABCNEWS.com,

December 18. World Wide Web, http://www.abcnews.aol.com/sections/world/bosnia1120/index.html

BENNETT, CHRISTINE. 1989. "Preservice Multicultural Teacher Education: Predictors of Student Readiness." Paper presented at the annual meeting of the American Educational Research Association, March 27–31, San Francisco.

BENOKRAITIS, NIJOLE V. 1993. *Marriages and Families: Changes, Choices, and Contrasts.* Englewood Cliffs, NJ: Prentice Hall.

BERG, BARBARA J. 1986. *The Crisis of the Working Mother.* New York: Summit Books.

BERG, IVAR. 1975. "Rich Man's Qualifications for Poor Man's Jobs." Pp. 306–13 in Scott G. McNall (ed.), *The Sociological Perspective,* 4th ed. Boston: Little, Brown. (Reprinted from *Transaction* 6 [1969].)

———. 1971. *Education and Jobs: The Great Training Robbery.* Boston: Beacon Paperbacks.

BERGEN, TIMOTHY J., JR. 2001. "The Development of Prejudice in Children." *Education* 122, 1: 154–162.

BERGER, BRIGITTE. 1978. "A New Interpretation of IQ Controversy." *Public Interest* 50: 29–44.

BERNSTEIN, JARED and MARK GREENBERG. 2001. "Reforming Welfare Reform," *The American Prospect* 12, 1. Also available online at http://www.prospect.org/print/V12/1/bernstein-j.html (downloaded July 30, 2003).

BERRUETA-CLEMENT, J. R., L. J. SCHWEINHART, W. S. BARNETT, A. S. EPSTEIN, and D. P. WEIKART. 1984. "Changed Lives: The Effects of the Perry Preschool Program on Youths Through Age 19." *Monographs of the High/Scope Research Foundation* 8.

BERRY, BREWTON, and HENRY L. TISCHLER. 1978. *Racial and Ethnic Relations,* 4th ed. Boston: Houghton-Mifflin.

BERTRAND, MARIANNE, and SENDHIL MULLAINATHAN. 2002. "Are Emily and Brendan More Employable Than Lakisha and Jamal? A Field Experiment on Labor Market Discrimination." Paper presented at Yale University Seminar on Microeconomics, November 18. Also available online at http://www.econ.yale.edu/seminars/apmicro/am02/bertrand-021204.pdf (downloaded December 11, 2003).

BESHAROV, DOUGLAS J. 1993. "Fresh Start." *New Republic* (June 14): 14–16.

BESWICK, RICHARD. 1990. "Racism in America's Schools." *ERIC Digest Series,* no. EA 19. Eugene, OR: ERIC Clearinghouse on Educational Management.

BIANCHI, SUZANNE. 1981. *Household Composition and Racial Inequality.* New Brunswick, NJ: Rutgers University Press.

BIBLARZ, TIMOTHY J., and ADRIAN E. RAFTERY. 1999. "Family Structure, Educational Attainment, and Socioeconomic Success: Rethinking the 'Pathology of Matriarchy'." *American Journal of Sociology* 105: 321–65.

BIELBY, WILLIAM T., and DENISE D. BIELBY. 1992. "I Will Follow Him: Family Ties, Gender Role Beliefs, and Reluctance to Relocate for a Better Job." *American Journal of Sociology* 97: 1241–67.

BIENEN, LEIGH. 1987. "Of Race, Crime, and Punishment." *New York Times,* June 21.

BILLIG, MICHAEL. 2002. "Henri Tajfel's 'Cognitive Aspects of Prejudice' and the Psychology of Bigotry." *British Journal of Social Psychology* 41, 2: 171–88.

BILLIG, MICHAEL, and DUNCAN CRAMER. 1990. "Authoritarianism and Demographic Variables as Predictors of Racial Attitudes in Britain." *New Community* 16: 199–211.

BILLS, D. 1992. "A Survey of Employer Surveys: What We Know About Labor Markets from Talking with Bosses." *Research in Social Stratification and Mobility* 2: 3–31.

BINSTOCK, JEANNE. 1970. "Survival in the American College Industry." Ph.D. diss., Brandeis University.

BISHOP, J. 1987. "Information Externalities and the Social Payoff to Academic Achievement." Working paper, School of Industrial and Labor Relations, Cornell University, Ithaca, NY.

BLACK, DONALD J. 1970. "The Production of Crime Rates." *American Sociological Review* 35: 733–48.

BLACK, DONALD J., and ALBERT J. REISS, JR. 1967. "Patterns of Behavior in Police and Citizen Transactions." In President's Commission on Law Enforcement and Administration of Justice, *Studies in Crime and Law Enforcement in Major Metropolitan Areas.* Washington, DC: U.S. Government Printing Office.

BLACKER, COIT, and LAWRENCE J. KORB. 2000. "Military Tolerance Works." *New York Times* (January 13): A33.

BLAKE, R., and W. DENNIS. 1943. "The Development of Stereotypes Concerning the Negro." *Journal of Abnormal and Social Psychology* 38: 525–31.

BLAUNER, BOB. 1994. "Talking Past Each Other: Black and White Languages of Race." Pp. 18–28 in Fred L. Pincus and Howard J. Ehrlich (eds.), *Race and Ethnic Conflict.* Boulder, CO: Westview Press.

———. 1989. *Black Lives, White Lives: Three Decades of Race Relations in America.* Berkeley: University of California Press.

BLAUNER, ROBERT. 1972. *Racial Oppression in America.* New York: Harper & Row.

BLOCH, HERMAN D. 1969. *The Circle of Discrimination: An Economic and Social Study of the Black Man in New York.* New York: New York University Press.

BLOOM, DAN, JAMES J. KEMPLE, PAMELA MORRIS, SUSAN SCRIVENER, NANDITA VERMA, and RICHARD HENDRA. 2000. *FTP: Final Results of Florida's Initial Time-Limited Welfare Program.* New York: Manpower Demonstration Research Corporation.

BLUESTONE, BARRY, and TERESA GHILARDUCCI. 1996. "Rewarding Work: Feasible Antipoverty Policy." *The American Prospect* 26: 40–46. Also available via World Wide Web, http://epn.org/prospect/26/26blue.html

BLUMENTHAL, DAVID, and JAMES FALLOWS. 1974. "Health: The Care We Want and Need." Pp. 162–68 in Dushkin Publishing Group (eds.), *Annual Editions: Readings in Sociology '74–'75.* Guilford, CT: Dushkin Publishing Group.

BLUMER, HERBERT. 1965. "Industrialisation and Race Relations." Pp. 220–553 in Guy Hunter (ed.), *Industrialisation and Race Relations: A Symposium.* London: Oxford University Press.

BLUMSTEIN, ALBERT. 1993. "Racial Disproportionality of U.S. Prison Populations Revisited." *University of Colorado Law Review* 64: 743–60.

———. 1982. "On the Racial Disproportionality of U.S. Prison Populations." *Journal of Criminal Law and Criminology* 73: 1259–81.

BOBO, LAWRENCE. 1988. "Group Conflict, Prejudice, and the Paradox of Contemporary Racial Attitudes." Pp. 85–114 in P. A. Katz and D. A. Taylor (eds.), *Eliminating Racism: Profiles in Controversy.* New York: Plenum.

BOBO, LAWRENCE, and VINCENT L. HUTCHINGS. 1996. "Perceptions of Racial Group Competition: Extending Blumer's Theory of Group Position to a Multiracial Social Context." *American Sociological Review* 61: 951–72.

BOBO, LAWRENCE, JAMES R. KLUEGEL, and RYAN A. SMITH. 1998. "Laissez-Faire Racism: The Crystallization of a 'Kinder, Gentler' Anti-Black Ideology." In Steven A. Tuch and Jack K. Martin (eds.) *Racial Attitudes in the 1990s: Continuity and Change.* Westport, CT: Praeger.

BODENHAUSEN, G. V. 1990. "Stereotypes as Judgmental Heuristics: Evidence of Circadian Variations in Discrimination." *Psychological Science* 1: 319–22.

BODIPO-MEMBA, ALEJANDRO, and JAMIE BUTTERS. 2002. "Automakers Report That 3.8% of Their Key Officers Are African Americans." *Detroit Free Press,* February 27.

BOGARDUS, EMORY S. 1968. "Comparing Racial Distance in Ethiopia, South Africa, and the United States." *Sociology and Social Research* 52: 149–56.

BOLVIN, MICHAEL J., AMY J. DONKIN, and HAROLD W. DARLING. 1990. "Religiosity and Prejudice: A Case Study in Evaluating the Construct Validity of Christian Measures." *Journal of Psychology and Christianity* 9, 2: 41–55.

BONACICH, EDNA. 1976. "Advanced Capitalism and Black/White Relations in the United States: A Split Labor Market Interpretation." *American Sociological Review* 41: 34–51.

———. 1975. "Abolition, the Extension of Slavery, and the Position of Free Blacks: A Study of Split Labor Markets in the United States, 1830–1863." *American Journal of Sociology* 81: 601–28.

———. 1972. "A Theory of Ethnic Antagonism: The Split Labor Market." *American Sociological Review* 37: 547–59.

BONILLA-SILVA, EDWARDO. 2003a. "'It Wasn't Me!': How Will Race and Racism Work in 21st Century America?" in Betty A. Dobratz, Lisa K Waldner, and Tim Buzell (eds.), *Research in Political Sociology*, Vol. 12, *Political Sociology for the 21st Century*. New York: Elsevier.

———. 2003b. "Racial Attitudes or Racial Ideology?: An Alternative Paradigm for Examining Actors' Racial Views." *Journal of Political Ideologies* 8: 63–82.

———. 2003c. *Racism Without Racists: Color-Blind Racism and the Persistence of Racial Inequality in the United States*. Lanham, MD: Rowman & Littlefield.

———. 2002. "The Linguistics of Color-Blind Racism: How to Talk Nasty About Blacks Without Sounding 'Racist.' " *Critical Sociology* 28, 1–2: 41–64.

———. 1997. "Rethinking Racism: Toward a Structural Interpretation." *American Sociological Review* 62: 465–80.

BONILLA-SILVA, EDWARDO, and TYRONE A. FORMAN. 2000. "I'm Not a Racist, but . . . : Mapping White College Students' Racial Ideology in the U.S.A." *Discourse and Society* 11: 51–86.

BOOCOCK, SARANE SPENCE. 1978. "The Social Organization of the Classroom." Pp. 1–28 in Ralph H. Turner, James Coleman, and Renee C. Fox (eds.), *Annual Review of Sociology: 1978*. Palo Alto, CA: Annual Reviews.

BORNSCHIER, VOLKER, and CHRISTOPHER CHASE-DUNN. 1985. *Transnational Corporations and Underdevelopment*. New York: Praeger.

BOSITIS, DAVID. 2002. Black Elected Officials: A Statistical Summary, 2000. World Wide Web, http://www.jointcenter.org/whatsnew/beo-2002/beo-map-charts/BEO-00.pdf

———. 1998. "Political Report: Black Elected Officials, 1994–1997." *Focus Magazine* (September 1998): 9–10. Also available on World Wide Web, http://www.jointctr.org/focus/pdffiles/sept98.pdf

BOSKIN, JOSEPH. 1969. *Urban Racial Violence in the Twentieth Century*. Beverly Hills, CA: Glencoe Press.

———. 1965. "Race Relations in Seventeenth Century America: The Problem of the Origins of Negro Slavery." *Sociology and Social Research* 49: 446–55.

BOSWELL, JOHN. 1980. *Christianity, Social Tolerance, and Homosexuality: Gay People in Western Europe from the Beginning of the Christian Era to the Fourteenth Century*. Chicago: University of Chicago Press.

BOWEN, WILLIAM G., and DEREK CURTIS BOK. 1998. *The Shape of the River: Long-Term Consequences of Considering Race in College and University Admissions*. Princeton, NJ: Princeton University Press.

BOWER, BRUCE. 1992. "Genetic Clues to Female Homosexuality." *Science News* 142, 8: 117.

BOWKER, LEE H. 1972. "Red and Black in Contemporary History Texts: A Content Analysis." Pp. 101–10 in Howard M. Bahr, Bruce A. Chadwick, and Robert C. Day (eds.), *Native Americans Today: Sociological Perspectives*. New York: Harper & Row.

BOWLES, SAMUEL, and HERBERT GINTIS. 1999. "Comments on 'The Long Shadow of Work.' " *Critical Sociology* 25, 2–3: 281–85.

———. 1976. *Schooling in Capitalist America*. New York: Basic Books.

BOWLES, SAMUEL, HERBERT GINTIS, and PETER MEYER. 1999. "The Long Shadow of Work: Education, the Family, and the Reproduction of the Social Division of Labor." *Critical Sociology* 25, 2–3: 286–305.

BOYD, LAURA A. 1995. "Analyzing Postsecondary Returns: Does Educational Loan Default Play a Role?" *Contemporary Economic Policy* 13: 80–92.

BOYLE, MARY. 1997. "Denver Rocked by Series of Hate Crimes." (Associated Press report.) World Wide Web, http://www.athensnewspapers.com/1997/112297/1122a3denverhate.html

BRADDOCK, JOMILLS HENRY. 1985. "School Desegregation and Black Assimilation." *Journal of Social Issues* 41, 3: 9–22.

BRADDOCK, JOMILLS HENRY, ROBERT L. CRAIN, and JAMES M. MCPARTLAND. 1984. "A Long-Term View of School Desegregation.: Some Recent Studies of Graduates as Adults." *Phi Delta Kappan* 66: 259–264.

BRADDOCK, JOMILLS HENRY, MARVIN P. DAWKINS, and GEORGE WILSON. 1995. "Intercultural Contact and Race Relations Among American Youth." Pp. 237–56 in Willis D. Hawley and Anthony W. Jackson (eds.), *Toward a Common Destiny: Improving Race and Ethnic Relations in America*. San Francisco: Jossey-Bass.

BRAUNER, SARAH, and PAMELA LOPREST. 1999. "Where Are They Now? What States' Studies of People Who Left Welfare Tell Us." Washington, DC: The Urban Institute.

BRAZZIEL, WILLIAM F. 1969. "A Letter from the South." *Harvard Educational Review* 39: 348–56.

BREDEKAMP, SUE, and LORRIE SHEPARD. 1989. "How Best to Protect Children from Inappropriate School Expectations, Practices, and Policies." *Young Children* (March): 14–24.

BREWER, DOMINIC, et al. 1996. "The Reform Without Cost? A Reply to Our Critics." *Phi Delta Kappan* 77: 442–44.

BREWER, MARILYN, and RODERICK K. KRAMER. 1985. "The Psychology of Intergroup Attitudes and Behavior." Pp. 219–43 in Mark R. Rosenzweig and Lyman W. Porter (eds.), *Annual Review of Psychology* 36. Palo Alto, CA: Annual Reviews.

BREWER, MARILYN B., and NORMAN MILLER. 1984. "Beyond the Contact Hypothesis: Theoretical Perspectives on Desegregation." Pp. 281–302 in Norman Miller and Marilyn B. Brewer (eds.), *Groups in Contact: The Psychology of Desegregation*. Orlando, FL: Academic Press.

BRIEN, MICHAEL J. 1997. "Racial Differences in Marriage and the Role of Marriage Markets." *Journal of Human Resources* 32, 4: 741–78.

BRIMMER, ANDREW F. 1993. "The Economic Cost of Discrimination." *Black Enterprise* (November): 27.

BRINK, SUSAN. 1998. "Caring for the Neglected: Areas Untouched by a Physician Surplus." *U.S. News Online*. World Wide Web, http://www.usnews.com/usnews/edu/beyond/grad/gbmed.htm

BRISCHETTO, ROBERT, and TOMAS ARCINIEGA. 1973. "Examining the Examiner: A Look at Educators' Perspectives on the Chicano Student." In Rudolph O. de la Garza, Z. Anthony Kruzezewski, and Tomas A. Arciniega (eds.), *Chicanos and Native Americans: The Territorial Minorities*. Englewood Cliffs, NJ: Prentice Hall.

BRITTON, GWYNETH E., and MARGARET C. LUMPKIN. 1977. "For Sale: Subliminal Bias in Textbooks." *Reading Teacher* 31: 40–45.

BROBERG, ANDERS G., HOLGER WESSELS, MICHAEL E. LAMB, and C. PHILIP HWANG. 1997. "Effects of Day Care on the Development of Cognitive Abilities in 8-Year-Olds: A Longitudinal Study." *Developmental Psychology* 33: 62–69.

BRODY, DAVID. 1960. *Steelworkers in America: The Nonunion Era*. Cambridge, MA: Harvard University Press.

BROOKINGS INSTITUTION. 2000. *Moving Beyond Sprawl: The Challenge for Metropolitan America*. Washington, DC: Brookings Institution.

BROOKOVER, WILBUR, and L. W. LEZOTTE. 1979. *Changes in School Characteristics Coincident with Changes in Student Achievement: Executive Summary*. East Lansing: Institute for Research on Teaching, Michigan State University.

BROOKS, JAMES F. 2002. *Captives and Cousins: Slavery, Kinship, and Community in the Southwest Borderlands*. Chapel Hill: University of North Carolina Press.

BROPHY, JERE E. 1983. "Research on the Self-Fulfilling Prophecy and Teacher Expectations." *Journal of Educational Psychology* 75:631–61.

BROPHY, JERE E., and THOMAS GOOD. 1974. *Teacher-Student Relationships.* New York: Holt, Rinehart & Winston.

———. 1970. "Teacher's Communication of Differential Expectations for Children's Classroom Performance: Some Classroom Data." *Journal of Educational Psychology* 61: 365–74.

BROWN, ANITA, BEVERLY J. GOODWIN, BARBARA A. HALL, and HUBERTA JACKSON-LOWMAN. 1985. "A Review of Psychology of Women Textbooks: Focus on the Afro American Woman." *Psychology of Women Quarterly* 9: 29–38.

BROWN, BERNARD. 1985. "Head Start: How Research Changed Public Policy." *Young Children* 40:9–13.

BROWN, CLIFF. 2000. "The Role of Employers in Split Labor Markets: An Event-Structure Analysis of Racial Conflict and AFL Organizing, 1917–1919." *Social Forces* 79: 653–81.

BROWN, CLIFF, and TERRY BOSWELL. 1995. "Strikebreaking or Solidarity in the Great Steel Strike of 1919: A Split Labor Market, Game-Theoretic, and QCA Analysis." *American Journal of Sociology* 100:1479–1519.

BROWN, JODI M., and BERNARD A. LANGAN. 2001. "Policing and Homicide, 1976–98: Justifiable Homicide by Police, Police Officers Murdered by Felons." U.S. Department of Justice, Bureau of Justice Statistics. World Wide Web, http://www.ojp.usdoj.gov/bjs/pub/ascii/ph98.txt (downloaded August 6, 2003).

BROWN, LAWRENCE L., ALAN L. GINSBERG, J. NEIL KILLALEA, and ESTHER O. TRON. 1978. "School Finance Reform in the Seventies: Achievements and Failures." Pp. 57–110 in Esther O. Tron (ed.), *Selected Papers in School Finance.* Washington, DC: U.S. Department of Health, Education, and Welfare.

BROWN, ROGER. 1965. *Social Psychology.* New York: Free Press.

BROWNING, SANDRA LEE, FRANCIS T. CULLEN, LIQUN CAO, RENEE KOPACHE, and THOMAS J. STEVENSON. 1994. "Race and Getting Hassled by the Police: A Research Note." *Police Studies* 17: 1–11.

BROWNSBERGER, WILLIAM N. 2000. "Race Matters: Disproportionality of Incarceration for Drug Dealing in Massachusetts." *Journal of Drug Issues* 30: 345–74.

BRUCK, LILLY. 1978. *Access: The Guide to a Better Life for Disabled Americans.* New York: Random House.

BURCHINAL, MARGARET B., JOANNE E. ROBERTS, LAURA A. NABORS, and DONNA M. BRYANT. 1996. "Quality of Center Day Care and Infant Cognitive and Language Development." *Child Development* 67: 606–20.

BUREAU OF JUSTICE STATISTICS. 2002a. "National Criminal Victimization Survey, 2001. Criminal Victimization in the United States, Tables Index." World Wide Web, http://www.ojp.usdoj.gov/bjs/abstract/cvus/index.htm (downloaded August 5, 2003).

———. 2002b. "Police Departments in Large Cities, 1990–2000." World Wide Web, http://www.ojp.usdoj.gov/bjs/abstract/pdlc00.htm (downloaded August 5, 2003).

———. 2001a. *Contacts Between Police and the Public: Findings from the 1999 National Survey.* Washington, DC: U.S. Department of Justice.

———. 2001b. *Sourcebook of Criminal Justice Statistics: 2001.* Available online at http://www.albany.edu/sourcebook/ (downloaded August 4, 2003).

———. 1991. *National Update.* Washington, DC: U.S. Department of Justice.

BURNELL, BARBARA S., and JAMES D. BURNELL. 1989. "Community Interaction and Suburban Zoning Policies." *Urban Affairs Quarterly* 24: 470–82.

BUTLER, Y. G., J. E. ORR, M. B. GUTIERREZ, and K. HAKUTA. 2000. "Inadequate Conclusions from an Inadequate Assessment: What Can SAT-9 Scores Tell Us About the Impact of Proposition 227 in California?" *Bilingual Research Journal* 24: 141–54.

BUTTERFIELD, FOX. 1990. "Arab-Americans Face Wave of Threats in U.S." *Los Angeles Times,* August 29, sec. A.

BYNUM, TIM S. 1982. "Release on Recognizance: Substantive or Superficial Reform?" *Criminology* 20: 67–82.

BYNUM, TIM S., GARY W. CORDNER, and JACK R. GREENE. 1982. "Victim and Offense Characteristics: Impact on Police Investigative Decision-Making." *Criminology* 20: 301–18.

BYRNE, MICHELLE M. 2001. "Uncovering Racial Bias in Nursing Fundamentals Textbooks." *Nursing and Health Care Perspectives* 22, 6: 299–303.

BYRNES, DEBORAH, and GARY KIGER. 1990. "The Effect of a Prejudice Reduction Simulation on Attitude Change." *Journal of Applied Social Psychology* 20: 341–56.

CAMARILLO, ALBERT. 1979. *Chicanos in a Changing Society: From Mexican Pueblos to American Barrios in Santa Barbara and Southern California.* Cambridge, MA: Harvard University Press.

CAMAROTA, STEVEN A. 2003. "Back Where We Started: An Examination of Trends in Immigrant Welfare Use Since Welfare Reform." Center for Immigration Studies Report, March 2003. World Wide Web, http://www.cis.org/articles/2003/back503.html (downloaded December 18, 2003).

CAMIA, CATALINA. 1997. "Million Woman March Fills Streets of Philadelphia." *Dallas Morning News.* World Wide Web, http://www.dallasnews.com/national-nf/nat19.htm

CAMPBELL, ANGUS, and HOWARD SCHUMAN. 1968. "Racial Attitudes in Fifteen American Cities." Pp. 1–67 in Supplemental Studies for the National Advisory Commission on Civil Disorders. Washington, DC: U.S. Government Printing Office.

CAMPBELL, PAULETTE WALKER. 1997. "Minority Applications to Medical School Drop in States Without Affirmative Action." *Chronicle of Higher Education* (November 14).

CANNEDY, DANA. 1998. "Back at the Office." *Essence* 23, 11 (March): 80, 140.

CANTOR, JOEL C. et al. 1996. "Physician Service to the Underserved: Implications for Affirmative Action in Medical Education." *Inquiry* 33: 167–73.

CARD, DAVID, and ALAN B. KRUEGER. 1995. *Myth and Measurement: The New Economics of the Minimum Wage.* Princeton, NJ: Princeton University Press.

CARMICHAEL, STOKELEY, and CHARLES V. HAMILTON. 1967. *Black Power: The Politics of Liberation in America.* New York: Vintage Books.

CARTER, STEPHEN L. 1992. *Reflections of an Affirmative Action Baby.* New York: Basic Books.

CARTER, THOMAS P. 1968. "The Negative Self-Concept of Mexican-American Students." *School and Society* 95: 217–19.

CASE, CHARLES E., ANDREW M. GREELEY, and STEPHEN FUCHS. 1989. "Social Determinants of Racial Prejudice." *Sociological Perspectives* 32, 1: 469–83.

CASS, VIVIENNE C. 1984. "Homosexual Identity Formation: Testing a Theoretical Model." *Journal of Sex Research* 20: 143–67.

———. 1983–1984. "Homosexual Identity: A Concept in Need of Definition." *Journal of Homosexuality* 9: 2–3.

———. 1979. "Homosexual Identity Formation: A Theoretical Model." *Journal of Homosexuality* 4: 219–35.

CATALYST. 2002. "2001 Catalyst Census of Women Board Directors of the Fortune 1000." World Wide Web, http://www.catalystwomen.org/research/censuses.htm#2001wbd (downloaded July 22, 2003).

CATTON, WILLIAM J., JR. 1961. "The Functions and Disfunctions of Ethnocentrism: A Theory." *Social Problems* 8: 201–11.

CAUDRON, SHARI. 1998a. "Diversity Watch." *Black Enterprise* 28, 7 (February): 141–44.

———. 1998b. "Diversity Watch." *Black Enterprise* 29, 2 (September): 91–94.

CAUDRON, SHARI, and CASSANDRA HAYES. 1997. "Are Diversity Programs Benefiting African Americans?" *Black Enterprise* 27, 7 (February): 121–32.

CAVALLI-SFORZA, LUIGI LUCA, PAULO MENOZZI, and ALBERTO PIAZZA. 1994. *The History and Geography of Human Genes.* Princeton, NJ: Princeton University Press.

CECIL, NANCY LEE. 1988. "Black Dialect and Academic Success: A Study of Teacher Expectations." *Reading Improvement* 25: 34–38.

CENTER FOR THE AMERICAN WOMAN AND POLITICS, RUTGERS UNIVERSITY. 2003. "Women Serving in the 108th Congress 2003–05." World Wide Web, http://www.rci.rutgers.edu/~cawp/Facts/Officeholders/cong03.html (downloaded September 17, 2003).

CENTER FOR EDUCATION AND HUMAN DEVELOPMENT POLICY. 1981. *Current Knowledge About the Effects of School Desegregation Strategies, Vol. 1, Synthesis of Findings.* Nashville, TN: Vanderbilt University.

CENTER FOR MEDIA AND PUBLIC AFFAIRS. 1998. "Crime Most Common Story on Local Television News: Murders, Assaults, and Shootings Dominate Coverage." World Wide Web, http://www.cmpa.com/archive/healthtv.htm (downloaded August 6, 2003).

CENTERS FOR DISEASE CONTROL. 2003. "Adolescent and School Health, YRBSS, Youth Risk Behavior Surveillance System, Detailed Results, United States." World Wide Web, http://apps.nccd.cdc.gov/YRBSS/ListV.asp?site1=XX&Cat=4 (downloaded June 19, 2003).

CHACON, RAMON D. 1984. "Labor Unrest and Industrialized Labor in California : The Case of the San Joaquin Valley Cotton Strike." *Social Science Quarterly* 65, 2: 336–53.

CHARLES, JAMES P. 1989. "The Need for Textbook Reform: An American Indian Example." *Journal of American Indian Education* 28, 3: 1–13.

CHASE-LANSDALE, P. LINDSAY, ROBERT A. MOFFITT, BRENDA J. LOHMAN, ANDREW J. CHERLIN, REBEKAH LEVINE COLEY, LAURA D. PITTMAN, JENNIFER ROFF, and ELIZABETH VOTRUBA-DRZAL. 2003. "Mothers' Transitions from Welfare to Work and the Well-Being of Preschoolers and Adolescents." *Science* 299: 1548–52. Also available online at http://www.sciencemag.org/cgi/content/full/299/5612/1548?ijkey=.9z1C0Vo7k54s&keytype=ref&siteid=sci (downloaded July 30, 2003).

CHEBAT, JEAN CHARLES, PIERRE FILIATRAULT, and JEAN PERRIEN. 1990. "Limits of Credibility: The Case of Political Persuasion." *Journal of Social Psychology* 130: 157–67.

CHENOWETH, KARIN. 1998. "Growth Among the Credentialed Class." *Black Issues in Higher Education* 15, 11 (July 23): 14–17.

CHIRICOS, THEODORE G., and CHARLES CRAWFORD. 1995. "Race and Imprisonment: A Contextual Assessment of the Evidence." Pp. 281–309 in Darnell F. Hawkins (ed.), *Ethnicity, Race, and Crime: Perspectives Across Time and Place.* Albany: State University of New York Press.

CHRISTENSEN, KIMBERLY. 1997. "As if That Weren't Bad Enough: A Comment on Christopher Jencks' 'The Hidden Paradox of Welfare Reform.' " Cambridge, MA: The Electronic Policy Network. World Wide Web, http://epn.org/library/chri0620.html

CHRONICLE OF HIGHER EDUCATION. 2003a. "Almanac: The Nation—Proportion of Undergraduates Receiving Financial Aid, 1999–2000. World Wide Web, http://chronicle.com/weekly/almanac/2002/nation/0102103.htm (downloaded September 1, 2003).

———. 2003b. "Almanac: The Nation—Number of Full-Time Faculty Members by Sex, Rank, and Racial and Ethnic Group, Fall, 1999." World Wide Web, http://chronicle.com/weekly/almanac/2002/nation/0103202.htm (downloaded September 1, 2003).

———. 2003c. "Almanac: The Nation—College Enrollment by Racial and Ethnic Group, Selected Years." World Wide Web, http://chronicle.com/weekly/almanac/2002/nation/0102302.htm (downloaded September 1, 2003)

———. 2003d. "Almanac 2003–04: The Nation—College Enrollment by Racial and Ethnic Group, Selected Years." World Wide Web, http://chronicle.com/prm/weekly/almanac/2003/nation/0101503.htm (downloaded September 29, 2003).

———. 1997c. "Berkeley Law School to Enroll Only 1 Black First-Year Student." *Chronicle of Higher Education* (July 11): A11. Also available via World Wide Web, http://www.chronicle.com/che-data/articles.dir/art-44.dir/issue-44.dir/44a02302.htm

CHURCHILL, WARD. 1994. *Indians R Us? Culture and Genocide in Native North America.* Monroe, ME: Common Courage Press.

CICIRELLI, V. G., J. W. EVANS, and J. S. SCHILLER. 1969. *The Impact of Head Start: An Evaluation of the Effects of Head Start on Children's Cognitive and Affective Development,* Vols. 1, 2. Athens, OH: Westinghouse Learning Corporation and Ohio University.

CIULLO, ROSEMARY, and MARYANN V. TROIANI. 1988. "Resolution of Prejudice: Small Group Interaction and Behavior in Latency-Age Children." *Small Group Behavior* 19: 386–94.

CLAIBORNE, WILLIAM. 1993. "Labor Department Seeks Private Help as Summer Job Funds Fall Short." *Washington Post,* June 17, sec. A.

CLARK, KENNETH B., and MAMIE P. CLARK. 1958. "Racial Identification and Preference Among Negro Children." Pp. 602–11 in Eleanor Maccoby, Theodore M. Newcomb, and E. L. Hartley (eds.), *Readings in Social Psychology,* 3d ed. New York: Holt, Rinehart & Winston.

CLARK, WILLIAM A. V. 1991. "Residential Preferences and Neighborhood Racial Segregation: A Test of the Schelling Segregation Model." *Demography* 28: 1–19.

CLARK, WILLIAM A. V., and JULIAN WARE. 1997. "Trends in Residential Integration by Socioeconomic Status in Southern California." *Urban Affairs Review* 32: 825–43.

CLARKE-STEWART, ALISON, CHRISTIAN P. GRUBER, and LINDA MAY FITZGERALD. 1994. *Children at Home and in Day Care.* Mahwah, NJ: Lawrence Erlbaum.

CLAWSON, DAN. 1995. "From the Editor's Desk." *Contemporary Sociology* 24: ix.

CNN. 2003. "Hate Crimes Decrease in 2002." World Wide Web, http://www.cnn.com/2003/LAW/11/12/hate.crimes.ap/index.html (downloaded November 13, 2003).

———. 2003. "Illegal Immigrants Arrested in Raid Sue Walmart." Material posted November 9, World Wide Web, http://edition.cnn.com/2003/LAW/11/09/walmart.arrests.ap/ (downloaded December 11, 2003).

———. 2000. "Election 2000: Exit Polls." World Wide Web, http://www.cnn.com/ELECTION/2000/results/index.epolls.html (downloaded August 4, 2003).

———. 1998. "Election 98: Exit Poll. Washington Proposition 200: No Affirmative Action. 1375 Respondents." World Wide Web, http://www.cnn.com/ELECTION/1998/states/WA/I1/exit.poll.html

COCKERHAM, WILLIAM C. 1992. *Medical Sociology,* 5th ed. Englewood Cliffs, NJ: Prentice Hall.

———. 1978. *Medical Sociology.* Englewood Cliffs, NJ: Prentice Hall.

COE, RODNEY M. 1978. *Sociology of Medicine,* 2d ed. New York: McGraw-Hill.

COELHO, PHILIP R. P., and ROBERT A. McGUIRE. 1997. "African and European Bound Labor in the British New World: The Biological Consequences of Economic Choices." *Journal of Economic History* 57: 83–115.

COHEN, D., and M. LAZERSON. "Education and the Industrial Order." Unpublished manuscript.

COHEN, ELIZABETH G. 1993. "From Theory to Practice: The Development of an Applied Research Program." Pp. 385–415 in Joseph Berger and Morris Zelditch, Jr. (eds.), *Theoretical Research Programs: Studies in the Growth of Theory.* Stanford, CA: Stanford University Press.

———. 1984. "The Desegregated School: Problems in Status, Power, and Interethnic Climate." Pp. 77–96 in Norman

Miller and Marilyn B. Brewer (eds.), *Groups in Contact: The Psychology of Desegregation.* Orlando, FL.: Academic Press.

———. 1982. "Expectation States and Interracial Interaction in School Settings." Pp. 209–35 in Ralph H. Turner and James F. Short, Jr. (eds.), *Annual Review of Sociology,* Vol. 8. Palo Alto, CA: Annual Reviews.

———. 1972. "Interracial Interaction Disability." *Human Relations* 25: 9–24.

COHEN, ELIZABETH G., MARLAINE F. LOCKHEED, and MARK R. LOHMAN. 1976. "The Center for Interracial Cooperation: A Field Experiment." *Sociology of Education* 49: 47–58.

COHEN, ELIZABETH G., and RACHEL A. LOTAN. 1995. "Producing Equal-Status Interaction in the Heterogeneous Classroom." *American Educational Research Journal* 32: 99–120.

COHEN, ELIZABETH G., and S. S. ROPER. 1972. "Modification of Interracial Disability: An Application of Status Characteristic Theory." *American Sociological Review* 37: 643–57.

COHEN, FREDRIC. 1995. "Prom Pictures: Principals Look at Detracking." *Educational Leadership* 52: 85–86.

———. 1993. "Getting off the Tracks." *Executive Educator* 15: 29–31.

COHEN, SHIRLEY. 1977. *Special People.* Englewood Cliffs, NJ: Prentice Hall.

COHN, FREDERICK. 1974. *Understanding Human Sexuality.* Englewood Cliffs, NJ: Prentice Hall.

COHN, T. S. 1953. "The Relation of the F-Scale to a Response to Answer Positively." *American Psychologist* 8: 335.

COLEMAN, JAMES S. 1981. "Public Schools, Private Schools, and the Public Interest." *Public Interest* 64: 19–30.

COLEMAN, JAMES S., ERNEST Q. CAMPBELL, CAROL J. HOBSON, JAMES MCPARTLAND, ALEXANDER MOOD, FREDERICK D. WEINFIELD, and ROBERT L. YORK. 1966. *Equality of Educational Opportunity.* Washington, DC: U.S. Government Printing Office.

COLEMAN, JAMES S., THOMAS HOFFER, and SALLY KILGORE. 1982. *High School Achievement: Public, Catholic, and Private Schools Compared.* New York: Basic Books.

COLEY, REBEKAH LEVINE, and LOIS WLADIS HOFFMAN. 1996. "Relations of Parental Supervision and Monitoring to Children's Functioning in Various Contexts: Moderating Effects of Family and Neighborhood." *Journal of Applied Developmental Psychology* 17: 51–68.

COLLEGE BOARD. 1999. Measuring the SAT: A Short Defense by a Tall Man. World Wide Web, http://www.collegeboard.org/index_this/sat/html/admissions/measure/measure.html

COLLIER, JOHN. 1947. *The Indians of the Americas.* New York: Norton.

COLLIER, V. P. 1992. "A Synthesis of Studies Examining Long-term Language Minority Student Data on Academic Achievement." *Bilingual Research Journal* 16: 187–212.

COLLINS, PATRICIA HILL. 1991. *Black Feminist Thought: Knowledge, Consciousness, and the Politics of Empowerment.* New York: Routledge.

COLLINS, RANDALL. 1971. "A Conflict Theory of Sexual Stratification." *Social Problems* 19: 3–12.

COLLINS, SHARON M. 1997. *Black Corporate Executives: The Making and Breaking of a Black Middle Class.* Philadelphia: Temple University Press.

———. 1993. "Blacks on the Bubble: The Vulnerability of Black Executives in White Corporations." *Sociological Quarterly* 34: 429–47.

CONFLUENCE ST. LOUIS. 1985. "Health Care for the Indigent Population in the St. Louis Region: A Report of the Health Care Task Force." St. Louis: Confluence St. Louis.

CONLEY, DALTON. 2002. "Forty Acres and a Mule: What if America Pays Reparations?" *Contexts* 1, 3: 13–20.

———. *Being Black, Living in the Red: Race, Wealth, and Social Policy in America.* Berkeley: University of California Press.

CONNOLLY, PAUL. 2000. "What Now for the Contact Hypothesis? Towards a New Research Agenda." *Race, Ethnicity and Education* 3, 2: 169–93.

CONOT, ROBERT. 1967. *Rivers of Blood, Years of Darkness.* New York: Bantam Books.

CONSORTIUM FOR LONGITUDINAL STUDIES. 1983. *As the Twig Is Bent: Lasting Effects of Pre-School Programs.* Hillsdale, NJ: Erlbaum.

———. 1979. *Lasting Effects After Preschool, Summary Report.* Washington, DC: U.S. Department of Health and Human Services. Administration for Children, Youth, and Families.

CONSTABLE, PAMELA. 1995. "A Glass Ceiling of Misperceptions." *Washington Post* (October 10): A1. Also available via World Wide Web, http://www.washingtonpost.com/wp-srv/politics/special/affirm/stories/aa1001095.htm

CONYERS, JAMES E. 1986. "Toward the Achievement of Racial Progress in America, According to Black Doctorates in Sociology." Paper presented at the Annual Meeting of the North Central Sociological Association, April, Toledo, Ohio.

COOK, PHILIP J., and JENS LUDWIG. 1998. "The Burden of Acting White: Do Black Adolescents Disparage Academic Achievement?" Pp. 375–400 in Christopher Jencks and Meredeth Phillips (eds.), *The Black-White Test Score Gap.* Washington, DC: Brookings Institution Press.

COOK, STUART W. 1990. "Toward a Psychology of Improving Justice: Research on Extending the Equality Principle to Victims of Social Injustice." *Journal of Social Issues* 45: 147–61.

COOLEY, CHARLES HORTON. 1964 [1909]. *Human Nature and the Social Order.* New York: Schocken.

COOPER, E., and MARIE JAHODA. 1947. "The Evasion of Propaganda: How Prejudiced People Respond to Anti-Prejudiced Propaganda." *Journal of Psychology* 23: 15–25.

COOPER, JOEL, and ROBERT T. CROYLE. 1984. "Attitudes and Attitude Change." Pp. 395–426 in Mark R. Rosenzweig and Lyman W. Porter (eds.), *Annual Review of Psychology,* Vol. 34. Palo Alto, CA: Annual Reviews.

COOPER, ROBERT. 1997. "Detracking in a Racially Mixed Urban High School," Report 12. Baltimore, MD: Center for Research on the Education of Students Placed at Risk.

CORTES, CARLOS E. 1980. "Mexicans." Pp. 697–719 in Stephan Thernstrom, Ann Orlov, and Oscar Handlin (eds.), *Harvard Encyclopedia of American Ethnic Groups.* Cambridge, MA: Harvard University Press.

COTERA, MARTA. 1980. "Feminism: The Chicana and Anglo Versions, a Historical Analysis." Pp. 235–48 in Margarita B. Melville (ed.), *Twice a Minority: Mexican American Women.* St. Louis, MO: Mosby.

COTTER, DAVID A., JOAN M. HERMSON, SETH OVADIA, and REEVE VANNEMAN. 2001. "The Glass Ceiling Effect." *Social Forces* 80, 2: 655–81.

COUGHLIN, ELLEN K. 1991. "Amid Challenges to Classic Remedies for Race Discrimination, Researchers Argue Merits of Mandatory School Desegregation." *Chronicle of Higher Education* (October 9): A9, A11.

COUNCIL OF ECONOMIC ADVISORS, PRESIDENT'S INITIATIVE ON RACE. 1998. *Changing America: Indicators of Social and Economic Well-Being by Race and Hispanic Origin.* Washington, DC: U.S. Government Printing Office. Also available via World Wide Web, http://www.whitehouse.gov/WH/EOP/CEA/html/publications.html

COX, OLIVER CROMWELL. 1948. *Caste, Class, and Race.* Garden City, NY: Doubleday.

CRAIG, HOLLY K., and JULIE A. WASHINGTON. 2000. "An Assessment Battery for Identifying Language Impairments in African American Children." *Journal of Speech, Language, and Hearing Research* 43, 2: 366–79.

CRAIN, ROBERT L. 1981. *Some Social Policy Implications of the Desegregation Minority Achievement Literature.* Baltimore: Johns Hopkins University, Center for Social Organization of Schools.

CRAIN, ROBERT L., and RITA E. MAHARD. 1982. "Desegregation Plans That Raise Black Achievement: A Review of the Research." Rand Note, June. Santa Monica, CA: Rand Corporation.

CRAWFORD, BEVERLY. 1998a. "The Causes of Cultural Conflict: An Institutional Approach." In Beverly Crawford and Ronnie D. Lipschutz (eds.), *The Myth of "Ethnic Conflict": Politics, Economics, and "Cultural" Violence.* University of California Press/University of California International and Area Studies Digital Collection, Edited Volume 98: 3–43. World Wide Web, http://repositories.cdlib.org/uciaspubs/research/98/2

———. 1998b. "The Causes of Cultural Conflict: Assessing the Evidence." In Beverly Crawford and Ronnie D. Lipschutz (eds.), *The Myth of "Ethnic Conflict": Politics, Economics, and "Cultural" Violence.* University of California Press/University of California International and Area Studies Digital Collection, Edited Volume 98: 513–61. World Wide Web http://repositories.cdlib.org/uciaspubs/research/98/15

CRAWFORD, CHARLES, TED CHIRICOS, and GARY KLECK. 1998. "Race, Racial Threat, and Sentencing of Habitual Offenders." *Criminology* 36: 481–511.

CREECH, SUZANNAH. 1998. "A&M Minority Enrollment Also Low." *Daily Texan* (Student Newspaper), University of Texas, September 18.

CRONBACH, L. J. 1946. "Response Sets and Test Validity." *Educational and Psychological Measurement* 6: 475–94.

CROSBY, FAYE J., and SHARON D. HERZBERGER. 1996. "For Affirmative Action." Pp. 3–109 in R. J. Simon (ed.), *Affirmative Action: Pros and Cons of Policy and Practice.* Washington, DC: American University Press.

CROSS, H. 1990. "Employer Hiring Practices: Different Treatment of Hispanic and Anglo Job Seekers." Urban Institute Report 90, 4.

CROSS, THEODORE 1998. "The Thernstrom Fallacy: Why Affirmative Action is Not Responsible for High Dropout Rates of African American Students." *Journal of Blacks in Higher Education* 20: 91–98.

CROUTHAMEL, JAMES L. 1969. "The Springfield, Illinois, Race Riot of 1908." Pp. 8–19 in Joseph Boskin, *Urban Racial Violence in the Twentieth Century.* Beverly Hills, CA: Glencoe Press. (Reprinted from *Journal of Negro History,* [July 1960]: 164–75, 180–81.)

CUMMINGS, SCOTT. 1998. *Left Behind in Rosedale: Race Relations and the Collapse of Community Institutions.* Boulder, CO: Westview Press.

———. 1980. "White Ethnics, Racial Prejudice, and Labor Market Segmentation." *American Journal of Sociology* 85: 938–50.

CUMMINS, JAMES, and MICHAEL GENZUK. 1991. "Analysis of Final Report, Longitudinal Study of Structured English Immersion Strategy, Early Exit and Late-Exit Transitional Bilingual Education Programs for Language-Minority Children." *California Association for Bilingual Education Newsletter* 13, 5 (March–April). Also available via World Wide Web, http://www-rcf.usc.edu/~genzuk/Ramirez_report.html

CUNNINGHAM, JEAN A., STEPHEN J. DOLLINGER, MADELYN SATZ, and NANCY S. ROTTER. 1991. "Personality Correlates of Prejudice Against AIDS Victims." *Bulletin of the Psychonomic Society* 29, 2: 165–67.

CUNNINGHAM, PETER J. 2002. "Mounting Pressures: Physicians Serving Medicaid Patients and the Uninsured, 1997–2001." Tracking Report No. 6, Center for Studying Health System Change. World Wide Web, http://www.hschange.com/CONTENT/505/ (downloaded July 25, 2003).

CURTIN, PHILIP D. 1990. *The Rise and Fall of the Plantation Complex: Essays in Atlantic History.* Cambridge, England: Cambridge University Press.

CUTLER, BLAYNE. 1993. "When Cross Talks to the Boss." *American Demographics* 15, 5 (May): 12.

DAHL, ROBERT A. 1982. *Dilemmas of Pluralist Democracy: Autonomy vs. Control.* New Haven, CT: Yale University Press.

———. 1981. *Democracy in the United States,* 4th ed. Boston: Houghton Mifflin.

———. 1961. *Who Governs?* New Haven, CT: Yale University Press.

D'ALESSIO, STEWART J., and LISA STOLZENBERG. 1991. "Anti-Semitism in America: The Dynamics of Prejudice." *Sociological Inquiry* 61: 359–66.

DALMIA, SONIA. 2002. "Time Use Study." Allendale, MI: Grand Valley State University, Seidman School of Business.

DANNEFER, DALE, and RUSSELL K. SCHUTT. 1982. "Race and Juvenile Justice Processing in Court and Police Agencies." *American Journal of Sociology* 87: 1113–32.

DARDEN, JOE T. 1987. "Choosing Neighbors and Neighborhoods: The Role of Race in Housing Preferences." Pp. 15–42 in Gary Tobin (ed.), *Divided Neighborhoods: Changing Patterns of Racial Segregation,* Urban Affairs Annual Reviews, vol. 32. Newbury Park, CA: Sage.

DARDEN, JOE T., and SAMEH M. KAMEL. 2000. "Black Residential Segregation in the City and Suburbs of Detroit: Does Socioeconomic Status Matter?" *Journal of Urban Affairs* 22: 1–12.

DASKAL, JENNIFER. 1998. *In Search of Shelter: The Growing Shortage of Affordable Rental Housing.* Washington, DC: Center on Budget and Policy Priorities. Also available via World Wide Web, http://www.cbpp.org/615hous.htm

DAVILA, ALBERTO, JOSE A. PAGAN, and MONTSERRAT VILADRICH GRAU. 1998. "The Impact of IRCA on the Job-Opportunities and Earnings of Mexican-American and Hispanic-American Workers." *The International Migration Review* 32 (Spring): 79–95.

DAVINE, VALERIE R., and DAVID B. BILLS. 1992. "Changing Attitudes Toward Race-Related Issues: Is a Sociological Perspective Effective?" Paper presented at the annual meeting of the American Sociological Association, August 20–24, Pittsburgh, Pennsylvania.

DAVIS, ANGELA YVONNE. 1989. *Women, Culture, and Politics.* New York: Random House.

———. 1981. *Women, Race, and Class.* New York: Random House.

DAVIS, DAVID BRION. 1966. *The Problem of Slavery in Western Culture.* Ithaca, NY: Cornell University Press.

DAVIS, FRANK, and MARY WEST. 2003. "Evaluation Highlights." *Algebra Project Newsletter* (July): 2.

DAVIS, KINGSLEY, and WILBERT E. MOORE. 1945. "Some Principles of Stratification." *American Sociological Review* 10: 242–49.

DAY, ROBERT C. 1972. "The Emergence of Activism as a Social Movement." Pp. 506–31 in Howard M. Bahr, Bruce A. Chadwick, and Robert C. Day (eds.), *Native Americans Today.* New York: Harper & Row.

DEBO, ANGIE. 1970. *A History of the Indians in the United States.* Norman: University of Oklahoma Press.

DEBONO, KENNETH G., and RICHARD J. HARNISH. 1988. "Source Expertise, Source Attractiveness, and the Processing of Persuasive Information: A Functional Approach." *Journal of Personality and Social Psychology* 55: 541–45.

DEBREADUN, DEAGLAN. 1998. "NI Secretary Sees a 'Watershed.'" *The Irish Times* on the Web. World Wide Web, http://www.irish-times.com/irish-times/special/peace/assembly/news/news37.html

DEEGAN, MARY JO. 1991. *Women in Sociology: A Bio-Bibliographical Sourcebook.* New York: Greenwood Press.

DEFLEUR, MELVIN L., and F. R. WESTIE. 1958. "Verbal Attitudes and Overt Acts: An Experiment on the Salience of Attitudes." *American Sociological Review* 23: 667–73.

DEGLER, CARL N. 1980. *At Odds: Women and the Family in America from the Revolution to the Present.* New York: Oxford University Press.

———. 1959a. *Out of Our Past.* New York: Harper & Row.

———. 1959b. "Slavery and the Genesis of American Race Prejudice." *Comparative Studies in Society and History* 2: 49–66.

DELGADO, RICHARD and JEAN STEFANCIC. (Eds.). 2000. *Critical Race Theory: The Cutting Edge*, 2d ed. Philadelphia: Temple University Press.

DELORIA, VINE. 1981. "Native Americans: The American Indian Today." *Annals of the American Academy of Political and Social Science* 454: 139–49.

DEMO, DAVID H., and ALAN C. ACOCK. 1996. "Family Structure, Family Process, and Adolescent Well-Being." *Journal of Research on Adolescence* 6: 457–88.

———. 1988. "The Impact of Divorce upon Children." *Journal of Marriage and the Family* 50: 619–48.

DEMPSEY, VAN, and GEORGE NOBLIT. 1993. "The Demise of Caring in an African American Community: One Consequence of School Desegregation." *Urban Review* 25: 47–61.

DEMUTH, STEPHEN H. 2001. "The Processing of White, Black, and Hispanic Defendants in Large Urban Courts: Main and Interactive Effects of Race and Ethnicity on Case-Process Decision-Making" (Doctoral Dissertation, Pennsylvania State University). Available through Dissertation Abstracts International, order no. DA9982307.

DENT, PRESTON L. 1975. "The Curriculum as a Prejudice-Reduction Technique." *California Journal of Educational Research* 26: 167–77.

DEPALMA, ANTHONY. 1990. "The Culture Question." *New York Times*, November 4, 22–23.

DERVARICS, CHARLES. 1998. "Is Welfare Reform Reforming Welfare?" *Population Today* 26 (October):1–2.

DESFORGES, DONNA M., CHARLES G. LORD, et al. 1991. "Effects of Structured Cooperative Contact on Changing Negative Attitudes Toward Stigmatized Social Groups." *Journal of Personality & Social Psychology* 60: 531–44.

*DETROIT FREE PRESS*. 2001. "100 Questions and Answers About Arab Americans: A Journalist's Guide." World Wide Web, http://www.freep.com/jobspage/arabs/index.htm (downloaded July 3, 2003).

DEUTSCH, MARTIN. 1963. "The Disadvantaged Child and the Learning Process: Some Social and Developmental Considerations." In A. H. Passow (ed.), *Education in Depressed Areas*. New York: Teachers Press.

DEUTSCH, MORTON, and MARY EVANS COLLINS. 1951. *Interracial Housing: A Psychological Evaluation of a Social Experiment*. Minneapolis: University of Minnesota Press.

DIDHAM, CHERYL K. 1990. "Equal Opportunity in the Classroom: Making Teachers Aware." Paper presented at the annual meeting of the Association of Teacher Educators, February 5–8, Las Vegas.

DILLARD, J. L. 1972. *Black English*. New York: Random House.

DOBYNS, HENRY F. 1966. "Estimating Aboriginal American Population: An Appraisal of Techniques with a New Hemispheric Estimate." *Current Anthropology* 7: 395–416.

DOBZHANSKY, THEODOSIUS. 1962. *Mankind Evolving*. New Haven, CT: Yale University Press.

DODD, C. H., and M. E. SALES. 1970. *Israel and the Arab World*. London: Routledge & Kegan Paul.

DODGE, DIANE TRISTER. 1995. "The Importance of Curriculum in Achieving Quality Child Care Programs." *Child Welfare* 74: 1171–88.

DOHERTY, PAUL, and MICHAEL A. POOLE. 1997. "Ethnic Residential Segregation in Belfast, Northern Ireland, 1971–1991." *Geographical Review* 87, 4: 520–36.

DOMESTIC POLICY ASSOCIATION. 1986. *Immigration: What We Promised, Where to Draw the Line*. Dayton, OH: Domestic Policy Association.

DOMHOFF, G. WILLIAM. 2001. *Who Rules America? Power and Politics*. New York: McGraw-Hill.

———. 1983. *Who Rules America Now? A View for the Eighties*. Englewood Cliffs, NJ: Prentice Hall.

———. 1978. *Who Really Rules? New Haven and Community Power Reexamined*. New Brunswick, NJ: Transaction Books.

———. 1967. *Who Rules America?* Englewood Cliffs, NJ: Prentice Hall.

DORSEN, NORMA. 1969. *Discrimination and Civil Rights*. Boston: Little, Brown.

DOTY, R. M., B. E. PETERSON, and D. G. WINTER. 1991. "Threat and Authoritarianism in the United States: 1978–1987." *Journal of Personality and Social Psychology* 61: 629–40.

DOUGLAS-HOME, CHARLES. 1968. *The Arabs and Israel*. London: Bodley Head.

DOVIDIO, JOHN. 1993. "The Subtlety of Racism." *Training and Development* 47, 4 (April): 51–57.

DOVIDIO, JOHN F., J. C. BRIGHAM, B. T. JOHNSON, and S. L. GAERTNER. 1996. "Stereotyping, Prejudice, and Discrimination: Another Look." In C. N. MacRae, C. Stanger, and M. Hewstone (eds.), *Stereotypes and Stereotyping*. New York: Guilford.

DOWDALL, GEORGE W. 1974. "White Gains from Black Subordination in 1960 and 1970." *Social Problems* 22: 162–83.

DOWNING, LESLIE L., and NANCI RUSSO MONACO. 1986. "In-Group/Out-Group Bias as a Function of Differential Contact and Authoritarian Personality." *Journal of Social Psychology* 126, 4: 445–52.

DOWNS, ANTHONY. 1970. "Losses Imposed on Urban Households by Uncompensated Highway and Renewal Costs." Pp. 192–229 in Anthony Downs, *Urban Problems and Prospects*. Chicago: Markham.

DRAKE, ST. CLAIR, and HORACE R. CAYTON. 1945. *Black Metropolis*. New York: Harcourt Brace Jovanovich.

DREYFUSS, JOEL, and CHARLES LAWRENCE III. 1979. *The Bakke Case: The Politics of Inequality*. New York: Harcourt Brace Jovanovich.

DRIVER, HAROLD E. 1969. *Indians of North America*, 2d ed. Chicago: University of Chicago Press.

D'SOUZA, DINESH. 1996. "Improving Culture to End Racism." *Harvard Journal of Law and Public Policy* 19: 785–94.

———. 1995. *The End of Racism: Principles for a Multiracial Society*. New York: Free Press.

———. 1991. *Illiberal Education: The Politics of Race and Sex on Campus*. New York: Free Press.

DUBOIS, W. E. B. 1903. *The Souls of Black Folk: Essays and Sketches*. Chicago: A.C. McClurg. Electronic edition available at http://www.bartleby.com/114/ (downloaded June 30, 2003).

DUCKITT, JOHN. 1994a. "Conformity to Social Pressure and Racial Prejudice Among South Africans." *Genetic, Social, and General Psychology Monographs* 120: 121–43.

———. 1994b. "Are Subtle Racists Authoritarian?" *South African Journal of Psychology* 24: 232–33.

———. 1993a. "Further Validation of a Subtle Racism Scale in South Africa." *South African Journal of Psychology* 23: 116–19.

———. 1993b. "Prejudice and Behavior: A Review." *Current Psychology* 11, 4: 291–307.

DUNIER, MITCHELL. 1992. *Slim's Table: Race, Masculinity, and Respectability*. Chicago: University of Chicago Press.

DURKHEIM, EMILE. 1965 [1912]. *The Elementary Forms of Religious Life*. Joseph Wald Swain (tr.). New York: Free Press.

———. 1964 [1893]. *The Study of Society*. George Simpson (tr.). New York: Free Press.

DUSHKIN PUBLISHING GROUP. 1977. *The Study of Society*, 2d ed. Gilford, CT: Dushkin Publishing Group.

DUSTER, TROY. 2001. "Buried Alive: The Concept of Race in Science." *Chronicle of Higher Education* 48, 3.

———. 1995. "Review Symposium: The Bell Curve." *Contemporary Sociology* 24: 158–61.

DUTTON, DIANA B. 1986. "Social Class, Health, and Illness." Pp. 31–62 in L. Aiken and David Mechanic (eds.), *Applications of*

*Social Science to Clinical Medicine and Health Policy.* New Brunswick, NJ: Rutgers University Press.

DWYER, PAULA. 1989. "Legal Affairs: The Blow to Affirmative Action That May Not Hurt That Much." *Business Week* (July 3): 61–62.

DYE, THOMAS R. 1979. *Who's Running America?* Englewood Cliffs, NJ: Prentice Hall.

DYER, GWIN. 1992. "Ulster: 'Wait for 2037.' " *Washington Times* (July 24).

DYER, HERBERT, JR. 1992. "Why We Need Father Figures." *Essence* 23, 2: 132.

DYER, JAMES, ARNOLD VEDLITZ, and STEPHEN WORCHEL. 1989. "Social Distance Among Racial and Ethnic Groups in Texas: Some Demographic Correlates." *Social Science Quarterly* 70: 607–16.

DYG, INC. 1998. "Questionnaire and National Results: Study a6333, Campus Diversity." Survey conducted for Association of American Colleges and Universities and Ford Foundation Campus Diversity Initiative. Press Release, October 6.

EAGAN, ANDREA BOROFF. 1988. "The Damage Done: The Endless Saga of the Dalkon Shield." *Village Voice,* July 5.

EAGLY, ALICE H. 1992. "Uneven Progress: Social Psychology and the Study of Attitudes." *Journal of Personality and Social Psychology* 63: 693–710.

EAGLY, ALICE H., and S. CHAIKEN. 1993. *The Psychology of Attitudes.* Fort Worth, TX: Harcourt Brace Jovanovich.

ECONOMIC POLICY INSTITUTE. 1996. "The State of Working America 1996–97." Washington, DC: Economic Policy Institute. Also available via World Wide Web, http://epn.org/epi/epswa-in.html

*ECONOMIST.* 2003. "Out of Eden." (July 5): 31–32.

EDMONDS, RONALD. 1979. "Some Schools Work and More Can." *Social Policy* 9, 5 (March–April): 28–32.

EDWARDS, HARRY. 1994. "The Sociology of Sport." Pp. 100–103 in John E. Farley, *Sociology,* 3d ed. Englewood Cliffs, NJ: Prentice Hall.

———. 1979. "Camouflaging the Color Line: A Critique." Pp. 98–103 in Charles Vert Willie (ed.), *Caste and Class Controversy.* Bayside, NY: General Hall.

EGERTON, JOHN. 1970. "Black Executives in Big Businesses." *Race Relations Reporter* 1, 17: 5.

EHRLICH, ELIZABETH. 1990. "Anger, Shouting, and Sometimes Tears." *Business Week* (August 6): 55.

EHRLICH, HOWARD J. 1973. *The Social Psychology of Prejudice.* New York: Wiley Interscience.

EISENBERG, D. M., R. C. KESSLER, C. FOSTER, et al. 1993. "Unconventional Medicine in the United States." *New England Journal of Medicine* 328: 246–52.

ELIAS, MARILYN. 1997. "Racism and High Blood Pressure." *USA Today,* September 4. Also available via World Wide Web, http://www.usatoday.com/life/health/heartdis/pressure/lhhpr008.htm

———. 1996. "Racism May Shorten Life Span for Blacks." *USA Today,* March 17. Also available via World Wide Web, http://www.usatoday.com/life/health/lhs417.htm

ELKINS, STANLEY M. 1959. *Slavery: A Problem in American Institutional and Intellectual Life.* Chicago: University of Chicago Press.

ELLERMAN, SARAH. 1998. "Medicaid Managed Care." *Nurse Week* (August 17). Available online at http://www.nurseweek.com/features/98-8/medicaid.html (downloaded July 25, 2003).

ELLIOTT, DELBERT S., and SUZANNE S. AGETON. 1980. "Reconciling Race and Class Differences in Self-Reported and Official Estimates of Delinquency." *American Sociological Review* 45: 95–110.

ELLIOTT, DORINDA, ANDREW NAGORSKI, NATASHA LEBEDEVA, and CLINTON O'BRIEN. 1993. "After the Showdown: Yeltsin Sur-

vives a Power Struggle, but the Crisis May Only Speed Russia's Slide Toward a Crackup." *Newsweek* (April 5): 20–23.

ELLIS, ALBERT. 1992. "Rational-Emotive Approaches to Peace." *Journal of Cognitive Psychotherapy* 6, 2: 79–104.

ELWOOD, DANIEL T. 2000. "The Impact of the Earned Income Tax Credit and Social Policy Reforms on Work, Marriage, and Living Arrangements." Working Paper, Kennedy School of Government, Harvard University.

EMERY, ROBERT E. 1989. "Family Violence." *American Psychologist* 44: 321–28.

ENGLAND, ROBERT E., KENNETH J. MEIER, and LUIS RICARDO FRAGA. 1988. "Barriers to Equal Opportunity: Educational Practices and Minority Students." *Urban Affairs Quarterly* 23: 635–46.

EPP, FRANK H. 1970. *Whose Land Is Palestine?* Grand Rapids, MI: Erdmans.

EPSTEIN, JOYCE L. 1985. "After the Bus Arrives: Resegregation in Desegregated Schools." *Journal of Social Issues* 41, 3: 23–43.

EQUAL EMPLOYMENT OPPORTUNITY COMMISSION. 1998. "Americans with Disabilities Act of 1990 (ADA) Charges, FY1991–FY1997." World Wide Web, http://www.eeoc.gov/stats/ada.html

———. 1996. EEOC Notice Number 915.002 (May 22). Subject: Enforcement Guidance: Whether "Testers" Can File Charges and Litigate Claims of Employment Discrimination. World Wide Web, http://www.eeoc.gov/docs/testers.txt

EQUAL HOUSING OPPORTUNITY COUNCIL. 1998. "Gundaker Real Estate Co. Sued for Racial Steering." World Wide Web, http://www.siue.edu:80/~jfarley/florisrl.htm

ESCARCE, J. J., K. R. EPSTEIN, D. C. COLBY, and J. S. SCHWARTZ. 1993. "Health Care Reform and Minorities: Why Universal Insurance Won't Equalize Access." *Leonard Davis Institute Health Policy Research Quarterly* 3: 1–2.

ESPOSITO, D. 1973. "Homogeneous and Heterogeneous Ability Grouping: Principal Findings and Implications for Evaluating and Designing More Effective Educational Environments." *Review of Education Research* 43: 163–79.

ESSES, V. M., G. HADDOCK, and MARK P. ZANNA. 1992. "Values, Stereotypes, and Emotions as Determinants of Intergroup Attitudes." In D. M. Mackie and D. L. Hamilton (eds.), *Affect, Cognition, and Stereotyping: Interactive Processes in Group Perception.* New York: Academic Press.

ESTRADA, LEOBARDO F., F. CHRIS GARCIA, REYNALDO FLORES MACIAS, and LIONEL MALDONADO. 1985. "Chicanos in the United States: A History of Exploitation and Resistance." Pp. 162–84 in Norman R. Yetman (ed.), *Majority and Minority: The Dynamics of Race and Ethnicity in American Life,* 4th ed. Boston: Allyn & Bacon.

ETHNICMAJORITY. 2003. "Corporate Diversity for African, Hispanic (Latino), and Asian Americans." World Wide Web, http://www.ethnicmajority.com/corporate_diversity.htm

EUROPA PUBLICATIONS. 1989. *Europa World Yearbook, 1989.* London: Europa Publications.

EWENS, WILLIAM L., and HOWARD J. EHRLICH. 1969. "Reference Other Support and Ethnic Attitudes as Predictors of Intergroup Behavior." Revised version of paper presented at the joint meetings of the Midwest Sociological Society and Ohio Valley Sociological Society, May, Indianapolis, Indiana.

FAGAN, JEFFREY, MARTIN FORST, and T. SCOTT VIVONA. 1987. "Racial Determinants of the Judicial Transfer Decision: Prosecuting Violent Youth in Criminal Court." *Crime and Delinquency* 33: 259–86.

FAIR, BRYAN K. 1997. *Notes of a Racial Caste Baby: Color Blindness and the End of Affirmative Action.* New York: New York University Press.

FAIR HOUSING COUNCIL OF SUBURBAN PHILADELPHIA. 2001. "Homeowner's Insurance Discrimination & Redlining in the City of Chester." World Wide Web, http://www.fhcsp.com/Laws/insurance_study%202001.htm (downloaded May 14, 2004).

FAIRCHILD, HALFORD H. 1985. "Black, Negro, or Afro-American? The Differences Are Crucial." *Journal of Black Studies* 16: 47–55.

FAIRTEST. 1998. "FairTest Fact Sheet: The SAT." World Wide Web, http://www.bamn.com/resources/fairtest sat.htm

FARLEY, JOHN E. 2003a. "Race, Not Class: Explaining Racial Housing Segregation in the St. Louis Metropolitan Area, 2000." Paper presented at the annual meetings of the Midwest Sociological Society, Milwaukee, WI, April 16–19.

———. 2003b. "Residential Interracial Exposure Indices: Mean vs. Median Indices, and the Difference It Makes." Paper presented at annual meetings of the American Sociological Association, Atlanta, GA, August 15–19.

———. 2003c. *Sociology*, 5th ed. Upper Saddle River, NJ: Prentice Hall.

———. 2002a. "Contesting Our Everyday Work Lives: The Retention of Minority and Working Class Sociology Undergraduates" (2001 Midwest Sociological Society Presidential Address). *The Sociological Quarterly* 43 (Winter): 1–25.

———. 2002b. "Racial Housing Segregation in the St. Louis Metropolitan Area, 2000." *Edwardsville Journal of Sociology* 2, World Wide Web, http://www.siue.edu/SOCIOLOGY/journal/FARLEYV2.htm (downloaded July 23, 2003).

———. 2000. "Using the *Prime Time Live* 'True Colors' Video with a Survey on Beliefs About Race and Equal Opportunity." Pp. 100–108 in Howard J. Ehrlich and Regina Fidazzo (eds.), *Teaching About Ethnoviolence and Hate Crime: A Resource Guide*. Washington, DC: American Sociological Association.

———. 1995. "Race Still Matters: The Minimal Role of Income and Housing Cost as Causes of Housing Segregation in St. Louis, 1990." *Urban Affairs Review* (formerly *Urban Affairs Quarterly*) 31: 244–54.

———. 1994a. *Sociology*, 3d ed. Englewood Cliffs, NJ: Prentice Hall.

———. 1994b. "Twentieth Century Wars: Some Short-Term Effects on Intergroup Relations in the United States." *Sociological Inquiry* 64: 214–37.

———. 1993. "Racial Housing Segregation in the St. Louis Metropolitan Area: Comparing Trends at the Tract and Block Levels." *Journal of Urban Affairs* 15: 515–27.

———. 1992a. *American Social Problems: An Institutional Analysis*, 2d ed. Englewood Cliffs, NJ: Prentice Hall.

———. 1992b. "White Support for Black Political Candidates." Paper presented at the Annual Meeting of the Midwest Sociological Society, April, Kansas City, Missouri.

———. 1990. "The White Vote for Jesse Jackson in 1988 Democratic Primaries and Caucuses." Paper presented at the annual meeting of the Midwest Sociological Society, April, Chicago.

———. 1987a. *American Social Problems: An Institutional Analysis*. Englewood Cliffs, NJ: Prentice Hall.

———. 1987b. "Excessive Black and Hispanic Unemployment in U.S. Metropolitan Areas: The Roles of Racial Inequality, Segregation, and Discrimination in Male Joblessness." *American Journal of Economics and Sociology* 46: 129–50.

———. 1987c. "Segregation in 1980: How Segregated Are America's Metropolitan Areas?" In Gary A. Tobin (ed.), *Divided Neighborhoods*. Newbury Park, CA: Sage.

———. 1986. "Segregated City, Segregated Suburbs: To What Extent Are They Products of Black-White Socioeconomic Differentials?" *Urban Geography* 7: 180–87.

———. 1984. "Housing Segregation in the School Age Population and the Link Between Housing and School Segregation: A St. Louis Case Study." *Journal of Urban Affairs* 6, 4: 65–80.

———. 1983. "Metropolitan Housing Segregation in 1980: The St. Louis Case." *Urban Affairs Quarterly* 18: 347–59.

———. 1982. *Majority-Minority Relations*. Englewood Cliffs, NJ: Prentice Hall.

———. 1981. "Black Male Unemployment in U.S. Metropolitan Areas: The Role of Black Central City Segregation and Job Decentralization." Paper presented at the Annual Meeting of the Society for the Study of Social Problems, Toronto, Ontario.

———. 1977. "Effects of Residential Setting, Parental Lifestyle, and Demographic Characteristics on Children's Activity Patterns." Ph.D. diss., University of Michigan, Ann Arbor.

FARLEY, REYNOLDS. 1996. *The New American Reality: Who We Are. How We Got Here. Where We Are Going*. New York: Russell Sage Foundation.

———. 1991. "The Color Line and the Melting Pot: Racial and Ethnic Conflict in Twentieth-Century United States." Paper presented at Washington University, St. Louis, Missouri, October 28.

———. 1984. *Blacks and Whites: Narrowing the Gap?* Cambridge, MA: Harvard University Press.

———. 1979. "Racial Progress in the Last Two Decades: What Can We Determine About Who Benefited and Why?" Paper presented at the Annual Meeting of the American Sociological Association, Boston.

———. 1977. "Trends in Racial Inequalities: Have the Gains of the 1960s Disappeared in the 1970s?" *American Sociological Review* 42: 189–208.

FARLEY, REYNOLDS, SUZANNE BIANCHI, and DIANE COLASANTO. 1979. "Barriers to the Racial Integration of Neighborhoods: The Detroit Case." *Annals of the American Academy of Political and Social Science* 441 (January): 97–113.

FARLEY, REYNOLDS, and WILLIAM H. FREY. 1994. "Changes in the Segregation of Whites from Blacks During the 1980s: Small Steps Toward a More Integrated Society." *American Sociological Review* 59: 23–45.

———. 1992. "The Residential Segregation of Blacks, Latinos, and Asians: 1980 and 1990." Paper presented at the Annual Meeting of the American Sociological Association, August 21, Pittsburgh, Pennsylvania.

FARLEY, REYNOLDS, HOWARD SCHUMAN, SUZANNE BIANCHI, DIANE COLASANTO, and SHIRLEY HATCHETT. 1978. "Chocolate City, Vanilla Suburbs: Will the Trend Toward Racially Separate Communities Continue?" *Social Science Research* 7: 319–44.

FARLEY, REYNOLDS, CHARLOTTE STEEH, TARA JACKSON, MARIA KRYSAN, and KEITH REEVES. 1993. "Continued Racial Residential Segregation in Detroit: 'Chocolate City, Vanilla Suburbs' Revisited." *Journal of Housing Research* 4: 1–38.

FARLEY, REYNOLDS, CHARLOTTE STEEH, MARIA KRYSAN, TARA JACKSON, and KEITH REEVES. 1994. "Stereotypes and Segregation: Neighborhoods in the Detroit Area." *American Journal of Sociology* 100: 750–80.

FARRAKHAN, LOUIS. 1998. "A Message to the Grassroots." *The Final Call Online* (November 10). World Wide Web, http://www.finalcall.com/columns/mlfspks.html

FEAGIN, JOE R. 2001. "Social Justice and Sociology: Agendas for the Twenty-First Century" (2000 ASA Presidential Address). *American Sociological Review* 66: 1–20.

———. 2000. *Racist America: Roots, Current Realities, and Future Reparations*. New York: Routledge.

———. 1991. "The Continuing Significance of Race: Antiblack Discrimination in Public Places." *American Sociological Review* 56: 101–16.

———. 1984. *Racial and Ethnic Relations*, 2d ed. Englewood Cliffs, NJ: Prentice Hall.

———. 1972. "Poverty: We Still Believe That God Helps Those Who Help Themselves." *Psychology Today* (November).

FEAGIN, JOE R., and CLAIRECE BOOHER FEAGIN. 2003. *Racial and Ethnic Relations*, 7th ed. Upper Saddle River, NJ: Prentice Hall.

———. 1978. *Discrimination American Style: Institutional Racism and Sexism*. Englewood Cliffs, NJ: Prentice Hall.

FEAGIN, JOE R., and HARLAN HAHN. 1973. *Ghetto Riots: The Politics of Violence in American Cities.* New York: Macmillan.

FEAGIN, JOE R., VERA HERNAN, and NIKITAH IMANI. 1996. *The Agony of Education: Black Students at White Colleges and Universities.* New York: Routledge.

FEAGIN, JOE R., and MELVIN P. SIKES. 1994. *Living with Racism: The Black Middle-Class Experience.* Boston: Beacon Press.

FEARS, DARRYL. 1994. "Population Shifts Strain Unity Among Minorities." World Wide Web, http://www.afrinet.net/~hallh/afrotalk/afrosep94/0063.html. Reprinted from *Atlanta Journal-Constitution.*

FEATHERMAN, DAVID L., and ROBERT M. HAUSER. 1978. *Opportunity and Change.* New York: Academic Press.

FEDERAL BUREAU OF INVESTIGATION. 2003a. Tracking Crime Trends: New Hate Crime Statistics Published. World Wide Web, http://www.fbi.gov (downloaded November 13, 2003).

———. 2003b. *Uniform Crime Reports: Hate Crime Statistics, 2002.* Washington, DC: Federal Bureau of Investigation. Available online at http://www.fbi.gov/ucr/hatecrime2002.pdf (downloaded November 12, 2003).

———. 2002a. *Uniform Crime Reports: Crime in the United States, 2001.* World Wide Web, http://www.fbi.gov/ucr/01cius.htm (downloaded August 5, 2003).

———. 2002b. *Uniform Crime Reports: Crime in the United States, 2001: Hate Crime Statistics.* World Wide Web, http://www.fbi.gov/ucr/01hate.pdf (downloaded July 3, 2003).

———. 1990. *Uniform Crime Reports: Crime in the United States, 1989.* Washington, DC: U.S. Government Printing Office.

FENDRICH, J. M. 1967. "Perceived Reference Group Support: Racial Attitudes and Overt Behavior." *American Sociological Review* 32: 960–70.

FENTON, RAY, and DOUGLAS NANCARROW. 1986. "When Good Will Isn't Enough: Prejudice and Racism—Reactions to a Multicultural Unit on Alaska Native Land Claims." Paper presented at the Conference of Western Speech Communication Association, February 15–18, Tucson, Arizona.

FERDINAND, THEODORE N., and ELMER G. LUCHTERHAND. 1970. "Inner City Youth, the Police, the Juvenile Court, and Justice." *Social Problems* 17: 510–27.

FERGUSON, RONALD E. 1998. "Teachers' Perceptions and Expectations and the Black-White Test Score Gap." Pp. 273–317 in Christopher Jencks and Meredith Phillips (eds.), *The Black-White Test Score Gap.* Washington, DC: Brookings Institution.

FESTINGER, LEON. 1957. *A Theory of Cognitive Dissonance.* Stanford, CA: Stanford University Press.

FESTINGER, LEON, and J. M. CARLSMITH. 1959. "Cognitive Consequences of Forced Compliance." *Journal of Abnormal and Social Psychology* 58: 203–10.

FICARROTTO, THOMAS J. 1990. "Racism, Sexism, and Erotophobia: Attitudes of Heterosexuals Toward Homosexuals." *Journal of Homosexuality* 19, 1: 111–16.

FICKETT, JOAN G. 1975. "Merican: An Inner City Dialect—Aspects of Morphemics, Syntax, and Semiology." *Studies in Linguistics: Occasional Papers* 13.

FINE M., and A. ASCH. 1988. "Disability Beyond Stigma: Social Interaction, Discrimination, and Activism." *Journal of Social Issues* 44: 3–22.

FINEBERG, SOLOMON ANDHIL. 1949. *Punishment Without Crime.* New York: Doubleday.

FINN, CHESTER E. 1996. "Will 'Efficacy' Help New York's Schools?" *New York Times* (February 6). Also available via World Wide Web, http://edexcellence.net/issuespl/state/nyc/efficacy.html

FIREBAUGH, GLENN, and KENNETH E. DAVIS. 1988. "Trends in Antiblack Prejudice, 1972–1984: Region and Cohort Effects." *American Journal of Sociology* 94: 251–72.

FISCHER, PAUL B. 1995. "Housing Mobility: The Cincinnati Experience." *Journal of Housing and Community Development* 52: 15–17.

FISH, STANLEY. 1993. "Reverse Racism: Or How the Pot Got to Call the Kettle Black." *Atlantic Monthly* (November).

FISHBEIN, HAROLD D. 1996. *Peer Prejudice and Discrimination: Evolutionary, Cultural, and Developmental Dynamics.* Boulder, CO: Westview Press.

FISHBEIN, M., and I. AJZEN. 1975. *Belief, Attitude, Intention, and Behavior: An Introduction to Theory and Research.* Reading, MA: Addison-Wesley.

FISKE, S. T., and J. B. RUSCHER. 1992. "Negative Interdependence and Prejudicial: Whence the Affect?" In D. M. Mackie and D. L. Hamilton (eds.), *Affect, Cognition, and Stereotyping: Interactive Processes in Group Perception.* New York: Academic Press.

FITZGERALD, ANN K., and PAUL LAUTER. 1995. "Multiculturalism and Core Curricula." Pp. 729–746 in James A. Banks and Cherry A. McGee Banks (eds.), *Handbook of Research on Multicultural Education.* New York: Macmillan.

FIX, MICHAEL, and MARGERY AUSTIN TURNER. 1998a. "Executive Summary." In Michael Fix and Margery Austin Turner (eds.), *A National Report Card on Discrimination in America: The Role of Testing.* Washington, DC: Urban Institute. Available online at http://www.urban.org/urlprint.cfm?ID=5965 (downloaded November 24, 2003).

———. 1998b. "Measuring Racial and Ethnic Discrimination in America." Chapter 1 in Michael Fix and Margery Austin Turner (eds.), *A National Report Card on Discrimination in America: The Role of Testing.* Washington, DC: Urban Institute. Available online at http://www.urban.org/urlprint.cfm?ID=5965 (downloaded November 24, 2003).

FLEITAS, JOAN. 2000. "Sticks, Stones, and the Stigmata of Childhood Illness and Disability." *Reclaiming Children and Youth* 9, 3 (Fall): 146–50.

FLORES, SOLOMON HERNANDEZ. 1978. *The Nature and Effects of Bilingual Education Programs for the Spanish-Speaking Child in the United States.* New York: Arno Press.

FLOWERMAN, SAMUEL H. 1947. "Mass Propaganda in the War Against Bigotry." *Journal of Abnormal and Social Psychology* 42: 429–39.

FOGLEMAN, AARON S. 1998. "From Slaves, Convicts, and Servants to Free Passengers: The Transformation of Immigration in the Era of the American Revolution." *Journal of American History* 85: 43–76.

FOGELSON, ROBERT. 1971. *Violence as Protest: A Study of Riots and Ghettos.* New York: Doubleday.

FOGELSON, ROBERT, and R. B. HILL. 1968. "Who Riots? A Study of Participation in the 1967 Riots." Pp. 217–48 in *Supplemental Studies for the National Advisory Commission on Civil Disorders.* Washington, DC: U.S. Government Printing Office.

FOLEY, DOROTHY M. 1993. "Restructuring with Technology." *Principal* 72, 3: 22, 24–25.

FOLEY, NEIL. 1997. *The White Scourge: Mexicans, Blacks, and Poor Whites in Texas Cotton Culture.* Berkeley: University of California Press.

FOOTE, CALEB. 1958. "A Study of the Administration of Bail in New York City." *University of Pennsylvania Law Review* 106.

FORD, W. SCOTT. 1973. "Interracial Public Housing in a Border City: Another Look at the Contact Hypothesis." *American Journal of Sociology* 78: 1426–47.

FORDHAM, SIGNITHIA, and JOHN U. OGBU. 1986. "Black Students' School Success: Coping with the Burden of Acting White." *Urban Review* 18: 181.

FOSTER, WILLIAM Z. 1920. *The Great Steel Strike and Its Lessons.* New York: Huebsch.

FRANKENBERG, ERICA, CHUNGMEI LEE, and GARY ORFIELD. 2003. *A Multiracial Society with Segregated Schools: Are We Losing the Dream?* Cambridge, MA: The Civil Rights Project, Harvard

University. Available online at http://www.civilrightsproject. harvard.edu/research/reseg03/AreWeLosingtheDream.pdf (downloaded August 7, 2003).

FRANKENBERG, RUTH. 1993. *White Women, Race Matters: The Social Construction of Whiteness.* Minneapolis: University of Minnesota Press.

FRANKLIN, JOHN HOPE. 1969. *From Slavery to Freedom: A History of Negro Americans*, 3d ed. New York: Vintage Books.

FRANKLIN, JOHN HOPE, and ALFRED A. MOSS, JR. 2000. *From Slavery to Freedom: A History of African Americans*, 8th ed. New York: Knopf.

FRAZIER, E. FRANKLIN. 1966. *The Negro Family in the United States*, rev. ed. Chicago: University of Chicago Press.

FREDRICKSON, GEORGE M. 1988. *The Arrogance of Race: Historical Perspectives on Slavery, Racism, and Social Inequality.* Middletown, CT: Wesleyan University Press.

FREDRICKSON, GEORGE M., and DALE T. KNOBEL. 1980. "Prejudice and Discrimination, History of." Pp. 829–47 in Stephan Thernstrom, Ann Orlov, and Oscar Handlin (eds.), *Harvard Encyclopedia of American Ethnic Groups.* Cambridge, MA: Harvard University Press.

FREE, MARVIN D., JR. 1997. "The Impact of Sentencing Reforms on African Americans." *Journal of Black Studies* 28: 268–86.

FREEMAN, JO. 1979. "Resource Mobilization and Strategy." In Mayer N. Zald and John D. McCarthy (eds.), *The Dynamics of Social Movements.* Cambridge, MA: Winthrop.

———. 1973. "The Origins of the Women's Liberation Movement." *American Journal of Sociology* 78: 782–811.

FREUD, SIGMUND. 1962 [1930]. *Civilization and Its Discontents.* James Strachey (tr.). New York: Norton.

FRIEDENBERG, E. Z. 1965. *Coming of Age in America.* New York: Random House.

FRIEDMAN, RAYMOND A, and DAVID KRACKHARDT. 1997. "Social Capital and Career Mobility." *Journal of Applied Behavioral Science* 33: 316–34.

FRISBIE, W. PARKER. 1977. "The Scale and Growth of World Urbanization." Pp. 44–58 in John Walton and Donald E. Carns (eds.), *Cities in Change: Studies on the Urban Condition.* Boston: Allyn & Bacon.

FUCHS, ESTELLE, and ROBERT J. HAVIGHURST. 1972. *To Live on This Earth.* Garden City, NY: Doubleday.

FUERST, J. S. 1981. "Report Card: Chicago's All-Black Schools." *Public Interest* 64: 79–91.

FUKURAI, HIROSHI, EDGAR W. BUTLER, and RICHARD KROOTH. 1991a. "Cross-Sectional Jury Representation or Systematic Jury Representation? Simple Random and Cluster Sampling Strategies in Jury Selection." *Journal of Criminal Justice* 19: 31–48.

———. 1991b. "Where Did the Black Jurors Go? A Theoretical Synthesis of Racial Disenfranchisement in the Jury System and Jury Selection." *Journal of Black Studies* 22: 196–215.

FURSTENBERG, FRANK F., THEODORE HERSHBERG, and J. MODELL. 1975. "The Origins of the Female-Headed Black Family: The Impact of the Urban Experience." *Journal of Interdisciplinary History* 6: 211–33.

FYFE, JAMES J. 1982. "Blind Justice: Police Shootings in Memphis." *Journal of Criminal Law and Criminology* 73: 707–22.

GAINES, MARGIE L., and MARGARET DAVIS. 1990. "Accuracy of Teacher Prediction of Elementary Student Achievement." Paper presented at the Annual Meeting of the American Educational Research Association, April 16–20, Boston.

GALAGAN, PATRICIA A. 1993. "Trading Places at Monsanto." *Training and Development* 47, 4 (April): 45–49.

GALLUP ORGANIZATION. 2004. Poll Topics and Trends: Race Relations. World Wide Web, http://www.gallup.com/content/default. aspx?ci=1687&pg=3 (premium content, downloaded April 25, 2004).

———. 2003a. "Poll Topics and Trends: Race Relations." World Wide Web, http://www.gallup.com/poll/topics/race3.asp (premium content, downloaded June 5, 2003).

———. 2003b. "Poll Topics and Trends: Taxes." World Wide Web, http://www.gallup.com/poll/topics/taxes2.asp (premium content, downloaded June 5, 2003).

———. 2003c. "Focus on Election, 2004," July 1 release. World Wide Web, http://www.gallup.com/poll/focus/sr030701.asp (premium content, downloaded July 2, 2003).

———. 2003d. "Lieberman Continues to Pace Democratic Field; Sharpton Is Top Choice Among Black Democrats." World Wide Web, http://www.gallup.com/poll/releases/pr030625.asp (premium content, downloaded August 4, 2003).

———. 2003e. "Poll Topics and Trends: Homosexual Relations." World Wide Web, http://www.gallup.com/poll/topics/ homosexual.asp (premium content, downloaded September 29, 2003).

———. 2001. "Election Polls: Vote by Group, 2000." World Wide Web, http://www.gallup.com/poll/topics/ptgrp2000.asp (premium content, downloaded August 4, 2003).

———. 1997. "Special Reports: Black/White Relations in the U.S." World Wide Web, http://www.gallup.com/Special_ Reports/black-white.htm

GALLUP, GEORGE, JR. 1990. *The Gallup Poll: Public Opinion, 1989.* Wilmington, DE: Scholarly Resources.

GALLUP, GEORGE, JR., and FRANK NEWPORT. 1991. "Blacks and Whites Differ on Civil Rights Progress." *Gallup Poll Monthly* (August): 54–59.

GAMORAN, ADAM. 1992a. "Is Ability Grouping Equitable?" *Educational Leadership* (October): 11–17.

———. 1992b. "The Variable Effects of High School Tracking." *American Sociological Review* 57: 812–29.

GAMORAN, ADAM, and MATTHEW WEINSTEIN. 1998. "Differentiation and Opportunity in Restructured Schools." *American Journal of Education* 106, 3: 385–415.

GANS, HERBERT. 1979. "Symbolic Ethnicity: The Future of Ethnic Groups and Cultures in America." *Ethnic and Racial Studies* 2: 1–20.

———. 1974. "Foreword." In Neil C. Sandberg, *Ethnic Identity and Assimilation: The Polish American Community.* New York: Praeger.

———. 1973. *More Equality.* New York: Pantheon Books.

———. 1971. "The Uses of Poverty: The Poor Pay All." *Social Policy* (July–August).

———. 1967. "The Negro Family: Reflections on the Moynihan Report." Pp. 445–57 in Lee Rainwater and William L. Yancey (eds.), *The Moynihan Report and the Politics of Controversy.* Cambridge, MA: MIT Press.

GARBARINO, MERWYN S. 1976. *American Indian Heritage.* Boston: Little, Brown.

GARCIA, E. E. 1991. *Education of Linguistically and Culturally Diverse Students: Effective Instructional Practices.* National Center for Research on Cultural Diversity and Second Language Learning. Educational Practice Report No. 1.

GARCIA, JESUS. 1993. "The Changing Image of Minorities in Textbooks." *Phi Delta Kappan* 75: 29–35.

GARCIA-COLL, CYNTHIA T., and HEIDIE A. VAZQUEZ-GARCIA. 1995. "Developmental Processes and Their Influence on Interethnic and Intercultural Relations." In Willis D. Hawley and Anthony Jackson (eds.), *Toward a Common Destiny: Improving Race and Ethnic Relations in America.* San Francisco: Jossey-Bass.

GARFINKEL, HAROLD. 1949. "Research Note on Inter- and Intraracial Homicides." *Social Forces* 27: 369–81.

GARTRELL, JOHN, and STEPHANIE AMADEO MARQUEZ. 1995. "The Spurious Relationship Between IQ and Social Behavior: Ethnic Abuse, Gender Ignorance, and Confounded Education." *Alberta Journal of Educational Research* 41: 277–82.

GAY RIGHTS INFO HOMEPAGE. 2003. "Gay Rights Info." World Wide Web, http://www.actwin.com/eatonohio/gay/GAY.htm (downloaded May 10, 2004).

GEDICKS, AL. 2001. *Resource Rebels: Native Challenges to Mining and Oil Corporations.* Cambridge, MA: South End Press.

———. 1993. *The New Resource Wars: Native and Environmental Struggles Against Multinational Corporations.* Boston: South End Press.

GEHRKE, ROBERT. 2001. "GAO: Students at BIA Schools Lagging." *Washington Post* Associated Press Online Web site, http://www.washingtonpost.com/wp-srv/aponline/20011026/aponline192859_000.htm (downloaded September 11, 2003).

GEIGER, H. JACK. 1996. "Race and Health Care: An American Dilemma?" *New England Journal of Medicine* 335, 11.

GENERAL ACCOUNTING OFFICE. 1998. *School Finance: State Efforts to Reduce Funding Gaps Between Wealthy and Poor Districts.* Washington, DC: U.S. Government Printing Office.

———. 1994. "Information on Minority-Targeted Scholarships." Washington, DC: U.S. Government Printing Office.

———. 1990. "Report and Recommendations of the Task Force on IRCA-Related Discrimination." Washington, DC: U.S. Government Printing Office.

GENNETIAN, LISA A. , GREG J. DUNCAN, VIRGINIA W. KNOX, WANDA G. VARGAS, ELIZABETH CLARK-KAUFFMAN, and ANDREW S. LONDON. 2000. "How Welfare and Work Policies for Parents Affect Adolescents: A Synthesis of Research." New York: MDRC. Available online at http://www.mdrc.org/Reports2002/ng_adolescent/ng_adolescentsynthesis_overview.htm (downloaded July 30, 2003).

GERARD, HAROLD B. 1988. "School Desegregation: The Social Science Role." In Phyllis Katz and Dalmas Taylor (eds.), *Eliminating Racism.* New York: Plenum.

GERMOND, JACK W., and JULES WITCOVER. 1996. "Another Affirmative-Action Test for Clinton." *Baltimore Sun* (December 13). Also available via World Wide Web, http://www.sunspot.net/columnists/data/germond/1213germond.html

GESCHWENDER, JAMES A. 1964. "Social Structure and the Negro Revolt." *Social Forces* 43: 248–56.

GESCHWENDER, JAMES A., and B. D. SINGER. 1968. "Deprivation and the Detroit Riot." *Social Problems* 17: 457–63.

GETTMAN, JON. 2000. "United States Marijuana Arrests, Part 2: Racial Differences in Drug Arrests." Washington, DC: NORML Foundation. World Wide Web, http://www.norml.org/index.cfm?Group_ID=5328 (downloaded May 10, 2004).

GIBSON, GEOFFREY, GEORGE BUGBEE, and ODIN W. ANDERSON. 1970. *Emergency Medical Services in the Chicago Area.* Chicago: University of Chicago, Center for Health Administration.

GIBSON, JAMES L., and RAYMOND M. DUCH. 1992. "Anti-Semitic Attitudes of the Mass Public: Estimates and Explanations Based on a Survey of the Moscow Oblast." *Public Opinion Quarterly* 56, 1: 1–28.

GIBSON, MARGARET A., and JOHN U. OGBU (EDS.). 1992. *Minority Status and Schooling: Immigrant vs. Nonimmigrant.* New York: Garland.

GILBERT, G. M. 1951. "Stereotype Persistence and Change Among College Students." *Journal of Abnormal and Social Psychology* (April): 245–54.

GILENS, MARTIN. 1995. "Racial Attitudes and Opposition to Welfare." *Journal of Politics* 57: 994–1014.

GINTIS, HERBERT. 1971. "Education, Technology, and Worker Productivity." *American Economic Review* 61 (American Economic Association proceedings): 266–79.

GITLIN, TODD. 1995. *The Twilight of Common Dreams: Why America Is Wracked by Culture Wars.* New York: Metropolitan Books.

GLAESER, EDWARD L., and JACOB L. VIGDOR. 2001. *Racial Segregation in the 2000 Census: Promising News.* Washington, DC: Brookings Institution.

GLAZER, NATHAN. 2002. "Do We Need the Census Race Question?" *Public Interest* 149.

———. 1976. *Affirmative Discrimination.* New York: Basic Books.

———. 1971. "Blacks and Ethnic Groups: The Difference, and the Political Difference It Makes." *Social Problems* 18: 444–61.

GLAZER, NATHAN, and DANIEL PATRICK MOYNIHAN. 1970. *Beyond the Melting Pot.* Cambridge, MA: MIT Press.

GLENN, EVELYN MAKANO. 1980. "Dialectics of Wage Work: Japanese American Women and Domestic Service, 1905–1940." *Feminist Studies* 6: 432–71.

GLENN, NORVAL. 1997a. *Closed Hearts, Closed Minds: The Textbook Story of Marriage.* New York: Institute for American Values. Available online at http://www.americanvalues.org/html/a-closed_hearts_closed_minds_.html.

———. 1997b. "A Critique of Twenty Marriage and the Family Textbooks." *Family Relations* 46, 3: 197–208.

———. 1966. "White Gains from Negro Subordination." *Social Problems* 14: 159–78.

———. 1963. "Occupational Benefits to Whites from the Subordination of Negroes." *American Sociological Review* 28: 443–48.

GLIEDMAN, JOHN. 1979. "The Wheelchair Rebellion." *Psychology Today* (August).

GLOVER, REBECCA J. 1994. "Using Moral and Epistemological Reasoning as Predictors of Prejudice." *Journal of Social Psychology* 134: 633–40.

GOBINEAU, ARTHUR DE. 1915 [1853–1855]. *The Inequality of Human Races.* Adrian Collins (tr.). New York: Putnam.

GOERING, JOHN M. 1971. "The Emergence of Ethnic Interests: A Case of Serendipity." *Social Forces* 49: 379–84.

GOLDBERG, K. C., A. J. HATZ, S. J. JACOBSEN, H. KRAKAUER, and A. A. RIMM. 1992. "Racial and Community Factors Influencing Coronary Artery Bypass Graft Surgery Rates for All 1986 Medicare Patients." *JAMA* 267: 1473–77.

GOLDEN, MARK, and B. BIRNS. 1968. "Social Class and Cognitive Development in Infancy." *Merrill-Palmer Quarterly* 14: 139–49.

GOLDSTEIN, JOSEPH. 1960. "Police Discretion Not to Invoke the Criminal Process: Low Visibility Decisions in the Administration of Justice." *Yale Law Journal* 69 (March).

GOLEMAN, DANIEL. 1990. "Anger over Racism Seen as Cause of Blacks' High Blood Pressure." *New York Times*, April 24: C3.

GOLUB, ELLEN. 1989. "Making a World of Difference." *Education and Society* 1, 1: 5–9.

GONZALES, NANCIE L. 1967. *The Spanish Americans of New Mexico: A Distinctive Heritage.* Advance Report 9. Los Angeles: University of California, Mexican-American Study Project.

GONZALES, NANCY A., and ANA MARI CAUCE. 1995. "Ethnic Identity and Multicultural Competence: Dilemmas and Challenges for Minority Youth." Pp. 131–62 in Willis D. Hawley and Anthony W. Jackson (eds.), *Toward a Common Destiny: Improving Race and Ethnic Relations in America.* San Francisco: Jossey-Bass.

GONZALEZ, GUSTAVO and LENTO F. MAEZ. 1995. "Advances in Research in Bilingual Education." *Directions in Language & Education, National Clearinghouse for Bilingual Education* 1, 5.

GORDON, MILTON M. 1978. *Human Nature, Class, and Ethnicity.* New York: Oxford University Press.

———. 1964. *Assimilation in American Life.* New York: Oxford University Press.

GOREN, ARTHUR A. 1980. "Jews." Pp. 571–98 in Stephan Thernstrom, Ann Orlov, and Oscar Handlin (eds.), *Harvard Encyclopedia of American Ethnic Groups.* Cambridge, MA: Harvard University Press.

GORNICK, MARIAN E., PAUL W. EGGERS, THOMAS W. REILLY, RENEE M. MENTNECH, LESLYE K. FITTERMAN, LAWRENCE E. KUCKEN, BRUCE C. VLADECK. 1996. "Effects of Race and Income on Mortality and Use of Services Among Medicare Beneficiaries." *New England Journal of Medicine* 335: 791–99.

GOSSETT, THOMAS F. 1963. *Race: The History of an Idea in America.* Dallas, TX: Southern Methodist University Press.

GOTTFREDSON, MICHAEL R., and TRAVIS HIRSCHI. 1990. *A General Theory of Crime.* Stanford: CA: Stanford University Press.

GOTTFREDSON, STEPHEN D., and G. ROGER JARJOURA. 1996. "Race, Gender, and Guidelines-Based Decision Making." *Journal of Research in Crime and Delinquency* 33: 49–69.

GOULDNER, HELEN, and MAYR SYMONS STRONG. 1978. *Teachers' Pets, Troublemakers, Nobodies: Black Children in Elementary School.* Westport, CT: Greenwood Press.

GRAMS, ROBERT, and RACHEL ROHDE. 1976. Unpublished report to Judges Committee. Hennepin County, Minnesota District Court.

GRANOVETTER, MARK. 1995. *Getting a Job*, 2d ed. Chicago: University of Chicago Press.

GRANT, MADISON. 1916. *The Passing of the Great Race or the Racial Basis of European History.* New York: Scribner's.

GREBLER, LEO, JOAN W. MOORE, and RALPH C. GUZMAN. 1970. *The Mexican-American People.* New York: Free Press.

GREELEY, ANDREW M. 1982. *Catholic High Schools and Minority Students.* New Brunswick, NJ: Transaction Books.

———. 1977. *The American Catholic: A Social Portrait.* New York: Basic Books.

———. 1974. *Ethnicity in the United States: A Preliminary Reconnaissance.* New York: Wiley.

———. 1971. *Why Can't They Be Like Us?* New York: Dutton.

———. 1970. "Religious Intermarriage in a Denominational Society." *American Journal of Sociology* 75: 949–52.

GREELEY, ANDREW M., and PAUL B. SHEATSLEY. 1971. "Attitudes Toward Racial Integration." *Scientific American* 225, 6: 13–19.

GREEN, RAYMOND J., and ROBERT MANZI, JR. 2002. "A Comparison of Methodologies for Uncovering the Structure of Racial Stereotype Subgrouping." *Social Behavior and Personality* 30, 7: 709–28.

GRIMSHAW, ALLEN D. 1969. "Three Major Cases of Racial Violence in the United States." Pp. 105–15 in Allen D. Grimshaw (ed.), *Racial Violence in the United States.* Chicago: Aldine.

———. 1959a. "Lawlessness and Violence in America and Their Special Manifestations of Changing Negro-White Relationships." *Journal of Negro History* 64: 52–72.

———. 1959b. "A Study of Social Violence: Urban Race Riots in the United States." Ph.D. diss., University of Pennsylvania, Philadelphia.

GRISCOM, JOAN L. 1992. "The Case of Sharon Kowalski and Karen Thompson: Ableism, Heterosexism, and Sexism." Pp. 215–25 in Paula S. Rothenberg (ed.), *Race, Class, and Gender in the United States: An Integrated Study.* New York: St. Martin's Press.

GRODZINS, MORTON. 1949. *Americans Betrayed: Politics and the Japanese Evacuation.* Chicago: University of Chicago Press.

GROGGER, JEFFREY. 2003. "The Effects of Time Limits, the EITC, and Other Policy Changes on Welfare Use, Work, and Income Among Female-Headed Families." *Review of Economics and Statistics.* 85, 2: 394–408. Also available online at http://www.sppsr.ucla.edu/faculty/grogger/tlwwi_rev.pdf

GROSS, JANE. 1990. "Men and Women in Office: On Parity and Equality." *New York Times*, August 21, sec. A.

GROSS, SAMUEL, and ROBERT MAURO. 1989. *Death and Discrimination: Racial Disparities in Capital Sentencing.* Boston: Northeastern University Press.

GROSSARTH-MATICEK, R., HANS J. EYSENCK, and H. VETTER. 1989. "The Causes and Cures of Prejudice: An Empirical Study of the Frustration-Aggression Hypothesis." *Personality and Individual Differences* 10: 547–59.

GROSSMAN, BARRY A. 1974. "The Discretionary Enforcement of Law." In Sawyer F. Sylvester and Edward Sagarin (eds.), *Politics and Crime.* New York: Praeger.

GRUBE, J. W., and M. MORGAN. 1990. "Attitude–Social Support Interactions: Contingent Consistency Effects in the Predic-

tion of Adolescent Smoking, Drinking, and Drug Use." *Social Psychology Quarterly* 53: 329–39.

GRUBEN, WILLIAM C. 1998. "NAFTA Revisited: The Impact of the North American Free Trade Agreement on Maquiladora Employment." *Texas Business Review* (December).

GRUNWALD, MICHAEL. 1997. "Welfare-to-Work Isn't Cheap: How She Got a Job." *The American Prospect* 33: 25–29. Also available via World Wide Web, http://epn.org/prospect/33/33grunfs.html

GUEST, AVERY M., GUNNAR ALMGREN, and JON M. HUSSEY. 1998. "The Ecology of Race and Socioeconomic Distress: Infant and Working-Age Mortality in Chicago." *Demography* 35: 23–34.

GUEST, AVERY M., and JAMES A. WEED. 1976. "Ethnic Residential Segregation: Patterns of Change." *American Journal of Sociology* 81: 1088–1111.

GUILLEMIN, JEANE. 1978. "The Politics of National Integration: A Comparison of United States and Canadian Indian Administrations." *Social Problems* 25: 319–32.

GUINIER, LANI. 1998. "An Equal Chance." *New York Times*, op-ed page, April 23. Also available via World Wide Web, http://humanitas.ucsb.edu/projects/aa/docs/guinier.html

GURIN, PATRICIA. 1999. Expert report of Patricia Gurin, in "The Compelling Need for Diversity in Higher Education," presented in *Gratz et al. v. Bollinger et al.* and *Grutter et al. v. Bollinger et al.* Washington, DC: Wilmer, Cutler, Pickering.

GUTERL, MATTHEW PRATT. 2001. *The Color of Race in America, 1900–1940.* Cambridge, MA: Harvard University Press.

GUTMAN, HERBERT. 1976. *The Black Family in Slavery and Freedom, 1750–1925.* New York: Pantheon.

HACKER, ANDREW. 1992. *Two Nations: Black and White, Separate, Hostile, Unequal.* New York: Scribner's.

HAERTEL, EDWARD H. 1987. "Comparing Public and Private Schools Using Longitudinal Data from the HSB Study." Pp. 9–32 in Edward H. Haertel, Thomas James, and Henry M. Levin (eds.), *Comparing Public and Private Schools*, Vol. 2, *School Achievement.* New York: Falmer.

HAGAN, JOHN. 1985. *Modern Criminology: Crime, Criminal Behavior, and Its Control.* New York: McGraw-Hill.

———. 1974. "Extra-Legal Attributes and Criminal Sentencing: An Assessment of a Sociological Viewpoint." *Law and Society Review* 8: 357–83.

HAGGARD, ERNEST A. 1954. "Social Status and Intelligence." *Genetic Psychology Monographs* 49: 141–86.

HAIMOWITZ, MORRIS L., and NATALIE R. HAIMOWITZ. 1950. "Reducing Ethnic Hostility Through Psychotherapy." *Journal of Social Psychology* (May): 231–41.

HALEY, ALEX (ED.). 1964. *The Autobiography of Malcolm X.* New York: Grove Press.

HALL, EDWIN L., and ALBERT A. SIMKUS. 1975. "Inequality in Types of Sentence Received by Native Americans and Whites." *Criminology* 13, 2: 199–222.

HALL, RAYMOND L. 1978. *Black Separatism in the United States.* Hanover, NH: University Press of New England.

HALL, ROBERT L., MARK RODEGHIER, and BERT USEEM. 1986. "Effects of Education on Attitudes to Protest." *American Sociological Review* 51: 564–73.

HALL, THOMAS D. 1993. "Bound Labor: The Spanish Borderlands." Pp. 35–44 in Jacob Ernest Cooke (ed.), *Encyclopedia of the North American Colonies.* New York: Charles Scribner's Sons.

———. 1989. *Social Change in the Southwest, 1350–1880.* Lawrence: University of Kansas Press.

HALLER, EMIL J. 1985. "Pupil Race and Elementary School Ability Grouping: Are Teachers Biased Against Black Children?" *American Educational Research Journal* 22: 465–83.

HALLINAN, MAUREEN T. 1992. "The Organization of Students for Instruction in the Middle School." *Sociology of Education* 65: 114–27.

HAMER, DEAH H., STELLA HU, VICTORIA L. MAGNUSON, NAN HU, and ANGELA M. L. PATTATUCCI. 1993. "A Linkage Between DNA Markers on the X Chromosome and Male Sexual Orientation." *Science* 261, 519: 321–27.

HAMER, JENNIFER. 2001. *What It Means to Be a Daddy: Fatherhood for Black Men Living Away from Their Children.* New York: Columbia University Press.

HAMILTON, DAVID L. 1981. *Cognitive Processes in Stereotyping and Intergroup Behavior.* Hillsdale, NJ: Erlbaum.

HAMILTON, GLORIA, and J. DAVID ROESNER. 1972. "How Employers Screen Disadvantaged Workers." *Monthly Labor Review* (September).

HAMILTON, PHILIP. 1998. "Revolutionary Principles and Family Loyalties: Slavery's Transformation in the St. George Tucker Household of Early National Virginia." *William and Mary Quarterly* 55, 3: 531–56.

HAMNETT, BRIAN R. 1996. "Liberalism Divided: Regional Politics and the National Project During the Mexican Restored Republic, 1867–1876." *Hispanic American Historical Review* 76: 659–89.

HANDLIN, OSCAR, and MARY F. HANDLIN. 1950. "Origins of the Southern Labor System." *William and Mary Quarterly* 7: 199–222.

HANE, MIKISO. 1990. "Wartime Internment." *Journal of American History* 77: 569–75.

HANKS, ROMA STOVALL, and MARJORIE ICENOGLE. 2001. "Preparing for an Age-Diverse Workforce: Intergenerational Service-Learning in Social Gerontology and Business Curricula." *Educational Gerontology* 27, 1: 49–70.

HANSEN, MARCUS L. 1966. "The Third Generation." Pp. 255–72 in Oscar Handlin (ed.), *Children of the Uprooted.* New York: Harper & Row.

———. 1952. "The Third Generation in America." *Commentary* 14: 492–500.

HANSEN, MARK. 1998. "A Road No Longer Taken." *ABA Journal* 84: 28–29.

HANUSHEK, ERIC A. 1998. "Conclusions and Controversies About the Effectiveness of School Resources." *Economic Policy Review* 4: 11–27.

———. 1992. "The Trade-off Between Child Quantity and Quality." *Journal of Political Economy* 100: 84–117.

HARDING, JOHN, HAROLD PROSHANSKY, BERNARD KUTNER, and ISADOR CHEIN. 1969. "Prejudice and Ethnic Relations." Pp. 1–77 in Gardner Lindzey and Elliott Aronson (eds.), *The Handbook of Social Psychology,* 2d ed., Vol. 5. Reading, MA: Addison-Wesley.

HARKINS, STEPHEN G., and RICHARD E. PETTY. 1987. "Information Utility and the Multiple Source Effect." *Journal of Personality and Social Psychology* 52: 260–68.

HARRIS, KATHLEEN MULLAN. 1993. "Work and Welfare Among Single Mothers in Poverty." *American Journal of Sociology* 99: 317–52.

HARRIS-WARRICK, RONALD M., and EVE MARDER. 1991. "Modulation of Neural Networks for Behavior." *Annual Review of Neuroscience* 14: 39–57.

HARRISON, BENNETT. 1972. *Education, Training, and the Urban Ghetto.* Baltimore, MD: Johns Hopkins University Press.

HARRISON, RODERICK J., and DANIEL H. WEINBERG. 1992a. "Changes in Racial and Ethnic Segregation, 1980–1990." Paper presented at the Annual Meeting of the American Statistical Association, August 9–13, Boston.

———. 1992b. "Racial and Ethnic Residential Segregation in 1990." Paper presented at the Annual Meeting of the Population Association of America, May, Denver, Colorado.

HARTLEY, E. M. 1946. *Problems in Prejudice.* New York: King's Crown Press.

HARTLEY, RUTH E. 1974. "Sex-Role Pressures and the Socialization of the Male Child." Pp. 185–98 in Judith Stacey, Susan Bereaud, and Joan Daniels (eds.) *And Jill Came Tumbling After: Sexism in American Education.* New York: Dell. [Reprinted from *Psychological Reports* 5 (1959).]

HARVEY, D. G., and G. T. SLATIN. 1975. "The Relationship as Hypothesis." *Social Forces* 54: 140–59.

HASIAN, MAROUF, JR., and FERNANDO DELGADO. 1998. "The Trials and Tribulations of Racialized Critical Rhetorical Theory: Understanding the Rhetorical Ambiguities of Proposition 187." *Communication Theory* 8: 245–70.

HASLAM, NICK, LOUIS ROTHSCHILD, and DONALD ERNST. 2002. "Are Essentialist Beliefs Associated with Prejudice?" *British Journal of Social Psychology* 41, 1: 87–100.

HASSO, FRANCES S. 2001. "Feminist Generations? The Long-Term Impact of Social Movement Involvement on Palestinian Women's Lives." *American Journal of Sociology* 107: 586–611.

HASSAN, M. K. 1987. "Parental Behavior, Authoritarianism, and Prejudice." *Manas* 34, 1–2: 41–50.

HASSAN, M. K., and A. KHALIQUE 1987. "Impact of Parents on Children's Religious Prejudice." *Indian Journal of Current Psychological Research* 2, 1: 47–55.

HAUSER, ROBERT M. 1995. "Review Symposium: The Bell Curve." *Contemporary Sociology* 24: 149–53.

HAUSER, ROBERT M., WILLIAM H. SEWELL, and DUANE F. ALWIN. 1976. "High School Effects on Achievement." Pp. 309–41 in William H. Sewell, Robert M. Hauser, and David L. Featherman (eds.), *Schooling and Achievement in American Society.* New York: Academic Press.

HAWKINS, HUGH. 1962. *Booker T. Washington and His Critics: The Problem of Negro Leadership.* Boston: Heath.

HAWLEY, WILLIS D., JAMES A. BANKS, AMADO M. PADILLA, DONALD B. POPE-DAVIS, and JANET WARD SCHOFIELD. 1995. "Strategies for Reducing Racial and Ethnic Prejudice: Essential Principles for Program Design." Pp. 423–33 in Willis D. Hawley and Anthony W. Jackson (eds.), *Toward a Common Destiny: Improving Race and Ethnic Relations in America.* San Francisco: Jossey-Bass.

HAWORTH, KARLA. 1998. "Minority Admissions Fall on 3 U. of California Campuses." *Chronicle of Higher Education* (March 27): A41. Also available on World Wide Web, http://www.chronicle.com/che-data/articles.dir/art-44.dir/issue-29.dir/29a04101.htm

HAYES, CHERYL D. 1987a. "Adolescent Pregnancy and Childbearing: An Emerging Research Focus." Pp. 1–6 in Sandra Hofferth and Cheryl D. Hayes (eds.), *Risking the Future: Adolescent Sexuality, Pregnancy, and Childbearing,* Vol. 2, *Working Papers and Statistical Appendices.* Washington, DC: National Academy Press.

———. 1987b. *Risking the Future: Adolescent Sexuality, Pregnancy, and Childbearing. Report of the Panel on Adolescent Pregnancy and Childbearing, National Research Council,* Vol. 1. Washington, DC: National Academy Press.

HAYES, CHERYL D., and SHEILA KAMERMAN (EDS.), 1983. *Children of Working Parents: Experiences and Outcomes.* Washington, DC: National Academy Press.

HAYNES, M. ALFRED, and MICHAEL R. GARVEY. 1969. "Physicians, Patients, and Hospitals in the Inner City." Pp. 117–24 in John C. Norman (ed.), *Medicine in the Ghetto.* New York: Appleton-Century-Crofts.

HEALY, PATRICK. 1998a. "Admissions Law Changes the Equations for Students and Colleges in Texas." *Chronicle of Higher Education* (April 3): A29–31.

———. 1998b. "Berkeley Struggles to Stay Diverse in Post–Affirmative-Action Era." *Chronicle of Higher Education* (May 29): A31. Also available via World Wide Web, http://www.chronicle.com/che-data/articles.dir/art-44.dir/issue-38.dir/38a03101.htm

HEAVEN, PATRICK C., and ADRIAN FURNHAM. 1987. "Race Prejudice and Economic Beliefs." *Journal of Social Psychology* 127: 483–89.

HELEM, LISA. 2001. "Poll: Racial Split Widens, Blacks, Whites in U.S. See Two Americas." *Atlanta Constitution,* July 11.

HELLER, DANIEL A. 1998. "Support for Ebonics." *English Journal* 87, 4: 89.

HELMICH, EDITH. 1985. *The Effectiveness of Preschool for Children from Low-Income Families: A Review of the Literature.* Springfield: Illinois State Board of Education, Department of Planning, Research, and Evaluation.

HELMS, L. JAY, JOSEPH P. NEWHOUSE, and CHARLES E. PHELPS. 1978. *Copayments and Demand for Medical Care: The California Medicaid Experience.* Report no. R-2167-HEW. Santa Monica, CA: Rand Corporation.

HEMPHILL, HELLEN, and RAY HAINES. 1997. *Discrimination, Harassment, and the Failure of Diversity Training: What to Do Now?* Westport, CT: Quorum Books.

HENSHAW, STANLEY K. 1998. "Unintended Pregnancy in the United States." *Family Planning Perspectives* 30: 24–29, 46.

HERMALIN, ALBERT I., and REYNOLDS FARLEY. 1973. "The Potential for Residential Integration in Cities and Suburbs: Implications for the Busing Controversy." *American Sociological Review* 38: 595–610.

HERRING, CEDRIC, HAYWARD DERRICK HORTON, VERNA KEITH, and MELVIN THOMAS. 2000. "Race Traitors, Self-Haters, or Equal Opportunists?: Explaining Support for the 'Wrong Views' on Affirmative Action." Paper presented at annual meetings of the American Sociological Association, Washington, DC, August 12–16.

HERRNSTEIN, RICHARD J., and CHARLES MURRAY. 1994. *The Bell Curve: Intelligence and Class Structure in American Life.* New York: Free Press.

HERSHBERG, THEODORE, HANS BURSTEIN, EUGENE P. ERICKSEN, STEPHANIE GREENBERG, and WILLIAM L. YANCEY. 1978. "A Tale of Three Cities: Blacks and Immigrants in Philadelphia: 1850–1880, 1930, and 1970." *Annals of the American Academy of Political and Social Science* 441 (January): 55–81.

HEWSTONE, MILES, MARK RUBIN, and HAZEL WILLIS. 2002. "Intergroup Bias." *Annual Review of Psychology* 53: 575–604.

HIGGENBOTHAM, ELIZABETH. 1992. "We Were Never on a Pedestal: Women of Color Continue to Struggle with Poverty, Racism, and Sexism." Pp. 183–90 in Margaret L. Anderson and Patricia Hill Collins (eds.), *Race, Class, and Gender: An Anthology.* Belmont, CA: Wadsworth.

HIGGENBOTHAM, JOHN C., FERNANDO M. TREVINO, and LAURA A. RAY. 1990. "Utilization of *Curanderos* by Mexican Americans: Prevalence and Predictors. Findings from HHANES 1982–84." *American Journal of Public Health* 80 (suppl): 32–35.

HIGHAM, JOHN. 1974. "Integration vs. Pluralism: Another American Dilemma." *Center Magazine* 7 (July–August): 67–73.

HILDEBRAND, KAREN. 1998. "Allstate, Hispanics Connect." *Colorado Business Magazine* 25, 1 (January): SS8.

HILL, ROBERT. 1972. *The Strengths of Black Families.* New York: Emerson Hall.

HILLIARD, ASA G. 1988. "Conceptual Confusion and the Persistence of Group Oppression Through Education." *Equity and Excellence* 24, 1: 36–43.

HINDELANG, MICHAEL J. 1969. "Equality Under the Law." *Journal of Criminal Law, Criminology, and Police Science* 60: 306–13.

HINES, RALPH. 1972. "The Health Status of Black Americans: Changing Perspectives." Pp. 40–50 in E. Jaco (ed.), *Patients, Physicians, and Illness,* 2d ed. New York: Free Press.

HITLER, ADOLF. 1940 [1925–1927]. *Mein Kampf.* New York: Reynmal and Hitchcock, 1940.

HOCHSCHILD, ARLIE. 1989. *The Second Shift: Working Parents and the Revolution at Home.* New York: Viking Penguin.

HODGSON, SUSAN. 1979. "Childrearing Systems: The Influence of Shared Childrearing on the Development of Competence." In William Michelson, Saul V. Levine, and Anna-Rose Spina (eds.), *The Child in the City: Changes and Challenges.* Toronto: University of Toronto Press.

HOFFER, THOMAS, ANDREW M. GREELEY, and JAMES S. COLEMAN. 1987. "Catholic High School Effects on Achievement Growth." Pp. 67–88 in Edward H. Haertel, Thomas James, and Henry M. Levin (eds.), *Comparing Public and Private Schools,* Vol. 2, *School Achievement.* New York: Falmer.

———. 1985. "Achievement Growth in Public and Catholic Schools." *Sociology of Education* 58: 74–97.

HOFFMAN, C., and N. HURST. 1990. "Gender Stereotypes: Perception or Rationalization?" *Journal of Personality and Social Psychology* 58: 197–208.

HOFFMANN, LOIS WLADIS. 1989. "Effects of Maternal Employment in the Two-Parent Family." *American Psychologist* (February): 283–92.

HOFFMAN, LOIS W., and LISA M. YOUNGBLAD. 1999. *Mothers at Work: Effects on Children's Well-Being.* Cambridge, UK: Cambridge University Press.

HOFFMAN, SAUL D., and GREG J. DUNCAN. 1995. "The Effect of Income, Wages, and AFDC Benefits on Marital Disruption." *Journal of Human Resources* 30, 1: 19–41.

HOLCOMB, PAMELA A., TERRI S. THOMPSON, CAROLINE E. RATCLIFFE, DAVID J. FEIN, ERIK BEECROFT, WILLIAM HAMILTON, and WANG S. LEE. 1998. "The Indiana Welfare Reform Evaluation: Program Implementation and Economic Impacts After Two Years." Washington, DC: The Urban Institute and Abt Associates.

HOLLINGER, RICHARD C. 1984. "Race, Occupational Status, and Proactive Police Arrest for Drinking and Driving." *Journal of Criminal Justice* 12: 173–83.

HOLMES, MALCOLM D., and HOWARD C. DAUDISTEL. 1984. "Ethnicity and Justice in the Southwest: The Sentencing of Anglo, Black, and Mexican Origin Defendants." *Social Science Quarterly* 65: 265–77.

HOLMES, MALCOLM D., HOWARD C. DAUDISTEL, and RONALD A. FARRELL. 1987. "Determinants of Charge Reductions and Final Dispositions in Cases of Burglary and Robbery." *Journal of Research in Crime and Delinquency* 24: 233–54.

HOLZER, HARRY J. 1996. *What Employers Want: Job Prospects for Less-Educated Workers.* New York: Russell Sage Foundation.

HOLZER, HARRY J., and KEITH R. IHLANFELDT. 1996. "Spatial Factors and the Employment of Blacks at the Firm Level." *New England Economic Review* (May–June): 65.

HOLZER, HARRY J., and DAVID NEUMARK. 2000. "Assessing Affirmative Action." *Journal of Economic Literature* 38: 483–568.

———. 1999. "Are Affirmative Action Hires Less Qualified? Evidence from Employer-Employee Data on New Hires." *Journal of Labor Economics* 17: 534–69.

HONEMAN, BOB. 1990. "Rationale and Ideas for Emphasizing Afrocentricity in the Public Schools." Paper presented at the Conference on Rhetoric and Teaching of Writing, July 10–11, Indiana, Pennsylvania.

HOOKS, BELL. 1991. "Black Women Intellectuals." Pp. 147–64 in bell hooks and Cornell West, *Breaking Bread: Insurgent Black Intellectual Life.* Boston: South End Press.

———. 1989. *Talking Back: Thinking Feminist, Thinking Black.* Boston: South End Press.

———. 1981. *Ain't I a Woman: Black Women and Feminism.* Boston: South End Press.

HORTON, JOHN. 1966. "Order and Conflict Theories of Social Problems as Competitive Ideologies." *American Journal of Sociology* 71: 701–13. Reprinted in Norman R. Yetman and C. Hoy Steele, 1975, *Majority and Minority,* 2d ed. Boston: Allyn & Bacon.

HOVLAND, CARL I., IRVING L. JANIS, and HAROLD H. KELLEY. 1953. *Communication and Persuasion.* New Haven, CT: Yale University Press.

HOWARD, JEFF. 1995. "You Can't Get There from Here: The Need for a New Logic in Education Reform." *Daedalus, Journal of the American Academy of Arts and Sciences* 124, 4.

HUDSON-WEEMS, CLENORA. 2001. "Africana Womanism: The Flip Side of a Coin." *The Western Journal of Black Studies* 25, 3: 137–45.

———. 1993. *Africana Womanism: Reclaiming Ourselves.* Troy, MI: Bedford Publishers.

HUMM, ANDREW. 1980. "The Personal Politics of Lesbian and Gay Liberation." *Social Policy* 11, 2: 40–45.

HUMPHREY, JOHN A., and TIMOTHY J. FOGARTY. 1987. "Race and Plea-Bargained Outcomes: A Research Note." *Social Forces* 66: 176–82.

HUMPHREYS, DEBRA. 2000. "National Survey Finds Diversity Requirements Common Around the Country." *Diversity Digest* (Fall). World Wide Web, http://www.diversityweb.org/Digest/F00/survey.html

HUNT, CHESTER, and LEWIS WALKER. 1974. *Ethnic Dynamics: Patterns of Intergroup Relations in Various Societies.* Homewood, IL: Dorsey Press.

HUNTER, ANDREA, JANE L. PEARSON, NICHOLAS S. IALONGO, and SHEPPARD G. KELLAM. 1998. "Parenting Alone to Multiple Caregivers: Child Care and Parenting Arrangements in Black and White Urban Families." *Family Relations* 47, 4: 343–53.

HUNTER, GUY. 1965. *Industrialisation and Race Relations.* London: Oxford University Press.

HURD, HILARY. 2000. "Corporations Lend Support to U-Michigan's Diversity Efforts." *Black Issues in Higher Education* (November 9): 18–19.

HURN, CHRISTOPHER. 1978. *The Limits and Possibilities of Schooling: An Introduction to the Sociology of Education.* Boston: Allyn & Bacon.

HURTADO, ALBERT L. 1988. *Indian Survival on the California Frontier.* New Haven, CT: Yale University Press.

HURTADO, SYLVIA. 2001. "Linking Diversity and Educational Purpose: How Diversity Affects the Classroom Environment and Student Development." In Gary Orfield (ed.), *Diversity Challenged: Evidence on the Impact of Affirmative Action.* Cambridge, MA: Harvard Education Publishing Group.

HUTCHINSON, PETER M. 1974. "The Effects of Accessibility and Segregation on the Employment of the Urban Poor." Pp. 74–96 in George M. von Furstenberg, Bennett Harrison, and Ann R. Horowitz (eds.), *Patterns of Racial Discrimination,* Vol. 1, *Housing.* Lexington, MA: Lexington Books.

HUTTENBACH, HENRY R. 1990. "Conclusion: Towards a Multiethnic Soviet State: Managing a Multinational Society Since 1985." Pp. 286–91 in Henry R. Huttenbach (ed.), *Soviet Nationality Policies: Ruling Ethnic Groups in the U.S.S.R.* London: Mansell Publishing.

HWANG, SEAN-SHONG, and STEVE H. MURDOCK. 1983. "Segregation in Nonmetropolitan and Metropolitan Texas in 1980." *Rural Sociology* 48: 607–23.

———. 1982. "Residential Segregation in Texas in 1980." *Social Science Quarterly* 63: 737–48.

HYMAN, HERBERT H., and PAUL B. SHEATSLEY. 1964. "Attitudes Toward Desegregation." *Scientific American* 211: 2–9.

IBISH, HUSSEIN, and ANNE STEWART. 2003. *Report on Hate Crime and Discrimination Against Arab Americans: The Post–September 11 Backlash: September 11, 2001–October 11, 2002.* Washington, DC: American-Arab Anti Discrimination Committee.

ICHIHASHI, YAMATO. 1969. *Japanese in the United States.* New York: Arno Press and the *New York Times.* (First published by Stanford University Press, 1932.)

IGNATIEV, NOEL. 1995. *How the Irish Became White.* New York: Routledge.

IHLANFELDT, KEITH R. 1993. "Intra-Urban Job Accessibility and Hispanic Youth Unemployment Rates." *Journal of Urban Economics* 33: 254–71.

———. 1992. *Job Accessibility and the Employment and School Enrollment of Teenagers.* Kalamazoo, MI: W.E. Upjohn Institute for Employment Research.

IHLANFELDT, KEITH R., and BENJAMIN SCAFIDI. 2004. "Whites' Neighborhood Preferences and Neighborhood Racial Com-

position in the United States: Evidence from the Multi-City Study of Urban Inequality." Forthcoming in *Urban Studies.*

———. 2002. "Black Self-Segregation as a Cause of Housing Segregation: Evidence from the Multi-City Study of Urban Inequality." *Journal of Urban Economics* 51: 366–90.

IHLANFELDT, KEITH R., and DAVID L. SJOQUIST. 1998. "The Spatial Mismatch Hypothesis: A Review of Recent Studies." *Housing Policy Debate* 9: 849–92. Also available online at http://www.fanniemaefoundation.org/programs/hpd/pdf/hpd_0904_ihlanfeldt.pdf

———. 1991. "The Effect of Job Access on Black and White Youth Unemployment: A Cross-Sectional Analysis." *Urban Studies* 28: 255–65.

———. 1990. "Job Accessibility and Racial Differences in Youth Unemployment Rates." *American Economic Review* 80: 267–76.

ILLINOIS BOARD OF HIGHER EDUCATION. 2001. *Gateway to Success: Rethinking Access and Diversity for a New Century. Report of the Committee on Access and Diversity.* Springfield: Illinois Board of Higher Education.

ILLINOIS CAPITAL DEVELOPMENT BOARD. 1977. *The East St. Louis Area: An Overview of State Capital Projects and Policies.* Springfield: Illinois Capital Development Board.

INDIAN HEALTH SERVICE. 2002. "Facts on Indian Health Disparities." Available online at http://info.ihs.gov/Health/Health11.pdf (downloaded May 1, 2004).

INSTITUTE FOR THE STUDY OF SOCIAL CHANGE. 1991. *The Diversity Project: Final Report.* Berkeley: University of California.

JABIN, NORMA. 1987. "Attitudes Toward Disability: Horney's Theory Applied." *American Journal of Psychoanalysis* 47: 143–53.

JACKMAN, MARY R., and MARIE CRANE. 1986. " 'Some of My Best Friends Are Black . . . ': Interracial Friendship and Whites' Racial Attitudes." *Public Opinion Quarterly* 50: 459–86.

JACKMAN, MARY R., and MICHAEL J. MUHA. 1984. "Education and Intergroup Attitudes: Moral Enlightenment, Superficial Democratic Commitment, or Ideological Refinement?" *American Sociological Review* 49: 751–69.

JACKMAN, MARY R. and MARY S. SENTER. 1983. "Different, Therefore Unequal: Beliefs about Trait Differences Between Groups of Unequal Status." *Research in Social Stratification and Mobility* 2: 309–35.

JACKSON, AURORA P. 2003. "Mothers' Employment and Poor and Near-Poor African-American Children's Development: A Longitudinal Study." *Social Service Review* (March): 93–109.

JAEGER, RICHARD M., and JOHN A. HATTIE. 1995. "Detracking America's Schools: Should We Really Care?" *Phi Delta Kappan* 77: 218–19.

JAKUBS, JOHN F. 1986. "Recent Racial Segregation in U.S. SMSAs." *Urban Geography* 7: 146–63.

JANYES, GERALD, and ROBIN WILLIAMS (EDS.). 1989. *A Common Destiny: Blacks and American Society.* Washington, DC: National Academy Press.

JASCHIK, SCOTT. 1993. "Backed by 1990 Law, People with Disabilities Press Demands on Colleges." *Chronicle of Higher Education* (February 3): A26.

———. 1992. "Education Department Says Affirmative Action Policies of Berkeley's Law School Violated Federal Anti-Bias Laws." *Chronicle of Higher Education* (October 7): A21, A25.

JEFFRIES, JUDSON L. 2002. "Police Use of Excessive Force Against Black Males: Aberrations or Everyday Occurrences." *Journal of Mundane Behavior* 3, 3. World Wide Web, http://mundanebehavior.org/issues/v3n3/jeffries.htm (downloaded August 6, 2003).

JEKIELEK, SUSAN M. 1998. "Parental Conflict, Marital Disruption, and Children's Emotional Well-Being." *Social Forces* 76: 905–36.

JENCKS, CHRISTOPHER. 2002. "Liberal Lessons from Welfare Reform." *The American Prospect* 13, 13. Available online at http://www.prospect.org/print/V13/13/jencks-c.html (downloaded July 30, 2003).

———. 1998. "Racial Bias in Testing." Pp. 55–85 in Christopher Jencks and Meredith Phillips (eds.), *The Black-White Test Score Gap.* Washington, DC: Brookings Institution.

———. 1997. "The Hidden Paradox of Welfare Reform: Why Single Mothers May Earn More But Do Worse." *The American Prospect* 32: 33–40. Also available via World Wide Web, http://epn.org/prospect/32/32jenkfs.html

———. 1991. "Is the American Underclass Growing?" Pp. 28–100 in Christopher Jencks and Paul E. Peterson (eds.), *The Urban Underclass.* Washington, DC: Brookings Institution.

———. 1985. "How Much Do High School Students Learn?" *Sociology of Education* 58: 128–35.

JENCKS, CHRISTOPHER, and MEREDETH PHILLIPS. 1998. *The Black-White Test Score Gap.* Washington, DC: Brookings Institution Press.

JENCKS, CHRISTOPHER, MARSHALL SMITH, HENRY ACLAND, MARY JO BANE, DAVID COHEN, HERBERT GINTIS, BARBARA HEYNS, and STEPHAN MICHELSON. 1972. *Inequality: A Reassessment of the Effect of Family and Schooling in America.* New York: Basic Books.

JENKINS, J. CRAIG, and CRAIG M. ECKERT. 1986. "Channeling Black Insurgency: Elite Patronage and Professional Social Movement Organization in the Development of the Black Movement." *American Sociological Review* 51: 812–29.

JENKINS, J. CRAIG, and CHARLES PERROW. 1977. "Insurgency of the Powerless: Farm Workers' Movements (1946–1972)." *American Sociological Review* 42: 249–68.

JENSEN, ARTHUR. 1980. *Bias in Mental Testing.* New York: Free Press.

———. 1973. *Educability and Group Differences.* New York: Harper & Row.

———. 1969. "How Much Can We Boost IQ and Scholastic Achievement?" *Harvard Educational Review* 39: 1–123.

JESILOW, PAUL, GILBERT GEIS, and HENRY PONTELL. 1991. "Fraud by Physicians Against Medicaid." *JAMA* 266: 3318–22.

*JET.* 1993a. "Many Schools Continue to Separate Kids by Ability." *Jet* 83, 18 (March 1): 22.

———. 1993b. "Minority Directors Scarce in Corporate Boardrooms." *Jet* 83, 11 (January 11): 16.

JOFFE, JOSEF. 1992. "Bosnia: The Return of History." *Commentary* (October): 24–29.

JOHANSEN, BRUCE, and ROBERTO MAESTAS. 1979. *Wasi'chu: The Continuing Indian Wars.* New York: Monthly Review Press.

JOHNSON, CHARLES S. 1943. *Patterns of Negro Segregation.* New York: Harper & Row.

JOHNSON, D. A. 1990. "The Relationship Between School Integration and Student Attitude Toward Residential Racial Integration." Ph.D. dissertation, Pennsylvania State University, University Park. *Dissertation Abstracts International* 51: 2527.

JOHNSON, D. W., R. T. JOHNSON, and G. MARUYAMA. 1984. "Goal Interdependence and Interpersonal Attraction in Heterogeneous Classrooms: A Meta-Analysis." Pp. 187–212 in N. Miller and Marilyn B. Brewer (eds.), *Groups in Contact: The Psychology of Desegregation.* San Diego: Academic Press.

JOHNSON, GUY B. 1941. "The Negro and Crime." *The Annals of the American Academy of Political and Social Science* 217: 93–104.

JOHNSON, STEPHEN D. 1992. "Anti-Arabic Prejudice in 'Middletown.' " *Psychological Reports* 70: 811–18.

JOHNSTON, ROBERT C. 1998a. "Michigan." *Education Week* Online, World Wide Web, http://www.edweek.org/sreports/qc98/states/min.htm

JOINT CENTER FOR POLITICAL STUDIES. 2000. "Black Elected Officials: Number of Black Elected Officials in the United States by State and Office." World Wide Web, http://www.jointcenter.org/DB/detail/BEO.htm (downloaded July 17, 2003).

———. 1985. *Black Elected Officials: A National Roster, 1985.* Washington, DC: Joint Center for Political Studies.

———. 1977. *National Roster of Black Elected Officials, Vol. 7.* Washington, DC: Joint Center for Political Studies.

JONES, AISHA. 2002. "Homemaker and Homeworker: How the New Black Domestic Servant Manages the Care of Family and the Paid Care of Others." Paper presented at 2002 annual meeting of the Midwest Sociological Society, Milwaukee, WI, April 4–7.

JONES, ELISE F., JAQUELINE DARROCH FORREST, NOREEN GOLDMAN, STANLEY HENSHAW, RICHARD LINCOLN, JEANNE I. ROSOFF, CHARLES F. WESTOFF, and DIERDRE WULF. 1986. *Teenage Pregnancy in Industrialized Countries.* New Haven, CT: Yale University Press.

JONES, JAMES M. 1972. *Prejudice and Racism.* Reading, MA: Addison-Wesley.

JONES, JAQUELINE. 1985. *Labor of Love, Labor of Sorrow: Black Women, Work, and the Family from Slavery to the Present.* New York: Basic Books.

JONES DE ALMEIDA, ADJOA FLORENCIA. 2003. "Unveiling the Mirror: Afro-Brazilian Identity and the Emergence of a Community School Movement." *Comparative Education Review* 47: 41–63.

JORDAN, WINTHROP D. 1968. *White over Black.* Chapel Hill: University of North Carolina Press.

———. 1962. "Modern Tensions and the Origins of American Slavery." *Journal of Southern History* 18: 18–30.

JORGENSEN, JOSEPH G. 1972. *The Sun Dance Religion: Power for the Powerless.* Chicago: University of Chicago Press.

JOSEPHY, ALVIN M. (ED.). 1992. *America in 1492: The World of the Indian Peoples Before the Arrival of Columbus.* New York: Alfred A. Knopf.

JOSEPHY, ALVIN M., JR. 1968. *The Indian Heritage of America.* New York: Alfred A. Knopf. (Bantam Ed. 1969.)

*JOURNAL OF BLACKS IN HIGHER EDUCATION.* 2003. "Jeb Bush Ducks the Truth About Black Enrollments in Florida's Public Universities." *Journal of Blacks in Higher Education* 41: 48–49.

———. 1996/97. "News and Views: The Banneker Ruling: Two Years Later Scholarships for Blacks Are Drying Up." *Journal of Blacks in Higher Education* 14: 38–40.

JUNG, MOON-KIE. 2002. "Different Racisms and the Differences They Make: *Race* and 'Asian Workers' of Prewar Hawai'i." *Critical Sociology* 28: 77–102.

———. 1999. "No Whites, No Asians: Race, Marxism, and Hawai'i's Preemergent Working Class." *Social Science History* 23, 3: 357–93.

JUSSIM, LEE, JACQUELYNNE ECCLES, and STEPHANIE MADON. 1996. "Social Perception, Social Stereotypes, and Teacher Expectations: Accuracy and the Quest for the Powerful Self-Fulfilling Prophecy." *Advances in Experimental Social Psychology* 28: 281–387.

KADISH, MORTIMER R., and SANFORD H. KADISH. 1973. *Discretion to Disobey.* Palo Alto, CA: Stanford University Press.

KAGAN, JEROME. 1971. "The Magical Aura of the IQ." *Saturday Review of Literature* (December 4): 92–93.

KAHLENBERG, RICHARD D. 1996. *The Remedy: Class, Race, and Affirmative Action.* New York: Basic Books.

KAIN, JOHN F. 1992. "The Spatial Mismatch Hypothesis: Three Decades Later." *Housing Policy Debate* 3, 2: 371–462.

———. 1987. "Housing Market Discrimination and Black Suburbanization in the 1980s." In Gary A. Tobin (ed.), *Divided Neighborhoods.* Beverly Hills, CA: Sage.

———. 1968. "Housing Segregation, Negro Employment, and Metropolitan Decentralization." *Quarterly Journal of Economics* (May): 175–97.

KALMIJN, MATTHIJS. 1998. "Intermarriage and Homogamy: Causes, Patterns, Trends." *Annual Review of Sociology* 24: 395–421.

KAMIN, LEON J. 1974. *The Science and Politics of IQ.* New York: Wiley.

KAMO, YOSHINORI, and ELLEN L. COHEN. 1998. "Division of Household Work Between Partners: A Comparison of Black and White Couples." *Journal of Comparative Family Studies* 29, 1: 131–45.

KANE, MICHAEL B. 1970. *Minorities in Textbooks: A Study of Their Treatment in Social Science Texts.* Chicago: Quadrangle.

KANE, THOMAS J. 1998. "Racial and Ethnic Preferences in College Admission." In Christopher Jencks and Meredith Phillips (eds.), *The Black-White Test Score Gap.* Washington, DC: Brookings Institution.

KANTROWITZ, NATHAN. 1979. "Racial and Ethnic Residential Segregation in Boston 1930–1970." *Annals of the American Academy of Political and Social Science* 441 (January): 41–54.

KAPLAN, DAVID H. 1994. "Population and Politics in a Plural Society: The Changing Geography of Canada's Linguistic Groups." *Annals of the Association of American Geographers* 84: 46–67.

KARLEN, A. 1971. *Sexuality and Homosexuality.* New York: Norton.

KARLINS, MARVIN, THOMAS COFFMAN, and GARY WALTERS. 1969. "On the Fading of Social Stereotypes: Studies in Three Generations of College Students." *Journal of Personality and Social Psychology* 13: 1–6.

KASARDA, JOHN D. 1990. "Structural Factors Affecting the Location and Timing of Underclass Growth." *Urban Geography* 11: 234–64.

———. 1989a. "Urban Change and Minority Opportunities." Pp. 147–67 in D. Stanley Eitzen and Maxine Baca Zinn (eds.), *The Reshaping of America: Social Consequences of the Changing Economy.* Englewood Cliffs, NJ: Prentice Hall.

———. 1989b. "Urban Industrial Transition and the Underclass." *Annals of the American Academy of Political and Social Science* 501: 26–47.

———. 1976. "The Changing Occupational Structure of the American Metropolis: Apropos the Urban Problem." Pp. 113–36 in Barry Schwartz (ed.), *The Changing Face of the Suburbs.* Chicago: University of Chicago Press.

KATZ, DONALD, and KENNETH BRALY. 1933. "Racial Stereotypes of One Hundred College Students." *Journal of Abnormal Psychology.* (October–December): 280–90.

KATZ, DONALD, I. SARNOFF, and C. McCLINTOCK. 1956. "Ego Defense and Attitude Change." *Human Relations* 9: 27–46.

KATZ, JESSE. 1991. "Gulf Tensions Seen as Factor in Record Level of Hate Crimes." *Los Angeles Times,* March 2, sec. B.

KATZ, PHYLLIS A., and SUE R. ZALK. 1974. "Doll Preferences: Index of Racial Attitudes?" *Journal of Educational Psychology* 66: 663–68.

KEIL, THOMAS J., and GENNARO F. VITO. 1995. "Race and the Death Penalty in Kentucky Murder Trials." *American Journal of Criminal Justice* 20: 17–36.

KELMAN, H. C. 1958. "Compliance, Identification, and Internalization: Three Processes of Attitude Change." *Journal of Conflict Resolution* 2: 51–60.

KENDALL, PATRICIA L., and KATHERINE M. WOLF. 1949. "The Analysis of Deviant Cases in Communication Research." In Paul F. Lazarsfeld and Frank N. Stanton (eds.), *Communications Research, 1948–1949.* New York: Harper & Row.

KENNEDY, MARGARET A. 1992. "Testing to Uncover Unfair Hiring." *Nation's Business* (February): 36–37.

KENNEDY, RUBY JO REEVES. 1952. "Single or Triple Melting Pot? Intermarriage in New Haven, 1870–1950." *American Journal of Sociology* 58: 56–69.

———. 1944. "Single or Triple Melting Pot? Intermarriage Trends in New Haven, 1870–1940." *American Journal of Sociology* 49: 331–39.

KIER, ELIZABETH. 1998. "Homosexuals in the U.S. Military: Open Integration and Combat Effectiveness." *International Security* 23, 2: 5–39. Also available online at http://mitpress.mit.edu/journals/pdf/isec_23_02_5_0.pdf (downloaded October 10, 2003).

KIEV, ARI. 1968. *Curanderismo: Mexican-American Folk Psychiatry.* New York: Free Press.

KILLIAN, LEWIS M. 1975. *The Impossible Revolution, Phase 2: Black Power and the American Dream.* New York: Random House.

———. 1968. *The Impossible Revolution?* New York: Random House.

KILSON, MARTIN, and CLEMENT COTTINGHAM. 1991. "Thinking About Race Relations: How Far Are We Still from Integration?" *Dissent* 38: 520–30.

KIM, MYUNGOAK. 1997. "NAACP to Look at New Strategies: Delegates Will Debate the School Issue of 'To Bus or Not to Bus.'" *Houston Chronicle* (July 12).

KINDER, DONALD R., and LYNN M. SANDERS. 1996. *Divided by Color: Racial Politics and Democratic Ideals.* Chicago: University of Chicago Press.

KINDER, DONALD R., and D. O. SEARS. 1981. "Symbolic Racism Versus Racial Threats to the Good Life." *Journal of Personality and Social Psychology* 40: 414–31.

KING, DESMOND. 1995. *Separate and Unequal: Black Americans and the U.S. Federal Government.* New York: Clarendon Press, Oxford University Press.

KING, JOYCE. 2002. *Hate Crime: The Story of a Dragging in Jasper, Texas.* New York: Pantheon.

KINGSLEY, G. THOMAS, and KATHRYN L. S. PETTIT. 2003. "Concentrated Poverty: A Change in Course." *Neighborhood Change in Urban America* 2 (May): 1–11, A1–2. Available online at http://www.urban.org/UploadedPDF/310790_NCUA2.pdf (downloaded August 5, 2003).

KINLOCH, GRAHAM C. 1979. *The Sociology of Minority Group Relations.* Englewood Cliffs, NJ: Prentice Hall.

———. 1974. *The Dynamics of Race Relations: A Sociological Analysis.* New York: McGraw-Hill.

KIRBY, DOUGLAS. 2001. *Emerging Answers: Research Findings on Programs to Reduce Teenage Pregnancy.* Washington, DC: The National Campaign to Prevent Teen Pregnancy. Summary available online at http://www.teenpregnancy.org/resources/data/report_summaries/emerging_answers/default.asp (downloaded June 19, 2003).

KIRP, DAVID L. 1991. "Textbooks and Tribalism in California." *Public Interest* 104: 20–36.

KIRSCHENMAN, JOLENE. 1990. "Tales from the Survivors: Business Relocation in a Restructured Urban Economy." Paper presented at the Joint Annual Meetings of the North Central Sociological Association and Southern Sociological Society, March, Louisville, Kentucky.

———. 1989. "From Steel to Software, from Boardroom to Beyond the Expressway: Employers Consider the Inner City Economy." Paper presented at the Annual Meeting of the Midwest Sociological Society, April, St. Louis, Missouri.

KIRSCHENMAN, JOLENE, and KATHRYN M. NECKERMAN. 1991. "'We'd Love to Hire Them, but . . .': The Meaning of Race for Employers." Pp. 203–32 in Christopher Jencks and Paul E. Peterson (eds.), *The Urban Underclass.* Washington, DC: Brookings Institution.

KIRSCHT, JOHN P., and RONALD C. DILLEHAY. 1967. *Dimensions of Authoritarianism: A Review of Research and Theory.* Lexington: University of Kentucky Press.

KISELICA, MARK S., and PATRICIA MABEN. 1999. "Do Multicultural Education and Diversity Appreciation Training Reduce Prejudice Among Counseling Trainees?" *Journal of Mental Health Counseling* 21, 3: 240–54.

KITANO, HARRY H. L. 1985. *Race Relations,* 3d ed. Englewood Cliffs, NJ: Prentice Hall.

KLECK, GARY. 1985. "Life Support for an Ailing Hypothesis: Modes of Summarizing the Evidence for Racial Discrimination in Sentencing." *Law and Human Behavior* 9: 271–85.

KLEG, MILTON, and KAORU YAMAMOTO. 1998. "As the World Turns: Ethno-Racial Distances After 70 Years." *Social Science Journal* 35, 2: 183–90.

KLEIN, STEPHEN, JOAN PETERSILLA, and SUSAN TURNER. 1990. "Race and Imprisonment Decisions in California." *Science* 247: 812–16.

KLOSS, ROBERT MARSH, RON E. ROBERTS, and DEAN S. DORN. 1976. *Sociology with a Human Face.* St. Louis, MO: Mosby.

KLUEGEL, JAMES R. 1990. "Trends in Whites' Explanation of the Black-White Gap in Socioeconomic Status, 1977–1989." *American Sociological Review* 55: 512–25.

KLUEGEL, JAMES R., and LAWRENCE BOBO. 1991. "Modern American Prejudice: Stereotypes of Blacks, Hispanics, and Asians." Paper presented at the Annual Meetings of the American Sociological Association, Cincinnati, Ohio, August 23–27.

KLUEGEL, JAMES R., and ELIOT R. SMITH. 1986. *Beliefs About Inequality: American Views of What Is and What Ought to Be.* Hawthorne, NY: Aldine de Gruyter.

———. 1982. "Whites' Beliefs About Blacks' Opportunity." *American Sociological Review* 47: 518–32.

KNAPP, MICHAEL S., and PATRICK M. SHIELDS. 1990. "Reconceiving Academic Instruction for the Children of Poverty." *Phi Delta Kappan* (June): 753–58.

KNOWLTON, CLARK S. 1985. "Reies L. Tijerina and the Alianza Federal de Mercedes: Seekers After Justice." *Wisconsin Sociologist* 22: 133–44.

KOBLER, ARTHUR L. 1975. "Police Homicide in a Democracy." *Journal of Social Issues* 31: 163–84.

KOHLBERG, LAWRENCE. 1969. "Stage and Sequence: The Cognitive-Developmental Approach to Socialization." Pp. 347–480 in David A. Goslin (ed.), *Handbook of Socialization Theory and Research.* Chicago: Rand McNally.

KOMAROMY, MIRIAM, KEVIN GRUMBACH, MICHAEL DRAKE, KAREN VRANIZAN, NICOLE LURIE, DENNIS KEANE, and ANDREW B. BINDMAN. 1996. "The Role of Black and Hispanic Physicians in Providing Health Care for Underserved Persons." *New England Journal of Medicine* 334: 1305–10.

KORFHAGE, DARLENE W. 1972. "Differential Treatment in the Municipal Court System." Master's thesis, Washington State University, Pullman.

KOZOL, JONATHAN. 1991. *Savage Inequalities: Children in America's Schools.* New York: Crown.

KRAMER, BERNARD M. 1949. "The Dimensions of Prejudice." *Journal of Psychology* (April): 389–451.

KRAMER, MICHAEL. 1995. "The Myth About Welfare Mothers." *Time* (July 3). Also available via World Wide Web, http://www.pathfinder.com/time/magazine/archive/1995/950703/950703.politicalinterest.html

———. 1993. "Getting Smart About Head Start." *Time* (March 8): 43.

KRAMER, RONALD L. 1984. "Corporate Criminality: The Development of an Idea." In Ellen Hochs (ed.), *Corporations as Criminals.* Beverly Hills, CA: Sage.

KRAUSS, CLIFFORD. 1993. "Senate Passes a Smaller Stimulus Bill." *New York Times,* June 23, sec. A.

KRASHEN, STEPHEN D. 1991. "Bilingual Education: A Focus on Current Research." *NCBE Focus: Occasional Papers in Bilingual Education* 3 (Spring). Also available via World Wide Web, http://www.ncbe.gwu.edu/ncbepubs/focus/focus3.html

KROEBER, ALFRED L. 1939. "Cultural and Natural Areas of Native North America." *University of California Publications in American Archeology and Ethnology* 38.

KUNEN, JAMES S. 1996. "The End of Integration." *Time* 147, 18 (April 29). Also available via World Wide Web, http://www.pathfinder.com/time/magazine/archive/1996/dom/96049/cover.html

KUTNER, B., C. WILKINS, and P. R. YARROW. 1952. "Verbal Attitudes and Overt Behavior Involving Racial Prejudice." *Journal of Abnormal and Social Psychology* 47: 649–52.

KUYKENDALL, JACK L. 1970. "Police and Minority Groups: Toward a Theory of Negative Contact." *Police* 15: 47–56.

LAABS, JENNIFER J. 1993. "First Person: Employees Manage Conflict and Diversity." *Personnel Journal* (December): 30–36.

LABICH, KENNETH. 1996. "Making Diversity Pay." *Fortune* 134, 5 (September 9): 177–80.

LABOV, WILLIAM. 1972. "Academic Ignorance and Black Intelligence." *Atlantic Monthly* (June): 59–67.

LABOV, WILLIAM, and P. COHEN. 1967. "Systematic Relations of Standard and Nonstandard Rules in the Grammars of Negro Speakers." In *Project Literacy Reports,* no. 8. Ithaca, NY: Cornell University.

LA FAVE, WAYNE R. 1965. *Arrest: The Decision to Take a Suspect into Custody.* Boston: Little, Brown.

LAIRD, BOB. 2002. "Bending Admissions to Political Ends." *Chronicle of Higher Education,* May 17. Available online at http://chronicle.com/prm/weekly/v48/i36/36b01101.htm (premium content, downloaded November 26, 2003).

LAIRD, THOMAS F. NELSON, MARK E. ENGBERG, and SYLVIA HURTADO. 2002. "Modeling the Effects of a Diversity Course on Students' Preparation for a Diverse Democracy." Paper presented at the Annual Meeting of the Association for the Study of Higher Education, Sacramento, CA, November 21–24. Also available online at http://www.umichedu/~divdemo/2002ASHE_CBS.pdf

LAKE, ROBERT. 1981. *The New Suburbanites: Race and Housing in the Suburbs.* New Brunswick, NJ: Rutgers University, Center for Urban Policy Research.

LAMMERMEIER, P. J. 1973. "The Black Family in the Nineteenth Century: A Study of Black Family Structure in the Ohio Valley, 1850–1880." *Journal of Marriage and the Family* 35: 440–56.

LA PIERE, R. T. 1934. "Attitudes Versus Actions." *Social Forces* 13: 230–37.

LAPORTE, SUZANNE B. 1991. "Cultural Diversity: 12 Companies That Do the Right Thing." *Working Woman* 16, 1 (January): 57–59.

LARSEN, KNUD S., REIDAR OMMUNDSEN, and ROBERT ELDER. 1991. "Acquired Immune Deficiency Syndrome: International Attitudinal Comparisons." *Journal of Social Psychology* 131: 289–91.

LARSON, CALVIN J., and STAN R. NIKKEL. 1979. *Urban Problems: Perspectives on Corporations, Governments, and Cities.* Boston: Allyn & Bacon.

LASCH-QUINN, ELIZABETH. 2001. *Race Experts: How Racial Etiquette, Sensitivity Training, and New Age Therapy Hijacked the Civil Rights Revolution.* New York: W.W. Norton.

LAUTER, PAUL, and FLORENCE HOWE. 1970. *The Conspiracy of the Young.* New York: Crowell.

LAVILLE-WILSON, DEBRA, and JUDI ANNE CARON SHEPPARD. 2001. "Explaining Concern About Police Brutality: How Important Is Race?" Paper presented at annual meeting of the Society for the Study of *Social Problems,* Anaheim, CA.

LAYTHE, BRIAN, DEBORAH FINKEL, and LEE. A. KIRKPATRICK. 2001. "Predicting Prejudice from Religious Fundamentalism and Right-Wing Authoritarianism: A Multiple-Regression Approach." *Journal for the Scientific Study of Religion* 40, 1: 1–10.

LAZAR, IRVING. 1981. "Early Intervention Is Effective." *Educational Leadership* 38: 303–5.

LAZAR, IRVING, R. DARLINGTON, H. MURRAY, J. ROYCE, and A. SNIPPER. 1982. "Lasting Effects of Early Childhood Education." *Monographs of the Society for Research in Child Development* 47, 1–2, serial no. 194.

LAZAR, IRVING, V. R. HUBBEL, H. MURRAY, M. ROSCHE, and J. ROYCE. 1977. *The Persistence of Pre-School Effects: A Long-Term Follow-Up of Fourteen Infant and Pre-School Experiments, Summary.* Washington, DC: U.S. Department of Health and Human Services, Administration for Children, Youth, and Families.

LEACOCK, E. B. 1969. *Teaching and Learning in City Schools.* New York: Basic Books.

LEAL, DAVID, and FREDERICK M. HESS. 2000. "The Politics of Bilingual Education Expenditures in Urban Districts." *Social Science Quarterly* 81: 1064–72.

LEARY, WARREN E. 1991. "Social Links Are Seen in Black Stress." *New York Times*, February 6, sec. A.

LEATHERMAN, COURTNEY. 1994a. "All Quiet on the Western Front, at Least for Now: A West Coast Accrediting Group Approves Controversial Diversity Guidelines." *Chronicle of Higher Education* (March 2): A17.

———. 1994b. "North Carolina A&T Decides to Require Black Studies Course." *Chronicle of Higher Education* (March 9): A19.

———. 1994c. "Professors at U. of Oregon Will Try Again to Expand Multicultural Requirement." *Chronicle of Higher Education* (March 9): A18.

LEDERMAN, DOUGLAS, MICHAEL CRISSEY, and BRYAN MEALER. 1997. "Impact of Affirmative Action Ruling in Texas Is Less Clear-Cut Than Predicted." *Chronicle of Higher Education* (September 26).

LEDUC, DANIEL. 1996, "Union? Yes! No? In Uncertain Economy, Maybe." *Philadelphia Enquirer*, October 20. Also available via World Wide Web, http://www.phillynews.com/packages/labor/lab20.htm

LEE, MIN-WEI. 1992. " 'Programming' Minorities for Medicine." *JAMA* 267, 17: 2391, 2394.

LEGUM, COLIN. 1975. "Color and Race in the South African Situation." Pp. 98–105 in Norman R. Yetman and C. Hoy Steele (eds.), *Majority and Minority: The Dynamics of Racial and Ethnic Relations.* Boston: Allyn & Bacon. (Reprinted from Daedalus 96 [1967]: 483–95.)

LEHRMAN, SALLY. 2003. "The Reality of Race." *Scientific American* 288, 2.

LEIPPE, M. R., and D. EISENSTADT. 1994. "Generalization of Dissonance Reduction: Decreasing Prejudice Through Induced Compliance." *Journal of Personality and Social Psychology* 67: 395–413.

LENIN, V. I. 1960–1970. *Collected Works.* Moscow and London: Marx-Engels-Lenin Institute.

LESLIE, JOHN C. 1998. "Emerging Ethnic Politics in Germany: Far Right Parties and Violence." In *The Myth of "Ethnic Conflict": Politics, Economics, and "Cultural" Violence,* edited by Beverly Crawford and Ronnie D. Lipschutz. University of California Press/University of California International and Area Studies Digital Collection, Edited Volume 98: 353–93. World Wide Web, http://repositories.cdlib.org/uciaspubs/research/98/11

LESSING, ELISE E., and CHESTER C. CLARKE. 1976. "An Attempt to Reduce Ethnic Prejudice and Assess Its Correlates in a Junior High School Sample." *Educational Research Quarterly* 1, 2: 3–16.

LEVAY, SIMON. 1993. *The Sexual Brain.* Cambridge, MA: MIT Press (Bradford Books).

LEVE, LESLIE D., and BEVERLY I. FAGOT. 1997. "Gender-Role Socialization and Discipline Processes in One- and Two-Parent Families." *Sex Roles* 36: 1–21.

LEVIN, C. L., J. T. LITTLE, H. O. NOURSE, and P. B. REED. 1976. *Neighborhood Change: Lessons in the Dynamics of Urban Decay.* New York: Praeger.

LEVIN, R. J. 1975. "The Redbook Report on Premarital and Extramarital Sex." *Redbook* (October): 38–44, 190.

LEVY, JERROLD E. 1983. "Traditional Navajo Health Beliefs and Practices." Pp. 118–78 in J. Kunitz (ed.), *Disease Change and the Role of Medicine: The Navajo Experience.* Berkeley: University of California Press.

LEWIN, KURT. 1948. *Resolving Social Conflicts.* New York: Harper & Row.

LEWIS, ANNE C. 1992. "Head Start." *Education Digest* 57, 9 (May): 52.

———. 1991. "Washington News: Bilingual Education." *Education Digest* (January): 63–64.

LEWIS, OSCAR. 1965. *La Vida: A Puerto Rican Family in the Culture of Poverty.* New York: Random House.

———. 1959. *Five Families: Mexican Case Studies in the Culture of Poverty.* New York: Basic Books.

LEWIS MUMFORD CENTER. 2002. "Metropolitan Racial and Ethnic Change: 2000: Metropolitan Area Data." World Wide Web, http://mumford1.dyndns.org/cen2000/WholePop/WPseg data.htm (downloaded July 23, 2003)

LICHT, HANS. 1932. *Sexual Life in Ancient Greece.* London: Routledge.

LICHTER, DANIEL. 1988. "Racial Differences in Unemployment in American Cities." *American Journal of Sociology* 993: 772–92.

LICHTER, DANIEL, FELICIA B. LECLERE, and DIANE K. MCLAUGHLIN. 1991. "Local Marriage Markets and the Marital Behavior of Black and White Women." *American Journal of Sociology* 96: 843–67.

LICHTER, DANIEL, DIANE K. MCLAUGHLIN, and DAVID C. RIBAR. 1997. "Welfare and the Rise in Female-Headed Families." *American Journal of Sociology* 103: 112–43.

LIEBERMAN, LEONARD, and LARRY T. REYNOLDS. 1991. "Race and Racism in the Academy and on the Streets." *Michigan Sociological Review* 5: 19–30.

LIEBERSON, STANLEY. 1980. *A Piece of the Pie: Blacks and White Immigrants Since 1880.* Berkeley: University of California Press.

———. 1961. "A Societal Theory of Race Relations." *American Sociological Review* 26: 902–10.

LINK, BRUCE G., and JO C. PHELAN. 2001. "Conceptualizing Stigma." *Annual Review of Sociology,* 2001 Edition: 363–85.

LINN, L. 1965. "Verbal Attitudes and Overt Behavior: A Study of Racial Discrimination." *Social Forces* 43: 353–64.

LINTON, SIMI. 1998. *Claiming Disability: Knowledge and Identity.* New York: New York University Press.

LIPSET, SEYMOUR MARTIN. 1992. "The Politics of Race: The Meaning of Equality." *Current* 343: 10–15.

———. 1959. "Democracy and Working Class Authoritarianism." *American Sociological Review* 24: 498–501.

LIPSET, SEYMOUR MARTIN, and EARL RAAB. 1973. "An Appointment with Watergate." *Commentary* (September): 35–43.

LISKA, ALLEN E., and MARK TANSIG. 1979. "Theoretical Interpretations of Social Class and Racial Differentials in Legal Decision-Making for Juveniles." *Sociological Quarterly* 20: 197–207.

LITCHER, J. H., and D. W. JOHNSON. 1969. "Changes in Attitudes Toward Negroes of White Elementary School Students After Use of Multiethnic Readers." *Journal of Educational Psychology* 60: 148–52.

LITRAS, MARIKA. 2002. "Civil Rights Complaints in U.S. District Courts: 2000." Bureau of Justice Statistics Special Report. Available online at http://www.ojp.usdoj.gov/bjs/pub/pdf/crcus00.pdf

———. 2000. "Civil Rights Complaints in U.S. District Courts: 1990–98." Bureau of Justice Statistics Special Report. Available online at http://www.ojp.usdoj.gov/bjs/pub/pdf/crcusdc.pdf

LITTLE, ALLAN, and GEORGE SMITH. 1971. *Strategies of Compensation: A Review of Educational Projects for the Disadvantaged in the United States.* Paris: Organization for Economic Cooperation and Development.

LITWACK, LEON F. 1961. *North of Slavery: The Negro in the Free States, 1790–1860.* Chicago: University of Chicago Press.

LIVINGSTON, ABBY. 1991. "What YOUR Department Can Do." *Working Woman* (January): 59–60.

LOCKWOOD, ANDREW. 2002. *School Finance Reform in Michigan—Proposal A: A Retrospective.* Lansing, MI: Office of Revenue and Tax Analysis. Also available online at http://www.michigan.gov/documents/propa_3172_7.pdf (downloaded August 13, 2003).

LOCKWOOD, ANNE TURNBAUGH. 1996. *Tracking: Conflicts and Resolutions.* Thousand Oaks, CA: Corwin Press.

LOFLAND, JOHN. 1985. *Protest: Studies of Collective Behavior and Social Movements.* New Brunswick, NJ: Transaction Books.

LOGAN, JOHN R. 2001. "Ethnic Diversity Grows, Neighborhood Integration Lags Behind," Report by the Lewis Mumford Center, April 3, 2001 (revised December 18, 2001, to include 1980 data). World Wide Web, http://mumford1.dyndns.org/cen2000/WholePop/WPreport/page1.html (downloaded June 3, 2003).

LOGAN, JOHN R., and M. SCHNEIDER. 1984. "Racial Segregation and Racial Change in American Suburbs, 1970–1980." *American Journal of Sociology* 89: 875–88.

LOGAN, JOHN R., and LINDA STEARNS. 1981. "Suburban Racial Segregation as a Nonecological Process." *Social Forces* 60: 61–73.

LONG, HARRY H., and PAUL C. GLICK. 1976. "Family Patterns in Suburban Areas: Recent Trends." Pp. 39–68 in Barry Schwartz (ed.), *The Changing Face of the Suburbs.* Chicago: University of Chicago Press.

LOPEZ, G. E. 1993. "The Effect of Group Contact and Curriculum on White, Asian American, and African American Students' Attitudes." Ph.D. dissertation, University of Michigan.

LOPEZ, MANUEL MARIANO. 1981. "Patterns of Interethnic Residential Segregation in the Urban Southwest." *Social Science Quarterly* 62: 50–63.

LOPEZ, MARK HUGO. 1998. "Statement at Hearing of the House Committee on Equal Economic Opportunity." World Wide Web, http://www.house.gov/eeo/hearings/ecyf/bilingual43098/lopez.htm

———. 1996. "The Educational and Labor Market Impacts of Bilingual Education in the Short Run and Long Run: Evidence from the National Education Longitudinal Study of 1988 and High School and Beyond." Unpublished Ph.D. dissertation, Princeton University, Princeton, NJ.

LOPEZ, MARK HUGO, and MARIE T. MORA. 1998. "The Labor Market Effects of Bilingual Education Among Hispanic Workers." *READ Perspectives* (Fall).

LORANT, RICHARD. 1995. "Experts Lower Estimate for Million Man March to 837,000" (Associated Press report). World Wide Web, http://sddt.com/files/librarywire/DN95_10_27_lo.html

LORD, JANE T., and STEPHEN K. SANDERSON. 1999. "Current Theoretical and Political Perspectives of Western Sociological Theorists." *American Sociologist* 30, 3: 42–66.

LORD, LEWIS. 1997. "How Many People Were Here Before Columbus?" *U.S. News and World Report* (August 18): 68–70.

LORDE, AUDRE. 1992. "Age, Race, Class, and Sex: Women Redefining Difference." Pp. 401–7 in Paula S. Rothenberg (ed.), *Race, Class, and Gender in the United States: An Integrated Study.* New York: St. Martin's Press.

LOUW-POTGIETER, J. 1988. "The Authoritarian Personality: An Inadequate Explanation for Intergroup Conflict in South Africa." *Journal of Social Psychology* 128: 75–87.

LOWENSTEIN, L. F. 1985. "Investigating Ethnic Prejudice Among Boys and Girls in a Therapeutic Community for Maladjusted Children and Modifying Some Prejudices: Can Basic Prejudices Be Changed?" *School Psychology International* 6: 239–43.

LUBOVE, SETH. 1997. "Damned if You Do, Damned if You Don't." *Forbes* (December 15): 122–34.

LUCAS, SAMUEL ROUNDFIELD. 1999. *Tracking Inequality: Stratification and Mobility in American High Schools.* New York: Teachers College Press, 1999.

LUDWIG, JACK. 2003a. "Blacks and Whites Still Perceive Local Treatment of Blacks Differently." *Gallup Poll Tuesday Briefing,* May 27. World Wide Web, http://www.gallup.com/poll/tb/religValue/20030527b.asp (premium content, downloaded June 4, 2003).

———. 2003b. "Q and A: Black-White Relations in the U.S.A." *Gallup Poll Tuesday Briefing,* June 10. World Wide Web, http://www.gallup.com/poll/tb/religValue/20030610b.asp (premium content, downloaded July 2, 2003).

LUNDMAN, RICHARD J. 1996. "Demeanor and Arrest: Additional Evidence from Previously Unpublished Data." *Journal of Research in Crime and Delinquency* 33: 306–23.

———. 1980. *Police and Policing: An Introduction.* New York: Holt, Rinehart & Winston.

LURIE, NANCY OESTREICH. 1991. "The American Indian: Historical Background." Pp. 132–45 in Norman R. Yetman (ed.), *Majority and Minority: The Dynamics of Race and Ethnicity in American Life,* 5th ed. Needham Heights, MA: Allyn & Bacon.

———. 1985. "The American Indian: Historical Background." Pp. 136–49 in Norman R. Yetman, *Majority and Minority: The Dynamics of Race and Ethnicity in American Life,* 4th ed. Boston, MA: Allyn & Bacon.

LYNCH, FREDERICK R., and WILLIAM R. BEER. 1990. " 'You Ain't the Right Color, Pal': White Resentment of Affirmative Action." *Policy Review* 51: 61–67.

LYNCH, JAMES. 1988. "Pedagogical Strategies to Reduce Prejudice: Towards Middle Range Theories." Paper presented at the annual meeting of the American Educational Research Association, April, New Orleans.

———. 1987. *Prejudice Reduction and the Schools.* New York: Nichols.

LYND, ROBERT S., and HELEN MERRELL LYND. 1929. *Middletown: A Study in Contemporary American Culture.* New York: Harcourt Brace Jovanovich.

LYONS, LINDA. 2002. "Is Tolerance a Non-Issue for Teens?" *Gallup Poll Tuesday Briefing,* Education and Youth, February 26, 2002. World Wide Web, http://www.gallup.com/poll/tb/educaYouth/20020226b.asp (premium content, downloaded July 3, 2003).

MAASS, A., D. SALVI, L. ARCURI, and G. SEMIN. 1989. "Language Use in Intergroup Contexts: The Linguistic Ingroup Bias." *Journal of Personality and Social Psychology* 57: 981–93.

McADAM, DOUG. 1982. *Political Process and the Development of Black Insurgency, 1930–1970.* Chicago: University of Chicago Press.

McADAM, DOUG, JOHN D. McCARTHY, and MAYER N. ZALD. 1988. "Social Movements." Pp. 695–737 in Neil J. Smelser (ed.), *Handbook of Sociology.* Newbury Park, CA: Sage.

McCARTHY, JOHN D., and MAYER N. ZALD. 1977. "Resource Mobilization and Social Movements: A Partial Theory." *American Journal of Sociology* 82: 1212–41.

———. 1973. *The Trend of Social Movements in America: Professionalization and Resource Mobilization.* Morristown, NJ: General Learning Press.

McCARTHY, KEVIN F., and R. B. VALDEZ. 1997. *Immigration in a Changing Economy: California's Experience.* Santa Monica, CA: Rand Corporation.

———. 1985. *Current and Future Effects of Mexican Immigration in California.* Santa Monica, CA: Rand Corporation.

McCARY, JAMES LESLEY. 1978. *McCary's Human Sexuality,* 3d ed. New York: Van Nostrand Reinhold.

McCONAHAY, J. B. 1982. "Self-Interest Versus Racial Attitudes as Correlates of Anti-busing Attitudes in Louisville: Is It the Buses or the Blacks?" *Journal of Politics* 44: 692–720.

McCONAHAY, J. B., B. B. HARDEE, and V. BATES. 1981. "Has Racism Declined in America? It Depends on Who Is Asking and What Is Asked." *Journal of Conflict Resolution* 25: 563–79.

McCUTCHEON, GAIL, DIANE KYLE, and ROBERT SKOVIRA. 1979. "Characters in Basal Readers: Does 'Equal' Now Mean 'Same'?" *Reading Teacher* 32: 438–41.

McDERMOTT, KEVIN. 1999. "Illinois State Police Target Hispanics, Suit Alleges." *St. Louis Post-Dispatch* (March 15).

McDERMOTT, PETER, et al. 1995. " 'Should We Do It the Same Way?' Teaching in Tracked and Untracked High School Classes." Paper presented at the Annual Meeting of the Northeast Educational Research Association, Portsmouth, New Hampshire, October 25–27.

McFarlane, Bruce. 1988. *Yugoslavia: Politics, Economics, and Society*. London and New York: Pinter.

McGarrell, Edmond F. 1993. "Trends in Racial Disproportionality in Court Processing: 1985–1989." *Crime and Delinquency* 39: 29–48.

McGauley, Clark, Mary Wright, and Mary E. Harris. 2000. "Diversity Workshops on Campus: A Survey of Current Practice at U.S. Colleges and Universities." *College Student Journal*, 34(1), 100–114.

McGinley, P., and H. McGinley. 1970. "Reading Groups as Psychological Groups." *Journal of Experimental Education* 39: 36–42.

McGuire, William J. 1968. "Personality and Susceptibility to Social Influence." Pp. 1130–87 in Edgar F. Borgatta and William W. Lambert (eds.), *Handbook of Personality Theory and Research*. Chicago: Rand McNally.

McKee, James B. 1993. *Sociology and the Race Problem: The Failure of a Perspective*. Urbana: University of Illinois Press.

McKeever, Matthew, and Nicholas H. Wolfinger. 2001. "Reexamining the Economic Costs of Marital Disruption for Women." *Social Science Quarterly*. 82, 1: 202–17.

McKey, Ruth, Larry Condelli, Harriet Ganson, Barbara Barrett, Catherine McConkey, and Margaret Plantz. 1985. *The Impact of Head Start on Children, Families, and Communities: Head Start Synthesis Project*. DHHS Publication no. (OHDS) 85-31193. Washington, DC: U.S. Government Printing Office.

MacKinnon, William, and Richard Centers. 1956. "Authoritarianism and Urban Stratification." *American Journal of Sociology* 61: 610–20.

McLanahan, Sara. 1994. "The Consequences of Single Motherhood." *The American Prospect* 18 (Summer): 48–58. Also available via World Wide Web, http://www.prospect.org/web/page.ww?section=root&name=ViewPrint&articleId=5064

———. 1988. "The Consequences of Single Parenthood for Subsequent Generations." *Focus* 11: 16–21.

McLanahan, Sara, and Larry Bumpass. 1988. "Intergenerational Consequences of Family Disruption." *American Journal of Sociology* 94: 130–52.

McLanahan, Sara, and Gary D. Sandefur. 1994. *Growing Up with a Single Parent*. Cambridge, MA: Harvard University Press.

McLaughlin, Barry, and Beverly McLeod. 1996. *The Impact Statement on Practice and Knowledge—Educating All Our Students: Improving Education for Children from Culturally and Linguistically Diverse Backgrounds*. Final Report of the National Center for Research on Cultural Diversity and Second Language Learning, Vol. I. Santa Cruz: University of California–Santa Cruz.

McLaughlin, Diane K., and Daniel T. Lichter. 1997. "Poverty and the Marital Behavior of Young Women." *Journal of Marriage and the Family* 59: 582–94.

McManus, Patricia A., and Thomas A. Diprete. 2001. "Losers and Winners: The Financial Consequences of Separation and Divorce for Men." *American Sociological Review* 66: 246–68.

McMorris, Michael Anthony. 2002. "Perceptions of Criminality: Michigan Police Recruits Rank Likely Criminal Types. Year 2000 Exploratory Study" (doctoral dissertation). Available through Dissertation Abstracts International, Order No. DA3027410.

McMurray, Coleen. 2003. "Public Split in Federal Role on Affirmative Action." *Gallup Poll Tuesday Briefing*, Government and Public Affairs, May 6. World Wide Web, http://www.gallup.com/poll/tb/goverPubli/20030506b.asp (premium content, downloaded June 5, 2003).

McPhail, Clark. 1994. "The Dark Side of Purpose: Individual and Collective Violence in Riots." *Sociological Quarterly* 35: 1–32. Presidential address at the 1993 Annual Meeting of the Midwest Sociological Society, April 7–10, Chicago.

McWhirter, J. Jeffries, Rosie Paluch, and Rose M. Ohm. 1988. "Anytown: A Human Relations Experience." *Journal for Specialists in Group Work* 13, 3: 117–23 (special issue: *Group Work and Human Rights*, Vol. 2).

McWilliams, Carey. 1951. *Brothers Under the Skin*, rev. ed. Boston: Little, Brown.

———. 1949. *North from Mexico*. Philadelphia: Lippincott.

Madsen, William. 1973. *The Mexican-Americans of South Texas*, 2d ed. New York: Holt, Rinehart & Winston.

Maheswaran, D., and S. Chaiken. 1991. "Promoting Systematic Processing in Low-Motivation Settings: Effect of Incongruent Information on Processing and Judgment." *Journal of Personality and Social Psychology* 61: 13–25.

Majors, Richard, and Janet Mancini Billson. 1992. *Cool Pose: The Dilemmas of Black Manhood in America*. New York: Lexington Books.

Makepeace, J. M. 1981. "Courtship Violence Among College Students." *Family Relations* 30: 97–102.

Mandelbaum, D. G. 1952. *Soldier Groups and Negro Soldiers*. Berkeley: University of California Press.

Mangan, Katherine S. 1999. "Minority Numbers Down Sharply at California Medical Schools, Report Says." *Chronicle of Higher Education*, April 2. Available online at http://chronicle.com/prm/weekly/v45/i30/30a05001.htm (premium content, downloaded November 26, 2003).

———. 1998. "Minority Groups Are 'Critically Underrepresented' in Medical Education, Report Concludes." *Chronicle of Higher Education* (June 25). Also available via World Wide Web http://www.chronicle.com/daily/98/06/98062502n.shml

Mann, Coramae Richey. 1993. *Unequal Justice: A Question of Color.* Bloomington: Indiana University Press.

Marcuse, Peter. 1997. "The Ghetto of Exclusion and the Fortified Enclave: New Patterns in the United States." *American Behavioral Scientist* 41: 311–26.

Mare, Robert D., and Christopher Winship. 1991. "Socioeconomic Change and the Decline of Marriage for Blacks and Whites." Pp. 175–202 in Christopher Jencks and Paul E. Peterson (eds.), *The Urban Underclass*. Washington, DC: Brookings Institution.

Marketti, James. 1990. "Estimated Present Value of Income Diverted During Slavery." In Richard F. America (ed.), *The Wealth of Races: The Present Value of Benefits from Past Injustices*. New York: Greenwood.

Marmor, Judd. 1992. "Cultural Factors in the Darker Passions." *Journal of the American Academy of Psychoanalysis* 20: 325–34.

Marrett, Cora Bagley. 1980. "The Precariousness of Social Class in Black America." *Contemporary Sociology* 9: 16–19.

Marshall, Ray. 1965. *The Negro and Organized Labor*. New York: Wiley.

Martin, Douglas. 1985. "Parti Quebecois Is Ousted After Nine Years in Power." *New York Times*, December 3, sec. 1.

Martz, Larry, Mark Starr, and Todd Barrett. 1990. "A Murderous Hoax." *Newsweek* (January 22): 16–21.

Marx, Karl. 1971 [1859]. *A Contribution to the Critique of Political Economy*. Maurice Dobb (ed. and tr.). New York: International Publishers.

———. 1967 [1867–1894]. *Capital, a Critique of Political Economy*. Three vols., Friedrich Engels (ed.), Samuel Moore and Edward Aveling (trs.). New York: International Publishers.

———. 1964 [1867–1894]. *Selected Works in Sociology and Social Philosophy*. Thomas B. Bottomore and Maximilien Rubel (eds. and trs.). New York: McGraw-Hill.

Mason, Heather. 2003. "Equal-Opportunity Education: Is It Out There?" *Gallup Poll Tuesday Briefing*, July 1. World Wide Web, http://www.gallup.com/poll/tb/educayouth/20030701.asp (downloaded July 2, 2003).

Mason, Margie. 2002. "Military Boots 9 Gay Linguists Despite Shortage." *Napa Valley Register* (November 15). Also available online at http://www.napanews.com/templates/index.cfm?template=story_full&id=C0B7EDD6-A874-4437-91DB-CE6F958DF838 (downloaded October 10, 2003).

MASON, PHILIP. 1971. *Patterns of Dominance*. London: Oxford University Press.

MASSEY, DOUGLAS S. 1995. "Review Essay: The Bell Curve: Intelligence and Class Structure in American Life." *American Journal of Sociology* 101: 747–53.

———. 1990. "American Apartheid: Segregation and the Making of the Underclass." *American Journal of Sociology* 96: 239–57.

MASSEY, DOUGLAS S., GRETCHEN A. CONDRAN, and NANCY A. DENTON. 1987. "The Effect of Residential Segregation on Black Social and Economic Well-Being." *Social Forces* 66: 29–56.

MASSEY, DOUGLAS S., and NANCY A. DENTON. 1993. *American Apartheid: Segregation and the Making of the Underclass*. Cambridge, MA: Harvard University Press.

———. 1989. "Hypersegregation in U.S. Metropolitan Areas: Black and Hispanic Segregation Along Five Dimensions." *Demography* 26: 373–91.

———. 1988. "Suburbanization and Segregation in U.S. Metropolitan Areas." *American Journal of Sociology* 94: 592–626.

———. 1987. "Trends in the Segregation of Blacks, Hispanics, and Asians, 1970–1980." *American Sociological Review* 52: 802–25.

MASSEY, DOUGLAS S., and MITCHELL L. EGGERS. 1990. "The Ecology of Inequality: Minorities and the Concentration of Poverty." *American Journal of Sociology* 95: 1153–88.

MASSEY, DOUGLAS S., and ANDREW B. GROSS. 1991. "Explaining Trends in Racial Segregation, 1970–1980." *Urban Affairs Quarterly* 27: 13–35.

MASTERS, STANLEY H. 1975. *Black-White Income Differentials: Empirical Studies and Policy Implications*. New York: Academic Press.

MATHEWS, JAY. 1992. "Undercover Bias Busters." *Newsweek* (November 23): 88.

MATHEWS, TOM. 1992. "The Siege of L.A." *Newsweek* (May 11): 30–38.

MATTHIESSEN, PETER. 1983. *In the Spirit of Crazy Horse*. New York: Viking Press.

MATUTE-BIANCHI, MARIA EUGENIA. 1986. "Ethnic Identities and Patterns of School Success and Failure Among Mexican-Descent and Japanese American Students in a California High School: An Ethnographic Analysis." *American Journal of Education* 95: 233–55.

MAZÓN, MAURICIO. 1984. *The Zoot Suit Riots: The Psychology of Symbolic Annihilation*. Austin: University of Texas Press.

MEAD, GEORGE HERBERT. 1967 [1934]. *Mind, Self, and Society*. Chicago: University of Chicago Press.

MEANS, BARBARA, and MICHAEL S. KNAPP. 1991. "Cognitive Approaches to Teaching Advanced Skills to Educationally Disadvantaged Students." *Phi Delta Kappan* (December): 282–89.

MEDINA, MARCELLO, MACARIO SALDATE, and SHILALA P. MISHRA. 1985. "The Sustaining Effects of Bilingual Education: A Followup Study." *Journal of Instructional Psychology* 12: 132–39.

MEDINA, Z., and D. M. NEILL. 1988. *Fallout from the Testing Explosion: How 100 Million Standardized Exams Undermine Equity and Excellence in America's Public Schools*. Cambridge, MA: National Center for Fair and Open Testing.

MEHAN, HUGH, et al. 1992. *Untracking and College Enrollment*, Research Report: 4. Santa Cruz, CA: National Center for Research on Cultural Diversity and Second Language Learning.

MEIER, AUGUST, and ELLIOTT RUDWICK (EDS.). 1970a. *Black Protest in the Sixties*. Chicago: Quadrangle Books.

———. 1970b. *From Plantation to Ghetto: The Interpretative History of American Negroes*, rev. ed. New York: Atheneum.

———. 1969. "The Boycott Against Jim Crow Streetcars in the South." *Journal of American History* 55: 756–59.

MEIER, MATT S., and FELICIANO RIVERA. 1972. *The Chicanos: A History of Mexican Americans*. New York: Hill & Wang.

MEKOSH-ROSENBAUM, VICTORIA, JOAN Z. SPADE, and GEORGE P. WHITE. 1996. "Effects of Homogeneous and Heterogeneous Grouping on Classroom Environment and Achievement in Middle Schools." Paper presented at the Annual Meetings of the American Sociological Association.

MERTON, ROBERT K. 1949. *Social Theory and Social Structure*. New York: Free Press. (Reprint of "The Self-Fulfilling Prophecy," 1948. *Antioch Review* (Summer).

MEYER, BRUCE D., and DAN T. ROSENBAUM. 2001. "Welfare, Earned Income Tax Credit, and the Labor Supply of Single Mothers." *Quarterly Journal of Economics* 116: 1063–1114.

MEYER, BRUCE D., and JAMES SULLIVAN. 2001. "The Effects of Welfare and Tax Reform: The Material Well-Being of Single Mothers in 1980s and 1990s." in Bruce Meyer and Greg Duncan (eds.), *The Incentives of Government Programs and the Well-Being of Families*. Chicago: Joint Center for Poverty Research (University of Chicago and Northwestern University). Book available online at http://www.jcpr.org/book/ (downloaded July 30, 2003).

MICHELSON, STEPHAN. 1972. "The Political Economy of School Finance." In Martin Carnoy (ed.), *Schooling in Corporate Society*. New York: McKay.

MICHIGAN STATE BOARD OF EDUCATION. 1989. *Michigan Social Studies Textbook Study (1988): A Review and Evaluation of Selected Middle School Textbooks*. Lansing: Michigan State Board of Education.

MIDDLETON, RUSSELL. 1960. "Ethnic Prejudice and Susceptibility to Persuasion." *American Sociological Review* 25: 679–86.

MIELENZ, CECILE C. 1979. "Non-Prejudiced Caucasian Parents and Attitudes of Their Children Toward Negroes." *Journal of Negro Education* 48: 84–91.

MILETI, DENNIS, JOANNE DARLINGTON, COLLEEN FITZPATRICK, and PAUL W. O'BRIEN. 1993. *Communicating Earthquake Risk: Societal Response to Revised Probabilities in the Bay Area*. Fort Collins: Colorado State University, Hazards Assessment Laboratory and Department of Sociology.

MILETI, DENNIS, and COLEEN FITZPATRICK. 1993. *The Great Earthquake Experiment*. Boulder, CO: Westview Press.

MILLER, JOHN J. 1998. *The Unmaking of Americans: How Multiculturalism Has Undermined the Assimilation Ethic*. New York: Simon & Schuster.

MILLER, KAREN A., MELVIN L. KOHN, and CARMI SCHOOLER. 1986. "Educational Self-Direction and Personality." *American Sociological Review* 51: 372–90.

MILLER, RANDI L. 1990. "Beyond Contact Theory: The Impact of Community Affluence on Integration Efforts in Five Suburban High Schools." *Youth and Society* 22: 12–34.

———. 1989. "Desegregation Experiences of Minority Students: Adolescent Coping Strategies in Five Connecticut High Schools." *Journal of Adolescent Research* 4: 173–89.

MILLER, SARAH RAFIULLAH, and JAMES E. ROSENBAUM. 1997. "Hiring in a Hobbesian World: Social Infrastructure and Employers' Use of Information." *Work and Occupations* 24: 498–523.

MILLS, C. WRIGHT. 1956. *The Power Elite*. New York: Oxford University Press.

MINCY, RONALD B., and HELEN OLIVER. 2003. "Age, Race, and Children's Living Arrangements: Implications for TANF Reauthorization." Urban Institute Report No. B-53 in Series, "New Federalism: National Survey of America's Families." World Wide Web, http://www.urban.org/url.cfm?ID=310670 (downloaded June 27, 2003).

MIRANDE, ALFREDO. 1987. *Gringo Justice*. Notre Dame, IN: University of Notre Dame Press.

———. 1985. *The Chicano Experience: An Alternative Perspective*. Notre Dame, IN: University of Notre Dame Press.

MISHEL, LAWRENCE. 1997."Capital's Gain." *The American Prospect* 33: 71–73. Also available via World Wide Web, http://epn.org/prospect/33/33mishf.html

MITTNICK, LEONARD, and ELLIOTT McGINNIES. 1958. "Influencing Ethnocentrism in Small Discussion Groups Through a Film Communication." *Journal of Abnormal and Social Psychology* 56: 423–41.

MLADENKA, KENNETH R. 1991. "Public Employee Unions, Reformism, and Black Employment in 1,200 American Cities." *Urban Affairs Quarterly* 26: 532–48.

MOFFIT, ROBERT. 1992. "Incentive Effects of the U.S. Welfare System." *Journal of Economic Literature* 30: 1–61.

MOLOTCH, HARVEY. 1972. *Managed Integration: Dilemmas of Doing Good in the City*. Berkeley: University of California Press.

MONAGLE, KATIE. 1992. "Race and the Courts." *Scholastic Update* 125, 1 (Teachers' ed.): 3.

MONTAGU, M. F. ASHLEY. 1964. *Man's Most Dangerous Myth: The Fallacy of Race*, 4th ed. Cleveland, OH: World.

———. 1963. *Race, Science and Humanity*. Princeton, NJ: D. Van Nostrand.

MONTEIRO, TONY. 1994. "The New Face of Racism." *Peace Review* 6: 139–147.

MOONEY, JOSEPH D. 1969. "Housing Segregation, Negro Unemployment, and Metropolitan Decentralization: An Alternative Perspective." *Quarterly Journal of Economics* (May): 299–311.

MOORE, DAVID W. 2003a. "Half of Young People Expect to Strike It Rich." Gallup Organization poll analysis, March 11. World Wide Web, http://www.gallup.com/poll/releases/pr030311.asp (premium content, downloaded June 20, 2003).

———. 2003b. "How Question Order Affects Attitudes on Affirmative Action." Gallup Organization poll talk, July 1, 2003. World Wide Web, http://www.gallup.com/poll/talk/default.asp?pw=7/1/2003 (downloaded November 26, 2003).

MOORE, JOAN W. 1970. "Colonialism: The Case of the Mexican Americans." *Social Problems* 17: 463–72.

MOORE, JOAN, and HARRY PACHON. 1985. *Hispanics in the United States*, 2d ed. Englewood Cliffs, NJ: Prentice Hall.

———. 1976. *Mexican Americans*. Englewood Cliffs, NJ: Prentice Hall.

MOORE, L. AUBREY, and PAUL M. ROESTI. 1980. "Race and Two Juvenile Justice System Decision Points: The Filing of a Petition and Declaration of Wardship." Paper presented to the annual meeting of the Midwest Sociological Society, Milwaukee, Wisconsin.

MOORE, ROBERT. 1972. "Race Relations in the Six Counties: Colonialism, Industrialization, and Stratification in Ireland." *Race* 14. (Reprinted in Norman R. Yetman, and C. Hoy Steele (eds.), 1975, *Majority and Minority: The Dynamics of Racial and Ethnic Relations*. Boston: Allyn & Bacon.)

MOORE, STEPHEN. 1998. *A Fiscal Portrait of the Newest Americans*. Washington, DC: Immigration Forum.

MORGAN, S. PHILIP, ANTONIO McDANIEL, ANDREW T. MILLER, and SAMUEL H. PRESTON. 1993. "Racial Differences in Household and Family Structures at the Turn of the Century." *American Journal of Sociology* 98: 798–828.

MORGANTHAU, TOM. 1993. "America: Still a Melting Pot?" *Newsweek* (August 9): 16–23.

MORRIS, ALDON. 1984. *The Origins of the Civil Rights Movement: Black Communities Organizing for Change*. New York: Free Press.

MORRIS, JOHN W., and PATRICK C. HEAVEN. 1986. "Attitudes and Behavioral Intentions Toward Vietnamese in Australia." *Journal of Social Psychology* 126: 513–20.

MORRIS, PAMELA, GREG J. DUNCAN, and LINDSAY CHASE-LANSDALE. 2001. "Welfare Reform's Effects on Children." *Poverty Research News* 5, 4 (July–August). Chicago: Joint Center for Poverty Research (University of Chicago and Northwestern University). Available online at http://www.jcpr.org/newsletters/vol5_no4/articles.html#story1footone (downloaded July 30, 2003).

MORRISON, ANN. 1993. "Diversity. Interview by Patricia Galagan." *Training and Development* 47, 4 (April): 39–43.

MOSER, BOB. 2003. "Hate for Sale." *Intelligence Report* (Summer). Available online at http://www.splcenter.org/intel/intelreport/article.jsp?aid=51 (downloaded May 10, 2004).

MOSES, ROBERT P., and CHARLES E. COBB, JR. 2001. *Radical Equations: Civil Rights from Mississippi to the Algebra Project*. Boston: Beacon Press.

MOSKOS, CHARLES. 1991. "How Do They Do It?" *New Republic* 205, 6: 16–19.

MOSS, PHILIP, and CHRIS TILLY. 2001a. *Stories Employers Tell: Race, Skill, and Hiring in America*. New York: Russell Sage Foundation.

———. 2001b. "Why Opportunity Isn't Knocking: Racial Inequality and the Demand for Labor." Pp. 444–95 in Alice O' Conner, Chris Tilly, and Lawrence D. Bobo (eds.), *Urban Inequality: Evidence from Four Cities*. New York: Russell Sage Foundation.

MOUSTAFA, A. TAHER, and GERTRUD WEISS. 1968. *Health Status and Practices of Mexican Americans*. Advance Report 2, Mexican American Study Project. Los Angeles: University of California at Los Angeles.

MOY, EARNEST, and BARBARA A. BARTMAN. 1995. "Physician Race and Care of Minority and Medically Indigent Patients" *JAMA* 273: 1515–17.

MOYNIHAN, DANIEL PATRICK. 1995a. Press Release, "Moynihan Introduces Welfare Reform Legislation." Also available via World Wide Web, http://www.epn.org/library/moyn01pr.html

———. 1995b. Speech on U.S. Senate floor, introducing alternative welfare reform proposal, May 18, 1995. Available on World Wide Web, http://www.epn.org/library/moyn01lg.html

———. 1986. *Family and Nation*. San Diego: Harcourt Brace Jovanovich.

MULLER, KLAUS. 1993. "A Dark Past Brought to Light." *10 Percent* 1 (Winter): 36.

MULLER, THOMAS. 1985. "Economic Effects of Immigration." In Nathan Glazer (ed.), *Clamor at the Gates*. San Francisco: Institute for Contemporary Studies.

MURGUIA, EDWARD. 1975. *Assimilation, Colonialism, and the Mexican American People*. Austin: University of Texas.

MURRAY, CHARLES. 1984. *Losing Ground: American Social Policy, 1950–1980*. New York: Basic Books.

MYRDAL, GUNNAR. 1944. *An American Dilemma: The Negro Problem and Modern Democracy*. New York: Harper & Row.

NAGEL, JOANE. 1995. "American Indian Ethnic Renewal: Politics and the Resurgence of Identity." *American Sociological Review* 60: 947–65.

NAGEL, STEWART. 1969. *The Legal Process from a Behavioral Perspective*. Homewood, IL: Dorsey Press.

NAGORSKI, ANDREW. 1993. "The Laws of Blood: Neo-Nazi Attacks Pressure Germany to Change Its Citizenship Rules." *Newsweek* (June 14): 38–39.

NAHAYLO, BOHDAN, and VICTOR SWOBODA. 1989. *Soviet Disunion: A History of the Nationalities Problem in the Soviet Union*. New York: Free Press.

N.A.M.I. 2001. "U.S. Supreme Court Cuts Back Protections of the ADA." World Wide Web http://web.nami.org/update/ada_cut.html (downloaded October 10, 2003).

NANDI, PROSHANTA K., and HUGH HARRIS. 1997."The Social World of Female-Headed Black Families: A Study of the Quality of Life in a Marginalized Neighborhood." Paper presented at the Annual Meeting of the American Sociological Association, Toronto.

NASH, GARY B. 1970. "Red, White, and Black: The Origins of Racism in Colonial America." Chap. 1 in Gary B. Nash and Richard Weiss, *The Great Fear: Race in the Mind of America.* New York: Holt, Rinehart & Winston.

NASH, ROY. 1976. *Teacher Expectations and Pupil Learning.* London: Routledge & Kegan Paul.

NATIONAL CENTER FOR EDUCATION STATISTICS. 2003a. "Average Writing Scale Scores, by School-Reported Race/Ethnicity, Grades 4, 8, and 12: 1998 and 2002." World Wide Web, http://nces.ed.gov/nationsreportcard/writing/results2002/raceethnicity.asp (downloaded August 13, 2003).

————. 2003b. *The Condition of Education 2003 in Brief.* Washington, DC: U.S. Government Printing Office. Also available online at http://nces.ed.gov/pubs2003/2003068.pdf (downloaded August 13, 2003).

————. 2003c. *Digest of Education Statistics, 2002.* Available online at http://nces.ed.gov/pubs2003/digest02/list_tables2.asp#c2_3 (downloaded September 5, 2003).

————. 2002a. *Digest of Education Statistics, 2001.* Washington, DC: U.S. Government Printing Office. Also available online at http://nces.ed.gov/pubs2002/digest2001/index.asp (downloaded May 28, 2003).

————. 2002b. "Results over Time: NAEP 1999 Long-Term Summary Tables." World Wide Web, http://nces.ed.gov/nationsreportcard/tables/Ltt1999/ (downloaded August 13, 2003).

————. 2001. "Enrollment Rates of 18- to 24-Year-Olds in Colleges and Universities: Selected Years 1980 to 2000." World Wide Web, http://nces.ed.gov/Pubs2003/Hispanics/figures.asp?FigureNumber=7_1a

————. 1998. *The Condition of Education, 1998.* Washington, DC: U.S. Government Printing Office. Also available via World Wide Web, http://nces.ed.gov/pubs98/condition98

————. 1997. *Digest of Education Statistics 1997.* Washington, DC: U.S. Government Printing Office. Also available via World Wide Web, http://nces.ed.gov/pubs/digest97/listtables.html

————. 1992a. *The Condition of Education, 1992.* Washington, DC: U.S. Government Printing Office.

————. 1992b. *Digest of Education Statistics, 1992.* Washington, DC: U.S. Government Printing Office.

NATIONAL CENTER FOR HEALTH STATISTICS. 2003. "Data Warehouse: Mortality Tables." World Wide Web, http://www.cdc.gov/nchs/datawh/statab/unpubd/mortabs.htm (downloaded July 18, 2003).

————. 2002a. "Births: Final Data for 2001." *National Vital Statistics Report* 51, 2. Hyattsville, MD: National Center for Health Statistics. Also available online at http://www.cdc.gov/nchs/releases/02news/precare.htm (downloaded July 18, 2003).

————. 2002b. "Deaths: Final Data for 2000." *National Vital Statistics Report* 51, 3. Hyattsville, MD: National Center for Health Statistics. Also available online at http://www.cdc.gov/nchs/data/nvsr/nvsr51/nvsr51_03.pdf (downloaded July 18, 2003).

————. 2002c. *Health: United States, 2002.* Hyattsville, MD: National Center for Health Statistics. Also available online at http://www.cdc.gov/nchs/data/hus/hus02.pdf (downloaded July 18, 2003).

————. 2002d. "Summary Health Statistics for U.S. Adults: National Health Interview Survey, 1997." *Vital and Health Statistics,* Series 10, No. 205. World Wide Web, http://www.cdc.gov/nchs/data/series/sr_10/sr10_205.pdf (downloaded October 10, 2003).

————. 1997a. *Monthly Vital Statistics Report* 46, 1(S)2, "Births and Deaths: United States, 1996." Hyattsville, MD: Public Health Service. Also available via World Wide Web, http://www.cdc.gov/nchswww/data/mv46_1s2.pdf

————. 1997b. Report of Final Natality Statistics, 1995. Hyattsville, MD: Public Health Service.

————. 1992. *Health, United States: 1991.* Hyattsville, MD: Public Health Service.

NATIONAL COMMISSION ON MARIHUANA AND DRUG ABUSE. 1972. *Marihuana: A Signal of Misunderstanding,* appendix, part 4. *Technical Papers of the National Commission on Marihuana and Drug Abuse.* Washington, DC: U.S. Government Printing Office.

NATIONAL INSTITUTE ON DRUG ABUSE. 2003. *Monitoring the Future: National Results on Adolescent Drug Use.* "Overview of Key Findings, 2002." World Wide Web, http://www.drugabuse.gov/PDF/overview2002.pdf (downloaded August 5, 2003).

————. 1989. *National Household Survey on Drug Abuse, 1988.* Rockville, MD: National Institute on Drug Abuse.

NATIONAL LEGAL AID AND DEFENDER ASSOCIATION. 2002. "History of Civil Legal Aid." World Wide Web, http://www.nlada.org/About/About_HistoryCivil (downloaded August 7, 2003).

NATIONAL LEGAL RESEARCH GROUP, INC. 1999. "Domestic Violence/Violence Against Women Act/Constitutionality." World Wide Web, http://www.divorcesource.com/research/dl/domestic/99mar60.shtml (downloaded May 10, 2004).

NATIONAL OPINION RESEARCH CENTER. 2003. "General Social Survey Codebook." World Wide Web, http://www.icpsr.umich.edu:8080/GSS/homepage.htm (downloaded June 5, 2003).

————. 1991. "General Social Survey, 1990." Press release issued January 8. Chicago: National Opinion Research Center.

NATIONAL ORGANIZATION ON DISABILITY. 2001. "Life Satisfaction of People with Disabilities." World Wide Web, http://www.nod.org/content.cfm?id=136 (downloaded May 10, 2004).

NATIONAL RESEARCH COUNCIL. 1999. *Evaluating Welfare Reform: A Framework and Review of Current Work,* edited by Robert Moffitt and Michele Ver Ploeg. Washington, DC: National Academy Press.

NATIONAL RESEARCH COUNCIL, PANEL ON ADOLESCENT PREGNANCY AND CHILDBEARING. 1987. *Risking the Future: Adolescent Sexuality, Pregnancy, and Childbearing.* Washington, DC: National Academy Press.

*NATIONAL REVIEW.* 1994. "Institutionalized Racism." *National Review* (September 12). Also available via World Wide Web, http://humanitas.ucsb.edu/projects/aa/docs/NR-v46-n17.html

NATIONAL WOMEN'S LAW CENTER. 1998. "Anti-Poverty Programs Are No Substitute for Affirmative Action." World Wide Web, http://humanitas.ucsb.edu/projects/aa/docs

NATION OF ISLAM. 1998. "The Muslim Program: What the Muslims Want." World Wide Web, http://www.noi.org//main.html

*NEA TODAY.* 1996. "A Bridge from Math to Algebra." *NEA Today* 15, 4 (November): 19–22.

NEFF, JOSEPH, JOHN WAGNER and KARIN RIVES. 2003. "Leaders Scramble While Job Losses Mount." *Raleigh News and Observer* (March 7). Also available at http://www.newsobserver.com/trade/story/1651741p-1677888c.html

NEIDERT, LISA J., and REYNOLDS FARLEY. 1985. "Assimilation in the United States: An Analysis of Ethnic and Generation Differences in Status." *American Sociological Review* 50: 840–50.

NELKIN, DOROTHY, and MICHAEL POLLAK. 1981. *The Atom Besieged.* Cambridge, MA: MIT Press.

NELSON, LORI, et al. 1994. "Effects of Participation in an Intergroup Communication Program: An Assessment of Shippensburg University's Building Bridges Program." Paper presented at Annual Meeting of the Eastern Psychological Association, Providence, Rhode Island, April 14–17.

NEWMAN, BERNIE SUE, and PETER GERARD MUZZONIGRO. 1993. "The Effects of Traditional Family Values on the Coming Out Process of Gay Male Adolescents." *Adolescence* 28, 109: 213–26.

NEWPORT, FRANK. 1998. "Americans Support Elimination of Bilingual Education: U.S. Public Agrees with California Voters." Gallup Poll Archives (June 6). World Wide Web, http://www.gallup.com/POLL_ARCHIVES/980606.htm

NEWPORT, JOHN PAUL, JR. 1992. "Steps to Help the Urban Black Man." Pp. 140–43 in John A. Kromkowski (ed.), *Race and Ethnic Relations 92/93.* Guilford, CT: Dushkin Publishing Group.

*NEWSWEEK.* 1979. "A New Racial Poll." February 26, pp. 48, 53.

*NEW YORK TIMES.* 1985. Editorial. September 30, sec. A.

———. 1980. "3 Ex-Houston Policemen Begin Terms for Civil Rights Violations." April 12, p. 30.

———. 1979a. June 29. Pp. 14, 11B, 12B.

———. 1979b. "A Tale of Two Cities," by Tom Wicker. November 2, p. 31.

———. 1973. February, 1973, p. 5.

NICHOLS, ANDREA. 2001. "Veiling Practices of Muslim Immigrant Women in the US." Paper presented at annual meeting of the Illinois Sociological Association, October 11–12, Rockford, IL.

NICHOLS, DONALD. 2003. "The Impact of Racial Segregation in Hospitals on Racial Differences in Medical Treatment." Paper presented at Baylor University Department of Economics Spring Research Seminar Series, February 13. Available online at http://business.baylor.edu/Tisha_Nakao/Seminar/nichols.pdf (downloaded July 25, 2003).

NICKENS, HERBERT W. 1992. "The Rationale for Minority-Targeted Programs in Medicine in the 1990s." *JAMA* 267, 7: 2390, 2395.

NICKLIN, JULIE L. 1992. "Helping to Manage Diversity in the Work Force." *Chronicle of Higher Education* (September 30): A5.

NISBET, LEE. 1977. "Affirmative Action: A Liberal Program?" Pp. 50–53 in Barry R. Gross (ed.), *Reverse Discrimination.* Buffalo: Prometheus Books.

NISBETT, RICHARD. 1998. "Race, Genetics, and IQ." Pp. 86–102 in Christopher Jencks and Meredith Phillips (eds.), *The Black-White Test Score Gap.* Washington, DC: Brookings Institution Press.

———. 1995. "Race, IQ, and Scientism." Pp. 36–57 in Steven Fraser (ed.), *The Bell Curve Wars: Race, Intelligence, and the Future of America.* New York: Basic Books.

NOCK, S. L., and P. W. KINGSTON. 1988. "Time with Children: The Impact of Couples' Work-Time Commitments." *Social Forces* 67: 59–85.

NOEL, DONALD L. (ED.) 1972a. *The Origins of American Slavery and Racism.* Columbus, OH: Merrill.

———. 1972b. "Slavery and the Rise of Racism." Pp. 153–74 in Donald L. Noel (ed.), *The Origins of American Slavery and Racism.* Columbus, OH: Merrill.

———. 1968. "A Theory of the Origin of Ethnic Stratification." *Social Problems* 16: 157–72.

NOLAN, PATRICK D. 1987. "World System Status, Income Inequality, and Economic Growth: A Criticism of Recent Criticism." *International Journal of Comparative Sociology* 28(1–2): 69–75.

NOLEN, SUSAN BOBBITT, and THOMAS M. HALADYNA. 1990. "Personal and Environmental Influences on Students' Beliefs About Effective Study Strategies." *Contemporary Educational Psychology* 15, 2: 116–30.

NORMENT, LYNN. 2002. "Black Women on Corporate Boards." *Ebony* (March): 42–48.

NOSTRAND, RICHARD L. 1992. *The Hispano Homeland.* Norman: University of Oklahoma Press.

NOVAK, MICHAEL. 1971. *The Rise of the Unmeltable Ethnics.* New York: Macmillan.

NTIRI, DAPHNE W. 2001. "Reassessing Africana Womanism: Continuity and Change." *The Western Journal of Black Studies* 25, 3: 163–67.

NUNES, ANA P., and BRAD SELIGMAN. 1999. "Testing Project Final Report: Treatment of Caucasian and African-American Applicants by San Francisco Bay Area Employment Agencies; Results of a Study Utilizing 'Testers.' " Berkeley, CA: The Impact Fund. Available online at http://www.impactfund. org/testing_project_final_report.html (downloaded November 24, 2003).

OAKES, JEANNINE, ADAM GAMORAN, and R. N. PAGE. 1992. "Curriculum Differentiation: Opportunities, Outcomes, and Meanings." In P. W. Jackson (ed.), *Handbook of Research on Curriculum.* Washington, DC: American Educational Research Association.

OFFICE OF APPLIED STUDIES. 2001. "Illicit Drug Use Tables: 1.1 to 1.110 (Prevalence Estimates)." World Wide Web, http://www. samhsa.gov/oas/nhsda/2kdetailedtabs/Vol_1_Part_1/sect1v1. htm#1.26b (downloaded August 5, 2003).

OFFICE OF MANAGEMENT and BUDGET. 1997. "Revisions to the Standards for the Classification of Federal Data on Race and Ethnicity." World Wide Web, http://www.whitehouse.gov/WH/ EOP/OMB/html/fedreg/Ombdir15.html

OFFICE OF POSTSECONDARY EDUCATION. 1998. "High Hopes for College for America's Youth." World Wide Web, http:// www.ed.gov/offices/OPE/PPI/highhopes.html (downloaded August 22, 2003).

OGBU, JOHN U. 1988a. "Diversity and Equity in Public Education: Community Forces and Minority School Adjustment and Performance." In Ron Haskins and Duncan MacRae (eds.), *Policies for America's Schools: Teachers, Equity, and Indicators.* Norwood, NJ: Ablex.

———. 1988b. "The Individual in Collective Adaptation: A Framework for Focusing on Academic Underperformance and Dropping Out Among Involuntary Minorities." Paper presented at the Annual Meeting of the American Educational Research Association, April 5–9, New Orleans.

———. 1978. *Minority Education and Caste: The American System in Cross Cultural Perspective.* New York: Academic Press.

O'HARE, WILLIAM P. 1992. "America's Minorities: The Demographics of Diversity." *Population Bulletin* 47, 4.

O'HARE, WILLIAM P., and USDANSKY, MARGARET L. 1992. "What the 1990 Census Tells Us About Segregation in 25 Large Cities." *Population Today* (September): 6–7.

OLIVER, J. ERIC, and TALI MENDELBERG. 2000. "Reconsidering the Environmental Determinants of White Racial Attitudes." *American Journal of Political Science* 44, 3: 574–89.

OLIVER, MELVIN L., and THOMAS M. SHAPIRO. 1995. *Black Wealth/White Wealth: A New Perspective on Racial Inequality.* New York: Routledge.

———. 1990. "Wealth of a Nation: A Reassessment of Asset Inequality in America Shows at Least One-Third of Households Are Asset-Poor." *American Journal of Economics and Sociology* 49: 129–51.

OLOJEDE, DELE. 1991. "Can I Quota You?" *Mother Jones* (July–August): 17, 19.

OLSEN, MARVIN E. 1990. "The Affluent Prosper While Everyone Else Struggles." Presidential address delivered at the 1990 Annual Meeting of the North Central Sociological Association, Louisville, Kentucky. (Reprinted in *Sociological Focus* 23: 73–87.)

OLSON, JAMES M., and MARK P. ZANNA. 1993. "Attitudes and Attitude Change." *Annual Review of Psychology* 44: 117–54.

OMI, MICHAEL, and HOWARD WINANT. 1994. *Racial Formation in the United States: From the 1960s to the 1990s,* 2d ed. New York: Routledge.

OREGON STATE UNIVERSITY LIBRARIES. 2002. "Govstats: 1992 Economic Census." World Wide Web, http://govinfo.kerr.orst.edu/ php/econ_census_92/home.php (data downloaded July 22, 2003).

ORFIELD, GARY. 1997. "Does Desegregation Help Close the Gap?" (Testimony of Gary Orfield, March 22, 1996). *Journal of Negro Education* 66: 241–54.

———. 1983. *Public School Desegregation in the United States, 1968–1980.* Washington, DC: Joint Center for Political Studies.

ORFIELD, GARY, and SUSAN E. EATON. 1996. *Dismantling Desegregation: The Quiet Reversal of Brown v. Board of Education.* New York: New Press.

ORFIELD, GARY, and FRANKLIN MONFORT. 1992. *Status of School Desegregation: The Next Generation*. Alexandria, VA: National School Boards Association.

ORFIELD, GARY, et al. 1991. "Interdisciplinary Social Science Statement to U.S. Supreme Court Concerning Research on the Effects of School Desegregation." Submitted as appendix to friend-of-court brief in DeKalb County, Georgia, school desegregation case.

OSSENBERG, RICHARD J. 1975. "Social Pluralism in Quebec: Continuity, Change, and Conflict." Pp. 112–25 in Norman R. Yetman and C. Hoy Steele (eds.), *Majority and Minority: The Dynamics of Racial and Ethnic Relations*. Boston: Allyn & Bacon.

OVANDO, MARTHA N., and BETTY J. ALFORD. 1997."Creating a Culture of Detracking in a Learner-Centered School: Issues, Problems, and Possibilities." Paper presented at the Annual Meeting of the American Association of School Administrators.

OVERBY, ANDREW. 1972. "Discrimination in the Administration of Justice." Pp. 264–76 in Charles E. Reasons and Jack L. Kuykendall (eds.), *Race, Crime, and Justice*. Pacific Palisades, CA: Goodyear.

OWEN, CAROLYN, HOWARD C. EISNER, and THOMAS R. MCFAUL. 1981. "A Half-Century of Social Distance Research: National Replication of the Bogardus Studies." *Sociology and Social Research* 66: 80–98.

OWENS, REGINALD. 1997."Diversity: A Bottomless Issue." *Workforce* (Workforce Tools Supplement) (March): 3–5.

OYER, PAUL, and SCOTT SCHAEFER. 2002. "Sorting, Quotas, and the Civil Rights Act of 1991: Who Hires When It's Hard to Fire?" *Journal of Law and Economics* 45: 41–68.

PACHON, HARRY P., and JOAN W. MOORE. 1981. "Mexican Americans." *Annals of the American Academy of Political and Social Science* 454: 111–24.

PADILLA, FELIX M. 1985. *Latino Ethnic Consciousness: The Case of Mexican Americans and Puerto Ricans in Chicago*. Notre Dame, IN: University of Notre Dame Press.

PAGER, DEVAH. 2003a. "The Mark of a Criminal Record." *American Journal of Sociology* 108(5): 937–75.

———. 2003b. "Blacks and Ex-Cons Need Not Apply." *Contexts* 2(4).

———. 2002. *The Mark of a Criminal Record: The Consequences of Incarceration for the Employment Opportunities of Black and White Job Seekers*. Doctoral dissertation, University of Wisconsin–Madison.

PALMER, BETSY. 2000. "The Impact of Diversity Courses: Research from Pennsylvania State University." *Diversity Digest* (Winter). World Wide Web, http://www.diversityweb.org/Digest/W00/research.html (downloaded May 28, 2003).

PALMER, FRANCIS H. 1970. "Socioeconomic Status and Intellective Performance Among Negro Pre-School Boys." *Developmental Psychology* 3: 1–9.

PANAYI, PANIKOS. 1999. *The Impact of Immigration: A Documentary History of the Effects and Experiences of Immigrants in Britain Since 1945*. Manchester, England: University of Manchester Press.

———(ed.). 1996. *Racial Violence in Britain in the Nineteenth and Twentieth Centuries*. Leicester, England: Leicester University Press.

PARENT, WAYNE. 1980. "A Liberal Legacy: Blacks Blaming Themselves for Economic Failures." *Journal of Black Studies* 16: 3–20.

PARISH, NORM. 2001. "Advocacy Group, Florissant, MO, Reach Agreement in Housing Lawsuit." *St. Louis Post-Dispatch* (April 26).

PARISI, NICOLETTE, MICHAEL R. GOTTFREDSON, MICHAEL J. HINDELANG, and TIMOTHY J. FLANIGAN (EDS.). 1979. *Sourcebook of Criminal Justice Statistics—1978*. Washington, DC: U.S. Government Printing Office.

PARSONS, TALCOTT. 1959. "The School Class as a Social System." *Harvard Education Review* 29: 297–318.

PARSONS, TALCOTT, and ROBERT F. BALES. 1955. *Family, Socialization, and Interaction Process*. Glencoe, IL: Free Press.

PASCHALL, MALLIE J., SUSAN T. ENNETT, and ROBERT L. FLEWELLING. 1996. "Relationships Among Family Characteristics and Violent Behavior by Black and White Male Adolescents." *Journal of Youth and Adolescence* 25: 177–97.

PATERNOSTER, RAYMOND. 1983. "The Decision to Seek the Death Penalty in South Carolina." *Journal of Criminal Law and Criminology* 74: 754–87.

PATTEN, CHRISTI A., CHRISTIAN J. GILLIN, ARTHUR J. FARKAS, and ELIZABETH A. GILPIN. 1997."Depressive Symptoms in California Adolescents: Family Structure and Parental Support." *Journal of Adolescent Health* 20: 271–78.

PATTERSON, ORLANDO. 1982. *Slavery and Social Death: A Comparative Study*. Cambridge, MA: Harvard University Press.

———. 1977. *Ethnic Chauvinism: The Reactionary Impulse*. New York: Stein & Day.

PAVEL, D. MICHAEL. 1999. "Schools, Principals, and Teachers Serving American Indian and Alaska Native Students." *ERIC Digest*, ERIC Identifier: ED425895. Available online at http://www.ericfacility.net/ericdigests/ed425895.html (downloaded September 11, 2003).

PAYNE, CHARLES. 1979. "On the Declining—and Increasing—Significance of Race." Pp. 117–39 in Charles Vert Willie (ed.), *Caste and Class Controversy*. Bayside, NY: General Hall.

PAXTON, SUSAN. 2002. "The Impact of Utilizing HIV-Positive Speakers in AIDS Education." *AIDS Education and Prevention* 14, 4: 282–94.

PEAR, ROBERT. 2004. "Despite the Sluggish Economy, Welfare Rolls Actually Shrank." *New York Times*, March 22.

———. 1990. "Study Finds Bias, Forcing a Review of 1986 Alien Law." *New York Times*, March 3, sec. 1.

PEARCE, DIANA. 1980. *Breaking Down the Barriers: New Evidence on the Impact of Metropolitan School Desegregation on Housing Patterns*. Washington, DC: National Institute of Education.

———. 1976. "Black, White, and Many Shades of Gray: Real Estate Brokers and Their Racial Practices." Ph.D. dissertation, University of Michigan, Ann Arbor.

PEARCE, DIANA, ROBERT L. CRAIN, and REYNOLDS FARLEY. 1984. "Lessons Not Lost: The Effect of School Desegregation on the Rate of Residential Desegregation in Large Center Cities." Paper presented at the Annual Meeting of the American Educational Research Association, New Orleans.

PEARL, D. 1954. "Ethnocentrism and the Self-Concept." *Journal of Social Psychology* 40: 137–47.

PEDERSON, WILLY. 1996. "Working Class Boys at the Margin: Ethnic Prejudice, Cultural Capital, and Gender." *Acta Sociologica* 39: 257–79.

PERLMANN, JOEL, and MARY C. WATERS. 2002. "Introduction." Pp. 1–30 in Joel Perlmann and Mary C. Waters (eds.), *The New Race Question: How the Census Counts Multiracial Individuals*. New York: Russell Sage Foundation.

PERRONE, VITO. 1991. "On Standardized Testing." *Childhood Education* (Spring): 132–42.

PESKIN, JANICE. 1982. "Measuring Household Production for the GNP." *Family Economics Review* (Summer): 16–25.

PETERSDORF, ROBERT G., K. S. TURNER, HERBERT W. NICKENS, and TIMOTHY READY. 1990. "Minorities in Medicine: Past, Present, and Future." *Academic Medicine* 65: 663–70.

PETERSILLA, JOAN. 1983. *Racial Disparities in the Criminal Justice System*. Santa Monica, CA: Rand Corporation.

PETERSON, E. D., S. M. WRIGHT, J. DALEY, and G. E. THIBAULT. 1994. "Racial Variation in Cardiac Procedure Use and Survival Following Acute Myocardial Infarction in the Department of Veterans Affairs." *JAMA* 271: 1175–89.

PETERSON, JAMES L., and NICHOLAS ZILL. 1986. "Marital Disruption, Parent-Child Relationships, and Behavior Problems in Children." *Journal of Marriage and the Family* 48: 295–307.

PETERSON, KAREN. 1997."Teenage Dating Shows Racial Barriers Falling." *Detroit News* (November 3). Also available via World Wide Web, http://detnews.com/1997/nation/9711/030094.htm

PETERSON, RICHARD R. 1996. "A Re-Evaluation of the Economic Consequences of Divorce." *American Sociological Review* 61: 528–36.

PETROCELLI, MATTHEW, ALEX R. PIQUERO, and MICHAEL R. SMITH. 2003. "Conflict Theory and Racial Profiling: An Empirical Analysis of Police Traffic Stop Data." *Journal of Criminal Justice* 31: 1–11.

PETTIGREW, THOMAS F. 1998."Intergroup Contact Theory." *Annual Review of Psychology* 49: 65–85.

———. 1985. "New Black-White Patterns: How Best to Conceptualize Them." Pp. 329–46 in Ralph H. Turner and James F. Short (eds.), *Annual Review of Sociology*, Vol. 11. Palo Alto, CA: Annual Reviews.

———. 1980. "The Changing—Not Declining—Significance of Race." *Contemporary Sociology* 9: 19–21.

———. 1976. "Race and Intergroup Relations." Pp. 459–510 in Robert K. Merton and Robert Nisbet (eds.), *Contemporary Social Problems*, 4th ed. New York: Harcourt Brace Jovanovich.

———. 1973. "Attitudes on Race and Housing: A Social-Psychological View." Pp. 21–84 in Amos H. Hawley and V. P. Rock (eds.), *Segregation in Residential Areas*. Washington, DC: National Academy of Sciences.

———. 1971. *Racially Separate or Together*. New York: McGraw-Hill.

———. 1969a. "The Negro and Education: Problems and Proposals." Pp. 49–112 in Irwin Katz and Patricia Gurin (eds.), *Race and the Social Sciences*. New York: Basic Books.

———. 1969b. "Race and Equal Educational Opportunity." Pp. 69–79 in Harvard Educational Review Editors (eds.), *Equality of Educational Opportunity*. Cambridge, MA: Harvard University Press.

PETTIGREW, THOMAS F., ELIZABETH L. USEEM, CLARENCE NORMAND, and MARSHALL S. SMITH. 1973. "Busing: A Review of the Evidence." *Public Interest* 30: 88–118.

PETTY, RICHARD E., and JOHN T. CACIOPPO. 1986. "The Elaboration Likelihood Model of Persuasion." *Advanced Experimental Social Psychology* 19: 123–205.

PETTY, RICHARD E., JOHN T. CACIOPPO, and RACHEL GOLDMAN. 1981. "Personal Involvement as a Determinant of Argument-Based Persuasion." *Journal of Personality and Social Psychology* 41: 847–55.

PHARR, SUZANNE. 1992. "Homophobia as a Weapon of Sexism." Pp. 431–40 in Paula S. Rothenberg (ed.), *Race, Class, and Gender in the United States: An Integrated Study*. New York: St. Martin's Press.

PHILLIPS, MEREDETH, JAMES CROUSE, and JOHN RALPH. 1998. "Does the Black-White Test Score Gap Widen After Children Enter School?" Pp. 229–72 in Christopher Jencks and Meredeth Phillips (eds.), *The Black-White Test Score Gap*. Washington, DC: Brookings Institution Press.

PIAGET, JEAN. 1965 [1932]. *The Moral Judgment of the Child*. Marjorie Gabain (tr.). New York: Free Press.

PIERSON, DONALD. 1942. *Negroes in Brazil*. Chicago: University of Chicago Press.

PILIAVIN, IRVING, and SCOTT BRIAR. 1964. "Police Encounters with Juveniles." *American Journal of Sociology* 70: 206–14.

PILLARD, RICHARD C., and J. MICHAEL BAILEY. 1998."Human Sexual Orientation Has a Heritable Component." *Human Biology* 70, 2: 347–65.

PINKNEY, ALPHONSO. 1976. *Red, Black, and Green: Black Nationalism in the United States*. New York: Cambridge University Press.

———. 1975. *Black Americans*. Englewood Cliffs, NJ: Prentice Hall.

PISKO, VALENA WHITE, and JOYCE D. STERN (EDS.). 1985. *The Condition of Education*, 1985 edition. Statistical Report, National Center for Education Statistics. Washington, DC: U.S. Government Printing Office.

PIVEN, FRANCES FOX. 1977. "The Urban Crisis: Who Got What and Why." Pp. 132–44 in Roger E. Alcaly and David Mermelstein (eds.), *The Fiscal Crisis of American Cities*. New York: Vintage Books.

PLANT, RICHARD. 1986. *The Pink Triangle: The Nazi War Against Homosexuals*. New York: Henry Holt.

POLLETTA, FRANCESCA, and JAMES M. JASPER. 2001. "Collective Identity and Social Movements." *Annual Review of Sociology* 27: 283–305.

PONTEROTTO, JOSEPH G., PAUL B. PEDERSEN, and CLEMMONT E. VONTRESS. 1993. *Preventing Prejudice: A Guide for Counselors and Educators*. Newbury Park, CA: Sage.

POOL, ROBERT. 1993. "Evidence for Homosexuality Gene." *Science* 261, 5119 (July 16): 291–92.

POPENOE, DAVID. 1996. *Life Without Father*. New York: Free Press.

———. 1988. *Disturbing the Nest: Family Change and Decline in Modern Societies*. New York: Aldine de Gruyter.

POPULATION REFERENCE BUREAU. 2003. "2003 World Population Data Sheet." Washington, DC: Population Reference Bureau. Available online at http://www.prb.org/pdf/WorldPopulationDS03_Eng.pdf

———. 2002. "2002 World Population Data Sheet." Washington, DC: Population Reference Bureau. Available online at http://www.prb.org/pdf/WorldPopulationDS02_Eng.pdf

PORTER, JUDITH D. R. 1971. *Black Child, White Child*. Cambridge, MA: Harvard University Press.

PORTER, ROSALIE PEDELINO. 1991. "Language Choice for Latino Students." *Public Interest* 105: 48–60.

POTOK, MARK. 2003. "The Year in Hate." *Intelligence Report* 109 (Spring), Southern Poverty Law Center. Also available on World Wide Web, http://www.splcenter.org/intelligenceproject/ip-index.html (downloaded May 26, 2003).

POTTINGER, J. STANLEY. 1972. "The Drive Toward Equality." *Change* 4, 8: 24.

POUSSAINT, ALVIN. 1977. Presentation to Intergroup Relations Week Program, Concordia College, Moorhead, Minnesota.

POWELL, RICHARD R., and JESUS GARCIA. 1985. "The Portrayal of Minorities and Women in Selected Elementary Science Series." *Journal of Research in Science Teaching* 22: 519–33.

POWELL, STEWART M. 1998."Poll Shows Power of Hispanics as Swing Vote in Midterm Elections." *Latinolink News*, World Wide Web, http://www.latinolink.com/news/news98/0423ncis.htm

POWELL, STEWART M., and MARK HELM. 1998."Hispanic Clout Emerging at Polls." *Times Union*, Albany, Nov. 8.

PRATTE, ANDRE. 2003. "Can We Talk, Canada?" *The Globe and Mail* (April 16): A17.

PRATTO, F., and J. A. BARGH. 1991. "Stereotyping Based on Apparently Individuating Information: Trait and Global Components of Sex Stereotypes Under Attention Overload." *Journal of Experimental Social Psychology* 27: 26–47.

PRIMUS, WENDELL, and KATHRYN PORTER. 1998. *Strengths of the Safety Net: How the EITC, Social Security, and Other Government Programs Affect Poverty*. Washington, DC: Center for Budget and Policy Priorities. Also available via World Wide Web, http://www.cbpp.org/snd98-rep.htm

PRIMUS, WENDELL, LYNETTE RAWLINGS, KATHY LARIN, and KATHRYN PORTER. 1999. "The Initial Impacts of Welfare Reform on the Incomes of Single-Mother Families." Washington, DC: Center on Budget and Policy Priorities.

PROTHRO, E. T. 1952. "Ethnocentrism and Anti-Negro Attitudes in the Deep South." *Journal of Abnormal and Social Psychology* 47: 105–8.

PUBLIC BROADCASTING SERVICE. 1985. "Frontlines: A Class Divided."

QUILLIAN, LINCOLN. 1996. "Group Threat and Regional Change in Attitudes Toward African Americans." *American Journal of Sociology* 102: 816–60.

QUINNEY, RICHARD. 1979. *Criminology.* Boston: Little, Brown.

QUINONES, SAM. 1998."Mexico Slow to Capitalize Along Border; Maquiladoras Are of Little Benefit So Far." *The San Diego Union-Tribune*, Dec 8.

QUINTON, WENDY J., GLORIA COWAN, and BRETT D. WATSON. 1996. "Personality and Attitudinal Predictors of Support for Proposition 187: California 's Anti-illegal Immigrant Initiative." *Journal of Applied Social Psychology* 26: 2204–23.

RAAB, EARL R. 1978. "Son of Coalition." Paper presented to the Twenty-Eighth Annual Meeting of the Society for the Study of Social Problems, San Francisco.

RAAB, EARL, and SEYMOUR MARTIN LIPSET. 1959. *Prejudice and Society.* New York: Anti-Defamation League.

RADELET, MICHAEL, and GLENN L. PIERCE. 1985. "Race and Prosecutorial Discretion in Homicide Cases." *Law and Society Review* 19: 587–621.

RADEN, DAVID. 1994. "Are Symbolic Racism and Traditional Prejudice Part of a Contemporary Authoritarian Attitude?" *Political Behavior* 16: 365–84.

RADKE, MARIAN J., and HELEN G. TRAGER. 1950. "Children's Perceptions of the Social Roles of Negroes and Whites." *Journal of Psychology* 29: 3–33.

RAKOWSKA-HARMSTONE, TERESA. 1992. "Chickens Coming Home to Roost: A Perspective on Soviet Ethnic Relations." *Journal of International Affairs* 45: 519–48.

RAMIREZ, J. D. 1991. *Executive Summary to the Final Report: Longitudinal Study of Structured English Immersion Strategy, Early-Exit and Late-Exit Transitional Bilingual Education Programs for Language-Minority Children.* San Mateo, CA: Aquirre International.

RAND CORPORATION AND URBAN INSTITUTE. 1990. *The Effect of Employer Sanctions on the Flow of Undocumented Immigrants to the United States.* Report no. JRI-03. Santa Monica, CA: Rand Corporation.

RANSFORD, H. EDWARD. 1972. "Blue-Collar Anger: Reactions to Student and Black Protest." *American Sociological Review* 37: 333–46.

RAPHAEL, STEVEN. 1998. "The Spatial Mismatch Hypothesis and Black Youth Joblessness: Evidence from the San Francisco Bay Area." *Journal of Urban Economics* 43: 79–111.

RATTERAY, JOAN DAVIS. 1988. *Freedom of the Mind: Essays and Policy Studies.* Washington, DC: Institute for Independent Education.

RAY, JOHN J. 1988. "Why the F Scale Predicts Racism: A Critical Review." *Political Psychology* 9: 671–79.

———. 1980. "Authoritarianism in California 30 Years Later—With Some Cross-Cultural Comparisons." *Journal of Social Psychology* (June): 9–17.

REDMOND, EUGENE B., SHERMAN FOWLER, and MARCUS ATKINS. 1998. "Visible Glory: The Million Man March." Special Issue, *Drumvoices Revue: A Confluence of Literary, Cultural, and Visionary Arts* 7, 1–2.

REED, ADOLPH. 1996. "Dissing the Underclass." *Progressive* 60, 12: 20–21.

REICH, MICHAEL. 1986. "The Political-Economic Effects of Racism." Pp. 304–11 in Richard C. Edwards, Michael Reich, and Thomas E. Weisskopf (eds.), *The Capitalist System: A Radical Analysis of American Society*, 3d ed. Englewood Cliffs, NJ: Prentice Hall.

———. 1981. *Racial Inequality: A Political-Economic Analysis.* Princeton, NJ: Princeton University Press.

REICHMANN, REBECCA (ED.). 1999. *Race in Contemporary Brazil: From Indifference to Inequality.* University Park: The Pennsylvania State University Press.

REIMAN, PAUL. 2004. *The Rich Get Richer and the Poor Get Prison*, 7th ed. Boston: Allyn & Bacon.

REIMERS, CORDELIA W. 1984. "Sources of the Family Income Differentials Among Hispanics, Blacks, and White Non-Hispanics." *American Journal of Sociology* 89: 889–903.

REISS, ALBERT J., JR. 1968. "Police Brutality: Answers to Key Questions." *Transaction* 5: 10–19.

RENNISAN, CALLIE MARIE, and SARAH WELCHANS. 2000. "Intimate Partner Violence." Washington, DC: U.S. Department of Justice, Bureau of Justice Statistics. World Wide Web, http://www.ojp.usdoj.gov/bjs/pub/ascii/ipv.txt. (downloaded September 25, 2003).

RENO, JANET. 1998. Address to American-Arab Anti-Discrimination Committee Conference on "Shaping the Future," June 12.

———. 1997. Address to Governors' Conference on Racial Reconciliation, Charlotte, North Carolina, October 27.

RESKIN, BARBARA F. 1998. *The Realities of Affirmative Action in Employment.* Washington, DC: American Sociological Association.

———. 1988. "Bringing the Men Back In: Sex Differentiation and the Devaluation of Women's Work." *Gender and Society* 2: 58–81.

REYNOLDS, ROBERT E., and THOMAS W. RICE. 1971. "Attitudes of Medical Interns Toward Patients and Health Professionals." *Journal of Health and Social Behavior* 12: 307–11.

RHODES, N., and W. WOOD. 1992. "Individual Differences in Influenceability: Self-Esteem and Intelligence." *Psychological Bulletin* 111: 156–71.

RICH, YISRAEL, PERI KEDEM, and AVIVA SHLESINGER. 1995. "Enhancing Intergroup Relations Among Children: A Test of the Miller-Brewer Model" *International Journal of Intercultural Relations* 19: 539–53.

RICHERT, JEAN PIERRE. 1974. "The Impact of Ethnicity on the Perception of Heroes and Historical Symbols." *Canadian Review of Sociology and Anthropology* 11, 2 (May): 156–63.

RICHMAN, CHARLES L., M. L. CLARK, and KATHRYN P. BROWN. 1985. "General and Specific Self-Esteem in Late Adolescent Students: Race × Sex × Gender Effects." *Adolescence* 20: 555–66.

RICHMOND, ANTHONY H. 1986. "Racial Conflict in Great Britain. Review Essay." *Contemporary Sociology* 15: 184–87.

RIDLEY, C. R. 1989. "Racism in Counseling as an Adverse Behavioral Process." Pp. 55–77 in Paul B. Pederson, J. G. Draguns, W. J. Lonner, and J. E. Trimble (eds.), *Counseling Across Cultures*, 3d ed. Honolulu: University of Hawaii Press.

RIEDER, JONATHAN. 1985. *Canarsie: The Jews and Italians of Brooklyn Against Liberalism.* Cambridge, MA: Harvard University Press.

RIESMAN, DAVID. 1961. *The Lonely Crowd.* New Haven, CT: Yale University Press.

RIGBY, KEN. 1988. "Sexist Attitudes and Authoritarian Personality Characteristics Among Australian Adolescents." *Journal of Research in Personality* 22: 465–73.

RIORDAN, CORNELIUS, and JOSEPHINE RUGGIERO. 1980. "Producing Equal Status Interracial Interaction: A Replication." *Social Psychology Quarterly* 43: 131–36.

RIST, RAY C. 1978. *The Invisible Children: School Integration in American Society.* Cambridge, MA: Harvard University Press.

———. 1970. "Student Social Class and Teacher Expectations: The Self-Fulfilling Prophecy in Ghetto Education." *Harvard Educational Review* 40: 411–51.

ROBINSON, JERRY W., and JAMES D. PRESTON. 1976. "Equal-Status Contact and Modification of Racial Prejudice: A Reexamination of the Contact Hypothesis." *Social Forces* 54: 911–24.

ROBINSON, JOHN. 1977. *How Americans Use Their Time: A Social Psychological Analysis of Everyday Behavior.* New York: Praeger.

RODDY, DENNIS B. 1990. "Perceptions Still Segregate Police, Black Community." *Pittsburgh Press*, August 29, sec. B.

RODRIQUEZ, DANIEL. 1998."Diversity Training Brings Staff Closer." *Education Digest* 64, 1 (September): 28–31.

ROEBUCK, JULIAN, and ROBERT QUAN. 1976. "Health-Care Practices in the American Deep South." Pp. 141–61 in R. Wallis and P. Morely (eds.), *Marginal Medicine.* New York: Free Press.

ROEDIGER, DAVID R. 1991. *The Wages of Whiteness.* London: Verso Books.

ROMERO, ANN, and DON ZANCANELLA. 1990. "Expanding the Circle: Hispanic Voices in American Literature." *English Journal* 79, 1: 24–29.

RONCAL, JOAQUIN. 1944. "The Negro Race in Mexico." *Hispanic American Historical Review* 24: 530–40.

ROONEY-REBEK, PATRICIA, and LEONARD JASON. 1986. "Prevention of Prejudice in Elementary School Students." *Journal of Primary Prevention* 7: 63–73.

ROSE, R. 1971. *Governing Without Consensus.* London: Faber & Faber.

ROSEN, ILENE S. 1996. "Good News About Day Care." *Parents* 71, 11: 168–70.

ROSENBAUM, JAMES E. 1976. *Making Inequality: The Hidden Curriculum of High School Teaching.* New York: Wiley.

ROSENBAUM, JAMES E., and AMY BINDER. 1997. "Do Employers Really Need More Educated Youth?" *Sociology of Education* 70: 68–85.

ROSENBAUM, JAMES E., and TAKEHIKO KARIYA. 1991. "Do School Achievements Affect the Early Jobs of High School Graduates in the United States and Japan?" *Sociology of Education* 64: 78–95.

ROSENBAUM, JAMES E., and SUSAN J. POPKIN. 1991. "Employment and Earnings of Low-Income Blacks Who Move to Middle-Class Suburbs." Pp. 342–56 in Christopher Jencks and Paul E. Peterson (eds.), *The Urban Underclass.* Washington, DC: Brookings Institution.

ROSENBAUM, ROBERT J., and ROBERT W. LARSON. 1987. "Mexicano Resistance to the Expropriation of Grant Lands in New Mexico." Pp. 269–310 in Charles L. Briggs and John R. Van Ness (eds.), *Land, Water, and Culture: New Perspectives on Hispanic Land Grants.* Albuquerque: University of New Mexico Press.

ROSENBERG, MORRIS, and ROBERTA G. SIMMONS. 1971. *Black and White Self-Esteem: The Urban School Child.* Washington, DC: American Sociological Association.

ROSENTHAL, BERNARD G. 1974. "Development of Self-Identification in Relation to Attitudes Toward the Self in the Chippewa Indians." *Genetic Psychology Monographs* 90: 43–141.

ROSENTHAL, ROBERT, and LENORE JACOBSON. 1968. *Pygmalion in the Classroom: Teacher Expectation and Pupils' Intellectual Development.* New York: Holt, Rinehart & Winston.

ROSS, CATHERINE E., and JOHN MIROWSKY. 1999. "Parental Divorce, Life-Course Disruption, and Adult Depression." *Journal of Marriage and the Family* 61: 1034–45.

ROSSELL, CHRISTINE H. 1991. "The Effectiveness of Educational Alternatives for Limited English Proficient Children." In G. Imhoff (ed.), *The Social and Cultural Context of Instruction in Two Languages: From Conflict and Controversy in Cooperative Reorganization of Schools.* New York: Transaction Books.

———. 1990. *The Carrot or the Stick for School Desegregation Policy: Magnet Schools or Forced Busing.* Philadelphia: Temple University Press.

ROSSELL, CHRISTINE H., and CHARLES L. GLENN. 1988. "The Cambridge Controlled Choice Plan." *Urban Review* 20, 2: 75–94.

ROSSELL, CHRISTINE H., and J. M. ROSS. 1986. "The Social Science Evidence on Bilingual Education." *Journal of Law and Education* 15, 385–418.

ROTHENBERG, JULIA JOHNSON, et al. 1997. "Challenges in Pedagogy: A Qualitative Result of Teaching Heterogenous Classes." Paper presented at the Annual Meeting of the American Educational Research Association, March 24–28, Chicago.

ROTHSTEIN, R. 2000. "Equalizing Education Resources on Behalf of Disadvantaged Children." Pp. 31–92 in R. D. Kahlenberg (ed.), *A Notion at Risk: Preserving Public Education as an Engine for Social Mobility.* New York: The Century Foundation Press.

RUBACK, R. BARRY, and PAULA VARDAMAN. 1997. "Decision Making in Delinquency Cases: The Role of Race and Juveniles' Admission/Denial of the Crime." *Law and Human Behavior* 21: 47–69.

RUBENSTEIN, ROSS. 2003. "National Evidence on Racial Disparities in School Finance Adequacy." Pp. 93–107 in William J. Fowler (ed.), *Developments in School Finance: 2001–02: Fiscal Proceedings from the Annual State Data Conferences of July 2001 and July 2002.* Washington, DC: National Center for Education Statistics.

RUBIN, I. M. 1967. "Increased Self-Acceptance: A Means of Reducing Prejudice." *Journal of Personality and Social Psychology* 5: 133–238.

RUDWICK, ELLIOTT M. 1964. *Race Riot at East St. Louis, July 2, 1917.* Carbondale: Southern Illinois University Press.

RUGGLES, STEVEN. 1997a. "The Effects of AFDC on American Family Structure." *Journal of Family History* 22: 307–25.

———. 1997b. "The Rise of Divorce and Separation in the United States, 1880–1990." *Demography* 34: 455–66.

RUNDALL, THOMAS G., and JOHN R. C. WHEELER. 1979. "The Effect of Income on Use of Preventive Care: An Evaluation of Alternative Explanations." *Journal of Health and Social Behavior* 20: 397–406.

RYAN, WILLIAM. 1971. *Blaming the Victim.* New York: Vintage Books.

———. 1967. "Savage Discovery: The Moynihan Report." Pp. 457–66 in Lee Rainwater and William L. Yancey (eds.), *The Moynihan Report and the Politics of Controversy.* Cambridge, MA: MIT Press.

SAHA, SOMNATH, et al. 1999. "Patient-Physician Racial Concordance and the Perceived Quality and Use of Health Care." *ARCH Internal Medicine* 159: 997 –1000.

ST. JOHN, NANCY H. 1975. *School Desegregation: Outcomes for Children.* New York: Wiley.

ST. LOUIS POST-DISPATCH. 1998a. "Number of Unmarried Couples Sets a Record. Census Bureau Says: 4 Million and Rising Figures Show Trend to Live Together Before Marriage." July 27.

———. 1998b. "Protestant Group Insists It Will March, Despite Ban." June 30, p. A3.

———. 1993d. "U.S. School Segregation Called Highest Since '60s." December 14, p. 3a.

SALTZMAN, AMY, and TED GEST. 1991. "Your New Civil Rights." *U.S. News and World Report* (November 18): 93–95.

SAMPSON, ROBERT J. 1987. "Urban Black Violence: The Effect of Male Joblessness and Family Disruption." *American Journal of Sociology* 93: 348–82.

SANDBERG, NEIL C. 1974. *Ethnic Identity and Assimilation: The Polish-American Community.* New York: Praeger.

SANDHU, DAYA SINGH, and CHERYL BLALOCK ASPY. 1997. *Counseling for Prejudice Prevention and Reduction.* Alexandria, VA: American Counseling Association.

SANDOVAL, J. 1979. "The WISC-R and Internal Evidence of Test Bias with Minority Groups." *Journal of Counselling and Clinical Psychology* 47: 919–27.

SAN FRANCISCO CHRONICLE 2003. "SAVAGE TALK: A Former Herbalist Has Remade Himself into the Vitriol-Spewing King of the Bay Area's Afternoon Drive Time." February 6. Available online at http://www.sfgate.com/cgi-bin/article.cgi?file=/chronicle/archive/2003/02/06/DD165846.DTL

SARD, BARBARA, and WILL FISCHER. 2003. "Funding Level Approved by House Subcommittee Would Reduce, but Not Eliminate, Shortfall in Housing Voucher Funding." Washington, DC: Center on Budget and Policy Priorities. World Wide Web, http://www.cbpp.org/7-21-03hous.htm

SATIN, GEORGE D. 1973. "Help? The Hospital Emergency Unit Patient and His Presenting Picture." *Medical Care* 11: 328–37.

SATIN, GEORGE, and FREDERICK J. DUHL. 1972. "Help? The Hospital Emergency Unit as Community Physician." *Medical Care* 10: 248–60.

SATTLER, JEROME M. 1982. *Assessment of Children's Intelligence and Special Abilities*, 2d ed. Boston: Allyn & Bacon.

SAUL R. LEVEN MEMORIAL FOUNDATION. 1959. Unpublished report of study of Detroit Recorder's Court over 20-month period, November 1, 1957 through June 30, 1959.

SCAGLION, RICHARD, and RICHARD CONDON. 1980. "Determinants of Attitudes Toward City Police." *Criminology* 17: 485–94.

SCHAEFER, RICHARD T. 1996. "Education and Prejudice: Unraveling the Relationship." *Sociological Quarterly* 37: 1–16.

SCHAFER, WALTER E., CAROL OLEXA, and KENNETH POLK. 1972. "Programmed for Social Class: Tracking in High School." Pp. 34–54 in Kenneth Polk and Walter E. Schafer (eds.), *Schools and Delinquency*. Englewood Cliffs, NJ: Prentice Hall.

SCHAICH, WARREN. 1975. "A Relationship Between Collective Racial Violence and War." *Journal of Black Studies* 5: 374–94.

SCHERMERHORN, RICHARD A. 1978. *Comparative Ethnic Relations: A Framework for Theory and Research*, Phoenix ed. Chicago: University of Chicago Press.

SCHIRALDI, VINCENT. 1995. "Blacks Are Target of 57 Percent of 'Three Strikes' Prosecutions in Los Angeles." *Overcrowded Times* 6, 2: 7.

SCHLACHTER, ANNE, and JOHN DUCKITT. 2002. "Psychopathology, Authoritarian Attitudes, and Prejudice." *South African Journal of Psychology* 32, 2, 1–7.

SCHMALZ, JEFFREY. 1993. "Survey Stirs Debate on Number of Gay Men in U.S." *New York Times*, April 16, sec. A.

SCHMIDT, PETER. 1992. "Gap Cited in Awareness of Students' Home Languages." *Education Week* (April 29): 11.

SCHMIDT, WILLIAM E. 1991. "Oslo Journal: Who's in Charge Here? Chances Are It's a Woman." *New York Times* (May 22): A4.

SCHNAIBERG, LYNN. 1997. "The Politics of Language." *Education Week* on the Web, March 7. World Wide Web, http://www.edweek.org/ew/vol-16/23bilin1.h16

SCHNARE, ANN B. 1977. *Residential Segregation by Race in U.S. Metropolitan Areas: An Analysis Across Cities and over Time*. Washington, DC: Urban Institute.

SCHNEIDER, MARK, and THOMAS PHELAN. 1990. "Blacks and Jobs: Never the Twain Shall Meet?" *Urban Affairs Quarterly* 26: 299–312.

SCHOEN, ROBERT, NAN MARIE ASTONE, KENDRA ROTHERT, NICOLA J. STANDISH, and YOUNG J. KIM. 2002. "Women's Employment, Marital Happiness, and Divorce." *Social Forces* 81, 2: 643–62.

SCHOFIELD, JANET WARD. 1995. "Review of Research on School Segregation's Impact on Elementary and Secondary School Students." Pp. 597–616 in James A. Banks and Cherry A. McGee Banks (eds.), *Handbook of Research on Multicultural Education*. New York: Macmillan.

SCHORR, LISBETH B., and DANIEL SCHORR. 1988. *Within Our Reach: Breaking the Cycle of Disadvantage*. New York: Anchor Doubleday.

SCHRAG, PETER. 1995. "So You Want to Be Color-Blind: Alternative Principles for Affirmative Action." *The American Prospect* 22 (September): 38–43. Also available via World Wide Web, http://epn.org/prospect/22/22schr.html

SCHUCHARDT, THOMAS. 1980. "A Study of the Disabled in the Role of Social Deviant." Master's thesis, Southern Illinois University, Edwardsville.

SCHULMAN, KEVIN A., J. A. BERLIN, W. HARLESS, J. F. KERNER, S. SISTRUNK, B. J. GERSH, R. DUBE, C. K. TALEGHANI, J. E. BURKE, S. WILLIAMS, J. M. EISENBERG, and J. J. ESCARCE. 1999. "The Effect of Race and Sex on Physicians' Recommendations for Cardiac Catheterization." *New England Journal of Medicine* (February 25).

SCHUMAN, HOWARD. 1975. "Free Will and Determinism in Public Beliefs About Race." Pp. 375–80 in Norman R. Yetman and C. Hoy Steele (eds.), *Majority and Minority: The Dynamics of Racial and Ethnic Relations*. Boston: Allyn & Bacon. (Earlier version appeared in *Transaction* 7, 2 [1969]: 44–48.)

SCHUMAN, HOWARD, and LAWRENCE BOBO. 1988. "Survey-Based Experiments on White Racial Attitudes Toward Residential Integration." *American Journal of Sociology* 94: 273–99.

SCHUTTE, GERALD. 1995. *What Racists Believe: Race Relations in South Africa and the United States*. Thousand Oaks, CA: Sage.

SCHWARTZ, BARRY, and ROBERT DISCH. 1975. *White Racism: Its History, Pathology, and Practice*. New York: Dell.

SCOTT, R. R., and J. M. McPARTLAND. 1982. "Desegregation as National Policy: Correlates of Racial Attitudes." *American Educational Research Journal* 19: 397–414.

SCRUGGS, OTEY M. 1971. "The Economic and Racial Components of Jim Crow." Pp. 70–87 in Nathan I. Huggins, Martin Kilson, and Daniel M. Fox (eds.), *Key Issues in the Afro-American Experience*, Vol. 2. New York: Harcourt Brace Jovanovich.

SEABURY, PAUL. 1977. "HEW and the Universities." Pp. 97–112 in Barry R. Gross (ed.), *Reverse Discrimination*. Buffalo: Prometheus Books. (Earlier version appeared in *Commentary* [February, 1972].)

SEARS, D. O., R. R. LAU, T. R. TAYLOR, and H. M. ALLEN. 1980. "Self-Interest or Symbolic Politics in Policy Attitudes and Presidential Voting?" *American Political Science Review* 74: 670–84.

SEDER, RICHARD C. 1998. *Bilingual Education: Reading, Writing, and Rhetoric*. Los Angeles: Reason Foundation.

SEE, KATHERINE O'SULLIVAN. 1986. *First World Nationalisms: Class and Ethnic Politics in Northern Ireland and Quebec*. Chicago: University of Chicago Press.

SEEBORG, MICHAEL C., and KRISTIN JAEGER. 1993. "The Impact of Local Labor Markets on Black and White Family Structure." *Journal of Socio-Economics* 22: 115–30.

SEIFER, NANCY. 1973. *Absent from the Majority: Working Class Women in America*. New York: American Jewish Committee.

SELIGMAN, DANIEL. 1992. "Keeping Up: The Curious Case of the Missing Data." *Fortune* (June 15): 159–60.

SELINGO, JEFFERY. 2003. "What Americans Think About Higher Education: Poll Finds Strong Support for Colleges, but Many Questions About Their Priorities." *Chronicle of Higher Education* (May 2): A10–A15.

SELVIN, PAUL. 1992. "Math Education: Multiplying the Meager Numbers." *Science* 28: 1200–1201.

SERVICEMEMBERS' LEGAL DEFENSE NETWORK. 1997. "Conduct Unbecoming: Third Annual Report on 'Don't Ask, Don't Tell, Don't Pursue.'" World Wide Web, http://www.sldn.org/scripts/sldn.ixe?page5article_0008a

SEYMOUR, D. Z. 1972. "Black English." *Intellectual Digest* 2.

SFGATE.COM. 2004. Text of Gov. George Ryan's speech announcing his commutation of all of Illinois' death sentences. World Wide Web, http://www.sfgate.com/cgi-bin/article.cgi?file=/gate/archive/2003/01/11/ryan.DTL&type=printable (downloaded May 10, 2004).

SHAHEEN, JACK G. 2001. *Reel Bad Arabs: How Hollywood Vilifies a People*. Northampton, MA: Interlink Publishing.

———. 1990. "Our Cultural Demon: The 'Ugly Arab.'" *Washington Post* (August 19): C1.

———. 1984. *The TV Arab*. Bowling Green, OH: Bowling Green State University Popular Press.

SHANAHAN, J. L. 1976. "Impaired Access of Black Inner-City Residents to the Decentralized Workplaces." *Journal of Economics and Business* 28, 2: 156–60.

SHARMA, RAMA, and SAEEDUZ ZAFAR. 1989. "A Study of Prejudice in Relation to Feelings of Security-Insecurity." *Journal of Personality and Clinical Studies* 5: 73–75.

SHAW, BARRETT. 1994. *The Ragged Edge: The Disability Experience from the Pages of the First Fifteen Years of the Disability Rag*. Louisville, KY: Advocado Press.

SHEATSLEY, PAUL B. 1966. "White Attitudes Toward the Negro." *Daedalus* 95: 217–38.

SHENKER, JOSEPH. 1992. "Preparing Teachers for Democratic Schools: A Response." *Teachers College Record* 94, 1: 45–47.

SHEPPARD, B. H., J. HARTWICK, and P. R. WARSHAW. 1988. "The Theory of Reasoned Action: A Meta-Analysis of Past Research with Recommendations for Modifications and Future Research." *Journal of Consumer Research* 15: 325–43.

SHERIF, MUZAFER, O. J. HARVEY, B. JACK WHITE, WILLIAM R. HOOD, and CAROLYN W. SHERIF. 1961. *Intergroup Conflict and Cooperation: The Robbers Cave Experiment.* Norman, OK: University Book Exchange.

SHERMAN, LAWRENCE. 1980. "Causes of Police Behavior: The Current State of Quantitative Research." *Journal of Research in Crime and Delinquency* 17: 69–100.

SHILTS, RANDY. 1993a. *Conduct Unbecoming: Gays and Lesbians in the U.S. Military.* New York: St. Martin's Press.

———. 1993b. "What's Fair in Love and War." *Newsweek* (February 1): 58–59.

SHIN, FAY H. 2000. "Parent Attitudes Toward the Principles of Bilingual Education and Their Children's Participation in Bilingual Programs." *Journal of Intercultural Studies* 21: 93–99.

SHIRLOW, PETER. 2002. "Devolution, Identity and the Reproduction of Ethno-Sectarianism in Northern Ireland." Paper presented at the annual meeting of the Royal Geographical Society and Institute of British Geographers, Belfast, Northern Ireland, January 5.

SHOCKLEY, WILLIAM. 1971a. "Models, Mathematics, and the Moral Obligation to Diagnose the Origin of Negro IQ Deficits." *Review of Educational Research* 41: 369–77.

———. 1971b. "Negro IQ Deficit: Failure of a 'Malicious Coincidence' Model Warrants New Research Proposals." *Review of Educational Research* 41: 227–28.

SIA, TIFFINY L., CHARLES G. LORD, KENNETH A. BLESSUM, CHRISTOPHER D. RATCLIFF, and MARK R. LEPPER. 1997. "Is a Rose Always a Rose? The Role of Social Category Exemplar Change in Attitude Stability and Attitude-Behavior Consistency." *Journal of Personality & Social Psychology* 72, 3: 501–14.

SILVERSTEIN, BARRY, and RONALD KRATE. 1975. *Children of the Dark Ghetto: A Developmental Psychology.* New York: Praeger.

SILVERSTEIN, LEE. 1966. "Bail in the State Courts: A Field Study and Report." *Minnesota Law Review* 50.

SIMMONS, WENDY W. 2000. "Black Americans Feel 'Cheated' by Election 2000." Poll analysis, Gallup Organization, December 20. World Wide Web, http://www.gallup.com/poll/releases/pr001220.asp (downloaded July 2, 2003).

SIMON, DAVID R., and D. STANLEY EITZEN. 1993. *Elite Deviance,* 4th ed. Boston: Allyn & Bacon.

SIMON, JULIAN. 1990. *The Economic Consequences of Immigration.* Cambridge, MA: Basil Blackwell.

SIMPKINS, G., and C. SIMPKINS. 1981. "Cross-Cultural Approach to Curriculum Development." In Geneva Smitherman (ed.), *Black English and the Education of Black Children and Youth.* Detroit: Wayne State University Center for Black Studies.

SIMPSON, GEORGE EATON, and J. MILTON YINGER. 1985. *Racial and Cultural Minorities: An Analysis of Prejudice and Discrimination,* 5th ed. New York: Plenum.

SINDLER, ALLAN P. 1978. *Bakke, DeFunis, and Minority Admissions: The Quest for Equal Opportunity.* New York: Longman.

SINGER, DAVID (ED.). 2002. *American Jewish Year Book, 2002.* New York: American Jewish Committee.

SINNOTT, RICHARD. 1998. "Vote Shows Peace Optimists Are on the Increase." *Irish Times* on the Web. World Wide Web, http://www.irish-times.com/irish-times/special/peace/assembly/analysis/analysis6.html

SKOLNICK, JEROME H. 1969. *The Politics of Protest.* New York: Simon & Schuster.

SLAVIN, ROBERT E. 1995a. "Cooperative Learning and Intergroup Relations." Pp. 628–34 in James A. Banks and Cherry A.

McGee Banks (eds.), *Handbook of Research on Multicultural Education.* New York: Macmillan.

———. 1995b. "Detracking and Its Detractors: Flawed Evidence, Flawed Values." *Phi Delta Kappan* 77: 220–21.

———. 1985. "Cooperative Learning: Applying Contact Theory in Desegregated Schools." *Journal of Social Issues* 41, 3: 43–62.

SMITH, D. G., GUY L. GERBICK, MARK A. FIGUEROA, GAYLE HARRIS WATKINS, THOMAS LEVITAN, LEESHAWN CRADOC MOORE, PAMELA A. MERCHANT, HAIM DOV BELIAK, and BENJAMIN FIGUEROA. 1997. *Diversity Works: The Emerging Picture of How Students Benefit.* Washington, DC: Association of American Colleges and Universities.

SMITH, DONALD. 1984. *Saving the African American Child.* Report of the National Alliance of Black School Administrators, Inc.

SMITH, DOUGLAS A., and CHRISTY A. VISHER. 1981. "Street Level Justice: Situational Determinants of Police Arrest Decisions." *Social Problems* 29: 167–77.

SMITH, DOUGLAS A., CHRISTY A. VISHER, and LAURA A. DAVIDSON. 1984. "Equity and Discretionary Justice: The Influence of Race on Police Arrest Decisions." *Journal of Criminal Law and Criminology* 75: 234–49.

SMITH, JAMES P., and BARRY EDMONSTON. 1997. *The New Americans: Economic, Demographic, and Fiscal Effects of Immigration.* Report of the Panel on the Demographic and Economic Impacts of Immigration, Committee on Population and Committee on National Statistics, Commission on Behavioral and Social Sciences and Education, National Research Council. Washington, DC: National Academy Press.

SMITH, M. DWAYNE. 1987. "Patterns of Discrimination in Assessments of the Death Penalty: The Case of Louisiana." *Journal of Criminal Justice* 15: 279–86.

SMITH, TOM W. 1999. "Measuring Inter-Racial Friendships: Experimental Comparisons." GSS Methodological Report No. 91. Chicago: National Opinion Research Center.

———. 1998. "American Sexual Behavior: Trends, Socio-Demographic Differences, and Risk Behavior." GSS Topical Report No. 25. Chicago: National Opinion Research Center, University of Chicago. World Wide Web, http://cloud9.norc.uchicago.edu/dlib/t-25.htm (downloaded September 29, 2003).

SMITH, W. C. 1942. "Minority Groups in Hawaii." *Annals of the American Academy of Political and Social Science* 233: 41.

SMITHERMAN, GENEVA. 1997. "Black Language and the Education of Black Children: One Mo Once." *Black Scholar* 27: 28–35.

SMOCK, PAMELA J., WENDY D. MANNING, and SANJIV GUPTA. 1999. "The Effect of Marriage and Divorce on Women's Economic Well-Being." *American Sociological Review* 64: 794–812.

SNIDERMAN, PAUL M., and MICHAEL GRAY HAGEN. 1985. *Race and Inequality: A Study in American Values.* Chatham, NJ: Chatham House.

SNIDERMAN, PAUL M., and THOMAS PIAZZA. 1993. *The Scar of Race.* Cambridge, MA: Belknap Press, Harvard University Press.

SNIDERMAN, PAUL M., THOMAS PIAZZA, PHILIP E. TETLOCK, and ANN KENDRICK. 1991. "The New Racism." *American Journal of Political Science* 35: 423–47.

SNIPP, C. MATTHEW. 1988. "Public Policy and American Indian Economic Development." Pp. 1–22 in C. Matthew Snipp (ed.), *Public Policy Impacts on American Indian Economic Development.* Santa Fe: Native American Studies, University of New Mexico.

SNIPP, C. MATTHEW. 1986a. "American Indians and Natural Resource Development." *American Journal of Economics and Sociology* 45: 457–74.

———. 1986b. "The Changing Political and Economic Status of American Indians: From Captive Nations to Internal Colonies." *American Journal of Economics and Sociology* 45: 145–57.

SNOW, DAVID A., E. BURKE ROCHFORD, JR., STEVEN K. WORDEN, and ROBERT D. BENFORD. 1986. "Frame Alignment Processes, Micromobilization, and Movement Participation." *American Sociological Review* 78: 537–61.

SNOW, LOUDELL F. 1978. "Sorcerers, Saints, and Charlatans: Black Folk Healers in Urban America." *Culture, Medicine, and Psychiatry* 2: 69–106.

SNYDER, THOMAS D. 1991. *Youth Indicators 1991: Trends in the Well-Being of American Youth.* Office of Research and Improvement, U.S. Department of Education. Washington, DC: U.S. Government Printing Office.

SNYDERMAN, MARK, and STANLEY ROTHMAN. 1987. "Survey of Expert Opinion on Intelligence and Aptitude Testing." *American Psychologist* 42: 137–44.

SOLOMON, CHARLENE MARMER. 1992. "Keeping Hate Out of the Workplace." *Personnel Journal* (July): 30–36.

SOLORZANO, DANIEL G. 1991. "Mobility Aspirations Among Racial Minorities, Controlling for SES." *Sociology and Social Research* 75: 182–88.

SOMMERFELD, MEG. 1995. "Employers Discount School Factors in Hiring Decisions, Study Concludes." *Education Week* 14, 23 (March 1): 7.

SOUTH, SCOTT J., and GLENNA SPITZE. 1994. "Housework in Marital and Nonmarital Households." *American Sociological Review* 59: 327–47.

SOUTHERN POVERTY LAW CENTER. 2004. "Hate Group Web Site List." *Intelligence Report* 113 (Spring): 443–49.

———. 1998a. "Klanwatch Documents Increase in Skinhead Violence." World Wide Web, http://www.splcenter.org/klanwatch/kw-7.html

———. 1998b. "A Skinhead's Story: An Interview with a Former Racist." *Intelligence Report* (Winter). Also available via World Wide Web, http://www.splcenter.org/klanwatch/kw-4e8.html

———. 1997. "Patriot Movement Poses Continued Threat: Groups Are Growing in Number, Hardening in Attitude." World Wide Web, http://www.splcenter.org/klanwatch/kw-5.html

———. 1993a. "For the Record." *Intelligence Report* (September): 11–17.

———. 1993b. "Klanwatch Reports Hate Violence at Record Levels Last Year." *SPLC Report* 23, 2 (April): 1, 5.

———. 1988. *Special Report: The Ku Klux Klan: A History of Racism and Violence,* 3d ed. Montgomery, AL: Southern Poverty Law Center.

SOWELL, THOMAS. 1990. *Preferential Policies.* New York: Morrow.

———. 1977. " 'Affirmative Action' Reconsidered." Pp. 113–31 in Barry R. Gross (ed.), *Reverse Discrimination.* Buffalo, NY: Prometheus.

SPEAR, ALLAN. 1971. "The Origins of the Urban Ghetto, 1870–1915." Pp. 153–66 in Nathan I. Huggins, Martin Kilson, and Daniel M. Fox (eds.), *Key Issues in the Afro-American Experience,* Vol. 2. New York: Harcourt Brace Jovanovich.

SPENCER, MARGARET BEALE, ELIZABETH NOLL, JILL STOLTZFUS, and VINAY HARPALANI. 2001. "Identity and School Adjustment: Revisiting the 'Acting White' Assumption." *Educational Psychologist* 36: 21–30.

SPENCER, METTA. 1979. *Foundations of Modern Sociology.* Englewood Cliffs, NJ: Prentice Hall.

SPOHN, CASSIA, and MIRIAN DELONE. 2000. "When Does Race Matter? An Analysis of the Conditions Under Which Race Affects Sentence Severity." *Sociology of Crime, Law, and Deviance* 2: 3–37.

STACK, STEVEN. 1994. "Divorce." Pp. 153–63 in *Encyclopedia of Human Behavior,* Vol. 2. New York: Academic Press.

STAMPP, KENNETH M. 1959. *The Peculiar Institution: Slavery in the Ante-bellum South.* New York: Knopf.

———. 1956. *The Peculiar Institution: Slavery in the Ante-bellum South.* New York: Vintage Books.

STANGOR, CHARLES, and C. DUAN. 1991. "Effects of Multiple Task Demands upon Memory for Information About Social Groups." *Journal of Experimental Social Psychology* 27: 357–78.

STANGOR, CHARLES, LINDA A. SULLIVAN, and THOMAS E. FORD. 1991. "The Affective and Cognitive Dimensions of Prejudice." *Social Cognition* 9: 359–80.

STANLEY, JULIAN C. (ED.). 1973. *Compensatory Education for Children, Ages 2 to 8, Recent Studies of Environmental Intervention.* Baltimore, MD: Johns Hopkins University Press.

STAPLES, ROBERT. 1973. *The Black Woman in America.* Chicago: Nelson-Hall.

STEEH, CHARLOTTE, and MARIA KRYSAN. 1996. "The Polls-Trends: Affirmative Action and the Public, 1970–1995." *Public Opinion Quarterly* 60: 128–58.

STEELE, C. HOY. 1985. "The Acculturation/Assimilation Model in Urban Indian Studies: A Critique." Pp. 332–39 in Norman R. Yetman (ed.), *Majority and Minority: The Dynamics of Race and Ethnicity in America,* 4th ed. Boston: Allyn & Bacon.

———. 1972. "American Indians and Urban Life: A Community Study." Ph.D. diss., University of Kansas, Lawrence.

STEELE, CLAUDE M. 1999. "Thin Ice: 'Stereotype Threat' and Black College Students." *Atlantic Online* (*Atlantic Monthly* digital edition) (August 1999). World Wide Web, http://www.theatlantic.com/issues/99aug/9908stereotype.htm

STEELE, CLAUDE M., and JOSHUA ARONSON. 1998. "Stereotype Threat and Test Performance." Pp. 401–27 in Christopher Jencks and Meredith Phillips (eds.), *The Black-White Test Score Gap.* Washington, DC: Brookings Institution Press.

———. 1995. "Stereotype Threat and the Intellectual Test Performance of African Americans." *Journal of Personality and Social Psychology* 69: 797–811.

STEELE, SHELBY. 1990. *The Content of Our Character: A New Vision of Race in America.* New York: St. Martin's Press.

STEINBERG, LAURENCE. 1996. "Failure Outside the Classroom." *Wall Street Journal,* eastern edition (July 11): A14.

STEINBROOK, ROBERT. 1996. "Diversity in Medicine." *New England Journal of Medicine* 334, 20. Also available via World Wide Web, http://www.nejm.org/content/1996/0334/0020/1327.asp

STEPHAN, WALTER G., VLADIMIR AGEYEV, LISA COATES-SHRIDER, and COOKIE WHITE STEPHAN. 1994. "On the Relationship Between Stereotypes and Prejudice: An International Study." *Personality and Social Psychology Bulletin* 20: 277–84.

STERNLIEB, GEORGE, and JAMES W. HUGHES. 1976. *Post-Industrial America: Metropolitan Decline and Inter-Regional Job Shifts.* New Brunswick, NJ: Rutgers University Center for Urban Policy Research.

STERTZ, BRADLEY, and KRYSTAL MILLER. 1991. "Chaldeans in Detroit Are Prime Targets of Threats, Violence." *Wall Street Journal,* January 21, sec. A.

STEVENS, ROSEMARY. 1971. *American Medicine and the Public Interest.* New Haven, CT: Yale University Press.

STEVENSON, RICHARD W. 1990. "Study Finds Mild Gain in Drive on Illegal Aliens." *New York Times,* April 21, p. 24.

STOCKARD, JEAN, and MIRIAM M. JOHNSON. 1992. *Sex and Gender in Society,* 2d ed. Englewood Cliffs, NJ: Prentice Hall.

STODDARD, LOTHROP. 1920. *The Rising Tide of Color Against White World-Supremacy.* New York: Scribner's.

STOKES, RANDALL, and ALBERT CHEVAN. 1996. "Female-Headed Families: Social and Economic Context of Racial Differences." *Journal of Urban Affairs* 18: 245–68.

STOTLAND, E., DONALD KATZ, and M. PATCHEN. 1959. "The Reduction of Prejudice Through the Arousal of Self-Insight." *Journal of Personality* 27: 507–31.

STOUFFER, SAMUEL A., E. A. SUCHMAN, L. C. DEVINNEY, S. A. STAR, and R. N. WILLIAMS. 1949. *The American Soldier,* Vol. 1, *Adjustment During Army Life.* Princeton, NJ: Princeton University Press.

STRAUS, MURRAY A. 1980. "A Sociological Perspective on the Causes of Family Violence." In Maurice R. Green (ed.), *Violence and the Family.* Boulder, CO: Westview Press.

STRONG, JAMES. 1994. "The Resurgence of Black Nationalism." *St. Louis American* (March 10–16): 7A, 8A.

STUBBINS, JOSEPH (ED.). 1977. *Social and Psychological Aspects of Disability: A Handbook for Practitioners*. Baltimore, MD: University Park Press.

STUCKERT, ROBERT S. 1958. "The African Ancestry of the White American Population." *Ohio Journal of Science* (May): 155–60.

SUDARKASA, NIARA. 1991. "Absent: Black Men on Campus." *Essence* 22, 7: 140.

SUH, TONGWOO, CHRISTIAN G. SCHUTZ, and CHRIS ELLYN JOHANSON. 1996. "Family Structure and Initiating Non-Medical Drug Use Among Adolescents." *Journal of Child and Adolescent Substance Abuse* 5, 3: 21–36.

SULLIVAN, ANDREW. 1990. "Racism 101." *New Republic* (November 26): 18–21.

SUMMERS, ANITA, and BARBARA L. WOLFE. 1977. "Do Schools Make a Difference?" In *Sociological Inventory* Sample Issue. Washington, DC: American Sociological Association.

SUMNER, WILLIAM GRAHAM. 1906. *Folkways*. Boston: Ginn.

SUPER, DONALD E., and JOHN O. CRITES. 1962. *Appraising Vocational Fitness*. New York: Harper & Row.

SUPLEE, C. 1991. "Brain May Determine Sexuality." *Washington Post*, August 30, sec. A.

SZYMANSKI, ALBERT. 1976. "Racial Discrimination and White Gain." *American Sociological Review* 41: 403–14.

TAEUBER, KARL E. 1979. "Housing, Schools, and Incremental Segregative Effects." *Annals of the American Academy of Political and Social Science* 441: 157–67.

TAEUBER, KARL E., and ALMA F. TAEUBER. 1965. *Negroes in Cities*. Chicago: Aldine.

TAJFEL, HENRI. 1981. *Human Groups and Social Categories*. Cambridge, UK: Cambridge University Press.

———. 1969. "Cognitive Aspects of Prejudice." *Journal of Biosocial Sciences*, Supplement No. 1, 173–91.

TAKAGI, PAUL. 1979. "Death by 'Police Intervention.' " In U.S. Department of Justice, *A Community Concern: Police Use of Deadly Force*. Washington, DC: U.S. Government Printing Office.

TANAKA, G. K. 1996. "The Impact of Multiculturalism on White Students." Ph.D. dissertation, University of California at Los Angeles.

TAYLOR, D. GARTH. 1981. "Racial Preferences, Housing Segregation, and the Causes of School Segregation: Recent Evidence from a Social Survey Used in Civil Litigation." *Review of Public Data Use* 9: 267–82.

———. 1979. "Housing, Neighborhoods, and Race Relations: Recent Survey Evidence." *Annals of the American Academy of Political and Social Science* 441 (January): 26–40.

TAYLOR, EDWARD. 2000. "Critical Race Theory and Interest Convergence in the Backlash Against Affirmative Action: Washington State and Initiative 2000." *Teachers College Record* 102, 3: 339–60.

TAYLOR, HOWARD F. 1995. "Review Symposium: The Bell Curve." *Contemporary Sociology* 24: 153–58.

TAYLOR, KARYN J. 1978. "A Black Perspective on the Melting Pot." *Social Policy* 8, 5: 31–37.

TAYLOR, LIZ. 2003. "Patients Struggle to Find Doctors Who Will Take Medicare, Medicaid." *Seattle Times* (January 18). Available online at http://seattletimes.nwsource.com/text/134617683_liztaylor20.html (downloaded July 25, 2003).

TAYLOR, MARYLEE C. 1995. "White Backlash to Workplace Affirmative Action: Peril or Myth?" *Social Forces* 73: 1385–1414.

TAYLOR, PAUL S., and CLARK KERR. 1935. "Uprising on the Farm." *Survey Graphic* 24: 19–22.

TAYLOR, RONALD L. 1998. "On Race and Society." *Race and Society* 1: 1–3.

TERRY, ROBERT M. 1967. "Discrimination in the Handling of Juvenile Offenders by Social Control Agencies." *Journal of Research in Crime and Delinquency* 4: 218–30.

TESSER, ABRAHAM, and DAVID R. SHAFFER. 1990. "Attitudes and Attitude Change." *Annual Review of Psychology* 41: 479–523.

THEISING, ANDREW J. 2003. *East St. Louis: Made in U.S.A.* St. Louis, MO: Virginia Publishing Co.

THERNSTROM, ABIGAIL. 1991. "Beyond the Pale." *New Republic* 205, 25: 22–24.

———. 1980. "E Pluribus Plura: Congress and Bilingual Education." *Public Interest* 60 (Summer): 3–22.

THERNSTROM, STEPHAN, ANN ORLOV, and OSCAR HANDLIN (EDS.). 1980. *The Harvard Encyclopedia of American Ethnic Groups*. Cambridge, MA: Harvard University Press.

THOMAS, CLARENCE. 2003. Opinion in *Barbara Grutter, Petitioner v. Lee Bollinger et al.*, United States Supreme Court, 539 U.S. (2003).

THOMAS, R. ROOSEVELT, JR. 1990. "From Affirmative Action to Affirming Diversity." *Harvard Business Review* 68, 2 (March–April): 107–17.

THOMAS, RICHARD. 1996. *Understanding Racial Unity: A Study of U.S. Race Relations*. Thousand Oaks, CA: Sage.

THOMAS, WAYNE, and VIRGINIA COLLIER. 1997. *School Effectiveness for Language Minority Students*. Washington, DC: National Clearinghouse for Bilingual Education.

THOMLINSON, RALPH. 1976. *Population Dynamics: Causes and Consequences of World Demographic Change*, 2d ed. New York: Random House.

THOMPSON, LEONARD MONTIETH, and LEONARD L. THOMPSON. 2001. *A History of South Africa*, 3d ed. New Haven, CT: Yale University Press.

THOMPSON, MARILYN S., KRISTEN E. DICERBO, KATE MAHONEY, and JEFF MACSWAN. 2002. "*¿Exito en California?* A Validity Critique of Language Program Evaluations and Analysis of English Learner Test Scores." *Education Policy Analysis Archives*, 10(7). Available online at http://epaa.asu.edu/epaa/v10n7/ (downloaded August 28, 2003).

THOMPSON, WILBUR. 1976. "Economic Processes and Employment Problems in Declining Metropolitan Areas." Pp. 187–96 in George Sternlieb and James W. Hughes (eds.), *Post-Industrial America: Metropolitan Decline and Interregional Job Shifts*. New Brunswick, NJ: Rutgers University Center for Urban Policy Research.

THOMSON, ERNIE. 1997. "Discrimination and the Death Penalty in Arizona." *Criminal Justice Review* 22: 65–76.

THOMSON, RANDALL J., and MATTHEW T. ZINGRAFF. 1981. "Detecting Sentencing Disparity: Some Problems and Evidence." *American Journal of Sociology* 86: 869–80.

———. 1978. "A Longitudinal Analysis of Crime Sentencing Patterns." Paper presented at the Annual Meeting of the Society for the Study of *Social Problems*, San Francisco.

THORNBERRY, TERENCE P. 1974. "Race, Socioeconomic Status, and Sentencing in the Juvenile Justice System." *Journal of Criminal Law and Criminology* 64: 90–98.

THORNDIKE, ROBERT C. 1969. "Review of Pygmalion in the Classroom." *Teachers College Record* 70: 805–7.

THORNTON, ARLAND, and DEBORAH FREEDMAN. 1984. "The Changing American Family." *Population Bulletin* 38, 4.

THORNTON, JOHN. 1992. *Africa and Africans in the Making of the Atlantic World, 1400–1680*. Cambridge, England: Cambridge University Press.

THORNTON, RUSSELL. 1997. "Aboriginal North American Population and Rates of Decline, ca. A.D. 1500–1900." *Current Anthropology* 38: 310–15.

———. 1987. *American Indian Holocaust and Survival*. Norman: University of Oklahoma Press.

TIENDA, MARTA, KATHARINE M. DONATO, and HECTOR CORDERO-GUZMAN. 1992. "Schooling, Color, and the Labor Force Activity of Women." *Social Forces* 71: 365–95.

TILLY, CHARLES. 1998. *Durable Inequality.* Berkeley: University of California Press.

———. 1974. "The Chaos of the Living City." Pp. 86–108 in Charles Tilly (ed.), *An Urban World.* Boston: Little, Brown.

TILLY, CHRIS, PHILIP MOSS, JOLEEN KIRSCHENMAN, and IVY KENNELLY. 2001. "Space as a Signal: How Employers Perceive Neighborhoods in Four Metropolitan Labor Markets." Pp. 304–38 in Alice O'Conner, Chris Tilly, and Lawrence D. Bobo (eds.), *Urban Inequality: Evidence from Four Cities.* New York: Russell Sage Foundation.

TINDALL, DAVID B. 2002. "Social Networks, Identification and Participation in an Environmental Movement: Low-Medium Cost Activism Within the British Columbia Wilderness Preservation Movement." *Canadian Review of Sociology and Anthropology* 39: 413–52.

TOLNAY, STUART E. 1997. "The Great Migration and Changes in the Northern Black Family, 1940–1990." *Social Forces* 75: 1213–38.

TOMAS RIVERA CENTER. 1998. "TRC Announces Key Findings on Attitudes of U.S. Latinos Toward Major Social and Political Issues of the Day." World Wide Web, http://www.cgs.edu/inst/trc_hispanicperspectives.html

TONRY, MICHAEL. 1995. *Malign Neglect: Race, Crime, and Punishment in America.* New York: Oxford University Press.

TOOMER, JETHRO W. 1977. "Intergroup Relations in the Urban Education Setting: Lessons from the Literature." *Urban Education* 12: 217–22.

TOWNSEND, LINDA, and ALEXIS J. WALKER. 1990. "American Women Get Mad: Women's Attitudes Are Changing: Here's What You Can Expect in the 1990s." *American Demographics* (August): 26–32.

TOWSON, KAROLYN. 2002. "Weighing In: Elementary-Age Students and the Debate on Attitudes Toward School Among Black Students." *Social Forces* 80, 4: 1157–89.

TRAVER, NANCY. 1990. "Opening Doors for the Disabled." *Time* (June 4): 54.

TREANOR, RICHARD BRYANT. 1993. *We Overcame: The Story of Civil Rights for Disabled People.* Falls Church, VA: Regal Direct Publishing.

TRENT, WILLIAM T. 1997. "Why the Gap Between Black and White Performance in School?: A Report on the Effects of Race on Student Achievement in the St. Louis Public Schools." *Journal of Negro Education* 66: 320–29.

———. 1991. *Desegregation Analysis Report.* New York: Legal Defense and Education Fund.

TRIANDIS, HARRY C. 1971. *Attitude and Attitude Change.* New York: Wiley; Princeton, NJ: Princeton University Press.

TRIPP, LUKE. 1992. "The Political Views of Black Students During the Reagan Era." *Black Scholar* 22, 3: 45–52.

TRITELLI, DAVID. 2001. "Diversity Workshops: New Research." *Diversity Digest* (Winter). World Wide Web, http://www.diversityweb.org/Digest/W01/research.html (downloaded May 29, 2003).

TUCH, STEVEN A. 1988. "Race Differences in the Antecedents of Social Distance Attitudes." *Sociology and Social Research* 72: 181–84.

TUMIN, MELVIN M. 1953. "Some Principles of Stratification: A Critical Analysis." *American Sociological Review* 18: 387–93.

TURKHEIMER, ERIC, ANDREANA HALEY, MARY WALDRON, BRIAN D'ONOFRIO, and IRVING I. GOTTESMAN. 2003. "Socioeconomic Status Modifies Heritability of IQ in Young Children." *Psychological Science* 14, 6: 623–8.

TURNER, LORENZO DOW. 1949. *Africans in the Gullah Dialect.* Chicago: University of Chicago Press.

TURNER, MARGERY AUSTIN, and STEPHEN L. ROSS. 2003. "Discrimination in Metropolitan Housing Markets: Phase 2—Asians and Pacific Islanders." Final Report. Washington, DC: U.S. Department of Housing and Urban Development. Available online at http://www.huduser.org/publications/pdf/phase2_final.pdf (downloaded November 13, 2003).

TURNER, MARGERY AUSTIN, STEPHEN L. ROSS, GEORGE C. GALSTER, and JOHN YINGER. 2002. "Discrimination in Metropolitan Housing Markets: National Results from Phase I HDS 2000." Final Report. Washington, DC: U.S. Department of Housing and Urban Development. Available online at http://www.huduser.org/Publications/pdf/Phase1_Report.pdf (downloaded November 13, 2003).

TURQUE, BILL. 1992. "Gays Under Fire." *Newsweek* (September 14): 34–40.

ULMER, JEFFREY T., and JOHN H. KRAMER. 1996. "Court Communities Under Sentencing Guidelines: Dilemmas of Formal Rationality and Sentencing Disparity." *Criminology* 34: 383–407.

UNESCO. 1952. "Statement on the Nature of Race and Race Differences—by Physical Anthropologists and Geneticists." New York: UNESCO. (Reprinted in Ashley Montagu, 1963, *Race, Science, and Humanity*, pp. 178–83. Princeton, NJ: D. Van Nostrand.)

———. 1950. "The UNESCO Statement by Experts on Race Problems." New York: UNESCO. (Reprinted in Ashley Montagu, 1963, *Race, Science, and Humanity*, pp. 172–78. Princeton, NJ: D. Van Nostrand.)

UNITED CEREBRAL PALSY ASSOCIATIONS. 1996. *1996 ADA Snapshot of America: ADA Changes Lives of People with Disabilities.* Washington, DC: United Cerebral Palsy Associations.

UNITED NATIONS POPULATION DIVISION. 2003. *World Population Prospects: The 2002 Revision.* World Wide Web, http://esa.un.org/unpp/p2k0data.asp (downloaded December 11, 2003.)

———. 1995. *World Urbanization Prospects, 1994 Revision.* New York: United Nations.

UNIVERSITY OF MARYLAND, OFFICE OF HUMAN RELATIONS. 1994. "Policy on Inclusive Language." World Wide Web, http://www.inform.umd.edu/Student/Diversity_Resources/What_is_Diversity/inclusive_language

UNNEVER, JAMES D., and LARRY A. HEMBROFF. 1988. "The Prediction of Racial/Ethnic Sentencing Disparities: An Expectation States Approach." *Journal of Research in Crime and Delinquency* 25: 53–82.

UPCHURCH, DAWN M., CAROL S. ANESHENSEL, CLEA A. SUCOFF, and LENE LEVY-STORMS. 1999. "Neighborhood and Family Contexts of Adolescent Sexual Activity." *Journal of Marriage and the Family* 61: 920–33.

*USA TODAY.* 1997. "Black-White Gap over O.J.'s Guilt Narrows." World Wide Web, http://www.usatoday.com/news/index/nns168.htm

———. 1991. "By the Numbers, Tracking Segregation in 219 Metro Areas." *USA Today,* November 11, p. 3a.

U.S. BUREAU OF LABOR STATISTICS. 2003. "Bureau of Labor Statistics News: Employment Situation." World Wide Web, http://www.bls.gov/news.release/empsit.toc.htm (downloaded July 17, 2003).

———. 1984. *Employment and Earnings, January.* Washington, DC: U.S. Government Printing Office.

U.S. BUREAU OF THE CENSUS. 1999. "Historical Income Tables: People." World Wide Web, http://www.census.gov/hhes/income/histinc/incperdet.html

———. 1998a. "Resident Population of the United States: Estimates, by Sex, Race, and Hispanic Origin, with Median Age." World Wide Web, http://www.census.gov/population/estimates/nation/intfile3–1.txt

———. 1998b. "1990 Census Data Lookup." World Wide Web, http://venus.census.gov/cdrom/lookup

———. 1998c. "March, 1996 CPS: Employment Status by Race-Ethnicity, Age 16 and Over: Both Sexes—Values/Percents." World Wide Web, http://www.census.gov/population/socdemo/hispanic/cps96/tab07-2.txt

———. 1998d. "Table 1. Selected Characteristics of the Population by Sex, Region, and Race, March, 1997." World Wide Web, http://www.census.gov/population/socdemo/race/black/tabs97/tab01.txt

———. 1998e. "United States State and Local Government Finances by Level of Government, 1994–95," World Wide Web, http://www.census.gov/estimate/95stlus.txt

———. 1997a. *Current Population Reports, Consumer Income.* Series P-60, no. 199, "Health Insurance Coverage, 1996." Washington, DC: U.S. Government Printing Office. Also available via World Wide Web, http://www.census.gov/prod/3/97pubs/P60–199.pdf

———. 1997b. *Statistical Abstract of the United States, 1997.* Washington, DC: U.S. Government Printing Office. Also available via World Wide Web, http://www.census.gov/prod/3/97pubs/97statab/

———. 1993a. *Statistical Abstract of the United States, 1993.* Washington, DC: U.S. Government Printing Office.

———. 1993b. *We, the Americans: Blacks.* Washington, DC: U.S. Government Printing Office.

———. 1993c. *We, the Americans: First Americans.* Washington, DC: U.S. Government Printing Office.

———. 1992a. "1990 Census of Population. General Population Characteristics, United States." Report no. 1990CP-1–1. Washington, DC: U.S. Government Printing Office.

———. 1992b. *1990 Census of Population.* "Summary Social, Economic, and Housing Characteristics, United States." Report no. CPH-5–1. Washington, DC: U.S. Government Printing Office.

———. 1992c. *Statistical Abstract of the United States, 1992.* Washington, DC: U.S. Government Printing Office.

———. 1990. *Statistical Abstract of the United States, 1990.* Washington, DC: U.S. Government Printing Office.

———. 1986 *Statistical Abstract of the United States,* 1986 Edition. Washington, DC: U.S. Government Printing Office.

———. 1983. *1980 Census of Population. Characteristics of the Population, General Population Characteristics, United States Summary.* Report no. PC80-1-B1. Washington, DC, U.S. Government Printing Office.

———. 1979a *Current Population Reports: Consumer Income.* "Money Income in 1977 of Families and Persons in the United States." Series P-60, no. 118. Washington, DC: U.S. Government Printing Office.

———. 1979b. *The Social and Economic Status of the Black Population in the United States: An Historical View, 1970–1978.* "Current Population Reports, Special Studies." Series P-23, no. 80. Washington, DC: U.S. Government Printing Office.

———. 1972. *1970 Census of Population.* "General Characteristics: United States Summary." PC(1)-B1. Washington, DC: U.S. Government Printing Office.

———. 1953. *A Report of the Seventeenth Decennial Census of the United States,* Vol. II, *Characteristics of the Population.* Washington, DC: U.S. Government Printing Office.

U.S. CENSUS BUREAU. 2004a. *U.S. Interim Projections by Age, Sex, Race, and Hispanic Origin.* World Wide Web, http://www.census.gov/ipc/www/usinterimproj/ (downloaded March 28, 2004).

———. 2003a. *2000 Census of Population,* "National Population Characteristics, Table 2. Resident Population Estimates of the United States by Sex, Race, and Hispanic or Latino Origin: April 1, 2000/1, July 1, 2000 and July 1, 2001." World Wide Web, http://eire.census.gov/popest/data/national/tables/asro/US-EST2001-ASRO-02.xls (downloaded May 15, 2003).

———. 2004b. Annual Estimates of the Population by Sex, Race and Hispanic or Latino Origin for the United States: April 1, 2000 to July 1, 2003. World Wide Web, http://eire.census.gov/popest/data/national/tables/NC-EST2003-03.xls (Downloaded June 23, 2004).

———. 2003b. "American Fact Finder. Census 2000, Summary File 1, Detailed Tables." World Wide Web, http://factfinder.census.gov/servlet/DTGeoSearchByListServlet?ds_name=EC_2000_SF1_U&_lang=en&_ts=76352123460

———. 2003c. "American Fact Finder. Census 2000, Summary File 3, Detailed Tables." World Wide Web, http://factfinder.census.gov/servlet/DTGeoSearchByListServlet?ds_name=DEC_2000_SF3_U&_lang=en&_ts=76438156180

———. 2003d. "American Fact Finder, Census 2000 Summary File 4 (SF 4): Sample Data, Detailed Tables." World Wide Web, http://factfinder.census.gov/servlet/DTGeoSearchByListServlet?ds_name=DEC_2000_SF4_U&_lang=en&_ts=82573275750 (downloaded September 25, 2003).

———. 2003e. "American Fact Finder, Economic Censuses and Surveys, Economic-Wide Key Statistics, Geography Quick Reports." World Wide Web, http://factfinder.census.gov/servlet/DatasetMainPageServlet?_program=ECN&_lang=en

———. 2003f. "American Fact Finder: Geographic Comparison Tables." World Wide Web, http://factfinder.census.gov/servlet/GCTGeoSearchByListServlet?ds_name=DEC_2000_SF2_U&_lang=en&_ts=76349903870 (downloaded July 15, 2003).

———. 2003g. "Asset Ownership of Households: 1998 and 2000, Detailed Tables." World Wide Web, http://www.census.gov/hhes/www/wealth/1998_2000/wealth98_00.html

———. 2003h. *The Black Population in the United States: March 2002* (PPL-164). World Wide Web, http://www.census.gov/population/www/socdemo/race/ppl-164.html (downloaded June 27, 2003).

———. 2003i. *Current Population Reports,* Report P20-547, "Children's Living Arrangements and Characteristics, March, 2002." Washington, DC: U.S. Government Printing Office. Available online at http://www.census.gov/prod/2003pubs/p20-547.pdf.

———. 2003j. "Educational Attainment in the United States: March, 2002, Detailed Tables." World Wide Web, http://www.census.gov/population/www/socdemo/education/ppl-169.html (downloaded July 18, 2003).

———. 2003k. *The Hispanic Population in the United States: March 2002* "Detailed Tables" (PPL-165). World Wide Web, http://www.census.gov/population/www/socdemo/hispanic/ppl-165.html (downloaded June 27, 2003).

———. 2003l. "Historical Income Tables." World Wide Web, http://www.census.gov/hhes/income/histinc/ineqtoc.html (downloaded November 7, 2003).

———. 2003m. "Housing Patterns: Racial and Ethnic Residential Segregation in the United States: 1980–2000." World Wide Web, http://www.census.gov/hhes/www/housing/resseg/papertoc.html

———. 2003n. "Income in the United States, 2002. Current Population Reports, Consumer Income," Report No. P60-271. World Wide Web, http://www.census.gov/prod/2003pubs/p60-221.pdf (downloaded November 7, 2003).

———. 2003o. *National Population Estimates: Characteristics.* World Wide Web, http://eire.census.gov/popest/data/national/asro.php (downloaded July 15, 2003).

———. 2003p. "School Enrollment—Social and Economic Characteristics of Students: October 2001—Detailed Tables" World Wide Web, http://www.census.gov/population/www/socdemo/school/cps2001.html

———. 2003q. *Statistical Abstract of the United States, 2002.* Washington, DC: U.S. Government Printing Office. Available online at http://www.census.gov/prod/www/statistical-abstract-02.html

———. 2003r. *Technical Summary of A.C.E. Revision II for the Committee on National Statistics.* Available online, http://www.census.gov/Press-Release/www/2003/ExecSumm.pdf

———. 2002a. *Census 2000 Brief: The American Indian and Native Alaskan Population, 2000.* World Wide Web, http://www.census.gov/prod/2002pubs/c2kbr01-15.pdf

———. 2002b. *Census 2000 Brief: The Asian Population: 2000.* World Wide Web, http://www.census.gov/prod/2002pubs/c2kbr01-16.pdf

———. 2002c. "Cumulative Births, Deaths, and Migration by State: Estimated Components of State Population Change: April 1, 2000 to July 1, 2002." World Wide Web, http://eire.census.gov/popest/data/states/tables/ST-EST2002-07.php

———. 2002d. *Current Population Survey*, "Annual Demographic Survey, March Supplement, Detailed Person Income." World Wide Web,http://ferret.bls.census.gov/macro/032002/perinc/toc.htm (downloaded July 17, 2003). Printed Version, *Current Population Survey*, Report P-60, No. 218. Washington, DC: U.S. Government Printing Office.

———. 2002e. *Current Population Survey*, "Annual Demographic Survey, March Supplement, Family Income." World Wide Web, http://ferret.bls.census.gov/macro/032002/faminc/toc.htm (downloaded June 9, 2003). Printed Version, *Current Population Survey*, Report P-60, No. 218. Washington, DC: U.S. Government Printing Office.

———. 2002f. *Current Population Survey*, "Annual Demographic Survey, March Supplement, Poverty." World Wide Web, http://ferret.bls.census.gov/macro/032002/pov/toc.htm (downloaded June 9, 2003). Printed version, *Current Population Survey*, Report P-60, No. 219. Washington, DC: U.S. Government Printing Office.

———. 2002g. "Detailed Health Insurance (P-60 Package): 2001 Annual Demographic Survey, March Supplement." World Wide Web, http://ferret.bls.census.gov/macro/032002/health/toc.htm

———. 2002h. "Historical Income Tables: People." World Wide Web, http://www.census.gov/hhes/income/histinc/incperdet.html

———. 2002i. *Income 2001*. World Wide Web, http://www.census.gov/hhes/www/income01.html (downloaded July 17, 2003).

———. 2002j. "National Population Projections: Total Population by Race, Hispanic Origin, and Nativity." World Wide Web, http://www.census.gov/population/www/projections/natsum-T5.html

———. 2001a. *Census 2000*, Summary File 1, P-10, "Hispanic or Latino by Race (Total Races Tallied)." World Wide Web, http://factfinder.census.gov/servlet/DTTable?_ts=71116323 5370

———. 2001b. *Census 2000*, PHC-T-6, Table 1, "Population by Race and Hispanic or Latino Origin, for the United States, Regions, Divisions, and States, and for Puerto Rico: 2000." World Wide Web, http://www.census.gov/population/cen2000/phc-t6/tab01.txt

———. 2001c. "America's Family and Living Arrangements, March 2000." Detailed Tables for *Current Population Report*, P20-537. World Wide Web, http://www.census.gov/population/www/socdemo/hh-fam/p20-537_00.html (downloaded July 3, 2003).

———. 2001d. "ESCAP II: Demographic Analysis Results." World Wide Web, http://www.census.gov/dmd/www/pdf/Report1.PDF (downloaded December 11, 2003).

———. 2001e. *The Hispanic Population 2000*. Census 2000 Brief. World Wide Web, http://www.census.gov/prod/2001pubs/c2kbr01-3.pdf

———. 2001f. "Overview of Race and Hispanic Origin, 2000." World Wide Web, http://www.census.gov/prod/2001pubs/c2kbr01-1.pdf

———. 2001g. "School Enrollment Social and Economic Characteristics of Students: October 2000." World Wide Web, http://www.census.gov/population/www/socdemo/school/ppl-148.html (downloaded July 18, 2003).

———. 2000. "Projections of the Resident Population by Race, Hispanic Origin, and Nativity: Middle Series, 2050 to 2070." World Wide Web, http://www.census.gov/population/projections/nation/summary/np-t5-g.txt (downloaded May 15, 2003).

U.S. CITIZENSHIP AND IMMIGRATION SERVICE. 2003a. "Estimates of the Unauthorized Immigrant Population Residing in the United States: 1990 to 2000." World Wide Web, http://uscis.gov/graphics/shared/aboutus/statistics/2000ExecSumm.pdf (downloaded December 11, 2003).

———. 2003b. "Fiscal Year 2002 Supplemental Tables." World Wide Web, http://uscis.gov/graphics/shared/aboutus/statistics/SupplementalTables.htm (downloaded December 11, 2003).

———. 2003c. *Fiscal Year 2002 Yearbook of Immigration Statistics*. World Wide Web, http://uscis.gov/graphics/shared/aboutus/statistics/IMM02yrbk/IMM2002list.htm (downloaded December 11, 2003).

U.S. COMMISSION ON CIVIL RIGHTS. 2001. *Voting Irregularities in Florida During the 2000 Presidential Election*. World Wide Web, http://www.usccr.gov/pubs/vote2000/report/main.htm (downloaded July 28, 2003).

———. 2000. *Sharing the Dream: Is the ADA Accommodating All?* World Wide Web, http://www.usccr.gov/pubs/ada/main.htm (downloaded October 15, 2003).

———. 1976. *Fulfilling the Letter and Spirit of the Law: Desegregation of the Nation's Schools*. Washington, DC: U.S. Government Printing Office.

———. 1975. *The Voting Rights Act: Ten Years Later*. Washington, DC: U.S. Government Printing Office.

———. 1974. *Toward Quality Education for Mexican Americans*. Mexican American Study Report no. 4. Washington, DC: U.S. Government Printing Office.

———. 1970a. *Mexican Americans and the Administration of Justice in the Southwest*. Washington, DC: U.S. Government Printing Office.

———. 1970b. *Racism in America and How to Combat It*. Clearinghouse Publication, Urban Series no. 1. Washington, DC: U.S. Government Printing Office.

———. 1968. *Political Participation*. Washington, DC: U.S. Government Printing Office.

———. 1965. *Law Enforcement: A Report on Equal Protection in the South*. Washington, DC: U.S. Government Printing Office.

U.S. DEPARTMENT OF EDUCATION. 1987. *Schools That Work: Educating Disadvantaged Children*. Washington, DC: U.S. Government Printing Office.

U.S. DEPARTMENT OF HOUSING AND URBAN DEVELOPMENT. 1991. *1989 Housing Discrimination Study*. Washington, DC: U.S. Government Printing Office.

———. 1979. *Measuring Racial Discrimination in American Housing Markets: The Housing Market Practices Survey*. Washington, DC: U.S. Government Printing Office.

U.S. DEPARTMENT OF LABOR. 2003. "Fact Sheet #30: The Federal Wage Garnishment Law, Consumer Credit Protection Act's Title 3 (CCPA)." World Wide Web, http://www.dol.gov/esa/regs/compliance/whd/whdfs30.htm (downloaded August 7, 2003).

———. 1987. *Workforce 2000: Work and Workers for the 21st Century*. Washington, DC: U.S. Government Printing Office.

———. 1965. *The Negro Family: The Case for National Action* (The Moynihan Report). Washington, DC: U.S. Government Printing Office.

USEEM, ELIZABETH L. 1992. "Middle Schools and Math Groups: Parents' Involvement in Children's Placement." *Sociology of Education* 65: 263–79.

———. 1991. "Tracking Students out of Mathematics." *Education Digest* (May): 54–58.

U.S. IMMIGRATION AND NATURALIZATION SERVICE. 1998. "Immigration to the United States in Fiscal Year 1996, Table 2." World Wide Web, http://www.ins.usdoj.gov/stats/annual/fy96/993.html

U.S. NATIONAL ADVISORY COMMISSION ON CIVIL DISORDERS. 1968. *Report of the National Advisory Commission on Civil Disorders*. New York: New York Times Company, Bantam Books.

VALDES, FRANCISCO, JEROME, MCCRISTAL CULP and ANGELA P. HARRIS. (EDS.) 2002. *Crossroads, Directions, and a New Critical Race Theory*. Philadelphia: Temple University Press.

VALENTINE, CHARLES A. 1968. *Culture and Poverty: Critique and Counter-Proposals.* Chicago: University of Chicago Press.

VALENZUELA DE LA GARZA, JESUS, and MARCELLO MEDINA. 1985. "Academic Achievement as Influenced by Bilingual Instruction for Spanish-Dominant Mexican-American Children." *Hispanic Journal of Behavior Science* 7: 247–59.

VAN AUSDALE, DEBRA, and JOE R. FEAGIN. 2001. *The First R: How Children Learn Race and Racism.* Lanham, MD: Rowman & Littlefield.

VAN DEN BERGHE, PIERRE L. 1978. *Race and Racism: A Comparative Perspective,* 2d ed. New York: Wiley.

———. 1965. *South Africa: A Study in Conflict.* Middletown, CT: Wesleyan University Press.

———. 1958. "The Dynamics of Racial Prejudice: An Ideal-Type Dichotomy." *Social Forces* 37: 138–41.

VAN DER HORST, SHEILA T. 1967. "The Effects of Industrialisation on Race Relations in South Africa." Pp. 97–140 in Guy Hunter (ed.), *Industrialisation and Race Relations: A Symposium.* London: Oxford University Press.

VERHOVEK, SAM HOWE. 1997. "In Poll, Americans Reject Means but Not Ends of Racial Diversity." *New York Times,* December 14: 1, 32.

VERNON, P. E. 1969. *Intelligence and Cultural Environment.* London: Methuen.

VIADERO, DEBRA. 1997. "Intellectual Development Linked to Quality of Day Care." *Education Week* (April 16): 7.

VIDAL, GORE. 1992. "Get Gay and Save the Planet." *New Statesman and Society* 5, 215: 12–13.

VILLALPANDO, O. 1994. "Comparing the Effects of Multiculturalism and Diversity on White and Minority Students' Satisfaction with College." Paper presented at Annual Meeting of the Association for the Study of Higher Education, Tucson, Arizona, November.

VINING, DANIEL R. 1979. "Net Migration by Air: A Lower-Bound on Total Net Migration into the United States." *Working Papers in Regional Science and Transportation,* no. 15. Philadelphia: University of Pennsylvania.

VOSE, CLEMENT E. 1959. *Caucasians Only.* Berkeley: University of California Press.

WAHLSTEN, DOUGLAS. 1995. "Increasing the Raw Intelligence of a Nation Is Constrained by Ignorance, Not Its Citizens' Genes." *Alberta Journal of Educational Research* 41: 257–64.

WAITE, LINDA J. 1981. "U.S. Women at Work." *Population Bulletin* 36, 2.

WAITE, LINDA J., and LEE A. LILLARD. 1991. "Children and Marital Disruption." *American Journal of Sociology* 96: 930–53.

WALKER, ALICE. 1983. *In Search of Our Mothers' Gardens.* San Diego: Harcourt.

WALKER, MARY. 2001. "A World Where Womanhood Reigns Supreme (The Seeds of My Own Re-Evaluations)." World Wide Web, http://www.islamfortoday.com/mary_walker.htm Originally published in *Impact Magazine* (downloaded July 3, 2003).

WALLECHINSKY, DAVID, and IRVING WALLACE. 1975. *The People's Almanac.* Garden City, NY: Doubleday.

WALLERSTEIN, JUDITH S., and SANDRA BLAKESLEE. 1989. *Second Chances: Men, Women, and Children a Decade After Divorce.* New York: Ticknor and Fields.

WALLERSTEIN, JUDITH, and JOAN B. KELLY. 1980. "California's Children of Divorce." *Psychology Today* 13, 8: 67–76.

WALTON, HANES, JR. 1985. *Invisible Politics: Black Political Behavior.* Albany: State University of New York Press.

WAQUANT, LOIC. 2002. "Scrutinizing the Street: Poverty, Morality, and the Pitfalls of Urban Ethnography." *American Journal of Sociology* 107: 1468–1532.

WARNER, W. LLOYD, and LEO SROLE. 1945. *The Social Systems of American Ethnic Groups.* New Haven, CT: Yale University Press.

WARREN ELIZABETH, TERESA SULLIVAN, and MELISSA JACOBY. 2000. "Medical Problems and Bankruptcy Filings." *Norton's Bankruptcy Advisor* (May).

WASHINGTON, BOOKER T. 1900. *Up from Slavery: An Autobiography.* Garden City, NY: Doubleday. Electronic edition available at http://docsouth.unc.edu/washington/washing.html (downloaded June 30, 2003).

WASHINGTON, JULIE A., and HOLLY K. CRAIG. 1992. "Articulation Test Performance of Low-Income, African American Preschoolers with Communication Impairments." *Language, Speech, and Hearing Services in Schools* 23: 203–7.

*WASHINGTON POST.* 1998a. "$100M Judgment Against Nationwide." World Wide Web, http://search.washingtonpost.com/wp-srv/WPlate/1998-10/27/152l-102798-idx.html

———. 1998b. "The Road to Peace." World Wide Web, http://www.washingtonpost.com/wp-srv/inatl/longterm/nireland/roadtopeace.htm

WATSON, BRUCE. 1996. "A Freedom Summer Activist Becomes a Math Revolutionary." *Smithsonian* 26, 11 (February): 114–25.

WATSON, WARREN, KAMALESH KUMAR, and LARRY MICHEALSEN. 1993. "Cultural Diversity's Impact on Interaction Process and Performance: Comparing Homogeneous and Diverse Task Groups." *Academy of Management Journal* 36: 590–602.

WEBER, C. U., P. W. FOSTER, and D. P. WEIKART. 1978. "An Economic Analysis of the Ypsilanti Perry Preschool Project." *Monographs of High/Scope Educational Research Foundation* 5.

WEBER, G. 1971. *Inner City Children Can Be Taught to Read: Four Successful Schools.* Washington, DC: Center for Basic Education.

WEBER, MAX. 1968 [1922]. *Economy and Society: An Outline of Interpretive Sociology.* Guenther Roth and Claus Wittich (eds.), Ephraim Fischoff et al. (trs.). New York: Bedminster Press.

WEBSTER, PAMELA S., TERRI L. ORBUCH, and JAMES S. HOUSE. 1995. "Effects of Childhood Family Background on Adult Marital Quality and Perceived Stability." *American Journal of Sociology* 101: 404–32.

WEEKS, JOHN R. 1992. *Population: An Introduction to Concepts and Issues,* 5th ed. Belmont, CA: Wadsworth.

WEIL, ALAN. 2002. "Ten Things Everyone Should Know About Welfare Reform." Number A-52 in Urban Institute Series, *New Federalism: Issues and Options for States.* World Wide Web, http://www.urban.org/Template.cfm?NavMenuID=24&template=/TaggedContent/ViewPublication.cfm&PublicationID=7692 (downloaded July 30, 2003).

WEINBERG, MARTIN S., and COLIN J. WILLIAMS. 1974. *Male Homosexuals: Their Problems and Adaptations.* New York: Oxford University Press.

WEINER, M. J., and F. E. WRIGHT. 1973. "Effects of Undergoing Arbitrary Discrimination upon Subsequent Attitudes Toward a Minority Group." *Journal of Applied Social Psychology* 3: 94–102.

WEINSTEIN, RICHARD P. 2001. "Should Public Schools Address Diversity?" In Ethical Issues in Education: Practicing Educators Reflect on Professional Concerns, World Wide Web, http://www2.widener.edu/~egr0001/EDControversy/ControPalette.html (downloaded May 28, 2003).

WEISBURD, DAVID, ROSANN GREENSPAN, EDWIN E. HAMILTON, HUBERT WILLIAMS and KELLIE A. BRYANT. 2000. *Police Attitudes Toward Abuse of Authority: Findings from a National Study.* Washington, DC: National Institute of Justice: Research in Brief.

WEISS, RANDALL. 1968. "The Effects of Scholastic Achievement on the Earnings of Blacks and Whites." Honors thesis, Harvard University, Cambridge, Massachusetts.

WEITZER, RONALD, and STEVEN A. TUCH. 2002. "Perceptions of Racial Profiling: Race, Class, and Personal Experience." *Criminology* 40: 435–56.

WEITZMAN, LENORE. 1985. *The Divorce Revolution: The Unexpected Social and Economic Consequences for Women and Children in America.* New York: Free Press.

WELCH, FINIS. 1967. "Labor Market Discrimination in the Rural South." *Journal of Political Economy* 75: 225–40.

WELCH, SUSAN, JOHN GRUHL, and CASSIA SPOHN. 1984. "Dismissal, Conviction, and Incarceration of Hispanic Defendants: A

Comparison with Anglos and Blacks." *Social Science Quarterly* 65: 257–64.

WELLEN, JACKIE M., MICHAEL A. HOGG, and DEBORAH J. TERRY. 1998."Group Norms and Attitude-Behavior Consistency: The Role of Group Salience and Mood." *Group Dynamics: Theory, Research, & Practice* 2, 1, 48–56.

WELLMAN, D. T. 1993. *Portraits of White Racism.* New York: Cambridge University Press.

WELLS, AMY STUART, and ROBERT L. CRAIN. 1997. *Stepping over the Color Line: African American Students in White Suburban Schools.* New Haven, CT: Yale University Press.

WELLS, AMY STUART, and IRENE SERNA. 1996. "The Politics of Culture: Understanding Local Political Resistance to Detracking in Racially Mixed Schools." *Harvard Educational Review* 66: 93–118.

WERNER, NORMA E., and IDELLA M. EVANS. 1968. "Perceptions of Prejudice in Mexican-American Pre-School Children." *Perceptual and Motor Skills* 27: 1039–46.

WESLEY, CHARLES H. 1927. *Negro Labor in the United States: 1850–1925.* New York: Vanguard.

WEST, CORNELL. 1993. *Race Matters.* Boston: Beacon Press.

WHEELER, DAVID L. 1995. "A Growing Number of Scientists Reject the Concept of Race." *Chronicle of Higher Education* (February 17): A8.

———. 1993. "Study Suggests X Chromosome Is Linked to Homosexuality." *Chronicle of Higher Education* (July 21): A6.

———. 1992. "Studies Linking Homosexuality to Genes Draw Criticism from Researchers." *Chronicle of Higher Education* (February 5): A7–A9.

———. 1991. "A Genetic Component of Homosexuality Is Strongly Indicated." *Chronicle of Higher Education* (December 18): All.

WHITAKER, CHARLES. 1991. "Do Black Males Need Special Schools?" *Ebony* 23, 1: 17–22.

WHITE, SHELDON. 1970. "The National Impact of Head Start." *Disadvantaged Child* 3: 163–84.

WHITELY, B. E., JR. 1990. "The Relationship of Heterosexuals' Attributions for the Causes of Homosexuality to Attitudes Toward Lesbian and Gay Men." *Personality and Social Psychology Bulletin* 16: 369–77.

WILDER, D. A., and J. E. THOMPSON. 1980. "Intergroup Contact with Independent Manipulations of In-Group and Out-Group Interaction." *Journal of Personality and Social Psychology* 38: 764–72.

WILENSKY, HAROLD L., and HUGH EDWARDS. 1959. "The Skidder: Ideological Adjustments of Downward Mobile Workers." *American Sociological Review* (April): 215–31.

WILHELM, SIDNEY M. 1980. "Can Marxism Explain America's Racism?" *Social Problems* 28: 98–112.

WILINKSON, DORIS. 2002. "The Clinical Irrelevance and Scientific Invalidity of the 'Minority' Notion: Deleting It from the Social Science Vocabulary." *Journal of Sociology and Social Welfare* 29, 2: 21–34.

WILLIAMS, CHARLES. 1992. "The Relationship Between the Affective and Conative Dimensions of Prejudice." *College Student Journal* 26, 1: 50–54.

WILLIAMS, PATRICIA J. 1997."The Hidden Meanings of Black English." *Black Scholar* 27: 7–8.

WILLIAMS, ROBIN. 1977. "Competing Models of Multiethnic and Multiracial Societies: An Appraisal of Possibilities and Performances." Paper presented at the plenary session of the American Sociological Association, 72nd Annual Meeting, Chicago.

———. 1975. "Race and Ethnic Relations." Pp. 125–64, in Alex Inkeles, James Coleman, and Neil Smelser (eds.), *Annual Review of Sociology.* Palo Alto, CA: Annual Reviews.

WILLIAMSON, JOEL. 1984. *The Crucible of Race: Black-White Relations in the American South Since Emancipation.* New York: Oxford University Press.

WILLIE, CHARLES VERT. 1979. *The Caste and Class Controversy.* Bayside, NY: General Hall.

WILLIG, ANN. 1985. "A Meta-Analysis of Selected Studies on the Effectiveness of Bilingual Education." *Review of Educational Research* 55: 269–317.

WILLMS, J. DOUGLAS. 1987. "Patterns of Academic Achievement in Public and Private Schools: Implications for Public Policy and Future Research." Pp. 113–34 in Edward H. Haertel, Thomas James, and Henry M. Levin (eds.), *Comparing Public and Private Schools*, Vol. 2, *School Achievement.* New York: Falmer.

WILNER, DANIEL M., ROSABELLE P. WALKLEY, and STUART W. COOK. 1955. *Human Relations in Interracial Housing.* Minneapolis: University of Minnesota Press.

WILSON, FRANKLIN D., and KARL E. TAEUBER. 1978. "Residential and School Segregation: Some Tests of Their Association." Pp. 51–78 in F. D. Bean and W. Parker Frisbie (eds.), *The Demography of Racial and Ethnic Groups.* New York: Academic Press.

WILSON, JAMES Q. 1978. *Varieties of Police Behavior: The Management of Law and Order in Eight Communities.* Cambridge, MA: Harvard University Press.

WILSON, WILLIAM JULIUS. 2001. *The Bridge over the Racial Divide: Rising Inequality and Coalition Politics.* Berkeley: University of California Press.

———. 1996. *When Work Disappears: The New World of the Urban Poor.* New York: Alfred A. Knopf.

———. 1991. "Public Policy Research and the Truly Disadvantaged." Pp. 460–81 in Christopher Jencks and Paul E. Peterson (eds.), *The Urban Underclass.* Washington, DC: The Brookings Institution.

———. 1987. *The Truly Disadvantaged: The Inner City, the Underclass, and Public Policy.* Chicago: University of Chicago Press.

———. 1981. "The Black Community in the 1980s: Questions of Race, Class, and Public Policy." *The Annals of the American Academy of Political and Social Science* 454: 26–41.

———. 1979. "The Declining Significance of Race: Revisited but Not Revised." Chapter 14 in Charles Vert Willie (ed.), *Caste and Class Controversy.* Bayside, NY: General Hall. (Reprinted from *Society* [July–August, 1978].)

———. 1978. *The Declining Significance of Race: Blacks and Changing American Institutions.* Chicago: University of Chicago Press.

———. 1973. *Power, Racism and Privilege.* New York: Free Press.

WIMBERLEY, DALE W. 1990. "Investment Dependence and Alternative Explanations of Third World Mortality: A Cross National Study." *American Sociological Review* 55: 75–91.

WINANT, HOWARD. 1997."Behind Blue Eyes: Contemporary White Racial Politics." in Michelle Fine et al., eds., *Off White: Readings on Race, Power, and Society.* New York: Routledge. Also available via World Wide Web, http://blue.temple.edu/~winant/whitness.html

———. 1994. *Racial Conditions: Politics, Theory, Comparisons.* Minneapolis: University of Minnesota Press.

WINSBERG, MORTON D. 1983. "Changing Distribution of the Black Population: Florida Cities, 1970–1980." *Urban Affairs Quarterly* 18: 361–70.

WITT, L. ALLEN. 1989. "Authoritarianism, Knowledge of AIDS, and Affect Toward Persons with AIDS: Implications for Health Education." *Journal of Applied Psychology* 19: 599–607.

WOLFE, ALAN. 1995. "Has There Been a Cognitive Revolution in America?" Pp. 109–23 in Steven Fraser (ed.), *The Bell Curve Wars: Race, Intelligence, and the Future of America.* New York: Basic Books.

WOMACK, HELEN. 1997."Capturing the Palace but Not the Country." *Irish Times* on the Net, January 28. World Wide Web, http://www.irish-times.com/irish-times/paper/1997/0128/for9.html

WOOD, BARBARA SUDENE, and JULIA CURRY. 1969. "Everyday Talk and School Talk of the City Black Child." *Speech Teacher* 18: 282–96.

WOOD, PETER B., and BARRETT A. LEE. 1991. "Is Neighborhood Racial Succession Inevitable? Forty Years of Evidence." *Urban Affairs Quarterly* 26: 610–20.

WOOD, PETER B., and NANCY SONLEITNER. 1996. "The Effect of Childhood Interracial Contact on Adult Antiblack Prejudice." *International Journal of Intercultural Relations* 20: 1–17.

WOOD, W., and A. M. EAGLY. 1981. "Stages in the Analysis of Persuasive Messages: The Role of Causal Attribution and Message Comprehension." *Journal of Personality and Social Psychology* 40: 246–59.

WOODWARD, C. VAN. 1971. *American Counterpoint: Slavery and Racism in the North-South Dialogue.* Boston: Little, Brown.

———. 1966. *The Strange Career of Jim Crow,* 2d rev. ed. New York: Oxford University Press.

WORLD JEWISH CONGRESS. 1998."Jewish Communities of the World," abridged Internet ed., United States page. World Wide Web, http://virtual.co.il/communities/wjcbook/usa/index.htm

WORTMAN, PAUL M., and FRED B. BRYANT. 1985. "School Desegregation and Black Achievement: An Integrative Review." *Sociological Methods and Research* 13: 289–324.

WRIGHT, J. SKELLY. 1969. "The Courts Have Failed the Poor." *New York Times Magazine* (March 9).

WRIGHT, LAWRENCE. 1994. "One Drop of Blood." *New Yorker* (July 25).

WU, CHENGHUAN, and DAVID R. SHAFFER. 1987. "Susceptibility to Persuasive Appeals as a Function of Source Credibility and Prior Experience with the Attitude Object." *Journal of Personality and Social Psychology* 52: 677–88.

YANCEY, GEORGE, and SHERELYN YANCEY. 1998."Interracial Dating: Evidence from Personal Advertisements." *Journal of Family Issues* 19: 334–48.

YANG, ALAN S. 1998. *From Wrongs to Rights: Public Opinion on Gay and Lesbian Americans Moves Toward Equality.* Washington, DC: Policy Institute of the National Gay and Lesbian Task Force. Also available via World Wide Web, http://www.ngltf.org/downloads/yang.pdf

YETMAN, NORMAN R. 1991. *Majority and Minority: The Dynamics of Race and Ethnicity in American Life,* 5th ed. Boston: Allyn & Bacon.

———. 1985. *Majority and Minority: The Dynamics of Race and Ethnicity in American Life,* 4th ed. Boston: Allyn & Bacon.

YINGER, JOHN. 1995. *Closed Doors, Opportunities Lost: The Continuing Costs of Housing Discrimination.* New York: Russell Sage Foundation.

ZALD, MAYER N., and JOHN D. MCCARTHY. 1975. "Organizational Intellectuals and the Criticism of Society." *Social Service Research* 49: 344–62.

ZANNA, MARK P. 1994. "On the Nature of Prejudice." *Canadian Psychology* 35: 11–23.

ZEICHNER, KENNETH M. 1995. "Preparing Educators for Cross-Cultural Teaching." Pp. 397–419 in Willis D. Hawley and Anthony W. Jackson (eds.), *Toward a Common Destiny: Improving Race and Ethnic Relations in America.* San Francisco: Jossey-Bass.

ZENGERLE, JASON GRAY. 1997."Welfare as Vermont Knows It." *The American Prospect* 30: 54–55. Also available via World Wide Web, http://epn.org/prospect/30/zeng.html

ZHANG, CUI-XIA, and JOHN E. FARLEY. 1995. "Gender and the Distribution of Household Work: A Comparison of Self-Reports by Female College Faculty in the United States and China." *Journal of Comparative Family Studies* 26: 195–205.

ZIGLER, EDWARD, E. F. ABELSON, and V. SEITZ. 1973. "Motivational Factors in the Performance of Economically Disadvantaged Children on the Peabody Picture Vocabulary Test." *Child Development* 44: 294–303.

ZIGLER, EDWARD, and SUSAN MUENCHOW. 1992. *Head Start: The Inside Story of America's Most Successful Educational Experiment.* New York: Basic Books.

ZIMRING, FRANKLIN E., JOEL EIGEN, and SHIELA O'MALLEY. 1976. "Punishing Homicide in Philadelphia: Perspectives on the Death Penalty." *University of Chicago Law Review* 43: 227–52.

ZINN, MAXINE BACA, LYNN WEBER CANNON, ELIZABETH HIGGENBOTHAM, and BONNIE THORNTON DILL. 1986. "The Costs of Exclusionary Practices in Women's Studies." *Signs* 11: 290–303.

ZIRKEL, PERRY A. 1971. "Self-Concept and the 'Disadvantage' of Ethnic Group Membership and Mixture." *Review of Educational Research* 41: 211–25.

ZIRKEL, PERRY A., and GNANARAJ E. MOSES. 1971. "Self-Concept and Ethnic Group Membership Among Public School Students." *American Educational Research Journal* 8: 253–65.

ZUBRINSKY CHARLES, CAMILLE. 2001. "Processes of Racial Residential Segregation." Pp. 217–71 in Alice O'Conner, Chris Tilly, and Lawrence D. Bobo (eds.), *Urban Inequality: Evidence from Four Cities.* New York: Russell Sage Foundation.

ZWEIGENHAFT, RICHARD L., and G. WILLIAM DOMHOFF. 2003. *Blacks in the White Elite: Will Progress Continue?* Lanhan, MD: Rowman & Littlefield.

———. 1991. *Blacks in the White Establishment? A Study of Race and Class in America.* New Haven, CT: Yale University Press.

# PHOTO CREDITS

# NAME INDEX

# SUBJECT INDEX